DATE DUE

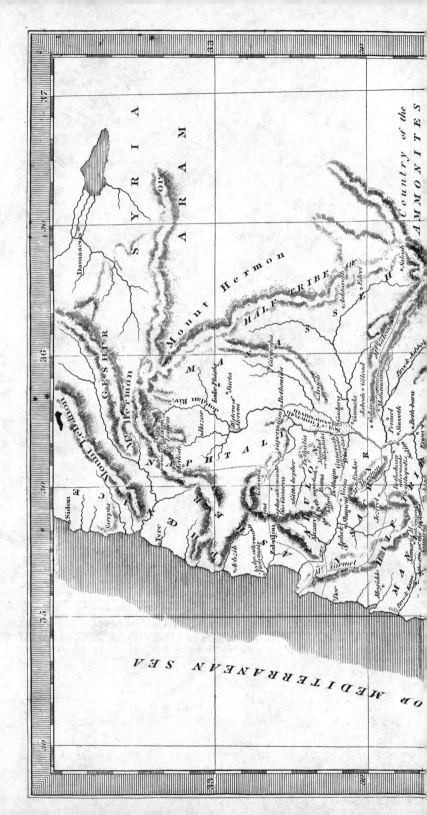

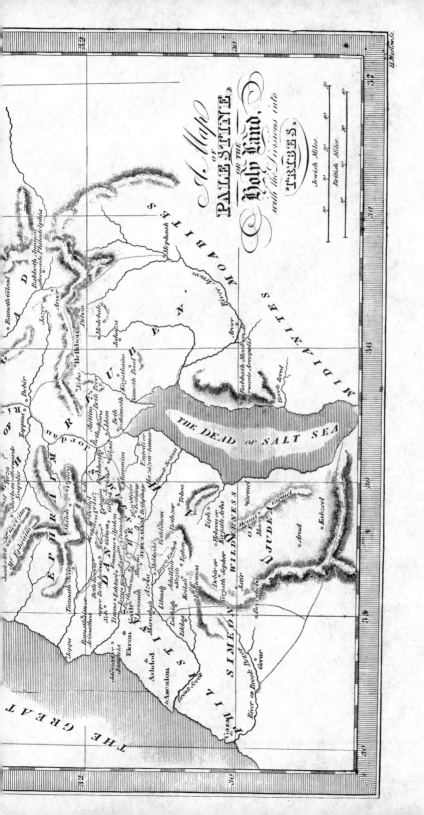

AN

INTRODUCTION

TO THE

Critical Study and Knowledge

OF THE

HOLY SCRIPTURES.

BY

THOMAS HARTWELL HORNE, B.D.

OF SAINT JOHN'S COLLEGE, CAMBRIDGE;

RECTOR OF THE UNITED PARISHES OF SAINT EDMUND THE KING AND
MARTYR AND SAINT NICHOLAS ACONS, LOMBARD STREET;
PREBENDARY OF SAINT PAUL'S.

14600

EIGHTH EDITION, CORRECTED AND ENLARGED.

ILLUSTRATED WITH NUMEROUS MAPS AND FACSIMILES OF BIBLICAL
MANUSCRIPTS.

VOLUME III.

BAKER BOOK HOUSE
Grand Rapids, Michigan

Standard Book Number: 8010-4003-5

Library of Congress Catalog Card Number: 76-132693

Reprinted 1970 by
Baker Book House Company

Reprinted 1970 by
Baker Book House Company
from the Eighth Edition, Corrected and Enlarged,
printed in Edinburgh in 1839

CONTENTS

OF

THE THIRD VOLUME.

SUMMARY OF BIBLICAL GEOGRAPHY AND ANTIQUITIES,

PART I.

A SKETCH OF THE HISTORICAL AND PHYSICAL GEOGRAPHY OF
THE HOLY LAND.

A 2

PART II.

POLITICAL ANTIQUITIES OF THE JEWS.

CHAPTER I. *Different Forms of Government, and Political
State of the Hebrews, or Jews, from the Patriarchal Times
to the Babylonian Captivity.*

CHAPTER II. *Political State of the Jews, from their Return
from the Babylonish Captivity to the Subversion of their Civil
and Ecclesiastical Polity.*

SECTION I. *Political State of the Jews under the Maccabees, and the
Sovereigns of the Herodian Family.*

A 3

PART III.

SACRED ANTIQUITIES OF THE JEWS, AND OF OTHER NATIONS INCI-
DENTALLY MENTIONED IN THE SCRIPTURES.

PART IV.

DOMESTIC ANTIQUITIES OF THE JEWS, AND OF OTHER NATIONS, INCIDENTALLY MENTIONED IN THE SCRIPTURES.

INTRODUCTION

TO THE

CRITICAL STUDY AND KNOWLEDGE

OF

THE HOLY SCRIPTURES.

SUMMARY OF BIBLICAL GEOGRAPHY AND ANTIQUITIES.

PART I.

A SKETCH OF THE HISTORICAL AND PHYSICAL GEOGRAPHY
OF THE HOLY LAND.[1]

CHAPTER I.

HISTORICAL GEOGRAPHY OF THE HOLY LAND.

I. *Names.* — II. *Boundaries.* — III. *Inhabitants before the Conquest of Canaan by the Israelites.* — IV. *Division by Joshua.* — *Allotments of the Twelve Tribes.* — V. *The Kingdom under David and Solomon.* — VI. *The Kingdoms of Judah and Israel.* — VII. *Divisions in the Time of Jesus Christ.* — VIII. *Account of the City of* JERUSALEM: — 1. *Its Situation;* — 2. *Names;* — 3. *Fortifications and Walls;* — 4. *State of the City before the fatal War of the Jews with the Romans;* — 5. *Remarkable Buildings;* — 6. *Notice of the successive Captures of the City;* — 7. *Sketch of its Present State.* — IX. *Later Divisions of Palestine:* — 1. *Under the Romans;* — 2. *In the Time of the Crusades;* — 3. *Modern Divisions under the Turkish Government.*

I. THIS country has in different ages been called by various NAMES, which have been derived either from its inhabitants, or from the extraordinary circumstances attached to it. Thus, in Ruth i. 1. and Jer. iv. 20. it is termed generally *the land :* and hence, both in the Old and New Testament, the word Γη, which is sometimes rendered *earth,* is by the context in many places determined to mean the promised land of Israel; as in Josh. ii. 3. *They be come to search out all* THE COUNTRY (Sept. την γην) ; Matt. v. 5. *The meek shall inherit the* EARTH (γην, the land) ; and in Luke iv. 25. where a great famine is said to have pre-

---

[1] As this portion of the present work is designed to exhibit only an *outline* of the Geography of the Holy Land, and not a complete system of Biblical Geography ; the reader will find, in the Historical, Biographical, and Geographical Index, annexed to this volume, a concise notice of the principal countries and places, both in and out of Palestine, which are mentioned in the Scriptures.

vailed throughout all the LAND (επι πασαν την γην). In like manner, οικουμενη, which primarily means the inhabited world, and is often so rendered, is by the connection of the discourse restrained to a particular country, as in Isa. xiii. 5. (Sept.) ; and to the land of Judæa, as in Luke ii. 1. xxi. 26. Acts xi. 28. and James v. 17. But the country occupied by the Hebrews, Israelites, and Jews, is in the sacred volume more particularly called,

1. The LAND OF CANAAN, from Canaan, the youngest son of Ham, and grandson of Noah, who settled here after the confusion of Babel, and divided the country among his eleven children, each of whom became the head of a numerous tribe, that ultimately became a distinct nation. (Gen. x. 15. *et seq.*) It continued to bear this name until the Israelites took possession of it. (Lev. xxv. 38. Psal. cv. 11.) But, in strictness, only the countries on the west of the river Jordan were thus called; those on the east being denominated Gilead. (Num. xxxiii. 51. xxxiv. 2. 11, 12. xxxv. 10. Josh. xxii. 9—11. 13. 15. 32.)

2. The LAND OF ISRAEL, from the Israelites, or posterity of Jacob, having settled themselves there. This name is of most frequent occurrence in the Old Testament: it is also to be found in the New Testament (as in Matt. ii. 20, 21.); and in its larger acceptation comprehended all that tract of ground on each side the river Jordan, which God gave for an inheritance to the children of Israel. Within this extent lay all the provinces or countries visited by Jesus Christ, except Egypt, and, consequently, almost all the places mentioned or referred to in the four Gospels.

3. The LAND OF JEHOVAH, or, the LORD'S LAND (Hos. ix. 3.) ; that is, *the land which the* LORD *sware . . . . . to Abraham, to Isaac, and to Jacob, to give them* (Deut. xxx. 20.); and which he did accordingly give to the Israelites, their descendants, still reserving the ownership of it unto himself. (See Lev. xxv. 23.)[1] With reference to this circumstance, we meet with the appellation of the LAND OF GOD, in various parts of the Old Testament. But, of all the names given to this country, the most delightful in the eyes of a Christian Believer is that of IMMANUEL'S LAND. (Isa. viii. 8.)

4. The LAND OF PROMISE (Heb. xi. 9.), from the promise made by Jehovah to Abraham, that his posterity should possess it (Gen. xii. 7. and xiii. 15.); who being termed Hebrews, this region was thence called the *Land of the Hebrews.*[2] (Gen. xl. 15.) And the same appellation may still be given to it; because the people of Israel, though at present exiled from it, have the promise of returning thither again, and of resuming possession of it when they shall be wholly converted to the Lord Jesus Christ. (Deut. xxx. 3—5. Isa. xi. 11—13. and especially Ezek. xxxvi. and xxxvii.)

5. The HOLY LAND; which appellation is to this day conferred on it by all Christians, because it was chosen by God to be the immediate seat of his worship, and was consecrated by the presence, actions, miracles, discourses, and sufferings of the Lord Jesus Christ, and also

---

[1] Dr. Pocock, on Hos. ix. 3.

[2] This appellation (the Land of the Hebrews) is recognised by Pausanias (lib. vi. c. 24. *in fine*). By heathen writers the Holy Land is variously termed, Syrian Palestine, Syria, and Phœnicia; but as these appellations are not applied *generally* in the Scriptures to that country, any further notice of them is designedly omitted.

because it was the residence of the holy patriarchs, prophets, and apostles. This name does not appear to have been used by the Hebrews themselves, until after the Babylonish Captivity, when we find the prophet Zechariah applying it to his country. (ii. 12.) After this period it seems to have become a common appellation: we meet with it in the apocryphal book of Wisdom (xii. 3.), and also in the second book of Maccabees. (i. 7.) The whole world was divided by the ancient Jews into two general parts, *the land of Israel,* and the *land out of Israel,* that is, all the countries inhabited by the *nations of the world,* or the Gentiles : to this distinction there seems to be an allusion in Matt. vi. 32. All the rest of the world, together with its inhabitants (Judæa excepted), was accounted as profane, *polluted,* and *unclean* (see Isa. xxxv. 8. lii. 1. with Joel iii. 17. Amos. vii. 17. and Acts x. 14.); but though the whole land of Israel was regarded as *holy,* as being the place consecrated to the worship of God, and the inheritance of his people, whence they are collectively styled *saints,* and a holy nation or people in Exod. xix. 6. Deut. vii. 6. xiv. 2. xxvi. 19. xxxiii. 3. 2 Chron. vi. 41. Psal. xxxiv. 9. l. 5. 7. and lxxix. 2.; yet the Jews imagined particular parts to be vested with more than ordinary sanctity, according to their respective situations. Thus the parts situated beyond Jordan were considered to be less holy than those on this side : walled towns were supposed to be more clean and holy than other places, because no lepers were admissible into them, and the dead were not allowed to be buried there. Even the very dust of the land of Israel was reputed to possess such a peculiar degree of sanctity, that when the Jews returned from any heathen country they stopped at its borders, and wiped the dust of it from their shoes, lest the sacred inheritance should be polluted with it : nor would they suffer even herbs to be brought to them from the ground of their Gentile neighbours, lest they should bring any of the mould with them, and thus defile their pure land. To this notion our Lord unquestionably alluded when he commanded his disciples to shake off the dust of their feet (Matt. x. 14.) on returning from any house or city that would neither receive nor hear them; thereby intimating to them, that when the Jews had rejected the Gospel they were no longer to be regarded as the people of God, but were on a level with heathens and idolaters.[1]

6. The LAND OF JUDAH. Under this appellation was at first comprised only that part of the region which was allotted to the tribe of Judah; though the whole land of Israel appears to have been occasionally thus called in subsequent times, when that tribe excelled all the others in dignity. After the separation of the ten tribes, that portion of the land which belonged to the tribes of Judah and Benjamin, who formed a separate kingdom, was distinguished by the appellation of *the land of Judah* (Psal. lxxvi. 1.) or of Judæa; which last name

---

[1] Lightfoot, Hor. Heb. in Matt. x. 14.; Reland, Antiquitates Hebraicæ, pp. 1. 17. Beausobre's Introduction to the New Testament. (Bp. Watson's Collection of Theological Tracts, vol. iii. p. 141.) This distinction of holy and unholy places and persons throws considerable light on 1 Cor. i. 28. where the Apostle, speaking of the calling of the Gentiles and the rejection of the Jews, says, that God hath chosen *base things of the world, and things that are despised, yea, and things which are not,* (that is, the Gentiles) *to bring to nought* (Gr. *to abolish*) *things that are ;* in other words, to become God's church and people, and so to cause the Jewish church and economy to cease. See Whitby in loc.

the whole country retained during the existence of the second temple, and under the dominion of the Romans.

7. The appellation of PALESTINE, by which the whole land appears to have been called in the days of Moses (Exod. xv. 14.), is derived from the Philistines, a people who migrated from Egypt, and having expelled the aboriginal inhabitants, settled on the borders of the Mediterranean; where they became so considerable as to give their name to the whole country, though they, in fact, possessed only a small part of it. Herodotus[1] called the whole tract of country from Syria to Egypt by the name of Palestine; and Philo, in his book concerning Abraham, expressly says, that the region inhabited by the Canaanites was, by the Syrians, termed Palestine. The same region is also called the Syrian Palestine (*Syria Palæstina*) by Tacitus[2] and other antient geographers.[3]

II. The antient geographers placed the Holy Land in the centre of the then known world. Its extent has been variously estimated; some geographers making it not to exceed one hundred and seventy or eighty miles in length, from north to south, and one hundred and forty miles from east to west in its broadest parts (or towards the south), and about seventy miles in breadth, where narrowest, towards the north. From the latest and most accurate maps, however, it appears to have extended nearly two hundred miles in length, and to have been about eighty miles in breadth about the middle, and ten or fifteen, more or less, where it widens or contracts.

By the Abrahamic covenant, recorded in Gen. xv. 18., the original grant of the Promised Land to the Israelites was *from the river of Egypt unto the river Euphrates*. The *Boundaries* of it are thus accurately described by Moses (Numb. xxxiv. 1—16.), before the Israelites entered into it: " *When ye come into the land of Canaan, (this is the land that shall fall unto you for an inheritance, even the land of Canaan, with the coasts thereof,) your* SOUTH QUARTER *shall be from the wilderness of Zin, along by the coast of Edom,*" or Idumæa. This was its general description. The boundary itself is next traced: " *And your south border shall be the utmost coast of the Salt Sea eastward ;* or, as explained by Joshua's description afterwards, (xv. 2—4.) " *the south border of the tribe of Judah began from the bay of the Salt Sea that looketh southward ;*" or, by combining both, from the south·east corner of the Salt Sea or Asphaltite Lake. " *From thence, your border shall turn southwards to the ascent of Akrabbim,*" or the mountains of Accaba, (signifying " ascent" in Arabic,) which run towards the head of the Elanitic, or Eastern gulf of the Red Sea; passing (we may presume) through the sea-ports of Elath and Eziongeber, on the Red Sea, which belonged to Solomon (1 Kings ix. 26.), though they are not noticed in this place. " *Thence it shall pass on to* [the wilderness of] *Zin,*" on the east side of Mount Hor, including that whole mountainous region within the boundary; " *and the going forth thereof shall be to Kadesh Barnea southwards ; and it shall go on to Hazar Addar , and pass on to*

---

[1] Hist. lib. viii. c. 89.
[2] Annal. lib. ii. c. 42.
[3] Alber, Hermeneutica Vet. Test. tom. i. p. 60.
[4] Joshua (xv. 3.) interposes two additional stations, Hezron and Karkaa, before and after Addar, or Hazar Addar, which are not noticed by Moses.

Azmon."   " And the border shall fetch a compass," or form an angle,
" from Azmon," or turn westwards " towards the river of Egypt," or
Pelusiac branch of the Nile ; " and its outgoings shall be at the sea,"
the Mediterranean. [1]

" *And as for the* WESTERN BORDER, *ye shall have the Great Sea for a
border. This shall be your west border.*" The Great Sea is the
Mediterranean, as contrasted with the smaller seas or lakes, the Red
Sea, the Salt Sea, and the Sea of Tiberias, or Galilee.

And this shall be your NORTH BORDER : *from the Great Sea you shall
point out Hor ha-hor,* (not " Mount Hor," as rendered in our English
Bible, confounding it with that on the southern border, but) " *the
mountain of the mountain* [2]," or " *the double mountain,*" or Mount
Lebanon, which formed the northern frontier of Palestine, dividing it
from Syria ; consisting of two great parallel ranges, called Libanus
and Antilibanus, and running eastwards from the neighbourhood of
Sidon to that of Damascus.

" *From Hor ha-hor ye shall point your border to the entrance of
Hamath,*" which Joshua, speaking of the yet unconquered land,
describes, " *All Lebanon, towards the sun rising, from* (the valley of)
Baal Gad, under Mount Hermon, unto the entrance of Hamath." (Josh.
xiii. 5.) This demonstrates, that Hor ha-hor corresponded to all
Lebanon, including Mount Hermon, as judiciously remarked by
Wells [3], who observes, that it is not decided which of the two ridges,
the northern or the southern, was properly Libanus ; the natives at
present call the southern so, but the Septuagint and Ptolemy called it
Antilibanus. — " *From Hamath it shall go on to Zedad, and from thence
to Ziphron, and the goings out of it shall be at Hazar Enan,*" (near Damascus, Ezek. xlviii. 1.) This shall be your north border.

" *And ye shall point out your* EAST BORDER *from Hazar Enan to
Shephan, and the coast shall go down to Riblah on the east side of Ain*
(" the fountain" or springs of the river Jordan), *and the border shall
descend and shall reach unto the* [east] *side of the sea of Chinnereth.
And the border shall go down to Jordan on the east side, and the goings
out of it shall be at the Salt Sea.*" There it met the southern border,
at the south-east corner of that sea, or the Asphaltite lake.

" This shall be your land, with the coasts thereof round about" in
circuit. [4]

Such was the admirable geographical chart of the Land of Promise,
dictated to Moses by the God of Israel, and described with all the
accuracy of an eye-witness. Of this region, however, the Israelites
were not put into immediate possession. In his first expedition
Joshua subdued all the southern department of the Promised Land,
and in his second the northern, having spent five years in both (Josh.
xi. 18.): what Joshua left unfinished of the conquest of the whole
was afterwards completed by David and Solomon. (2 Sam. viii. 3—14.

---

[1] This termination of the southern border westwards, is exactly conformable to the accounts of Herodotus and Pliny : the former represents Mount Casius lying between Pelusium
and the Sirbonic lake, as the boundary between Egypt and Palestine Syria, (iii. 5.) the latter
reckoned the Sirbonic lake itself as the boundary. (Nat. Hist. v. 13.)

[2] The Septuagint Version has judiciously rendered it, παρα το ὄρος το ὄρος, " the mountain
beside the mountain."

[3] Sacred Geography, vol. ii. p. 271.

[4] Dr. Hales's Analysis of Chronology, vol. i. pp. 414—416.

2 Chron. ix. 26.) In the reign of the latter was realised the Abrahamic covenant in its full extent. *And Solomon reigned over all the kingdoms from the river* (Euphrates) *unto the land of the Philistines, and the border of Egypt: — for he had dominion over all the region on this side the river* (Euphrates), *from Tipsah* (or Thapsacus situated thereon) *even to Azzah* (or Gaza with her towns and villages), " *unto the river*" of Egypt, southward, " and the Great Sea," *westward* (Josh. xv. 47.), *even over all the kings on this side the river* (Euphrates). 1 Kings iv. 21. 24.[1]

But the Israelites did not always retain possession of this tract, as is shown in the succeeding pages. It lies far within the temperate zone, and between 31 and 33 degrees of north latitude, and was bounded on the west by the Mediterranean or Great Sea, as it is often called in the Scriptures; on the east by Arabia; on the south by the river of Egypt (or the river Nile, whose eastern branch was reckoned the boundary of Egypt, towards the great Desert of Shur, which lies between Egypt and Palestine[2],) and by the desert of Sin, or Beersheba, the southern shore of the Dead Sea, and the river Arnon; and on the north by the chain of mountains termed Labanon, near which stood the city of Dan: hence in the Sacred Writings we frequently meet with the expression, *from Dan to Beersheba*, in order to denote the whole length of the land of Israel.[3]

III. The Land of Canaan, previously to its CONQUEST by the Israelites, was possessed by the descendants of Canaan, the youngest son of Ham, and grandson of Noah; who divided the country among his eleven sons, each of whom was the head of a numerous clan or tribe. (Gen. x. 15—19.) Here they resided upwards of seven centuries, and founded numerous republics and kingdoms. In the days of Abraham, this region was occupied by ten nations; the Kenites, the Kenizzites, and the Kadmonites, to the east of Jordan; and westward, the Hittites, Perizzites, Rephaims, Amorites, Canaanites, Girgashites, and the Jebusites. (Gen. xv. 18—21.) These latter in the days of Moses were called the Hittites, Girgashites, Amorites, Canaanites, Perizzites, Hivites, and Jebusites (Deut. vii. 1. Josh. iii. 10. xxiv. 11.); the Hivites being substituted for the Rephaims. These seven nations were thus distributed : —

The *Hittites* or sons of Heth, the *Perizzites*, the *Jebusites, and the Amorites, dwelt in the mountains*, or hill country of Judæa, southward; the *Canaanites* dwelt in the midland *by the sea*, westward, and *by the coast of Jordan* eastward; and the *Girgashites*, or Gergesenes, along the eastern side of the Sea of Galilee; and the *Hivites* in Mount Lebanon, under Hermon, in the land of Mizpeh or Gilead, northward. (Compare Numb. xiii. 29. Josh. xi. 3. Judges iii. 3. and Matt. viii. 28.) Of all these nations the Amorites became the most powerful, so as to extend their conquests beyond the river Jordan over the

---

[1] Dr. Hales's Analysis of Chronology, vol. i. pp. 416, 417.

[2] It is a point much in dispute among writers on the geography of the Bible, whether the " river of Egypt " means the Nile, or the Sichor mentioned in Josh. xiii. 3. and Jer. ii. 18. Dr. Hales, however, has shown at length that the Nile is the river intended; and upon his authority we have considered " the river of Egypt," and the Nile, as the same river. See his Analysis of Chronology, vol. i. pp. 413, 414.

[3] For a full investigation of the boundaries of the promised land, see Michaelis's Commentaries on the Law of Moses, vol. i. pp. 55—97.

Kadmonites; whence they are sometimes put for the whole seven nations, as in Gen. xv. 16. Josh. xxiv. 15. and 2 Sam. xxi. 2. These nations were the people whom the children of Israel were commanded to extirminate. Within the period of seven years Moses conquered two powerful kingdoms on the east, and Joshua thirty-one smaller kingdoms, on the west of Jordan, and gave their land to the Israelites; though it appears that some of the old inhabitants were permitted by Jehovah to remain there, *to prove* their conquerors, *whether they would hearken to the commandments of the Lord, which he commanded their fathers by the hand of Moses :* and the nations thus spared were afterwards suffered to oppress the Israelites with great severity. (Numb. xxi. 21—35. xxxii. and xxxiv. Deut. ii. 26—37. iii. 1—20. Josh. vi. 21. Judges i. 4.) Nor were they finally subdued until the reigns of David and Solomon, who reduced them to the condition of slaves: the latter employed 153,600 of them in the most servile parts of his work, in building his temple, palace, &c. (2 Sam. v. 6—8. 1 Chron. xi. 4—8. 1 Kings ix. 20. 2 Chron. ii. 17, 18. and viii. 7, 8.)

Besides these devoted nations there were others, either settled in the land at the arrival of the Israelites, or in its immediate environs, with whom the latter had to maintain many severe conflicts: they were six in number.

1. The PHILISTINES were the descendants of Mizraim, the second son of Ham; who, migrating from Caphtor or the north-eastern part of Egypt, very early settled in a small strip of territory along the sea-shore, in the south-west of Canaan, having expelled the Avites, who had before possessed it. (Deut. ii. 23. Amos ix. 7. Jer. xlvii. 4.) The district occupied by the Philistines was in the time of Joshua distinguished into five lordships, denominated, from the chief towns, Gaza, Ashdod, Askelon, Gath, and Ekron. They were the most formidable enemies, perhaps, whom the children of Israel had to encounter: and of the inveteracy of their enmity against the latter, we have abundant evidence in the Sacred Writings. Though they were subdued by David, and kept in subjection by some succeeding monarchs, yet they afterwards became so considerable, that from them the Holy Land was called by the Greeks Palestine, which appellation it retains to this day. The country was finally subdued about the year of the world 3841 (B. C. 159.) by the illustrious general, Judas Maccabæus; and about sixty-five years afterwards Jannæus burnt their city Gaza, and incorporated the remnant of the Philistines with such Jews as he placed in their country.

2. The MIDIANITES were the descendants of Midian, the fourth son of Abraham by Keturah. (Gen. xxv. 2.) In the Scriptures two different places are assigned as the territory of the Midianites: the one almost the north-east point of the Red Sea, where Jethro the father-in-law of Moses was a prince or priest. These western or southern Midianites were also called Cushites, because they occupied the country that originally belonged to Cush. They retained the knowledge of the true God, which appears to have been lost among the eastern or northern Midianites who dwelt on the east of the Dead Sea. (Gen. xxv. 2—6. xxxvii. 28. Exod. ii. iii. xviii.) These northern Midianites were either subject to or allied with the Moabites; and their women were particularly instrumental in seducing the Israelites

to idolatry and other crimes; which wickedness was punished by
Jehovah with the almost total destruction of their nation (Numb. xxii.
4—7. xxv. xxxi. Josh. xiii. 21.); although they afterwards recovered
so much of their former strength as to render the Israelites their tributaries, and for seven years greatly oppressed them. From this bondage,
Gideon delivered his countrymen with a very inferior force, and
almost annihilated the Midianites, whose surviving remnants are supposed to have been incorporated with the Moabites or Ammonites.

3, 4. The MOABITES and AMMONITES were the descendants of the
incestuous offspring of Lot. (Gen. xix. 30—38.) The Moabites dwelt
on the east of the Jordan, in a tract whence they had expelled the
Emims, a gigantic aboriginal race. The Ammonites had their residence north-east of the Moabites, which territory they had wrested
from the Zamzummim, another gigantic tribe. The country occupied
by these two tribes was exceedingly pleasant and fertile; they were
violently hostile to the Israelites, whom they at different times terribly
oppressed. They were conquered by David, and for about 150 years
continued in subjection to the Israelites. On the division of the kingdom they fell to the share of the ten tribes; and after several attempts
to regain their liberty under succeeding kings of Israel, (some of whom
severely chastised them, and imposed heavy tributes upon them,) they
are supposed to have effected their complete liberation during the
unhappy reign of Ahaz.

5. The AMALEKITES were descended from Amalek the son of
Ham, and grandson of Noah, and were very formidable enemies to
the Israelites. They were settled on the south coast westward of
Jordan, and first opposed the Israelites after their departure from
Egypt, but were defeated and doomed to destruction (Exod. xvii.
8—16. Deut. xxv. 17—19.); which was commenced by Saul, and
finished by David.

6. The EDOMITES were the descendants of Esau or Edom: they
possessed themselves of the country southward of Judæa and the Red
Sea, which was originally occupied by the Horites, who are supposed
to have been finally blended with their conquerers. It was a mountainous tract, including the mountains of Seir and Hor, and the provinces of Dedan, Teman, &c. They were governed by dukes or
princes, and afterwards by their own kings. (Gen. xxxvi. 31.) Inveterate foes to Israel, they continued independent until the time of
David, by whom they were subdued and rendered tributary, in completion of Isaac's prophecy, that Jacob should rule Esau. (Gen. xxvii.
29.) The Edomites bore their subjection with great impatience; and,
at the end of Solomon's reign, Hadad the Edomite, who had been
carried into Egypt during his childhood, returned into his own country, where he procured himself to be acknowledged king. (1 Kings xi.
21, 22.) It is probable, however, that he reigned only in the eastern
part of Edom; for that part which lay directly to the south of Judæa
continued subject to the kings of Judah until the reign of Jehoram,
against whom the Edomites rebelled. (2 Chron. xxi. 8—10.) They
were also discomfited by Amaziah king of Judah, who slew one thousand men, and cast ten thousand more from a precipice. But their
conquests were not permanent. When Nebuchadnezzar besieged
Jerusalem, the Edomites joined him, and encouraged him to raze the

very foundations of the city (Ezek. xxv. 12—14. xxxv. 3—5. Obad. 10—16. Psal. cxxxvi. 7. Lam. iv. 21.): but their cruelty did not continue long unpunished. Five years after the capture of Jerusalem, Nebuchadnezzar humbled all the states around Judæa, and particularly the territory of the Edomites.[1]

IV. On the conquest of Canaan by the children of Israel, JOSHUA DIVIDED IT INTO TWELVE PARTS, which the twelve tribes drew by lot, according to their families : so that in this division every tribe and every family received their lot and share by themselves, distinct from all the other tribes. Thus each tribe remained a distinct province, in which all the freeholders were not only Israelites, but of the same tribe, or descendants from the same patriarch : and the several families were placed together in the same neighbourhood, receiving their inheritance in the same part or subdivision of the tribe. Or, each tribe may be said to live together in one and the same county, and each family in one and the same hundred; so that the inhabitants of every neighbourhood were relations to each other, and of the same families. Nor was it permitted that an estate in one tribe should become the property of any person belonging to another tribe.

In order to preserve as nearly as possible the same balance, not only between the tribes, but between the heads of families and the families of the same tribes, it was further provided that every man's possession should be unalienable.

The wisdom of this constitution had provided for a release of all debts and servitudes every seventh year (Deut. xv. 1, 2. 12.), that the Hebrew nation might not moulder away from so great a number of free subjects, and be lost to the public in the condition of slaves. It was moreover provided, by the law of jubilee, which was every fiftieth year, that then all lands should be restored, and the estate of every family, being discharged from all incumbrances, should return to the family again. For this there was an express law. (Lev. xxv. 10.) *Ye shall hallow the fiftieth year, and proclaim liberty throughout all the land, unto all the inhabitants thereof : it shall be a jubilee unto you, and ye shall return every man to his possession, and ye shall return every man unto his family.* It is further enacted, *And the land shall not be sold for ever;* (or, as in the margin, *be quite cut off,* or alienated from the family;) *for the land is mine, for ye are strangers and sojourners with me.*

By this agrarian law of the Hebrews, all estates were to be kept in the same families, as well as the same tribes to which they originally belonged at the first division of the land by Joshua; so that how often soever a man's estate had been sold or alienated from one jubilee to another, or through how many hands soever it had passed, yet in fifty years every estate must return to the heirs of the persons who were originally possessed of it.

It was at first an excellent constitution, considering the design of this government, to make so equal a division of the land among the whole Hebrew nation, according to the poll; it made provision for settling and maintaining a numerous and brave militia of six hundred thou-

---

[1] See an interesting and accurately compiled history of the Edomites in the Biblical Repository, vol. iii. pp. 250—266. Andover, Massachussetts, 1833.

sand men, which, if their force was rightly directed and used, would be a sufficient defence not only against any attempts of their less powerful neighbours to deprive them of their liberty or religion; but, considering, moreover, the natural security of their country, into which no inroads could be made but through very difficult passes, it was a force sufficient to defend them against the more powerful empires of Egypt, Assyria, or Babylon.

The wisdom of this constitution is yet further observable, as it provided against all ambitious designs of private persons, or persons in authority, against the public liberty; for no person in any of the tribes, or throughout the whole Hebrew nation, had such estates and possessions, or were allowed by the constitution to procure them, that could give any hopes of success in oppressing their brethren and fellow-subjects. They had no riches to bribe indigent persons to assist them, nor could there, at any time, be any considerable number of indigent persons to be corrupted. They could have no power to force their fellow-subjects into a tame submission to any of their ambitious views. The power in the hands of so many freeholders in each tribe was so unspeakably superior to any power in the hands of one or of a few men, that it is impossible to conceive how any such ambitious designs should succeed, if any person should have been found so weak as to attempt them. Besides, this equal and moderate provision for every person wisely cut off the means of luxury, with the temptations to it from example. It almost necessarily induced the whole Hebrew nation to be both industrious and frugal, and yet gave to every one such a property, with such an easy state of liberty, that they had sufficient reason to esteem and value them, and endeavour to preserve and maintain them.[1]

In this division of the land into twelve portions the posterity of Ephraim and Manasseh (the two sons of Joseph) had their portions, as distinct tribes, in consequence of Jacob having adopted them. The *northern* parts of the country were allotted to the tribes of Asher, Naphtali, Zebulon, and Issachar; the *middle* parts to that of Ephraim, and one half of the tribe of Manasseh; the *southern* parts to those of Judah, Benjamin, Dan, and Simeon; and the *Country beyond Jordan* (which was first conquered by the Israelites, before the subjugation of the whole land of Canaan,) was allotted to the tribes of Reuben, Gad, and the other half tribe of Manasseh. The tribe of Levi, indeed (which formed in effect a thirteenth tribe), possessed no lands. By divine command there were assigned to the Levites, who were appointed to minister in holy things, without any secular incumbrance, the tenths and first-fruits of the estates of their brethren. Forty-eight cities were appropriated to their residence, thence called Levitical cities: these were dispersed among the twelve tribes, and had their respective suburbs, with land surrounding them. Of these cities the Kohathites received twenty-three, the Gershonites thirteen, and the Merarites twelve; and six of them, three on each side of Jordan[2], were appointed

---

[1] Lowman on the Civil Government of the Hebrews, pp. 46—49.

[2] The cities of refuge on the *eastern* side of Jordan were Bezer, in the tribe of Reuben; Ramoth Gilead, in that of Gad; and Golan, in the half tribe of Manasseh. Those on the *western* side of Jordan were Hebron, in the tribe of Judah; Shechem, in that of Ephraim; and Kadish-Naphtali, in that of Naphtali.

to be Cities of Refuge, whither the inadvertent man-slayer might flee, and find an asylum from his pursuers, and be secured from the effects of private revenge, until cleared by a legal process. (Numb. xxxv. 6—15. Deut. xix. 4—10. Josh. xx. 7, 8.)[1] The way to these cities the Israelites were commanded to make good, so that the man-slayer might flee thither without impediment, and with all imaginable expedition; and, according to the Rabbins, there was an inscription set up at every cross road — " Asylum, Asylum." It has been thought that there is an allusion to this practice in Luke iii. 4—6., where John the Baptist is described *as the voice of one crying in the wilderness, Prepare ye the way of the Lord, make his path straight.* He was the Messiah's forerunner, and in that character was to remove the obstacles to men fleeing to him as their asylum, and obtaining the salvation of God.[2]

It is remarkable that all the sacerdotal cities lay within the southern tribes, eight belonging to Judah and four to Benjamin, and only one to Simeon, which is supposed to have been situated on the frontier of Judah, and to have remained under the control of the latter tribe. This was wisely and providentially designed to guard against the evils of schism between the southern and northern tribes. For by this arrangement all the sacerdotal cities (except one) lay in the faithful tribes of Judah and Benjamin, to maintain the national worship in them, in opposition to the apostasy of the other tribes. Otherwise the kingdom of Judah might have experienced a scarcity of priests, or have been burdened with the maintenance of those who fled from the kingdom of Israel (2 Chron. xi. 13, 14.), when the base and wicked policy of Jeroboam made priests of the lowest of the people to officiate in their room.

Of the country beyond Jordan, which was given by Moses to the tribes of Reuben and Gad, and to the half tribe of Manasseh (Deut. iii. 12—17. Josh. xii. 1—6. xiii.), the tribe of Reuben obtained the southern part, which was bounded on the south from Midian by the river Arnon; on the north, by another small river; on the east, by the Ammonites and Moabites; and on the west, by the river Jordan. Its principal cities were Ashdod-Pizgah, Bethabara, Beth-peor, Bezer, Heshbon, Jahaz, Kedemoth, Medeba, Mephaath, and Midian. The territory of the tribe of Gad was bounded by the river Jordan on the west, by the canton of the half tribe of Manasseh on the north, by the Ammonites on the east, and by the tribe of Reuben on the south. Its chief cities were Betharan (afterwards called Julias), Debir, Jazer, Mahanaim, Mizpeh, Penuel, Rabbah, or Rabboth (afterwards called Philadelphia), Succoth, and Tishbeh. The region allotted to the half tribe of Manasseh, on the eastern side of the Jordan, was bounded on the south by the territory of the tribe of Gad; by the sea of Cinnereth (afterwards called the lake of Gennesareth and the sea of Galilee), and the course of the river Jordan from its source towards that sea, on the west; by Mount Lebanon, or more properly Mount Hermon, on the north and north-east; and by Mount Gilead on the

---

[1] Most of the North American nations had similar places of refuge (either a house or a town), which afforded a safe asylum to a man-slayer, who fled to it from the revenger of blood. Adair's History of the American Indians, pp. 158, 159. 416.

[2] Godwin's Moses and Aaron, p. 78. Jenning's Jewish Antiquities, book ii. ch. 5. p. 295. Edinb. 1808.

east. Its principal cities were Ashtaroth-Carnaim, Auran, Beesh-terah, Bethsaida, Gadara, Gerasa, Geshur, and Jabesh-Gilead. This tribe was greatly indebted to the bravery of Jair, who took *threescore cities*, besides several small towns or villages, which he called Havoth-Jair, or the *Dwellings of Jair.* (1 Chron. ii. 23. Numb. xxxii. 41.) The remaining nine tribes and a half were settled on the western side of the Jordan.

The canton of the tribe of JUDAH was bounded on the east by the Dead Sea; on the west, by the tribes of Dan and Simeon, both of which lay between it and the Mediterranean Sea; on the north, by the canton of the tribe of Benjamin; and on the south, by Kadesh-Barnea, and the Desert of Paran or Zin. Judah was reckoned to be the largest and most populous of all the twelve tribes; and its inha-bitants were the most valiant; it was also the chief and royal tribe, from which, in subsequent times, the whole kingdom was denomi-nated. The most remarkable places or cities in this tribe were Adullam, Azekah, Bethlehem, Bethzor, Debir, or Kiriath-sepher, Emmaus, Engedi, Kiriath-arba or Hebron, Libnah, Makkedah, Maon, Massada, Tekoah, and Ziph.

The inheritance of the tribes of DAN and of SIMEON was within the inheritance of the tribe of Judah, or was taken out of the portion at first allotted to the latter. The boundaries of these two tribes are not precisely ascertained; though they are placed by geographers to the north and south-west of the canton of Judah, and consequently bordered on the Mediterranean Sea. The principal cities in the tribe of Dan, were Ajalon, Dan or Lesham, Eltekeh, Eshtaol, Gath-rimmon, Gibbethon, Hirshemesh, Joppa, Modin, Timnath, and Zorah. The chief cities in the tribe of Simeon were Ain, Beersheba, Hormah, and Ziklag.

The canton allotted to the tribe of BENJAMIN lay between the tribes of Judah and Joseph, contiguous to Samaria on the north, to Judah on the south, and to Dan on the west, which last parted it from the Mediterranean. It did not contain many cities and towns, but this defect was abundantly supplied by its possessing the most considerable, and the metropolis of all, — the city of Jerusalem. The other places of note in this tribe were Anathoth, Beth-el, Gibeah, Gibeon, Gilgal, Hai, Mizpeh, Ophrah, and Jericho.

To the north of the canton of Benjamin lay that allotted to the tribe of EPHRAIM, and that of the other HALF TRIBE OF MANASSEH. The boundaries of these two districts cannot be ascertained with pre-cision. The chief places in Ephraim were Bethoron the Nether and Upper, Gezer, Lydda, Michmash, Naioth, Samaria, Schechem, Shiloh, and Timnath-Serah. After the schism of the ten tribes, the seat of the kingdom of Israel being in Ephraim, this tribe is frequently used to signify the whole kingdom. The chief places in the half tribe of Manasseh were Abel-meholath, Bethabara, Bethshan (afterwards called Scythopolis), Bezek, Endor, Enon, Gath-rimmon, Megiddo, Salim, Ophrah, and Tirzah.

To the north, and more particularly to the north-east of the half tribe of Manasseh, lay the canton of ISSACHAR, which was bordered by the celebrated plain of Jezreel, and its northern boundary was Mount Tabor. The chief cities of Issachar were Aphek, Bethshemesh, Do-than, Kishon, Jezreel, Naim or Nain, Ramoth, and Shunem.

On the north and west of Issachar resided the tribe of ZEBULUN. Its chief places were Bethlehem, Cinnereth or Chinnereth, Gath-hepher, Jokneam, Remmon-Methoar, and Shimroncheron.

The tribe of ASHER was stationed in the district to the north of the half tribe of Manasseh, and west of Zebulun: consequently it was a maritime country. Hence it was said (Judg. v. 17.) that *Asher continued on the sea-shore, and abode in his creeks.* Its northern boundary was Mount Libanus or Lebanon; and on the south it was bounded by Mount Carmel, and the canton of Issachar. Its principal cities were Abdon, Achshaph, Helkath, Mishal, and Rehob. This tribe never possessed the whole extent of district assigned to it, which was to reach to Libanus, to Syria, and Phœnicia, and included the celebrated cities of Tyre and Sidon.

Lastly, the tribe of NAPHTALI or Nephtali occupied that district in the northern part of the land of Canaan, which lay between Mount Lebanon to the north, and the sea of Cinnereth (or Gennesareth) to the south, and between Asher to the west, and the river Jordan to the east. Its chief places were Abel or Abel-Beth-Maachah, Hamoth-dor, Harosheth of the Gentiles, Kedesh, and Kiriathaim.

V. The next remarkable division was made by king SOLOMON, who divided the kingdom, which he had received from his father David, into twelve provinces or districts, each under a peculiar officer. These districts, together with the names of their respective presidents, are enumerated in 1 Kings iv. 7—19. From the produce of these districts every one of these officers was to supply the king with provisions for his household, in his turn, that is, each for one month in the year. The dominions of Solomon extended *from the river unto the land of the Philistines, and unto the border of Egypt: they brought presents, and served Solomon all the days of his life.* (1 Kings iv. 21.) Hence it appears that the Hebrew monarch reigned over all the provinces from the river Euphrates to the land of the Philistines, even to the frontiers of Egypt. The Euphrates was the *eastern* boundary of his dominions; the Philistines were *westward*, on the Mediterranean Sea; and Egypt was on the *south*. Solomon therefore had, as his tributaries, the kingdoms of Syria, Damascus, Moab, and Ammon; and thus he appears to have possessed all the land which God had covenanted with Abraham to give to his posterity.

VI. Under this division the Holy Land continued till after the death of Solomon, when ten tribes revolted from his son Rehoboam, and erected themselves into a separate kingdom under Jeroboam, called the KINGDOM OF ISRAEL. The two other tribes of Benjamin and Judah, continuing faithful to Rehoboam, formed the KINGDOM OF JUDAH. This kingdom comprised all the southern parts of the land, consisting of the allotments of those two tribes, together with so much of the territories of Dan and Simeon as were intermixed with that of Judah: its royal city or metropolis was Jerusalem, in the tribe of Benjamin. The kingdom of Israel included all the northern and middle parts of the land, occupied by the other ten tribes; and its capital was Samaria, in the tribe of Ephraim, situated about thirty miles north-east of Jerusalem. But this division ceased, on the subversion of the kingdom of Israel by Shalmaneser, king of Assyria, after it had subsisted two hundred and fifty-four years.

VII. The Holy Land fell successively into the hands of the Syrian kings, the Greeks, and Romans. IN THE TIME OF JESUS CHRIST it was divided into five separate provinces, viz. Galilee, Samaria, Judæa, Peræa, and Idumæa.

1. GALILEE.—This portion of the Holy Land is very frequently mentioned in the New Testament: its limits seem to have varied at different times. It comprised the country formerly occupied by the tribes of Issachar, Naphtali, and Asher, and by part of the tribe of Dan; and is divided by Josephus into *Upper* and *Lower Galilee.*

Upper Galilee abounded in mountains; and from its vicinity to the cities of Tyre and Sidon, it is called the *Coasts of Tyre and Sidon.* (Mark vii. 31.) The principal city in this region was Cæsarea Philippi; through which the main road lay to Damascus, Tyre, and Sidon.

Lower Galilee was situated in a rich and fertile plain, between the Mediterranean Sea and the lake of Gennesareth: according to Josephus, this district was very populous, containing upwards of two hundred cities and towns. The principal cities of Lower Galilee, mentioned in the New Testament, are Tiberias, Chorazin, Bethsaida, Nazareth, Cana, Capernaum, Nain, Cæsarea of Palestine, and Ptolemais.

Galilee was most honoured by our Saviour's presence. " Hither Joseph and Mary returned with him out of Egypt, and here he resided until his baptism by John (Matt. ii. 22, 23. Luke ii. 39—51. Matt. iii. 13. Luke iii. 21.) Hither he returned after his baptism and temptation (Luke iv. 14.): and, after his entrance on his public ministry, though he often went into other provinces, yet so frequent were his visits to this country, that he was called a Galilean. (Matt. xxvi. 69.) The population of Galilee being very great, our Lord had many opportunities of doing good; and, being out of the power of the priests at Jerusalem, he seems to have preferred it as his abode. To this province our Lord commanded his apostles to come and converse with him after his resurrection (Matt. xxviii. 7. 16.) : and of this country most, if not the whole, of his apostles were natives, whence they are all styled by the angels *men of Galilee.*"[1] (Acts i. 11.)

The Galileans spoke an unpolished and corrupt dialect of the Syriac, compounding and using ע (*ain*) for א (*aleph*), כ (*caph*) for ב (*beth*), ת (*tau*) for ד (*daleth*); and also frequently changed the gutturals.[2] This probably proceeded from their great communication and intermixture with the neighbouring nations. It was this corrupt dialect that led to the detection of Peter as one of Christ's disciples. (Mark xiv. 70.) The Galileans are repeatedly mentioned by Josephus as a turbulent and rebellious people, and upon all occasions ready to

---

[1] Wells's Geography of the Old and New Testament, vol. ii. p. 137.

[2] Dr. Lightfoot, to whom we are indebted for the above remark, has given several instances in Hebrew and English, which are sufficiently amusing. One of these is as follows: A certain woman intended to say before the judge, *My Lord, I had a picture, which they stole ; and it was so great, that if you had been placed in it, your feet would not have touched the ground.* But she so spoiled the business with her pronunciation, that, as the glosser interprets it, her words had this sense:—*Sir, slave, I had a beam, and they stole thee away ; and it was so great, that if they had hung thee on it, thy feet would not have touched the ground.* Lightfoot's Chorographical Century of the Land of Israel, ch. lxxxvii. (Works, vol. ii. p. 79.) See additional examples in Buxtorf's Lexicon Chaldaicum, Talmudicum et Rabbinicum, p. 434.

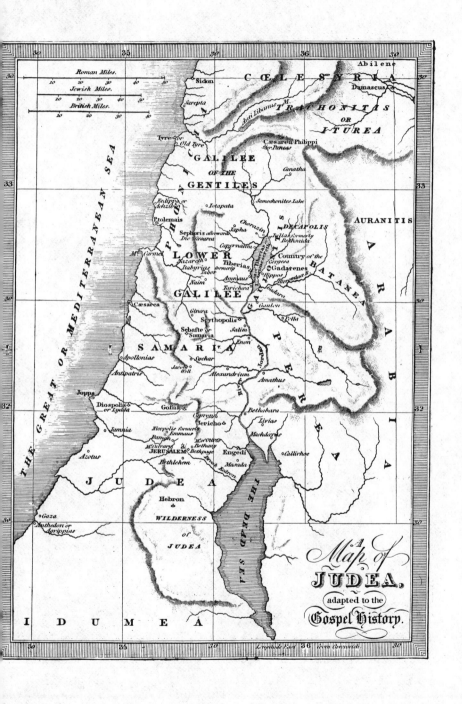

A Map of JUDEA, adapted to the Gospel History.

disturb the Roman authority. They were particularly forward in an insurrection against Pilate himself, who proceeded to a summary mode of punishment, causing a party of them to be treacherously slain, during one of the great festivals, when they came to sacrifice at Jerusalem.[1] This character of the Galileans explains the expression in St. Luke's Gospel (xiii. 1.) *whose blood Pilate mingled with their sacrifices;* and also accounts for his abrupt question, *when he heard of Galilee,* and asked if Jesus *were a Galilean?* (Luke xxiii. 6.) Our Redeemer was accused before him of seditious practices, and of exciting the people to revolt; when, therefore, it was stated, among other things, that he had been in Galilee, Pilate caught at the observation, and enquired if he were a Galilean; having been prejudiced against the inhabitants of that district by their frequent commotions, and being on this account the more ready to receive any charge which might be brought against any one of that obnoxious community.[2]

Galilee of the Nations, or *of the Gentiles,* mentioned in Isa. ix. 1. and Matt. iv. 15., is by some commentators supposed to be Upper Galilee, either because it bordered on Tyre and Sidon, or because the Phœnicians, Syrians, Arabs, &c. were to be found among its inhabitants. Others, however, with better reason, suppose, that the *whole* of Galilee is intended, and is so called, because it lay adjacent to idolatrous nations.[3]

2. SAMARIA. — The division of the Holy Land, thus denominated, derives its name from the city of Samaria, and comprises the tract of country which was originally occupied by the two tribes of Ephraim and Manasseh within Jordan, lying exactly in the middle between Judæa and Galilee; so that it was absolutely necessary for persons who were desirous of going expeditiously from Galilee to Jerusalem to pass through this country. This sufficiently explains the remark of St. John, (iv. 4.) which is strikingly confirmed by Josephus.[4] The three chief places of this district, noticed in the Scriptures, are Samaria, Sichem, or Schechem, and Antipatris.

3. JUDÆA. — Of the various districts into which Palestine was divided, Judæa was the most distinguished. It comprised the territories which had formerly belonged to the tribes of Judah, Benjamin, Simeon, and to part of the tribe of Dan; being nearly co-extensive with the antient kingdom of Judah. Its metropolis was JERUSALEM; and of the other towns or villages of note contained in this region, the most remarkable were Arimathea, Azotus or Ashdod, Bethany, Bethlehem, Bethphage, Emmaus, Ephraim, Gaza, Jericho, Joppa, Lydda, and Rama.

4. The district of PERÆA comprised the six cantons of Abilene, Trachonitis, Ituræa, Gaulonitis, Batanæa, and Peræa, strictly so called, to which some geographers have added Decapolis.

(1.) ABILENE was the most northern of these provinces, being

---

[1] Josephus, Antiq. book xviii. c. 3. § 2. and Mr. Whiston's note there. In another place (book xvii. c. 10. § 2.), after describing a popular tumult, he says, *A great number of these were* GALILEANS *and Idumæans.*

[2] Gilly's Spirit of the Gospel, or the Four Evangelists elucidated, p. 328.

[3] Kuinöel in loc. Robinson's Greek and English Lexicon to the New Testament, *voce* Γαλιλαια.

[4] Antiq. book xx. c. 5. § 1. De Bell. Jud. book ii. c. 12. § 3.

situated between the mountains of Libanus and Anti-Libanus, and deriving its name from the city Abila, or Abela. It is supposed to have
been within the borders of the tribe of Naphtali, although it was never
subdued by them. This canton or territory had formerly been governed as a kingdom (βασιλεια) by a certain Lysanias, the son of
Ptolemy and grandson of Mennæus; but he was put to death B.C. 36,
through the intrigues of Cleopatra, who took possession of his province.
After her death it fell to Augustus, who hired it out to one Tenodorus;
but, as he suffered the country to be infested with robbers, the province
was taken from him and given to Herod, misnamed the great, on whose
death part of the territory was given to Philip. But the greater part,
with the city Abila, seems then, or afterwards, to have been bestowed
on another Lysanias, a descendant (as it appears) of the former, with
the title of Tetrarch. (Luke iii. 1.)   The emperor Claudius afterwards
made a present of this district to king Agrippa, or at least confirmed
him in the possession of it.[1]

(2.) TRACHONITIS was bounded by the Desert Arabia on the east,
Batanæa on the west, Ituræa on the south, and the country of Damascus on the north. It abounded with rocks, which afforded shelter
to numerous thieves and robbers.

(3.) ITURÆA antiently belonged to the half tribe of Manasseh, who
settled on the east of Jordan: it stood to the east of Batanæa, and to
the south of Trachonitis. Of these two cantons Philip the son of
Herod the Great was tetrarch at the time John the Baptist commenced
his ministry. (Luke iii. 1.)   It derived its name from Jetur the son of
Ishmael (1 Chron. i. 31.), and was also called Auranitis, from the city
of Hauran. (Ezek. xlvii. 16. 18.)   This region exhibits vestiges of its
former fertility, and is most beautifully wooded and picturesque.[2] The
Ituræans are said to have been skilful archers and dexterous robbers.

(4.) GAULONITIS was a tract on the east side of the lake of Gennesareth and the river Jordan, which derived its name from Gaulan
or Golan, the city of Og, king of Bashan. (Josh. xx. 8.)   This canton
is not mentioned in the New Testament.

(5.) BATANÆA, the antient kingdom of Bashan, was situated to the
north-east of Gaulonitis, and was celebrated for its excellent breed of
cattle, its rich pastures, and for its stately oaks: the precise limits of
this district are not easy to be defined.   A part of it is now called the
Belka, and affords the finest pasturage, being every where shaded with
groves of noble oaks and pistachio trees.   It was part of the territory
given to Herod Antipas, and is not noticed in the New Testament.

(6.) PERÆA, in its restricted sense, includes the southern part of
the country beyond Jordan, lying south of Ituræa, east of Judæa and
Samaria; and was antiently possessed by the two tribes of Reuben
and Gad. Its principal place was the strong fortress of Machærus,
erected for the purpose of checking the predatory incursions of the
Arabs.   This fortress, though not specified by name in the New

---

[1] Josephus, Ant. Jud. lib. xiv. c. 13. xv. c. 4. xix. c. 5.   Bell. Jud. lib. i. c. 13.   Robinson's Lexicon, cvii. 'Αβιλήνη.
[2] Buckingham's Travels in Palestine, pp. 408, 409. London, 1821. 4to. Mr. Burckhardt,
who visited this region in the years 1810 and 1812, has described its present state, together
with the various antiquities which still remain.   See his Travels in Syria and the Holy Land,
pp. 51—119. 211—310. London, 1822. 4to.

Testament, is memorable as the place where John the Baptist was put to death. (Matt. xiv. 3—12.)

(7.) The canton of DECAPOLIS (Matt. iv. 25. Mark v. 20. and vii. 31.), which derives its name from the ten cities it contained, is considered by Reland and other eminent authorities as part of the region of Peræa. Concerning its limits, and the names of its ten cities, geographers are by no means agreed; but, according to Josephus (whose intimate knowledge of the country constitutes him an unexceptionable authority), it contained the cities of Damascus, Otopos, Philadelphia, Raphana, Scythopolis (the capital of the district), Gadara, Hippos, Dios, Pella, and Gerasa.

5. IDUMÆA. — This province was added by the Romans, on their conquest of Palestine. It comprised the extreme southern part of Judæa, together with some small part of Arabia.[1] During the Babylonish captivity, being left destitute of inhabitants, or not sufficiently inhabited by its natives, it seems to have been seized by the neighbouring Idumæans; and though they were afterwards subjugated by the powerful arms of the Maccabees and Asmonæan princes, and embraced Judaism, yet the tract of country, of which they had thus possessed themselves, continued to retain the appellation of Idumæa in the time of Christ, and, indeed, for a considerable subsequent period. Ultimately, the Idumæans became mingled with the Ishmaelites, and they were jointly called Nabathæans, from Nebaioth, a son of Ishmael.[2]

VIII. Of the whole country thus described, JERUSALEM was the metropolis during the reigns of David and Solomon: after the secession of the ten tribes, it was the capital of the kingdom of Judah, but during the time of Christ and until the subversion of the Jewish polity, it was the metropolis of Palestine.

1. Jerusalem is frequently styled in the Scriptures the *Holy City*, (Isa. xlviii. 2. Dan. ix. 24. Nehem. xi. 1. Matt. iv. 5. Rev. xi. 2.) because *the Lord chose it out of all the tribes of Israel to place his name there*, his temple and his worship (Deut. xii. 5. xiv. 23. xvi. 2. xxvi. 2.); and to be the centre of union in religion and government for all the tribes of the commonwealth of Israel. It is held in the highest veneration by Christians for the miraculous and important transactions which happened there, and also by the Mohammedans, who to this day never call it by any other appellation than *El-Kods*[3], or *El Khoudes*, that is, The Holy, sometimes adding the epithet *Al-Sherif*, or The Noble. The most antient name of the city was *Salem*, or Peace (Gen. xiv. 18.): the import of Jerusalem is, the *vision* or *inheritance of peace*[4]; and to this it is not improbable that our Saviour alluded in his beautiful and pathetic

[1] For a copious and interesting illustration of the fulfilment of prophecy concerning Idumæa, from the statements of modern travellers, see Dr. Keith's Evidence of the Truth of the Christian Religion from Prophecy, pp. 172—220.

[2] Besides the authorities incidentally cited in the preceding pages, the following works have been consulted for this chapter, viz. Relandi Palæstina, tom. i. pp. 1—204. (Traj. ad Rhen. 1714); Antient Universal History, vol. ii. pp. 452—465. 476—486. (Lond. 1748); Pritii Introductio ad Lectionem Novi Testamenti, pp. 497—518.; Beausobre's and L'Enfant's Introduction to the New Testament (Bp. Watson's Collection of Theological Tracts, vol. iii. pp. 262—278.); Pareau, Antiquitas Hebraica breviter descripta, pp. 44—52.; Spanhemii Introductio ad Geographiam Sacram, pp. 1—81.

[3] This is a contraction from *Medinet-el-*KADESS, that is, the *Sacred City*. Capt. Light's Travels in Egypt, Nubia, &c. p. 177. Burckhardt in his map terms Jerusalem *Khodess*.

[4] Relandi Palæstina, tom. ii. p. 833. Schulzii Archæologia Biblica, p. 20.

lamentation over the city. (Luke xix. 41.) It was also formerly called *Jebus* from one of the sons of Canaan. (Josh. xviii. 28.) After its capture by Joshua (Josh. x.) it was jointly inhabited both by Jews and Jebusites (Josh. xv. 63.) for about five hundred years, until the time of David ; who having expelled the Jebusites, made it his residence (2 Sam. v. 6—9.), and erected a noble palace there, together with several other magnificent buildings, whence it is sometimes styled the *City of David* (1 Chron. xi. 5.).[1] By the prophet Isaiah (xxix. 1.) Jerusalem is termed *Ariel*, or the Lion of God ; but the reason of this name, and its meaning, as applied to Jerusalem, is very obscure and doubtful. It *may* possibly signify the strength of the place, by which the inhabitants were enabled to resist and overcome their enemies[2] ; in the same manner as the Persians term one of their cities *Shiráz*, or the *Devouring Lion*. Being situated on the confines of the two tribes of Benjamin and Judah, Jerusalem sometimes formed a part of the one, and sometimes of the other ; but, after Jehovah had appointed it to be the place of his habitation and temple, it was considered as the metropolis of the Jewish nation, and the *common property* of the children of Israel. On this account it was, that the houses were not let, and all strangers of the Jewish nation had the liberty of lodging there gratis, by right of hospitality. To this custom our Lord probably alludes in Matt. xxvi. 18. and the parallel passages.[3]

2. The name of the whole mountain, on the several hills and hollows of which the city stood, was called MORIAH, or *Vision ;* because it was high land, and could be seen afar off, especially from the south (Gen. xxii. 2—4.) ; but afterwards that name was appropriated to the most elevated part on which the temple was erected, and where Jehovah appeared to David. (2 Chron. iii. 1. 2 Sam. xxiv. 16, 17.) This mountain is a rocky limestone hill, steep of ascent on every side, except the north ; and is surrounded on the other sides by a group of hills, in the form of an amphitheatre (Psal. cxxv. 2.), which situation rendered it secure from the earthquakes that appear to have been frequent in the Holy Land (Psal. xlvi. 2, 3.), and have furnished the prophets with many elegant allusions. On the east, stands the MOUNT OF OLIVES, fronting the temple, of which it commanded a noble prospect, (Matt. xxiv. 2, 3. Luke xix. 37—41.) as it does to this day of the whole city, over whose streets and walls the eye roves as if in the survey of a model. This mountain, which is frequently noticed in the evangelical history, stretches from north to south, and is about a mile in length. The olive is still found growing in patches at the foot of this mountain, to which it gives its name. About half way up this mountain is a ruined monastery, built on the spot where we have every reason to conclude that Jesus Christ sat, when he beheld the city and wept over its impending miseries, when he delivered his prediction concerning the downfall of Jerusalem (Luke xix. 41—44.) ; and the army of Titus encamped upon the very spot where its destruction had been foretold.[4] The panoramic view from the Mount of Olives is truly

---

[1] Beausobre and L'Enfant, in Bp. Watson's Tracts, vol. iii. p. 142.
[2] Bp. Lowth, on Isaiah, vol. ii. p. 206.
[3] Schulzii Archæologia Biblica, p. 21. Beausobre and L'Enfant, in Bp. Watson's Tracts, vol. iii. p. 143.
[4] Josephus, de Bell. Jud. lib. vi. c. 5. " It is not difficult to conceive,"—says the Rev.

magnificent. While its summit commands a view extending as far as the Dead Sea, and the mountains beyond Jordan, the whole city lies before it so completely exposed to view, that the eye of the beholder can *walk about Zion, and go round about her, tell the towers thereof and mark well her bulwarks.* (Psal. xlviii. 12, 13.) Dr. Clarke discovered some Pagan remains on this mountain; and at its foot he visited an olive ground always noticed as the garden of Gethsemane. " This place," says he, " is, not without reason, shown as the scene of our Saviour's agony the night before his crucifixion (Matt. xxvi. Mark xiv. Luke xxii. John xviii.), both from the circumstance of the name it still retains, and its situation with regard to the city." Here he found a grove of olives of immense size covered with fruit, almost in a mature state.[1] Between Olivet and the city lies the deep valley of Kedron, through which flows the brook of that name which is noticed in a subsequent page.

On the south side stood the MOUNT OF CORRUPTION, where Solomon, in his declining years, built temples to Moloch, Chemosh, and Ashtaroth (1 Kings xi. 7. 2 Kings xxiii. 13.): it was separated from the city by the narrow valley of Hinnom (Josh. xviii. 16.   Jer. xix. 2.), where the Israelites burnt their children in the fire to Moloch (Jer. vii. 31. and xxxii. 35.): thence made the emblem of hell, GEHENNA, or the place of the damned. (Matt. v. 22. xxiii. 33. Mark ix. 43.)

Towards the north, according to Eusebius and Jerome, and without the walls of the city, agreeably to the law of Moses[2] (Levit. iv.), lay CALVARY or GOLGOTHA, that is, the place of a skull (Matt. xxvii. 33.), so called by some from its fancied resemblance to a skull, but more probably because criminals were executed there.[3] Calvary, which now groans beneath the weight of monastic piles, was probably open ground, cultivated for gardens (John xix. 41.), at the time when He,

---

W. Jowett, who, in December 1823, surveyed Jerusalem from this mountain, —" observing from this spot the various undulations and slopes of the ground, that when Mount Zion, Acra, and Mount Moriah, constituted the bulk of the city, with a deep and steep valley surrounding the greater part of it, it must have been considered by the people of that age as nearly impregnable. It stands *beautiful for situation !* It is, indeed, *builded* as a city that is compact together. (Ps. cxxii. 3.) *The Kings of the earth, and all the inhabitants of the world would not have believed, that the adversary and the enemy should have entered into the Gates of Jerusalem.* (Lam. iv. 12. B.C. 588.) This was said nearly two thousand four hundred years ago. And when, 650 years after, Titus besieged and took this devoted city, he exclaimed on viewing the vast strength of the place, — ' We have certainly had God for our assistant in this war; and it was no other than God who ejected the Jews out of these fortifications: for what could the hands of men, or any machines do, towards overthrowing these towers?'" Josephus, de Bell. Jud. lib. vi. c. 9. (Jowett's Christian Researches in Syria, &c. p. 256. London, 1825. 8vo.)

[1] Dr. Clarke's Travels, vol. iv. pp. 355. 365, 366. 8vo. edit.   In 1818, however, the gardens of Gethsemane were of a miserable description, surrounded with a dry stone fence, and provided with a few olive trees, without either pot-herbs or vegetables of any kind. Richardson's Travels along the Mediterranean and Parts adjacent, in 1816-17-18. vol. ii. p. 366. London, 1822. 8vo. Mr. Carne, who visited Palestine a few years later, describes this spot as being " of all gardens the most interesting and hallowed, but how neglected and decayed ! It is surrounded by a kind of low hedge, but the soil is bare; no verdure grows on it, save six fine venerable olive trees, which have stood here for many centuries." Letters from the East, p. 290.

[2] To this St. Paul delicately alludes in his Epistle to the Hebrews, (xiii. 12, 13.) where he says that Christ, as a sacrifice for sin, *suffered without the gate ;* and when he exhorts the Hebrew Christians *to go forth unto him without the camp,* that is, out of Jerusalem, this city being regarded by the Jews as the camp of Israel. (Bp. Watson's Tracts, vol. iii. p. 156.)

[3] Schulzii Archæologia Biblica, p. 23. Relandi Palæstina, tom. ii. p. 860.

who suffered without the gate (Heb. xiii. 12.), there *poured out his soul unto death*.[1]

The southern quarter, originally "the city of David," built on Mount Zion[2], Josephus calls the *upper city;* and the house of Millo was what he calls the *upper market*.[3]

3. We have no particulars recorded concerning the nature of the fortifications of Jerusalem, previously to the time of the pious and patriotic governor Nehemiah; though such there undoubtedly must have been, from the importance and sanctity of the city, as the metropolis of the country, and the seat of the Jewish worship. After the return of the Jews from the Babylonish captivity, they rebuilt Jerusalem, which had been destroyed by the Chaldæans; and in the account of the rebuilding of the wall, under the direction of Nehemiah, ten gates are distinctly enumerated, viz. three on the south, four on the east, and three on the western side of the wall.

The three gates on the *south* side were, 1. The *Sheep Gate* (Neh. iii. 1.), which was probably so called from the victims, intended for sacrifice, being conducted through it to the second temple. Near this gate stood the towers of Meah and Hananeel. The pool of Bethesda was at no great distance from this gate, which was also called the *Gate of Benjamin.*—2. The *Fish Gate* (Neh. iii. 3. xii. 39.), which was also called the *First Gate.*—3. The *Old Gate*, also called the *Corner Gate.* (Neh. iii. 6. xii. 39. 2 Kings xiv. 13. Jer. xxxi. 38.)

The gates on the *eastern* side were, 1. The *Water Gate* (Neh. iii. 26.), near which the waters of Etam passed, after having been used in the temple service, in their way to the brook Kedron, into which they discharged themselves.—2. The *Horse Gate* (Neh. iii. 28. Jer. xxxi. 40.), which is supposed to have been so called, because horses went through it in order to be watered.—3. The *Prison Gate* (xii. 39.), probably so called from its vicinity to the prison.—4. The Gate *Miphkad.* (Neh. iii. 31.)

The gates on the *western* side were, 1. The *Valley Gate* (Neh. iii. 13.), also termed the *Gate of Ephraim*, above which stood the *Tower of Furnaces* (Neh. iii. 11. xii. 38.); and near it was the *Dragon Well* (Neh. ii. 13.), which may have derived its name from the representation of a dragon, out of whose mouth the stream flowed that issued from the well.— 2. The *Dung Gate* (Neh. iii. 13.), which is supposed

---

[1] Jowett's Christian Researches in Syria, &c. p. 255.

[2] When Dr. Richardson visited this sacred spot in 1818, he found one part of Mount Zion supporting a crop of barley, another was undergoing the labour of the plough; and the soil turned up consisted of stone and lime mixed with earth, such as is usually met with in the foundations of ruined cities. " It is nearly a mile in circumference, is highest on the west side, and towards the east falls down in broad terraces on the upper part of the mountain, and narrow ones on the side, as it slopes down towards the brook Kedron. Each terrace is divided from the one above it by a low wall of dry stone, built of the ruins of this celebrated spot. The terraces near the bottom of the hill are still used as gardens, and are watered from the pool of Siloam. They belong chiefly to the small village of Siloa, immediately opposite. We have here another remarkable instance of the special fulfilment of prophecy : — *Therefore shall Zion for your sakes be plowed as a field, and Jerusalem shall become heaps.* (Micah iii. 12.)" Dr. Richardson's Travels along the Mediterranean, &c. vol. ii. p. 348. " The sides of the Hill of Zion have a pleasing aspect, as they possess a few olive trees and rude gardens; and a crop of corn was growing there." Carne's Letters, p. 265.

[3] Dr. Hales's Analysis of Chronology, vol. i. pp. 425—429. Josephus, de Bell. Jud. lib. v. c. 4.

to have received its name from the filth of the beasts that were sacrificed, being carried from the temple through this gate.—The *Gate of the Fountain* (Neh. iii. 15.), had its name either from its proximity to the fountain of Gihon, or to the spot where the fountain of Siloam took its rise.   We have no account of any gates being erected on the northern side.[1]

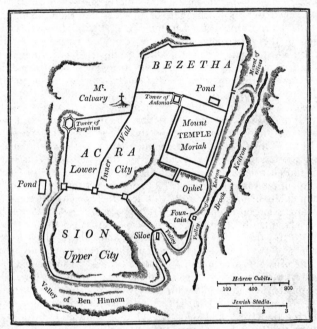

Plan of Jerusalem, in the time of the Romans, from D'Anville.

4. Previously to the fatal war of the Jews with the Romans, we learn from Josephus[2], that the city of Jerusalem was erected on two hills, opposite to one another, with a valley between them, which he subsequently calls the Valley of the Cheesemongers.   The loftiest of these hills contained the *Upper City* (ἡ ἄνω πόλις); and the other called *Acra*, contained the *Lower City* (ἡ κάτω πόλις), which seems to have been the most considerable part of the whole city.   Over against this was a third hill, lower than Acra, and formerly divided from the other by a broad valley[3]; which was filled up with earth during the reign of the Asmonæans or Maccabæan princes, in order to join the city to the temple.   As population increased, and the city crept beyond its old limits, Agrippa joined to it a fourth hill (which was situated to the north of the temple), called Bezetha, and thus still further enlarged Jerusalem.

---

[1] Observationes Philologicæ ac Geographicæ. Amstelædami, 1747. 8vo. pp. 21—29.

[2] De Bell. Jud. lib. vi. c. 6.

[3] Πλατεια φαραγγι διεργομενος ἄλλη προτερον, are the words of Josephus; which Pritius renders *alia lata valle ante divisus* (Introd. ad Nov. Test. p. 522.), "formerly divided by another broad valley."   The rendering above given is that of Mr. Whiston.

c 3

At this time the city was surrounded by three walls on such parts as were not encompassed with impassable valleys, where there was only one wall. The first wall began on the north side, at the tower called Hippicus, whence it extended to the place called the *Xistus*, and to the council-house, and it terminated at the western cloister of the temple. But, proceeding westward, in a contrary direction, the historian says, that it began at the same place, and extended through a place called Bethso, to the gate of the Essenes, then taking a turn towards the south, it reached to the place called Ophlas, where it was joined to the eastern cloister of the temple. The *second* wall commenced at the gate Gennath, and encompassed only the northern quarter of the city, as far as the tower Antonia. The *third* wall began at the tower Hippicus, whence it reached as far as the north quarter of the city, passed by the tower Psephinus, till it came to the monument of Helena, queen of Adiabene. Thence it passed by the sepulchres of the kings; and, taking a direction round the south-west corner, passed the Fuller's monument, and joined the old wall at the valley of Kedron. This third wall was commenced by Agrippa, to defend the newly erected part of the city called Bezetha; but he did not finish it, from apprehension of incurring the displeasure of the emperor Claudius. His intention was to have erected it with stones, twenty cubits in length by ten cubits in breadth; so that no iron tools or engines could make any impression on them. What Agrippa could not accomplish, the Jews subsequently attempted: and, when Jerusalem was besieged by the Romans, this wall was twenty cubits high, above which were battlements of two cubits, and turrets of three cubits, making in all an altitude of twenty-five cubits. Numerous towers, constructed of solid masonry were erected at certain distances: in the third wall, there were ninety; in the middle wall, there were forty; and in the old wall, sixty. The towers of Hippicus, Phasaelus, and Mariamne, erected by Herod the Great, and dedicated to the memories of his friend, his brother, and his wife, were pre-eminent for their height, their massive architecture, their beauty, and the conveniences with which they were furnished. According to Josephus the circumference of Jerusalem, previously to its siege and destruction by the Romans, was thirty-three furlongs, or nearly four miles and a half: and the wall of circumvallation, constructed by order of Titus, he states to have been thirty-nine furlongs, or four miles eight hundred and seventy-five paces.[1] At present, a late traveller states that the circumference of Jerusalem cannot exceed *three* miles.[2]

5. During the time of Jesus Christ, Jerusalem was adorned with numerous edifices, both sacred and civil, some of which are mentioned or alluded to in the New Testament. But its chief glory was the temple, described in a subsequent part of this volume; which magnificent structure occupied the northern and lower top of Sion, as we learn from the Psalmist (xlviii. 2.) ; *Beautiful for situation, the joy* (or *delight*) *of the whole earth, is Mount Sion. On her north side is the city*

---

[1] M. D'Anville has elaborately investigated the extent of Jerusalem, as described by Josephus, in his learned " Dissertation sur l'Etendue de l'ancienne Jerusalem et de son Temple," the accuracy of whose details Viscount Chateaubriand has attested in his Itinerary to and from Jerusalem. This very rare dissertation of D'Anville is reprinted in the Bible de Vence, tom. vi. pp. 43—84. 5th edition.

[2] Jolliffe's Letters from Palestine, p. 103.

of the great king. Next to the temple in point of splendour, was the very superb palace of Herod, which is largely described by Josephus[1]; it afterwards became the residence of the Roman procurators, who for this purpose generally claimed the royal palaces in those provinces which were subject to kings.[2] These dwellings of the Roman procurators in the provinces were called *Prætoria*[3]: Herod's palace therefore was Pilate's prætorium (Matt. xxvii. 27. John xviii. 28.): and in some part of this edifice was the armoury or barracks of the Roman soldiers that garrisoned Jerusalem[4], whither Jesus was conducted and mocked by them. (Matt. xxvii. 27. Mark xv. 16.) In the front of this palace was the tribunal, where Pilate sat in a judicial capacity to hear and determine weighty causes; being a raised pavement of mosaic work (λιθοστρωτον), the evangelist informs us that in the Hebrew language it was on this account termed *Gabbatha* (John xix. 13.), i. e. an elevated place. In this tribunal the procurator Florus sat, A. D. 66; and, in order to punish the Jews for their seditious behaviour, issued orders for his soldiers to plunder the upper market-place in Jerusalem, and to put to death such Jews as they met with; which commands were executed with savage barbarity.[5]

On a steep rock adjoining the north-west corner of the temple stood the *Tower of Antonia,* on the site of a citadel that had been erected by Antiochus Epiphanes[6] in order to annoy the Jews; and which, after being destroyed by them[7], was rebuilt by the Maccabæan prince John Hyrcanus, B. C. 135.[8] Herod the Great repaired it with great splendour, uniting in its interior all the conveniences of a magnificent palace, with ample accommodations for soldiers. This citadel (in which a Roman legion was always quartered) overlooked the two outer courts of the temple, and communicated with its cloisters by means of secret passages, through which the military could descend and quell any tumult that might arise during the great festivals. This was the guard to which Pilate alluded, as already noticed. (Matt. xxvii. 65.) The tower of Antonia was thus named by Herod, in honour of his friend Mark Antony: and this citadel is "the castle" into which St. Paul was conducted (Acts xxi. 34, 35.) and of which mention is made in Acts xxii. 24. As the temple was a fortress that guarded the whole city of Jerusalem, so the tower of Antonia was a fortress that entirely commanded the temple.[9]

Besides the preceding edifices, Josephus mentions a house or palace at the extremity of the upper city, which had been erected by the princes of the Asmonæan family, from whom it was subsequently called the Asmonæan Palace. It appears to have been the residence of the princes of the Herodian family (after the Romans had reduced Judæa into a province of the empire), whenever they went up to Jerusalem. In this palace, Josephus mentions Berenice and Agrippa as residing[10],

---

1 Antiq. Jud. lib. xv. c. 9. § 3.   De Bell. Jud. lib. i. c. 21. § 1. et lib. v. c. 4. § 3.
2 Cicero contra Verrem, action. ii. lib. v. c.12. (op. tom. iv. p. 96. ed. Bipont.)
3 Ibid. lib. v. c. 35. et 41. (tom. iv. pp. 125. 142.
4 Compare Josephus, de Bell. Jud. lib. v. c. 15. § 5. c. 17. § 8.
5 Josephus, de Bell. Jud. lib. ii. c. 14. § 8.
6 Ibid Ant. Jud. lib. xii. c. 5. § 4.   7 Ibid. lib. xiii. c. 6. § 6.
8 Ibid. lib. xv. c. 11. § 4.   9 De Bell. Jud. lib. v. c. 5. § 8.
10 De Bell. Jud. lib. ii. c. 15. § 1. and c. 16. § 3.

and it is not improbable that it was the residence of Herod the tetrarch of Galilee when he went to keep the solemn festivals at that city; and that it was here that our Saviour was exposed to the wanton mockery of the soldiers, who had accompanied Herod thither, either as a guard to his person, or from ostentation. (Luke xxiii. 7—11.)[1]

There were several pools at Jerusalem (κολυμβηθραι), two of which are mentioned in the New Testament, viz.

(1.) The *Pool of Bethesda,* which was situated near the sheep-gate or sheep-market, (John v. 2.) not far from the temple. It had five porticoes, for the reception of the sick; and it was most probably called Bethesda, or the *house of mercy,* from the miraculous cures there mercifully vouchsafed by God to persons labouring under the most desperate diseases.[2]

(2.) The *Pool of Siloam* (John ix. 7.) was twofold, viz. *Upper* and *Lower.* The *Upper* Reservoir or Pool (Isa. vii. 3.), called the King's Pool in Neh. ii. 14., probably watered the king's gardens (Neh. iii. 15.), while the *Lower* Pool seems to have been designed for the use of the inhabitants. Both these reservoirs were supplied from the fountain of Siloam: but which of them is to be understood in John ix. 7., it is now impossible to determine.[3]

6. During the reigns of David and Solomon, Jerusalem was the metropolis of the land of Israel; but, after the defection of the ten tribes under Jeroboam, it was the capital of the kings of Judah, during whose government it underwent various revolutions. It was captured four times without being demolished, viz. by Shishak, sovereign of Egypt (2 Chron. xii.), from whose ravages it never recovered its former splendour; by Antiochus Epiphanes, who treated the Jews with singular barbarity; by Pompey the Great, who rendered the Jews tributary to Rome; and by Herod, with the assistance of a Roman force under Sosius. It was first entirely destroyed by Nebuchadnezzar, and again by the Emperor Titus, the repeated insurrections of the turbulent Jews having filled up the measure of their iniquities, and drawn down upon them the implacable vengeance of the Romans. Titus ineffectually endeavoured to save the temple: it was involved in the same ruin with the rest of the city, and after it had been reduced to ashes, the foundations of that sacred edifice were ploughed up by the Roman soldiers. Thus literally was fulfilled the prediction of our Lord, that not one stone should be left upon another that should not be thrown down. (Matt. xxiv. 2.)[4] On his return to Rome, Titus was honoured with a triumph, and to commemorate his conquest of Judæa, a triumphal arch was erected, which is still in existence. Numerous medals of Judæa vanquished were struck in honour of the same event. The Emperor Adrian erected a city on part of the former site of Jerusalem, which he called Ælia Capitolina: it was

---

[1] Schulzii Archæologia Biblica, pp. 27—30.

[2] Parkhurst's Lexicon voce. Bp. Pearce, (and after him, Dr. Boothroyd,) Jahn, Rosenmüller, Kuinoel, and othern modern commentators, have supposed the pool of Bethesda to have been a medicinal bath. The reader will find a brief statement, and satisfactory refutation of this notion in Dr. Bloomfield's Annotations on the New Testament, vol. iii. pp. 148—156.

[3] Robinson's Gr. Lexicon to the New Test., voce Σιλωαμ.

[4] For a full view of the predictions of Jesus Christ concerning the destruction of Jerusalem and their literal fulfilment, see Vol. I. Appendix, No. VI. pp. 507—515.

afterwards greatly enlarged and beautified by Constantine the Great, who restored its antient name. During that emperor's reign the Jews made various efforts to rebuild their temple; which, however, were always frustrated: nor did better success attend the attempt made, A. D. 363, by the apostate emperor Julian. An earthquake, a whirlwind, and a fiery eruption, compelled the workmen to abandon their design.

From the destruction of Jerusalem by the Romans to the present time, that city has remained, for the most part, in a state of ruin and desolation; "and has never been under the government of the Jews themselves, but oppressed and broken down by a succession of foreign masters — the Romans, the Saracens, the Franks, the Mamelukes, and last by the Turks, to whom it is still subject. It is not, therefore, only in the history of Josephus, and in other antient writers, that we are to look for the accomplishment of our Lord's predictions: — we see them verified at this moment before our eyes, in the desolate state of the once celebrated city and temple of Jerusalem, and in the present condition of the Jewish people, not collected together into any one country, into one political society, and under one form of government, but dispersed over every region of the globe, and every where treated with contumely and scorn."[1]

7. The modern city of Jerusalem contains within its walls several of the hills, on which the antient city is supposed to have stood; but these are only perceptible by the ascent and descent of the streets. When seen from the Mount of Olives, on the other side of the valley of Jehoshaphat, it presents an inclined plane, descending from west to east. An embattled wall, fortified with towers and a Gothic castle, encompasses the city all round, excluding, however, part of Mount Sion, which it formerly inclosed. Notwithstanding its seemingly strong position, it is incapable of sustaining a severe assault, because, on account of the topography of the land, it has no means of preventing the approaches of an enemy; and, on the other hand, it is commanded at the distance of a gun-shot, by the Djebel Tor, or the Mount of Olives, from which it is seen to the best advantage.[2] Imposing, however, as the appearance of Jerusalem is, when viewed from that mountain, — and exhibiting a compactness of structure like that alluded to by the Psalmist (cxxii. 3.) the allusion vanishes on entering the town. No "streets of palaces and walks of state,"—no high-raised arches of triumph—no fountains to cool the air, or porticoes—not a single vestige meets the traveller, to announce its former military greatness or commercial opulence: but in the place of these, he finds himself encompassed by walls of rude masonry, the dull uniformity of which is only broken by the occasional protrusion of a small grated window. All the streets are wretchedness, and the houses of the Jews, more especially, are as dunghills. *From the daughter of Zion, all her beauty is departed.* (Lam. i. 6.) The finest section of the city is that inhabited by the Armenians; in the other quarters, the streets are much narrower, being scarcely wide enough to admit three camels to stand

---

[1] Bp. Porteus's Lectures on the Gospel of Saint Matthew, vol. ii. p. 215.
[2] Travels of Ali Bey, in Morocco, Egypt, Arabia, Syria, &c. between 1803 and 1807, vol. ii. p. 245.

abreast. In the western quarter and in the centre of Jerusalem, towards Calvary, the low and ill-built houses (which have flat terraces or domes on the top, but no chimneys or windows) stand very close together; but in the eastern part, along the brook Kedron, the eye perceives vacant spaces, and amongst the rest that which surrounds the mosque[1] erected by the Khalif Omar, A.D. 637, on the site of the temple, and the nearly deserted spot where once stood the tower of Antonia and the second palace of Herod.

The modern population of Jerusalem is variously estimated by different travellers. Professor Carlyle, at the commencement of the nineteenth century, computed it at about 15,000; and Capt. Light, who visited Jerusalem in 1814, estimated it at twelve thousand. Mr. Buckingham, who was there in 1816, from the best information he could procure, states, that the *fixed residents* (more than one half of whom are Mohammedans) are about eight thousand: but the continual arrival and departure of strangers make the total number of *persons present* in the city from ten to fifteen thousand generally, according to the season of the year. The proportions which the numbers of persons of different sects bear to each other in this estimate, he found it difficult to ascertain. The Mohammedans are unquestionably the most numerous. Next, in point of numbers, are the Greek Christians, who are chiefly composed of the clergy, and of devotees. The Armenians follow next in order as to numbers, but their body is thought to exceed that of the Greeks in influence and in wealth. Of Europeans there are only the few monks of the *Convento della Terra Santa*, and the Latin pilgrims who occasionally visit them. The Copts, Abyssinians, Nestorians, &c. are scarcely perceptible in the crowd: and even the Jews are more remarkable from the striking peculiarity of their features and dress, than from their numbers as contrasted with other bodies. Mr. Jolliffe, who visited Jerusalem in 1817, states that the highest estimate makes the total number amount to twenty-five thousand. Dr. Richardson, who was at Jerusalem in 1818, computed the population at 20,000 persons; Dr. Scholz, in 1821, at 18,000; and the Rev. Mr. Fisk[2], an Anglo-American Missionary in Palestine, in 1823, at 20,000. The Rev. William Jowett, who was at Jerusalem in December 1823, is of opinion that 15,000 are the utmost which the city would contain in ordinary circumstances, that is, exclusive of the pilgrims, who are crowded into the convents, and fill up many spaces in the convents which are vacant nine months in the year, thus augmenting the population by some few thousands; and he is disposed to estimate the resident population at 12,000.

Upon the whole, it does not appear that the number of the *ordinary* inhabitants of Jerusalem can be rated higher than from 12 to 14,000. This is, indeed, a very slender aggregate, compared with the flourishing population which the city once supported; but the numerous

---

[1] In the travels of Ali Bey, (vol. ii. pp. 214—227.) there is a minute description, illustrated with three large plates, of this mosque, or rather group of mosques, erected at different periods of Islamism, and exhibiting the prevailing taste of the various ages when they were severally constructed. This traveller states that they form a very harmonious whole : the edifice is collectively termed, in Arabic, *Al Haram*, or the *Temple*.

[2] Missionary Register for 1824, p. 503.

sieges it has undergone, and the spoliations consequent on them, have left no vestige of its original power. " Jerusalem, under the government of a Turkish aga, is still more unlike Jerusalem, as it existed in the reign of Solomon, than Athens during the administration of Pericles, and Athens under the dominion of the chief of the black eunuchs. We have it upon judgment's record, that *before a marching army, a land has been as the garden of Eden, behind it a desolate wilderness.* (Joel ii. 3.) The present appearance of Judæa has embodied the awful warnings of the prophet in all their terrible reality."[1]

IX. LATER DIVISIONS OF PALESTINE.

1. UNDER THE ROMANS, Palestine was dependent on the government of Syria; and, about the commencement of the fifth century, was divided into three parts; viz.

(1.) *Palæstina Prima* comprised the antient regions of Judæa and Samaria. It contained thirty-five episcopal cities, and its metropolis was Cæsarea-Palæstina. In this division were Jerusalem and Sychar or Neapolis.

(2.) *Palæstina Secunda* included the antient districts of Galilee and Trachonitis. Scythopolis or Bethshan was its capital; and it contained twenty-one episcopal cities.

(3.) *Palæstina Tertia*, or *Salutaris*, comprised the antient Peræa and Idumæa, strictly so called: its metropolis was Petra, and it contained eighteen episcopal cities.[2] Most of these bishoprics were destroyed in the seventh century, when the Saracens or Arabs conquered Palestine or Syria.

2. IN THE TIME OF THE CRUSADES, after the Latins had conquered Jerusalem from the Saracens, they established a patriarch of their own communion in that city, and gave him three suffragan bishops, whose sees were at Bethlehem, Hebron, and Lydda. They also re-established the antient capitals, viz. Cæsarea, with a suffragan bishop at Sebaste or Samaria; Scythopolis, and afterwards Nazareth, with a suffragan bishop at Tiberias; Petra, with a suffragan bishop at Mount Sinai; and for Bostra, the suffragan-episcopal sees were established at Ptolemais or Acre, Seyde or Sidon, and Beyroot or Berytus in the northern part of Phœnicia.

3. MODERN DIVISIONS of Palestine under the Turkish government.

At present, Palestine does not form a distinct country. The Turks include it in Sham or Syria, and have divided it into pachaliks or governments. "That of Acre or Akka extends from Djebail nearly to Jaffa; that of Gaza comprehends Jaffa and the adjacent plains; and, these two being now united, all the coast is under the jurisdiction of the pacha of Acre. Jerusalem, Hebron, Nablous, Tiberias, and, in

---

1 Jolliffe's Letters from Palestine, written in 1817, Lond. 1820, 8vo. p. 102. The sketch of the modern state of Jerusalem, above given, has been drawn up, from a careful comparison of this intelligent writer's remarks, with the observations of Professor Carlyle (Walpole's Memoirs, p. 187.); of M. Chateaubriand, made in 1806 (Travels, vol. ii. pp. 53. 83, 84. 179, 180.), of Ali Bey, made in 1803—1807 (Travels, vol. ii. pp. 240—245.), of Capt. Light, made in 1814 (Travels in Egypt, &c. pp. 178—187.): and of Mr. Buckingham, made in 1816 (Travels in Palestine, pp. 260—262.). See also Dr. Richardson's Travels along the Mediterranean, &c. vol. ii. pp. 238—368.; Jowett's Christian Researches in Syria, pp. 238. 290., and Mr. Carne's Letters from the East, p. 62.

2 Relandi Palæstina, tom. i. pp. 204—214.

3 Abrégé de la Geographie Sacrée, p. 41, (Paris, 1827. 12mo.)

fact, the greater part of Palestine, are included in the pachalik of Damascus, now held in conjunction with that of Aleppo, which renders the present pacha, in effect, the viceroy of Syria. Though both pachas continue to be dutiful subjects of the grand seignior in appearance, they are to be considered as tributaries rather than as subjects of the Porte; and it is supposed to be the religious supremacy of the sultan, as caliph and vicar of Mohammed, more than any apprehension of his power, which prevents them from declaring themselves independent." [1]

Mount Tabor, as seen from the Plain of Esdraelon.

CHAPTER II.

PHYSICAL GEOGRAPHY OF THE HOLY LAND.

SECTION I.

CLIMATE, SEASONS, AND PHYSICAL APPEARANCE OF THE COUNTRY.

I. *Climate.* — II. *Seasons.* — 1. *Seed Time.* — 2. *Winter.* — 3. *The Cold Season, or Winter Solstice.* — 4. *Harvest.* — 5. *Summer.* — 6. *The Hot Season.* — *Heavy Dews.* — *Winds.* — III. *Rivers and Lakes.* — IV. *Wells and Fountains.* — *Cisterns, and Pools of Solomon.* — V. *Mountains.* — VI. *Vallies.* — VII. *Caves.* — VIII. *Plains.* — IX. *Deserts.* — *Horrors and Dangers of travelling in the Great Desert of Arabia.*[2]

I. THE surface of the Holy Land being diversified with mountains and plains, its CLIMATE varies in different places; though in general it is more settled than in our westerly countries. From Tripoli to Sidon, the country is much colder than the rest of the coast further to the north and to the south, and its seasons are less regular. The

---

[1] Modern Traveller: — Palestine, p. 6. In the Abrégé de la Geographie Sacrée (pp. 42—44.) there is an account of the Turkish Divisions of Palestine, professing to be drawn from a Turkish treatise printed at Constantinople, and somewhat different from the divisions above noticed; which have been preferably adopted, because they exhibit the actual government of Palestine, as described by the most recent travellers.

[2] Besides the researches of modern travellers and the other authorities, cited for particular facts, the following treatises have been consulted for the present section, viz. Relandi Palestina, tom. i. pp. 234—379.; Jahn, et Ackermann, Archæologia Biblica, §§ 14—21.; Schulzii Archæologia Hebraica, pp. 4—9; Pareau, Antiquitas Hebraica, pp. 57—64.; and Alber, Hermeneutica Sacra, tom. i. pp. 64—72.

same remark applies to the mountainous parts of Judæa, where the vegetable productions are much later than on the sea-coast or in the vicinity of Gaza. From its lofty situation, the air of Saphet in Galilee is so fresh and cool, that the heats are scarcely felt there during the summer; though in the neighbouring country, particularly at the foot of Mount Tabor and in the plain of Jericho, the heat is intense.[1] Generally speaking, however, the atmosphere is mild: the summers are commonly dry, and extremely hot[2] : intensely hot days, however, are frequently succeeded by intensely cold nights; and these sudden vicissitudes, which an Arab constitution alone can endure, together with their consequent effects on the human frame, verify the words of the patriarch Jacob to his father-in-law, *that in the day the drought consumed him, and the frost by night.* (Gen. xxxi. 40.)[3]

II. Six several SEASONS of the natural year are indicated in Gen. viii. 22. viz. *seed-time* and *harvest, cold* and *heat, summer* and *winter;* and as agriculture constituted the principal employment of the Jews, we are informed by the rabbinical writers, that they adopted the same division of seasons, with reference to their rural work.[4] These divisions also exist among the Arabs to this day.[5] A brief statement of the natural phenomena occurring in these several seasons, will enable us to form a tolerably correct idea of the climate and weather of the Holy Land.

1. SEED-TIME, by the rabbins termed זרע (zerô), comprised the latter half of the Jewish month Tisri, the whole of Marchesvan, and the former half of Kisleu or Chisleu, that is, from the beginning of October to the beginning of December. During this season the weather is various, very often misty, cloudy, with mizzling or pouring rain. Towards the close of October or early in November, the *former* or early autumnal rains begin to fall; when they usually ploughed their land, and sowed their wheat and barley, and gathered the latter grapes. The rains last for three or four days; they do not fall without intermission, but in frequent showers. The air at this season is frequently warm, sometimes even hot; but is much refreshed by cold in the night, which is so intense as to freeze the very heavy dews that fall. Towards the close it becomes cooler, and at the end of it snow begins to fall upon the mountains. The channels of the rivulets are sometimes dry, and even the large rivers do not contain much water. In the latter part of November the leaves lose their foliage. Towards the end of that month the more delicate light their fires (Jer. xxxvi. 22.),

---

[1] Harmer's Observations, vol. i. pp. 2—4. London, 1808.

[2] Of the intensity of the heat in Palestine, during the summer, some idea may be formed, when it is known that the mercury of Dr. E. D. Clarke's thermometer, *in a subterraneous recess perfectly shaded* (the scale being placed so as not to touch the rock), remained at *one hundred* degrees of Fahrenheit. Travels, vol. iv. p. 190. 8vo. edit.

[3] The same vicissitudes of temperature exist to this day at Smyrna (Emerson's Letters from the Ægean, vol. i. p. 94.), also in the Desert of Arabia (Capt. Keppel's Narrative of a Journey from India to England, vol. i. p. 140. London, 1827. 8vo.) in the Desert between Damascus and the ruins of Palmyra (Carne's Letters from the East, p. 585.), in Persia (Morier's Second Journey, p. 97. London, 1818, 4to.), and in Egypt. (Capt. Light's Travels, p. 20.; Dr. Richardson's Travels along the Mediterranean, &c. vol. i. pp. 181, 182. London, 1822. 8vo.) Harmer has collected several testimonies to the same effect, from the earlier travellers in the East. Observations on Scripture, vol. i. pp. 61—65. London, 1808.

[4] Bava Metsia, fol. 106. cited by Dr. Lightfoot, in his Hebrew and Talmudical Exercitations on John iv. 36. (Works, vol. ii. p. 543.)

[5] See Golius's Lexicon Arabicum, col. 934.

which they continue, almost to the month of April; while others pass the whole winter without fire.

2. WINTER, by the rabbins termed חוֹרֶף (CHOReP), included the latter half of Chisleu, the whole of Tebeth, and the former part of Sebat, that is, from the beginning of December to the beginning of February. In the commencement of this season, snows rarely fall, except on the mountains, but they seldom continue a whole day; the ice is thin, and melts as soon as the sun ascends above the horizon. As the season advances, the north wind and the cold, especially on the lofty mountains, which are now covered with snow, is intensely severe, and sometimes even fatal: the cold is frequently so piercing, that persons born in our climate can scarcely endure it. The roads become slippery, and travelling becomes both laborious and dangerous, especially in the steep mountain-paths (Jer. xiii. 16. xxiii. 12.); and on this account our Lord, when predicting the calamities that were to attend the siege at Jerusalem, told his disciples to pray that their *flight might not be in the winter.* (Matt. xxiv. 20.) The cold, however, varies in severity according to the local situation of the country. On high mountains (as we have just remarked) it is extreme; but in the plain of Jericho it is scarcely felt, the winter there resembling spring; yet, in the vicinity of Jerusalem, the vicissitudes of a winter in Palestine were experienced by the crusaders at the close of the twelfth century, in all its horrors. Many persons of both sexes perished in consequence of want of food, the intenseness of the cold, and the heaviness of the rains, which kept them wet for four successive days. The ground was alternately deluged with rain, or encrusted with ice, or loaded with snow; the beasts of burden were carried away by the sudden torrents, that descended (as they still do) from the mountains, and filled the rivers, or sank into the boggy ground. So vehement were the rains, storms of hail, and winds, as to tear up the stakes of the tents, and carry them to a distance. The extremity of the cold and wet killed the horses, and spoiled their provisions.[1]

The hail-stones which fall during the severity of the winter season are very large, and sometimes fatal to man and beast. Such was the storm of hail that discomfited the Amorites (Josh. x. 10.); and such also the *very grievous hail* that destroyed the cattle of the Egyptians. (Exod. ix. 18. 23, 24.) A similar hail-storm fell upon the British fleet in Marmorice Bay, in Asiatic Turkey, in the year 1801[2], which affords a fine comment on that expression of the psalmist, *He casteth forth his* ICE *like morsels; who can stand before his cold?* (Psal. cxlvii. 17.) The snow, which falls in Judæa, is by the same elegant inspired writer compared to wool (Psal. cxlvii. 16.); and we are informed that in countries,

---

[1] Harmer's Observations, vol. i. pp. 36—42.

[2] " On the 8th of February commenced the most violent thunder and hail storm ever remembered, and which continued two days and nights intermittingly. The hail, or rather the *ice-stones*, were as big as large walnuts. The camps were deluged with a torrent of them two feet deep, which, pouring from the mountains, swept everything before it. The scene of confusion on shore, by the horses breaking loose, and the men being unable to face the storm, or remain still in the freezing deluge, surpasses description. It is not in the power of language to convey an adequate idea of such a tempest." Sir Robert Wilson's History of the British Expedition to Egypt, vol. i. p. 8. 8vo. edit. Hail-storms are so violent in some parts of Persia, as frequently to destroy the cattle in the fields. Kinneir's Geographical Memoir, p. 158.

which are at no great distance from Palestine, the snow falls in flakes as large as walnuts: but not being very hard or very compact, it does no injury to the traveller whom it covers.[1]

But, however severe the cold weather sometimes is in these countries, there are intervals even in the depth of winter when the sun shines and there is no wind, and when it is perfectly warm—sometimes almost hot—in the open air. At such seasons the poorer classes in the East enjoy the conversation of their friends, sauntering about in the air, and sitting under the walls of their dwellings; while the houses of the more opulent inhabitants, having porches or gateways, with benches on each side, the master of the family receives visitors there, and despatches his business—few persons (not even the nearest relations) having further admission except on extraordinary occasions.[2] These circumstances materially illustrate a difficult passage in the prophet Ezekiel (xxxiii. 30.)—*Also, thou son of man, the children of thy people are still talking concerning thee* [3], *by the WALLS AND IN THE DOORS of the houses, and speak one to another, every one to his brother, saying, Come, I pray you, and hear what is the word that cometh forth from the Lord.* It appears from Ezek. xxxiii. 21. that these things were transacted in the tenth month, corresponding with the close of our December or the commencement of January. The poorer people, therefore, sat under their walls for the benefit of the sun, while those in better circumstances sat in their porchways or gateways to enjoy its genial rays.[4]

It appears, therefore, that one part of the winter is, by the inhabitants of the East, distinguished from the rest by the severity of the cold, which may be denominated the depth of their winter.

3. The COLD SEASON or Winter Solstice, by the rabbins termed קור (KOR), comprises the latter half of Sebat, the whole of Adar, and the former half of Nisan, from the beginning of February to the beginning of April. At the commencement of this season, the ground is frequently covered with a thick hoar frost, and the weather is cold; but it gradually becomes warm and even hot, particularly in the plain of Jericho. Thunder, lightning, and hail are frequent. Vegetable nature now revives; the almond tree blossoms, and the gardens assume a delightful appearance. Barley is ripe at Jericho, though but little wheat is in the ear. The *latter* rains sometimes begin to fall in the end of this season, swelling the rising crops, with which the vallies are covered.

4. The HARVEST, by the rabbins denominated קציר (KETSIR), includes the latter half of Nisan, the whole of Jyar (or Zif), and the former half of Sivan, that is, from the beginning of April to the beginning of June. In the first fortnight of this season, the *latter rains* are frequent, but cease towards the end of April, when the sky is generally fair and serene. In the plain of Jericho the heat of the sun is ex-

---

[1] Harmer's Observations, vol. i. p. 45. note.

[2] The same usage still obtains at Smyrna. Emerson's Letters from the Ægean, vol. i. pp. 96, 97.

[3] In our authorised version, the proposition בך (BAK) is rendered *against thee*, which is erroneous, as the context shows that the Jews were talking *of* or *concerning* the prophet, and so it is properly rendered in Psal. lxxxvii. 3. *Glorious things are spoken of thee, O city of God.*

[4] Harmer's Observations, vol. i. pp. 50—53.

cessive, though in other parts of Palestine the weather is most delightful ; and on the sea-coast the heat is tempered by morning and evening breezes from the sea.   As the harvest depends on the duration of the rainy season, the *early* or autumnal rains, and the *latter* or spring rains, are absolutely necessary to the support of vegetation, and were consequently objects greatly desired by the Israelites and Jews.[1] These rains, however, were always chilly (Ezra x. 9. and Sol. Song ii. 11.), and often preceded by whirlwinds (2 Kings iii. 16, 17.) that raised such quantities of sand as to darken the sky, or, in the words of the sacred historian, to make *the heavens black with clouds and wind.* (1 Kings xviii. 45.)   In Egypt the barley harvest precedes the summer.   This may explain Jer. viii. 20. where the harvest is put first in the description, — *The harvest is past, the summer is ended, and we are not saved.*[2]

The rains descend in Palestine with great violence ; and as whole villages in the East are constructed only with palm branches, mud, and tiles baked in the sun (perhaps corresponding to and explanatory of the untempered mortar noticed in Ezek. xiii. 11.), these rains not unfrequently dissolve the cement, such as it is, and the houses fall to the ground.   To these effects our Lord probably alludes in Matt. vii. 25—27.   Very small clouds are likewise the forerunners of violent storms and hurricanes in the east as well as in the west: they rise *like a man's hand*, (1 Kings xviii. 44.) until the whole sky becomes black with rain, which descends in torrents, that rush down the steep hills, and sweep every thing before them.[3]   In our Lord's time, this phenomenon seems to have become a certain prognostic of wet weather. *He said to the people, When ye see* THE *cloud* (THN Νεφελην)[4] *rise out of the west, straightway ye say,* There cometh a shower; AND SO IT IS.   (Luke xii. 54.)

5. The SUMMER, by the rabbins termed קַיִץ (KYITS), comprehends the latter half of Sivan, the whole of Thammuz, and the former half of Ab, that is, from the beginning of June to the beginning of August.   The heat of the weather increases, and the nights are so warm that the inhabitants sleep on their house-tops in the open air.

6. The HOT SEASON, by the rabbins called חוֹם (CHUM), or the

---

[1] The following are a few among the many allusions in the Scripture to the importance of the early and latter rains, and the earnestness with which they were desired. Deut. xi. 14. Job xxix. 23.   Prov. xvi. 15.   Jer. iii. 3. v. 24.   Hos. vi. 3.   Joel ii. 23.   Zech. x. 1. " From these bountiful showers of heaven, indeed, the fertility of every land springs : but how dreadful in this country would be such a three years' drought, as was inflicted upon Israel in the days of Ahab, may easily be conceived, when it is remembered that in summer the richest soil is burnt to dust ; so that a traveller, riding through the plain of Esdraelon in July or August, would imagine himself to be crossing a desert." (Jowett's Christian Researches in Syria, p. 306. London, 1825. 8vo.)

[2] Jowett's Christian Researches in the Mediterranean, &c. p. 144. London, 1822. 8vo.

[3] A similar phenomenon is noticed by Homer (Iliad, lib. iv. 275—278.) and also takes place in Abyssinia.   Mr. Bruce, speaking of the phenomena attending the inundation of the Nile, says, — Every morning, " about nine, a small cloud, not above four feet broad, appears in the east, whirling violently around, as if upon an axis ; but, arrived near the zenith, it first abates its motion, then loses its form, and extends itself greatly, and seems to call up vapours from all opposite quarters.   These clouds having attained nearly the same height, rush against each other with great violence, and put me always in mind of Elisha foretelling rain on Mount Carmel." Travels, vol. v. p. 336. 8vo.

[4] The article here is unquestionably demonstrative. See Bp. Middleton's Doctrine of the Greek Article, p. 327. (first edit.)

great heat, includes the latter half of Ab, the whole of Elul, and the former half of Tisri, that is, from the beginning of August to the beginning of October. During the chief part of this season the heat is intense, though less so at Jerusalem than in the plain of Jericho: there is no cold, not even in the night, so that travellers pass whole nights in the open air without inconvenience. Lebanon is for the most part free from snow, except in the caverns and defiles where the sun cannot penetrate. During the hot season, it is not uncommon in the East Indies for persons to die suddenly, in consequence of the extreme heat of the solar rays (whence the necessity of being carried in a palanquin). This is now commonly termed a *coup-de-soleil*, or stroke of the sun. The son of the woman of Shunem appears to have died in consequence of a coup-de-soleil (2 Kings iv. 19, 20.)[1]; and to this fatal effect of the solar heat the psalmist alludes (Psal. cxxi. 6.), as he also does to the effect of the lunar rays, which in Arabia (as well as in Egypt) are singularly injurious to the eyes of those who sleep in the open air. "The moon here really strikes and affects the sight when you sleep exposed to it much more than the sun: indeed, the sight of a person, who should sleep with his face exposed at night, would soon be utterly impaired or destroyed."[2]

From the time of harvest, that is, from the middle of April to the middle of September, it neither rains nor thunders. (Prov. xxvi. 1. 1 Sam. xii. 17.) During the latter part of April, or about the middle of the harvest, the *morning cloud* is seen early in the morning, which disappears as the sun ascends above the horizon. (Hos. vi. 4. xiii. 3.) These light fleecy clouds are without water ($\nu\epsilon\phi\epsilon\lambda\alpha\iota$ $\overset{,}{\alpha}\nu\upsilon\delta\rho\sigma\iota$); and to them the apostle Jude (verse 12.) compares the false teachers, who even then began to contaminate the church of Christ. In Deut. xxxii. 2. the doctrine of Jehovah is compared to the rain, and clouds are the instruments by which rain is distilled upon the earth. In arid or parched countries, the very appearance of a cloud is delightful, because it is a token of refreshing showers; but when sudden winds arise, and disperse these clouds, the hope of the husbandman and shepherd is cut off. The false teachers alluded to, are represented as *clouds*; they have the *form* and *office* of teachers of righ-

---

[1] Egmont and Heyman (who travelled in Palestine in the beginning of the eighteenth century), found the air about Jericho extremely hot, and say that it destroyed several persons the year before they were there. The army of King Baldwin IV. suffered considerably from this circumstance near Tiberias. The heat at the time was so unusually great, that as many died by that as by the sword. After the battle, in their return to their former encampment, a certain ecclesiastic, of some distinction in the church and in the army, not being able to bear the vehemence of the heat, was carried in a litter, but expired under Mount Tabor.—Harmer's Observations, vol. i. p. 4.

[2] Carne's Letters from the East, p. 77. A nearly similar account is given by Mr. R. R. Madden, who travelled in the East, between the years 1824 and 1827. Travels in Turkey, &c. vol. ii. pp. 197, 198. The deadly influence of the moon is equally felt in the East and West Indies. Thus, in the East Indies, meat hung up, if exposed to moonlight, will not take the salt, but taints and spoils speedily: whereas the same kind of meat, if kept from the moonlight, will take salt and keep good for some time. (Christian Observer for 1808, p. 754. Roberts's Oriental Illustrations of Scripture, p. 355.) And at Demerara the moon strikes (similarly to the sun) with a *coup-de-lune;* so that people walk out at night with umbrellas or *paralunes.* Such, indeed, are the effects of the lunar rays upon fish, as to make it part from the bones. (From information communicated to the author by the Rev. Mr. Elliott, missionary at Demerara.)

teousness, and from such appearances pure doctrine may naturally be expected. But these are *clouds without water ;* they distil no refreshing showers, because they contain none; and they are *carried about by* their passion, as those light and fleecy clouds in question are carried by the winds.[1]

From the Jewish month Sivan, through the entire months of Tammuz, Ab, and the former part of Elul, corresponding with our months of May, June, July, and August, not a single cloud is to be seen; but during the night, the earth is moistened by a copious DEW, which in the sacred volume is frequently made a symbol of the divine goodness. (Compare Gen. xxvii. 28. and xlix. 25. where the *blessing from above* is equivalent with dew, Deut. xxxii. 2. xxxiii. 13. Job. xxix. 19. Mic. v. 7.) In Arabia Petræa the dews are so heavy, as to wet to the skin those who are exposed to them: but as soon as the sun arises, and the atmosphere becomes a little warmed, the mists are quickly dispersed, and the abundant moisture, which the dews had communicated to the sands, is entirely evaporated. What a forcible description is this of the transiently good impressions, felt by many, to which the prophet Hosea alludes! (vi. 4.) Other references to the refreshing nature of the dews of Palestine occur in Psal. cxxxiii. 3. and Hos. xiv. 5.[2] These dews fall, as in other countries, very fast as well as very suddenly, upon every blade of grass and every spot of earth: whence an active and expeditious soldiery is, in 2 Sam. xvii. 12. by a beautiful figure compared to dew. But, however copious the dews are, they nourish only the more robust or hardy plants; and as the season of heat advances, the grass withers, the flowers fade, every green herb is dried up by the roots and dies, unless watered by the rivulets or by the labour of man.[3] To this appearance of the fields, during an eastern summer, the royal psalmist alludes. (Psal. xxxii. 4.) If, at this season, a single spark falls upon the grass, a conflagration immediately ensues, especially if there should be any briars or thorns, low shrubs, or woods contiguous. (Psal. lxxxiii. 14. Isa. ix. 18. x. 17, 18. Jer. xxi. 14. Compare also Exod. xxii. 6. and Joel i. 19, 20.) The face of the country becomes entirely changed; the fields, so lately clothed with the richest verdure and adorned with the loveliest flowers, are converted into a brown and arid wilderness; *the grass withereth, the flower fadeth* (Isa. xl. 6, 7.)[4]; the fountains and rivulets are dried up; and the soil becomes so hard as to exhibit large fissures or clefts.

---

[1] Dr. A. Clarke, on Jude 12.

[2] Shaw's Travels, vol. ii. p. 325. The very heavy dews which fall in the Holy Land, are noticed by almost every one who has travelled in that country. We shall adduce the testimonies of two or three. Maundrell, travelling near Mount Hermon, in the year 1697, says, " We were instructed by experience, what the Psalmist means by the *dew of Hermon* (Psal. cxxxiii. 3.), *our tents being as wet with it as if it had rained all night.*" (Travels from Aleppo to Jerusalem, p. 77.) Dr. E. D. Clarke, when on his journey from Aboukir to Rosetta, in 1801, says, " We had a tent allotted to us for the night; it was double lined; yet so *copious are the dews of Egypt*" (the climate of which country is similar to that of the Holy Land), " *after sunset, that the water ran copiously down the tent-pole.*" (Travels, vol. iii. p. 365. 8vo.) Mr. Carne says, " The dews had fallen heavily for some nights, and the clothes that covered us were quite wet in the morning." Letters from the East, p. 178.

[3] Harmer's Observations, vol. i. p. 6.

[4] " The very affecting images of Scripture, which compare the short-living existence of man to the decay of the vegetable creation, are scarcely understood in this country. The verdure is perpetual in England. It is difficult to discover a time when it can be said, ' *The grass*

The WINDS which prevail in Palestine, are either land winds or sea breezes. The last are cooler, and commonly bring on rain. (Luke xii. 54, 55.): the east wind on the contrary, which blows from the desert, is hot : and as it ordinarily produces a blight, it becomes fatal to the corn and vines (Job xv. 2. Gen. xli. 6. 23. Ezek. xvii. 10. xix. 12. Hos. xiii. 15. Jonah iv. 8. Psal. ciii. 15, 16.); and is particularly dangerous to navigators in the Mediterranean sea. This is alluded to in Psal. xlviii. 7. and Ezek. xxvii. 26. The people of the East generally term every wind an east wind, that blows between the east and north and the east and south. The Euroclydon, which caused the wreck of the vessel in which Paul was sailing to Rome, was one of these tempestuous east winds, ἄνεμος τυφονικος, that drove every thing before it. (Acts xxvii. 14.) Such winds are common in the Mediterranean to this day, where they are called *Levanters,* the term *Levant* meaning that country which lies at the eastern extremity of that sea.[1] The north-west winds prevail from the autumnal equinox till November; the south-west and west winds from November till February; the east wind usually prevails from February until June, which are succeeded by the north wind.

III. In consequence of the paucity of showers in the East, WATER is an article of great importance to the inhabitants. Hence, in Lot's estimation, it was a principal recommendation of the plain of Jordan that it was *well watered every where* (Gen. xiii. 10.); and the same advantage continued in later ages to be enjoyed by the Israelites, whose country was intersected by numerous brooks and streams; whence it is not more emphatically than beautifully described as a *land of brooks of water, of fountains and depths, that spring out of valleys and hills.* And the same preference is given to this day by the Eelauts (a Tartar tribe occupying a district in the northern part of the Persian empire), who carry their flocks to the highest parts of the mountains, where the blessings of pasturage and of good water are to be found in abundance. The knowledge of this circumstance will, perhaps, impart new force to the promises made to the Gentiles by the evangelical prophet. *Their pastures shall be in all high places, they shall not hunger nor thirst; neither shall the sun or heat smite them; for he that hath mercy on them shall lead them, even by the springs of water shall he guide them.* (Isa. xlix. 9—11.)[2] See also Rev. vii. 16, 17.

Although RIVERS are frequently mentioned in the Sacred Writings, yet, strictly speaking, the only river in the Holy Land is the Jordan, which is sometimes designated in the Scripture as *the river* without any addition; as also is the Nile (Gen. xli. 1. Exod. i. 22. ii. 5. iv. 9. vii. 18. and viii. 3. 9. 11.), and, occasionally, the Euphrates

---

withereth.' But, let the traveller visit the beautiful plain of Smyrna, or any other part of the East, in the month of May, and revisit it towards the end of June, and he will perceive the force and beauty of these allusions. In May, an appearance of fresh verdure and of rich luxuriance every where meets the eye : the face of nature is adorned with a carpet of flowers and herbage, of the most elegant kind. But, a month or six weeks subsequently, how changed is the entire scene! The beauty is gone ; the grass is withered ; the flower is faded ; a brown and dusty desert has taken place of a delicious garden. It is, doubtless, to this rapid transformation of nature that the Scriptures compare the fate of man."— Hartley's Researches in Greece, p. 237.

[1] Shaw's Travels in Barbary, &c. vol. ii. pp. 127—133.
[2] Morier's Second Journey through Persia, p. 121.

(as in Jer. ii. 18.); in these cases, the tenor of the discourse must determine which is the river actually intended by the sacred writers. The name of river is also given to inconsiderable streams and rivulets, as to the Kishon (Judges iv. 7. and v. 21.) and the Arnon. (Deut. iii. 16.) [1]

1. The principal river which waters Palestine is the JORDAN or *Yar-Dan*, i. e. the river of Dan, so called because it takes its rise in the vicinity of the little city of Dan. Its true source is in two fountains at Paneas (a city better known by its subsequent name of Cæsarea Philippi), at the foot of Anti-Libanus; its apparent source flows from beneath a cave at the foot of a precipice, in the sides of which are several niches with Greek inscriptions.[2] During several hours of its course, it continues to be a small and insignificant rivulet.[3] It flows due south through the centre of the country, intersecting the lake Merom and the sea or lake of Galilee, and (it is said) without mingling with its waters; and it loses itself in the lake Asphaltites or the Dead Sea, into which it rolls a considerable volume of deep water, with such rapidity as to prevent a strong, active, and expert swimmer, from swimming across it. The course of the Jordan is about one hundred miles; its breadth and depth are various. Dr. Shaw computed it to be about thirty yards broad, and three yards or nine feet in depth; and states that it discharges daily into the Dead Sea about 6,090,000 tons of water.[4] Viscount Chateaubriand (who travelled nearly a century after him) found the Jordan to be six or seven feet deep close to the shore, and about fifty paces in breadth. The late Count Volney asserts it to be scarcely sixty paces wide at its embouchure. Messrs. Banks and Buckingham, who crossed it in January, 1816, pretty nearly at the same ford over which the Israelites passed on their first entering the promised land, found the stream extremely rapid; and as it flowed at that part over a bed of pebbles, its otherwise turbid waters were tolerably clear, as well as pure and sweet to the taste.[5] It is here fordable, being not more than four feet deep, with a rapid current.[6]

Antiently the Jordan overflowed its banks about the time of barley harvest (Josh. iii. 15. iv. 18. 1 Chron. xii. 15. Jer. xlix. 19.), or the feast of the passover; when, the snows being dissolved on the mountains, the torrents discharged themselves into its channel with great impetuosity. When visited by Mr. Maundrell, at the beginning of the eighteenth century, he could discern no sign or probability of such inundations, though so late as the 30th of March; and so far was the river from overflowing, that it ran almost two yards below the brink of its channel. It may be said to have two banks, — the first, that of the river in its natural state; the second, that of its overflowings. After descending the outermost bank, the traveller proceeds about a furlong upon a level strand, before he comes to the immediate bank of the river. This second bank is now (as it antiently was) so beset with

---

1 In a few instances, the *sea* is called a *river*, as in Hab. iii. 8., where the Red Sea is intended.

2 Capt. Irby's and Mangles' Travels in Egypt, &c. pp. 287—289.

3 Carne's Recollections of Travels in the East, p. 38. London, 1830. 8vo.

4 Shaw's Travels, vol. ii. pp. 156, 157.

5 Buckingham's Travels, p. 315.   6 Three Weeks in Palestine, p. 90.

bushes, reeds, tamarisks, willows, oleanders, and other shrubs and trees, which form an asylum for various wild animals, that no water is perceptible until the traveller has made his way through them.[1] In this thicket, several kinds of wild beasts used formerly to conceal themselves, until the swelling of the river drove them from their coverts. To this fact the prophet Jeremiah alludes, when he compares the impatience of Edom and Babylon under the divine judgments, to the *coming up of a lion from the swellings of Jordan*. (Jer. xlix. 19.) On the level strand above noticed, it probably was, that John the Baptist stood, and pointed to the stones of which it was composed, when he exclaimed, *I say unto you, that God is able of* THESE STONES *to raise up* children unto Abraham: and turning to the *second* bank, which was overgrown with various shrubs and trees that had been suffered to grow wild for ages, he added, *and now also the axe is laid unto the root of* THE TREES: *therefore every tree which bringeth not forth good* FRUIT, *is hewn down, and cast into the fire.* (Matt. iii. 9, 10.) The passage of this deep and rapid river by the Israelites, at the most unfavourable season, when augmented by the dissolution of the winter snows, was more manifestly miraculous, if possible, than that of the Red Sea; because here was no natural agency whatever employed; no mighty winds to sweep a passage as in the former case; no reflux in the tide on which minute philosophers might fasten to depreciate the miracle. It seems, therefore, to have been providentially designed to silence cavils respecting the former: it was done at noonday, in the presence of the neighbouring inhabitants; and it struck terror into the kings of the Amorites and Canaanites westward of the river, *whose hearts melted, neither was there any spirit in them any more, because of the children of Israel.* (Josh. v. 1.) The place where the Israelites thus miraculously passed this river, is supposed to be the *fords of Jordan* mentioned in Judg. iii. 26.

The other remarkable streams or rivulets of Palestine are the following: —

2. The ARNON, which descends from the mountains of the same name, and discharges itself into the Dead Sea. It separated the Amorites, and subsequently the tribe of Reuben, from the Moabites, and formed the southern limit of the eastern part of Palestine.

3. The SIHOR (the Belus of antient geographers, at present called the Kardanah) has its source about four miles to the east of the head of the river Kishon. It waters the plains of Acre and Esdraelon, and falls into the sea at the gulph of Keilah.[2]

4. The brook JABBOK takes its rise in the same mountains, and falls into the river Jordan. It is a rapid stream, flowing over a rocky bed; its waters are clear, and agreeable to the taste, and its banks are very thickly wooded with oleander and plane trees, wild olives, wild almonds, and numerous other trees. By the Arabs it is now

---

[1] Maundrell's Journey, p. 110. Dr. Macmichael's Travels from Moscow to Constantinople, in the years 1817, 1818, p. 191. Lond. 1819. 4to.) The Jordan is annually frequented by many thousand pilgrims, chiefly of the Greek church, under the protection of the Moosillim, or Turkish governor of Jerusalem, and a strong military escort. Ibid. pp. 191, 192. Richardson's Travels, vol. ii. p. 387. Irby's and Mangles' Travels, pp. 329, 330.

[2] Shaw's Travels, vol. ii. p. 33.

termed *Nahr-el-Zerkah*, or the river of Zerkah, from a neighbouring station or village of that name.[1]

5. The KANAH, or *Brook of Reeds*, springs from the mountains of Judah, but only flows during the winter, and it falls into the Mediterranean Sea near Cæsarea: it formerly separated the tribe of Ephraim from that of Manasseh. (Josh. xvii. 8, 9.)

6. The brook BESOR (1 Sam. xxx. 9.) falls into the same sea between Gaza and Rhinocorura.

7. The KISHON, now called the Moukattoua, issues from the mountains of Carmel, at the foot of which it forms two streams; one flows eastward into the sea of Galilee, and the other, taking a westerly course through the plain of Jezreel or Esdraelon, discharges itself into the Mediterranean Sea, at a short distance to the south of Acro or Acre. This is the stream noticed in Judg. v. 20, 21. and 1 Kings xviii. 40.: when swollen by heavy rains it is impassable.[2]

8. The KEDRON, KIDRON, or CEDRON, as it is variously termed (2 Sam. xv. 23. 1 Kings xv. 13. 2 Kings xxiii. 6. 12. 2 Chron. xxix. 16. Jer. xxxi. 40. John xviii. 1.), runs in the valley of Jehoshaphat, eastward of Jerusalem, between that city and the Mount of Olives. Except during the winter, or after heavy rains, its channel is generally dry, but, when swollen by torrents, it flows with great impetuosity[3]; its waters are said to become dark and turbid, probably because it collects the waste of the adjacent hills; and, like other brooks in cities, it is contaminated with the filth, of which it is the receptacle and common sewer. The blood and offal of the victims sacrificed in the temple are said, in later times, to have been carried off by a drain into the Kedron.[4] As no mention is made of bridges in Palestine, it is probable that the inhabitants forded the rivers and brooks wherever it was practicable (in the same manner as persons of both sexes do to this day in Bengal), which is alluded to in Isa. xlvii. 2.

Of the LAKES mentioned in the Scriptures, three are particularly worthy of notice; that of *Galilee* or *Gennesareth*, the *Lake Merom*, and the *Lake of Sodom*, both of which are termed *seas*[5], agreeably to the Hebrew phraseology, which gives the name of sea to any large body of water.

1. The SEA OF GALILEE (so called from its situation on the eastern borders of that division of Palestine), through which the Jordan flows, was antiently called the *Sea of Chinnereth* (Numb. xxxiv. 11.), or Chinneroth (Josh. xii. 3.), from its vicinity to the town of that name; afterwards *the Water of Gennesar* (1 Macc. xi. 67.), and in the time of Jesus Christ, *the Lake of Genesareth* or *Gennesareth* (Luke v. 1.), from the neighbouring land of the same name (Matt. xiv. 34. Mark vi. 53.); and also the *Sea of Tiberias* (John vi. 1. xxi. 1.), from the contiguous

---

[1] Buckingham's Travels, p. 325.

[2] Carne's Letters, p. 250. Richter's Pilgrimages in the East, in 1815-1816. (Cabinet of Foreign Voyages, vol. i. pp. 159, 160. London, 1825.)

[3] In like manner the rivers of Cyprus (which island lies to the north-west of the Holy Land) are dry during the summer months, and are swollen into torrents by sudden rains. Dr. Clarke's Travels, vol. iv. p. 75.

[4] Lightfoot's Chorographical Century, on Matthew, chap. 38. fine. (Works, vol. i. p. 80.)

[5] This appellation is retained by the modern inhabitants, who reside in its vicinity, "who, like the earliest ones, call their water a *sea*, and reckon it and the Dead Sea to the south of them to be the two largest known except the great ocean." Buckingham's Travels, p. 471.

city of Tiberias. This capacious lake, almost equal in the grandeur of its appearance to that of Geneva, spreads its transparent waters over all the lower territory, extending from the north-east to the south-west. The waters of the northern part of this lake abound with fish : this circumstance marks the propriety of our Lord's parable of the net cast into the sea (Matt. xiii. 47, 48.) which was delivered by him from a vessel near the shore. The fish are said to be most delicious. There is not much variety, but the best sort is the most common; it is a species of bream, equal to the finest perch. It is remarkable, that there is not a single boat of any description on the lake at present; and the fish are caught, partly by the fishermen going into the water, up to their waist, and throwing in a hand net, and partly with casting nets from the beach: a method which must yield a very small quantity, compared to what they would get with boats.[1]

Pliny states this lake to be sixteen miles in length by six miles in breadth. Josephus, whose intimate knowledge of his country gives his descriptions a high claim to attention, says that " its breadth is forty furlongs, and its length one hundred and forty. Its waters are sweet and very agreeable for drinking, for they are finer than the thick waters of other fens. The lake is also pure, and on every side ends directly at the shores, and at the sand: it is also of a temperate nature, when drawn up, and softer than river or fountain water: and it is so cold, that the people of the place cannot warm it by setting it in the sun, in the hottest season of the year. There are several kinds of fish in it, different both to the taste and sight from those elsewhere. It is divided into two parts by the river Jordan."[2]

The fidelity of Josephus's description is attested by two learned and acute modern travellers. Mr. Buckingham, who beheld it in 1816, observes that "all these features are drawn with an accuracy that could only have been attained by one resident in the country. The size is still nearly the same, the borders of the lake still end at the beach or the sands, at the feet of the mountains which environ it. Its waters are still as sweet and temperate as ever, and the lake abounds with great numbers of fish of various sizes and kinds. The appearance of the lake as seen from Capernaum," Mr. Buckingham states, " is still grand; its greatest length runs nearly north and south from twelve to fifteen miles; and its breadth seems to be, in general, from six to nine miles. The barren aspect of the mountains on each side, and the total absence of wood, give, however, a cast of dulness to the picture; and this is increased to melancholy by the dead calm of its waters, and the silence which reigns throughout its whole extent, where not a boat or vessel of any kind is to be found."[3]

Dr. Clarke, by whom this lake was visited a few years before Mr. Buckingham's arrival, describes it as longer and finer than our Cumberland and Westmorland lakes, although it yields in majesty to the stupendous features of Loch Lomond in Scotland. Like our Winder-

---

[1] Travels in Egypt, &c. by Captains Irby and Mangles, p. 295. Madden's Travels in Turkey, &c. vol. ii. p. 312. See also Carne's Letters from the East, pp. 254—363. Richter's Pilgrimages in the East. (Cabinet of Foreign Voyages, vol. i. p. 157.)

[2] Josephus de Bell. Jud. lib. iii. c. 10. § 7.   Pritii Introd. in Nov. Test. p. 503.

[3] Buckingham's Travels, pp. 470, 471. Mr. Jowett's estimate nearly coincides with that of Mr. Buckingham, (Christian Researches in Syria, p. 175.), as also does that of Mr. Rae Wilson. (Travels in the Holy Land, vol. ii. pp. 13, 14. 3d edition.)

mere, the lake of Gennesareth is often greatly agitated by winds.
(Matt. viii. 23—27.) A strong current marks the passage of the Jordan through the middle of this lake; and when this is opposed by contrary winds, which blow here with the force of a hurricane from the
south-east, sweeping into the lake from the mountains, a boisterous
sea is instantly raised: this the small vessels of the country are ill
qualified to resist. " The wind," he says, " rendered its surface rough,
and called to mind the situation of our Saviour's disciples; when,
in one of the small vessels, which traversed these waters, they were
tossed in a storm, and saw Jesus in the fourth watch of the night
walking to them upon the waves." (Matt. xiv. 24—26.) These agitations, however, do not last for any length of time. — Its broad and
extended surface, covering the bottom of a profound valley, environed
by lofty and precipitous eminences (excepting only the narrow entrance
and outlet of the Jordan at each extremity), added to the impression
of a certain reverential awe under which every Christian pilgrim approaches it, give it a character of dignity unparalleled by any similar
scenery.[1] When not agitated by tempests, the water is stated to be
as clear as the purest crystal, sweet, cool, and most refreshing to the
taste.

2. The WATERS OF MEROM, mentioned in Josh. xi. 5. 7., are
generally supposed to be the lake, afterwards called Samochonitis,
which lies between the head of the river Jordan and the Sea of Tiberias. Its modern name is Houle. According to Josephus, it is
thirty furlongs broad, and sixty furlongs in length; and its marshes
extend to the place called Daphne[2], where the Jordan issues from it.
Though its waters are no longer bitter, this lake derives no small
interest from the illustrations and allusions so often made to it by the
prophets.[3]

3. The LAKE or SEA OF SODOM, or the DEAD SEA, has been
celebrated not only by the sacred writers, but also by Josephus, and
several profane authors.[4] It was antiently called in the Scriptures the
Sea of the Plain (Deut. iii. 17. iv. 49.), being situated in a valley, with
a plain lying to the south of it, where once flourished the cities of
Sodom and Gomorrah, with the other cities of the plain; — the *Salt
Sea* (Deut. iii. 17. Josh. xv. 5.) from the extremely saline, and bitter,
taste of its waters; — the *Salt Sea eastward* (Numb. xxxiv. 3.) — and
the *East Sea* (Ezek. xlvii. 18. Joel ii. 20.), from its situation relatively
to Judæa. By Josephus and other writers it was called the *Lake
Asphaltites,* from the abundance of bitumen found in it; and by Jerome,
the *Dead Sea,* that is the Bituminous Lake, from antient traditions,
erroneously though generally received, that no living creature can
exist in its stagnant and hydro-sulphuretted waters; which, though
they look remarkably clear and pure, are in the highest degree salt,

---

[1] Dr. Clarke's Travels, vol. iv. pp. 209, 210. 225.   Buckingham's Travels, pp. 468. 471.
[2] De Bell. Jud. lib. iv. c. 1. § 1.   Reland conjectures that, for *Daphne*, in this passage
of Josephus, we ought to read *Dan*, as there is no mention of any place called Daphne in this
vicinity, and Daphne near Antioch was far distant from the waters of Merom.   Palæstina,
tom. i. p. 263.
[3] Carne's Recollections of the East, p. 39.
[4] Josephus de Bell. Jud. lib. iv. c. 8. § 4.;   Pliny, Hist. Nat. lib. v. c. 16.;   Tacitus,
Hist. lib. v. c. 6.;   Justin. lib. xxxvi. c. 3.;   Strabo, lib. xvi. pp. 1087, 1088. edit. Oxon.

bitter, and nauseous in the extreme, and of such a degree of specific gravity as will enable a man to float on their surface without motion.[1] The acrid saltness of its waters is much greater than that of the sea; and the land, which surrounds this lake, being equally impregnated with that saltness, refuses to produce any plants except a few stunted thorns, which wear the brown garb of the desert. To this circumstance Moses alludes in Deut. xxix. 23.—" *The whole land thereof is* brimstone *and* salt." [2] The air itself, which is by evaporation loaded with it, and which is impregnated with the sulphureous and bituminous vapours, is fatal to vegetation; hence arises the *deadly* aspect which reigns around the lake. [3] Here formerly stood the cities of Sodom and Gomorrah, which, with three other cities of the plain, were consumed by fire from heaven; to this destruction there are numerous allusions in the Scriptures, as displaying most signally the certainty and suddenness of the divine anger, which sooner or later overtakes the impenitently wicked. Viewing this sea (which has never been navigated since those cities were engulphed) from the spot where the Jordan discharges its waters into it, this body of water takes a south-easterly direction visible for ten or fifteen miles, when it disappears in a curve towards

---

[1] Irby's and Mangles' Travels, p. 330.   Quarterly Journal of Science, Literature, and the Arts, vol. viii. p. 164.   An analysis of the water of the Dead Sea, (a phial of which had been brought to England by Mr. Gordon of Clunie, at the request of the late Sir Joseph Banks,) conducted by Dr. Marcet, gave the following results : — This water is perfectly transparent, and does not deposit any crystals on standing in close vessels. — Its taste is peculiarly bitter, saline, and pungent. — The application of tests or re-agents proves that it contains the muriatic and sulphuric acids.   There is no alumina in it, nor does it appear to be saturated with marine salt or muriate of soda.—On summing up the contents of 150 grains of the water, they were found to hold in solution the following substances, and in the undermentioned proportions : —

	Salts.	Acid.
Muriate of lime - - -	5,88 grains.	3,89 grains.
Muriate of magnesia - -	15,37 —	8,61
Muriate of soda - - -	15,54 —	7,15
Selenite - - - -	0,08 —	- - -
	36,87	18,65

And, consequently, the proportions of these salts in 100 grains of the water would be : —

	Grains.
Muriate of lime - - - - -	3,920
Muriate of magnesia - - - - -	10,246
Muriate of soda - - - - -	19,360
Sulphate of lime - - - - -	0,054
	24,580

Philosophical Transactions of the Royal Society of London, for 1807, part ii. pp. 298—312.   Another Analysis, made by the eminent French chemist, M. Gay-Lussac in 1819, gave nearly similar results.   (See Quarterly Journal of Science, &c. vol. viii. p. 165.) " Hence it appears that the Dead Sea water *now* contains about *one fourth* of its weight of salt supposed in a state of perfect desiccation; or, if they be desiccated at the temperature of 180° on Fahrenheit's scale, they will amount to *forty-one per cent.* of the water.   If any person wish for a stronger confirmation of the Scripture account of the origin of the Dead Sea than this furnishes, we can only pity the miserable state of incredulity to which he is reduced, and commit him to the influences of that power which can cause the ' wilderness to blossom as the rose,' and from ' stones raise up children unto Abraham.'"   Eclectic Review for 1809, vol. v. part i. p. 134.

[2] In the vicinity of this sea Captains Irby and Mangles collected lumps of nitre and fine sulphur, from the size of a nutmeg to that of a small hen's egg, which had been brought down from the surrounding cliffs by the rain.   Travels in Egypt, &c. p. 453.

[3] Volney's Travels in Egypt and Syria, vol. i. p. 288. 8vo. 3d edit. ; Turner's Tour in the Levant, vol. ii. p. 227.

the east. Its surface is generally unruffled, from the hollow of the
basin in which it lies, scarcely admitting the free passage necessary for
a strong breeze; it is, however, for the same reason, subject to whirlwinds or squalls of short duration.[1] The expanse of water at this point
has been supposed not to exceed five or six miles; though the mountains, which skirt each side of the valley of the Dead Sea, are apparently separated by a distance of eight miles.[2] These mountains
present to the eye of the spectator granite, and those other rocks, which
(according to the Wernerian system of geology) characterise the oldest
or primitive formation. It is probable that this region, at a remote
period, was the theatre of immense volcanoes, the effects of which may
still be traced along the banks of the Lower Jordan, and more especially on the lake itself, on the shores of which bitumen, lava, and
pumice stones, continue to be thrown by the waves.[3] As the Dead
Sea advances towards the south, it evidently increases in breadth.[4]
Pliny states the total length to be one hundred miles, and its greatest
breadth twenty-five. But Dr. Shaw and other modern travellers who
appear to have ascertained its dimensions with accuracy, have estimated its length to be about seventy-two English miles, and its greatest
breadth to be nearly nineteen.[5] A profound silence, awful as death,
hangs over the lake: not a ripple is to be seen on its surface; its shores
are rarely visited by any footsteps but those of the wild Arab; and
not a vessel of any kind ploughs its waters: not a bird builds its
nest, or pours forth its strains in the vicinity of this sea: nor is any thing
to be found near it but a few dry and stunted shrubs; and "its desolate though majestic features are well suited to the tales related
concerning it by the inhabitants of the country, who all speak of it
with terror."[6] M. Cornille, who advanced upwards of fifty paces into

---

[1] Buckingham's Travels in Palestine, p. 293.

[2] "The mountains on the Judæan side are lower than those of the Arabian, and also of
a lighter colour; the latter chain, at its southern extremity, is said to consist of dark granite,
and of various colours. The hills, which branch off from the western end, are composed
entirely of white chalk: bitumen abounds most on the opposite shore. There is no outlet to
this lake, though the Jordan flows into it, as did formerly the Kedron, and the Arnon to the
south. It is not known that there has been any visible increase or decrease of its waters.
Some have supposed that it finds a subterraneous passage to the Mediterranean, or that there
is a considerable suction in the plain, which forms its western boundary." (Carne's Letters,
pp. 317, 318.) But the uniform level of its waters is sufficiently accounted for by the
quantity which is evaporated. (See Dr. Shaw's Travels, vol. ii. pp. 157, 158.)

[3] Volney's Travels in Syria, vol. i. pp. 281, 282. Travels of Ali Bey (M. Badhia),
vol. ii. p. 263. Buckingham's Travels, pp. 443. 448. Russell's Palestine, p. 412.

[4] Jolliffe's Letters from Palestine, p. 118.

[5] Shaw's Travels, vol. i. p. 157. Mr. Carne, however, who visited the Dead Sea in 1825,
estimates its length to be about sixty miles, and its general breadth eight. On his arrival at
its shore, where the waters lay like lead, there was not a breath of wind. "Whoever," says
this intelligent traveller, "has seen the Dead Sea, will ever after have its aspect impressed
upon his memory; it is, in truth, a gloomy and fearful spectacle. The precipices, in general descend abruptly into the lake, and on account of their height it is seldom agitated by
the winds. Its shores are not visited by any footstep, save that of the wild Arab, and he
holds it in superstitious dread. No unpleasant effluvia are perceptible round it, and birds are
seen occasionally flying across . . . . . A few inches beneath the surface of the mud are found
those black sulphureous stones, out of which crosses are made, and sold to the pilgrims. The
water has an abominable taste, in which that of salt predominates; and we observed incrust-
ations of salt on the surface of some of the rocks." Letters from the East, pp. 316, 317.

[6] For an account and refutation of the antient traditions concerning the Dead Sea, see
Dr. Clarke's Travels, vol. iv. pp. 400—406. 8vo. New Monthly Magazine, vol. lii. p. 354.
A comprehensive digest of nearly all that has been written concerning this sea will be found
in the Modern Traveller, Palestine, pp. 204—224.

this sea, found that its depth did not exceed two feet. He states that he walked, not upon sand, but upon a reddish bituminous earth, covered with a hard crust, which shook at the slightest motion over it.[1]

4. The GREAT SEA, mentioned in Numb. xxxiv. 6. and elsewhere in the Sacred Volume, is the Mediterranean Sea, so called by way of eminence. In Exod. xxiii. 31. it is called the *Sea of the Philistines*, because their country bordered on its shores: in Josh. xxiii. 4. the *Great Sea westward;* and in Deut. xi. 24. Joel. ii. 20. and elsewhere, the *Uttermost*, or *Utmost* Sea.

5. The RED SEA, so often noticed, is now known by the appellation of the Arabian Gulph.[2]

IV. Besides the preceding rivers and lakes, the Scriptures mention several FOUNTAINS and WELLS. In a country where these are of rare occurrence, it is no wonder that they should antiently have given rise to strife and contention.[3] (Gen. xxi. 25. xxvi. 20.) The most remarkable of these fountains and wells are the *Fountain* or *Pool of Siloam*, and *Jacob's Well.*

1. SILOAM was a fountain under the walls of Jerusalem, east, between the city and the brook Kedron: it is supposed to be the same as the fountain En-Rogel, or the Fuller's Fountain (Josh. xv. 7. and xviii. 16. 2 Sam. xvii. 17. and 1 Kings i. 9.), and also the Gihon. (1 Kings i. 33.) The spring issues from a rock, and runs in a silent stream, according to the testimony of Isaiah. (viii. 6.) The modern descent to this fountain is by fifteen or sixteen steps. Being defended from the sun, it is deliciously cool, and clear as crystal: it has a kind of ebb and flood, sometimes discharging its current like the fountain of Vaucluse; at others, retaining and scarcely suffering it to run at all. The pool, or rather the two pools of the same name, are quite close to the spring. They are still used for washing linen as formerly.[4] Antiently, its waters were conducted into the two large reservoirs or pools, already noticed in page 24. Modern travellers relate that people still bathe their eyes with the waters of this fountain, in memory of the miracle performed on the man who had been born blind. At this fountain, the antient Jews were wont to draw water with great solemnity on the last day of the Feast of Tabernacles: an account of this ceremony will be found in Part III. Chap. IV. § VII. of this volume.

2. JACOB'S WELL or fountain is situated at a small distance from Sichem or Shechem, also called Sychar, and at present Napolose: it was the residence of Jacob before his sons slew the Shechemites. It has been visited by pilgrims of all ages, but especially by Christians, to whom it has become an object of veneration from the memorable discourse of our Saviour with the woman of Samaria. (John iv.

---

1 Souvénirs d'Orient, par Henri Cornille, pp. 345, 346. Paris, 1836. 8vo.

2 See the article RED SEA, in the Historical and Geographical Index, infra.

3 When Capt. Light descended in 1814, into the beautiful plain of Sephora, or Sephoury, at a short distance from Nazareth, he saw in the centre a band of herdsmen, *armed* with muskets, watering their cattle in a large stone reservoir. With them he was obliged to have an altercation before they would permit him to water his horse, without paying for the privilege. Travels, p. 196. Three Weeks in Palestine, p. 68.

4 Chateaubriand's Travels, vol. ii. pp. 34. 36. Mr. Buckingham, who visited the fountain of Siloam in 1816, describes it as a dirty little brook ; which even in the rainy season is said to be an insignificant muddy stream. Travels in Palestine, p. 188. See also Richardson's Travels, vol. ii. p. 357.

5—30.) The spot is so distinctly marked by the evangelist John, and is so little liable to uncertainty, from the circumstance of the well itself and the features of the country, that, if no tradition existed for its identity, the site of it could scarcely be mistaken.[1]

In consequence of the scarcity of water in the East, travellers are careful to stop as often as possible near some river, fountain, or well: this will probably account for Jacob's halting with his family at the ford Jabbok (Gen. xxxii. 22.); for the Israelites assembling their forces near the fountains of Jezreel (1 Sam. xxix. 1.), as the celebrated Moslem warrior Saladin afterwards did[2]; and for David's men that were unable to march with him, waiting for him by the brook Besor. (1 Sam. xxx. 21.) It is not improbable that the antient wells, mentioned in Gen. xvi. 14. xxiv. 20. and Exod. ii. 16., were furnished with some conveniences for drawing water to refresh the fainting traveller, and with troughs or other contrivances for supplying cattle with water, similar to those which are to this day found in Persia, Arabia, and other countries in the East.[3] In Eccl. xii. 6. Solomon alludes to a wheel as being employed for the purpose of raising water.[4] Great precautions were taken antiently, as well as in modern times, to prevent the moving sands from choking up their wells, by placing a stone over the mouth (Gen. xxix. 2—8.) after the requisite supply had been drawn up; or by *locking* them up, which Sir John Chardin thinks was done at Laban's well, of which Rachel, perhaps, kept the key. (Gen. xxix. 6. 9.) The stopping up of wells is to this day an act of hostility in the East, as it was in the days of Abraham and Isaac (Gen. xxvi. 15—18.), and of Hezekiah (2 Chron. xxxii. 3, 4.), and also long after among several antient nations. Thus, the Scythians, in their retreat before the Persians, under Darius, filled up the wells and fountains which lay in their way[5]: and Arsaces ordered the wells to be broken and filled up, upon the advance of Antiochus from Ecbatana; while the latter, who was fully aware of their consequence to himself and his army, sent a detachment of a thousand

---

[1] Dr. Clarke's Travels, vol. iv. pp. 278—280. Some learned men have conjectured that Jacob's well was only a cistern or reservoir for rain water; but the whole of the surrounding scenery confirms the evangelist's narrative, and the antiquity of the well. Such cisterns, indeed, are common in the oriental deserts to this day; and it is perhaps to conveniences of this kind, made or renewed by the devout Israelites, in the valley of Baca, to facilitate their going up to Jerusalem, that the Psalmist refers (lxxxiv. 6, 7.) where he speaks of going from strength to strength till they appeared in Zion. Harmer's Observations, vol. ii. p. 184. To prevent accidents by the owners of such cisterns leaving them uncovered, Moses enacted various regulations. See Exod. xxi. 33, 34.

[2] Harmer's Observations, vol. iii. p. 401. The Christian kings of Jerusalem, in the close of the twelfth century, also assembled their forces at a fountain between Nazareth and Sephoris. Ibid.

[3] In the villages of Ethiopia Messrs. Waddington and Hanbury frequently met with huts by the road-side, containing large jars of water for travellers. When there is no hut, the jar is generally placed under a pine tree. Journal of a Visit to Ethiopia, p. 35.

[4] In Smyrna and many other places in the East, a large wheel is fixed over the mouth of a well in a vertical position: to this wheel a number of pitchers is attached in such a manner, that by means of its revolution, which is effected by a horse, they are continually descending and filling and ascending and discharging themselves. (Hartley's Researches in Greece, pp. 235, 236.) In the Russian Government of Iver, Dr. Henderson was struck with the number of wells which he saw, over each of which is built a large wooden apparatus, consisting chiefly of a windlass, with a wheel about six feet in diameter, which is turned round by the hand, and thus the water is drawn up in a bucket. He is of opinion that it is obviously to a machine of this kind that Solomon refers in his highly figurative picture of old age. Biblical Researches, p. 32.

[5] Herodotus, lib. iv. c. 120. tom. i. p. 292. Oxon. 1809.

horse, to drive away the Persian cavalry who were employed upon this service.[1] Dry wells were used as places of concealment. (2 Sam. xvii. 19.) as they are still in India.[2] Wells and fountains were also lurking-places of robbers and assassins, and enemies were accustomed to lie in ambush at them, as they are now. To this Deborah alludes in her song. (Judg. v. 11.) The Crusaders suffered much from the Saracens, who lay in ambush for them in like manner; and Dr. Shaw mentions a beautiful well in Barbary, the water of which is received into a large basin for the accommodation of travellers; and which is called *Shrub we krub*, that is, *Drink and away*, from the danger which they incur of meeting with assassins there.[3]

In our own time it is the custom for the oriental women, particularly those who are unmarried, to fetch water from the wells, in the mornings and evenings; at which times they go forth adorned with their trinkets. This will account for Rebecca's fetching water (Gen. xxiv. 15.), and will further prove that there was no impropriety in Abraham's servant presenting her with more valuable jewels than those she had before on her hands. (Gen. xxiv. 22—47.)[4]

3. As the cities were mostly erected on eminences, and (as we have already seen) the rains fall only in the spring and autumn, the inhabitants of Palestine constructed CISTERNS, or reservoirs for water, both in cities and in private houses. Allusions to the latter occur in 2 King's xviii. 31. Prov. v. 15. and Isa. xxxvi. 16. Uzziah, king of Judah, cut out many cisterns (2 Chron. xxvi. 10.) for the supply of his cattle. Cisterns of very large dimensions exist, at this day, in Palestine. In the vicinity of Bethlehem, in particular, there are three capacious pools, known by the name of SOLOMON'S POOLS. They are in the shape of a long square, covered with a thick coat of plaster in the inside, and supported by abutments : the workmanship throughout, like every thing Jewish, is more remarkable for strength than beauty.

[1] Polybius, lib. x. c. 29. tom. iii. p. 253. edit. Schweighaeuser.
[2] Roberts's Oriental Illustrations of Scripture, p. 189.
[3] Harmer's Observations, vol. iii. p. 409. Shaw's Travels, vol. i. p. 63. 8vo. Burckhardt's Travels in Syria, &c. p. 627. Captains Irby and Mangles stopped at some wells of fresh water, where they found a great assemblage of camels and many Arabs, who appeared to stop all passengers. They entered into a violent dispute with the conductors of those gentlemen ; and presently levied a contribution on the Arabs who accompanied them. A similar fate would certainly have awaited them, had it not been for the appearance of their arms ; as the chief followed them all the way to El Arish, surveying their baggage " with the most thieving inquisitiveness." Travels in Egypt, &c. pp. 173, 174.
[4] Harmer's Observations, vol. i. pp. 198, 199. vol. ii. pp. 125. 184. 193. vol. iii. p. 401. " In the valley of Nazareth," says Dr. Clarke, " appeared one of those fountains, which, from time immemorial, have been the halting place of caravans, and sometimes the scene of contention and bloodshed. The women of Nazareth were passing to and from the town, with pitchers upon their heads. We stopped to view the group of camels with their drivers who were there reposing ; and calling to mind the manners of the most remote ages, we renewed the solicitations of Abraham's servant unto Rebecca, by the well of Nahor. Gen. xxiv. 17." (Travels, vol. iv. p. 165.) A similar custom was observed by the same traveller in the Isle of Syros. (vol. vi. pp. 152, 153.) And by Mr. Emerson. (Letters from the Ægean, vol. ii. p. 45.) At Cana, Mr. Rae Wilson, (Travels in the Holy Land, vol. ii. pp. 3, 4.) and also Mr. Carne, observed several of the women bearing stone watering-pots on their heads as they returned from the well. (Letters from the East, p. 253.) In Bengal it is the universal practice for the women to go to pools and rivers to fetch water. Companies of four, six, ten, or more, may be seen in every town, daily, going to fetch water, with the pitchers resting on their sides. (Ward's View of the History, &c. of the Hindoos, vol. ii. p. 316. Roberts's Oriental Illustrations of Scripture, p. 27.) In the island of Goza, which is eighteen miles from Malta, Mr. Jowett says, that the women, as they go to the wells for water, carry their empty pitchers horizontally on their heads, with the mouth looking backwards. (Missionary Register for 1818, p. 297.) May not this illustrate Jer. xiv. 3.?

They are situated at the south end of a small valley; and, from the slope of the ground, the one falls considerably below the level of the other. That on the west is nearest the source of the spring, and is the smallest, being about four hundred and eighty feet long; the second is about six hundred feet, and the third about six hundred and sixty feet long. The breadth of them all is nearly the same, about two hundred and seventy feet. The fountains communicate freely with each other, and are capable of holding a great quantity of water; which they discharge into a small aqueduct, that conveys it to Jerusalem. Both fountains and aqueduct are said to have been made by Solomon the son and successor of David, and the antiquity of their appearance bears testimony to the truth of the statement.[1]

V. Palestine is a mountainous country, especially that part of it which is situated between the Mediterranean or Great Sea and the river Jordan. The principal MOUNTAINS are those of Lebanon, Carmel, Tabor, the mountains of Israel, and of Gilead: those which are either within the limits, or in the immediate vicinity of Jerusalem, have been noticed in pp. 18, 19, *supra*.

1. LEBANON, by the Greeks and Latins termed Libanus, is a long chain of limestone mountains, on the summits of which fossilised antediluvian fishes were formerly discovered[2]; extending from the neighbourhood of Sidon on the west to the vicinity of Damascus eastward, and forming the extreme northern boundary of the Holy Land. Antiently, it abounded with odoriferous trees of various descriptions, from which the most curious gums and balsams were extracted.[3] It is divided into two principal ridges or ranges parallel to each other, the most westerly of which is known by the name of LIBANUS, and the opposite or eastern ridge by the appellation of Anti-Libanus: but the Hebrews do not make this distinction of names, denominating both summits by the common name of Lebanon. These mountains may be seen from a very considerable distance, and some part or other of them is covered with snow throughout the year. From this circumstance probably the modern natives term it Gibl Leban or the White Mountain. On the loftiest summit of all, Dr. Clarke observed the snow lying, not in patches, as he had seen it during the summer upon the tops of very elevated mountains, but investing all the higher part with that perfect white and smooth velvet-like appearance which snow only exhibits when it is very deep — a striking spectacle in such a climate, where the beholder seeking protection from a burning sun, almost considers the firmament to be on fire.[4] Petrified sea shells and other marine substances have been discovered in Lebanon.

These mountains are by no means barren; but are almost all well cultivated, and well peopled: their summits are, in many parts, level, and form extensive plains, in which are sown corn, and all kinds of pulse. They are watered by numerous cold flowing springs, rivulets, and streams of excellent water, which diffuse on all sides a freshness and fertility even in the most elevated regions. To these Solomon

---

[1] Dr. Richardson's Travels, vol. ii. pp. 379, 380.
[2] See the authorities in Reland's Palæstina, tom. i. p. 321.
[3] *The heights of* ODOROUS *Lebanon* are eulogised by Musǽeus: — Λιβανου Ṣυοεντος ενι πτερυγεσσι. Good's Sacred Idyls, p. 122.
[4] Dr. Clarke's Travels, vol. iv. pp. 201, 202.

has a beautiful allusion. (Song iv. 15.) Vineyards, and plantations of mulberry, olive, and fig-trees, are also cultivated on terraces formed by walls, which support the earth from being washed away by the rains from the sides of the acclivities.[1] The soil of the declivities and of the hollows that occur between them is most excellent, and produces abundance of corn, oil, and wine; which is as much celebrated in the East in the present day as it was in the time of the prophet Hosea, who particularly alludes to it. (Hos. xiv. 7.) Lebanon was antiently celebrated for its stately cedars, which are now less numerous than in former times[2]; they grow among the snow near the highest part of the mountain, and are remarkable, as well for their age and size, as for the frequent allusions made to them in the Scriptures. (See 1 Kings iv. 33. Psal. lxxx. 10. and xcii. 12, &c. &c.) These trees form a little grove by themselves, as if planted by art, and are seated in a hollow amid rocky eminences all around them, and form a small wood, at the foot of the ridge, which forms the highest peak of Lebanon. The number of the largest trees has varied at different times. To omit the varying numbers stated by the earlier travellers : — the Rev. Henry Maundrell, who travelled in this region in 1696, reckoned sixteen of the largest size, one of which he measured, and found it to be twelve yards and six inches in girth, and yet sound; and thirty-seven yards in the spread of the boughs. Dr. Pocock, in 1738, found fifteen standing, and one which had been recently blown down. The celebrated oriental traveller, Mr. Burckhardt, who traversed Mount Libanus in 1810, counted eleven or twelve of the oldest and best looking trees, twenty-five very large ones, about fifty of middling size, and more than three hundred smaller and young ones. Mr. Buckingham, in 1816, computed them to be about two hundred in number, twenty of which were very large.[3] In 1817–18, Captains Irby and Mangles stated that there might be about fifty of them, not one of which had much merit either for dimensions or beauty; the largest among them appearing to be the junction of four or five trunks into one tree.[4] Dr. Richardson, in 1818, and Mr. Robinson in 1830, stated the oldest trees to be no more than seven or eight.[5] The oldest trees are distinguished by having the foliage and small branches at the top only, and by four, five, or even seven trunks springing from one base; the branches and trunks of the others are lower: the trunks of the old trees are covered with the names of travellers and other persons who have visited them, some of which are dated as far back as 1640. The trunks of the oldest trees (the wood of which is of a grey tint) seemed to be quite dead.[6] These cedars were the resort of eagles (Ezek. xvii. 3.); as the lofty summits of the mountains were the haunts of lions and other beasts of prey (Sol.

---

[1] Light's Travels, p. 219.

[2] Mr. Kinneir, who visited this country at the close of the year 1813, says, that the once celebrated cedars are now only to be found in one particular spot of the great mountainous range which bears the name of Libanus, and that in so scanty a number as not to exceed four or five hundred. Journey through Asia Minor, &c. p. 172. 8vo. 1818.

[3] Buckingham's Travels among the Arab Tribes, pp. 475, 476.

[4] Irby's and Mangles' Travels, pp. 209, 210.

[5] Maundrell's Journey, p. 191. La Roque, Voyage de Syrie et du Mont Liban, p. 88. See also Dr. Richardson's Travels, vol. ii. pp. 512, 513. Robinson's Travels in Palestine and Syria, vol. ii. pp. 86, 87.

[6] Burckhardt's Travels in Syria and the Holy Land, pp. 20, 21. London, 1822. 4to.

Song iv. 8.), which used to descend and surprise the unwary traveller. But instead of these, the traveller may now frequently see the hart or the deer issue from his covert to slake his thirst in the streams that issue from the mountains.   To this circumstance David beautifully alludes in Psal. xlii. 1., which was composed when he was driven from Jerusalem by the rebellion of Absalom, and was wandering among these mountains.   Finally, Mr. Carne, in 1825, states that the forests, the cedar-trees, the glory of Lebanon, have in a great measure disappeared, to make way for innumerable plantations of vines.[1]   In the course of another century it is probable that not a vestige of them will remain, and the predictions of the prophets Isaiah (xxxiii. 9. x. 33, 34.), Ezekiel (xxxi. 12. 14.), and Zechariah (xi. 1, 2.), will then be most literally fulfilled.

ANTI-LIBANUS or ANTI-LEBANON is the more lofty ridge of the two, and its summit is clad with almost perpetual snow, which was carried to the neighbouring towns for the purpose of cooling liquors (Prov. xxv. 13. and perhaps Jer. xviii. 14.); a practice[2] which has obtained in the East to the present day.   Its rock is primitive calcareous, of a fine grain, with a sandy slate upon the higher parts: it affords good pasturage in many spots where the Turkmans feed their cattle, but the western declivity towards the district of Baalbec is quite barren.[3] The most elevated summit of this ridge was by the Hebrews called HERMON; by the Sidonians SIRION; and by the Amorites, SHENIR (Deut. iii. 9.): it formed the northern boundary of the country beyond Jordan.   Very copious dews fall here[4], as they also did in the days of the Psalmist. (See Psal. cxxxiii. 3.) The mountain of AMANA, mentioned in Sol. Song iv. 8., is the southern part or summit of Anti-Libanus, probably so called because the river Amana descended from it, which waters the territories of Damascus.[5]   In Deut. iv. 48. this mountain is called SION, which has been supposed to be either a contraction, or a faulty reading for Sirion: but Bishop Pococke thinks it probable, that Hermon was the name of the highest summit of this mountain, and that a lower part of it had the name of Sion.   This obviates the geographical difficulty which some interpreters have imagined to exist in Psal. cxxxiii. 3. where Mount Sion is mentioned in connection with Hermon, and is generally understood to be Mount Sion in Jerusalem, which was more than thirty miles distant. According to the bishop's supposition, the dew falling from the top of Hermon down to the lower parts, might well be compared in every respect to the *precious ointment upon the head that ran down unto the beard, even Aaron's beard, and went down to the skirts of his garments* (Psal. cxxxiii. 2.), and that both of them, in this sense, are very proper emblems of the blessings of unity and friendship, which diffuse themselves throughout the whole society.[6]

Both Lebanon and Anti-Lebanon are computed to be about fifteen or sixteen hundred fathoms in height, and offer a grand and magnifi-

---

[1] Letters from the East, p. 411.
[2] Harmer's Observations, vol. ii. pp. 156, 157.
[3] Burckhardt's Travels in Syria and the Holy Land, pp. 20, 21.
[4] Maundrell, p. 77.   [5] Gesenius's Heb. and Engl. Lexicon by Robinson, p. 73.
[6] Pococke's Description of the East, vol. ii. part. i. pp. 74, 75.   Bp. Pococke's explanation is approved by Mr. Buckingham.   Travels among the Arab Tribes, p. 395.

cent prospect to the beholder; from which many elegant metaphors are derived by the sacred writers. (See Isa. x. 34. xxix. 17. and xxxv. 2.) Lebanon was justly considered as a very strong barrier to the Land of Promise, and opposing an almost insurmountable obstacle to the movements of cavalry and to chariots of war. "When, therefore, Sennacherib, in the arrogance of his heart, and the pride of his strength, wished to express the ease with which he had subdued the greatest difficulties, and how vain was the resistance of Hezekiah and his people, he says, *By the multitude of my chariots have I come to the height of the mountains, to the side of Lebanon! and I will cut down the tall cedars thereof, and the choice fir-trees thereof; and I will enter into the height of his border, and the forest of his Carmel.* (Isa. xxxvii. 24.) What others accomplish on foot, with much labour and the greatest difficulty, by a winding path cut into steps, which no beast of burden, except the cautious and sure-footed mule, can tread, that haughty monarch vaunted he could perform with horses and a multitude of chariots."[1] During the latter period of the Roman empire, Lebanon afforded an asylum to numerous robbers, who infested the neighbouring regions, so that the eastern emperors found it necessary to establish garrisons there.[2]

2. Mount Carmel is situated about ten miles to the south of Acre or Ptolemais, on the shore of the Mediterranean Sea: it is a range of hills extending six or eight miles nearly north and south, coming from the plain of Esdraelon, and ending in the promontory or cape which forms the bay of Accho or Acre. It is very rocky, and is composed of a whitish stone, with flints imbedded in it. On the east is a fine plain watered by the river Kishon; and on the west a narrower plain descending to the sea. Its greatest height does not exceed fifteen hundred feet.[3] The summits of this mountain are said to abound with oaks, pines, and other trees; and, among brambles, wild vines and olive trees are still to be found, proving that industry had formerly been employed on this ungrateful soil: nor is there any deficiency of fountains and rivulets, so grateful to the inhabitants of the East. There are many caves in this mountainous range, particularly on the western side, the largest of which, called the school of Elijah, is much venerated both by Mohammedans and Jews. On the summit, facing the sea, tradition says, that the prophet stood when he prayed for rain, and beheld the cloud arise out of the sea[4]: and on the side next the sea is a lofty and spacious cave, to which, tradition states that the prophet Elijah desired Ahab to bring Baal's prophets, when celestial fire descended on his sacrifice. (1 Kings xviii. 19—40.) Carmel appears to have been the name, not of the hill only distinguished as Mount Carmel, on the top of which the faithful prophet Elijah offered sacrifice, but also of the whole district, which afforded the richest pasture: and shepherds with their flocks are to be seen on its long

---

[1] Paxton's Illustrations of Scripture, vol. i. p. 134. First edition.
[2] Glycæ Annal. lib. xiv. p. 91. Procopius de Bell. Pers. lib. i. c. 13. lib. ii. c. 16. 19. cited in Reland's Palæstina, tom. i. p. 322.
[3] Buckingham's Travels in Palestine, pp. 119, 120. Mr. Rae Wilson, however, estimates its height at two thousand feet. Travels in the Holy Land, vol. ii. p. 51. Third edition.
[4] Scholz's Travels in Egypt, &c. cited in the Brit. Crit. and Theol. Review, vol. i. p. 372. Carne's Letters, p. 249.

grassy slopes, which at present afford as rich a pasture ground, as in the days when Nabal fed his numerous herds on Carmel.[1] This was *the excellency of Carmel* which Isaiah (xxxv. 2.) opposes to the barren desert. It is mentioned by Amos (i. 2.) as *the habitations of the shepherds.* The expression, *forest of his Carmel* (2 Kings xix. 23. Isa. xxxvii. 24.), implies that it abounded at one time with wood: but its remoteness, as the border country of Palestine, and the wilderness characteristic of pastoral highlands, rather than its loftiness or its inaccessibility, must be alluded to by the prophet Amos. (ix. 2, 3.) There was another Mount Carmel, with a city of the same name, situated in the tribe of Judah, and mentioned in Joshua xv. 55. 1 Sam. xxv. 2. and 2 Sam. iii. 3., which was rich in pasturage.

3. TABOR or THABOR is a calcareous mountain of a conical form, entirely detached from any neighbouring mountain, and stands on one side of the great plain of Esdraelon : the sides are rugged and precipitous, but clothed with luxuriant trees and brushwood, except on the southern side of the mountain. Here Barak was encamped, when, at the suggestion of Deborah, he descended with ten thousand men, and discomfited the host of Sisera. (Judg. iv.) The mountain is steep of ascent, and is computed to be nearly one mile in height. To a person standing at its foot, it appears to terminate in a point; but when arrived at the top, he is agreeably surprised to find an oval plain of about a quarter of a mile in its greatest length, covered with a bed of fertile soil on the west, and having on its eastern side a mass of ruins, seemingly the vestiges of churches, grottoes, and strong walls, all decidedly of some antiquity, and a few appearing to be the works of a very remote age.[2] The prospects from this mountain are singularly delightful and extensive. To the south lie the MOUNTAINS OF ENGEDDA AND SAMARIA; to the north-east, about six miles off, appears MOUNT HERMON, beneath which were Nain and Endor. To the north lie the MOUNT OF THE BEATITUDES[3], where Christ delivered his divine sermon to the multitude (who were miraculously fed in its vicinity), and the MOUNTAINS OF GILBOA so fatal to Saul. The latter are still called by the natives *Djebel Gilbo,* or Mount Gilbo. They are a lengthened ridge, rising up in peaks about eight hundred feet above the level of the road, probably about one thousand feet above the level of the Jordan, and about twelve hundred above that of the sea ; and bounding the plain of the Jordan on the west. Utter solitude is on every side of these mountains, which afford no dwelling places for men, except for the wandering shepherd, whose search for pasturage must often be in vain; as a little withered grass and a few scanty shrubs, dispersed in different places, constitute the whole produce of the mountains of Gilboa.[4] The Sea of Tiberias is clearly discovered towards the north-

---

1 Monro's Summer Ramble in Syria, vol. i. p. 6. Carne's Recollections of the East, p. 43.

2 Jolliffe's Letters from Palestine, p. 140.   Buckingham's Travels in Palestine, p. 104. Burckhardt's Travels in Syria, &c. p. 334.   Monro's Ramble in Syria, vol. i. p. 297.   The vignette of this mountain in p. 28. is copied from Dr. E. D. Clarke's Travels, vol. iv. p. 234.   It represents the mountain as seen in crossing the plain of Jezreel or Esdraelon.

3 This hill may have an elevation of from two to three hundred feet. The prospect from its summit, which is an area of many acres containing scattered ruins, is both extensive and beautiful. Wilson's Travels in Egypt and the Holy Land, p. 343. (London, 1822, 8vo.)

▶ 4 Richardson's Travels, vol. ii. p. 425. Carne's Recollections of the East, p. 19. (London, 1830, 8vo.)

east, terminated by the snow-capped Hermon.[1] On the eastern side
of Tabor there is a small height, which by antient tradition is supposed
to have been the scene of our Lord's transfiguration. On the anniversary of the transfiguration of Jesus Christ, according to the ritual
of the Romish section of the universal Christian church, there is a
great procession, and mass is performed at the altars, which superstition has erected where the three tabernacles are supposed to have been
made. They are in a subterraneous vault.[2] (Matt. xvii. 1—8. Mark
ix. 2—9.) During the greater part of the summer, the mountain is
covered in the morning with thick clouds, which disperse towards
mid-day. MOUNT CARMEL is to the south-west, and conceals the
Mediterranean from view: and at the foot of this mountain the spacious and cultivated plain of Esdraelon spreads itself.

4. The MOUNTAINS OF ISRAEL, also called the MOUNTAINS OF
EPHRAIM, were situated in the very centre of the Holy Land, and
opposite to the MOUNTAINS OF JUDAH. The soil of both ridges is
fertile, excepting those parts of the mountains of Israel which approach
the region of the Jordan, and which are both rugged and difficult of
ascent, and also with the exception of the chain extending from the
Mount of Olives near Jerusalem to the plain of Jericho, which has
always afforded lurking places to robbers. (Luke x. 30.) The most
elevated summit of this ridge, which appears to be the same that was
antiently called the *Rock of Rimmon* (Judg. xx. 45. 47.), is at present
known by the name of *Quarantania*, and is supposed to have been the
scene of our Saviour's temptation. (Matt. iv. 8.) It is described by
Maundrell[3], as situated in a mountainous desert, and as being a most
miserably dry and barren place, consisting of high rocky mountains,
torn and disordered, as if the earth had here suffered some great con-
vulsion. The celebrated Mountains of EBAL (sometimes written
Gebal) and GERIZIM (Deut. xi. 29. xxvii. 4. 12. Josh. viii. 30—35.)
are separated from each other merely by an intervening valley; they
are situate, the former to the north, and the latter to the south of
Sichem or Napolose, whose streets run parallel to the latter mountain,
which overlooks the town. In the Mountains of Judah there are
numerous caves, some of a considerable size: the most remarkable of
these is the CAVE OF ADULLAM, mentioned in 1 Sam. xxii. 1, 2. —
" There is a kind of sublime horror in the lofty, craggy, and barren
aspect of these two mountains, which seem to face each other with an
air of defiance ; especially as they stand contrasted with the rich valley
beneath, where the city [of Shechem or Napolose] appears to be
embedded on either side in green gardens and extensive olive grounds,

---

[1] Light's Travels, p. 200.
[2] Major Skinner's Overland Journey to India, vol. i. p. 131. — From the silence of the
evangelists as to the mountain of transfiguration, and from the circumstance of Jesus Christ
being just before at Cæsarea Philippi, some learned men have contended that Tabor could
not have been the scene of that great event. No mountain, it is true, is specified by the
evangelist, nor is the fact of Tabor being a mountain *apart by itself* any argument in point;
but, as the sacred writers expressly state it to have happened six days *after* our Saviour's
discourse at Cæsarea Philippi, he had time enough to return into Galilee, which was not
above twenty-five leagues' distance from Tabor. It is, therefore, not improbable that this
mountain was the scene of his transfiguration. Beausobre and L'Enfant's Introduction.
(Bp. Watson's Tracts, vol. iii. pp. 271, 272.)
[3] Maundrell, pp. 106, 107. A later traveller, however (Mr. Jolliffe) is of opinion that
the view from this mountain is not sufficiently extensive. Letters from Palestine, p. 129.

E 2

— rendered more verdant by the lengthened periods of shade which they enjoy from the mountains on each side. Of the two, Gerizim is not wholly without cultivation."[1]

5. The MOUNTAINS OF GILEAD are situated beyond the Jordan, and extend from Anti-Libanus or Mount Hermon southward into Arabia Petræa. The *northern* part of them, known by the name of BASHAN, was celebrated for its stately oaks[2], and numerous herds of cattle pastured on its fertile soil, to which there are many allusions in the Scriptures. (See, among other passages, Deut. xxxii. 14. Psal. xxii. 12. and lxviii. 15. Isa. ii. 13. Ezek. xxxix. 18. Amos iv. 1.) The hair of the goats that browsed about Mount Gilead, appears from Cant. iv. 1. to have been as fine as that of the oriental goat, which is well known to be possessed of the fineness of the most delicate silk, and is often employed in modern times for the manufacture of muffs. The *middle* part of this mountainous range, in a stricter sense, was termed *Gilead;* and in all probability is the mountain now called *Djebel Djelaad* or *Djebel Djelaoud,* on which is the ruined town of Djelaad, which may be the site of the antient city Gilead (Hos. vi. 8.) elsewhere called Ramoth Gilead. In the *southern* part of the same range, beyond the Jordan, were, —

6. The MOUNTAINS OF ABARIM[3], a range of rugged hills, forming the northern limits of the territory of Moab, which are conjectured to have derived their name from the passes between the hills, of which they were formed, or, perhaps, from the Israelites having passed the river Jordan into the promised land, opposite to these mountains. According to Dr. Shaw, they are a long ridge of frightful, rocky, and precipitous hills, which are continued all along the eastern coast of the Dead Sea, as far as the eye can reach. Near these mountains the Israelites had several encampments. The most eminent among them are PISGAH and NEBO, which form a continued chain, and command a view of the whole land of Canaan. (Deut. iii. 27. xxxii. 48—50. xxxiv. 1, 2, 3.) From Mount Nebo Moses surveyed the promised land, before he was *gathered to his people.* (Numb. xxvii. 12, 13.) The Hebrews frequently give the epithet of *everlasting* to their mountains, because they are as old as the earth itself. See, among other instances, Gen. xlix. 26. and Deut. xxxiii. 15.

The mountains of Palestine were antiently places of refuge to the inhabitants when defeated in war (Gen. xiv. 10.); and modern travellers assure us that they are still resorted to for the same purpose.[4] The rocky summits found on many of them appear to have been not unfrequently employed as altars, on which sacrifices were offered to Jehovah (Judg. vi. 19—21. and xiii. 15—20.); although they were afterwards converted into places for idol worship, for which the prophets Isaiah (lvii. 7.) and Ezekiel (xviii. 6.) severely reprove their degenerate countrymen. And as many of the mountains of Palestine were situated in desert places, the *shadow* they project has furnished

---

[1] Jowett's Christian Researches in Syria, &c. p. 102. (London, 1825. 8vo.)

[2] The oak, which in antient times supplied the Tyrians with oars (Ezek. xxvii. 6.) is still frequently to be found here : the soil is most luxuriantly fertile ; and the nomadic Arab inhabitants are as robust and comely as we may conceive its antient possessors to have been, according to the notices which incidentally occur in the Sacred Volume. See Mr. Buckingham's interesting description of this region. Travels, pp. 325—329.

[3] *Abarim* denotes passes or passages.   [4] Harmer's Observations, vol. iii. pp. 429, 430.

the prophet Isaiah with a pleasing image of the security that shall be enjoyed under the kingdom of Messiah.[1] (xxxii. 2.)

VI. From the mountains, the transition to the VALLIES is natural and easy. Of those which are mentioned in the Sacred Writings, the following are the most celebrated; viz.

1. The VALLEY OF BLESSING (in Hebrew, the Valley of Berachah), in the tribe of Judah, on the west side of the lake of Sodom, and in the wilderness of Tekoah. It derived its name from a signal victory which God granted to the pious king Jehoshaphat over the combined forces of the Moabites, Edomites, and Ammonites. (2 Chron. xx. 22—26.)

2. The VALE OF SIDDIM, memorable for the overthrow of Chedorlaomer and his confederate emirs or kings. (Gen. xiv. 2—10.) In this vale stood the cities of Sodom and Gomorrah, which were afterwards destroyed by fire from heaven, on which account this vale is also termed the *Salt Sea.* (Gen. xiv. 3.)

3. The VALLEY OF SHAVEH, also called the *King's Dale.* (Gen. xiv. 17. 2 Sam. xviii. 18.), derived its name from a city of the same name that stood in it. Here Melchisedek, king of Salem, met the victorious Abraham after the defeat of the confederate kings. (Gen. xiv. 18.)

4. The VALE OF SALT is supposed to have been in the land of Edom, east of the Dead Sea, between Tadmor and Bozrah. Here both David and Amaziah discomfited the Edomites. (2 Sam. viii. 13. 2 Kings xiv. 7.)

5. The VALLEY OF MAMRE received its name from Mamre an Amorite, who was in alliance with Abraham: it was celebrated for the *oak* (or as some critics render it terebinth-) *tree,* under which the patriarch dwelt (Gen. xiii. 18.), in the vicinity of Hebron.

6. The VALLEY OF AJALON is contiguous to the city of the same name, in the canton allotted to the tribe of Dan: it is memorable as the scene of the miracle related in Josh. x. 12. It is said to be of sufficient breadth and compass to allow a numerous host to engage thereon. This valley is better inhabited and cultivated than most other places in the territory, and seems to enjoy a more equal and healthful temperature.[2]

7. The VALLEY OF THE REPHAIM (or the Giant's Valley) was so called from its gigantic inhabitants: it was situated on the confines of the territories allotted to the tribes of Judah and Benjamin. It was memorable, as oftentimes being the field of battle between the Philistines and the Jews under David and his successors. (2 Sam. v. 18. 22. xxiii. 13. 1 Chron. xi. 15. and xiv. 9.) This valley also appears antiently to have been distinguished for its abundant harvests. (Isa. xvii. 5.) Like all the country about Jerusalem, it is now stony, and scantily furnished with patches of light red soil.[3]

---

1 " Ascending a sand-hill that overlooked the plain, we saw Jericho, contrary to our hopes, at a great distance; and the level tract we must pass to arrive at it was exposed to a sultry sun, without a single tree to afford us a temporary shade. The simile of ' the shadow of a great rock in a weary land ' was never more forcibly felt. (Carne's Letters, p. 320.) — " The shadow of a great projecting rock is the most refreshing that is possible in a hot country, not only as most perfectly excluding the rays of the sun, but also having in itself a natural coolness, which it reflects and communicates to every thing about it." Bishop Lowth's Isaiah, vol. ii. p. 221. See also Dr. Henderson's Travels in Iceland, vol. i. p. 206. and Dr. Richardson's Travels along the Mediterranean, &c. vol. ii. p. 186.

2 Carne's Recollections of the East, pp. 137. 140.   3 Buckingham's Travels, p. 216.

8. The VALLEY OF BÒCHIM (or of *Weeping*) was thus denominated from the universal mourning of the Israelites, on account of
the denunciations there made against them, for their disobedience
to the divine commands respecting the nations whom they had invaded. (Judg. ii. 5.)

9. Three miles from Bethlehem, on the road to Jaffa, lies the celebrated *Terebinthine Vale*, or VALLEY OF ELAH, not above half a mile
in breadth, and memorable as the field of the victory gained by the
youthful David over the uncircumcised champion of the Philistines,
who had *defied the armies of the living God.* (1 Sam. xvii. 2, 3.) "It
is a pretty and interesting looking spot; the bottom covered with olive
trees. Its present appearance answers exactly to the description
given in Scripture : for nothing has ever occurred to alter the appearance of the country. The two hills, on which the armies of the
Israelites and Philistines stood, entirely confine it on the right and
left. The very brook, whence David *chose him five smooth stones,*
(which has been noticed by many a thirsty pilgrim, journeying from
Jaffa to Jerusalem,) still flows through the vale, which is varied with
banks and undulations. The ruins of goodly edifices attest the religious veneration entertained in later periods for the hallowed spot:
but even these are now become so insignificant, that they are scarcely
discernible; and nothing can be said to interrupt the native dignity
of this memorable scene." [1]

10. The narrow VALLEY OF HINNOM lies at the foot of Mount
Zion, just south of Jerusalem; it was well watered, and in antient
times was most verdant and delightfully shaded with trees. This
valley is celebrated for the inhuman and barbarous, as well as idolatrous worship, here paid to Moloch; to which deity parents sacrificed their smiling offspring by making them pass through the fire.
(2 Kings xxiii. 10. 2 Chron. xxviii. 3.) To drown the lamentable
shrieks of the children thus immolated, musical instruments (in Hebrew named *Tuph*) were played; whence the spot, where the victims
were burnt, was called *Tophet.* After the captivity, the Jews regarded
this spot with abhorrence on account of the abominations which had
been practised there: and, following the example of Josiah (2 Kings
xxiii. 10.), they threw into it every species of filth, as well as the
carcasses of animals, and the dead bodies of malefactors, &c. To
prevent the pestilence which such a mass would occasion, if left to
putrefy, constant fires were maintained in the valley, in order to consume the whole: hence the place received the appellation of Γεέννα
του πυρος. (Matt. v. 26.) By an easy metaphor, the Jews, who could
imagine no severer torment than that of fire, transferred this name
to the *infernal fire,* — to that part of ᾍδης or the Invisible World,
in which they supposed that demons and the souls of wicked men
were punished in eternal fire. The place now shown as the Valley
of Hinnom "is a deep ravine, closed in on the right by the steep
acclivity of Mount Zion, and on the left by a line of cliffs more or
less elevated. From some point in these cliffs tradition relates that
the apostate betrayer of our Lord sought his desperate end : and the

position of the trees, which in various parts overhang the brow of the cliff, accords with the manner of his death." [1]

11. The VALE OF SHARON (Song of Sol. ii. 1. Isa. lxv. 10.) was, as it is to this day, a spacious and fertile plain of arable land, extending from Cæsarea to Joppa. How valuable this land must have been to Solomon when he made his engagement with Hiram king of Tyre, — and to Herod when he marked his displeasure *against them of Tyre and Sidon,* — may be inferred from 1 Kings v. 7—11. and Acts xii. 20.[2]   At present, this plain is only partially cultivated: the grinding exactions of the Turk, and the predatory incursions of the Arab, prevent the wretched inhabitants from tilling more than is absolutely necessary for their support.[3]

12. The VALLEY OF JEHOSHAPHAT mentioned in Joel iii. 2—12., is situated a short distance to the east of Jerusalem: it is supposed to have derived its name from the circumstance of Jehoshaphat king of Judah tbeing interred here.   It has also been called the *Valley of the Kedron,* because the brook Kedron flows through it, and (in Joel iii. 2. 12. 14.) the *Valley of Decision,* in which the Almighty will gather all nations, in order to be judged.   Aben Ezra, however, imagines it to be the Valley of Blessing above noticed: and some commentators consider the word to be symbolical, signifying the judgment of God; or, Jehovah judgeth.   They are of opinion, that it may mean some place where Nebuchadnezzar should gain a great battle, which would utterly discomfit the antient enemies of the Jews, and resemble the victory obtained by Jehoshaphat over the Ammonites, Moabites, and Edomites.[4]   This narrow valley has, from a very early period, served as a burial place for the inhabitants of Jerusalem; as we may infer from the account of the destruction of idolatry in Judah and of the vessels made for Baal, when the bones of the priests were burned to ashes at the brook Kedron, and were cast upon the graves of the children of the people. (1 Kings xiii. 2. 2 Kings xxiii. 6. 2 Chron. xxxiv. 4.)   The Hebrew population of Jerusalem still inter their dead in this valley, in which there are numerous tomb-stones: and as a strong inclination still exists among the Jews to have their remains entombed in the country of their ancestors, many of them arrive here with this view, in the course of the year, from the most distant lands.[5] One day in the year the Jews purchase from their oppressors the permission to assemble in this place, which they pass in weeping and mourning over the desolation of Jerusalem, and their lengthened captivity.[6]   It was on this side, that the city was carried by assault by the besiegers in the first crusade.

---

[1] Robinson's Gr. Lex. to New Testament, voce. Γεέννα.   Jowett's Christian Researehes in Syria, &c. p. 262.
[2] Jowett's Researches, p. 305.
[3] Three Weeks' Residence in Palestine, p. 11.
[4] Archbp. Newcome, and Dr. A. Clarke, on Joel iii. 2.
[5] Mr. Rae Wilson's Travels in the Holy Land, vol. i. p. 220.   The same intelligent traveller continues : — "Observing many Jews, whom I could easily recognise by their yellow turbans, black eyebrows, and bushy beards, walking about the place, and reposing along the brook Kedron in a pensive mood, the pathetic language of the Psalmist occurred to me, as expressing the subject of their meditation, — *By the rivers we sat down and wept, when we remembered Zion.*   Upon frequently enquiring the motive that prompted them in attempting to go to Jerusalem, the answer was, ' To die in the land of our fathers.' " Ibid.
[6] **Three Weeks' Residence in Palestine, p. 39.**

VII. The country of Judæa, being mountainous and rocky, is full of CAVERNS; to which the inhabitants were accustomed to flee for shelter from the incursions of their enemies. (Josh. x. 16. Judg. vi. 2. 1 Sam. xiii. 6. xiv. 11.) Some of these appear to have been on low grounds, and liable to inundations, when the rivers, swollen by torrents or dissolving snows, overflowed their banks, and carried all before them with resistless fury. To the sudden destruction thus produced Isaiah probably alludes. (xxxviii. 17.) Therefore, to enter *into the holes of the rocks, and into the caves of the earth, for fear of the Lord,* (Isa. ii. 19.) was to the Jews a very proper image to express terror and consternation. The prophet Hosea has carried the same image further, and added great strength and spirit to it (x. 8.); which image, together with these of Isaiah, is adopted by the sublime author of the Revelation (vi. 15, 16.), who frequently borrows his imagery from the prophet Isaiah.[1]

Some of these caves were very capacious: that of ADULLAM afforded an asylum to David and four hundred men, including his family, who resorted thither to him. (1 Sam. xxii. 1, 2.) The cave of ENGEDI was so large, that David and six hundred men concealed themselves in its sides; and Saul entered the mouth of the cave without perceiving that any one was there. " At first, it appears neither lofty nor spacious; but a low passage on the left leads into apartments, where a party could easily remain concealed from those without. The face of the hill around it corresponds to the description, — *he came to the rocks of the wild goats.*" (1 Sam. xxiv. 2.)[2] Bishop Poc.cke has described a cave, which he thinks may be this of Engedi; concerning which there is a tradition, that thirty thousand people retired into it to avoid a bad air.[3] Josephus[4] has taken particular notice of similar caverns, which in his time were the abode of robbers. Maundrell[5] has described a large cavern under a high rocky mountain in the vicinity of Sidon, containing two hundred smaller caverns, which are supposed to have been the residence of the original inhabitants. Numerous caves were noticed by Mr. Buckingham[6] in the rock to the south of Nazareth; several of which now, as antiently, serve as dwellings to the Nazarenes. Mr. Hartley has described a similar cavern, capable of holding a thousand men by actual enumeration, whither the Greeks fled, and found a secure asylum from their Mohammedan enemies.[7] Captain Lyon has described similar residences occupied by a tribe of Troglodytes in northern Africa.[8]

[1] Bishop Lowth's Isaiah, vol. ii. p. 37.   [2] Carne's Letters, p. 307.
[3] Pococke's Travels, vol. ii. part i. p. 41.   [4] Antiq. lib. xiv. c. 15. § 5.
[5] Travels, pp. 158, 159.   [6] Travels in Palestine, p. 113.
[7] Journal of a Tour in Greece, in 1828. (Missionary Register, May 1830, p. 231.)
[8] " As the natives live under ground, a person unacquainted with the circumstance might cross the mountain without once suspecting that it was inhabited. All the dwelling-places being formed in the same manner, a description of the scheik's may suffice for the rest. The upper soil is sandy earth of about four feet in depth; under this sand, and in some places lime-stone, a large hole is dug to the depth of twenty-five or thirty feet, and its breadth in every direction is about the same, being as nearly as can be made, a perfect square. The rock is then smoothed, so as to form perpendicular sides to this space, in which doors are cut through, and arched chambers excavated, so as to receive their light from the doors: these rooms are sometimes three or four of a side; in others, a whole side composes one: the arrangements depending on the number of the inhabitants. In the open court is generally a well, water being found at about ten or twelve feet below the base of the square. The entrance to the house is about thirty-six yards from the pit, and opens above ground. It is

It was probably in some such cave that Lot and his two daughters dwelt after the destruction of Sodom (Gen. xix. 30.); and in similar caverns, excavated by primeval shepherds as a shelter from the scorching beams of the sun, Dr. Clarke and his fellow-travellers found a grateful protection from the intense heat of the solar rays[1]; as Captains Irby and Mangles subsequently did from a violent storm.[2] These caves were sometimes the haunts or strongholds of robbers (as the excavations in the rocks near Bethlehem are to this day[3], and to them our Lord probably alludes in Matt. xxi. 13., where he reproaches the Jews with having profaned the temple of God, and made it *a den of thieves.*

VIII. Numerous fertile and level tracts are mentioned in the Sacred Volume, under the title of PLAINS. Three of these are particularly worthy of notice; viz.

1. The PLAIN OF THE MEDITERRANEAN SEA, which reached from the river of Egypt to Mount Carmel. The tract between Gaza and Joppa was simply called the *Plain;* in this stood the five principal cities of the Philistine satrapies, Ascalon, Gath, Gaza, Ekron or Accaron, and Azotus or Ashdod. The tract from Joppa to Mount Carmel was called Saron or *Sharon;* which however is a different place from the Sharon that lies between Mount Tabor and the Sea of Tiberias, and from another place of the same name, which was celebrated for its pastures, and was situated in the tribe of Gad beyond Jordan.

2. The PLAIN OF JEZREEL, or of ESDRAELON, also called the GREAT PLAIN (the Armageddon of the Apocalypse), extends from Mount Carmel and the Mediterranean to the place where the Jordan issues from the Sea of Tiberias, through the middle of the Holy Land. Here, in the most fertile part of the land of Canaan, the tribe of Issachar *rejoiced in their tents.* (Deut. xxxiii. 18.) In the first ages of Jewish history, as well as during the Roman empire and the crusades, and even in later times, it has been the scene of many a memorable contest. " Here it was that Barak, descending with his ten thousand men from Mount Tabor, discomfited Sisera and *all his chariots, even nine hundred chariots of iron, and all the people that were with him,* gathered *from Harosheth of the Gentiles unto the river of Kishon;* when *all the host of Sisera fell upon the sword, and there was not a man left;* when *the kings came and fought, the kings of Canaan in Taanach by the waters of Megiddo.* (Judg. iv. 13. 15, 16. v. 19.) Here also it was that Josiah, king of Judah, fought in disguise against Necho king of Egypt, and fell by the arrows of his antagonist. (2 Kings

---

arched over head ; is generally cut in a winding direction, and is perfectly dark. Some of these passages are sufficiently large to admit a loaded camel. The entrance has a strong wall built over it, something resembling an ice-house. This is covered over-head, and has a very strong heavy door, which is shut at night, or in cases of danger. At about ten yards from the bottom is another door equally strong, so that it is almost impossible to enter these houses, should the inhabitants determine to resist. Few Arab attacks last long enough to end in a siege. All their sheep and poultry being confined in the house at night, the bashaw's army, when here, had recourse to suffocating the inmates, being unable to starve them out." — See Capt. Lyon's Travels in Northern Africa, p. 25.

[1] Travels in Greece, &c. vol. iv. pp. 189, 190.   [2] Travels, p. 217.

[3] Clarke's Travels, vol. iv. p. 421. See also Sir R. K. Porter's Travels in Georgia, Persia, &c. vol. ii. pp. 540—544. for a description of the caves in the mountain of Kerefto (in the province of eastern Courdistan), which tradition states to have been antiently used for the same purpose.

xxiii. 29.) So great were the lamentations for his death, that the
mourning of Josiah became *an ordinance* in Israel (2 Chron. xxxv.
24, 25.) : and *the great mourning in Jerusalem,* foretold by Zechariah
(xii. 11.), is said to be as the lamentations in the plain of Esdraelon,
or, according to the prophet's language, *as the mourning of Hadad-
rimmon in the valley of Megiddo.* Josephus often mentions this very
remarkable part of the Holy Land, and always under the appellation
of the *Great Plain :* and under the same name it is also mentioned by
Eusebius and by Jerome. It has been a chosen place for encampment
in every contest carried on in this country, from the days of Nabu-
chadonosor king of the Assyrians, in the history of whose war with
Arphaxad it is mentioned as *the Great Plain of Esdrelom*[1], until the
disastrous march of the late Napoleon Buonaparte from Egypt into
Syria. Jews, Gentiles, Saracens, Christian crusaders, and anti-christian
Frenchmen, Egyptians, Persians, Druses, Turks, and Arabs, warriors
out of every nation which is under heaven, have pitched their tents in
the Plain of Esdraelon, and have beheld the various banners of their
nation wet with the dews of Tabor and of Hermon." [2]   This plain is
inclosed on all sides by mountains : the hills of Nazareth to the north,
— those of Samaria to the south, — to the east, the mountains of
Tabor and Hermon, and Carmel to the south-west. The Rev. Mr.
Jowett, in November, 1823, counted in his road across this plain only
five very small villages, consisting of wretched mud hovels, chiefly in
ruins, and only a very few persons moving on the road; so that to
this scene the words of Deborah might again be truly applied : — *The
highways were unoccupied; the inhabitants of the villages ceased ; — they
ceased in Israel.* (Judg. v. 6, 7.) The soil is stated to be extremely
rich ; and in every direction are the most picturesque views.[3]   Cotton is raised here, the quality of which is supposed to be superior to
any in the east. The fertility of this plain is chiefly to be attributed
to its being watered by the river Kishon, which flows through it. The
plain of Esdraelon now bears the name of *Fooli,* and has been celebrated in modern times by the victory which Murat gained over the
Mamelukes and Arabs, in their attempt to relieve Acri or Acre, in
April 1799.[4] Mr. Jowett computes this plain to be at least fifteen
miles square, making allowances for some apparent irregularities.
Though it bears the title of " Plain," yet it abounds with hills, which
in the view of it from the adjacent mountains shrink into nothing.[5]

3. The REGION ROUND ABOUT JORDAN, (Matt. iii. 5.) comprised
the level country on both sides of that river, from the lake of Gennesareth to the Dead Sea. Of this district the *Plain of Jericho,* celebrated for its fertility and the intense heat that prevails there during
the hot season, forms a part; as also do the *Valley of Salt* near the
Salt or Dead Sea, (where David defeated the Syrians (1 Chron. xviii.
3—8.) and Amaziah discomfited the Edomites[6]), and the *Plains of
Moab,* where the Israelites encamped[7], and which are also called

---

[1] Judith i. 8.   [2] Clarke's Travels, vol. iv. pp. 255—258.
[3] Jowett's Christian Researches in Syria, pp. 191, 192.   A later traveller estimates the
length of the valley of Esdraelon at twenty-four miles, and its breadth from ten to twelve
miles.   Madden's Travels in Turkey, &c. vol. ii. p. 305.
[4] Light's Travels, p. 201.
[5] Jowett's Researches in Syria, pp. 301, 302.
[6] 2 Kings, xiv. 7.   2 Chron. xxv. 11.   [7] Numb. xxii. 1. xxvi. 3.

Shittim in Numb. xxv. 1. Josh. ii. 1. and iii. 1., the *Plains of Shittim*, in Numb. xxxiii. 49. (marginal rendering), and the *Valley of Shittim*, in Joel iii. 18.

IX. Frequent mention is made in the Scriptures of WILDER-NESSES or DESERTS, by which we usually understand desolate places, equally devoid of cities and inhabitants. The deserts noticed in the Bible, however, are of a different description; as the Hebrews were accustomed to give the name of desert or wilderness to all places that were not cultivated[1], but which were chiefly appropriated to the feeding of cattle, and in many of them trees and shrubs grew wild. Hence this term is frequently applied to the commons (as they would be called in England) which were contiguous to cities or villages, and on which the plough never came. The wildernesses or deserts of Palestine, therefore, are twofold : some are mountainous and well-watered, while others are sterile sandy plains, either destitute of water, or affording a very scanty supply from the few brackish springs that are occasionally to be found in them; yet even these afford a grateful though meagre pasturage to camels, goats, and sheep.

The Deserts of the Hebrews frequently derive their appellations from the places to which they were contiguous. Thus,

1. The DESERT or WILDERNESS OF SHUR lay towards the north-eastern point of the Red Sea. In this wilderness, Hagar wandered, when unjustly driven from Abraham's house by the jealousy of Sarah. (Gen. xvi. 7.). Being the most direct communication between Egypt and Palestine, it has been traversed from the earliest times (Exod. xiii. 17.) to the present, by caravans, armies, and people. The Israelites marched through this wilderness after they had miraculously crossed the Red Sea (Exod. xv. 22.), as they also did subsequently through,

2. The WILDERNESS or DESERT OF PARAN, which lay considerably more to the south. (Numb. x. 12.) In this desert (which was situated in Arabia Petræa, near a city of the same name,) Ishmael resided : and hence Moses sent out spies to bring intelligence concerning the promised land. (Numb. xiii. 3.) The Desert of Paran " is in many parts intersected by numerous ravines and glens, and broken by lofty barriers. Among these, the noble mountain of Paran, with its enormous precipices, is only a long day's journey distant, and always in sight from the neighbourhood : it is capable of ascent only on the farthest side, and that not without difficulty. Around its base are flat plains of sand, well adapted to large encampments : here and there, at long intervals, a clump of palm-trees is seen, and in their vicinity water is generally found."[2]

3. The DESERT OF SINAI was that in the vicinity of Mount Sinai in Arabia : here the Israelites were for a long time encamped, and received the chief part of the laws delivered to them by Jehovah, through the ministry of Moses.

4. The WILDERNESS OF ZIPH was contiguous to a town or village of the same name, and here David concealed himself for some time. (1 Sam. xxiii. 14, 15.) But the most celebrated of all is,

---

[1] The Arabs to this day give the appellation of *Desert* to any solitude, whether barren or fertile. Clarke's Travels, vol. iv. p. 422.
[2] Carne's Recollections of the East, p. 278.

5. The WILDERNESS or DESERT OF JUDAH. (Psal. lxiii. title) The Desert of Judæa in which John the Baptist abode till the day of his showing unto Israel (Luke i. 80.), and where he first taught his countrymen (Matt. iii. 1. Mark i. 4. John x. 39.), was a mountainous, wooded, and thinly inhabited tract of country, but abounding in pastures; it was situated adjacent to the Dead Sea, and the River Jordan. In the time of Joshua it had six cities, with their villages. (Jos. xv. 61, 62.) It is now one of the most dreary and desolate regions of the whole country.

6. The vast DESERT OF ARABIA, reaching from the eastern side of the Red Sea to the confines of the land of Canaan, in which the children of Israel sojourned after their departure from Egypt, is in the Sacred Writings particularly called THE DESERT; very numerous are the allusions made to it, and to the divine protection and support, which were extended to them during their migration. Moses, when recapitulating their various deliverances, terms this desert *a desert land and waste howling wilderness* (Deut. xxxii. 10.) — and *that great and terrible wilderness,* wherein were *fiery serpents, scorpions*[1]*, and drought, where* there was *no water.* (Deut. viii. 15.) The prophet Hosea describes it as a *land of great drought* (Hos. xiii. 5.); but the most minute description is that in Jer. ii. 6. — *a land of deserts and of pits, a land of drought, and of the shadow of death*[2]*, a land that no man passed through, and where no man dwelt.* These characteristics of the desert, particularly the want of water, will account for the repeated murmurings of the Israelites both for food and water (especially the latter[3]): and the extremity of their sufferings is thus concisely, but most emphatically portrayed by the Psalmist (cvii. 5.)[4]

Hungry and thirsty, THEIR SOUL FAINTED *in them.*

In this our temperate climate, surrounded as we are with perpetual verdure, and with every object that can delight the eye, we can scarcely conceive the horrors encountered by the hapless traveller when crossing the trackless sands, and exposed to all the ardours of a vertical sun. The most recent as well as the most graphic description of a desert (which admirably illustrates the passages above cited), is that

---

[1] Scorpions are numerous in the desert as well as in all the adjacent parts of Palestine; the malignity of their venom is in proportion to their size; and serpents of fiery bites (as the Arabic version renders Deut. viii. 15.) are not unfrequent. Burckhardt's Travels in Syria, &c. pp. 499, 500.

[2] This expression has exercised the ingenuity of commentators, whose opinions are recited by Mr. Harmer (Observations, vol. iv. pp. 115, 116.); but the correctness of the prophetic description is confirmed by the existence of a similar desert in Persia. It is a tract of land broken into *deep ravines, destitute of water, and of dreariness without example.* The Persians have given to it the extraordinary but emphatic appellation of *Malek-Moatderch,* or *the Valley of the Angel of Death.* (Morier's Second Journey, p. 168.) At four hours' distance from the promontory of Carmel, keeping along the coast, Mr. Buckingham entered a dreary pass cut out of the rock, called *Waad-el-Ajal,* literally, *the Valley of the Shadow of Death.* Here were the appearances of a gate having once closed it, as places for hinges were still visible; and while the centre was just broad enough to admit a wheeled carriage or loaded camel, there were on each side raised causeways hewn out of the rock, as if for benches of repose, or for foot passengers. (Buckingham's Travels, p. 122.) It was, in all probability, from some similar pass, that the son of Jesse borrowed the figure of which he makes so sublime a use in the twenty-third psalm.

[3] See particularly Numb. xx. 2—5. and xxi. 5.

[4] In the Christian Observer for 1810, pp. 1—9. there is a new and elegant version of the hundred and seventh psalm, accompanied with critical and explanatory notes, from the pen of Bishop Jebb.

given by the enterprising traveller, Mr. Belzoni, whose researches have contributed so much to the elucidation of the Sacred Writings. Speaking of a desert crossed by him in Upper Egypt, on the western side of the Red Sea, and which is parallel with the great desert tra-versed by the Israelites on the *eastern* side of that sea, he says, " It is difficult to form a correct idea of a desert, without having been in one : it is an endless plain of sand and stones, sometimes intermixed with mountains of all sizes and heights, without roads or shelter, without any sort of produce for food. The few scattered trees and shrubs of thorns, that only appear when the rainy season leaves some moisture, barely serve to feed wild animals, and a few birds. Every thing is left to nature; the wandering inhabitants do not care to cultivate even these few plants, and when there is no more of them in one place they go to another. When these trees become old and lose their vegetation, the sun, which constantly beams upon them, burns and reduces them to ashes. I have seen many of them entirely burnt. The other smaller plants have no sooner risen out of the earth than they are dried up, and all take the colour of straw, with the exception of the plant *harack ;* this falls off before it is dry.

" Generally speaking, in a desert, there are few springs of water, some of them at the distance of four, six, and eight days' journey from one another, and not all of sweet water : on the contrary, it is gene-rally salt or bitter; so that if the thirsty traveller drinks of it, it increases his thirst, and he suffers more than before. But, when the calamity happens, that the next well, which is so anxiously sought for, is found dry, the misery of such a situation cannot be well described. The camels, which afford the only means of escape, are so thirsty, that they cannot proceed to another well : and if the travellers kill them, to extract the little liquid which remains in their stomachs, they themselves cannot advance any farther. The situation must be dread-ful, and admits of no resource. Many perish, *victims of the most horrible thirst.* It is then that the value of a cup of water is really felt. He that has a *zenzabia* of it is the richest of all. In such a case there is no distinction. If the master has none, the servant will not give it to him ; for very few are the instances, where a man will volun-tarily lose his life to save that of another, particularly in a caravan in the desert, where people are strangers to each other. *What a situa-tion for a man, though a rich one, perhaps the owner of all the caravans! He is dying for a cup of water — no one gives it to him — he offers all he possesses — no one hears him — they are all dying* — though by walking a few hours farther they might be saved. — If the camels are lying down, and cannot be made to rise — *no one has strength to walk* — only he that has a glass of that precious liquor lives to walk a mile farther, and, perhaps, dies too. If the voyages on seas are dangerous, so are those in the deserts. At sea, the provisions very often fail ; in the desert it is worse : at sea, storms are met with ; in the desert there cannot be a greater storm than to find a dry well : at sea, one meets with pirates—we escape—we surrender—we die ; in the desert they rob the traveller of all his property and water; they let him live, per-haps, but what a life ! to die the most barbarous and agonising death. In short, *to be thirsty in a desert, without water, exposed to the burn-ing sun, without shelter, and* NO HOPES *of finding either, is the most terrible situation that a man can be placed in, and one of the greatest suffer-ings that a human being can sustain: the eyes grow inflamed; the tongue and lips swell; a hollow sound is heard in the ears, which brings on deafness, and the brains appear to grow thick and inflamed:* all these feelings arise from the want of a little water. In the midst of all this misery the deceitful morasses appear before the traveller at no great distance, something like a lake or river of clear fresh water.[1] If, per-chance, a traveller is not undeceived, he hastens his pace to reach it sooner: the more he advances towards it, the more it recedes from him, till at last it vanishes entirely, and the deluded passenger often asks, where is the water he saw at no great distance? He can scarcely believe that he was so deceived; he protests that he saw the waves running before the wind, and the reflection of the high rocks in the water.

" If unfortunately any one falls sick on the road, there is no alter-native; he must endure the fatigue of travelling on a camel, which is troublesome even to healthy people, or he must be left behind on the sand, without any assistance, and remain so till a slow death come to relieve him. What horror! What a brutal proceeding to an unfor-tunate sick man! No one remains with him, not even his old and faithful servant; no one will stay and die with him; all pity his fate, but no one will be his companion." [2]

The phenomenon, here described, is produced by a diminution of the density of the lower stratum of the atmosphere, which is caused by the increase of heat, arising from that communicated by the rays of

---

[1] Terrific as the above description is, it is confirmed in most of its details by Quintus Curtius; who, describing the passage of Alexander the Great and his army across the deserts of Sogdiana, thus graphically delineates its horrors: — " Amidst a dearth of water, despair of obtaining any kindled thirst before nature excited it. Throughout four hundred stadia not a drop of moisture springs. As soon as the fire of summer pervades the sands, every thing is dried up, as in a kiln always burning. *Steaming from the fervid expanse, which appears like a surface of sea, a cloudy vapour darkens the day...... The heat,* which commences *at dawn, exhausts the animal juices, blisters the skin, and causes internal inflammation.* The soldiers sunk under depression of spirits caused by bodily debility." Quint. Curt. lib. vii. c. 5.

[2] Belzoni's Narrative of his Operations and Researches in Egypt, &c. (4to. London, 1820,) pp. 341—343. In another part of his volume, Mr. B. more particularly describes the *mirage* (for such is the appellation by which this phenomenon is now commonly known), in the following terms:—" It generally appears like a still lake, so unmoved by the wind, that every thing above is to be seen most distinctly reflected by it. If the wind agitate any of the plants that rise above the horizon of the mirage, the motion is seen perfectly at a great distance. If the traveller stand elevated much above the mirage, the apparent water seems less united and less deep; for, as the eyes look down upon it, there is not thickness enough in the vapour on the surface of the ground to conceal the earth from the sight; but, if the traveller be on a level with the horizon of the mirage, he cannot see through it, so that it appears to him clear water. By putting my head first to the ground, and then mounting a camel, the height of which from the ground might have been about ten feet at the most, I found a great difference in the appearance of the mirage. On approaching it, it becomes thinner, and appears as if agitated by the wind, like a field of ripe corn. It gradually vanishes, as the traveller approaches, and at last entirely disappears, when he is on the spot." (p. 196.) Dr. Clarke has described the mirage, as it appeared to him on his journey to Rosetta, in 1801. (Travels, vol. iii. p. 371.) Similar descriptions, but none so full as that of Mr. Belzoni, may be seen in Sir J. Malcolm's Hist. of Persia, vol. ii. p. 512.; in El-phinstone's Account of the Kingdom of Caubul (p. 16. 4to. London, 1815); Kinneir's Geographical Memoir of the Persian Empire (p. 223. 4to. London, 1813); Lieut. Pot-tinger's Travels in Beloochistan and Sinde (p. 185. 4to. London, 1816); in Dr. Della Cella's Narrative of the Bey of Tripoli's Expedition, in 1817, to the Western Frontier of Egypt, (p. 58. London, 1822, 8vo.); in Mr. Madden's Travels in Turkey, &c. vol. ii. pp. 199, 200. London, 1829; and Mr. Rae Wilson's Travels in the Holy Land, Egypt, &c. vol. i. p. 67. Dr. Henderson has described the Seráb as it appeared on his journey towards Kherson in the Crimea, Biblical Researches, pp. 278, 279. (London, 1826. 8vo.)

the sun to the sand with which this stratum is in immediate contact. This phenomenon existed in the great desert of Judæa, and is expressly alluded to by the sublime and elegant Isaiah [1], who, when predicting the blessings of the Messiah's spiritual kingdom, says, —

> *The glowing sand [2] shall become a pool,*
> *And the thirsty soil bubbling springs.*

And it is not improbable that Jeremiah refers to the serâb or mirage when, in pouring forth his complaint to God for mercies deferred, he says, *Wilt thou be altogether unto me as waters that be not sure?* (marginal rendering of Jer. xv. 18.) that is, *which have no reality*, as the Septuagint translators have rendered it, ὕδωρ ψευδὲς οὐκ ἔχον πίστιν.

Frightful as the horrors of the deserts are, they are augmented beyond description, should the traveller be overtaken by one of those sand storms, which prevail during the dry seasons. Sometimes the high winds raise into the air thick clouds of dust and sand, which, descending like a shower of rain, most grievously annoy all among whom they fall, and penetrate the eyes, nostrils, ears, in short, every part of the human frame that is exposed to it. At other times the sands are drifted into such heaps, that, if any storm of wind should arise, the track is lost, and whole caravans perish in the inhospitable wilderness. Such are the showers of *powder and dust*, with which Moses denounced that God would *scourge* the disobedient Israelites, in Deut. xxviii. 24. [3]

SECTION II.

ON THE FERTILITY AND PRODUCTIONS OF THE HOLY LAND.

I. *Fertility of the Holy Land.* — II. *Its Productions* ; — 1. *Vegetables* ; — 2. *Cattle* ; — 3. *Mines.* — III. *Testimonies of Antient and Modern Authors to its Fertility and Populousness.* — IV. *Calamities with which this Country was visited* ; — 1. *The Plague* ; — 2. *Earthquakes* ; — 3. *Whirlwinds* ; — 4. *The Devastations of Locusts* ; — 5. *Famine* ; — 6. *The Simoom or Pestilential Blast of the Desert.* [4]

I. MOSES, addressing the Israelites a short time before his death, characterised the country whither they were going to reside, as a *good*

---

[1] Isa. xxxv. 7. Bp. Lowth's translation.

[2] The phenomenon referred to by Isaiah, is termed by the Arabs, as well as by the Hebrews שׁרב (SERÁB) ; and to this day the Persians and Arabs make use of it, by an elegant metaphor, to express disappointed hope.

[3] Fragments supplementary to Calmet's Dictionary, No. 172. In the London Weekly Review, No. I. (June 9th, 1827,) there is an animated and graphic delineation of one of these terrific sand-storms in the desert, extracted from the manuscript Journal of the intelligent traveller Mr. Buckingham, who was exposed to its fury for several hours, and, with his companions, was providentially preserved from destruction.

[4] Besides the authorities cited in the course of this section, the following works have been consulted for it ; viz. Relandi Palæstina, tom. i. pp. 378—391. ; Schulzii Archæologia Hebraica, pp. 9—16. ; Pareau, Antiquitas Hebraica, pp. 63—66. ; Jahn et Ackermann, Archæologia Biblica, §§ 16. 22, 23. ; Hasselquist's Travels, vol. ii. pp. 138—153. ; and Volney's Travels in Egypt and Syria, vol. i. pp. 290—297. The testimony of Volney is the more valuable, as he was through life an inveterate enemy of the Bible, and directed his great talents to the fruitless task of destroying its credibility. To these are to be added the " Economical Calendar of Palestine," translated from the Latin of John Gottlieb Buhle

land — *a land of brooks of water, of fountains and depths that spring out of vallies and hills.* How justly this corresponded with the actual state of the country, the preceding pages have shown : — Moses further added, that it was *a land of wheat and barley, and vines and fig-trees, and pomegranates, a land of oil olive, and honey, whose stones were iron, and out of whose hills they might dig brass.* The enemies of Revelation, forming their notions of its former exuberant fertility from the *present* state of the Holy Land under the Turkish government, have insinuated that it never could have been the lovely and fertile spot which the Sacred Writings affirm it to have been: but a concise statement of its productions, as we may collect them from the Scriptures, together with the attestations of antient profane writers, as well as of modern voyagers and travellers, will all concur to establish the unimpeachable veracity of the inspired writers.

II. The Holy Land is said to have exceeded even the very celebrated land of Egypt, in the abundance of its PRODUCTIONS. To this wonderful fertility many circumstances are supposed to have contributed; such as the generally excellent temperature of the air, which was never subject to excessive heats (except in the plain of Jericho), or colds; the regularity of its seasons, especially of the former and the latter rain: and the natural richness of the soil, which is a fine mould without stones, and almost without a pebble.

1. A plenty of WHEAT was promised to the Israelites on their obedience (Psal. lxxxi. 16. and cxlvii. 14.); and so abundant was the produce of the wheat and barley, that *sixty* and *a hundred fold* rewarded the toil of the cultivator. (Gen. xxvi. 12. and Matt. xiii. 8.) This was sometimes stored in subterraneous granaries, which in 1 Chron. xxvii. 25. are termed storehouses in the fields. Such granaries are still in use among the Moors.[1] The wheat of Minnith and Pannog was particularly celebrated, and so plentiful that it was exported to Tyre. (Ezek. xxvii. 17.) In the treaty concluded between Solomon and Hiram king of Tyre, for the building of the temple, the Hebrew monarch was to supply the latter annually with *twenty thousand measures of wheat for food to his household* (1 Kings v. 11.), and the same quantity for the hewers that cut timber (2 Chron. ii. 10.), together with an equal number of measures of barley. More than a thousand years after this time, the coasts of Tyre and Sidon were supplied with corn from Palestine. (Acts xii. 20.)

This country also abounded with HONEY, not only that made by the domesticated or hived bees, but also with honey made by bees in a wild state, and deposited on rocks and in the hollows of trees (1 Sam. xiv. 25. Deut. xxxii. 13. Psal. lxxxi. 16.), which formed a part of the food of John the Baptist in the wilderness. (Matt. iii. 4.) The Mount of Olives and other districts in Judæa and Galilee produced the finest OLIVES; and the red wines of Lebanon were particularly celebrated for their fragrance. (Hos. xiv. 7.) The wines of Helbon furnished a profitable article of export to Damascus (Ezek. xxvii. 18.): and modern travellers attest the size and weight of the

---

by the editor of Calmet's Dictionary, and inserted in the Fragments supplementary to that work. See also an elaborate and pleasing Disquisition on the Agriculture of the Israelites, by the Rev. J. Plumptre, in Nos. I. II. and IV. of the Investigator.

[1] Chenier, Recherches Historiques sur les Maures, tom. iii. p. 219.

clusters of GRAPES still produced in Palestine, which will account for the spies carrying the cluster of grapes cut down in the valley of Eshcol (Numb. xiii. 23.) between two upon a staff.

Various herbs, shrubs, and trees, imparted beauty and fragrance to this highly-favoured land. Among the herbs and shrubs, the aloe (Psal. xlv. 8. Prov. vii. 17. Sol. Song iv. 14.), the hyssop [1] (1 Kings iv. 33. Matt. xxvii. 48. Mark xv. 36.), the rose, especially the rose of Sharon (Sol. Song ii. 1.), the lily (Ibid. ii. 16. iv. 5. v. 13. Matt. vi. 28.[2]), the spikenard (Mark xiv. 3. 5. Sol. Song i. 12.) the carob-tree (κερατιον, Luke xv. 6.[3]), the *spina Christi* or thorn of Christ [4], the mandrake (a species of melon) (Gen. xxx. 14. Sol. Song vii. 13.), the myrtle (Isa. xli. 19. and lv. 13. Zech. i. 8.[5]), and the mustard tree (Matt. xiii. 31, 32.), may be distinctly noticed.[6]

Although modern travellers do not mention the existence of any woods or forests, or, indeed, any considerable number of trees, yet it appears that, antiently, the Holy Land was well covered with wood. We read of several FORESTS and WOODS in the Sacred Writings, particularly, —

(1.) The FOREST OF CEDARS on Mount Lebanon. See 1 Kings vii. 2. 2 Kings xix. 23. Hos. xiv. 5, 6. These noble and beautiful trees, which are unrivalled in grandeur and beauty in the vegetable kingdom, have furnished the inspired writers with numerous exquisite similitudes. " To break the cedars, and shake the enormous mass in which they grow, occur among the figures which David selects to express the

---

[1] The hyssop is a low shrubby plant, growing in the east, and also in the south of Europe, the stem of which usually rises to about a foot and a half in height. In Palestine, its altitude sometimes exceeds two feet. This plant was much used in the antient Hebrew ritual for ceremonial sprinklings, &c. (Heb. ix. 16. compared with Exod. xii. 22. and Numb. xix. 18.) The sponge filled with vinegar, which was presented to Jesus Christ upon the cross (John xix. 29.) was most probably fastened around a rod of hyssop, two or more feet in length, which was sufficiently long to enable a person to reach the mouth of a man upon the cross. Robinson's Lexicon, voce Υσσωπος.

[2] In this passage Jesus Christ is commonly supposed to have referred to the white lily or to the tulip; but neither of these grows wild in Palestine. It is natural to presume that, according to his usual custom, he called the attention of his hearers to some object at hand; and as the fields of the Levant are overrun with the *amaryllis lutea*, whose golden liliaceous flowers, in autumn, afford one of the most brilliant and gorgeous objects in nature, the expression of *Solomon in all his glory not being arrayed like one of these*, is peculiarly appropriate. Should this conjecture prove correct, we learn a chronological fact, respecting the season of the year when the Sermon on the Mount was delivered.

[3] " The modern Greeks still call this fruit by the same name, κερατια, and sell them in the markets. They are given to swine, but not rejected as food even by man." (Hartley's Researches in Greece, p. 241.)

[4] This shrub is supposed, and not without reason, to be the plant which supplied the crown of thorns, with which mockery decked the Saviour's brow before his crucifixion. For this purpose it must have been very fit; as its thorns, which are an inch in length, are very strong and sharp. It is not unlike a willow in growth and flexibility; and as the leaves greatly resemble those of the ivy, it is not improbable that the enemies of Christ chose it, on account of its similarity to the plant with which it was usual to crown emperors and generals: so that calumny, insult, and derision might be meditated in the very act of punishment. Hasselquist's Voyages in the Levant, p. 288. Three Weeks in Palestine, p. 83.

[5] From the passages above referred to, it should seem that the myrtle tree attained a considerable size. In the Morea, an intelligent traveller (Mr. Emerson) states that he travelled for hours through an uncultivated track, while the groves of myrtle form an almost continuous arbour overhead, " covered here and there with its delicate white flowers, and exhaling at every motion the most delicious perfume, whilst its dark polished leaves combined coolness with beauty." Letters from the Ægean, vol. i. p. 113.

[6] For copious accounts of these and other vegetables, as well as of the animal and mineral productions mentioned in the Scriptures (many of which it falls not within the limits of this work to notice), the reader is referred to Dr. Harris's Natural History of the Bible.

power and majesty of Jehovah (Psal. xxix. 4, 5.), to the full understanding of which their countless number at one period, and vast bulk,
ought to be kept in view. By the planting of a cedar the prophet
(Ezek. xvii. 22. 24.) has described the kingdom of Christ : the growth
and extent of the New Testament church, and the prodigious increase
of her converts, are also beautifully set forth by the Psalmist under
this emblem. (Psal. xcii. 12.) Of this particular wood, we find that
Solomon made himself a chariot. (Song iv. 11.) . . . . . The prosperity
of the righteous is compared to the cedar ; and it is further employed
to denounce the judgments of God on men of proud and high minds.
(Psal. xxix. 4.) The conversion of the Gentiles also to the worship
of the true God is expressed in terms highly beautiful (Isa. xxix. 17.
xxxii. 15.), as also the prosperity of the kingdom of Christ. (Isa.
ii. 2.) Those who encompassed the priests at the altar are also compared to them, as also the glory of wisdom. (Ecclus. xxiv. 15.) It
may be further added, that cedar trees, uniting so many qualities well
adapted for building, afforded ample materials for the structure of the
temple, and were sent by king Hiram to Solomon for that purpose.
(1 Kings v. 10—15.)"[1] Every thing about the cedar tree has a strong
balsamic odour : this probably is the *smell of Lebanon,* mentioned in
Sol. Song iv. 11. and Hos. iv. 16.

(2.) The FOREST OF OAKS on the mountains of Bashan (Zech.
xi. 2.) : we may judge of the high estimation in which these oaks were
held, from an incidental expression of the prophet Ezekiel ; who,
speaking of the power and wealth of antient Tyre, says, — *Of the oaks
of Bashan they have made thine oars.* (Ezek. xxvii. 6.) Groves of
oaks, it is well known, were the scenes of idolatry in those remote
times, on account of the grateful shelter which they afforded to the
deluded worshippers. The prophet Ezekiel expressly alludes to this
practice. (Ezek. vi. 13.)

(3.) The FOREST or WOOD *of Ephraim,* which the children of
Ephraim began to cut down (Josh. xvii. 15.), was still standing in the
time of David : here Absalom was suspended from an oak, and was
slain. (2 Sam. xviii. 6. 8. 17.) The wood in the vicinity of Bethel
mentioned in 2 Kings ii. 24. appears to have been part of the wood
of Ephraim.

(4.) The spacious FOREST *of Hareth* in the tribe of Judah, to which
David withdrew in order to avoid the fury of Saul. (1 Sam. xxii. 5.)
To these, perhaps, may be added, —

(5.) The THICKETS on the banks of the Jordan, in Zech. xi. 3.
termed *the pride of Jordan,* which antiently were the coverts of wild
beasts, and are to this day composed of oleanders, tamarisks, and
other shrubs.

Among the trees, which adorn Palestine, the PALM TREE claims
the precedence of notice, on account of its singular utility ; it affords
a grateful shelter, an agreeable fruit, and a most delicious wine.[2] The
finest palm trees grew in the vicinity of Jordan and Engeddi ; and
they still flourish in the plain of Jericho, which city was antiently termed
by way of distinction the *City of Palm Trees.* In 1818, however, its

---

[1] Rae Wilson's Travels in the Holy Land, &c. vol. ii. p. 105. 3d edition.
[2] On the various products of the palm tree, see Kæmpfer's Amœnitates Exoticæ, p. 665.

plantations of palm trees were reduced to about one dozen[1]; and, in 1825, the " City of Palms" could not boast of one of these beautiful trees around it.[2]   The palm trees of Judæa are celebrated by Strabo[3], and by Josephus[4], who has particularly noticed the palm trees of Jericho.   The palm tree was the common symbol of Palestine, many coins of Vespasian and other emperors[5] being extant, in which Judæa is personified by a disconsolate woman sitting under a palm tree.   A vignette of one of these is given in Vol. I. page 199.   As the momentary prosperity of the wicked is frequently compared to the transient verdure of grass; so the durable felicity of the righteous is in Psalm xcii. 12. likened to the lasting strength and beauty of the palm tree.   " But chiefly is the comparison applicable to that Just One, the King of Righteousness and Tree of Life; eminent and upright; ever verdant and fragrant; under the greatest pressure and weight of sufferings, still ascending towards Heaven; affording both fruit and protection; incorruptible and immortal." [6]

Besides the palm trees, Jericho was celebrated for its fragrant balsam, mentioned in the Scriptures under the name of the BALM OF GILEAD. (Jer. viii. 22. xlvi. 11. li. 8.)   This balsam, which exudes from the opobalsamum or balsam tree, was mentioned by Strabo[7]; and two plantations of it existed during the last war of the Jews with the Romans, for which both parties fought desperately,—the Jews, that they might destroy them;—the Romans, that they might prevent them from destruction.   Since the country has been under the government of the Turks, the balm of Gilead has ceased to be cultivated in Palestine, though it is found in different parts of Arabia and Egypt.   At present, it is collected chiefly in Arabia, between Mecca and Medina, and is therefore sometimes called the balm of Mecca.   Its odour is exquisitely fragrant and pungent.   It is very costly, and is still in the highest esteem among the Turks and other oriental nations, both as a cosmetic and as a medicine for the cure of external wounds.

OLIVE TREES are now, as antiently, abundant and fruitful; and the culture of them continues to form a particular object of attention. The expression — *Oil out of the flinty rock* (Deut. xxxii. 13.) plainly denotes, that this most valuable tree grew not only in rich land; but that even the tops of the rocks would afford sufficient support for olive trees, from which they should extract abundance of oil. Accordingly we are informed that, although the immediate vicinity of Jerusalem is rugged and unpromising, yet even there the olive and vine might thrive under proper culture.[8]   The olive tree flourishes two hundred years before it begins to decay; and even while it is living, young trees spring up around it, which occupy its place when dead.[9]   Various similitudes are derived from the olive tree by the inspired writers; as well as from the vine, which affords a triple produce in each year.

---

1 Dr. Macmichael's Travels from Moscow to Constantinople, p. 205. *note.*
2 Carne's Letters, p. 323.
3 Lib. xvi. vol. ii. p. 1085. Oxon. 1807. folio.
4 De Bell. Jud. lib. i. c. 6. § 6. lib. iv. c. 8. § 3.
5 Dr. Shaw has enumerated them.   Travels, vol. ii. p. 151.
6 Bp. Horne's Commentary on Psal. xcii. 12.   (Works, vol. ii. p. 145).
7 Lib. xvi. vol. ii. p. 1085.
8 Jowett's Researches in Syria, p. 305.   Dr. A. Clarke on Deut. xxxii. 13.
9 Robinson's Travels in Palestine, vol. i. p. 125.

Pomegranate and Apple trees were likewise cultivated to a considerable extent (Numb. xiii. 23. Deut. viii. 8. Joel. i. 12.), as also was the almond tree, whose fruit is ripe and fit to gather about the middle of April.   The citron tree was in great request for its fragrant and refreshing shade, as well as for its delicious fruit.   (Sol. Song ii. 3. where it is mis-translated apple tree.)

Fig trees are very common in Palestine, and flourish in a dry and sandy soil: although in our climate they are little more than shrubs, yet in the East they attain a considerable height, and some of them are capable of affording shelter to a large number of horsemen. The shade of the fig tree is very pleasant; and to *sit under it* is an emblem of security and peace. (Mic. iv. 4.) Fig trees begin to sprout at the time of the vernal equinox. (Luke xxi. 29, 30. Matt. xxiv. 32.) The fruit makes its appearance before the leaves and flowers, and the foliage expands about the end of March.   The fig trees of Palestine are of three kinds:—1. The *Untimely fig*, which puts forth at the vernal equinox, and before it is ripe is called the *green* fig, but when it is ripe the *untimely* fig. (Sol. Song ii. 13. Jer. xxiv. 2. Hos. ix. 3.) It comes to maturity towards the end of June (Matt. xxi. 19. Mark xi. 13.), and in flavour surpasses the other kinds.—2. The *Summer* or *dry* fig: it appears about the middle of June, and is ripe in August.—3. The *Winter* fig, which germinates in August, and does not ripen until about the end of November: it is longer and of a browner colour than the others.   All figs, when ripe, but especially the untimely, fall spontaneously. (Nahum iii. 12.)   The early figs are eaten, but some are dried in the sun, and preserved in masses which are called *cakes of figs* in 1 Sam. xxv. 18. xxx. 12. 1 Chron. xii. 40.   It is well known that the fruit of these prolific trees always precedes the leaves: consequently, when Jesus Christ saw one of them in full vigour *having leaves* (Mark xi. 13.), he might, according to the common course of nature, very justly *look for fruit*, and *haply* find some boccores or early figs, if not some winter figs, likewise upon it.   The parable in Luke xiii. 6—9. is founded on the oriental mode of gardening; and the method of improving the palm (whose barrenness may be remedied in the way there mentioned) is transferred to the fig tree.

The Sycamore tree flourished in Palestine as well as in Egypt: its leaves are like those of the mulberry tree; and its sweetish, watery, but somewhat aromatic and not disagreeable fruit, comes to maturity several times in the year, without observing any certain seasons. It resembles that of the fig tree in appearance, but differs from it in having no seeds within.   This tree does not grow from the seed, but is propagated by the branch: it produces abundance of fruit, which grows in a peculiar manner,— not on the extremities of the boughs as in other trees, but near the trunk.   It is a large tree, attaining a considerable height, which circumstance will account for Zacchæus's climbing up into a sycamore tree, in order that he might see Jesus. Its timber appears to have been antiently used in building. (Isa. ix. 10.)   It affords a very grateful shade.   From its fruit the Arabs extract an oil, which they sell to travellers, who keep it among their other holy things, and pretend that it possesses a singular virtue in curing wounds, for which reason they call it the oil of Zacchæus, attributing its virtue to the stay which Zacchæus made upon the tree ! (Luke xix. 4.)

The PRICKLY PEAR, which most probably is the *thorns* mentioned in Hos. ii. 6., is a cumbrous shrub, which grows to a prodigious size, and affords one of the firmest and most secure fences imaginable.[1]

2. But the Holy Land was eminently distinguished for its abundance of CATTLE, to the management and rearing of which the inhabitants chiefly applied themselves.[2]   The hilly country not only afforded them variety and plenty of pasture, but also of water, which descending thence, carried fertility into the low lands and vallies.   The most celebrated pasture grounds were on each side of the river Jordan, besides those of Sharon, the plains of Lydda, Jamnia, and some others of less note.   The breed of cattle reared in Bashan, and on the mountains of Gilead and Carmel, were remarkable for their size, their strength, and fatness, to which there are frequent allusions in the Scriptures.   The cattle of the Israelites comprised every sort of animal that afforded either food or clothing, or was applicable to other useful purposes, as sheep, oxen, goats, camels, and asses.   The last-mentioned animals were of a more handsome form than are seen in our colder climate; hence they were chiefly used in travelling in this hilly country, even by persons of rank.   Horses do not appear to have been in use, until after the establishment of the monarchy. The various rivers, especially the Jordan, the Lake of Tiberias, and the Mediterranean Sea, afforded great variety and plenty of FISH, vast quantities of which were carried to Jerusalem, and, according to Jerome, one of the gates of that city was from this circumstance denominated the *Fish-gate*.   The Dead Sea furnished abundance of salt for curing their fish, for which purpose it was said to be superior to every other kind of salt.

3. Although we have no evidence that the Jews wrought any MINES of iron or copper; yet the researches of modern travellers have ascertained that the mountains of Palestine contain iron, particularly those whose summits and sides are occupied by the industrious Druses. A vein of coal has also been discovered: but there is no one to sink a mine. Report says, that there was antiently a copper-mine at Aleppo, which (M. Volney is of opinion) must have long since been abandoned.   These facts, however, substantiate the accuracy of Moses in his description of the Promised Land — as a *land whose stones are iron, and out of whose mountains thou mayest dig copper* (Deut. viii. 9.), as the Hebrew ought to be rendered, there being no such thing in nature as a *brass* mine.

III. In perusing the Scripture accounts of this highly-favoured country it ought to be considered that it was then inhabited by an industrious people, who knew how to improve every inch of their land,

---

[1] Rae Wilson's Travels in the Holy Land, &c. vol. i. p. 177. 3d edition.   For a particular account of the vegetable productions of the Holy Land, the reader is referred to the Hiero-Botanicon of Celsius (Upsalæ, 1745 — 1747, in two parts or vols. 8vo.); and for its zoology to the Hierozoïcon of Bochart (folio, Lug. Bat. 1714, or in three vols. 4to. Lipsiæ, 1793 and following years).   The reader who may not be able to consult these elaborate works, will find much useful information concerning the plants and animals of the Holy Land, in Professor Paxton's Illustrations of Scripture, part ii. vol. i. pp. 297—567. vol. ii. pp. 1 — 359.; and particularly in Dr. Harris's Natural History of the Bible, already referred to.

[2] " The whole of the scenery (says Dr. Richardson), since we entered Palestine, amply confirms the language of Scripture, that this is a land flowing with milk and honey,—a land for flocks, and herds, and bees, and fitted for the residence of men, whose trade, like the patriarchs of old, was in cattle." Travels along the Mediterranean, &c. vol. ii. p. 374.

and by their good husbandry had made even the most desert and barren places to yield some kind of production; so that the very rocks, which *now* appear quite naked, then yielded either corn, pulse, or pasture. Every man had his own land to improve; and when, in addition to these facts, it is considered that a warm country will support more people than a cold one, the people in southern climates being satisfied with less food than in northern; and that the dominions of David and Solomon comprised a greater extent of territory than many apprehend; — we can be at no loss to account for the vast multitude of inhabitants[1], which the Scriptures assert that Palestine antiently supported, especially when their statements of its fertility and population are confirmed by the testimonies of profane historians.

Thus, Tacitus describes the climate as dry and sultry; the natives as strong and patient of labour; the soil, as fruitful, exuberant in its produce, like that of Italy, and yielding the palm and balm tree. Libanus or Lebanon is stated to be the loftiest mountain in the country, and to rise to a great height, affording a grateful shade under its verdant groves, and even in the ardent heat of that sultry region as being covered at the top with perpetual snow.[2] Justin confirms the account of Tacitus, respecting the exuberant produce of Palestine, its beautiful climate, its palm and fragrant balsam trees.[3] The palms of Judæa are celebrated by the elder Pliny[4]; and Ammianus Marcellinus commends the beauty of the country, and its large and handsome cities.[5] But the most memorable testimony is that of Josephus the Jewish historian, which appears in various parts of his writings. Not to multiply unnecessary examples, we may state briefly, that, after describing the boundaries of the regions of Upper and Lower Galilee, of Peræa and Samaria, he speaks of their fertility and produce in the following terms: —

The two Galilees have always been able to make a strong resistance on all occasions of war: for the Galileans are inured to war from their infancy, and have always been very numerous. Their soil is universally rich, and fruitful, and full of plantations of all sorts of trees; so that its fertility invites the most slothful to take pains in its cultivation. Accordingly the whole of it is cultivated by its inhabitants, and no part of it lies idle. Although the greater part of Peræa, he continues, is desert and rough, and much less disposed for the production of the milder sorts of fruits, yet in other parts it has a moist soil, and produces all kinds of fruits. Its plains are planted with trees of all sorts; the olive tree, the vine, and the palm trees are principally cultivated there. It is also sufficiently watered with torrents, that issue from the mountains, and with springs which never fail to run, even when the torrents fail them, as they do in the dog-days. Samaria is entirely of the same nature with Judæa. Both countries are composed of hills and vallies; they are moist enough for agriculture, and are very fertile. They have abundance of trees, and are full of autumnal fruit, both of that which grows wild, and also that which is the effect of

---

[1] On the population of the Holy Land, see Michaelis's Commentaries on the Laws of Moses, vol. i. pp. 98 — 110.
[2] Taciti Historia, lib. v. c. 6.
[3] Justin. Hist. Philipp. lib. xxxvi. c. 3.   [4] Hist. Nat. lib. xiii. c. 6.
[5] Lib. xiv. c. 8. vol. i. p. 29. edit. Bipont.

cultivation. They are not naturally watered by many rivers, but derive their chief moisture from rain water, of which they have no want. The waters of such rivers as they have, are exceedingly sweet; and in consequence of the excellence of their grass, the cattle reared in these countries yield more milk than do those of other places.[1]

On the division of the land of Canaan, we are informed (Josh. xv. 20—62.) that not fewer than *one hundred and twelve walled cities* fell to the lot of the tribe of Judah. Many centuries afterwards, Josephus states that the regions of Samaria and Judæa were very full of people, which he notices as the greatest sign of their excellency[2]; that in the two Galilees the villages were extremely numerous and thickly inhabited; and that there also were great numbers of the larger cities, the smallest of which contained a population of fifteen thousand souls.[3] From the two small provinces of Upper and Lower Galilee alone, Josephus collected an army of more than one hundred thousand men.[4] These statements abundantly confirm the narratives of the sacred historian relative to the fertility and vast population of the Holy Land. Compare Numb. xi. 21. Judg. xx. 17. 1 Sam. xv. 4. 1 Chron. xxvii. 4—15. 2 Sam. xxiv. 9. and 2 Chron. xvii. 14—19. Nor are the testimonies less satisfactory, which have been given by Maundrell, Shaw, Hasselquist, and other modern travellers[5], who have visited this country, and especially by Dr. Clarke[6], who thus describes its appearance between Napolose or Sichem and Jerusalem: — " The road," says he, " was mountainous, rocky and full of loose stones; yet the cultivation was every where marvellous: it afforded one of the most striking pictures of human industry which it is possible to behold. The limestone rocks and vallies of Judæa were entirely covered with plantations of figs, vines, and olive trees; not a single spot seemed to be neglected. The hills, from their bases to their upmost summits, were entirely covered with gardens: all of these were free from weeds, and in the highest state of agricultural perfection. Even the sides of the most barren mountains had been rendered fertile by being divided into terraces, like steps rising one above another, whereon soil had been accumulated with astonishing labour. Under a wise and beneficial government, the produce of the Holy Land would exceed all calculation. Its perennial harvest; the salubrity of its air; its limpid springs; its rivers, lakes, and matchless plains; its hills and vales, — all these, added to the serenity of its climate, prove this land to be indeed *a field which the Lord hath blessed* (Gen. xxvii. 27.): *God hath given it of the dew of heaven, and the fatness of the earth, and plenty of corn and wine.*" [7]

---

[1] Josephus de Bell. Jud. lib. iii. c. 3. §§ 2, 3, 4.   [2] Ibid. lib. iii. c. 3. § 4.
[3] Ibid. lib. iii. c. 3. § 2.   [4] Ibid. lib. ii. c. 20. § 6.
[5] The most important facts relative to the fertility of Palestine, recorded by Maundrell and Dr. Shaw, are collected by Dr. Macknight in discourses vi. and vii. prefixed to the first volume of his Harmony, and the testimonies of Hasselquist and others are collected by Mr. Harmer. (Observations, vol. i. pp. 243 — 250.) Their accounts are corroborated by Mr. Buckingham, in his Travels among the Arab Tribes, p. 141.
[6] Travels, vol. iv. pp. 283 — 285.
[7] " In the north of Palestine," says a recent traveller, " there are many beautiful and fertile spots, but not so in Judæa. The breath of Jehovah's wrath seems in a peculiar manner to have blasted and withered the territory of the daughter of Zion. What a change has been wrought in the land, once flowing with milk and honey!"— See the Journal of the Rev. J. Connor (who was in Palestine in the spring of the year 1820), in the Appendix

Such being the state of the Holy Land, at least of that part of it which is properly cultivated, we can readily account for the vast population it antiently supported: and although this country, generally speaking, by no means corresponds with the statements we have of its former exuberant fertility and population, yet this is no contradiction to the narrative of the sacred writers. The devastations of the Holy Land by the Assyrians, Chaldees, Syrians, Romans, Saracens, the European crusaders, and Turks,—together with the oppressions of the inhabitants by the Turks in our own time, (who not only do not encourage agricultural industry, but also extort to the uttermost from the husbandmen[1],)—to which are to be added the depredations of robbers, and the predatory incursions of the Arabs,—all concur satisfactorily to account for the present state of this country: and, so far is it from contradicting the assertions of the Sacred Writings, that it confirms their authority; for, in the event of the Israelites proving unfaithful to their covenant engagements with Jehovah, all these judgments were predicted and denounced against them (Lev. xxvi. 32. Deut. xxix. 22. *et seq.*); and the exact accomplishment of these prophecies affords a permanent comment on the declaration of the royal Psalmist, that a righteous God *turneth a fruitful land into barrenness, for the wickedness of them that dwell therein.* (Psal. cvii. 34.) " But it has been through the instrumentality of this very wickedness,—the increasing wickedness of the inhabitants,—that the awful change has been effected. Were good government, good faith, and good manners to flourish in this land for half a century, it would literally become again a *land flowing with milk and honey:* the proper fruits of the mountains, honey and wax, would be collected by the industrious bee from myriads of fragrant plants: the plains, the vallies, and the upland slopes, would yield corn for man, and pasturage for innumerable flocks and herds. Such a stupendous and delightful change might well gladden not only every child of Israel, but the heart of every Christian."[2]

IV. Yet lovely as Palestine confessedly was, its beauty and the comforts it afforded were not unalloyed: among the CALAMITIES of various kinds, which at different times visited the inhabitants, the pestilence, earthquakes, whirlwinds, the devastations of locusts, famines, and the pestilential Simoom, demand to be distinctly noticed.

1. Palestine is now, as it antiently was, often afflicted with the PLAGUE; which makes its entrance from Egypt and the neighbouring countries. This tremendous scourge is frequently mentioned in the Sacred Writings. From the insidious manner in which it is first introduced into a country, it is, perhaps, termed the *pestilence that walketh in darkness.* (Psal. xci. 6.)

2. This region being mountainous and near the sea, is often shaken by EARTHQUAKES[3], from which, however, Jerusalem seems to have

---

to the Rev. Mr. Jowett's Christian Researches in the Mediterranean, p. 441. (London, 1822. 8vo.)

[1] Volney has given some painfully interesting details on the oppression of the agricultural inhabitants of Palestine, by their barbarous masters, the Turks. Travels in Egypt, &c. vol. ii. pp. 341 — 347.

[2] Jowett's Christian Researches in Syria, p. 309.

[3] The coast in general, and indeed the whole of Asia Minor, is still subject to earthquakes. In 1759 there happened one, which caused the greatest ravages, destroying upwards of 20,000 persons in the valley of Balbec. For three months the shocks of it terrified the in-

suffered little if at all. (Psal. xlvi. 2—5.) Sometimes these earthquakes were accompanied by land-slips, in which pieces of ground,
lying on a declivity, are removed from their place. To these (which
occasionally happen in the present day[1], and which are not uncommon
in Barbary[2],) the Psalmist alludes when he speaks of the *mountains
being carried into the midst of the sea* (Psal. xlvi. 2.), of their *skipping
like rams, and the little hills like young sheep* (Ps. cxiv. 4. 6.) ; and also
the prophet Isaiah (xxiv. 20.) when he says that *the earth shall reel to
and fro like a drunkard, and shall be removed like a cottage.* These
terrible concussions have supplied the sacred prophets and poets with
numerous figures, by which they have represented the concussions
and subversions of states and empires. See particularly Isa. xxix. 6.
liv. 10. Jer. iv. 24. Hag. ii. 6, 7. 22. Matt. xxiv. 7.

3. TORNADOES or WHIRLWINDS, followed by thunder, lightning, and
rains, were also very frequent during the winter and cold seasons.
Whirlwinds often preceded rain. In the figurative language of the
Scriptures, these are termed the *commandment* and the *word* of God
(Psal. cxlvii. 15. 18.)[3] ; and, as they are sometimes fatal to travellers
who are overwhelmed in the deserts, the rapidity of their advance is
elegantly employed by Solomon to show the certainty as well as the
suddenness of that destruction which will befall the impenitently
wicked. (Prov. i. 27.) They are alluded to by Isaiah, as occurring in
the deserts which border on the south of Judæa (Isa. xxi. 1.); and
they appear to blow from various points of the compass. The prophet
Ezekiel speaks of one that came from the north (Ezek. i. 4.); but more
frequently it blows from the south (Job xxxvii. 9.), in which case it is
generally attended with the most fatal consequences to the hapless traveller. Mr. Morier, describing the whirlwinds of Persia, says, that
they swept along the country in different directions, in a manner truly
terrific. " They carried away in their vortex sand, branches, and the
stubble of the fields, and really appeared to make a communication
between the earth and the clouds. The correctness of the imagery
used by the prophet Isaiah, when he alludes to this phenomenon, is
very striking. *The whirlwind shall take them away as stubble.* (Isa.
xl. 24.) *Chased as the chaff of the mountains before the wind, and like a
rolling thing before the whirlwind.* (Isa. xvii. 13.) In the Psalms
(lxxxiii. 13.) we read, *Make them like a wheel ; as the stubble before the
wind.* This is happily illustrated by the rotatory action of the whirlwind, which frequently impels a bit of stubble over a waste, just like
a wheel set in a rapid motion."[4] From these phenomena, the sacred

---

habitants of Lebanon so much, that they abandoned their houses and dwelt under tents.
(Volney's Travels, vol. i. p. 283.) In the autumn of 1822 this region was desolated by
another earthquake, or rather by a succession of earthquakes ; and, on the 1st of January,
1837, by another tremendous earthquake, which was further attended with the loss of
nearly seven thousand lives, besides wounding many hundreds. Full particulars of this
calamity are given in Mr. Calman's " Description " of this earthquake. London, 1837. 8vo.

1 See a description of one in the same work, vol. i. p. 278.

2 Shaw's Travels in Barbary, &c. vol. i. pp. 277,278.

3 The Arabs, to this day, call them *good news* or *messengers :* and in the Koran they are
termed the *sent* of God, c. 77. p. 477. of Sale's translation, 4to. edit.

4 Morier's Second Journey, p. 202. Mr. Bruce, in his Travels to discover the source of
the Nile, was surprised by a whirlwind in a plain near that river, which lifted up a camel
and threw it to a considerable distance, with such violence as to break several of its ribs ;
whirled himself and two of his servants off their feet, and threw them violently to the ground ;
and partly demolished a hut, the materials of which were dispersed all over the plain, leaving

writers have borrowed many very expressive figures and allusions. Compare Psal. xviii. 8—15. xxix. 1—10. lv. 8. lxxxiii. 15. Isa. v. 30. viii. 7, 8. xi. 15. xxviii. 2. xxix. 6. Jer. xxiii. 19. Matt. vii. 25.

What tornadoes are on land water-spouts are at sea, the vacuum being filled with a column of water, instead of earth, sand, &c. — To this phenomenon the Psalmist refers. (xlii. 7.)

4. Frequently the country was laid waste by vast bodies of migrating Locusts, whose depredations are one of the most terrible scourges with which mankind can be afflicted. By the prophet Joel (ii. 11.) they are termed the *army of the Lord*, from the military order which they appear to observe : disbanding themselves and encamping in the evening, and in the morning resuming their flight in the direction of the wind, unless they meet with food. (Nah. iii. 17. Prov. xxx. 27.) They fly in countless hosts (Jer. xlvi. 23. Judg. vi. 5.), so as to obscure the sun, and bring a temporary darkness upon the land. (Joel ii. 2. 10. Exod. x. 15.) The noise made by them is compared to the noise of chariots (Joel ii. 5.) : and wherever they settle, they darken the land. (Exod. x. 15.) If the weather be cold, they *encamp in the hedges*, until the sun rises, when they resume their progress (Nah. iii. 17.), climbing or creeping in perfect order. Regardless of every obstacle, they mount the walls of cities and houses, and enter the very apartments. (Joel ii. 7—9.)[1] They devour every green herb, and strip the bark off every tree (Exod. x. 12. 15. Joel i. 4. 7. 10. 12. 16. 18. 20.), so as to render the land which before was as the garden of Eden, a desolate wilderness, as if it had been laid waste by fire. (Joel ii. 3.) The noise made by them, when committing their ravages, is compared to the crackling noise of fire among the dry stubble, or a mighty host set in battle array. (Ibid. 5.) So fearful are the effects of their devastations, that every one was filled with dismay (Ibid. 6.), and vainly attempted to prevent them from settling on their grounds by making loud shouts (Jer. li. 14.), as the inhabitants of Egypt[2], and the Nogai Tartars[3] do to this day. What aggravates this tremendous calamity is, that when one host is departed, it is succeeded by a second, and sometimes even by a third or a fourth, by which every thing that has escaped the ravages of the preceding is inevitably consumed by the last company. As Arabia is generally considered

the other half standing. Mr. B. and his attendants were literally plastered with mud ; if dust and sand had arisen with the whirlwind in the same proportion, instead of mud, they would inevitably have been suffocated (Travels, vol. vi. p. 346.) ; — a disaster which the late enterprising traveller Mr. Park with difficulty escaped, when crossing the great desert of Sahara in his way to explore the sources of the Niger. Destitute of provisions and water, his throat pained with thirst, and his strength nearly exhausted, he heard a wind scourging from the east, and instinctively opened his parched mouth to receive the drops of rain which he confidently expected, but it was instantly filled with sand drifted from the desert. So immense was the quantity raised into the air and wafted upon the wings of the wind, and so great the velocity with which it flew, that he was compelled to turn his face to the west to prevent suffocation, and continued motionless till it had passed. Park's Travels, p. 178.

[1] The Rev. Mr. Hartley, an English clergyman, who visited Thyatira in June 1826, thus describes the ravages of these destructive insects: — " I am perfectly astonished at their multitudes. They are, indeed, as *a strong people, set in battle array : they run like mighty men ; they climb the walls like men of war.* I actually saw them *run to and fro* in the city of Thyatira ; they *ran upon the wall ; they climbed up upon the houses ; they entered into the windows like a thief.* (Joel ii. 5. 7. 9.) This is, however, by no means one of the most formidable armies of locusts which are known in these countries." Missionary Register, July 1827, p.328.

[2] Light's Travels, p. 56. Belzoni's Narrative, p. 197.

[3] Baron De Tott's Memoirs, extracted in Harmer's Observations, vol. iii. p. 319.

as the native country of these depredators, they were carried thence
into Egypt by an east wind (Exod. x. 13.), and were removed by a
westerly wind (19.) which blew from the Mediterranean Sea (that lay
to the north-west of that country), and wafted them into the Red Sea,
where they perished.   On their departure from a country, they leave
their fetid excrements behind them, which pollute the air, and myriads
of their eggs deposited in the ground, whence issues in the following
year a new and more numerous army.   They are generally carried
off by the wind into the sea, where they perish ; and their dead
bodies putrefying on the shore, emit a most offensive, and (it is said)
sometimes even fatal smell.   The plague of locusts, predicted by Joel,
entered Palestine from Hamath, one of the northern boundaries,
whence they are called the *northern* army, and were carried away by the
wind, some into the dreary plain on the coast of the *East* (or Dead)
Sea, and others into the *utmost* (or Mediterranean) *Sea.*   (Joel ii. 20.)
These predatory locusts are larger than those which sometimes visit
the southern parts of Europe, being five or six inches long, and
as thick as a man's finger.   From their heads being shaped like
that of a horse, the prophet Joel says, that they *have the appearance of horses ;* and on account of their celerity they are compared
to horsemen on full gallop (ii. 4.), and also to horses prepared
for battle.   (Rev. ix. 7.)   The locust has a large open mouth; and
in its two jaws it has four incisive teeth, which traverse each other
like scissors, and from their mechanism are calculated to grasp and
cut every thing of which they lay hold.   These teeth are so sharp
and strong, that the prophet, by a bold figure, terms them the *teeth of
a great lion.* (Joel i. 6.)   In order to mark the certainty, variety, and
extent of the depredations of the locusts, not fewer than eight or nine
different appellations, expressive of their nature, are given to them in
the Sacred Writings.

Such are the Scripture accounts of this tremendous scourge, which
are corroborated by every traveller who has visited the East.   The
quantity of these insects (to whose devastations Syria, Egypt, and
Persia, together with the whole middle part of Asia, are subject), is
incredible to any person who has not himself witnessed their astonishing numbers.   Their numerous swarms, like a succession of
clouds, sometimes extend a mile in length, and half as much in
breadth, darken the horizon, and intercept the light of the sun.
Should the wind blow briskly, so that the swarms are succeeded by
others, they afford a lively idea of that similitude of the Psalmist (cix.
23.) of being *tossed up and down as the locusts.*   Wherever they alight,
the land is covered with them for the space of several leagues, and
sometimes they form a bed six or seven inches thick.   The noise
which they make in browsing on the trees and herbage may be heard
at a great distance, and resembles that of an army foraging in secret,
or the rattling of hail-stones : and, whilst employed in devouring the
produce of the land, it has been observed, that they uniformly proceed
one way, as regularly as a disciplined army upon its march.   The
Tartars themselves are a less destructive enemy than these little
animals ; one would imagine that fire had followed their progress.
Fire itself, indeed, consumes not so rapidly.   Wherever their myriads
spread, the verdure of the country disappears as if a covering had

been removed; trees and plants, stripped of their leaves, and reduced to their naked boughs and stems, cause the dreary image of winter to succeed, in an instant, to the rich scenery of the spring. They have a government among them, similar to that of the bees and ants; and, when their king or leader rises, the whole body follow him, not one solitary straggler being left behind to witness the devastation. When these clouds of locusts take their flight, to surmount any obstacle, or to traverse more rapidly a desert soil, the heavens may literally be said to be obscured by them. In Persia, as soon as they appear, the gardeners and husbandmen make loud shouts, to prevent them from settling on their grounds. To this custom the prophet Jeremiah, perhaps, alludes, when he says, —*Surely I will fill thee with* MEN *as with locusts, and* THEY SHALL LIFT UP THEIR VOICE AGAINST THEE. (Jer. li. 14.) Should the inhabitants dig pits and trenches, and fill them with water, or kindle fires of stubble therein, to destroy them, rank presses on rank, fills up the trenches, and extinguishes the fires. Where these swarms are extremely numerous, they climb over every thing in their way, entering the inmost recesses of the houses, adhering to the very clothes of the inhabitants, and infesting their food.[1] Pliny relates that, in some parts of Ethiopia, the inhabitants lived upon nothing but locusts salted, and dried in the smoke; and that the Parthians also accounted them a pleasant article of food.[2] The modern Arabs catch great quantities of locusts, of which they prepare a dish by boiling them with salt, and mixing a little oil, butter, or fat; sometimes they toast them before a fire, or soak them in warm water, and without any other culinary process, devour almost every part except the wings.[3] They are also said to be sometimes pickled in vinegar. The locusts which formed part of John the Baptist's food (Mark i. 6.) were these insects, and not the fruit of the locust tree.[4]

5. The devastations caused by the locusts, together with the absence of the former and latter rains, were generally followed by a scarcity of provisions, and not unfrequently by absolute FAMINE, which also often prevailed in besieged cities to such a degree, that the starving inhabitants have been reduced to the necessity of devouring not only unclean animals, but also human flesh. Compare Deut. xxviii. 22—42. 56, 57. 2 Sam. xxi. 1. 2 Kings vi. 25—28. xxv. 3. Jer. xiv. 15. xix. 9. xlii. 17. Lam. ii. 20. iv. 10. Ezek. v. 10—12. 16. vi. 12. vii. 15.

6. But the greatest of all the calamities that ever visited this highly-favoured country is the pestilential blast, by the Arabs termed the SAM wind, by the Persians, SAMOUN, by the Turks, SIMOOM or SAMIEL,

---

[1] Volney's Travels in Egypt and Syria, vol. i. p. 286. Harmer's Observations, vol. iii. p. 319. Shaw's Travels, vol. i. pp. 340—343. Morier's Second Journey, p. 100. Sir Wm. Ouseley's Travels in Persia from 1810 to 1812, vol. i. pp. 195—200. (4to. London, 1819.) Mr. Dodwell has given an interesting account of the ravages of the locusts in Greece; where, however, they are smaller than those of the Levant. See his Classical and Topographical Tour, vol. i. pp. 214, 215.

[2] Pliny, Hist. Nat. lib. vi. c. 30. and lib. x. c. 28.

[3] At Busheher [or Bushire] in Persia, Mr. Price saw "many Arab women employed in filling bags with locusts, to be preserved and eaten like shrimps." Journal of the British Embassy to Persia, p. 6. London, 1825. folio.

[4] Sir Wm. Ouseley's Travels, vol. i. p. 197. Dodwell's Tour, vol. i. p. 215. Dr. Della Cella's Travels from Barbary to the Western Frontier of Egypt, p. 78. Jackson's Account of the Empire of Marocco, pp. 51—54.

and by the prophet Jeremiah, a *dry wind of the high places in the wilderness.* (Jer. iv. 11.) It blows in Persia, Arabia, and the deserts of Arabia, during the months of June, July, and August; in Nubia during March and April, and also in September, October, and November. It rarely lasts more than seven or eight minutes, but so poisonous are its effects, that it instantly suffocates those who are unfortunate enough to inhale it, particularly if it overtake them when standing upright. Thevenot mentions such a wind, which in 1658 suffocated *twenty thousand* men in one night; and another, which in 1655 suffocated *four thousand* persons. As the principal stream of this pestilential blast always moves in a line, about twenty yards in breadth, and twelve feet above the surface of the earth, travellers in the desert, when they perceive its approach, throw themselves upon the ground, with their faces close to the burning sands, and wrap their heads in their robes, or in a piece of carpet, till the wind has passed over them. The least mischief which it produces is the drying up their skins of water, and thus exposing them to perish with thirst in the deserts. When this destructive wind advances, which it does with great rapidity, its approach is indicated by a redness in the air; and, when sufficiently near to admit of being observed, it appears like a haze, in colour resembling the purple part of the rainbow, but not so compressed or thick. When travellers are exposed to a second or third attack of this terrible blast, it produces a desperate kind of indifference for life, and an almost total prostration of strength. Camels and other animals instinctively perceive its approach, and bury their mouths and nostrils in the ground. The effects of this blast on the bodies of those whom it destroys are peculiar. At first view, its victims appear to be asleep: but if an arm or leg be smartly shaken or lifted up, it separates from the body, which soon after becomes black.[1] In Persia, in the district of Dashtistan a *sam* or *simoon* blew during the summer months, which so totally burnt up all the corn (then near its maturity), that no animal would eat a blade of it, or touch any of its grain.[2] The image of *corn blasted before it be grown up,* used by the sacred historian in 2 Kings xix. 26., was most probably taken from this or some similar cause. The Psalmist evidently alludes (Psal. ciii. 15, 16.) to the desolating influence of the simoom.

---

[1] Bruce's Travels, vol. vi. pp. 462, 463. 484. Harmer's Observations, vol. i. pp. 94—96. Sir R. K. Porter's Travels in Georgia, Persia, &c. vol. ii. p. 230.
[2] Morier's Second Journey, p. 43.

PART II.

POLITICAL ANTIQUITIES OF THE JEWS.

CHAPTER I.

DIFFERENT FORMS OF GOVERNMENT, AND POLITICAL STATE OF THE HEBREWS, OR JEWS, FROM THE PATRIARCHAL TIMES TO THE BABYLONIAN CAPTIVITY.

I. *Patriarchal Government.* — II. *Government under Moses — a Theocracy; — its nature and design.* — 1. *Notices of the Heads or Princes of tribes and families.* — 2. *Of the Jethronian Prefects or Judges appointed by Moses.* — 3. *Of the Senate or Council of Seventy Assessors.* — 4. *Scribes.* — III. *Government of the Judges.* — IV. *Regal Government instituted;* — 1. *The Functions and Privileges of the Kings;* — 2. *Inauguration of the Kings;* — 3. *Chief Distinctions of Majesty;* — 4. *Scriptural Allusions to the Courts of Sovereigns and Princes explained.* — V. *Revenues of the Kings of Israel.* — VI. *Magistrates under the Monarchy.* — VII. *Officers of the Palace.* — VIII. *The Royal Harem.* — IX. *Promulgation of Laws.* — X. *Schism between the Twelve Tribes;* — *its latent causes;* — *the Kingdoms of Israel and Judah founded;* — *their Duration and End.* — XI. *Reasons why the Kingdom of Judah subsisted longer than that of Israel.* — XII. *State of the Hebrews during the Babylonish Captivity.*

I. OF the forms of Government which obtained among mankind from the earliest ages to the time of Moses, we have but little information communicated in the Scriptures. The simplicity of manners which then prevailed would render any complicated form of government unnecessary; and accordingly we find that the PATRIARCHS, that is, the Heads or Founders of Families, exercised the chief power and command over their families, children, and domestics, without being responsible to any superior authority. Such was the government of Abraham, Isaac, and Jacob. So long as they resided in the land of Canaan, they were subject to no foreign power, but tended their flocks and herds wherever they chose to go (Gen. xiii. 6—12.), and vindicated their wrongs by arms whensoever they had sustained any injury. (Gen. xiv.) They treated with the petty kings who reigned in different parts of Palestine as their equals in dignity, and concluded treaties with them in their own right. (Gen. xiv. 13. 18—24. xxi. 22—32. xxvi. 16. 27—33. xxxi. 44—54.)

The patriarchal power was a sovereign dominion: so that parents may be considered as the first kings, and children the first subjects. They had the power of disinheriting their children (Gen. xlix. 3, 4. 1 Chron. v. 1.), and also of punishing them with death (Gen. xxxviii. 24.), or of dismissing them from home without assigning any reason. (Gen. xxi. 14.) Further, the patriarchs could pronounce a solemn blessing or curse upon their children, which at that time was regarded as a high privilege and of great consequence. Thus Noah cursed his son Canaan (Gen. ix. 25.); Isaac blessed Jacob (Gen. xxvii. 28, 29.

33.) ; and Jacob blessed his sons. (Gen. xlix.) On the decease of the
father, the eldest son, by a natural right of succession, inherited the
paternal power and dominion, which in those days was one of the rights
of primogeniture. To this right the sacerdotal dignity, in the first
ages, seems to have been annexed ; so that the heads of families not
only possessed a secular power, but also officiated as priests in the
families to which they belonged. (Gen. viii. 20. xii. 7, 8. xxxv. 1—3.)

Although the sons of Jacob exercised, each, the supreme power in
his own family, during their father's life (Gen. xxxviii. 24.), yet the
latter appears to have retained some authority over them. (Gen. xlii.
1—4. 37, 38. xliii. 1—13. l. 15—17.) Afterwards, however, as the
posterity of Jacob increased, in Egypt, it became necessary to have
magistrates or governors, invested with more extensive authority ;
these are termed *Elders* (Exod. iii. 16.), being probably chosen on
account of their age and wisdom. The *Shoterim* or " officers of the
children of Israel" (Exod. v. 14, 15. 19.) have been conjectured to be a
kind of magistrates elected by them ; but, from the context of the sacred
historian, they rather appear to have been appointed by the Egyptians,
and placed over the Israelites in order to oversee their labour.[1]

II. On the departure of the Israelites from the land of their oppressors, under the guidance of Moses, Jehovah was pleased to institute a
new form of government, which has been rightly termed a Theocracy ; the supreme legislative power being exclusively vested in God
or in his oracle, who alone could enact or repeal laws. The Hebrew
government appears not only designed to subserve the common and
general ends of all good governments ; — viz. the protection of the
property, liberty, safety, and peace of the several members of the
community (in which the true happiness and prosperity of states will
always consist), but also to set apart the Hebrews or Israelites as *a
holy people to Jehovah, and a kingdom of priests.* For thus Moses is
directed to tell the children of Israel, *Ye have seen what I did unto the
Egyptians, and how I bore you on eagles' wings, and brought you unto
myself. Now, therefore, if ye will hear my voice indeed, and keep my
covenant, then ye shall be a peculiar treasure unto me above all people ;
for all the earth is mine, and ye shall be unto me a kingdom of priests
and an holy nation.* (Exod. xix. 3, 4, 5, 6.) We learn what this covenant was in a further account of it. *Ye stand this day all of you before
the Lord your God, your captains of your tribes, your elders and your
officers, and all the men of Israel ; that you should enter into covenant
with the Lord thy God, and into his oath which the Lord thy God maketh
with thee this day ; that he may establish thee to-day for a people unto
himself, and that he may be unto thee a God, as he hath said unto thee,
and as he hath sworn unto thy fathers, to Abraham, Isaac, and to Jacob :
for ye know,* adds Moses, *how we have dwelt in the land of Egypt, and
how we came through the nations which ye passed by ; and ye have seen
their abominations and their idols, wood and stone, silver and gold, which
were among them, lest there should be among you, man, or woman, or
family, or tribe, whose heart turneth away this day from the Lord our
God to go and serve the gods of these nations.* (Deut. xxix. 10—18.)

From these passages it is evident that the fundamental principle of

---

[1] Pareau Antiquitas Hebraica, pp. 231—233.

the Mosaic Law was the maintenance of the doctrine and worship of one true God, and the prevention, or rather the proscription, of polytheism and idolatry. The covenant of Jehovah with the Hebrew people, and their oath by which they bound their allegiance to Jehovah, their God and King, was, that they should receive and obey the laws which he should appoint as their supreme governor, with a particular engagement to keep themselves from the idolatry of the nations round about them, whether the idolatry they had seen while they dwelt in the land of Egypt, or that which they had observed in the nations by which they passed into the promised land. In keeping this allegiance to Jehovah, as their immediate and supreme Lord, they were to expect the blessings of God's immediate and particular protection in the security of their liberty, peace, and prosperity, against all attempts of their idolatrous neighbours; but if they should break their allegiance to Jehovah, or forsake the covenant of Jehovah, by going and serving other gods, and worshipping them, then they should forfeit these blessings of God's protection, and the anger of Jehovah should be kindled against the land, to bring upon it all the curses that are written in the book of Deuteronomy. (xxix. 25—27.) The substance, then, of this solemn transaction between God and the Israelites (which may be called the original contract of the Hebrew government) was this:—If the Hebrews would voluntarily consent to receive Jehovah as their Lord and King, to keep his covenant and laws, to honour and worship him as the one true God, in opposition to all idolatry; then, though God as sovereign of the world rules over all the nations of the earth, and all nations are under the general care of his providence, he would govern the Hebrew nation by peculiar laws of his particular appointment, and bless it with a more immediate and particular protection; he would secure to them the invaluable privileges of the true religion, together with liberty, peace, and prosperity, as a favoured people above all other nations. This constitution, it will be observed, is enforced chiefly by temporal sanctions, and with singular wisdom, for temporal blessings and evils were at that time the common and prevailing incitements to idolatry: but by thus taking them into the Hebrew constitution, as rewards to obedience and punishments for disobedience, they became motives to continuance in the true religion, instead of encouragements to idolatry.[1]

In the Theocracy of the Hebrews, the laws were given to them by God, through the mediation of Moses, and they were to be of perpetual force and obligation so long as their polity subsisted. The judges by whom these laws were administered were represented as holy persons, and as sitting in the place of God (Deut. i. 17. xix. 17.): they were usually taken from the tribe of Levi; and the chief expounder of the law was the high priest. In this there was a singular propriety; for the Levites, being devoted to the study of the law, were (as will be shown in a subsequent page) the *literati* among the Israelites. In difficult cases of law, however, relating both to government and war, God was to be consulted by Urim and Thummim; and in matters, which concerned the welfare of the state, God frequently

---

[1] Lowman on the Civil Government of the Hebrews, pp. 8—10. See also Dr. Graves's Lectures on the Pentateuch, vol. ii. pp. 141—185. for some masterly observations on the introduction of temporal sanctions into the Mosaic law.

made known his will by prophets whose mission was duly attested, and the people were bound to hearken to their voice. In all these cases, Jehovah appears as sovereign king, ruling his people by his appointed ministers.[1]

A subordinate design of this constitution of the Hebrew government was, the prevention of intercourse between the Israelites and foreign nations. The prevalence of the most abominable idolatry among those nations, and the facility with which the Israelites had, on more than one occasion, adopted their idolatrous rites, during their sojourning in the wilderness, rendered this seclusion necessary, in order to secure the fundamental principle of the Mosaic law above mentioned: and many of the peculiar laws will, on this principle, be found both wisely and admirably adapted to secure this design.[2]

The form of the Hebrew republic was unquestionably democratical. Its head admitted of change as to the name and nature of his office, and at certain times it could even subsist without a general head. When Moses promulgated his laws, he convened the whole congregation of Israel, to whom he is repeatedly said to have *spoken*, but as he could not possibly be heard by six hundred thousand men, we must conclude that he only addressed a certain number of persons who were deputed to represent the rest of the Israelites. Accordingly in Numb. i. 16. these delegates or representatives are termed קרואי העדה (KERUAY HOËDAH), that is, *those wont to be called to the convention;* in our version called the *renowned of the congregation;* and in Numb. xvi. 2. they are denominated נשיאי עדה קרואי מועד (NESIAY EDAH KERUAY MUOED), that is, *chiefs of the community,* or congregation, *that are called to the convention,* in our version termed, *famous in the congregation, men of renown.* By comparing Deut. xxix. 10. with Josh. xxiii. 2. it appears that these representatives were the head of *tribes or families,* and *judges* and *officers;* and Michaelis is of opinion that, like the independent members of our British House of Commons, they acted in the plenitude of their own power, without taking instruction from their constituents.[3]

1. HEADS OR PRINCES OF TRIBES AND FAMILIES.—All the various branches of Abraham's descendants, like the antient Germans or the Scottish clans, kept together in a body according to their tribes and families; each tribe forming a lesser commonwealth, with its own peculiar interests, and all of them at last uniting into one great republic.[4] The same arrangement, it is well known, obtained among the Israelites, who appear to have been divided into twelve great tribes, previously to their departure from Egypt. By Moses, however, they were subdivided into certain greater families, which are called משפחות (MISHPACHOTH) or *families,* by way of distinction, and בתי אבות (BATEY ABOTH) or *houses of fathers* (Numb. i. 2. Josh. vii. 14.); each

---

[1] Michaelis's Commentaries on the Laws of Moses, vol. i. pp. 190—196.

[2] Ibid. vol. i. pp. 202—225. Brunings, Antiq. Heb. pp. 91—93. Mr. Lowman (Civil Government of the Hebrews, pp. 17—31.) has illustrated the wisdom of this second design of the Jewish theocracy by several pertinent examples.

[3] Commentaries on the Laws of Moses, vol. i. p. 231.

[4] In this manner were the Ishmaelites governed by twelve princes according to the number of Ishmael's sons (Gen. xxv. 16.); and the Bedouins their descendants have always preserved some traces of this patriarchal government. Their families continue together; and, under the name of *Emir,* one is prince among people, who are all his kindred within a certain degree of affinity. Michaelis's Commentaries, vol. i. p. 232.

of whom, again, had their heads, which are sometimes called *heads of houses of fathers*, and sometimes simply *heads*. These are likewise the same persons, who in Josh. xxiii. 2. and xxiv. 1. are called *Elders*. (Compare also Deut. xix. 12. and xxi. 1—9.) It does not appear in what manner these heads or elders of families were chosen, when any of them died. The princes of tribes do not seem to have ceased with the commencement, at least, of the monarchy: from 1 Chron. xxvii. 16—22. it is evident that they subsisted in the time of David; and they must have proved a powerful restraint upon the power of the king.

It will now be readily conceived how the Israelitish state might have subsisted not only without a king, but even occasionally without that magistrate who was called a *Judge*, although we read of no supreme council of the nation. Every tribe had always its own independent chief magistrate, who may not inaptly be compared to the lords lieutenants of our British counties; subordinate to them, again, were the heads of families, who may be represented as their deputy-lieutenants: and, if there were no *general* ruler of the whole people, yet there were twelve smaller commonwealths, who in certain cases united together, and whose general convention would take measures for their common interest. In many cases particular tribes acted as distinct and independent republics, not only when there was neither king nor judge, but even during the times of the kings. Instances of wars being carried on by one or more particular tribes, both before and after the establishment of the regal government, may be seen in Josh. xvii. 15—17. Judg. iv. 10. and xviii—xx. 1 Chron. v. 18—23. 41—43. It appears from 1 Chron. xxiii. 11. that a certain number of persons was necessary to constitute a family, and to empower such a family to have a representative head; for it is there said that the four sons of Shimei had not a numerous progeny, and were therefore reckoned only as one family. Hence we may explain why, according to Micah v. 2., Bethlehem may have been too small to be reckoned among the families of Judah. It is impossible to ascertain, at this distance of time, what number of individuals was requisite to constitute a house or family; but probably the number was not always uniform.[1]

2. The JUDGES, who were appointed by Moses, had also a right, by virtue of their office, to be present in the *congregation*, or convention of the state. After the departure of the Israelites from Egypt, Moses, for some time, was their sole judge. Jethro, his father-in-law, observing that the daily duties of his office were too heavy for him, suggested to him (subject to the approbation of Jehovah) the institution of *Judges* or rulers, *of tens*, *of fifties*, *of hundreds*, and *of thousands*, who determined every affair of little importance among themselves, but brought the *hard causes* to Moses. (Exod. xviii. 14—26.) Of the judges of *tens*, therefore, there must have been *sixty thousand*; of the judges of *fifties*, *twelve thousand*; of the judges of *hundreds*, *six thousand*; and of the judges of *thousands*, *six hundred*. These Judges, or Jethronian prefects (as they have been called), seem to have been a sort of justice of the peace in several divisions, probably taken from the military division of an host into thousands, hundreds, fifties, and tens; this was

a model proper for them as an army marching, and not unsuitable to their settlement as tribes and families, in a sort of counties, hundreds, and tithings.   Perhaps our old Saxon constitution of *sheriffs* in *counties, hundredors* or centgraves in *hundreds,* and *deciners in decennaries,* may give some light to this constitution of Moses.   Some of our legal antiquaries have thought that those constitutions of the Saxons were taken from these laws of Moses, introduced by Alfred, or by his direction.[1]   It is not probable, that in the public deliberative assemblies the whole sixty thousand judges of tens had seats and voices. Michaelis conjectures that only those of hundreds, or even those only of thousands, are to be understood, when mention is made of judges in the Israelitish conventions.[2]

But, after the establishment of the Hebrews in the land of Canaan, as they no longer dwelt together in round numbers, Moses ordained that judges should be appointed in every city (Deut. xvi. 18.), and it should seem that they were chosen by the people.   In succeeding ages these judical offices were filled by the Levites, most probably because they were the persons best skilled in the law of the Hebrews.   (See 1 Chron. xxiii. 4. xxvi. 29—32. 2 Chron. xix. 8—11. xxxiv. 13.)[3]

3. During the sojourning of the Israelites in the wilderness, Moses established a council or SENATE of seventy, to assist him in the government of the people.   The Jewish rabbinical writers, who have exercised their ingenuity in conjecturing why the number was limited to seventy, have pretended that this was a permanent and supreme court of judicature; but as the sacred writers are totally silent concerning such a tribunal, we are authorised to conclude that it was only a temporary institution.   *After* their return from the Babylonish captivity, it is well known that the Jews did appoint a sanhedrin or council of seventy at Jerusalem, in imitation of that which Moses had instituted.[4]   In the New Testament, very frequent mention is made of this supreme tribunal, of which an account will be found in a subsequent chapter of this volume.

4. Among the persons who appear in the Israelitish congregation or diet (as Michaelis terms it), in addition to those already mentioned, we find the שׁוֹטְרִים (SHOTeRIM) or *Scribes.*   It is evident that they were different from the Jethronian prefects or judges; for Moses expressly ordained that they should not only appoint judges in every city, but also *shoterim* or scribes.   What their functions were, it is now difficult to ascertain.   Michaelis conjectures, with great probability, that they kept the genealogical tables of the Israelites, with a faithful record of births, marriages, and deaths; and that to them was assigned the duty of apportioning the public burthens and services on the people individually.   Under the regal government, these scribes were generally taken from the tribe of Levi.   (1 Chron. xxiii. 4. 2 Chron. xix. 8—11. and xxxiv. 13.)   In Deut. xxix. 10. xxxi. 28. Josh. viii. 33. and xxiii. 2. we find them as representatives of the people in the diets, or when they entered into covenant with God.   In time of war they were charged with the duty of conveying orders to the army

---

[1] Bacon on English Government, part i. p. 70.   Lowman's Civil Government of the Hebrews, p. 162.

[2] Michaelis's Commentaries, vol. i. p. 245.

[3] Ibid. p. 246.   [4] Ibid. pp. 247—249.

(Deut. xx. 5.); and in 2 Chron. xxvi. 11. we meet with a *scribe*, who appears to have been what is now termed the *muster-master-general.*[1]

III. On the death of Moses, the command of the children of Israel was confided to JOSHUA, who had been his minister (Exod. xxiv. 13. Josh. i. 1.); and under whom the land of Canaan was subdued, and divided agreeably to the divine injunctions. On the death of Joshua and of the elders of his council, it appears that the people did not choose any chief magistrate or counsellors in their place. The consequence (as might naturally be expected) was a temporary anarchy, in which we are told that every man did what was right in his own eyes. (Judg. xxi. 25.) This state of things occasioned the government of Israel to be committed to certain supreme magistrates, termed JUDGES. Their dignity was, in some cases, for life, but not always: and their office was not hereditary, neither was their succession constant. There also were anarchies, or intervals of several years' continuance, during which the Israelites groaned under the tyranny of their oppressors, and had no governors. But though God himself did regularly appoint the judges of the Israelites, the people nevertheless, on some occasions, elected him who appeared to them most proper to deliver them from their immediate oppression: thus Jephthah was chosen by the Israelites beyond Jordan. As, however, it frequently happened that the oppressions which rendered the assistance of judges necessary, were not felt equally over all Israel, so the power of those judges, who were elected in order to procure their deliverance from such servitudes, did not extend over all the people, but only over that district which they had delivered. Thus Jephthah did not exercise his authority on this side Jordan, neither did Barak exercise his judicial power beyond that river. The authority of the judges was not inferior to that, which was afterwards exercised by the kings: it extended to peace and war. They decided causes without appeal; but they had no power to enact new laws, or to impose new burthens upon the people. They were protectors of the laws, defenders of religion, and avengers of crimes, particularly of idolatry, which was high treason against Jehovah their Sovereign. Further, these judges were without pomp or splendour, and destitute of guards, train, or equipage: unless indeed their own wealth might enable them to make an appearance suitable to their dignity. Their income or revenue arose solely from presents. This form of administration subsisted from Joshua to Saul, during a period of about 339 years.[2]

IV. At length, the Israelites, weary of having God for their sovereign, and provoked by the misconduct of the sons of the judge and prophet Samuel, who in his old age had associated them with himself for the administration of affairs, desired a KING to be set over them, *to judge them like all the nations* (1 Sam. viii. 5.), thus undesignedly fulfilling the designs of the Almighty, who had ordained that in the fulness of time the Messiah should be born of a royal house.

1. Such a change in their government Moses foresaw, and accord-

---

[1] Michaelis's Commentaries, vol. i. pp. 249—251.

[2] Tappan's Lectures on Jewish Antiquities, p. 77. Michaelis's Commentaries, vol. i. pp. 262—264. Dr. Graves's Lectures on the Pentateuch, vol. ii. pp. 95—104. Biographical notices of the several judges, as well as of the sovereigns who succeeded them, will be found in the historical index at the end of this volume.

ingly, by divine command, he prescribed the following laws, both concerning their election of a king, and also for the direction of their
future sovereigns, which are recorded in Deut. xvii. 14—20.

(1.) The *right* of choice was left to the people, but with this limitation, that they must always elect a native Israelite, and not a foreigner.
One *from among thy brethren shalt thou set king over thee : thou mayest
not set a stranger over thee, which is not thy brother.*

This was a wise and patriotic law, well adapted to inspire a just
dread of foreign intriguers and invaders, and an united vigilance in
repulsing such persons from the government. " One who is born and
educated in a community, is its natural brother : his habits, attach-
ments, and interests strongly link him to it; while the sentiments, feelings, and interests of a stranger do often as naturally connect him with
a foreign country, and alienate him from that in which he resides."
But this statute did not apply to the case of the nation being at any
time subjected, by force of arms, to a foreign prince; though the
Pharisees afterwards so explained it.[1]

(2.) The Israelites were on no account to appoint any one to be
their king, who was not chosen by God. *Thou shalt in any wise set*
him *king over thee whom the* LORD *thy God shall choose.*

Accordingly, he appointed Saul, by lot, to be their first king; David,
by name, to be their second ; Solomon, his son, to be his successor :
and then made the regal government hereditary in David's family.
But this law did not extend to their subsequently electing every individual king : for, so long as the reigning family did not violate the
fundamental laws of the theocracy, they would continue to possess the
throne, but if they tyrannized, they would forfeit it.

With regard to the external qualifications which the Jews appear
to have demanded in their kings : — comeliness of person and tallness
of stature seem to have been the principal requisites. Thus, although
Saul was constituted King of Israel by the special appointment of God,
yet it appears to have been no inconsiderable circumstance in the eyes
of the people that he was a *choice young man and goodly, and* that there
was *not among the children of Israel a goodlier person than he : from the
shoulders and upwards* he was *higher than any of the people.* (1 Sam.
ix. 2.)   And therefore Samuel said to the people, when he presented
Saul to them : *See ye him whom the* LORD *hath chosen, that* there is
none like him among all the people. (1 Sam. x. 24.)   Hence, also, David
is said to have been *ruddy, withal of a beautiful countenance, and goodly
to look to.* (1 Sam. xvi. 12.)   The people of the East seem to have had
a regard to these personal qualities in the election of their kings, in
addition to those of strength, courage, and fortitude of mind; and it
was such a king as their neighbours had, whom the Israelites desired.

(3.) The king was not to *multiply horses to himself, nor cause the
people to return to Egypt to the end that he should multiply horses.*[2]

---

[1] It was on the ground of this law that the Pharisees and Herodians proposed that insidious question to Jesus Christ, — *Is it lawful to give tribute to* CÆSAR, *or* No ? (Matt. xxii.
17.) for, at that time, they were under the authority of a foreign power which they detested.
Had Christ replied, YES, then they would have condemned him by this law.   Had he
answered, No, then they would have accused him to Cæsar. (Dr. A. Clarke on Deut. xvii.
15.   In his Commentary on Matt. xxii. 16—22. he has discussed this important subject in
great detail and with equal ability.)

[2] This law was to be a standing trial of prince and people, whether they had trust and

This prohibition was intended to prevent all commercial intercourse with Egypt, and, consequently, to preserve them from being contaminated with idolatry; and also, by restraining the Jews from the use of cavalry in war, to lead them to trust implicitly in the special protection of the Almighty, from whose pure worship they might be seduced by extending their dominions among the neighbouring idolatrous nations by means of cavalry.

(4.) The king was, further, prohibited from *multiplying wives to himself, that his heart turn not away* from the law and worship of the God of Israel, by his being seduced into idolatry in consequence of foreign alliances. How grossly this law was violated by Solomon and other monarchs the history of the Jews and Israelites abundantly records, together with the fatal consequences of such disobedience.

(5.) In order to prevent or restrain that royal avarice or luxury, for which oriental monarchs have always been distinguished, the king was forbidden *greatly to multiply to himself silver and gold;* lest the circulation of money should be obstructed, industry discouraged, or his subjects be impoverished.

(6.) In order that they might not be ignorant of true religion, and of the laws of the Israelites, the king was enjoined to write out, for his own use, a correct copy of the divine law; which injunction was intended to rivet this law more firmly in his memory, and to hold him in constant subjection to its authority. For the same purpose he was required to read in this copy *all the days of his life, that he may learn to fear the LORD his God, to keep all the words of this law, and these statutes, to do them.*

Thus the power of the Israelitish kings was circumscribed by a code of fundamental and equal laws, provided by infinite wisdom and rectitude. With regard to actual facts, it appears from 1 Sam. x. 25. compared with 2 Sam. v. 3. 1 Kings xii. 22—24. and 2 Kings xi. 17. that the Israelitish kings were by no means possessed of unlimited power, but were restricted by a solemn stipulation; although they on some occasions evinced a disposition leaning towards despotism. (1 Sam. xi. 5—7. and xxii. 17, 18.)[1] They had, however, the right of making war and peace, as well as the power of life and death; and could on particular occasions put criminals to death, without the formalities of justice (2 Sam. i. 5—15. iv. 9—12.); but, in general they administered justice; sometimes in a summary way by themselves where the case appeared clear, as David did (see 2 Sam. xii. 1—5. xiv. 4—11. and 1 Kings ii. 5—9.), or by judges duly constituted to hear and determine causes in the king's name. (1 Chron. xxiii. 4. xxvi. 29—32.) Michaelis thinks it probable that there were superior courts established at Jeru-

---

confidence in God their deliverer.   See Bp. Sherlock's Discourses on Prophecy, Disc. iv.; where he has excellently explained the reason and effect of the law, and the influence which the observance or neglect of it had in the affairs of the Israelites.

[1] That the Israelitish monarchs, even in the worst times, were considered not as above law, but as restrained by it, is evident from the history of Ahab, a most abandoned prince. Though he earnestly coveted the Vineyard of Naboth, one of his subjects, and offered to purchase it, yet because the law prohibited the alienation of lands from one tribe or family to another, he could not obtain it, until, by bribing false witnesses, he had procured the legal condemnation and death of Naboth, as a traitor and blasphemer.   (See 1 Kings xxi. 1—14.) Tappan's Lectures on Jewish Antiquities, pp. 81, 82.   The preceding regulations concerning the Hebrew monarchs are also fully considered and illustrated by Michaelis, Commentaries, vol. i. pp. 266—283.

salem, in which David's sons presided, and that in Psal. cxxii. 5. there
is an allusion to them; but no mention is made of a supreme tribunal
in that city earlier than the reign of Jehoshaphat. (2 Chron. xix. 8—11.)
Although the kings enjoyed the privilege of granting pardons to
offenders at their pleasure, without consulting any person; and in
ecclesiastical affairs exercised great power, sometimes deposing or
condemning to death even the high priest himself (1 Sam. xxii. 17, 18.
1 Kings ii. 26, 27.), and at other times reforming gross abuses in religion, of which we have examples in the zealous conduct of Hezekiah
and Josiah; yet this power was enjoined by them not as *absolute* sovereigns in their own right. They were merely the viceroys of Jehovah,
who was the sole legislator of Israel : and, therefore, as the kings
could, on no occasion, either enact a new law or alter or repeal an old
one, the government continued to be a *theocracy*, as well under their
permanent administration, as we have seen that it was under the occasional administration of the judges. The only difference, that can be
discovered between the two species of government, is, that the conduct
of the judges was generally directed by *urim*, and that of the kings,
either by the inspiration of God vouchsafed to themselves, or by prophets raised up from time to time to reclaim them when deviating
from their duty, as laid down by the law.

(7.) Lastly, the monarch was charged, *that his heart be not lifted up
above his brethren ;* in other words, to govern his subjects with mildness and beneficence, not as slaves, but as brothers. So, David styled
his subjects his *brethren* in 1 Chron. xxviii. 2. ; and this amiable model
was, subsequently, imitated by the first Christian emperors, particularly
by Constantine the Great.[1]

Thus the regal government, though originating in the perverse impiety and folly of the Israelites, was so regulated and guarded by the
divine law, as to promise the greatest public benefits. It is to be observed that the preceding enactments relate to the election of a *king*,
not of a queen. Athaliah, indeed, reigned, but she was an usurper;
and, long afterwards, Alexandra, the daughter of Jannæus, also
reigned. She, however, reigned as a queen only in name, being under
the influence of the Pharisees.

It was customary for the Jewish kings sometimes to nominate
their successors, and sometimes to assume them as partners with them
in the government during their own lifetime. Thus David caused
Solomon to be anointed (1 Kings i. 32—40.) ; so that Solomon reigned
conjointly with his father during the short remainder of David's life,
for it does not appear that the latter resigned his sceptre, till he
resigned his breath. In like manner Rehoboam, though a prince of no
great merit, appointed his youngest son Abijah to be *ruler among his
brethren*, (2 Chron. xi. 22.) designing that he should reign after him ;
and accordingly Abijah succeeded him on the throne. (2 Chron. xiii. 1.)
So, among the sons of Josiah, Jehoahaz, the younger, was preferred
to Jehoiakim the elder. (2 Kings xxiii. 31—36.) This practice of the
Jewish sovereigns serves to elucidate some supposed chronological
difficulties in Sacred History.

2. The INAUGURATION OF THE KINGS was performed with various

---

[1] Tappan's Lectures, p. 83.

ceremonies and with great pomp. The principal of these was anointing with holy oil (Psal. lxxxix. 20.), which was sometimes privately performed by a prophet (1 Sam. x. 1. xvi. 1—13. 1 Kings xix. 16. 2 Kings ix. 1—6.), and was a symbolical prediction that the person so anointed would ascend the throne; but after the monarchy was established, this unction was performed by a priest (1 Kings i. 39.), at first in some public place (1 Kings i. 32—34.), and afterwards in the temple, the monarch elect being surrounded by his guards. (2 Kings xi. 11, 12. 2 Chron. xxiii.) [1] It is probable, also, that he was at the same time girded with a sword. (Psalm xlv. 3.) After the king was anointed he was proclaimed by the sound of the trumpet. In this manner was Solomon proclaimed (1 Kings i. 34. 39.), and (it should seem) also the rebel Absalom. (2 Sam. xv. 10.) When Jehovah proclaimed his law, and himself to be the King of Israel, the sound of the trumpet preceded with great vehemence. (Exod. xix. 16.) The knowledge of this circumstance will explain the many passages in the Psalms, in which God is said to have *gone up with a shout; the Lord, with the sound of a trumpet;* and the Israelites are called upon, *with trumpets* to *make a joyful noise before the Lord the King.* (See Psal. xlvii. 5. xcviii. 6, &c.) From this ceremony of anointing, kings are in the Scriptures frequently termed the *anointed of the Lord, and of the God of Jacob.* (1 Sam. xxiv. 6. 10. xxvi. 9. 11. 16. 23. 2 Sam. xxiii. 1. Psal. ii. 2. lxxxix. 38. Habak iii. 13.) A diadem or crown was also placed upon the sovereign's head, and a sceptre put into his hand (Ezek. xxi. 26. Psal. xlv. 6. 2 Kings xi. 12.), after which he entered into a solemn covenant with his subjects that he would govern according to its conditions and to the law of Moses. (2 Sam. v. 3. 1 Chron. xi. 3. 2 Kings xi. 12. 2 Chron. xxiii. 11. compare Deut. xvii. 18.) The nobles in their turn promised obedience, and appear to have confirmed this pledge with a kiss, either of the knees or feet. (Psal. ii. 12.) Loud acclamations accompanied with music then followed, after which the king entered the city. (1 Kings i. 39, 40. 2 Kings xi. 12. 19. 2 Chron xxiii. 11.) To this practice there are numerous allusions both in the Old Testament (Psal. xlvii. 1—9. xcvii. 1. xcix. 1, &c.) as well as in the New (Matt. xxi. 9, 10. Mark xi. 9, 10. Luke xix. 35—38.); in

---

[1] Where the kingdom was hereditary, as that of Judah was, every king was not anointed, but only the first of the family; who being anointed for himself and all his successors of the same family, they required no other unction. If, however, any difficulty arose concerning the succession, then the person who obtained the throne, though of the same family, was anointed in order to terminate the dispute; after which, the title was not to be questioned. This was the case with Solomon, Joash, Jehoahaz, and others. The kingdom was not made hereditary in the family of Saul; and, therefore, Ishbosheth's seizing on the crown was only an usurpation. The power of nominating a successor to Saul was reserved by God to himself, by whom David (who was no relation to Saul by blood, 1 Sam. xvi. 12.) was appointed king. David, therefore, had no other title but by divine appointment, first signified by the prophet Samuel's anointing him, and afterwards by the voluntary ratification of this appointment on the part of the people: so that the anointing of David was necessary for the confirmation of his title. But the kingdom being made hereditary in David's family, his being anointed served for him and all his successors, except when the right to the throne was disputed. Thus, when Solomon's right to the throne was contested by his elder brother Adonijah, it was necessary that he should be crowned, in order to quash that claim. In like manner, Joash, the seventh king of Judah, was anointed, because Athaliah had usurped and possessed the throne for six years. (2 Kings xi. 12.) So, Jehoahaz, the younger son of Josiah, was anointed king (2 Kings xxiii. 30.) and reigned three months: after which, he was succeeded by his elder brother Jehoiakim, who ought first to have ascended the throne of Judah. Thus it appears, that in all cases of disputed succession, anointing was deemed to give a preference. Home's Scripture History of the Jews, vol. i. p. 343.

which last-cited passages the Jews, by welcoming our Saviour in the same manner as their kings were formerly inaugurated, manifestly acknowledged him to be the Messiah whom they expected. Lastly, after entering the city, the kings seated themselves upon the throne, and received the congratulations of their subjects. (1 Kings i. 35. 47, 48. 2 Kings xi. 19, 20.) On the inauguration of Saul, however, when there was neither sceptre, diadem, nor throne, these ceremonies were not observed. After the establishment of royalty among the Jews, it appears to have been a maxim in their law, that *the king's person was inviolable, even though he might be tyrannical and unjust* (1 Sam. xxiv. 5—8.); a maxim which is necessary not only to the security of the king, but also to the welfare of the subject. On this principle, the Amalekite, who told David the improbable and untrue story of his having put the mortally wounded Saul to death, that he might not fall into the hands of the Philistines, was merely on this his own statement, ordered by David to be instantly despatched, *because he had laid his hand on the Lord's Anointed.* (2 Sam. i. 14.)

3. The CHIEF DISTINCTIONS OF MAJESTY mentioned in Scripture, were the Royal Apparel, the crown, the throne, and the sceptre. The *Royal Apparel* was splendid (Matt. vi. 29.), and the retinue of the sovereigns was both numerous and magnificent. (1 Kings iv. 1—24.) That the apparel of the Jewish monarchs was different from that of all other persons, is evident from Ahab's changing his apparel before he engaged in battle, and from Jehoshaphat's retaining his. (1 Kings xxii. 30.) It is most probable, after the example of other oriental sovereigns, that their garments were made of purple and fine white linen (Esth. viii. 15.): in after-times, it appears from Luke xvi. 19. that the rich and great were clad in purple and fine linen : and this circumstance may account for Pilate's soldiers clothing Christ with purple (Mark xv. 17.), and for Herod the tetrarch, with his men of war, arraying him in a gorgeous, most probably a white robe (Luke xxiii. 11.), thereby in derision clothing him as a king. Further, their *Crowns* or diadems glittered with gold, silver, and precious stones, (2 Sam. xii. 30. Zech. vi. 11.) Their arms were decorated with bracelets (2 Sam. i. 10.) as those of the Persian sovereigns are to this day[1]; and their thrones were equally magnificent. The throne of Solomon is particularly described in 1 Kings x. 18—20. Similar to this was the throne on which the sovereign of Persia was seated to receive his late Majesty's ambassador, Sir Gore Ouseley, Bart. It was ascended by steps, on which were painted dragons (that of Solomon was decorated with carved lions; and was also overlaid with fine gold). [2] The *Royal Sceptre* seems to have been various at different times. That of Saul was a javelin or spear (1 Sam. xviii. 10. xxii. 6.), as Justin informs us was antiently the practice among the early Greek sovereigns.[3] Sometimes the sceptre was a walking-stick, cut from the branches of trees, decorated with gold or studded with golden nails. Such sceptres were carried by judges, and by such a sceptre Homer introduces Achilles as swearing[4], and to a sceptre of this description the prophet Ezekiel unquestionably alludes. (xix. 11.)

---

[1] Morier's Second Journey, p. 173.   [2] Ibid. p. 174.
[3] Hist. lib. xliii. c. 3.   [4] Iliad, lib. i. v. 234—239.

The sceptres of the antient Persian monarchs were of solid gold. (Esth. v. 2.) [1]

In time of peace, as well as of war, it was customary to have watchmen set on high places, wherever the king was, in order to prevent him from being surprised.   Thus David, at Jerusalem, was informed by the watchmen of the approach of the messengers, who brought him tidings of Absalom's defeat. (2 Sam. xviii. 24—27.)   And Jehoram king of Israel, who had an army lying before Ramoth-Gilead, kept a watchman on the tower of Jezreel where he was, who *spied the company of Jehu as he came*, and accordingly announced it to the King. (2 Kings ix. 17. 20.) [2]

It is well known that the tables of the modern oriental sovereigns are characterised by luxurious profusion; and vast numbers are fed from the royal kitchen.[3]   This fact serves to account for the apparently immense quantity of provisions stated in 1 Kings iv. 22, 23. 28. to have been consumed by the household of Solomon, whose vessels were for the most part of massive gold (1 Kings x. 21.), and which were furnished throughout the year from the twelve provinces into which he divided his dominions.   A similar custom obtains in Persia to this day.[4]   Splendid banquets were given by the kings (Dan. v. 1. Matt. xxii. 1. Mark vi. 21.); but it does not appear that women were admitted to them, except in Persia, when the queen was present, until the men grew warm with wine. (Dan. v. 2, 3. 23. Esther i. 11. v. 4. 8. vii. 1.) [5]

4. Numerous are the ALLUSIONS IN THE SACRED WRITINGS TO THE COURTS OF PRINCES, and to the regal state which they antiently enjoyed.   "The eastern monarchs were ever distinguished for studiously keeping up the majesty of royalty, and thus inspiring their subjects with the most reverential awe.   They were difficult of access [6], very rarely showing themselves to their people, and lived in the depth of their vast palaces, surrounded with every possible luxury, and gratifying every desire as it arose.   In these kingdoms of slaves it was accounted the summit of human grandeur and felicity to be admitted into that splendid circle which surrounded the person of their sovereign [7];" whence the expression of seeing God (Matt. v. 8.) is to be explained of the enjoyment of the highest possible happiness, namely, his favour and protection, especially in the life to come.   And as only a select few in the oriental courts were permitted to behold the face of the monarch, it is in reference to this custom that the angel Gabriel

---

1 Pareau, Antiquitas Hebraica, pp. 277—279. Schulzii Archæologia Hebraica, pp. 45, 46. Jahn, Archæologia Biblica, §§ 223—227.   Ackermann, Archæologia Biblica, §§ 217—220.

2 Home's Scripture History, vol. i. p. 352.

3 Not fewer than *two thousand* are said to be employed about the palace of the reigning Emir of the Druses.   "We saw," says Mr. Jowett, "many professions and trades going on in it,— soldiers, horse-breakers, carpenters, blacksmiths, scribes, cooks, tobacconists, &c. There was, in the air of this mingled assemblage, something which forcibly brought to my recollection the description of an eastern royal household, as given to the Israelites by Samuel.   1 Sam. viii. 11—17."   Jowett's Christian Researches in Syria, p. 84.

4 Morier's Second Journey, p. 274.

5 This is confirmed by Herodotus, lib. v. c. 18.   Jahn, Archæologia Biblica, § 227. Ackermann, Archæologia Biblica, § 221.

6 Among the Persians it was death to enter the royal presence without being called for, Esther iv. 11.   Herodotus (book i. c. 99.) states Deioces the Mede to have been the first who instituted this ordinance.

7 Harwood's Introduction to the New Testament, vol. ii. pp. 322, 323.

replied to Zechariah (who hesitated to believe his annunciation of the Baptist's birth), that he was Gabriel that stood in the presence of God; thus intimating that he stood in a state of high favour and trust with Jehovah. (Luke i. 19.)   *To dwell,* or *to stand in the presence of a sovereign,* is an oriental idiom, importing the most eminent and dignified station at court.[1]

This allusive phraseology beautifully illustrates another very striking passage of Scripture. When the disciples, from their very low conceptions of the nature of Christ's kingdom, were contending among themselves who should be the greatest, our Saviour, in order to dispel these animosities, took a child; and, placing him before them, in the most solemn manner assured them that, *unless they were converted,* and purified their minds from all ambition and worldly thoughts, *they should not enter the kingdom of heaven,* should not be deemed proper subjects of the spiritual kingdom of the Messiah. But, continued Jesus Christ, *whosoever therefore shall humble himself as this little child, the same is greatest in the kingdom of heaven;* and, after urging various cautions against harshly treating sincere and humble Christians, he added, *Take heed that ye despise not one of these little ones; for I say unto you, That in heaven their angels do always* BEHOLD THE FACE OF MY FATHER WHICH IS IN HEAVEN. (Matt. xviii. 1—10.); referring to the custom of oriental courts, where the great men, those who are highest in office and favour, are most frequently in the prince's palace and presence. (Esth. i. 14. 1 Kings x. 8. xii. 6. 2 Kings xxv. 19.)[2] On another occasion, after our Lord had promised the apostles that they should sit on twelve thrones to judge the tribes of Israel, still mistaking the spiritual nature of his kingdom, the mother of James and John came to Jesus with her sons, and requested that he would grant that they might sit, the one on his right hand, and the other on his left hand, in his kingdom. (Matt. xx. 20—23.)   This alludes to the custom which in those times obtained in the courts of princes; where two of the noblest and most dignified personages were respectively seated, one on each side, next the sovereign himself, thus enjoying the most eminent places of dignity. (Compare 1 Kings ii. 19. Psal. xlv. 9. and Heb. i. 3.)   In reply to the request of Salome, our Saviour stated that seats of distinguished eminence in his kingdom were not to be given through favour or partiality, but to those only whom God should deem to be properly prepared for them.

The eastern monarchs were never approached but with presents of some kind or other, according to the ability of the individual, who accompanied them with expressions of the profoundest reverence, prostrating themselves to the ground[3]; and the same practice con-

---

[1] Harwood's Introduction to the New Testament, vol. ii. p. 323.

[2] Ibid. pp. 324, 325.   Among the antient Persians, to sit *next* the person of the king was the highest possible honour.   See 1 Esdras iii. 7. iv. 42.   Josephus, Ant. Jud. lib. xi. c. 3. § 2.

[3] It was (says Ælian) the law of Persia, that, whenever their king went abroad, the people should, according to their abilities and occupations, present him, as he passed along, with some gift, — as an ox, a sheep, a quantity of corn, or wine, or with some fruit.   It happened one day, when Artaxerxes was taking the air, that he was met by one Sinætus.   The man being at a great distance from home, was in the greatest distress, having nothing to offer, and observing others crowding with their presents.   At length he ran to the river Cyrus, and taking up some water in both his hands, he approached the monarch, and thus accosted him: — "O king, reign for ever! I now pay my respects in the best manner I am able.

tinues to this day. Thus Jacob instructed his sons to carry a present
to Joseph, when they went to buy food of him as governor of Egypt.
(Gen. xliii. 11. 26.) In like manner the magi, who came from the
East to adore Jesus Christ, as king of the Jews, brought him presents
of gold, frankincense, and myrrh. (Matt. ii. 11.) Allusions to this
practice occur in Gen. xxxii. 13. 1 Kings x. 2. 10. 25. 2 Kings v. 5.;
see also 1 Sam. ix. 7. and 2 Kings viii. 8. The prostrations were made,
with every demonstration of reverence, to the ground. Thus David
stooped with his face to the earth, and bowed himself before Saul. (1 Sam.
xxiv. 8.) The mode of doing reverence to the sovereign, among the
antient Persians, was little short of absolute idolatry [1]; and similar
prostrations are made by their descendants in the present day.[2] On
these occasions, it was usual to address them with some compliment,
or with wishes for their long life. Thus the widow of Tekoah, after
prostrating herself before David, addressed him with—*My lord is wise
according to the wisdom of an angel of God* [3] (2 Sam. xiv. 20.); and the
Chaldæan magi accosted Nebuchadnezzar with—*O king, live for ever!*
(Dan. ii. 4.) [4] The all but idolatrous homage thus rendered to their
monarchs, was exacted by their chief courtiers and favourites of all
who approached them; and such was their pride, that the refusal of
this homage never failed to involve the refractory individual in ruin.
Thus Orsines, a descendant of Cyrus, who had refused to worship the
eunuch Bagoas (who had enslaved Alexander by his abominable obse-
quiousness), fell a victim to the revengeful minion's wounded pride.[5]
In like manner, Mordecai's refusal to prostrate himself before Haman
(Esth. iii. 2.) would have proved fatal not only to himself but also to
the Jewish nation, had not the malignant design of the crafty but mortified Agagite (Esth. iii. 3—6. v. 13.) been providentially frustrated.

Those who rendered personal services to the sovereign had their
names inscribed in the public registers (Esth. vi. 1.) [6]; and were
rewarded by distinguished marks of the royal favour. Thus Mordecai
was arrayed with the royal vestments and led in state on horseback
through the street of the city, with the royal diadem on his head.
(Esth. vi. 8—11.) On such occasions the person raised to dignity
was invested with a new name or title expressive of his deserts. This
was the case with Joseph (Gen. xli. 45.), Solomon (2 Sam. xii. 25.),

---

I present to thee some of the waters of the river Cyrus : should your majesty ever pass by,
or near my house, I hope to vie with the best of these in my donatives." The monarch was
highly pleased with the man, commanded his present to be received into a golden vial, and
afterwards handsomely rewarded him. Ælian, Var. Hist. lib. i. cc. 31, 32.

[1] Quintus Curtius, lib. vi. c. 6. tom. ii. p. 23. (edit. Bipont): lib. viii, c. 5. (p. 118.)

[2] Morier's Second Journey, p. 172. ; where an engraving is given, illustrative of the
oriental prostrations.

[3] This is very similar to the hyperbolical language, which is addressed by the Hindoos to
an European, when they are desirous of obtaining something from him. " *Saheb*, say they,
can do every thing. No one can prevent the execution of Saheb's commands. Saheb is God."
(Ward's View of the History, &c. of the Hindoos, vol. ii. p. 323)

[4] A similar salutation is to this day given in India. When a poor man goes into the presence of a king, to solicit a favour, he says, " O Father! thou art the support of the destitute
—*Mayest thou live to old age!*" Ibid. p. 333. See also Roberts's Oriental Illustrations,
p. 501.

[5] Quintus Curtius, lib. x. c. 1. vol. ii. pp. 199—201. (edit. Bipont.)

[6] Herodotus, lib. viii. c. 85. Thucydides, lib. i. c. 129. Josephus, Ant. Jud. lib. xi.
c. 6. The same practice continues to obtain at the Ottoman Porte Baron de Tott's Mem.
vol. ii. p. 15.), and also in Abyssinia, and other parts of the East. Burder's Oriental
Customs, vol. i. p. 311. 5th edit.

Daniel and his companions (Dan. i. 7.); and to this there is an evident allusion in Rev. ii. 17.

The sovereigns of the East, it is well known, are very fond of displaying their gorgeous splendour. The present sovereign of Persia, and (after his example) his sons, generally appoint for the reception of ambassadors such an hour as, according to the season, or the intended room of audience, will best enable them to display the brilliancy of their jewels in full sunshine. The title of *bright* or *resplendent* was added to the name of one sovereign, who lived upwards of eight centuries ago; because his regal ornaments, glittering in the solar rays on a solemn festival, so dazzled the eyes of all beholders that they could scarcely bear the effulgence: and some knew not which was the monarch, or which the great luminary of the day. Thus Theophylact Simocatta[1] (a Greek historian who flourished in the seventh century of the Christian æra) relates that the Persian king, Hormisdas, sitting on his throne, astonished all spectators by the blazing glories of his jewels. Thus also king Agrippa was almost regarded as a god, so powerfully did his ornamented dress reflect the morning sun-beams[2]; and it was probably the splendour of Solomon " *in all his glory*," when seated on the throne, in addition to the magnificence of his establishment, which so struck the queen of Sheba on beholding them, that " *there was no more spirit in her.*" (1 Kings x. 4, 5.)

Further, whenever the oriental sovereigns go abroad, they are uniformly attended by a numerous and splendid retinue: the Hebrew kings and their sons either rode on asses or mules (2 Sam. xiii. 29. 1 Kings i. 33. 38.) or in chariots (1 Kings i. 5. 2 Kings ix. 21. x. 15.), preceded or accompanied by their royal guards (who, in 2 Sam. viii. 18. and xv. 18., are termed Cherethites and Pelethites); as the oriental sovereigns do to this day. For greater state they had footmen to run before them. Thus, the rebel Absalom had *fifty men to run before him.* (2 Sam. xv. 1.) And in this manner, the prophet Elijah, though he detested the crimes of Ahab, was desirous of paying him all that respect which was due to his exalted station; girded up his loins *and ran before Ahab to the entrance of Jezreel.* (1 Kings xviii. 46.) In India, when a person wishes to do honour to an European, he will run before his palanquin for miles.[3] Further, the approach of a king was often announced by the sound of trumpets. (1 Kings i. 34. 39.) Hence the presence of God is described in the same manner. (Heb. xii. 19. compared with Exod. xix. 13.), and also the final advent of the Messiah. (Matt. xxiv. 31. 1 Cor. xv. 52. 1 Thess. iv. 15.)[4]

Whenever the Asiatic monarchs entered upon an expedition, or took a journey through desert and untravelled countries, they sent harbingers before them to prepare all things for their passage, and pioneers to open the passes, level the ways, and remove all impediments. The antient sovereigns of Hindoostan used to send persons to precede them in their journies, and command the inhabitants to clear the roads; a

---

[1] Theophylact, lib. iv. c. 3. cited by Sir Wm. Ouseley, to whom we are indebted for the above remark, in his Travels in various Countries of the East, more particularly Persia, vol. ii. p. 36. (London, 1821. 4to.)

[2] Acts xii. 21, 22. See Vol. I. pp. 167, 168. where Josephus's account of Agrippa's gorgeous array is given in illustration of the sacred historian.

[3] Statham's Indian Recollections, pp. 116, 117.

[4] Robinson's Lexicon to the Greek Testament, p. 742.

very necessary step in a country where there are scarcely any public
roads. And, when a modern Hindoo of rank has to pass through a
town or village, a messenger is despatched to tell the people to prepare the way, and to await his orders.[1]   To this practice the prophet
Isaiah manifestly alludes (Isa. xl. 3. compared with Mal. iii. 1. Matt.
iii. 3. and Mark i. 3.) ; and we shall obtain a clear notion of the
preparation of the way for a royal expedition, and the force and
beauty of the prophetic declaration will fully appear, if we attend to
the following narrative of the marches of Semiramis in Media, recorded
by Diodorus Siculus.[2]   " In her march to Ecbatane, she came to the
Zarcean mountain, which extending many furlongs, and being full of
craggy precipices and *deep hollows*, could not be passed without making
a long circuit.   Being desirous, therefore, of leaving an everlasting
memorial of herself, as well as to make a shorter way, she ordered the
precipices to be digged down, and *the hollow places to be filled up ;* and at
a great expense she made a shorter and more expeditious road, which
to this day is called the road of Semiramis.   Afterwards she made a
progress through Persia, and all her other dominions in Asia ; and
wherever she came, she commanded the *mountains* and *craggy precipices to be cut down*, and, at a vast expense, made the *ways level and
plain.*   On the other hand, in *low places* she raised *mounds*, on which
she erected monuments in honour of her deceased generals, and sometimes whole cities."   The writer of the apocryphal book of Baruch
(v. 7.) expresses the same subject by the same images, either taking
them from Isa. xl. 3. (or perhaps from lxii. 10—12.), or from the
common notions of his countrymen : " For God," says he, " hath
appointed that every high *hill*, and banks of long continuance, shall be
cast down and *vallies filled up*, to *make even the ground*, that Israel may
go safely in the glory of God."   The " Jewish church was that desert country to which John the Baptist was sent (Matt. iii. 1—4.),
to announce the coming of the Messiah.   It was at that time destitute
of all religious cultivation, and of the spirit and practice of piety ; and
John was sent to *prepare the way of the Lord* by preaching the doctrine
of repentance.   The desert is therefore to be considered as a proper
emblem of the rude state of the Jewish church, which was the true
wilderness meant by the prophet, and in which John was to prepare
the way of the promised Messiah."[3]

V. With regard to the REVENUES OF THE KINGS OF ISRAEL, as none
were appointed by Moses, so he left no ordinances concerning them :

---

[1] Ward's View of the History, &c. of the Hindoos, vol. iii. p. 339.   Roberts's Oriental
Illustrations, p. 555.
[2] Bibliotheca Historica, lib. ii. cc. 13, 14. (vol. ii. pp. 44— 46. edit. Bipont.)
[3] Bishop Lowth on Isaiah xl. 3. vol. ii. pp. 252—254.   Dr. Clarke's Commentary on
Matt. iii. 3.   A practice similar to that above described, is recorded by the chaplain to Sir
Thomas Roe, ambassador to the Mogul court in the reigns of James I. and Charles I. ; who
says (p. 128.) that, making a progress with the ambassador and emperor, they came to a
wilderness, " where (*by a very great company sent before us, to make those passages and places
fit for us*) a WAY WAS CUT OUT AND MADE EVEN, broad enough for our convenient passage.
And in the place where we pitched our tents, a great compass of ground was rid and made
plain for them, by grubbing a number of trees and bushes : yet there we went as readily to
our tents, as we did when they were set up in the plains."   Fragments supplemental to
Calmet's Dictionary, No. 171.   See similar instances in Dr. Clarke's Travels, vol. viii.
p. 277. 8vo.   Mr. Forbes's Oriental Memoirs, vol. ii. p. 450. and Mr. Ward's View of
the History, &c. of the Hindoos, vol. iii. p. 132.

we may, however, collect from the Sacred Writings, that they were derived from the following sources : —

1. Voluntary offerings, or presents, which were made to them conformably to the oriental custom. (1. Sam. x. 27. xvi. 20.) Michaelis is of opinion that they were confined to Saul only, as no trace of them is to be found after his time.

2. The produce of the royal flocks (1 Sam. xxi. 7. 2 Sam. xiii. 23. 2 Chron. xxxii. 28, 29.) ; and as both king and subjects had a common of pasture in the Arabian deserts, Michaelis thinks that David kept numerous herds there (1 Chron. xxvii. 29—31.), which were partly under the care of Arabian herdsmen.

3. The produce of the royal demesnes, consisting of arable lands, vineyards, olive and sycamore grounds, &c. which had originally been uninclosed and uncultivated, or were the property of state criminals confiscated to the sovereign : these demesnes were cultivated by bondsmen, and, perhaps, also by the people of conquered countries (1 Chron. xxvii. 26—31. 2 Chron. xxvi. 10.) ; and it appears from 1 Sam. viii. 14. xxii. 7. and Ezek. xlvi. 17. that the kings assigned part of their domains to their servants in lieu of salary.

4. Another source of the royal revenue was the tenth part of all the produce of the fields and vineyards, the collection and management of which seem to have been confided to the officers mentioned in 1 Kings iv. 7. and 1 Chron. xxvii. 25. It is also probable from 1 Kings x. 14. that the Israelites likewise paid a tax in money. These imposts Solomon appears to have increased ; and Rehoboam's refusal to lessen them is stated by the sacred historian as the cause of the rebellion of the ten tribes against him. (1 Kings xii. 14. 18.) There is an allusion in Mal. i. 8. and Neh. v. 18. to the custom of paying dues in kind to governors, which obtains to this day in Abyssinia.[1]

5. Not only did the most precious part of the plunder of the conquered nations flow into the royal treasury (2 Sam. viii.), but the latter also had tributes imposed on them, which were termed MINCHA, or presents, and were paid partly in money, and partly in agricultural produce. (1 Kings iv. 21. Psal. lxxii. 10. compared with 1 Chron. xxvii. 25—31.)

6. Lastly, the customs paid to Solomon by the foreign merchants who passed through his dominions (1 Kings x. 15.) afforded a considerable revenue to that monarch ; who, as the Mosaic laws did not encourage foreign commerce, carried on a very extensive and lucrative trade (1 Kings x. 22.), particularly in Egyptian horses and the byssus or fine linen of Egypt. (1 Kings x. 28, 29.)[2]

VI. On the introduction of the regal government among the Israelites, the princes of the tribes, heads of families, scribes or genealogists, and judges, retained the authority which they had previously exercised, and constituted a senate or legislative assembly for the cities, in or near which they respectively resided. (1 Kings xii. 1—24. 1 Chron. xxiii. 4. xxvi. 29, 30. xxviii. and xxix. 6.) The judges and scribes or genealogists were appointed by the sovereign, together with other officers, of whom the following were the principal : —

---

[1] Bruce's Travels, vol. i. p. 353. 8vo.
[2] Jahn, Archæologia Biblica, § 234. Ackermann, Archæologia Biblica, § 228. Michaelis's Commentaries, vol. i. pp. 299—307.

1. The most important officer was the PRIME MINISTER, or *Second to the King*, as he is termed in Scripture. Such was Elkanah, who in our version of 2 Chron. xxviii. 7. is said to have been *next* (literally *second*) *to the king* Ahaz; Joseph was prime minister to Pharaoh, king of Egypt (Gen. xli. 40—43.); and Haman, to Ahasuerus. (Esth. iii. 1.) Jonathan, speaking to David, says, — " *Thou shalt be king over Israel, and I shall be next unto thee.* (1 Sam. xviii. 17.) From 1 Chron. xviii. 17., it should seem that this office was sometimes held by one or more of the king's sons.

2. The ROYAL COUNSELLORS, or Privy Council, as we perhaps should term them. (Isa. iii. 3. xix. 11, 12. Jer. xxvi. 11.) Such were *the old men that stood before Solomon while he lived*, and whom the headstrong Rehoboam consulted (1 Kings xii. 6.); and such also was *Jonathan, David's uncle.* (1 Chron. xxvii. 32.)

3. The PROPHETS, though holding a divine commission as prophets, may, nevertheless, be noticed among the royal officers; as they were consulted by the pious monarchs of Israel and Judah. Thus Nathan was consulted by David (2 Sam. vii. 2.); Micaiah, by Jehoshaphat (1 Kings xxii. 7, 8.); Isaiah, by Hezekiah (2 Kings xix. 2.); and the prophetess Huldah, by Josiah. (2 Kings xxii. 14—20.) But the idolatrous and profligate kings imitated the heathen monarchs, and summoned to their council soothsayers and false prophets. Ahab, for instance, consulted the pseudo-prophets of Baal (1 Kings xviii. 22. and xxii. 6.); as Pharaoh had before called in the wise men and the sorcerers or magicians (Exod. vii. 11. and viii. 18.); and Nebuchadnezzar afterwards consulted the *magicians and astrologers in his realm.* (Dan. i. 20.)

4. The מַזְכִּיר (MAZKIR) or RECORDER (2 Sam. viii. 16.), who in the margin of our larger English Bibles is termed a *remembrancer* or *writer of chronicles*. His office was of no mean estimation in the eastern world, where it was customary with kings to keep daily registers of all the transactions of their reigns. Whoever discharged this trust with effect, it was necessary that he should be acquainted with the true springs and secrets of action, and consequently be received into the greatest confidence. Ahilud was David's recorder or historiographer (2 Sam. viii. 16.), and appears to have been succeeded in this office by his son Jehoshaphat (2 Sam. xx. 24.), who was retained by Solomon. (1 Kings iv. 3.) Joah, the son of Asaph, was the recorder of the pious king Hezekiah. (2 Kings xviii. 18. 37. Isa. xxxvi. 3.) In Esther vi. 1. and x. 2. mention is made of the *records of the chronicles*, written by this officer.

5. The סוֹפֵר (SOPHER) or *Scribe* (Sept. Γραμματεύς) seems to have been the king's secretary of state, who issued all the royal commands : he also registered all acts and decrees. Seraiah (2 Sam. viii. 17.) and Sheva (2 Sam. xx. 25.) were David's secretaries. This officer is also mentioned in 1 Kings iv. 3. 2 Kings xviii. 18. and Isa. xxxvi. 3.

6. The HIGH PRIEST, as one would naturally expect in a theocracy, is likewise to be reckoned among the royal counsellors. Zadok the son of Ahitub, and Ahimelech the son of Abiathar, are particularly mentioned among the principal officers of David. (2 Sam. viii. 17. 1 Chron. xviii. 16.)

VII. Mention has already been incidentally made of the numerous retinue that attended the oriental monarchs: the principal officers, who thus composed the domestic establishment of the Israelitish and Jewish kings, were as follow: —

1. The GOVERNOR OF THE PALACE, who was over the household, seems to have answered, as to his employment and rank, to the stewards whom the rich men engaged to superintend their affairs. To him was committed the charge of the servants, and indeed of every thing which belonged to the palace. Ahishar held this office under David (1 Kings iv. 6.); Obadiah, under Ahab (1 Kings xviii. 3.); and Eliakim, under Hezekiah. (2 Kings xviii. 18.) From Isa., xxii. 22. it appears that this officer wore, as a mark of his office, a robe of a peculiar make, bound with a precious girdle, and carried on his shoulder a richly ornamented key.

2. The *Officers*, mentioned in 1 Kings iv. 5. 7 — 19. and 1 Chron. xxvii. 25 — 31., are in 1 Kings xx. 15. called the PRINCES OF THE PROVINCES. They supplied the royal table, and must not be confounded with those who collected the tribute. In 2 Sam. xx, 24. and 1 Kings iv. 6. Adoram, who is enumerated among David's and Solomon's officers of state, is said to be *over the tribute:* he was, probably, what we call *chancellor of the exchequer.* He received and brought into the royal treasury all the proceeds of taxes and tributes.

3. The KING'S FRIEND, or COMPANION, was the person with whom the sovereign conversed most familiarly and confidentially. Thus, Hushai was the friend of David (2 Sam. xv. 37. xvi. 16.); and Zabud the son of Nathan, of Solomon. (1 Kings iv. 5.) In the time of the Maccabees, this appellation admitted of a broader meaning, and was applied to any one who was employed to execute the royal commands, or who held a high office in the government. See 1 Macc. x. 65. xi. 26, 27.

4. The KING'S LIFE-GUARD, whose commander was termed the Captain of the Guard. This office existed in the court of the Pharaohs (Gen. xxxvii. 36. xxxix. 1.), as well as in that of the Israelitish and Jewish monarchs. The captain of the guard appears to have been employed in executing summary justice on state criminals. See 1 Kings ii. 25. 34. In the time of David the royal life-guards were called Cherethites and Pelethites, concerning the origin of whose names commentators and critics are by no means agreed. The Chaldee Targum, on the second book of Samuel, terms them the *archers* and *slingers:* and as the Hebrews were expert in the use of the bow and the sling, it is not improbable that the royal guards were armed with them.[1]

The life-guards of the Maccabæan sovereigns, and subsequently of Herod and his sons, were foreigners: they bore a lance or long spear, whence they were denominated in Greek Σπεκουλατορες. Among the other duties of these guards was that of putting to death condemned persons (Mark vi. 27.), in the same manner as the *capidgis* among the Turks and other Orientals are the bearers of the sovereign's commands for punishing any one, whether by decapitation or otherwise; an office which is very honourable in the East, though considered degrading among us.

---

[1] Calmet, Dissertations, tom. ii. pp. 508—512. Jahn, Archæologia Biblica, §§ 235, 236. Ackermann, Archæologia Biblica, §§ 229, 230.

VIII. The women of the king's HAREM are to be considered as
forming part of the royal equipage: as, generally speaking, they were
principally destined to augment the pomp, which was usually attached
to his office. Notwithstanding Moses had prohibited the multipli-
cation of women in the character of wives and concubines (Deut. xvii.
17.): yet the Hebrew monarchs, especially Solomon, and his son
Rehoboam, paid but little regard to his admonitions, and too readily
as well as wickedly exposed themselves to the perils which Moses had
anticipated as the result of forming such improper connections.
(1 Kings xi. 1—3. 2 Chron. xi. 21. xiii. 21.) The Israelitish and
Jewish monarchs spared no expense in decorating the persons of their
women, and of the eunuchs who guarded them: and who, as the Mosaic law prohibited castration (Lev. xxii. 24. Deut. xxiii. 1), were
procured from foreign countries at a great expense. In proof of the
employment of eunuchs in the Hebrew court see 1 Kings xxii. 9.
(Heb.) 2 Kings viii. 6. (Heb.) ix. 32, 33. xx. 18. xxiii. 11. (Heb.)
xxxix. 16. and xli. 16. Black eunuchs appear to have been preferred,
as they still are in the East; at least, we find one in the court of Zedekiah. (Jer. xxxviii. 7.) [1] The maids of the harem, at the king's pleasure, became his concubines; but the successor to the throne, though
he came into possession of the harem, was not at liberty to have any
intercourse with the inmates of it. Hence Adonijah, who in his zeal
to obtain Abishag, a concubine of David's, for his wife, had dropt
some intimations of his right to the kingdom, was punished with death,
as a seditious person. (1 Kings ii. 13—25.) But though the king had
unlimited power over the harem, yet the queen, or wife who was
chiefly in favour, and especially the mother of the king, enjoyed great
political influence. (1 Kings xi. 3. 2 Chron. xxi. 6. and xxii. 3.)
Hence it is that we find the mother of the king so frequently and particularly mentioned in the books of Kings and Chronicles. She
evidently held the station of first matron in the kingdom, which in
modern times is enjoyed by a queen consort. The similar influence
of the reigning sultana, as well as of the mother of the sovereign, in
modern oriental courts, is attested by almost every traveller in the
East.[2] The king's mother appears to have retained that dignified
title, even though she should survive her son; for Maachah, the grandmother of Asa, king of Judah, is in one passage called his mother, and
held the dignity of queen till she was degraded by her descendant on
account of her idolatry. (1 Kings xv. 2—10. 13.)

IX. The PROMULGATION OF THE LAWS was variously made at different times. Those of Moses, as well as the commands or temporary
edicts of Joshua, were announced to the people by the שׁוֹטְרִים
(SHOTERIM), who in our authorised English version are termed *officers.*
Afterwards, when the regal government was established, the edicts,
and laws of the kings were publicly proclaimed by criers. (Jer. xxxiv.

---

[1] As, however, in the East, eunuchs often rose to stations of great power and trust, and
were even privy counsellors to kings, the term ultimately came to signify a court-officer
generally. The eunuch mentioned in Acts viii. 27. was an officer of great power and
influence at the court of Candace, queen of Ethiopia. Bloomfield's Annotations on the
New Testament, vol. iv. p. 294.

[2] Pareau, Antiquitas Hebraica, pp. 279, 280. Jahn, Archæologia Biblica, § 237. Ackermann, Archæologia Biblica, § 231.

8, 9. Jonah iii. 5—7.) [1] But in the distant provinces, towns, and cities, they were made known by messengers or couriers, specially sent for that purpose (1 Sam xi. 7.), who were afterwards termed *posts.* (Esth. viii. 10. 14. Jer. li. 31.) Cyrus, or, according to Herodotus, Xerxes, was the first who established relays of horses and couriers at certain distances on all the great roads, in order that the royal messages and letters might be transmitted with the greatest possible speed. These *Angari,* or couriers, had authority to impress into their service men, horses, and ships, or any thing that came in their way, and which might serve to accelerate their journey. From the Persians this custom passed to the Romans (who, it may be inferred from Matt. v. 41., commonly pressed men into their service), and it is still retained in the East.[2] These proclamations were made at the gates of the cities, and in Jerusalem at the gate of the temple, where there was always a great concourse of people. On this account it was that the prophets frequently delivered their predictions in the temple (and also in the streets and at the gates) of Jerusalem, as being the edicts of Jehovah, the supreme King of Israel. (Jer. vii. 2, 3. xi. 6. xvii. 19, 20. xxxvi. 10.) In later times, both Jesus Christ and his apostles taught in and at the gate of the temple. (Luke ii. 46. Matt. xxvi. 55. Mark xii. 35. Acts iii. 11. v. 12.)[3]

X. The kingdom which had been founded by Saul, and carried to its highest pitch of grandeur and power by David and Solomon, subsisted entire for the space of 120 years; until Rehoboam, the son and successor of Solomon, refused to mitigate the burthens of his subjects, when a division of the twelve tribes took place: ten of these (of which Ephraim was the principal) adhered to Jeroboam, and formed the kingdom of Israel, while the tribes of Judah and Benjamin, continuing faithful in their allegiance to Rehoboam, constituted the kingdom of Judah. The causes of this revolution in the commencement of Rehoboam's reign, may, as in all similar commotions, be traced to anterior events: the impolicy of that monarch was only the immediate occasion of it ; and in the successive periods of the history of the Hebrews, we may discern vestiges of hereditary jealousy, which terminated only in the division of the posterity of Abraham into two distinct nations, one of whom has since disappeared. The limits necessarily assigned to this portion of our work, will only allow us to attempt a rapid sketch of this long series of discord and hatred.

---

[1] The edicts of the antient kings of Egypt "appear to have been issued in the form of a *firmán,* or written order, as in all oriental countries : and from the expression used by Pharaoh, in granting power unto Joseph, we may infer, that the people who received that order adopted the usual eastern mode of acknowledging their obedience and respect for the sovereign. (The expression in the Hebrew is, *according to thy word shall my people* KISS — be ruled — alluding evidently to the custom of kissing a *firmán.* Gen. xlv. 40.) Nor can there be any doubt that, besides the custom of kissing the signature attached to those documents, they were expected to *bow the knee* (Gen. xli. 43.) in the presence of the monarchs and chiefs of the country." Joseph's brethren *bowed themselves to him to the earth.* (Wilkinson's Manners, &c. of the Antient Egyptians, vol. ii. p. 24.)

[2] Xenoph. Cyr. lib. viii. 6. 17. Herod. viii. 98. Robinson's Lexicon, voce Αγγαρευω. Among the Turks, these Angari or couriers are called *Tatars ;* and in Persia *Chappars.* "When a chappar sets out, the master of the horse furnishes him with a single horse : and when that is weary, he dismounts the first man he meets and takes his horse. There is no pardon for a traveller that should refuse to let a chappar have his horse, nor for any other who should deny him the best horse in his stable." Chardin's Travels, vol. i. p. 257.

[3] Jahn, Archæologia Biblica, § 223. Ackermann, Archæologia Biblica, § 227.

From the very beginning of the Israelitish nation, the two tribes of Judah and Ephraim had disputed for the pre-eminency. The former, whose glory had been predicted by the dying patriarch Jacob (Gen. xlix. 10.), flourished in the number of its families, as well as by its power and wealth ; being allied to the blood of the Pharoahs during the residence of the Israelites in Egypt, where the two remarkable establishments of Er and of Jokim had been formed, which this tribe carried into Palestine. (1 Chron. v. 2. iv. 18.) Judah also marched first during the sojourning in the desert (Numb. x. 14.), and reckoned upon a dominion which had been promised by so many oracles. The latter, or tribe of Ephraim, depending on the great name of Joseph, and on the right of primogeniture which it had acquired in consequence of being adopted by Jacob (1 Chron. v. 2. Gen. xlviii. 5. 19.), confided in that numerous posterity which had been predicted to it; became powerful during the residence in Egypt, as is evident from the buildings erected by Sherah (1 Chron. vii. 24.); and afterwards rapidly increased in strength and prosperity. (Josh. xvii. 14. Judg. i. 35.) One very remarkable proof, that Ephraim and Judah were the two preponderating tribes, is, that when the land of Canaan was divided (Josh.xviii. 2.), they each received their allotments before the western tribes. As the southern part of the Holy Land, which was apportioned to Judah, proved too large for that tribe, the Simeonites were added to them. (Josh. xix. 1. 9.) The Ephraimites, on the contrary, and the half tribe of Manasseh, which were sister and neighbouring tribes, pleaded that their allotment was not sufficiently extensive for them; and enlarged it by force of arms, and by cutting down the forests which abounded in the mountainous districts of the land of Canaan. (Josh. xvii. 14—18.)

In this state of things, with such recollections and mutual pretensions, it was impossible that a spirit of rivalry and jealousy should not break forth. The tribe of Ephraim was distinguished for its proud, turbulent, and warlike spirit, as is evident not only from the remonstrances addressed by them to Joshua, but also by their discontented murmuring against Gideon, notwithstanding he was of the tribe of Manasseh (Judg. viii. 1.), and in the civil war with Jephthah in which their envy and hatred were so severely punished. (xii. 1—4.) The tribe of Judah, on the contrary, more pacific in its temper and more sedentary in its pursuits, appears always to have cherished a coolness towards the northern tribes. It never assisted them in their wars; its name does not occur in the triumphal hymn of Deborah, in which so many others are mentioned ; and (what is particularly deserving of attention) it took no part in the exploits of Gideon, although the enemies whom he was going to fight had made incursions as far as Gaza (Judg. vi. 4.), whither they could not have penetrated without entering on its territory. It was the men of Judah, also, who were desirous of delivering up Samson, a Danite, to the Philistines. (xv. 11.) This old grudge subsisted in all its force, when the elevation of Saul, a Benjamite, to the throne of Israel, still further chagrined the proud tribe of Ephraim : it is not improbable that the discontent manifested in the assembly of the Israelites at Mizpeh, which induced Samuel to renew the kingdom at Gilgal (1 Sam. x. 27. xi. 12—14.), was excited by the Ephraimites ; and at the very commencement of Saul's reign we observe a census, in which the troops of Judah are reckoned separately from those of Israel. (18.)   At length, the elevation of David completed the mortification of the jealous and envious tribe of Ephraim, and of the northern tribes which ordinarily followed the fortune of so powerful a neighbour; while Simeon and Benjamin, from necessity as well as choice, were more disposed in favour of Judah.   Hence David, during the whole of his long-continued flight from Saul, never quitted the territory of Judah and Benjamin, but when he took refuge in a foreign country; and he sent presents only to the cities of his own tribe. (1 Sam. xxx. 26.)   On the death of Saul, two thrones arose in Israel; which gave rise to a civil war, that lasted seven years; and, had it not been for the defection of Abner, and the timidity of Ishbosheth, the tribes might never have been united under one sceptre. (2 Sam. ii. 10. iii. 1. 9—12. v. 5.)   David himself felt the weakness of his power. (iii. 39.)   The choice of Jerusalem for his capital and for the centre of worship, to the exclusion of Shiloh, a town of Ephraim where the tabernacle and ark had formerly been kept (Josh. xviii. 1.), could not but displease the malecontents, whose pride was wounded by hearing that advantage celebrated in one of the sacred hymns. (Psal. lxxviii. 67, 68.)   During David's reign, the dispute at the passage of the river Jordan showed how a small spark kindled a flame (2 Sam. xix. 41.), which Sheba, retiring towards the north, was at hand to excite. (xx. 1.)

Finally, the erection of the temple, the immoveable sanctuary, which secured the supremacy of the tribe of Judah, — the taxes levied and personal services required by Solomon, who employed them for the most part in the embellishment of Jerusalem, — the little commercial advantage which Ephraim could derive during his reign, in comparison of Judah, which tribe was more commodiously situated for profiting by the transit of commodities between Egypt, Idumæa, and Arabia, — the intrigues of Jeroboam who had been imprudently nominated to the command of the *house of Joseph* (2 Kings xi. 26. 28.) ; — all these circumstances contributed secretly to mature that revolution, which only awaited his death to break forth, and which the folly of Rehoboam rendered inevitable.

The KINGDOM OF ISRAEL subsisted under various sovereigns during a period of 254 years, according to some chronologers; its metropolis Samaria being captured by Shalmaneser king of Assyria, B. c. 721, after a siege of three years.   Of the Israelites, whose numbers had been reduced by immense and repeated slaughters, some of the lower sort were suffered to remain in their native country; but the nobles and all the more opulent persons were carried into captivity beyond the Euphrates.[1]

[1] It was the belief of some of the antient fathers of the Christian church, that the descendants of the ten tribes did afterwards return into their own country : and the same notion has obtained among some modern Jews, but neither of these opinions is supported by history.   In the New Testament, indeed, we find mention of the twelve tribes (Matt. xix. 28. Luke xxii. 30. Acts xxvi. 7.): and St. James (i, 1.) directs his epistle to them; but it cannot be concluded from these passages, that they were at that time gathered together; all that can be inferred from them is, that they were still in being.   Perhaps the whole body of the Jewish nation retained the name of the *twelve tribes* according to the antient division; as we find the disciples called the *twelve* after the death of Judas, and before the election of Matthias.   This conjecture becomes the more probable, as it is certain from the testimony of the Sacred Writers and of Josephus, that there were considerable numbers of Israelites mingled with the

The KINGDOM OF JUDAH continued 388 years; Jerusalem its capital being taken, the temple burnt, and its sovereign Zedekiah being carried captive to Babylon by Nebuchadnezzar; the rest of his subjects (with the exception of the poorer classes who were left in Judæa) were likewise carried into captivity beyond the Euphrates, where they and their posterity remained seventy years, agreeably to the divine predictions.

XI. The kingdom of Judah subsisted one hundred and thirty-three years after the subversion of the Israelitish monarchy; and for this longer duration various reasons may be adduced.

1. *The geographico-political situation of Judah was more favourable than that of Israel.*

In point of extent, indeed, Israel far surpassed Judah, the latter kingdom being scarcely equal to the third part of Israel, which also exceeded Judah both in the fertility of its soil and the amount of its population. But the kingdom of Judah was more advantageously situated for commerce, and further possessed greater facilities of defence from hostile attacks, than the kingdom of Israel. The Syrians, being separated from the Jews by the intervening kingdom of Israel, once only laid waste the lower regions of Judah; while, for upwards of a century, they made incursions into and devastated the kingdom of Israel. The Assyrians, also, being more remote from the Jews, could not observe them so narrowly as they watched the Israelites, whom they in a manner continually threatened. Further, the naturally strong situation of Jerusalem (which city the Assyrians vainly attempted to reduce by famine) contributed much to the preservation of the kingdom, as it enabled Hezekiah to hold out successfully against the forces of Sennacherib, who besieged it in the eighth year after the subversion of the kingdom of Israel.

2. *The people were more united in the kingdom of Judah than in that of Israel.*

The religious worship, which was solemnised at Jerusalem, the metropolis of Judah, not only united the Jews and Benjaminites more closely together, but also offered a very powerful attraction to every pious person of the other tribes to emigrate into Judah. Hence the priests and Levites, as well as many other devout Israelites, enriched the kingdom of Judah with piety, learning, and wealth. In the kingdom of Israel, on the contrary, in consequence of the expulsion of the priests and Levites, by whom its civil affairs had for the most part been administered, tumults and internal discord necessarily arose, from its very commencement under Jeroboam I.; and, with regard to the other Israelites, the history of later ages abundantly attests the very great loss sustained in states and kingdoms by the compulsory emigration of virtuous and industrious citizens, in consequence of changes made in religion. Thus, Spain has never recovered the expulsion of the Moors; and the unprincipled repeal of the edict of Nantes by Louis XIV. against the faith of the most solemn treaties, inflicted a loss upon France, from the effects of which that country has scarcely yet recovered. In like manner, in antient times, the kingdom of Israel

Jews, sufficient indeed to authorise the former to speak of the twelve tribes as constituting but one body with the Jewish nation. Beausobre's Introd. to the New Test. (Bishop Watson's Tracts, vol. iii. pp. 114—116.)

fell into decay, in consequence of the oppression of the faithful worshippers of Jehovah after the introduction of the worship of the calves.
But this new idolatrous religion was of no advantage to the apostates :
on the contrary, it was detrimental to them, for the worship of the
calves had the effect of disuniting more and more the provinces of
Galilee and Samaria, which naturally were too much separated ; and
the idolatrous worship of Baal, established at Samaria, was so repugnant to the manners of the Hebrews, as to prove the chief cause — not
of concord, but of civil wars.

To this union among the Jews is principally to be ascribed the
brilliant victory which in the reign of Abijah gave them a decided
superiority over the Israelites ; and the same unanimity and affection
for true religion, in the time of Hezekiah, disposed them all promptly
to shake off the yoke of the Assyrians, and rendered them sufficiently
strong to accomplish their deliverance without any foreign aid. The
Israelites, on the contrary, being for the most part torn by factions,
and despairing of being able to recover their affairs, were irresolute
under almost every circumstance.

3. *The succession to the throne of Judah was more regular ; and the
character of its sovereigns was more exemplary than in the kingdom of
Israel.*

Although the authority of the kings of Judah was unquestionably
much lessened in point of extent by the revolt of the ten tribes, yet, if
we consider its internal power and stability, we shall find that it was
rather increased than diminished by that defection. From the very
commencement of the separation it is evident that the prophets, in
obedience to former oracles (see 2 Kings viii. 19.) were so attached to
the family of David, that no wickedness or contempt of the laws on
the part of individual kings could lessen their fidelity to the royal
lineage. Hence no Jew ever thought of seizing the throne of David,
no prophet ever foretold the ruin of the royal family. For, though
some of the Jewish monarchs more than once followed strange gods ;
though Asa, disregarding the counsels of Hanani, called the Syrians
to his aid ; though Jehoshaphat, by forming an alliance with the wicked
Ahab, king of Israel, was the cause of the greatest calamities both to
his kingdom and to his family ; though Athaliah destroyed all the seed
royal of the house of Judah, Joash alone excepted, who afterwards put
to death the innocent high priest Zechariah, the son of the very man
to whom he was indebted for the preservation of his life and kingdom ;
though, finally, Ahaz, disregarding the advice of the prophet Isaiah,
voluntarily called to his aid the Assyrians, and shut up the doors of
the house of the Lord ; yet, notwithstanding all these circumstances,
the Jews never thought of expelling the royal family from the throne.
Some of the Jewish monarchs, indeed, came to violent deaths in various
ways [1] ; but no civil wars ensued, no ambitious princes ever disturbed
the state ; on the contrary, that kingdom, being always restored to the
lawful heir, derived advantage, rather than suffered injury, from such
changes. Thus the kingdom of Judah continued in peaceable sub-

---

[1] Thus, Ahaziah, king of Judah, was slain by Jehu, king of Israel (2 Chron. xxii. 7—9.) ;
Athaliah, who succeeded Ahaziah, by the command of Jehoiada the priest (2 Chron. xxiii.
14—16.) ; Joash, by his own servants (2 Chron. xxiv. 25, 26.) ; and Amaziah, by some of
his subjects who conspired against him (2 Chron. xxv. 27.).

jection to its legitimate sovereigns ; and all orders in the state consulted its welfare.   Many of the kings maintained the worship of Jehovah from motives of sincere piety, and others from a conviction of the utility of religion to a state ; while the priests and prophets, who vigilantly watched over the religion of their country, influenced their sovereigns to the adoption of sage counsels.

To this circumstance we may ascribe the fact, that the *characters of the kings of Judah were more exemplary* than those of the kings of Israel : for, although there were not wanting wicked and imprudent Jewish sovereigns, yet their errors and misconduct were for the most part corrected or avoided by their successors, who were instructed by the advice and example of wise and virtuous men, and thus were enabled to repair the injuries which their kingdom had sustained. The reverse of all this was the case in the kingdom of Israel; in which the royal dignity, polluted by continual murders and seditions, gradually fell into decay, and with the regal power declined all regard for the welfare of the state.   Distracted by civil wars and by the contests of ambitious aspirants to the throne, the Israelites became disunited; the provinces, which at the commencement of the Israelitish monarchy had been tributary to it, revolted; and almost all the kings, who swayed the sceptre of Israel, governed so ill, as scarcely to deserve the name of sovereigns. While the sacred historians repeatedly record of various kings of Judah that they did that which was right in the sight of the Lord, according to all that their father David had done, the ordinary character of the kings of Israel is related with this stigma, — that they departed not from all the sins of Jeroboam the son of Nebat, who made Israel to sin.

4. Lastly, and principally, *pure and undefiled religion was most carefully preserved and cultivated in the kingdom of Judah, while the vilest idolatry was practised in the kingdom of Israel.*

This fact is so clearly narrated in the histories of the two kingdoms, that it is needless to adduce any examples.   As a necessary consequence of true piety, the Jews far surpassed the Israelites in the purity of their moral character, and in the implicit confidence with which they left all their affairs to the Divine Protection: for, at the very time, when abominations of every kind were practised in Israel, when scarcely a crime was left unattempted, and when the Israelites sought all their safety and protection from foreign aid, in Judah, the " Law of the LORD" was most diligently studied ; and the Jews, strengthened by their unshaken trust in Jehovah, voluntarily risked every thing to promote the welfare of their country.[1]   In short, the histories of the two kingdoms of Judah and Israel furnish a perpetual illustration of the truth of Solomon's declaration, that " *righteousness exalteth a nation, but sin is a reproach to any people.* Prov. xiv. 34.

XII. STATE OF THE HEBREWS DURING THE BABYLONISH CAPTIVITY.

The condition of the Hebrews, during the captivity, was far from being one of abject wretchedness.   " This is manifest from the circumstance, that a pious Hebrew prophet held the first office at the court of Babylon ; that three devout friends of this prophet occupied important

---

[1] Bernhardi, Commentatio de Caussis quibus effectum sit, ut Regnum Judæ diutius persisteret quam Regnum Israel, pp. 96—104. 120—122.

political stations; and that Jehoiachin, the former king of Judah, in the forty-fourth year of the captivity, was released from an imprisonment which had continued for thirty-six years, and was preferred in point of rank to all the kings who were then at Babylon, either as hostages, or for the purpose of paying homage to the Chaldæan monarch. He was treated as the first of the kings; he ate at the table of his conqueror, and received an annual allowance, corresponding to his royal rank. These circumstances of honour must have reflected a degree of dignity on all the exiles, sufficient to prevent their being ill-treated or despised. They were probably viewed as respectable colonists, enjoying the peculiar protection of the sovereign. In the respect paid to Jehoiachin, his son Shealtiel and his grandson Zerubbabel undoubtedly partook. If that story[1] of the discussion before Darius, in which Zerubbabel is said to have won the prize, be a mere fiction, still it is at least probable that the young prince, though he held no office, had free access to the court; a privilege which must have afforded him many opportunities of alleviating the unhappy circumstances of his countrymen. It is therefore not at all surprising, that, when Cyrus gave the Hebrews permission to return to their own country, many, and perhaps even a majority of the nation, chose to remain behind, believing that they were more pleasantly situated where they were, than they would be in Judæa. It is not improbable that the exiles (as is implied in the story of Susanna, and as the tradition of the Jews affirms), had magistrates and a prince from their own number. Jehoiachin, and after him Shealtiel and Zerubbabel, might have been regarded as their princes, in the same manner as Jozadak and Joshua were as their high priests. At the same time it cannot be denied that their humiliation, as a people punished by their God, was always extremely painful, and frequently drew on them expressions of contempt. The peculiarities of their religion afforded many opportunities for the ridicule and scorn of the Babylonians and Chaldæans, a striking example of which is given in the profanation of the sacred vessels of the temple. (Dan. v.) By such insults they were made to feel so much the more sensibly the loss of their homes, their gardens, and fruitful fields; the burning of their capital and temple; and the cessation of the public solemnities of their religion. Under such circumstances, it is not strange that an inspired minstrel breaks out into severe imprecations against the scornful foes of his nation. (Psal. cxxxvii. 8, 9.)

" If the Israelites were ill-treated in Assyria after the overthrow of Sennacherib in Judæa, as the book of Tobit intimates, this calamity was of short duration; for Sennacherib was soon after assassinated. The Israelites of Media appear to have been in a much better condition, since Tobit advised his son to remove thither. (Tobit, xiv. 4. 12, 13.) This is the more probable, as the religion of the Medes was not grossly idolatrous, and bore considerable resemblance to that of the Jews." [2]

---

[1] 1 Esdras iii. iv.   Josephus, Ant. Jud. lib. xi. c. 3.
[2] Jahn's History of the Hebrew Commonwealth, vol. i. pp. 161. 163.

CHAPTER II.

POLITICAL STATE OF THE JEWS, FROM THEIR RETURN FROM
THE BABYLONISH CAPTIVITY, TO THE SUBVERSION OF THEIR
CIVIL AND ECCLESIASTICAL POLITY.

SECTION I.

POLITICAL STATE OF THE JEWS UNDER THE MACCABEES, AND THE
SOVEREIGNS OF THE HERODIAN FAMILY.

I. *Brief Account of the Maccabees.* — II. *Sovereigns of the Herodian Family:*
— 1. *Herod the Great.* — *St. Matthew's Narrative of the Murder of the
Infants at Bethlehem confirmed.* — 2. *Archelaus.* — 3. *Herod Antipas.* —
4. *Philip.* — 5. *Herod Agrippa.* — 6. *Agrippa junior.* — 7. *Bernice and
Drusilla.*

I. ON the subversion of the Babylonian empire by Cyrus the founder
of the Persian monarchy (B. c. 543), he authorised the Jews by an
edict to return into their own country, with full permission to enjoy
their laws and religion, and caused the city and temple of Jerusalem
to be rebuilt.   In the following year, part of the Jews returned under
Zerubbabel, and renewed their sacrifices : the theocratic government,
which had been in abeyance during the captivity, was resumed ; but
the re-erection of the city and temple being interrupted for several
years by the treachery and hostility of the Samaritans or Cutheans,
the avowed enemies of the Jews, the completion and dedication of the
temple did not take place until the year 511 B. c., six years after the
accession of Cyrus.   The rebuilding of Jerusalem was accomplished,
and the reformation of their ecclesiastical and civil polity was effected
by the two divinely inspired and pious governors, Ezra and Nehemiah.
After their death the Jews were governed by their high priests, in
subjection, however, to the Persian kings, to whom they paid tribute
(Ezra iv. 13. vii. 24.), but with the full enjoyment of their other magistrates, as well as their liberties, civil and religious.   Nearly three
centuries of uninterrupted prosperity ensued, until the reign of Antiochus Epiphanes, king of Syria, when they were most cruelly oppressed,
and compelled to take up arms in their own defence.

Under the able conduct of Judas, on account of his heroic exploits
surnamed Maccabæus, (מכבי MAKABI the Hammerer) [1] the son of
Mattathias, surnamed Asmon (from whom is derived the appellation
Asmonæans, borne by the princes descended from him), and his valiant
brothers, the Jews maintained a religious war for twenty-six years
with five successive kings of Syria ; and after destroying upwards of
200,000 of their best troops, the Maccabees finally established the in-

---

[1] He is, however, most generally supposed to have derived this name from a cabalistical
word, formed of M. C. B. I. the initial letters of the Hebrew Text, *Mi Chamoka Baelim
Jehovah, i. e. who among the gods is like unto thee, O Jehovah ?* (Exod. xv. 11.) which letters
might have been displayed on his sacred standard, as the letters S. P. Q. R. (*Senatus,
Populus Que Romanus,*) were on the Roman ensigns.   Dr. Hales's Analysis of Chronology,
vol. i. p. 599.

dependence of their own country and the aggrandisement of their family. This illustrious house, whose princes united the regal and pontifical dignity in their own persons, administered the affairs of the Jews during a period of one hundred and twenty-six years; until, disputes arising between Hyrcanus II. and his brother Aristobulus, the latter was defeated by the Romans under Pompey, who captured Jerusalem, and reduced Judæa to a tributary province of the republic. (B.C. 59.)

II. SOVEREIGNS OF THE HERODIAN FAMILY. — 1. Julius Cæsar, having defeated Pompey, continued Hyrcanus in the high priesthood, but bestowed the government of Judæa upon Antipater, an Idumæan by birth, who was a Jewish proselyte, and the father of Herod surnamed the Great, who was subsequently king of the Jews. Antipater divided Judæa between his two sons Phasael and Herod, giving to the former the government of Jerusalem, and to the latter the province of Galilee; which being at that time greatly infested with robbers, HEROD signalised his courage by dispersing them, and shortly after attacked Antigonus the competitor of Hyrcanus in the priesthood, who was supported by the Tyrians. In the mean time, the Parthians having invaded Judæa, and carried into captivity Hyrcanus the high priest and Phasael the brother of Herod; the latter fled to Rome, where Mark Antony, with the consent of the senate, conferred on him the title of king of Judæa. By the aid of the Roman arms Herod kept possession of his dignity; and after three years of sanguinary and intestine war with the partisans of Antigonus, he was confirmed in his kingdom by Augustus.[1]

This prince is characterised by Josephus as a person of singular courage and resolution, liberal and even extravagant in his expenditure, magnificent in his buildings, especially in the temple of Jerusalem, and apparently disposed to promote the happiness of every one. But under this specious exterior he concealed the most consummate duplicity; studious only how to attain and to secure his own dignity, he regarded no means, however unjustifiable, which might promote that object of his ambition; and in order to supply his lavish expenditure, he imposed oppressive burdens on his subjects. Inexorably cruel, and a slave to the most furious passions, he imbrued his hands in the blood of his wife, his children, and the greater part of his family[2]; such,

---

1 Beausobre, Introd. to the New Test. (Bp. Watson's Tracts, vol. iii. p. 119.)

2 "When Herod," says the accurate Lardner, "had gained possession of Jerusalem by the assistance of the Romans, and his rival Antigonus was taken prisoner, and in the hands of the Roman general Sosius, and by him carried to Mark Antony, Herod, by a large sum of money, persuaded Antony to put him to death. Herod's great fear was, that Antigonus might sometime revive his pretensions, as being of the Asmonæan family. Aristobulus, brother of his wife Mariamne, was murdered by his directions at eighteen years of age, because the people at Jerusalem had shown some affection for his person. In the seventh year of his reign from the death of Antigonus, he put to death Hyrcanus, grandfather of Mariamne, then eighty years of age, and who had saved Herod's life when he was prosecuted by the Sanhedrin; a man who, in his youth and in the vigour of his life, and in all the revolutions of his fortune, had shown a mild and peaceable disposition. His beloved wife, the beautiful and virtuous Mariamne, had a public execution, and her mother Alexandra followed soon after. Alexander and Aristobulus, his two sons by Mariamne, were strangled in prison by his order upon groundless suspicions, as it seems, when they were at man's estate, were married, and had children. I say nothing of the death of his eldest son Antipater. If Josephus's character of him be just, he was a miscreant, and deserved the worst death that could be inflicted; in his last sickness, a little before he died, he sent orders throughout Judæa, requiring the presence of all the chief men of the nation at Jericho. His orders were obeyed, for they were enforced

indeed, were the restlessness and jealousy of his temper, that he spared neither his people, nor the richest and most powerful of his subjects, not even his very friends.   It is not at all surprising that such a conduct should procure Herod the hatred of his subjects, especially of the Pharisees, who engaged in various plots against him : and so suspicious did these conspiracies render him, that he put the innocent to the torture, lest the guilty should escape.   These circumstances sufficiently account for Herod and all Jerusalem with him being troubled at the arrival of the Magi, to inquire where the Messiah was born. (Matt. ii. 1—3.)   The Jews, who anxiously expected the Messiah " the Deliverer," were moved with an anxiety made up of hopes and fears, of uncertainty and expectation, blended with a dread of the sanguinary consequences of new tumults; and Herod, who was a foreigner and usurper, was apprehensive lest he should lose his crown by the birth of a rightful heir.   Hence we are furnished with a satisfactory solution of the motive that led him to command all the male children to be put to death, who were under two years of age, in Bethlehem and its vicinity. (Matt. ii. 16.)

No very long time after the perpetration of this crime, Herod died, having suffered the most excruciating pains, in the thirty-seventh year of his being declared king of the Jews by the Romans.   The tidings of his decease were received by his oppressed subjects with universal joy and satisfaction.

Herod had a numerous offspring by his different wives, although their number was greatly reduced by his unnatural cruelty in putting many of them to death : but, as few of his descendants are mentioned in the Sacred Volume, we shall notice only those persons of whom it is requisite that some account should be given for the better understanding of the New Testament.   The annexed table [1] will, perhaps, be found useful in distinguishing the *particular persons* of this family, whose names occur in the Evangelical histories.

---

with no less penalty than that of death.   When these men were come to Jericho, he had them all shut up in the circus, and calling for his sister Salome, and her husband Alexas, he told them, My life is now but short ; I know the dispositions of the Jewish people, and nothing will please them more than my death.   ' You have these men in your custody ; as soon as ' the breath is out of my body, and before my death can be known, do you let in the soldiers ' upon them and kill them.   All Judæa and every family will then, though unwillingly, ' mourn at my death.'   Nay, Josephus says, ' That with tears in his eyes he conjured them ' by their love to him, and their fidelity to God, not to fail of doing him this honour ; and ' they promised they would not fail ; ' these orders, indeed, were not executed.   But as a modern historian of very good sense observes, ' the history of this his most wicked design ' takes off all objection against the truth of murdering the innocents, which may be made from ' the incredibility of so barbarous and horrid an act.   For this thoroughly shows, that there ' can nothing be imagined so cruel, barbarous, and horrid, which this man was not capable ' of doing.'   It may also be proper to observe, that almost all the executions I have instanced, were sacrifices to his state jealousy, and love of empire." Josephus, Ant. Jud. lib. xiv. c. 23. 25, 26. 28. lib. xvi. c. 7, 8. 11, 12. lib. xvii. c. 6.   Lardner's Credibility, part i. book ii. c. 2. § 1.

[1] From Schulz's Archæologia Hebraica, p. 54.   Reland has given a genealogical table of the *entire* Herodian family.   (Palæstina, tom. i. p. 174.)

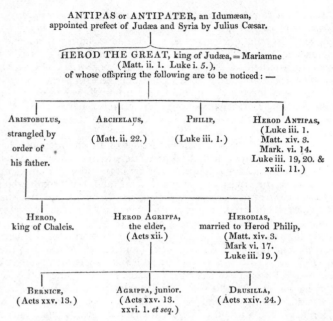

ANTIPAS or ANTIPATER, an Idumæan,
appointed prefect of Judæa and Syria by Julius Cæsar.

HEROD THE GREAT, king of Judæa, = Mariamne
(Matt. ii. 1. Luke i. 5.),
of whose offspring the following are to be noticed : —

| ARISTOBULUS, strangled by order of his father. | ARCHELAUS, (Matt. ii. 22.) | PHILIP, (Luke iii. 1.) | HEROD ANTIPAS, (Luke iii. 1. Matt. xiv. 3. Mark. vi. 14. Luke iii. 19, 20. & xxiii. 11.) |

| HEROD, king of Chalcis. | HEROD AGRIPPA, the elder, (Acts xii.) | HERODIAS, married to Herod Philip, (Matt. xiv. 3. Mark vi. 17. Luke iii. 19.) |

| BERNICE, (Acts xxv. 13.) | AGRIPPA, junior. (Acts xxv. 13. xxvi. 1. *et seq.*) | DRUSILLA, (Acts xxiv. 24.) |

HEROD, misnamed the Great, by his will divided his dominions among his three sons, Archelaus, Herod Antipas, and Herod Philip.

2. To ARCHELAUS he assigned Judæa, Samaria, and Idumæa, with the regal dignity, subject to the approbation of Augustus, who ratified his will as it respected the territorial division, but conferred on Archelaus the title of *Ethnarch,* or chief of the nation, with a promise of the regal dignity, if he should prove himself worthy of it. Archelaus entered upon his new office amid the loud acclamations of his subjects, who considered him as a king; hence the evangelist, in conformity with the Jewish idiom, says that he *reigned.* (Matt. ii. 22.) His reign, however, commenced inauspiciously: for, after the death of Herod, and before Archelaus could go to Rome to obtain the confirmation of his father's will, the Jews having become very tumultuous at the temple in consequence of his refusing them some demands, Archelaus ordered his soldiers to attack them; on which occasion upwards of three thousand were slain.[1] On Archelaus going to Rome to solicit the regal dignity (agreeably to the practice of the tributary kings of that age, who received their crowns from the Roman emperor), the Jews sent an embassy, consisting of fifty of their principal men, with a petition to Augustus that they might be permitted to live according to their own laws, under a Roman governor.   To this circumstance our Lord evidently alludes in the parable related by Saint Luke. (xix. 12—27.) *A certain nobleman* (ευγενης, a man of birth or rank, the son of Herod,) *went into a far country* (Italy), *to receive for himself a kingdom* (that of

---

[1] This circumstance probably deterred the Holy Family from settling in Judæa on their return from Egypt, and induced them by the divine admonition to return to their former residence at Nazareth in Galilee. (Matt. ii. 22, 23.) Dr. Hales's Analysis of Chronology, vol. ii. p. 717.

Judæa) *and to return. But his citizens* (the Jews) *hated him, and sent a message* (or embassy) *after him* (to Augustus Cæsar), *saying, " We will not have this man to reign over us."* The Jews, however, failed in their request, and Archelaus, *having received the kingdom* (or ethnarchy), on his return inflicted a severe vengeance on those *who would not that he should reign over them.*[1] The application of this parable is to Jesus Christ, who foretells, that, on his ascension, he would go into a distant country, to receive the kingdom from his Father; and that he would return, at the destruction of Jerusalem, to take vengeance on those who rejected him.[2] The subsequent reign of Archelaus was turbulent, and disgraced by insurrections of the Jews against the Romans, and also by banditti and pretenders to the crown: at length, after repeated complaints against his tyranny and mal-administration, made to Augustus by the principal Jews and Samaritans who were joined by his own brothers, Archelaus was deposed and banished to Vienne in Gaul, in the tenth year of his reign; and his territories were annexed to the Roman province of Syria.[3]

3. HEROD ANTIPAS (or Antipater), another of Herod's sons, received from his father the district of Galilee and Peræa, with the title of *Tetrarch*.[4] He is described by Josephus as a crafty and incestuous prince, with which character the narratives of the evangelists coincide; for, having deserted his wife, the daughter of Aretas king of Arabia, he forcibly took away and married Herodias the wife of his brother Herod Philip, a proud and cruel woman, to gratify whom he caused John the Baptist to be beheaded (Matt. xiv. 3. Mark vi. 17. Luke iii. 19.), who had provoked her vengeance by his faithful reproof of their incestuous nuptials; though Josephus ascribes the Baptist's death to Herod's apprehension, lest the latter should by his influence raise an insurrection among the people. It was this Herod that laid snares for our Saviour; who, detecting his insidious intentions, termed him *a fox* (Luke xiii. 32.), and who subsequently ridiculed by him and his soldiers. (Luke xxiii. 7—11.) Some years afterwards, Herod aspiring to the regal dignity in Judæa was banished together with his wife, first to Lyons in Gaul, and thence into Spain.[5]

4. PHILIP, tetrarch of Trachonitis, Gaulonitis, and Batanæa, is mentioned but once in the New Testament. (Luke iii. 1.) He is represented by Josephus as an amiable prince, beloved by his subjects, whom he governed with mildness and equity[6]: on his decease without

---

[1] Josephus, Ant. Jud. lib. xvii. c. 9. § 3. c. 11. Harwood's Introduction, vol. i. p. 294.

[2] There is an impressive application of this parable in Mr. Jones's Lectures on the figurative Language of Scripture, lect. v. near the beginning. (Works, vol. iii. pp. 35, 36.)

[3] Josephus, Ant. Jud. lib. xvii. c. 11. (al. xii.) § 2. c. 13. (al. xiv.)

[4] Concerning the meaning of this term learned men are by no means agreed. In its primary and original signification it implies a governor of the fourth part of a country; and this seems to have been the first meaning affixed to it. But afterwards it was given to the governors of a province, whether their government was the fourth part of a country or not: for Herod divided his kingdom only into three parts. The Tetrarchs, however, were regarded as princes, and sometimes were complimented with the title of *king*. (Matt. xiv. 9.) Beausobre's Introd. to the New Test. (Bp. Watson's Tracts, vol. iii. p. 123.) The Romans conferred this title on those princes whom they did not choose to elevate to the regal dignity; the Tetrarch was lower in point of rank than a Roman governor of a province. Schulzii Archæol. Hebr. pp. 18, 19. Jahn, Archæol. Bibl. § 240.

[5] Josephus, Ant. Jud. lib. xviii. c. 7.

[6] Ibid. lib. xvii. c. 8. § 1. lib. xviii. c. 5. § 4.   De Bell. Jud. lib. i. c. 33. § 8. lib. ii. c. 6. § 3.

issue, after a reign of thirty-seven years, his territories were annexed to the province of Syria.[1]

5. AGRIPPA, or Herod Agrippa I., was the son of Aristobulus, and grandson of Herod the Great, and sustained various reverses of fortune previously to his attaining the royal dignity. At first he resided at Rome as a private person, and ingratiated himself into the favour of the emperor Tiberius; but being accused of wishing him dead that Caligula might reign, he was thrown into prison by order of Tiberius. On the accession of Caligula to the empire, Agrippa was created king of Batanæa and Trachonitis, to which Abilene, Judæa, and Samaria were subsequently added by the emperor Claudius. Returning home to his dominions, he governed them much to the satisfaction of his subjects (for whose gratification he put to death the apostle James, and meditated that of St. Peter, who was miraculously delivered, Acts xii. 2—17.); but, being inflated with pride on account of his increasing power and grandeur, he was struck with a noisome and painful disease of which he died at Cæsarea in the manner related by St. Luke. (Acts xii. 21—23.) [2]

6. HEROD AGRIPPA II., or *Junior*, was the son of the preceding Herod Agrippa, and was educated under the auspices of the emperor Claudius: being only seventeen years of age, at the time of his father's death, he was judged to be unequal to the task of governing the whole of his dominions. These were again placed under the direction of a Roman procurator or governor, and Agrippa was first king of Chalcis, and afterwards of Batanæa, Trachonitis, and Abilene, to which other territories were subsequently added, over which he seems to have ruled, with the title of King.[3] It was before this Agrippa and his sister Bernice that St. Paul delivered his masterly defence (Acts xxvi.), where he is expressly termed a king. He was the last Jewish prince of the Herodian family, and for a long time survived the destruction of Jerusalem.

7. Besides Herodias, who has been mentioned in page 110., the two following princesses of the Herodian family are mentioned in the New Testament; viz.

(1) BERNICE, the eldest daughter of king Herod Agrippa I. and sister to Agrippa II. (Acts xxv. 13. 23. xxvi. 30.), was first married to her uncle Herod king of Chalcis; after whose death, in order to avoid the merited suspicion of incest with her brother Agrippa, she became the wife of Polemon, king of Cilicia. This connection being soon dissolved, she returned to her brother, and became the mistress, first of Vespasian, and then of Titus, who would have married her, but that he was unwilling to displease the Romans, who were averse to such a step.[4]

(2) DRUSILLA, her sister, and the youngest daughter of Herod Agrippa, was distinguished for her beauty, and was equally celebrated with Bernice, for her profligacy. She was first espoused to Epiphanes, the son of Antiochus, king of Comagena, on condition of his embracing

[1] Josephus, Ant. Jud. lib. xviii. c. 4. § 6.
[2] Ibid. lib. xviii. cc. 5—8.
[3] Ibid. lib. xix. c. 9. De Bell. Jud. lib. ii. cc. 12, 13.
[4] Ibid. lib. xix. c. 1. § 1. lib. xx. c. 7. § 3. Tacitus, Hist. lib. ii. c. 81. Suetonius in Tito, c. 7. Juvenal, Sat. vi. 155.

the Jewish religion; but as he afterwards refused to be circumcised, she was given in marriage, by her brother, to Azizus king of Emessa, who submitted to that rite. When Felix came into Judæa, as procurator or governor of Judæa, he persuaded her to abandon her husband and marry him. Josephus [1] says that she was induced to transgress the laws of her country, and become the wife of Felix, in order to avoid the envy of her sister Bernice, who was continually doing her ill offices on account of her beauty.[2]

SECTION II.

POLITICAL STATE OF THE JEWS UNDER THE ROMAN PROCURATORS, TO THE SUBVERSION OF THEIR CIVIL AND ECCLESIASTICAL POLITY.

I. *Powers and Functions of the Roman Procurators.* — II. *Political and Civil State of the Jews under their Administration.* — III. *Account of Pontius Pilate.* — IV. *And of the Procurators Felix and Festus.*

I. THE Jewish kingdom, which the Romans had created in favour of Herod the Great, was of short duration; expiring on his death, by the division of his territories, and by the dominions of Archelaus, which comprised Samaria, Judæa, and Idumæa, being reduced to a Roman province annexed to Syria, and governed by the ROMAN PROCURATORS.

These officers not only had the charge of collecting the imperial revenues, but also had the power of life and death in capital causes: and on account of their high dignity they are sometimes called governors (Ηγεμονες). They usually had a council, consisting of their friends and other chief Romans in the province; with whom they conferred on important questions.[3] During the continuance of the Roman republic, it was very unusual for the governors of provinces to take their wives with them. Augustus [4] disapproved of the introduction of this practice, which, however, was in some instances permitted by Tiberius. Thus Agrippina accompanied Germanicus [5] into Germany and Asia, and Plancina was with Piso, whose insolence towards Germanicus she contributed to inflame [6]: and though Cæcina Severus afterwards offered a motion to the senate, to prohibit this indulgence (on account of the serious inconveniences, — not to say abuses, that would result from the political influence which the wives might exercise over their husbands), his motion was rejected [7], and they continued to attend the procurators to their respective provinces. This circumstance will account for Pilate's wife being at Jerusalem. (Matt.

---

[1] Ant. Jud. lib. xx. c. 7. § 1, 2. Acts xxiv. 24.

[2] Schulzii Archæologia Hebraica, pp. 49—59. Pritii Introd. ad Nov. Test. pp. 429—444. Dr. Lardner's Credibility, vol. i. book i. ch. i. §§ 1—11. (Works, vol. i. pp. 11—30. 8vo. or vol. i. pp. 9—18. 4to.) Carpzovii Antiquitates Hebrææ Gentis, pp. 15—19.

[3] Josephus (Ant. Jud. lib. xx. c. 4. § 4. and de Bell. Jud. lib. ii. c. 16. § 1.) mentions instances in which the Roman procurators thus took council with their assessors.

[4] Suetonius, in Augusto, c. 24.

[5] Tacitus, Annal. lib. ii. cc. 54, 55. lib. i. cc. 40, 41.

[6] Ibid. lib. i. c. 40.

[7] Ibid. lib. iii. cc. 33, 34.

xxvii. 19.) The procurators of Judæa resided principally at Cæsarea[1], which was reputed to be the metropolis of that country, and occupied the splendid palace which Herod the Great had erected there. On the great festivals, or when any tumults were apprehended, they repaired to Jerusalem, that, by their presence and influence, they might restore order. For this purpose they were accompanied by *cohorts* (Σπειραι, Acts x. 1.) or bands of soldiers, not legionary cohorts, but distinct companies of military : each of them was about one thousand strong.[2] Six of these cohorts were constantly garrisoned in Judæa; five at Cæsarea, and one at Jerusalem, part of which was quartered in the tower of Antonia, so as to command the temple, and part in the prætorium or governor's palace.

These procurators were Romans, sometimes of the equestrian order, and sometimes freedmen of the emperor : Felix (Acts xxiii. 24—26. xxvi. 3. 22—27.) was a freedman of the emperor Claudius[3], with whom he was in high favour. These governors were sent, not by the senate, but by the Cæsars themselves, into those provinces which were situated on the confines of the empire, and were placed at the emperor's own disposal. Their duties consisted in collecting and remitting tribute, in the administration of justice, and the repression of tumults ; some of them held independent jurisdictions, while others were subordinate to the proconsul or governor of the nearest province. Thus Judæa was annexed to the province of Syria.

II. The Jews endured their subjection to the Romans with great reluctance, on account of the tribute which they were obliged to pay : but in all other respects they enjoyed a large measure of national liberty. It appears from the whole tenor of the New Testament (for the particular passages are too numerous to be cited[4]), that they practised their own religious rites, worshipped in the temple and in their synagogues, followed their own customs, and lived very much according to their own laws. Thus they had their high priests, and council or senate; they inflicted lesser punishments; they could apprehend men and bring them before the council; and if a guard of soldiers was necessary, could be assisted by them, on requesting them of the governor. Further, they could bind men and keep them in custody; the council could likewise summon witnesses and take examinations; they could excommunicate persons, and they could inflict scourging in their synagogue (Deut. xxv. 3. Matt. x. 17. Mark xiii. 9.) ; they enjoyed the privilege of referring litigated questions to arbitrators, whose decisions in reference to them the Roman prætor was bound to see put in execution.[5] Beyond this, however, they were not allowed to go; for, when they had any capital offenders, they carried them before the procurator, who usually paid a regard to what they stated, and, if

---

[1] Josephus, Ant. Jud. lib. xviii. c. 3. § 1. lib. xx. c. 5. § 4.   De Bell. Jud. lib. ii. c. 9. § 2.   Tacit. Hist. lib. ii. c. 79.

[2] Biscoe on the Acts, vol. i. pp. 330—335.

[3] Suetonius in Claudio, c. 28.

[4] See Dr. Lardner's Credibility, part i. book ii. c. 2. where the various passages are adduced and fully considered.

[5] Cod. lib. i. tit. 9. l. 8. de Judæis. — As the Christians were at first regarded as a sect of the Jews, they likewise enjoyed the same privilege. This circumstance will account for Saint Paul's blaming the Corinthian Christians for carrying their causes before the Roman prætor, instead of leaving them to referees chosen from among their brethren. (1 Cor. vi. 1—7.)

they brought evidence of the fact, pronounced sentence according to their laws. He was the proper judge in all capital causes; for, after the council of the Jews had taken under their consideration the case of Jesus Christ, which they pretended was of this kind, they went with it immediately to the governor, who re-examined it and pronounced sentence. That they had not the power of life and death is evident from Pilate's granting to them the privilege of judging, but not of condemning Jesus Christ, and also from their acknowledgment to Pilate — *It is not lawful for us to put any man to death* (John xviii. 31.); and likewise from the power vested in Pilate of releasing a condemned criminal to them at the passover (John xviii. 39, 40.), which he could not have done if he had not had the power of life and death, as well as from his own declaration that he had power to crucify and power to release Jesus Christ.[1] (John xix. 10.)

III. Of the various procurators that governed Judæa under the Romans, PONTIUS PILATE is the best known, and most frequently mentioned in the Sacred Writings. — He is supposed to have been a native of Italy, and was sent to govern Judæa about the year A.D. 26 or 27. Pilate is characterised by Josephus as an unjust and cruel governor, sanguinary, obstinate, and impetuous; who disturbed the tranquillity of Judæa by persisting in carrying into Jerusalem the effigies of Tiberius Cæsar that were upon the Roman ensigns, and by other acts of oppression, which produced tumults among the Jews.[2] Dreading the extreme jealousy and suspicion of Tiberius he delivered up the Redeemer to be crucified, contrary to the conviction of his better judgment; and in the vain hope of conciliating the Jews whom he had oppressed. After he had held his office for ten years, having caused a number of innocent Samaritans to be put to death, that injured people sent an embassy to Vitellius, proconsul of Syria; by whom he was ordered to Rome, to give an account of his mal-administration to the emperor. But Tiberius being dead before he arrived there, his successor Caligula banished him to Gaul, where he is said to have committed suicide about the year of Christ 41.[3]

IV. On the death of king Herod Agrippa, Judæa being again reduced to a Roman province, the government of it was confided to ANTONIUS FELIX; who had originally been the slave, then the freedman of Nero, and, through the influence of his brother Pallas, also a

---

[1] The celebrated Roman jurist, Ulpian, states that the governors of the Roman provinces *had the right of the sword ;* which implied the authority of punishing malefactors ; — an authority which was personal, and not to be transferred. (Lib. vi. c. 8. de Officio Proconsulis.) And Josephus states (De Bell. Jud. lib. ii. c. 8. § 1.) that Coponius, who was sent to govern Judæa as a province after the banishment of Archelaus, was invested by Augustus with the power of life and death. (Bp. Gray's Connection of Sacred and Profane Literature, vol. i. p. 273. See also Dr. Lardner's Credibility, c. 2. § 6.) The case of the Jews stoning Stephen (Acts vii. 56, 57.) has been urged by some learned men as a proof that the former had the power of life and death, but the circumstances of that case do not support this assertion. Stephen, it is true, had been examined before the great council, who had heard witnesses against him, but no where do we read that they had collected votes or proceeded to the giving of sentence, or even to pronounce him guilty : all which ought to have been done, if the proceedings had been regular. Before Stephen could finish his defence, a sudden tumult arose; the people who were present rushed with one accord upon him, and casting him out of the city, stoned him before the affair could be taken before the Roman procurator. Pritii Introd. ad Nov. Test. p. 592.

[2] Josephus, Ant. Jud. lib. xviii. c. 3. §§ 1, 2.

[3] Ibid. lib. xviii. c. 4. Eusebius, Hist. Eccl. lib. ii. cc. 7, 8.

freedman of that emperor, was raised to the dignity of procurator of
Judæa. He liberated that country from banditti and impostors (the
very worthy deeds alluded to by Tertullus, Acts xxiv. 2.); but he was
in other respects a cruel and avaricious governor, incontinent, intemperate, and unjust. So oppressive at length did his administration
become, that the Jews accused him before Nero, and it was only
through the powerful interposition of Pallas that Felix escaped condign punishment. His *third*[1] wife, Drusilla, has already been mentioned. It was before these persons that St. Paul, with singular
propriety, reasoned of righteousness, temperance, and a judgment to
come. (Acts xxiv. 25.)   On the resignation of Felix, A.D. 60, the
government of Judæa was committed to PORTIUS FESTUS, before whom
Paul defended himself against the accusations of the Jews (Acts xxv.),
and appealed from his tribunal to that of Cæsar. Finding his province
over-run with robbers and murderers, Festus strenuously exerted himself in suppressing their outrages. He died in Judæa about the year 62.[2]

The situation of the Jews under the two last-mentioned procurators
was truly deplorable. Distracted by tumults, excited on various occasions, their country was over-run with robbers that plundered all
the villages whose inhabitants refused to listen to their persuasions to
shake off the Roman yoke. Justice was sold to the highest bidder;
and even the sacred office of high priest was exposed to sale. But, of
all the procurators, no one abused his power more than GESSIUS
FLORUS, a cruel and sanguinary governor, and so extremely avaricious
that he shared with the robbers in their booty, and allowed them to
follow their nefarious practices with impunity. Hence considerable
numbers of the wretched Jews, with their families, abandoned their
native country; while those who remained, being driven to desperation, took up arms against the Romans[3], and thus commenced that
war, which terminated in the destruction of Judæa, and the *taking
away of their name and nation.*[4]

CHAPTER III.

COURTS OF JUDICATURE, LEGAL PROCEEDINGS, AND CRIMINAL LAW OF THE JEWS.

SECTION I.

JEWISH COURTS OF JUDICATURE, AND LEGAL PROCEEDINGS.[5]

I. *Seat of Justice.* — II. *Inferior Tribunals.* — III. *Appeals.* — *Constitution
of the Sanhedrin or Great Council.*—IV. *Time of Trials.*—*Form of Legal
Proceedings among the Jews.*— 1. *Citation of the Parties.*—2, 3. *Form of
Pleading in Civil and Criminal Cases.*— 4. *Witnesses.*—*Oaths.*—5. *The*

---

1 Claudii Commentatio de Felice, pp. 62, 63.
2 Josephus, Ant. Jud. lib. xx. c. 8. §§ 9, 10.   De Bell. Jud. lib. ii. c. 14. § 1.
3 Ibid. lib. xx. cc. 8. 11.   Ibid. lib. ii. cc. 9, 10.
4 Schulzii Archæologia Hebraica, pp. 59—66.
5 Besides the authorities incidentally cited in the course of this section, the following
works have been consulted for it, throughout; viz. Schulzii Archæologia Hebraica, pp. 66

Lot, in what Cases used judicially.—6. Forms of Acquittal.—7. Summary Justice, sometimes clamorously demanded.— V. Execution of Sentences, by whom, and in what manner performed.

I. IN the early ages of the world, the *Gate of the City* was the SEAT OF JUSTICE, where conveyances of titles and estates were made, complaints were heard and justice done, and all public business was transacted.   Thus Abraham made the acquisition of his sepulchre in the presence of all those who entered in *at the gate of the city* of Hebron. (Gen. xxiii. 10. 18.)   When Hamor and his son Schechem proposed to make an alliance with Jacob and his sons, they spoke of it to the people at the *gate of the city.* (Gen. xxxiv. 24.)   In later times Boaz, having declared his intention of marrying Ruth, *at the gate* of Bethlehem caused her kinsman to resign his pretensions, and give him the proper conveyance to the estate. (Ruth iv. 1—10.)   From the circumstance of the gates of cities being the seat of justice, the judges appear to have been termed the *Elders of the Gate* (Deut. xxii. 15. xxv. 7.); for, as all the Israelites were husbandmen, who went out in the morning to work, and did not return until night, the city gate was the place of greatest resort.   By this antient practice, the judges were compelled, by a dread of public displeasure, to be most strictly impartial, and most carefully to investigate the merits of the causes which were brought before them.   The same practice obtained after the captivity. (Zech. viii. 16.)   The Ottoman Court, it is well known, derived its appellation of the *Porte,* from the distribution of justice and the despatch of public business at its gates.   During the Arabian monarchy in Spain, the same practice obtained; and the magnificent gate of entrance to the Moorish palace of Alhamrā at Grenada to this day retains the appellation of the *Gate of Justice* or *of Judgment.*[1]   To the practice of dispensing justice at the gates of cities, there are numerous allusions in the Sacred Volume.   For instance, in Job v. 4. the children of the wicked are said to be *crushed in the gate;* that is, they lose their cause, and are condemned in the court of judgment.   The Psalmist (cxxvii. 5.), speaking of those whom God has blessed with many children, says that *they shall not be ashamed, but they shall speak with the enemies in the gate;* that is, those who are thus blessed, shall courageously plead their cause, and need not fear the want of justice when they meet their adversaries in the court of judicature.   Compare Prov. xxii. 22 and xxxi. 23. Lament. v. 14. Amos. v. 12., in all which passages the *gate,* and *elders of the land* or *of the gate,* respectively denote the seat of justice and the judges who presided there.   And as the gates of a city constituted its strength, and as the happiness of a people depended much upon the wisdom and integrity of the judges who sat there, it may be that our Saviour alluded to this circumstance, when he said, *The gates of hell shall not prevail against* his church (Matt. xvi. 18.); that is, neither the strength nor policy of Satan or his instruments shall ever be able to overcome it.

—81. ; Calmet, Dissertation sur la Police des Hébreux, (Dissertations, tom. i. pp. 187—204.); Alber, Hermeneutica Vet. Test. pp. 234—238. ; Pritii Introd. ad Nov. Test. pp. 575—594. ; Brunings, Antiq. Hebr. pp. 99—107.; Home's Hist. of the Jews, vol. ii. pp. 30—41. ; Jahn, Archæol. Biblica, §§ 243—248. ; Ackermann, Archæol. Bibl. §§ 237—243.

[1] Murphy's Arabian Antiquities of Spain, plates xiv. xv. pp. 8, 9.

In the time of Jesus Christ the Jews held courts of judicature in their *synagogues,* where they punished offenders by scourging. (Matt. x. 17. Acts xxii. 19. xxvi. 11.) After their example, Dr. Macknight thinks it probable, that the first Christians held courts for determining civil causes, in the places where they assembled for public worship, called *your synagogue* in the epistle of James. (ii. 2. Gr.) It is evident, he adds, that the Apostle speaks not of their assembly, but of the place where their assembly was held, from his mentioning the litigants as sitting in a more honourable or less honourable place in the synagogue. And the context shows, that judges and judicial causes were the subjects of the Apostle's thoughts.[1]

II. On the settlement of the Israelites in the land of Canaan, Moses commanded them to *appoint judges and officers in all their gates, throughout their tribes* (Deut. xvi. 18.); whose duty it was to exercise judicial authority in the neighbouring villages; but weighty causes and appeals were carried before the supreme judge or ruler of the commonwealth. (Deut. xvii. 8, 9.) According to Josephus, these inferior judges were seven in number, men zealous in the exercise of virtue and righteousness. To each judge (that is, to each college of judges in every city) two officers were assigned out of the tribe of Levi.[2] These judges existed in the time of that historian[3]; and, although the rabbinical writers are silent concerning them, yet their silence neither does, nor can outweigh the evidence of an eye-witness and magistrate, who himself appointed such judges.

The Priests and Levites, who, from their being devoted to the study of the law, were, consequently, best skilled in its various precepts, and old men, who were eminent for their age and virtue, administered justice to the people: in consequence of their age, the name of *elders* became attached to them. Many instances of this kind occur in the New Testament; they were also called *rulers,* αρχοντες. (Luke xii. 58. where ruler is synonymous with judge.)[4] The law of Moses contained the most express prohibitions of bribery (Exod. xxiii. 8.), and partiality; enjoining them to administer justice without respect of persons, and reminding them, that a judge sits in the seat of God, and, consequently, that no man ought to have any pre-eminence in his sight, neither ought he to be afraid of any man in declaring the law. (Exod. xxiii. 3. 6, 7. Lev. xix. 15. Deut. i. 17. xvi. 18, 19.) The prophet Amos (viii. 6.) reproaches the corrupt judges of his time, with taking not only silver, but even so trifling an article of dress as a pair of (wooden) sandals, as a bribe, to condemn the innocent poor who could not afford to make them a present of equal value. Turkish officers and their wives in Asia, to this day, go richly clothed in costly silks given them by those who have causes depending before them.[5] It is probable, at least in the early ages after the settlement of the Jews in Canaan, that their judges rode on *white* asses, by way of distinction (Judges v. 10.), as the *Mollahs* or men of the law do to this day in

---

1 Macknight on James ii. 2.

2 Josephus, Ant. Jud. lib. iv. c. 14.   Schulzii Prolusio de variis Judæorum erroribus in Descriptione Templi II. § xv. pp. 27—32., prefixed to his edition of Reland's Treatise De Spoliis Templi Hierosolymitani Trajecti ad Rhenum, 1775. 8vo.

3 Josephus, de Bell. Jud. lib. ii. c. 20. § 5.

4 Ernesti Institutio Interpretis Novi Testamenti, part iii. c. 10. § 73. p. 356.

5 Morier's Second Journey, p. 136.

Persia[1], and the heads of families returning from their pilgrimage to Mecca.[2]

III. From these inferior tribunals, appeals lay to a higher court, in cases of importance. (Deut. xvii. 8—12.) In Jerusalem, it is not improbable that there were superior courts in which David's sons presided. Psalm cxxii. 5. seems to allude to them: though we do not find that a supreme tribunal was established at Jerusalem earlier than in the reign of Jehoshaphat. (2 Chron. xix. 8—11.) It was composed of priests and heads of families, and had two presidents,—one in the person of the high priest, and another who sat in the name of the king. The judicial establishment was re-organised after the captivity, and two classes of judges, inferior and superior, were appointed. (Ezra vii. 25.) But the more difficult cases and appeals were brought, either before the ruler of the state, or before the high priest; until, in the age of the Maccabees, a supreme judicial tribunal was instituted, which is first mentioned under Hyrcanus II.[3]

This tribunal (which must not be confounded with the seventy-two counsellors, who were appointed to assist Moses in the civil administration of the government, but who never fulfilled the office of judges), is by the Talmudists denominated SANHEDRIN, and is the great Council so often mentioned in the New Testament. It was most probably instituted in the time of the Maccabees, and was composed of seventy or seventy-two members, under the chief presidency of the high priest, under whom were two vice-presidents; the first of whom, called the *Father of the Council*, sat on the right, as the second vice-president, who was called *Chakam*, or the *Wise Man*, did on the left hand of the president. The other assessors, or members of this council, comprised three descriptions of persons, viz. 1. The Αρχιερεις, or *Chief Priests*, who were partly such priests as had executed the Pontificate, and partly the princes or chiefs of the twenty-four *courses* or classes of priests, who enjoyed this honourable title:—2. The Πρεσβυτεροι, or *Elders*, perhaps the princes of tribes or heads of families;—and, 3. The Γραμματεις, *Scribes*, or men learned in the law. It does not appear that *all* the elders and scribes were members of this tribunal: most probably, those only were assessors, who were either elected to the office, or nominated to it by royal authority. They are reported to have sat in a semicircular form; and to this manner of their sitting in judgment Jesus Christ is supposed to refer in Matt. xix. 28., and St. Paul in 1 Cor. vi. 2.

The Sanhedrin held its daily sittings early in the morning, and (according to the Talmudists) in the Temple; but they are contradicted by Josephus[4], who speaks of a council-house in the immediate vicinity

---

[1] Harmer's Observations, vol. ii. p. 317.

[2] " We met, one day, a procession, consisting of a family returning from the Pilgrimage to Mecca. Drums and pipes announced the joyful event. A white-bearded old man, riding on a *white ass*, led the way with patriarchal grace ; and the men who met him, or accompanied him, were continually throwing their arms about his neck, and almost dismounting him with their salutations. He was followed by his three wives, each riding on a high camel ; their female acquaintances running on each side, while they occasionally stooped down to salute them. The women continually uttered a remarkably shrill whistle. It was impossible, viewing the old man who led the way, not to remember the expression in Judges v. 10." — Jowett's Christian Researches, p. 163.

[3] Josephus, Ant. Jud. lib. xiv. c. 9. § 3.

[4] De Bell. Jud. lib. v. c. 4. § 2. lib. vi. c. 6. § 3.

of the Temple, where this council was in all probability convened; though in extraordinary emergencies it was assembled in the high priest's house, as was the case in the mock trial of Jesus Christ. The authority of this tribunal was very extensive. It decided all causes, which were brought before it, by appeal from inferior courts; and also took cognisance of the general affairs of the nation. *Before* Judæa was subject to the Roman power, the Sanhedrin had the right of judging in capital cases, but not afterwards; the stoning of Stephen being (as we have already observed) a tumultuary act, and not in consequence of sentence pronounced by this Council.[1]

Besides the Sanhedrin, the Talmudical writers assert that there were other smaller councils, each consisting of twenty-three persons, who heard and determined petty causes: two of these were at Jerusalem, and one in every city containing one hundred and twenty inhabitants. Josephus is silent concerning these tribunals, but they certainly appear to have existed in the time of Jesus Christ; who, " by images taken from these two courts, in a very striking manner represents the different degrees of future punishments, to which the impenitently wicked will be doomed according to the respective heinousness of their crimes. *But I say unto you, that whosoever is angry with his brother without a cause, shall be in danger of the* JUDGMENT; *and whosoever shall say to his brother, Raca, shall be in danger of the* COUNCIL; *but whosoever shall say, Thou fool, shall be in danger of* HELL FIRE. (Matt. v. 22.) That is, whosoever shall indulge causeless and unprovoked resentment against his Christian brother, shall be punished with a severity similar to that which is inflicted by the *court of judgment.* He, who shall suffer his passions to transport him to greater extravagances, so as to make his brother the object of derision and contempt, shall be exposed to a still severer punishment, corresponding to that which the *Council* imposes. But he who shall load his fellow-Christian with odious appellations and abusive language, shall incur the severest degree of all punishments, — equal to that of being burnt alive in the valley of Hinnom[2]:" — which, having formerly been the scene of those horrid sacrifices of children to Moloch by causing them to pass through the fire, the Jews in our Saviour's time used to denote the place of the damned.

Where there were not one hundred and twenty inhabitants in a town or village, according to the Talmudists, there was a tribunal of three judges: and to this tribunal some writers have erroneously imagined that Joseph of Arimathea belonged, rather than to the great Sanhedrin. But both the writers of the New Testament and Josephus are silent concerning the existence of such a tribunal. Jahn is of opinion that this court was merely a session of three arbitrators, which the Roman laws permitted to the Jews in civil causes; as the Talmudists themselves state that one judge was chosen by the accuser, another by the party accused, and a third by both parties. It appears, however, that only petty affairs were cognisable by this tribunal. The reference to arbitrators, recommended to Christians by St. Paul in 1 Cor. vi. 1—5., has been supposed to be derived from this tribunal.

---

[1] Dr. Lightfoot has given a list of sixteen presidents who directed the Sanhedrin from the captivity till its dissolution. (Prospect of the Temple, ch. xxii. § 1. Works, vol. ix. pp. 342—346. 8vo. edit.)

[2] Harwood's Introduction to the New Test. vol. ii. pp. 188, 189.

It is essential to the ends of justice, that the proceedings of the courts should be committed to writing, and preserved in archives or registries : Josephus informs us that there was such a repository at Jerusalem, which was burnt by the Romans [1], and which was furnished with scribes or notaries, for recording the proceedings. From this place, probably, St. Luke derived his account of the proceedings against the protomartyr Stephen, related in Acts vi. and vii. These tribunals also had inferior *ministers* or *officers* (υπηρεται, Matt. v. 25.), who probably corresponded with our apparitors or messengers; and others whose office it was to carry the decrees into execution, viz. 1. The πρακτορες, or *exactors*, whose business it was to levy the fines imposed by the court; and, 2. The βασανισται, or *tormentors*, those whose office it was to examine by torture : as this charge was devolved on gaolers, in the time of Christ, the word βασανιστης came to signify a gaoler.[2]

IV. It appears from Jer. xxi. 12., that causes were heard, and judgment was executed in the morning. According to the Talmud [3] capital causes were prohibited from being heard in the night, as also were the institution of an examination, the pronouncing of sentence, and the carrying of it into execution, on one and the same day; and it was enjoined that at least the execution of a sentence should be deferred until the following day. How flagrantly this injunction was disregarded in the case of Jesus Christ, it is scarcely necessary to mention. According to the Talmud, also, no judgments could be executed on festival days; but this by no means agrees with the end and design of capital punishment expressed in Deut. xvii. 13. viz. *That all the people might hear and fear.* It is evident from Matt. xxvi. 5. that the chief priests and other leading men among the Jews were at first afraid to apprehend Jesus, lest there should be a tumult among the people : it is not improbable that they feared the Galilæans more than the populace of Jerusalem, because they were the countrymen of our Lord. Afterwards, however, when the traitor Judas presented himself to them, their fears vanished away.

In the early ages of the Jewish history, judicial procedure must have been summary, as it still is in Asia.[4] Of advocates, such as ours, there is no appearance in any part of the Old Testament. Every one pleaded his own cause; of this practice we have a memorable instance in 1 Kings iii. 16—28. As causes were heard at the city gate, where the people assembled to hear news or to pass away their time, Michaelis thinks that men of experience and wisdom might be asked for their opinions in difficult cases, and might sometimes assist with their advice those who seemed embarrassed in their own cause, even when it was a good one. Probably this is alluded to in Job xxix. 7—17. and Isa. i. 17.[5] From the Romans, the use of advocates, or patrons who pleaded the cause of another, might have passed to the Jews. In this view the word Παρακλητος, or advocate, is applied to Christ, our *intercessor, who*

---

[1] Josephus, De Bell. Jud. lib. vi. c. 3. § 3.

[2] Schleusner's and Parkhurst's Lexicon, in voce.   [3] Sanhedrin, IV.

[4] And also among the Marootzee, a nation inhabiting the interior of South Africa.— Campbell's Travels in the interior of South Africa, vol. ii. p. 236. (London, 1822. 8vo.) From this, and other coincidences with Jewish observances, Mr. C. thinks it probable that the Marootzee are of Jewish or Arabian origin.

[5] Michaelis's Commentaries on the Laws of Moses, vol. iv. pp. 320—323.

pleads the cause of sinners with his Father. (1 John ii. 1.) The form of proceeding appears to have been as follows : —

1. Those who were summoned before courts of judicature, were said to be προγεγραμμενοι εις κρισιν, because they were cited by posting up their names in some public place, and to these judgment was published or declared in writing. The Greek writers applied the term προγεγραμμενους, to those whom the Romans called *proscriptos* or *proscribed,* that is, whose names were posted up in writing in some public place, as persons doomed to die, with a reward offered to whoever would kill them. To this usage there is an allusion in the Epistle of Jude (verse 4.), where the persons who are said to be προγεγραμμενοι εις τουτο το κριμα, *fore written to,* or *before described for, this condemnation,* denote those who were long before described, in the examples of their wickedness contained in the writings of Moses and the Prophets, such as the angels that sinned, the antediluvians, the people of Sodom, &c. And in the condemnation of these sinners God has shown what he will do to all others like them.[1] In the Sacred Writings all false teachers and impure practices have been most openly proscribed and condemned, and in the following verses of the same epistle the Apostle distinctly specifies who these persons are.

2. He, who entered the action, went to the judges, and stated his affair to them ; and then they sent officers with him to seize the party and bring him to justice. To this our Lord alludes, when he says, (Matt. v. 25.) *Agree with thine adversary while thou art in the way with him,* before thou art brought before the judge, lest thou be condemned. On the day appointed for hearing the cause, the plaintiff and defendant presented themselves before the judges; who at first sat alone. (Deut. xxv. 1.) In later times, the Jewish writers inform us, that there were always two notaries belonging to the court, one of whom stood on the right hand of the judge, who wrote the sentence of acquittal; and the other, on his left hand, who wrote the sentence of condemnation. To this custom, probably, our Saviour referred, (Matt. xxv. 33.) when, speaking of the last judgment, he says, that he will *set the sheep on his right hand,* in order to be acquitted, *and the goats on his left,* in order to be condemned. It appears that the judicial decrees were (as they still are in the East) first written by a notary, and then authenticated or annulled by the magistrate. To this the prophet Isaiah alludes when he denounces a *woe unto them that decree unrighteous decrees, and to the writers that write grievousness.* (Isa. x. 1. marginal rendering.)[2] The judges sat, while the defendants stood, particularly during the examination of witnesses. Thus, *Jesus stood before the governor.* (Matt. xxvii. 11.)

3. In criminal cases, when the trial came on, the judge's first care was to exhort the criminal to confess his crime, if he really were guilty : thus Joshua exhorted Achan to *give glory to the Lord God of Israel, and make confession unto him.* (Josh. vii. 19.) To this custom of the Jews, St. Paul seems to allude, when he says, *Happy is he that condemneth not himself in that thing which he alloweth* (Rom. xiv. 22.); that is, who, being convinced of the truth of a thing, does not really

---

[1] Parkhurst's and Schleusner's Lexicon to the New Testament, voce Προγραφω. Booth-royd on Jude, 4.

[2] Harmer's Observations, vol. ii. pp. 519—521.

and effectually condemn himself in the sight of God by denying it. After the accusation was laid before the court, the criminal was heard in his defence, and therefore Nicodemus said to the chief priests and Pharisees, *Doth our law judge any man before it hear him, and know what he doth?* (John vii. 51.) If, during the trial, the defendant, or supposed criminal, said any thing that displeased either the judge or his accuser, it was not unusual for the latter to smite him on the face. This was the case with St. Paul (Acts xxiii. 2.), and the same brutal conduct prevails in Persia to this day.[1]

4. In matters of life and death, the evidence of one witness was not sufficient : in order to establish a charge, it was necessary to have the testimony of two or three credible and unimpeachable witnesses. (Numb. xxxv. 30. Deut. xvii. 6, 7. xix. 15.) Though the law of Moses is silent concerning the evidence of women, Josephus says that it was prohibited on account of the levity and boldness of their sex! He also adds that the testimony of servants was inadmissible, on account of the probability of their being influenced to speak what was untrue, either from hope of gain or fear of punishment. Most likely, this was the exposition of the scribes and Pharisees, and the practice of the Jews, in the last age of their political existence.[2] The party sworn held up his right hand, which explains Psal. cxliv. 8., *Whose mouth speaketh vanity, and their right hand is a right hand of falsehood.* In general, the witnesses to be sworn did not pronounce the formula of the oath, either when it was a judicial one, or taken on any other solemn occasion. A formula was read, to which they said *Amen.* (Lev. v. 1. 1 Kings viii. 31.) Referring to this usage when Jesus Christ was abjured or put upon his oath, he immediately made an answer. (Matt. xxvi. 63.) All manner of false witness was most severely prohibited. (Exod. xx. 16. xxiii. 1—3.)[3]

5. In questions of property, in default of any other means of decision, recourse was had to the lot. In this manner, it will be recollected that the land of Canaan was divided by Joshua, to which there are so many allusions in the Old Testament, particularly in the book of Psalms. And it should seem, from Prov. xvi. 33. and xviii. 18. that it was used in courts of justice, in the time of Solomon, though, probably, only with the consent of both parties. In *criminal* cases, recourse was had to the sacred lot, called Urim and Thummim, in order to *discover,* not to convict the guilty party (Josh. vii. 14—18. 1 Sam. xiv. 37—45.) ; but it appears to have been used only in the case of an oath being transgressed, which the whole people had taken, or the leader of the host in their name.[4]

A peculiar mode of eliciting the truth was employed in the case of a woman suspected of adultery. She was to be brought by her husband to the tabernacle, — afterwards to the temple ; where she took an oath of purgation, imprecating tremendous punishment upon herself. The form of this process (which was the foundation of the trial by

---

[1] Morier's Second Journey, p. 95. Hanway's Travels, vol. i. p. 299.

[2] Michaelis's Commentaries on the Laws of Moses, vol. iv. p. 325. Schulzii Archæol. Hebr. p. 74. Josephus, Ant. Jud. lib. iv. c. 8. § 15.

[3] Michaelis's Commentaries, vol. iv. pp. 342, 343. Brunings says, that in cases of idolatry, the Jews assert the admissibility of false witnesses ; but he gives no authority for this statement.

[4] Michaelis's Commentaries, vol. iv. pp. 357—359.

ordeal that so generally prevailed in the dark ages) is detailed at length in Numb. v. 11—31., to which the rabbinical writers have added a variety of frivolous ceremonies. If innocent, the woman suffered no inconvenience or injury; but if guilty, the punishment which she had imprecated on herself immediately overtook her.[1]

6. Sentences were only pronounced in the day-time; of which circumstance notice is taken in Saint Luke's narrative of our Saviour's mock trial. (xxii. 66.) It was the custom among the Jews to pronounce sentence of condemnation in this manner: — *He is guilty of death.* (Matt. xxvi. 66.) In other countries, a person's *condemnation* was announced to him by giving him a *black* stone, and his *acquittal* by giving him a *white* stone. Ovid mentions this practice thus: —

> *Mos erat antiquus, niveis atrisque lapillis,*
> *His damnare reos, illis absolvere culpâ.*
> *Nunc quoque sic lata est sententia tristis* ——
>   Met. lib xv. 41—43.

> A custom was of old, and still obtains,
> Which *life* or *death* by suffrages ordains:
> *White stones* and *black* within an urn are cast;
> The *first* absolve, but fate is in the *last.*
>   Dryden.

In allusion to this custom, some critics[2] have supposed that our Saviour (Rev. ii. 17.) promises to give the spiritual conqueror *a white stone, and on the stone a new name written, which no man knoweth, saving he that receiveth it;* which may be supposed to signify — *Well done, thou good and faithful servant.* The white stones of the antients were inscribed with characters; and so is the white stone mentioned in the Apocalypse. According to Persius, the letter Θ was the token of condemnation:

> Et potis es *nigrum* vitio prefigere *Theta.*
>   Sat. iv. 13.
> Fixing thy stigma on the brow of vice.
>   Drummond.

But, as there was a *new name* inscribed on the white stone given by our Lord, *which no man knoweth but he who receiveth it,* it should rather seem that the allusion in this passage is to the *tesseræ hospitales,* of which the reader will find an account *infra,* in the close of Chap. VI. of Part IV. of this volume.

7. Such were the judicial proceedings in ordinary cases, when the forms of law were observed. On some occasions, however, when particular persons were obnoxious to the populace, it was usual for them to demand prompt justice upon the supposed delinquents. It is well known that in Asia, to this day, those who demand justice against a criminal, repair in large bodies to the gate of the royal residence, where they make horrid cries, tearing their garments and throwing dust into the air. This circumstance throws great light upon the conduct of the Jews towards Saint Paul, when the chief captain of the Roman garrison at Jerusalem presented himself to them. (Acts xxii. 28—36.) When they found the Apostle in the temple, prejudiced as they were against him in general, and at that time particularly irritated

---

[1] Schulzii Archæologia Hebraica, pp. 79, 80.
[2] Wetstein, Doddridge, and Dean Woodhouse on Rev. ii. 17.

by the mistaken notion that he had polluted the holy place by the introduction of Greeks into it, they raised a tumult, and were on the point of inflicting summary vengeance on Saint Paul. As soon as the chief captain of the Roman soldiers, who resided in a castle adjoining the temple, heard the tumult, he hastened thither. They then ceased beating the Apostle, and addressed themselves to him as the chief official person there, exclaiming, *Away with him.* Permission being at length given to Paul to explain the affair in their hearing, they became still more violently enraged; but not daring to do themselves justice, they demanded it nearly in the same manner as the Persian peasants now do, by loud vociferations, tearing off their clothes and throwing up dust into the air.[1]

V. As soon as sentence of condemnation was pronounced against a person, he was immediately dragged from the court to the place of execution. Thus our Lord was instantly hurried from the presence of Pilate to Calvary: a similar instance of prompt execution occurred in the case of Achan; and the same practice obtains to this day in the east. At Damascus, for instance, the law is administered in the most summary manner. The criminal is sometimes arrested, tried, and executed within a very few hours after the perpetration of his offence; his head being struck off in the presence of the governor at a given signal, which is often unknown to any other person besides the executioner.[2] In Turkey and Persia, when the enemies of a great man have sufficient influence to procure a warrant for his death, a *capidgi* or executioner is despatched with it to the victim, who quietly submits to his fate.[3] Nearly the same method of executing criminals was used by the antient Jewish princes. It is evidently alluded to in Prov. xvi. 14. Thus, Benaiah was the capidgi (to use the modern Turkish term) who was sent by Solomon to put to death Adonijah, a prince of the blood royal (1 Kings ii. 25.), and also Joab the commander-in-chief of the army. (29—31.) John the Baptist was put to death in like manner. (Matt. xiv. 10.) Previously, however, to executing the criminal, it was usual, among the antient Persians, to cover his head, that he might not behold the face of the sovereign. Thus, the head of Philotas, who had conspired against Alexander the Great, was covered[4]; and in conformity with this practice, the head of Haman was veiled or covered. (Esth. vii. 8.)

So zealous were the Jews for the observance of their law, that they were not ashamed themselves to be the executioners of it, and to punish criminals with their own hands. In stoning persons, the witnesses threw the first stones, agreeably to the enactment of Moses. (Deut. xvii. 7.) Thus, the witnesses against the protomartyr Stephen, after laying down their clothes at the feet of Saul, stoned him (Acts vii. 58, 59.); and to this custom our Saviour alludes, when he said to

---

[1] Harmer's Observations, vol. iii. pp. 367—369.

[2] Hardy's Notices of the Holy Land, p. 256.

[3] Harmer's Observations, vol. ii. pp. 372—376. Captains Irby and Mangles have related a singular instance of similar rapidity of executing a condemned person. In this case " the sufferer had been appointed to the command of the hadj " (or pilgrims to Mecca), " and had set off from Constantinople. While he was on his return from Mecca, a Khat-sheriffe was despatched from the capital, ordering his head to be cut off, and sent immediately to Constantinople. His sentence was carried into execution before he reached Damascus." Travels in Egypt, &c. p. 257.

[4] Quintus Curtius, lib. vi. c. 8. tom. ii. p. 34. edit. Bipont.

the Pharisees, who had brought to him a woman who had been taken in adultery, — *He that is without sin among you, let him first cast a stone at her.* (John viii. 7.) As there were no public executioners in the more antient periods of the Jewish history, it was not unusual for persons of distinguished rank themselves to put the sentence in execution upon offenders. Thus, Samuel put Agag to death (1 Sam. xv. 33.); and in like manner Nebuchadnezzar ordered Arioch the commander-in-chief of his forces to destroy the wise men of Babylon, because they could not interpret his dream. (Dan. ii. 24.) Previously, however, to inflicting punishment, it was a custom of the Jews, that the witnesses should lay their hands on the criminal's head. This custom originated in an express precept of God, in the case of one who had blasphemed the name of Jehovah, who was ordered to be brought without the camp: when all, who had heard him, were appointed to lay their hands upon his head, and afterwards the congregation were to stone him. By this action they signified, that the condemned person suffered justly, protesting that, if he were innocent, they desired that his blood might fall on their own head. In allusion to this usage, when sentence was pronounced against Jesus Christ, the Jews exclaimed, — *His blood be upon us and our children.* (Matt. xxvii. 25.) From the above-noticed precept of bringing the criminals without the camp, arose the custom of executing them without the city.

But in whatever manner the criminal was put to death, according to the Talmudical writers, the Jews always gave him some wine with incense in it, in order to stupify and intoxicate him. This custom is said to have originated in the precept recorded in Prov. xxxi. 6., which sufficiently explains the reason why wine, mingled with myrrh, was offered to Jesus Christ when on the cross. (Mark xv. 23.) In the latter ages of the Jewish polity, this medicated cup of wine was so generally given before execution, that the word *cup* is sometimes put in the Scriptures for *death* itself. Thus, Jesus Christ, in his last prayer in the garden of Gethsemane, said — *If it be possible let this* CUP *pass from me.* (Matt. xxvi. 39. 42.)

SECTION II.

OF THE ROMAN JUDICATURE, MANNER OF TRIAL, TREATMENT OF PRISONERS, AND OTHER TRIBUNALS MENTIONED IN THE NEW TESTAMENT.

I. *Judicial Proceedings of the Romans.* — II. *Privileges and Treatment of Roman Citizens, when Prisoners.*—III. *Appeals to the Imperial Tribunal.* —IV. *The Roman Method of fettering and confining Criminals.*—V. *The Roman Tribunals.*—VI. *Other Tribunals mentioned in the New Testament:* — 1. *The Areopagus at Athens.* — 2. *The Assembly at Ephesus.*

WHEREVER the Romans extended their power, they also carried their laws; and though, as we have already seen, they allowed their conquered subjects to enjoy the free performance of their religious worship, as well as the holding of some inferior courts of judicature, yet in all cases of a capital nature the tribunal of the Roman prefect or president was the last resort. Without his permission, no person could be put to death, at least in Judæa. And as we find numerous allusions in the new Testament to the Roman judicature, manner of trial, treatment of prisoners, and infliction of capital punishment, a brief account of these subjects so intimately connected with the political state of Judæa under the Romans, naturally claims a place in the present sketch.[1]

I. " The judicial proceedings of the Romans were conducted in a manner worthy the majesty, honour, and magnanimity of that people. Instances, indeed, occur of a most scandalous venality and corruption in Roman judges, and the story of Jugurtha and Verres will stand, a lasting monument of the power of gold to pervert justice and shelter the most atrocious villany. But, in general, in the Roman judicatures, both in the imperial city and in the provinces, justice was administered with impartiality; a fair and honourable trial was permitted; the allegations of the plaintiff and defendant were respectively heard; the merits of the cause weighed and scrutinised with cool unbiassed judgment; and an equitable sentence pronounced. The Roman law, in conformity to the first principle of nature and reason, ordained that no one should be condemned and punished without a previous public trial. This was one of the decrees of the twelve tables : *No one shall be condemned before he is tried.*[2] Under the Roman government, both in Italy and in the provinces, this universally obtained. After the cause is heard, says Cicero, a man may be acquitted : but, his cause unheard, no one can be condemned.[3] To this excellent custom among the Romans, which the law of nature prescribes, and all the principles of equity, honour, and humanity dictate, there are several allusions in Scripture. We find the holy apostles, who did not, like frantic enthusiasts and visionaries, court persecution, but embraced every legal method which the usages and maxims of those times had established to avoid it, and to extricate themselves from calamities and sufferings, pleading this privilege, reminding the Romans of it when they were going to infringe it, and in a spirited manner upbraiding their persecutors with their violation of it. When Lysias, the Roman tribune, ordered Saint Paul to be conducted into the castle, and to be examined by scourging, that he might learn what he had done that

---

[1] The materials of this section are principally derived from Dr. Harwood's Introduction to the New Testament (a work now of rare occurrence), vol. ii. section xvi. the texts cited being carefully verified and corrected. The subjects of this and the following section are also discussed by Dr. Lardner, Credibility, part i. book i. c. 10. §§ 9—11. ; and especially by Calmet in his elaborate *Dissertation sur les supplices dont il est parlé dans l'Ecriture*, inserted in his Commentaire Littérale, tom. i. part ii. pp. 387—402., and in his Dissertations, tom. i. p. 241. *et seq.* See also Merill's Notæ Philologicæ in passionem Christi, and Wyssenbach's Notæ Nomico-Philologicæ in passionem, in vol. iii. of Crenius's Fasciculus Opusculorum, pp. 583—691. and Lydius's Florum Sparsio ad Historiam Passionis Jesu Christi, 18mo. Dordrechti, 1672.

[2] Interfici indemnatum quemcunque hominem, etiam xii Tabularum decreta vetuerant. Fragment. xii.   Tab. tit. 27.

[3] Causâ cognitâ multi possunt absolvi : incognitâ quidem condemnari nemo potest.   In Verrem, lib. i. c. 25.   " Producing the laws which ordain that no person shall suffer death without a legal trial." Dion. Halicarn. lib. iii. p. 153. Hudson.   " He did not allow them to inflict death on any citizen uncondemned." Ibid. lib. vi. p. 370. lib. vii. p. 428. edit. Hudson, Oxon. 1704.   " They thought proper to call him to justice, as it is contrary to the Roman customs to condemn any one to death without a previous trial." Appian. Bell. Civil. lib. iii. p. 906. Tollii, 1670. " Did not you miserably murder Lentulus and his associates, without their being either judged or convicted ? " Dion Cassius, lib. 46. p. 463. Reimar.

enraged the mob thus violently against him, as the soldiers were fastening him with thongs to the pillars to inflict this upon him, Paul said to the centurion who was appointed to attend and see this executed, Doth the Roman law authorise you to scourge a freeman of Rome uncondemned, to punish him before a legal sentence hath been passed upon him? (Acts xxii. 25.) The centurion hearing this went immediately to the tribune, bidding him be cautious how he acted upon the present occasion, for the prisoner was a Roman citizen! The tribune upon this information went to him, and said, Tell me the truth, Are you a freeman of Rome? He answered in the affirmative. It cost me an immense sum, said the tribune, to purchase this privilege.[1] But I was the son of a freeman[2], said the Apostle. Immediately, therefore, those who were ordered to examine him by torture desisted; and the tribune was extremely alarmed that he had bound a Roman citizen. In reference to this also, when Paul and Silas were treated with the last indignity at Philippi by the multitude abetted by the magistrates, were beaten with rods, thrown into the public gaol, and their feet fastened in the stocks, the next morning upon the magistrates sending their lictors to the prison with orders to the keeper for the two men whom they had the day before so shamefully and cruelly treated to be dismissed, Paul turned to the messengers and said, We are Roman citizens. Your magistrates have ordered us to be publicly scourged without a legal trial. They have thrown us into a dungeon. And would they now have us steal away in a silent and clandestine manner? No! Let them come in person and conduct us out themselves. The lictors returned and reported this answer to the governors, who were greatly alarmed and terrified when they understood they were Roman citizens. Accordingly, they went in person to the gaol, addressed them with great civility, and begged them in the most respectful terms that they would quietly leave the town. (Acts xvi. 37.)[3]

" Here we cannot but remark the distinguished humanity and honour which St. Paul experienced from the tribune Lysias. His whole conduct towards the Apostle was worthy a Roman. This most generous and worthy officer rescued him from the sanguinary fury of the mob, who had seized the Apostle, shut the temple doors, and were in

---

[1] Dion Cassius confirms what the tribune here asserts, that this honour was purchased at a very high price. " The freedom of Rome formerly," says the historian, " could only be purchased for a large sum;" but he observes, "that in the reign of Claudius, when Messalina and her freedmen had the management of every thing, this honour became so cheap that any person might buy it for a little broken glass." Dion Cassius, lib. lx. p. 955. Reimar.

[2] " But I was free born." Probably St. Paul's family was honoured with the freedom of Rome for engaging in Cæsar's party, and distinguishing themselves in his cause during the civil wars. Appian informs us, that " He made the Laodiceans and Tarsensians free, and exempted them from taxes; and those of the Tarsensians who had been sold for slaves, he ordered by an edict to be released from servitude." Appian de Bell. Civil. p. 1077. Tollii. 1670.

[3] It was deemed a great aggravation of an injury by the Roman law, that it was done in public before the people. The Philippian magistrates, therefore, conscious of the iniquity which they had committed, and of the punishment to which they were liable, might well be afraid : for Paul and Silas had their option, either to bring a civil action against them, or to indict them criminally for the injury which they had inflicted on the Apostle and his companion. In either of which cases, had they been cast, they would be rendered infamous, and incapable of holding any magisterial office, and subjected to several other legal incapacities, besides the punishment they were to undergo at the discretion of the judge, which in so atrocious an injury would not have been small. Biscoe on the Acts, vol. i. pp. 352—354.

a tumultuous manner dragging him away instantly to shed his blood. Afterwards, also, when above forty Jews associated and mutually bound themselves by the most solemn adjurations, that they would neither eat nor drink till they had assassinated him; when the tribune was informed of this conspiracy, to secure the person of the Apostle from the determined fury of the Jews, he immediately gave orders for seventy horsemen and two hundred spearmen to escort the prisoner to Cæsarea, where the procurator resided; writing a letter, in which he informed the president of the vindictive rage of the Jews against the prisoner, whom he had snatched from their violence, and whom [1] he afterwards discovered to be a Roman citizen. In consequence of this epistle Felix gave the Apostle a kind and candid reception : when he read it, he turned to him and said, When your accusers come hither before me, I will gave your cause an impartial hearing.[2] And accordingly when the high priest Ananias and the Sanhedrin went down to Cæsarea with one Tertullus an orator, whose eloquence they had hired to aggravate the Apostle's crimes before the procurator, Felix, though a man of a mercenary and profligate character[3], did not depart from the Roman honour in this regard ; and would not violate the usual processes of judgment to gratify this body of men, though they were the most illustrious personages of the province he governed, by condemning the Apostle unheard, and yielding him, poor and friendless as he was, to their fury, merely upon their impeachment. He allowed the Apostle to offer his vindication and exculpate himself from the charges they had alleged against him; and was so far satisfied with his apology as to give orders for him to be treated as a prisoner at large, and for all his friends to have free access to him; disappointing those who thirsted for his blood, and drawing down upon himself the relentless indignation of the Jews, who, undoubtedly, from such a disappointment, would be instigated to lay all his crimes and oppressions before the emperor.

"The same strict honour, in observing the usual forms and processes of the Roman tribunal, appears in Festus the successor of Felix. Upon his entrance into his province, when the leading men among the Jews waited upon him to congratulate him upon his accession, and took that opportunity to inveigh with great bitterness and virulence against the Apostle, soliciting it as a favour (Acts xxv. 3.) that he would send him to Jerusalem, designing, as it afterwards appeared, had he complied with their request, to have hired ruffians to murder him on the road, Festus told them, that it was his will that Paul should remain in custody at Cæsarea ; but that any persons whom they fixed upon might go down along with him, and produce at his tribunal what they had to allege against the prisoner. This was worthy the Roman honour and spirit. How importunate and urgent the priests and principal magistrates of Jerusalem, when Festus was in this capital, were with him to pass sentence of death upon the Apostle,

---

[1] Acts xxiii. 27. " I have since learned that he is a Roman citizen."

[2] Acts xxiii. 35. Literally, " Hear it through; give the whole of it an attentive examination." Similar expressions occur in Polybius, lib. i. pp. 39.170. 187. lib. iv. p. 328. edit. Hanov. 1619. See also Dion. Halicarn. lib. x. p. 304.

[3] Felix per omne sævitium ac libidinem, jus regium servili ingenio exercuit. Tacitus Hist. lib. v. p. 397. edit. Dublin. Felix cuncta maleficia impune ratus. Annal. xii. 54. He hoped also that money, &c. Acts xxiv. 26.

merely upon their impeachment, and upon the atrocious crimes with which they loaded him, appears from what the procurator himself told king Agrippa and Bernice upon a visit they paid him at Cæsarea, to congratulate him upon his new government. I have here, said he, a man whom my predecessor left in custody when he quitted this province. During a short visit I paid to Jerusalem, upon my arrival I was solicited by the priests and principal magistrates to pass sentence of death upon him. To these urgent entreaties I replied, that it was not customary for the Romans to gratify (xxv. 16.) any man with the death of another; that the laws of Rome enacted that he who is accused should have his accuser face to face; and have licence to answer for himself concerning the crimes laid against him.[1]

II. " It appears from numberless passages in the classics that a Roman citizen could not legally be scourged.[2] This was deemed to the last degree dishonourable, the most daring indignity and insult upon the Roman name. ' A Roman citizen, judges!' exclaims Cicero in his oration against Verres, ' was publicly beaten with rods in the forum of Messina: during this public dishonour, no groan, no other expression of the unhappy wretch was heard amidst the cruelties he suffered, and the sound of the strokes that were inflicted, but this, I am a Roman citizen! By this declaration that he was a Roman citizen, he fondly imagined that he should put an end to the ignominy and cruel usage to which he was now subjected.'[3] The orator afterwards breaks forth into this pathetic prosopopœia: ' O transporting name of liberty! O the distinguished privilege of Roman freedom! O Porcian and Sempronian laws! Are things at last come to this wretched state, that a Roman citizen, in a Roman province, in the most public and open manner, should be beaten with rods!'[4] The historian Appian, after relating how Marcellus, to express his scorn and contempt of Cæsar, seized a person of some distinction, to whom Cæsar had given his freedom, and beat him with rods, bidding him go and show Cæsar the marks of the scourges he had received, observes, that this was an indignity which is never inflicted upon a Roman citizen for any enormity whatever.[5] Agreeably to this custom, which also obtained at Athens, in the Adelphi of Terence, one of the persons of the drama says to another, If you continue to be troublesome and impertinent, you shall be instantly seized and dragged within, and there you shall be torn and mangled with scourges within an inch of

---

[1] " Senators," saith Piso, " the law ordains that he who is accused should hear his accusation, and after having offered his defence, to wait the sentence of the judges." Appian, Bell. Civil. lib. iii. p. 911. Tollii, Amst. 1670. " He said, that what he now attempted to do was the last tyranny and despotism, that the same person should be both accuser and judge, and should arbitrarily dictate the degree of punishment." Dion. Halicarn. lib. vii. p. 428. Hudson.

[2] Facinus est vinciri civem Romanum: scelus verberari. In Verrem, lib. v. 70.

[3] Cædebatur virgis in medio foro Messinæ civis Romanus, judices; cum interea nullus gemitus, nulla vox alia istius miseri, inter dolorem crepitumque plagarum audiebatur, nisi hæc, Civis Romanus sum. Hac se commemoratione civitatis omnia verbera depulsurum cruciatumque a corpore dejecturum arbitrabatur. Cicero in Verrem, lib. v. 162.

[4] O nomen dulce libertatis! O jus eximium nostræ civitatis! O lex Porcia, legesque Semproniæ! Huccine tandem omnia recederunt, ut civis Romanus in provincia populi Romani, delegatis in foro virgis cæderetur. Ibid. 163.

[5] Appian. Bell. Civil. lib. ii. p. 731. Tollii.

your life. What! a freeman scourged, replies Sannio.[1] To this privilege of Roman citizens, whose freedom exempted them from this indignity and dishonour, there are several references in Scripture. St. Paul pleads this immunity. He said to the centurion, as they were fastening him to the pillar with thongs to inflict upon him this punishment, Is it lawful for you to scourge a Roman?[2] So also at Philippi he told the messengers of the magistrates, They have beaten us openly uncondemned, being Romans, and have cast us into prison, and now do they thrust us out privately; no, verily, but let them come themselves and fetch us out. And the sergeants told these words to the magistrates, and they feared when they heard that they were Romans, and were conscious they had used them with a contumely and dishonour which subjected them to the just displeasure of the Roman senate.

 "Neither was it lawful for a Roman citizen to be bound[3], to be examined by the question, or to be the subject of any ingenious and cruel arts of tormenting to extort a confession from him. These punishments were deemed servile; torture was not exercised but upon slaves[4]; freemen were privileged from this inhumanity and ignominy. It is a flagrant enormity, says Cicero, for a Roman citizen to be bound[5]: not meaning by that, that it was unlawful for a Roman to be fettered and imprisoned; but it was in the highest degree unjustifiable and illegal for a freeman of Rome to be bound in order to be tortured for the discovery of his crimes. Dion Cassius, particularising the miseries of Claudius's government, observes, that Messalina and Narcissus, and the rest of his freemen, seized the occasion that now offered to perpetrate the last enormities. Among other excesses they employed slaves and freedmen to be informers against their masters. They put to the torture several persons of the first distinction, not merely foreigners, but citizens; not only of the common people, but some even of the Roman knights and senators: though Claudius, when he first entered upon his government, had bound himself under a solemn oath that he would never apply the torture to any Roman citizen.[6] These two passages from Cicero and Dion illustrate what St. Luke relates concerning Lysias the tribune. This officer, not knowing the dignity of his prisoner, had, in violation of this privilege of Roman citizens, given orders for the Apostle to be bound, and examined by scourging. (Acts xxii. 24, 25.) When he was afterwards informed by his centurion that St. Paul was a freeman of Rome, the sacred historian observes, that upon receiving this intelligence, the chief captain was afraid, after he knew that he was a Roman, and because he had bound him. (xxii. 29.)

III. "We find that St. Paul, when he discovered that Festus his

---

1 Nam si molestûs pergis esse, jam intro abripiere, atque ibi
   Usque ad necem operiere loris.   S. loris liber.   Adelphi, act. ii. scena 1. ver. 28.

2 Acts xxii. 25. The consul Marcellus scourged with rods one of the magistrates of that place who came to Rome, declaring he inflicted this as a public token that he was no Roman citizen.   Plutarch, in Cæsar. p. 1324. edit. Gr. Stephan.

3 Facinus est vinciri civem Romanum.   Cicero in Verr. lib. v. 170.

4 Q. Gallium prætorem, servilem in modum torsit.   Sueton. in vita Augusti, cap. 27. p. 192. Variorum Edit.

5 See the last note but one.

6 Dion Cassius, lib. lx. p. 953.   Reimar.

judge was disposed to gratify the Jews, appealed from a provincial court to the imperial tribunal; transferred his cause, by appeal, from the jurisdiction of the Roman procurator to the decision of the emperor. This appears to be another singular privilege which a freeman of Rome enjoyed. The sacred historian relates, that after Festus had stayed about ten days in the metropolis, he went down to Cæsarea, and the next day after his arrival he summoned a court, ascended the bench, and ordered Paul to be brought before him. Here, as he stood at the bar, his prosecutors from Jerusalem with great virulence charged him with many heinous and atrocious crimes, none of which, upon strict examination, they were able to prove against him. For in his apology he publicly declared, in the most solemn terms, that they could not convict him of any one instance of a criminal behaviour, either to the law, the temple, or to the Roman emperor. Festus then, being (Acts xxv. 9.) desirous to ingratiate himself with the Jews, asked him if he was willing his cause should be tried at Jerusalem. To this proposal Paul replied, I am now before Cæsar's tribunal, where my cause ought to be impartially canvassed and decided. You yourself are conscious that I have been guilty of nothing criminal against my countrymen. If I have injured them, if I have perpetrated any capital crime, I submit without reluctance to capital punishment. But if all the charges they have now brought against me are proved to be absolutely false and groundless, no person can condemn me to death merely to gratify them. I appeal to the emperor. Festus, after deliberating with the Roman council, turned and said to him, Have you appealed to the emperor? You shall then go and be judged by the emperor. From the above-mentioned particulars, which are corroborated by several other similar incidents in the Roman history, it appears that a Roman citizen could by appeal remove his cause out of the provinces to Rome. ' It was,' says Mr. Melmoth, ' one of the privileges of a Roman citizen, secured by the Sempronian law, that he could not be capitally convicted but by the suffrage of the people, which seems to have been still so far in force as to make it necessary to send the person here mentioned to Rome.'[1] We are informed by Dionysius of Halicarnassus that the ever-memorable Poplicola enacted this law, that if any Roman governor showed a disposition to condemn any one to death, to scourge him, or despoil him of his property, that any private person should have liberty to appeal from his jurisdiction to the judgment of the people, that in the mean time he should receive no personal harm from the magistracy till his cause was finally decided by the people.[2] This law, which was instituted at the first establishment of the commonwealth, continued in force under the emperors. If a freeman of Rome, in any of the provinces, deemed himself and his cause to be treated by the president with dishonour and injustice, he could by appeal remove it to Rome to the determination of the emperor. Suetonius informs us that Augustus delegated a number of consular persons at Rome to receive the appeals of people in the provinces, and that he appointed one person to superintend the affairs of

---

[1] Mr. Melmoth's note on the 97th letter in the 10th book of Pliny's Epistles, vol. ii. p. 672. 3d edit.

[2] Dion. Halicarn. lib. v. p. 281. edit. Oxon. 1704. See also p. 334. ejusdem edit.

each province.[1] A passage in Pliny's epistle confirms this right and privilege which Roman freemen enjoyed of appealing from provincial courts to Rome, and, in consequence of such an appeal, being removed, as St. Paul was, to the capital to take their trial in the supreme court of judicature. In that celebrated epistle to Trajan, who desired to be informed concerning the principles and conduct of the Christians, he thus writes: 'The method I have observed towards those who have been brought before me as Christians is this — I interrogated them whether they were Christians: if they confessed, I repeated the question twice again, adding threats at the same time, when, if they still persevered, I ordered them to be immediately punished; for I was persuaded, whatever the nature of their opinions might be, a contumacious and inflexible obstinacy certainly deserved correction. There were others, also, brought before me, possessed with the same infatuation, but, being citizens of Rome, I directed them to be carried thither.'[2]

IV. "The Roman method of fettering and confining criminals was singular. One end of a chain, that was of commodious length, was fixed about the right arm of the prisoner, and the other end was fastened to the left arm of a soldier. Thus a soldier was coupled to the prisoner, and every where attended and guarded him.[3] This manner of confinement is frequently mentioned, and there are many beautiful allusions to it in the Roman writers. Thus was St. Paul confined. Fettered[4] in this manner, he delivered his apology before Festus, king Agrippa, and Bernice. And it was this circumstance that occasioned one of the most pathetic and affecting strokes of true oratory that ever was displayed either in the Grecian or Roman senate. *Would to God that not only* THOU, *but also* ALL *that hear me this day, were both almost and altogether such as I am, except these bonds!* What a prodigious effect must this striking conclusion, and the sight of the irons held up[5] to enforce it, make upon the minds of the audience! During the two years that St. Paul was a prisoner at large, and lived at Rome in his own hired house, he was subjected to this confinement. Paul was suffered to dwell with a soldier that kept him. The circumstance of publicly wearing this chain, and being thus coupled to a soldier, was very disgraceful and dishonourable, and the ignominy of it would naturally occasion the desertion of former friends and acquaintance. Hence the apostle immortalises the name of Onesiphorus, and fervently intercedes with God to bless his family, and to remember him in the day of future recompense, for a rare instance of distinguished fidelity and affection to him when all had turned away from him and forsaken

---

[1] Appellationes quotannis urbanorum quidem litigatorum prætori delegavit; ac provincialium consularibus viris, quos singulos cujusque provinciæ negotiis reposuisset. Sueton. vit. August. cap. 33. p. 208. edit. var. Lug. Bat. 1662.

[2] Plinii Epistolæ, lib. x. epist. 97. pp. 722, 723. ed. var. 1669.

[3] Quemadmodum eadem catena et custodiam et militem copulat, sic ista quæ tam dissimilia sunt, pariter incedunt. Senecæ Epist. 5. tom. ii. p. 13. Gronovii, 1672. So also Manilius.

Vinctorum dominus, sociusque in parte catenæ,
Interdum pœnis innoxia corpora servat.   Lib. V. v. 628, 629.

[4] In like manner the brave but unfortunate Eumenes addressed a very pathetic speech to his army, with his fetters on. Plutarch, Eumenes. Justin, lib. xiv. cap. 3.

[5] Prolatam, sicut erat catenatus, manum ostendit. Justin, lib. xiv. cap. 3. p. 395. Gronovii.

him. *The Lord give mercy to the house of Onesiphorus, for he oft refreshed me, and was not* ASHAMED *of my* CHAIN, *but immediately upon his arrival in Rome he sought me out very diligently till he found me! The Lord grant unto him that he may find mercy of the Lord in that day.* (2 Tim. i. 16, 17, 18.)

" Sometimes the prisoner was fastened to two soldiers, one on each side, wearing a chain both on his right and left hand. St. Paul at first was thus confined. When the tribune received him from the hands of the Jews, he commanded him to be bound with two chains. (Acts xxi. 33.) In this manner was Peter fettered and confined by Herod Agrippa. *The same night Peter was sleeping between two soldiers, bound with* TWO CHAINS. (Acts xii. 6.)

" It further appears, that if the soldiers, who were thus appointed to guard criminals, and to whom they were chained, suffered the prisoner to escape, they were punished with death. Thus when Peter was delivered out of prison by a miracle, the next morning we read there was no small confusion among the soldiers who were appointed his guards, and to whom he had been chained, what was become of Peter.

" Whence it appears that his deliverance had been effected, and his shackles had been miraculously unloosed, without their knowledge, when they were sunk in repose. Upon which Herod, after making a fruitless search for him, ordered all those who had been entrusted with the custody of Peter to be executed. (Acts xii. 19.) In like manner also keepers of prisons were punished with death, if the confined made their escape. This is evident from what is related concerning the imprisonment of Paul and Silas at Philippi. These, after their bodies were mangled with scourges, were precipitated into the public dungeon, and their feet were made fast in the stocks. At midnight these good men prayed and sang praises to God in these circumstances; when suddenly a dreadful earthquake shook the whole prison to its foundation, all the doors in an instant flew open, and the shackles of all the prisoners dropped to the ground. This violent concussion awakening the keeper, when he saw the doors of the prison wide open, he drew his sword, and was going to plunge it in his bosom, concluding that all the prisoners had escaped. In that crisis Paul called to him with a loud voice, entreating him not to lay violent hands upon himself, assuring him all the prisoners were safe.

V. " The Roman tribunal, if we may judge of it from what is related concerning Pilate's, was erected on a raised stage, the floor of which was embellished with a tesselated pavement. This consisted of little square pieces of marble, or of stones of various colours, which were disposed and arranged with great art and elegance, to form a chequered and pleasing appearance.[1] Pliny informs us that this refinement was first introduced among the Romans by Sylla.[2] Their great men were so fond of this magnificence, and thought it so essential to the elegance and splendour of life, that they appear to have carried with them these splendid materials to form and compose these elaborate floors, for their

---

[1] Opus tessellatum ex parvulis coloris varii lapillis quadratis constabat, quibus solum pavimenti incrustabatur.   Varro de re rustica, lib. iii. 1.
[2] Lithostrota acceptavere sub Sylla.   Plinii Hist. Nat. lib. xxxvi. p. 60.

tents, for their houses, and for their tribunals, wherever they removed [1] — from a depraved and most wretchedly vitiated taste, at last deeming them a necessary and indispensable furniture, not merely a vain and proud display of grandeur and greatness. With this variegated pavement, composed of pieces of marble or stone thus disposed and combined, the evangelist informs us that the floor of Pilate's tribunal was ornamented. (John xix. 13.) Such an embellishment of a tribunal was only a proud ostentatious display to the world of Italian greatness and magnificence, calculated less for real use than to strike the beholders with an idea of the boundless prodigality and extravagance of the Romans.

" Having mentioned Pilate the Roman procurator, we cannot close this section without remarking the efforts he repeatedly made, when he sat in judgment upon Jesus, to save him from the determined fury of the Jews. Five successive attempts are enumerated by commentators and critics. He had the fullest conviction of his innocence — that it was merely through malice, and a virulence which nothing could placate, that they demanded his execution. Yet though the governor for a long time resisted all their united clamour and importunity, and, conscious that he had done nothing worthy of death, steadily refused to pronounce the sentence of condemnation upon him ; yet one argument, which in a menacing manner they addressed to him, at last totally shook his firmness and induced him to yield to their sanguinary purpose. The Jews, after aggravating his guilt, and employing every expedient in vain to influence the president to inflict capital punishment upon him, at last cried out: *If thou let this man go, thou art not Cæsar's friend ; whosoever maketh himself a king, speaketh against Cæsar.* Upon hearing this, all his former firmness instantly vanished ; he could stem the torrent of popular fury no longer ; to this he yielded, and immediately ordered his execution. *Then delivered he him, therefore, to them to be crucified.* This conduct of Pilate arose from his perfect knowledge of the character and temper of his master Tiberius, who was a gloomy old tyrant, day and night incessantly haunted with the fiends of jealousy and suspicion — who would never forgive any innovations in his government, but punished the authors and abettors of them with inexorable death.[2] Pilate, therefore, hearing the Jews reiterating this with menaces, that if he let him go he was not Cæsar's friend — knowing the jealousy and cruelty of Tiberius[3], and fearing that the disappointed rage of the Jews would instigate them to accuse him to the old tyrant, as abetting and suffering a person to escape with impunity, who had assumed the regal title and character in one of his provinces, was alarmed for his own safety ; and rather than draw down upon his devoted head the resentment of the sovereign, who would never forgive or forget an injury, real or imaginary, contrary to his own judgment and clear persuasion of the innocence of Jesus, sentenced him to be crucified."

VI. As the Romans allowed the inhabitants of conquered countries

---

[1] In expeditionibus tessella et sectilia pavimenta circumtulisse. Suetonius vita J. Cæsaris. cap. 46. p. 74. edit. variorum Lug. Bat. 1662. Vid. etiam not. Salmasii in loc.
[2] See Suetonius, Tacitus, Dion Cassius.
[3] Philo makes the very same remark concerning Pilate, p. 390. edit. Mangey.

to retain their local tribunals, we find incidental mention made in the
New Testament, of provincial courts of justice.   Two of these are of
sufficient importance to claim a distinct notice in this place : viz.
1. The Areopagus, at Athens; and, 2. The Assembly, at Ephesus.

1. The tribunal of the AREOPAGUS is *said* to have been instituted
at Athens, by Cecrops the founder of that city, and was celebrated for
the strict equity of its decisions.   Among the various causes of which
it took cognizance, were matters of religion, the consecration of new
gods, erection of temples and altars, and the introduction of new ceremonies into divine worship.   On this account St. Paul was brought
before the tribunal of Areopagus as a *setter forth of strange gods, because
he preached* unto the Athenians, Jesus and Αναστασις, or *the Resurrection.* (Acts xvii. 18.)   Its sittings were held on the Αρειος Παγος, or
Hill of Mars (whence its name was derived), which is situated in the
midst of the city of Athens, opposite to the Acropolis or citadel, and is
an insulated precipitous rock, broken towards the south, and on the
north side sloping gently down to the temple of Theseus.   Its appearance is thus described by Dr. E. D. Clarke : — " It is not possible to
conceive a situation of greater peril, or one more calculated to prove
the sincerity of a preacher, than that in which the Apostle was here
placed : and the truth of this, perhaps, will never be better felt than
by a spectator, who from this eminence actually beholds the monuments of pagan pomp and superstition, by which he, whom the Athenians considered as the *setter forth of strange gods,* was then surrounded:
representing to the imagination the disciples of Socrates and of Plato,
the dogmatist of the porch, and the sceptic of the academy, addressed
by a poor and lowly man, who, *rude in speech,* without the *enticing
words of man's wisdom,* enjoined precepts contrary to their taste, and
very hostile to their prejudices.   One of the peculiar privileges of the
Areopagitæ seems to have been set at defiance by the zeal of Saint
Paul on this occasion; namely, that of inflicting extreme and exemplary
punishment upon any person, who should slight the celebration of the
holy mysteries, or blaspheme the gods of Greece.   We ascended to the
summit by means of steps cut in the natural stone.   The sublime scene
here exhibited, is so striking, that a brief description of it may prove how
truly it offers to us a commentary upon the apostle's words, as they
were delivered upon the spot.   He stood upon the top of the rock,
and beneath the canopy of heaven.   Before him there was spread a
glorious prospect of mountains, islands, seas, and skies : behind him
towered the lofty Acropolis, crowned with all its marble temples.
Thus every object, whether in the face of nature, or among the works
of art, conspired to elevate the mind, and to fill it with reverence
towards that BEING, *who made and governs the world* (Acts xvii. 24. 28.) ;
who sitteth in that light which no mortal eye can approach, and yet is
nigh unto the meanest of his creatures ; *in whom we live and move and
have our being.*" [1]

2. The ASSEMBLY mentioned in Acts xix. 39. is, most probably,
that belonging to the district of Ephesus, Asia Minor being divided
into several districts, each of which had its appropriate legal assembly.

---

[1] Dr. Clarke's Travels, vol. vi. pp. 263—265.   See also Mr. Dodwell's Classical and
Topographical Tour through Greece, vol. i. pp. 361, 362.

Some of these are referred to by Cicero[1], and many others are mentioned by Pliny[2], particularly this of Ephesus. The Γραμματευς or chief officer says, that if Demetrius had any claim of property to make, there were civil courts in which he might sue: if he had crimes to object to any person, the proconsul was there, to take cognizance of the charge: but, if he had complaints of a political nature to prefer, or had any thing to say which might redound to the honour of their goddess, there was the usual legal assembly of the district belonging to Ephesus, in which it ought to be proposed. The regular periods of such assemblies, it appears, were three or four times a month; although they were convoked extraordinarily for the despatch of any pressing business.[3]

SECTION III.[4]

ON THE CRIMINAL LAW OF THE JEWS.

I. CRIMES AGAINST GOD: — 1. *Idolatry.* — 2. *Blasphemy.* — 3. *Falsely prophesying.* — 4. *Divination.* — 5. *Perjury.* — II. CRIMES AGAINST PARENTS AND MAGISTRATES. — III. CRIMES AGAINST PROPERTY: — 1. *Theft.* — 2. *Man-stealing.* — 3. *The Crime of denying any thing taken in trust, or found.* — 4. *Regulations concerning Debtors.* — IV. CRIMES AGAINST THE PERSON: — 1. *Murder.* — 2. *Homicide.* — 3. *Corporal Injuries.* — 4. *Crimes of Lust.* — V. CRIMES OF MALICE.

I. IT has been shown in a preceding chapter[5], that the maintenance of the worship of the only true God was a fundamental object of the Mosaic polity. The government of the Israelites being a *Theocracy*, that is, one in which the supreme legislative power was vested in the Almighty, who was regarded as their king, it was to be expected that, in a state confessedly religious, crimes against the Supreme Majesty of Jehovah should occupy a primary place in the statutes given by Moses to that people. Accordingly,

1. IDOLATRY, that is, the worship of other gods, in the Mosaic law occupies the first place in the list of crimes. It was, indeed, a crime not merely against God, but also against a fundamental law of the state, and, consequently, was a species of *high treason*, which was capitally punished. This crime consisted not in ideas and opinions, but in the overt act of worshipping other gods. An Israelite, therefore, was guilty of idolatry: —

(1.) When he actually worshipped other gods besides JEHOVAH, the only true God. This was, properly speaking, the state crime just noticed; and it is, at the same time, the greatest of all offences against sound reason and common sense. This crime was prohibited in the first of the ten commandments. (Exod. xx. 3.)

(2.) *By worshipping images*, whether of the true God under a visible

---

[1] Cicero, Epist. ad Atticum, lib. v. ep. 20.
[2] Pliny, Hist. Nat. lib. v. cc. 25. 29, 32, 33. See also Cellarii Geographia Antiqua, vol. ii. p. 127.
[3] Biscoe on the Acts, vol. i. p. 312., and Bloomfield's Annotations, vol. iv. p. 657.
[4] This section is wholly an abridgment of Michaelis's Commentaries, vol. iv. pp. 1—312.
[5] See pp. 79, 80. *supra.*

form, to which the Israelites were but too prone (Exod. xxxii. 4, 5. Judg. xvii. 3. xviii. 4—6. 14—17. 30, 31. vi. 25—33. viii. 24—27. 1 Kings xii. 26—31.), or of the images of the gods of the Gentiles of which we have so many instances in the sacred history. All *image-worship* whatever is expressly forbidden in Exod. xx. 4, 5.: and a curse is denounced against it in Deut. xxvii. 15.

(8.) *By prostration before, or adoration of, such images,* or of any thing else revered as a god, such as the sun, moon, and stars. (Exod. xx. 5. xxxiv. 14. Deut. iv. 19.) This prostration consisted in falling down on the knees, and at the same time touching the ground with the forehead.

(4.) *By having altars or groves dedicated to idols, or images thereof;* all which the Mosaic law required to be utterly destroyed (Exod. xxxiv. 13. Deut. vii. 5. xii. 3.) ; and the Israelites were prohibited, by Deut. vii. 25, 26., from keeping, or even bringing into their houses, the gold and silver that had been upon any image, *lest it should prove a snare,* and lead them astray: because, having been once consecrated to an idol-god (considering the then prevalent superstition as to the reality of such deities), some idea of its sancity, or some dread of it, might still have continued, and have thus been the means of propagating idolatry afresh among their children.

(5.) *By offering sacrifices to idols,* which was expressly forbidden in Levit. xvii. 1—7., especially human victims, the sacrifices of which (it is well known) prevailed to a frightful extent. Parents immolated their offspring: this horrid practice was introduced among the Israelites, from the Canaanites, and is repeatedly reprobated by the prophets in the most pointed manner. The offering of human victims was prohibited in Levit. xviii. 21. compared with 2, 3. 24—30. xx. 1—5. Deut. xii. 30. and xviii. 10.

(6.) *By eating of offerings made to idols, made by other people,* who invited them to their offering-feasts. Though no special law was enacted against thus attending the festivals of their gods, it is evidently presupposed as unlawful in Exod. xxxiv. 15.

Idolatry was punished by stoning the guilty *individual.* When a whole city became guilty of idolatry, it was considered in a state of rebellion against the government, and was treated according to the laws of war. Its inhabitants and all their cattle were put to death; no spoil was made, but every thing which it contained was burnt, together with the city itself; nor was it ever allowed to be rebuilt. (Deut. xiii. 13—18.) This law does not appear to have been particularly enforced; the Israelites (from their proneness to adopt the then almost universally prevalent polytheism) in most cases overlooked the crime of a city that became notoriously idolatrous; whence it happened, that idolatry was not confined to any one city, but soon overspread the whole nation. In this case, when the people, *as a people,* brought guilt upon themselves by their idolatry, God reserved to himself the infliction of the punishments denounced against that national crime; which consisted in wars, famines, and other national judgments, and (when the measure of their iniquity was completed) in the destruction of their polity, and the transportation of the people as slaves into other lands. (Lev. xxvi. Deut. xxviii. xxix. xxxii.) For the crime of seducing others to the worship of strange gods, but more especially where a pretended prophet (who might often naturally anticipate what would come to pass) uttered predictions tending to lead the people into idolatry, the appointed punishment was stoning to death. (Deut. xiii. 2—12.) In order to prevent the barbarous immolation of infants, Moses denounced the punishment of stoning upon those who offered human sacrifices; which the by-standers might instantly execute upon the delinquent when caught in the act, without any judicial inquiry whatever. (Levit. xx. 2.)

2. God being both the sovereign and the legislator of the Israelites, BLASPHEMY (that is, the speaking injuriously of his name, his attributes, his government, and his revelation,) was not only a crime against Him, but also against the state; it was, therefore, punished capitally by stoning. (Levit. xxiv. 10—14.)

3. It appears from Deut. xviii. 20—22. that a FALSE PROPHET was punished capitally, being stoned to death; and there were two cases in which a person was held as convicted of the crime, and consequently liable to its punishment, viz. (1.) If he had prophesied any thing in the name of any other god, — whether it took place or not, — he was at all events considered as a false prophet, and, as such, stoned to death. (Deut. xiii. 2—6.) — (2.) If a prophet spoke in the name of the true God, he was tolerated, so long as he remained unconvicted of imposture, even though he threatened calamity or destruction to the state, and he could not be punished: but when the event which he had predicted did *not* come to pass, he was regarded as an audacious impostor, and, as such, was stoned. (Deut. xviii. 21, 22.)

4. DIVINATION is the conjecturing of future events from things which are supposed to presage them. The eastern people were always fond of divination, magic, the curious arts of interpreting dreams, and of obtaining a knowledge of future events. When Moses gave the law which bears his name to the Israelites, this disposition had long been common in Egypt and the neighbouring countries. Now, all these vain arts in order to pry into futurity, and all divination whatever, unless God was consulted by prophets, or by Urim and Thummim (the sacred lot kept by the high priest), were expressly prohibited by the statutes of Lev. xix. 26. 31. xx. 6. 23. 27. and Deut. xviii. 9—12. In the case of a person transgressing these laws, by *consulting* a diviner, God reserved to himself the infliction of his punishment; the transgressor not being amenable to the secular magistrate. (Lev. xx. 6.) The *diviner* himself was to be stoned. (Lev. xx. 27.)

5. PERJURY is, by the Mosaic law, most peremptorily prohibited as a most heinous sin against God; to whom the punishment of it is left, and who in Exod. xx. 7. expressly promises that he will inflict it, without ordaining the infliction of any punishment by the temporal magistrate; except only in the case of a man falsely charging another with a crime, in which case the false witness was liable to the same punishment which would have been inflicted on the accused party if he had been found to have been really guilty (as is shown in p. 144. *infra*); not indeed as the punishment of perjury against God, but of false witness.

II. CRIMES AGAINST PARENTS *and* MAGISTRATES constitute an important article of the criminal law of the Hebrews.

1. In the form of government among that people, we recognise much of the patriarchal spirit; in consequence of which fathers enjoyed great

rights over their families.   The CURSING OF PARENTS, — that is, not only the imprecation of evil on them, but probably also all *rude* and *reproachful language* towards them, was punished with death.   (Exod. xxi. 17. Levit. xx. 9.); as likewise was the *striking* of them.   (Exod. xxi. 15.)   An example of the crime of cursing of a parent, which is fully in point, is given by Jesus Christ in Matt. xv. 4—6. or Mark vii. 9—12.; " where he upbraids the Pharisees with their giving, from their deference to human traditions and doctrines, such an exposition of the divine law, as converted an action, which, by the law of Moses, would have been punished with death,into a vow, both obligatory and acceptable in the sight óf God. It seems, that it was then not uncommon for an undutiful and degenerate son, who wanted to be rid of the burden of supporting his parents, and in his wrath, to turn them adrift upon the wide world, to say to his father or mother, *Korban*, or, *Be that Korban* (consecrated) *which I should appropriate to thy support;* that is, *Every thing wherewith I might ever aid or serve thee*, and, of course, *every thing, which I ought to devote to thy relief in the days of helpless old age, I here vow unto God.* — A most abominable vow, indeed! and which God would, unquestionably, as little approve or accept, as he would a vow to commit adultery.   And yet some of the Pharisees pronounced on such vows this strange decision ; that they were absolutely obligatory, and that the son, who uttered such words, was bound to abstain from contributing, in the smallest article, to the use of his parents, because every thing, that should have been so appropriated, had become consecrated to God, and could no longer be applied to their use, without sacrilege and a breach of his vow.   But on this exposition, Christ not only remarked, that it abrogated the fifth commandment, but he likewise added, as a counter-doctrine, that Moses, their own legislator, had expressly declared, that *the man who cursed father or mother deserved to die.* Now, it is impossible for a man to curse his parents more effectually, than by a vow like this, when he interprets it with such rigour, as to preclude him from doing any thing in future for their benefit.   It is not imprecating upon them a curse in the common style of curses, which evaporate into air ; but it is fulfilling the curse, and making it to all intents and purposes effectual." [1]

Of the two crimes above noticed, the act of striking a parent evinces the most depraved and wicked disposition : and severe as the punishment was, few parents would apply to a magistrate, until all methods had been tried in vain.   Both these crimes are included in the case of the stubborn, rebellious, and drunkard son ; whom his parents were unable to keep in order, and who, when intoxicated, endangered the lives of others.   Such an irreclaimable offender was to be punished with stoning. (Deut. xxi. 18—21.)   Severe as this law may *seem*, we have no instance recorded of its being carried into effect ; but it must have had a most salutary operation in the prevention of crimes, in a climate like that of Palestine, where (as in all southern climates) liquor produces more formidable effects than with us, and where also it is most probable that at that time, the people had not the same efficacious means which we possess, of securing drunkards, and preventing them from doing mischief.

---

[1] Michaelis's Commentaries, vol. iv. p. 300.

2. Civil government being an ordinance of God, provision is made in all well regulated states for respecting the persons of MAGISTRATES. We have seen in a former chapter[1], that when the regal government was established among the Israelites, the person of the king was inviolable, even though he might be tyrannical and unjust. It is indispensably necessary to the due execution of justice that the persons of magistrates be sacred, and that they should not be insulted in the discharge of their office. All reproachful words or curses uttered against persons invested with authority, are prohibited in Exod. xxii. 28. No punishment, however, is specified; probably it was left to the discretion of the judge, and was different according to the rank of the magistrate and the extent of the crime.

III. The CRIMES or offences AGAINST PROPERTY, mentioned by Moses, are theft, man-stealing, and the denial of any thing taken in trust, or found.

1. On the crime of THEFT, Moses imposed the punishment of double (and in certain cases still higher) restitution; and if the thief were unable to make it, (which, however, could rarely happen, as every Israelite by law had his paternal field, the crops of which might be attached,) he was ordered to be sold for a slave, and payment was to be made to the injured party out of the purchase-money. (Exod. xxii. 1. 3.) The same practice obtains, according to Chardin, among the Persians. The wisdom of this regulation is much greater than the generality of mankind are aware of; for, as the desire of gain and the love of luxuries are the prevalent inducements to theft, restitution, varied according to circumstances, would effectually prevent the unlawful gratification of that desire, while the idle man would be deterred from stealing by the dread of slavery, in which he would be compelled to work by the power of blows. If, however, a thief was found breaking into a house in the night season, he might be killed (Exod. xxii. 2.) but not if the sun had arisen, in which case he might be known and apprehended, and the restitution made which was enjoined by Moses. When stolen oxen or sheep were found in the possession of a thief, he was to make a *two-fold* restitution to the owner, who thus obtained a profit for his risk of loss. (Exod. xxii. 4.) This punishment was applicable to every case in which the article stolen remained unaltered in his possession. But if it was already alienated or slaughtered, the criminal was to restore *four-fold* for a *sheep*, and *five-fold* for an *ox* (Exod. xxii. 1.), in consequence of its great value and indispensable utility in agriculture, to the Israelites, who had no horses. In the time of Solomon, when property had become more valuable from the increase of commerce, the punishment of restitution was increased to *seven-fold*. (Prov. vi. 30, 31.) When a thief had nothing to pay, he was sold as a slave (Exod. xxii. 3.), probably for as many years as were necessary for the extinction of the debt, and of course, perhaps, for life; though in other cases the Hebrew servant could be made to serve only for six years. If, however, a thief — after having denied, even upon oath, any theft, with which he was charged, — had the honesty or conscience to retract his perjury, and to confess his guilt, instead of double restitution, he had only to repay the amount stolen, and one *fifth* more. (Levit. vi. 2—5.)

---

[1] See p. 89. *supra.*

2. MAN-STEALING, that is, the seizing or stealing of the person of a free-born Israelite, either to use him as a slave himself, or to sell him as a slave to others, was absolutely and irremissibly punished with death. (Exod. xxi. 16. Deut. xxiv. 7.)

3. " Where a person was judically convicted of having DENIED ANY THING COMMITTED TO HIS TRUST, or found by him, his punishment, as in the case of theft, was double restitution ; only that it never, as in that crime, went so far as quadruple, or quintuple restitution ; at least nothing of this kind is ordained in Exod. xxii. 8. If the person accused of this crime had sworn himself guiltless, and afterwards, from the impulse of his conscience, acknowledged the commission of perjury, he had only one-fifth beyond the value of the article denied to refund to its owner." (Levit. vi. 5.)

4. The Mosaic laws respecting DEBTORS were widely different from those which obtain in European countries : the mode of procedure sanctioned by them, though simple, was very efficient. Persons, who had property due to them, might, if they chose, secure it either by means of a mortgage, or by a pledge, or by a bondsman or surety.

(1.) The creditor, when about to receive a pledge for a debt, was not allowed to enter the debtor's house, and take what he pleased; but was to wait before the door, till the debtor should deliver up that pledge with which he could most easily dispense. (Deut. xxiv. 10, 11. Compare Job xxii. 6. xxiv. 3. 7—9.)

(2.) When a mill or mill-stone, or an upper garment, was given as a pledge, it was not to be kept all night. These articles appear to be specified as examples for all other things, with which the debtor could not dispense without great inconvenience. (Exod. xxii. 26, 27. Deut. xxiv. 6. 12.)

(3.) The debt which remained unpaid until the seventh or sabbatic year (during which the soil was to be left without cultivation, and, consequently, a person was not supposed to be in a condition to make payments,) could not be exacted during that period. (Deut. xv. 1—11.) But, at other times, in case the debt was not paid, the creditor might seize, first, the *hereditary land* of the debtor, and enjoy its produce until the debt was paid, or at least until the year of jubilee; or, secondly, his *houses*. These might be sold in perpetuity, except those belonging to the Levites. (Levit. xxv. 14—32.) Thirdly, in case the house or land was not sufficient to cancel the debt, or if it so happened that the debtor had none, the *person* of the debtor might be sold, together with his wife and children, if he had any. This is implied in Lev. xxv. 39.: and this custom is alluded to in Job xxiv. 9. It existed in the time of Elisha (2 Kings iv. 1.); and on the return of the Jews from the Babylonish captivity, some rich persons exercised this right over their poor debtors. (Nehem. v. 1—13.) Our Lord alludes to the same custom in Matt. xviii. 25. As the person of the debtor might thus be seized and sold, his *cattle* and *furniture* were, consequently, liable for his debts. This is alluded to by Solomon, in Prov. xxii. 27. It does not appear that imprisonment for debt existed in the age of Moses, but it seems to have prevailed in the time of Jesus Christ. (Matt. xviii. 34.)

(4.) If a person had become bondsman, or surety for another, he was liable to be called upon for payment in the same way with the original debtor. But this practice does not appear to have obtained before the time of Solomon (in whose Proverbs there are several references to it), when it was attended with serious consequences. It seems that the formality observed was, for the person who became surety *to give his hand to the debtor*, and not to the creditor, to intimate that he became, in a legal sense, one with the debtor; for Solomon cautions his son against giving his hand to a *stranger*, to a person whose circumstances he did not know: and intreats him to go and urge the person to whom he had given his hand, or for whom he had become surety, to pay his own debt; so that it must have been to the debtor that the hand was given. See Prov. xi. 15. xvii. 18. and xxii. 26.

IV. Among the CRIMES which may be committed AGAINST THE PERSON,

1. MURDER claims the first place. As this is a crime of the most heinous nature, Moses has described four accessory circumstances or marks, by which to distinguish it from simple homicide or manslaughter; viz. (1.) When it proceeds from *hatred* or enmity. (Numb. xxxv. 20, 21. Deut. xix. 11.) — (2.) When it proceeds from *thirst* of blood, or a desire to satiate revenge with the blood of another. (Numb. xxxv. 20.) — (3.) When it is committed *premeditatedly and deceitfully.* (Exod. xxi. 14.) — (4.) When a man lies in wait for another, falls upon him, and slays him. (Deut. xix. 11.) In order to constitute wilful murder, besides enmity, Moses deemed it essential, that the deed be perpetrated by a blow, a thrust, or a cast, or other thing of such a nature as inevitably to cause death. (Numb. xxxv. 16—21.): such as, the use of an iron tool, — a stone, or piece of wood, that may probably cause death, — the striking of a man with the fist, out of enmity, — pushing a man down in such a manner that his life is endangered,— and throwing any thing at a man, from sanguinary motives, so as to occasion his death. The punishment of murder was death, without all power of redemption.

2. HOMICIDE or MANSLAUGHTER is discriminated by the following adjuncts or circumstances: — (1.) That it takes place *without* hatred or enmity. (Numb. xxxv. 22. Deut. xix. 4—6.) — (2.) *Without* thirst for revenge. (Exod. xxi. 13. Numb. xxxv. 22.) — (3.) When it happens by mistake. (Numb. xxxv. 11. 15.) — (4.) By *accident* or (as it is termed in the English law) *chance-medley*. (Deut. xix. 5.) The punishment of homicide was confinement to a city of refuge, as will be shown in the following section.

Besides the two crimes of murder and homicide, there are two other species of homicide, to which no punishment was annexed; viz. (1.) If a man caught a thief breaking into his house by night, and killed him, *it was not blood-guiltiness*, that is, he could not be punished; but if he did so when the sun was up, it was *blood-guiltiness;* for the thief's life ought to have been spared, for the reason annexed to the law (Exod. xxii. 2, 3.), viz. because then the person robbed might have it in his power to obtain restitution; or, at any rate, the thief, if he could not otherwise make up his loss, might be sold, in order to repay him. — (2.) If the Goël or avenger of blood overtook the innocent homicide before he reached a city of refuge, and killed him while his *heart was hot*, it was considered as done in justifiable zeal (Deut.

xix. 6.) ; and even if he found him without the limits of his asylum, and slew him, he was not punishable. (Numb. xxxv. 26, 27.) The taking of pecuniary compensation for murder was prohibited ; but the *mode* of punishing murderers was undetermined : and, indeed, it appears to have been left in a great degree to the pleasure of the Goël. An exception, however, was made to the severity of the law in the case of a perfect slave, (that is, one not of Hebrew descent,) whether male or female. Although a man had struck any of his slaves, whether male or female, with a stick, so as to cause their death, unless that event took place immediately, and under his hand, he was not punished. If the slave survived one or two days, the master escaped with impunity : it being considered that his death might not have proceeded from the beating, and that it was not a master's interest to kill his slave, because, as Moses says (Exod. xxi. 20, 21.), *they are his money.* If the slave died under his master's hand while beating him, or even during the same day, his death was to be avenged ; but in what manner Moses has not specified. Probably the Israelitish master was subjected only to an arbitrary punishment, regulated according to circumstances by the pleasure of the judge.

In order to increase an abhorrence of murder, and to deter them from the perpetration of so heinous a crime, — when it had been committed by some person unknown, the city nearest to which the corpse was found was to be ascertained by mensuration : after which the elders or magistrates of that city were required to declare their utter ignorance of the affair in the very solemn manner prescribed in Deut. xxi. 1—9.

3. For other CORPORAL INJURIES of various kinds, different statutes were made, which show the humanity and wisdom of the Mosaic law. Thus, if a man injured another in a *fray*, he was obliged to pay the expenses of his cure, and of his bed, that is, the loss of his time arising from his confinement. (Exod. xxi. 18, 19.) By this admirable precept, most courts of justice still regulate their decisions in such cases. — If a pregnant woman was hurt, in consequence of a fray between two individuals, — as posterity among the Jews was among the peculiar promises of their covenant, — in the event of her premature delivery, the author of the misfortune was obliged to give her husband such a pecuniary compensation as he might demand, the amount of which, if the offender thought it too high, was to be determined by the decision of arbitrators. On the other hand, if either the woman or her child was hurt or maimed, the law of retaliation took its full effect, as stated in Exod. xxi. 22—25. — The law of retaliation also operated, if one man hurt another by either assaulting him openly, or by any insidious attack, whether the parties were both Israelites, or an Israelite and a foreigner. (Levit. xxiv. 19—22.) This equality of the law, however, did not extend to slaves : but if a master knocked out the eye or tooth of a slave, the latter received his freedom as a compensation for the injury he had sustained. (Exod. xxi. 26, 27.) If this noble law did not teach the unmerciful slave-holder *humanity*, at least it taught him caution ; as one rash blow might have deprived him of all right to the future services of his slave, and, consequently, self-interest would oblige him to be cautious and circumspect.

4. The crime, of which decency withholds the name, as nature abo-

minates the idea, was punished with death (Levit. xviii. 22, 23. xx. 13. 15, 16.), as also was adultery [1] (Levit. xx. 10.), — it should seem by stoning (Ezek. xvi. 38. 40. John viii. 7.), except in certain cases which are specified in Levit. xix. 20—22. Other crimes of lust, which were common among the Egyptians and Canaanites, are made capital by Moses. For a full examination of the wisdom of his laws on these subjects, the reader is referred to the Commentaries of Michaelis.[2]

V. In nothing, however, were the wisdom and equity of the Mosaic law more admirably displayed, than in the rigour with which CRIMES OF MALICE were punished. Those pests of society, malicious informers, were odious in the eye of that law (Levit. xix. 16—18.), and the publication of false reports, affecting the characters of others, is expressly prohibited in Exod. xxiii. 1.: though that statute does not annex any punishment to this crime. One exception, however, is made, which justly imposes a very severe punishment on the delinquent. See Deut. xxii. 13—19. All manner of false witness was prohibited (Exod. xx. 16.), even though it were to favour a poor man. (Exod. xxiii. 1—3.) But in the case of false testimony against an innocent man, the matter was ordered to be investigated with the utmost strictness, and, as a species of wickedness altogether extraordinary, to be brought before the highest tribunal, where the priests and the judges of the whole people sat in judgment: and, after conviction, the false witness was subjected to punishment, according to the law of retaliation, and beyond the possibility of reprieve; so that he suffered the very same punishment which attended the crime of which he accused his innocent brother. (Deut. xix. 16—21.) No regulation can be more equitable than this, which must have operated as a powerful prevention of this crime. Some of those excellent laws, which are the glory and ornament of the British Constitution, have been made on this very ground. Thus, in the 37 Edw. III. c. 18., it is enacted, that all those who make suggestion, shall suffer the same penalty to which the other party would have been subject, if he were attainted, in case his suggestions be found evil. A similar law was made in the same reign. (38 Edw. III. c. 9.) By a law of the twelve tables, false witnesses were thrown down the Tarpeian rock. In short, false witnesses have been deservedly execrated by all nations, and in every age.

---

[1] As the Jewish law inflicted such heavy punishments on those who committed fornication and adultery, it is probable, from Prov. ii. 16., that the Jews had harlots among them from the neighbouring nations, who seduced them into impurity and idolatry, and who might be tolerated in some corrupt periods of their state. The case was the same at Athens, where foreign harlots were tolerated. Hence the term *strange women*, came to be applied to all bad women, whether foreigners or Israelites. Orton's Exposition, vol. v. p. 6.

[2] Vol. iv. pp. 163—203.

SECTION IV.

ON THE PUNISHMENTS MENTIONED IN THE SCRIPTURES.[1]

Design of Punishments. — Classification of Jewish Punishments. — I. Pu-
NISHMENTS, NOT CAPITAL.— 1. *Scourging.* — 2. *Retaliation.* — 3. *Pecuniary Fines.*—4. *Offerings in the Nature of Punishment.*—5. *Imprisonment.*
—6. *Banishment.* — *Oriental Mode of treating Prisoners.* — 7. *Depriving
them of Sight.* — 8. *Cutting or Plucking off the Hair.* — 9. *Excommunication.* — II. CAPITAL PUNISHMENTS. — 1. *Slaying with the Sword.* —
2. *Stoning.* — 3. *Burning to Death.* —4. *Decapitation.* — 5. *Precipitation.*
—6. *Drowning.* — 7. *Bruising in a Mortar.* — 8. *Dichotomy, or cutting
asunder.* — 9. Τυμπανισμος, *or beating to Death.* — 10. *Exposing to wild
Beasts.*— 11. *Crucifixion.*— (1.) *Prevalence of this Mode of Punishment
among the Antients.* (— 2.) *Ignominy of Crucifixion.* — (3.) *The Circumstances of our Saviour's Crucifixion considered and illustrated.*

THE end of punishment is expressed by Moses to be the determent
of others from the commission of crimes. His language is, that *others
may hear and fear, and may shun the commission of like crimes.* (Deut.
xvii. 13. xix. 20.) By the wise and humane enactments of this legislator, parents are not to be put to death for their children, nor children
for their parents (Deut. xxiv. 16.) as was afterwards the case with the
Chaldæans (Dan. vi. 24.), and also among the kings of Israel (1 Kings
xxi. and 2 Kings ix. 26.), on charges of treason.[2] Of the punishments
mentioned in the sacred writers, some were inflicted by the Jews in
common with other nations, and others were peculiar to themselves.
They are usually divided into two classes, *non-capital* and *capital.*

I. The NON-CAPITAL or inferior PUNISHMENTS, which were inflicted
for smaller offences, are eight in number; viz.

1. The most common corporal punishment of the antient Mosaic
law was SCOURGING. (Lev. xix. 20. Deut. xxii. 18. xxv. 2, 3.) After
the captivity it continued to be the usual punishment for transgressions
of the law, so late indeed as the time of Josephus[3]; and the Apostle
tells us that he suffered it *five* times.[4] (2 Cor. xi. 24.) In the time of
our Saviour it was not confined to the judicial tribunals, but was also
inflicted in the synagogues. (Matt. x. 17. xxiii. 34. Acts xxii. 19.
xxvi. 11.) The penalty of scourging was inflicted by judicial sentence.
The offender having been admonished to acknowledge his guilt, and
the witnesses produced against him as in capital cases, the judges commanded him to be tied by the arms to a low pillar : the culprit being
stripped down to his waist, the executioner, who stood behind him
upon a stone, inflicted the punishment both on the back and breast

---

[1] The general authorities for this section are, Schulzii Archæologia Hebraica, pp. 82.—
92. Calmet, Dissertation sur les Supplices des Hébreux, Dissert. tom. i. pp. 241—276. ;
Brunings, Antiq. Hebr. pp. 107—114. ; Alber, Hermeneut. Vet. Test. tom. i. pp. 225
—233. C. B. Michaelis, de judiciis, poenisque capitalibus Hebræorum, in Pott's and
Ruperti's Sylloge Commentationum, vol. iv. pp. 177—239. ; Jahn, Archæologia Biblica,
§§ 249—255. ; Ackermann, Archæologia Biblica, §§ 243—258.

[2] Michaelis's Commentaries, vol. iv. p. 371. vol. iii. pp. 400—402. 404.

[3] Ant. Jud. lib. iv. c. 8. § 11.

[4] In inflicting the punishment of whipping, the Jews sometimes, for notorious offences,
tied sharp bones, pieces of lead, or thorns to the end of the thongs, called by the Greeks,
αστραγαλωλας μαστιγας, *flagra taxillata ;* but in the Scriptures termed scorpions. To these
Rehoboam alludes in 1 Kings xii. 11.—Burder's Oriental Literature, vol. i. p. 414.

with thongs ordinarily made of ox's hide or leather. The number of stripes depended upon the enormity of the offence. According to the talmudical writers [1], while the executioner was discharging his office, the principal judge proclaimed these words with a loud voice : *If thou observest not all the words of this law, &c. then the Lord shall make thy plagues wonderful, &c.* (Deut. xxviii. 58, 59.) ; adding, *Keep therefore the words of this covenant, and do them, that ye may prosper in all that ye do* (Deut. xxix. 9.) ; and concluding with these words of the Psalmist (lxxviii. 38.) : — *But he being full of compassion forgave their iniquities ;* which he was to repeat, if he had finished these verses before the full number of stripes was given. It was expressly enacted that no Jew should suffer more than forty stripes for any crime, though a less number might be inflicted. In order that the legal number might not be exceeded, the scourge consisted of three lashes or thongs : so that, at each blow, he received three stripes : consequently when the full punishment was inflicted, the delinquent received only thirteen blows, that is, *forty stripes save one ;* but if he were so weak, as to be on the point of fainting away, the judges would order the executioner to suspend his flagellation. Among the Romans, however, the number was not limited, but varied according to the crime of the malefactor and the discretion of the judge. It is highly probable that, when *Pilate took Jesus and scourged him,* he directed this scourging to be unusually severe, that the sight of his lacerated body might move the Jews to compassionate the prisoner, and desist from opposing his release. This appears the more probable ; as our Saviour was so enfeebled by this scourging, that he afterwards had not strength enough left to enable him to drag his cross to Calvary. Among the Jews, the punishment of scourging involved no sort of ignominy, which could make the sufferer infamous or an object of reproach to his fellow-citizens. It consisted merely in the physical sense of the pain.[2]

2. RETALIATION, or the returning of like for like, was the punishment inflicted for corporal injuries to another,—*eye for eye, tooth for tooth, hand for hand, foot for foot.* (Exod. xxi. 24.) It appears, however, to have been rarely, if ever, strictly put in execution : but the injurious party was to give the injured person satisfaction. In this sense the ταυτοπαθεια among the Greeks, and the *Lex Talionis* among the Romans, was understood ; and an equivalent was accepted, the value of an eye, a tooth, &c. for the eye or tooth itself. It should seem that in the time of Jesus Christ, the Jews had made this law (the execution of which belonged to the civil magistrate) a ground for authorising private resentments, and all the excesses committed by a vindictive spirit. Revenge was carried to the utmost extremity, and more evil returned than what had been received. On this account our Saviour prohibited retaliation in his divine sermon on the mount. (Matt. v. 38, 39.)

3. RESTITUTION. — Justice requires that those things which have been stolen or unlawfully taken from another should be restored to the party aggrieved, and that compensation should be made to him by the aggressor. Accordingly, various fines or pecuniary payments were enacted by the Mosaic law ; as,

---

[1] Cited by Dr. Lightfoot, Works, vol. i. p. 901. folio edit.
[2] Michaelis's Commentaries, vol. iii. pp. 444—448.

(1.) *Fines,* עֹנֶשׁ (oNesh), strictly so called, went commonly to the injured party; and were of two kinds,—*Fixed,* that is, those of which the amount was determined by some statute, as for instance, that of Deut. xxii. 19. or xxii. 29.;—and *Undetermined,* or where the amount was left to the decision of the judges. (Exod. xxi. 22.)

(2.) Two-fold, four-fold, and even five-fold, *restitution* of things stolen, and restitution of property unjustly retained, with twenty per cent. over and above. Thus, if a man killed a beast, he was to make it good, beast for beast. (Levit. xxiv. 18.)—If an ox pushed or gored another man's servant to death, his owner was bound to pay for the servant thirty shekels of silver. (Exod. xxi. 32.)—In the case of one man's ox pushing the ox of another man to death, as it would be very difficult to ascertain which of the two had been to blame for the quarrel, the two owners were obliged to bear the loss. The living ox was to be sold, and its price, together with the dead beast, was to be equally divided between them. If, however, one of the oxen had previously been notorious for pushing, and the owner had not taken care to confine him, in such case he was to give the loser another, and to take the dead ox himself. (Exod. xxi. 36.)—If a man dug a pit and did not cover it, or let an old pit remain open, and another man's beast fell into it, the owner of such pit was obliged to pay for the beast, and had it for the payment. (Exod. xxi. 33, 34.)—When a fire was kindled in the fields and did any damage, he who kindled it was to make the damage good. (Exod. xxii. 6.)[1]

(3.) *Compensation,* not commanded, but only allowed, by law, to be given to a person injured, that he might depart from his suit, and not insist on the legal punishment, whether corporal or capital. It is termed either כֹּפֶר (kopheR), that is *Compensation* or פִּדְיוֹן נֶפֶשׁ (pidjon Nephesh), that is, *Ransom of Life.* In one case it is most expressly permitted (Exod. xxi. 30.); but it is prohibited in the case of murder and also in homicide. (Numb. xxxv. 31, 32.) The highest fine leviable by the law of Moses, was *one hundred shekels* of silver, a great sum in those times, when the precious metals were rare.[2]

4. To this class of punishments may be referred the *Sin* and *Trespass* OFFERINGS, which were IN THE NATURE OF PUNISHMENTS. They were in general extremely moderate, and were enjoined in the following cases : —

(1.) For every unintentional transgression of the Levitical law, even if it was a sin of *commission,* (for in the Mosaic doctrine concerning sin and trespass offerings, all transgressions are divided into sins of *commission,* and sins of *omission,*) a sin-offering was to be made, and thereupon the legal punishment was remitted, which, in the case of wilful transgression, was nothing less than extirpation. (Lev. iv. 2. v. 1. 4—7.)

(2.) Whoever had made a rash oath, and had not kept it, was obliged to make a sin-offering; for his inconsideration, if it was an oath to do evil, and for his neglect, if it was an oath to do good. (Lev. v. 4.)

(3.) Whoever had, as a witness, been guilty of perjury—not, however, to impeach an innocent man (for in that case the *lex talionis*

---

[1] Michaelis's Commentaries, vol. ii. pp. 365—367. 477, 478.
[2] Ibid. pp. 478, 479.

operated), but — in not testifying what he knew against a guilty person, or in any other respect concerning the matter in question; and in consequence thereof felt disquieted in his conscience, might, without being liable to any farther punishment, or ignominy, obtain remission of the perjury, by a confession of it, accompanied with a trespass-offering. (Lev. v. 1.)

(4.) Whoever had incurred debt to the sanctuary, that is, had not conscientiously paid his tithes, had his crime cancelled by making a trespass-offering, and making up his deficiencies with twenty per cent. over and above. (Lev. v. 14, 15.)

(5.) The same was the rule, where a person denied any thing given him in trust, or any thing lost, which he had found, or any promise he had made; or again, where he had acquired any property dishonestly, and had his conscience awakened on account of it, — even where it was a theft, of which he had once cleared himself by oath, but was now moved by the impulse of his conscience to make voluntary restitution, and wished to get rid of the guilt. (Lev. vi. 1—7.) By the offering made on such an occasion, the preceding crime was wholly cancelled; and because the delinquent would otherwise have had to make restitution from *two* to *five* fold, he now gave twenty per cent. over and above the amount of his theft.

(6.) In the case of adultery committed with a slave, an offering was appointed by Lev. xix. 20—22.: which did not, however, wholly cancel the punishment, but mitigated it from death, which was the established punishment of adultery, to that of stripes for the woman, the man bringing the trespass-offering in the manner directed by Moses.[1]

Such measures as these, Michaelis remarks, must have had a great effect in prompting to the restitution of property unjustly acquired: but in the case of crimes, of which the good of the community expressly required that the legal punishment should uniformly and actually be put in execution, no such offering could be accepted.[2]

5. IMPRISONMENT does not appear to have been imposed by Moses as a punishment, though he could not be unacquainted with it; for he describes it as in use among the Egyptians. (Gen. xxxix. 20, 21.) The only time he mentions it, or more properly *arrest*, is solely for the purpose of keeping the culprit safe until judgment should be given on his conduct. (Lev. xxiv. 12.) In later times, however, the punishment of the prison came into use among the Israelites and Jews; whose history, under the monarchs, abounds with instances of their imprisoning persons, especially the prophets, who were obnoxious to them for their faithful reproofs of their sins and crimes. Thus, Asa committed the prophet Hanani to prison, for reproving him (2 Chron. xvi. 10.)[3]; Ahab committed Micaiah (1 Kings xxii. 27.), as Zedekiah did the prophet Jeremiah, for the same offence. (Jer. xxxvii. 21.) John the Baptist was imprisoned by Herod, misnamed the Great (Matt. iv. 12.); and Peter, by Herod Agrippa. (Acts xii. 4.) Debtors (Matt.

---

[1] Michaelis's Commentaries, vol. iii. pp. 482—487.

[2] Ibid. p. 488.

[3] This place is termed the *prison-house :* but it appears that suspected persons were sometimes confined in part of the house which was occupied by the great officers of state, and was converted into a prison for this purpose. In this manner Jeremiah was at first confined (Jer. xxxvii. 15.), and probably Joseph in the same manner (see Gen. xl. 3.): a similar practice obtains in the East to this day. See Harmer's Observations, vol. iii. p. 503.

xviii. 30.) and murderers (Luke xxiii. 19.) were also committed to prison. We read also of Τηρησις Δημοσια, a common prison, a public gaol (Acts v. 18.), which was a place of durance and confinement for the worst sort of offenders. In their prisons, there was usually a dungeon (Jer. xxxviii. 6.) or a *pit* or *cistern*, as the word בּוֹר (BOR) is rendered in Zech. ix. 11. where it unquestionably refers to a prison: and from this word we may conceive the nature of a dungeon, viz. that it was a place, in which indeed there was no water, but in its bottom *deep mud;* and, accordingly, we read that Jeremiah, who was cast into this worst and lowest part of the prison, *sunk into the mire.* (Jer. xxxviii. 6.)[1]

In the prisons also were *Stocks,* for detaining the person of the prisoner more securely. (Job xiii. 27. xxxiii. 11.)[2] Michaelis conjectures that they were of the sort by the Greeks called Πεντεσυριγγον, wherein the prisoner was so confined, that his body was kept in an unnatural position, which must have proved a torture truly insupportable.[3] The Εσωτερα Φυλακη, or *Inner Prison,* into which Paul and Silas were *thrust* at Philippi, is supposed to have been the same as the pit or cistern above noticed; and here *their feet were made fast in the wooden stocks* (Acts xvi. 24.), το ξυλον. As this prison was under the Roman government, these stocks are supposed to have been the *cippi* or large pieces of wood in use among that people, which not only loaded the legs of prisoners, but sometimes distended them in a very painful manner. Hence the situation of Paul and Silas would be rendered more painful than that of an offender sitting in the stocks, as used among us; especially if (as is very possible) they lay on the hard or dirty ground, with their bare backs, lacerated by recent scourging.[4]

The keepers of the prison antiently had, as in the East they still have, a discretionary power to treat their prisoners just as they please; nothing further being required of them, than to produce them when called for. According to the accurate and observant traveller, Chardin, the gaoler is master, to do as he pleases; to treat his prisoner well or ill; to put him in irons or not, to shut him up closely, or to hold him in easier restraint; to admit persons to him, or to suffer no one to see him. If the gaoler and his servants receive large fees, however base may be the character of the prisoner, he shall be lodged in the best part of the gaoler's own apartment: and, on the contrary, if the persons, who have caused the prisoner to be confined, make the gaoler greater presents, he will treat his victim with the utmost inhumanity. Chardin illustrates this statement by a narrative of the treatment received by a very great Armenian merchant. While he bribed the gaoler, the latter treated him with the greatest lenity; but afterwards, when the adverse party presented a considerable sum of money, first to the judge, and afterwards to the gaoler, the hapless Armenian first felt his privileges retrenched: he was next closely confined, and then was treated with such inhumanity, as not to be permitted to drink

---

[1] Michaelis's Commentaries, vol. iii. pp. 439—442.. Schulzii Archæol. Hebr. pp. 84, 85.
[2] The word rendered *stocks* in our authorised version of Jer. xx. 2. and xxix. 26. ought to have been rendered *house of correction.* See Dr. Blayney's notes on those passages.
[3] Michaelis's Commentaries, vol. iii. p. 443.
[4] Doddridge's Expositor, and Kuinöel, on Acts xvi. 24. Biscoe on Acts, vol. i. p. 348.

oftener than once in twenty-four hours, even during the hottest time
in the summer. No person was allowed to approach him but the
servants of the prison : at length he was thrown into a dungeon, where
he was in a quarter of an hour brought to the point to which all this
severe usage was designed to force him.[1] What energy does this
account of an Eastern prison give to those passages of Scripture, which
speak of the *soul coming into iron* (Psal. cv. 17. marginal rendering),
of *the sorrowful* SIGHING *of the prisoner coming before God* (Psal. lxxix.
11.), and of Jeremiah's being kept in a dungeon many days, and supplicating that he might not be remanded thither lest he should die !
(Jer. xxxvii. 16—20.)

6. BANISHMENT was not a punishment enjoined by the Mosaic law;
but after the captivity, both exile and forfeiture of property were introduced among the Jews : and it also existed under the Romans, by
whom it was called *diminutio capitis*, because the person banished lost
the right of a citizen, and the city of Rome thereby lost a head.[2] But
there was another kind of exile, termed *disportatio*, which was accounted
the worst kind. The party banished forfeited his estate; and being
bound was put on board ship, and transported to some island specified
exclusively by the emperor, there to be confined in perpetual banishment. In this manner the apostle John was exiled to the little island
of Patmos (Rev. i. 9.), where he wrote his Revelation.

7. In the East, antiently, it was the custom to PUT OUT THE EYES
OF PRISONERS. Thus Samson was deprived of sight by the Philistines
(Judg. xvi. 21.), and Zedekiah by the Chaldees. (2 Kings xxv. 7.)
It is well known that cutting out one or both of the eyes has been
frequently practised in Persia and other parts of the East, as a punishment for treasonable offences.[3] To the great work of restoring eye-
balls to the sightless by the Messiah, the prophet Isaiah probably
alludes in his beautiful prediction cited by our Lord, and applied to
himself in Luke iv. 18.[4]

8. CUTTING OFF THE HAIR of criminals seems to be rather an ignominious than a painful mode of punishment: yet it appears that pain
was added to the disgrace, and that the hair was violently plucked off,
as if the executioner were plucking a bird alive. This is the literal
meaning of the original word, which in Neh. xiii. 25. is rendered
plucked off their hair; sometimes hot ashes were applied to the skin
after the hair was torn off, in order to render the pain more exquisitely
acute. In the spurious book, commonly termed the fourth book of
Maccabees, is is said that the tyrant Antiochus Epiphanes caused the
hair and skin to be entirely torn off the heads of some of the seven
Maccabean brethren. As an historical composition this book is utterly
destitute of credit; but it shows that the mode of punishment under

---

1 Harmer's Observations, vol. iii. pp. 504, 505.

2 Dr. Adam's Roman Antiquities, pp. 66, 67.

3 In 1820, Mr. Rae Wilson met, at Acre, with numerous individuals, who exhibited
marks of the vengeance of the late pacha Hadjee Achmet, from his sanguinary cruelties
fitly surnamed *Djezzar*, or the Butcher. They were disfigured in various ways, by a hand
amputated, *an eye torn out*, or a nose which had been split, or partly or totally cut off. (Travels in the Holy Land, vol. ii. p. 43.) In the winter of 1826, two emirs had *their eyes burnt
out*, and their tongues in part cut off, by the emir Bechir, the prince of Mount Lebanon, their
uncle ; on account of their having been concerned in some disturbances against his government. (Missionary Register, July 1827, p. 333.)

4 Fragments supplementary to Calmet, No. 192.

consideration was not unusual in the East. This sort of torture is said to have been frequently inflicted on the early martyrs and confessors for the Christian faith.

9. EXCLUSION FROM SACRED WORSHIP, or EXCOMMUNICATION, was not only an ecclesiastical punishment, but also a civil one; because in this theocratic republic there was no distinction between the divine and the civil right. The fancies of the Rabbins, relative to the origin of excommunication, are endless. Some affirm, that Adam excommunicated Cain and his whole race; others, that excommunication began with Miriam, for having spoken ill of Moses; others, again, find it in the song of Deborah and Barak (Judg. v. 23. *Curse ye Meroz*), interpreting Meroz as a person who had refused to assist Barak. But it is most probable, that the earliest positive mention of this punishment occurs after the return from the Babylonish captivity, in Ezra. x. 7, 8., or in the anathema of Nehemiah (xiii. 5.) against those who had married strange women. In later times, according to the rabbinical writers, there were three degrees of excommunication among the Jews. The *first* was called נִדּוּי (N*i*DUI), removal or separation from all intercourse with society: this is, in the New Testament, frequently termed casting out of the synagogue. (John ix. 22. xvi. 2. Luke vi. 22, &c.) This was in force for thirty days, and might be shortened by repentance. During its continuance, the excommunicated party was prohibited from bathing, from shaving his head, or approaching his wife or any other person nearer than four cubits: but if he submitted to this prohibition, he was not debarred the privilege of attending the sacred rites. If, however, the party continued in his obstinacy after that time, the excommunication was renewed with additional solemn maledictions. This *second* degree was called חֵרֶם (CH*e*R*e*M), which signifies to *anathematise* or devote to death: it involved an exclusion from the sacred assemblies. The *third*, and last degree of excommunication was termed שֵׁם אָתָא (SH*a*M-*a*THA) or מָרָן אָתָא (M*a*R*a*N-ATHA), that is, *the Lord cometh*, or *may the Lord come;* intimating that those against whom it was fulminated, had nothing more to expect but the terrible day of judgment.[1]

The condition of those who were excommunicated was the most deplorable that can be imagined. They were excluded from all the rights and privileges of the Jewish people, were debarred from all social intercourse, and were excluded from the temple and the synagogues, on pain of severe corporal punishment. Whoever had incurred this sentence was loaded with imprecations, as appears from Deut. xxvii. where the expression *cursed* is *he*, is so often repeated : whence to *curse* and to *excommunicate* were equivalent terms with the Jews. And therefore St. Paul says, that *no man, speaking by the Spirit of God, calleth Jesus anathema* or *accursed* (1 Cor. xii. 3.), that is, curses Him as the Jews did, who denied him to be the Messiah, and excommunicated the Christians. In the second degree, they delivered the excommunicated party over to Satan, devoting him by a solemn curse : to this practice St. Paul is supposed to allude (1 Cor. v. 5.); and in this sense he expresses his desire even to be *accursed for his brethren*

---

[1] Robinson's Lexicon to the Gr. Test. voce Αποσυναγωγος. Jahn, Archæologia Biblica, § 258. Ackermann, Archæol. Bibl. § 252. Encyclopædia Metropolitana, vol. xxi. p. 703.

(Rom. ix. 3.), that is, to be excommunicated, laden with curses, and to suffer all the miseries consequent on the infliction of this punishment, if it could have been of any service to his brethren the Jews. In order to impress the minds of the people with the greater horror, it is said that, when the offence was published in the synagogue, all the candles were lighted, and when the proclamation was finished, they were extinguished, as a sign that the excommunicated person was deprived of the light of Heaven; further, his goods were confiscated, his sons were not admitted to circumcision; and if he died without repentance or absolution, by the sentence of the judge a stone was to be cast upon his coffin or bier, in order to show that he deserved to be stoned.[1]

II. The Talmudical writers have distinguished the CAPITAL PUNISHMENTS of the Jews into *lesser deaths*, and such as were *more grievous :* but there is no warrant in the Scriptures for these distinctions, neither are these writers agreed among themselves what particular punishments are to be referred to these two heads. A capital crime was termed, generally, a *sin of death* (Deut. xxii. 26.), or a *sin worthy of death* (Deut. xxi. 22.); which mode of expression is adopted, or rather imitated, by the apostle John, who distinguishes between a *sin unto death*, and a *sin* NOT *unto death*. (1 John v. 16.) Criminals, or those who were deemed worthy of capital punishment, were called *sons* or *men of death* (1 Sam. xx. 31. xxvi. 16. 2 Sam. xix. 29. marginal rendering); just as he who had incurred the punishment of scourging was designated a *son of stripes*. (Deut. xxv. 2. Heb.) Those who suffered a capital punishment, were said to be *put to death for their own sin*. (Deut. xxiv. 16. 2 Kings xiv. 6.) A similar phraseology was adopted by Jesus Christ, when he said to the Jews, *Ye shall die in your sins*. (John viii. 21. 24.) Eleven different sorts of capital punishments are mentioned in the Sacred Writings; viz.

1. SLAYING WITH THE SWORD is commonly confounded with decapitation or beheading. They were, however, two distinct punishments. The laws of Moses are totally silent concerning the latter practice, and it appears that those who were slain with the sword were put to death in any way which the executioner thought proper. See 1 Kings ii. 25. 29. 31. 34. 46. This punishment was inflicted in two cases:— (1.) When a murderer was to be put to death; and (2.) When a whole city or tribe was hostilely attacked for any common crime, *they smote all* (as the Hebrew phrase is) *with the edge of the sword*. (Deut. xiii. 13—16.) Here, doubtless, the sword was used by every one as he found opportunity.[2]

With respect to the case of murder, frequent mention is made in the Old Testament of the גֹאֵל (GOËL) or *blood-avenger;* various regulations were made by Moses concerning this person.

The inhabitants of the East, it is well known, are now, what they antiently were, exceedingly revengeful. If, therefore, an individual should unfortunately happen to lay violent hands upon another person and kill him, the next of kin is bound to avenge the death of the latter,

---

[1] Grotius's Note, or rather Dissertation, on Luke vi. 22. Lightfoot's Works, vol. ii. pp. 747—749. Selden, de Jure Naturæ et Gentium, lib. iv. c. 8. Lamy's Apparatus Biblicus, vol. i. pp. 279—284.

[2] Michaelis's Commentaries, vol. iii. pp. 418, 419.

and to pursue the murderer with unceasing vigilance until he have caught and killed him, either by force or by fraud. The same custom exists in Arabia and Persia [1], and also among the Circassians [2], Ingush Tartars [3], Nubians [4], and Abyssinians [5], and it appears to have been alluded to by Rebecca: when she learned that Esau was threatening to kill his brother Jacob, she endeavoured to send the latter out of the country, saying, *Why should I be bereft of you both in one day?* (Gen. xxvii. 15.) She could not be afraid of the magistrate for punishing the murder, for the patriarchs were subject to no superior in Palestine: and Isaac was much too partial to Esau, for her to entertain any expectation that *he* would condemn him to death for it. It would, therefore, appear that she dreaded lest he should fall by the hand of the *blood-avenger*, perhaps of some Ishmaelite. The office, therefore, of the Goël was in use before the time of Moses, and it was probably filled by the nearest of blood to the party killed, as the right of redeeming a mortgaged field is given to him. To prevent the unnecessary loss of life through a sanguinary spirit of revenge, the Hebrew legislator made various enactments concerning the blood-avenger. In most ages and countries, certain reputed sacred places enjoyed the privileges of being asylums: Moses, therefore, taking it for granted that the murderer would flee to the altar, commanded that when the crime was deliberate and intentional, he should be torn even from the altar, and put to death. (Exod. xxi. 14.) But in the case of unintentional murder, the man-slayer was enjoined to flee to one of the

---

[1] " The interest of the common safety has, for ages, established a law among them" (the Arabians), "which decrees that the blood of every man, who is slain, must be avenged by that of his murderer. This vengeance is called *tar*, or retaliation ; and the right of exacting it devolves on the nearest of kin to the deceased. So nice are the Arabs on this point of honour, that, if any one neglects to seek his retaliation, he is disgraced for ever. He therefore watches every opportunity of revenge : if his enemy perishes from any other cause, still he is not satisfied, and his vengeance is directed against the nearest relation. These animosities are transmitted, as an inheritance, from father to children, and never cease but by the extinction of one of the families, unless they agree to sacrifice the criminal, or *purchase the blood* for a stated price, in money or in flocks. Without this satisfaction there is neither peace, nor truce, nor alliance between them ; nor, sometimes, even between whole tribes. *There is blood between us*, say they, on every occasion ; and this expression is an insurmountable barrier." (Volney's Travels in Egypt and Syria, vol. i. p. 367. See also Niebuhr, Description de l'Arabie, pp. 26—30.) In Turkey and in Persia murder is never prosecuted by the officers of the government. It is the business of the next relations, and of them only, to revenge the slaughter of their kinsmen ; and if they rather choose, as they generally do, to compound the matter for money, nothing more is said about it. — Lady M. W. Montague's Letters, let. 42. Sir R. K. Porter's Travels, vol. ii. pp. 75, 76.

[2] Among the Circassians, all the relatives of the murderers are considered as guilty. This customary infatuation to avenge the blood of relations, generates most of the feuds, and occasions great bloodshed among all the tribes of Caucasus ; for, unless pardon be purchased, or obtained by intermarriage between the two families, the principle of revenge is propagated to all succeeding generations. If the thirst of vengeance is quenched by a price paid to the family of the deceased, this tribute is called *Thlil- Uasa*, or *the price of blood ;* but neither princes nor usdens (or nobles) accept of such a compensation, as it is an established law among them, to *demand blood for blood.* — Pallas, Voyages dans les Gouvernemens Méridionaux de l'Empire de Russie, tome i. p. 441. Paris, 1805.

[3] Dr. Henderson, in describing the operation of the oriental law, of "blood for blood" among the Ingush Tartars, mentions the case of "a young man of amiable disposition, who was worn down almost to a skeleton, by the constant dread in which he lived, of having avenged upon him a murder committed by his father before he was born. He can reckon up more than a hundred persons who consider themselves bound to take away his life, whenever a favourable opportunity shall present itself."—Biblical Researches and Travels in Russia, p. 485.

[4] Light's Travels in Egypt, Nubia, &c. p. 95. Burckhardt's Travels in Nubia, p. 138.

[5] Salt's Voyage to Abyssinia, pp. 345, 346.

six cities of refuge which (we have already seen) were appropriated for his residence. The roads to these cities, it was enacted, should be kept in such a state that the unfortunate individual might meet with no impediment whatever in his way. (Deut xix. 3.) If the Goël overtook the fugitive before he reached an asylum, and put him to death, he was not considered as guilty of blood: but if the man-slayer had reached a place of refuge, he was immediately protected, and an inquiry was instituted whether he had a right to such protection and asylum, that is, whether he had caused his neighbour's death *undesignedly*, or was a *deliberate murderer*. In the latter case he was judicially delivered to the Goël, who might put him to death in whatever way he chose: but in the former case the homicide continued in the place of refuge until the high priest's death, when he might return home in perfect security. If, however, the Goël found him without the city or beyond its suburbs, he might slay him without being guilty of blood. (Numb. xxxv. 26, 27.) Further to guard the life of man, and prevent the perpetration of murder, Moses positively prohibited the receiving of a sum of money from a murderer in the way of compensation. (Numb. xxxv. 31.) It should seem that if no avenger of blood appeared, or if he were dilatory in the pursuit of the murderer, it became the duty of the magistrate himself to inflict the sentence of the law; and thus we find that David deemed this to be his duty in the case of Joab, and that Solomon, in obedience to his father's dying entreaty, actually discharged it by putting that murderer to death. (1 Kings ii. 5, 6. 28—34.) [1] There is a beautiful allusion to the blood-avenger in Heb. vi. 17, 18.

Hewing in pieces with the sword may be referred to this class of punishments. Thus Agag was executed, as a criminal, by the prophet Samuel (1 Sam. xv. 33.); and recent travellers inform us that criminals are literally hewed in pieces in Abyssinia, Persia, and in Asiatic Turkey. [2]

2. STONING was denounced against idolaters, blasphemers, sabbath-breakers, incestuous persons, witches, wizards, and children who either cursed their parents or rebelled against them. (Lev. xx. 2. 27. xxiv. 14. Deut. xiii. 10. xvii. 5. xxi. 21. and xxii. 21. 24.) It was the most general punishment denounced in the law against notorious criminals; and this kind of punishment is intended by the indefinite term of *putting to death.* (Lev. xx. 10. compared with John viii. 5.) Michaelis supposes that the culprit was bound, previously to the execution of his sentence. The witnesses threw the first stones, and the rest of the people then followed their example. Instances of persons being stoned in the Old Testament occur in Achan (Josh. vii. 25.), Adoram (1 Kings xii. 18.), Naboth (1 Kings xxi. 10.), and Zechariah. (2 Chron. xxiv. 21.) [3]

In the New Testament we meet with vestiges of a punishment, which has frequently been confounded with lapidation: it originated in the latter times of the Jewish commonwealth, and was termed the *rebel's beating.* It was often fatal, and was inflicted by the mob with their

---

[1] Michaelis's Commentaries, vol. ii. pp. 221—225.

[2] Bruce's Travels, vol. iv. p. 81. Harmer's Observations, vol. iv. pp. 229, 230. Capt. Light's Travels in Egypt, Nubia, &c. p. 194.

[3] Michaelis's Commentaries, vol. iii. p. 421.

fists, or staves, or stones, without mercy, or the sentence of the judges. Whoever transgressed against a prohibition of the wise men, or of the scribes, which had its foundation in the law, was delivered over to the people to be used in this manner, and was called *a son of rebellion*.[1] The frequent taking up of stones by the Jews against our Saviour, mentioned in the New Testament, and also the stoning of Stephen (Acts vii. 59.), were instances of this kind, to which some have referred the stoning of St. Paul at Lystra. (Acts xiv. 19.) But this appears to be a mistake. The people of Lystra were Gentiles, though they stoned Paul at the instigation of the Jews who came from Antioch and Iconium: and it appears from various passages of Greek authors, that stoning was a Grecian punishment. The inconstancy of a populace, easily persuaded by any plausible demagogues, will sufficiently account for the sudden change in the mind of the Lystrians towards the Apostle.[2]

Although the law of Moses punished no one with infamy, during life, yet three marks of infamy are denounced against those who were punished capitally; viz. — (1.) *Burning* the criminal who had been stoned, agreeably to the antient consuetudinary law. (Gen. xxxviii. 24. Lev. xx. 14. xxi. 9.) — (2.) *Hanging*, either on a tree or on a gibbet (for the Hebrew word signifies both) ; which was practised in Egypt (Gen. xl. 17—19.), and also enjoined by Moses. (Numb. xxv. 4, 5. Deut. xxi. 22.) The five Canaanitish kings were first slain and then hanged. (Josh. x. 26.) Persons who were hanged were considered as *accursed of God*, that is, punished by him and abominable; on which account they were to be taken down and buried the same day. (Deut. xxi. 23.) The hanging of Saul's sons, recorded in 2 Sam. xxi. 6., was done *not* by the Israelites, but by the *Gibeonites*, who were of Canaanitish origin, and probable retained their old laws. The hanging mentioned by Moses was widely different from crucifixion, which was a Roman punishment; on account of its ignominy, however, the Jews subsequently extended the declaration of Moses to it, and accounted the crucified person as accursed. (John xix. 31—34. Gal. iii. 13.) — (3.) The *Heaping of Stones* on the bodies of criminals, who had been already stoned to death, or slain by the sword, or upon their remains, when consumed by fire.[3] Such a heap was accumulated over Achan (Josh. vii. 25, 26.), and also over Absalom. (2 Sam. xviii. 17.) The Arabs, long after the time of David, expressed their detestation of deceased enemies in the same manner.[4] Similar heaps were raised over persons murdered in the highways in the time of the prophet Ezekiel (xxxix. 15.); as they also are to this day, in Palestine, an' other parts of the East.[5]

3. BURNING OFFENDERS ALIVE is a punishment which Moses commanded to be inflicted on the daughters of priests, who should be guilty of fornication (Lev. xxi. 9.), and upon a man who should marry both the mother and the daughter. (Lev. xx. 14.) This punishment seems to have been in use in the East, from a very early period. When Judah was informed that his daughter-in-law Tamar was pregnant, he condemned her to be burnt. (Gen. xxxviii. 24.) Many ages afterwards

---

[1] Michaelis's Commentaries, vol. iii, pp. 422—429.
[2] Biscoe on the Acts, vol. i. pp. 315, 316.
[3] Michaelis has given some instances of this practice, see his Commentaries, vol. iii. p. 430.
[4] Dr. Lightfoot's Works, vol. i. pp. 901, 902.
[5] Dr. Shaw's Travels in Barbary, vol. i. Pref. p. xviii. 8vo. edit.

we find the Babylonians or Chaldæans burning certain offenders alive (Jer. xxix. 22. Dan. iii. 6.) ; and this mode of punishment was not uncommon in the East so lately as the seventeenth century.[1]

The preceding are the only capital punishments denounced in the Mosaic law : in subsequent times others were introduced among the Jews, as their intercourse increased with foreign nations.

4. DECAPITATION, or beheading, though not a mode of punishment enjoined by Moses, was certainly in use before his time. It existed in Egypt (Gen. xl. 19.), and it is well known to have been inflicted under the princes of the Herodian family. Thus John the Baptist was beheaded (Matt. xiv. 8—12.) by one of Herod's life-guards, who was despatched to his prison for that purpose. (Mark vi. 27.)

5. PRECIPITATION, or casting headlong from a window, or from a precipice, was a punishment rarely used; though we meet with it in the history of the kings, and in subsequent times. Thus, the profligate Jezebel was precipitated out of a window (2 Kings ix. 30. 33.), and the same mode of punishment still obtains in Persia.[2] Amaziah, king of Judah, barbarously forced ten thousand Idumæan prisoners of war to leap from the top of a high rock. (2 Chron. xxv. 12.) The Jews attempted to precipitate Jesus Christ from the brow of a mountain. (Luke iv. 29.) James, surnamed the Just, was thrown from the highest part of the temple into the subjacent valley. The same mode of punishment, it is well known, obtained among the Romans, who used to throw certain malefactors from the Tarpeian rock.[3] The same practice obtains among the Moors at Constantine, a town in Barbary.[4]

6. DROWNING was a punishment in use among the Syrians, and was well known to the Jews in the time of our Saviour, though we have no evidence that it was practised by them. It was also in use among the Greeks and Romans. The Emperor Augustus, we are told, punished certain persons, who had been guilty of rapacity in the province (of Syria or of Lycia), by causing them to be thrown into a river, with a heavy weight about their necks.[5] Josephus[6] also tells us that the Galileans revolting, drowned the partisans of Herod in the sea of Gennesareth. To this mode of capital punishment Jesus Christ alludes in Matt. xviii. 6.[7] It is still practised in India: a large stone is tied round the neck of the criminal, who is cast into the sea or into deep water.[8]

7. BRUISING, OR POUNDING IN A MORTAR, is a punishment still in use among the Turks. The ulema or body of lawyers are, in Turkey, exempted from confiscation of their property, and from being put to death, except by the pestle and mortar. Some of the Turkish guards,

---

[1] Chardin, in his Travels, (vol. vi. p. 118. of Langlés' edition,) after speaking of the most common mode of punishing with death, says, " But there is still a particular way of putting to death such as have transgressed in civil affairs, either by causing a dearth, or by selling above the tax by a false weight, or who have committed themselves in any other manner. The cooks are put upon a spit and roasted over a slow fire (see Jeremiah xxix. 22.), bakers are thrown into a hot oven. During the dearth in 1688, I saw such ovens heated on the royal square in Ispahan, to terrify the bakers, and deter them from deriving advantage from the general distress." — Burder's Oriental Literature, vol. ii. p. 204.

[2] Sir R. K. Porter's Travels in Persia, vol. ii. pp. 28—30.

[3] Livy, Hist. lib. vi. c. 20.

[4] Pitt's Religion and Manners of the Mahometans, pp. 311, 312.   London edit. 1810.

[5] Suetonius, in Augusto, c. 67.

[6] Ant. Jud. lib. xiv. c. 15. § 10.

[7] Grotius in loc.   [8] Roberts's Illustrations, p. 543.

who had permitted the escape of the Polish prince Coreski in 1618, were pounded to death in great mortars of iron.[1] This horrid punishment was not unknown in the time of Solomon, who expressly alludes to it in Prov. xxvii. 22.

8. DICHOTOMY, or CUTTING ASUNDER, was a capital punishment antiently in use in the countries contiguous to Judæa. The rabbinical writers report that Isaiah was thus put to death by the profligate Manasseh; and to this Saint Paul is supposed to allude. (Heb. xi. 37.) Nebuchadnezzar threatened it to the Chaldee magi, if they did not interpret his dream (Dan. ii. 5.), and also to the blasphemers of the true God. (Dan. iii. 29.) Herodotus says, that Sabacho had a vision, in which he was commanded to *cut in two* all the Egyptian priests: and that Xerxes ordered one of the sons of Pythias to be cut in two, and one half placed on each side of the way, that his army might pass between them.[2] Trajan is said to have inflicted this punishment on some rebellious Jews. It is still practised by the Moors of Western Barbary, and also in Persia.[3]

9. BEATING TO DEATH (Τυμπανισμος) was practised by Antiochus towards the Jews (2 Macc. vi. 19. 28. 30.), and is referred to by Saint Paul. (Heb. xi. 35. Gr.) This was a punishment in use among the Greeks, and was usually inflicted upon slaves. The real or supposed culprit was fastened to a stake, and beaten to death with sticks. The same punishment is still in use among the Turks, under the appellation of the bastinado: with them, however, it is seldom mortal.

10. HANGING does not appear to have been a punishment among the Jews after their settlement in Palestine. Joshua hung the king of Ai on a tree until evening. (Josh. viii. 29.) In Egypt however it was a customary punishment for many capital crimes; and the criminals were kept bound in prison till their fate was decided; being confined under the immediate superintendence, and within the house of the chief of the police.[4]

11. EXPOSING TO WILD BEASTS appears to have been a punishment among the Medes and Persians. It was inflicted first on the exemplary prophet Daniel, who was miraculously preserved, and afterwards on his accusers, who miserably perished. (Dan. vi. 7. 12. 16—24.) From them it appears to have passed to the Romans.[5] In their theatres they had two sorts of *amusements*, each sufficiently barbarous. Sometimes they cast men naked to the wild beasts, to be devoured by them: this punishment was inflicted on slaves and vile persons. Sometimes persons were sent into the theatre, armed, to fight with wild beasts: if they conquered, they had their lives and liberty: but if not, they fell a prey to the beasts. To this latter usage (concerning which some further particulars are given in a subsequent page) Saint Paul refers in 2 Tim. iv. 17. and 1 Cor. xv. 32.

In the case of certain extraordinary criminals, besides inflicting upon

---

[1] Knolles's History of the Turks, vol. ii. p. 947. London, 1687.
[2] Raphelii Annotationes in Nov. Test. ex Herodoto, tom. i. p. 376. Other instances from antient writers are given by Dr. Whitby, on Matt. xxiv. 51. and Kuinoël, Comment. in Hist. Lib. Nov. Test. vol. i. p. 633.
[2] Shaw's Travels, vol. i. p. 457. Morier's Second Journey, p. 96.
[4] Wilkinson's Manners, &c. of the Antient Egyptians, vol. ii. p. 45.
[5] This barbarous mode of punishment still exists in Morocco. See an interesting **extract** from Höst's Account of Morocco and Fez, in Burder's Oriental Literature, vol. ii. p. 207.

them the sentence to which they had been condemned, it was not un-usual to demolish their houses, and reduce them to a common place for filth and dung. Among other things, Nebuchadnezzar denounced this disgrace to the diviners of Chaldæa, if they did not declare his dream to him (Dan. ii. 5.); and afterwards to all such as should not worship the God of Shadrach, Meshech, and Abednego. (Dan. iii. 29.) And Darius threatened the same punishment to those who should molest the Jews. (Ezra vi. 11.) In this way the Romans destroyed the house of Spurius Cassius, after they had precipitated him from the Tarpeian rock, for having (as they said) aimed at tyranny.[1] Fur-ther, the heads, hands, and feet of state criminals, were also frequently cut off, and fixed up in the most public places, as a warning to others. This punishment obtains among the Turks, and was inflicted on the sons of Rimmon (who had treacherously murdered Ishbosheth), by command of David: who commanded that the assassins' hands and feet should be hung up over the pool of Hebron, which was probably a place of great resort.[2] Among the antient Chaldæans, cutting off the nose and ears was a common punishment of adulterers. To this the prophet Ezekiel alludes. (xxiii. 25.)

11. CRUCIFIXION was a punishment which the antients inflicted only on the most notorious criminals and malefactors. The cross was made of two beams, either crossing at the top at right angles, or in the middle of their length like an X. There was, besides, a piece on the centre of the transverse beam, to which was attached the accusation, or state-ment of the culprit's crime; together with a piece of wood that projected from the middle, on which the person sat as on a kind of saddle, and by which the whole body was supported. Justin Martyr, in his dia-logue with Trypho the Jew, gives this description; and it is worthy of note, that he lived in the former part of the second century of the Christian æra, before the punishment of the cross was abolished. The cross, on which our Lord suffered, was of the former kind, being thus represented on all antient monuments, coins, and crosses.

Crucifixion is one of the most cruel and excruciating deaths, which the art of ingeniously tormenting and extinguishing life ever devised. The naked body of the criminal was fastened to the upright beam by nailing or tying the feet to it, and on the transverse beam by nailing and sometimes tying the hands to it. Those members, being the grand instruments of motion, are provided with a greater quantity of nerves, which (especially those of the hands) are peculiarly sensible. As the nerves are the instruments of all sensation or feeling, wounds in the parts where they abound must be peculiarly painful; especially when inflicted with such rude instruments as large nails, forcibly driven through the exquisitely delicate tendons, nerves, and bones of those parts. The horror of this punishment will appear, when it is considered that the person was permitted to hang (the whole weight of his body being borne up by his nailed hands and feet, and by the

---

1 Dionys. Halicarnass. lib. viii. cc. 78, 79.

2 Harmer's Observations, vol. i. pp. 501, 502. This kind of punishment was in use in the time of Mohammed, who introduces Pharaoh as saying, *I will surely cut off your hands and your feet on the opposite sides ;* that is, first the right hand, and then the left foot; next the left hand, and then the right foot. Koran, ch. xx. 74. and xxvi. 49. (Sale's translation, pp. 259. 304. 4to. edit.) See additional examples of such mutilations in Burder's Oriental Literature, vol. ii. p. 186. Wilson's Travels in Egypt and the Holy Land, pp. 375—377.

projecting piece in the middle of the cross,) until he perished through agony and want of food. There are instances of crucified persons living in this exquisite torture several days.[1] " The wise and adorable Author of our being has formed and constituted the fabric of our bodies in such a merciful manner, that nothing violent is lasting. Friendly death sealed the eyes of those wretches generally in three days. Hunger, thirst, and acute pain dismissed them from their intolerable sufferings. The rites of sepulture were denied them. Their dead bodies were generally left on the crosses on which they were first suspended, and became a prey to every ravenous beast and carnivorous bird.[2]

(1.) " Crucifixion obtained among several antient nations, the Egyptians[3], Persians, Greeks[4], and Carthaginians. The Carthaginians generally adjudged to this death their unfortunate and unsuccessful commanders.[5] There are many unhappy instances of this. They crucified Bomilcar[6], whom Justin calls their king, when they detected his intended design of joining Agathocles. They erected a cross in the midst of the forum, on which they suspended him, and from which, with a great and unconquered spirit, amidst all his sufferings, he bitterly inveighed against them, and upbraided them with all the black and atrocious crimes they had lately perpetrated. But this manner of executing criminals prevailed most among the Romans. It was generally a servile punishment, and chiefly inflicted on vile, worthless, and incorrigible slaves.[7] In reference to this, the Apostle, describing the condescension of Jesus, and his submission to this most opprobrious death, represents him as taking upon him the form of a servant (Phil. ii. 7, 8.), and becoming obedient to death, even the death of the cross.

(2.) " It was universally and deservedly reputed the most shameful and ignominious death to which a wretch could be exposed. In such an exit were comprised every idea and circumstance of odium, disgrace, and public scandal." Hence the Apostle magnifies and extols the great love of our Redeemer, *in that while we were yet sinners, Christ died for us,* and *for the joy set before him, endured the cross, despising the shame* (Rom. v. 8. Heb. xii. 2.) ; disregarding every circum-

---

[1] Dr. Adam Clarke on Matt. xxvii. 35. For the remainder of this account of the crucifixion the author is indebted to Dr. Lardner's Credibility of the Gospel History, part i. book i. c. 7. §§ ix.—xvii., and Dr. Harwood's Introduction to the New Testament, vol. ii. pp. 336—353.

[2] Pasces in cruce corvos. Horat. Epist. lib. i. epist. 16. ver. 48.
    Vultur, jumento et canibus, crucibusque relictis
    Ad fœtus properat, partemque cadaveris affert. Juvenal, Satyr. 14. ver. 77, 78.

[3] Thucydides, lib. i. sect. 110. p. 71. edit. Duker. Justin, treating of the affairs of Egypt, says : Concursu multitudinis et Agathocles occiditur, et mulieres in ultionem Eurydices patibulis suffiguntur. Justin, lib. xxx. cap. 2. p. 578. edit. Gronovii. Herodoti Erato. p. 451. edit. Wesseling, 1763. See also Thalia, p. 260. and Polyhymnia. p. 617.

[4] Alexander crucified two thousand Tyrians. Triste deinde spectaculum victoribus ira præbuit regis; duo millia, in quibus occidendi defecerat rabies, crucibus adfixi per ingens litoris spatium, dependerunt. Q. Curtii, lib. iv. cap. 4. p. 187. edit. Snakenburgh, 1724. See also Plutarch in vita Alex. and Justin, lib. xviii. cap. 3.

[5] Duces bella pravo consilio gerentes, etiamsi prospera fortuna subsecuta esset, cruci tamen suffigebantur. Valerius Maximus, lib. ii. cap. 7. p. 191. edit. Torren. Leidæ, 1726.

[6] Bomilcar rex Pœnorum in medio foro a Pœnis patibulo suffixus est. De Summa cruce, veluti de tribunali, Pœnorum scelera concionaretur. Justin, lib. xxii. cap. 7. p. 505. ed. Gronovii.

[7] Pone crucem servo. Juvenal, Sat. 6. ver. 218.

stance of public indignity and infamy with which such a death was loaded. " It was from the idea they connected with such a death, that the Greeks treated the apostles with the last contempt and pity for publicly embarking in the cause of a person who had been brought to this reproachful and dishonourable death by his own countrymen. The preaching of the cross was to them foolishness (1 Cor. i. 23.); the promulgation of a system of religion that had been taught by a person who, by a national act, had publicly suffered the punishment and death of the most useless and abandoned slave, was, in their ideas, the last infatuation; and the preaching of Christ crucified, publishing in the world a religion whose founder suffered on a cross, appeared the last absurdity and madness.[1] The Heathens looked upon the attachment of the primitive Christians to a religion whose publisher had come to such an end, as an undoubted proof of their utter ruin, that they were destroying their interest, comfort, and happiness, by adopting such a system founded on such a dishonourable circumstance.[2] The same inherent scandal and ignominy had crucifixion in the estimation of the Jews. They indeed annexed more complicated wretchedness to it, for they esteemed the miscreant who was adjudged to such an end not only to be abandoned of men, but forsaken of God. He that is hanged, says the law, is accursed of God. (Deut. xxi. 23.) Hence St. Paul, representing to the Galatians the grace of Jesus, who released us from that curse to which the law of Moses devoted us, by being made a curse for us, by submitting to be treated for our sakes as an execrable malefactor, to show the horror of such a death as Christ voluntarily endured, adds, *It is written in the law, Cursed is every one that hangeth on a tree!* (Galat. iii. 13.) And from this express declaration of the law of Moses concerning persons thus executed, we may account for that aversion the Jews discovered against Christianity, and perceive the reason of what St. Paul asserts, that their preaching of Christ crucified was to the Jews a stumbling block. (1 Cor. i. 23.) The circumstance of the cross caused them to stumble at the very gate of Christianity.[3]

(3.) " The several circumstances related by the four evangelists as accompanying the crucifixion of Jesus were conformable to the Roman

---

[1] " From this circumstance," says Justin Martyr, " the Heathens are fully convinced of our madness for giving the second place after the immutable and eternal God, and Father of all, to a person who was crucified!" Justin Martyr, Apol. 2. pp. 60, 61. edit. Paris, 1636. Et qui hominem summo supplicio pro facinore punitum, et crucis ligna feralia ceremonias fabulatur, congruentia perditis sceleratisque tribuit altaria : ut id colant quod merentur. Minucius Felix, p. 57. edit. Davis. Cantab. 1712. Nam quod religioni nostræ hominem noxium et crucem ejus adscribitis, longe de vicinia veritatis erratis. Min. Felix, p. 147.

[2] That this was the sentiment of the Heathens concerning the Christians, St. Paul informs us, and he exhorts the Philippians not to be discouraged by it. Philip. i. 28. Not intimidated in any thing by your adversaries ; for though they look upon your attachment to the Gospel as an undoubted proof of your utter ruin, yet to you it is a demonstration of your salvation — a salvation which hath God for its author.

[3] Trypho the Jew every where affects to treat the Christian religion with contempt, on account of the crucifixion of its author. He ridicules its professors for centering all their hopes in a man who was crucified! Dialog. cum Tryphone, p. 33. The person whom you call your Messiah, says he, incurred the last disgrace and ignominy, for he fell under the greatest curse in the law of God ; he was crucified! p. 90. Again, we must hesitate, says Trypho, with regard to our believing a person, who was so ignominiously crucified, being the Messiah ; for it is written in the law, Cursed is every one who is hanged on a cross. Justin Martyr, Dialog. cum Tryphone, p. 271. edit. Jebb. London, 1719. See also pages 272. 283. 378. 392. See also Eusebii Hist. Eccl. pp. 171. 744. Cantab.

custom in such executions; and, frequently occurring in antient authors, do not only reflect beauty and lustre upon these passages, but happily corroborate and confirm the narrative of the sacred penmen." We will exhibit before our readers a detail of these as they are specified by the evangelists.

Every mark of infamy that malice could suggest was accumulated on the head of our Redeemer. While he was in the high priest's house, *they did spit in his face and buffeted him, and others smote him with the palms of their hands, saying, Prophesy unto us, thou Christ, who is he that smote thee?* (Matt. xxvi. 67, 68. Mark xiv. 65.) Pilate, hearing that our Lord was of Galilee, sent him to Herod; and before he was dismissed by him, *Herod, with his men of war, set him at nought; and mocked him, and arrayed him in a gorgeous robe.* (Luke xxiii. 11.) He was insulted and mocked by the soldiers, when Pilate ordered him to be scourged the first time; that by that lesser punishment he might satisfy the Jews and save his life, as is related by St. John. After Pilate had condemned him to be crucified, the like indignities were repeated by the soldiers, as we are assured by two evangelists. (Matt. xxvii. 27—31. Mark xv. 16—20.) *And they stripped him, and put on him a scarlet robe, and when they had platted a crown of thorns[1], they put it on his head, and a reed in his right hand: and they bowed the knee before him, and mocked him, saying, Hail! king of the Jews. And they spit upon him, and took the reed, and smote him on the head.*

These are tokens of contempt and ridicule which were in use at that time. Dio, among the other indignities offered to Sejanus the favourite of Tiberius (in whose reign our Saviour was crucified), as they were carrying him from the senate-house to prison, particularly mentions this, — "That they struck him on the head." But there is one instance of ridicule which happened so soon after this time, and has so great a resemblance to that to which our Saviour was exposed, that it deserves to be stated at length. Caligula, the successor of Tiberius, had, in the very beginning of his reign, given Agrippa the tetrarchy of his uncle Philip, being about the fourth part of his grandfather Herod's dominions, with the right of wearing a diadem or crown. When he was setting out from Rome to make a visit to his people, the emperor advised him to go by Alexandria as the best way. When he came thither he kept himself very private: but the Alexandrians having got intelligence of his arrival there, and of the design of his journey, were filled with envy, as Philo says, at the thoughts of a Jew having the title of king. They had recourse to various expedients, in order to manifest their indignation: one was the following: — "There

---

[1] Various opinions have been offered concerning the species of thorn, intended by the sacred writers. Bartholin wrote an elaborate dissertation *De Spinea Corona*, and Lydius has collected the opinions of several writers in his Florum Sparsio ad Historiam Passionis Jesu Christi. (Analect. pp. 13—17.) The intelligent traveller Hasselquist says, that the *naba* or *nabka* of the Arabians " is in all probability the tree which afforded the crown of thorns put on the head of Christ: it grows very commonly in the East. *This plant was very fit for the purpose; for it has many* SMALL AND SHARP SPINES, *which are well adapted to give pain.* The crown might easily be made of these soft, round, and pliant branches: and what in my opinion seems to be the greatest proof is, that the leaves very much resemble those of ivy, as they are of a very deep green. Perhaps the enemies of Christ would have a plant somewhat resembling that with which emperors and generals were used to be crowned, that there might be calumny even in the punishment." Hasselquist's Voyages and Travels in the Levant, pp. 288, 289.

was," says Philo[1], "one Carabas, a sort of distracted fellow, that in all seasons of the year went naked about the streets. He was somewhat between a madman and a fool, the common jest of boys and other idle people. This wretch they brought into the theatre, and placed him on a lofty seat, that he might be conspicuous to all; then they put a thing made of paper on his head for a crown, the rest of his body they covered with a mat instead of a robe, and for a sceptre one put into his hand a little piece of a reed which he had just taken up from the ground. Having thus given him a mimic royal dress, several young fellows with poles on their shoulders came and stood on each side of him as his guards. Then there came people toward him, some to pay their homage to him, others to ask justice of him, and some to know his will and pleasure concerning affairs of state; and in the crowd were loud and confused acclamations of Maris, Maris; that being, as they say, the Syriac word for Lord, thereby intimating whom they intended to ridicule by all this mock show: Agrippa being a Syrian, and king of a large country in Syria."

When Pilate had pronounced the sentence of condemnation on our Lord, and publicly adjudged him to be crucified, he gave orders that he should be scourged. *Then Pilate took Jesus and scourged him. And when he had scourged Jesus,* says another of the evangelists, *he delivered him to be crucified.* Among the Romans, scourging was always inflicted previously to crucifixion. Many examples might be produced of this custom. Let the following suffice. Livy, speaking of the fate of those slaves who had confederated and taken up arms against the state, says, that many of them were slain, many taken prisoners, and others, after they had been whipped or scourged[2], were suspended on crosses. Philo, relating the cruelties which Flaccus the Roman prefect exercised upon the Jews of Alexandria, says, that after they were mangled and torn with scourges[3] in the theatres, they were fastened to crosses. Josephus also informs us, that at the siege of Jerusalem great numbers of the Jews were crucified, after they had been previously whipped, and had suffered every wanton cruelty.[4]

" After they had inflicted this customary flagellation, the evangelist informs us that they obliged our Lord to carry to the place of execution the cross, or, at least, the transverse beam of it, on which he was to be suspended. Lacerated, therefore, with the stripes and bruises he had received, faint with the loss of blood, his spirits exhausted by the cruel insults and blows that were given him when they invested him with robes of mock royalty, and oppressed with the incumbent weight of his cross; in these circumstances our Saviour was urged along the road. We doubt not but in this passage to Calvary every indignity was offered him. This was usual.[5] Our Lord, fatigued and spent with the treatment he had received, could not support his cross. The soldiers, therefore, who attended him, compelled one

---

1 In Flacc. p. 970.

2 Multi occisi, multi capti, alii verberati crucibus affixi. Livii, lib. xxxiii. 36.

3 Philo in Flac. p. 529. edit. Mangey. See also pages 527, 528. ejusdem editionis. The Roman custom was to scourge before all executions. The magistrates bringing them out into the forum, after they had scourged them according to custom, they struck off their heads. Polybii Hist. lib. i. p. 10. tomi i. edit. Gronovii. 1670.

4 Josephus de Bello Jud. lib. v. c. 2. p. 353. Havercamp. Bell. Judaic. lib. ii. cap. 14. § 9. p. 182. Haverc.

5 Vid. Justi Lipsii de Cruce, lib. ii. cap. 6. p. 1180. Vesaliæ.

Simon, a Cyrenean, who was coming from the country to Jerusalem, and happened then to be passing by them, to carry it for him. The circumstance here mentioned of our Lord bearing his cross was agreeable to the Roman custom. Slaves and malefactors, who were condemned to this death, were compelled to carry the whole or part of the fatal gibbet on which they were destined to die. This constituted a principal part of the shame and ignominy of such a death. Cross-bearer was a term of the last reproach among the Romans. The miserable wretch, covered with blood, from the scourges that had been inflicted upon him, and groaning under the weight of his cross, was, all along the road to the place of execution, loaded with every wanton cruelty. So extreme were the misery and sufferings of the hapless criminals who were condemned to this punishment, that Plutarch makes use of it as an illustration of the misery of sin, that every kind of wickedness produces its own particular torment; just as every malefactor, when he is brought forth to execution, carries his own cross.[1] He was pushed, thrown down, stimulated with goads, and impelled forwards by every act of insolence and inhumanity that could be inflicted.[2] There is great reason to think that our blessed Redeemer in his way to Calvary experienced every abuse of this nature, especially when he proceeded slowly along, through languor, lassitude, and faintness, and the soldiers and rabble found his strength incapable of sustaining and dragging his cross any farther. On this occasion we imagine that our Lord suffered very cruel treatment from those who attended him. Might not the scourging that was inflicted, the blows he had received from the soldiers when in derision they paid him homage, and the abuse he suffered on his way to Calvary, greatly contribute to accelerate his death, and occasion that speedy dissolution at which one of the evangelists tells us Pilate marvelled?

"When the malefactor had carried his cross to the place of execution, a hole was dug in the earth, in which it was to be fixed; the criminal was stripped, a stupefying potion was given him, the cross was laid on the ground, the wretch distended upon it, and four soldiers, two on each side, at the same time were employed in driving four large nails through his hands and feet. After they had deeply fixed and rivetted these nails in the wood, they elevated the cross with the agonising wretch upon it; and in order to fix it the more firmly and securely in the earth, they let it violently fall into the cavity they had dug to receive it. This vehement precipitation of the cross must give the person that was nailed to it a most dreadful convulsive shock, and agitate his whole frame in a dire and most excruciating manner. These several particulars the Romans observed in the crucifixion of our Lord. Upon his arrival at Calvary he was stripped: a stupefying draught was offered him, which he refused to drink. This, St. Mark says, was a composition of myrrh and wine. The design of this potion

---

[1] Plutarch de tardâ Dei vindictâ, p. 982. edit. Gr. 8vo. Steph. Dionysii Halicar. lib. vii. tom. i. p. 456. Oxon. 1704.
　　　O carnificium cribrum, quod credo fore :
　　Ita te forabunt patibulatum per vias
　　Stimulis, si huc reveniat senex.
　　　　　　Plautus Mostel. Act. i. sc. 1. ver. 53. edit. var. 1684.
[2] Nec dubium est quin impulerint, dejecerint, erexerint, per sævitiam aut per lusum. Lipsius de Cruce, tom. vi. p. 1180. Vesaliæ.

was, by its inebriating and intoxicating quality, to blunt the edge of pain, and stun the quickness of sensibility.[1] Our Lord rejected this medicated cup, offered him perhaps by the kindness of some of his friends, it being his fixed resolution to meet death in all its horrors; not to alleviate and suspend its pains by any such preparation, but to submit to the death, even this death of crucifixion, with all its attendant circumstances." He had the joy that was set before him, in procuring the salvation of men, in full and immediate view. He wanted not, therefore, on this great occasion, any thing to produce an unnatural stupor, and throw oblivion and stupefaction over his senses.[2] He cheerfully and voluntarily drank the cup with all its bitter ingredients, which his heavenly Father had put into his hands. Our Lord was fastened to his cross, as was usual, by four soldiers[3], two on each side, according to the respective limbs they severally nailed. While they were employed in piercing his hands and feet, it is probable that he offered to Heaven that most compassionate and affecting prayer for his murderers, in which he pleaded the only circumstance that could possibly extenuate their guilt: *Father, forgive them, for they know not what they do!* It appears from the evangelist that our Lord was crucified without the city. *And he bearing his cross went forth to a place called the place of a skull, which is called in the Hebrew Golgotha.* (John xix. 17.) *For the place where Jesus was crucified was nigh to the city.* (ver. 20.) And the Apostle to the Hebrews has likewise mentioned this circumstance: *Wherefore Jesus also — suffered without the gate.* (Heb. xiii. 12.) This is conformable to the Jewish law, and to examples mentioned in the Old Testament. (Numb. xv. 35.) *And the Lord said unto Moses, The man shall surely be put to death: all the congregation shall stone him with stones without the camp.* (1 Kings xxi. 13.) *Then they carried him* [Naboth] *forth out of the city, and stoned him with stones that he died.* This was done at Jezreel, in the territories of the king of Israel, not far from Samaria. And if this custom was practised there, we may be certain the Jews did not choose that criminals should be executed within Jerusalem, of the sanctity of which they had so high an opinion, and which they were very zealous to preserve free from all ceremonial impurity, though they defiled it with the practice of the most horrid immoralities. It is possible, indeed, that they might, in their sudden and ungoverned rage (to which they were subject in the extreme at this time), upon any affront offered to their laws or customs, put persons who thus provoked them to death, upon the spot, in the city, or the temple, or wherever they found them; but whenever they were calm enough to admit the form of a legal process, we may be assured that they did not approve of an execution within

---

[1] Sese multimodis conculcat ictibus, myrrhæ contra præsumptione munitus. Apuleii Metamorph. lib. viii. Again: Obfirmatus myrrhæ presumptione nullis verberibus, ac ne ipsi quidem succubuit igni. Lib. x. Apuleii Met. Usque hodie, says St. Jerome, Judæi omnes increduli Dominicæ resurrectionis aceto et felle potant Jesum, et dant ei vinum myrrhatum, ut dum consopiant, et mala eorum non videant. Hieronymus ad Matt. xxvii.

[2] See Dr. Benson's Life of Christ, p. 508.

[3] Monet nos quoque non parum evangelista, qui quatuor numerat milites crucifigentes, scilicet juxta quatuor membra figenda. Quod clarum etiam est ex tunicæ partitione, quæ quatuor militibus facienda erat. Cornelii Curtii de Clavis Dominicis, p. 35. edit. Antwerpiæ, 1670. The four soldiers who parted his garments, and cast lots for his vesture, were the four who raised him to the cross, each of them fixing a limb, and who, it seems, for this service had a right to the crucified person's clothes. Dr. Macknight, p. 604. second edition, 4to.

the city. And among the Romans this custom was very common[1], at least in the provinces. The robbers of Ephesus, whom[2] Petronius Arbiter mentions, were crucified by order of the governor of the province without the city. This was the custom, likewise, in Sicily, as appears from Cicero.[3]

" It was customary for the Romans, on any extraordinary execution, to put over the head of the malefactor an inscription denoting the crime for which he suffered. Several examples of this occur in the Roman history."[4] It was also usual at this time, at Jerusalem, to post up advertisements, which were designed to be read by all classes of persons, in several languages. Titus, in a message which he sent to the Jews when the city was on the point of falling into his hands, and by which he endeavoured to persuade them to surrender, says: Did you not erect pillars, *with inscriptions on them in the* GREEK *and in our* (the LATIN) *language,* " Let no one pass beyond these bounds ?"[5] " In conformity to this usage, an inscription by Pilate's order was fixed above the head of Jesus, written in Hebrew, Greek and Latin, specifying what it was that had brought him to this end. This writing was by the Romans called *titulus,* a *title*[4], and it is the very expression made use of by the evangelist John: *Pilate wrote a* TITLE (εγραψε TITΛON), *and put it on the cross.* (John xix. 19.)[7] After the cross was erected, a party of soldiers was appointed to keep guard[8], and to attend at the place of execution till the criminal breathed his last; thus also we read that a body of Roman soldiers, with a centurion, were deputed to guard our Lord and the two malefactors that were crucified with him. (Matt. xxvii. 54.)

" While they were thus attending them, it is said, our Saviour complained of thirst. This is a natural circumstance. The exquisitely sensible and tender extremities of the body being thus perforated, the person languishing and faint with loss of blood, and lingering under such acute and excruciating torture, — these causes must necessarily produce a vehement and excessive thirst. One of the guards, hearing this request, hasted and took a sponge, and filled it from a vessel that stood by, that was full of vinegar. The usual drink of the Roman soldiers was vinegar and water.[9] The knowledge of this custom illustrates this passage of sacred history, as it has sometimes been inquired,

---

[1] Credo ego istoc exemplo tibi esse eundum actutum extra portam, dispessis manibus patibulum quem habebis. Plautus in Mil. Glor. act. ii. scen. 4.

[2] Quum interim imperator provinciæ latrones jussit crucibus adfigi, secundum illam eandem casulam, in qua recens cadaver matrona deflebat. Satyr. c. 71.

[3] Quid enim attinuit, cum Mamertini more atque instituto suo crucem fixissent post urbem in via Pompeia; te jubere in ea parte figere, quæ ad fretum spectaret? In Verr. lib. v. c. 66. n.169.

[4] Dion Cassius, lib. liv. p. 732. edit. Reimar, 1750. See also Suetonius in Caligula, c. 32. Eusebius, Hist. Eccl. lib. v. p. 206. Cantab. 1720.

[5] Josephus, de Bell. Jud. lib. vi. c. 2. § 4.

[6] See instances in Suetonius, in Caligula, c. 34. ; and in Domitian, c. 10.

[7] " It is with much propriety that Matthew calls this αιτια *accusation :* for it was false, that ever Christ pretended to be king of the Jews, in the sense the inscription held forth : he was accused of this, but there was no proof of the accusation ; however, it was affixed to the cross." Dr. A. Clarke on Matt. xxvii. 37.

[8] Miles cruces asservabat, ne quis corpora ad sepulturam detraheret. Petronius Arbiter, cap. 111, p. 513. edit. Burman. Traject. ad Rhen. 1709. Vid. not. ad loc.

[9] The Roman soldiers, says Dr. Huxham, drank posca (viz. water and vinegar) for their common drink, and found it very healthy and useful. Dr. Huxham's Method for preserving the Health of Seamen, in his Essay on Fevers, p. 263. 3d edition. See also Lamy's Apparatus Biblicus, vol. ii. p. 278., and Macknight in loc.

for what purpose was this vessel of vinegar? Considering, however, the derision and cruel treatment which Jesus Christ had already received from the soldiers, it is by no means improbable that one of them gave him the vinegar with the design of augmenting his unparalleled sufferings. After receiving this, Jesus cried with a loud voice, and uttered with all the vehemence he could exert, that comprehensive word on which a volume might be written, *It is finished!* the important work of human redemption is finished; after which he reclined his head upon his bosom, and dismissed his spirit." (John xix. 30. Matt. xxvii. 50.)

The last circumstance to be mentioned relative to the crucifixion of our Saviour, is the petition of the Jews to Pilate, that the death of the sufferers might be accelerated, with a view to the interment of Jesus. All the four evangelists have particularly mentioned this circumstance. *Joseph of Arimathea went to Pilate, and begged the body of Jesus; then Pilate commanded the body to be delivered. And when Joseph had taken the body, he laid it in his own new tomb.* (Matt. xxvii. 58—60. Mark xv. 45, 46. Luke xxiii. 50—53. John xix. 38—40.) And it may be fairly concluded, the rulers of the Jews did not disapprove of it: since they were solicitous that the bodies might be taken down, and not hang on the cross the next day. (John xix. 31.) *The Jews therefore,* says St. John, *because it was the preparation, that the bodies should not remain on the cross on the Sabbath-day (for that Sabbath-day was an high day), besought Pilate that their legs might be broken, and that they might be taken away.*

Burial was not always allowed by the Romans in these cases. For we find that sometimes a soldier was appointed to guard the bodies of malefactors, that they might not be taken away and buried.[1] However it seems that it was not often refused unless the criminals were very mean and infamous. Cicero reckons it one of the horrid crimes of Verres's administration in Sicily, that he would take money of parents for the burial of their children whom he had put to death.[2] Both Suetonius[3] and Tacitus[4] represent it as one of the uncommon cruelties of Tiberius, in the latter part of his reign, that he generally denied burial to those who were put to death by his orders at Rome. Ulpian, in his treatise on the duty of a pro-consul, says, "The bodies of those who are condemned to death are not to be denied to their relations:" and Augustus writes, in the tenth book of his own life, " that he had been wont to observe this custom[5];" that is, to grant the bodies to relations. Paulus says, " that the bodies of those who have been punished [with death] are to be given to any that desire them in order to burial."[6]

It is evident, therefore, from these two lawyers, that the governors of provinces had a right to grant burial to the bodies of those who had

---

[1] See the passage cited from Petronius Arbiter, in note [8], p. 165.

[2] Rapiunt eum ad supplicium, dii patrii : quod iste inventus est, qui e complexu parentum abreptos filios ad necem duceret, et parentes pretium pro sepultura posceret.   In Ver. lib. i. cap. 3.

[3] Nemo punitorum non et in Gemonias adjectus uncoque tractus.   Vit. Tiber. c. 61.

[4] Et quia damnati, publicatis bonis, sepulturâ prohibebantur.   Ann. lib. 6. c. 29.

[5] Corpora eorum qui capite damnantur cognatis ipsorum neganda non sunt : et id se observasse etiam D. Aug. lib. x. de vitâ suâ, scribit.   Hodie autem eorum, in quos animadvertitur, corpora non aliter sepeliuntur, quam si fuerit petitum et permissum ; et nonnunquam non permittitur, maxime majestatis causâ damnatorum. 1. i. ff. de cadaver. Punit.

[6] Corpora animadversorum quibuslibet petentibus ad sepulturam danda sunt. 1. iii. eod.

been executed by their order: nay, they seem to intimate that it ought not usually to be denied when requested by any.

Hence it appears, that burial was ordinarily allowed to persons who were put to death in Judæa: and the subsequent conduct of Pilate shows that it was seldom denied by the Roman governors in that country. There is, moreover, an express command in the law (of which we know that the latter Jews were religiously observant), that the bodies of those who were hanged should not be suffered to remain all night upon the tree. (Deut. xxi. 23.) [1] " On this account it was, that, after the crucifixion, a number of leading men among the Jews waited on Pilate in a body, to desire that he would hasten the death of the male-factors hanging on their crosses. (John xix. 31.) Pilate, therefore, despatched his orders to the soldiers on duty, who broke the legs of the two criminals who were crucified along with Christ; but when they came to Jesus, finding he had already breathed his last, they thought this violence and trouble unnecessary; but one of the soldiers pierced his side with a spear, whose point appears to have penetrated into the pericardium, or membrane surrounding the heart; for St. John, who says he was an eye-witness of this, declares that there issued from the wound a mixture of blood and water. This wound, had he not been dead, must necessarily have been fatal. This circumstance St. John saw, and has solemnly recorded and attested." [2]

CHAPTER IV.

ON THE JEWISH AND ROMAN MODES OF COMPUTING TIME, MENTIONED IN THE SCRIPTURES.

I. *Days.*—II. *Hours.*— *Watches of the Night.*—III. *Weeks.*—IV. *Months.* — V. *Years, Civil, Ecclesiastical, and Natural.*— *Jewish Calendar.* — VI. *Parts of the Time taken for the Whole.* — VII. *Remarkable Æras of the Jews.*

IT is well known that, in the perusal of antient authors, we are liable to fall into many serious mistakes, if we consider their modes of computing time to be precisely the same as ours: and hence it becomes necessary that we observe their different notations of time, and carefully adjust them to our own. This remark is particularly applicable to the sacred writers, whom sceptics and infidels have charged with various contradictions and inconsistencies, which fall to the ground as soon as the various computations of time are considered and adapted to our own standard. The knowledge of the different divisions of time mentioned in the Scriptures will elucidate the meaning of a multitude of passages with regard to seasons, circumstances, and ceremonies.

I. The Hebrews computed their DAYS from evening to evening, according to the command of Moses.[3] (Lev. xxiii. 32.) It is remark-

---

[1] See an instance, incidentally mentioned by Josephus. De Bell. Jud. lib. iv. c. 5. § 2.

[2] *And he that saw it bare record, and his record is true ; and he knoweth that he saith true, that ye might believe.* John xix. 35.

[3] Tacitus, speaking of the antient Germans, takes notice that their account of time differs from that of the Romans; and that instead of days they reckoned the number of nights. De Mor. Germ. c. 11. So also did the antient Gauls (Cæsar de Bell. Gall. lib. vi. c. 17.); and vestiges of this antient practice still remain in our own country. We say last *Sunday*

able that the evening or natural night precedes the morning or natural day in the account of the creation (Gen. i. 5, &c.) : whence the prophet Daniel employs the compound term *evening-morning* (Dan. viii. 14. marginal reading) to denote a civil day in his celebrated chronological prophecy of the 2300 days; and the same portion of time is termed in Greek νυχθημερον.

The Romans had two different computations of their days, and two denominations for them. The one they called the *civil,* the other the *natural* day; the civil day was from midnight to midnight; and the natural day was from the rising to the setting sun.[1] The natural day of the Jews varied in length according to the seasons of the year : the longest day in the Holy Land is only fourteen hours and twelve minutes of our time; and the shortest day, nine hours and forty-eight minutes. This portion of time was at first divided into *four* parts (Nehem. ix. 3.) ; which, though varying in length according to the seasons, could nevertheless be easily discerned from the position or appearance of the sun in the horizon. Afterwards the natural day was divided into twelve hours, which were measured from dials constructed for that purpose. Among these contrivances for the measurement of time, the sun-dial of Ahaz is particularly mentioned in 2 Kings xx. 11.[2] Jahn thinks it probable that Ahaz first introduced it from Babylon.[3]

II. The *earliest* mention of HOURS in the Sacred Writings occurs in the prophecy of Daniel (iii. 6. 15. v. 5.) : and as the Chaldæans, according to Herodotus[4], were the inventors of this division of time, it is probable that the Jews derived their hours from them. It is evident that the division of hours was unknown in the time of Moses (compare Gen. xv. 12. xviii. 1. xix. 1. 15. 23.) ; nor is any notice taken of them by the most antient of the profane poets, who mentions only the *morning* or *evening* or *mid-day.*[5] With Homer corresponded the notations of time referred to by the royal Psalmist, who mentions them as the times of prayer. (Psal. lv. 17.) The Jews computed their hours of the civil day from six in the morning till six in the evening : thus their *first* hour corresponded with our *seven* o'clock ; their *second* to our *eight ;* their *third* to our *nine,* &c. The knowledge of this circumstance will illustrate several passages of Scripture, particularly Matt. xx., where the third, sixth, ninth, and eleventh hours (ver. 3. 5. 6. 9.) respectively denote nine o'clock in the morning, twelve at noon, three and five in the afternoon; see also Acts ii. 15. iii. 1. x. 9. 30. The first three hours (from six to nine) were their morning : during

---

se'nnight, or *this day fortnight.* The practice of computing time by nights, instead of days, obtains among the Mashoos, an inland nation, dwelling in the interior of South Africa. Travels by the Rev. John Campbell, vol. i. p. 182. (London, 1822. 8vo.)

[1] Pliny, Hist. Nat. lib. ii. c. 77. ; Censorinus de Die Natali, c. 23.; Macrobius Saturnal. lib. iii. c. 3. See also Dr. Ward's Dissertations on several passages of Scripture, p. 126. ; and Dr. Macknight's Harmony, vol. i. Prelim. Obs. v. Adam's Roman Antiquities, p. 305.

[2] Few topics have caused more discussion among biblical commentators than the sun-dial of Ahaz. As the original word signifies, properly, steps or stairs, many have imagined that it was a kind of ascent to the gate of the palace, marked at proper distances with figures showing the division of the day, rather than a regular piece of dial-work. On this subject the reader will find some very ingenious and probable illustrations, together with a diagram, in Dr. A. Clarke's Commentary, on 2 Kings xx.

[3] Jahn, Archæol. Hebr. § 101.

[4] Lib. ii. c. 109.

[5] ——— 'Ηως, η δειλη, η μεσον ημαρ. Hom. Il. lib. xxi. 3.

the *third* hour, from eight to nine, their morning sacrifice was prepared, offered up, and laid on the altar precisely at nine o'clock; this
interval they termed the *preparation* (παρασκευη). Josephus confirms
the narrative of the evangelists.[1]   As the Israelites went out of Egypt
at the vernal equinox, the morning watch would answer to our four
o'clock in the morning.[2]

Before the Captivity the night was divided into three parts or
WATCHES. (Psal. lxiii. 6. xc. 4.)   The *first* or beginning of watches
is mentioned in Lam. ii. 19.; the *middle-watch* in Jud. vii. 19.; and the
morning-watch, or *watch of day-break,* in Exod. xiv. 24.   It is probable
that these watches varied in length according to the seasons of the
year: consequently those, who had a long and inclement winter watch
to encounter, would ardently *desire* the approach of morning light to
terminate their watch.   This circumstance would beautifully illustrate
the fervour of the Psalmist's devotion (Psal. cxxx. 6.) as well as serve
to explain other passages of the Old Testament.[3]   These *three* watches
are also mentioned by various profane writers.[4]

During the time of our Saviour, the night was divided into four
watches, a fourth watch having been introduced among the Jews from
the Romans, who derived it from the Greeks.   The second and third
watches are mentioned in Luke xii. 38.; the fourth in Matt. xiv. 25.;
and the four are all distinctly mentioned in Mark xiii. 35.   *Watch,
therefore, for ye know not when the master of the house cometh ; at* EVEN,
(οψε, or the late watch,) *or at* MIDNIGHT (μεσονυκτιον), *or at the* COCK-
CROWING (αλεκτοροφωνιας)[5], *or in the* MORNING (πρωι, the early watch).
Here, the *first* watch was at even, and continued from six till nine;
the *second* commenced at nine and ended at twelve, or midnight; the
third watch, called by the Romans *gallicinium,* lasted from twelve to
three; and the *morning watch* closed at six.   A double cock-crowing,
indeed, is noticed by St. Mark (xiv. 30.), where the other evangelists
mention only one. (Matt. xxvi. 34. Luke xxii. 34. John xiii. 38.)
But this may be easily reconciled.   The Jewish doctors divided the
cock-crowing into the first, second, and third; the heathen nations in
general observed only *two.*   As the cock crew the *second* time after
Peter's third denial, it was this second or principal cock-crowing (for
the Jews seem in many respects to have accommodated themselves to

---

1 During the siege of Jerusalem, the Jewish historian relates that the priests were not interrupted in the discharge of their sacred functions, but continued twice a day, in the morning,
and at the ninth hour (or at three o'clock in the afternoon), to offer up sacrifices at the altar.
The Jews rarely, if ever, ate or drank till after the hour of prayer (Acts x. 30.), and on
Sabbath-days not till the sixth hour (twelve at noon, Josephus, de vita sua, § 54.): which
circumstance well explains the apostle Peter's defence of those on whom the Holy Spirit
had miraculously descended on the day of Pentecost. (Acts ii. 15.)

Dr. A. Clarke on Exod. xiv. 11.

3 Thus the 134th psalm gives an instance of the temple watch : the whole psalm is nothing
more than the alternate cry of two different divisions of the watch. The first watch addresses
the second (v. 1. 2.), reminding them of their duty; and the second answers (v. 3.) by a
solemn blessing.   The address and the answer seem both to be a set form, which each individual proclaimed or sung aloud, at stated intervals, to notify the time of the night.   Bishop
Lowth's Isaiah, vol. ii. p. 357.

4 See Homer, Iliad. lib. x. v. 252, 253.   Livy, lib. vii. c. 35. and Xenophon, Anab.
lib. iv. p. 250. (edit. Hutchinson.)

5 In India it is very common for the people to regulate their time in the night by the
crowing of the cock.   They attach a high value to those birds, which crow with the
greatest regularity; and some of them keep the time with astonishing precision.   Roberts's
Oriental Illustrations, p. 572.

the Roman computation of time) to which the evangelists Matthew, Luke, and John refer. Or, perhaps, the second cock-crowing of the Jews might coincide with the second of the Romans.[1]

It may be proper to remark that the word *hour* is frequently used with great latitude in the Scriptures, and sometimes implies the space of time occupied by a whole watch. Matt. xxv. 13. xxvi. 40. Mark xiv. 37. Luke xxii. 59. Rev. iii. 3.) Perhaps the third *hour* mentioned in Acts xxiii. 23. was a military *watch* of the night.[2]

The Jews reckoned two evenings: the former began at the ninth hour of the natural day, or three o'clock in the afternoon; and the latter at the eleventh hour. Thus the paschal lamb was required to be sacrificed *between the evenings* (Exod. xii. 6. Lev. xxiii. 4.); which Josephus tells us, the Jews in his time did, from the ninth hour until the eleventh.[3] Hence the law, requiring the paschal lamb to be sacrificed "at even, at the going down of the sun," (Deut. xvi. 6.) expressed both evenings. It is truly remarkable, that "Christ our passover," the antitype of the paschal lamb, "expired at the ninth hour, and was taken down from the cross at the eleventh hour, or sunset." [4]

III. Seven nights and days constituted a WEEK; six of these were appropriated to labour and the ordinary purposes of life, and the *seventh* day or *Sabbath* was appointed by God to be observed as a day of rest, *because that on it he had rested from all his work which God had created and made.* (Gen. ii. 3.) This division of time was universally observed by the descendants of Noah; and some eminent critics have conjectured that was lost during the bondage of the Israelites in Egypt, but was revived and enacted by Moses agreeably to the divine command. This conjecture derives some weight from the word *Sabbat* or *Sabbata,* denoting a week among the Syrians, Arabians, Christian Persians, and Ethiopians, as in the following antient Syriac Calendar, expressed in Hebrew characters [5]:

חד־שבתא	- *One of the Sabbath,* or *Week.*	-	Sunday.
תהי־שבתא	- *Two of the Sabbath*	-	- Monday.
תלת־שבתא	- *Three of the Sabbath*	-	- Tuesday.
ארבעא־שבתא	- *Four of the Sabbath*	-	- Wednesday.
חמשא־שבתא	- *Five of the Sabbath*	-	- Thursday.
ער־שבתא	- *Eve of the Sabbath*	-	- Friday.
שבתא	- *The Sabbath.*	-	- Saturday.

The high antiquity of this calendar is evinced by the use of the cardinal numbers, *one, two, three,* &c. instead of the ordinals, *first, second, third,* &c. following the Hebrew idiom; as in the account of the creation, where we read in the original, "*one* day — *two* day — *three* day," &c.; where the Septuagint retains it in the first, calling it, ἡμερα μια. It is remarkable that all the evangelists follow the Syriac calendar,

---

[1] Lightfoot, Hor. Heb. on John xiii. 38. (Works, vol. ii. p. 597.) Grotius and Whitby on Matt. xxvi. 34. Dr. Hales's Analysis of Chronology, vol. i. p. 112. By which writers various passages of classical authors are cited. See also Mr. Townsend's Harmony of the New Testament, vol. i. pp. 480—482.

[2] Fragments annexed to Calmet's Dictionary, No. cclxiii. p. 164.

[3] De Bell. Jud. lib. vi. c. 9. § 3.

[4] Dr. Hales's Analysis of Chronology, vol. i. p. 114. In the two following pages, he illustrates several apparently chronological contradictions between the evangelists with equal felicity and learning.

[5] This calendar is taken from Bp. Marsh's Translation of Michaelis's Introduction to the New Testament, vol. i. p. 136

both in the word σαϐϐατα, used for "*a week*," and also in retaining the cardinal number μια σαϐϐατων, "*one of the week*," to express the day of the resurrection. (Matt. xxviii. 1. Mark xvi. 2. Luke xxiv. 1. John xx. 1.) Afterwards Mark adopts the usual phrase, πρωτη σαϐϐατου, "*the first of the week*" (Mark xvi. 9.), where he uses the singular σαϐϐατον for *a week ;* and so does Luke, as Νηστευω δις του σαϐϐατου, "I fast twice in *the week*." (Luke xviii. 12.)

The Syriac name for Friday, or the sixth day of the week, is also adopted by Mark, who renders it προσαϐϐατον "*sabbath-eve*," (xv. 42.) corresponding to παρασκευη, "*preparation-day*." (Matt. xxvii. 62. Mark. xv. 42. Luke xxiii. 54. John xix. 31.) And Josephus also conforms to this usage, except that he uses σαϐϐατα in the singular sense, for the *sabbath-day*, in his account of a decree of Augustus, exempting the Jews of Asia and Cyrene from secular services, εν σαϐϐασι, η τη προ ταυτης παρασκευη, απο της ωρας εννατης. "On the *sabbath*-day, or *on the preparation*-day before it, from the *ninth hour*."[1] The first three evangelists also use the plural σαϐϐατα, to denote the sabbath day. (Matt. xii. 5—11. Mark i. 21. and ii. 23. Luke iv. 16, &c.) Whereas John, to avoid ambiguity, appropriates the singular σαϐϐατον to the *sabbath*-day, and the plural σαϐϐατα to *the week*. (John v. 9—16. vii. 22, &c. xx. 1.)

The *second sabbath after the first* (Luke vi. 1.), δευτεροπρωτον, or rather the *second prime sabbath*, concerning which commentators have been so greatly divided, appears to have been the first sabbath after the second day of unleavened bread or of the passover week. Besides weeks of days, the Jews had *weeks of seven years* (the seventh of which was called the *sabbatical year*); and weeks of seven times seven years, or of forty-nine years, which were reckoned from one jubilee to another. The fiftieth or *jubilee* year was celebrated with singular festivity and solemnity.[2]

IV. The Hebrews had their MONTHS, which, like those of all other antient nations, were lunar ones, being measured by the revolutions of the moon, and consisting alternately of twenty-nine and thirty days. While the Jews continued in the land of Canaan, the commencement of their months and years was not settled by any astronomical rules or calculations, but by the *phasis* or actual appearance of the moon. As soon as they saw the moon, they began the month. Persons were therefore appointed to watch on the tops of mountains for the first appearance of the moon after the change: as soon as they saw it, they informed the Sanhedrin, and public notice was given, first, by the sounding of trumpets, to which there is an allusion in Psal. lxxxi. 3.; and afterwards lighting beacons throughout the land; though (as the mishnical rabbins tell us) after they had frequently been deceived by the Samaritans who kindled false fires, they used to announce the appearance by sending messengers. As, however, they had no months longer than thirty days, if they did not see the new moon the night following the thirtieth day, they concluded that the appearance was obstructed by the clouds; and, without watching any longer, made the next day the first day of the following month. But, on the dispersion of the Jews throughout all nations, having no opportunities of

---

[1] Antiq. lib. xvi. c. 6. § 2.
[2] Dr. Hales's Analysis of Chronology, vol. i. p. 120.

being informed of the appearance of the new moons, they were obliged to have recourse to astronomical calculations and cycles, in order to fix the beginning of their months and years. At first, they employed a cycle of eighty-four years: but this being discovered to be defective, they had recourse to the Metonic cycle of nineteen years; which was established by the authority of rabbi Hillel, prince of the Sanhedrin, about the year 360 of the Christian æra. This they still use, and say that it is to be observed until the coming of the Messiah. In the compass of this cycle there are twelve common years, consisting of twelve months, and seven intercalary years, consisting of thirteen months.[1]

Originally, the Jews had no particular names for their months, but called them the *first, second,* &c. Thus the Deluge began in the *second* month, and came to its height in the *seventh* month, at the end of 150 days (Gen. vii. 11—24. viii. 4.); and decreased until the *tenth* month, when the tops of the mountains were seen. (viii. 5.) Afterwards they acquired distinct names; thus Moses named the *first* month of the year *Abib* (Exod. xii. 2. xiii. 4.); signifying *green,* from the green ears of corn at that season; for it began about the vernal equinox. The second month was named *Zif,* signifying in Chaldee *glory* or *splendour;* in which the foundation of Solomon's temple was laid. (1 Kings vi. 1.) The seventh month was styled *Ethanim,* which is interpreted *harvests* by the Syriac version. (1 Kings viii. 2.) The eighth month *Bul;* from *the fall* of the leaf. (1 Kings vi. 38.) But concerning the origin of these appellations critics are by no means agreed: on their return from the Babylonish captivity, they introduced the names which they had found among the Chaldæans and Persians. Thus, the first month was also called *Nisan,* signifying *flight;* because in that month the Israelites were thrust out of Egypt (Exod. xii. 39.); the third month, *Sivan,* signifying *a bramble* (Esth. iii. 7. Nehem. ii. 1.); and the sixth month *Elul,* signifying *mourning,* probably because it was the time of preparation for the great day of atonement, on the tenth day of the seventh month. (Neh. vi. 15.) The ninth month was called *Chisleu,* signifying *chilled;* when the cold weather sets in, and fires are lighted. (Zech. vii. 1. Jer. xxxvi. 22.) The tenth month was called *Tebeth,* signifying *miry.* (Esth. ii. 16.) The eleventh, *Shebet,* signifying a *staff* or a *sceptre.* (Zech. i. 7.) And the twelfth. *Adar,* signifying a *magnificent mantle,* probably from the profusion of flowers and plants with which the earth then begins to be clothed in warm climates. (Ezra vi. 15. Esther iii. 7.) It is said to be a Syriac term. (2 Mac. xvi. 36.)[2]

V. The Jews had four sorts of YEARS,—one for plants, another for beasts, a third for sacred purposes, and the fourth was civil and common to all the inhabitants of Palestine.

1. The *year of Plants* was reckoned from the month corresponding with our January; because they paid tithe-fruits of the trees which budded at that time.

2. The second year was that of *Beasts;* for when they tithed their

---

[1] Dr. A. Clark, at the end of his commentary on Deuteronomy, has given six elaborately constructed tables explanatory of the Jewish calendar. Mr. Allen has also given six tables; which, though less extensive than the preceding, are well calculated to afford a clear idea of the construction and variations of the Jewish calendar. See Modern Judaism, pp. 369—377.

[2] Dr. Hales's Analysis of Chronology, vol. i. p. 127.

lambs, the owner drove all the flock under a rod, and they marked the tenth, which was given to the Levites. They could, however, only take those which fell in the year, and *this* year began at the month Elul, or the beginning of our August.

But the two years which are the most known are the *Civil* and *Ecclesiastical Years.*

3. The *Civil Year* commenced on the fifteenth of our September, because it was an old tradition that the world was created at that time. From this year the Jews computed their jubilees, dated all contracts, and noted the birth of children, and the reign of kings. It is said also that this month was appointed for making war; because, the great heats being passed, they then went into the field. In 2 Sam. xi. 1. we read that *David sent Joab and his servants with him, and all Israel, to destroy the Ammonites, at the return of the year* (marginal rendering), *at the time when kings go forth to battle*, that is, in the month of September. The annexed table exhibits the months of the Jewish civil year with the corresponding months of our computation: —

1. Tisri	corresponds with part of	September and October.
2. Marchesvan		October and November.
3. Chisleu or Kisleu		November and December.
4. Thebet		December and January.
5. Sebat		January and February.
6. Adar		February and March.
7. Nisan or Abib.		March and April.
8. Jyar or Zif		April and May.
9. Sivan.		May and June.
10. Thammuz		June and July.
11. Ab		July and August.
12. Elul		August and September.

Some of the preceding names are still in use in Persia.

4. The *Ecclesiastical* or *Sacred Year* began in March, or on the first day of the month Nisan, because at that time they departed out of Egypt. From that month they computed their feasts, and the prophets also occasionally dated their oracles and visions. Thus Zechariah (vii. 1.) says, that *the word of the Lord came unto him in the fourth* day *of the ninth month*, even in *Chisleu;* which answers to our November, whence it is evident that he adopted the ecclesiastical year, which commenced in March. The month Nisan is noted in the Old Testament for the *overflowings of Jordan* (Jos. iii. 15. 1 Chron. xii. 15.); which were common at that season, the river being swollen by the melted snows that poured in torrents from Mount Lebanon. The following table presents the months of the Jewish ecclesiastical year, compared with our months: —

1. Nisan or Abib (Neh. ii. 1. Esth. iii. 7.)	answers to part of March and April.
2. Jyar or Zif	April and May.
3. Sivan (Esth. viii. 9.)	May and June.
4. Thammuz	June and July.
5. Ab	July and August.
6. Elul (Neh. vi. 15.)	August and September.
7. Tisri	September and October.
8. Marchesvan	October and November.
9. Kisleu or Chisleu (Zech. vii. 1. Neh. i. 1.)	November and December.
10. Thebet	December and January.
11. Sebat (Zech. i. 7.)	January and February.
12. Adar (Ezr. vi. 15. Esth. iii. 7.)	February and March.[1]

---

[1] The preceding view of the sacred and civil years of the Jews is that generally adopted by the most eminent writers on Jewish antiquities, after the opinions of the Jewish rabbins,

The Jewish months being regulated by the phases or appearances of the moon, their years were consequently lunar years, consisting of twelve lunations, or 354 days and 8 hours; but as the Jewish festivals were held not only on certain fixed days of the month, but also at certain seasons of the year, consequently great confusion would, in process of time, arise by this method of calculating; the *spring* month sometimes falling in the middle of *winter*, it became necessary to accommodate the lunar to solar years, in order that their months, and consequently their festivals, might always fall at the same season. For this purpose, the Jews added a whole month to the year, as often as it was necessary; which occurred commonly once in three years, and sometimes once in two years. This intercalary month was added at the end of the ecclesiastical year after the month Adar, and was therefore called Ve-Adar, or the second Adar: but no vestiges of such intercalation are to be found in the Scriptures.

As agriculture constituted the principal employment of the Jews, they also divided their *natural* year into seasons with reference to their rural work. These, we have seen, were six in number, each of two months' duration, including one whole month and the halves of two others. See an account of them in pp. 29—34, of this volume.

To this natural division of the year there are several allusions in the Sacred Writings: as in Jer. xxxvi. 22. where king Jehoiakim is said to be sitting in the winter-house in the ninth sacred month Chisleu, the latter half of which fell in the winter or rainy season; so, in Ezra x. 13. it is said that the congregation of the people which had been convened on the twentieth day of the same month, were not able to stand out in the open air, because it was "a time of much rain." The knowledge of this mode of dividing the year illustrates John x. 22, 23. and accounts for our Lord's walking in the portico of the temple at the feast of dedication, which was celebrated towards the close of the same month.

Further, the Jews divided their solar year into four parts, called by them *Tekuphat* (that is, *revolutions of time,*) or quarters, which they distinguished by the names of the months with which they commenced: thus, the vernal equinox is termed *Tekuphat Nisan;* the autumnal equinox, *Tekuphat Tisri;* the winter solstice, *Tekuphat Tebeth;* and the summer solstice, *Tekuphat Thammuz.* Some critics have conjectured that our Lord refers to the intervening space of four months, from the conclusion of seed-time to the commencement of the harvest, in John iv. 35.

---

who affirm that March and September were the initial months of these two years, instead of April and October. That this was the case at a late period is admitted by Jahn and Ackermann, after J. D. Michaelis. But after the destruction of Jerusalem by the Romans, who commenced their year with the month of March, it appears that the Jews adopted the practice of their conquerors. In confirmation of this remark it may be observed that the rabbinical opinion is opposed not only by Josephus, but also by the genius of the Syriac and Arabic languages, and by the fact that the ceremonies prescribed to be observed on the three great festival days do not agree with the months of March and September. For a further investigation of this curious question, which cannot be discussed within the limits of a note, the reader is referred to Michaelis's Commentatio de Mensibus Hebræorum, in the Commentationes Regiæ Societatis Goettingensi per annos 1763-68, pp. 10. *et seq.*, or to Mr. Bowyer's translation of this disquisition in his " Select Dicourses" on the Hebrew months, &c. pp. 1—32.

The following CALENDAR will present to the reader a view of the entire JEWISH YEAR. It is abridged from Father Lamy's *Apparatus Biblicus*[1], with additions from the Calendar printed by Calmet, at the end of his Dictionary of the Bible. In it are inserted the festivals and fasts celebrated by the Jews; including not only those enacted by the law of Moses, and which are described in a subsequent part of this work, but likewise those which were not established until after the destruction of the temple, and those which are observed by the Jews to the present time. The lessons also are introduced which they were accustomed to read in the synagogues. Those days, on which no festival or fast was celebrated, are designedly omitted.

1. TISRI, FORMERLY CALLED ETHANIM.

The FIRST *month of the civil year, the* SEVENTH *month of the ecclesiastical year; it has thirty days, and corresponds with part of our September and October.*

1. Rosch Haschana, the beginning of the civil year. The feast of trumpets commanded in Leviticus. (Lev. xxiii. 24, 25. Numb. xxix. 1. Jer. xli. 1.)

3. The fast of Gedaliah; because Gedaliah, the son of Ahikam, and all the Jews that were with him, were slain at Mizpah. (2 Kings xxv. 25.) This is the fast that Zechariah calls the fast of the seventh month. (Zech. viii. 19.)

5. A fast. Twenty Israelites were killed: Rabbi Akiba, the son of Joseph, was loaded with irons, and died in prison.

7. A fast appointed on account of the golden calf. (Exod. xxxii. 6, 7, 8.) The lessons for this day were from Deut. xxvi. 1. to Deut. xxix. and the lxth chapter of Isaiah.

10. The fast of expiation. (Lev. xxiii. 27.)

14. The lessons for this day were from Deut. xxix. 10. to Deut. xxxi. 1. when the year had most Sabbaths; and when fewest, the book was finished on this day. And from Isa. lxi. 1. to Isa. lxiii. 10.

15. The feast of tabernacles. (Lev. xxiii. 34, 35.) It lasted seven days, exclusive of the octave or eighth day.

21. Hosanna Rabba, the seventh day of the feast of tabernacles; or the feast of branches. The lessons for this day were from Gen. i. 1. to Gen. vi. 9. and from Isa. xlii. 5. to Isa. xliii. 11.

22. The octave of the feast of tabernacles. (Lev. xxiii. 36.)

23. The solemnity of the law, in memory of the covenant and death of Moses. On this day Solomon's dedication was finished. (1 Kings viii. 65.)

28. The lessons were from Gen. vi. 9. to Gen. xii. 1. and from Isa. liv. 1. to Isa. lv. 5.

30. On this day the lessons were from Gen. xii. 1. to Gen. xviii. 1. and from Isa. xl. 27. to Isa. xli. 17. (This day is the fast held in commemoration of the murder of Gedaliah, whom Nebuchadnezzar made governor of Judæa, after he had destroyed Jerusalem, according to Dr. Prideaux.)[2]

2. MARCHESVAN.

The SECOND *month of the civil year, the* EIGHTH *month of the ecclesiastical year, it has only twenty-nine days, and corresponds with part of our October and November.*

1. The new moon. (Calmet observes, in the Jewish Calendar, at the end of his Dictionary of the Bible, that the Jews always made two new moons for every month; the first of which

---

[1] Lamy's Apparatus Biblicus, vol. i. pp. 155. *et seq.*
[2] Prideaux's Connection, part i. book. i. under the year 588.

was the last day of the preceding month ; and the first day of the month was the second new moon of that month.

3. The lessons for this day were from Gen. xviii. 1. to Gen. xxiii. 1. and from 2 Sam. iv. 1. to 2 Sam. iv. 38.

6. A fast, appointed on account of Zedekiah's having his eyes put out by the command of Nebuchadnezzar, after he had seen his children slain before his face. (2 Kings xxv. 7. Jer. lii. 10.)

8 The lessons for this day were from Gen. xxiii. 1. to Gen. xxv. 19. and from 1 Sam. i. 1. to 1 Sam. i. 32.

15. The lessons for this day were from Gen. xxv. 19. to Gen. xxviii. 10. and from Mal. i. 1. to Mal. ii. 8.

19. Fast to expiate the crimes committed on account of the feast of tabernacles.

23. A fast in memory of the stones of the altar which the Gentiles profaned, 1 Mac. iv. 46. The lessons for this day were from Gen. xxviii. 10. to Gen. xxxii. 3. and from Hos. xi. 7. to Hos. xiv. 3.

25. A fast in memory of some places which the Cuthæans seized, and were recovered by the Israelites after the captivity.

In this month the Jews prayed for the rain, which they call Jore, or the autumnal rain, which was very seasonable for their seed. Genebrard pretends that they did not ask for this rain till the next month. Perhaps there might be no stated time for asking for it ; that might depend upon their want of it. The Jews say it was in October ; and it was called in general the autumnal rain, which season lasted three months.

---

3. CHISLEU, or CASLEU.

The THIRD *month of the civil year, the* NINTH *month of the ecclesiastical year; it has thirty days, and corresponds with part of our November and December.*

1. The new moon.

2. Prayers for rain.

3. A feast in memory of the idols, which the Asmonæans threw out of the temple.

6. The lessons for this day were from Gen. xxxii. 3. to Gen. xxxvii. 1. and the whole book of Obadiah, or from Hos. xii. 12. to the end of the book.

7. A fast, instituted because king Jehoiakim burned the prophecy of Jeremiah, which Baruch had written. (Jer. xxxvi. 23.) This fast Dr. Prideaux places on the 29th of this month.[1] But Calmet places it on the sixth of this month, and makes the seventh of this month a festival, in memory of the death of Herod the Great, the son of Antipater. Scaliger will have it that it was instituted on account of Zedekiah's having his eyes put out, after his children had been slain in his sight.

10. The lessons for this day were from Gen. xxxvii. 1. to Gen. xli. 1. and from Amos ii. 6. to Amos iii. 9.

17. The lessons for this day were from Gen. xli. 1. to Gen. xliv. 18. and from 1 Sam. iii. 15. to the end of the chapter.

25. The dedication of the temple. This feast lasted eight days.

The lessons for this day were from Gen. xliv. 18. to Gen. xlvii. 27. and from Ezek. xxxvii. 15. to the end of the chapter.

---

4. THEBETH, or TEBETH.

The FOURTH *month of the civil year, the* TENTH *month of the ecclesiastical year ; it has but twenty-nine days, and corresponds with part of our December and January.*

1. The new moon.

3. The lessons for this day were from Gen. xlvii. 27. to the end of the book, and the thirteen first verses of the second chapter of the first book of Samuel.

8. A fast on account of the translation of the Bible into Greek. Philo, in his Life of Moses, says, that the Jews of Alexandria celebrated a feast on this day, in memory of the 72 Interpreters. But the Jews at present abominate that version.

---

[1] Connection, part. i. book i. under the year 685.

9. A fast, the reason of which is not mentioned by the Rabbins.

10. A fast on account of the siege which the king of Babylon laid to Jerusalem. 2 Kings xxv.

11. The lessons were the five first chapters of Exodus, and with them from Isa. xxvii. 6. to Isa. xxvii. 14. or else from Jer. i. 1. to Jer. ii. 4.

17. The lessons for this day were from Exod. vi. 1. to Exod. x. 1. and from Ezek. xxviii. 25. to Ezek. xxx. 1.

25. The lessons for this day were from Exod. x. 1. to Exod. xiii. 17. and from Jer. xlvi. 13. to the end of the chapter.

28. A fast in memory of Rabbi Simeon's having driven the Sadducees out of the Sanhedrin, where they had the upper hand in the time of Alexander Jannæus; and his having introduced the Pharisees in their room.

---

5. SEBAT, SHEVET, or SHEBAT.

The FIFTH *month of the civil year, the* ELEVENTH *month of the ecclesiastical year ; it has thirty days, and corresponds with part of our January and February.*

1. The new moon. In this month the Jews began to reckon the years of the trees which they planted, whose fruit was not to be eaten till after they had been planted three years. Calmet fixes the beginning of this year of trees to the 15th day of this month.

2. A rejoicing for the death of Alexander Jannæus.

3. Now is read from Exod. xiii. 17. to Exod. xviii. 1. and from Judg. iv. 4. to Judg. vi. 1. A fast in memory of the death of the elders who succeeded Joshua. (Judg. ii. 10.)

8. A fast, because on this day died the just men who lived in the days of Joshua. (Judg. ii. 10.)

10. The lessons were from Exod. xviii. 1. to Exod. xxi. 1. and the whole sixth chapter of Isaiah.

17. The lessons for this day were from Exod. xxi. 1. to Exod. xxv. 1. and Jer. xxxiv. from v. 8. to the end of the chapter.

23. A fast in memory of the insurrection of the other tribes against that of Benjamin, on account of the death of the Levite's wife. (Judg. xx.)

26. Now is read, from Exod. xxv. 1. to Exod. xxvii. 20. and from 1 Sam. v. 12. to 1 Sam. vi. 14.

29. Now is read, from Exod. xxvii. 20. to Exod. xxx. 11. and Ezek. xliii. from the 10th verse to the end of the chapter.

---

6. ADAR.

The SIXTH *month of the civil year, the* TWELFTH *month of the ecclesiastical year ; it has only twenty-nine days, and corresponds with part of our February and March.*

1. The new moon Genebrard places the first fruits on this day.

3. The lessons for this day were from Exod. xxx. 11. to Exod. xxxv. 1. and from 1 Sam. xviii. 1. to 1 Sam. xviii. 39.

7. A fast on account of the death of Moses, the lawgiver of the Jews. (Deut. xxxiv. 5, 6.)

9. A fast. The schools of Schammai and Hillel began to be divided on this day.

12. The lessons are from Exod. xxxv. 1. to Exod. xxxviii. 21. and from 1 Sam. xvii. 13. to 1 Sam. xvii. 26. (This day is also a feast in memory of the death of Hollianus and Pipus, two proselytes and brothers, who chose rather to die than violate the law.) [1]

13. A festival on account of the death of Nicanor. (2 Macc. xv. 37.) Genebrard places the fast of Esther (Esth. iv. 16.) on this day.

14. Purim the first, or the Little Feast of Lots.

15. Purim the second, or the Great Feast of Lots. (Esth. ix. 18.) An account of these festivals is given in a subsequent part of this volume.

The dedication of the temple of Zorobabel (Ezra vi. 16.) was made in this month, but the day is not known.

18. Now is read from Exod. xxxviii. 21. to the end of the book ; and from 1 Sam. vii. 50. to 1 Sam. viii. 21.

20. A fast in memory of the rain obtained of God, by one Onias Hammagel, in a time of great dearth.

---

[1] Selden, l. iii. c. 13. de Syned. ex Megill. Taanith. Calmet's Calend.

25. The lessons were the five first chapters of Leviticus, and from Isa. xliii. 21. to Isa. xliv. 24.

28. A feast. The Grecian edict, which forbad the Jews the use of circumcision, recalled. The intercalary month was inserted here, when the year was to consist of thirteen lunar months; and the month so added was called Ve-Adar, that is, the second Adar.

---

7. ABIB, OR NISAN.

The SEVENTH *month of the civil year, the* FIRST *month of the ecclesiastical year; it has thirty days, and corresponds with part of our March and April.*

1. The new moon. A fast on account of the death of the children of Aaron. (Levit. x. 1.)
3. The lessons were from Lev. vi. 1. to Lev. ix. 1. and from Jer. vii. 21. to Jer. viii. 4.
10. A fast on account of the death of Miriam. (Numb. xx. 1.) On this day every one provided himself with a lamb against the fourteenth.
12. The lessons were from Lev. ix. 1. to Lev. xii. 1. and from 2 Sam. vi. 1. to 2 Sam. vii. 17.
14. The passover. The Jews now burn all the leavened bread they have in their houses.
15. The feast of unleavened bread.
16. The morrow after the feast of the passover. On this second day the Jews offered up to God the Omer, that is, the sheaf of the new barley harvest, which was cut and carried into the temple with much ceremony. The fifty days of Pentecost were reckoned from this day.
19. The lessons were from Lev. xii. 1. to Lev. xiv. 1. and from 2 Sam. iv. 42. to 2 Sam. v. 20.
21. The last day of the feast of unleavened bread.
26. A fast for the death of Joshua. (Josh. xxiv. 29.)
27. The lessons were from Lev. xiv. 1. to Lev. xvi. 1. and 2 Sam. vii. 3. to the end of the chapter.
29. Genebrard observes, that the Jews in this month prayed for the spring rain, or the latter rain, which was seasonable for their harvest. (Deut. xi. 14. Zech. x. 1.) This is that rain which the Hebrews call Malkosh, that is, the rain which prepares for the harvest, and makes the grain swell.

---

8. JYAR, OR ZIF.

The EIGHTH *month of the civil year, the* SECOND *month of the ecclesiastical year; it has only twenty-nine days, and corresponds with part of our April and May.*

1. The new moon.
3. The lessons were from Lev. xvi. 1. to Lev. xix. 1. and 17 verses of Ezek. xxii.
10. A fast for the death of Eli, and the taking of the ark. (1 Sam. iv. 18.)
11. The lessons were from Lev. xix. 1. to Lev. xx. 1. and from Amos ix. 7. to the end; or else from Ezek. xx. 2. to Ezek. xxi. 21.
14. The second passover (Numb. ix. 10, 11.) in favour of those who could not, or were not suffered to celebrate the passover the last month.
19. The lessons were from Lev. xxi. 1. to Lev. xxv. 1. and from Ezek. iv. 15. to the end of the chapter.
23. A feast. Simon takes Gaza, according to Scaliger.
26. The lessons were from Lev. xxv. 1. to Lev. xxvi. 3. and from Jer. xxxii. 6. to Jer. xxxii. 28.
28. A fast for the death of Samuel, who was lamented by all the people. (1 Sam. xxv. 1.)

---

9. SIVAN, OR SIUVAN.

The NINTH *month of the civil year, the* THIRD *month of the ecclesiastical year; it has thirty days, and corresponds with part of our May and June.*

1. The new moon.
3. The lessons were from Lev. xxvi. 3. to the end of the book, and from Jer. xvi. 19. to Jer. xvii. 15.

6. The Feast of Pentecost, which is also called the feast of weeks, because it fell just seven weeks after the morrow after the feast of the passover.

10. Numbers is begun and read to ch. iv. v. 21. and from Hosea ii. 10. to Hosea ii. 21.

13. A feast in memory of the victories of the Maccabees over the Bathsurites, 1 Macc. v. 52.

17. A feast for the taking of Cæsarea by the Asmonæans.

19. The lessons were from Numb. iv. 21. to Numb. viii. 1. and from Judg. ii. 2. to the end of the chapter.

23. A fast, because Jeroboam forbad the ten tribes, which obeyed him, to carry up their first fruits to Jerusalem. (1 Kings xii. 27.)

25. A fast, on account of the murder of the Rabbins, Simon the son of Gamaliel, Ishmael the son of Elisha, and Ananias the Sagan, that is, the high-priest's vicar.

26. The lessons were from Numb. viii. to Numb. xiii. 1. and from Zech. ii. 10. to Zech. iv. 8.

27. A fast, because Rabbi Hanina, the son of Tardion, was burnt, and with him the book of the law.

10. THAMMUZ, or TAMMUZ.

The TENTH *month of the civil year, the* FOURTH *month of the ecclesiastical year; it has only twenty-nine days, and corresponds with part of our June and July.*

1. The new moon.

3. The lessons were from Numb. xiii. 1. to Numb. xvi. 1. and the 2d chapter of Joshua.

10. The lessons were from Numb. xvi. 1. to Numb. xix. 1. and from 1 Sam. xi. 14. to 1 Sam. xii. 23.

14. A feast for the abolition of a pernicious book of the Sadducees against the oral law and tradition.

17. The fast of the fourth month, because the tables of the law were broken, the perpetual sacrifice ceased, Epistemon burned the law, and set up an idol in the temple.[1] (Exod. xxxii. 19.)

19. The lessons were from Numb. xix. 1. to Numb. xxii. 2. and the eleventh chapter of Judges to the 34th verse.

26. The lessons were from Numb. xxii. 2. to Numb. xxv. 10. and from Mic. v. 7. to Mic. vi. 9.

29. The lessons were from Numb. xxv. 10. to Numb. xxx. 2. and from 1 Sam. xviii. 46. to the end of the chapter.

11. AB.

The ELEVENTH *month of the civil year, the* FIFTH *month of the ecclesiastical year; it has thirty days, and corresponds with part of our July and August.*

1. The new moon. A fast on account of the death of Aaron the high-priest. (Numb. xxxiii. 38.)

3. The lessons were from Numb. xxx. 2. to Numb. xxxiii. 1. and from Jer. i. 1. to Jer. ii. 4.

9. The fast of the fifth month, because the temple was first burnt by the Chaldees, and afterwards by the Romans, on this day; and because God on this day declared in the time of Moses that none of those who came out of Egypt should enter into the land of promise. (Numb. xiv. 29. 31.)

12. The book of Numbers is now finished; and from Jer. ii. 4. to Jer. ii. 29. is also read.

18. A fast, because in the time of Ahaz the evening lamp went out. Genebrard calls this lamp the Western Lamp.

20. Deuteronomy is begun, and read from i. 1. to iii. 23. and the first chapter of Isaiah to verse 28.

21. Selden asserts that this was the day that all the wood which was wanted in the temple was brought into it; but others think that this was done in the next month.

24. A feast for the Maccabees having abolished that law of the Sadducees whereby sons and daughters inherited alike.

28. The lessons were from Deut. iii. 23. to Deut. vii. 12. and Isa. xl. to verse 27.

---

[1] See Prideaux's Con. p. i. b. 1. under the year 588.

12. ELUL.

The TWELFTH *month of the civil year, the* SIXTH *month of the ecclesiastical year; it has but twenty-nine days, and corresponds with part of our August and September.*

1. The new moon.
3. The lessons were from Deut. vii. 12. to Deut. xi. 26. and from Isa. xlix. 14. to Isa. li. 4.
7. The dedication of the walls of Jerusalem by Nehemiah.
12. The lessons were from Deut. xi. 27. to Deut. xvi. 18. and from Isa. liv. 11. to Isa. lv. 4.
17. A fast, because of the death of the spies who brought up the evil report of the land of promise. (Numb. xiv. 36, 37.)
20. The lessons were from Deut. xvi. 18. to Deut. xxi. 10. and from Isa. li. 12. to Isa. lii. 18.
21. The festival of wood offering (*xylophoria*).
22. A fast in memory of the punishment of the wicked and incorrigible Israelites.
28. The lessons were from Deut. xxi. 10. to Deut. xxvi. 1. and Isa. liv. to verse 11.
29. This is the last day of the month, on which the Jews reckoned up the beasts that had been born, the tenths of which belonged to God. They chose this day on which to do it, because the first day of the month Tisri was a festival, and therefore they could not tithe a flock on that day.

VI. In common with other nations, the Jews reckoned any *part* of a period of time for the whole, as in Exod. xvi. 35. An attention to this circumstance will explain several apparent contradictions in the Sacred Writings : thus, a part of the day is used for the whole, and part of the year for an entire year.

In Gen. xvii. 12. circumcision is enjoined to be performed when a child is *eight days old*, but in Lev. xii. 3. on the *eighth day ;* accordingly, when Jesus Christ is said to have been circumcised *when eight days were accomplished* (Luke ii. 21.) and John the Baptist *on the eighth day* (Luke i. 59.), the last, which was the constant usage, explains the former passage. Abenezra, an eminent Jewish commentator (on Levit. xii. 3.), says, that if an infant were born in the *last* hour of the day, such hour was counted for one *whole* day. This observation critically reconciles the account of our Lord's resurrection in Matt. xxvii. 63. and Mark viii. 31., "*three days after*," with that of his resurrection "*on the third day*," according to Matt. xvi. 21. Luke ix. 22., and according to fact; for, as our Lord was crucified on Good Friday, about the sixth hour, or noon, the remainder of that day to sunset, according to the Jewish computation, was reckoned as one day. Saturday, it is universally admitted, formed the *second* day; and as the third day began on Saturday at sunset, and our Saviour rose about sunrise on the following morning, that part of a day is justly reckoned for the third day: so that the interval was "*three days and three nights*," or three calendar days current, not exceeding 42 hours, and, consequently, not two entire days.[1] This observation also illustrates 2 Chron. x. 5. 12.; and the same mode of computing time obtains in the East, to this day.[2]

---

[1] Dr. Hales, to whom we are partly indebted for the above remark, has cited several passages from profane authors, who have used a similar phraseology. (Analysis of Chronology, vol. i. pp. 121, 122.) Similar illustrations from rabbinical writers are collected by Bp. Beveridge, (on the 39 Articles, in Art. IV. Works, vol. ix. p. 159. note f.) by Dr. Lightfoot (Hor. Heb. in Matt. xii. 40.), and by Reland. (Antiq. Heb. lib. iv. c. 1.)

[2] Shortly before the philanthropic Mr. Howard arrived at Constantinople, the grand chamberlain of the city (whose province it was to supply the inhabitants with bread) had been beheaded in a summary way, in the public street, for having furnished, or permitted to be furnished, loaves short of weight; and his body was exposed for a day and a half, with three light loaves beside it to denote his crime. " When Mr. Howard was told that the body had

In like manner, in some parts of the East, the year ending on a certain day, any portion of the foregoing year is taken for a whole year; so that, supposing a child to be born in the last week of our December, it would be reckoned one year old on the first day of January, because born in the old year. If this mode of computation obtained among the Hebrews, the principle of it easily accounts for those anachronisms of single years, or parts of years taken for whole ones, which occur in sacred writ: it obviates the difficulties which concern the half years of several princes of Judah and Israel, in which the latter half of the deceased king's last year has hitherto been supposed to be added to the former half of his successor's first year.

" We are told," (1 Sam. xiii. 1. marg. reading,) " a son of one year was Saul in his kingdom : and two years he reigned over Israel," that is, say he was crowned in June: he was consequently *one year* old on the first of January following, though he had only reigned six months, — *the son* of a year. But, after this so following first of January he was in the second year of his reign; though, according to our computation, the first year of his reign wanted some months of being completed; in this, his *second* year, he chose three thousand military, &c. guards.

" The phrase (απο διετης) used to denote the age of the infants slaughtered at Bethlehem (Matt. ii. 16.) 'from two years old and under,' is a difficulty that has been deeply felt by the learned. Some infants *two weeks* old, some *two months*, others *two years*, equally slain ! Surely those born so long before could not possibly be included in the order, whose purpose was to destroy a child, certainly born within *a few* months. This is regulated at once by the idea that they were *all* of nearly equal age, being recently born; some not long *before* the close of the old year, others a little time *since* the beginning of the new year. Now, those born *before* the close of the old year, though only a few months or weeks, would be reckoned not merely *one year* old, but also in their second year, as the expression implies; and those born *since* the beginning of the year, would be well described by the phrase ' *and under*,' that is, under one year old;—some, *two years* old, though not born a complete twelvemonth (perhaps, in fact, barely six months) ; others, *under* one year old, yet born three, four, or five months, and, therefore, a trifle younger than those before described: according to the time which Herod had diligently inquired of the wise men, IN *their second year and* UNDER." [1]

VII. Besides the computation of years, the Hebrews first and the Jews afterwards, were accustomed to reckon their time from some RE- MARKABLE ÆRAS or epochas. Thus, 1. From Gen. vii. 11. and viii. 13., it appears that they reckoned from the lives of the patriarchs or other illustrious persons: 2. From their departure out of Egypt, and the first institution of their polity (Exod. xix. 1. xl. 17. Numb. i. 1. ix. 1. xxxiii. 38. 1 Kings vi. 1.) : 3. Afterwards, from the building of

---

lain there for three days, he expressed his surprise that it had not bred a contagion. He learnt, however, that in point of fact it had not been left so long, as they were *not* entire days: for, it being the evening when the head was struck off, it remained the whole of the second, and was removed early in the succeeding morning, which was accounted the third ; thus" (as Mr. H.'s biographer very properly remarks) " the manner of computation, in use at the time of our Saviour's crucifixion and burial, still subsists among the eastern nations." (Brown's Life of John Howard, Esq. pp. 437, 438. 8vo. edit.)

[1] Calmet's Dictionary, 4to. edit. vol. ii. Supplementary Addenda.

the temple (1 Kings ix. 10. 2 Chron. viii. 1.), and from the reigns of the kings of Judah and Israel: 4. Then from the commencement of the Babylonian captivity (Ezek. i. 1. xxxiii. 21. xl. 1.); and, perhaps, also from their return from captivity, and the dedication of the second temple. In process of time they adopted, 5. The Æra of the Seleucidæ, which in the books of Maccabees is called the Æra of the Greeks, and the Alexandrian Æra: it began from the year when Seleucus Nicanor attained the sovereign power, that is, about 312 years before the birth of Jesus Christ. This æra the Jews continued to employ for upwards of thirteen hundred years.[1]   6. They were further accustomed to reckon their years from the years when their princes began to reign. Thus, in 1 Kings xv. 1. Isa. xxxvi. 1. and Jer. i. 2, 3., we have traces of their antiently computing according to the years of their kings; and in later times, (1 Macc. xiii. 42. xiv. 27.) according to the years of the Asmonæan princes. Of this mode of computation we have vestiges in Matt. ii. 1. Luke i. 5. and iii. 1. Lastly, ever since the compilation of the Talmud, the Jews have reckoned their years from the creation of the world.[2]

CHAPTER V.

ON THE TRIBUTE AND TAXES MENTIONED IN THE SCRIPTURES.[3]

I. *Annual Payments made by the Jews for the support of their Sacred Worship.*— II. *Tributes paid to their own Sovereigns.* — III. *Tributes and Customs paid by them to Foreign Powers.*—*Notice of the Money-Changers.* — IV. *Account of the Publicans or Tax-Gatherers.*

As no government can be supported without great charge, it is but just that every one who enjoys his share of protection from it, should contribute towards its maintenance and support.

---

[1] There are in fact two dates assigned to the æra of the Seleucidæ in the two books of Maccabees. As Seleucus did not obtain permanent possession of the city of Babylon (which had been retaken from him by Demetrius, surnamed Poliorcetes, or the vanquisher of cities,) until the spring of the year 311 before Christ, the Babylonians fixed the commencement of this æra in the latter year. " The *first* book of Maccabees computes the years from April, B. c. 311, as Michaelis has shown in his note on 1 Macc. x. 21.; while the *second* book dates from October, B. c. 312.; consequently, there is often the difference of a year in the chronology of these books. (Compare 2 Macc. xi. 21. with 1 Macc. vi. 16., and 2 Macc. xiii. 1. with 1 Macc. vi. 20.) This æra continued in general use among the orientals, with the exception of the Mohammedans, who employed it together with their own æra from the flight of Mohammed, B. c. 622. The Jews had no other epoch until A.D. 1040.; when, being expelled from Asia by the caliphs, and scattered about in Spain, England, Germany, Poland, and other western countries, they began to date from the creation, though still without entirely dropping the æra of the Seleucidæ. The orientals denominate this epoch the *æra of the two-horned;* by which it is generally supposed they mean Alexander the Great. But perhaps the name had primary reference to Seleucus; for on some coins he is represented with two horns. See Froelich, Annales Syriæ, Tab. ii. Seleuc. Nic. 1. et Tab. iii. 29."— (Jahn's History of the Hebrew Commonwealth, vol. i. pp. 249, 250.)

[2] Reland, Antiq. Hebr. pp. 203—215. Schulzii Compendium Archæologiæ Hebraicæ, lib. i. c. 11. pp. 94—107. Lamy's Apparatus Biblicus, book i. ch. 5. vol. i. pp. 138—154. Calmet's Dictionary, articles Day, Week, Month, Year. Jahn. et Ackermann, Archæologia Biblica, §§ 101—103. Jennings' Jewish Antiquities, book iii. ch. 1. See also Waehner's Antiquitates Hebræorum, part ii. p. 5. et seq. Pritii Introd. in Nov. Test. pp. 566—575.; Pareau, Antiquitas Hebraica, pp. 310—318.

[3] The materials of this chapter, where other authorities are not cited, are derived from Schulz's Archæologia Hebraica, c. 13. de vectigalibus et tributis, and Pareau's Antiquitas Hebraica, part iii. sect. ii. c. 5. de tributis et vectigalibus.

I. On the first departure of the Israelites from Egypt, before any regulation was made, the people contributed, on any extraordinary occasion, according to their ability, as in the case of the voluntary donations for the tabernacle. (Exod. xxv. 2. xxxv. 5.) After the tabernacle was erected, a payment of half a shekel was made by every male of twenty years of age and upwards (Exod. xxx. 13. 14.), when the census, or *sum of the children of Israel,* was taken : and on the return of the Jews from the Babylonian captivity, an annual payment of the *third part* of a shekel was made, for the maintenance of the temple-worship and service. (Neh. x. 32.) Subsequently, the enactment of Moses was deemed to be of perpetual obligation[1], and in the time of our Saviour two drachmæ, or half a shekel, were paid by every Jew, whether native or residing in foreign countries : besides which, every one, who was so disposed, made voluntary offerings, according to his ability. (Mark xii. 41—44.)[2] Hence vast quantities of gold were annually brought to Jerusalem into the temple[3], where there was an apartment called the *Treasury* (Γαζοφυλακιον), specially appropriated to their reception. After the destruction of Jerusalem, Vespasian, by an edict, commanded that the half shekel should in future be brought by the Jews, wherever they were, into the capitol.[4] In addition to the preceding payments for the support of their sacred worship, we may notice the first fruits and tenths, of which an account is found in Part III. Chap. IV. *infra.*

II. Several of the Canaanitish tribes were tributary to the Israelites even from the time of Joshua (Josh. xvi. 10. xvii. 13. Judg. i. 28. 33.) whence they could not but derive considerable wealth. The Moabites and Syrians were tributary to David (2 Sam. viii. 2. 6.) : and Solomon at the beginning of his reign compelled the Amorites, Hittites, Perizzites, Hivites, and Jebusites, who were left in the country, to pay him tribute, and to perform the drudgery of the public works which he had undertaken, and from which the children of Israel were exempted. (1 Kings ix. 21. 22. 33. 2 Chron. viii. 9.) But towards the end of his reign he imposed a tribute on them also (1 Kings v. 13. 14. ix. 15. xi. 27.), which alienated their minds, and sowed the seeds of that discontent, which afterwards ripened into open revolt by the rebellion of Jeroboam the son of Nebat.

III. Afterwards, however, the Israelites being subdued by other nations, were themselves compelled to pay tribute to their conquerors. Thus Pharaoh-Necho, king of Egypt, imposed a tribute of one hundred talents of silver and a talent of gold. (2 Kings xxiii. 33. 35.) After their return from captivity, the Jews paid tribute to the Persians, under whose government they were (Ezra iv. 13.), then to the Greeks, from which, however, they were exonerated, when under the Maccabees they had regained their liberty.[5] In later times, when they were con-

---

[1] Josephus de Bell. Jud. lib. vii. c. 6. § 6. Philonis Judæi Opera, tom. ii. p. 224.
[2] A singular law was in force in the time of Jesus Christ, prohibiting *one* mite (λεπτον) from being cast into the treasury. The poor widow, therefore, who in Mark xii. 42. is said to have cast in *two* mites, gave the smallest sum permitted by the law. Schœtgen, Horæ Hebraicæ, vol. i. p. 250. Townsend's Harmony of the New Testament, vol. i. p. 114
[3] Josephus, Ant. Jud. lib. xiv. c. 7. § 2. Cicero, Orat. pro Flacco, c. 28.
[4] Josephus, de Bell. Jud. lib. vii. c. 6. § 6.
[5] 1 Macc. x. 29, 30. xi. 35, 36. xv. 5. Josephus, Ant. Jud. lib. xiii. c. 2. § 3. c. 4. § 9. c. 6. § 6.

quered by the Roman arms under Pompey, they were again subjected
to the payment of tribute, even though their princes enjoyed the honours
and dignities of royalty, as was the case with Herod the Great (Luke
ii. 1—5.) : and afterwards, when Judæa was reduced into a Roman
province, on the dethronement and banishment of his son Archeläus,
the Romans imposed on the Jews not only the annual capitation tax of
a denarius (φορος) but also a tax on goods imported or exported (τελος),
and various other taxes and burthens. To this capitation tax the evangelists allude in Matt. xxii. 17. and Mark xii. 14. where it is termed
νομισμα κηνσου (*numisma census*), or the tribute money; and as this tax
appears from Matt. xxii. 20,21. to have been paid in Roman coin, the
Jews paid it with great reluctance; and raised various insurrections on
account of it. Among these malcontents, Judas, surnamed the Gaulonite or Galilæan, distinguished himself: he pretended that it was not
lawful to pay tribute to a foreigner; that it was the badge of actual
servitude, and that they were not allowed to own any for their master
who did not worship the Lord. These sentiments animated the Pharisees, who came to Christ with the insidious design of ensnaring him
by the question, whether it was lawful to pay tribute to Cæsar or not?
Which question he answered with equal wisdom and regard for the
Roman government. (Matt. xxii. 17—21.) With these sentiments the
Jews continued to be animated long after the ascension of Jesus Christ;
and it should seem that some of the first Hebrew Christians had imbibed their principles. In opposition to which, the apostles Paul and
Peter in their inimitable epistles strenuously recommend and inculcate
on all sincere believers in Jesus Christ, the duties of submission and
obedience to princes, and a conscientious discharge of their duty, in
paying tribute. (Rom. xiii. 7. 1 Pet. ii. 13.)

To supply the Jews who came to Jerusalem from all parts of the
Roman empire to pay the half-shekel with coins current there, the
money changers (κολλυβισται) stationed themselves at tables, in the
courts of the temple, and chiefly, it should seem, in the court of the
Gentiles, for which they exacted a small fee, *kolbon* (κολλυβος). It was
the tables on which these men trafficked for this unholy gain, which
were overturned by Jesus Christ. (Matt. xxi. 12.)[1]

The money-changers (called τραπεζιται in Matt. xxi. 12. and κερ-
ματισται in John ii. 14.) were also those who made a profit by exchanging money. They supplied the Jews who came from distant parts of
Judæa and other parts of the Roman empire, with money, to be received back at their respective homes, or which, perhaps, they had paid
before they commenced their journey. It is likewise probable that
they exchanged foreign coins for such as were current at Jerusalem.

IV. Among the Romans, the censors let their taxes by *public* auction; and those who farmed them were called *Publicani*, or PUBLICANS.
These farmers-general were usually Roman knights[2], who had under

---

[1] Grotius, Hammond, and Whitby, on Matt. xxi. 12. Dr. Lightfoot's Works, vol. ii.
p. 225. In Ceylon, " Moormen, whose business it is to give cash for notes, may be seen
sitting in public places, with heaps of coin before them. On observing a person with a note,
or in want of their services, they earnestly solicit his attention." Callaway's Oriental Observations, p. 68.

[2] Cicero, in Verrem, lib. iii. c. 72. Orat. pro Planco, c. 9. De Petitione Consulatûs
c. 1. Tacit. Annal. lib. iv. c. 6. Adam's Roman Antiquities, pp. 25. 60.

them inferior collectors: Josephus has made mention of several Jews who were Roman knights[1], whence Dr. Lardner thinks it probable that they had merited the equestrian rank by their good services in collecting some part of the revenue. The collectors of ·these tributes were known by the general name of Τελωναι, that is, tax-gatherers, in our authorised version rendered PUBLICANS. Some of them appear to have been receivers-general for a large district, as Zaccheus, who is styled a *chief publican* (Αρχιτελωνης). Matthew, who is termed simply a *publican* (Τελωνης), was one who sat at the receipt of custom where the duty was paid on imports and exports. (Matt. ix. 9. Luke v. 29. Mark ii. 14.) These officers, at least the inferior ones, (like the *rahdars*, or toll-gatherers, in modern Persia[2], and the *mirigees*, or collectors of customs, in Asia Minor[3], were generally rapacious, extorting more than the legal tribute; whence they were reckoned infamous among the Greeks, and various passages in the gospels show how odious they were to the Jews (Mark ii. 15, 16. Luke iii. 13.), insomuch that the Pharisees would hold no communication whatever with them, and imputed it to our Saviour as a crime that he *sat at meat* with publicans. (Matt. ix. 10, 11. xi. 19. xxi. 31, 32.) The payment of taxes to the Romans was accounted by the Jews an intolerable grievance; hence those who assisted in collecting them were detested as plunderers in the cause of the Romans, as betrayers of the liberties of their country, and as abettors of those who had enslaved it; this circumstance will account for the contempt and hatred so often expressed by the Jews in the evangelical histories against the collectors of the taxes or tribute.[4]

The parable of the Pharisee and the Publican (Luke xviii. 10—13.) will derive considerable illustration from these circumstances. Our Saviour, in bringing these two characters together, appears to have chosen them as making the strongest contrast between what, in the public estimation, were the extremes of excellence and villany. The

---

[1] De Bell. Jud. lib. ii. c. 14. § 9.

[2] The *rahdars*, or toll-gatherers, are appointed to levy a toll upon *Kafilehs* or caravans of merchants: "who in general exercise their office with so much brutality and extortion, as to be execrated by all travellers. The police of the highways is confided to them, and whenever any goods are stolen, they are meant to be the instruments of restitution; but when they are put to the test, are found to be inefficient. None but a man in power can hope to recover what he has once lost.......The collections of the toll are farmed, consequently extortion ensues; and as most of the rahdars receive no other emolument than what they can exact over and above the prescribed dues from the traveller, their insolence is accounted for on the one hand, and the detestation in which they are held on the other." Morier's Second Journey, p. 70.

[3] At Smyrna, the mirigee sits in the house allotted to him, as Matthew *sat at the receipt of custom* (or in the custom-house of Capernaum); "and receives the money which is due from various persons and commodities, entering into the city. The exactions and rude behaviour of these men," (says Mr. Hartley, who experienced both) "are just in character with the conduct of the publicans mentioned in the New Testament."......" When men are guilty of such conduct as this, no wonder that they were detested in antient times, as were the publicans; and in modern times, as are the mirigees." (Hartley's Researches in Greece, p. 239.)

[4] Lardner's Credibility, part i. book i. c. 9. §§ 10, 11. Carpzovii Apparatus Antiquitatum Sacri Codicis, pp. 29, 30. As the Christians subsequently were often termed Galilæans, and were represented as a people hostile to all government, and its necessary supports, St. Paul in Rom. xiii. 6. studiously obviates this slander; and enjoins the payment of tribute to civil governors, because, as all governments derive their authority from God, rulers are His ministers, attending upon this very t hing, viz. the public administration, to protect the good and to punish the evil doer. (Gilpin and Valpy on Rom. xiii. 6.)

Pharisees, it is well known, were the most powerful sect among the Jews, and made great pretences to piety; and when the account of the Persian rahdars, given in the preceding page, is recollected, it will account for the Pharisee, in addressing God, having made *extortioners,* and *the unjust* almost synonymous terms with publicans; because, from his peculiar office, the rahdar is almost an extortioner by profession.[1]

CHAPTER VI.

ON THE GENEALOGICAL TABLES OF THE HEBREWS, AND PUBLIC MEMORIALS OF EVENTS.

I. *On the Genealogical Tables of the Hebrews.*—II. *Public Memorials of Events.*

I. THE Hebrews were very careful in preserving their GENEALO-GIES, or the history of the successions of families. Vestiges of these histories of families appear in Gen. v. and x. In proportion as the Hebrews increased in numbers during their residence in Egypt, it became an object of growing importance carefully to preserve the genealogical tables of the whole nation, in order that each tribe might be kept perfectly distinct. The charge of these genealogies was, most probably, confided, in the first instance, to the *shoterim,* or scribes, of whom a short account is given in p. 83. *supra,* and afterwards to the Levites: at least in the time of the kings, we find that the scribes were generally taken from the tribe of Levi. (1 Chron. xxiii. 4. 2 Chron. xix. 8—11. xxxiv. 13.) "This was a very rational procedure, as the Levites devoted themselves particularly to study; and, among husbandmen and unlearned people, few were likely to be so expert in writing, as to be intrusted with keeping registers so important. In later times the genealogical tables were kept in the temple."[2]

Whatever injury the public genealogies might have sustained in consequence of the Babylonish captivity, it was repaired on the restoration of the Jewish polity, as far at least as was practicable. (Ezra ii. viii. 1—14. Nehem. vii. xii.) Hence it is, that a very considerable portion of the first book of Chronicles is composed of genealogical tables: the comparison of which, as well as of the genealogy recorded in Gen. v. with the tables in Matt. i. and Luke iii., will contribute materially to show the fulfilment of the prophecies relative to the advent of the Messiah. Josephus states that the Jews had an uninterrupted succession of their high-priests preserved in their records for the space of nearly two thousand years; and that the priests in Judæa, and even in Egypt and Babylon, or in any other place whithersoever their priests were carried, were careful to preserve their genealogies.[3] Such priests after the captivity as could not produce their genealogies, were excluded from the sacerdotal office. Hence, when in Heb. vii. 3.

---

[1] Morier's Second Journey, p. 71,
[2] Michaelis's Commentaries, vol. i. p. 250.
[3] Josephus against Apion, book i. § 7.

Melchizedek is said to have been *without descent*, (ἀγενεαλογητος, that is, without genealogy,) the meaning is, that his name was not found in the public genealogical registers: his father and mother, and ancestors, were unknown, whence his priesthood was of a different kind, and to be regarded differently from that of Aaron and his sons.

From similar public registers Matthew and Luke derived the genealogies of our Saviour; the former of which, from Abraham to Jesus Christ, embraces a period of nearly two thousand years, while the genealogy of Luke, from Adam to Christ, comprises a period of about four thousand years. It is well known that the Jews carried their fondness for genealogies to great excess, and prided themselves on tracing their pedigrees up to Abraham. Jerome says that they were as well acquainted with genealogies from Adam to Zerubbabel as they were with their own names.[1] Against such unprofitable genealogies Paul cautions Timothy (1 Tim. i. 4.) and Titus (iii. 9.) Since the total dispersion of the Jews in the reign of Adrian, the Jews have utterly lost their antient genealogies.

In exhibiting genealogical tables with any specific design, some of the sacred writers, for the sake of brevity, omitted names which were of less importance, and distributed the genealogies into certain equal classes. Examples of this kind occur in Exod. vi. 14—24. 1 Chron. vi. 12—15. compared with Ezra i. 5. and in Matt. i. 17. The Arabs have not unfrequently taken a similar liberty in their genealogies.[2]

II. From the remotest ages, mankind have been desirous of perpetuating the memory of remarkable events, not only for their own benefit, but also in order to transmit them to posterity; and in proportion to the antiquity of such events has been the simplicity of the PUBLIC MEMORIALS employed to preserve the remembrance of them. When, therefore, any remarkable event befell the patriarchs, they raised either a rude stone or a heap of stones in the very place where such event had happened. (Gen. xxviii. 18. xxxi. 45, 46.) Sometimes, also, they gave names to places importing the nature of the transactions which had taken place (Gen. xvi. 14. xxi. 31. xxii. 14. xxviii. 19. xxxi. 47—49.): and symbolical names were sometimes given by them to individuals. (Gen. xxv. 26. 30.) To this usage the Almighty is represented as vouchsafing to accommodate himself, in Gen. xvii. 5. 15. and xxxii. 28, 29.

Conformably to this custom, Moses enjoined the Israelites to erect an altar of great stones on which the law was to be inscribed, after they had crossed the river Jordan (Deut. xxvii. 1—4.), and also gave to those places, which had been signalised by the previous conduct of the Israelites, significant names which would be perpetual memorials of their rebellion against God. (Exod. xvii. 7.) The same custom obtained after their arrival in the land of Canaan. (Josh. iv.) In like manner, Samuel erected a stone at Mizpeh, to commemorate the discomfiture of the Philistines. (1 Sam. vii. 12.)

---

[1] Valpy's Gr. Test. vol. iii. p. 117.
[2] Pareau, Antiq. Hebr. pp. 318—320. Schulzii Archæol. Hebr. p. 41. The ecclesiastical historian Eusebius, on the authority of Julius Africanus, a writer of the third century, relates that Herod, misnamed the Great, committed to the flames all the records of the Jewish genealogies; but Carpzov has shown that this narrative is not worthy of credit. Antiquitates Gentis Hebrææ, p. 36.

In progress of time more splendid monuments were erected (1 Sam. xv. 12. 2 Sam. viii. 13. xviii. 18.); and symbolical memorial names were given both to things and persons. Thus, the columns which were erected in the temple of Solomon,—*Jachin*, he shall establish, *Boaz*, in it is strength, — most probably denoted the devout monarch's hope, that Jehovah would firmly establish that temple in the entrance of which they were placed. To the same practice Pareau ascribes the origin of the name of Maccabæus with which Judas was first distinguished (1 Macc. ii. 4.), (who was surnamed מקבא, MACABA, or the *Hammer*, on account of his singular valour and success against the enemies of his nation)[1]; and also the new name given by our Lord to Peter (Matt. xvi. 18. John i. 43.), and the name given to the field which was bought with the purchase-money of Judas's treason. (Matt. xxvii. 8. Acts i. 19.) The great festivals, prescribed by Moses to the Jews, as well as the feasts and fasts instituted by them in later times, and the tables of the law which were to be most religiously preserved in the ark, were so many memorials of important national transactions.

In more antient times proverbs sometimes originated from some remarkable occurrence. (Gen. x. 9. xxii. 14. 1 Sam. x. 12. xix. 24.)[2]

CHAPTER VII.

ON THE TREATIES OR COVENANTS, CONTRACTS, AND OATHS OF THE JEWS.

I. *Whether the Jews were prohibited from concluding Treaties with Heathen Nations.* — II. *Treaties, how made and ratified.* — *Covenant of Salt.* — III. *Contracts for the Sale and Cession of Alienable Property, how made.* — IV. *Of Oaths.*

I. A TREATY is a pact or covenant made with a view to the public welfare by the superior power. It is a common mistake, that the Israelites were prohibited from forming alliances with Heathens: this would in effect have amounted to a general prohibition of alliance with any nation whatever, because at that time all the world were Heathens. In the Mosaic law, not a single statute is enacted, that prohibits the conclusion of treaties with heathen nations in general; although, for the reasons therein specified, Moses either commands them to carry on eternal war against the Canaanites and Amalekites (but not against the Moabites and Ammonites), or else forbids all friendship with these particular nations. It is however clear, from Deut. xxiii. 4—9., that he did not entertain the same opinion with regard to *all* foreign nations: for in that passage, though the Moabites are pronounced to be an abomination to the Israelites, no such declaration is made respecting

---

[1] In like manner Charles, mayor of the palace to the king of France, received the name of *Martel*, or the *Hammer*, from the irresistible blows he is said to have given to the Saracens or Moors, who were utterly discomfited in the memorable battle fought near Poictiers, in 733.—Another, and more generally received origin of the appellation Maccabees, has been given in p. 106. *supra*.

[2] Pareau, Antiq. Hebr. pp. 320—322.

the Edomites.   Further, it is evident that they felt themselves bound religiously to observe treaties when actually concluded; though one of the contracting parties had been guilty of fraud in the transaction, as in the case of the treaty with the Gibeonites. (Josh. ix.)   David and Solomon lived in alliance with the king of Tyre; and the former with the King of Hamath (2 Sam. viii. 9, 10.) ; and the Queen of Sheba cannot be regarded in any other light than as an ally of Solomon's.   Even the Maccabees, who were so laudably zealous for the law of Moses, did not hesitate to enter into a compact with the Romans.   The only treaties condemned by the prophets are those with the Egyptians, Babylonians, and Assyrians, which were extremely prejudicial to the nation, by involving it continually in quarrels with sovereigns more powerful than the Jewish monarchs; and the event always showed, in a most striking manner, the propriety of their reproofs.

II. Various solemnities were used in the conclusion of treaties; sometimes it was done by a simple junction of the hands. (Prov. xi. 21.) Ezek. xvii. 18.)   The Hindoos to this day ratify an engagement by one person laying his right hand on the hand of the other.[1]   Sometimes, also, the covenant was ratified by erecting a heap of stones, to which a suitable name was given, referring to the subject-matter of the covenant (Gen. xxxi. 44—54.) ; that made between Abraham and the king of Gerar was ratified by the oath of both parties, by a present from Abraham to the latter of seven ewe-lambs, and by giving a name to the well which had given occasion to the transaction. (Gen. xxi. 22—32.)   It was, moreover, customary to cut the victim (which was to be offered as a sacrifice upon the occasion) into two parts, and so placing each half upon two different altars, to cause those who contracted the covenant to pass between both.   (Gen. xv. 9, 10. 17. Jer. xxxiv. 18.)   This rite was practised both by believers and heathens at their solemn leagues; at first, doubtless, with a view to the great Sacrifice, who was to purge our sins in his own blood; and the offering of these sacrifices, and passing between the parts of the divided victim, was symbolically staking their hopes of purification and salvation on their performance of the conditions on which it was offered.[2]

The editor of the Fragments supplementary to Calmet[3] is of opinion that what is yet practised of this ceremony may elucidate that passage in Isa xxviii. 15. : — *We have made a covenant with death, and with hell are we at agreement ; when the overflowing scourge shall pass through, it shall not come unto us, for we have made lies our refuge, and under falsehood have we hid ourselves.*   As if it had been said : — We have cut off a covenant Sacrifice, a purification offering with death, and with the grave we have settled, so that the scourge shall not injure us.   May not such a custom have been the origin of the following superstition related by Pitts ? — " If they (the Algerine corsairs) at any time hap-

---

[1] Ward's View of the History, &c. of the Hindoos, vol. ii. p. 328.

[2] This remarkable practice may be clearly traced in the Greek and Latin writers.   Homer has the following expression :—

Ορκια πιστα ταμοντες.   Iliad, lib. ii. ver. 124.
Having cut faithful oaths.

Eustathius explains the passage by saying, they were oaths relating to important matters, and were made by the division of the victim.   See also Virgil, Æn. viii. ver. 640.

[3] No. 129.

pen to be in a very great strait or distress, as being chased, or in a storm, they will gather money, light up candles in remembrance of some dead marrabot (saint) or other, calling upon him with heavy sighs and groans. If they find no succour from their before-mentioned rites and superstitions, but that the danger rather increases, then they go to sacrificing a sheep, (two or three upon occasion, as they think needful,) which is done after this manner: having cut off the head with a knife, they immediately take out the entrails, and throw them and the head overboard; and then, with all the speed they can (without skinning), they cut the body into two parts by the middle, and throw one part over the right side of the ship, and the other over the left, into the sea, as a kind of propitiation. Thus those blind infidels apply themselves to imaginary intercessors, instead of the living and true God." [1]   In the case here referred to, the ship passes between the parts thus thrown on each side of it. This behaviour of the Algerines may be taken as a pretty accurate counterpart to that of making *a covenant with death* and with imminent danger of destruction, by appeasing the angry gods.

Festivities always accompanied the ceremonies attending covenants. Isaac and Abimelech feasted at making their covenant (Gen. xxvi. 30.), *And he made them a feast, and they did eat and drink.* (Gen. xxxi. 54.) *Jacob offered sacrifice upon the mount, and called his brethren to eat bread.* This practice was also usual amongst the heathen nations.[2]

Afterwards, when the Mosaic law was established, and the people were settled in the land of Canaan, the people feasted, in their peace offerings, on a part of the sacrifice, in token of their reconciliation with God (Deut. xii. 6, 7.): and thus, in the sacrament of the Lord's supper, we renew our covenant with God, and (in the beautiful language of the communion office of the Anglican church) "we offer and present ourselves, our souls and bodies, to be a reasonable, holy, and lively sacrifice" unto Him, being at His table feasted with the bread and wine, the representation of the sacrifice of Christ's body and blood; who by himself once offered upon the cross has made a full, perfect, and sufficient sacrifice, oblation, and atonement for the sin of the whole world.

Sometimes the parties to the covenant were sprinkled with the blood of the victim. Thus Moses, after sprinkling part of the blood on the altar, to show that Jehovah was a party to the covenant, sprinkled part of it on the Israelites, and said unto them, *Behold the blood of the covenant which the Lord hath made with you.* (Exod. xxiv. 6. 8.)   To this transaction Saint Paul alludes in his Epistle to the Hebrews (ix. 20.), and explains its evangelical meaning.

The Scythians are said to have first poured wine into an earthen vessel, and then the contracting parties, cutting their arms with a knife, let some of the blood run into the wine, with which they stained their armour. After which they themselves, together with the other persons present, drank of the mixture, uttering the direst maledictions on the party who should violate the treaty.[3]

---

[1] Travels, p. 18.
[2] Burder's Oriental Customs, vol. ii. p. 84.—Fifth edition. See examples of the antient mode of ratifying covenants, in Homer. Il. lib. iii. verses 103—107. 245. *et seq.*   Virgil, Æn. lib. viii. 641. xii. 169. *et seq.* Dionysius Halicarnassensis, lib. v. c. 1.   Hooke's Roman History, vol. i. p. 67.
[3] Herodotus, lib. iv. c. 70. vol. i. p. 273. Oxon. 1809.   Doughtæi Analecta, 1. p. 69.

Another mode of ratifying covenants was by the superior contracting party presenting to the other some article of his own dress or arms. Thus, *Jonathan stripped himself of the robe that was upon him, and gave it to David, and his garments, even to the sword, and to his bow, and to his girdle.* (1 Sam. xviii. 4.)   The highest honour, which a king of Persia can bestow upon a subject, is to cause himself to be disapparelled, and to give his robe to the favoured individual.[1]

In Numb. xviii. 19. mention is made of a *covenant of salt.*   The expression appears to be borrowed from the practice of ratifying their federal engagements by salt; which, as it not only imparted a relish to different kinds of viands, but also preserved them from putrefaction and decay, became the emblem of incorruptibility and permanence.   It is well known, from the concurrent testimony of voyagers and travellers, that the Asiatics deem the eating together as a bond of perpetual friendship: and as salt is now (as it antiently was) a common article in all their repasts, it may be in reference to this circumstance that a perpetual covenant is termed *a covenant of salt;* because the contracting parties ate together of the sacrifice offered on the occasion, and the whole transaction was considered as a league of endless friendship.[2]   In order to assure those persons to whom the divine promises were made, of their certainty and stability, the Almighty not only willed that they should have the force of a covenant; but also vouchsafed to accommodate Himself (if we may be permitted to use such an expression) to the received customs.   Thus, he constituted the rainbow a sign of his covenant with mankind that the earth should be no more destroyed by a deluge (Gen. ix. 12—17.); and in a vision appeared to Abraham to pass between the divided pieces of the sacrifice, which the patriarch had offered. (Gen. xv. 12—17.   Jehovah further instituted the rite of circumcision, as a token of the covenant between himself and Abraham (Gen. xvii. 9—14.); and sometimes sware by Himself (Gen. xxii. 16. Luke i. 73), that is, pledged his eternal power and godhead for the fulfilment of his promise, there being no one superior to Himself to whom he could make appeal, or by whom he could be bound.   Saint Paul beautifully illustrates this transaction in his Epistle to the Hebrews. (vi. 13—18.)   Lastly, the whole of the Mosaic constitution was a mutual covenant between Jehovah and the Israelites; the tables of which being preserved in an ark, the latter was thence termed the *ark of the covenant,* and as (we have just seen) the blood of the victims slain in ratification of that covenant, was termed the *blood of the covenant.* (Exod. xxiv. 8. Zech. ix. 11.)   Referring to this, our Saviour, when instituting the Lord's supper, after giving the cup, said, *This is* (signifies or represents) *my blood of the New Covenant, which is shed for many, for the remission of sins.* (Matt. xxvi. 28.)   By this very remarkable expression, Jesus Christ teaches us, that as his body was to be *broken* or crucified, ὑπερ ἡμων, *in our stead,* so his blood was to be *poured out* (εκχυνομενον, a sacrificial term) to make an *atonement,* as the words *remission* of sins evidently imply; for *without shedding of blood* there *is no remission* (Heb. ix. 22.), nor any remission by shedding of blood but in a sacrificial way. Compare Heb. ix. 20. and xiii. 12.

---

[1] Harmer's Observations, vol. ii. p. 94.   Burder's Or. Cust. vol. i. p. 206.
[2] Some pleasing facts from modern history, illustrative of the covenant of salt, are collected by the industrious editor of Calmet, Fragments, No. 130.

III. What treaties or covenants were between the high contracting powers who were authorised to conclude them, that contracts of bargain and sale are between private individuals.

Among the Hebrews, and long before them among the Canaanites, the purchase of any thing of consequence was concluded and the price paid, at the gate of the city, as the seat of judgment, before all who went out and came in. (Gen. xxiii. 16—20. Ruth iv. 1, 2.) As persons of leisure, and those who wanted amusement, were wont to sit in the gates, purchases there made could always be testified by numerous witnesses. From Ruth iv. 7—11. we learn another singular usage on occasion of purchase, cession, and exchange, viz. that in earlier times, the transfer of alienable property was confirmed by the proprietor plucking off his shoe at the city gate, in the presence of the elders and other witnesses, and handing it over to the new owner. The origin of this custom it is impossible to trace: but it had evidently become antiquated in the time of David, as the author of the book of Ruth introduces it as an unknown custom of former ages.

In process of time the joining or striking of hands, already mentioned with reference to public treaties, was introduced as a ratification of a bargain and sale. This usage was not unknown in the days of Job (xvii. 3.), and Solomon often alludes to it. (See Prov. vi. 1. xi. 15. xvii. 18. xx. 16. xxii. 26. xxvii. 13.) The earliest vestige of written instruments, sealed and delivered for ratifying the disposal and transfer of property, occurs in Jer. xxxii. 10—12., which the prophet commanded Baruch to bury in an earthen vessel in order to be preserved for production at a future period, as evidence of the purchase. (14, 15.) No mention is expressly made of the manner in which deeds were antiently cancelled. Some expositors have imagined that in Col. ii. 14. Saint Paul refers to the cancelling of them by blotting or drawing a line across them, or by striking them through with a nail: but we have no information whatever from antiquity to authorise such a conclusion.[1]

IV. It was customary for those who appealed to the Deity in attestation of any thing, to hold up their right hand towards heaven; by which action the party swearing, or making OATH, signified that he appealed to God to witness the truth of what he averred. Thus Abram said to the king of Sodom — *I have* LIFT UP MY HAND *unto the* LORD *the most high God, the possessor of heaven and earth, ... that I will not take any thing that is thine.* (Gen. xiv. 22, 23.) Hence the expression, "to lift up the hand," is equivalent to making oath. In this form of scriptural antiquity, the angel in the Apocalypse is represented as taking a solemn oath. (Rev. x. 5.) [2]

Among the Jews, an oath of fidelity was taken by the servant's putting his hand under the thigh of his lord, as Eliezer did to Abraham (Gen. xxiv. 2.): whence, with no great deviation, is perhaps

[1] Schulzii Archæologia Hebraica, cap. 14. de Fœderibus et Contractibus, pp. 130—132.; Pareau, Antiquitas Hebraica, part. iii. § 2. cap. 3. de Fœderibus et Contractibus, pp. 322—325. Bruning, Antiquitates Hebrææ, cap. 26. pp. 242—245. Michaelis's Commentaries, vol. i. pp. 310—313.

[2] " This mode of swearing has descended even to our own times and nation, being still used in Scotland, and there allowed by act of Parliament to those dissenters who are styled Seceders. The Solemn League and Covenant, in the time of Charles I., was taken in this form." Dean Woodhouse, on Rev. x. 5.

derived the form of doing homage at this day, by putting the hands between the knees, and within the hands of the liege.[1] Sometimes an oath was accompanied with an imprecation, as in 2 Sam. iii: 9. 35. Ruth i. 17. 1 Kings ii. 23. 2 Kings vi. 31.: but sometimes the party swearing omitted the imprecation, as if he were afraid, and shuddered to utter it, although it was, from other sources, sufficiently well understood. (Gen. xiv. 22, 23. Ezek. xvii. 18.)   At other times he merely said, "*Let God be a witness;*" and sometimes affirmed, saying, "*As surely as God liveth.*" (Jer. xlii. 5. Ruth iii. 13. 1 Sam. xiv. 45. xx. 3. 21.)

These remarks apply to the person who uttered the oath himself of his own accord.   When an oath was *exacted*, whether by a judge or another, the person who exacted it put the oath in form; and the person to whom it was put, responded by saying, *Amen, Amen, so let it be :* or gave his response in other expressions of like import, such as συ ειπας, Thou hast said it. (Numb. v. 19—22. 1 Kings xxii. 16. Deut. xxvii. 15—26.)   Sometimes the exacter of the oath merely used the following adjuration, viz. *I adjure you by the living God to answer, whether this thing be so or not.*   And the person sworn accordingly made answer to the point inquired of. (Numb. v. 22. Matt. xxvi. 64.)   It should be remarked here, that although the formulary of assent on the part of the respondent to an oath was frequently AMEN, AMEN, yet this formulary did not always imply an oath, but, in some instances, was merely a protestation.   As the oath was an appeal to God (Lev. xix. 12. Deut. vi. 13.), the taking of a false oath was deemed a heinous crime; and perjury, accordingly, was forbidden in those words, *Thou shalt not take the name of the Lord thy God in vain,* that is, thou shalt not call God to witness in pretended confirmation of a falsehood. (Exod. xx. 6.)

It was also common to swear by those whose life and prosperity were dear to the party making oath.   Thus, Joseph swore by the *life of the king* (Gen. xlii. 15.); and this practice prevailed subsequently among the Hebrews. (1 Sam. xxv. 26. 2 Sam. xi. 11. xiv. 19. comp. Psal. lxiii. 11.)   A person sometimes swore *by himself,* and sometimes by the *life of the person* before whom he spoke, as in 1 Sam. i. 26. 2 Kings ii. 2. Judges vi. 13. 15. 1 Kings iii. 17. 26.; a practice which obtains in Syria to this day.[2]   In some instances, persons adjured others by the beasts of the field (Sol. Song ii. 7.), a sort of adjuration which still makes its appearance in the writings of the Arabian poets.[3]

In the time of Christ, the Jews were in the habit of swearing by the *altar,* by *Jerusalem,* by *heaven,* by the *earth,* by *themselves,* by their *heads,* by the *gold of the temple,* by *sacrifices,* &c.   Because the name of God was not mentioned in these oaths, they considered them as imposing but small, if *any* obligation[4]; and we, accordingly, find, that our Saviour takes occasion to inveigh, in decided terms, against such arts of deception. (Matt. v. 33.—37. xxiii. 16—22.)   It is against

---

1 Paley's Mor. and Polit. Philosophy, Book iii. ch. 16. § I.

2 "*By your life*" is still a common oath in Syria (Burckhardt's Travels in Syria, p. 40.), but the *most* common oath in that country is,—"*On my head.*" (Jowett's Christian Researches in Syria, p. 269.)

3 Consult the Koran, Sura lxxxv. 1—3. lxxxvi. 1. 11—13. lxxxix. 1—4. xci. 1—8, &c.

4 Martialis Epigrammat. XI. 95.

oaths of this kind, and *these alone* (not against an oath uttered in sincerity), that he expresses his displeasure, and prohibits them. This is clear, since he himself consented to take upon him the solemnity of an oath (Matt. xxvi. 64.); and since Paul himself, in more than one instance, utters an adjuration. Compare Rom. ix. 1. 2 Cor. i. 23.

In the primitive periods of their history, the Hebrews religiously observed an oath (Josh. ix. 14, 15.), but we find, that, in later times, they were often accused by the prophets of perjury. After the captivity, the Jews became again celebrated for the scrupulous observance of what they had sworn to, but corruption soon increased among them : they revived the old forms, the words without the meaning; and acquired among all nations the reputation of perjurers.[1]

CHAPTER VIII.

LAWS RESPECTING STRANGERS, AGED, DEAF, BLIND, AND POOR PERSONS.

I. *Of Strangers.* — II. *Of the Aged, Blind, and Deaf.* — III. *Of the Poor.*

ALL wise legislators have deemed it an important branch of political economy, to direct their attention towards aliens and to the poor : and the humanity and wisdom of the Mosaic regulations in this respect will be found not unworthy of a divinely inspired legislator.

I. STRANGERS are frequently mentioned in the laws of Moses, who specifies two different descriptions of them, viz. 1. תושבים (TOSCHaBIM), or those who had no home, whether they were Israelites or foreigners; and, 2. גרים (GeRIM), or those who were strangers generally, and who possessed no landed property, though they might have purchased houses. Towards both of these classes the Hebrew legislator enforced the duties of kindness and humanity, by reminding the Israelites that they had once been strangers in Egypt. (Lev. xix. 33, 34. Deut. x. 19. xxiii. 7. xxiv. 18.) Hence he ordained the same rights and privileges for the Israelites, as for strangers. (Lev. xxiv. 19—22. Numb. ix. 14. xv. 5.) Strangers might be naturalised, or permitted to *enter into the congregation* of the LORD, by submitting to circumcision, and renouncing idolatry. (Deut. xxiii. 1—9.) The Edomites and Egyptians were capable of becoming citizens of Israel after the third generation. Doeg the Edomite (1 Sam. xxi. 8. Psal. lii.) was thus naturalised; and, on the conquest of Idumæa by the Jews, about 129 years before the birth of Christ, the Jews and Idumæans became one people. It appears, also, that other nations were not entirely excluded from being incorporated with the people of Israel : for *Uriah the Hittite,* who was of Canaanitish descent, is represented as being a fully naturalised Israelite. But the "Ammonites and Moabites, in consequence of the hostile disposition which they

------

[1] Alber, Hermeneut. Vet. Test. pp. 210, 211. Jahn's Archæologia Biblica, translated by Mr. Upham, pp. 494, 495.

had manifested to the Israelites in the wilderness, were absolutely
excluded from the right of citizenship." [1]

" In the earlier periods of the Hebrew state, persons who were
natives of another country, but who had come, either from choice or
necessity, to take up their residence among the Hebrews, appear to
have been placed in favourable circumstances. At a later period, viz.
in the reigns of David and Solomon, they were compelled to labour
on the religious edifices, which were erected by those princes; as we
may learn from such passages as these:—*And Solomon numbered all the
strangers that were in the land of Israel, after the numbering wherewith
David his father had numbered them ; and they were found an hundred
and fifty thousand and three thousand and six hundred ; and he set threescore and ten thousand of them to be bearers of burdens, and fourscore
thousand to be hewers in the mountain.* (2 Chron. ii. 1. 17, 18. compared
with 1 Chron. xxii. 2.) The exaction of such laborious services from
foreigners was probably limited to those who had been taken prisoners
in war; and who, according to the rights of war as they were understood at that period, could be justly employed in any offices, however
low and however laborious, which the conqueror thought proper to
impose.   In the time of Christ, the degenerate Jews did not find it
convenient to render to the strangers from a foreign country those
deeds of kindness and humanity, which were not only their due, but
which were demanded in their behalf by the laws of Moses.   They
were in the habit of understanding by the word *neighbour*, their friends
merely, and accordingly restricted the exercise of their benevolence
by the same narrow limits that bounded in this case their interpretation; contrary as both were to the spirit of those passages, which
have been adduced in the preceding paragraph." [2]

II. In a monarchy or aristocracy, birth and office alone give rank,
but in a democracy, where all are on an equal footing, the right discharge of official duties, or the arrival of OLD AGE, are the only sources
of rank.   Hence the Mosaic statute in Lev. xix. 32. (*before the hoary
head thou shalt stand up, and shalt reverence the aged,*) will be found
suited to the republican circumstances of the Israelites, as well as conformable to the nature and wishes of the human heart : for no man
has any desire to sink in honour, or to be of less consequence than he
was before ; and to allow precedence to old age cannot be a matter
that will ever affect a young man very sensibly.   Nor does Moses confine his attention to the aged.   He extends the protection of a special
statute to the DEAF and the BLIND, in Levit. xix. 14., which prohibits
reviling the one or putting a stumbling-block in the way of the other.
In Deut. xxvii. 18. a curse is denounced against him who misleads
the blind.

III. With regard to those whom misfortune or other circumstances
had reduced to poverty, various humane regulations were made : for
though Moses had, by his statutes relative to the division of the land,
studied to prevent any Israelite from being born poor, yet he nowhere
indulges the hope that there would actually be no poor.   On the contrary, he expressly says (Deut. xv. 11.), THE POOR *shall never cease out
of thy land ;* and he enjoins the Hebrews to open wide their hands to

---

[1] Michaelis's Commentaries, vol. ii. pp. 233—239.
[2] Jahn's Archæologia Biblica, by Upham, p. 197.

their brethren, to the poor and to the needy in their land. He exhorts the opulent to assist a decayed Israelite with a loan, and not to refuse even though the sabbatical year drew nigh (Deut. xv. 7—10.); and no pledge was to be detained for the loan of money that served for the preservation of his life or health (Deut. xxiv. 12, 13.), or was necessary to enable him to procure bread for himself and family, as the upper and nether mill-stones. During harvest, the owner of a field was prohibited from reaping the corn that grew in its corners, or the after-growth : and the scattered ears, or sheaves carelessly left on the ground, equally belonged to the poor. After a man had once shaken or beaten his olive-trees, he was not permitted to gather the olives that still hung on them: so that the fruit, which did not ripen until after the season of gathering, belonged to the poor. (Lev. xix. 9, 10. Deut. xxiv. 19, 20, 21. Ruth ii. 2—19.) Further, whatever grew during the sabbatical year, in the fields, gardens, or vineyards, the poor might take at pleasure, having an equal right to it with the owners of the land. Another important privilege enjoyed by the poor was, what were called *second tenths* and second firstlings. " Besides the tenth received by the Levites, the Israelites were obliged to set apart *another* tenth of their field and garden produce; and, in like manner, of their cattle, a second set of offerings, for the purpose of presenting as thank offerings at the high festivals." Of these thank offerings only certain fat pieces were consumed on the altar : the remainder, after deducting the priest's portion, was appropriated to the sacrifice-feasts, to which the Israelites were bound to invite the stranger, the widow, and the orphan. " When any part of these tenths remained, which they had not been able to bring to the altar or to consume as offerings, they were obliged every three years to make a conscientious estimate of the amount, and, without presenting it as an offering to God, employ it in benevolent entertainments in their native cities." (Deut. xii. 5—12. 17—19. xiv. 22—29. xvi. 10, 11. xxvi. 12. 13.) [1]

But though Moses had made such abundant provision for the poor, yet it does not appear that he has said any thing respecting beggars. The earliest mention of beggars occurs in Psal. cix. 10. In the New Testament, however, we read of beggars, blind, distressed, and maimed, who lay at the doors of the rich, by the waysides, (as they still do in India,[2]) and also before the gate of the temple. (Mark x. 46. Luke xvi. 20, 21. Acts iii. 2.)[3] But " we have no reason to suppose, that there existed in the time of Christ that class of persons called *vagrant beggars,* who present their supplications for alms from door to door, and who are found at the present day in the East, although less frequently than in the countries of Europe. That the custom of seeking alms by sounding a trumpet or horn, which prevails among a class of Mohammedan monastics, called *Kalendar* or *Karendal,* prevailed also in the time of Christ, may be inferred from Matt. vi. 2.; where the verb σαλπισης, which possesses the shade of signification, that would be attached to a corresponding word in the Hiphil form of the Hebrew verbs, is to be rendered transitively, as is the case with many other

---

[1] Michaelis's Commentaries, vol. ii. pp. 254—259.

[2] Roberts's Oriental Illustrations, p. 558. Sturdy beggars (the same intelligent observer states) not unfrequently make use of expressions similar to that uttered by the unfaithful steward in Luke xvi. 3. Ibid. p. 564.

[3] Michaelis's Commentaries, vol. ii. p. 249.

verbs in the New Testament. There is one thing characteristic of those orientals, who are reduced to the disagreeable necessity of following the vocation of mendicants, which is worthy of being mentioned; they do not appeal to the pity, or to the alms-giving spirit, but to the justice of their benefactors." (Job xxii. 7. xxxi. 16. Prov. iii. 27, 28.) "[1]

CHAPTER IX.

OF THE MILITARY AFFAIRS OF THE JEWS AND OTHER NATIONS MENTIONED IN THE SCRIPTURES.

SECTION I.

ON THE MILITARY DISCIPLINE OF THE JEWS.

I. *The earliest Wars, predatory Excursions.* — II. *Character of the Wars of the Israelites.* — *Their Levies how raised.* — *Mosaic Statutes concerning the Israelitish Soldiers.* — III. *Divisions, and Officers of the Jewish Armies;— which were sometimes conducted by the Kings in Person.* — *Military Chariots.* — IV. *Encampments.* — V. *Military Schools and Training.* — VI. *Defensive Arms.* — VII. *Offensive Arms.* — VIII. *Fortifications.* — IX. *Mode of declaring War.* — X. *Military Tactics.* — *Order of Battle.* — *Treatment of the Slain, of captured Cities, and of Captives.* — XI. *Triumphant Reception of the Conquerors.* — XII. *Distribution of the Spoil.* — *Military Honours conferred on eminent Warriors.* — *A military Order established by David.* — XIII. *Trophies.*

I. THERE were not wanting in the earliest ages of the world men who, abusing the power and strength which they possessed to the purposes of ambition, usurped upon their weaker neighbours. Such was the origin of the kingdom founded by the plunderer Nimrod (Gen. x. 8—10.), whose name signifies a *rebel ;* and it was most probably given him, from his rejection of the laws both of God and man, and supporting by force a tyranny over others. As mankind continued to increase, quarrels and contests would naturally arise, and, spreading from individuals to families, tribes and nations, produced wars. Of the military affairs of those times we have very imperfect notices in the Scriptures. These wars, however, appear to have been nothing more than predatory incursions, like those of the Modern Wahabees and Bedouin Arabs, so often described by oriental travellers. The patriarch Abraham, on learning that his kinsman Lot had been taken captive by Chedorlaomer and his confederate emirs or petty kings, mustered his trained servants, three hundred and eighteen in number ; and coming against the enemy by night, he divided his forces, and totally discomfited them. (Gen. xiv. 14—16.) The other patriarchs also armed their servants and dependents when a conflict was expected. (Gen. xxxii. 7—12. xxxiii. 1.) [2]

---

[1] Jahn's Archæologia, by Upham, p. 198.
[2] This section is chiefly translated from Calmet's Dissertation sur la Milice des anciens

II. Although the Jews are now the very reverse of being a military people (in which circumstance we may recognise the accomplishment of prophecy[1]), yet antiently they were eminently distinguished for their prowess.   But the notices concerning their discipline, which are presented to us in the Sacred Writings, are few and brief.

The wars in which the Israelites were engaged, were of two kinds, either such as were expressly enjoined by divine command, or such as were voluntary and entered upon by the prince for revenging some national affronts, and for the honour of the sovereignty.   Of the first sort were those undertaken against the seven nations of Canaan, whom God had devoted to destruction, viz. the Hittites, the Amorites, the Canaanites (strictly so called), the Perizzites, the Hivites, the Jebusites, and the Girgashites.   These the Israelites were commanded to extirpate, and to settle themselves in their place. (Deut. vii. 1, 2. and xx. 16, 17.) There were indeed other nations who inhabited this country in the days of Abraham, as may be seen in Gen. xv. 19, 20. But these had either become extinct since that time, or being but a small people were incorporated with the rest.   To these seven nations no terms of peace could be offered; for, being guilty of gross idolatries and other detestable vices of all kinds, God thought them unfit to live any longer upon the face of the earth.   These wars, thus undertaken by the command of God, were called the *wars of the Lord,* of which a particular record seems to have been kept, as mentioned in Numb. xxi. 14.

In the voluntary wars of the Israelites, which were undertaken upon some national account, such as most of those were in the times of the Judges, when the Moabites, Philistines, and other neighbouring nations invaded their country, and such as that of David against the Ammonites, whose king had violated the law of nations by insulting his ambassadors, — there were certain rules established by God, which were to regulate their conduct, both in the undertaking and carrying on of these wars.   As, first, they were to proclaim peace to them, which, if they accepted, these people were to become tributaries to them; but if they refused, all the males, upon besieging the city, were allowed to be slain, if the Israelites thought fit; but the women and little ones were to be spared, and the cattle with the other goods of the city were to belong, as spoil, to the Israelites. (Deut. xx. 10—15.)   Secondly, in besieging a city, they were not to commit unnecessary waste and depredations; for though they were allowed to cut down barren trees of all sorts, to serve the purposes of their approaches, yet they were obliged to spare the fruit trees, as being necessary to support the lives of the inhabitants in future times, when the little rancour, which was the

---

Hebreux, inserted in the third volume of his Commentaire Littérale sur la Bible, and also in vol. i. pp. 205—240. of his Dissertations qui peuvent servir de Prolegomènes de l'Ecriture; which, in the judgment of the celebrated tactician, the Chevalier Folard, discusses the military affairs of the Hebrews with so much accuracy and knowledge, as to leave scarcely any room for additions.   (Dissertation on the Military Tactics of the Hebrews, in vol. iii. p. 535. of the folio English translation of Calmet's Dictionary.)   The Dissertation of the Chevalier Folard has also been consulted; together with Alber's Inst. Herm. Vet. Test. tom. i. pp. 239—247.; Schulzii Archæologia Hebraica, pp.132—146.; Jahn, Archæologia Biblica, §§ 266—296.; Ackermann, Archæologia Biblica, §§ 260—288.; Home's Hist. of the Jews, vol. ii. pp. 303—316.; Bruning, Antiq. Hebr. pp. 74—91.; Carpzovii Antiquitates Gentis Hebrææ, pp. 665—671.

[1] See Levit. xxvi. 36.   Deut. xxviii. 65, 66.

occasion of their present hostilities, should be removed and done away (Deut. xx. 19, 20.)

The Israelites, in the beginning of their republic, appear to have been a timorous and cowardly people; their spirits were broken by their bondage in Egypt; and this base temper soon appeared upon the approach of Pharaoh and his army, before the Israelites passed through the Red Sea, which made them murmur so much against Moses. (Exod. xiv. 10, 11, 12.)   But in no instance was their cowardice more evident, than when they heard the report of the spies concerning the inhabitants of the lands, which threw them into a fit of despair, and made them resolve to return into Egypt, notwithstanding all the miracles wrought for them by God. (Numb. xiv. 1—6.)   It was on this account that David, who was well acquainted with their disposition, says, that *they got not the land in possession by their own sword, neither did their own arm save them, but thy right hand and thine arm, and the light of thy countenance, because thou hadst a favour unto them.* (Psal. xliv. 3.)

After their departure from Egypt, the whole of the men, from twenty years and upwards, until the age of fifty (when they might demand their discharge if they chose), were liable to military service, the priests and Levites not excepted. (Numb. i. 3. 22. 2 Sam. xxiii. 20. 1 Kings ii. 35.)   Like the militia in some countries, and the hardy mountaineers of Lebanon at this day[1], they were always ready to assemble at the shortest notice. If the occasion were extremely urgent, affecting their existence as a people, all were summoned to war; but ordinarily, when there was no necessity for convoking the whole of their forces, a selection was made. Thus Joshua chose twelve thousand men, in order to attack the Amalekites (Exod. xvii. 9, 10.) : in the war with the Midianites, one thousand men were selected out of each tribe (Numb. xxxi. 4, 5.), and in the rash assault upon the city of Ai, three thousand men were employed. (Josh. vii. 3, 4.)   The book of Judges furnishes numerous instances of this mode of selection. Hence we read in the Scriptures of *choosing* the men, not of levying them. In like manner, under the Roman republic, all the citizens of the military age (seventeen to forty-six years) were obliged to serve a certain number of campaigns, when they were commanded.   On the day appointed the consuls held a levy (*delectum habebant*), by the assistance of the military or legionary tribunes; when it was determined by lot in what manner the tribes should be called. The consuls ordered such as they pleased to be cited out of each tribe, and every one was obliged to answer to his name under a severe penalty. On certain occasions some of the most refractory were put to death.[2] To the above described mode of selecting troops, our Saviour alluded, when he said that *many are called, but few chosen* (Matt. xx. 16.); the great mass of the people being convened, choice was made of those who were the most fit for service.

---

[1] A recent learned traveller in the Holy Land, describing the present state of Mount Lebanon, says, that, " of the peasants, great numbers carry arms.   In fact, *every* young man may in some sense be called a soldier, and would in case of need muster as such: the gun which serves him for field sport and sustenance is ready for the call of war; and his discipline consists in the bracing, hardy habits of a mountaineer." Rev. W. Jowett's Christian Researches in Syria, p. 74. (London, 1825, 8vo.)

[2] Dr. Adam's Roman Antiquities, pp. 362, 363. fifth edit.

This mode of selecting soldiers accounts for the formation of those vast armies, in a very short space of time, of which we read in the Old Testament. The men of Jabesh Gilead, who, in the beginning of Saul's reign, were besieged by the Ammonites, had only seven days' respite given them to send messengers to the coasts of Israel, after which, if no relief came to them, they were to deliver up the city and have their eyes put out, which was the best condition, it seems, they could procure. (1 Sam. xi. 1, 2, 3.) As soon as Saul was informed of it, he, by a symbolical representation of cutting a yoke of oxen in pieces, and sending them all over Israel, signified what should be done to the oxen of such as did not appear upon this summons. In consequence of this summons, we find that an army of *three hundred and thirty thousand men* was formed, who relieved the place within the seven days allowed them. In like manner, when the children of Israel had heard of the crime that was committed by the inhabitants of Gibeah against the Levite's concubine, it is said, that they resolved not to return to their houses till they had fully avenged this insult (Judg. xx. 8.), and accordingly, upon the tribe of Benjamin refusing to deliver up these men, an army was soon gathered together of four hundred thousand men of war. (verse 17.) Nor was the providing of their armies with necessaries any impediment to these sudden levies ; for in the beginning of the Jewish republic, their armies consisting altogether of infantry, every one served at their own expense, and ordinarily carried their own arms and provisions along with them. And thus we find that Jesse sent a supply of provisions by David to his other three sons that were in Saul's camp (1 Sam. xvii. 13. 17.), which gave David an opportunity of engaging Goliath; and this was the chief reason why their wars in those days were ordinarily but of a short continuance, it being hardly possible that a large body could subsist long upon such provisions as every one carried along with him. After the time of Solomon, their armies became vastly numerous : we read that Abijah king of Judah had an army of four hundred thousand men, with which he fought Jeroboam king of Israel, who had double that number (2 Chron. xiii. 3.), and it is said there were five hundred thousand killed of Jeroboam's army. (ver. 17.) Asa king of Judah had an army of nearly six hundred thousand men, when he was attacked by Zerah the Ethiopian with an host of a million of men. (2 Chron. xiv. 8, 9.) Jehoshaphat king of Judah had eleven hundred and sixty thousand men, without reckoning the garrisons in his fortified places. (2 Chron. xvii. 14—19.)

Various regulations were made by Moses concerning the Israelitish soldiers, which are characterised by equal wisdom and humanity. Not to repeat what has already been noticed in p. 198. we may remark that the following classes of persons were wholly exempted from military service (Deut. xx. 5—8. xxiv. 5.); viz.

1. He, who had built a new house, and had not dedicated it, was to return home, lest he should die in battle, and another man dedicate it. From the title of Psal. xxx. — *A Psalm or Song at the dedication of the house of David,* — it was evidently a custom in Israel to dedicate a new house to Jehovah, with prayer, praise, and thanksgiving, in order to obtain the divine blessing.

2. Those who had planted a vine or olive yard, and who had not yet eaten of its produce.

3. Every man who had betrothed a wife, and had not taken her home. It is well known, that among the Jews a considerable time sometimes elapsed between the espousal or betrothing of the parties and the celebration of a marriage. When the bridegroom had made proper preparations, the bride was conducted to his house, and the nuptials were consummated.

4. Every newly married man, during the first year after his marriage. The humanity of these exemptions will be the more evident, when it is recollected that, antiently, it was deemed an excessive hardship for a person to be obliged to go to battle (in which there was a probability of his being slain) who had left a new house unfinished, a newly purchased heritage half tilled, or a wife with whom he had just contracted marriage. Homer represents the case of Protesilaus as singularly afflicting, who was obliged to go to the Trojan war, leaving his wife in the deepest distress, and his house unfinished.[1]

5. The last exemption was in favour of the *fearful and faint-hearted;* an exemption of such a disgraceful nature, that one would think it never would have been claimed. Such, however, was the case in Gideon's expedition against the Midianites. Ten thousand only remained out of *thirty-two thousand,* of which number his army originally consisted; twenty-two thousand having complied with his proclamation, that *whosoever was fearful and afraid* might return and depart early from Mount Gilead. (Judg. vii. 3.) [2]

Before the regal government was established, the Israelitish army was entirely disbanded at the conclusion of a war. The earliest instance recorded of any military force being kept in time of peace, is in the reign of Saul, who retained two thousand for his body guard, and one thousand for his son Jonathan's guard. (1 Sam. xiii. 1, 2.) David had a distinct guard, called Cherethites and Pelethites, concerning the origin of whose name various contradictory opinions have been offered. Josephus, however, expressly says, that they were his guards, and the Chaldee paraphrast terms them *archers* and *slingers.*[3] Besides these he had twelve bodies of twenty-four thousand men each, who were on duty for one month, forming an aggregate of two hundred and eighty-eight thousand men. (1 Chron. xxvii. 1—15.) Subsequently, when the art of war was improved, a regular force seems to have been kept up both in peace and war; for, exclusive of the vast army which Jehoshaphat had in the field, we read that he had troops throughout all the fenced cities, which, doubtless, were garrisoned in time of peace as well as during war.

III. The Officers who were placed at the head of the Hebrew forces appear not to have differed materially from those whom we find in antient and modern armies.

The *Division* of the army into *three bands* or companies, mentioned in Gen. xiv. 14, 15. Job i. 17. Judg. vii. 16. 20. 1 Sam. xi. 11. and 2 Sam. xviii. 2., was probably no other than the division into the *centre, left,* and *right wing,* which obtains in the modern art of war. The Hebrews, when they departed from Egypt, marched in military order, צִבְאֹתָם עַל (AL TSeBOTaM) *by their armies* or *hosts*[4] (Exod. xii. 51.),

---

[1] Iliad, lib. ii. 700—702.   [2] Michaelis's Commentaries, vol. iii. pp. 34—37.

[3] On this subject the reader may consult the Dissertations of Ikenius, De Crethi et Plethi (Lug. Bat. 1749), and of Lakemacher, Observationes Philologicæ, part ii. pp. 11—44., and also Michaelis's Commentaries on the Law of Moses, § 232.

[4] It is from this circumstance " that the Divine Being calls himself the Lord of Hosts,

and וַחֲמֻשִׁים (ve-CHAMUSHIM), which word in our English Bibles (Exod. xiii. 18.) is rendered *harnessed,* and in the margin, *by five in a rank.* It is probable, from these expressions, that they followed each other in ranks fifty deep, and that at the head of each rank or file of fifty was the captain of fifty. (1 Sam. viii. 12. 2 Kings i. 9—14.) The other divisions consisted of tens, hundreds, thousands, &c.; and the officers that commanded them are styled captains of thousands, captains of hundreds, captains of fifties, and captains of tens; of these mention is made in 1 Chron. xii. 14. 20. xiii. 1. xxviii. 1. and 2 Kings i. 9. 11. 13. These, probably, were of the same rank with those whom Moses constituted in the wilderness, rulers of thousands, &c. (Exod. xviii. 25.) and who at first acted in a double capacity, being at the same time civil magistrates and military officers. The captains of thousands seem to have been much the same as colonels of regiments with us; and the captains of hundreds might probably answer to those who in our army have the command of troops and companies; the captains of fifties and tens to our subalterns, sergeants, and corporals. During the Mosaic commonwealth, in conformity to the law in Deut. xx. 9., all these officers were appointed by the *Shoterim,* genealogists or officers (as they are termed in our version), who probably chose the *heads of families;* but after the monarchy took place, they received their commissions either from the king in the same manner as at present, as appears from 2 Sam. xviii. 1. and 2 Chron. xxv. 5.; or from the commander in chief (2 Sam. xviii. 11.): and it should seem that a captain's commission was denoted by giving a military girdle or sash. (2 Sam. xviii. 11.)

The first and principal Head of the armies of Israel was the Almighty himself, who is so frequently termed in Scripture the Lord of Hosts. The whole nation marched forth under the superintending guidance of their God. Subordinate to Him, and as his lieutenant-general, was the principal officer, or leader of the whole army, who, in the Scriptures, is termed the Captain of the Lord's Host, and who appears to have been of the same rank with him, who is now called the commander in chief of an army. Such were Joshua and the Judges under the primitive constitution of their government as settled by God himself: such was Abner under Saul (2 Sam. ii. 8.), Joab under David (2 Sam. xx. 23.), and Amasa under Absalom, when he was raising a rebellion against his father. (2 Sam. xvii. 25.) The command and authority of this captain of the host appear to have been very great, sometimes, indeed, nearly equal to that of the sovereign. David seems to have been afraid of Joab his commander in chief; otherwise he would never have suffered him to live after the sanguinary assassinations which he had perpetrated. It is evident that the captain of the host enjoyed great influence in the time of Elisha: for we read, that the prophet having been hospitably entertained by an opulent woman at Shunem, and being desirous of making her some acknowledgment for her kindness, ordered his servant Gehazi to inquire what she would wish to have done for her. *Wouldest thou be*

---

or armies; because the Israelites were brought out of Egypt under his direction, marshalled and ordered by himself, guided by his wisdom, supported by his providence, and protected by his might. This is the true and simple reason, why God is so frequently styled in Scripture the Lord of Hosts: *for the* Lord *did bring the children of Israel out of Egypt by their armies.*" Dr. A. Clarke's Commentary, on Exod. xii. 51.

spoken for to the king, or to the CAPTAIN OF THE HOST? (2 Kings iv. 13.)

After the establishment of the monarchy, the kings went to war in person, and at first fought on foot, like the meanest of their soldiers. Thus David fought, until the danger to which he exposed himself became so great, that his people would no longer allow him to lead them on to battle. (2 Sam. xxi. 17.) It does not appear that there were any horse in the Israelitish army before the time of Solomon. In the time of David there were none; for the rebel Absalom was mounted on a mule in the battle in which he lost his life. (2 Sam. xviii. 9.) Solomon, who had married the daughter of the king of Egypt, procured horses from that country at a great expense (1 Kings x. 28, 29.); and afterwards had four thousand stalls for horses and chariots, and twelve thousand horsemen. (2 Chron. ix. 25.) From Zech. xiv. 20. it should seem, that bells formed a part of the caparison of war-horses. Subsequent kings of Judah and Israel went into the battle in chariots, arrayed in their royal vestments, or sometimes in disguise. They generally had a spare chariot to attend them: thus we read that king Josiah, after he was mortally wounded, was taken out of his war-chariot, and put into another, in which he was carried to Jerusalem. (2 Chron. xxxv. 23, 24. 1 Kings xxii. 34.) Both kings and generals had *armour-bearers*, who were chosen from the bravest of the soldiery, and not only bore the arms of their masters, but were also employed to give his commands to the subordinate captains, and were present at his side in the hour of peril. (1 Sam. xiv. 6. xvii. 7.)

Military chariots were much in use among the Egyptians, Canaanites, and other oriental nations.[1] Two sorts are mentioned in the Scriptures; one in which princes and generals rode, the other to break the enemy's battalions by rushing in among them, armed with iron scythes, which caused terrible havoc. The most antient war-chariots, of which we read, are those of Pharoah, which were destroyed in the Red Sea (Exod. xiv. 7.): his infantry, cavalry, and war-chariots were so arranged as to form separate divisions of his army. (Exod. xiv. 6, 7.) The Canaanites, whom Joshua engaged at the waters of Merom, had cavalry and a multitude of chariots. (Josh. xi. 4.) Sisera, the general of Jabin, king of Hazor, had nine hundred chariots of iron in his army. (Judg. iv. 3.) The tribe of Judah could not obtain possession of part of the lands allotted to them, because the inhabitants of the country were strong in chariots of iron. (Judg. i. 19.) The Philistines, in their war with Saul, had thirty thousand chariots, and six thousand horsemen. (1 Sam. xiii. 5.) David, having taken a thousand war-chariots from Hadadezer, king of Damascus, ham-strung the horses, and burnt nine hundred chariots, reserving only one hundred. (2 Sam. viii. 4.) It does not appear that the Hebrews ever used chariots in war, though Solomon had a considerable number; but we know of no military expedition in which he employed them. In the second book of Maccabees, mention is made of chariots armed with scythes, which the king of Syria led against the Jews. (2 Macc. xiii. 2.) These chariots were generally placed on the whole front of the infantry, ranged in a straight line, parallel sometimes to the cavalry. Some of them were with four, others with two wheels only: these

---

[1] They were also used among the antient Britons.

were driven against the enemy, whom they never failed to put into disorder, when they were followed closely by the line. There were two ways of rendering them useless: first, by opening a passage for them through the battalions; secondly, by killing the horses before they were too far advanced: in which case they were of the greatest disservice to those who employed them, because they not only embarrassed them, but, further, broke the closeness of the line, and checked all the force of the onset. The infantry were divided into *light-armed troops*, and into *spear-men*. (Gen. xlix. 19. 1 Sam. xxx. 8, 15. 23. 2 Sam. iii. 22. iv. 2. xxii. 30. Psalm. xviii. 30. in the Hebrew, 29. of our English version, 2 Kings v. 2. Hos. vii. 1.) The light-armed troops of infantry were furnished with a sling and javelin, with a bow, arrows, and quiver, and also, at least in later times, with a buckler: they fought the enemy at a distance. The spear-men, on the contrary, who were armed with spears, swords, and shields, fought hand to hand. (1 Chron. xii. 24. 34. 2 Chron. xiv. 8. xvii. 17.) The light-armed troops were commonly taken from the tribes of Ephraim and Benjamin. (2 Chron. xiv. 8. xvii. 17.)

IV. No information is given us in the Scriptures, concerning the order of ENCAMPMENT adopted by the Israelites after their settlement in Canaan. During their sojourning in the wilderness, the form of their camp, according to the account given in Numb. ii., appears to have been quadrangular, having three tribes placed on each side, under one general standard, so as to inclose the tabernacle, which stood in the centre. Between these four great camps and the tabernacle were pitched four smaller camps of the priests and Levites, who were immediately in attendance upon it; the camp of Moses and of Aaron and his sons (who were the ministering priests, and had the charge of the sanctuary) was on the east side of the tabernacle, where the entrance was. From Isa. liv. 2. it appears that the tents, under which they lived, were nearly the same as those which are now in use in the East. Every family and household had their particular ensign; under which they encamped or pursued their march. Rabbinical writers assert that the standard of Judah was a lion; that of Reuben, the figure of a man; that of Ephraim, an ox; that of Dan, an eagle, with a serpent in his talons[1]: but for these assertions there is no foundation. They are probably derived from the patriarch's prophetic blessing of his children, related in Gen. xlix. It is far more likely, that the names of the several tribes were embroidered in large letters on their respective standards, or that they were distinguished by appropriate colours. The following diagram, after Ainsworth, Roberts, and Dr. A. Clarke[2], will, perhaps, give the reader a tolerable idea of the beautiful order of the Israelitish encampment; the sight of which, from the mountains of Moab, extorted from Balaam (when *he saw Israel abiding* in his tents *according to their tribes*) the following exclamation: — *How goodly are thy tents, O Jacob*, and *thy tabernacles, O Israel! As the vallies are they spread forth, as gardens by the river's side, as the trees of lign aloes which the Lord hath planted*, and *as cedar trees beside the waters.* (Numb. xxiv. 2. 5, 6.)

---

[1] Lamy de Tabernaculo, lib. iii. c. 2. Carpzov has given at length the rabbinical descriptions of the Israelitish standard. Antiq. Hebr. Gentis. pp. 667, 668.

[2] In their Commentaries, on Numb. ii. Roberts's Clavis Bibliorum, p. 24. folio edit.

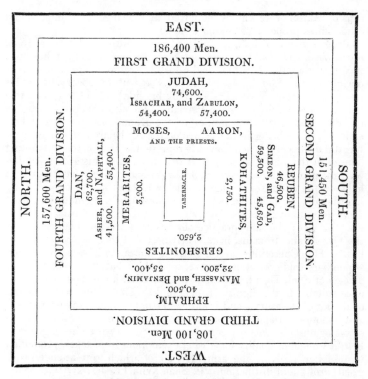

During the encampment of the Israelites in the wilderness, Moses made various salutary enactments, which are recorded in Deut. xxiii. 10—15., for guarding against the vice and uncleanliness that might otherwise have prevailed among so large a body of people, forming an aggregate of upwards of three millions. The following was the order of their march, which was not much unlike that in which the caravans or assemblages of oriental travellers still continue to move: — When they were to remove (which was only when the cloud was taken off the tabernacle), the trumpet was sounded, and upon the first alarm the standard of Judah being raised, the three tribes which belonged to it set forward; then the tabernacle being taken down, which was the proper office of the Levites, the Gershonites and the Merarites (two families of that order) attended the waggons with the boards, staves, &c. When these were on their march a second alarm was sounded, upon which the standard of Reuben's camp advanced with the three tribes under it. After them followed the Kohathites (the third family of the Levites) bearing the sanctuary, that is, the Holy of Holies and the utensils thereto belonging; and because this was less cumbersome than the boards, pillars, and other parts of the tabernacle, and more holy, it was on that account not put into a waggon, but carried on their shoulders. Next followed the standard of Ephraim's camp with the tribes belonging to it: and last of all the other three tribes under the standard of Dan brought up the rear; Moses and Aaron overseeing the whole, that every thing was done as God had directed, while the sons of Aaron were chiefly employed in blowing the trumpets, and other offices properly belonging to them.

From 1 Sam. xxvi. 5., as rendered in our authorised version, (*Saul lay in the trench, and the people pitched round about him,*) it has been imagined that the Israelites had a fortified camp. The proper rendering is, that *Saul lay among the baggage,* with his spear stuck at his head, *and a cruse* or vessel *of water* by his side[1], (7. 11.) in the same manner as is usual among the Persians[2], and also among the Arabs to this day, wherever the disposition of the ground will permit it: their emir or prince being in the centre of the Arabs around him at a respectful distance.[3] When David is represented as sometimes secreting himself in the night, when he was with his armies, instead of lodging with the people (2 Sam. xvii. 8, 9.), it probably means that he did not lodge in the middle of the camp, which was the proper place for a king, in order that he might the better avoid any surprise from his enemies.[4]

V. In antient times the Hebrews received no pay, during their military service: the same practice of gratuitous service obtained among the Greeks and Romans, in the early period of their respective republics.[5] The Cherethites and Pelethites appear to have been the first stipendiary soldiers: it is however probable, that the great military officers of Saul, David, Solomon, and the other kings, had some allowance suitable to the dignity of their rank. The soldiers were paid out of the king's treasury: and in order to stimulate their valour, rewards and honours were publicly bestowed on those who distinguished themselves against the enemy; consisting of pecuniary presents, a girdle or belt, a woman of quality for a wife, exemptions from taxes, promotion to a higher rank in the army, &c. all of which were attended with great profit and distinction. (2 Sam. xviii. 11. Jos. xv. 16. 1 Sam. xviii. 25. 1 Chron. xi. 6.) In the age of the Maccabees, the patriot Simon both armed and paid his brave companions in arms, at his own expense. (1 Macc. xiv. 32.) Afterwards, it became an established custom, that all soldiers should receive pay. (Luke iii. 14. 1 Cor. ix. 7.)

It appears from various passages of Scripture, and especially from Isa. ii. 4. and Mic. iv. 3., that there were military schools, in which the Hebrew soldiers *learned war*, or, in modern language, were trained, by proper officers, in those exercises which were in use among the other nations of antiquity. Swiftness of foot was an accomplishment highly valued among the Hebrew warriors, both for attacking and pursuing an enemy, as well as among the antient Greeks and Romans. In 2 Sam. i. 19. Saul is denominated the *roe* (in our version rendered *the beauty*) *of Israel;* the force of which expression will be felt, when it is recollected that in the East, to this day, the hind and roe, the hart and antelope, continue to be held in high estimation for the delicate elegance of their form, or their graceful agility of action. In 2 Sam. ii. 18. we are told that *Asahel was as light of foot as a wild*

---

[1] In the same way do all eastern travellers sleep at this day. "The bolster is round, about eight inches in diameter, and twenty in length. In travelling, it is carried rolled up in the mat on which the owner sleeps. In a hot climate a draught of water is very refreshing in the night: hence a vessel filled with water is always near where a person sleeps." (Roberts's Oriental Illustrations of Scripture, p. 177.

[2] Morier's Second Journey into Persia, pp. 115, 116.

[3] Captains Irby's and Mangles' Travels in Egypt, &c. p. 395. Dr. Della Cella's Narrative of an Expedition from Tripoli in Barbary to the Western Frontiers of Egypt, p. 11.

[4] Harmer's Observations, vol. iii. pp. 430, 431.

[5] Livy, lib. iv. c. 59. Bruning's Antiquit. Græc. p. 102.

roe; — a mode of expression perfectly synonymous with the epithet of
Ποδας ωκυς Αχιλλευς, *the swift-footed Achilles,* which is given by Homer
to his hero, not fewer than thirty times in the course of the Iliad.
David expressed his gratitude to God for making his feet *like hind's feet*
for swiftness, and teaching his hands to war, so that a bow of steel was
broken by his arms. (Psal. xviii. 33, 34.) The tribe of Benjamin
could boast of a great number of brave men, who could use their right
and left hands with equal dexterity (Judg. xx. 16. 1 Chron. xii. 2.),
and who were eminent for their skill in the use of the bow and the
sling. The *men of war,* out of the tribe of Gad, who came to David
when persecuted by Saul, are described as being *men of war, fit for the
battle, that could handle shield and buckler, whose faces were like the faces
of lions, and* who were as *swift as the roes* upon the mountains. (1 Chron.
xii. 8.)

VI. The Hebrews do not appear to have had any peculiar military
habit: as the flowing dress which they ordinarily wore, would have
impeded their movements, they girt it closely around them, when preparing for battle, and loosened it on their return. (2 Sam. xx. 8. 1
Kings xx. 11.) They used the same arms as the neighbouring nations,
both defensive and offensive, and these were made either of iron or of
brass, principally of the latter metal. In the Scriptures we read of
brazen shields, helmets, and bows : the helmet, greaves, and target of
the gigantic Goliath were all of brass, which was the metal chiefly used
by the antient Greeks.[1] The national museums of most countries
contain abundant specimens of brazen arms, which have been rescued
from the destroying hand of time. Originally, every man provided
his own arms: but after the establishment of the monarchy, depôts
were formed, whence they were distributed to the men as occasion required. (2 Chron. xi. 12. xxvi. 14, 15.)

Of the DEFENSIVE ARMS of the Hebrews, the following were the
most remarkable; viz.

1. The HELMET כּוֹבַע (KOBaNG), for covering and defending the
head. This was a part of the military provision made by Uzziah for
his vast army (2 Chron. xxvi. 14.): and long before the time of that
king, the helmets of Saul and of the Philistine champion were of brass.
(1 Sam. xvii. 38. 5.) This military cap was also worn by the Persians,
Ethiopians, and Lybians (Ezek. xxxviii. 5.), and by the troops which
Antiochus sent against Judas Maccabeus. (1 Macc. vi. 35.)

2. The BREAST-PLATE or CORSLET, שִׁרְיוֹן (SHiRION), was another
piece of defensive armour. Goliath, and the soldiers of Antiochus
(1 Sam. xvii. 5. 1 Macc. vi. 35.) were accoutred with this defence,
which, in our authorised translation, is variously rendered *habergeon,
coat of mail,* and *brigandine.* (1 Sam. xvii. 38. 2 Chron. xxvi. 14.
Isa. lix. 17. Jer. xlvi. 4.) Between the joints of his *harness* (as it is
termed in 1 Kings xxii. 34.), the profligate Ahab was mortally wounded
by an arrow shot at a venture. From these various renderings of the
original word, it should seem that this piece of armour covered both
the back and breast, but principally the latter. The corslets were made
of various materials : sometimes they were made of flax or cotton, woven
very thick, or of a kind of woollen felt : others again were made of iron

---

[1] Calmet, in his elaborate Dissertation sur la Milice des Anciens Hebreux, has collected
numerous examples from Homer, Hesiod, Virgil, and various other classic writers, in which
brazen arms and armour are mentioned. Dissertations, tom. i. pp. 220—222.

or brazen scales, or laminæ, laid one over another like the scales of a fish; others were properly what we call coats of mail; and others were composed of two pieces of iron or brass, which protected the back and breast. All these kinds of corslets are mentioned in the Scriptures. Goliath's *coat of mail* (1 Sam. xvii. 5.) was literally, a *corslet of scales*, that is, composed of numerous laminæ of brass, crossing each other. It was called by the Latin writers *squamea lorica*.[1] Similar corslets were worn by the Persians and other nations. The breast-plate worn by the unhappy Saul, when he perished in battle, is supposed to have been of flax, or cotton, woven very close and thick. (2 Sam. i. 9. marginal rendering.)

3. The SHIELD defended the whole body during the battle. It was of various forms, and made of wood or ozier, covered with tough hides, or of brass, and sometimes was overlaid with gold. (1 Kings x. 16, 17. xiv. 26, 27.) Two sorts are mentioned in the Scriptures, viz. the צִנָּה (TSin̄naH) great shield or buckler, and the מָגֵן (MaGeN) or smaller shield. It was much used by the Jews, Babylonians, Chaldeans, Assyrians, and Egyptians. David, who was a great warrior, often mentions a shield and buckler in his divine poems, to signify that defence and protection of heaven which he expected and experienced, and in which he reposed all his trust. (Psal. v. 12.) And when he says, *God will with favour compass the righteous as with a shield,* he seems to allude to the use of the great shield *tsinnah* (which is the word he uses) with which they covered and defended their whole bodies. King Solomon caused two different sorts of shields to be made, viz. the tsinnah (which answers to the clypeus of the Latins), such a large shield as the infantry wore, and the maginnim or scuta, which were used by the horsemen, and were of a much less size. (2 Chron. ix. 15, 16.) The former of these are translated targets, and are double in weight to the other. The Philistines came into the field with this weapon: so we find their formidable champion was appointed. (1 Sam xvii. 7.) One bearing a shield went before him, whose proper duty it was to carry this and some other weapons, with which to furnish his master upon occasion.[2]

A shield-bearer was an office among the Jews as well as the Philistines, for David when he first went to court was made king Saul's armour-bearer (1 Sam. xvi. 21.), and Jonathan had a young man who bore his armour before him. (1 Sam. xiv. 1.) Besides this tsinnah, or great massy shield, Goliath was furnished with a less one (1 Sam. xvii. 6. and 45.), which is not expressed by one of the fore-mentioned words, but is called *cidon,* which we render a target in one place and a shield in another, and was of a different nature from the common shields. He seems not only to have held it in his hand when he had occasion to

---

[1] Æneid, lib. ix. 707.

[2] The chevalier Folard is of opinion that the brazen shield, with which Goliath covered his shoulders, consisted only of brass plates fastened upon the wood; similar to the bucklers which Solomon afterwards enriched with gold plates, and deposited in the temple (1 Kings x. 16, 17.), and which, having been carried away by Shishak, king of Egypt, were replaced by Rehoboam, with other brazen shields. An additional reason for concluding Goliath's shield to have been composed of brass plates affixed to wood, is, that if it had been wholly composed of this metal, and had been of a size proportionable to his body, it is doubtful whether this giant, and still more whether his squire, would have been able to support its weight.

use it, but could also at other times conveniently hang it about his neck and turn it behind, on which account it is added, that it was between his shoulders.   The loss of the shield in fight was excessively resented by the Jewish warriors, as well as lamented by them, for it was a signal ingredient of the public mourning, that *the shield of the mighty was vilely cast away.* (2 Sam. i. 21.) David, a man of arms, who composed the beautiful elegy on the death of Saul related in 2 Sam. i. 19 —27., was sensible how disgraceful a thing it was for soldiers to quit their shields in the field, yet this was the deplorable case of the Jewish soldiers in that unhappy engagement with the Philistines (1 Sam. xxxi. 7.), they fled away and left their shields behind them; this vile and dishonourable casting away of that principal article of their armour is deservedly the subject of the royal poet's lamentation.

But these honourable sentiments were not confined to the Jews. We find them prevailing among most other antient nations, who considered it infamous to cast away or lose their shield.   With the Greeks it was a capital crime, and punished with death. The Lacedemonian women, it is well known, in order to excite the courage of their sons, used to deliver to them their fathers' shields, with this short address : " This shield thy father always preserved; do thou preserve it also, or perish." Alluding to these sentiments, Saint Paul, when exhorting the Hebrew Christians to steadfastness in the faith of the Gospel, urges them not to *cast away their confidence,* their confession of faith, which *hath great recompense of reward,* no less than the approbation of God, the peace which passeth all understanding *here,* and the glories of heaven as their *eternal* portion. (Heb. x. 35.)

It may be further observed, that they used to scour and polish their arms, as may be inferred from the prophet's expressions of *furbishing the spears and making bright the arrows* (Jer. xlvi. 4. and li. 11.) ; and it should seem that such shields as were covered with leather, were oiled in order to keep them clean, and prevent them from becoming too dry.   To this custom there is an allusion in 2 Sam. i. 21. and Isa. xxi. 5.   When the shields were not in use, they were covered with a case, in order to preserve them from being rusty and soiled; hence we read of *uncovering the shield,* which signifies preparing for war, and having that weapon especially in readiness. (Isa. xxii. 6.)

4. Another defensive provision in war, was the MILITARY GIRDLE, or BELT, which answered a twofold purpose, viz. first, in order to wear the sword, which hung at the soldier's girdle or belt (1 Sam. xvii. 39.) ; secondly, it was necessary to gird their clothes and armour together, and thus David girded his sword upon his armour.   To *gird* and to *arm* are synonymous words in Scripture; for those who are said to be able to put on armour, are, according to the Hebrew and the Septuagint, girt with a girdle, and hence comes the expression of girding to the battle. (1 Kings xx. 11. Isa. viii. 9. 2 Sam. xxii. 40.)   The military girdle was the chief ornament of a soldier, and was highly prized among all antient nations; it was also a rich present from one chieftain to another.   Thus, Jonathan gave his girdle to David, as the highest pledge of his esteem and perpetual friendship. (1 Sam. xviii. 4.)[1]

5. BOOTS or GREAVES, were part of the antient defensive harness,

---

[1] In like manner, Ajax gave his girdle to Hector as a token of the highest respect. (Iliad, vii. 305.)   Dr. A. Clarke, on 2 Sam. xviii. 11.

because it was the custom to cast certain εμποδια, impediments (so called because they entangle the feet, afterwards known by the name of gall-traps, which since, in heraldry, are corruptly called call-trops), in the way before the enemy : the military boot or shoe was, therefore, necessary to guard the legs and feet from the iron stakes placed in the way to gall and wound them ; and thus we are enabled to account for Goliath's greaves of brass which were upon his legs.

VII. The OFFENSIVE ARMS were of two sorts, viz. such as were employed when they came to a close engagement ; and those with which they annoyed the enemy at a distance. Of the former description were the sword and the battle-axe.

1. The SWORD is the most antient weapon of offence mentioned in the Bible. With it Jacob's sons treacherously assassinated the She-chemites. (Gen. xxxiv. 25.) It was worn on the thigh (Psal. xlv. 3. Exod. xxxii. 27.), and it should seem, on the left thigh; though it is particularly mentioned that Ehud, a Benjamite, put a dagger or short sword under his garments on his right thigh. (Judg. iii. 16.) The palanquin, or travelling couch of Solomon, (Song iii. 7, 8. where our version terms it a bed,) was surrounded by threescore valiant Israel-itish soldiers, every one of whom had his sword girt upon his thigh. There appear to have been two kinds of swords in use, a larger one with one edge, which is called in Hebrew the *mouth* of the sword (Josh. vi. 21.) ; and a shorter one with two edges, like that of Ehud. The modern Arabs, it is well known, wear a sabre on one side, and a *can-giar* or dagger in their girdles.

2. Of the BATTLE-AXE we have no description in the Sacred Vo-lume : it seems to have been a most powerful weapon in the hands of cavalry, from the allusion made to it by Jeremiah :—*Thou art my battle-axe and weapons of war ; for with thee will I break in pieces the nations, and with thee will I destroy kingdoms : and with thee will I break in pieces the horse and his rider, and with thee will I break in pieces the chariot and his rider.* (Jer. li. 20, 21.)

The other offensive weapons for annoying the enemy at a distance, were the spear or javelin, the sling, and the bow and arrow.

3. The SPEAR or JAVELIN (as the words רמה (ROMACH), and חנית (CHANITH), are variously rendered in Numb. xxv. 7. 1 Sam. xiii. 19. and Jer. xlvi. 4.) was of different kinds, according to its length or make. Some of them might be thrown or darted (1 Sam. xviii. 11.); and it appears from 2 Sam. ii. 23. that some of them were pointed at both ends. When armies were encamped, the spear of the general or com-mander-in-chief was stuck into the ground at his head.[1]

4. SLINGS are enumerated among the military stores collected by Uzziah. (2 Chron. xxvi. 14.) In the use of the sling, David eminently excelled, and slew Goliath with a stone from one (1 Sam. xvii. 40. &c.) : he had been accustomed to use it, in keeping off the enemies of his flock. In the East, to this day, shepherds carry a sling and stones for the same purpose.[2] The Benjamites were celebrated in battle because they had attained to a great skill and accuracy in handling this wea-pon; *they could sling stones to a hair's breadth, and not miss* (Judg. xx. 16.) ; and where it is said that they were left-handed, it should rather

---

[1] See p. 206. *supra*, for examples of this custom.
[2] Roberts's Oriental Illustrations, p. 169.

be rendered ambidexters, for we are told, they could use *both the right hand and the left* (1 Chron. xii. 2.) ; that is, they did not constantly use their right hand as others did, when they shot arrows or slung stones, but they were so expert in their military exercises, that they could perform them with their left hand as well as with their right.

5. Bows and Arrows are of great antiquity : indeed, no weapon is mentioned so early. Thus Isaac said to Esau, *Take thy weapons, thy quiver and thy bow* (Gen. xxvii. 3.) ; though it is true, these are not spoken of as used in war, but in hunting, and so they are supposed and implied before this : where it is said of Ishmael, that he became an archer, and used bows and arrows in shooting wild beasts. (Gen. xxi. 20.) This afterwards became so useful a weapon, that care was taken to train up the Hebrew youth to it betimes. When David had in a solemn manner lamented the death of king Saul, he gave orders for teaching *the young men the use of the bow* (2 Sam. i. 18.), that they might be as expert as the Philistines, by whose bows and arrows Saul and his army were slain. These were part of the military ammunition (for in those times bows were used instead of guns, and arrows supplied the place of powder and ball). From Job xx. 24. and from Psal. xviii. 34. it may be collected, that the military bow was made of steel, and, consequently, was very stiff and hard to bend, on which account they used their foot in bending their bows ; and therefore when the prophets speak of *treading the bow*, and of *bows trodden*, they are to be understood of *bows bent*, as our translators rightly render it (Jer. l. 14. Isa. v. 28. xxi. 15.) ; where the Hebrew word, which is used in these places, signifies *to tread upon*. This weapon was thought so necessary in war, that it is called *the bow of war*, or the *battle-bow*. (Zech. ix. 10. x. 4.)

VIII. Many of the cities of Palestine being erected on eminences, were fortified by nature ; but most frequently they were surrounded with a lofty wall, either single or double (Deut. xxviii. 52. 2 Chron. xxxiii. 14. Isa. xxii. 11.) ; on which were erected towers or bulwarks. (2 Chron. xiv. 7. xxiv. 9. Psal. xlviii. 13.) These towers were furnished with machines from which the besieged could discharge arrows and great stones. (2 Chron. xxvi. 15.) It was also usual to erect towers on the confines of a country, to repress the incursions of troublesome neighbours, and which also served as occasional places of refuge. The tower of Peniel (Judg. viii. 9. 17.), and those erected by Uzziah (2 Chron. xxvi. 9, 10.), appear to have been of this description ; and similar towers were afterwards erected by the crusaders.[1] When the Israelites were about to besiege a city, they dug trenches, drew a line of circumvallation, erected ramparts, built forts against it, and cast a mount against it ; they also set the camp against it, and set battering rams against it round about. (2 Sam. xx. 15. Lam. ii. 8. Ezek. iv. 2.) These engines of *shot*, as our margin renders it in the prophecy of Jeremiah (vi. 6.), in all probability, resembled in some measure the balistæ and catapultæ among the Romans ; which were used for throwing stones and arrows, and antiently served instead of mortars and carcasses. Further, in order to give notice of an approaching enemy, and to bring the dispersed inhabitants of the country together, they used

---

[1] Harmer's Observations, vol. iii. pp. 415—418. 425—428.

to set up beacons on the tops of mountains, as a proper alarm upon those occasions.

Such were the various instruments of offence and defence in use among the antient Israelites. Sometimes, however, they were very badly provided with military weapons: for, after the Philistines had gained many considerable advantages over them, and in effect had subdued their country, they took care that no smith should be left throughout the land of Israel, to prevent them from making swords and spears; so that the Israelites were obliged to go down to the Philistines whenever they had occasion to sharpen their instruments of husbandry. (1 Sam. xiii. 19, 20. 22.) Long before the reign of Saul we read that there *was not a shield or spear seen among forty thousand in Israel* (Judg. v. 8.); though it is probable that they had other military weapons which are not mentioned. After Nebuchadnezzar had captured Jerusalem, he adopted the policy of the Philistines, and took all the craftsmen and smiths with him to Babylon, that the poorest of the people, whom he had left behind, might be in no condition to rebel. (2 Kings xxiv. 14.)

It was an antient custom to *shoot an arrow* or *cast a spear* into the country which an army intended to invade. As soon as Alexander had arrived on the coasts of Ionia, he threw a dart into the country of the Persians.[1] The throwing of a dart was considered as an emblem of the commencement of hostilities among the Romans.[2] Some such custom as this appears to have obtained among the eastern people; and to this the prophet Elisha alluded when he termed the arrow shot by the king of Israel, *the arrow of deliverance* from Syria (2 Kings xiii. 17.): meaning, that as surely as that arrow was shot towards the lands which had been conquered from the Israelites by the Syrians, so surely should those lands be reconquered and restored to Israel.

IX. Previously to undertaking a war, the heathens consulted their oracles, soothsayers, and magicians; and after their example, Saul, when forsaken by God, had recourse to a witch to know the result of the impending battle (1 Sam. xxviii. 7.): they also had recourse to divination by arrows, and inspection of the livers of slaughtered victims. (Ezek. xxi. 21.) The Israelites, to whom these things were prohibited, formerly consulted the urim and thummim, or the sacred lot. (Judg. i. 1. xx. 27, 28.) After the establishment of the monarchy, the Hebrew kings, as they were piously or impiously disposed, consulted the prophets of the Lord, or the false prophets, the latter of whom (as it was their interest) failed not to persuade them that they should succeed. (1 Kings xxii. 6—13. 2 Kings xix. 2. 20.) Their expeditions were generally undertaken in the spring (2 Sam. xi. 1.), and carried on through the summer. Previously to the engagement, the combatants anointed their shields, and took food that their strength might not fail them. (Isa. xxi. 5. Jer. xlvi. 3, 4.) The law and usage of civilised nations require, that no war should be undertaken without a previous declaration, and without a previous demand of satisfaction for the injury complained of. Hence, in the voluntary wars of the Jews, Moses ordained that certain conditions of peace should be offered before the Israelites attacked any place. (Deut. xx. 10—20.) There

---

[1] Justin, Hist. Philipp. lib. ii.
[2] Livy, lib. i. c. 32. Other instances from the Roman history may be seen in Adam's Roman Antiquities, p. 362.

does not, however, appear to have been any uniform mode of declaring war. When Jephthah was appointed judge of the Israelites beyond the Jordan, he sent messengers (or ambassadors) to the king of the Ammonites, saying, *What hast thou to do with me, that thou art come against me, to fight in my land?* (Judg. xi. 12.) On the Ammonites complaining that the Israelites had forcibly seized their lands, Jephthah, after justifying his people from the charge, concluded by saying, *The* Lord, *the Judge, be judge this day between the children of Israel and the children of Ammon* (27.); after which he attacked and totally discomfited them. When the Philistines invaded the territory of the tribe of Judah, to avenge the injury committed by Samson in burning their corn, in reply to the question of the men of Judah, *Why are ye come up against us?* and on their promising to deliver up Samson, the Philistines withdrew their forces. (Judg. xv. 9, 10, &c.) After the detestable crime committed by certain Benjamites of the town of Gibeah, upon the Levite's concubine, all the assembled Israelites sent to the tribe of Benjamin, to demand that the guilty parties should be delivered up, that they might *put them to death, and put away evil from Israel.* (Judg. xx. 12, 13.) Nor did they resolve upon war, until after the refusal of the Benjamites.

In later times, we may observe a kind of defiance, or declaration of war between David's army under the command of Joab, and that of Ishbosheth under Abner, who said to Joab, *Let the young men now arise and play before us. And Joab said, Let them arise;* and immediately the conflict began between twelve men of each army. (2 Sam. ii. 14, 15.) Amaziah, king of Judah, proud of some advantages which he had obtained over the Edomites, sent a challenge to Jehoash king of Israel, saying, *Come, let us look one another in the face.* Jehoash, in a beautiful parable, dissuaded him from going to war; to which Amaziah refused to listen. The two kings did *look one another in the face at Bethshemesh,* where the king of Judah was totally defeated. (2 Kings xiv. 8—12.) Ben-Hadad, king of Syria, declared war against Ahab in a yet more insolent manner. Having laid siege to Samaria, he sent messengers, saying, *Thy silver and thy gold is mine; thy wives also and thy children are mine.* Ahab, who felt his weakness, replied, *My Lord, O king, according to thy saying, I am thine and all that I have.* Then Ben-Hadad, more insolent than before, rejoined, *Although I have sent unto thee, saying, Thou shalt deliver me thy silver, and thy gold, and thy wives, and thy children; yet I will send my servants unto thee to-morrow about this time, and they shall search thine house, and the houses of thy servants, and whatsoever is pleasant in thine eyes, they shall put it in their hand, and take it away.* These exorbitant demands being rejected by Ahab and his council, who resolved to defend themselves and sustain the siege, Ben-Hadad was obliged to abandon it, after having lost the greater part of his army. (1 Kings xx. 4—21.) When Pharaoh Necho, king of Egypt, on his way to Carchemish against the Assyrians was desirous of crossing the dominions of the king of Judah, Josiah, who was the ally or tributary of the Assyrian monarch, opposed his passage with an army. Then Necho sent ambassadors to him, saying, *What have I to do with thee, thou king of Judah? I come not against thee this day, but against the house wherewith I have war, for God commanded me to make haste. Forbear thou from meddling with God, who is with me, that he destroy thee not.* Josiah persisted, and was mortally wounded in a battle which he lost. (2 Chron. xxxv. 20—24.)

X. Of the precise mode in which the earliest Jewish armies were drawn up, the Scriptures gives us no information: but, as the art of war was then comparatively imperfect, much reliance was placed in the multitude of combatants, — a notion, the fallacy of which is exposed in Psal. xxxiii. 16.

Subsequently, however, under the kings, when the Jews had cavalry, they threw them upon the wings (according to the chevalier Folard), in large squadrons of six or eight hundred horse, with a depth equal to the front, and with little intervals between them. But this order was not always observed. John the son of Simon Maccabæus, in the battle which he fought with Cendebeus, placed his horse in the centre, and threw his foot upon the wings; to which successful stratagem he was, under Providence, indebted for a complete victory (1 Macc. xvi. 7, 8.) : for the novelty of this order of battle amazed the enemy's infantry, and confounded Cendebeus, when he found that he had to encounter the whole of John's cavalry, which bore down his foot, while the infantry of the Jews broke through his horse, and put them to flight.

From the time of Moses to that of Solomon, the ark of the covenant was present in the camp, the symbol of the divine presence, and an incitement to valiant achievements. It was taken by the Philistines in the time of the high-priest Eli (1 Sam. iv. 11.), but subsequently restored. In like manner the Philistines carried their deities into the field of battle (1 Chron. xiv. 12.); and it appears that Jeroboam and the Israelites of the ten tribes had their golden calves with them in the field. (2 Chron. xiii. 8.) Before they engaged in battle, the law of Moses appointed two priests to blow with two silver trumpets (Numb. x. 9.) which are described by Josephus[1] to have been a cubit long, and narrow like a pipe, but wider, as ours are, at the bottom; no more than two were at first ordered for present use, but more were afterwards made when the priests and the people were increased. There were others called trumpets of rams' horns (Josh. vi. 4.), probably from their shape, which were used in war, to incite the soldiers to the conflict. These instruments were blown to call the people to the sanctuary to pay their devotion, and pray to God before they engaged; and they were sounded with a particular blast, that they might know the meaning of the summons: then *the anointed for the war*, going from one battalion to another, was to exhort the soldiers to fight valiantly. (Deut. xx. 2.) There were officers whose duty it was to make proclamation, that those whose business it was should make sufficient provision for the army before they marched; and every tenth man was appointed for that purpose. (Josh. i. 10, 11. Judg. xx. 10.) Sometimes they advanced to battle singing hymns (2 Chron. xx. 21, 22.); and the signal was given by the priests sounding the trumpets. (Numb. x. 9. Judg. vi. 34. 2 Chron. xiii. 14. 1 Macc. iii. 54. iv. 13.) It should seem that a notion prevailed among the antient idolatrous nations of the East, of the efficacy of devoting an enemy to destruction. Under this persuasion Balak engaged Balaam to curse the Israelites, because they were too mighty for him (Numb. xxii. 6.); and Goliath cursed David by his gods. (1 Sam xvii. 43.)[2] The Romans in later times

---

[1] Antiq. lib. iii. c. 11.

[2] In like manner, the Cingalese frequently utter imprecations in the name of the most

had a peculiar form of evoking or calling out the gods, under whose protection a place was supposed to be, and also of devoting the people, which is fully described by Macrobius [1]; and many accounts are related in the Hindoo puranas of kings employing sages to curse their enemies when too powerful for them. It was customary for the Hebrew kings or their generals (in common with other antient nations) to deliver an address to their armies. (2 Chron. xiii. 4—12. xx. 21. 1 Macc. iv. 8—11.) These harangues had a great share in the success of the day, and often contributed to the gaining of a battle. The Greek and Roman historians abound with pieces of this kind; but they are too long, and too elaborate, to be originals. Those only which are recorded in the Scriptures appear to be natural: the terms in which they are conceived, carry certain marks of truth, which cannot fail to strike the reader : they are short, but lively, moving, and full of pious sentiments.

The onset of the battle, after the custom of the Orientals, was very violent (Numb. xxiii. 24. xxiv. 8, 9.), and was made with a great shout. (Exod. xxxii. 17. 1 Sam. xvii. 20. 52. 2 Chron. xiii. 15. Jer. l. 42.)   The same practice obtained in the age of the Maccabees (1 Macc. iii. 54.), as it does to this day among the Cossacks, Tartars, and Turks. All the wars, in the earliest times, were carried on with great cruelty and ferocity ; of which we may see instances in Judg. viii. 7. 16. 2 Kings iii. 27. viii. 12. xv. 16. 2 Chron. xxv. 12. Amos i. 3. 13. and Psal. cxxxvii. 8, 9. Yet the kings of Israel were distinguished for their humanity and lenity towards their enemies. (1 Kings xx. 31. 2 Kings vi. 21—23. 2 Chron. xxviii. 8—15.) When the victory was decided, the bodies of the slain were interred. (1 Kings xi. 15. 2 Sam. ii. 32. xxi. 14. Ezek. xxxix. 11, 12. 2 Macc. xii. 39.) Sometimes, however, the heads of the slain were cut off, and deposited in heaps at the palace gate (2 Kings x. 7, 8.), as is frequently done to this day in Turkey, and in Persia [2]; and when the conquerors were irritated at the obstinacy with which a city was defended, they refused the rites of burial to the dead, whose bodies were cast out, a prey to carnivorous birds and beasts. This barbarity is feelingly deplored by the Psalmist (lxxix. 1—3.) And on some occasions the remains of the slain were treated with every mark of indignity. Thus the Philistines *cut off the head of Saul, and stripped off his armour, which they put in the house of* their deity, *Ashtaroth* or Astarte; *and they fastened his body and the bodies of his sons to the wall of Beth-shan ;* whence they were soon taken by the brave inhabitants of Jabesh Gilead. (1 Sam. xxxi. 9—12.) A heap of stones was raised over the grave of princes, as in the case of Absalom. (2 Sam. xviii. 17.) The daily diminishing cairn of pebble-stones, situated about two miles from the lake of Grasmere, in Cumberland, and known by the appellation of *Dunmail Raise-stones,* was raised in a like manner to commemorate the name and defeat of Dunmail, a petty king of Cumbria, A.D. 945 or 946, by the Anglo-Saxon monarch Edmund I.

When a city was taken, after being rased to the foundation, it was sometimes sowed with salt, and ploughed up, in token of perpetual desolation. In this manner Abimelech, after putting the inhabitants

---

malignant of their deities. Callaway's Oriental Observations, p. 20.   During the war with the Burmese, several magicians were much engaged in cursing the British troops. Roberts's Oriental Illustrations, p. 102.

[1] Saturnalia, lib. iii. c. 9.   [2] Morier's Second Journey, p. 186.

of Shechem to the sword, levelled it with the ground, and sowed it with salt : and thus many centuries after, the emperor Frederick Barbarossa (A.D. 1163) irritated at the long and strenuous defence made by the besieged inhabitants of Milan, on capturing that city, abandoned it to pillage, and sparing nothing but the churches, ordered it to be entirely rased to the ground, which *was ploughed and sown with salt*, in memory of its rebellion.[1] The prophet Micah (iii. 12.) foretold that Jerusalem should be *ploughed as a field*, and his prediction (as we have seen in another part of this work) was most literally fulfilled after Jerusalem was taken by the Roman army under Titus. It was not unusual in remote antiquity to pronounce a curse upon those who should rebuild a destroyed city. Thus Joshua denounced a curse upon the man who should rebuild Jericho (Josh. vi. 26.), the fulfilment of which is recorded in 1 Kings xvi. 34. In like manner Crœsus uttered a curse on him who should rebuild the walls of Sidene which he had destroyed; and the Romans also upon him who should rebuild the city of Carthage.[2]

Various indignities and cruelties were inflicted on those who had the misfortune to be taken captive. On some occasions particular districts were marked out for destruction. (2 Sam. viii. 2.) Of those whose lives were spared, the victors set their feet upon the necks (Josh. x. 24.) or mutilated their persons[3] (Judg. i. 7. 2 Sam. iv. 12. Ezek. xxiii. 25.[4]), or imposed upon them the severest and most laborious occupations. (2 Sam. xii. 31.) It was the barbarous custom of the conquerors of those times, to suspend their unhappy captives by the hand (Lam. v. 12.[5]), and also to make them bow down in order that they might go over them (Isa. li. 23.[6]), and also to strip them naked, and make

---

[1] Modern Universal History, vol. xxvi. p. 11. 8vo. edit.

[2] Burder's Oriental Literature, vol. i. p. 301.

[3] That the cutting off the thumbs and toes of captured enemies was an antient mode of treating them, we learn from Ælian (Var. Hist. lib. ii. c. 9.), who tells us, that the " Athenians, at the instigation of Cleon, son of Cleænatus, made a decree that all the inhabitants of the island of Ægina should have the thumb cut off from the right hand, so that they might ever after be disabled from holding a spear, yet might handle an oar." It was a custom among those Romans who disliked a military life, to cut off their own thumbs, that they might not be capable of serving in the army. Sometimes the parents cut off the thumbs of their children, that they might not be called into the army. According to Suetonius, a Roman knight, who had cut off the thumbs of his two sons to prevent them from being called to a military life, was, by the order of Augustus, publicly sold, both he and his property. *Equitem Romanum, quod duobus filiis adolescentibus, causa detractandi sacramenti, pollices amputasset, ipsum bonaque subjecit hastæ.* Vit. August. c. 24. Calmet remarks, that the Italian language has preserved a term, *poltrone*, which signifies one whose thumb is cut off, to designate a soldier destitute of courage. Burder's Oriental Literature, vol. i. p. 310.

[4] Ezek. xxiii. 25. *They shall take away thy nose and thine* EARS. This cruelty is still practised under some of the despotic governments of the eastern countries. One of the most recent instances is thus related by Messrs. Waddington and Hanbury, during their visit to some parts of Ethiopia :—" Our servants, in their expedition into the village, found only an old woman alive, *with her ears off*. The pasha buys human ears at fifty piastres apiece, which leads to a thousand unnecessary cruelties, and barbarises the system of warfare ; but enables his highness to collect a large stock of ears, which he sends down to his father, as proofs of his successes." Journal of a Visit, &c. p. 118. (London, 1822. 4to.)—Similar instances of this kind of cruelty may be seen in Dodwell's Classical Tour through Greece, vol. i. p. 20. Sir James Malcolm's Hist. of Persia, vol. i. p. 555. ; and Burckhardt's Travels in Nubia, p. 35.

[5] Suspending by the hand is a punishment very common in the East ; especially for slaves and refractory children. Roberts's Oriental Illustrations, p. 485.

[6] A similar barbarous instance is recorded long after the time of Isaiah. The Roman emperor Valerian, being through treachery betrayed to Sapor, king of Persia, was treated by him as the basest and most abject slave : for the Persian monarch commanded the unhappy Roman to *bow himself down*, and offer him his back, on which he set his foot, in order to mount his chariot or his horse, whenever he had occasion. (Lactantius, de Morte Perse-

them travel in that condition, exposed to the inclemency of the weather, and, which was worst of all, to the intolerable heat of the sun. Nor were women, as appears from Isa. iii. 17., exempted from this treatment. To them this was the height of indignity, as well as of cruelty, especially to those described by the prophets, who had indulged themselves in all manner of delicacies of living, and all the superfluities of ornamental dress; and even whose faces had hardly ever been exposed to the sight of men. This is always mentioned as the hardest part of the lot of captives. Nahum (iii. 5, 6.), denouncing the fate of Nineveh, paints it in very strong colours.[1] Women and children were also exposed to treatment at which humanity shudders. (Zech. xiv. 2. Esth. iii. 13. 2 Kings viii. 12. Psal. cxxxvii. 9. Isa. xiii. 16. 18. 2 Kings xv. 16. Hos. xiii. 16. Amos i. 13.) And whole nations were carried into captivity, and transplanted to distant countries : this was the case with the Jews (2 Kings xxiv. 12—16. Jer. xxxix. 9, 10. xl. 7.), as Jeremiah had predicted (Jer. xx. 5.), and instances of similar conduct are not wanting in the modern history of the East.[2] In some cases, indeed, the conquered nations were merely made tributaries, as the Moabites and Syrians were by David (2 Sam. viii. 4. 6.) : but this was considered a great ignominy, and was a source of reproach to the idol deities of the countries which were thus subjected. (2 Kings xix. 12, 13.) Still further to show their absolute superiority, the victorious sovereigns used to change the names of the monarchs whom they subdued. Thus we find the king of Babylon changing the name of Mattaniah into Zedekiah, when he constituted him king of Judah. (2 Kings xxiv. 17.) Archbishop Usher remarks, that the king of Egypt gave to Eliakim the name of Jehoiakim (2 Chron. xxxvi. 4.), thereby to testify that he ascribed his victory over the Babylonians to Jehovah the God of Israel, by whose command, as he pretended (2 Chron. xxxv. 21, 22), he undertook the expedition. Nebuchadnezzar also ordered his eunuch to change the name of Daniel, who afterwards was called Belteshazzar ; and the three companions of Daniel, whose names formerly were Hananiah, Mishael, and Azariah, he called Shadrach, Meshach, and

---

cutorum, c. 5.   Aurelius Victor, Epitome, c. 32.)   Bp. Lowth's Isaiah, vol. ii. p. 315. In p. 307. he has given another similar instance.

[1] Bp. Lowth's Isaiah vol. ii. p. 45.

[2] In the thirteenth century, when the Moguls or Tartars under Zinghis Khan, overran and conquered Asia, " the inhabitants, who had submitted to their discretion, were ordered to evacuate their houses, and to assemble in some plain adjacent to the city, where a division was made of the vanquished into three parts.   The first class consisted of the *soldiers of the garrison, and of the young men capable of bearing arms ;* and their fate was instantly decided : they were either enlisted among the Moguls, or they were massacred on the spot by the troops, who with pointed spears and bended bows had formed a circle round the captive multitude.   The second class, composed of the *young and beautiful women,* of the *artificers* of every rank and profession, and *of the more wealthy* or *honourable citizens,* from whom a private ransom might be expected, was distributed in equal or proportionable lots. The remainder, whose life or death was alike useless to the conquerors, were permitted to return to the city, which in the mean while had been stripped of its valuable furniture ; and a tax was imposed on those wretched inhabitants for the indulgence of breathing their native air." (Gibbon's Decline and Fall of the Roman Empire, vol. iii. pp. 367, 368. 4to., or vol. vi. p. 55. 8vo. edit.)   Here we evidently see the distinction made by Jeremiah (xx. 5.) of the *strength* of the city (that is, the men of war who constitute the strength of a city or state) ; its *labours* or industry (that is, the industrious artizans and mechanics) ; and *all the precious things thereof,* all that is valuable in it, or the honourable and respectable members of the community not included in the two former classes ; and also of those poorer and meaner citizens who, according to Jer. xxxix. 18. and xl. 7., were left in Judæa, but still tributary to the Chaldæans, first under Zedekiah, and next under Gedaliah. Dr. Blayney, on Jer. xx. 5.

Abednego. (Dan. i. 7.) It was likewise a custom among the heathens
to carry in triumph the images of the gods of such nations as they had
vanquished : Isaiah prophesies of Cyrus, that in this manner he would
treat the gods of Babylon, when he says, *Bel boweth, Nebo stoopeth,
their idols were upon the beasts, and upon the cattle, and themselves have
gone into captivity.* (Isa. xlvi. 1, 2.) Daniel foretells that the gods of
the Syrians, with their princes, should be carried captive into Egypt
(Dan. xi. 8.) ; and similar predictions are to be met with in Jeremiah
(xlviii. 7.) and in Amos (i. 15.)

XI. On their return home, the VICTORS were received with every
demonstration of joy. The women preceded them with instruments of
music, singing, and dancing. In this manner Miriam and the women
of Israel joined in chorus with the men, in the song of victory which
Moses composed on occasion of the overthrow of Pharaoh and his
Egyptian host in the Red Sea, and which they accompanied with timbrels and dances. (Exod. xv. 1—21.) Thus, also, Jephthah was hailed
by his daughter, on his return from discomfiting the children of Ammon (Judg. xi. 34.) ; and Saul and David were greeted, in like manner,
on their return from the defeat of the Philistines. *The women came
out of all the cities of Israel, singing and dancing, to meet king Saul, with
tabrets, with joy, and with instruments of music. And the women answered
one another as they played, and said, Saul hath slain his thousands, and
David his ten thousands !* (1 Sam. xviii. 7, 8.) The victorious army of
Jehoshaphat, the pious king of Judah, long afterwards, *returned, every
man of Judah and Jerusalem with the king at their head, to go again to
Jerusalem with joy : for the Lord had made them to rejoice over their
enemies. And they came to Jerusalem with psalteries and harps, and
trumpets unto the house of the Lord.* (2 Chron. xx. 27, 28.) The same
custom still obtains in India and in Turkey.[1] In further commemoration of signal victories, it was a common practice, both among the
antient heathen nations and the Jews, to hang up the arms that were
taken from their enemies in their temples. Thus we find, that the
sword with which David cut off Goliath's head, being dedicated to the
Lord, was kept as a memorial of his victory, and of the Israelites' deliverance, and was deposited in the tabernacle ; for we find that when
David came to Abimelech at Nob, where the tabernacle was, Abimelech
acknowledged it was there, and delivered it to David. (1 Sam. xxi.
8, 9.) For when occasions of state required it, it was no unusual thing
to take such trophies down, and employ them in the public service.
Thus when Joash was crowned king of Judah, Jehoiada, the high
priest (who had religiously educated him), *delivered to the captains of
hundreds spears, and bucklers, and shields, that had been king David's,
which were in the house of God.* (2 Chron. xxiii. 9.)

XII. By the law of Moses (Numb. xxxi. 19—24.) the whole army
that went out to war were to stay without, seven days before they were
admitted into the camp, and such as had had their hands in blood, or
had touched a dead body, though killed by another, were to be purified
on the third and on the seventh day by the water of separation. All
spoil of garments, or other things that they had taken, were to be purified in the same manner, or to be washed in running water, as the

---

[1] Forbes's Oriental Memoirs, vol. ii. p. 295. Roberts's Oriental Illustrations, p. 484,
485. Lady Mary Wortley Montague's Letters, vol. i. p. 197.

method was in other cases. All sorts of metals had, besides sprinkling with the water of separation, a purification by fire, and what would
not bear the fire passed through the water before it could be applied
to use.

In the DISTRIBUTION OF THE SPOIL, the king antiently had the tenth
part of what was taken. Thus Abraham gave a tenth to Melchisedec
king of Salem. (Gen. xiv. 20. Heb. vii. 4.) And if any article of peculiar beauty or value was found among the spoil, it seems to have
been reserved for the commander-in-chief. To this Deborah alludes
in her triumphal ode. (Judg. v. 30.) After the establishment of the
monarchy, the rabbinical writers say (but upon what authority it is
impossible now to ascertain) that the king had all the gold, silver, and
other precious articles, besides one half of the rest of the spoil, which
was divided between him and the people. In the case of the Midianitish
war (Numb. xxxi. 27.), the whole of the spoil was, by divine appointment, divided into two parts: the army that won the victory had one,
and those that staid at home had the other, because it was a common
cause in which they engaged, and the rest were as ready to fight as
those that went out to battle. This division was by a special direction,
but was not the rule in after ages; for, after the general had taken
what he pleased for himself, the rest was divided among the soldiers,
as well those who kept the baggage, or were disabled by wounds or
weariness, as those who were engaged in the fight, but the people had
no share; and this was ordained, as a statute to be observed throughout their generations (1 Sam. xxx. 24.): but in the time of the Maccabees the Jewish army thought fit to recede from the strictness of this
military law, for when they had obtained a victory over Nicanor, under
the conduct of Judas, they divided *among themselves many spoils, and
made the maimed, orphans, widows, yea, and the aged also, equal in spoils
with themselves.* (2 Macc. viii. 28. 30.) In the Midianitish war, after
the distribution of the spoils among the army and the people, there was
another division made for the service of the priesthood, and the Levitical ministry. (Numb. xxxi. 28—30.) The priests, out of the share
that fell to the army, were allotted one out of five hundred of all women
and children, and cattle that were taken; and the Levites, from the
part that fell to the people, received one out of fifty, so that the priests
had just a tenth part of what was allowed to the Levites, as they had
a tenth part of the Levitical tithes, which was paid them for their
constant support: but whether this was the practice in future wars is
uncertain. Sometimes all the spoils were, by divine appointment, ordered to be destroyed; and there is an instance in the siege of Jericho,
when all the silver and the gold, (except the gold and the silver of their
images, which were to be consumed utterly,) and vessels of brass and
iron, were devoted to God, and appropriated to his service. They
were to be brought into the treasury which was in the tabernacle, after
they were purified by making them pass through the fire according to
the law; the Jews conceive that these spoils (called in the Scripture
the accursed thing on the account of their being devoted with a curse
upon him who should take them for his own use) were given to God,
because the city was taken upon the Sabbath-day. But in succeeding
ages, it appears to be an established rule that the spoil was to be divided among the army actually engaged in battle; those who had the

charge of the baggage (as already noticed) being considered intitled to an equal share with the rest. (1 Sam. xxx. 24.)

Besides a share of the spoil and the honours of a triumph, various military rewards were bestowed on those warriors who had pre-eminently distinguished themselves. Thus Saul promised to confer great riches on the man who should conquer Goliath, and further to give his daughter in marriage to him, and to exempt his father's house from all taxes in Israel. (1 Sam. xvii. 25.) How reluctantly the jealous monarch fulfilled his promise is well known. David promised the command in chief of all his forces to him who should first mount the walls of Jerusalem, and expel the Jebusites out of the city. (2 Sam. v. 8. 1 Chron. xi. 6.); which honour was acquired by Joab. In the rebellion of Absalom against David, Joab replied to a man who told him that the prince was suspended in an oak, — *Why didst thou not smite him to the ground, and I would have given thee ten* shekels *of silver and a girdle?* (2 Sam. xviii. 11.) Jephthah was constituted *head and captain* over the Israelites beyond Jordan, for delivering them from the oppression of the Ammonites. Judg. xi. 11. compared with xii. 7.

From 2 Sam. xxiii. 8—39. it appears that the heroes or "mighty men," during the reign of David, were thirty-seven in number, including Joab, who was commander-in-chief of all his forces. These warriors were divided into three classes, the first and second of which consisted, each, of three men, Jashobeam, Eleazar, and Shammah; Abishai, Benaiah, and Asahel; and the third class was composed of the remaining thirty, of whom Asahel appears to have been the head. Such is the list according to 2 Sam. xxiii.; but in 1 Chron. xi. 10—47. the list is more numerous, and differs considerably from the preceding. The most probable solution of these variations is, that the first list contains the worthies who lived in the former part of David's reign, and that it underwent various changes in the course of his government of the kingdom of Israel. At the head of all these "mighty men" was Jashobeam the son of Hachmoni (1 Chron. xi. 11.), who from his office in 2 Sam. xxiii. 8. (Hebr. and marginal rendering) is termed *Joseb-Bassebet, the Tachmonite, head of the three;* and whose military appellation was *Adino-He-Ezni* (*the lifting up — or striking with — a spear*) because he lifted up his spear against, or encountered, three hundred soldiers at once. However extraordinary it may seem, we may here clearly perceive a distinct order of knighthood, similar to our modern orders, and presenting the same honorary degrees, and of which Jashobeam, according to modern parlance, was the grand-master. An institution of this kind was in every respect adapted to the reign, the character, and the policy of David.[1]

After the return of the Jewish armies to their several homes, their military dress was laid aside. The militia, which had been raised for the occasion, were disbanded; their warlike instruments, with the exception of such as were private property, were delivered up as the property of the state, until some future war should call them forth; and the soldiers themselves returned (like Cincinnatus) to the plough, and the other avocations of private life. To this suspension of their arms, the prophet Ezekiel alludes (xxvii. 10, 11.) when he says, that

---

[1] Coquerel, Biographie Sacrée, tom. ii. p. 167.

they of *Persia, and of Lud, and of Phut, and of Arvad,* were in the Tyrian army *as men of war,* and *hanged their shields upon the walls of
Tyre.* To the same custom also the bridegroom refers in the sacred
idyls of Solomon (Song iv. 4.), when he compares the neck of his bride
to *the tower of David builded for an armoury, whereon there hang a
thousand bucklers, all shields of mighty men.*

XIII. It does not certainly appear from the Sacred Writings, that
the Hebrews were accustomed to erect TROPHIES or monuments for
commemorating their victories. In 1 Sam. xv. 12. Saul is said to *have
set him up a place on Mount Carmel;* which some expositors understand to be a column, or other monument, while others imagine it to
have been simply a hand, pointing out the place where he had obtained
his decisive victory over the Amalekites. Far more devout was the
conduct of Moses, who, after discomfiting Amalek, erected an altar
to the Lord, with this inscription, *Jehovah-nissi,* that is, *The* LORD *is
my banner.* (Exod. xvii. 15.) Under the influence of similar devout
affections, David consecrated the sword and other arms of Goliath
in the tabernacle, and subsequently deposited in the sacred treasury
the rich spoils won in battle, as Samuel and Saul had done before
him (1 Chron. xxvi. 26—28.), and as several of his pious successors
on the throne of Judah also did. Thus they gratefully acknowledged
that they were indebted to the Lord of Hosts alone for all their
strength and victories.

SECTION II.

ALLUSIONS IN THE NEW TESTAMENT TO THE MILITARY DISCIPLINE AND TRIUMPHS OF THE ROMANS.

I. *Division of the Roman Army, and Roman Military Officers mentioned in
the New Testament.*—II. *Allusions to the Armour of the Romans.*—III. *To
their Military Discipline. — Strict Subordination. — Rewards to Soldiers
who had distinguished themselves.*—IV. *Allusions to the Roman Triumphs.*

I. AT the time the evangelists and apostles wrote, the Romans had
extended their empire almost to the utmost boundaries of the then
known world, principally by their unparalleled military discipline and
heroic valour. Judæa was at this time subject to their sway, and their
troops were stationed in different parts of that country.

The Roman army was composed of Legions (Λεγεωνες), each of
which was divided into ten *cohorts,* each cohort into three *maniples,*
and each maniple (Σπειρα) into two centuries. The number of men in
a legion was different at different times. But besides the cohorts which
were formed into legions, there were certain others separate and distinct
from any legion; such were the Cohortes Urbanæ, and Prætoriæ, &c.
Such appears to have been the *Italian Band* (Σπειρα Ιταλικη) mentioned in Acts x. 1., which was in attendance on the Roman governor,
who at that time was residing at Cæsarea. It was probably called the
Italian cohort, because most of the soldiers belonging to it were Italians,
and also to distinguish it from the other troops which were drawn

from Syria and the adjacent regions.   The Italian legion was not in existence at this time.[1]   Of the same description also was the *Augustan Band* or *Cohort* (Acts xxvi. 1.), (Σπειρα Σεϐαστη), which, most probably, derived its name from 'Sebaste, the capital of Samaria.   The commanding officer of the Prætorian Cohorts at Rome, (a body of troops instituted by Augustus to guard his person, and to whom the care of the city was subsequently committed,) was termed *Præfectus Prætorio.*   This last officer was the *Captain of the Guard* (Στρατοπεδαρχης), to whose custody Paul was committed, it being a part of his office to take the charge of accused persons. (Acts xxviii. 16.)   The commanding officer of an ordinary cohort was called *Tribunus Cohortis,* if it was composed of Roman citizens; or *Præfectus Cohortis,* if composed of auxiliary troops.   The officer, intended by both these words, is in the New Testament termed Χιλιαρχος, or Captain of a Thousand, most probably because each tribune had under him ten centuries of troops. This was the officer who commanded the legion of soldiers that garrisoned the tower of Antonia, which overlooked the temple at Jerusalem, in the porticoes of which a company kept guard (κουστωδιαν) to prevent any tumult at the great festivals.[2]   Claudius Lysias was the tribune or Roman captain of this fort, who rescued Paul from the tumultuous attack of the murderous Jews. (Acts xxi. 31. xxii. 34. xxiii. 26.)   Under the command of the tribune was the centurion (Κεντυριων or Έκατονταρχος), who, as his name implies, had one hundred men under him.[3]

The Roman infantry were divided into three principal classes, the *Hastati,* the *Principes,* and the *Triarii,* each of which was composed of thirty *manipuli* or companies, and each manipulus contained two *centuries* or hundreds of men: over every company were placed two centurions, who, however, were very far from being *equal* in rank and honour though possessing the same office.   The Triarii and Principes were esteemed the most honourable, and had their centurions elected *first,* and these took presidency of the centurions of the Hastati, who were elected *last.*   The humble centurion, who in Matt. viii. 8, 9. besought the aid of the compassionate Redeemer, appears to have been of this last order.   He was a *man under authority,* that is, of the Principes or Triarii, and had none *under* him but the hundred men, who appear to have been in a state of the strictest military subordination, as well as of loving subjection to him.   *I am,* said the centurion, *a man under authority, having soldiers under me, and I say to this* man, *Go, and he goeth, and to another, Come, and he cometh ; and to my* slave (Τῳ δουλῳ μου), *Do this, and he doeth it.*   The application of his argument, addressed to Christ, seems to be this:—If I, who am a person subject to the controul of others, yet have some so completely subject to myself, that I can say to one, *Come, and he cometh,* &c., how much more then canst *thou* accomplish whatsoever thou willest, being under no controul, and having all things under thy command?[4]

The Δεξιολαϐοι or *Spearmen,* mentioned in Acts xxiii. 23., were sol-

---

1 Biscoe on the Acts, vol. i. pp. 328—332.   Doddridge on Acts x. 1. and Kuinöel on Acts x. 1. and xxvii. 1.

2 Josephus, de Bell. Jud. lib. v. c. 5. § 8.   Ant. Jud. lib. xx. c. 4. § 3.

3 Biscoe on the Acts, vol. i. pp. 328, 329. Adam's Roman Antiquities, pp. 336. 339. 352.

4 Dr. A. Clarke, on Matt. viii. 9.

diers, carrying spears or lances in their right hand, whose duty it was, not only to attend as guards upon their sovereign or commander, but also to guard prisoners, who were bound by a chain to their right hand.[1] The Σπεκουλατορες (in Latin, *Spiculatores* or *Speculatores*, from the spiculum, a javelin or spear which they carried), were a kind of soldiers who formed the body-guard of princes. Among other duties of these guards, was that of putting condemned persons to death.[2] (Mark, vi. 27.)

II. The allusions in the New Testament to the military discipline, armour, battles, sieges, and military honours of the Greeks, and especially of the Romans, are very numerous; and the sacred writers have derived from them metaphors and expressions of singular propriety, elegance, and energy, for animating Christians to fortitude against temptations, and to constancy in the profession of their holy faith under all persecutions, and also for stimulating them to persevere unto the end, that they may receive those final honours and that immortal crown which await victorious piety.

In the following very striking and beautiful passage of St. Paul's Epistle to the Ephesians (vi. 11—17.), the various parts of the panoply-armour of the heavy troops among the Greeks and Romans (those who had to sustain the rudest assaults) "are distinctly enumerated, and beautifully applied to those moral and spiritual weapons with which the believer ought to be fortified. *Put on the whole armour of God, that ye may be able to stand against the wiles of the devil. For we wrestle not against flesh and blood, but against principalities, against powers, against the rulers of the darkness of this world, against spiritual wickedness in high places. Wherefore, take unto you the whole armour of God, that ye may be able to withstand in the evil day, and having done[3] all to stand. Stand, therefore, having your loins girt about with truth, and having on the breast-plate of righteousness: and your feet shod with the preparation of the gospel of peace; above all[4], taking the shield[5] of*

---

[1] Valpy's Gr. Test. vol. iii. p. 255.

[2] Robinson's Gr. Lex. to the New Test. in voce.

[3] Ephes. vi. 13. 'Απανία καίεργασαμενοι. This verb frequently signifies to *despatch* a foe, totally to vanquish and subdue an adversary. So it should be translated in this place. 'Ον αυίοχειρια καίειργασατο: Whom he *despatched* with his own hand. Dion. Halicarn. tom. i. p. 99. Oxon. 1704. Πανία πολεμια καίεργασαμενοι: Having quelled all hostilities. Idem, p. 885. Μεθ' ής ηδη πολλους πολεμιους καίειργασθε: By which you have vanquished many enemies. Polyæni Stratag. p. 421. Lugd. 1589. Πείρας αβαίους σιδηρω καίειργασαμην. Idem, p. 599. Casaubon. Ταυρον αγριον—ταις χερσι μοναις καίειργασμενω: He despatched a wild bull only with his hands. Appian, vol. i. p. 201. Amst. 1670. See also pp. 5. 291. 410. 531. Tollii. The word here used by the Apostle has also this signification in Dion Cassius, Josephus, and Philo.

[4] Επι πασιν, after all, or besides all: it never signifies above all. Αυίος δε χαλεπως επι πασι διαβαινων: After all, he himself passed with difficulty. Plutarch, Cæsar, p. 1311. edit. Gr. Stephan. Αγονία πρωίον την φαλαγγα, μεία ταυία τους ιππεις, επι πασι δε το σκενοφορον: First, he led up the phalanx, next the cavalry, after all the baggage. Polybius, p. 664. Casaubon. Επι πασι δε Ασσις εννεα και τεσσαρακονία και μηνας δυο: After all, Assis reigned forty-nine years and two months. Josephus contra Apion. p. 445. Havercamp.

[5] The shield here intended (Θυρεος) is the *scutum*, or large oblong shield of the Romans, which was made of wood covered with hides, and derived its name from its resemblance to a door (Θυρα). As faith is that Christian grace, by which all the others are preserved and rendered active, it is here properly represented under the figure of a shield; which covered and protected the whole body; and enables the believer to *quench* — to intercept, blunt, and extinguish, as on a shield — *the fiery darts of the wicked one*, that is, all those evil thoughts, and strong injections, as they are termed, which inflame the passions of the unrenewed, and excite the soul to acts of transgression.

faith wherewith you shall be able to quench all the fiery darts[1] *of the wicked, and take the helmet*[2] *of salvation, and the sword of the Spirit, which is the word of God.*"[3]

Having thus equipped the spiritual soldier with the divine panoply, the Apostle proceeds to show him how he is to use it: he therefore subjoins — *Praying always with all prayer and supplication in the Spirit, and watching thereunto with all perseverance.* The Greeks and other antient nations, we have already observed, offered up prayers before they went into the battle. Alluding to this, Saint Paul adds the exhortation to believers, *praying always*, at all seasons and on all occasions, *with all prayer* (more correctly, *supplication* for what is good) and *deprecation* of evil; *and watching thereunto* — being always on their guard lest their spiritual enemies should surprise them — *with all perseverance*, being always intent on their object, and never losing sight of their danger or of their interest.[4]

" In the Epistle to the Romans, the Apostle, exhorting men to renounce those sins to which they had been long accustomed, and to enter upon a new and holy life, uses a beautiful similitude, borrowed from the custom of soldiers throwing off their ordinary habit in order to put on a suit of armour. *The night is far spent, the day is at hand : let us therefore* CAST OFF *the works of darkness, and let us* PUT ON *the* ARMOUR *of light.*[5] (Rom. xiii. 12.) In another passage he represents, by a striking simile, in what manner the apostles were fortified against the opposition with which they were called to conflict in this world. *By the word of truth, by the power of God, by the* ARMOUR *of righteousness* ON THE RIGHT HAND AND ON THE LEFT." (2 Cor. vi. 7.)[6]

---

[1] Βελη σεπυρωμενα. These dreadful weapons were frequently employed by the antients. Πυρφορα τοξευμαῖα. Appian. p. 329. Πυρφοροις οἴστοις βαλλεσθαι. Thucydides, tom. ii. lib. xi. p. 202. Glasg.

Τοιους, αγριε δαιμον, εχεις σπυροενῖας οἴστους. Oppian. Κυνηγ. lib. ii. ver. 425.

According to Ammianus Marcellinus (lib. xxiii. c. 4.) these fiery darts consisted of a hollow reed, to the lower part of which, under the point or barb, was fastened a round receptacle, made of iron, for combustible materials, so that such an arrow had the form of a distaff. This was filled with burning naphtha; and when the arrow was shot from a slack bow (for if discharged from a tight bow the fire went out), it struck the enemies' ranks and remained infixed, the flame consuming whatever it met with; water poured on it increased its violence; there were no other means to extinguish it but by throwing earth upon it. Similar darts or arrows, which were twined round with tar and pitch, and set fire to, are described by Livy (lib. xxi. c. 8.), as having been made use of by the inhabitants of the city of Saguntum, when besieged by the Romans.

[2] On the tops of the antient helmets, as well as on those now in use, is a crest or ridge, furnished with ornaments; some of the antient helmets had emblematic figures, and it is probable that Saint Paul, who in 1 Thess. v. 8. terms the helmet *the hope of salvation*, refers to such helmets as had on them the emblematic representation of hope. His meaning therefore is, that as the helmet defended the head from deadly blows, so the *hope of salvation*, (of conquering every adversary, and of surmounting every difficulty, through Christ strengthening the Christian,) built on the promises of God, will ward off, or preserve him from the fatal effects of all temptations, from worldly terrors and evils, so that they shall not disorder the imagination or pervert the judgment, or cause men to desert the path of duty, to their final destruction.

[3] Dr. Harwood's Introd. to the New Test. vol. ii. pp. 49, 50.

[4] Drs. Chandler, Macknight, and A. Clarke, on Eph. vi. 11—17. In the fifth of Bishop Horne's Discourses (Works, vol. v. pp. 60—72.) the reader will find an admirable and animated exposition of the Christian armour.

[5] Αποθωμεθα τα εργα τοῦ σκολους και ενδυσωμεθα τα ὅπλα του φωλος. Fulgentiaque induit arma. Virgil, Æneid. ii. ver. 747. Πρωῖον τοινυν αποδυσωμεν, αναγκη γαρ τους μελλουῖας ὁπλιζεσθαι, γυμνουσθαι σρολερον. Lucian. tom. ii. p. 256. edit. Grævii.

[6] Harwood's Introd. vol. ii. p. 52.

III. It is well known that the strictest subordination and obedience were required of every Roman soldier.   An allusion to this occurs in the speech of the centurion to Jesus Christ (Matt. viii. 8, 9.) which has already been noticed in page 222., and which is greatly illustrated by two striking passages in Arrian's Discourses of Epictetus: — speaking of the Saturnalia, he says, — " We agreed to play Agamemnon and Achilles.   He who is appointed for Agamemnon says to me — ' Go *to Achilles, and force away Briseis.*' — I GO. — ' COME.' — *I come.*"[1]   Again, discoursing on all things being under the divine inspection, he says, — " When God *commands* the plants to *blossom*, they *bear blossoms*.   When he *commands* them to *bear seed*, they *bear seed*.   When he *commands* them to *bring forth fruit*, they *put forth their fruit*.   When he *commands* them to *ripen*, they *grow ripe*.   When he *commands* them to *fade* and *shed their leaves*, and to remain inactive, and involved (or contracted) within themselves, they thus remain and are inactive."[2]

Nor is the military subordination adverted to by the centurion, without its (almost *verbal*) parallel in modern times in the East: — Kirtee-Ranah, a captive Ghoorkha chief, who was marching to the British head-quarters, — on being interrogated concerning the motives that induced him to quit his native land and enter into the service of the Rajah of Nepāl, — replied in the following very impressive manner : — " *My master, the rajah, sent me : He says to his people,* — *to one,* ' Go *you to Gurwhal;*' *to another,* ' Go *you to Cashmire, or to any distant part.*' — ' *My Lord, thy slave* OBEYS; *it is* DONE.' — None ever inquires into the reason of an order of the rajah."[3]

In his Epistle to Timothy, who appears to have been greatly dejected and dispirited by the opposition he met with, St. Paul animates him to fortitude, and among other directions encourages him to ENDURE HARDSHIP as a good soldier of Jesus Christ (2 Tim. ii. 3.) — and what hardship a Roman soldier supported, the following passage in Josephus will abundantly evince.   It is the most striking commentary upon this text that ever was written.   " When they march out of their encampment, they advance in silence and in great decorum, each man keeping his proper rank just as in battle.   Their infantry are armed with breast-plates and helmets, and they carry a sword on each side.   The sword they wear on their left side is by far the longest, for that on the right is not above a span's length.   That select body of infantry, which forms part of the general's lifeguards, is armed with lances and bucklers, but the rest of the phalanx have a spear and a long shield, besides which they bear a saw and a basket, a spade and a hatchet; they also carry with them a cord, a sickle, a chain, and provisions for three days ! so that a Roman foot-soldier is but very little different from a BEAST OF BURDEN."[4]

---

[1] Arrian's Epictetus, book i. c. 25. § 1.   (Mrs. Carter's translation, vol. i. p. 113.)

[2] Arrian's Epictetus, book i. c. 14.   Raphelii Annotationes in Sacram Scripturam, ex Herodoto, &c. vol. i. pp. 242, 243.

[3] Frazer's Notes on the Hills at the Foot of the Himala Mountains, p. 226.   London, 1820. 4to.

[4] Josephus, De Bell. Jud. lib. iii. c. 5. §.5.   Harwood's Introduction, vol. ii. p. 52. The following particulars, collected from Roman authors, will confirm and illustrate the statements of Josephus :—" The load which a Roman soldier carried is almost incredible (Virg. Georg. iii. 346. Horat. Sat. ii. 10.); victuals (*cibaria*) for *fifteen* days (Cic. Tusc. ii. 15, 16.), sometimes more (Liv. Epit. 57.), usually corn, as being lighter, sometimes drest

According to a military custom, established in an early period of the commonwealth, every Roman soldier chose his favourite comrade; and by that tie of friendship all were mutually bound to share every danger with their fellows.[1] Saint Paul, alluding to this practice, terms Epaphroditus his *companion in labour and fellow-soldier.* (Phil. ii. 25.) Further, "it is well known that the Roman soldiers were not allowed to marry; by this prohibition the Roman providence, as much as possible, studying to keep their military disembarrassed from the cares and distractions of secular life. To this law the Apostle refers; *no one that warreth,* ENTANGLETH HIMSELF WITH THE AFFAIRS OF THIS LIFE; that he *may please him who hath chosen him to be a soldier.* (2 Tim. ii. 4.)[2]

"The names of those who died or were cashiered for misconduct were expunged from the muster-roll. To this custom, probably, the following text alludes; in this view the similitude is very striking, *I will not* BLOT OUT *his* NAME *out of the* BOOK *of life.* (Rev. iii. 5.)[3]

"The triumphant advancement of the Christian religion through the world, St. Paul compares to the irresistible *progress* of a victorious *army,* before which every *fortified place,* and all *opposition,* how *formidable* soever, yielded and fell. (2 Cor. x. 4.) *For the weapons of our warfare are not carnal, but mighty through God*[4] *to the pulling down of strong holds; casting down imaginations, and every thing that exalteth itself against the knowledge of God, and bringing into captivity every thought to the obedience of Christ.*[5] *Having spoiled principalities and powers, he made a show of them openly, triumphing over them.*

"By a very striking metaphor, taken from the *pay* of a soldier, he represents the *wages* with which SIN rewards those who *fight* under her *banners,* to be certain and inevitable *death.* The WAGES[6] of SIN is DEATH.

---

food (*coctus cibus,* Liv. iii. 27.), utensils (*utensilia,* ib. 42.) a saw, a basket, a mattock, an axe, a hook, and leather thong, a chain, a pot, &c. (Liv. xxviii. 45. Horat. Epod. ix. 13.), stakes usually three or four, sometimes twelve (Liv. iii. 27.); the whole amounting to *sixty* pounds weight, besides arms; for a Roman soldier considered these not as a burden but as a part of himself (arma membra milites ducebant. Cic. Tusc. ii. 16.)."—Adam's Roman Antiquities, p. 377.

[1] Livy, lib. ix. c. 39. Tacitus, Hist. lib. i. c. 18.—Murphy's note, in his translation of Tacitus, vol. v. p. 356. 8vo. edit.

[2] Τοις δε στρα]ευομενοις, επειδη γυναικας ουκ εδυναν]ο εκ γε των νομων εχειν. Dion. Cassius, lib. lx. p. 961. Reimar. Tacitus, speaking of some Roman veterans, says, Neque conjugiis suscipiendis neque alendis liberis sueti. Taciti Annales, tom. ii. lib. xiv. cap. 27. p. 210. Dublin.

[3] It is, however, possible that this allusion may be drawn from *civil* life, in which case the meaning of the above-cited passage will be this: — As in states and cities, those who obtained freedom and fellowship were enrolled in the public registers, which enrolment was their title to the privileges of citizens; so the King of Heaven, of the New Jerusalem, engages to preserve in his register and enrolment, in the book of life, the names of those, who, like the faithful members of the church of Sardis, in a corrupted and supine society, shall preserve allegiance, and a faithful discharge of their Christian duties. He will own them as his fellow-citizens, before men and angels. Compare Matt. xx. 32. Luke xii. 8. See also Psal. lxix. 28. Ezek. xiii. 9. Exod. xxxiii. 33. Dan. xii. 1. Mal. iii. 16. Luke x. 20. Dr. Woodhouse on the Apocalypse, p. 84.

[4] Δυνα]α τω Θεω, exceeding powerful. Moses is called αστειος τω θεω, exceeding beautiful. Acts viii. 20.

[5] See the conquest of the Gospel, and its triumph over idolatry in a very striking manner represented by Eusebius, lib. x. p. 468. Cantab.

[6] Rom. vi. 23. Οψωνια, the pay of a soldier. Οψωνιον τη στραλεια, — καλενεγκανλες αργυριον: Bringing money to pay the army. Dion. Halicarn. tom. i. p. 568. Oxon. Λαβων οψωνια τε και τ' αλλα οσων εδει τη στραλια. p. 587.

" Our Lord in that wonderful prophecy of the destruction of Jeru-salem accurately represents the Roman manner of besieging and taking towns, — which was by investing the place, digging a deep trench round it, and encompassing it with a strong wall, to prevent escape, and consume the inhabitants by famine. *The days shall come upon thee, that thine enemies shall cast a* TRENCH *about thee, and* COM-PASS *thee* ROUND, *and keep thee in on every side : and shall lay thee even with the ground, and thy children within thee, and they shall not leave in thee one stone upon another ; because thou knewest not the time of thy visitation.* (Luke xix. 43, 44.)

" In expatiating upon the difficulties and distresses with which the first preachers of the Gospel conflicted, the apostle Paul in a strong figure compares their situation to that of an *army pent up* in a *narrow* place — *annoyed* on *every* side — but not totally *precluded* from an *escape* [1] — their condition to the last degree *perplexed* and *wretched*, yet not altogether *desperate* and *forlorn*. (2 Cor. iv. 8.) We are *troubled* on *every side*, yet not *distressed :* we are *perplexed*, but not in *despair.*"

Once more, " as among the other military honours and recom-penses, rich and splendid *crowns* [2], frequently of *gold*, were publicly bestowed upon the illustrious conqueror, and upon every man who, acting worthy of the Roman name, had distinguished himself by his valour and his virtue — in allusion to *this* custom how beautiful and striking are those many passages of Sacred Scripture, which represent Jesus Christ, before *angels* and the whole assembled *world*, acknow-ledging and applauding distinguished piety, and publicly conferring *crowns* of immortal *glory* upon *persevering* and *victorious* holiness. *Be thou faithful unto death : I will give thee a* CROWN *of life.* (Rev. ii. 10.) *Blessed is the man that endureth temptation ; for when he is tried, he shall receive the* CROWN *of life* (James i. 12.), *which the Lord hath promised to them that love him. When the chief shepherd shall appear, ye shall receive a* CROWN *of glory that fadeth not away.* (1 Pet. v. 4.) *I have fought a good fight, I have finished my course, I have kept the faith : Henceforth there is laid up for me a* CROWN *of righteousness, which the Lord the righteous judge shall give me at that day ; and not to* ME *only, but unto* ALL *them also that love his appearing.*" (2 Tim. iv. 8.)

IV. But the highest military honour that could be conferred in the Roman state was a *triumph*, or solemn procession, with which a victo-rious general and his army advanced through the city to the capitol; and which was the most grand and magnificent spectacle ever beheld in antient times.

" After a decisive battle gained, and the complete conquest of a kingdom, the most illustrious captives in war, kings, princes, and nobles, with their wives and children, to the perpetual infamy of this

---

[1] Harwood's Introd. vol. ii. pp. 53—58.

[2] Στεφανους επι ταις νικαις—χρυσους ελαβε: He received several *crowns of gold* on account of his victories. Dion. Cassius, lib. xlii. p. 334. edit. Reimar. Vid. etiam notas Fabricii ad loc. Τοις δε δη ναυκραιησασι και στεφανον ελαιας εδωκε: To those who had conquered in the naval engagement he gave *crowns of olive.* Lib. xlix. p. 597. See also pp. 537. 580. So also Josephus says that Titus gave *crowns of gold* to those who had dis-tinguished themselves in the siege of Jerusalem ; στεφανους επειθει χρυσους. Bell. Jud. lib. vii. p. 404. See also p. 412. Havercamp.

people, were, with the last dishonour and ignominy, led in fetters before the general's chariot, through the public streets of Rome: scaffolds being every where erected, the streets and public places crowded, and this barbarous and uncivilised nation all the while in the highest excess of joy, and in the full fruition of a spectacle that was a reproach to humanity. Nor was only the [1] sovereign of large and opulent kingdoms, the magnanimous hero [2] who had fought valiantly for his country and her liberties, the weak and tender sex, born to a happier fate, and young children [3] insensible of their wretched condition, led in triumph; but vast numbers of waggons, full of rich furniture, statues, pictures, plate, vases, vests [4], of which they had stripped palaces and the houses of the great; and carts loaded with the arms they had taken from the enemy, and with the coin [5] of the empires they had conquered, pillaged, and enslaved, preceded the triumphal car. On this most splendid occasion, imperial Rome was a scene of universal festivity: the temples were all thrown open, were adorned with garlands, and filled with clouds of incense and the richest perfumes [6]: the spectators were clothed in white garments [7]: hetacombs of victims were slain [8], and the most sumptuous entertainments [9] were given. The illustrious captives, after having been dragged through the city in this procession, and thus publicly exposed, were generally imprisoned, frequently strangled and despatched [10] in dungeons, or

---

[1] Behind the children and their train walked Perseus himself [the captive king of Macedon], and wearing sandals of the fashion of his country. He had the appearance of a man overwhelmed with terror, and whose reason almost staggered under the load of his misfortunes. He was followed by a great number of friends and favourites, whose countenances were oppressed with sorrow; and who, by fixing their weeping eyes continually upon their prince, testified to the spectators that it was his lot which they lamented, and that they were regardless of their own. Plutarchi Vitæ, in Æmil. tom. ii. pp. 186, 187. edit. Briani.

[2] Thus, at the conclusion of the second Punic war, the Numidian and Carthaginian captive generals were led in triumph. Appian. tom. i. p. 58. edit. Tollii. Amst. 1670. Several kings, princes, and generals were also led in Pompey's triumph. Appian. tom. i. p. 417.

[3] Plutarch, in his account of the triumph of Æmilius at the conquest of Macedon, represents this tragical circumstance in a very affecting manner. The king's *children* were also led captive, and along with them a train of nurses, and tutors, and governors; all bathed in tears, stretching out their hands to the spectators, and teaching the children to entreat and supplicate their mercy. There were two boys and a girl, whose tender age rendered them insensible to the greatness of their calamity, and this their insensibility was the most affecting circumstance in their unhappy condition. Plutarch. Æmil. tom. ii. p. 186. See also Appian. p. 417. edit. Amst. 1670.

[4] Κρατηρας αργυρους, και κεραῖα, και φιαλας και κυλικας. Plutarch, ibid. p. 497. Αιχμαλωτοις ανδριασι και γραφαις και κολοσσοις. κ. λ. p. 496. See also Appian. tom i. p. 58. and p. 417. Tollii.

[5] Ανδρες επεπορευονῖο τρισχιλιοι, νομισμα φερονῖες αργυρουν κ. λ. Ειτα μετα τουῖους οἱ το νομισμα φεροντες. Plutarch. tom. ii. p. 184. Appian, p. 417.

[6] Πας δε ναος ανεωκῖο, και στεφανων και θυμιαμαῖων ην ϖληρης. Plutarch. tom. i. p. 496. Gr. 8vo.

[7] Niveos ad fræna Quirites. Juvenal. Sat x. ver. 45. Καθαραις εσθησι κεκοσμημενοι. Plutarch. p. 496. Steph.

[8] Μετα τουτους ηγονῖο χρυσοκερω τροφιαι βους, ἑκατον εικοσι, μιῖραις ησκημενοι και στεμμασι. After these were led one hundred and twenty fat oxen, which had their horns gilded, and which were adorned with ribands and garlands. Plutarch. ii. p. 885.

[9] Αφικομενος δε ες το Καπιῖωλιον ὁ Σκιπιων, την μεν ϖομπην κατεπαυσεν, εἱστια δεῖ τους φιλους, ὡσπερ εθος εστιν, ες το ἱερον. Appian. tom. i. p. 59. edit. Amst. 1670.

[10] Παρελθων δ᾽ ες Καπιῖωλιον, ουδενα των αιχμαλωτων, ὡς ἑτεροι των θριαμβοις παραγαγοντων [ανειλετο]. Appian. p. 418. For example, Aristobulus king of the Jews, after having been exposed, and dragged through the city in Pompey's triumph, was immediately, after the procession was concluded, put to death : Tigranes, some time afterwards, Αριστοβουλος ευθυς ανηρεθη, και Τιγρανης ὑστερον. Appian. de Bellis Mithrid. p. 419. Amst. 1670. See also p. 403.

sold for slaves.[1] — To *several* of these well known circumstances attending a *Roman triumph*, the sacred writers evidently allude in the following passages. In the *first* of which Jesus Christ is represented as a great *conqueror*, who, after having totally *vanquished* and *subjugated* all the *empires* and kingdoms of false religion, and *overturned* the mighty *establishment* of *Judaism* and *Paganism,* supported by the *great* and *powerful,* celebrates a most magnificent TRIUMPH over them, *leads* them in *procession,* openly *exposing* them to the *view* of the WHOLE WORLD, as the captives of his omnipotence, and the trophies of his Gospel! *Having spoiled principalities and powers, he made a show of them openly, triumphing over them!* [2] — The *second* passage, whose beautiful and striking imagery is taken from a *Roman triumph,* occurs in 2 Cor. ii. 14—16. *Now thanks be unto God, who always causeth us to triumph in Christ, and maketh manifest the savour of his knowledge by us in every place. For we are unto God a sweet savour of Christ, in them that are saved, and in them that perish: to the one we are a savour of death unto death; and to the other, of life unto life.* In this passage God Almighty, in very striking sentiments and language, is represented as *leading the apostles in triumph* [3] through the world, showing them every where as the monuments of his grace and mercy, and by their means *diffusing* in every place the *odour* of the knowledge of God — in reference to a triumph, when all the temples were filled with fragrance, and the whole air breathed perfume; — and the apostle, continuing the allusion, adds, that this *odour* would prove the means of the *salvation* of some, and *destruction* of others — as in a triumph, after the pomp and procession was *concluded,* some of the captives were *put to death,* others *saved alive.*" [4]

---

[1] Longe plurimos captivos ex Etruscis ante currum duxit, quibus sub hasta venumdatis, Livy, lib. vi. p. 409. edit. Elz. 1634.

[2] Coloss. ii. 15. Θριαμβευσας αυτους, Leading them in triumph.

[3] Θριαμβευοντι ἡμας, Causeth us to triumph; rather, Leadeth us about in triumph. Εθριαμβευθη και απηρεθη, He was led in triumph and then put to death. Appian. p. 403. Amst. 1670. " The Greek word, Θριαμβευοντι, which we render *causeth us to triumph,* properly signifies to *triumph over,* or to *lead in triumph,* as our translators themselves have rightly rendered it in another place, Coloss. ii. 15. And so the Apostle's true meaning is plainly this: Now thanks be to God, who always triumpheth over us in Christ: *leading us about in triumph,* as it were in solemn procession. This yields a most congruous and beautiful sense of his words. And in order to display the force of his fine sentiment, in its full compass and extent, let it be observed, that when St. Paul represents himself and others, as being led about in triumph, like so many captives by the prevailing power and efficacy of Gospel grace and truth, his words naturally imply and suggest three things worthy of particular notice and attention; namely, a contest, a victory, and an open show of his victory." (Brekell's Discourses, pp. 141, 142.) "While God was leading about such men in triumph, he made them very serviceable and successful in promoting Christian knowledge in every place wherever they came." (Ibid. p. 151.)

[4] Harwood's Introduction to the New Testament, vol. ii. pp. 29—34. collated with Brunings's disquisition De Triumpho Romanorum in the Appendix to his Compendium Antiquitatum Græcarum (pp. 415—434.), which seems to have guided Dr. Harwood in his manner of illustrating a Roman triumph. He has, however, greatly improved upon Brunings's Dissertation.

PART III.

SACRED ANTIQUITIES

OF THE JEWS, AND OF OTHER NATIONS INCIDENTALLY
MENTIONED IN THE SCRIPTURES.

CHAPTER I.

OF SACRED PLACES.

THE whole world being the workmanship of God, there is no place, in which men may not testify their reverence for His supreme Majesty. From the very beginning of time some place was always appropriated to the solemn duties of religious worship. Adam, even during his continuance in Paradise, had some place where to present himself before the Lord; and, after his expulsion thence, his sons in like manner had whither to bring their oblations and sacrifices. This, probably, was the reason why Cain did not immediately fall upon his brother, when his offering was refused, because perhaps the solemnity and religion of the place, and the sensible appearance of the divine Majesty there, struck him with a reverential awe that might cause him to defer his villainous design till he came into the field where he slew him.

The patriarchs, both before and after the flood, used altars and mountains and groves for the same purpose: thus we read of Noah's building an altar to the Lord, and offering burnt offerings upon it. (Gen. viii. 20.) Abraham, when he was called to the worship of the true God, erected altars wherever he pitched his tent (Gen. xii. 8. and xiii. 4.): he planted a grove in Beersheba, and called there on the name of the Lord (Gen. xxi. 33.): and it was upon a mountain that God ordered him to offer up his son Isaac. (Gen. xxii. 2.) Jacob in particular called a place by the name of God's House, where he vowed to pay the tithes of all that God should give him. (Gen. xxviii. 22.)

There were several public places appropriated to the religious worship of the Jews, viz. 1. The *Tabernacle*, which in time gave place to, 2. The *Temple*, both of which are oftentimes in Scripture called the Sanctuary; between which there was no other difference as to the principal design (though there was in beauty and workmanship) than that the tabernacle was a moveable temple, as the temple was an immoveable tabernacle; on which account the tabernacle is sometimes called the temple (1 Sam. i. 9. and iii. 3.), as the temple is sometimes called the tabernacle. (Jer. x. 20. Lam. ii. 6.) 3. There were also places of worship called in Scripture *High Places*, used promiscuously during the times of both the tabernacle and temple until the captivity; and, lastly, there were *Synagogues* among the Jews, and other places, used only for prayer, called *Proseuchæ* or *Oratories*, which chiefly obtained after the captivity; of these various structures some account will be found in the following sections.

SECTION I.

OF THE TABERNACLE.

I. *Different Tabernacles in use among the Israelites.*—II. THE TABERNACLE, *so called by way of Eminence, not of Egyptian Origin. — Its Materials.—* III. *Form and Construction of the Tabernacle. — Its Contents. — IV. Its Migrations.*

I. MENTION is made in the Old Testament of three different tabernacles previously to the erection of Solomon's temple. The *first*, which Moses erected, is called the *Tabernacle of the Congregation* (Exod. xxxiii. 7.); here he gave audience, heard causes, and inquired of Jehovah, and here also, at first, perhaps the public offices of religion were solemnised. The *second* tabernacle was that erected by Moses for Jehovah, and at his express command, partly to be a palace of his presence as the king of Israel (Exod. xl. 34, 35.) and partly to be the medium of the most solemn public worship, which the people were to pay to him. (26—29.) This tabernacle was erected on the first day of the first month in the second year after the departure of the Israelites from Egypt. The *third* public tabernacle was that erected by David in his own city, for the reception of the ark, when he received it from the house of Obed-Edom. (2 Sam. vi. 7. 1 Chron. xvi. 1.) Of the second of these tabernacles we are now to treat, which was called THE TABERNACLE by way of distinction. It was a moveable chapel, so contrived as to be taken to pieces and put together again at pleasure, for the convenience of carrying it from place to place.

II. It has been imagined that this tabernacle, together with all its furniture and appurtenances, was of Egyptian origin: that Moses projected it after the fashion of some such structure which he had observed in Egypt, and which was in use among other nations; or that God directed it to be made with a view of indulging the Israelites in a compliance with their customs and modes of worship, so far as there was nothing in them directly sinful. The heathen nations, it is true, had such tabernacles or portable shrines as are alluded to by the prophet Amos (v. 26.), which might bear a great resemblance to that of the Jews; but it has neither been proved, nor is it probable, that they had them *before* the Jews, and that the Almighty so far condescended to indulge the Israelites, a wayward people, and prone to idolatry, as to introduce them into his own worship. It is far more likely that the heathens derived their tabernacles from that of the Jews, who had the whole of their religion immediately from God, than that the Jews, or rather that God should take them from the heathens.[1]

The materials of the tabernacle were provided by the people; every one brought his oblation according to his ability: those of the first quality offered gold, those of a middle condition brought silver and brass, and shittim-wood [2] ; and the offerings of the meaner sort consisted of yarn, fine linen, goats' hair, and skins; nor were the women backward in contributing to this work, for they willingly brought in their bracelets, ear-rings, and other ornaments, and such of them as were skilful in spinning made yarn and thread. In short, the liberality of the people on this occasion was so great, that Moses was obliged by proclamation to forbid any more offerings, and thereby restrain the excessive zeal of the people for that service. (Exod. xxxv. and xxxvi.)

This tabernacle was set up in the wilderness of Sinai, and carried along with the Israelites from place to place as they journeyed towards Canaan, and is often called the *Tabernacle of the Congregation.* In form it appears to have closely resembled our modern tents, but it was much larger, having the sides and roof secured with boards, hangings, and coverings, and was surrounded on all sides by a large outer court, which was inclosed by pillars, posted at equal distances, whose spaces were filled up with curtains fixed to these pillars : whence it is evident that this tabernacle consisted first of the tent or house itself which was covered, and next of the court that surrounded it, which was open : all which are minutely and exactly described in Exod. xxv.—xxx. xxxvi.—xl. from which chapters the following particulars are abridged.

III. The tent itself was an oblong square, thirty cubits in length, and ten in height and breadth. The inside of it was divided by a veil or hanging, made of rich embroidered linen, which parted the Holy Place, which is called the *first tabernacle* in Heb. ix. 2. 6., from the *Holy of Holies*, called the *second tabernacle* in Heb. ix. 7. In the former stood the altar of incense overlaid with gold, the table of shew-bread, consisting of twelve loaves, and the great candlestick of pure gold, containing seven branches : none of the people were allowed to go into the holy place, but only the priests. The Holy of Holies (so called because it was the most sacred place of the tabernacle, into which none went but the high priest,) contained in it the ark, called the ark of the testimony (Exod. xxv. 22.) or the ark of the covenant. (Josh iv. 7.) This was a small chest or coffer made of shittim-wood, overlaid with gold, into which were put the two tables of the law (as well the broken ones, say the Jews, as the whole,) with the pot of manna, and Aaron's rod that budded. (Heb. ix. 4.) This was the most holy of all the sacred furniture. None but the

---

[1] The hypothesis above noticed was advanced by Spencer in his learned, but in many respects fanciful, treatise, De Legibus Hebræorum, lib. iii. diss. i. c. 3. and diss. vi. c. 1. His arguments were examined and refuted by Buddeus in his Historia Ecclesiastica Veteris Testamenti, part i. pp. 310. 548.

[2] This *shittim-wood* is supposed to have been either the acacia or the cedar, both which grow in Egypt and in Syria. The acacia is delineated by Prosper Alpinus, De Plantis Ægyptiacis, c. 4. Hasselquist found it in Palestine (Tour in the Levant, p. 250.), and Dr. Pococke found it both on Mount Sinai and in Egypt. The cedar has been already mentioned.

priests were allowed to touch it; and only the Kohathites, the sacerdotal family, were permitted to carry it, with poles made of shittim-wood
also overlaid with gold inserted in two golden rings at each end
(1 Kings viii. 8.) Hence Uzzah the *Levite* was punished with death
for touching it. (2 Sam. vi. 7.)

The lid or covering of the ark was wholly of solid gold, and called
the mercy-seat: at the two ends of it were two cherubim (or hieroglyphic figures, the form of which it is impossible now to ascertain),
looking inwards towards each other, with wings expanded, which,
embracing the whole circumference of the mercy-seat, met on each
side in the middle. Here the Shechinah or Divine Presence rested,
both in the tabernacle and temple, and was visibly seen in the appearance of a cloud over it. (Lev. xvi. 2.) From this the divine oracles
were given out by an audible voice, as often as Jehovah was consulted
on behalf of his people. (Exod. xxv. 22. Numb. vii. 89.) And hence
it is that the ark is called the footstool of God (Psal. xcix. 5.), who
is so often said in Scripture, *to dwell between the cherubim.* (2 Kings
xix. 15. Psal. lxxx. 1.) The roof of the tabernacle was a square
frame of planks, resting upon their basis, and over these were coverings or curtains of different kinds; of which the first on the inside
was made of fine linen, curiously embroidered in various colours of
crimson and scarlet, purple and hyacinth. The next was made of
goats' hair curiously wove together; and the last, or outmost, was of
sheep and badgers' skins (some dyed red, and others of azure blue,)
which served to preserve the other rich curtains from the rain, and to
protect the tabernacle itself from the injuries of the weather.

The tabernacle was surrounded by a large oblong court, an hundred cubits long, and fifty broad, nearly in the centre of which stood
a vessel, called the *Brazen Laver,* in which the priests washed their
hands and feet, whenever they were to offer sacrifices, or go into the
tarbernacle; and directly opposite to the entrance of the tabernacle
stood the *Brazen Altar* of burnt-offerings, in the open air, in order
that the interior might not be spoiled by the fire, which was at first
miraculously kindled [1], (Lev. ix. 24.) and which was kept perpetually
upon it, and by the smoke arising from the victims that were there
consumed.

There is no precept in the law to make the altar a privileged place,
but in conformity to the custom of other nations the Jews seem to
have made it such; for, from the words in Exod. xxi. 14. where God
ordered the wilful murderer *to be taken from his altar, that he may die,*
it seems unquestionably true, that both in the wilderness and afterwards in Canaan, this altar continued a sanctuary for those who fled
unto it; and very probably it was the horns of this altar (then at Gibeon)

---

1 God had previously ordered that the fire on this altar, when once kindled, should never
go out. (Levit. vi. 12, 13.) It was reckoned an impious presumption to make use of any
other but this sacred fire in burning incense before the Lord ; which was sufficiently notified
to Aaron by an injunction given him, that he was to light the incense offered to God, in the
most holy place on the great day of expiation, at this fire only. (Lev. xvi. 12, 13.) Notwithstanding which prohibition Nadab and Abihu, two unhappy sons of Aaron, forgetful of
their duty, took their censers, and putting common fire in them, laid incense thereon, and
offered strange fire before the Lord, in their daily ministrations, which profane approach God
immediately resented; for we are told that *a fire went out from the Lord, and devoured them,
so that they died.* (Levit. x. 1.)

that Adonijah and Joab took hold of (1 Kings i. 50. and ii. 28.), for the temple of Solomon was not then erected.[1]

After the Israelites were settled in the land of promise, it appears that this tabernacle was surrounded with a great many other tents or cells, which were placed about it in the same manner as the buildings were afterwards placed round the temple. These were absolutely necessary for the reception of the priests during the time of their ministration, and for laying up the utensils and provisions which were used in the tabernacle. This circumstance explains what is related of Eli's sons going into the kitchen where the peace-offerings were dressing, and taking out of the pots whatever the flesh-hook brought up. (1 Sam. ii. 14.) And thus Eli is said to be laid down in his place (iii. 2.), that is, was gone to bed in one of these tents near the tabernacle, next to which Samuel lay, which made him (being then a child) run to Eli, when he heard the voice of the Lord, thinking that Eli had called (4, 5, &c.) : and this also explains what is said of David (Matt. xii. 4.), that *he entered into the house of God and did eat the shewbread*, that is, he came to the priest's habitation, which was among these tents round the tabernacle, and which were reckoned as parts of the house of God.

When the tabernacle was finished, it was consecrated, with all the furniture therein, by being anointed with a peculiar oil, prepared by divine command for that very purpose (Exod. xxx. 22, &c.), after which God made His people sensible of His special presence in it, covering it with a thick cloud which overshadowed it by day, and by night gave light, as if it had been a fire, and by giving answers in an audible manner from the ark when consulted by the high priest. Whenever the Israelites changed their camp the tabernacle was taken down, and every Levite knew what part he was to carry, for this was a part of their office; and sometimes, upon extraordinary occasions, the priests themselves bore the ark, as when they passed over Jordan, and besieged Jericho. (Josh. iii. 14. and vi. 6.) Concerning the manner of carrying the several parts of it, see Numb. iv. When they encamped, the tabernacle stood always in the midst, being surrounded by the army of the Israelites on all sides in a quadrangular form, divided according to their several tribes; the Israelitish camp being at the distance of two thousand cubits from the tabernacle, which by computation is reckoned a mile, and is called *a Sabbath-day's journey* (Acts i. 12.),

---

[1] It is evident from this and other passages of Scripture, that the altar was considered as an asylum ; and it is well known that, among almost all the heathen nations of antiquity, the altar of their deities were accounted so sacred that the vilest miscreant found safety, if he once reached an altar. Hence arose many abuses, and justice was greatly perverted : so that it became a maxim that the guilty should be punished even though they should have taken refuge there. We have remarked above that the presumptuous murderer was, by divine command, to be dragged thence and put to death. Euripides thus alludes to a similar ordinance among the heathen nations in his time : —

Εγω, γαρ όστις μη δικαιος ων ανηρ
Βωμον προσιξει, τον νομον χαιρειν εων,
Προς την δικην αγοιμ' αν, ου τρεσας θεους·
Κακον γαρ ανδρα χρη κακως πασχειν αει.

Eurip. Frag. 42. edit. Musgrave.

In English thus : —

"If an unrighteous man, availing himself of the law, should claim the protection of the altar, I would drag him to justice, nor fear the wrath of the gods : for it is necessary that a wicked man should always suffer for his crimes." Dr. A. Clarke on 1 Kings ii. 30.

being the distance they had to go on that day to the place of worship. Moses and Aaron, with the priests and Levites, encamped in their tents next the tabernacle, between it and the army; as represented in the diagram inserted in p. 205. *suprà*.

IV. The tabernacle being so constructed as to be taken to pieces and put together again as occasion required, it was removed as often as the camp of the Israelites moved from one station to another ; and thus accompanied them in all their marches, until they arrived at the land of Canaan. It was at first set up at Gilgal, being the first en-campment of the Israelites in Canaan ; and here it continued for about seven years, during which Joshua was occupied in the conquest of that country. Afterwards, it was pitched in Shiloh, being nearly in the centre of the country then subdued; on being restored by the Philistines, who had taken it and deposited it in the temple of one of their idols, as related in 1 Sam. iv. 10, 11. v. vi., it remained for twenty years in the custody of Abinadab of Gibeah, and afterwards (for three months) in the house of Obed-Edom, whence David brought it with great solemnity into that part of Jerusalem which was called the city of David. (2 Sam. vi. 17. 1 Chron. xv. 25. xvi. 1.) Here it remained until it was deposited in the temple of Solomon, where (having been subsequently removed) it was again replaced by order of the pious king Josiah. (2 Chron. xxxv. 3.) It is supposed to have been consumed in the destruction of Jerusalem by Nebuchadnezzar.[1]

---

[1] Schulzii Archæol. Hebr. pp. 183—204. ; Pareau, Antiq. Hebr. pp. 94—101. ; Relandi Antiq.,Hebr. pp. 11—24. ; Home's Hist. of the Jews, vol. ii. pp. 129—138. ; Brunings, Antiq. Hebr. pp. 145—159.

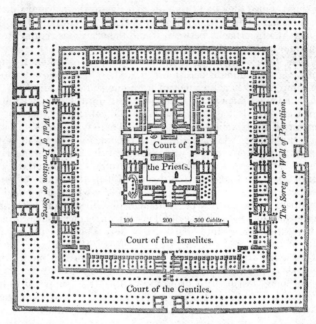

The Wall of Partition or Soreg.

The Soreg or Wall of Partition.

Court of
the Priests.

100   200   300 *Cubits.*

Court of the Israelites.

Court of the Gentiles.

Plan of the Temple at Jerusalem, according to Lamy and Calmet.

SECTION II.

OF THE TEMPLE.

I. *The Temple of Solomon.*—II. *The Second Temple.*—*Its various Courts.*—
Reverence of the Jews for it.—III. *Notice of the Temples at Heliopolis and
Gerizim.*

ACCORDING to the opinion of some writers, there were *three*
temples, viz. the first, erected by Solomon; the second, by Zerubbabel
and Joshua, the high priest; and the third, by Herod a few years before the birth of Christ.   But this opinion is very properly rejected by
the Jews: who do not allow the third to be a new temple, but only
the second temple rebuilt: and this opinion corresponds with the prophecy of Haggai (ii. 9.), that *the glory of this latter house* — the
temple built by Zerubbabel, *should be greater than that of the former;*
which prediction was uttered with reference to the Messiah's honour-
ing it with his presence and ministry.

   I. The first temple is that which usually bears the name of SOLO-
MON; the materials for which were provided by David before his
death, though the edifice was raised by his son.   It stood on Mount
Moriah, an eminence of the mountainous ridge in the Scriptures

termed Mount Sion (Psal. cxxxii. 13, 14.), which had been purchased
of Araunah or Ornan the Jebusite. (2 Sam. xxiv. 23, 24. 1 Chron.
xxi. 25.) The plan and whole model of this superb structure were
formed after that of the tabernacle, but of much larger dimensions. It
was surrounded, except at the front or east end, by three stories of
chambers, each five cubits square, which reached to half the height of
the temple: and the front was ornamented with a magnificent portico,
which rose to the height of one hundred and twenty cubits: so that
the form of the whole edifice was not unlike that of some antient
churches which have a lofty tower in the front, and a low aisle running
along each side of the building. The utensils for the sacred service
were the same; excepting that several of them, as the altar, candlestick, &c. were larger, in proportion to the more spacious edifice to
which they belonged. Seven years and six months were occupied in
the erection of the superb and magnificent temple of Solomon; by
whom it was dedicated[1] with peculiar solemnity to the worship of the
Most High, who on this occasion vouchsafed to honour it with the
Shechinah, or visible manifestation of His presence. The prayer of
the Hebrew monarch on this occasion, is one of the noblest and most
sublime compositions in the Bible, exhibiting, in the prophetic spirit
of Moses, the most exalted conceptions of the omnipresence of the
Deity, of his superintending Providence, and of his peculiar protection
of the Israelites from the time of their departure out of Egypt; and
imploring pardon and forgiveness for all their sins and transgressions
in the land, and during the captivities which might ensue.[2] Various
attempts have been made to describe the proportions and several parts
of this structure; but as no two writers scarcely agree on this subject, a
minute description of it is designedly omitted.[3] It retained its pristine splendour only thirty-three or thirty-four years, when Shishak
king of Egypt took Jerusalem, and carried away the treasures of the
temple[4]; and after undergoing subsequent profanations and pillages,
this stupendous building was finally plundered and burnt by the Chaldæans under Nebuchadnezzar in the year of the world 3416, or before
Christ, 584. (2 Kings xxv. 13—15. 2 Chron. xxxvi. 17—20.)

II. After the captivity the temple emerged from its ruins, being
rebuilt by Zerubbabel[5], but with vastly inferior and diminished glory;
as appears from the tears of the aged men who had beheld the former
structure in all its grandeur. (Ezra iii. 12.) The second temple was
profaned by order of Antiochus Epiphanes (A. M. 3837, B. C. 163.);
who caused the daily sacrifice to be discontinued, and erected the
image of Jupiter Olympius on the altar of burnt-offering. In this condition it continued three years (2 Macc. x. 1—8.), when Judas Maccabæus purified and repaired it, and restored the sacrifices and true
worship of Jehovah. (A.M. 3840, B.C. 160.)

Some years before the birth of our Saviour, the repairing or rather

---

[1] In the year of the world 3001 ; before Christ 999.
[2] Hales's Chronology, vol. ii. p. 393.
[3] The reader will find a copious description of what the first temple is supposed to have
been, in Home's Hist. of the Jews, vol. ii. pp. 144—158.
[4] In the year of the world 3033 ; before Christ 967. 1 Kings xiv. 25, 26. 2 Chron.
xii. 9.
[5] Ezra i.—vi. Josephus, Ant. Jud. lib. xi. c. 4.

gradual rebuilding of this second temple, which had become decayed in the lapse of five centuries, was undertaken by Herod the Great, who for nine years employed eighteen thousand workmen upon it, and spared no expense to render it equal, if not superior, in magnitude, splendour, and beauty to any thing among mankind. Josephus calls it a work the most admirable of any that had ever been seen or heard of, both for its curious structure and its magnitude, and also for the vast wealth expended upon it, as well as for the universal reputation of its sanctity.[1]   But though Herod accomplished his original design in the time above specified, yet the Jews continued to ornament and enlarge it, expending the sacred treasure in annexing additional buildings to it : so that they might with great propriety assert that their temple had been forty and six years in building.[2]

Before we proceed to describe this venerable edifice, it may be proper to remark, that by the temple is to be understood not only the fabric or house itself, which by way of eminence is called the *The Temple,* viz. the holy of holies, the sanctuary, and the several courts both of the priests and Israelites ; but also all the numerous chambers and rooms which this prodigious edifice comprehended, and each of which had its respective degree of holiness, increasing in proportion to its contiguity to the holy of holies. This remark it will be necessary to bear in mind, lest the reader of the Scriptures should be led to suppose that whatever is there said to be transacted in the temple was actually done in the interior of that sacred edifice. To this infinite number of apartments into which the temple was disposed our Lord refers (John xiv. 2.) : and by a very striking and magnificent simile borrowed from them, he represents those numerous seats and mansions of heavenly bliss which his *Father's house* contained, and which were prepared for the everlasting abode of the righteous. The imagery is singularly beautiful and happy, when considered as an allusion to the temple, which our Lord not unfrequently called *his Father's house.*

The second temple, originally built by Zerubbabel, after the captivity, and repaired by Herod, differed in several respects from that erected by Solomon, although they agreed in others.

The temple erected by Solomon was more splendid and magnificent than the second temple, which was deficient in five remarkable things that constituted the chief glory of the first :— these were the ark and mercy-seat, — the shechinah or manifestation of the divine presence in the holy of holies, — the sacred fire on the altar, which had been first kindled from heaven, — the urim and thummim, — and the spirit of

---

[1] De Bell. Jud. lib. vi. c. 4. § 8.

[2] John ii. 20.   There is, therefore, no real contradiction between the sacred writer and Josephus. The words of the evangelist are, " Forty and six years was this temple in building." This, as Calmet well observes, is not saying that Herod had employed forty-six years in erecting it.   Josephus acquaints us that Herod began to rebuild the temple, yet so as not to be esteemed a new edifice, in the eighteenth year of his reign (Antiq. lib. xv. c. 14.), computing from his being declared king by the Romans, or in the fifteenth year (Bell. Jud. lib. i. c. 16.), reckoning from the death of Antigonus.   He finished it for use in about nine years (Ant. xv. 14.) ; but it continued increasing in splendour and magnificence through the pious donations of the people (Bell. Jud. v. 14.) to the time of Nero, when it was completed, and 18,000 workmen were dismissed from that service during the procuratorship of Albinus.   From the eighteenth of Herod, who reigned thirty-seven years, to the birth of Christ, more than a year before the death of that prince, was above sixteen years, added to which, the age of Christ, now thirty, gives forty-six complete years.   Calmet's Comment. in loc.

prophecy. But the second temple surpassed the first in glory, being honoured by the frequent presence of our divine Saviour, agreeably to the prediction of Haggai. (ii. 9.) Both, however, were erected upon the same site, a very hard rock encompassed by a very frightful precipice; and the foundation was laid with incredible expense and labour. The superstructure was not inferior to this great work; the height of the temple wall, especially on the south side, was stupendous, in the lowest places it was three hundred cubits, or four hundred and fifty feet, and in some places even greater. This most magnificent pile was constructed with hard white stones of prodigious magnitude.[1]

The temple itself, strictly so called, (which comprised the portico, the sanctuary, and the holy of holies,) formed only a small part of the sacred edifice on Mount Moriah; being surrounded by spacious courts, making a square of half a mile in circumference. It was entered through nine magnificent gates; one of which, called the *Beautiful Gate* in Acts iii. 2., was more splendid and costly than all the rest: it was composed of Corinthian brass, the most precious metal in antient times.

1. The first or outer court, which encompassed the holy house and the other courts, was named the COURT OF THE GENTILES; because the latter were allowed to enter into it, but were prohibited from advancing further: it was surrounded by a range of porticoes or cloisters, above which were galleries or apartments supported by pillars of white marble, each consisting of a single piece, and five and twenty cubits in height. One of these was called SOLOMON's PORCH or PIAZZA, because it stood on a vast terrace, which he had originally raised from a valley beneath, four hundred cubits high, in order to enlarge the area on the top of the mountain, and make it equal to the plan of his intended building; and as this terrace was the only work of Solomon's that remained in the second temple, the piazza which stood upon it retained the name of that prince. Here it was that our Lord was walking at the feast of dedication (John x. 23.)[2]; and the lame man, when healed by Peter and John, glorified God before all the people.[3] (Acts iii. 11.) This superb portico is termed the ROYAL PORTICO by Josephus, who represents it as the noblest work beneath the sun, being elevated to such a prodigious height that no one could look down from its flat roof to the valley below without being seized with dizziness, the sight not reaching to such an immeasurable depth. The south-east corner of the roof of this portico, where the height was greatest, is supposed to have been the πτερυγιον, pinnacle, or extreme angle, whence Satan tempted our Saviour to precipitate himself. (Matt. iv. 5. Luke iv. 9.) This also was the spot where it was predicted that the abomination of desolation, or the Roman ensigns, should stand. (Dan. ix. 27. Matt. xxiv. 15.) Solomon's portico was situated in the eastern front of the temple, opposite to the Mount of Olives, where our Lord is said to have sat when his disciples came to show him the grandeur of its various buildings, of which, grand as they were, he said, the time was approaching

---

[1] Antiq. Jud. lib. xv. § 5.   [2] Antiq. Jud. lib. xv. c. 11. § 3.
[3] Of the same kind with these porticoes, cloisters, or piazzas, were doubtless the five porticoes which surrounded the pool of Bethesda. (John v. 2.) The pool was probably a pentagon, and the piazzas round it were designed to shelter from the weather the multitude of diseased persons who lay waiting for a cure by the miraculous virtue of those waters. Jennings's Jewish Antiq. p. 267.

when one stone should not be left upon another. (Matt. xxiv. 1—3.) This outermost court being assigned to the Gentile proselytes, the Jews, who did not worship in it themselves, conceived that it might be lawfully put to profane uses : for here we find that the buyers and sellers of animals for sacrifices, and also the moneychangers, had stationed themselves; until Jesus Christ, awing them into submission by the grandeur and dignity of his person and behaviour, expelled them, telling them that it was the house of prayer *for all nations*, and that it had a relative sanctity, and was not to be profaned.   It is not improbable, that the captains of the temple, who were officers that had the care and charge of it, let out this court for profit and advantage; and that the sellers, to compensate themselves for what they paid for their tables and seats, made an unjust and exorbitant gain ; and that this circumstance occasioned its being called a den of thieves.[1] (Matt. xxi. 12, 13.   Mark xi. 15—17.   Luke xix. 45, 46.)

2. Within the court of the Gentiles stood the Court of the Is-raelites divided into two parts or courts, the outer one being appropriated to the women, and the inner one to the men.   The *Court of the Women* was separated from that of the Gentiles by a low stone wall or partition, of elegant construction, on which stood pillars at equal distances, with inscriptions in Greek and Latin, importing that no alien should enter into the holy place.   To this wall St. Paul most evidently alludes in Eph. ii. 13, 14.   *But now in Christ Jesus, ye, who sometimes were afar off, are made nigh by the blood of Christ : for he is our peace, who hath made both one* (united both Jews and Gentiles into one church), *and hath broken down* the middle wall of partition *between us ;* having abolished the law of ordinances by which, as by the wall of separation, both Jews and Gentiles were not only kept asunder, but also at variance.   In this court was the treasury, over against which Christ sat, and beheld how the people threw their voluntary offerings into it for furnishing the victims and other things necessary for the sacrifices. (Mark xii. 41.   John viii. 20.)

From the court of the women, which was on higher ground than that of the Gentiles, there was an ascent of fifteen steps into the *Inner* or *Men's Court :* and so called because it was appropriated to the worship of the male Israelites.   In these two courts, collectively termed the *Court of the Israelites*, were the people praying, each apart by himself, for the pardon of his sins, while Zechariah was offering incense within the sanctuary. (Luke i. 10.)

3. Within the court of the Israelites was that of the Priests, which was separated from it by a low wall, one cubit in height.   This inclosure surrounded the altar of burnt-offerings, and to it the people brought their oblations and sacrifices : but the priests alone were permitted to enter it.   From this court twelve steps ascended to the Temple strictly so called, which was divided into three parts, the portico, the outer sanctuary, and the holy place.

(1.) In the Portico were suspended the splendid votive offerings made by the piety of various individuals.   Among its other treasures, there was a golden table given by Pompey, together with several golden vines of exquisite workmanship as well as of immense size : for Jose-

---

[1] Bp. Pearce's Commentary, vol. i. on Matt. xxi. 13.

phus relates that there were clusters as tall as a man. And he adds, that all around were fixed up and displayed the spoils and trophies taken by Herod from the Barbarians and Arabians. These votive offerings, it should seem, were visible at a distance; for when Jesus Christ was sitting on the Mount of Olives, and his disciples called his attention to the temple, they pointed out to him the *gifts* with which it was adorned. (Luke xxi. 5.) This porch had a very large portal or gate, which, instead of folding doors, was furnished with a costly Babylonian veil, of many colours, that mystically denoted the universe.

(2.) The SANCTUARY or Holy Place was separated from the holy of holies by a double veil, which is supposed to have been the veil that was rent in twain at our Saviour's crucifixion: thus emblematically pointing out that the separation between Jews and Gentiles was abolished, and that the privilege of the high priest was communicated to all mankind, who might henceforth have access to the throne of grace through the one great mediator, Jesus Christ. (Heb. x. 19—22.) This corresponded with the Holy Place in the Tabernacle. In it were placed the Golden Candlestick, the Altar of Incense, and the Table of Shew-Bread, which consisted of twelve loaves, according to the number of the tribes of Israel. Various fanciful delineations have been given of these articles: in the subjoined engraving is represented the form of the GOLDEN CANDLESTICK as it was actually carried in the triumphal procession of the Roman General Titus;

and the following engraving exhibits the TABLE OF SHEW-BREAD, with a cup upon it, and with two of the sacred trumpets, which were used to proclaim the year of Jubilee, as they were also carried in the same triumph. They are copied from the plates in Reland's Treatise on the Spoils of the Temple of Jerusalem[1], the drawings for which were made at Rome, upwards of a century since, when the triumphal Arch of Titus was in a much better state of preservation than it now is.

(3.) The HOLY OF HOLIES was twenty cubits square. No person was ever admitted into it but the high priest, who entered it once a year on the great day of atonement. (Exod. xxx. 10. Levit. xvi. 2. 15. 34. Heb. ix. 2—7.)[2]

Magnificent as the rest of the sacred edifice was, it was infinitely surpassed in splendour by the *Inner Temple* or *Sanctuary*. "Its appearance," according to Josephus, "had every thing that could strike the mind or astonish the sight: for it was covered on every side with plates of gold, so that when the sun rose upon it, it reflected so strong and dazzling an effulgence, that the eye of the spectator was obliged to turn away, being no more able to sustain its radiance than the splendour of the sun. To strangers who were approaching, it appeared at a distance like a mountain covered with snow, for where it was not decorated with plates of gold, it was extremely white and glistering. On the top it had sharp-pointed spikes of gold, to prevent any bird from resting upon it and polluting it. There were," continues the Jewish historian, "in that building several stones which were forty-five cubits in length, five in height, and six in breadth.[3] When all these things are considered, how natural is the exclamation of the disciples when viewing this immense building at a distance:

---

[1] Hadr. Relandus de Spoliis Templi in Arcu Titiano Romæ conspicuis. Trajecti ad Rhenum, 1775. 8vo.

[2] Godwin's Moses and Aaron, book ii. ch. 1.; Jennings's Jewish Antiquities, book ii. ch. 1.; Schulzii Archæologia Hebraica, pp. 204—220.; Beausobre's and L'Enfant's Introduction. (Bp. Watson's Theol. Tracts, vol. iii. pp. 145—150.) Pareau, Antiquitas Hebraica, pp. 196—203.; Brunings, Antiq. Hebr. pp. 165—172.

[3] Josephus, Antiq. Jud. lib. xv. c. 11. § 3. De Bell. Jud. lib. v. c. 5. §§ 1—6.

Master, see what MANNER *of* STONES, (ποταποι λιθοι, what very large stones,) *and what* BUILDINGS *are here!* (Mark xiii. 1.) ; and how wonderful is the declaration of our Lord upon this, how unlikely to be accomplished before the race of men who were then living should cease to exist. *Seest thou these great buildings? There shall not be left one stone upon another that shall not be thrown down.*" (Mark xiii. 2.)[1] Improbable as this prediction must have appeared to the disciples at that time, in the short space of thirty-seven years after, it was exactly accomplished; and this most magnificent temple, which the Jews had literally turned into a den of thieves, through the righteous judgments of God upon that wicked and abandoned nation, was utterly destroyed by the Romans A.M. 4073 (A.D. 73), in the same month, and on the same day of the month, on which Solomon's temple had been rased to the ground by the Babylonians!

Both the first and second temples were contemplated by the Jews with the highest reverence : of their affectionate regard for the first temple, and for Jerusalem, within whose walls it was built, we have several instances in those psalms which were composed during the Babylonish captivity ; and of their profound veneration for the second temple we have repeated examples in the New Testament. " They could not bear any disrespectful or dishonourable thing to be said of it. The least injurious slight of it, real or apprehended, instantly awakened all the choler of a Jew, and was an affront never to be forgiven. Our Saviour, in the course of his public instructions, happening to say, *Destroy this temple, and in three days I will raise it up again* (John i. 19.), it was construed into a contemptuous disrespect, designedly thrown out against the temple; his words instantly descended into the heart of a Jew, and kept rankling there for several years; for upon his trial, this declaration, which it was impossible for a Jew ever to forget or to forgive, was immediately alleged against him as big with the most atrocious guilt and impiety : they told the court they had heard him publicly assert, I am able to destroy this temple.[2] The rancour and virulence they had conceived against him for this speech, which they imagined had been levelled against the temple, was not softened by all the affecting circumstances of that excruciating and wretched death they saw him die: even as he hung upon the cross, with infinite triumph, scorn, and exultation, they upbraided him with it, contemptuously shaking their heads, and saying, *Thou that destroyest the temple, and buildest it in three days, save thyself! If thou be the Son of God, come down from the cross.* (Matt. xxvii. 40.) The superstitious veneration, which this people had for their temple, further appears from the account of Stephen. When his adversaries were baffled and confounded by that superior wisdom and those distinguished gifts which he possessed, they were so exasperated at the victory he had gained over them, that they suborned persons to swear that they had heard him speak blasphemy against Moses and against God. These inflaming the populace, the magistrates, and the Jewish clergy, the holy man was seized, dragged away, and brought before the Sanhedrin. Here the false witnesses, whom

---

[1] Dr. Harwood's Introd. to the New Test. vol. ii. pp. 159. 161.

[2] Matt. xxvi. 61. " This fellow said, I am able to destroy the temple of God and to build it in three days."

they had procured, stood up and said, This person before you is continually uttering the most reproachful expressions against this sacred
place [1], meaning the temple. This was blasphemy not to be pardoned.
A judicature composed of high priests and scribes would never forgive
such impiety.

" Thus, also, when St. Paul went into the temple to give public
notice, as was usual, to the priests, of his having purified and bound
himself by a religious vow along with four other persons, declaring
the time when this vow was made, and the oblations he would offer for
every one of them at his own expense, when the time of their vow was
accomplished, some Jews of Asia Minor, when the seven days prescribed by the law were almost completed, happening to see him in
the temple, struck with horror at the sight of such apprehended profanation, immediately excited the populace, who all at once rushed
upon him and instantly seized him, vehemently exclaiming, *Men of
Israel, help! This is the man that teacheth all men every where against
the people* (the Jews), *and the law, and this place; and, further, brought
Greeks into the temple, and hath polluted this holy place.* (Acts xxi. 28.)
They said this, because they had a little before seen Trophimus an
Ephesian along with him in the city, and they instantly concluded he
had brought him into the temple. Upon this the whole city was
immediately raised; all the people at once rushed furiously upon him,
and dragged him out of the temple, whose doors were instantly shut.
Being determined to murder him, news was carried to the Roman
tribune, that the whole city was in a commotion. The uproar now
raised among the Jews, and their determined resolution to imbrue
their hands in the blood of a person who had spoken disrespectfully of
the temple, and who they apprehended had wantonly profaned it by
introducing Greeks into it, verify and illustrate the declaration of Philo;
that it was certain and inevitable death for any one who was not a Jew
to set his foot within the inner courts of the temple." [2]

It only remains to add, that it appears from several passages of
Scripture, that "the Jews had a body of soldiers who guarded the
temple, to prevent any disturbance during the ministration of such an
immense number of priests and Levites. To this guard Pilate referred,
when he said to the chief priests and Pharisees who waited upon him
to desire he would make the sepulchre secure. *Ye have a watch, go
your way, and make it as secure as ye can.* (Matt. xxvii. 65.) Over
these guards one person had the supreme command, who in several
places is called the CAPTAIN OF THE TEMPLE (Στρατηγος τοῦ Ἱεροῦ), or
officer of the temple guard. ' And as they spake unto the people, the
priests and the captain of the temple and the Sadducees came upon
them.' (Acts iv. 1. v. 25, 26. John xviii. 12.) Josephus mentions such
an officer." [3] It should seem that this officer was a Jew, from the circumstance of his assisting the high-priest in arresting those who were
deemed to be seditious, without the intervention of the Roman
procurator.

---

[1] Acts i. 13.　　　　　　　　　[2] Harwood's Introd. vol. ii. pp. 166—169.
[3] Τον στρατηγον Ανανον, Ananias, the commander of the temple. Antiq. Jud. lib. xx.
c. 6. § 2. Bell. Jud. lib. ii. c. 17. § 2. Αφορωντες εις τον Ελεαζαρον στρατηγοντα, having
the chief regard to Eleazar, the governor of the temple. Bell. Jud. lib. ii. c. 17. § 2. edit.
Hudson. Harwood's Introd. vol. ii. p. 169. and Dr. Lardner's Credibility, book i. ch. xi.
§ 1. ch. ix. § 4.

III. Besides the temple at Jerusalem, two others were erected, viz. one in Egypt, and another on Mount Gerizim, of which the following notice may not be unacceptable to the reader : —

1. The HELIOPOLITAN TEMPLE, also called the temple of Onias, was erected in imitation of that at Jerusalem by Onias, the son of Onias the high priest; who, finding that no hope remained of his being restored to the pontifical dignity which had been held by his ancestors, fled into Egypt in the time of Antiochus Epiphanes. "Having acquired great favour with the then reigning sovereign, Ptolemy Philometor, and his queen Cleopatra, by his skill in political and military affairs, Onias represented to them, that it would be productive of great advantage to their kingdom, if the numerous Jewish inhabitants of Egypt and Cyrene could have a temple of their own, which would supersede the necessity of their repairing to Jerusalem in the dominions of a foreign monarch, to perform their religious services; and that, if such a temple were built, many more Jews would be induced to settle in the country, as Judæa was continually exposed to the evils of war. By such representations he at length obtained permission to erect a temple for the Jews, on the site of an antient temple of Bubastis or Isis, in the city of Leontopolis in the Heliopolitan nome (or district), over which he was governor."[1] To the Jews he justified his undertaking, on the plea that the buildingof such a temple had been predicted by the prophet Isaiah, who lived about six hundred years before.[2] Accordingly, the temple was completed on the model of that at Jerusalem. Onias was invested with the high priesthood; the subordinate priests were furnished from the descendants of Aaron; Levites were employed in the sacred services; and the whole of their religious worship was performed in the same manner as at Jerusalem. Though the Heliopolitan temple was smaller in its dimensions than the temple at Jerusalem, it was made comformable to the latter in every respect, except that a golden lamp suspended by a golden chain was substituted for a candlestick. It was also adorned with votive gifts. This temple continued until the time of Vespasian, who, in consequence of a tumult which had been raised by the Jews in Egypt, commanded Lupus the governor to demolish it. Accordingly, the gates were effectually closed, so that no vestiges remained of any divine worship having been there performed. This occurrence took place three hundred and forty-three years after the building of the temple.[3] In 2 Macc. i. 1—9. there is an epistle from the Jews at Jerusalem to those in Egypt.

2. The TEMPLE ON MOUNT GERIZIM was erected by Sanballat, under the authority of Alexander the Great, for the use of the Samaritans; who on the return of the Jews from the Babylonish captivity, pretended that they were of the stock of the true and antient Hebrews, and that their mountain was the most proper place of worship. (Upon this principle the Samaritan woman argued with Jesus Christ in

---

[1] Jahn's Hist. of Hebr. Commonwealth, vol. i. p. 348.

[2] There is a considerable diversity of opinion among commentators concerning the interpretation of Isa. xix. 18, 19., which is the prediction above alluded to. See Bp. Lowth's Isaiah, and Dr. Boothroyd's translation of the Bible on that passage.

[3] Josephus, Ant. Jud. lib. xiii. c. 3. Bell. Jud. lib. vii. c. 10. Schulzii Archæol. Hebr. pp. 221, 222. Pareau, Antiq. Hebr. p. 203.

John iv. 20.)   Sanballat constituted his son-in-law Manasseh the first high priest. This temple was destroyed about two hundred years afterwards by Hyrcanus, and was rebuilt by the Samaritans, between whom and the Jews there subsisted the bitterest animosity.[1] Representations of this temple are to be seen on the coins of the city of Sichem or Neapolis.[2]

SECTION III.

OF THE HIGH PLACES, AND PROSEUCHÆ, OR ORATORIES OF THE JEWS.

I. *Of the High Places.* — II. *Of the Proseuchæ, or Oratories.*

I. BESIDES the tabernacle, which has been described in a former section, frequent mention is made, in the Old Testament, of places of worship, called HIGH PLACES, which were in use both before and after the building of the temple. In the early ages of the world, the devotion of mankind seems to have delighted greatly in groves, woods, and mountains, not only because these retired places were naturally fitted for contemplation, but probably also because they kindled a certain sacred dread in the mind of the worshipper. It is certain that nothing was more antient in the East, than altars surrounded by groves and trees, which made the place very shady and delightful in those hot countries. The idolaters in the first ages of the world, who generally worshipped the sun, appear to have thought it improper to straiten and confine the supposed infinity of this imaginary deity within walls, and therefore they generally made choice of hills and mountains, as the most convenient places for their idolatry; and when in later times they had brought in the use of temples, yet for a long time they kept them open-roofed. Nay, the patriarchs themselves, who worshipped the true God, generally built their altars near to some adjacent grove of trees, which, if nature denied, were usually planted by the religious in those days. When Abraham dwelt at Beersheba, in the plains of Mamre, it is said, *He planted a grove there, and called upon the name of the Lord the everlasting God* (Gen. xxi. 33.), and doubtless that was the place to which the patriarch and his family resorted for public worship.[3]

But at length these hills and groves of the heathen idolaters, as they were more retired and shady, became so much the fitter for the exercise of their unholy rites, and for the commission of the obscene and horrid practices that were usually perpetrated there. (See 1 Kings xv. 12. 2 Kings xxiii. 7.) In many passages of Scripture it is recorded of the Israelites (who in this respect imitated the heathens) that they secretly did the things which were not right, that they set up images and groves in every high hill, and under every green tree, and there

---

1 Josephus, Ant. Jud. lib. x. c. 8. §§ 2—4. lib. xiii. c. 9. § 1.
2 Schulzii Archæol. Hebr. p. 221. Pareau, Ant. Hebr. p. 229.
3 Many antient nations used to erect altars and offer sacrifices to their gods upon high places and mountains. See the examples adduced in Burder's Oriental Literature, vol. i. p. 233.

burnt incense in all the high places, and *wrought wickedness to provoke the Lord, as did the heathen.* (2 Kings xvii. 9—13.) On this account, therefore, God expressly commanded the Israelites utterly to destroy all the places wherein the nations of Canaan, whose land they should possess, served their gods upon the high mountains and upon the hills; and to pay their devotions and bring their oblations to that place only which God should choose. (Deut. xii. 2—15.) Nay, to prevent every approach to the idolatrous customs of the heathens, they were forbidden to plant any trees near the altar of the Lord. (Deut. xvi. 21.) Hence it is clear, that after God should fix upon a place for his public worship, it was entirely unlawful to offer sacrifices upon high places, or any where else but in the place God did choose; so that after the building of the temple, the prohibition of high places and groves (so far at least as concerned the sacrificing in them) unquestionably took place. And it was for their disobedience to this command, by their sacrificing upon high places and in groves, even after the temple was erected (2 Kings xv. 35.), and for not destroying the high places of the heathens, where their idol gods were worshipped, which by that command and in many other places of Scripture (Numb. xxxiii. 52.), they were expressly appointed to do;—that the prophets with so much holy zeal reproached the Israelites. We have, indeed, several instances in Scripture besides that of Abraham, where the prophets and other good men are said to have made use of these high places for sacrificing, as well as other less solemn acts of devotion, and which are not condemned. Thus, Samuel, upon the uncertain abode of the ark, fitted up a place of devotion for himself and his family in a high place, and built an altar there, and sacrificed upon it. (1 Sam. ix. 12. 19. 25.) Gideon also built an altar and offered a sacrifice to God upon the top of a rock (Judg. vi. 25, 26.); and the tabernacle itself was removed to the high place that was at Gibeon. (1 Chron. xvi. 39. and xxi. 29.) But all this was *before* the temple was erected, which was the first fixed place that God appointed for his public worship; after which other places for sacrificing became unlawful.

That the Israelites, both kings and people, offered sacrifices upon these high places even after the temple was built, will evidently appear by noticing a few passages in their history; for (not to mention Jeroboam and his successors in the kingdom of Israel, whose professed purpose was to innovate every thing in matters of religion, and who had peculiar priests whom they termed prophets of the groves, 1 Kings xviii. 19.) it is clear that most of the kings of Judah, — even such of them who were otherwise zealous for the observance of the law, — are expressly recorded as blameable on this head, and but few have the commendation given them of destroying these high places. No sooner had Rehoboam the son of Solomon, after the revolt of the ten tribes from him, strengthened himself in his kingdom, but we read that Judah *did evil in the sight of the Lord, and built them high places, and images, and groves on every high hill, and under every green tree.* (1 Kings xiv. 22, 23.)

Of the exemplary sovereigns, Asa and Jehoshaphat, indeed, it is recorded that they took away the high places and groves (2 Chron. xiv. 3. xv. 16. xvii. 6.); but Jehoshaphat's son and successor, Jehoram, is said to have *made high places in the mountains of Judah.* (2 Chron.

xxi. 11.) And though Joash, one of his sons, set out well, yet in the latter part of his life he was perverted by his idolatrous courtiers, who served groves and idols, to whom it appears that he gave a permission for that purpose; for, after making their obeisance, we are told *that he hearkened to them, and then they left the house of God.* (2 Chron. xxiv. 17, 18.) Nor was the reign of Amaziah the son of Joash any better, for still the people *sacrificed and burnt incense on the high places* (2 Kings xiv. 4.); and though Uzziah his son is said to have done *that which was right in the sight of God,* yet this exception appears against him, *that the high places were not removed, but the people still sacrificed there* (2 Kings xv. 3, 4.); the same observation is made of Jotham and Ahaz. (2 Chron. xxviii. 4.) But Hezekiah who succeeded him was a prince of extraordinary piety: he *removed the high places, and brake the images, and cut down the groves* (2 Kings xviii. 4.), *which his son Manasseh again built up.* (2 Kings xxi. 2.) At length good king Josiah, a prince very zealous for the true religion, utterly cleared the land from the high places and groves, and purged it from idolatry: but as the four succeeding reigns before the Babylonian captivity were very wicked, we may presume that the high places were again revived, though there is no mention of them after the reign of Josiah.[1]

II. From the preceding facts and remarks, however, we are not to conclude, that the prohibition relating to high places and groves, which extended chiefly to the more solemn acts of sacrificing there, did on any account extend to the prohibiting of other acts of devotion, particularly *prayer,* in any other place besides the temple, the high places and groves of the heathen (which were ordered to be rased) only excepted. For we learn from the Sacred Writings, that prayers are always acceptable to God in every place, when performed with that true and sincere devotion of heart, which alone gives life and vigour to our religious addresses. And therefore it was that in many places of Judæa, both before and after the Babylonian captivity, we find mention made in the Jewish and other histories of places built purposely for prayer, and resorted to only for that end, called PROSEUCHÆ or ORATORIES.

These places of worship were very common in Judæa (and it should seem in retired mountainous or elevated places) in the time of Christ; they were also numerous at Alexandria, which was at that time a large and flourishing commercial city, inhabited by vast numbers of Jews: and it appears that in heathen countries they were erected in sequestered retreats, commonly on the banks of rivers, or on the sea-shore. The proseucha or oratory at Phillippi, where *the Lord opened the heart of Lydia, that she attended unto the things which were spoken by Paul,* was *by a river side.* (Acts xvi. 13, 14, 15.)[2]

It is a question with some learned men, whether these proseuchæ were the same as the synagogues (of which an account will be found

---

[1] Home's Hist. of the Jews, vol. ii. pp. 161—166.   Croxall's Scripture Politicks, pp. 90—99.

[2] Josephus has preserved the decree of the city of Halicarnassus, permitting the Jews to erect oratories, part of which is in the following terms:—" We ordain, that the Jews who are willing, both men and women, do observe the sabbaths and perform sacred rites according to the Jewish law, and *build proseuchæ by the sea-side, according to the custom of their country ;* and if any man, whether magistrate or private person, give them any hinderance or disturbance, he shall pay a fine to the city." Ant. Jud. lib. xiv. c. 10. § 23.

in the following section), or distinct edifices from the latter. Both Josephus and Philo, to whom we may add Juvenal, appear to have considered them as synonymous; and with them agree Grotius, Ernesti, Drs. Whitby, Doddridge, and Lardner[1]; but Calmet, Drs. Prideaux and Hammond, and others, have distinguished between these two sorts of buildings, and have shown that though they were *nearly* the same, and were sometimes confounded by Philo and Josephus, yet that there was a real difference between them; the synagogues being in cities, while the proseuchæ were without the walls, in sequestered spots, and (particularly in heathen countries) were usually erected on the banks of rivers, or on the sea-shore (Acts xvi. 13.), without any covering but galleries or the shade of trees. Dr. Prideaux thinks the proseuchæ were of greater antiquity than the synagogues, and were formed by the Jews in open courts, in order that those persons who dwelt at a distance from Jerusalem might offer up their private prayers in them as they were accustomed to do in the courts of the temple or of the tabernacle. In the synagogues, he further observes, the prayers were offered up in public forms, while the proseuchæ were appropriated to private devotions: and from the oratory, where our Saviour spent a whole night in prayer, being erected on a mountain (Luke vi. 12.), it is highly probable that these proseuchæ were the same as the high places, so often mentioned in the Old Testament.[2]

---

[1] Philo de Legatione ad Caium, p. 1011.   Josephus de Vita sua, § 54.   Juvenal, Sat. iii. 14.   Grotius, Whitby, and Doddridge, on Luke vi. 12.   Ernesti Institutio Interpretis Novi Testamenti, pp. 363, 364. edit. 4ta. 1792.   Lardner's Credibility, book i. c. 3. § 3. Dr. Harwood's Introduction to the New Testament, vol. ii. pp. 171—180.

[2] Dr. Hammond on Luke vi. 12. and Acts xvi. 13—16.   Calmet's Dict. voce Proseucha. Prideaux's Connection, part. i. book vi. sub anno 444. vol. i. pp. 387—390. edit. 1720.

SECTION IV.

ON THE SYNAGOGUES.

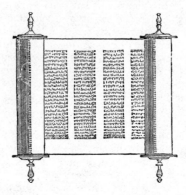

Form of a SYNAGOGUE ROLL of the Pentateuch.

I. *Nature and Origin of Synagogues. — The Synagogue of the Libertines explained.* — II. *Form of the Synagogues.* — III. *The Officers or Ministers.* — IV. *The Service performed in the Synagogues.* — V. *Ecclesiastical Power of the Synagogues.* — VI. *The Shemoneh Esreh, or Nineteen Prayers used in the Synagogue Service.*

I. THE SYNAGOGUES were buildings in which the Jews assembled for prayer, reading and hearing the Sacred Scriptures, and other instructions. Though frequently mentioned in the historical books of the New Testament, their origin is not very well known; and many learned men are of opinion that they are of recent institution.

Although sacrifices could only be offered at the holy tabernacle or temple, yet it does not appear that the Jews were restricted to any particular place for the performance of other exercises of devotion. Hence formerly, the praises of Jehovah were sung in the schools of the prophets, which the more devout Israelites seem to have frequented on sabbath-days and new moons for the purpose of instruction and prayer. (1 Sam. x. 5—11. xix. 18—24. 2 Kings iv. 23.) During the Babylonish captivity, the Jews, being deprived of the solemn ordinances of divine worship, resorted to the house of some prophet, or other holy man, who was in the practice of giving religious instruction to his own family, and of reading the Scriptures. (Compare Ezek. xiv. 1. and xx. 1. with Neh. viii. 18.) At length these domestic congregations became fixed in certain places, and a regular order of conducting divine worship was introduced. Philo[1] thinks these edifices were originally instituted by Moses: but as no mention is made of them during the time of Antiochus Epiphanes, their origin in Jerusalem is referred to the reigns of the Asmonæan princes, under whom they were

---

[1] Philo, De Vita Mosis, lib. iii. p. 685.

first erected, and were soon greatly multiplied; though in Alexandria, and other foreign places where the Jews were dispersed, they were certainly of much greater antiquity.[1] There appears to be an allusion to them in Psal. lxxiv. 4. 8.

In the time of the Maccabees, synagogues became so frequent, that they were to be found in almost every place in Judæa: but the Jews were not permitted to build one in a town, unless there were ten persons of leisure in it. Not fewer than four hundred and eighty synagogues are said to have been erected in Jerusalem, previously to its capture and destruction by the Romans. In the evangelical history we find, that wherever the Jews resided, they had one or more synagogues, constructed after those at Jerusalem: hence we find, in Acts vi. 9. synagogues belonging to the Alexandrians, the Asiatics, the Cilicians, the Libertines, and the Cyrenians, which were erected for such Jewish inhabitants of those countries or cities, as should happen to be at Jerusalem.

With regard to the synagogue of the LIBERTINES, a considerable difference of opinion exists among the learned, whether these Libertines were the children of freed men (Italian Jews or proselytes), or African Jews from the city or country called Libertus, or Libertina, near Carthage. The former opinion is supported by Grotius and Vitringa; the latter (which was first hinted by Oecumenius, a commentator in the close of the tenth century) by Professor Gerdes, Wetstein, Bishop Pearce, and Schleusner.

It is well known that the antient Romans made a distinction between the *Liberti* and the *Libertini.* The *Libertus* was one who had been a slave, and obtained his freedom [2]; the *Libertinus* was the son of a Libertus.[3] But this distinction in after ages was not strictly observed; and Libertinus also came to be used for one not born but made free, in opposition to *Ingenuus* or *one born free.*[4] Whether the *Libertini,* mentioned in this passage of the Acts, were Gentiles, who had become proselytes to Judaism, or native Jews, who having been made slaves to the Romans were afterwards set at liberty [5], and in remembrance of their captivity called themselves Libertini, and formed a synagogue by themselves, is differently conjectured by the learned. It is probable,

---

[1] Josephus, De Bell. Jud. lib. vii. c. 3. § 3.

[2] Cives Romani sunt Liberti, qui vindictâ, censu aut testamento, nullo jure impediente, manumissi sunt. Ulpian. tit. i. § 6.

[3] This appears from the following passage of Suetonius concerning Claudius, who, he says, was, ignarus temporibus Appii, et deinceps aliquamdiu Libertinos dictos, non ipsos, qui manumitterentur, sed ingenuos ex his procreatos. In vita Claudii, cap. 24. § 4. p. 78. Pitisci.

[4] Quintilian. de Institutione Oratoria, lib. 5. cap. 10. p. 246. edit. Gibson, 1693. Qui servus est, si manumittatur, fit Libertinus—Justinian. Institut. lib. i. tit. v. Libertini sunt, qui ex justa servitute manumissi sunt. Tit. iv. Ingenuus est is, qui statim ut natus est, liber est; sive ex duobus ingenuis matrimonio aditus est, sive ex libertinis duobus, sive ex altero libertino, et altero ingenuo.

[5] Of these there were great numbers at Rome. Tacitus informs us (Anal. lib. ii. cap. 85.) that four thousand Libertini, of the Jewish superstition, as he styles it, were banished at one time, by order of Tiberius, into Sardinia; and the rest commanded to quit Italy, if they did not abjure, by a certain day. See also Suetonius in vita Tiberii, cap. 36. Josephus (Antiq. lib. xviii. cap. 3. § 5. edit. Haverc.) mentions the same fact. And Philo (Legat. ad Caium. p. 785. C. edit. Colon. 1613.) speaks of a good part of the city beyond the Tiber, as inhabited by Jews, who were mostly Libertini, having been brought to Rome as captives and slaves, but, being made free by their masters, were permitted to live according to their own rites and customs.

that the Jews of Cyrene, Alexandria, &c. erected synagogues at Jerusalem at their own charge, for the use of their brethren who came from those countries, as the Danes, Swedes, &c. built churches for the use of their own countrymen in London; and that the Italian Jews did the same; and because the greatest number of them were *Libertini*, their synagogue was therefore called the synagogue of the Libertines.

In support of the second opinion above noticed, viz. that the Libertines derived their name from Libertus or Libertina, a city in Africa, it is urged that Suidas in his Lexicon, on the word Λιϐερτινος, says, that it was ονομα εθνους, a national appellative; and that the *Glossa interlinearis*, of which Nicholas de Lyra made great use in his notes, has, over the word Libertini, *e regione*, denoting that they were so styled from a country. Further, in the acts of the celebrated conference with the Donatists at Carthage, *anno* 411, there is mentioned one Victor, bishop of the church of *Libertina;* and in the acts of the Lateran council, which was held in 649, there is mention of *Januarius gratia Dei episcopus sanctæ ecclesiæ Libertinensis*, Januarius, by the grace of God, bishop of the holy church of Libertina; and therefore Fabricius in his Geographical Index of Christian Bishoprics, has placed Libertina in what was called *Africa propria*, or the proconsular province of Africa. Now, as all the other people of the several synagogues, mentioned in this passage of the Acts, are called from the places whence they came, it is probable that the Libertines were denominated in like manner; and as the Cyrenians and Alexandrians, who came from Africa, are placed next to the Libertines in that catalogue, the supporters of this opinion think it probable, that they also belonged to the same country. But we have no evidence to show that there were any natives of this place at Jerusalem, at the period referred to in the Acts of the Apostles. On the contrary, as it is well known that, only about 15 years before, great numbers of Jews, emancipated slaves, or their sons, were banished from Rome, it is most likely that the Libertines mentioned by Luke were of the latter description, especially as his account is corroborated by two Roman historians.

II. It does not appear from the New Testament that the synagogues had any peculiar FORM. The building of them was regarded as a mark of piety (Luke vii. 5.); and they were erected within or without the city, generally in an elevated place, and were distinguished from the proseuchæ by being roofed. Each of them had an altar, or rather table, on which the book of the law was spread; and on the east side there was an ark or chest, in which the volume of the law was deposited. The seats were so disposed that the people always sat with their faces towards the elders, and the place where the law was kept; and the elders sat in the opposite direction, that is to say, with their backs to the ark and their faces to the people. The seats of the latter, as being placed nearer the ark, were accounted the more holy, and hence they are in the New Testament termed the *chief seats in the synagogue;* which the Pharisees affected; and for which our Lord inveighed against them. (Matt. xxiii. 6.) A similar precedency seems to have crept into the places of worship even of the very first Christians, and hence we may account for the indignation of the apostle James (ii. 3.) against the undue preference that was given to the rich. The women were separated from the men, and sat in a gallery inclosed with lattices, so that they could distinctly see and hear all that passed in the synagogue, without themselves being exposed to view.

III. For the maintenance of good order, there were in every synagogue certain OFFICERS, whose business it was to see that all the duties of religion were decently performed therein. These were,—

1. The Αρχισυναγωγος, or *Ruler of the synagogue.* (Luke xiii. 14. Mark v. 22.) It appears from Acts xiii. 15., collated with Mark v. 22. and John vi. 59., that there were several of these rulers in a synagogue. They regulated all its concerns, and gave permission to persons to preach. They were always men advanced in age, and respectable for their learning and probity. The Jews termed them *Hacamim,* that is, *sages or wise men,* and they possessed considerable influence and authority. They were judges of thefts, and similar petty offences: and to them St. Paul is supposed to allude in 1 Cor. vi. 5., where he reproaches the Corinthian Christians with carrying their differences before the tribunals of the Gentiles, as if they had no persons among them who were capable of determining them. *Is it so,* says he, *that there is not a* WISE MAN *among you? no, not one that shall be able to judge between his brethren?* These rulers, likewise, had the power of inflicting punishment on those whom they judged to be rebellious against the law; in allusion to which circumstance Christ forewarned his disciples that they *should be scourged in the synagogues.* (Matt. x. 17.)

2. Next to the Αρχισυναγωγος, or ruler of the synagogue, was an officer, whose province it was to offer up public prayers to God for the whole congregation: he was called *Sheliach Zibbor,* or the angel of the church, because, as their messenger, he spoke to God for them. Hence also, in Rev. ii. iii. the presiding ministers of the Asiatic churches are termed angels.

3. The *Chazan* appears to have been a different officer from the *Sheliach Zibbor,* and inferior to him in dignity. He seems to have been the person, who in Luke iv. 20. is termed υπηρετης, the *minister,* and who had the charge of the sacred books.

IV. The service performed in the synagogue, on the sabbath and on other holy days, consisted of three parts, viz. prayer, reading the Scriptures, and preaching, or exposition of the Scriptures.

1. The first part of the synagogue service is *Prayer;* for the performance of which, according to Dr. Prideaux, they had liturgies, in which are all the prescribed forms of the synagogue worship. The most solemn part of these prayers are the שמונה עשרה (SHeMONeH ESReH), or the eighteen prayers, which, according to the rabbies, were composed and instituted by Ezra, in order that the Jews, whose language after the captivity was corrupted with many barbarous terms borrowed from other languages, might be able to perform their devotions in the pure language of their own country. Such is the account which Maimonides gives, out of the Gemara, of the origin of the Jewish liturgies; and the eighteen collects, in particular, are mentioned in the Mishna. However, some better evidence than that of the talmudical rabbies is requisite, in order to prove their liturgies to be of so high an antiquity; especially since some of their prayers, as Dr. Prideaux acknowledges, seem to have been composed after the destruction of Jerusalem, and to have reference to it. It is evident they were composed when there was neither temple nor sacrifice; since the seventeenth

collect prays, that God would restore his worship to the inner part of his house, and make haste, with fervour and love, to accept the burnt sacrifices of Israel[1], &c. They could not, therefore, be the composition of Ezra, who did not receive his commission from Artaxerxes to go to Judæa, till more than fifty years after the second temple was built, and its worship restored. The probability is, that the forms of prayer for the synagogue worship were at first very few, and that *some were in use in the time of Jesus Christ*, the number of which was subsequently increased. To the eighteen prayers above mentioned, another was added, a short time before the destruction of the second temple, by Rabbi Gamaliel, or, according to some writers, by Rabbi Samuel, one of his scholars. It is directed against apostates and heretics, appellations which the Jews liberally employ to designate all Christians, whether of Jewish or of Gentile descent. This additional prayer is now inserted as the twelfth, and the number is nineteen. They are required to be said by all Jews without exception, who are of age, three times every day, either in public, at the synagogue, or at their own houses, or wherever they may happen to be. As some readers may be curious to see them, they are subjoined, at the end of this section.[2]

2. The second part of this synagogue service is the *Reading of the Scriptures*, which is of three sorts, — *the Kirioth-Shema*, the reading of the whole law of Moses, and portions out of the prophets, and the Hagiographa or holy writings.

(1.) The *Kirioth-Shema* consists of three portions of Scripture, viz. Deut. vi. 6—9. Deut. xi. 13—21. Numb. xv. 37—41. As the first of these portions commences with the word *shema*, that is, *hear*, they are collectively termed the Shema, and the reading of them is called *kirioth-shema*, or the reading of the Shema. This reading or recital is preceded and followed by several prayers and benedictions; and, next to the saying of the nineteen prayers above noticed, is the most solemn part of the religious service of the Jews; who, believing the commands in Deut. vi. 7. and xi. 19. to be of perpetual obligation, repeat the Shema daily, every morning and evening.

(2.) The *Law* was divided into fifty-three, according to the Masorets, or, according to others, fifty-four *Paraschioth* or sections: for the Jewish year consisted of twelve lunar months, alternately of twenty-nine or thirty days, that is, of fifty weeks and four days. The Jews, therefore, in their division of the law into *Paraschioth* or sections, had a respect to their intercalary year, which was every second or third, and consisted of thirteen months; so that the whole law was read over this year, allotting one *Paraschioth* or section to every Sabbath; and in common years they reduced the fifty-three or fifty-four sections to the number of the fifty Sabbaths, by reading two shorter ones together, as often as there was occasion. They began the course of

---

[1] The fifth, tenth, eleventh, and fourteenth collects have the same allusion and reference as the seventeenth. See the original prayers in Maimonides de Ordine Precum, or in Vitringa, (de Synag. vetere, lib. iii. part ii. cap. 14. pp. 1033—1038.) who observes that the Talmudists will have the seventeenth collect, which prays for the restoration of the temple worship, (reduc ministerium Leviticum in Adytum Domus tuæ, as he translates it,) to have been usually recited by the king in the temple at the feast of tabernacles; which is such an absurdity that it confutes itself, and shows how little the Jewish traditions concerning the antiquity and use of their liturgies are to be depended upon.

[2] See pp. 260—263. *infrà.*

reading the first Sabbath after the feast of tabernacles; or rather, indeed, on the Sabbath day before that, when they finished the last course of reading, they also made a beginning of the new course; that so, as the rabbies say, the devil might not accuse them to God of being weary of reading his law.

(3.) The portions selected out of the prophetical writings are termed *Haphtoroth.* When Antiochus Epiphanes conquered the Jews about the year 163 before the Christian æra, he prohibited the public reading of the law in the synagogues, on pain of death. The Jews, in order that they might not be wholly deprived of the word of God, selected from other parts of the Sacred Writings *fifty-four* portions, which were termed HAPHTORAS, חפטורת (HαPHTOROTH), from פטר (PαTαR), he *dismissed, let loose, opened* — for though the Law was *dismissed* from their synagogues, and was *closed* to them by the edict of this persecuting king, yet the *prophetic writings,* not being under the *interdict,* were left *open;* and therefore they used them in place of the others. It was from this custom of the Jews, that the primitive Christians adopted theirs, of reading a lesson every Sabbath out of the Old and New Testaments. The following tables exhibit the paraschioth or sections of the law, and the haphtoroth or sections of the prophets (which were substituted for the former), as they have been read together ever since the days of the Asmonæans or Maccabees, and as they continue to be read in the various synagogues belonging to the English, Portuguese, Italian, Dutch, and German Jews.

A GENERAL VIEW OF ALL THE SECTIONS OF THE LAW, AND
SYNAGOGUES FOR EVERY

PARASCHIOTH, or *Sections* of the LAW.

SECT.

GENESIS.

i.	ברשית Bereshith,	- - -	i. 1. to vi. 8.
ii.	תלרות נח Toledoth noach,	-	vi. 9. to xi. 32.
iii.	לך לך Lec leca,	- -	xii. 1. to xvii. 27.
iv.	וירא Vaiyera,	- -	xviii. 1. to xxii. 24.
v.	חייה שרה Chaiyeh Sarah,	-	xxiii. 1. to xxv. 18.
vi.	תלרת Toledoth,	- - -	xxv. 19. to xxviii. 9.
vii.	ויצא Vaiyetse,	- - -	xxviii. 10. to xxxii. 3.
viii.	וישלח Vaiyishlach,	- -	xxxii. 4. to xxxvi. 43.
ix.	וישב Vaiyesheb,	- - -	xxxvii. 1. to xl. 23.
x.	מקץ Mikkets,	- - -	xli. 1. to xliv. 17.
xi.	ויגש Vaiyiggash,	- -	xliv. 18. to xlvii. 27.
xii.	ויחי Vayechei,	- - -	xlvii. 28. to l. 26.

EXODUS.

xiii.	שמות Shemoth,	- -	i. 1. to vi. 1.
xiv.	וארה Vaera,	- -	vi. 2. to ix. 35.
xv.	בא אל פרעה Bo el Paraôh,	-	x. 1. to xiii. 16.
xvi.	בשלח Besholach,	-	xiii. 17. to xvii. 16.
xvii.	יתרו Yithro,	-	xviii. 1. to xx. 26.
xviii.	משפטים Mishpatim,	-	xxi. 1. to xxiv. 18.
xix.	תרומה Terumah,	-	xxv. 1. to xxvii. 19.
xx.	תצוה Tetsaveh,	-	xxvii. 20. to xxx. 10.
xxi.	כי תשא Kei tissa,	-	xxx. 11. to xxxiv. 35.
xxii.	ויקהל Vaiyakhel,	-	xxxv. 1. to xxxviii. 20.
xxiii.	פקודי Pekudey,	-	xxxviii. 21. to xl. 38.

LEVITICUS.

xxiv.	ויקרא Vaiyikra,	- -	i. 1. to vi. 7.
xxv.	ויקרא צו Vaiyikra Tsau,	-	vi. 8. to viii. 36.
xxvi.	שמיני Shemini,	-	ix. 1. to xi. 47.
xxvii.	תזריע Tazriâ,	-	xii. 1. to xiii. 59.
xxviii.	מצרע Metsorâ,	-	xiv. 1. to xv. 33.
xxix.	אחרי מות Acharey Moth,	-	xvi. 1. to xviii. 30.
xxx.	קדשים Kedushim,	-	xix. 1. to xx. 27.
xxxi.	אמר Emor,	-	xxi. 1. to xxiv. 23.
xxxii.	בהר סיני Behar Sinai,	-	xxv. 1. to xxvi. 2.
xxxiii.	בחקתי Bechukkotai,	-	xxvi. 3. to xxvii. 34.

NUMBERS.

xxxiv.	במדבר Bemidbar,	-	i. 1. to iv. 20.
xxxv.	נשא Naso,	-	iv. 21. to vii. 89.
xxxvi.	בהעלתך Behaâlotica,	-	viii. 1. to xii. 16.
xxxvii.	שלח Shelach,	-	xiii. 1. to xv. 41.
xxxviii.	קרח Korach,	-	xvi. 1. to xviii. 32.
xxxix.	חקת Chukkath,	-	xix. 1. to xxii. 1.
xl.	בלק Balak,	-	xxii. 2. to xxv. 9.
xli.	פינחס Pinchas,	-	xxv. 10. to xxx. 1.
xlii.	מטות Mattoth,	-	xxx. 2. to xxxii. 42.
xliii.	מסעי Masêy,	-	xxxiii. 1. to xxxvi. 13.

DEUTERONOMY.

xliv.	דברים Debarim,	-	i. 1. to iii. 22.
xlv.	ואתחנן Vaethchanan,	-	iii. 23. to vii. 11.
xlvi.	עקב Ekeb,	-	vii. 12. to xi. 25.
xlvii.	ראה Reeh,	-	xi. 26. to xvi. 17.
xlviii.	שפטים Shophetim,	-	xvi. 18. to xxi. 9.
xlix.	תצא Tetse,	-	xxi. 10. to xxv. 19.
l.	תבוא Tabua,	-	xxvi. 1. to xxix. 8.
li.	נצבים Nitsabim,	-	xxix. 9. to xxx. 20.
lii.	וילך Vaiyelec,	-	xxxi. 1. to xxxi. 30.
liii.	האזינו Haazinu,	-	xxxii. 1. to xxxii. 52.
liv.	וזות הברכה Vezot Habaracah,	-	xxxiii. 1. to xxxiv. 12.

SECTIONS OF THE PROPHETS, AS READ IN THE DIFFERENT JEWISH
SABBATH OF THE YEAR.

HAPHTOROTH, or *Sections* of the PROPHETS.

Portuguese and Italian Jews.					*German and Dutch Jews.*
Isa. xlii. 5—21.					Isa. xlii. 5—25. xliii. 10.
Isa. liv. 1—10.	-	-	-	-	Isa. liv. 1—17. lv. 1—5.
Isa. xl. 27—31. xli. 1—16.		-	-	-	Ditto.
2 Kings iv. 1—23.	-		-	-	2 Kings iv. 1—37.
1 Kings i. 1—31.	-		-	-	Ditto.
Mal. i. 1—14. ii. 1—7		-	-	-	Ditto.
Hos. xi. 7—12. xii. 1—11.		-		-	Ditto.
Obad. i. 1—21.	-		-	-	Hos. xii. 12—14. xiii. 1—16.
Amos ii. 1—16. iii. 1—8			-	-	Ditto.
1 Kings iii. 15—28. iv. 1.		-	-	-	Ditto.
Ezek. xxxvii. 15—28.	-		-	-	Ditto.
1 Kings ii. 1—12.	-		-	-	Ditto.
Jer. i. 1—19. ii. 1—3.		-	-	-	Isa. xxvii. 6. to xxix. 23.
Ezek. xxviii. 25. to xxix. 21.	-		-	-	Ditto.
Jer. xlvi. 13—28.	-		-	-	Ditto.
Judg. v. 1—31.	-		-	-	Judg. iv. 4. to v. 1—31.
Isa. vi. 1—31.		-		-	Isa. vi. 1—13. vii. 1—6. ix. 6, 7.
Jer. xxxiv. 8—22. and xxxiii. 25, 26.		-	-		Ditto.
1 Kings v. 12—18. vi. 1—13.		-	-		Ditto.
Ezek. xliii. 10—27.	-		-		1 Kings xviii. 1—39.
1 Kings xviii. 20—39.		-	-		1 Kings vii. 40—50.
1 Kings vii. 13—26.		-	-		1 Kings vii. 51. viii. 1—21.
1 Kings vii. 40—50.		-	-		
Isa. xliii. 21—28. xliv. 1—25.		-	-		Ditto.
Jer. vii. 21—34. viii. 1—3. ix. 23, 24.		-	-		Ditto.
2 Sam. vi. 1—19.	-		-	-	2 Sam. vi. 1—23. vii. 1—17.
2 Kings iv. 42—44. v. 1—19.	-		-	-	Ditto.
2 Kings vii. 3—20.	-		-	-	Ditto.
Amos ix. 7—15.	-		-	-	Ezek. xxii. 1—19.
Ezek. xx. 2—20.	-		-	-	Amos ix. 7—15.
Ezek. xliv. 15—31.		-	-	-	Ditto.
Jer. xxxii. 6—27.	-		-	-	Ditto.
Jer. xvi. 19—21. xvii. 1—14.		-	-	-	Ditto.
Hos. i. 10, 11. ii. 1—20.		-	-	-	Ditto.
Judg. xiii. 2—25.	-		-	-	Ditto.
Zech. ii. 10—13. iii. 1—13. iv. 1—7.		-	-	-	Ditto.
Josh. ii. 1—24.	-		-	-	Amos ix. 7—15.
1 Sam. xi. 14, 15. xii. 1—22.	-		-	-	Ditto.
Judg. xi. 1—33.	-		-	-	Ditto.
Micah v. 7—15. vi. 1—8		-	-	-	Ditto.
1 Kings xx. 46. xix. 1—21.		-	-	-	Ditto.
Jer. i. 1—19. ii. 1—3.		-	-	-	Ditto.
Jer. ii. 4—28. iv. 1, 2.		-	-	-	Jer. ii. 4—28. iii. 4.
Isa. i. 1—27.	-		-	-	Ditto.
xl. 1—26.	-		-	-	Ditto.
xlix. 14—26. l. 1—3.		-	-	-	Ditto.
liv. 11—17. lv. 1—5.		-	-	-	Ditto.
li. 12—23. lii. 1—12.		-	-	-	Ditto.
liv. 1—10.	-		-	-	Ditto.
lx. 1—22.	-		-	-	Ditto.
lxi. 10, 11. lxii. 1—12. lxiii. 1—9.		-		-	Isa. lv. 6—13. lvi. 1—8.
Hos. xiv. 1—9. Mic. vii. 18—20.					
2 Sam. xxii. 1—51. Some say Ezek. xvii. 22—24.					Hos. xiv. 1—9. Joel ii. 1—27.[1]
xviii. 1—32.	-		-	-	
Josh. i. 1—18. Eccles. i—xii. inclusive.			-		Ditto.[2]

---

[1] It is a circumstance highly deserving of notice, that the celebrated prophecy, quoted by the apostle Peter on the day of Pentecost from the prophet Joel (ii. 28—32.) forms a part of the Pentecostal service of the Karaite Jews in the Crimea, "Such, however, is the fact; and may we not conclude, from the pertinacity with which this antient sect have adhered to their primitive institutions, that the same coincidence took place in the apostolic age?" Dr. Henderson's Biblical Researches, &c. p. 326.

[2] The above tables are copied from Dr. A. Clarke's Commentary on Deut. xxxiv., who states that he has in general followed the divisions in the best Masoretic Bibles, from which our common English Bibles in some cases will be found to vary a little. On the above

In the synagogues of the Hellenists or Greek Jews, the law was always read in the Alexandrian or Greek version[1] : but in those of the native Jews, the law was always read in Hebrew; whence it became necessary, as soon as that language ceased to be vernacular among the Jews, to establish an interpreter, by whom the Jewish Scriptures were expounded in the Chaldee dialect, which was spoken by them after the return from the Babylonian captivity.[2] The doctor or reader, therefore, having the interpreter always by him, softly whispered in his ears what he said, and this interpreter repeated aloud to the people what had thus been communicated to him. To this custom our Saviour is supposed to have alluded when he said to his disciples, *What ye hear in the ear, that preach ye upon the housetops.* (Matt. x. 27.)[3]

3. The third and last part of the synagogue service is, *Exposition of the Scriptures*, and *Preaching to the people from them.* The first was performed *at* the time of reading them, and the other *after* the reading of the law and the prophets. In Luke iv. 15—22. we have an account of the service of the synagogue in the time of Christ; from which it appears that he taught the Jews in both these ways : *And he taught in their synagogues, being glorified of all. And he came to Nazareth, where he had been brought up ; and as his custom was, he went into the synagogue on the Sabbath-day, and stood up for to read. And there was delivered unto him the book of the prophet Esaias : and when he had unrolled the volume*[4] *he found the place where it was written, " The Spirit of the Lord is upon me, because he hath anointed me to preach the Gospel to the poor ; he hath sent me to heal the broken-hearted, to preach deliverance to the captives, and recovering of sight to the blind ; to set at liberty them that are bruised ; to preach the acceptable year of the Lord !" And he folded the volume*[5] *and he gave it again to the minister and sat down: and the eyes of all them that were in the synagogue were fastened on him. And he began to say unto them : This day is the Scripture fulfilled in your ears. And all bare him witness, and wondered at the gracious words that proceeded out of his mouth.*

From this passage we learn, that when Jesus Christ came to Nazareth, his own city, he was called out, as a member of that synagogue, to read the haphtorah, that is, the section or lesson out of the prophets for that day; which appears to have been the fifty-first haphtorah, and to have commenced with the *first* verse of Isa. lxi. and not with the tenth, as in the table above given. "Have the Jews," asks an eminent

---

tables, Dr. Clarke remarks, that though the Jews are agreed in the sections of the law that are read every sabbath ; yet they are not agreed in the hapthoroth, or sections from the prophets; as it appears above, that the Dutch and German Jews differ in several cases from the Italian and Portuguese ; and there are some slighter variations besides those above, which he has not noticed.   [1] Tertulliani Apologia, c. 18.

[2] From this practice originated the Chaldee-Paraphrases, of which an account has been given in Vol. II. pp. 198—203.

[3] Dr. Lightfoot's Horæ Hebraicæ, on Matt. x. 27.

[4] " Αναπτυξας το βιβλιον. This word signifies to *unfold, unroll.* The books of the antients were written on parchment and rolled up. Hence the word *volume.* Αλλ' ουκ αναπτυξαντες αυτους και τω χειρε περιβαλοντες αλληλοις; Why do we not unfold our arms, and clasp each other in them? Dion. Halicarn. lib. vi. p. 392. Hudson. Την επιστολην ΑΝΑΠΤΥΞΑΣ, unfolding the letter. Josephus de vitâ sua, p. 21. Havercamp. Γραψας ες βιβλιον τα εβουλετο, ἀλιην των Περσων εποιησατο, μετα δε, ΑΝΑΠΤΥΞΑΣ ΤΟ ΒΙΒΛΙΟΝ." [the very expression of the evangelist]. Herodotus, lib. i. c. 125. tom. i. p. 158. edit. Oxon. 1809. Dr. Harwood's Introduction, vol. ii. p. 181.   [5] Πτυξας το βιβλιον.

commentator, "altered this haphtorah, knowing the use which our blessed Lord made of it among their ancestors?"[1] Further he stood up (as it was customary, at least for the officiating minister to do out of reverence for the word of God) to read the Scriptures; and unrolled the manuscript until he came to the lesson appointed for that day; which having read he rolled it up again, and gave it to the proper officer; and then he sat down and expounded it, agreeably to the usage of the Jews.[2] But when Christ entered any synagogue of which he was not a member, (as it appears from Luke iv. 16. he always did on every sabbath-day, wherever he was,) he taught the people in sermons after the law and the prophets had been read. The Sacred Writings, used to this day in all the Jewish synagogues, are written on skins of parchment or vellum, and (like the antient copies) rolled on two rollers, beginning at each end: so that, in reading from right to left, they roll off with the *left*, while they roll *on* with the *right* hand.[3] The vignette, at the head of this section, will convey some idea of the manner in which the Synagogue Rolls are unrolled. It is taken from the original and very valuable manuscript in the British Museum, which is described in Vol. II. page 77.

"It should seem also, at least in foreign countries where places of worship were established, that when strangers, who were Jews, arrived at such towns, and went to offer their devotions, it was usual for the presidents of the synagogue, after the appointed portion out of the law and the prophets was read, to send a servant to them, and in a very respectful manner to request that if they could impart any thing that might contribute to the religious instruction and edification of the audience, they would deliver it. This token of respect and politeness shown to strangers, appears from the following passage in the Acts of the Apostles. (Acts xiii. 14, 15.) When Paul and his companions, on their arrival at Antioch in Pisidia, went into the Jewish synagogue on the sabbath-day, and sat down after the reading of the law and the prophets, the rulers of the synagogue sent to them, saying, *Men and brethren, if ye have any word of exhortation for the people, say on. Upon which Paul stood up, and beckoning with his hand said, Men of Israel, and ye that fear God, give audience.*"[4]

The synagogues, however, were not only places set apart for prayer; they were also schools where youth were instructed. The sages (for so were the teachers called) sat upon elevated benches, while the pupils stood at their feet or before them[5]; which circumstance explains

---

[1] Dr. A. Clarke, on Deut. xxxiv.

[2] In like manner, according to the custom of their public instructors, we find our Saviour *sitting down* (Matt. v. 1.) before he began to deliver his sermon on the mount to the assembled multitudes; and upon another occasion *sitting down*, and out of the ship teaching the people who were collected on the shore. (Matt. xiii. 1.) So also it is said of the scribes, who were the Jewish clergy, that they *sat* (Matt. xxiii. 2.) in *Moses' chair : whatever therefore they bid you observe, that observe and do, but do not after their works, for they say and do not.*

[3] Dr. A. Clarke, on Luke vi. 17.

[4] Dr. Harwood's Introd. vol. ii. p. 182.

[5] Fleury, Lamy, and other eminent critics, have supposed that the Jewish youth *sat* on low seats or on the ground, at the feet of their preceptors, who occupied a lofty chair; but Vitringa has shown, from Jewish authority, that the disciples of the rabbins *stood* before them in the manner above represented. See his treatise de Synag. Vet. lib. i. p. 1. c. 7. Kypke (Observ. Sacræ, in Nov. Fœd. Libros, vol. ii. pp. 114, 115.) has collected a variety of passages from Greek writers, to show that the expression παρα τους ποδας *at the feet*, is equivalent to πλησιον, *near* or *before*.

St. Paul's meaning (Acts xxii. 3.) when he says that he was *brought up* AT THE FEET *of* Gamaliel.

V. Those who had been guilty of any notorious crime, or were otherwise thought unworthy, were cast out of these synagogues, that is, excommunicated, and excluded from partaking with the rest in the public prayers and religious offices there performed; so that they were looked upon as mere Heathens, and shut out from all benefit of the Jewish religion, which exclusion was esteemed scandalous. We are told that the Jews came to a resolution, that *whoever confessed that Jesus was the Christ, he should be put out of the synagogue.* (John ix. 22.) And, therefore, when the blind man, who had been restored to sight, persisted in confessing that he believed the person who had been able to work such a miracle could not have done it, if *he were not of God, they cast him out.* (ver. 33, 34.)[1]

VI. The following are the *Shemoneh Esreh,* or nineteen prayers of the Jews, referred to in page 254. as translated by Dr. Prideaux. That which was formerly the *nineteenth* is now the *twelfth* in the order in which they stand in the Jewish liturgies. The first or *precatory* part of each article was pronounced by the priest, and the last or *eucharistical* part was the response of the people.

" 1. Blessed be thou, O LORD our GOD, the GOD of our fathers, the GOD of Abraham, the GOD of Isaac, the GOD of Jacob, the great GOD, powerful and tremendous, the high GOD, bountifully dispensing benefits, the creator and possessor of the universe, who rememberest the good deeds of our fathers, and in thy love sendest a Redeemer to those who are descended from them, for thy name's sake, O King our LORD and helper, our Saviour and our shield. — *Blessed art thou, O LORD, who art the shield of Abraham!*

" 2. Thou, O LORD, art powerful for ever; thou raisest the dead to life, and art mighty to save; thou sendest down the dew, stillest the winds, and makest the rain to come down upon the earth, and sustainest with thy beneficence all that are therein; and of thy abundant mercy makest the dead again to live. Thou raisest up those who fall; thou healest the sick, thou loosest them who are bound, and makest good thy word of truth to those who sleep in the dust. Who is to be compared to thee, O thou LORD of might! and who is like unto thee, O our King, who killest and makest alive, and makest salvation to spring as the grass in the field! Thou art faithful to make the dead to rise again to life. — *Blessed art thou, O LORD, who raisest the dead again to life!*

" 3. Thou art holy, and thy name is holy, and thy saints do praise thee every day. Selah. For a great king and a holy art thou, O GOD. — *Blessed art thou, O LORD GOD, most holy!*

---

[1] The preceding account of the Jewish Synagogues has been compiled from Lamy's Apparatus Biblicus, vol. ii. pp. 219—221. Prideaux's Connections, (book vi. sub anno 444.) vol. i. pp. 374—391. Fleury's Manners of the Israelites by Dr. Clarke, pp. 336—338. Pictet, Antiq. Judaiques, pp. 12—14. (Theol. Chret. tom. iii.) Schulzii Archæol. Hebr. pp. 225, 226. Reland's Antiq. Hebr. part i. c. 10. pp. 126—140. Ikenii Antiq. Hebr. part i. c. 9. pp. 100—105. Schachtii Animadversiones ad Ikenii Antiq. Hebr. pp. 452 —470. Lardner's Credibility, book i. c 9. § 6. Pritii Introd. ad Nov. Test. pp. 447. 595—608. ; and Dr. Jennings's Jewish Antiquities, book ii. c. 2. Pareau, Antiq. Hebr. pp. 204—208. Beausobre's and L'Enfant's Introd. Bp. Watson's Theol. Tracts, pp. 158 —169. On the synagogue-worship of the modern Jews, see Mr. Allen's Modern Judaism, pp. 319—354.

" 4. Thou of thy mercy givest knowledge unto men, and teachest them understanding: give graciously unto us knowledge, wisdom, and understanding. — *Blessed art thou, O LORD, who graciously givest knowledge unto men !*

" 5. Bring us back, O our Father, to the observance of thy law, and make us to adhere to thy precepts, and do thou, O our King, draw us near to thy worship, and convert us to thee by perfect repentance in thy presence. — *Blessed art thou, O LORD, who vouchsafest to receive us by repentance !*

" 6. Be thou merciful unto us, O our Father: for we have sinned: pardon us, O our King, for we have transgressed against thee. For thou art a God, good and ready to pardon. — *Blessed art thou, O LORD most gracious, who multipliest thy mercies in the forgiveness of sins !*

" 7. Look, we beseech thee, upon our afflictions. Be thou on our side in all our contentions, and plead thou our cause in all our litigations; and make haste to redeem us with a perfect redemption for thy name's sake. For thou art our GOD, our King, and a strong Redeemer. — *Blessed art thou, O LORD, the Redeemer of Israel !*

" 8. Heal us, O LORD our GOD, and we shall be healed; save us, and we shall be saved. For thou art our praise. Bring unto us sound health, and a perfect remedy for all our infirmities, and for all our griefs, and for all our wounds. For thou art a GOD who healest and art merciful. — *Blessed art thou, O LORD our GOD, who curest the diseases of thy people Israel !*

" 9. Bless us, O LORD our GOD, in every work of our hands, and bless unto us the seasons of the year, and give us the dew and the rain to be a blessing unto us, upon the face of all our land, and satiate the world with thy blessings, and send down moisture upon every part of the earth that is habitable. — *Blessed art thou, O LORD, who givest thy blessing to the years !*

" 10. Gather us together by the sound of the great trumpet, to the enjoyment of our liberty; and lift up thy ensign to call together all the captivity, from the four quarters of the earth into our own land.— *Blessed art thou, O LORD, who gatherest together the exiles of the people of Israel !*

" 11. Restore unto us our judges as at the first, and our counsellors as at the beginning; and remove far from us affliction and trouble, and do thou only reign over us in benignity, and in mercy, and in righteousness, and in justice. — *Blessed art thou, O LORD our king, who lovest righteousness and justice !*

" 12. [1] Let there be no hope to them, who apostatise from the true religion; and let heretics, how many soever they be, all perish as in a moment. And let [2] the kingdom of pride be speedily rooted out and broken in our days. — *Blessed art thou, O LORD our GOD, who destroyest the wicked, and bringest down the proud !* [3]

---

[1] This is the prayer which was added by Rabbi Gamaliel against the Christians, or as others say by Rabbi Samuel the little, who was one of his scholars.

[2] The Roman empire.

[3] The twelfth prayer, as now used by the Jews, varies considerably from that above given. In the Prayer Book of the *German* and *Polish* Jews, it stands thus: — " O let the slanderers have no hope, all the wicked be annihilated speedily, and all the tyrants be cut off quickly ; humble thou them quickly in our days.—*Blessed art thou, O Lord, who destroyest*

"13. Upon the pious and the just, and upon [1] the proselytes of justice, and upon the remnant of thy people of the house of Israel, let thy mercies be moved, O Lord our God, and give a good reward unto all who faithfully put their trust in thy name; and grant us our portion with them, and for ever let us not be ashamed, for we put our trust in thee. — *Blessed art thou, O Lord, who art the support and confidence of the just!*

"14. Dwell thou in the midst of Jerusalem, thy city, as thou hast promised: build it with a building to last for ever, and do this speedily even in our days. — *Blessed art thou, O Lord, who buildest Jerusalem!*

"15. Make the offspring of David thy servant speedily to grow up, and flourish; and let our horn be exalted in thy salvation. For we hope for thy salvation every day. — *Blessed art thou, O Lord, who makest the horn of our salvation to flourish!*

"16. Hear our voice, O Lord our God, most merciful Father, pardon and have mercy upon us, and accept of our prayers with thy mercy and favour, and send us not away from thy presence, O our king. For thou hearest with mercy the prayer of thy people Israel.— *Blessed art thou, O Lord, who hearest prayer!*

"17. Be thou well pleased, O Lord our God, with thy people Israel; and have regard unto their prayers; restore thy worship to [2] the inner part of thy house, and make haste with favour and love to accept of the burnt sacrifices of Israel, and their prayers; and let the worship of Israel thy people be continually well pleasing unto thee.— *Blessed art thou, O Lord, who restorest thy divine presence to Zion!*

"18. We will give thanks unto thee with praise. For thou art the Lord our God, the God of our fathers, for ever and ever. Thou art our rock, and the rock of our life, and the shield of our salvation. To all generations will we give thanks unto thee, and declare thy praise, because of our life which is always in thy hands, and because of thy signs, which are every day with us, and because of thy wonders, and marvellous loving-kindness, which are morning, and evening, and night before us. Thou art good, for thy mercies are not consumed; thou art merciful, for thy loving kindnesses fail not. For ever we hope in thee. And for all these mercies be thy name, O king, blessed and exalted, and lifted up on high for ever and ever; and let all that live give thanks unto thee. Selah. And let them in truth and sincerity praise thy name, O God of our salvation, and our help. Selah. — *Blessed art thou, O Lord, whose name is good, and to whom it is fitting always to give praise!*

"19. Give peace, beneficence, and benediction, grace, benignity,

---

enemies and humblest tyrants!" In the Prayer Book of the Spanish and Portuguese Jews, this prayer runs thus:—" Let slanderers have no hope, and all presumptuous apostates perish as in a moment; and may thine enemies, and those who hate thee, be suddenly cut off, and all those who act wickedly be suddenly broken, consumed, and rooted out; and humble thou them speedily in our days.—*Blessed art thou, O Lord, who destroyest the enemies and humblest the proud!*" Allen's Modern Judaism, p. 329.

[1] Concerning these supposed proselytes of justice, see p. 266. *infrà.*

[2] *i. e.* The Adytum Templi, which in the Temple of Jerusalem was the holy of holies, into which none ever entered but the high priest once a year, on the great day of expiation. From this place, after the Babylonish captivity, were wanting the ark, the mercy-seat, the Shechinah of the divine presence, and the Urim and Thummim, which causing an imperfection in their worship in respect of what it was formerly, a restoration of them seems to be the subject of this petition.

and mercy unto us, and to Israel thy people. Bless us, our Father, even all of us together as one man, with the light of thy countenance. For in the light of thy countenance hast thou given unto us, O Lord our God, the law of life, and love, and benignity, and righteousness, and blessing, and mercy, and life, and peace. And let it seem good in thine eyes, to bless thy people Israel with thy peace at all times, and in every moment. — *Blessed art thou, O Lord, who blessest thy people Israel with peace!* Amen."

CHAPTER II.

SACRED PERSONS.

SECTION I.[1]

OF THE JEWISH CHURCH AND ITS MEMBERS.

I. *The whole Nation accounted holy.*—II. *Members of the Jewish Church; Hebrews of the Hebrews.*—III. *Proselytes.*—IV. *Jews of the Dispersion.* — V. *Hellenists.* — VI. *The Libertines.* — VII. *Devout Men.* — VIII. *Circumcision.*

I. JEHOVAH, in his infinite wisdom and goodness, having been pleased to prefer the posterity of Abraham, Isaac, and Jacob, before every other nation, and to select them from every other people, for the purposes of imparting to them the revelation of his will, and of preserving the knowledge and worship of the true God; He is thence said to have chosen them, and they are in many passages of Scripture represented as his chosen and elect people.[2] And because they were by the will of God set apart, and appropriated in a special manner to his honour and obedience, and furnished with extraordinary motives to holiness, God is therefore said to have sanctified them. (Lev. xx. 8. xxi. 8. xxii. 9. 16. 32.) For these reasons they are termed a HOLY NATION, a kingdom of priests, and also saints[3]; and their covenant relation to God is urged upon them as a motive to holiness of heart and practice. (Lev. xix. 2. xx. 7, 8. 26. xi. 45. Exod. xxii. 31.) But the Jews of later times becoming proud of these titles, and of their ecclesiastical privileges, extended their charity only to those of their

---

[1] This section is principally derived from Schulzii Archæologia Hebraica, lib. ii. c. 1. de Ecclesia Judaica ejusque Membris; together with Beausobre and L'Enfant's Introd. to the New Test. (Bishop Watson's Coll. of Tracts, vol. iii. pp. 205, 206.) Ikenii Antiq. pp. 343—347. Stosch. Compend. Archæol. Œconomicæ Nov. Test. §§ 32—36. Edwards on the Authority, &c. of Scripture, vol. ii. pp. 313—330. Alber, Inst. Herm. Vet. Test. tom. i. pp. 181—186. ; Carpzovii Antiq. Hebr. Gentis, pp. 39—50. ; Jennings's Jewish Antiquities, book i. ch. 3. Mr. Allen has given an interesting account of the mode of circumcision that obtains among the Jews of the present time in his " Modern Judaism," pp. 283—296.

[2] Compare Deut. iv. 37. vii. 6. x. 15. 1 Kings viii. 22. *et seq.* 1 Chron. xvi. 13. Psal. cv. 6. xxxiii. 12. cv. 43. cvi. 5. cxxxv. 4. Isa. xli. 8, 9. xliii. 20. xliv. 1, 2. xlv. 4. and Ezek. xx. 5.

[3] Compare Exod. xix. 6. Lev. xi. 44, 45. xix. 2. xx. 26. Deut. vii. 6. xiv. 2. 21. xxvi. 19. xxviii. 9. xxxiii. 3. 2 Chron. vi. 41. Psal. xxxiv. 9. l. 5. 7. lxxix. 2. cxxxii. 9. cxlviii. 14.

own faith; while towards the rest of mankind they cherished a sullen and inveterate hatred, accounting them to be profane persons and sinners.[1] This relative or imputed holiness of the Jews as a covenant people, separated and consecrated to the worship of the true God, was perpetual (in other words it was to subsist until the institution of the Gospel dispensation); although the Jews were often extremely corrupt in their manners, as the numerous denunciations of the prophets sufficiently indicate. Hence some of the rabbinical writers call the most wicked kings of Israel and Judah holy,—holy, or righteous, and Israelite, being with them convertible terms (compare Wisd. x. 15. 17. 20. xviii. 1. 7. 9. 20.); and in the time of our Lord the Jews held the preposterous notion, that though they should continue in their sins, yet, because they were the offspring of Abraham, God would not impute their sins to them.[2]

The Apostles being Jews by birth, though they wrote in Greek, have retained their national idiom, and have borrowed the Old Testament phraseology, which they have applied to Christians, in order to convey to them accurate ideas of the magnitude of God's love to them in Christ. Thus the Apostles not only call them disciples and brethren, that is, friends united in the same profession of faith by bonds equally close as those of brothers, *having one Lord, one faith, one baptism*, but, because all true Christians are by the will of God set apart and appropriated in an especial manner to his honour, service, and obedience, and are furnished with extraordinary helps and motives to holiness, they are, therefore, said to be *sanctified* (1 Cor. i. 2. vi. 11. Heb. ii. 11. x. 29. Jude 1.); and are further, styled *holy, holy brethren, a holy nation* and *saints*.[3]

II. The first MEMBERS OF THE JEWISH CHURCH were the immediate descendants of Abraham by Isaac and Jacob, whom God, having delivered from their oppressive bondage in Egypt, chose for himself to be his peculiar people, and their direct issue, without any intermixture of Gentile blood or language. These are termed by St. Paul *Hebrews of the Hebrews* (Phil. iii. 5.), as opposed to the *Hellenistic Jews*, or those who lived among the Greeks, whose language they spoke, and who were called *Hellenists*. (Acts vi. 1. ix. 29. xi. 20.) Many of the latter were descended from parents, *one* of whom only was a Jew. Of this description was Timothy. (Acts xvi. 1.) Those who were born in Judæa, of parents rightly descended from Abraham, and who received their education in Judæa, spoke the language of their forefathers, and were thoroughly instructed in the learning and literature of the Jews, were reckoned more honourable than the Hellenists[4]; and, to mark the excellence of their lineage and language,

---

[1] Apud ipsos fides obstinata, misericordia in promptu, sed adversus omnes alios hostile odium. Such is the character of the Jews given by the Roman historian, as they were in the time of our Saviour (Tacit. Hist. lib. v. c. 5. tom. iii. p. 267. edit. Bipont.); which is abundantly confirmed by the sacred writers. See Matt. ix. 10, 11. xxvi. 45. Gal. ii. 15. 17. 1 Thess. ii. 15, 16.

[2] See Whitby on Matt. iii. 9.

[3] See Col. iii. 12. 1 Thess. v. 27. Heb. iii. 1. 1 Pet. ii. 9. Acts ix. 32. 41. xxvi. 10. Rom. i. 7. xii. 13. xv. 25, 26. xvi. 15. 1 Cor. i. 2. 2 Cor. i. 1. xiii. 13. Phil. iv. 22. Eph. i. 1. Phil. i. 1. and Col. i. 2.

[4] It has been remarked that Greek words ending in ιστης imply inferiority. Thus the Ἕλληνες (*Hellenes*) were distinguished from the Ἑλληνισται (*Hellenistæ*); the *former* imply *pure* or *native* Greeks, who spoke the Greek tongue in its purity; and the *latter*,

they were called *Hebrews ;* — a name the most antient, and therefore the most honourable, of all the names borne by Abraham's descendants; for it was the name given to Abraham himself, by the Canaanites, to signify that he had come from the other side of the Euphrates. A *Hebrew*, therefore, possessing the character and qualifications above described, was more honourable than an *Israelite;* as that name indicated only that a person was a member of the commonwealth of Israel, which a Jew might be, though born and educated in a foreign country. St. Paul, indeed, was born at Tarsus, in Cilicia; yet being a Hebrew of the Hebrews, who received his education at Jerusalem, spoke the language used there, and understood the Hebrew in which the antient oracles of God were written, he was a Jew of the most honourable class; and, therefore, when cautioning the Philippians against Judaising teachers and unbelieving Jews, he enumerates this privilege among those of which (if salvation were to be obtained by them) he *might have confidence in the flesh.* (Phil. iii. 4, 5.)   The privileges of the Israelites, which were very highly esteemed by all Jews, are enumerated by St. Paul in his Epistle to the Romans, in a very animated manner.[1]

All the posterity of Jacob were antiently called *Israel*, or *Children of Israel*, from the surname of that patriarch, until the time of king Rehoboam; when ten tribes, revolting from this prince and adhering to Jeroboam, were thenceforth denominated the *House of Israel :* while the two tribes of Judah and Benjamin, who remained faithful to the family of David, were styled the *House of Judah.* After the captivity, most of those who returned and rebuilt Jerusalem and the temple, and restored the rites of the Mosaic worship, having sprung from the kingdom of Judah, the term Jews became a general appellation for all the inhabitants of Palestine, and afterwards for those who were descended from them. (Dan. iii. 8. Esth. iii. 3. 2 Macc. ix. 17.) And in this extensive sense the word is employed in the New Testament.[2]

III. Although the constitution of the Jewish polity and the laws of Moses allowed no other nations to participate in their sacred rites, yet they did not exclude from them such persons as were willing to qualify themselves for conforming to them.   Hence they admitted PROSE-LYTES, who renounced the worship of idols, and joined in the religious services of the Jews; although they were not held in the same estimation as Jews by birth, descent, and language, who, we have just seen, were termed Hebrews of the Hebrews.   During the time of Jesus

---

Jews or others sojourning among the Greeks, who spoke the Greek language according to the Hebrew idiom. These were the Ἑλλενιϲται, Hellenists or *Grecians* who *murmured against the Hebrews.* (Acts vi. 1.) " Pythagoras divided his disciples into two classes. Those, who were capable of entering into the spirit and mystery of his doctrine, he called Πυθαγορειοι, *Pythag* OREANS; those, who were of a different cast, he termed Πυθαγοριϲται, or *Pythag*ORISTS. The former were eminent and worthy of their master; the latter, but *indifferent.*   The same distinction is made between those who were called Αττικους, or *Attic*s, and Αττικιϲτας, or *Attic*ISTS, — the pure and less pure Greeks, as between those called Ἑλληνας and Ἑλληνιϲτας, *Hellen*ES and *Hellen*ISTS, pure Greeks, and Græcising Jews." Iamblichus de vita Pythag. c. 18. and Schoettgen, cited by Dr. A. Clarke on Acts vi. 1.

[1] See Drs. Whitby, Doddridge, Macknight, A. Clarke, or Messrs. Scott, Henry, &c. on Rom. ix. 4. and Phil. iii. 5.

[2] Robinson's and Parkhurst's Lexicons, voce Ιουδαιος.

Christ, the Jews, especially the Pharisees, greatly exerted themselves in making proselytes to their religion and sect.[1]

Calmet, and some other learned men after him, have distinguished two kinds of proselytes, namely, 1. *Proselytes of the gate,* who dwelt either in or out of the land of Israel, and worshipped the true God, observing the seven precepts of Noah[2], but without obliging themselves to circumcision or any other legal ceremony; and, 2. *Proselytes of justice or of righteousness,* who were converts to Judaism, and engaged themselves to receive circumcision, as well as to observe the whole of the Mosaic law. There does not, however, appear to be any foundation in the Scriptures for such a distinction: nor can any with propriety be termed proselytes, except those who *fully* embraced the Jewish religion. The Scriptures mention only two classes of persons, viz. the Israelites or Hebrews of the Hebrews above mentioned, and the Gentile converts to Judaism, which last are called by the names of strangers and sojourners, or proselytes.[3]

In the initiation of proselytes to the Jewish religion, according to the rabbinical writers, the three following observances were appointed, namely, circumcision, baptism, and the offering of sacrifice; all of which, except circumcision, were performed by the women, as well as by the men, who became proselytes.

1. *Circumcision* (the import of which is more fully explained in pp. 269—271.) was the seal of the covenant into which the proselyte entered with God, and of the solemn profession which he made to observe the entire law of Moses: and if the proselyte were a Samaritan, or of any other nation that used that rite, blood was to be drawn afresh from the part circumcised.

2. The second ceremony was *Washing* or *Baptism;* which must be performed in the presence of at least three Jews of distinction, and in the day-time that nothing might be done in secret. At the time of its performance the proselyte declared his abhorrence of his past life, and

---

[1] Compare Acts vi. 5. xiii. 43. and Matt. xxiii. 15. with Josephus, Ant. Jud. lib. xiii. c. 9. § 1. and lib. xx. c. 3. § 4.

[2] These precepts are by the Jewish doctors termed the seven precepts of Noah, and (they pretend) were given by God to the sons of Noah. They are as follows: — 1. That man should abstain from idolatry; — 2. That they should worship the true God alone; — 3. That they should hold incest in abhorrence; — 4. That they should not commit murder; — 5. Nor rob or steal; — 6. That they should punish a murderer with death; — 7. That they should not eat blood, nor any thing in which blood is, consequently, nothing strangled. " Every one," says a living Jewish writer, " that observes these seven commandments, is entitled to happiness. But to observe them merely from a sense of their propriety, is deemed by Maimonides insufficient to constitute a pious Gentile, or to confer a title to happiness in the world to come ; it is requisite that they be observed, *because* they are divine commands." See Allen's Modern Judaism, p. 107.

[3] These two classes are very frequently mentioned in the books of Moses; thus in Levit. xxv. we have " the children of Israel " (ver. 2.) and " the strangers that sojourn " among them."(ver. 45.) See also Ezek. xiv. 7.—" Every one of the house of Israel, or of the stranger that sojourneth in Israel, that separateth himself from me, and setteth up idols in his heart."—It is evident that, by the " stranger," in this passage, is meant a proselyte who had been converted to the worship of Jehovah, otherwise he could not have been separated from him. Schulzii Archæol. Hebr. *ut suprà.* Jennings's Jewish Antiquities, book i. ch. iii. pp. 63—80. Dr. Lardner has remarked that the notion of two sorts of proselytes is not to be found in any Christian writer before the *fourteenth* century ; see his arguments at large, Works, vol. vi. pp. 522—533. 8vo. or vol. iii. pp. 397—400. 4to. and vol. xi. pp. 313—324. 8vo. or vol. v. pp. 485—493. 4to. This observation renders it probable that the twelfth prayer of the Jews in p. 261. *suprà,* is not of so early a date as is commonly supposed.

that no secular motives, but a sincere love for the law of Moses, induced him to be baptised; and he was then instructed in the most essential parts of the law. He promised, at the same time, to lead a holy life, to worship the true God, and to keep his commandments.

Baptism was also administered to the children of proselytes who were born *before* their parents became proselytes, and generally at the same time with their parents: but it was not administered to children born *after* that event, because the parents and their offspring were considered as Israelites, clean from their birth, and therefore were brought into covenant by circumcision alone.[1]

3. The third ceremony to be performed was that of *offering Sacrifice.*

It was a common notion among the Jews, that every person who had duly performed all the preceding ceremonies was to be considered as a new-born infant. Thus Maimonides expressly says[2]:—"A Gentile who is become a proselyte, and a servant who is set at liberty, are both as it were new-born babes[3]; and all those relations which he had while either Gentile or servant, now cease from being so."

On the proselytism of the Jews, Jesus Christ appears to have formed the principal qualities which he required in the proselytes of *his* covenant. "The *first* condition of proselytism among the Jews was, that he, who came to embrace their religion, should come voluntarily, and that neither force nor influence should be employed in this business. This, also, is the *first* condition required by Jesus Christ, and which he considers as the foundation of all the rest. *If any man be willing* (ει τις θελει) *to come after me.* (Matt. xvi. 24.) The *second* condition required in the Jewish proselyte was, that he should perfectly renounce all his prejudices, his errors, his idolatry, and every thing that concerned his false religion, and that he should entirely separate himself from his most intimate friends and acquaintances. It was on this ground that the Jews called proselytism a new birth, and proselytes *new born* and *new men;* and our Lord requires men to be born again, not only of water but by the Holy Ghost. (John iii. 5.) All this our Lord includes in this word, *let him renounce himself*— απαρνησασθω εαυτον. (Mark viii. 34.) To this the following scriptures refer; Matt. x. 33. John iii. 3. 5. 2 Cor. v. 17.—The *third* condition, on which a person was admitted into the Jewish church as a proselyte, was, that he should submit to the yoke of the Jewish law; and patiently bear the inconve-

---

[1] Lightfoot's Hor. Hebr. on Matt. iii. 6.

[2] Ibid. ; Wetstein on John iii. 2. ; and Whitby on John iii. 4,5,6. Some learned men have supposed that our Lord alluded to this rabbinical tradition when he reproached Nicodemus with being a master in Israel (John iii. 10.), and yet being at the same time ignorant how a man could be born a second time. But it is most probable that Jesus Christ referred to that spiritual meaning of circumcision which is noticed in p. 270. note [2] *infrà.* The arguments on the much disputed question, Whether baptism was in use, or not, before the time of our Saviour, are reviewed by Carpzov in his Apparatus Antiquitatum Sacrarum, p. 49. and by Dr. Jennings in his Jewish Antiquities, book i. c. 3. It may not be irrelevant to remark that the learned Dr. Campbell refers our Lord's censure of Nicodemus, not to the rabbinical custom above mentioned, but rather to his entire ignorance of that effusion of the Spirit which was to take place under the Messiah, and which had been so clearly foretold by the prophets. Translation of the Four Gospels, vol. ii. p. 515. 3d edit.

[3] In allusion most probably to this custom, St. Peter addresses the Hebrews who had recently embraced Christianity, as *new-born* babes (1 Ep. ii. 2.), because they had been born again not of corruptible seed, but of incorruptible, even the word of God which liveth and abideth for ever. (i. 23.)

niences and sufferings, with which a profession of the Mosaic religion might be accompanied. Christ requires the same condition, but, instead of the yoke of the law, he brings in his own doctrine, which he calls his *yoke* (Matt. xi. 29.) and his *cross* (Matt. xvi. 24. Mark viii. 34.), the taking up of which implies not only a bold profession of Christ crucified, but also a cheerful submitting to all the sufferings and persecutions to which he might be exposed, and even to death itself. — The *fourth* condition was, that they should solemnly engage to continue in the Jewish religion, faithful even unto death. This condition Christ also requires, and it is comprised in this word *let him follow me*."[1] (Matt. xvi. 24—26. Mark viii. 34—37.)

IV. In consequence of the Babylonish captivity, the Jews were dispersed among the various provinces of the great Babylonian empire; and though a large portion of them returned under Zerubbabel, it appears that a considerable part remained behind. From this circumstance, as well as from various other causes, it happened, in the time of our Lord, that great numbers of Jews were to be found in Greece, and all the other parts of the Roman empire, which at that time had no other limits but those of the then known world.[2] It was of the JEWS DISPERSED AMONG THE GENTILES OR GREEKS, that mention is made in John vii. 35.: and to them Jesus Christ is also supposed to have alluded when he said that he had other sheep (John x. 16.), but without excluding the Gentiles, who also were to enter into his sheepfold, or be admitted into his church. To these dispersed Jews it was, that Peter and James inscribed their respective epistles; the former to those who were scattered through Pontus, Galatia, Cappadocia, Asia Minor, and Bithynia (1 Pet. i. 1.); and the latter to the twelve tribes who were dispersed throughout the then known world. (James i. 1.) The Jews who were assembled at Jerusalem on the day of Pentecost, were of the dispersion. (Acts ii. 5—11.)

V. There were also Jews who lived in those countries where Greek was the living language, and perhaps spoke no other. These are distinguished in the New Testament from the Hebrews or *native* Jews, who spoke what was then called Hebrew (a kind of Chaldaico-Syriac), by the appellation of HELLENISTS, or Grecians as they are termed in our authorized English version. These in all other respects were members of the Jewish church; they are repeatedly mentioned in the Acts of the Apostles, and it was a party of the Hellenistic Jews that requested to see Jesus.[3]

VI. During the time of our Saviour there was a considerable number of Jews resident at Rome: Josephus estimates them at eight thousand; and Philo, who relates that they occupied a large quarter of the city, says, that they were chiefly such as had been taken captive at different times, and had been carried into Italy, where they had subsequently acquired their freedom, and were called LIBERTINES. The synagogue of the Libertines, mentioned in Acts vi. 9. is, by some critics, supposed to have belonged to this class of Jews.[4]

---

[1] Dr. A. Clarke, on Mark viii. 34.

[2] Philo, de Legatione ad Caium, p. 1031. et in Flaccum, p. 971. Josephus, Ant. Jud. lib. xvi. c. 6. lib. xii. c. 3. lib. xiv. c. 10. Cicero. Orat. pro Flacco, c. 28.

[3] John xii. 20. See also Acts vi. 1. ix. 29. and xi. 20. and the commentators on those passages.

[4] Josephus, Ant. Jud. lib. xvii. c. 11. (al. 13.) lib. xviii. c. 3. (al. 4.) §§ 4, 5. Philo

VII. In consequence of this dispersion of the Jews, throughout the Roman empire, and the extensive commerce which they carried on with other nations, their religion became known, and the result was the prevalence of a somewhat purer knowledge of the true God among the Gentiles. Hence we find, that there were many who, though they did not adopt the rite of circumcision, yet had acquired a better knowledge of the Most High than the Pagan theology furnished, and who in some respects conformed to the Jewish religion. Of this description appear to be the "DEVOUT MEN *who feared God,*" who are frequently mentioned in the New Testament[1], and particularly the pious centurion Cornelius, of whom the sacred writer has given us so pleasing an account. (Acts x.)

VIII. All these persons, with the exception of the last class, were members of the Jewish church, participated in its worship, and regulated themselves by the law of Moses (or at least professed to do so), and by the other inspired Hebrew books, whence their sacred rites and religious instruction were derived. No person, however, was allowed to partake of the sacred ordinances, until he had undergone the rite of CIRCUMCISION.[2] This rite is first mentioned in Gen. xvii. 10—12., where we read that it was a seal of the covenant which God made with Abraham and his posterity. Afterwards, when God delivered his law to the children of Israel, he renewed the ordinance of circumcision, which from that time became a sacrament of the Jewish religion. Hence the protomartyr Stephen calls it the "covenant of circumcision," (Acts vii. 8.); and Jesus Christ also ascribes its institution to Moses, though it was derived from the patriarchs. (John vii. 22.) Besides the design which God proposed to himself in establishing this ceremony, he appointed it for some other ends, suited to the circumstances of the Israelites; a brief consideration of which will illustrate many important passages of Scripture. In the first place, it included in it so solemn and indispensable an obligation to observe the whole law, that circumcision did not profit those who transgressed. (Rom. ii. 25.) Hence the Jews are in the Scriptures frequently termed the *circumcision,* that is, persons circumcised, as opposed to the uncircumcised Gentiles, who are styled the *uncircumcision* (Rom. iii. 1. 30. iv. 12. Gal. ii. 7—9. Eph. ii. 11. Phil. iii. 5.); the abstract being put for the concrete. Thus, our Saviour is called the minister of circumcision: and therefore St. Paul says, that whoever is circumcised, is bound to keep the whole law. (Gal. v. 3.) For the same reason Jesus Christ was circumcised, that he might be made under the law, to fulfil the promise of the Messiah, and redeem those who were under the law. (Gal. iv. 4.) Secondly, as only circumcised persons were deemed to be visible members of the Jewish church, so none but these were permitted to celebrate the great festivals, particularly the passover. On this account it was that Joshua commanded all the Israelites, who having been born in the wilderness remained uncircumcised, to undergo the rite of circumcision, pre-

---

de Legat. ad Caium, p. 1014.   Tacitus, Annal. lib. ii. c. 85.   Suetonius in Tiberio, c. 36. Wolfius on Acts vi. 1. has detailed the various opinions of learned men respecting the Libertines. — See pp. 251, 252. *suprà.*

[1] See Acts xiii. 43. 50. xvi. 14. xvii. 4. 17. and xviii. 7.

[2] Calmet has an elaborate disquisition on the origin and design of circumcision. Dissertations, tom. i. pp. 411—422.

viously to their entering the land of Canaan (Josh. v. 4. 6. 9.); on which occasion God told them that he had removed or rolled away the reproach of Egypt from them; in other words, that they should thenceforth be regarded as his peculiar people, and no longer as the slaves of Egypt. The knowledge of this circumstance beautifully illustrates Eph. ii. 11—13.; where St. Paul, describing the wretched state of the Gentiles before their conversion, represents them as aliens from the commonwealth of Israel, and, consequently, excluded from all its privileges and blessings. Thirdly, circumcision was an open profession of the worship of the true God, and, consequently, an abjuration of idolatry; on this account we are told that during the persecution of Antiochus the heathen put to death those Jewish women who had caused their children to be circumcised[1]; and such Jews as apostatised to heathenism took away as much as possible every vestige of circumcision. As this rite was an open profession of the Jewish religion, some zealous converts from that faith to Christianity strenuously urged its continuance, especially among those who were of Jewish origin; but this was expressly prohibited by St. Paul. (1 Cor. vii. 18.)

Lastly, circumcision was appointed for mystical and moral reasons: it was, as baptism is with us, an external sign of inward purity and holiness: hence these expressions of " circumcising the foreskin of the heart," the " circumcision of the heart," the " circumcision made without hands," the " uncircumcised in heart," &c. so often occurring in the Scriptures.[2]

The sacrament of circumcision was enjoined to be observed on the eighth day (Gen. xvii. 12.), including the day when the child was born, and that on which it was performed; and so scrupulous were the Jews in obeying the letter of the law, that they never neglected it, even though it happened on the sabbath-day. (John vii. 22, 23.) This

---

[1] 1 Macc. i. 63. Josephus, Ant. Jud. lib. xii. c. 7.
[2] See Lev. xxvi. 41, 42. Deut. x. 16. xxx. 6. Jer. iv. 4. ix. 25, 26. Rom. ii. 25—29. Col. ii. 11. Acts vii. 51. Circumcision was that rite of the law by which the Israelites were taken into God's covenant; and (in the spirit of it) was the same as baptism among Christians. For, as the form of baptism expresses the putting away of sin, circumcision was another form to the same effect. The Scripture speaks of a "circumcision made without hands," of which that made with hands was no more than an outward sign, which denoted "the putting off the body of the sins of the flesh," (Col. ii. 11.) and becoming a new creature; which is the sense of our baptism. Of this inward and spiritual grace of circumcision the apostle speaks expressly in another place; "He is not a Jew which is one outwardly, neither is that circumcision which is outward in the flesh; but he is a Jew which is one inwardly, and circumcision is that of the heart, in the spirit, and not in the letter." (Rom. ii. 28.) Some may suppose that this spiritual application of circumcision, as a sacrament, was invented after the preaching of the Gospel, when the veil was taken from the law; but this doctrine was only enforced to those who had it before, and had departed from the sense of their own law; for thus did Moses instruct the Jews, that there is a "foreskin of the heart" which was to be "circumcised" in a moral or spiritual way, before they could be accepted as the servants of God; and again, that the Lord would "circumcise their heart, to love him with all their heart, and with all their soul," (Deut. x. 16. and xxx. 6.); which was the same as to say, that he would give them what circumcision signified, making them Jews inwardly, and giving them the inward grace with the outward sign; without which the letter of baptism avails no more now than the letter of circumcision did then: and we may say of the one as is said of the other, "He is not a Christian which is one outwardly, and baptism is *not the putting away the filth of the flesh* by washing with water, but *the answer of a good conscience towards God.*" (1 Pet. iii. 21.) Rev. W. Jones on the Figurative Language of Scripture. (Works, vol. iii. pp. 77, 78.) On this subject Dr. Graves has some excellent remarks, in his Lectures on the Pentateuch, vol. i. pp. 241—250. See also an excellent discourse of Bishop Beveridge, entitled " The New Creature in Christianity." Works, vol. ii. Serm. xix. pp. 417. et seq. 8vo. edit.

they termed "driving away the sabbath." If they were obliged to perform circumcision, either sooner or later, it was considered as a misfortune, and the circumcision so administered, though valid, was not deemed equally good with that done on the eighth day: and when this ceremony was deferred, it was never used to drive away the sabbath. It was for this reason that St. Paul accounted it no small privilege to have been circumcised on the eighth day. Accordingly John the Baptist (Luke i. 59.) and Jesus Christ (Luke ii. 21.) were circumcised exactly on that day. There was a peculiar fitness in the circumcision of Jesus Christ: for, as the Jews reckoned it dishonourable to associate with uncircumcised persons (Acts xi. 3.), it was necessary that he should be circumcised in order to qualify him for conversing familiarly with them, and also for discharging the other duties of his ministry. Besides, as the Messiah was to be descended from Abraham, whose posterity were distinguished from the rest of mankind by this rite, he received the seal of circumcision to show that he was rightly descended from that patriarch: and as every person that was circumcised was "a debtor to the whole law" (Gal. v. 3.), it was further necessary, that Jesus Christ the true Messiah should be circumcised; because, being thus subjected to the law of Moses, he was put into a condition to fulfil all righteousness, and redeem those who were under the law.[1] (Gal. iv. 4, 5.)

At the same time that the child was circumcised, we learn from the Gospel, that it was usual for the father, or some near relation, to give him a name. Thus John the Baptist and Jesus Christ both received their names on that day. (Luke i. 59. ii. 21.) It appears, however, that the Jews had several names during the period comprised in the evangelical history. Thus it was customary with them, when travelling into foreign countries, or familiarly conversing with the Greeks and Romans, to assume a Greek or Latin name of great affinity, and sometimes of the very same signification with that of their own country, by which name they were usually called among the Gentiles. So Thomas was called Didymus (John xi. 16.); the one a Syriac and the other a Greek word, but both signifying *a twin.* (See Acts i. 23. xii. 12. 2 Pet. i. 1. Col. iv. 11, &c.) Sometimes the name was added from their country, as Simon the Canaanite, and Judas Iscariot (Matt. x. 4.); but more frequently from their assuming a new and different name upon particular occurrences in life. (See 2 Chron. xxxvi. 4. 2 Kings xxiv. 17. John i. 42.) The same practice obtains in the East to this day.[2]

However necessary circumcision was while the ceremonial law remained in force, it became equally indifferent and unnecessary on the abrogation of that law by the destruction of the temple. Until that time the apostles allowed it to be performed on the Jewish converts to Christianity; but they expressly prohibited the imposition of such a yoke on the necks of the Gentile converts: and therefore St. Paul, who has fully proved how unprofitable and unnecessary it is (1 Cor. vii. 19.), thought it proper to have Timothy circumcised, because his mother was of Jewish extraction (Acts xvi. 1—3.); though he would

---

[1] Macknight and Whitby on Luke ii. 21.
[2] See Harmer's Observations, vol. iv. pp. 431—433.

not, on the other hand, allow this ceremony to be performed on Titus, because he was a Greek (Gal. ii. 3.) : — thus giving to the church in all ages a most excellent pattern, either of condescension or resolution, in insisting upon or omitting things indifferent according to the difference of times and circumstances.

SECTION II.

ON THE MINISTERS OF THE TEMPLE AND OTHER ECCLESIASTICAL OR SACRED PERSONS.

I. *Of the Levites.*— II. *The Priests, their Functions, Maintenance, and Privileges.* — III. *The High Priest. —His Functions, Dress, and Privileges. —Succession to the Pontifical Dignity.*— IV. *Officers of the Synagogue.* —V. *The Nazarites ; Nature of their Vows.* — VI. *The Rechabites.*— VII. *The Prophets.*

THE Jews, on the establishment of their republic, had no king but Jehovah himself; and the place appointed for their sacrifices and prayers was at the same time both the temple of their God and the palace of their sovereign.   This circumstance will account for the pomp and splendour of their worship, as well as the number, variety, and gradations in rank of their ministers ; which were first established by Moses, and afterwards renewed by David, with increased splendour, for the service of the temple.   To this service the tribe of Levi was especially devoted, instead of the first-born of the tribes of Israel, and was disengaged from all secular labours.   The honour of the priesthood, however, was reserved to the family of Aaron alone, the rest of the tribe being employed in the inferior offices of the temple : so that all the priests were Levites, but all the Levites were not priests.

I. Originally, the tribe of Levi was divided into the three families and orders of Gershomites, Kohathites, and Merarites (1 Chron. vi. 16, &c.), but afterwards the LEVITES were divided by David (1 Chron. xxiii.) into four classes.   Their principal office was to wait upon the priests, and be assisting to them in the service of the tabernacle and temple ; so that they were properly the ministers and servants of the priests, and obliged to obey their orders. (Numb. iii. 9. 1 Chron. xxiii. 28.)   But the particular duties incumbent upon them were different in the time of Moses, while the Israelites were in the wilderness, from those which they had to discharge afterwards, in the days of David and Solomon. In the wilderness the tabernacle was always in a moveable condition as well as the Israelites : and at that time the chief business of the Levites was, when the Israelites journeyed, to take down the tabernacle, to carry it about as the host removed, to take care of all the instruments and sacred vessels belonging to it, and when the army pitched their tents to set them up again.

For the more regular performance of the several duties belonging to the tabernacle, the whole business was divided between the Kohathites, the Gershomites, and the Merarites.   The first were principally concerned in carrying the ark and sacred vessels belonging to the tabernacle under the conduct of Eleazar the priest (Numb. iv. 16.), which being the most honourable employment, was given to them, most probably out of respect to Moses, who was descended from this family. The Gershomites and Merarites, under the direction of Ithamar, had the burden and charge of every thing else belonging to the tabernacle, as the coverings, hangings, wood-work, cords, pins, &c. (ver. 24—34.) When the Israelites were encamped, these three families of Levites were to pitch their tents round three sides of the tabernacle, and Moses and Aaron with their sons round the fourth quarter; by which means they were so disposed, as to be each of them as near as conveniently they could to their respective charges. Such was the office of the Levites in the time of Moses. Afterwards, when the Israelites were settled in the promised land, this employment of the Levites, in carrying the tabernacle and its utensils ceased; and therefore David and Solomon appointed them to new offices. They were chiefly indeed employed about the service of the temple: but during their recess, while they were not in attendance there, they were dispersed through the whole country, and employed in the service of the state as well as of the church. David made six thousand of them officers and judges (1 Chron. xxiii. 4.); they also took care to instruct the people where they resided in the Mosaic law, by expounding the several parts of it; and, according to the Jews, they kept the public records and genealogies of the several tribes.

In the business about the temple some of the chief amongst them had the charge of the sacred treasures. (1 Chron. xxvi. 20.) Others of a lower rank were to prepare the shew-bread and unleavened cakes, with the proper quantity of flour for the morning and evening service. (1 Chron. xxiii. 29.) From which text it appears also that they had in their custody within the sanctuary the original standard for weights and measures, liquid and dry, according to which every thing of this kind was to be regulated. Hence it is we often read in Scripture of the shekel of the sanctuary, not that there were two sorts of shekels, one sacred and another civil, but because weights and measures, being reckoned among the sacred things, were kept in the sanctuary, as they were in the temples of the Pagans, and afterwards in Christian churches.[1] Many of the Levites were likewise employed as porters, to guard the gates and passages into the temple. (1 Chron. ix. 17.) Others were more honourably employed as singers, and were to stand every morning to thank and praise the Lord, and likewise in the evening (1 Chron. xxiii. 30.); and this we find they did in a very solemn manner at the dedication of the temple. (2 Chron. v. 12, 13.) The whole body of the Levites in David's time amounted to thirty-eight thousand, from thirty years old and upwards (1 Chron. xxii. 3.), of which number he appointed four and twenty thousand to attend the constant duty and work of the temple; and these being divided as the priests were into four and twenty courses (as appears from 1 Chron. xxiii. 24. and 2 Chron. xxxi. 17.), there were one thousand for each week. Six thousand again were to be officers and judges, as already mentioned, four thousand for porters, and four thousand for singers. (1 Chron. xxiii. 4, 5.) The four and twenty courses of singers are mentioned in 1 Chron. xxv. 8—31. This disposition of them was

---

[1] Novels of Justinian, nov. 128. cap. 15.

afterwards confirmed by Solomon when the temple was finished
(2 Chron. viii. 14.) ; and all these had their chiefs or overseers as well
as the priests. (Ezra viii. 29.) The duty of the porters was not only
to be a military guard upon the temple, but also to take care that no
person who was unclean or uncircumcised might enter the court of
the Israelites. (2 Chron. xxiii. 19.) And however mean their employment was, yet it was the pious desire of David, *rather to be a door-
keeper in the house of God, than to dwell in the tents of wickedness.*
(Psal. lxxxiv. 10.) The order of singers was instituted by David, and
it appears that the whole book of psalms was composed for this kind of
devotion. David (by whom the greatest number was composed) directed many of them to the chief musician, for this very purpose, that
they might be used in the service of the house of God. And we have
one particular instance in which it is said, that *David delivered this
psalm to thank the Lord into the hand of Asaph and his brethren.*
(1 Chron. xvi. 7.) The principal persons of this order who had the
superintendency over all the rest, were Heman and Asaph of the line
of Gershom, and Jeduthun of the line of Merari, of whom we have an
account in 1 Chron. xxv.

The mere circumstance of birth did not give the Levites a title to
officiate ; they were obliged to receive a sort of consecration, which
consisted chiefly in sprinkling them with water, in washing, and in
offering sacrifices. (Numb. viii. 6, 7, 8.) The usual age, at which
the Levites were to enter on their office, was at five and twenty years,
and they continued till fifty. (Numb. viii. 24, 25.) But there was a
particular precept which restrained the Kohathites (one of the three
branches) from being employed to carry the holy things belonging to
the sanctuary, till they were of the age of thirty (Numb. iv. 30.), probably, because these being the most valuable and important of all the
moveables belonging to the tabernacle, required therefore persons of
greater experience and strength. Afterwards, when David new-
moulded the constitution of the Levites, he (by the same authority
which empowered him to give directions about the building and situation of the house of God) ordered that for the future the Levites
should be admitted at the age of twenty years. (1 Chron. xxiii. 24.)
It does not appear by the first institution of the Levites that they had
any peculiar habit in the ceremonies of religion by which they were
distinguished from other Israelites. None of the Levites, of what
degree or order soever, had any right to sacrifice, for that was the
proper duty of the priests only: the Levites, indeed, were to assist the
priests in killing and flaying the sacrifices, and, during the time they
were offered up, to sing praises to God: and in this sense the two
passages in 1 Chron. xxiii. 31. and 2 Chron. xxxi. 2. are commonly
understood ; neither had they any title to burn incense to the Lord ;
and though the speech of Hezekiah (mentioned in 2 Chron. xxix.
particularly ver. 11.) seems to imply otherwise, yet we ought to consider that he is there speaking to the priests as well as to the Levites.
It was on account of their aspiring to the priest's office in this particular of burning incense, that Korah and his company (who were
Levites) were miraculously destroyed, and their censers ordered
to be beaten into broad plates, and fixed upon the altar, to be perpetual monuments of their presumptuous sacrilege, and a caution to all
the children of Israel, that none presume to offer incense before the

Lord, but the seed of Aaron, who alone were commissioned to the priestly office.

As the Levites were subordinate to the priests, so they (the Levites) had others under them, called NETHINIMS, whose business it was to carry the water and wood, that was wanted in the temple for the use of the sacrifices, and to perform other laborious services there. They were not originally of Hebrew descent, but are supposed to have been chiefly the posterity of the Gibeonites, who for their fraudulent stratagem in imposing upon Joshua and the Hebrew princes (Josh. ix. 3—27.) were condemned to this employment, which was a sort of honourable servitude. We read in Ezra, that the Nethinims were devoted by David and the other princes to the service of the temple (Ezra viii. 20.), and they are called the children of Solomon's servants (Ezra ii. 58.), being probably a mixture of the race of the Gibeonites, and some of the remains of the Canaanites, whom Solomon constrained to various servitudes. (1 Kings ix. 20, 21.) They had a particular place in Jerusalem where they dwelt, called Ophel, for the conveniency of being near the service of the temple. (Neh. iii. 26.)

In order to enable the Levites to devote themselves to that service, forty-eight cities were assigned to them for their residence, on the division of the land of Canaan ; thirteen of these were appropriated to the priests[1], to which were added the tithes of corn, fruit, and cattle. The Levites, however, paid to the priests a tenth part of all their tithes ; and as they were possessed of no landed property, the tithes which the priest received from them were considered as the first fruits which they were to offer to God. (Numb. xviii. 21—24.)[2]

II. Next to the Levites, but superior to them in dignity, were the ordinary PRIESTS, who were chosen from the family of Aaron exclusively. They served immediately at the altar, prepared the victims, and offered the sacrifices. They kept up a perpetual fire on the altar of the burnt sacrifices, and also in the lamps of the golden candlestick in the sanctuary ; they kneaded the loaves of shew-bread, which they baked, and offered on the golden altar in the sanctuary ; and changed them every sabbath-day. Every day, morning and evening, a priest (who was appointed at the beginning of the week by lot) brought into the sanctuary a smoking censer of incense, which he set upon the golden table, and which on no account was to be kindled with strange fire, that is, with any fire but that which was taken from the altar of burnt sacrifice. (Lev. x. 1, 2.) And as the number and variety of their functions required them to be well read in their law, in order that they might be able to judge of the various *legal* uncleannesses, &c. this circumstance caused them to be consulted as interpreters of the law (Hos. iv. 6. Mal. ii. 7., &c. Lev. xiii. 2. Numb. v. 14, 15.), as well as judges of controversies. Deut. xxi. 5. xvii. 8—13.) In the time of war, their business was to carry the ark of the covenant, to sound the holy trumpets, and animate the army to the performance of its duties. To them also it belonged publicly to bless the people in the name of the Lord.

---

[1] See pp. 10, 11, *suprà.*
[2] Home's Script. Hist. of Jews, vol. ii. pp. 214—221. Schulzii Archæol. Hebr. pp. 227—231.

The priests were divided by David into twenty-four classes (1 Chron. xxiv. 7—18.); which order was retained by Solomon (2 Chron. viii. 14.); and at the reformations of the Jewish religion by the kings Hezekiah and Josiah. (2 Chron. xxxi. 2. xxxv. 4, 5.) As, however, only four classes returned from the Babylonish captivity (Ezra ii. 36—39. Neh. vii. 39—42. xii. 1.), these were again divided into twenty-four classes, each of which was distinguished by its original appellation. This accounts for the introduction of the class or order of Abiah, mentioned in Luke i. 5., which we do not find noticed among those who returned from the captivity. One of these classes went up to Jerusalem every week to discharge the sacerdotal office, and succeeded one another on the sabbath-day, till they had all attended in their turn. To each order was assigned a president (1 Chron. xxiv. 6. 31. 2 Chron. xxxvi. 14.), whom some critics suppose to be the same as the *chief priests* so often mentioned in the New Testament, and in the writings of Josephus.[1] The prince or prefect of each class appointed an entire family to offer the daily sacrifices; and at the close of the week they all joined together in sacrificing. And as each family consisted of a great number of priests, they drew lots for the different offices which they were to perform. It was by virtue of such lot that the office of burning incense was assigned to Zacharias the father of John the Baptist, *when he went into the temple of the Lord.* (Luke i. 9.) According to some Jewish writers, there were three priests employed in the offering of the incense; one, who carried away the ashes left on the altar at the preceding service; another, who brought a pan of burning coals from the altar of sacrifice, and, having placed it on the golden altar, departed; a third, who went in with the incense, sprinkled it on the burning coals, and, while the smoke ascended, made intercession for the people. This was the particular office, which fell by lot to Zacharias; and it was accounted the most honourable in the whole service. This office could be held but once by the same person.[2]

The sacerdotal dignity being confined to certain families, every one who aspired to it was required to establish his descent from those families: on this account the genealogies of the priests were inscribed in the public registers, and were preserved in the archives of the temple.[3] Hence, in order to preserve the purity of the sacerdotal blood, no priest was permitted to marry a harlot or profane woman, or one who had been divorced; and if any one laboured under any bodily defect, this excluded him from serving at the altar. Purity of body and sanctity of life were alike indispensable; nor could any one undertake the priestly office, in the early period of the Jewish polity, before he had attained thirty years, or, in later times, the age of twenty years.[4] According to Maimonides, the priest, whose genealogy was defective in any respect, was clothed in black, and veiled in black, and sent without the verge of the court of the priests; but every one that

---

1 See Matt. xxvii. 1. Acts iv. 23. v. 24. ix. 14. 21. xxii. 30. xxiii. 14. xxv. 15. xxvi. 10.; and also Josephus, Ant. Jud. lib. xx. c. 8. § 8. De Bell. Jud. lib. iv. c. 3. § 7. c. 4. § 3. et de vita sua, §§ 2. 5.

2 Macknight, and Wetstein, on Luke i. 9.

3 Ezra ii. 62. Neh. vii. 64. Josephus contra Apion, lib. i. § 7. et in vita sua, § 1.

4 Levit. xxi. 7. 17—23. Numb. iv. 3. 2 Chron. xxxi. 17. Maimonides has enumerated not fewer than 140 bodily defects which disqualified persons for the priesthood. See Josephus, Ant. Jud. lib. iii. c. 12. § 2. and compare Carpzov's Apparatus Antiquitatum Sacrarum, pp. 89. *et seq.*

was found perfect and right was clothed in white, and went in and ministered with his brethren the priests. It is not improbable that St. John refers to this custom of the Jewish sanhedrin in Rev. iii. 5. Those priests, whose birth was pure, lived in certain apartments of the temple, in which was deposited wood for the altar, and were employed in splitting and preparing it, to keep up the sacred fire.[1] No particular ceremony appears to have taken place at the consecration of the ordinary priests, who were admitted to the exercise of their functions by "*filling their hands*," as the Scriptures term it,—that is, by making them perform the offices of their order. But when the priests had departed from their religion, or had been a long time without discharging their functions (which happened under some of the later kings of Judah), it was deemed necessary to sanctify anew such priests, as well as those who had never exercised their ministry. (2 Chron. xxix. 34.)

The priests were not distinguished by their sacerdotal habits, unless when engaged in the service of the altar. Of these garments there are four kinds mentioned in the books of Exodus (xxviii.) and Leviticus (viii.); viz.

1. *Linen Drawers.* These were prescribed for the express purpose of *covering their nakedness;* that is, to preserve the priests from an indecorous and ludicrous appearance, when they stood either above the heads of the people, or when their office required a variety of bodily gestures in the view of the multitude. This garment would prevent those indecent exposures of their persons, which some heathen idolaters esteemed honourable, and even religious, in the worship of their gods.

2. A *Linen Tunic,* which reached down to the ankles, fitting closely to the body, and the sleeves of which were tightly drawn round the arms: it was without seam, and woven from the top throughout. Such was the tunic worn by Jesus Christ, for which the soldiers cast lots.[2]

3. A *Girdle* or long sash, made of linen curiously embroidered, and intended to bind the coat closely around them, and thus to serve at once the purposes of warmth and strength, of convenience and ornament.

4. The *Tiara* was originally a pointed kind of bonnet or turban, made of several rolls of linen cloth twisted round the head, but in the time of Josephus it approached somewhat to a globular form.[3]

In order that the priests, as well as the Levites, might be wholly at liberty to follow their sacred profession, they were exempted from all secular burthens or labours. Of the Levitical cities already mentioned, thirteen were assigned for the residence of the priests, with their respective suburbs (Numb. xxxv.); the limits of which were confined to a thousand cubits beyond the walls of the city, which served for outhouses, as stables, barns, and perhaps for gardens of herbs and flowers.

---

[1] Lamy, Apparatus Biblicus, vol. i. p. 213.

[2] Josephus, Ant. Jud. lib. iii. c. 7. § 2. See also the Observations of Ernesti, Inst. Interp. Nov. Test. p. ii. c. 10. § 88. pp. 371—373. It was for a long time supposed that the art of making such vests was irrecoverably lost. Braunius, however, rediscovered it, and procured a loom to be made, in which tunics were woven all of one piece. See his treatise de Vestitu Sacerdotum Hebræorum, lib. i. c. 16. p. 264.

[3] Josephus, Antiq. Jud. lib. iii. c. 7. § 3. Tappan's Lect. on Jewish Antiquities, pp. 155—157.

T 3

Beyond this they had two thousand cubits more for their pasture, called properly the *fields of the suburbs.* (Levit. xxv. 34.) So that there were in the whole three thousand cubits round the city; and in this sense we are to understand Numb. xxxv. 4, 5. where the word suburbs comprehends both the houses, without the walls, and also the fields. But though the tribe of Levi had no portion in Canaan assigned them in the first division of it, yet they were not prevented from purchasing land, houses, goods, or cattle, out of their own proper effects. Thus we read that Abiathar had an estate of his own at Anathoth, to which Solomon banished and confined him (1 Kings ii. 26.); and the prophet Jeremiah, who was also a priest, purchased a field of his uncle's son in his own town. (Jer. xxxii. 8, 9.) Such were the residences allotted to the priests. Their maintenance was derived from the tithes offered by the Levites out of the tithes by them received, from the first fruits, from the first clip of wool when the sheep were shorn, from the offerings made in the temple, and from their share of the sin-offerings and thanksgiving-offerings sacrificed in the temple, of which certain parts were appropriated to the priests. Thus in the peace-offerings, they had the shoulder and the breast (Lev. vii. 33, 34.): in the sin-offerings, they burnt on the altar the fat that covered certain parts of the victim sacrificed; the rest belonged to the priest. (Lev. vii. 6. 10.) To him also was appropriated the skin or fleece of every victim; and when an Israelite killed an animal for his own use, there were certain parts assigned to the priest. (Deut. xviii. 3.) All the first-born also, whether of man or beast, were dedicated to God, and by virtue of that devotion belonged to the priests. The men were redeemed for five shekels (Numb. xviii. 15, 16.): the first-born of impure animals were redeemed or exchanged, but the clean animals were not redeemed. They were sacrificed to the Lord; their blood was sprinkled about the altar, and the rest belonged to the priest; who also had the first-fruits of trees, that is, those of the fourth year (Numb. xviii. 13. Lev. xix. 23, 24.), as well as a share in the tithes of the spoils taken in war. (Numb. xxxi. 28—41.) Such were the principal revenues of the priests, which, though they were sufficient to keep them above want, yet were not (as some writers have imagined) so ample as to enable them to accumulate riches, or to impoverish the laity; thus their political influence, arising from their sacred station, as well as from their superior learning and information, was checked by rendering them dependent on the people for their daily bread. By this wise constitution of Moses, they were deprived of all power, by which they might injure the liberty of the other tribes, or in any way endanger the Israelitish polity, by any ambitious views or prospects: for not only were all the estates of the Levites and priests, but also their persons, given into the hands of the other tribes, as so many hostages, and as a security for their good behaviour. They were so separated from one another, that they could not assist each other in any ambitious design; and they were so dispersed among the other tribes, that these could attach the whole subsistence as well as arrest all the persons of the Levites and priests at once, in the event of any national quarrel, or if they were suspected of forming any evil designs against the other tribes of Israel. Hence we may perceive, that, whatever power or influence the Mosaic constitution gave the Levites to do good, the same constitution carefully provided, that they should have no power, either to disturb the peace, or to endanger the liberties of their country.[1]

III. Over all the priests was placed the HIGH PRIEST, who enjoyed peculiar dignities and influence. He alone could enter the Holy of Holies in the temple : the supreme administration of sacred things was confined to him ; he was the final arbiter of all controversies ; in later times he presided over the sanhedrin, and held the next rank to the sovereign or prince. His authority, therefore, was very great at all times, especially when he united the pontifical and regal dignities in his own person. In the Old Testament he is sometimes called *the priest* by way of eminence (Exod. xxix. 30. Neh. vii. 65.), and some-times the head or chief of the high priests, because the appellation of *high priests* was given to the heads of the sacerdotal families or courses, who were members of the sanhedrin. This appellation, in the New Testament, includes not only the person who actually held the office of high priest of the Jews, but also those who, having once filled that office, still retained the name. (Matt. xxvi. 57, 58. Luke xxii. 50. 54. John xi. 49. 51.) When the high priest became old, or had acciden-tally been exposed to any pollution, a סָגָן (saGaN) or substitute was appointed to perform his duties. Zephaniah, the *second priest*, (Jer. lii. 24.) is supposed to have been the sagan or deputy of the high priest Seraiah. Such an officer seems to be intended in John xviii. 13. and Acts iv. 6.; in which passages Annas is called a chief priest, either as having formerly been high priest, or as then being actually his sagan.[2]

In order that the person of the high priest might be deemed more holy, he was inaugurated with great splendour ; being invested (after ablution was performed) with the sacred habiliments which conferred this dignity, and anointed with a precious oil prepared and preserved for this exclusive purpose. (Exod. xxix. 7. xxx. 23. *et seq.* Lev. viii. 12.) But, after the erection of the second temple, this anointing ceased, and the inauguration of the high priest was accomplished by arraying him with the pontifical robes worn by his predecessor.

Besides the garments which were common to the high priest, as well as to the inferior members of the sacerdotal order, there were four peculiar to himself; viz.

1. The *Coat or Robe of the Ephod*, which was made of blue wool; on its hem there were seventy-two golden bells[3], separated from one another by as many artificial pomegranates. As the pomegranates added to the beauty of the robe, so the sound of the bells gave notice to the people in the outer court of the high priest's entrance into the holy place to burn incense; in order that they might then apply them-selves to their devotions, as an expression of their concurrence with him in his offering, and of their hope that their prayers, accompanied with the incense offered by him, would ascend as a fragrant odour before God.

2. The *Ephod* was a vest, which was fastened on the shoulders, the

---

[1] Schulzii Archæologia Hebraica, pp. 231—236. Lowman's Civil Government of the Hebrews, p. 124.

[2] Godwin's Moses and Aaron, p. 18. Lightfoot's Horæ Hebraicæ, and Kuinöel, on Luke iii. 2.

[3] Similar bells are still in use in the East. See Hasselquist's Travels, p. 58., and D'Ar-vieux's Travels in Arabia the Desart, p. 226.

hinder part reaching down to the heels, while the fore part descended only a little below the waist. It was of fine twisted linen, splendidly wrought with gold and purple: to each of the shoulder-straps of this ephod was affixed a precious stone, on which were engraven the names of the twelve tribes of Israel.

3. The *Breast-plate of Judgment,* or oracle, was a piece of cloth doubled, one span square, and of similar texture and workmanship with the ephod: on it were set twelve precious stones, containing the engraved names of the twelve sons of Jacob, and also the words *Urim* and *Thummim,* signifying "lights and perfections," and emblematical of divine illumination. Concerning the nature of the Urim and Thummim, learned men are not agreed. All that we know with certainty is, that when the high priest went to ask counsel of Jehovah, he presented himself arrayed with this breast-plate, and received the divine commands. This mode of consultation subsisted under the tabernacle erected by Moses in the wilderness, and until the building of Solomon's temple. As God was the political sovereign of the Hebrews, the high priest was of course his minister of state: the names of the twelve tribes being worn at his breast, when he went to ask counsel of his sovereign, were a fit pledge and medium of divine direction. At the same time, these names being worn both on his breast and shoulders would forcibly instruct him to cherish the tenderest affection, and to exert his utmost power, for their welfare.[1]

4. The last peculiarity in the dress of the high priest was a *Crown* or *Mitre,* on the front of which was tied, by a blue riband, a plate of pure gold, on which were engraven the two Hebrew words קדש ליהוה (KODESH LAJEHOVAH), or *Holiness unto the Lord,* emblematical of that holiness which was the scope and end of the law.

With all these vestments the high priest was necessarily arrayed when he ministered in the tabernacle or temple, but at other times he wore the ordinary dress of the priests; and this, according to some learned persons, was the reason why St Paul, who had been long absent from Jerusalem, knew not that Ananias was the high-priest, when he appeared before him in the Sanhedrin.[2] (Acts xxiii. 5.) The frequent and violent changes in the pontifical office, which happened in those times, confirms the probability of this conjecture. The supreme pontiff was not allowed to rend his garments, as the other Jews did, on any occasions of domestic calamity (Levit. xxi. 10.); but in the time of Jesus Christ it had become lawful, or at least was tolerated as an expression of horror at hearing what was deemed blasphemy against God. This will explain the conduct of Caiaphas, who is said (Matt. xxvi. 65.) to have rent his garments.[3]

The Jewish writers have discovered much recondite meaning in the pontifical vestments. According to Josephus and Philo, the high priest's linen garment represented the body of the earth; the glorious robe which encompassed it, heaven; the bells and pomegranates, thunder and lightning. Or, the ephod of various colours is the

---

[1] Tappan's Lectures on Jewish Antiq. pp. 157—160.

[2] The dress and ornaments of the high priest above noticed, together with the mode of consecrating him, as directed by Moses, are described at length in Exod. xxviii. and xxix. 1—37.

[3] Tappan's Lectures, p. 164.

universe; the breast-plate, the earth in its centre; the girdle, the sea; the onyx-stone on each shoulder, the sun and moon; the twelve jewels in the breast-plate, the twelve signs of the zodiac; the mitre, heaven; and the golden plate, with the name of God engraven on it, the splendour of Jehovah in heaven. Some Christian divines have allegorised them in a manner equally extravagant; but such wild comments serve no other purpose than to throw an air of romance, of uncertainty, and of ridicule, over sacred things. It is sufficient for us to be assured, that these minute prescriptions were adapted to wise and excellent purposes, in the comparatively infant state of the church; and, particularly, that they served the general uses of an emblematical and typical religion, which was intended to impress moral and spiritual truth by sensible and striking representations.[1]

The high priest, who was the chief man in Israel, and appeared before God in behalf of the people in their sacred services, and who was appointed for sacrifice, for blessing, and for intercession, was a type of Jesus Christ, that great high priest, who offered himself a sacrifice for sin, who blesses his people, and who *evermore liveth to make intercession for them.* The term *priest* is also applied to every true believer, who is enabled to offer up himself a spiritual sacrifice acceptable to God through Christ. (1 Pet. ii. 5. Rev. i. 6.) [2]

The pontifical dignity, in its first institution, was held for life, provided the high priests were not guilty of crimes that merited deposition.   For we read that Solomon deprived Abiathar of this office for being concerned in treasonable practices with Adonijah, who aspired to the throne of Israel. (1 Kings ii. 27.)   At its first institution, also, the high priesthood was made hereditary in the family of Aaron (Numb. iii. 10.), who was the first person invested with this dignity. (Lev. viii. 1. *et seq.* Heb. v. 4, 5.)   From Aaron it descended to Eleazar, his eldest son, from whom it passed in long succession to Eli; from him, on account of the wickedness of his sons, the dignity subsequently devolved to the descendants of Ithamar, the second son of Aaron. (1 Sam. ii. 35, 36.)   In the reign of Solomon, however, it returned again into the family of Eleazar by Zadok (1 Kings ii. 35.); in which it remained until the Babylonian captivity.   During this period the high priest was elected by the other priests, or else by an assembly partly consisting of priests.

The first high priest, after the return from the captivity, was Joshua the son of Josedek, of the family of Eleazar; whence the succession went into a private Levitical family.   The office was then filled by some of the princes of the Maccabæan family.   According to the law, it was or ought to have been held for life; but this was very ill obeyed under the Roman government, especially during the time of our

---

[1] Besides the authorities already cited in the course of this article, the reader who is desirous of investigating the nature and functions of the Jewish priesthood is referred to Reland's Antiquitates veterum Hebræorum, part ii. cc. 1—6. pp. 141—238.; Ikenius's Antiquitates Hebraicæ, part i. cc. 10, 11. pp. 105—128.; and to Schacht's Animadversiones ad Ikenii Antiquitates, pp. 471—544.; Dr. Jennings's Jewish Antiquities, book i. c. 5. pp. 95—174.; Michaelis's Commentaries on the Law of Moses, vol. i. pp. 251—262.; Dr. Lightfoot's Works, vol. i. pp. 401. 915—918. and vol. ii. pp. 377—380. 397. 681.; Carpzovii Antiquitates Hebr. Gentis, pp. 64—110.

[2] The typical nature of the Jewish priesthood, especially of the high priest, is discussed by the Rev. W. Jones, in his Lectures on the Figurative Language of Scripture, and on the Epistle to the Hebrews. (Works, vol. iii. pp. 58—62. 223—227.)

Saviour, and in the latter years of the Jewish polity, when election and the right of succession were totally disregarded. The dignity, sanctity, and authority of the high priest were then almost annihilated; and this office was not unfrequently sold to the highest bidder, to persons who had neither age, learning, nor rank to recommend them; nay, even to individuals who were not of the sacerdotal race; and sometimes the office was made annual.[1] This circumstance will account for the variations in the lists of the succession to the high priesthood contained in the Scriptures, in Josephus, and in the Talmudical writers[2]; and will also explain the circumstance of several high priests being in existence at the same time, or, rather, of there being several pontifical men who, having once held the office for a short time, seem to have retained the original dignity attached to the name.[3]

The following TABLE exhibits a

CHRONOLOGICAL SERIES OF THE HIGH PRIESTS OF THE HEBREWS,

From the Commencement to the Subversion of their State and Government.

1. *Succession, taken from several places of the Holy Scriptures.*	2. *Succession, taken from* 1 Chron. vi. 3—15.	3. *Succession, taken from Josephus, Ant. Jud. lib.* x. *c.* 8. *lib.* xx. *c.* 10.	4. *Succession, taken from the Jewish Chronicle, intitled Seder Olam.*
1. Aaron, the brother of Moses, created high priest, A.M. 2514, died 2552.	1. Aaron.	1. Aaron.	1. Aaron.
2. Eleazar, created in 2552, and died about 2571.	2. Eleazar.	2. Eleazar.	2. Eleazar.
3. Phinehas, A.M. 2571, died 2590.	3. Phinehas.	3. Phinehas.	3. Phinehas.
4. Abiezer, or Abishua. These were under the judges.	4. Abishua.	4. Abiezer.	4. Eli.
5. Bukki.	5. Bukki.	5. Bukki.	5. Ahitub.
6. Uzzi.	6. Uzzi.	6. Uzzi.	6. Abiathar.
7. Eli, of the race of Ithamar, created in 2848, died in 2888.	7. Zerahiah.	7. Eli.	7. Zadok.
8. Ahitub I.	8. Meraioth.	8. Ahitub.	8. Ahimaaz, under Rehoboam.
9. Ahiah. He lived in 2911, or 2912.	9. Amariah.	9. Ahimelech.	9. Azariah, under Abiah.
10. Ahimelech, or Abiathar, he was murdered by Saul, 2944.	10. Ahitub I.	10. Abiathar.	10. Jehoachash, under Jehoshaphat.
11. Abiathar, Ahimelech, or Abimelech, under David, from 2944 to 2989.	11. Zadok I.	11. Zadok.	11. Jehoiarib, under Jehoram.
12. Zadok I. under Saul, David, and Solomon, from 2944 to about 3000.	12. Ahimaaz.	12. Ahimaaz.	12. Jehoshaphat, under Ahaziah.

---

[1] Josephus de Bell. Jud. lib. iv. c. 3. §§ 7, 8.

[2] That this was the case with Annas and Caiaphas, is fully proved by Dr. Lardner, Credibility, book ii. c. 4. § 1. (Works, vol. i. pp. 383—386.) The various successions of the high priests are given at length by Reland, Antiq. Hebr. part ii. c. 2. pp. 160—168. Utrecht, 12mo. 1717; and by Calmet, Dissertations, tom. i. pp. 487—490., and Dict. *voce* Priest, from whom we have copied the Table in the following pages.

[3] Antiq. Jud. lib. viii. c. 2. § 2. c. 4. § 3.

1. *Succession, taken from several places of the Holy Scriptures.*	2. *Succession, taken from* 1 Chron. vi. 3—15.	3. *Succession, taken from Josephus, Ant. Jud. lib. x. c. 8. lib. xx. c. 10.*	4. *Succession taken from the Jewish Chronicle, intitled Seder Olam.*
13. Ahimaaz, under Rehoboam, about A.M. 3030.	13. Azariah.	13. Azariah.	13. Jehoiadah, ⎫ under Joash.
14. Azariah, under Jehoshaphat; perhaps the same as Amariah. (2 Chron. xix. 11.)	14. Johanan. 1 Chron. vi. 9, 10.	14. Joram.	14. Phadaiah, ⎭
15. Johanan, perhaps Jehoida, in the reign of Joash, 2 Chron. xxiv. 15. in 3126. He died at the age of 130.	15. Azariah.	15. Issus.	15. Zedekiah, under Amaziah.
16. Azariah, perhaps the same with Zechariah, son of Jehoiadah, who was killed in 3164.	16. Amariah.	16. Axiora.	16. Joel, under Uzziah.
17. Amariah, perhaps Azariah, under Uzziah, in 3221.	17. Ahitub II.	17. Phideus.	17. Jotham, under Joatham.
18. Ahitub II. ⎫ Under Jotham,	18. Zadok II.	18. Sudeas.	18. Uriah, under Ahaz.
19. Zadok II. ⎭ king of Judah.	19. Shallum.	19. Julus.	19. Neriah, under Hezekiah.
20. Uriah, under Ahaz, 3265.	20. Hilkiah.	20. Jotham.	20. Hosaiah, under Manasseh.
21. Shallum, the father of Azariah, and grandfather to Hilkiah.	21. Azariah.	21. Uriah.	21. Shallum, under Amon.
22. Azariah, who lived in the time of Hezekiah (2 Chron. xxxi. 10.), 3278.	22. Seraiah.	22. Neriah.	22. Hilkiah, under Josiah.
23. Hilkiah, under Hezekiah.	23. Jehzadak.	23. Odeas.	23. Azariah, under Jehoiakim and Zedekiah.
24. Eliakim, or Joakim, under Manasseh, and at the time of the siege of Bethulia, in 3348. He continued to live under Josiah to 3380, and longer. He is also called Hilkiah. (Baruch i. 7.)	24. Joshua.	24. Saldam.	24. Jehozadak, after the taking of Jerusalem.
25. Azariah, perhaps Neriah, the father of Seraiah and of Baruch.		25. Hilkiah.	25. Jesus, son of Jozadak, after the captivity.
26. Seraiah, the last high priest before the captivity; put to death in 3414.		26. Seraiah.	
27. Jozadak, during the captivity of Babylon, from 3414 to 3469.		27. Jozadak.	
28. Joshua, or Jesus, the son of Jozadak: he returned from Babylon in 3468.		28. Jesus, or Joshua.	

The following succession is collected from Ezra, Nehemiah, and Josephus.

29. Joachim, under the reign of Xerxes, Jos. Ant. l. ii. c. 5.

30. Eliasib, Joasib, or Chasib, under Nehemiah, A.M. 3550.

31. Joiada, or Juda, Neh. xii. 10.

32. Jonathan, or John.

33. Jaddua, or Jaddus, who received Alexander the Great at Jerusalem in 3673, and died in 3682.

34. Onias I. made high priest in 3681, governed 21 years, and died in 3702.

35. Simon I. called the Just, made

high priest in 3702 or 3703, and died in 3711.

36. Eleazar, made in 3712. Under this pontiff, the translation of the Septuagint is said to have been made, about the year 3727 : he died in 3744.

37. Manasseh, made in 3745, died in 3771.

38. Onias II. made in 3771, died in 3785.

39. Simon II. made in 3785, and died in 3805.

40. Onias III. made in 3805, deposed 3829, died in 3834.

41. Jesus, or Jason, made in 3830, deposed in 3831.

42. Onias IV. otherwise called Menelaus, made in 3832, died in 3842.

43. Lysimachus, vicegerent of Menelaus, killed in 3834.

44. Alcimus, or Jacimus, or Joachim, made in 3842, died in 3844.

45. Onias V. He did not exercise his pontificate at Jerusalem, but retired into Egypt, where he built the temple Onion in 3854.

46. Judas Maccabæus, restored the altar and the sacrifices in 3840, died in 3843.

47. Jonathan, the Asmonæan, brother to Judas Maccabæus, created high priest in 3843, and died in 3860.

48. Simon Maccabæus made in 3860, died in 3869.

49. John Hyrcanus, made in 3869, died in 3898.

50. Aristobulus, king and pontiff of the Jews, died 3899.

51. Alexander Jannæus, also king and pontiff during 27 years, from 3899 to 3926.

52. Hyrcanus was high priest for the space of 32 years in the whole, from 3926 to 3958.

53. Aristobulus, brother to Hyrcanus, usurped the high priesthood, and held it three years and three months, from 3935 to 3940.

54. Antigonus, his son, also usurped the priesthood in prejudice to the rights of Hyrcanus, and possessed it for three years and seven months, from 3964 to 3967, when he was taken by Sosius.

55. Ananeel of Babylon, made high priest by Herod in 2968 till 3970.

56. Aristobulus, the last of the Asmonæans: he did not enjoy the pontificate a whole year. He died in 3970. Ananeel was made high priest a second time in 3971.

57. Jesus, the son of Phabis, deposed in 3981.

Succession of High Priests after the Captivity.

58. Simon, son of Botheus, made high priest in 3981, deposed in 3999.

59. Matthias, son of Theophilus, made high priest in 3999. Ellem was substituted in his place for a day, because of an accident that happened to Matthias, which hindered him from performing his office that day.

60. Joazar, son of Simon, son of Boethus, made high priest in 4000, the year of the birth of Jesus Christ, four years before the commencement of the vulgar era.

61. Eleazar, brother to Joazar, made high priest in 4004, of Christ 4, of the vulgar era 1.

62. Jesus, son of Siah, made high priest in the year of the vulgar era 6. Joazar was made a second time in 7, and deposed in 13.

63. Ananus, son of Seth, for 11 years, from 4016 to 4027, of the vulgar era 24.

64. Ishmael, son of Phabi, in 24.

65. Eleazar, son of Ananus, made in 24.

66. Simon, son of Camithus, made high priest in 25.

67. Joseph, surnamed Caiaphas, made in 26, and continued till 35.

68. Jonathan, son of Ananus, made in 35, and continued till 37.

69. Theophilus, son of Jonathan, made in 37, and continued till 41.

70. Simon, surnamed Cantharus, and son of Simon Boethus, was made high priest in 41.

71. Matthias, son of Ananus, made high priest in 42.

72. Elioneus, made in 44, and continued till 45. Simon, son of Cantharus, was a second time made high priest, A.D. 45, and deposed the same year.

73. Joseph, son of Caneus, was made high priest in A.D. 45, till 57.

74. Ananias, the son of Nebodeus, was made high priest in the year of the vulgar era 47, and enjoyed the priesthood till 63.

75. Ismael was ordained high priest, A.D. 63.

76. Joseph, surnamed Cabei, in 63.

77. Ananus, the son of Ananus, in 63.

78. Jesus, the son of Ananus, in 64.

79. Jesus, the son of Gamaliel, in 64.

80. Matthias, the son of Theophilus, was made high priest in the year of the vulgar Christian era 70.

81. Phannias, the son of Samuel, was made high priest in the year 70, in which year Jerusalem and the temple were destroyed by the Romans, and a final period was put to the Jewish priesthood.

Of those who discharged the functions of high priest during the decline of the Jewish polity, there are two particularly mentioned in the New Testament, namely, ANNAS (John xviii. 13. Acts iv. 6.), and CAIAPHAS. (Matt. xxvi. 3. 57. John xviii. 13. 24. 28.) The former is by Josephus called Ananus, of which name Annas is an abridgment: the latter he calls Joseph, intimating also that he was known by the name of Caiaphas.[1] Annas enjoyed the singular felicity (which indeed had never happened to any other of the Jewish high priests), not only of having himself held the supreme pontifical office for many years, but also of seeing it filled by several successors out of his own family, five of them being his sons, and others his sons-in-law. Hence, although he was deprived of the high priesthood by the Romans, he afterwards continued to take the chief sway in the administration of the Jewish affairs; and is represented in the sacred history, together with Caiaphas, as being chief priest and exercising supreme authority.

IV. Next to the Levites, priests, and high priests, the OFFICERS OF THE SYNAGOGUE may be mentioned here, as being in some degree sacred persons; since to them was confided the superintendence of those places which were set apart for prayer and instruction. Their functions and powers have been fully stated in p. 253. *suprà.*

V. The NAZARITES (as the Hebrew word Nazir implies) were persons separated from the use of certain things, and sequestered or consecrated to Jehovah. They are commonly regarded as sacred persons; a notice of their institute will be found *infrà* in Chapter V. Sect. I. § III. 2.

VI. The RECHABITES are by many writers considered as a class of holy persons, who, like the Nazarites, separated themselves from the rest of the Jews, in order that they might lead a more pious life. But this is evidently a mistake; for they were not Israelites or Jews, but Kenites or Midianites, who used to live in tents, and traverse the country in quest of pasture for their cattle, as the Nabathæan Arabs antiently did, and as the modern Arabians, and Crim-Tatars (or Tartars[2]) still do. Their manner of living was not the result of a religious institute, but a mere civil ordinance, grounded upon a national custom. They derived their name from Jonadab the son of Rechab, a man of eminent zeal for the pure worship of God against idolatry, who assisted king Jehu in destroying the house of Ahab and the worshippers of Baal. (2 Kings x. 15, 16. 23.) It was he who gave the rule of life to his children and their posterity, which is recorded by the prophet Jeremiah (xxxv. 5—7.); and which consisted of these three articles: 1. That they should drink no wine; 2. That they should neither possess nor occupy any houses, fields, or vineyards; and, 3. That they should dwell in tents. In these regulations he appears to have had no religious, but merely a prudential view, as is intimated in the reason assigned for them, viz. that they might live many days in the land where they were strangers. And such, in fact,

---

[1] Luke iii. 2. Acts iv. 6. In like manner Josephus (de Bell. Jud. lib. ii. c. 12. § 6.) places Jonathan, who had been high priest (Antiq. Jud. lib. xviii. c. 4. § 3.) and who still continued to possess great authority, before Ananias, who at that time discharged the functions of sovereign pontiff. (Ant. Jud. lib. xx. c. 5. § 2.) See also Lardner's Credibility, book i. c. 7. § 1. and book ii. c. 4. (Works, vol. i. pp. 143. 383—389.)

[2] See Mrs. Holderness's Notes relating to the Manners and Customs of the Crim-Tatars. London, 1821. 12mo.

would be the natural consequence of their temperate and quiet mode of living. On the first invasion of Nebuchadnezzar, with intent to besiege Jerusalem, these Rechabites, apprehending themselves in more danger in the open country, came to Jerusalem for safety; by these people God intended to convince the Jews of their disobedience to him; and, therefore, he ordered his prophet Jeremiah to bring them to an apartment of the temple, and there offer them wine to drink: which when they refused, on account of its being contrary to their institute, which they never had violated, the prophet, after due commendation of their obedience, addressed the Jews, and reproached them who were God's peculiar people, for being less observant of his laws, than these poor Rechabites had been of the injunctions of their ancestor. (Jer. xxxv.) Wherefore Jehovah declares (ver. 18, 19.) that, *because the Rechabites had obeyed the precepts of Jonadab their father, therefore Jonadab should not want a man to stand before him for ever.*[1] The Rechabites flourished as a community about one hundred and eighty years, and were supposed to have been dispersed after the captivity; but modern travellers have discovered their descendants in a tribe of Bedouin Arabs, who dwell alone in the vicinity of Mecca, and are called Beni Khaibr, or the sons of Khaibr (that is, of Heber). They continue to obey the injunctions of their ancestor Rechab. " To this moment they drink no wine, and have neither vineyard, nor field, nor seed; but dwell like Arabs in tents, and are wandering nomades. They believe and observe the law of Moses by tradition, for they are not in possession of the written law." [2]

VII. The PROPHETS were eminently distinguished among the persons accounted holy by the Jews: they were raised up by God in an extraordinary manner for the performance of the most sacred functions. Originally they were called *Seers:* they discovered things yet future, declared the will of God, and announced their divine messages, both to kings and people, with a confidence and freedom that could only be produced by the conviction that they were indeed authorised messengers of Jehovah. The gift of prophecy was not always annexed to the priesthood: there were prophets of all the tribes, and sometimes even among the Gentiles. The office of a prophet was not confined to the prediction of future events; it was their province to instruct the people, and they interpreted the law of God: hence the words *prophet* and *prophecy* are, in many passages of the Scriptures, synonymous with interpreter or teacher, and interpretation or teaching. It is unanimously agreed both by Jews and Christians that Malachi was the last of the prophets under the Old Testament dispensation; and it is a remarkable fact, that so long as there were prophets among the Jews, they were not divided by sects or heresies, although they often fell into idolatry. This circumstance may thus be accounted for: — As the prophets received their communications of the divine will *immediately* from God himself, there was no alternative for the Jews: either the people must obey the prophets, and

---

[1] Lamy's Apparatus Biblicus, vol. i. p. 223. Michaelis's Commentaries on the Law of Moses, vol. i. pp. 227, 228. Mede's Works, p. 127. Calmet, Commentaire Littérale, tome vi. p. xvii. The reader will find an instructive discourse on the history of the Rechabites, in Dr. Townson's Works, vol. ii. pp. 215—225.

[2] Wolff's Missionary Journal and Memoir, p. 257.; Carne's Recollections of the East, pp. 95, 96.

receive their interpretations of the law, or no longer acknowledge that God who inspired them. When, however, the law of God came to be explained by weak and fallible men, who seldom agreed in their opinions, sects and parties were the unavoidable result of such conflicting sentiments.[1]

CHAPTER III.

SACRED THINGS.

On the Sacrifices and other Offerings of the Jews.[2]

General Classification of Sacrifices and Offerings; — I. OFFERINGS OF BLOOD, *and the divine Origin of Sacrifices;*—1. *Different Kinds of Victims;* — 2. *Selection of Victims;* — 3. *Manner of presenting them;* — 4. *Immolation of the Sacrifice;* — 5. *The Place and Time appointed for sacrificing;*—6. *Different Kinds of Fire-sacrifices;*— i. *Burnt-offerings;* — ii. *Peace-offerings;* — iii. *Sin-offerings;* — iv. *Trespass-offerings.* — II. *National, regular, weekly, monthly, and annual Sacrifices.* — III. UN-BLOODY OFFERINGS. — IV. DRINK-OFFERINGS. — V. *Other Oblations made by the Jews :*—1. ORDINARY OBLATIONS;—(1.) *The Shew-bread.*— (2.) *Incense.* — 2. VOLUNTARY OBLATIONS. — *Corban.*—3. PRESCRIBED OBLATIONS;—(1.) *First-fruits;*—(2.) *Tithes.*—VI. *Fitness and Utility of the Jewish Sacrifices.*

A SACRIFICE is an offering made to God upon his altar by the hand of a lawful minister. *Sacrifice* differs from *oblation* in this respect, viz. in a sacrifice there must be a real change or destruction of the thing offered: whereas, an oblation is only a simple offering or gift.[3]

The sacrifices and oblations of the Jews demand particular notice in this sketch of their ecclesiastical state. " Such a ritual as they were enjoined to observe, the multiplicity of victims they were appointed statedly to offer, together with the splendour of that external worship in which they were daily engaged, — all tended to replenish and adorn their language with numerous allusions, and striking metaphors derived from the pomp of their religion. Hence it is that the writings of the Jews, more than of any other people, abound with phrases and terms borrowed from the temple worship and service. The psalms

---

1 For a more particular account of the sacred prophets, see Vol. IV. pp. 140—152.

2 General authorities from which this chapter is compiled : — Schulzii Archæol. Heb. pp. 250—280. Lamy, Apparatus Biblicus, vol. i. pp. 187—203. Relandi Antiq. Sacr. Hebræorum, part iii. cap. 1—5. pp. 290—368. Ikenii Antiq. Heb. part i. cap. 13, 14. pp. 152—191, Beausobre and L'Enfant's Introd. to the New Test. (Bishop Watson's Tracts, vol. iii. pp. 196—199.) Jennings's Jewish Antiquities, book i. chap. v. Michaelis's Commentaries, vol. iii. pp. 94—97. 109—115. 246—254. Dr. Hales's Analysis, vol. ii. book ii. pp. 270—272. Jahn, Archæol. Biblica, §§ 373—390. Dr. Owen on the Epistle to the Hebrews, vol. i. Exercit. xxiv. pp. 306—318. Dr. Lightfoot's Works, vol. i. pp. 926—941. folio edition, §§ 373—385. Ackermann, Archæol. Biblica, §§ 360—372. Tappan's Jewish Antiq. pp. 106—118. Brunings, Antiq. Hebr. pp. 172—192. Carpzovii Antiq. Hebr. Gentis, pp. 699—725.

3 Calmet's Dictionary, voce *Sacrifice.*

and prophetical writings may in particular be adduced in illustration of this remark. *Purge me with hyssop,* says David, *and I shall be clean.* — *Thou shalt be pleased with the sacrifices of righteousness.* (Psal. li. 7.19.) *Let my prayer come before thee as incense, and the lifting up of my hands as the evening sacrifice.* (Psal. cxli. 2.) *Therefore will I offer the sacrifice of joy.* (Psal. cxvi. 17.) *The sin of Judah,* says Jeremiah, *is - - - - graven upon the horns of your altars.* (Jer. xvii. 1.) *Take away all our iniquity and receive us graciously ; so will we render thee the calves of our lips.* (Hos. xiv. 2.)" Nor are similar examples wanting in the New Testament, whose inspired authors being educated in the Jewish religion, retain the same phraseology, which has enriched their writings with numerous beautiful and expressive allusions to the national sacrifices and ceremonies.[1]

Michaelis classes the offerings prescribed to the Israelites under three general heads—namely, offerings of *blood,* or sacrifices strictly so called; *unbloody* offerings, or those taken only from the vegetable kingdom; and *drink-offerings,* or libations, which were a kind of accompaniment to the two preceding. We shall follow this classification, as enabling us to present to our readers the most compendious account of the Jewish sacrifices.

I. OFFERINGS OF BLOOD were sacrifices properly and strictly so called; by which we may understand the infliction of death on a living creature, generally by the effusion of its blood in a way of religious worship, and the presenting of this act to God as a supplication for the pardon of sin, and as a supposed mean of compensation for the insult and injury offered by sin to his majesty and government. Sacrifices have in all ages, and by almost every nation, been regarded as necessary to appease the divine anger, and to render the Deity propitious[2]: but whether this universal notion derived its origin from divine revelation, or was suggested by conscious guilt and a dread of the divine displeasure, is a question that cannot be easily decided. It is, however, not improbable that it originated in the former, and prevailed under the influence of the latter. The Scripture account of sacrifices leads us to conclude, that they were instituted by divine appointment, immediately after the entrance of sin by the fall of Adam and Eve, to be a type or significant emblem of the great atonement or all-sufficient sacrifice of Christ.[3] Accordingly we find Abel, Noah, Abraham, Job, and others, offering sacrifices in the faith of the Messiah that was to be revealed; and the divine acceptance of their sacrifices is particularly recorded. This hypothesis, and this only,

---

[1] Harwood's Introd. to New Test. vol. ii. pp. 216, 217.

[2] To this notion of sacrifice our Saviour alluded in John xvi. 2. where he tells his disciples that such would be the enmity with which they should be pursued, that he who should kill them would be deemed to have slain a sacrifice highly *acceptable* to the Almighty — " He that killeth you shall *think he doeth God service.*" In reference also to this notion of sacrifice, the Apostle by a very beautiful and expressive figure represents Christ as loving us, and giving himself for us, *an offering and a sacrifice to God of a sweet-smelling savour.* (Eph. v. 2.) Harwood's Introd. to the New Test. vol. ii. p. 218.

[3] The divine origin of sacrifices is fully proved by Archbishop Magee, in his Discourses on the Atonement, vol. i. pp. 44—60. and vol. ii. pp. 22—46. 184—189., and by Mr. Jerram in his Treatise on the Doctrine of the Atonement, pp. 90—292. Mr. Davison has argued on the contrary side in his Inquiry into the Origin of Sacrifice. (London, 1825. 8vo.) Mr. Faber, in reply, has ably vindicated the divine origin of Sacrifices in a treatise published at London in 1827. 8vo.

satisfactorily accounts for the early prevalence of religious sacrifices, not only among the worshippers of the true God, but also among Pagan idolaters.

1. In all bloody sacrifices it was essential that the animals slaughtered should be clean; but it does not appear that all clean animals were to be offered indiscriminately. Fishes were not brought to the altar; and hence the Israelites are nowhere prohibited from eating their blood, but only that of birds and quadrupeds. (Lev. vii. 26.) It would seem that *all* clean birds might be offered, (Lev. xiv. 4—7.) though the dove was the most common offering of this class. Of quadrupeds, oxen, sheep, and goats were the only kinds which were destined for the altar. No wild beasts were admissible: and hence comes the expression in the law of Moses (Deut. xii. 15. 22. xv. 22.), *It shall be eaten like the roe or the hart;* by which he means to intimate that, in killing a beast, all religious intention and all idea of sacrifice was to be avoided.[1]

2. In the selection of the victims, the utmost care was taken to choose such only as were free from every blemish. Unless it were pure and immaculate, it was to be rejected, as a sacrifice unacceptable to Jehovah. (Lev. xxii. 22.) In a beautiful allusion to this circumstance, St. Paul beseeches Christians, by the mercies of God, to *present their bodies a living sacrifice, holy and acceptable,* which is their reasonable service. (Rom. xii. 1.) Hence also Jesus Christ is styled a *lamb without blemish and without spot.* (1 Pet. i. 19.) Further, it was a custom among nations contiguous to Judæa, and particularly among the Egyptians[2], to *set a seal* upon a victim that was deemed proper for sacrifice. With this custom the Jews could not be unacquainted; and it is possible that similar precautions were in use among themselves, especially as they were so strictly enjoined to have their sacrifices *without spot and without blemish.* To such a usage Jesus Christ is supposed to have alluded, when speaking of the sacrifice of himself, he says — *Him hath God the Father* SEALED. (John vi. 27. 51.) " Infinite justice found Jesus Christ to be without spot or blemish, and therefore *sealed,* pointed out and accepted him as a proper sacrifice and atonement for the sin of the whole world. Collate Heb. vii. 26—28. Eph. v. 27. 2 Pet. iii. 14., and especially Heb. ix. 13, 14. *For, if the blood of* BULLS *and of goats, and the ashes of an heifer, sprinkling the unclean, sanctifieth, — how much more shall the blood of Christ, who through the Eternal Spirit offereth himself* WITHOUT SPOT *to God, purge your consciences from dead works ?* "[3]

3. The victim thus chosen, being found immaculate, was led up to

---

1 Michaelis's Commentaries, vol. iii. p. 95.

2 The following account of the manner in which the Egyptians provided white bulls for their sacrifices, will materially explain the custom above alluded to : — " They sacrifice white bulls to Apis, and for that reason make the following trial. If they find one black hair upon him, they consider him as unclean. In order that they may know this with certainty, the priest appointed for this purpose views every part of the animal both standing and lying on the ground ; after this, he draws out his tongue, to see if he be clean by certain signs ; and in the last place he inspects the hairs of his tail, that he may be sure they are, as by nature they should be. If, after this search, the animal is found unblemished, he signifies it by *tying a label to his horns ;* then, having applied wax, he *seals it with his ring,* and they lead him away, for it is death to sacrifice one of these animals, unless he has been *marked with such a seal.*" Herodotus, lib. ii. c. 38. vol. i. p. 113. edit. Oxon.

3 Dr. A. Clarke, on John vi. 27.

the altar by the person offering the sacrifice; who laid his hand upon
its head, on which he leaned with all his strength[1]; and, while the
sacrifice was offering, said some particular prayers; and if several
persons united in offering the same victim, they put their hands upon
it in succession. (Lev. iv. 13—15.)[2] By this imposition of hands the
person presenting the victim acknowledged the sacrifice to be his own;
that he loaded it with his iniquities; that he offered it as an atonement
for his sins; that he was worthy of death because he had sinned, having
forfeited his life by violating the law of God; and that he entreated
God to accept the life of the innocent animal in the place of his
own. In this respect the victims of the Old Testament were types
of Jesus Christ, *the lamb of God that* TAKETH AWAY *the sin of the world*
(John i. 29.), and on whom Jehovah in the fulness of time *laid the
iniquity of us all.*[3] (Isa. liii. 6. with 1 Pet. ii. 24.)

Further, in certain cases it was required that the victim should be
one, *on which never came yoke* (Numb. xix. 2. Deut. xxi. 3. 1 Sam. vi.
7.); because any animal which had been used for a common purpose
was deemed improper to be offered in sacrifice to God.[4]

4. The animal thus conducted to the altar was next immolated, by
cutting the throat and windpipe entirely through at one stroke; the
blood being caught in a vessel, and sprinkled round about upon the
altar. By this sprinkling the atonement was made, for the blood was
the life of the beast, and it was always supposed that life went to redeem
life. (Lev. i. 5—7.) The blood remaining after these aspersions, was
poured out at the foot of the altar, either all at once, or at different
times, according to the nature of the sacrifice offered. Around the
altar there was a kind of trench into which the blood fell; whence it
was conveyed by subterraneous channels into the brook Kedron. This
altar, being very high, is considered by Lamy as a type of the cross to
which our Saviour was fixed, and which he washed with his precious
blood. The victim being thus immolated, the skin was stripped from
the neck; its breast was opened; its bowels were taken out, and the

---

[1] This ceremony, it is proper to remark, was omitted in respect to the turtle doves, and
young pigeons, which were allowed to be offered in certain cases.

[2] The nature and mystical import of laying hands on the head of the victim, are largely
considered by Archbishop Magee in his Discourses on the Atonement, vol. i. pp. 336
—377.

[3] On the vicarious import of the Mosaic sacrifices, see Archbishop Magee's Discourses
on the Atonement, vol. i. pp. 352—366.

[4] The heathens, who appear to have borrowed much from the Hebrews, were very scrupulous in this particular. Neither the Greeks, nor the Romans, (who had the same religion,
and, consequently, the same sacrifices with the Greeks,) nor indeed the Egyptians, would
offer an animal in sacrifice that had been employed in agriculture. Just such a sacrifice as
that prescribed here does Diomede vow to offer to Pallas. Iliad, x. 291—294. In the
very same words Nestor promises a similar sacrifice to Pallas. Odyss. iii. 382.

Thus also VIRGIL. Georg. iv. 550.

> Quatuor eximios præstanti corpore tauros,
> Ducit, et intacta totidem cervice juvencas.

> From his herd he culls,
> For slaughter, four the fairest of his bulls;
> Four heifers from his female stock he took,
> All fair, and all unknowing of the yoke.   DRYDEN.

It is very probable that the Gentiles learnt their first sacrificial rites from the Patriarchs;
and on this account we need not wonder to find so many coincidences in the sacrificial
system of the patriarchs and Jews, and of all the neighbouring nations. (Dr. A. Clarke, on
Numb. xix. 2.)

back bone was cleft. It was then divided into quarters; so that, both externally and internally, it was fully exposed to view. To this custom of laying open the victim, St. Paul has a very beautiful and emphatic allusion in one of the most animated descriptions ever written, of the mighty effects produced by the preached Gospel. (Heb. iv. 12, 13.) *The word of God is quick and powerful, sharper than any two-edged sword, piercing even to the dividing asunder of soul and spirit, and of the joints and marrow, and is a discerner of the thoughts and intents of the heart. Neither is there any creature that is not manifest in his sight; for all things are naked and* OPENED *to the eyes of him to whom we must give an account.* Previously to laying the sacrifice on the altar, it was salted *for the fire* (Lev. ii. 13. Ezek xliii. 24. Mark ix. 46.); the law prohibiting any thing to be offered there which was not salted: and according to the nature of the sacrifice, either the whole or part of the victim was consumed upon the altar, where the priests kept a fire perpetually burning.[1]

5. Before the building of the temple, sacrifices were offered at the door of the tabernacle; but after its erection it was not lawful to offer them elsewhere. (Deut. xii. 14.) This prohibition took from the Jews the liberty of sacrificing in any other place. The victims might indeed be slain *in* any part of the priest's court, but not without its precincts: and there they were also obliged to sacrifice the paschal lamb. All the victims were to be offered by day-light, and the blood was always to be sprinkled on the same day that they were slain; as it became polluted as soon as the sun was set. If, however, the sprinkling had been made in the day-time, the members and entrails of the victim might be consumed during the night. Subsequently to the time of Moses, indeed, altars were multiplied, but they fell under suspicion, although some of them, perhaps, were sacred to the worship of the true God. Nevertheless, on extraordinary occasions, some prophets, whose characters were above all suspicion, did offer sacrifices in other places than that prescribed by the Mosaic laws; as Samuel (1 Sam. xiii. 8—14. xvi. 1—5.), and Elijah. (1 Kings xviii. 21—40.)

6. The sacrifices of the altar were, in general, called by the Hebrews *Korbanim,* that is, offerings or oblations to God, from the Hebrew word *karab,* to approach or bring nigh. This term consequently denotes something *brought nigh,* in order to be dedicated, or offered to God, to whom the person offering thus had access in the way appointed by the law; and, therefore, at the close of the enumeration of all offerings by fire it is added (Lev. vii. 37, 38.), *This is the law . . . . . which the Lord commanded Moses in Mount Sinai, in the day that he commanded the children of Israel to offer or bring nigh their* KORBANIM, that is, offerings or sacrifices of all sorts.[2]

The Jewish fire-sacrifices were of three kinds; viz.

i. The BURNT-OFFERINGS, or *Holocausts,* were free-will offerings wholly devoted to God, according to the primitive patriarchal usage. The man himself was to bring them before the Lord, and they were offered in the manner described in the preceding page. The victim

---

[1] Harwood's Introd. to New Test. vol. ii. p. 220. Carpzov has assigned many devout and some fanciful reasons why salt was used in the Jewish sacrifices. Antiq. Heb. Gent. pp. 719—723.

[2] Dr. Owen on the Epistle to the Hebrews, vol. i. Exercitat. xxiv. p. 307.

to be offered was, according to the person's ability, a bullock without
blemish, or a male of the sheep or goats, or a turtle-dove or pigeon.
(Lev. i. 3. 10. 14.) If, however, he was too poor to bring either of
these, he was to offer a mincha or meat-offering, of which an account
is given in a subsequent page.[1] The Jews esteemed the burnt-offering
the most excellent of all their sacrifices, not only on account of its
superior antiquity, but also because it was *entirely* consecrated to God.
In allusion to this, St. Paul exhorts Christians to present their bodies,
or their whole selves, a living sacrifice to God. (Rom. xii. 1.) The
burnt-offerings are in Hebrew termed עלה (oLaH), which signifies to
ascend; because this offering, as being wholly consumed, ascended,
as it were, to God in smoke or vapour. It was a very expressive type
of the sacrifice of Christ, as nothing less than his *complete* and full
sacrifice could make atonement for the sins of the word.

ii. The PEACE-OFFERINGS (Levit. iii. 1.) were also free-will offerings,
in token of peace and reconciliation between God and man; they were
either *eucharistical,* that is, offered as thanksgivings for blessings received, or *votive,* that is, offered with prayers for the impetration of
mercies. These offerings consisted either of animals, or of bread or
dough; if the former, part of them was burnt upon the altar, especially
all the fat, as an offering to the Lord; and the remainder was to be
eaten by the priest and the party offering. To this sacrifice of praise
or thanksgiving St. Paul alludes in Heb. xiii. 15, 16. In this kind
of sacrifices the victims might be either male or female, provided they
were without blemish. The parts of both, which were appropriated
to the priests and Levites, were called *heave* or *wave-offerings;* because
they were *heaved* or lifted up towards heaven, and *waved* to and fro,
before they were eaten, in acknowledgment of the goodness and kindness of God, and also in token of their being consecrated to him.
(Lev. iii. 1—6. Exod. xxix. 26, 27. Numb. xviii. 24—28.)

The peace-offerings are in Hebrew termed שלמים (sHeLaMIM),
from שלם (sHaLaM), to complete or make whole: because, by
these offerings that which was *deficient* was considered as being now
made up; and that which was broken, viz. the covenant of God, by his
creature's transgression, was supposed to be made whole: so that, after
such an offering, the sincere and conscientious mind was authorised to
consider itself as reconciled to God, and that it might lay confident hold
on this covenant of peace. To this St. Paul alludes in that fine passage
contained in Eph. ii. 14—19.

The appointed seasons and occasions of the peace-offering were,
1. At the consecration of a priest. (Exod. xxix. 1—37.) 2. At the
expiration of the Nazarite vow. (Numb. vi. 13—21.) 3. At the
solemn dedication of the tabernacle and temple; and, 4. At the purification of a leper.

iii. SIN-OFFERINGS, in Hebrew termed חטאה (cHaTaAH), (from
the word חטא (cHaTa) to miss the mark,) were offered for sins committed either through ignorance, or wilfully against knowledge; and
which God always punished unless they were expiated. These offerings
in general consisted of a sin-offering to God, and a burnt-offering,
accompanied with restitution of damage (Levit. v. 2—19. vi. 1—7.,)

---

[1] See p. 294. *infrà.*

conformably to which our Lord requires previous reconciliation with an injured brother, including restitution, before the burnt-offering or gift would be acceptable to God. (Matt. v. 23, 24.) St. Paul (Eph. v. 2.) terms Christ's giving himself for us an offering (*i. e.* a peace-offering), and a *sacrifice* or sin-offering to God for a sweet-smelling savour. (Compare Lev. iv. 31.)   In warm climates nothing is more refreshing than fragrant odours: and as, in the highly figurative language of the antient Hebrews, *smelling* is used to denote the perception of a *moral quality* in another, God is said to smell a sweet savour from sacrifice, to signify that he perceived with pleasure the good disposition which the offerer expressed by such an act of worship.   When, therefore, the Apostle tells us that Christ gave himself for us, an offering and a sweet-smelling sacrifice to God, he teaches us that Christ's sacrifice for us was highly acceptable to God, not only as a signal instance of obedience to his Father's will, but also on account of its happy influence in establishing the moral government of God.[1]   The sacrifices offered for the purification of lepers, as well as of women after childbirth) Levit. xii. Luke ii. 24.), were reckoned among the sin-offerings, inasmuch as leprosy and the pains of child-bearing were considered as punishments for some particular sin ; though both were accompanied by eucharistic sacrifices for the recovery of the persons offering them. Maimonides adds, that if the person who offered this sacrifice did not repent, and make public confession of his sins, he was not cleansed or purified by it.[2]

iv. The TRESPASS-OFFERINGS were made, where the party offering had just reason to doubt whether he had violated the law of God or not. (Levit. v. 17, 18.) They do not appear to have differed materially from sin-offerings.[3]   In both these kinds of sacrifices, the person who offered them placed his hands on the victim's head (if a sin-offering), and confessed his sin over it, and his trespass over the trespass-offering; saying, " I have sinned, I have done iniquity, I have trespassed, and have done thus and thus, and do return by repentance before thee, and with *this* I make atonement." The animal was then considered as vicariously bearing the sins of the person who brought it.[4]   In Isa. liii. 10. Jesus Christ is said to make his soul an offering for sin, אשם (ASHaM), the very word used in the law of Moses to denote a trespass-offering.

II. All these sacrifices were occasional, and had reference to individuals; but there were others which were national and regular, DAILY, WEEKLY, MONTHLY, and ANNUAL.

1. The *Perpetual or Daily Sacrifice* was a burnt-offering, consisting of two lambs, which were offered every day, morning and evening, at the third and ninth hours. (Exod. xxix. 38—40. Levit. vi. 9—18. Numb. xxviii. 1—8.)   They were burnt as holocausts, but by a small fire, that they might continue burning the longer. With each of these victims was offered a bread-offering and a drink-offering of strong wine.   The morning sacrifice, according to the Jews, made atonement

---

[1] Macknight on Eph. v. 2.
[2] De Ratione Sacrificii, c. iii. n. 13.
[3] Michaelis is of opinion that sin-offerings were made for sins of *commission*, and trespass-offerings for sins of *omission*.   Commentaries, vol. iii. p. 96.
[4] Dr. A. Clarke on Exod. xxix. 10.

for the sins committed in the night, and the evening sacrifice expiated those committed during the day. This sacrifice was a daily expression of national as well as individual repentance, prayer, and thanksgiving.

2. The *Weekly Sacrifice* on every sabbath-day was equal to the daily sacrifice, and was offered in addition to it. (Numb. xxviii. 9, 10.)

3. The *Monthly Sacrifice*, on every new moon, or at the beginning of each month, consisted of two young bullocks, one ram, and seven lambs of a year old, together with a kid for a sin-offering, and a suitable bread and drink offering. (Numb. xxviii. 11—14.)

4. The *Yearly Sacrifices* were those offered on the great annual festivals; viz. (1.) The paschal lamb at the passover, which was celebrated at the commencement of the Jewish *sacred* year; (2.) On the day of pentecost, or day of first-fruits; (3.) On the new moon, or first day of the seventh month, which was the beginning of their *civil* year, or ingathering of the fruits and vintage; and all these stated burnt-offerings were to be accompanied with a sin-offering of a goat, to show their insufficiency to "make the comers thereunto perfect" (Numb. xxviii. Heb. x. 1.); (4.) Lastly, on the day of expiation, or great day of atonement. As a particular account is given of these solemn festivals in the following section, we proceed briefly to notice the second general class of sacrifice; viz.

III. The UNBLOODY OFFERINGS, or MEAT-OFFERINGS (Lev. ii.), which were taken solely from the vegetable kingdom. They consisted of meal, bread, cakes, ears of corn, and parched grain, with oil and frankincense prepared according to the divine command. Regularly they could not be presented as sin-offerings, except in the single case of the person who had sinned being so poor, that the offering of two young pigeons or two turtle doves exceeded his means. They were to be free from leaven or honey: but to all of them it was necessary to add pure salt, that is, saltpetre.

IV. DRINK-OFFERINGS were an accompaniment to both bloody and unbloody sacrifices: they were never used separately, and consisted of wine, which appears to have been partly poured upon the brow of the victim in order to consecrate it, and partly allotted to the priests, who drank it with their portions of both these kinds of offerings. The Psalmist shows how the use of drink-offerings degenerated amongst idolaters, who in their superstitious rage made use of the blood of living creatures, perhaps of men, in their libations. *Their* DRINK-OFFERINGS OF BLOOD, says he, *will I not offer.* (Psal. xvi. 4.)

V. Besides the various kinds of sacrifices above described, there were some oblations made by the Jews consisting of incense, bread, and other things: which have been divided by Lamy into three sorts, viz. such as were *ordinary* or *common*; *voluntary* or free oblations; and such as were *prescribed*.

1. The ORDINARY OBLATIONS were,

(1.) The *Shew-bread* (Heb. *bread of the face*), which consisted of twelve loaves, according to the number of the tribes of Israel. They were placed hot, every sabbath-day, by the priests, upon the golden table in the sanctuary, before the Lord; when they removed the stale loaves which had been exposed for the whole of the preceding week. The priests alone were to eat the bread thus removed. David, however, through necessity broke through this restriction (1 Sam. xxi. 3, 4.)

God preferring mercy to sacrifice, or, in the collision of duties, allowing a positive to give way to a natural law. (Matt. xii. 7.)

(2.) *Incense*, consisting of several fragrant spices, prepared according to the instructions given to Moses in Exod. xxx. 34—36. It was offered twice every day, morning and evening, by the officiating priest, upon an altar of gold, where no bloody sacrifice was to come, during which solemn rite the people prayed without in silence. (Luke i. 10.) But on the great day of expiation the high priest himself took fire from the great altar in a golden censer; and, on descending thence, he received incense from one of the priests, which he offered on the golden altar. During such offering the people prayed silently without; and to this most solemn silence St. John alludes in Rev. viii. 1., where he says that *there was silence in heaven about the space of half an hour*.[1] To this oblation of incense the Psalmist refers (cxli. 2.) in his devotions, and explains his meaning by his application of it: *Let my prayer be set forth in thy sight as the incense*. — "As the smoke and odour of this offering was wafted into the holy place, close by the veil of which stood the altar of incense, so do the prayers of the faithful ascend upwards and find admission to the highest heaven."[2] (Acts x. 4.)

2. The VOLUNTARY or FREE OBLATIONS were either the fruits of promises or of vows; but the former were not considered so strictly obligatory as the latter, of which there were two kinds.

(1.) The *vow of consecration*, when any thing was devoted either for sacrifice or for the service of the temple, as wine, wood, salt, &c.; and

(2.) The *vow of engagement*, when persons engaged to do something that was not in itself unlawful, as not to eat of some particular meat, nor to wear some particular habits, not to drink wine, nor to cut their hair, &c. When the Jews made a vow, they made use of one of these two forms: "*I charge myself with a burnt-offering;*" or "*I charge myself with the price of this animal for a burnt-offering.*" Besides these they had other shorter forms; for instance, when they devoted all they had, they merely said, "*All I have shall be corban,*" that is, "I make an oblation of it to God." Among other false doctrines taught by the Pharisees, who were the depositaries of the sacred treasury, was this, that as soon as a person had pronounced to his father or mother this form of consecration or offering, *Be it corban*, (that is, devoted,) *whatever of mine shall profit thee* (Mark vii. 11.), he thereby consecrated all he had to God, and must not thenceforth do any thing for his indigent parents if they solicited support from him. With great reason, therefore, does Jesus Christ reproach them with having destroyed, by their tradition, not only that commandment of the law which enjoins children

---

[1] Sir Isaac Newton on the Apocalypse, p. 264. See also Woodhouse on Rev. viii. 1. p. 199.

[2] Jones on the Fig. Lang. of Script. Lect. iv. towards the close. "The prayer of faith," adds this learned and pious writer, "is acceptable to God, as the fragrance of incense is agreeable to the senses of man; and, as the incense was offered twice a day, in the morning and evening, the spirit of this service is to be kept up at those times throughout all generations. The prophet Malachi (upon a *forced* and erroneous interpretation of whose words alone the church of Rome has founded and defended the use of incense in her worship) foretold that it should be observed throughout the world (Mal. i. 11.), and in the Revelation we hear of this incense as now actually carried up and presented in heaven (Rev. v. 8.) Happy are they who fulfil this service; and at the rising and going down of the sun send up this offering to heaven, as all Christians are supposed to do, at least twice in every day." Ibid. (Works, vol. iii. p. 66.)

to honour their fathers and mothers, but also another divine precept, which, under the severest penalty, forbad that kind of dishonour which consists in contumelious words. (Mark vii. 9, 10. 13.) They, however, proceeded even further than this unnatural gloss; for, though the son did not directly give, or mean to give, any thing to God at that time, yet if he afterwards should repent of his rashness, and wish to supply them with any thing, what he had formerly said precluded the possibility of doing so; for his property became eventually devoted to God, and according to the Pharisaic doctrine, the sacred treasury had a claim upon it, in preference to the parents. The words "be it corban," or devoted, consequently implied an imprecation against himself, if he should ever afterwards bestow any thing for the relief of his parents: as if he should say to them, "May I incur all the infamy of sacrilege and perjury if ever ye get any thing from me;" than which it is not easy to conceive of any thing spoken by a son to his parents more contemptuous or more barbarous, and therefore justly denominated κακολογια, "opprobrious language."[1]

3. The PRESCRIBED OBLATIONS were either first-fruits or tithes.

(1.) All the *First-Fruits*, both of fruit and animals, were consecrated to God (Exod. xxii. 29. Numb. xviii. 12, 13. Deut. xxvi. 2. Neh. x. 35, 36.)[2]; and the first-fruits of corn, wine, oil, and sheep's wool were offered for the use of the Levites. (Deut. xviii. 4.) The amount of this gift is not specified in the law of Moses, which leaves it entirely to the pleasure of the giver: the Talmudical writers, however, inform us, that liberal persons were accustomed to give the fortieth, and even the thirtieth; while such as were covetous or penurious gave only a sixtieth part. The first of these they called an oblation with a good eye, and the second an oblation with an evil eye. To this traditional saying our Lord is, by some learned men, supposed to have alluded in Matt. xx. 15. Among animals, the males only belong to God; and the Jews not only had a right, but were even obliged, to redeem them in the case of men and unclean animals, which could not be offered in sacrifice. These first-fruits were offered from the feast of pentecost until that of dedication, because after that time the fruits were neither so beautiful nor so good as before. Further, the Jews were prohibited from gathering in the harvest until they had offered to God the *omer*, that is, the new sheaf, which was presented the day after the great day of unleavened bread: neither were they allowed to bake any bread made of new corn until they had offered the new loaves upon the altar on the day of pentecost; without which all the corn was regarded as unclean and unholy. To this St. Paul alludes in Rom. xi. 16.; where he says, *If the* FIRST-FRUIT *be holy, the lump also is holy.* The presentation of the first-fruits was a solemn and festive ceremony. At the beginning of harvest, the sanhedrin deputed a number of priests to go into the fields and reap a handful of the first ripe corn; and these, attended by great crowds of people, went out of one of the gates of Jerusalem into the neighbouring corn-fields. The first-fruits thus

---

[1] Dr. Campbell's Translation of the Four Gospels, vol. ii. pp. 379—382. third edition. Michaelis's Commentaries, vol. iv. p. 300.

[2] From the Jewish custom of offering first-fruits to Jehovah, the heathens borrowed a similar rite. See Pliny, Nat. Hist. lib. xviii. c. 2. Horace, Sat. lib. ii. Sat. v. 12. Tibullus, Eleg. lib. i. El. i. 13.

reaped were carried with great pomp and universal rejoicing through the streets of Jerusalem to the temple. The Jewish writers say that an ox preceded them with gilded horns and an olive crown upon his head, and that a pipe played before them until they approached the city: on entering it they crowned the first-fruits, that is, exposed them to sight with as much pomp as they could, and the chief officers of the temple went out to meet them. They were then devoutly offered to God in grateful acknowledgment of his providential goodness in giving them the fruits of the earth. "These first-fruits, or handful of the first ripe grain, gave notice to all who beheld them that the *general* harvest would soon be gathered in. How beautiful and striking is St. Paul's allusion to this religious ceremony in that most consolatory and closely reasoned chapter, the fifteenth of his first Epistle to the Corinthians, in which, from the resurrection of Jesus Christ, he argues and establishes the certainty of the general resurrection; and represents Christ as the first-fruits of a glorious and universal harvest of all the sleeping dead! *Now is Christ risen, and become the* FIRST-FRUITS *of them that slept.*" (1 Cor. xv. 20.) The use which the apostle makes of this image is very extensive. "In the first place, the growing of grain from the earth where it was buried is an exact image of the resurrection of the body; for, as the one is *sown*, so is the other, and neither *is quickened* except it first die and be buried. Then the whole harvest, from its relation to the first-fruits, explains and ensures the order of our resurrection. For, is the sheaf of the first-fruits reaped? then is the whole harvest ready. Is Christ risen from the dead? then shall all rise in like manner. Is he accepted of God as an holy offering? then shall every sheaf that has grown up with him be taken from the earth and sanctified in its proper order:— *Christ the* FIRST-FRUITS, *and afterwards they that are Christ's at his coming.*" [1] (1 Cor. xv. 23.)

(2.) Besides the first-fruits, the Jews also paid the *Tenths* or *Tithes* of all they possessed. (Numb. xviii. 21.) They were in general collected of all the produce of the earth (Lev. xxvii. 30. Deut. xiv. 22, 23. Neh. xiii. 5. 10.), but chiefly of corn, wine, and oil, and were rendered every year except the sabbatical year. When these tithes were paid, the owner of the fruits further gave another tenth part, which was carried up to Jerusalem, and eaten in the temple at offering feasts, as a sign of rejoicing *and gratitude to God.* These are called *second tithes.*[2] The Levites paid a tenth of the tithes they received to the priests. Lastly, there were tithes allotted to the poor, for whom there was also a corner left in every field, which it was not lawful to reap with the rest (Lev. xix. 9. Deut. xxiv. 19.); and they were likewise allowed such ears of corn, or grapes, as were dropped or scattered about, and the sheaves that might be accidently forgotten in the field. Field-tithes might be redeemed by those who desired it, on

---

[1] Jones's Works, vol. iii. p. 64. Harwood's Introd. to the New Test. vol. ii. p. 307. Michaelis's Commentaries, vol. iii. pp. 146—149. Beausobre's Introd. to the New Test. (vol. iii. p. 200. of Bishop Watson's Collection of Tracts.) Dr. Lightfoot's Works, vol. i. p. 984. vol. ii. pp. 184. 306, 307. folio edit. Lamy's Apparatus, vol. i. p. 204. Ikenii Antiq. Hebr. part i. c. 15. pp. 210—224. Schulzii Archæol. Hebr. pp. 287—292. Lamy's Apparatus Biblicus, vol. i. pp. 203—206.

[2] On the application of these second tithes, see Michaelis's Commentaries, vol. iii. pp. 142, 143.

paying one fifth in addition: but all conversion of the tithes of cattle was prohibited. (Lev. xxvii. 32, 33.) The payment and appreciation of them Moses left to the consciences of the people, without subjecting them to judicial or sacerdotal visitations, but at the same time he did not prohibit the Levites from taking care that they duly received what was their own. The conscientious accuracy of the people, with respect to the second tithe, he secured merely by the declaration which they made every three years before God. From trifling articles he in no case required tithes; though we learn from the Gospel that the Pharisees affected to be scrupulously exact in paying tithes of every the least herb. (Matt. xxiii. 23.) If, however, a person had committed a trespass against the sanctuary, that is, had not paid the tithes of any particular things, and if, at any time afterwards, his conscience were awakened to a sense of his guilt, he had it in his power to make an atonement, without incurring any civil disgrace, by simply paying an additional fifth, with his tithe, and making a trespass-offering.[1] (Lev. v. 14—16.)

The custom of giving tithes to the Deity existed long before the time of Moses. Thus Abraham gave to Melchisedek king of Salem (who was at the same time the priest of the Most High God) the tithe of all that he had taken from the enemy, when he returned from his expedition against the four kings who were in alliance with Chedorlaomer. (Gen. xiv. 20.) And Jacob consecrated to God the tenth of all that he should acquire in Mesopotamia. (Gen. xxviii. 22.) The same custom obtained among various antient nations, who devoted to their gods the tenth part of every thing they obtained.

VI. From the preceding sketch of the Jewish Sacrifices, we may strongly infer their FITNESS AND UTILITY.

According to the refined ideas of modern times, animal sacrifices are a very absurd and savage mode of expressing and promoting devout sentiments and dispositions. But, if we steadily keep in view the genius and habits of antient nations, and the special circumstances of the Hebrews, these objections will vanish; and the propriety as well as expediency of the Jewish institutions will forcibly appear.

" When the practice of sacrificing was first appointed, the use of letters was probably unknown: consequently, the mode of instruction by visible emblems or symbols was both indispensable and highly beneficial. In such a state of things, the offering of animal victims was made to answer for that more simple and rational devotion, which words are now happily fitted to express. When we consider sacrifices, with all their attendant rites, as appointed by God in order to assist the religious instruction, improvement, and consolation of man, we must conclude that the Most High would, in the first instance, clearly explain every part of this institution; otherwise it could not answer its proposed ends. Now, if the moral import of sacrifices were thus explained, the utility of them to mankind in their rude and simple state is beyond calculation. In untutored man, reason is weak, the mental feelings are heavy and rough, while sense, imagination, and passion are the leading avenues both to the understanding and heart. To man thus situated, the appointment of sacrifices is peculiarly

---

[1] Michaelis's Commentaries, vol. iii. pp. 141—145.

adapted : for these convey a most pathetic and awful address to his very senses, and thus rouse him to the most serious and impressive reflections. The frequent spectacles of bleeding and smoking victims, suffering and atoning for the guilty offerers, would give them the deepest impressions of the purity, justice, and majesty of God, of the evil of transgression, of their own ill desert, and of the necessity of some adequate atonement, and of the readiness of the Deity to pardon the penitent. The numerous and diversified offerings of the antient Jews, with the striking pomp which preceded and attended them, were fitted not only to excite and express the most reverential, humble, and grateful devotion ; but also to give the best direction to the whole temper and conduct. The many washings and purifications, enjoined previous to the oblation of sacrifice, were not only physically beneficial in the eastern countries, but directly tended to impress a simple people with a scrupulous regard to inward and moral purity, especially in all their approaches to the Deity. That this was the primary intention of these ceremonies, was a maxim frequently and solemnly enforced. In those early ages, the language of these well-chosen emblems could not fail to be well understood and strongly felt. Above all, the frequent sacrifices of the Jewish law were intended to prefigure, and gradually to prepare men for, the great atoning sacrifice of the promised Messiah." Accordingly, " our Saviour, in allusion to those antient oblations, is called by way of eminence a sin-offering, a perfect sacrifice for the sins of the world. In a word, the religion of the Jews and that of Christians form one great and harmonious plan. The *Jews* saw gospel-truth in its early and gradual dawn ; *we* behold it in its meridian splendour. When Christ appeared, the candid and pious Jews embraced him ; because they saw in him a glorious counterpart, a perfect accomplishment of their antient rites and predictions. The Gentiles, on the other hand, were led to vene-rate and believe in the Hebrew law ; because they beheld in it an exact, though imperfect, figure and prophecy of the Gospel. What beauty and glory do these observations reflect both on the Jewish and Christian dispensations ! What admirable depth of wisdom do they discover in both !" [1]

CHAPTER IV.

SACRED TIMES AND SEASONS OBSERVED BY THE JEWS.

I. The Sabbath. — 1. *How observed.* — 2. *Jewish Worship on that Day ; particularly their Manner of worshipping in the Temple.*—II. New Moons. — III. *Annual Festivals. — Their important Design. —* IV. The Pass-over ; *when celebrated, and with what ceremonies ; its Mystical or Typical Reference.*—V. The Day of Pentecost. — VI. The Feast of Taber-nacles.—VII. *Other Annual Festivals.*—1. The Feast of Trumpets.— 2. The Day of Expiation. — VIII. *Annual Festivals instituted by the*

---

[1] Tappan's Lectures, pp. 116. 118.

In order to perpetuate the memory of the numerous wonders God had wrought in favour of his people, Moses, by the Divine command, instituted various festivals, which they were obliged to observe: these sacred seasons were either weekly, monthly, or annual, or recurred after a certain number of years.

I. Every *seventh day* was appropriated to sacred repose, and called the Sabbath; although this name is in some passages given to other festivals, as in Lev. xxv. 4., and sometimes it denotes a week, as in Matt. xxviii. 1.   Luke xxiv. 1.   Acts xx. 7. and 1 Cor. xvi. 2. (Gr.) It was originally instituted to preserve the memory of the creation of the world (Gen. ii. 3.); whether it continued to be observed by the Israelites as a day of rest and holy convocation during their residence in Egypt, is a question concerning which learned men are by no means agreed.[1]   When, however, God gave them rest in the land of Canaan, he gave them his sabbaths to be statedly kept (Exod. xx. 10, 11. and xvi. 23.); and its observance was specially enjoined on the Israelites in Deut. v. 15., because they were the redeemed people of God, and they were to make the sabbath a day of peculiar recognition of their deliverance from bondage.[2]

1. In the Observance of the Sabbath, the following circumstances were enjoined by divine command: — (1.) This day was to be held sacred as a day of worship, in memory of the creation of the world by Jehovah, and also of the deliverance of the Jews from Egyptian bondage, as well as a day of repose both for man and beast, that they might be refreshed, and not have their bodily strength exhausted by uninterrupted labour (Gen. ii. 1—3.   Deut. v. 13.   Exod. xx. 10, 11.   Ezek. xx. 20.); hence the celebration of the sabbath was the making of a weekly profession that they received and revered the Creator of heaven and earth, and was closely connected with the fundamental principle of the Mosaic law, whose object was to keep the people from idolatry, and to maintain the worship of the one true God; and hence, also, the punishment of death was denounced against the wilful profanation of this solemnity. (2.) On this day they were most religiously to abstain from all manner of work. (Exod. xx. 10. xxiii. 12. xxxi. 12—17. xxxv. 2. Deut. v. 14, 15. Jer. xvii. 22.) It was, therefore, unlawful to gather manna (Exod. xvi. 22—30.), to light a fire for culinary purposes (Exod. xxxv. 3. Numb. xv. 32—36.), and to sow or reap. (Exod. xxxiv. 21.)   To these enactments the Jewish doctors added a variety of other regulations, for which there is not the slightest foundation in the law of Moses.   Thus, it was formerly accounted unlawful to repel force by force on the sabbath-day[3]; and how much its observance was strained by the traditions of the elders

---

[1] For a minute and able discussion of this and every other question connected with the sabbath, the reader is referred to " The Christian Sabbath; or, an Inquiry into the Religious obligation of keeping Holy one Day in Seven.   By the Rev. Geo. Holden, M.A." London, 1825.   8vo.

[2] Stuart's Hebrew Chrestomathy, p. 175.

[3] 1 Macc. ii. 31—38.   See other examples in Josephus, Ant. Jud. lib. xii. c. 6. § 2. De Bell. Jud. lib. ii. c. 16. § 4. lib. iv. c. 2. § 3. and de vita sua, § 32.

in the time of our Lord, is sufficiently manifest. Hence, we find it was deemed unlawful to pluck ears of corn (Matt. xii. 2.) in order to satisfy the cravings of nature, because that was a species of reaping. We learn from the talmudical writers that it was unlawful to use oil medicinally, though they allowed it as a luxury; the anointing of the body with fragrant oils being then, as it is now, in the East, one of their highest enjoyments. It was a traditional rule of the antient Jewish doctors that " whatever could possibly be done on the day before, or might be deferred until the following day, ought not to drive out the sabbath ;" an excellent maxim when rightly understood, but when applied to cases of infirmity or sickness, they manifestly showed that they did not comprehend the meaning of the divine declaration — *I will have mercy and not sacrifice.* In *chronical diseases,* therefore, of which description were those cured by Jesus Christ on the sabbath-day, they conceived that the persons who had so long struggled with them might very well bear them a day longer, rather than prepare medicines or in any way attempt to be cured on that day. The knowledge of this circumstance will greatly illustrate the conduct of our Lord in healing the sick on the sabbath-day, and particularly the man who had been born blind. (John ix.) The rule above stated was made before he began to teach, and he gladly availed himself of the first opportunity to refute their erroneous notions, and expose their gross prevarication in interpreting many of the sabbatical laws. Further, seeing it was prohibited to put fasting spittle upon or into the eyes of a blind man on the sabbath-day, our Saviour effected a cure by using both clay and spittle (John ix. 6. 14.), to show his divine authority, in employing means to human reason the most improper, even on that sacred day, directly in opposition to the above rule; which was good and just in itself, but hypocritical, superstitious, and cruel, when applied to the case of healing on the sabbath.[1] The services of the temple, however, might be performed without profaning the sabbath, such as preparing the sacrifices (Lev. vi. 8—13. Numb. xxviii. 3—10. Matt. xii. 5.); and it was also lawful to perform circumcision on that day. (John vii. 23.) (3.) The sabbath was to be devoted to cheerful rest, that not only the Israelites, but also strangers living with them, as well as their cattle, might be refreshed. (Exod. xxiii. 12.) Hence, it is not improbable, that they celebrated sacrificial or offering feasts, to which, from the commencement of their polity, the poor were invited. In later times, at least, we know from history, that the Jews purchased and prepared the best viands they could procure for the sabbath-day, in order to do it honour; and that they actually had sabbath-feasts, to which they even invited persons with whom they were unacquainted.[2]

The sabbath commenced at sunset, and closed at the same time on

---

[1] Dr. Wotton's Misna, title Shabbath, pp. 101—103. 123. The sabbath, we may observe, was a type of that eternal rest, which all the true servants of God will hereafter enjoy in heaven. See Jones's Lectures on the Epistle to the Hebrews, Lect. ii. (Works, vol. iii. pp. 240—242.)

[2] Luke xiv. 1. and Lightfoot's Horæ Hebraicæ on that passage. (Works, vol. ii. pp. 445, 446.) See also Wetstein's Notes, vol. i. p. 750. Michaelis remarks that our Saviour's observation in Luke xiv. 12—14 can only be fully understood in reference to a feast that formed a part of divine worship, and, as such, might look for a recompense from God: for we do not in ordinary cases expect that God should reward us in another world for every entertainment we give. Commentaries, vol. iii. p. 158.

the following day. (Matt. viii. 16. Mark i. 32.) Whatever was necessary was prepared on the latter part of the preceding day, that is,
of our Friday : hence, the day preceding the sabbath (προσαββατον) is in
the New Testament termed the *preparation* (παρασκευη), in Matt.
xxvii. 62. Mark xv. 42. Luke xxiii. 54. and John xix. 14. 31. 42.[1]

2. We know not with certainty from the Mosaic writings what constituted the most antient WORSHIP of the Israelites on the sabbath-day.
It is, however, evident from the New Testament, that the celebration
of this day chiefly consisted in the religious exercises which were then
performed : though there is no injunction recorded, except that a burnt-
offering of two lambs should on that day be added to the morning and
evening sacrifices (Numb. xxviii. 9.); and that the shew-bread should
be changed. (Lev. xxiv. 8.) In the synagogues[2] the Sacred Writings
were read and expounded, to which was sometimes added a discourse
or sermon by some doctor or eminent teacher. (Luke iv. 16. Acts
xiii. 15.) Prayer also appears to have formed a part of their sacred
worship in the synagogue, and especially in the temple. (1 Sam. i. 9, 10.
1 Kings viii. 29, 30. 33. Psal. xxviii. 2. Luke xviii. 10. Acts ii. 15.
and iii. 1.)

With what reverence the Jews regarded their temple, we have
already seen[3] : and in proportion to the sanctity of the place was the
solemn and holy behaviour required of all who came to worship there.
The law, indeed, had prohibited the approach of all uncleanness ; but
to the enactments of Moses the great masters of traditions added a
variety of other trifling regulations, which the law had not named,
while they scrupled not to make the "house of prayer" a den of
thieves. Dr. Lightfoot has collected many of these traditions respecting the temple worship ; an abridgment of which will form a proper
supplement to the preceding observations.

(1.) No man might enter the "mountain of the house," for so they
called the temple, with his staff; weapons of offence being unsuited
to the house of peace; and it being reputed indecorous to lean, when
there, on any other staff than God. On this account it was, that our
Lord expelled the buyers and sellers of cattle from the temple, with a
whip of cords. (John ii. 15.) — (2.) No man was permitted to enter
with shoes on his feet[4], nor dust on his feet, which he was obliged to
wipe or wash (thus intimating the necessity of approaching the Most
High divested of all worldly cares and affections) ; nor with money in
his purse, nor with his purse about him. — (3.) Having arrived at the
temple, every worshipper was prohibited from spitting there, as well as
from using any irreverent gestures, or making it a thoroughfare to
shorten his distance in crossing from one part of the city to another ;
and on entering the court, he must walk leisurely and gravely to his
place, and there demean himself as in the presence of God. —
(4.) Having now entered to pray and attend the service, he was to
stand with his feet one even with the other; and, casting his eyes down-

---

1 Schulzii Archæologia Hebraica, pp. 311—314. ; Leusden's Philologus Hebræo-
Mixtus, pp. 240—262. ; Beausobre's and L'Enfant's Introduction (Bp. Watson's Theol.
Tracts, vol. iii. pp. 225—234.) ; the Mosaic statutes relative to the sabbath are fully dis-
cussed by Michaelis, Commentaries, vol. iii. pp. 150—181. ; vol. ii. pp. 399, 400.

2 See pp. 254—259. *suprà.*   3 See pp. 243, 244.

4 This prohibition was derived from the command of God to Moses (Exod. iii. 5.), and
Joshua. (v. 15.) The same usage obtains throughout the East to this day.

ward, while he raised his heart upward, must cross his hands upon his breast, and stand as a servant before his master with all reverence and fear. The practice of looking down in prayer the Jews derived from those passages of Scripture, which speak of being ashamed to look up towards heaven, on account of their sinfulness: to this position of looking down and laying his hands upon his heart, the demeanour of the devout publican (Luke xviii. 13.) seems to be parallel. Even the priests when they pronounced the blessing upon the people, neither looked up towards heaven, nor level upon the people, but down upon the ground; and the people were prohibited from looking upon them. — (5.) However weary the worshipper might be with standing, he might on no account sit down either in the Israelites' or priests' court: no person whatever being allowed that privilege, except the kings of the house of David. — (6.) Having offered their prayers, and performed the services, they were to depart in the same order in which they had entered: and as they were prohibited to turn their backs upon the altar, they went backward till they were out of the court, and departed from the temple by a different gate from that by which they had entered.[1]

II. The Jewish months being lunar were originally calculated from the first appearance of the moon, on which the Feast of the New Moon, or the beginning of the month (as the Hebrews termed it), was celebrated. (Exod. xii. 2. Numb. x. 10. xxviii. 11. Isa. i. 13, 14.) It seems to have been in use long before the time of Moses, who by the divine command prescribed what ceremonies were then to be observed. It was proclaimed by the sound of trumpets (Numb. x. 10. Psal. lxxxi. 3.); and several additional sacrifices were offered. (Numb. xxviii. 11—15.)

III. Besides the sabbath, Moses instituted three Annual Festivals, viz. the passover, the feast of pentecost, and the feast of tabernacles: these, which are usually denominated the *Great Festivals*, were distinguished from the sabbath, and indeed from all other holy days, by the circumstance of two of them lasting seven, and one for eight, successive days; during which the Jews were bound to rejoice before the Lord for all their deliverances and mercies. (Deut. xvi. 11—15.) All the males of the twelve tribes were bound to be present at these grand festivals (Exod. xxxiv. 23. Deut. xvi. 16.); and for their encouragement to attend they were assured that *no man should desire their land* during their absence (Exod. xxxiv. 24.) : in other words, that they should be secure from hostile invasion during their attendance on religious worship :—a manifest proof this of the divine origin of their religion, as well as of the power and particular providence of God in working thrice every year an especial miracle for the protection of his people; for it is a well-known fact that the Jews constantly attended these ceremonies without any fear of danger, and that their most vigilant enemies never invaded or injured them during these sacred seasons. The design of these meetings was partly to unite the Jews among themselves, and, teaching them to regard each other as brethren and fellow-citizens, to promote mutual love and friendship. To this the Psalmist probably refers in Psal. cxxii. 3, 4. ; and it was partly that,

---

[1] Lightfoot's Works, vol. ii. pp. 947—950.

as one church, they might make one congregation, join in solemn worship together, and renew their oath of allegiance to the one true God, and to their excellent constitution and religion. Further, so large a concourse of people would give the greater solemnity to these festivals : and as no Israelite was to present himself before the Lord without some offering (Deut. xvi. 16, 17.), ample provision was thus made for the support of the ministers of the sanctuary. On these occasions, although the men were required to attend, it does not appear that women were prevented from going if they chose, at least to the passover. (See 1 Sam. i. 3. 7. Luke ii. 41.) For greater security, however, against the attacks of robbers on the road, they used to travel in large companies, those who came from the same city, canton, or district, forming one company. They carried necessaries along with them, and tents for their lodging at night.[1] It was among such a " company" that Joseph and Mary sought Jesus Christ (Luke ii. 44.) : and to their journeying through a dreary valley on one of these festivals the Psalmist probably alludes. (lxxxiv. 6.) Further, as the Jewish sanctuary and service contained in them a shadow of good things to come, and were typical of the Christian church, this prescribed concourse from all parts of the country might be intended to typify the gathering of the people to Christ and into his church, from all parts of the world under the Christian dispensation. Hence St. Paul, alluding to these general assemblies of the Israelites on the three grand feasts, says, "We are come to the *general assembly and church of the first-born.*" (Heb. xii. 23.)

But besides the benefits to be derived from the religious celebration of these ordinances, Michaelis, to whom we are indebted for part of the preceding remarks, has pointed out several instances in which they produced a salutary effect on the community. Not only would their meeting together in one place for the purposes of religion and social intercourse tend to prevent a total alienation of rival tribes, as well as civil war, but it would also afford them an opportunity of being mutually reconciled. Further, it is not improbable that these annual meetings promoted the internal commerce of the Israelites, who were prohibited from carrying on traffic with foreigners ; and, lastly, they had an important influence on the Jewish calendar, inasmuch as the year was arranged, so that the various festivals should fall in their respective months without interfering with the labours of the field.[2]

IV. The first and most eminent of these festivals was the PASSOVER [3],

---

[1] Nearly similar to this is the mode of travelling in the East to this hour. Such companies they now call caravans ; and in many places there are buildings fitted up for their reception, called *caravanserais.* This account of the Israelites' mode of travelling furnishes a ready answer to the question, how Joseph and Mary could make a day's journey without discovering, before night, that Jesus was not in the " company." In the day-time, as circumstances might lead them, the travellers would probably mingle with their friends and acquaintance ; but in the evening, when they were about to encamp, every one would join the family to which he belonged. As Jesus then did not appear when it was growing late, his parents first sought him, where they supposed he would most probably be, among his relations and acquaintance : and not finding him, returned to Jerusalem. Dr. Campbell's Translation of the Gospels, vol. ii. p. 449. note on Luke ii. 44. See also Roberts's Oriental Illustrations, p. 561.

[2] Commentaries on the Law of Moses, vol. iii. pp. 182—189. Jennings's Jewish Antiquities, book iii. ch. 4. pp. 448, 449. Tappan's Lectures on Jewish Antiquities, pp. 127, 128.

[3] On the true meaning of the word *passover* Archbp. Magee has a learned disquisition in

instituted the night before the Israelites' departure from Egypt, for a perpetual memorial of their signal deliverance, and of the favour which God showed them in passing over and sparing their first-born, when he slew the first-born of the Egyptians. (Exod. xii. 12—14. 29—51.) This festival was also called the *feast* or *the days of unleavened bread* (Exod. xxiii. 15. Mark xiv. 1. Acts xii. 3.) ; because it was unlawful to eat any other bread during the seven days the feast lasted. The name was also by a metonymy given to the lamb that was killed on the first day of this feast (Ezra vi. 20. Matt. xxvi. 17.), whence the expressions to *eat the passover* (Mark xiv. 12. 14.)[1] and to *sacrifice* the passover.[2] (1 Cor. v. 7.) Hence also St. Paul calls Jesus Christ our passover (ibid.), that is, our true paschal lamb. But the appellation, passover, belongs more particularly to the second day of the feast, viz. the fifteenth day of the month Nisan.[3] It was ordained to be celebrated on the anniversary of the deliverance of the Israelites. This was an indispensable rite to be observed by every Israelite, except in particular cases enumerated in Numb. ix. 1—13., on pain of death[4]; and no uncircumcised person was allowed to partake of the passover.[5] On this festive occasion, it was the custom at Jerusalem for the inhabitants to give the free use of their rooms and furniture to strangers at the passover. This usage will explain the circumstance of our Saviour's sending to a man to prepare for his eating the passover, who, by the relation, appears to have been a stranger to him. Further, in order to render this grand festival the more interesting, a custom was introduced in the later times of the Jewish polity, of liberating some criminal. By whom or at what time this practice originated, it is now impossible accurately to determine : the most probable opinion is, that it was introduced by the Romans themselves, perhaps by Pilate at the commencement of his procuratorship of Judæa, with the permission of Augustus, in order to gratify the Jews by showing them this public mark of respect.[6] However this may be, it had become an established custom from which Pilate could not deviate (Matt. xxvii. 15. Luke xxiii. 17. John xviii. 39.), and therefore he reluctantly liberated the malefactor Barabbas.

---

vol. i. of his Discourses on the Atonement, pp. 309—321. That it was a kind of fœderal rite (as the Eucharist also is) between God and man, Dr. Cudworth has solidly proved in his " True Notion of the Lord's Supper," chap. vi. pp. 28—36. at the end of vol. ii. of his " Intellectual System," 4to. edit.

[1] Schulzii Archæologia Hebr. p. 318.

[2] That the passover was a proper and real sacrifice, see largely proved by Archbp. Magee, on the Atonement. vol. i. pp. 297—309.

[3] Lev. xxiii. 6.   Mark xiv. 1.   Josephus, Ant. Jud. lib. iii. c. 10. § 5.

[4] In like manner, Dr. Waterland has observed, a contempt and rejection of at least the thing signified by the sacrament of the Lord's supper, must necessarily exclude every man from the benefits of Christ's passion and death.

[5] So, in the early ages of Christianity, no person was permitted to come to the Lord's supper until he had been baptised. As soon, however, as the passover was celebrated, every one was at liberty to go home the very next morning if he pleased (Deut. xvi. 7.), of course while the festival lasted, in order that those Jews, who came from a distance, might return in time for getting in the harvest. Michaelis's Commentaries, vol. iii. pp. 183, 184.

[6] Hottinger has discussed the various opinions on the origin of this usage in a dissertation *De ritû dimittendi reum in festo Paschatis*, Tempe Helvetic. vol. iv. p. 264. From the Jews the custom proceeded to the Christians; Valentinian and several other emperors having issued their edict, that some prisoners should be liberated from their bonds at the annual commemoration of our Saviour's resurrection. This custom obtained among the Venetians till the close of the eighteenth century. (Schulzii Archæol. Hebr. p. 321.)

As the very interesting history of this most solemn of all the Jewish festivals is copiously related in the twelfth chapter of Exodus, it is unnecessary to detail it again in this place : but as various traditional observances were in after-times added to the Mosaic precepts concerning this sacrifice, to which there are manifest allusions in the New Testament, we shall trace them, as briefly as the important nature of the subject will admit, under the following heads : — 1. The time when it was to be kept ; — 2. The ceremonies with which it was to be celebrated ; — 3. The mystical signification of these rites.

1. *Of the time when the Passover was to be kept.* — This festival commenced on the evening subsequent to the fourteenth day of the month Nisan, the first in the Jewish sacred or ecclesiastical year (Exod. xii. 6. 8. 18. Lev. xxiii. 4—8. Numb. xxviii. 16—27.), with eating what was called the paschal lamb ; and it was to continue seven whole days, that is, until the twenty-first. The day preceding its commencement was called the *preparation of the passover.* (John xix. 14.) During its continuance no leavened bread was allowed to be used ; hence the fourteenth day of the month Nisan might with great propriety be called (as we find it is in Matt. xxvi. 17. Mark xiv. 12.) the first day of unleavened bread, because the passover began in the evening. The *fifteenth* day, however, might also be called the first day of unleavened bread [1] : since, according to the Hebrew computation of time, the evening of the fourteenth was the dawn or beginning of the fifteenth, on which day the Jews began to eat unleavened bread. (Exod. xii. 18.) But if any persons were prevented from arriving at Jerusalem in time for the feast, either by any uncleanness contracted by touching a dead body, or by the length of the journey, he was allowed to defer his celebration of the passover until the fourteenth day of the following month, in the evening. (Numb. ix. 10—12.) As it is not improbable that some difference or mistake might arise in determining the new moon, so often as such difference recurred, there would consequently be some discrepancy as to the precise time of commencing the passover. Such a discordance might easily arise between the rival and hostile sects of Pharisees and Sadducees ; and such a difference, it has been conjectured, did exist at the time Jesus Christ celebrated the passover with his disciples, one whole day before the Pharisees offered their paschal sacrifice.[2] Sacrifices peculiar to this festival were to be offered every day during its continuance ; but the first and last days were to be sanctified above all the rest, by abstaining from servile labour, and holding a sacred convocation. (Exod. xii. 16. Lev. xxiii. 7, 8.)

2. *Of the ceremonies with which the Passover was to be celebrated.* — The paschal lamb was to be a male, without blemish, of the first year,

---

[1] The fifteenth day is so called in Lev. xxiii. 6. and by Josephus, who expressly terms the *second day* of unleavened bread the sixteenth day of the month. Ant. Jud. lib. iii. c. 10. § 5.

[2] Schulzii Archæol. Hebr. pp. 318, 319. That a difference did exist as to the time of beginning the passover is intimated in John xiii. 1, 2. xviii. 28. and xix. 14. 31. The conjecture above noticed was made by Schulze ; and if it could be substantiated, it would reconcile the seeming differences occurring in the evangelists, respecting the time when Christ actually celebrated the passover. Dr. A. Clarke has collected the principal opinions on this much contested point, in his discourse on the Eucharist, pp. 5—24. See also Jennings's Jewish Antiquities, book iii. c. 4. pp. 455—458.

either from the sheep or the goats [1] (Exod. xii. 5.) : it was to be taken from the flocks four days before it was killed ; and one lamb was to be offered for each family ; and if its members were too few to eat a whole lamb, two families were to join together.   In the time of Josephus a paschal society consisted at least of ten persons to one lamb, and not more than twenty.[2]   Our Saviour's society was composed of himself and the twelve disciples. (Matt. xxvi. 20. Luke xxii. 14.) Next followed the killing of the passover : before the exode of the Israelites from Egypt, this was done in their private dwellings ; but after their settlement in Canaan, it was ordered to be performed "in the place which the Lord should choose to place his name there." (Deut. xvi. 2.) This appears to have been at first wherever the ark was deposited, and ultimately at Jerusalem in the courts of the temple.[3] Every particular person (or rather a delegate from every paschal society [4]) slew his own victim : according to Josephus, between the *ninth* hour, or *three* in the afternoon, and the *eleventh*, that is, about sunset ; and within that space of time it was, that Jesus Christ, our true paschal lamb, was crucified. (Matt. xxvii. 46.) The victim being killed, one of the priests received the blood into a vessel, which was handed from one priest to another, until it came to him who stood next the altar, and by whom it was sprinkled at the bottom of the altar.   After the blood was sprinkled, the lamb was hung up and flayed : this being done, the victim was opened, the fat was taken out and consumed on the altar, after which the owner took it to his own house.   The paschal lamb was to be roasted *whole*, which might be commanded as a matter of convenience at the first passover, in order that their culinary utensils might be packed up ready for their departure while the lamb was roasting ; no part of it was to be eaten either in a *raw* state, or boiled. (Exod. xii. 9.)

The propriety of the prohibition of eating any portion of the paschal lamb in a *raw* state will readily appear, when it is known that raw flesh and palpitating limbs were used in some of the old heathen sacrifices and festivals, particularly in honour of the Egyptian deity Osiris, and the Grecian Bacchus, who were the same idol under different names. That no resemblance or memorial of so barbarous a superstition might ever debase the worship of Jehovah, He made this early and express provision against it.   On the same ground, probably, He required the paschal lamb to be eaten privately and entire, in opposition to the bacchanalian feasts, in which the victim was publicly torn in pieces, carried about in pomp, and then devoured.   Further, the prohibition of boiling the paschal lamb was levelled against a superstitious practice of the Egyptians and Syrians, who were accustomed to boil their victims, and especially to seethe a kid or lamb in the milk of its dam ; as the command to roast and eat the *whole* of the lamb — not excepting its inwards — without leaving any portion until the following morning, was directed against another superstition of the antient heathens,

---

[1] The Hebrew word שה (seh) means either a lamb or a kid : either was equally proper. The Hebrews, however, in general preferred a lamb.

[2] De Bell. Jud. lib. vi. c. 9. § 3.

[3] The area of the three courts of the temple, besides the rooms and other places in it, where the paschal victim might be offered, contained upwards of 435,600 square cubits ; so that there was ample room for more than 500,000 men to be in the temple at the same time. Lamy, De Tabernaculo, lib. vii. c. 9. §§ 4, 5.

[4] See Lightfoot's Temple Service, ch. xii. § 5. (Works, vol. i. pp. 957—959.)

whose priests carefully preserved and religiously searched the entrails of their victims, whence they gathered their pretended knowledge of futurity. Those, likewise, who frequented pagan temples, were eager to carry away and devote to superstitious uses some sacred relics or fragments of the sacrifices. In short, the whole ceremonial of the passover appears to have been so adjusted as to wage an open and destructive war against the gods and idolatrous ceremonies of Egypt, and thus to form an early and powerful barrier around the true worship and servants of Jehovah.[1]

After the lamb was thus dressed, it was eaten by each family or paschal society.[2] " The FIRST passover was to be eaten standing, in the posture of travellers, who had no time to lose; and with unleavened bread and bitter herbs, and no bone of it was to be broken. (Exod. xii. 8. 11. 46.) The posture of travellers was enjoined them, both to enliven their faith in the promise of their then speedy deliverance from Egypt; and also, that they might be ready to begin their march presently after supper. They were ordered, therefore, to eat it with their loins girded; for as they were accustomed to wear long and loose garments, such as are generally used by the eastern nations to this day, it was necessary to tie them up with a girdle about their loins, when they either travelled or engaged in any laborious employment."[3] Further, " they were to eat the passover *with shoes on their feet,* for in those hot countries they ordinarily wore sandals, which were a sort of clogs, or went barefoot; but in travelling they used shoes, which were a kind of short boots, reaching a little way up the legs. Hence, when our Saviour sent his twelve disciples to preach in the neighbouring towns, designing to convince them by their own experience of the extraordinary care of Divine Providence over them, that they might not be discouraged by the length and danger of the journeys they would be called to undertake;—on this account he ordered them to make no provision for their present journey, particularly, not to take shoes on their feet, but to be shod with sandals. (Matt. x. 10. compared with Mark vi. 9.) Again they were to eat the passover with *staves in their hands,* such as were always used by travellers in those rocky countries, both to support them in slippery places, and defend them against assaults. (Gen. xxxii. 10.)[4] Of this sort was probably Moses's rod which he had in his hand, when God sent him with a message to Pharaoh (Exod. iv. 2.), and which was afterwards used as an instrument in working so many miracles. So necessary in these countries was a staff or walking-stick on a journey, that it was a usual thing for persons when they undertook long journeys to take a spare staff with them, for fear one should fail. When Christ, therefore, sent his apostles on the embassy above

---

[1] Tappan's Lectures on Jewish Antiquities, pp. 123, 124.

[2] Beausobre says that these sodalities were called *brotherhoods,* and the guests *companions* or *friends,* and that our Saviour's reproof of Judas by calling him friend or companion (Matt. xxvi. 50.) was both just and cutting, because he betrayed him after having eaten the passover with him.

[3] Thus when Elisha sent his servant Gehazi on a message in haste, he bade him "gird up his loins," 2 Kings iv. 29.; and when our Saviour set about washing his disciples' feet, " he took a towel and girded himself." John xiii. 4.

[4] David beautifully alludes to this custom in the twenty-third Psalm; where (ver. 4.), expressing his trust in the goodness of the Almighty, he exclaims, *Yea, though I walk through the valley of the shadow of death, I will fear no evil: for thou art with me, thy* ROD *and thy* STAFF *they comfort me.*

mentioned, he ordered them not to take staves (Luke ix. 3. Mark vi. 8.), that is, only one staff or walking-stick, without making provision of a spare one, as was common in long journeys.

" The paschal lamb was to be eaten with unleavened bread, on pain of being cut off from Israel, or excommunicated; though some critics understand this of being put to death. The reason of this injunction was, partly to remind them of the hardships they had sustained in Egypt, unleavened being more heavy and less palatable than leavened bread; on which account it is called the bread of affliction (Deut. xvi. 3.) ; and partly to commemorate the speed of their deliverance or departure from thence, which was such, that they had not sufficient time to leaven their bread; it is expressly said, that their " dough was not leavened, because they were thrust out of Egypt and could not tarry (Exod. xii. 39.); and on this account it was enacted into a standing law, 'Thou shalt eat unleavened bread, even the bread of affliction ; for thou camest forth out of Egypt in haste.' (Deut. xvi. 3.) This rite, therefore, was not only observed at the first passover, but in all succeeding ages." [1]   But from the metaphorical sense in which the term *leaven* is used [2], this prohibition is supposed to have had a moral view; and that the divine legislator's intention was, that the Israelites should cleanse their minds from malice, envy, and hypocrisy; in a word, from the leaven of Egypt. In consequence of this injunction, the Hebrews, as well as the modern Jews, have always taken particular care to search for all the leaven that might be in their houses, and to burn it. [3]

The passover was likewise to be eaten " with bitter herbs : " this was doubtless prescribed as "a memorial of their severe bondage in Egypt, which made their lives *bitter* unto them ; and possibly also to denote that the haste, in which they departed, compelled them to gather such wild herbs as most readily presented themselves. To this sauce the Jews afterwards added another, made of dates, raisins, and several ingredients beaten together to the consistence of mustard, which is called *charoseth,* and is designed to represent the clay in which their forefathers wrought while they were in bondage to the Egyptians.

" It was further prescribed, that they should eat the flesh of the lamb, without breaking any of his bones. (Exod. xii. 46.) This the latter Jews understand, not of the smaller bones, but only of the greater which had marrow in them. Thus was this rite also intended to denote their being in haste, not having time to break the bones and suck out the marrow."

---

[1] Jennings's Jewish Antiquities, book iii. ch. iv. pp. 468—470. (London, 1823, 8vo.)

[2] Lightfoot's Works, vol. i. pp. 953, 954. Allen's Modern Judaism, p. 381.

[3] See Matt. xvi. 6. St. Paul, writing to the Corinthians a short time before the passover, exhorts them to cleanse out the old leaven of lewdness by casting the incestuous person out of the church ; and to *keep the feast* (of the Lord's supper) *not with the old leaven* of sensuality and uncleanness, with which they were formerly corrupted, *neither with the leaven of malice and wickedness, but with the unleavened bread* (or qualities) *of sincerity and truth.* Macknight on 1 Cor. v. 7, 8. ; who observes, that it is probable from this passage that the disciples of Christ began very early to celebrate the Lord's supper with peculiar solemnity, annually, on the day on which the Redeemer suffered, which was the day of the Jewish passover, called in modern language *Easter.* It is with beautiful propriety, therefore, that this passage of Saint Paul is introduced by the Anglican Church among the occasional versicles for Easter Sunday.

Lastly, "it was ordered that nothing of the paschal lamb should remain till the morning; but, if it were not all eaten, it was to be consumed by fire. (Exod. xii. 10.) The same law was extended to all eucharistical sacrifices (Lev. xxii. 30.); no part of which was to be left, or set by, lest it should be corrupted, or converted to any profane or common use, — an injunction which was designed, no doubt, to maintain the honour of sacrifices, and to teach the Jews to treat with reverence whatever was consecrated more especially to the service of God." [1]

Such were the circumstances under which the first passover was celebrated by the Israelites; for, after they were settled in the land of Canaan, they no longer ate it standing, but the guests reclined on their left arms upon couches placed round the table. (John xiii. 23.) This posture, according to the talmudical writers, was an emblem of that rest and freedom which God had granted to the children of Israel by bringing them out of Egypt. This custom of reclining at table, over one another's bosom, was a sign of *equality* and strict union among the guests.[2]

Dr. Lightfoot has collected from the Talmud a variety of passages relative to the Jewish mode of celebrating the passover; from which we have abridged the following particulars, as they are calculated materially to illustrate the evangelical history of our Lord's last passover, recorded in Matt. xxvi. Mark xiv. Luke xxii. and John xiii.

(1.) The guests being placed around the table, they mingled a cup of wine with water, over which the master of the family (or, if two or more families were united, a person deputed for the purpose) gave thanks, and then drank it off. The thanksgiving for the wine was to this effect, "*Blessed be thou, O Lord, who hast created the fruit of the vine;*" and for the day, as follows — "*Blessed be thou for this good day, and for this holy convocation, which thou hast given us for joy and rejoicing! Blessed be thou, O Lord, who hast sanctified Israel and the times!*" Of these cups of wine they drank four in the course of the ordinance.

(2.) They then washed their hands, after which the table was furnished with the paschal lamb, roasted whole, with bitter herbs, and with two cakes of unleavened bread, together with the remains of the peace-offerings sacrificed on the preceding day, and the charoseth, or thick sauce, above mentioned.

(3.) The officiator, or person presiding, then took a small piece of salad, and having blessed God for creating the fruit of the ground, he ate it, as also did the other guests: after which all the dishes were removed from the table, that the children might inquire and be instructed in the nature of the feast. (Exod. xii. 25, 26.) The text on which they generally discoursed was Deut. xxvi. 5—11. In like manner our Saviour makes use of the sacrament of the Lord's supper, to declare the great mercy of God in our redemption; for it *shows forth the Lord's death till he come* to judge the world. The "continual re-

---

[1] Jennings's Jewish Antiquities, book iii. ch. iv. pp. 470, 471.

[2] This custom, Beausobre well observes, will explain several passages of Scripture, particularly those in which mention is made of Abraham's bosom (Luke xvi. 22.), and of the Son's being *in the bosom of the Father.* (John i. 18. compared with Phil. ii. 6. and John xiii. 23.)

membrance of the sacrifice of the death of Christ, and of the benefits we receive thereby," which has been observed ever since the time of the apostles, is a permanent and irrefragable argument for the reality of that "full, perfect, and sufficient sacrifice, oblation, and satisfaction for the sins of the whole world," which was made by Jesus Christ "by his one oblation of himself" upon the cross; in opposition to the opinion of those who deny the divinity of our Saviour, and the vicarious nature of his death.

(4.) Then replacing the supper, they explained the import of the bitter herbs and paschal lamb; and over the *second* cup of wine repeated the hundred and thirteenth and hundred and fourteenth psalms, with an eucharistic prayer.

(5.) The hands were again washed, accompanied by an ejaculatory prayer; after which the master of the house proceeded to break and bless a cake of the unleavened bread, which he distributed among the guests, reserving half of the cake beneath a napkin, if necessary, for the *aphicomen*, or last morsel; for the rule was, to conclude with eating a small piece of the paschal lamb, or, after the destruction of the temple, of unleavened bread.[1]   In like manner our Lord, upon instituting the sacrament of the eucharist, which was prefigured by the passover, took bread; and having blessed or given thanks to God, he brake it, and gave it to his disciples, saying, *Take, eat, this is* [that is, signifies] *my body, which is given for you.   This do in remembrance of me.* (Matt. xxvi. 26. Mark xiv. 22. Luke xxii. 19. 1 Cor. xi. 23, 24.)   In the communion service of the Anglican church, the spirit and design both of the type and antitype are most expressively condensed into one point of view in the following address to the communicant: — "*Take and eat this in remembrance that Christ died for thee, and feed upon him in thy heart by faith, with thanksgiving.*"

(6.) They then ate the rest of the cake with the bitter herbs, dipping the bread into the charoseth, or sauce. To this practice the evangelists Matthew (xxvi. 21—25.) and Mark (xiv. 18—21.) manifestly allude; and into this sauce our Saviour is supposed to have dipped the sop which he gave to Judas. (John xiii. 26.)

(7.) Next they ate the flesh of the peace-offerings which had been sacrificed on the fourteenth day, and then the flesh of the paschal lamb, which was followed by returning thanks to God, and a second washing of hands.

(8.) A third cup of wine was then filled, over which they blessed God, or said grace after meat (whence it was called the *cup of blessing*), and drank it off. To this circumstance St. Paul particularly alludes when he says, — *The cup of blessing which we bless, is it not the communion of the blood of Christ?* (1 Cor. x. 16.)   It was also at this part of the paschal supper that our Lord *took the cup, saying, This is the new testament* (rather *covenant*) *in my blood, which is shed for you, and for many, for the remission of sins.* (Luke xxii. 20. Matt.

---

[1] In this part of the paschal ceremony, among the modern Jews, after the master of the house has reserved the portion for the *aphicomen*, the bone of the lamb and the egg are taken off the dish, and all at table lay hold of the dish and say,—" *Lo! this is* [or signifies] *the bread of affliction, which our ancestors ate in the land of Egypt; let all those who are hungry eat thereof; and all who are necessitous, come, and celebrate the Passover.*" Form of prayers for the Festivals of Passover and Pentecost, according to the custom of the Spanish and Portuguese Jews, translated from the Hebrew by David Levi, p. 20.

xxvi. 27.) The *cup* here is put for *wine;* and *covenant* is put for the *token* or *sign* of the covenant. The *wine,* as representing Christ's *blood,* answers to the blood of the passover, which typified it; and the *remission of sins* here, answers to the passing over there, and preserving from death.[1]

(9.) Lastly, a fourth cup of wine was filled, called the cup of the hallel: over it they completed, either by singing or recitation, the great hallel, or hymn of praise, consisting of psalms cxv. to cxviii. inclusive, with a prayer, and so concluded.[2] In like manner our Lord and his disciples, when they had sung a hymn, departed to the Mount of Olives. (Matt. xxvi. 30, Mark xiv. 26.)

3. *With regard to the mystical signification of the passover,* we know generally from Saint Paul (1 Cor. v. 7.), who calls Jesus Christ *our passover,* that this Jewish sacrament had a typical reference to him: but, concerning the points of resemblance between the type and antitype, learned men are not agreed. Godwin[3] has enumerated *thirteen* points of coincidence; Dr. Lightfoot[4], *seventeen;* and Keach[5], *nineteen.* The most judicious arrangement of this subject which we have seen is that of Herman Witsius[6], who has treated it under four general heads, viz. the person of Christ, — the sufferings he bore for us, — the fruits of those sufferings, — and the manner in which we are made partakers of them. As, however, many of the analogies which Witsius has traced between the passover and the death of Christ are very fanciful, his arrangement only has been adopted in the following observations: —

(1.) THE PERSON OF CHRIST WAS TYPIFIED BY THE PASCHAL LAMB.

"The animal sacrificed at the passover was to be a lamb without blemish. (Exod. xii. 5.) Christ is styled the Lamb of God, which taketh away the sin of the world (John i. 29. 36.); a lamb without blemish and without spot. (1 Pet. i. 19. See Isa. liii. 7.) The paschal lamb was to be one of the flock. Christ the Word who was

---

[1] Clarke on the Eucharist, p. 39. On this part of the institution of the Lord's supper, Dr. Lightfoot has the following admirable remarks: — " *This is my blood of the New Testament.* Not only the seal of the covenant, but the sanction of the new covenant. The end of the Mosaic economy, and the confirming of a new one. The confirmation of the old covenant was by the *blood of bulls and of goats* (Exod. xxiv. Heb. ix.), because blood was still to be shed: the confirmation of the new was by a cup of wine; because under the new covenant there is no further shedding of blood. As it is here said of the cup, *This cup is the New Testament in my blood;* so it might be said of the *cup of blood.* (Exod. xxiv.) *That cup was the Old Testament in the blood of Christ:* there all the articles of that covenant being read over, Moses sprinkled all the people with blood, and said, *This is the blood of the covenant which God hath made with you;* and thus that old covenant, or testimony, was confirmed. In like manner, Christ, having published all the articles of the new covenant, he takes the cup of wine, and gives them to drink, and saith, *This is the New Testament in my blood,* and thus the new covenant was established."—(*Works,* vol. ii. p. 260.) Hor. Heb. on Matt. xxvi. 27.

[2] Lightfoot's Temple Service, c. xiii. (Works, vol. i. pp. 959—967.) See also Mr. Ainsworth's learned and interesting notes on Exod. xii. in his Annotations on the Pentateuch.

[3] Godwin's Moses and Aaron, pp. 114, 115.

[4] Lightfoot's Works, vol. i. pp. 1008, 1009.

[5] Keach's Key to Scripture Metaphors, pp. 979, 980. 2d. edit. See also M'Ewen on the Types, pp. 148—152.

[6] Witsius, de Œconomica Fœderum, lib. iv. c. 9. §§ 35—58. or vol. ii. pp. 275—282. of the English translation. Witsius's View of the Mystical Import of the Passover has been abridged by Dr. Jennings. Jewish Antiq. book iii. ch. iv. pp. 472—477.

made flesh, and dwelt among us (John i. 14.), was taken from the midst of the people, being in all things made like unto his brethren." (Heb. ii. 17.)[1]

(2.) THE SUFFERINGS AND DEATH OF CHRIST WERE ALSO TYPIFIED BY THE PASCHAL LAMB IN VARIOUS PARTICULARS.

" The sacrifice of the passover differed from other sacrifices, in being a public act of the whole people: it was to be slain by ' the whole assembly of the congregation of Israel.' (Exod. xii. 6.) The chief priests, and the rulers, and the people, were consenting to the death of Jesus. (Luke xxiii. 13.) The blood of the passover was, at its first institution, to be sprinkled upon the lintel, and the two side-posts (Exod. xii. 7. 22.), for the protection of the people; and in the subsequent celebration of the paschal sacrifice, ' the priests sprinkled the blood which they received of the hand of the Levites.' (2 Chron. xxx. 16. xxxv. 11.) It is by the sprinkling of the blood of Jesus Christ, that our consciences are purged (Heb. ix. 14.), and protection and salvation obtained. (Heb. xii. 24. 1 Pet. i. 2.) The passover was to be eaten by the Israelites, in the character of travellers, with their loins girded, their shoes upon their feet, and their staff in their hand. (Exod. xii. 11.) They, for whom Christ is sacrificed, are compared to strangers and pilgrims (1 Pet. ii. 11.), and are commanded to stand, having their loins girt about with truth, and having on the breast-plate of righteousness, and their feet shod with the preparation of the gospel of peace. (Eph. vi. 15.) The Israelites were to eat the passover in haste. (Exod. xii. 11.) We are to give diligence to make our calling and election sure (2 Pet. i. 10.); and to flee for refuge to lay hold upon the hope set before us. (Heb. vi. 18.) The passover was to be sacrificed only in the tabernacle, and afterwards only in the temple at Jerusalem. (Deut. xvi. 5, 6.) Neither could it be that Christ should perish out of Jerusalem. (Luke xiii. 33.) The month, and day of the month, on which the passover was to be sacrificed by the Israelites, is laid down with accuracy. And on the very day on which the passover *ought* to be slain, (Luke xxii. 7. Ἐν ᾗ ΕΔΕΙ θυεσθαι το πασχα,) and on which Christ celebrated the paschal feast with his disciples, he endured his agony and bloody sweat; and he suffered death upon the cross, on the day when, at least the scribes and Pharisees, and some of the principal men among the Jews, did ' eat the passover.' (John xviii. 28.) Further, not a bone of the paschal victim was to be broken, (Exod. xii. 46.) — a typical circumstance, which the evangelist specially notices as fulfilled in the person of Jesus Christ. (John xix. 32—36.)

" Another peculiarity in the paschal offering is the time of the *day* at which it was appointed to be slain. ' The whole assembly of the congregation shall kill it in the evening' (Exod. xii. 6.); or, as the expression is rendered in the margin, between the two evenings. — Now at the very time appointed for the sacrifice of the paschal lamb, between the two evenings, Christ our passover was sacrificed for us. The scene of suffering began at the third hour of the day. (Mark xv. 25.) And at the sixth hour there was darkness over all the land until the ninth hour. (Matt. xxvii. 45. Mark xv. 33. Luke xxiii. 44.) And about

---

[1] Chevallier's Hulsean Lectures, on the Historical Types of the Old Testament, p. 285.

the *ninth* hour, Jesus cried with a loud voice, and gave up the ghost. (Matt. xxvii. 46. 50. Mark xv. 34. 37.)"[1]

(3.) SEVERAL OF THE FRUITS OF CHRIST'S DEATH WERE REMARKABLY TYPIFIED BY THE SACRIFICE OF THE PASCHAL LAMB.

Such are " protection and salvation by his blood, of which the sprinkling of the door-posts with the blood of the lamb, and the safety which the Israelites by that means enjoyed from the plague that spread through all the families of the Egyptians, was a designed and illustrious emblem. In allusion to this type, the blood of Christ is called *the blood of sprinkling.* (1 Pet. i. 2. Heb. xii. 24.) Immediately upon the Israelites eating the first passover, they were delivered from their Egyptian slavery, and restored to full liberty, of which they had been deprived for many years; and such is the fruit of the death of Christ, in a spiritual and much nobler sense, to all that believe in him; for he hath thereby " obtained eternal redemption for us," and " brought us into the glorious liberty of the children of God." (Heb. ix. 12. Rom. viii. 21.)[2]

(4.) THE MANNER IN WHICH WE ARE TO BE MADE PARTAKERS OF THE BLESSED FRUITS OF THE SACRIFICE OF CHRIST, WERE ALSO REPRESENTED BY LIVELY EMBLEMS IN THE PASSOVER.

" The paschal lamb was ordered to be slain, and his blood was directed to be sprinkled upon the lintel and the door-posts of each dwelling occupied by God's chosen people; that, when the angel smote the Egyptians, he might pass over the houses of the Israelites and leave them secure from danger: in a similar manner, by the blood of Christ alone, shed for many for the remission of sins, can the impending wrath of heaven be averted from sinful man. Before the blood of our Lord was sprinkled upon his church, we stood (as it were) without, exposed, like the Egyptians, to the vengeance of a justly incensed God: but now his precious blood-shedding, like the sprinkled blood of the paschal lamb, is our safety and defence, so that the anger of Jehovah may pass over us. The death of the paschal lamb was for the deliverance of the Levitical church; yet, if any negligent or unbelieving Israelite availed not himself of the proffered refuge, he perished undistinguished with the Egyptians: thus likewise the death of the Lamb of God was for the deliverance of the Christian church; but, if any one claims to be a Christian in name, while yet he renounces the doctrine of pardon and acceptance through the sprinkled blood of the Messiah, he then places himself without the doors of the church, and will be strictly judged according to his works by a law which pronounces that man accursed who observes not with *undeviating* punctuality *all* the commandments which it has enjoined. (Gal. iii. 10.) From the creation to the day of judgment, there have been, and are, and can be, no more than two covenants; that of works, and that of grace. Under the one or the other of these compacts, every man must arrange himself."[3]

Lastly, the passover was to be eaten with unleavened bread: nor is it in vain that leaven is so often and so expressly forbidden to those who are invited to eat of the lamb; for in Scripture leaven is the

1 Chevallier's Lectures, pp. 287—289.
2 Jennings's Jewish Antiquities, book iii. ch. iv. pp. 474, 475.
3 Faber's Horæ Mosaicæ, vol. ii. p. 273.

symbol of corruption, and especially of hypocrisy.   Hence, St. Paul, speaking of Christ the true paschal lamb, exhorts Christians to *keep the feast, not with old leaven, neither with leaven of malice and wicked-ness, but with the unleavened* bread *of sincerity and truth.* (2 Cor. v. 7, 8.) [1]

On the second day of the festival (the sixteenth of the month Nisan) was offered the sheaf of the first-fruits of the barley-harvest which was usually ripe at this season, as a grateful acknowledgment of the good-ness of God, in bestowing upon them both the former and the latter rains (Jer. v. 24.), and also of his right to confer or withhold them as he pleases.   It was accompanied with a particular sacrifice, the cir-cumstances of which are detailed in Lev. xxiii. 9—14.

V. The second of the three great Jewish festivals was the FEAST OF PENTECOST, which is called by various names in the Sacred Writings; as the *feast of weeks* (Exod. xxxiv. 22. Deut. xvi. 10. 16.), because it was celebrated seven weeks or a week of weeks after the first day of unleavened bread ;—the *feast of harvest* (Exod. xxiii. 16.), and also the *day of first-fruits* (Numb. xviii. 26.), because on this day the Jews offered thanksgivings to God for the bounties of harvest, and presented to him the first-fruits of the wheat-harvest, in bread baked of the new corn. (Exod. xxiii. 16. Lev. xxiii. 14—21. Numb. xxviii. 26—31.) The form of thanksgiving for this occasion is given in Deut. xxvi. 5—10. On this day also was commemorated the giving of the law on Mount Sinai.   The Greek word Pentecost Πεντηκοστη (Acts ii. 1. xx. 16.), is derived from the circumstance of its being kept on the *fiftieth* day after the first day of unleavened bread. The number of Jews assembled at Jerusalem on this joyous occasion was very great. [2] This festival had a typical reference to the miraculous effusion of the Holy Spirit upon the apostles and first-fruits of the Christian church on the day of Pen-tecost (corresponding with our Whit-Sunday), on the fiftieth day after the resurrection of Jesus Christ. [3]

VI. The FEAST OF TABERNACLES, like the preceding festival, con-tinued for a week.   It was instituted to commemorate the dwelling of the Israelites in tents while they wandered in the desert. (Lev. xxiii. 34. 43.) Hence it is called by St. John the *feast of tents.* (σκηνοπηγια, John vii. 2.) [4] It is likewise termed the *feast of ingatherings.* (Exod. xxiii. 16. xxxiv. 22.) Further, the design of this feast was, to return thanks to God for the fruits of the vine, as well as of other trees, which were gathered about this time, and also to implore his blessing upon those of the ensuing year. The following were the principal ceremonies ob-served in the celebration of this feast : —

1. During the whole of this solemnity they were obliged to dwell in tents, which antiently were pitched on the flat terrace-like roofs of their houses. (Neh. viii. 16.)

2. Besides the ordinary daily sacrifices, there were several extra-ordinary ones offered on this occasion, which are detailed in Numb. xxix.

---

[1] Witsius on the Covenants, book vi. ch. ix. § 54. vol. ii. p. 280.

[2] Acts ii. 9—11. Josephus, Ant. Jud. lib. ii. c. 3. § 1.

[3] Schulzii Archæol. Hebr. pp. 321—323. Lamy's Apparatus Biblicus, vol. i. p. 179. Lightfoot's Works, vol. i. p. 960. Michaelis's Commentaries, vol. iii. p. 184. Relandi Antiq. Hebr. p. 472. Alber, Inst. Herm. Vet. Test. tom. i. pp. 172, 173.

[4] A similar appellation is given by Josephus, Ant. Jud. lib. xi. c. 5. § 5. lib. viii. c. 4. § 1.

3. During the continuance of this feast, they carried in their hands branches of palm-trees, olives, citrons, myrtles, and willows (Lev. xxiii. 40. Neh. viii. 15. 2 Macc. x. 7.) [1]; singing *Hosanna, save I beseech thee* (Psal. cxviii. 25.), in which words they prayed for the coming of the Messiah. These branches also bore the name of Hosanna, as well as all the days of the feast. In the same manner was Jesus Christ conducted into Jerusalem by the believing Jews, who, considering him to be the promised Messiah, expressed their boundless joy at finding in him the accomplishment of those petitions, which they had so often offered to God for his coming, at the feast of tabernacles. (Matt. xxi. 8, 9.) During its continuance, they walk in procession round the altar with the above-mentioned branches in their hands, amid the sound of trumpets, singing Hosanna; and on the last or seventh day of the feast, they compassed the altar seven times. This was called the Great Hosanna. To this last ceremony St. John probably alludes in Rev. vii. 9, 10., where he describes the saints as standing before the throne, *" clothed with white robes, and palms in their hands ; and saying, Salvation to our God which sitteth upon the throne, and unto the Lamb."*

4. One of the most remarkable ceremonies performed at this feast in the later period of the Jewish polity, was the libation or pouring out of water, drawn from the fountain or pool of Siloam, upon the altar. As, according to the Jews themselves [2], this water was an emblem of the HOLY SPIRIT, Jesus Christ applied the ceremony and the intention of it to himself, when he *" cried, saying, If any man thirst, let him come unto me and drink."* (John vii. 37. 39.)

On the last day, that great day of the feast (John vii. 37.), the Jews fetched water from that fountain in a golden pitcher, which they brought through the water-gate into the temple, with great rejoicing. The officiating priest poured it, mixed with wine, upon the morning sacrifice as it lay on the altar. The Jews seem to have adopted this custom (for it is not ordained in the law of Moses) as an emblem of future blessings, in allusion to this passage of Isaiah (xii. 3.), *With joy shall ye draw water out of the wells of salvation :* expressions that can hardly be understood of any benefits afforded by the Mosaic dispensation. Water was offered to God this day, partly in reference to the water which flowed from the rock in the wilderness (1 Cor. x. 4.), but chiefly to solicit the blessing of rain on the approaching seedtime. [3]

No festival was celebrated with greater rejoicings than this, which Josephus calls "a most holy and most eminent feast." [4] Dancing, music, and feasting were the accompaniments of this festival, together

---

[1] Lamy adds, that the Jews tied these branches with gold and silver strings, or with ribands, and did not lay them aside the whole day ; carrying them into their synagogues, and keeping them by them while they were at their prayers.   App. Bib. vol. i. p. 183.

[2] The sense of the Jews is in this matter plainly shown by the following passage of the Jerusalem Talmud:—" Why is it called the place or house of drawing ? because from thence they draw the Holy Spirit : as it is written, And ye shall draw water with joy from the wells of Salvation." Wolfii Curæ Philol. in N. T. on John vii. 37. 39. Lowth's Isaiah, vol. ii. p. 117.

[3] Bp. Lowth's Isaiah, vol. ii. p. 117.   Doyly's and Mant's Bible, on John vii. 37.

[4] Ant. Jud. lib. viii. c. 4. § 1.   The greatness of these rejoicings, and their happening at the time of vintage, led Tacitus erroneously to suppose that the Jews were accustomed to sacrifice to Bacchus.   Tacit. Hist. lib. v. c. 5. (tom. iii. p. 268. edit. Bipont.)

with such brilliant illuminations as lighted the whole city of Jerusalem. These rejoicings are supposed to have taken place in the court of the women, in order that they might be partakers of the general hilarity.[1] In every seventh year the law of Moses was also read in public, in the presence of all the people. (Deut. xxxi. 10—12. Neh. viii. 18.)

VII. To the three grand *annual* festivals above described, Moses added two others, which were celebrated with great solemnity, though the presence of every male Israelite was not absolutely required.

1. The first of these was the FEAST OF TRUMPETS, and was held on the first and second days of the month Tisri, which was the commencement of the civil year of the Hebrews: this feast derived its name from the blowing of trumpets in the temple with more than usual solemnity. (Numb. xxix. 1. Lev. xxiii. 24.) On this festival they abstained from all labour (Lev. xxiii. 25.), and offered particular sacrifices to God, which are described in Numb. xxix. 1—6.

2. The other feast alluded to was the FAST or FEAST OF EXPIATION, or DAY OF ATONEMENT; which day the Jews observed as a most strict fast, abstaining from all servile work, taking no food, and *afflicting their souls*. (Lev. xxiii. 27—30.) Of all the sacrifices ordained by the Mosaic law, the sacrifice of the atonement was the most solemn and important: it was offered on the tenth day of the month Tisri, by the high priest alone, for the sins of the whole nation.

" On this day only, in the course of the year, was the high priest permitted to enter the sanctuary[2], and not even then without due preparation, under pain of death; all others being excluded from the tabernacle during the whole ceremony. (Lev. xvi. 2. 17.) Previously to his entrance he was to wash himself in water, and to put on the holy linen garments, with the mitre; and to bring a young bullock into the outer sanctuary, and present it before the Lord to be a sin-offering for himself and his household, including the priests and Levites, and a ram also for a burnt-offering. (xvi. 3, 4.) Next, he was to take two young goats, and present them before the Lord, at the door of the tabernacle, to be a sin-offering for the whole congregation of Israel, and a ram also for a burnt-offering. (xvi. 5.) He was then to cast lots upon the two goats, which of them should be sacrificed as a sin-offering to the Lord, and which should be let go for a scape-goat into the wilderness. After this, he was first to sacrifice the bullock as a sin-offering for himself and his household, and to take some of the blood into the inner sanctuary, bearing in his hand a censer with incense burning, kindled at the sacred fire on the altar, and to sprinkle the blood with his finger upon the mercy-seat, and before it, seven times, to purify it from the pollution it might be supposed to have contracted from his sins and transgressions during the preceding year. He was then to sacrifice the allotted goat for the sins of the whole nation, and to enter the inner sanctuary a second time, and to sprinkle it with blood as before, to purify it from the pollution of the people's

---

[1] Schulzii Archæol. Heb. pp. 323—326.   Relandi Antiq. Heb. p. 477.   Ikenii Antiq. Heb. pp. 134, 135.   Lightfoot's Works, vol. i. p. 964. vol. ii. pp. 641—643.   Leusden's Philologus Hebræo-Mixtus, p. 295.   Beausobre's Introd. to the New Test. (Bp. Watson's Tracts, vol. iii. pp. 224, 225.)   Harmer's Observations, vol. i. p. 13.

[2] When the tabernacle was to be removed, and set up again, the inner sanctuary might safely be entered, but not at other times.

sins and transgressions of the foregoing year.   After which, he was to
purify, in like manner, the tabernacle and the altar.   He was next to
bring the live goat, and lay both his hands upon its head, and confess
over him all the iniquities, transgressions, and sins of the children of
Israel, putting them upon the head of the goat, and then to send him
away by the hand of a fit person into the wilderness, to bear away
upon him all their iniquities to a land of separation, where they should
be remembered no more.   After this atonement he was to put off his
linen garments, and leave them in the sanctuary, and to wash himself
again in water, and put on his usual garments; and then to offer
burnt-offerings for himself and for the people, at the evening sacrifice.
(Lev. xvi. 3—28.) The whole of this process seems to be typical or
prefigurative of the grand atonement to be made for the sins of the
whole world by Jesus Christ, *the high priest of our profession* (Heb. iii.
1.), and a remarkable analogy thereto may be traced in the course of
our Lord's ministry.   He began it with personal purification at his
baptism, *to fulfil all* legal *righteousness.* (Matt. iii. 13—15.) Immediately
after his baptism, he was led, by the impulse of the HOLY SPIRIT, into
the wilderness, as the true scape-goat, who *bore away our infirmities,
and carried off our diseases.* (Isa. liii. 4—6. Matt. viii. 17.) Immediately before his crucifixion, *he was afflicted,* and *his soul was exceeding
sorrowful unto death,* when he was to be made a sin-offering like the
allotted goat (Psal. xl. 12. Isa. liii. 7. Matt. xxvi. 38. 2 Cor. v. 21.
Heb. i. 3.) ; and *his sweat, as great drops of blood, falling to the ground,*
corresponded to the sprinkling of the mercy-seat (Luke xxii. 44.) ;
and when, to prepare for the sacrifice of himself, he consecrated himself in prayer to God (John xvii. 1—5. Matt. xxvi. 39—46.) ; and
then prayed for his household, his apostles, and disciples (John
xvii. 6—9.), and for all future believers on him by their preaching.
(John xvii. 20—26.) He put off his garments at his crucifixion, when
he became the sin-offering (Psal. xxii. 18. John xix. 23, 24.) ; and, as
our spiritual high priest, entered once for all into the most holy place,
heaven, to make intercession with God for all his faithful followers.
(Heb. vii. 24—28. ix. 7—15.) *Who died for our sins, and rose again
for our justification.*" [1] (Rom. iv. 25.)

VIII. Besides the annual festivals above described, the Jews in later
times introduced several fast and feast days in addition to those instituted by Moses.   The two principal festivals of this kind were the
Feast of Purim, and that of the Dedication of the Second Temple.

1. The FEAST OF PURIM, or of *Lots,* as the word signifies, is celebrated on the fourteenth and fifteenth days of the month of Adar
(or of Ve-Adar if it be an intercalary year), in commemoration of the
providential deliverance of the Jews from the cruel machinations of
Haman, who had procured an edict from Artaxerxes to extirpate them.
(Esth. iii.—ix.) On this occasion the entire book of Esther is read in

---

[1] Dr. Hales's Analysis, vol. ii. book i. pp. 274. 276.   See also Jennings's Jewish Antiquities, book iii. ch. viii.   Alber, Inst. Herm. Vet. Test. tom. i. pp. 174—176.   Lightfoot's Works, vol. i. pp. 961, 962.   Relandi, Antiq. Hebr. pp. 491. *et seq.*   Schulzii Archæol. Hebr. pp. 328—334.   The typical reference of the sacrifice offered on this day is
discussed at considerable length by Witsius, De Œcon. Fœd. lib. iv. c. 6. or vol. ii.
pp. 213—231. of the English translation.   On the manner in which this fast is observed by
the modern Jews, see Allen's Modern Judaism, pp. 391—399.

the synagogues of the modern Jews, not out of a printed copy, but from a roll which generally contains this book alone. All Jews, of both sexes, and of every age, who are able to attend, are required to come to this feast and to join in the reading, for the better preservation of the memory of this important fact. When the roll is unfolded, the chazan or reader says, " Blessed be God, the King of the world, who hath sanctified us by his precepts, and commanded us to read the Megillah ! Blessed be God, who in those days worked miracles for our fathers !" As often as the name of Haman occurs, the whole congregation clap their hands, stamp with their feet, and exclaim, " Let his name be blotted out ! May the memory of the wicked rot !" The children at the same time hiss, and strike loudly on the forms with little wooden hammers made for the purpose. When the reader comes to the seventh, eighth, and ninth chapters, where the names of Haman's ten sons occur, he pronounces them with great rapidity, and in one breath, to intimate that they were all hanged, and expired in the same moment. In most manuscripts and editions of the book of Esther, the ten names contained in the chapters just mentioned are written under each other in ten lines, no other word being connected with them, in order to exhibit the manner in which they were hanged, viz. on a pole fifty cubits, that is, seventy-five feet high; each of the brothers being immediately suspended, the one under the other, in one perpendicular line.

When the chazan has finished the reading, the whole congregation exclaim — " Cursed be Haman ! — Blessed be Mordecai ! — Cursed be Zeresh ! — Blessed be Esther ! — Cursed be all idolaters ! — Blessed be all the Israelites ! — And blessed likewise be Harbonah, at whose instance Haman was hanged !" In order to heighten the general joy on this festival, Buxtorf relates that some Jews wore party-coloured garments, and young foxes' tails in their hats, and ran about the synagogue exciting the congregation to laughter ! Further, to excite and increase mirth, the men and women exchange apparel; this, though positively forbidden by the law, they consider innocent, and allowable on this festive occasion, which is a season of peculiar gaiety. Alms are given to the poor; relations and friends send presents to each other; and all furnish their tables with every luxury they can command. These two days are the bacchanalia of the modern Jews ; who think it no sin to indulge themselves largely in their cups, some of them indeed to intoxication, in memory of Esther's banquet of wine; at which she succeeded in defeating the sanguinary designs of Haman.[1]

2. The FEAST OF DEDICATION (mentioned in John x. 22.) was instituted by Judas Maccabæus, in imitation of those by Solomon and Ezra, as a grateful memorial of the cleansing of the second temple and altar, after they had been profaned by Antiochus Epiphanes. (1 Macc. iv. 52—59.) It commenced on the twenty-fifth of the month Cisleu, corresponding with our December, and lasted eight days. This festival was also called the *feast of lights*, because the Jews illuminated their houses in testimony of their joy and gladness on this very important occasion.[2] The whole of this feast was spent in singing hymns, offering sacrifices,

[1] Buxtorf de Synagog. Jud. cap. 29. Iken. Antiq. Hebr. pp. 336—338. Schulzii Archæol. Hebr. pp. 334, 335. Allen's Modern Judaism, p. 405. Dr. Clarke's Commentary on Esther.
[2] Josephus, Ant. Jud. lib. xii. c. 7. §§ 6, 7.

and every kind of diversion [1]: it was celebrated with much solemnity in the time of Josephus.

Besides these two festivals, we find several others incidentally mentioned in the Old Testament, as being observed by the Jews in later ages, though not appointed by Moses. Such are the fast of the fourth month, on account of the taking of Jerusalem by the Chaldæans (Jer. lii. 6, 7.); the fast of the fifth month, on account of their burning the temple and city (2 Kings xxv. 8.); and that of the seventh month, on account of the murder of Gedaliah (2 Kings xxv. 25.); and the fast of the tenth month, when the Babylonian army commenced the siege of Jerusalem. (Jer. lii. 4.)   All these fasts are enumerated together in Zech. viii. 19.; and to them we may, perhaps, add the *xylophoria,* or feast of wood-offering, when the people brought and offered large quantities of wood for the use of the altar: it is supposed to have been celebrated in the time of Nehemiah (x. 34. xiii. 31.), in whose praises, on this occasion, the Jews largely expatiated, and related several wonderful tales concerning him and the fire lighted upon the altar. (2 Macc. i. 18—22.)   Nine days were appropriated to this festival, viz. The first of Nisan, the 20th of Tammuz, the 5th, 7th, 10th, 15th, and 20th, of Ab, the 20th of Elul, and the first of Tebeth.[2]

IX. The preceding are the chief annual festivals noticed in the Sacred Writings, that are particularly deserving of attention: the Jews have various others of more modern institution, which are here designedly omitted. We therefore proceed to notice those extraordinary festivals which were only celebrated after the recurrence of a certain number of years.

1. The first of these was the SABBATICAL YEAR. For, as the seventh day of the week was consecrated as a day of rest to man and beast, so this gave rest to the land; which, during its continuance, was to lie fallow, and the "sabbath of the land," or its spontaneous produce, was dedicated to charitable uses, to be enjoyed by the servants of the family, by the way-faring stranger, and by the cattle. (Lev. xxv. 1—7.   Exod. xxiii. 11.)   This was also the year of release from personal slavery (Exod. xxi. 2.), as well as of the remission of debts. (Deut. xv. 1, 2.)   Beausobre is of opinion that the frequent mention made in the New Testament of the remission of sins is to be understood as an allusion to the sabbatical year.   In order to guard against famine on this and the ensuing year, God was graciously pleased to promise a triple produce of the lands upon the sixth year, sufficient to supply the inhabitants till the fruits or harvest sown in the eighth year were ripe. (Lev. xxv. 2—22.)   This was a singular institution, peculiar to a theocracy.   And the breach of it was among the national sins that occasioned the captivity, that *the land might enjoy her sabbaths,* of which it had been defrauded by the rebellion of the inhabitants.[3] (Lev. xxvi. 34.   2 Chron. xxxvi. 21.)

---

[1] Schulzii Archæol. Hebr. pp. 335, 336.   Lamy, vol. i. p. 186.   Lightfoot's Works, vol. i. pp. 246. 979. vol. ii. pp. 576. 1033. 1039.   Relandi Antiq. Heb. p. 534.

[2] Schulzii Archæol. Hebr. p. 316.   Pictet, Antiq. Judaiques, p. 37.   (Théologie Chrétienne, tom. iii.)

[3] Schulzii Archæol. Hebr. pp. 337—339.   Michaelis's Commentaries, vol. i. pp. 387. *et seq.*   Leusden, Philol. Hebr. Mixt. p. 307.   Reland's Antiq. Hebr. p. 524.   Dr. Hales's Analysis, vol. ii. book i. p. 278.   Beausobre and L'Enfant, in Bp. Watson's Tracts, vol. iii. p. 124.   Jennings's Jewish Antiq. book iii. ch. 9.

2. The JUBILEE was a more solemn sabbatical year, held every seventh sabbatical year, that is, at the end of every forty-nine years, or the fiftieth current year. (Lev. xxv. 8—10.) Concerning the etymology of the Hebrew word *jobel* (whence our jubilee is derived) learned men are by no means agreed; the most probable of these conflicting opinions is that of Calmet, who deduces it from the Hebrew verb *hobil*, to recall, or bring back; because estates, &c. that had been alienated were then brought back to their original owners. Such appears to have been the meaning of the word, as understood by the Septuagint translators, who render the Hebrew word *jobel* by αφεσις, *remission*, and by Josephus, who says that it signified liberty.[1]

This festival commenced on the tenth day of the month Tisri, in the evening of the day of atonement (Lev. xxv. 9.) : a time, Bishop Patrick remarks, peculiarly well chosen, as the Jews would be better disposed to forgive their brethren their debts when they had been imploring pardon of God for their own transgressions. It was proclaimed by the sound of trumpet throughout the whole land, on the great day of atonement. All debts were to be cancelled; all slaves or captives were to be released. Even those who had voluntarily relinquished their freedom at the end of their six years' service, and whose ears had been bored in token of their perpetual servitude, were to be liberated at the jubilee: for then they were to *proclaim liberty throughout all the land, unto all the inhabitants thereof.* (Lev. xxv. 10.) Further, in this year all estates that had been sold, reverted to their original proprietors, or to the families to which they had originally belonged; this provision was made, that no family should be totally ruined, and doomed to perpetual poverty: for the family estate could not be alienated for a longer period than fifty years. The value and purchase-money of estates therefore diminished in proportion to the near approach of the jubilee. (Lev. xxv. 15.) From this privilege, however, houses in walled towns were excepted: these were to be redeemed within a year, otherwise they belonged to the purchaser, notwithstanding the jubilee. (ver. 30.) During this year, as well as in the sabbatical year, the ground also had its rest, and was not cultivated.[2]

The law concerning the sabbatical year, and especially the year of jubilee, affords a decisive proof of the divine legation of Moses. No legislator, unless he was conscious that he was divinely inspired, would have committed himself by enacting such a law: nor can any thing like it be found among the systems of jurisprudence of any other nations, whether antient or modern. "How incredible is it that any legislator would have ventured to propose such a law as this, except in consequence of the fullest conviction on both sides, that a peculiar providence would constantly facilitate its execution. When this law, therefore, was proposed and received, such a conviction must have existed in both the Jewish legislator and the Jewish people. Since, then, nothing could have produced this conviction, but the experience or the belief of some such miraculous interposition as the history of the Pentateuch details, the very existence of this law is a standing monu-

---

[1] Ant. Jud. lib. iii. c. 12. § 3.
[2] Leusden, Philol. Hebræo-Mixt. p. 309. Michaelis's Commentaries, vol. i. pp. 376 —386.

ment that, when it was given, the Mosaic miracles were fully believed. Now this law was coëval with the witnesses themselves. If, then, the facts were so plain and public, that those who witnessed them could not be mistaken as to their existence or miraculous nature, the reality of the Mosaic miracles is clear and undeniable." [1]

The reason and design of the law of the jubilee was partly political and partly typical. "It was *political*, to prevent the too great oppression of the poor as well as their liability to perpetual slavery. By this means the rich were prevented from accumulating lands upon lands, and a kind of equality was preserved through all the families of Israel. Never was there any people so effectually secure of their liberty and property as the Israelites were : God not only engaging so to protect those invaluable blessings by his providence, that they should not be taken away from them by others ; but providing, in a particular manner by this law, that they should not be thrown away through their own folly ; since the property, which every man or family had in their dividend of the land of Canaan, could not be sold or any way alienated for above half a century. By this means, also, the distinction of tribes was preserved, in respect both to their families and possessions ; for this law rendered it necessary for them to keep genealogies of their families, that they might be able when there was occasion, in the jubilee year, to prove their right to the inheritance of their ancestors. By this means it was certainly known from what tribe and family the Messiah sprung. Upon which Dr. Allix observes, that God did not suffer them to continue in captivity out of their own land for the space of two jubilees, lest by that means their genealogies should be lost or confounded. A further civil use of the jubilee might be for the easier computation of time. For, as the Greeks computed by olympiads, the Romans by lustra, and we by centuries, the Jews probably reckoned by jubilees ; and it might be one design of this institution to mark out these large portions of time for the readier computation of successive ages.

"There was also a *typical* design and use of the jubilee, which is pointed out by the prophet Isaiah, when he says, in reference to the Messiah, 'The Spirit of the Lord God is upon me, because the Lord hath anointed me to preach good tidings unto the meek ; he hath sent me to bind up the broken-hearted, to proclaim liberty to the captives, and the opening of the prison to them that are bound, to proclaim the acceptable year of the Lord.' (Isa. lxi. 1, 2.) Where 'the acceptable year of the Lord,' when 'liberty was proclaimed to the captives,' and 'the opening of the prison to them that were bound,' evidently refers to the jubilee ; but, in the prophetic sense, means the Gospel state and dispensation, which proclaims spiritual liberty from the bondage of sin and Satan, and the liberty of returning to our own possession, even the heavenly inheritance, to which, having incurred a forfeiture by sin, we had lost all right and claim." [2] That our Lord began his public ministry on a jubilee, Dr. Hales thinks, is evident from his declaration : "The LORD hath *anointed* me (as THE CHRIST) to preach the Gospel

---

[1] Dr. Graves's Lectures on the Pentateuch, vol. i. p. 171.
[2] Jennings's Jewish Antiq. book iii. ch. x. pp. 541, 542.   Schulzii Archæol. Hebr. pp. 341—344. Relandi Antiq. Hebr. p. 529.

to the poor: he hath sent me to heal the broken-hearted, to proclaim deliverance to the captives, and restoration of sight to the blind; to set at liberty the bruised; to *proclaim the acceptable year of* THE LORD."[1] (Luke iv. 18, 19.)

CHAPTER V.

SACRED OBLIGATIONS AND DUTIES.

SECTION I.

OF VOWS.

I. *Nature of Vows.* — *How far acceptable to God.* — II. *Requisites essential to the Validity of a Vow.* — III. *Different Sorts of Vows:* — 1. *The Cherem or Irremissible Vow.* — 2. *Other Vows, that might be redeemed.* — *Of the Nazareate.*

I. A VOW is a religious engagement or promise voluntarily undertaken by a person towards Almighty God. "Unless the Deity has expressly declared his acceptance of human vows, it can at best be but a very doubtful point, whether they *are* acceptable in his sight; and if they are not so, we cannot deduce from them the shadow of an obligation; for it is not from a mere offer alone, but from an offer of one party, and its acceptance by another, that the obligation to fulfil an engagement arises. The divine acceptance of vows, we can by no means take for granted; considering that from our vows God can derive no benefit, and that, in general, they are of just as little use to man."[2] In Matt. xv. 4—6. and Mark vii. 9—13. Christ himself notices the vow of *Korban* (already considered), which was common in his time, and by which a man *consecrated* to God what he was bound to apply to the support of his parents; and he declares it to be so impious that we cannot possibly hold it to be acceptable to God. In the New Testament, no vows whatever are obligatory, because God has nowhere declared that he will accept them from Christians. But the people of Israel *had* such a declaration from God himself; although even *they* were not counselled or encouraged to make vows. In consequence of this declaration, the vows of the Israelites were binding; and *that* not only in a moral view, but according to the national law; and the priest was authorised to enforce and estimate their fulfilment. The principal passages relating to this point are Lev. xxvii. Numbers xxx. and Deut. xxiii. 18. 21, 22, 23.[3]

II. In order to render a vow valid, Moses requires,

1. "That it be *actually uttered with the mouth*, and not merely made

---

[1] Dr. Hales's Analysis, vol. ii. book i. p. 279. Lightfoot's Works, vol. ii. p. 619. The best practical illustration which the author has seen, of the analogy between the Mosaic jubilee and the Gospel, is to be found in the Rev. Dr. Claudius Buchanan's "Three Sermons on the Jubilee," celebrated on the 25th October, 1809, on the occasion of King George III.'s entering on the fiftieth year of his reign.

[2] Michaelis's Commentaries on the Law of Moses, vol. ii. p. 263.

[3] Ibid. pp. 264—266.

in the heart. In Numb. xxx. 3. 7. 9. 13. and Deut. xxiii. 24. he repeatedly calls it *the expression of the lips,* or *what has gone forth from the mouth ;* and the same phrase occurs in Psal. lxvi. 14. If, therefore, a person had merely made a vow in his heart, without letting it pass his lips, it would seem as if God would not accept such a vow ; regarding it only as a resolution to vow, but not as a vow itself. This limitation is humane, and necessary to prevent much anxiety in conscientious people. If a vow made in the heart be valid, we shall often experience difficulty in distinguishing whether what we thought of was a bare intention, or a vow actually completed. Here, therefore, just as in a civil contract with our neighbour, words — *uttered* words — are necessary to prevent all uncertainty." [1]

2. The party making the vow must be in his own power, and competent to undertake the obligation. Therefore the vows of minors were void, unless they were ratified by the express or tacit consent of their fathers.[2] In like manner, neither unmarried daughters, so long as they were under the parental roof, nor married women, nor slaves, could oblige themselves by vow, unless it was ratified by their fathers, husbands, or masters; the authority being given to the head of the family in every thing which might produce advantage or injury.[3]

3. The things vowed to be devoted to God must be *honestly* obtained. It is well known, that in antient times, many public prostitutes dedicated to their gods a part of their impure earnings. This is most expressly forbidden by Moses. (Deut. xxiii. 18.)[4]

III. There are two sorts of vows mentioned in the Old Testament, viz. 1. The חרם (cheReM), which was the most solemn of all, and was accompanied with a form of execration and which could not be redeemed ; and, 2. The נדרים (neDeRiM), or common vows.

1. The cherem is nowhere enjoined by Moses; nor does he specify by what solemnities or expressions it was distinguished from other vows, but pre-supposes all this as already well known. The species of cherem with which we are best acquainted, was the previous devotement to God of hostile cities, against which they intended to proceed with extreme severity ; and *that* with a view the more to inflame the minds of the people to war. In such cases, not only were all the inhabitants put to death, but also, according as the terms of the vow declared, no booty was made by any Israelite; the beasts were slain; what would not burn, as gold, silver, and other metals, was added to the treasury of the sanctuary ; and every thing else, with the whole city, burnt, and an imprecation pronounced upon any attempt that should ever be made to rebuild it. Of this the history of Jericho (Josh. vi. 17—19. 21—24. and vii. 1. 12—26.) furnishes the most remarkable example. In Moses's lifetime we find a similar vow against the king of Arad. (Numb. xxi. 1—3.) If an Israelitish city introduced the worship of strange gods, it was (as we have already seen) in like manner, to be devoted or consecrated to God, and to remain un-rebuilt for ever. (Deut. xiii. 16—18.)[5] Jephthah's dedication of his daughter is generally supposed to

---

1 Michaelis's Commentaries on the Law of Moses, vol. ii. p. 269.
2 Alber, Inst. Herm. Vet. Test. tom. i. p. 214.
3 Maimonides' Reasons of the Law of Moses, by Dr. Townley, p. 308.
4 Schulzii Archæol. Hebr. p. 293.
5 Michaelis's Commentaries, vol. ii. pp. 272—275.

have been a cherem: but we have shown in another part of this work
that he did not sacrifice her.[1] The text (Judg. xi. 30.) says that *Jephthah vowed a vow* (נדר, NEDER), *unto the Lord,* and again, (verse 39.)
that *he did with her according to his vow* (נדר). There is no word in
either of these passages that either expresses or implies a cherem.

2. The common vows were divided into two sorts, viz. i. Vows of
dedication, and, ii. Vows of self-interdiction or abstinence.

i. The נדר (NEDER) or vow, in the stricter sense of the word, was
when a person engaged to do any thing, as, for instance, to bring an
offering to God; or otherwise to dedicate any thing unto him. Things
vowed in this way, were, 1. *Unclean beasts.* These might be estimated
by the priest, and redeemed by the vower, by the addition of one fifth
to the value. (Lev. xxvii. 11—13.)—2. *Clean beasts used for offerings.*
Here there was no right of redemption; nor could the beasts be exchanged for others under the penalty of both being forfeited, and
belonging to the Lord. (Lev. xxvii. 9, 10.)—3. *Lands and houses.*
These had the privilege of valuation and redemption. (Lev. xxvii.
14—24.) — To these we have to add, 4. *The person of the vower himself,* with the like privilege. (Lev. xxvii. 1—8.) To this species of
vow Michaelis thinks the *second tenths* may have belonged, as Moses
nowhere speaks of them as a new institution.[2] They most probably
derived their origin from the vow made by Jacob, which is recorded
in Gen. xxviii. 22.

ii. Vows of *self-interdiction* or *self-denial* were, when a person engaged to abstain from any wine, food, or any other thing. These are.
especially distinguished by Moses from other vows in Numb. xxx., and
are there termed אסר (ASSaR), or אסר על נפש (ASSaR AL NePHesH),
that is, a *bond upon the soul or person, a self-interdiction from some
desire of nature, or of the heart,* or, in other words, a *vow of abstinence,*
particularly from eating and drinking. Among this species of vows
may be classed those of the *Nazareate* or *Nazaritism;* which, Michaelis
is of opinion, was not instituted by Moses, but was of more antient,
and probably of Egyptian origin[3]; the Hebrew legislator giving certain injunctions for the better regulation and performance of these
vows. The statutes respecting the Nazareate are related in the sixth
chapter of the book of Numbers. Lamy, Calmet, and others, have
distinguished two classes of Nazarites: first, *those who were Nazarites
by birth,* as Samson and John the Baptist were; and, secondly, *those
who were Nazarites by vow and engagement;* who followed this mode of
living for a limited time, at the expiration of which they cut off their
hair at the door of the tabernacle, and offered certain sacrifices. The
Nazarites were required to abstain from wine, fermented liquors, and
every thing made of grapes, to let their hair grow, and not to defile
themselves by touching the dead; and if any person had accidentally
expired in their presence, the Nazarites of the second class were
obliged to recommence their Nazariteship.

Similar to the Nazareate was the vow frequently made by devout
Jews, on their recovery from sickness, or deliverance from danger or
distress; who, for thirty days before they offered sacrifices, abstained

---

1 See Vol. II. Part II. Chap. VII. Sect. V. § 13.
2 Michaelis's Commentaries, vol. ii. pp. 280, 281.
3 Ibid. p. 284.

from wine, and shaved the hair of their head.[1] This usage illustrates the conduct of Paul, as related in Acts xviii. 18. The Apostle, in consequence of a providential deliverance from some imminent peril not recorded by the sacred writer, bound himself by a vow, which the law in this case required him to pay at Jerusalem. In consequence of this transaction Luke relates, that he shaved his head at Cenchrea. Paul, in his intended journey afterwards to Judæa, says, *he must needs go to Jerusalem:* for the laws respecting the Nazarite's vow required the person who had entered into this engagement, if he were in a foreign country when he first laid himself under this solemn obligation, to go up to Jerusalem to accomplish it. Here several appointed sacrifices were offered, and a certain course of purifications and religious observances was prescribed and performed. This appears from another passage in the same sacred writer: (Acts xxi. 23, 24. 26, 27.) " *We have four men who have a* VOW *on them; them take and* PURIFY *thyself with them, and be at charges with them, that* THEY MAY SHAVE THEIR HEADS. *Then Paul took the men : and the next day purifying himself with them, entered into the temple, to signify the accomplishment of the days of purification ; and that an offering should be offered for every one of them. And when the* SEVEN *days were almost ended,*" &c. Josephus presents us with an instance parallel to this of Paul, in the person of Bernice, who went to Jerusalem, in order to perform a vow which she had made to God.[2]

SECTION II.

ON THE PRAYERS AND FASTS OF THE JEWS.

I. *Various Appellations given to Prayers.*—II. *Public Prayers.*—III. *Private Prayers. — Attitudes of the Jews during Prayer. —* IV. *Forms of Prayer in use among the Jews.*—V. *Fasts of the Jews.*—1. *Public Fasts.* — 2. *Private Fasts. —* 3. *Solemnities of the Jewish Fasts.*

I. PRAYERS, or petitions addressed to the Almighty, are closely connected with sacrifices and vows. (Psal. l. 14, 15.) VARIOUS APPELLATIONS are given to the prayers mentioned in the Scriptures. In Phil. iv. 6. and 1 Tim. ii. 1. five different terms are employed, viz. αιτηματα, or requests, which may be considered as a generic term,

---

[1] An usage similar to the vow of Nazariteship exists in Persia to this day. It frequently happens after the birth of a son, that if the parent be in distress, or the child be sick, or that there be any cause of grief, the mother makes a vow, that no razor shall come upon the child's head for a certain portion of time, and sometimes for his whole life, as Samuel was. (1 Sam. i. 11.) If the child recovers, and the cause of grief be removed, and if the vow be but for a time, so that the mother's vow be fulfilled, then she shaves his head at the end of the time prescribed, makes a small entertainment, collects money and other things from her relations and friends, which are sent as *Netzers* or offerings to the mosque at Kerbelah, and are there consecrated. Morier's Second Journey, p. 109.

[2] See Lamy's Apparatus Biblicus, vol. i. p. 221. Calmet's Dictionary, voce *Nazarite.* Fleury's Manners of the Israelites, pp. 338, 359. Lardner's Credibility, book i. c. 9. § 7. (Works, vol. i. pp. 208—212.) Jennings's Jewish Antiquities, book i. c. 8. Harwood's Introd. to the New Test. vol. ii. p. 298. Relands, Antiq. Hebr. part i. c. 10. pp. 284 —289. Schulzii Archæol. Hebr. pp. 294, 295. Bruning's Antiq. Hebr. pp. 198—204. Dr. Randolph's Discourse on Jepthah's Vow, in his View of Christ's Ministry, &c. vol. ii. pp. 166—195.

including προσευχαι, prayers for obtaining those things, whether temporal or spiritual, of which we feel our need; δεησεις, deprecations of evil of every kind; εντευξεις, intercessions or prayers in behalf of others; and ευχαριστιαι, thanksgivings or addresses of praise to God for all the blessings conferred upon us. The mode of praying was two-fold; 1. *Internal,* in which mental prayer is offered from the heart alone (such was the prayer of Hannah, 1 Sam. i. 13.); or, 2. *External,* being uttered aloud with the voice: hence, in Psal. cxlv. 19. it is termed a *cry.*

Prayers were either *public,* or *private,* or *stated,* that is, performed at a particular time. The STATED HOURS were at the time of offering the morning and evening sacrifice, or at the third and ninth hours (Acts ii. 15. and iii. 1.); although it was the custom of the more devout Jews, as David (Psal. lv. 17.) and Daniel (vi. 10.), to pray three times a day. Peter went up on the house-top to pray, about the *sixth hour.* (Acts x. 9.) A similar usage obtains among the Hindoos to this day.[1] Previously to offering up their supplications they washed their hands, to signify that they had put away sin and purposed to live a holy life. As the Jewish phylacterical prayers were long, and the canonical or stated hours obliged them to repeat these prayers wherever they happened to be, the proud, vain-glorious Pharisees contrived to be overtaken in the streets, in order that they might be observed by the people, and be applauded for their piety. Against this formal spirit Jesus Christ cautions his disciples in Matt. vi. 5.[2] The modern Hindoos and Mohammedans are guilty of the same ostentation.

II. PUBLIC PRAYERS were offered, at first, in the tabernacle, and afterwards in the temple and synagogues, by the minister appointed for that purpose, the people answering (*in the synagogues only*) at the conclusion with a loud Amen.[3] (Neh. viii. 6.)

III. PRIVATE PRAYERS were offered by individuals in a *low tone of voice* with the head covered[4]; either *standing* or kneeling, sometimes *bowing the head* towards the earth, and at others with the whole body prostrate on the ground. Sometimes they *smote upon the breast,* in token of their deep humiliation and penitence, or spread forth their hands, or lifted them up to heaven. Of these various postures in prayer many instances occur in the sacred writers. Thus Hannah, in her affliction, *spake in her heart; her lips only moved, but* HER VOICE *was* NOT HEARD (1 Sam. i. 13.); and the proud *Pharisee* STOOD[5] *and prayed with* (within) *himself.* (Luke xviii. 11.) David says, I STRETCH FORTH

---

[1] Ward's History, &c. of the Hindoos, vol. ii. p. 342.

[2] Drs. Lightfoot and A. Clarke on Matt. vi. 5.

[3] The Jews attribute a wonderful efficacy to this word; and have an idle tradition that the gates of Paradise will be open to him who says Amen with all his might.

[4] The reason of this custom was to profess themselves reverent and ashamed before God, and unworthy to appear before him. It was a maxim of the Jews,—" Let not the wise men, nor the scholars of the wise men, pray, unless they be covered." It appears that the Corinthians, though converted to the Christian faith, in this respect conformed to the Jewish practice; and therefore St. Paul remonstrated against it. 1 Cor. xi. 4. Lightfoot's Hor. Heb. in loc. (Works, vol. ii. pp. 769, 770.)

[5] The practice of *standing* during prayer obtained among the Arabs in the time of Mohammed, who, in his Koran, repeatedly commands his followers to *stand* when they pray. C. B. Michaelis de ritualibus S. S. ex Alcorano illustrandis, § XIV. in vol. ii. pp. 108, 109. of Pott's and Ruperti's Sylloge Commentationum Theologicarum. See also Dr. Richardson's Travels along the Shores of the Mediterranean, vol. i. pp. 463. *et seq.*

MY HANDS *unto thee.* (Psal. cxliii. 6.) *Solomon* KNEELED *down upon his knees before all the congregation of Israel, and* SPREAD FORTH HIS HANDS *towards heaven.* (2 Chron. vi. 13.) Ezra *fell upon his* KNEES, *and* SPREAD *out his* HANDS *to the Lord* his *God.* (Ezra ix. 5.) Our adorable Redeemer, in his agony in the Garden of Gethsemane, *fell on his face* (prostrated himself to the ground), KNEELED *down and prayed* (Matt. xxvi. 39. Luke xxii. 41.); and the proto-martyr Stephen KNEELED *down* and prayed for his murderers. (Acts vii. 60.) Moses, when interceding for the ungrateful Israelites, BOWED HIS HEAD *to the earth and worshipped.* (Exod. xxxiv. 8. Compare also Exod. ix. 29.) The humble and contrite *publican, standing afar off,* SMOTE ON HIS BREAST, and supplicated divine mercy. (Luke xviii. 13.) The prophet Isaiah, when reproving the hypocritical Jews, denounces that Jehovah would *hide his eyes* from them when they SPREAD FORTH their *hands,* (Isa. i. 15.); and the LIFTING UP OF THE HANDS to heaven, in prayer, is expressly noted by the Psalmist (cxli. 2.) and by the prophet Jeremiah. (Lam. iii. 41.)[1]

Similar postures were adopted by most of the heathen nations that pretended to any kind of worship, when approaching the objects of their adoration; which it is highly probable that they borrowed from the people of God. *Kneeling* was ever considered to be the proper posture of supplication, as it expressed *humility, contrition,* and *subjection.* If the person to whom the supplication was addressed was within reach, the supplicant caught him by the knees; for as, among the antients, the *forehead* was consecrated to *genius,* the *ear* to *memory,* and the *right hand* to *faith,* so the knees were consecrated to *mercy.* Hence those who entreated favour, fell at and caught hold of the knees of the person whose kindness they supplicated. This mode of supplication is particularly referred to in Homer.[2] In the same manner we find our Lord accosted, Matt. xvii. 14.— *There came to him a certain man, kneeling down to him,* γονυπετων αυτον, *falling down at his knees.*

As to the *lifting up,* or *stretching out, the hands* (often joined to kneeling), of which we have seen already several instances, and of which we have a very remarkable one in Exod. chap. xvii. 11. where the *lifting up,* or *stretching out* of the hands of Moses was the means of Israel's prevailing over Amalek; we find many examples of both in antient authors.[3] In some cases, the person petitioning came forward,

---

[1] Schulzii Archæol. Hebraica, pp. 298, 299. Brunings, Antiquitates Hebrææ, pp. 193 —198.

[2] Των νυν μιν μνησασα παρεξεο, και λαβε γουνων.   Iliad I. 407.

Now therefore, of these things reminding Jove,
Embrace his knees.   COWPER.

To which the following answer is made: —

Και τοτ' επειτα τοι ειμι Διος ποτι χαλκοβατες δω,
Και μιν γουνασομαι, και μιν πεισεσθαι οἴω.   Iliad I. 426, 427.

Then will I to Jove's brazen-floored abode,
That I may *clasp his knees;* and much misdeem
Of my endeavour, or my pray'r shall speed.   COWPER.

[3] The following instances are taken from Virgil: —

Corripio è stratis corpus, TENDOQUE SUPINAS
AD CŒLUM *cum voce* MANUS, *et munera libo.*   Æneid iii. 176, 177.

I started from my bed, and *raised on high*
My hands and voice in rapture to the sky;
And pour libations.   PITT.

and either sat in the dust or kneeled on the ground, placing his *left hand on the knee* of him, from whom he expected the favour, while he *touched the person's chin* with his *right.* We have an instance of this also in Homer.[1]

When the supplicant could not approach the person to whom he prayed, as where a *deity* was the object of the prayer, he washed his hands, made an offering, and kneeling down, either *stretched out both his hands to heaven,* or *laid them upon the offering* or *sacrifice,* or *upon the altar.* In this mode Homer represents the priest of Apollo as praying.[2]

The practice of standing with their hands spread out towards heaven, was adopted by the primitive Christians when offering their supplications: they stood up, says Tertullian, and directed their eyes towards heaven with expanded hands.[3] A similar testimony is given by Clement of Alexandria[4]: — " We lift up our head and elevate our hands towards heaven." So also, St. Paul, when exhorting Christians to pray for all classes of persons, describes the gesture then used in prayer (1 Tim. ii. 8.): — *Wherefore* LIFT UP *holy* HANDS *without wrath or doubting.* Those who affected superior sanctity, or who from motives of ostentation and hypocrisy, it appears, prayed in the streets[5], and *made long prayers,* were severely censured by our Lord for their for-

---

Dixerat : et GENUA AMPLEXUS, *genibusque volutans Hærebat.*	Æneid iii. 607, 608.
Then *kneeled* the wretch, and *suppliant clung around My knees,* with tears, and grovelled on the ground.	PITT.
——————————— *media inter numina divum, Multa Jovem* MANIBUS SUPPLEX *orasse* SUPINIS.	Ibid. iv. 204, 205.
Amidst the statues of the gods he stands, *And spreading forth* to Jove *his lifted hands* ——	Id.
Et DUPLICES *cum voce* MANUS *ad sidera* TENDIT.	Ibid. x. 667.
And *lifted both his hands* and voice *to heaven.*	Id.
[1] Και ρα παροιθ' αυτοιο καθεζετο, και λαβε γουνων Σκαιη· δεξιτερη δ' αρ' ύπ' ανθερεωνος ελουσα.	Iliad I. 500, 501.
Suppliant the goddess stood : *one hand she plac'd Beneath his chin,* and *one his knee embrac'd.*	POPE.
[2] Χερνιψαντο δ' επειτα, και ουλοχυτας ανελοντο. Τοισιν δε Χρυσης μεγαλ' ευχετο, χειρας ανασχων.	Iliad I. 449, 450.
With *water purify their hands,* and take The *sacred off'ring* of the salted cake, While thus with *arms* devoutly *rais'd in air,* And solemn voice, the priest *directs his pray'r.*	POPE.

Dr. A. Clarke on Exod. ix. 29. Other illustrations of the various attitudes in which the heathens offered up prayer to their deities are given by Brunings, Compendium Antiquitatum Græcarum, pp. 270—275.

[3] Apolog. c. 30.

[4] Stromata, lib. ii. p. 722. Dr. Harwood's Introd. vol. ii. p. 302. The practice of extending the hands in prayer still obtains in the East. See Harmer's Observations, vol. ii. pp. 511—513. Fragments supplementary to Calmet, No. cclxxviii.

[5] This practice is also general throughout the East. Both Hindoos and Musulmauns offer their devotions in the most public places; as, at the landing places of rivers, in the public streets, and on the roofs of boats, without the least modesty or effort at concealment. Ward's History of the Hindoos, vol. ii. p. 335. See also Fragments, No. cv. Morier's Second Journey, p. 208. Dr. Richardson's Travels, vol. i. p. 75. and Lightfoot's Horæ Hebraicæ on Matt. vi. 5. (Works, vol. ii. p. 156.)

mal and hypocritical devotion. (Matt. vi. 5. and xxiii. 14.) When at a distance from the temple, the more devout Jews turned themselves towards it when they prayed. We have an instance of this in the conduct of Daniel.[1] (Dan. vi. 10.) When the Orientals pray seriously, in a state of grief, they hide their faces in their bosom. To this circumstance, the Psalmist alludes (xxxv. 13.), when he says, *My prayer returned into my own bosom.*[2]

IV. Various FORMS OF PRAYER were in use among the Jews, from the earliest period of their existence as a distinct nation. The first piece of solemn worship recorded in the Scripture, is a hymn of praise composed by Moses, on occasion of the deliverance of the Israelites from the Egyptians, which was sung by all the congregation alternately; by Moses and the men first, and afterwards by Miriam and the women (Exod. xv. 1. 20, 21.); which could not have been done, unless it had been a precomposed set form. Again, in the expiation of an uncertain murder, the elders of the city which lay nearest to the party that was slain, were expressly commanded to say, and consequently to join in, the form of prayer appointed by God himself in Deut. xxi. 7, 8. In Numb. vi. 23—26. x. 35, 36. Deut. xxvi. 3. 5—11. and 13—15. there are several other divinely appointed forms of prayer, prescribed by Moses. On the establishment of the monarchy, David appointed the Levites to *stand every morning to thank and praise the Lord, and likewise at even* (1 Chron. xxiii. 30.); which rule was afterwards observed in the temple erected by Solomon, and restored at the building of the second temple after the captivity. (Neh. xii. 24.) And the whole book of Psalms was, in fact, a collection of forms of prayer and praise, for the use of the whole congregation; as is evident from the titles of several of those divinely inspired compositions[3], as well as from other passages of Scripture.[4]

What the stated public prayers were in the time of our Lord, it is now impossible exactly to ascertain: it is, however, probable that many of the eighteen prayers, which have been given in pp. 260—263. and which are said to have been collected by Rabbi Gamaliel the Elder, the master of St. Paul, were then in use; and as all persons were not able to commit them to memory, it is also probable that a summary of them was drawn up. But we know certainly that it was customary for the more eminent doctors of the Jews to compose forms of short prayers, which they delivered to their scholars. Thus John the Baptist gave his disciples such a form; and Jesus Christ, at the request of his disciples, gave them that most perfect model emphatically termed *The Lord's Prayer*, which Drusius and other eminent critics supposed was collected out of the Jewish euchologies: but this hypothesis has been refuted by Professor Tholuck in his "Exposition of Christ's Sermon on the Mount."[5]

---

[1] Lamy is of opinion that Hezekiah did so, and that we are to understand his *turning his face to the wall* (2 Kings xx. 2.) of his turning towards the temple. De Tabernaculo, lib. vii. c. 1. § 5.

[2] Burder's Oriental Literature, vol. ii. p. 20.

[3] See the titles of Psalms iv. v. vi. xlii. xliv. xcii. &c.

[4] See 1 Chron. xvi. 7. 2 Chron. xxix. 30. and Ezra iii. 10, 11. Wheatley on the Common Prayer, Introduction, p. 2.

[5] Vol. II. (Edinburgh Biblical Cabinet, vol. xx. pp. 141—147.) Drusius, in Critici Sacri, vol. vi. col. 259, 260. Dr. Hales has an excellent commentary on this prayer, in

V. To prayers the Jews sometimes added FASTS, or religious abstinence from food : these fasts were either public or private.

1. The PUBLIC FASTS were either ordinary or extraordinary. Moses
instituted only one ordinary annual public fast, which was solemnised
on the day of atonement[1], other public fasts being left to the discretion
of the nation. Of extraordinary fasts appointed by authority of the
civil magistrate, several instances are recorded in the Old Testament.
See 1 Sam. vii. 5, 6. 2 Chron. xx. 3. and Jer. xxxvi. 9. After the
return of the Jews from captivity, Ezra proclaimed a fast at the river
Ahava, in order to implore the direction and blessing of God (Ezra
viii. 21.) : and several other fasts were subsequently added, to commemorate particular melancholy events, of which we read in Zech. viii.
19.; viz. the fast of the fourth month, which was instituted in memory
of the famine in Jerusalem (Jer. lii. 6.) ; the fast of the fifth month, for
the destruction of the temple (Zech. vii. 3.) ; the fast of the seventh
month, on account of the murder of Gedaliah (2 Kings xxv. 28.) ; and
the fast of the tenth month, when Jerusalem was besieged. (Jer. lii. 4.)
Extraordinary public fasts were also held when the Jews were threatened with any imminent danger. (Joel i. 14. ii. 12.) In like manner
the people of Nineveh, on hearing the prophetic message of Jonah,
whom they believed to be truly sent by God, proclaimed a fast; and
by a decree of the king and his nobles, neither man nor beast, neither
herd nor flock, was permitted to taste any food, or even to drink any
water. (Jonah iii. 6, 7.) This was carrying their abstinence to a
greater degree of rigour than what we find recorded of the Jews : for
though, during seasons of public calamity, they made their children to
fast (as may be inferred from Joel ii. 15, 16.), yet we nowhere read of
their extending that severity to cattle.

2. PRIVATE FASTS were left to the discretion of individuals, who
kept them, in order that they might by prayer and fasting avert imminent calamities, and obtain the favour of God. So David fasted
and prayed during the sickness of his child by Bathsheba (2 Sam.
xii. 16.); Ahab, when he heard the divine judgments which were
denounced against him by the prophet Elijah (1 Kings xxi. 27.); and
the pious Jews, Ezra (x. 6.) and Nehemiah (i. 4.), on account of the
calamities of their country and of the Jews. In the time of Jesus
Christ, private fasts appear to have been deemed necessary, in order
to yield an acceptable worship to God : such at least was the case with
the Pharisees and their followers, who affected more than ordinary
devotion; and who fasted twice in the week, on the second and fifth
days (Luke xviii. 12.), to which acts of devotion they ascribed a marvellous efficacy.[1]

3. With regard to the SOLEMNITIES OF THE JEWISH FASTS, the
precept of the law simply enjoined that they should *afflict their souls*
(Lev. xvi. 29.) ; conformably to which the prophet Joel (ii. 13.) exhorts
his countrymen to *rend their hearts and not their garments.* From
various passages of Scripture, it appears that the Jewish fasts, whether

---

his Analysis of Chronology, vol. ii. book ii. pp. 1005—1011. The forms, &c. of prayer
of the modern Jews are described by Mr. Allen. Modern Judaism, pp. 326—354.

[1] See an account of this fast in pp. 317, 318. *suprà.*

[2] Lightfoot's Hor. Hebr. on Matt. ix. 14. Schulzii Archæologia Hebraica, pp. 301,
302. Home's Hist. of the Jews, vol. ii. pp. 279, 280.

public or private, were distinguished by every possible mark of grief; the people being clothed in sackcloth, with ashes strewed on their heads, downcast countenances, rent garments, and (on public occasions) with loud weeping and supplication. (2 Sam. xiii. 19. Psal. xxxv. 13. Isa. lviii. 5. Lam. ii. 10. Joel i. 13, 14. ii. 12, 13.) At these times they abstained from food until evening. The sanctimonious Pharisees affected the utmost humility and devotion, disfiguring their faces and avoiding every appearance of neatness; against this conduct our Lord cautions his disciples in Matt. vi. 16, 17.[1]

SECTION III.

ON THE PURIFICATIONS OF THE JEWS.

I. *Materials, with which the Purifications of the Jews were perrfomed.* — II. *Ceremonies of Purification.* — III. *Of the Persons lustrated.* — IV. *Account of the different Kinds of Legal Impurities, particularly,* — 1. *The Leprosy of the Person.* — 2. *The Leprosy of Clothes.* — 3. *The House Leprosy.* — V. *Minor legal Impurities, and their Lustrations.*

IT was requisite that every one who was about to make any offering to Jehovah should be cleansed from all impurities, or lustrated — to adopt an expression in common use among the Romans. The materials, form, and ceremonies of these lustrations, which were prescribed by Moses, were various, according to different circumstances. The design of them all was not only to preserve both the health and morals of the Israelites, but also to intimate how necessary it was to preserve inward purity, without which they could not be acceptable to God, though they might approach his sanctuary.

I. The purifications were for the most part performed with water, sometimes with blood (Heb. ix. 21, 22.), and with oil. (Exod. xxx. 26—29. Lev. viii. 10, 11.)[2] The water of purification was to be drawn from a spring or running stream, and was either pure, or mixed with blood (Heb. ix. 19.), or with the ashes of the red heifer. For preparing these ashes, a heifer of a red colour was burnt with great solemnity. This ceremony is described at length in the nineteenth chapter of the book of Numbers. As all the people were to be interested in it, the victim was to be provided at their charge. This Jewish rite certainly had a reference to things done under the Gospel, as St. Paul has remarked in his Epistle to the Hebrews — *For if the blood of bulls and of goats,* (alluding to the sin-offerings, and to the scape-goat,) *and* THE ASHES OF A HEIFER, *sprinkling the unclean, sanctifieth to the purifying of the flesh, how much more shall the blood of Christ . . . . purge* (or purify) *your conscience from dead works to serve the living God.* As the principal stress of allusion in this passage is to the ordinance of the red heifer, we may certainly conclude that it was designed to typify the sacrifice of our adorable Redeemer.

---

[1] See Lightfoot's Hor. Heb. on Matt. vi. 9—13. and Luke xviii. 12. Josephus, Ant. Jud. lib. iii. c. 10. § 3. Schulzii Archæol. Hebr. pp. 301, 302.
[2] Josephus, Ant. Jud. lib. iii. c. 8. § 6.

In the ordinance of the red heifer, we may perceive the wisdom of Moses (under the guidance of Jehovah) in taking every precaution that could prevent the Israelites from falling into idolatry. The animal to be selected was a *heifer*, in opposition to the superstition of the Egyptians, who held this animal to be sacred, and worshipped Isis under the form of a heifer: — it was also to be a *red heifer, without spot,* that is, altogether red, because *red bulls* were sacrificed to appease the evil demon Typhon, that was worshipped by the Egyptians; *wherein* was *no blemish,* so that it was free from every imperfection ; — *on which never came yoke,* because any animal that had been used for any common purpose was deemed improper to be offered in sacrifice to God.[1]

The animal being slain, and her blood sprinkled as directed in Numb. xix. 3, 4., was then reduced to ashes, which were to be collected and mixed with running water (ver. 9. 17.), for the purpose of lustration.

II. The Jews had two sorts of washing; one, — of the whole body by *immersion,* which was used by the priests at their consecration, and by the proselytes at their initiation; — the other, of the hands or feet, called *dipping* or *pouring of water,* and which was of daily use, not only for the hands and feet, but also for the cups and other vessels used at their meals. (Matt. xv. 2.   Mark vii. 3, 4.)   The six water-pots of stone, used at the marriage-feast of Cana, in Galilee (John ii. 6.), were set for this purpose.[2]   To these two modes of purification Jesus Christ seems to allude in John xiii. 10.; where the being *wholly washed* implies one who had become a disciple of Christ, and consequently had renounced the sins of his former life.   He who had so done, was supposed to be wholly washed, and not to need any immersion, in imitation of the ceremony of initiation, which was never repeated among the Jews.   All that was necessary in such case, was the dipping or rinsing of the hands and feet, agreeably to the customs of the Jews.   Sometimes the lustration was performed by sprinkling blood, or anointing with oil.   Sprinkling was performed either with the finger or with a branch of cedar and hyssop tied together with scarlet wool. (Lev. xiv. 4. 6.   Numb. xix. 18.   Psal. li. 7.)

III. The objects of lustration were either persons or things dedicated to divine worship.   The Levites, priests, and above all, the high priest, underwent a purification previously to undertaking their respective offices.   In like manner the Israelites were commanded to sanctify themselves by ablutions both of their persons and clothes, &c. previously to receiving the law (Exod. xix. 10, 11. 14, 15. Heb. ix. 19.); and after the giving of the law and the people's assent to the book of the covenant, Moses sprinkled them with blood. (Exod. xxiv.

---

[1] This opinion obtained among the antient Greeks.   See particularly Homer's Iliad, x. 291—293. and Odyssey, iii. 382., and Virgil's Georgics, iv. 550, 551.   Dr. A. Clarke on Numb. xix. 2.

[2] While Mr. W. Rae Wilson (who visited Palestine in 1819) was at Cana, "six women having their faces veiled came down to the well, each carrying on her head a pot for the purpose of being filled with water.   These vessels were formed of stone, and something in the shape of the bottles used in our country for containing vitriol, having great bodies and small necks, with this exception, they were not so large ; many had handles attached to the sides ; and it was a wonderful coincidence with Scripture, that the vessels appeared to contain much the same quantity as those, which the Evangelist informs [us] had been employed on occasion of the nuptial celebration," viz. " *three firkins,*" that is, about twelve gallons each. (Wilson's Travels in Egypt and the Holy Land, p. 339. first edition.)

5—8. Heb. ix. 19.) So also were the tabernacle, and all its sacred vessels anointed with oil (Exod. xxx. 26—28. xl. 9—11. Lev. viii. 10, 11.), and as Saint Paul further intimates, were sprinkled with the blood of the victims.

Those who were about to offer sacrifice unto Jehovah were also to be lustrated (1 Sam. xvi. 5.); as well as those who were repairing to divine worship to offer their prayers (Judith xii. 7, 8.); and especially the priest and the high priest, before they executed their respective offices. (Exod. xxx. 20.) Lastly, all who according to the Mosaic law were adjudged impure, were to be purified before they could be admitted into the congregation of the Lord. (Numb. xix. 20.)

IV. In the Mosaic law, those persons are termed *unclean*, whom others were obliged to avoid touching, or even meeting, unless they chose to be themselves defiled, that is, cut off from all intercourse with their brethren; and who, besides, were bound to abstain from frequenting the place where divine service and the offering-feasts were held, under penalties still more severe.

The duration and degrees of impurity were different. In some instances, by the use of certain ceremonies, an unclean person became purified at sunset; in others, this did not take place until eight days after the physical cause of defilement ceased. Lepers were obliged to live in a detached situation, separate from other people, and to keep themselves actually at a distance from them. They were distinguished by a peculiar dress; and if any person approached, they were bound to give him warning, by crying out, *Unclean! unclean!* Other polluted persons, again, could not directly touch those that were clean, without defiling them in like manner, and were obliged to remain without the *camp*, that they might not be in their way. (Numb. v. 1—4.) Eleven different species of impurity are enumerated in the Levitical law, to which the later Jews added many others. But the severest of all was,

1. The *Leprosy*, an infectious disease of slow and imperceptible progress, beginning very insidiously and gently, for the most part with one little bright spot, which causes no trouble, though no means will make it disappear: but increasing with time into furfuraceous scales that ultimately become a thick scab, it imperceptibly passes into a disease, which, though divested of its deadly nature in our temperate climates and by our superior cleanliness, is in the East attended with the most formidable symptoms: such as mortification and separation of whole limbs, and when arrived at a certain stage, it is altogether incurable. As the varieties and symptoms of this frightful malady are discussed at length in a subsequent part of this work, it will be sufficient to remark, for the present, that, among the heathens, the leprosy was considered as inflicted by their gods, by whom alone it could be removed, and the same notion appears to have prevailed among the Israelites; for when the king of Syria sent Naaman, his commander in chief, to the king of Israel, to heal him of his leprosy, the latter exclaimed,— *Am I* God, *to kill and to make alive, that this man doth send unto* me, *to recover a man of his leprosy?* (2 Kings v. 7.) Some instances are also recorded in which this disease is represented as a punishment immediately inflicted by God for particular sins; as in the cases of Miriam, Gehazi, and king Uzziah. This circumstance, con-

nected with the extreme foulness of the disorder, rendered it a very striking emblem of moral pollution; and the exclusion of persons infected with it from the worship and people of God was fitted not only to humble and reform the offenders, but also to impress upon the mind the most solemn and useful instructions.

The person who had been healed of leprosy was minutely examined by the priest, who proceeded to perform the rites and sacrifices of purification, which are minutely described in Lev. xiv. in order that the patient might be re-admitted into society and to the privileges of the Jewish church. Among these sacrifices and ceremonies, the following is very remarkable: — " The priest was required to take two small birds, and to kill one of them over an earthen vessel filled with river water, so that the blood might be mixed with the water. He was then to dip the other or living bird into the water, and sprinkle the leper with it seven times with a stick of cedar wood, upon which a bunch of *hyssop* was tied with a scarlet thread; after which the priest was to pronounce him purified, and let loose the living bird into the open air. (Lev. xiv. 2—7.) This ceremony seems to be typical of the purification of our sins by the sprinkling of the blood of Jesus Christ (Isa. lii. 15. 1 Pet. i. 2.), which flowed out of his wounded side mixed with water (John xix. 34.); while the dismissal of the living bird resembles that of the scape-goat into the wilderness, with the sins of the leper upon him. Our Lord expressly commanded the lepers, whom he healed, to conform to the law." (Matt. viii. 4. Mark i. 44. Luke v. 14. xvii. 14.) [1]

Besides the leprosy of the person, Moses mentions two other species of leprosy, viz. of clothes and of houses, which are in a great measure unknown in Europe.

2. The *Leprosy of Clothes* is described in Lev. xiii. 47—59. as consisting of green or reddish spots, which remain in spite of washing, and continue to spread; so that the cloth becomes bald or bare, sometimes on one side, and sometimes on the other. From the information which Michaelis received from a woollen manufacturer, he supposes this disease to arise in woollen cloth, from the use of the wool of sheep that have died of disease; which when worn next the skin (as in the East) is very apt to produce vermin. With respect to leather and linen, he could obtain no information.

Clothes suspected to be thus tainted were to be inspected by the priest; if they were found to be corroded by the leprosy, they were to be burnt; but if, after being washed, the plague was found to have departed from them, they were to be pronounced clean.

3. The *House Leprosy* is said in Lev. xiv. 33—37. to consist of greenish or reddish spots or dimples, that appear on the walls, and continually spread wider and wider. Michaelis considers it to be the same as the *saltpetre*, which sometimes attacks and corrodes houses that stand in damp situations. Although in Europe unattended with any injury to health, in Palestine it might be hurtful; so that the Mosaic regulations in this respect are both wise and provident.

When a house was suspected to be thus tainted, the priest was to examine it, and ordered it to be shut up seven days. If he found that

---

[1] Dr. Hales's Analysis of Chronology, vol. ii. book i. p. 273.

the plague or signs of the plague had not spread, he commanded it to be shut up seven days more.   On the thirteenth day he revisited it; and if he found the infected place *dim*, or gone away, he took out that part of the wall, carried it out to an unclean place, mended the wall, and caused the whole house to be newly plastered.   It was then shut up a third seven days: he once more inspected it on the nineteenth day; and if he found that the plague had broken out anew, he ordered the house to be pulled down.   If on the other hand it was pronounced to be clean, an offering was made on the occasion; in order that every one might certainly know that it was not infected, and the public might be freed from all apprehensions on that account.

V.   Various other legal impurities are enumerated in Lev. xii. 1—8. and xv. which it is not necessary to detail.   To which we may add, that all human corpses and the carcasses of beasts that died in any other way than by the knife, were regarded as unclean.   Whoever touched the *former*, or went into the *tent*, or *apartment* (after the Israelites had houses), where a corpse lay, was unclean for seven days; and whoever touched a dead body, or even a human bone, or a grave in the fields, was unclean for the same period.   The body of a clean beast that fell not by the knife, but died in any other way, defiled the person who touched it, until the evening (Lev. xi. 39.); and the carcasses of unclean beasts, by whatever means they died, did the same. (Lev. v. 2. xi. 8. 11. 24, 25. 27, 28. 31. Deut. xiv. 8.)   The consequence of this law was, that the carcasses of beasts were not suffered to remain above ground, but were put into the earth, that passengers might not be in danger of pollution from them.

By these wise enactments, the spreading of contagious diseases would be effectually prevented, which in hot climates are peculiarly rapid and fatal.   For the same reason, also, Michaelis is of opinion, that Moses commanded the Israelites to break earthen vessels, which were liable to be defiled by being left uncovered in a tent or apartment where a person died, or a corpse lay (Numb. xix. 15.), or by an unclean beast falling into them (Lev. xi. 33.), or by the touch of a diseased person. (Lev. xv. 12.)[1]

Such are the Mosaic statutes concerning purifications and impurities.   Profane scoffers, who deride those things, the reason and propriety of which they will not take the trouble to investigate, have ridiculed them as too minute,—especially those respecting the different species of leprosy,—and as unworthy to be made part of a divine law. But every well regulated mind surely must discern in them both the goodness and wisdom of Jehovah towards his chosen people, in giving them precepts which were calculated not only to preserve their health and regulate their morals, but also to accustom them to obedience to his will in every respect.   The leprosy has ever been considered as a lively emblem of that moral taint or " corruption of the nature of every man *that naturally is engendered of the offspring of Adam*[2];" as the sacrifices, which were to be offered by the healed leper, prefigured that spotless *Lamb of God that taketh away the sins of the world.*

---

[1] Schulzii Archæologia Hebraica, pp. 303—310.   Michaelis's Commentaries, vol. iii. pp. 254—335.

[2] Article IX. of the Confession of the Anglican Church.

CHAPTER VI.

ON THE CORRUPTIONS OF RELIGION AMONG THE JEWS.

SECTION I.

ON THE IDOLATRY OF THE JEWS.

I. *Origin and Progress of Idolatry. — Sketch of its History among the Israelites and Jews. —* II. *Idols worshipped by the Israelites alone. —* III. *Idols of the Ammonites, worshipped by the Israelites.—*IV. *Idols of the Canaanites or Syrians. —* V. *Phœnician Idols. —* VI. *Babylonian and Assyrian Idols.—*VII. *Idols worshipped in Samaria during the Captivity. — Hieroglyphic Stones, why prohibited to the Jews.—*VIII. *Idols of the Greeks and Romans mentioned in the New Testament. —* IX. *Allusions in the Scriptures to the Idolatrous Worship of the Heathen Nations.—*X. *Different Kinds of Divination.*

I. IDOLATRY is the superstitious worship of idols or false gods. From Gen. vi. 5. compared with Romans i. 23. there is every reason to believe that it was practised before the flood; and this conjecture is confirmed by the apostle Jude (ver. 4.), who, describing the character of certain men in his days that *denied the only Lord God,* adds, in the eleventh verse of his epistle, *Woe unto them, for they are gone into the way of Cain ;* whence it may be inferred that Cain and his descendants were the first who threw off the sense of a God, and worshipped the creature instead of the Creator.[1]

The heavenly bodies were the first objects of idolatrous worship; and Mesopotamia and Chaldæa were the countries where it chiefly prevailed after the deluge.[2]   Before Jehovah vouchsafed to reveal himself to them, both Terah and his son Abraham were idolaters (Josh. xxiv. 2.), as also was Laban, the father-in-law of Jacob (Gen. xxxi. 19. 30.) ; though he appears to have had some idea of the true God, from his mentioning the name of Jehovah on several occasions. (Gen. xxiv. 31. 50, 51.)   Previously to Jacob and his sons going into Egypt, idolatry prevailed in Canaan ; and while their posterity were resident in that country, it appears from Josh. xxiv. 14. and Ezek. xx. 7,8. that they worshipped the deities of Egypt.

On the departure of the Israelites from Egypt, although Moses by the command and instruction of Jehovah had given them such a religion as no other nation possessed, and notwithstanding all his laws were directed to preserve them from idolatry ; yet, so wayward were the Israelites, that almost immediately after their deliverance from bondage we find them worshipping idols. (Exod. xxxii. 1. Psal. cvi. 19, 20. Acts vii. 41—43.) Soon after their entrance into the land of Canaan, they adopted various deities that were worshipped by the Canaanites,

---

[1] The history of the origin and progress of idolatry are ably traced in Dr. Graves's Lectures on the Pentateuch, vol. i. pp. 183—190.

[2] On the subject of Zabianism, or the idolatrous worship of the stars, there is an interesting dissertation in Dr. Townley's Translation of Maimonides's Reasons of the Laws of Moses, pp. 38—47.

and other neighbouring nations (Judges ii. 13. viii. 33.); for which base ingratitude they were severely punished.   Shortly after the death of Joshua, the government became so unsettled, that *every man did that which seemed right in his own eyes.*   The prophet Azariah describes the infelicity of these times, when he says, *They were without the true God, without a teaching priest, and without the law* (2 Chron. xv. 3.); and as anarchy prevailed, so did idolatry, which first crept into the tribe of Ephraim in the house of Micah, and then soon spread itself amongst the Danites. (Judg. xvii. xviii.)   Nor were the other tribes free from this infection, during this dissolution of the government; for it is said, *They forsook the Lord and served Baal and Ashtaroth, and followed the other gods of the people round about them.* (Judg. ii. 13, 12.)

Under the government of Samuel, Saul, and David, the worship of God seems to have been purer than in former times.   Solomon is the first king, who, out of complaisance to the strange women he had married, caused temples to be erected in honour of their gods; and so far impiously complied with them himself, as to offer incense to these false deities (1 Kings xi. 5—8.): so fatal an evil is lust to the best understandings, which besots every one it overcomes, and reigns over them with uncontrolled power!   Solomon, it is true, did not arrive at that pitch of audacity which some of his successors afterwards did: but his giving the smallest countenance to the breach of the divine law, among a people so prone to idolatry, could not but be attended with the worst consequences; and accordingly, upon his death, the glory of his kingdom was speedily eclipsed by the revolt of the ten tribes and the division of his kingdom.   This civil defection was attended with a spiritual one, for Jeroboam the son of Nebat, who succeeded him in the government of the ten tribes which had revolted, (and who himself had probably been initiated in the idolatrous worship of the neighbouring nations, when he took refuge from Solomon's jealousy at the court of Shishak,) soon introduced the worship of two golden calves, the one at Dan and the other at Bethel.   He made choice of Bethel, because it had long been esteemed as a place sacred for the real appearance of God in antient times to Jacob, and might, therefore, induce the people to a more ready belief of the residence of the same Deity now; and Dan (as already observed) being at the extremity of the kingdom, was the place whither that part of the country resorted on account of Micah's teraphim.   Idolatry being thus established in Israel by public authority, and countenanced by all their princes, was universally adopted by the people, notwithstanding all the remonstrances against it by the prophets whom God sent to reclaim them from time to time, and who stood as a barrier against this growing wickedness, regardless of all the persecutions of impious Jezebel, who did what she could utterly to extinguish the worship of the true God.   At length this brought a flood of calamities upon that kingdom, and was the source of all the evils with which that people were afterwards afflicted; so that, after a continual scene of tragical deaths, civil wars, and judgments of various kinds, they were at length carried away captive by Shalmaneser into Assyria.

The people of Judah were little better.   One might justly have expected, that, if there had been no other reason than state policy for preserving the true religion in its native purity, that alone would have been sufficient to prevent any other false worship from being set up, and that the same motives, which induced the ten tribes to establish a strange worship, would have induced Judah to be jealous for the true one.   But the event proved otherwise; for notwithstanding the great strength added to the kingdom of Judah, by those who resorted thither out of other tribes for the sake of religion, prosperity inflated Rehoboam and soon ruined him.   It is said that he continued but *three years walking in the ways of David and Solomon.* (2 Chron. xi. 17.) After which these idolatrous inclinations began to appear, which probably were instilled into him by his mother Naamah, who was an Ammonitess. (1 Kings xiv. 21.)   In short, *he forsook the law of the Lord, and all Israel with him* (2 Chron. xii. 1.), and fell into the grossest idolatry *above all that their fathers had done.* (1 Kings xiv. 22.)   But God soon corrected him and his people, having delivered them into the hands of Shishak king of Egypt, who with a vast army entered the country, took their cities, and plundered Jerusalem and the temple of all the riches which David and Solomon had treasured up there. (2 Chron. xii. 2.)   Upon their repentance and humiliation, the anger of Jehovah was soon mitigated; and we do not find that the kingdom of Judah fell into any gross acts of idolatry till the reign of Ahaz, who was the most impious prince that ever sat upon that throne.   He was not content *with walking in the ways of the kings of Israel, and making molten images of Baalim* (2 Chron. xxviii. 2.), but he carried his wicked inclinations still farther, and imitated the old inhabitants of the land in their cruel and idolatrous practices; for it is said of him that *he burnt incense in the valley of the son of Hinnom, and burnt his children in the fire* (ver. 3.); or, as we read in 2 Kings xvi. 3., *He made his son to pass through the fire,* which doubtless was the *passing through the fire to Moloch,* so expressly prohibited in Lev. xviii. 21.   For these impieties Ahaz was justly punished by God, and after a constant course of all manner of wickedness, died in the flower of his age; but was happily succeeded by his son Hezekiah, who, among other reformations, it is said, *broke in pieces the brasen serpent that Moses had made, to which the children of Israel did burn incense.* (2 Kings xviii. 4.)   But Hezekiah's reformation was soon overturned upon the succession of his wicked son Manasseh, who seems to have made it his business to search out what God in his law had forbidden, and to make the practice of it his study. (2 Chron. xxxiii. 3—8.)

The princes who succeeded (Josiah only excepted) and their people seem to have lived in a kind of competition with one another in wickedness and idolatry, and to have given a loose to the wildness of their imaginations in the worship of God, which brought upon Judah and her people the utmost fury of God's wrath, and those judgments which had been decreed, and which ended in the captivity of king and people.[1]   At length, however, become wiser by the severe discipline they had received, the tribes that returned unto their native country from the Babylonian captivity wholly renounced idolatry; and thenceforth uniformly evinced the most deep-rooted aversion from all strange deities and foreign modes of worship.   This great reformation was accomplished by Ezra and Nehemiah, and the eminent men who accom-

---

[1] Home's Hist. of the Jews, vol. ii. pp. 282—291.

panied or succeeded them : but, in the progress of time, though the exterior of piety was maintained, the "power of godliness" was lost; and we learn from the New Testament, that, during our Saviour's ministry, the Jews were divided into various religious parties, which widely differed in opinion, and pursued each other with the fiercest animosity, and with implacable hatred.

Very numerous are the idols mentioned in the Scriptures, particularly in the Old Testament. It is proposed in the following pages of this section to offer, in the first place, a short notice of the idols which were peculiar to the Israelites; and, secondly, of those which they adopted from the Ammonites, Syrians, Phœnicians, Babylonians, and other nations of antiquity.[1]

II. IDOLS WORSHIPPED PARTICULARLY BY THE ISRAELITES. — Scarcely, as we have already observed, had the children of Israel been delivered from their cruel bondage in Egypt, when they returned to those idols, to which they had been accustomed.

1. The first object of their idolatrous worship was a GOLDEN CALF. (Exod. xxxii. 1—6.) Having been conducted through the wilderness by a pillar of cloud and fire, which preceded them in their marches, while that cloud covered the mountain where Moses was receiving the divine commands, they imagined that it would no longer be their guide; and therefore they applied to Aaron to make for them a sacred sign or symbol, as other nations had, which might visibly represent God to them. With this request Aaron unhappily complied : *the people offered burnt-offerings, and brought peace-offerings, and sat down to eat and to drink, and rose up to play.* The materials of this idol were the golden ear-rings of the people, worn in these eastern countries by men as well as women; and probably they were some of the jewels which they had demanded of the Egyptians. They were cast in a mould by Aaron, and subsequently chiselled into a calf, which is generally supposed to have been an exact resemblance of the celebrated Egyptian deity, Apis, who was worshipped under the form of an ox. This antient Egyptian superstition is still perpetuated on Mount Libanus, by those Druses who assume the name of Okkals, and who pay divine honours to a *calf*.[2]

2. In imitation of this were the two GOLDEN CALVES, made by Jeroboam, the first king of Israel, after the secession of the ten tribes. The Egyptians had two oxen, one of which they worshipped under the name of Apis, at Memphis, the capital of Upper Egypt, and the other under the name of Mnevis, at Hierapolis, the metropolis of Lower Egypt. In like manner, Jeroboam set up one of his calves at Bethel, and the other at Dan. (1 Kings xii. 28—32.) Like the idolaters in the wilderness, this leader of the rebels proclaimed before the idols upon the feast of their consecration, *These are thy gods, O Israel,*

---

[1] The following account of the idols worshipped by the Jews is abridged principally from Lamy's Apparatus Biblicus, vol. ii. pp. 176—188. Calmet's Dissertations in his Commentaire Littéral, tom. i. part ii. pp. 173—178. and tom. vi. pp. 745—752. and his Dictionary of the Bible under the several names of the idol deities. Lewis's Origines Hebrææ, vol. iii. pp. 1—102. Jahn's Archæologia Biblica, §§ 400—415. Ackermann's Archæologia Biblica, §§ 387—402. Millar's Hist. of the Propagation of Christianity, vol. i. pp. 227—340. Godwin's Moses and Aaron, book iv. pp. 140—178. and Alber, Inst. Herm. Vet. Test. tom. i. pp. 394—406.

[2] Dr. Clarke's Travels, vol. iv. p. 204.

which brought thee out of the land of Egypt! as if he had said, "God is every where in his essence, and cannot be included in any place : he dwells among you here as well as at Jerusalem, and if you require any symbols of his presence, behold here they are in these calves which I have set up ;" for they could not be so stupid as to believe, that the idols taken just before out of the furnace had been their deliverers, so many ages before. It is evident, that the worship of these calves was not regarded by the sacred writers and by the prophets, as an absolute *Pagan* idolatry, but only as a schism, which was indeed very criminal in itself, but did not come up to the degree of a total apostasy ; for the history of the revolt of the ten tribes introduces Jeroboam speaking not like a person whose intention was to make the people change their religion, but as representing to them that the true God, being every where, was not confined to any certain place, and, therefore, they might pay their devotions to him as well in Dan and Bethel as at Jerusalem.

The worship offered before these images is supposed to have been in imitation of the ceremonies of the Mosaic law.

As most of the priests of the family of Aaron, and the Levites, who had their cities and abodes among the ten revolted tribes, retired into the dominions of the king of Judah, to avoid joining in the schism, which proved a great additional strength to the house of David; Jeroboam seized their cities and estates, and he eased the people of paying their tithes, there being none to demand them ; so he gratified them by making priests out of every tribe and family, even in the extreme part of the country. The pontificate and supremacy over this schismatical priesthood he reserved in his own hands. These idols were at length destroyed by the kings of Assyria ; the calf in Bethel was carried to Babylon, with other spoils, by Shalmaneser, and the other in Dan was seized by Tiglath-Pileser, about ten years before, in the invasion which he made upon Galilee, in which province the city stood.

3. The BRASEN SERPENT was an image of polished brass, in the form of one of those fiery serpents (or serpents whose bite was attended with violent inflammation) which were sent to chastise the murmuring Israelites in the wilderness. By divine command *Moses made a serpent of brass,* or copper, and *put it upon a pole ; and it came to pass that if a serpent had bitten any man, when he beheld the serpent of brass, he lived.* (Numb. xxi. 6—9.) This brasen serpent was preserved as a monument of the divine mercy, but in process of time became an instrument of idolatry. When this superstition began, it is difficult to determine ; but the best account is given by the Jewish rabbi, David Kimchi, in the following manner. From the time that the kings of Israel did evil, and the children of Israel followed idolatry, till the reign of Hezekiah, they offered incense to it; for, it being written in the law of Moses, *whoever looketh upon it shall live,* they fancied they might obtain blessings by its mediation, and, therefore, thought it worthy to be worshipped. It had been kept from the days of Moses, in memory of a miracle, in the same manner as the pot of manna was: and Asa and Jehoshaphat did not extirpate it when they rooted out idolatry, because in their reign they did not observe that the people worshipped this serpent, or burnt incense to it; and, therefore, they

left it as a memorial. But Hezekiah thought fit to take it quite away, when he abolished other idolatry, because in the time of his father they adored it as an idol; and though pious people among them accounted it only as a memorial of a wonderful work, yet he judged it better to abolish it, though the memory of the miracle should happen to be lost, than suffer it to remain, and leave the Israelites in danger of committing idolatry hereafter with it.

On the subject of the serpent-bitten Israelites being healed by looking at the brasen serpent, there is a good comment in the book of Wisdom, chap. xvi. ver. 4—12. in which are these remarkable words:—" They were admonished, having a sign of salvation, (*i. e.* the brasen serpent) to put them in remembrance of the commandments of thy law. For he that turned himself towards it, was not saved by the THING that he saw, but by THEE that art the saviour of all." (ver. 6, 7.) To the circumstance of looking at the brasen serpent in order to be healed, our Lord refers (John iii. 14, 15.), *As Moses lifted up the serpent in the wilderness, even so must the Son of man be lifted up, that whosoever believeth in him, should not perish, but have eternal life:* from which words we may learn, 1. That *as* the serpent was lifted up on the pole or *ensign; so* Jesus Christ was lifted up on the cross. 2. That *as* the Israelites were to look at the brasen serpent; *so* sinners must look to Christ for salvation. 3. That *as* God provided no other remedy than this *looking,* for the wounded Israelites; *so* he has provided no other way of salvation than *faith* in the blood of his Son. 4. That *as* he who looked at the brasen serpent was *cured* and did *live; so* he that believeth on the Lord Jesus Christ shall *not perish,* but have *eternal life.* 5. That *as* neither the *serpent,* nor *looking at it,* but the invisible power of God, healed the people; *so* neither the *cross* of Christ, nor his merely *being crucified,* but the *pardon he has bought by his blood,* communicated by the *powerful energy of his Spirit,* saves the souls of men. May not all these things be plainly seen in the *circumstances* of this transaction, without making the *serpent* a type of Jesus Christ (the most exceptionable that could possibly be chosen), and running the parallel, as some have done, through ten or a dozen of particulars? [1]

4. In Judg. viii. 24—27. we read that Gideon made an EPHOD of gold from the spoils of the Midianites. This ephod is supposed to have been a rich sacerdotal garment, made in imitation of that worn by the high priest at Shiloh. But whether Gideon meant it as a commemorative trophy, or had a Levitical priest in his house, it is difficult to determine. It *became,* however, *a snare to all Israel,* who dwelt in Gilead, and on the eastern side of Jordan; who thus having an ephod and worship in their own country, would not so readily go over to the tabernacle at Shiloh, and, consequently, fell into idolatry, and worshipped the idols of their neighbours the Phœnicians. (Judg. viii. 27. 33.)

5. The TERAPHIM, it appears from 1 Sam xix. 13., were carved images in a human form, and household deities, like the *penates* and *lares* of the Romans many centuries afterwards (Gen. xxxi. 19. 34, 35. 1 Sam. xix. 13—17.), of which oracular inquiries were made. (Judg. xvii. 5.

---

[1] Dr. A. Clarke on Numb. xxi. 9. See also a pleasing and instructive contemplation of Bishop Hall on this subject.

xviii. 5, 6. 14—20. Zech. x. 2. Hos. iii. 4.) This is confirmed by
1 Sam. xv. 23. (marginal rendering), where the worship of teraphim
is mentioned in conjunction with divination. They appear to have been
introduced among the Israelites from Mesopotamia; and continued to
be worshipped until the Babylonish captivity.

6. The Jews were accused by the pagans of worshipping the HEAD
OF AN Ass; but from this calumny they have been completely vindicated by M. Schumacher.[1] " Apion, the grammarian, seems to be the
author of this slander. He affirmed that the Jews kept the head of
an ass in the sanctuary; that it was discovered there when Antiochus
Epiphanes took the temple and entered into the most holy place. He
added, that one Zabidus, having secretly got into the temple, carried
off the ass's head, and conveyed it to Dora. Suidas[2] says, that Da-
mocritus or Democritus the historian averred that the Jews adored the
head of an ass, made of gold, &c. Plutarch and Tacitus were imposed on by this calumny. They believed that the Hebrews adored
an ass, out of gratitude for the discovery of a fountain by one of these
creatures in the wilderness, at a time when the army of this nation was
parched with thirst and extremely fatigued. Learned men who have
endeavoured to search into the origin of this slander are divided in
their opinions. The reason which Plutarch and Tacitus gave for it
has nothing in the history of the Jews on which to ground it. Tanaquil
Faber has attempted to prove that this accusation proceeded from the
temple in Egypt called *Onion;* as if this name came from *onos,* an ass;
which is, indeed, very credible. The report of the Jews worshipping
an ass might originate in Egypt. We know that the Alexandrians
hated the Jews, and were much addicted to raillery and defamation.
But it was extremely easy for them to have known that the temple
Onion, at Heliopolis, was named from Onias, the High Priest of the
Jews, who built it in the reign of Ptolemy Philometer and Cleopatra.
Others have asserted that the mistake of the heathen proceeded from
an ambiguous mode of reading; as if the Greeks, meaning to say that
the Hebrews adored heaven, οὐρανον, might in abbreviation write
οὐνον; whence the enemies of the Jews concluded that they worshipped
ὄνος, an ass. Or, perhaps, reading in Latin authors that they worshipped
heaven, *cœlum,*

'Nil præter nubes et cœli numen adorant,'

instead of *cœlum,* they read *cillum,* an ass, and so reported that the
Jews adored this animal. Bochart is of opinion that the error arose
from an expression in Scripture 'the mouth of the Lord hath spoken
it;' in the Hebrew, *Pi-Jehovah,* or *Pi-Jeo.* Now, in the Egyptian
language, *pieo* signifies an ass; the Alexandrian Egyptians hearing the
Jews often pronounce this word *pieo,* believed that they appealed to
their God, and thence inferred that they adored an ass. These expli-
cations are ingenious, but not solid. It is doubtful whether any one
can assign the true reason for the calumny; which might have arisen
from a joke, or an accident. M. Le Moine seems to have succeeded
best, who says that in all probability the golden urn containing the
manna which was preserved in the sanctuary was taken for the head of

---

[1] De Cultu Animalium inter Ægyptios et Judæos Commentatio, ex recondita antiquitate
illustrata a M. Johann. Heinr. Schumacher. Sect. viii. *et seq.* (Brunsvigiis, 1773. 4to.)
[2] In Damocrito et in Juda.

an ass; and that the *omer* of manna might have been confounded with the Hebrew *hamor*, which signifies an ass." [1]

III. IDOL GODS OF THE AMMONITES, WORSHIPPED BY THE CHIL-DREN OF ISRAEL.

MOLOCH, also called Molech, Milcom, or Melcom, was the principal idol of the Ammonites (1 Kings xi. 7.), yet not so appropriated to them, but that it was adopted by other neighbouring nations for their god. Some writers have supposed that Moloch was the same as Saturn, to whom it is well known that human victims were offered. But he rather appears to have been Baal or the Sun (Jer. xxxii. 35.), and was the Adrammelech and Anammelech of the Sepharvaites, who burnt their children to them in the fire. There is great reason to think that the Hebrews were addicted to the worship of this deity before their departure from Egypt, since both the prophet Amos (v. 26.) and the proto-martyr Stephen (Acts vii. 43.) reproach them with having carried the tabernacle of their god Moloch with them in the wilderness. Solomon built a temple to Moloch on the Mount of Olives (1 Kings xi. 7.), and his impiety was followed by other kings, his successors, who had apostatised from the worship of Jehovah. The valley of Tophet and Hinnom, on the east of Jerusalem, was the principal scene of the horrid rites performed in honour of Moloch (Jer. xix. 5, 6.), who, it is probable, was the same as the Baal, Bel, or Belus of the Carthaginians, Sidonians, Babylonians, and Assyrians.

IV. IDOL GODS OF THE CANAANITES OR SYRIANS, WORSHIPPED BY THE ISRAELITES.

1. Mr. Selden, in his elaborate treatise on the Syrian gods [2], mentions a goddess, whom he terms GOOD FORTUNE, as the first idol mentioned in the Scriptures, and worshipped by the Hebrews. This opinion is founded on the exclamation of Leah (Gen. xxx. 11.), when her handmaid Zilpah bore a son to Jacob. *She said, I am prosperous* (or as some in the present day, who ascribe every thing to chance, would say — *Good luck to me*) *; and she called his name Gad*, that is, *prosperity.* Although this interpretation has been questioned, yet in Isa. lxv. 11. Gad is unquestionably joined with Meni (or the Moon), and both are names of idols, where the prophet says, —

> Ye . . . . . have deserted JEHOVAH,
> And have forgotten my holy mountain;
> Who set in order a table for Gad,
> And fill out a libation to Meni.   Bp. Lowth's Version.

What these objects of idolatrous worship were, it is now impossible exactly to ascertain: it is not improbable that Gad was the sun, and Meni the moon; the sun being the great source of plenty, which again is productive of prosperity. Jerome, as cited by bishop Lowth, gives an account of the idolatrous practice of the apostate Jews, which is alluded to by the prophet of making a feast, or a *lectisternium*, as the Romans called it, for these pretended deities. " It is," he says, " an antient idolatrous custom in every city in Egypt, and especially in Alexandria, that on the last day of the last month in the year they set out a table with various kinds of dishes, and with a cup filled with

---

[1] Dr. Harris's Nat. Hist. of the Bible, pp. 24, 25. (American edit.) or pp. 22, 23. of the London reprint.
[2] De Diis Syris, Syntag. i. c. 1. (Works, vol. ii. pp. 255, 256.)

a mixture of water, wine, and honey, indicating the fertility of the past or future year. This also the Israelites did."[1]

2. AHAD or ACHAD is the name of a Syrian deity, under which the sun was worshipped: it is mentioned in Isa. lxvi. 17. where the rites of this god are described:—

> They who sanctify themselves, and purify themselves
> In the gardens, after the rites of Achad;
> In the midst of those who eat swine's flesh,
> And the abomination, and the field mouse;
> Together shall they perish, saith JEHOVAH.   Bp. Lowth's Version.

3. BAAL-PEOR (Numb. xxv. 1—5.) was a deity of the Moabites and Midianites, supposed to be the same as the Priapus of the Romans, and worshipped with similar obscene rites. (Compare Hos. ix. 10.) Selden imagined that this idol was the same with Pluto, from Psal. cvi. 28. *They joined themselves unto Baal-peor, and ate the sacrifices of the dead.* But this may mean nothing more than the sacrifices and offerings made to idols, who are properly termed *dead*, in opposition to the true God, the Creator and Preserver of all things, who is in the Scriptures repeatedly and emphatically termed *the living God.* CHEMOSH, *the abomination of Moab*, to whom Solomon erected an altar on the Mount of Olives (1 Kings xi. 7.), is supposed to have been the same deity as Baal-peor. Servants are known by the name of their lord. As the Israelites were called by the name of the true God (2 Chron. vii. 14.), so the Moabites are called (Numb. xxi. 29.) by the name of their god, *the people of Chemosh;* and other idolatrous nations were designated in a similar manner. (See Mic. iv. 5.)

4. RIMMON was an idol of the Syrians, but not worshipped by the Israelites: it is mentioned in 2 Kings v. 8. and is supposed to have been the same as the Jupiter of the antients.

5. ASHTAROTH or ASTARTE (Judg. ii. 13. 1 Sam. xxxi. 10. 2 Kings xxiii. 13.) is generally understood to have been the moon; though in later times this idol became identified with the Syrian Venus, and was worshipped with impure rites. Astarte is still worshipped by the Druses of Mount Libanus.[2]

V. PHŒNICIAN IDOLS WORSHIPPED BY THE ISRAELITES.

1. None of the heathen deities, mentioned in the Old Testament, is more celebrated than BAAL.

The word signifies lord, master, and husband; a name which, doubtless, was given to their supreme deity, to him whom they regarded as the master of men and gods, and of the whole of nature. This name had its original from Phœnicia, Baal being a god of the Phœnicians: and Jezebel, daughter of Ethbaal king of the Zidonians, brought this deity from the city of Zidon; for he was the god of Tyre and Sidon, and was certainly the Ζευς of the Greeks, and the Jupiter of the Latins. This god was known under the same name all over Asia: it is the same as the Bel of the Babylonians; and the same name and the same god went to the Carthaginians, who were a colony of the Phœnicians[3]: witness the name of Hannibal, Asdrubal,

---

[1] Bp. Lowth's Isaiah, vol. ii. p. 375.
[2] Dr. Clarke's Travels, vol. v. pp. 32. 453—459.
[3] May it not be presumed that the antient inhabitants of Ireland were a Phœnician colony, from the appropriation of the round towers, found in that island, to the preservation of the

Adherbal, all consisting of Bel or Baal, being the name of the deity of that country, which was according to the custom of the East, where the kings, and great men of the realm, added to their own names those of their gods. In short, it seems to be a name common to all idols, to whatever country they belonged; and when it is mentioned in the Holy Writings without any explanatory circumstance annexed, it is usually understood to be the principal deity of that nation or place of which the sacred writer was speaking.

This false deity is frequently mentioned in Scripture in the plural number, *Baalim* (1 Sam. vii. 4.), which may either signify that the name of Baal was given to many different gods, or may imply a plurality of statues consecrated to that idol, and bearing several appellations, according to the difference of places: just as the antient heathens gave many surnames to Jupiter, as Olympian, Dodonæan, and others, according to the names of the places where he was worshipped.

The false gods of Palestine and the neighbouring nations were called Baal in general; but there were other Baals whose name was compounded of some additional word, such as Baal-peor, Baalberith, Baalzebub, and Baalzephon. The first of these has already been noticed in the preceding page.

2. BAALBERITH was the idol of the Shechemites (Judg. viii. 33.); and the temple of this deity was their arsenal and public treasury. As the Hebrew word Berith signifies a covenant or contract, this god is supposed to have had his appellation from his office, which was to preside over covenants, contracts, and oaths. In like manner, the Greeks had their Ζευς Ορχιος; and the Romans, their *Deus Fidius*.

3. BAALZEBUB or BELZEBUB was the god of the Ekronites (2 Kings i. 3.), but the origin of the name (which in Hebrew denotes the *god of flies*) it is difficult to ascertain: As the vicinity of this country was long after infested with minute flies that stung severely all on whom they settled, it is not improbable, that Ekron was infested in a similar manner, and that its inhabitants had a deity whom they supplicated for the prevention or removal of this plague.[1] The Jews, in the time of Christ, called the *prince of the devils* by the name of Beelzebub. (Matt. xii. 24. Luke xi. 15.)

4. BAALZEPHON is supposed to have been an idol, erected to guard the confines of the Red Sea, and also the name of a place, where a temple was erected for the use of mariners.

5. DAGON, the tutelary deity of the people of Ashdod or Azotus, was the *Derceto* of the heathens. Its name signifies a *fish;* and its figure is said to have been that of a man from the navel upwards, and that of a fish downwards. It is not improbable that this idol was commemorative of the preservation of Noah in the ark.

6. TAMMUZ or THAMMUZ, though an Egyptian deity, is the same as the Adonis of the Phœnicians and Syrians. For this idol the Jewish women are said to have sat weeping before the north gate of the temple. (Ezek. viii. 14.) Lucian[2] has given an account of the rites

---

Baal-Thinne, or sacred fire of Baal? On this subject, the further prosecution of which is foreign to the plan of the present work, much curious and antiquarian information is collected in the notes to " The Druid," a Dramatic Poem, by Thomas Cromwell. London, 1832, 8vo.

[1] See Harmer's Observations, vol. iii. pp. 323—325.

[2] In his treatise De Deâ Syriâ. Op. tom. ix. pp. 89—91. edit. Bipont.

of this deity, which illustrates the allusion of the prophet. " I saw,"
says he, " at Biblis, the great temple of Venus, in which are annually
celebrated the mysteries of Adonis in which I am initiated; for it is
said, that he was killed in the country by a wild boar, and in perpetual
remembrance of this event, a public mourning is solemnised every year
with doleful lamentations : then follows a funeral as of a dead body,
and next day is celebrated his resurrection, for it is said, he flew up
into heaven : one of the ceremonies is for women to have their heads
shaved in the same manner as the Egyptians at the death of Apis.
Those who refuse to be shaved are obliged to prostitute themselves a
whole day to strangers, and the money which they thus acquire is consecrated to the goddess. But some of the Biblians say, that all those
ceremonies are observed for Osiris, and that he is buried in their
country, not in Egypt. In order to which there comes yearly a head
made of papyrus, brought by sea, from Egypt to Biblis, and I myself
have seen it." Procopius, in his commentary on Isaiah, more particularly explains this rite, and observes that the inhabitants of Alexandria
annually prepare a pot in which they put a letter directed to the women
of Biblis, by which they are informed that the Adonis is found again.
This pot being sealed up, they commit it to the sea, after performing
some ceremonies over it, and command it to depart; accordingly, the
vessel immediately steers its course to Biblis, where it puts an end to
the women's mourning.

This Syrian Venus had a temple upon the top of a mountain, which
was built out of the way in a by-place, in the midst of a wood; it was
demolished by the emperor Constantine [1], who put an end to all the
filthy ceremonies which had been performed in it. The image of this
goddess, according to Macrobius [2], represented a woman in mourning
covered with a veil, having a dejected countenance, and tears seeming
to run down her face.

7. The BAITHYLIA or CONSECRATED STONES, adored by the early
Phœnicians, are supposed to have been the most antient objects of
idolatrous worship; and, probably, were afterwards formed into beautiful statues, when the art of sculpture became tolerably perfected.
They originated in Jacob's setting up and anointing with oil the stone
which he had used for a pillow, as a memorial of the heavenly vision
with which he had been favoured (Gen. xxviii. 18.), and also to serve
as a token to point out to him the place when God should bring him
back again.[3] The idolatrous unction of stones, consecrating them to
the memory of great men, and worshipping them after their death,
must have prevailed to a great extent in the time of Moses, who therefore prohibited the Israelites from erecting them. (Lev. xxvi. 1.) The
practice of setting up stones as a guide to travellers still exists in
Persia and other parts of the East.[4]

---

[1] Eusebius de Laudibus Constantini, pp. 736, 737. edit. Reading.
[2] Saturnalia, lib. i. c. 21.
[3] Dr. A. Clarke on Gen. xxviii. 18.
[4] In the course of Mr. Morier's journey in the interior of that country, he remarked that
his old guide " every here and there placed a stone on a conspicuous bit of rock, or two
stones one upon the other, at the same time uttering some words which" (says this intelligent traveller) " I learnt were a prayer for our safe return. This explained to me, what I
had frequently seen before in the East, and particularly on a high road leading to a great
town, whence the town is first seen, and where the eastern traveller sets up his stone, accompanied by a devout exclamation, as it were, in token of his safe arrival. The action of our

VI. BABYLONIAN AND ASSYRIAN IDOLS.

1, 2. BEL and NEBO are Babylonian deities mentioned in Isa. xlvi. 1. Bel (the Belus of profane historians) was most probably a contraction of Baal, or the Sun. The planet Mercury has the name of Nebo or Nebu among the Zabians : it is found also in the composition of several Chaldæan names of persons, as Nebuchadnezzar, Nebuzaradan, &c. &c.[1]

3. MERODACH is supposed to have been a Babylonish monarch, who was deified after his death.[2]

4. NISROCH was an Assyrian idol, adored by Sennacherib. (2 Kings xix. 37. Isa. xxxvii. 38.) Perhaps it was the solar fire, to whose anger he probably attributed the destruction of his army before Jerusalem ; and whom he was in the act of adoring, when he was assassinated by his sons.[3]

VII. IDOLS WORSHIPPED IN SAMARIA DURING THE CAPTIVITY.

The deities noticed in the preceding pages are the chief idols antiently adored in Palestine ; but there were other false gods worshipped there, which were imported into Samaria, after Shalmaneser had carried the ten tribes into captivity, by the colony of foreigners which he sent to occupy their country. These men brought their idols with them. The men of *Babylon* had their *Succoth-benoth*, which was the Babylonish Melitta, in honour of whom young women prostituted themselves. The men of *Cuth* or *Cutha* brought their *Nergal*, or the Sun : it was represented by a cock, which animal was dedicated to Apollo, or the Sun. The men of *Hamath* had *Ashima;* a deity of which nothing certain is known. The rabbinical writers say, that it was compounded of a man and a goat ; consequently it answered to the Pan of the Greek and Roman mythology. The people of *Sepharvaim* brought *Adrammelech* and *Anammelech*, already noticed. The *Avites* brought *Nibhaz* and *Tartak*, which probably are two different names of the same idol. As Nibhaz in Hebrew and Chaldee signifies *quick, swift, rapid;* and *Tartak*, in both languages, denotes a chariot, these two idols together may mean the Sun mounted on his car.

In Lev. xxvi. 1. Moses prohibits the Israelites from setting up any IMAGE OF STONE, literally, *figured stone*, or *stone of a picture*, in their land. This prohibition was directed against the hieroglyphic figures or stones of the Egyptians, the meaning of which was known only to the priests. With these stones idolatry was practised. In Egypt they were regarded as the god *Thoth*, the god of sciences ; and so late as the time of Ezekiel (viii. 8—11.) we find an imitation of this species of idolatry common among the Jews. According, therefore, to that fundamental principle of the Mosaic policy, which dictated the prevention

---

guide appears to illustrate the vow which Jacob made when he travelled to Padan-Aram. (Gen. xxviii. 18—22.) In seeing a stone on the road placed in this position, or one stone upon another, it implies that some traveller has there made a vow or a thanksgiving. Nothing is so natural in a journey over a dreary country, as for a solitary traveller to sit down, fatigued, and to make the vow that Jacob did : — *If God will be with me, and keep me in the way that I go, and will give me bread to eat and raiment to put on, so that I reach my father's house in peace,* &c. then I will give so much in charity : — or, again, that on first seeing the place which he has so long toiled to reach, the traveller should sit down and make a thanksgiving ; in both cases setting up a stone as a memorial." Morier's Second Journey, p. 84.

[1] Gesenius's Hebrew Lexicon, by Gibbs, p. 85. col. 2. p. 407. col. 2.
[2] W. Lowth, on Jer. l 2.   [3] Brown's Antiq. of the Jews, vol. ii. p. 32.

of idolatry, it became absolutely necessary to prohibit stones with hieroglyphic inscriptions. Besides, in an age when so great a propensity to idolatry prevailed, stones, with figures upon them which the people could not understand, would have been a temptation to idolatry, even though they had not been deified (as we know they actually were) by the Egyptians.[1] The walls of the antient temples, particularly that of Tentyra, and also the tombs of the kings in Egypt, are covered with such hieroglyphics; which it is impossible to see and not be struck with the necessity of the injunction contained in Deut. iv. 15—20.[2]

VIII. The idols mentioned in the New Testament are, doubtless, known to every classical reader. It will, therefore, suffice briefly to state here, that Jupiter was the supreme deity, or father of the gods, among the Greeks and Romans; Mercury was the god of eloquence, and the messenger of the other deities. The inhabitants of Lystra, in Lycaonia, struck with the miracle which had been wrought by St. Paul, considered him as Mercury, from his eloquence, and Barnabas as Jupiter, probably from his being the more majestic person of the two, and, consequently, answering to the prevalent notions which they had imbibed from statues concerning him. The Diana of the Greeks and Romans was worshipped with most solemnity at Ephesus, where she is said to have been represented as a woman, whose upper part was hung round with breasts, emblematic of the prolific powers of nature. Her image is said to have fallen down from Jupiter (Acts xix. 35.); whence some expositors have conjectured that it was an *aërolite* or *atmospheric stone*. But Pliny describes the image as having been made by one Caneti as from the wood of the vine.[3] This notion of certain statues having descended on earth from the clouds to represent particular divinities, and to inspire devotion in their temples, was very common in the heathen world. The palladium at Troy, and the statue of Minerva at Athens, like this of the Ephesian Diana, are said to have dropped from the skies. The avarice of priests forged these stories to dupe and fleece a blind and bigotted people. The same ridiculous tale the Romans were taught to believe concerning their *Ancilia*, or sacred shields, which their history represents to have fallen from heaven in the reign of Numa Pompilius.[4]

The Romans, also, it is well known, worshipped the virtues and affections of the mind, as *Justice*, *Fidelity*, or *Good Faith*, *Hope*, *Fortune*, *Fame*, &c.; and the same superstition prevailed among the inhabitants of Malta, on which island Paul was shipwrecked. When they saw a venomous serpent fasten on the hand of Paul, they concluded that he was a murderer, whom *vengeance* — more correctly the goddess Δικη (*Diké* or Vindictive Justice) — *had not permitted to live.* (Acts xxviii. 4.) We learn from the mythological poet Hesiod, that the Greeks had a female deity of this name.[5] Nay, the superstition of the Pagans went so far as to worship the gods and goddesses of all countries, even those which they knew not. Thus there was at Athens an altar consecrated to the gods and goddesses of Europe, Asia, Libya, and *to the unknown*

---

[1] Michaelis's Commentaries, vol. iv. pp. 54—59.

[2] Jowett's Christian Researches in the Mediterranean, pp. 132. 134.

[3] Pliny, Nat. Hist. lib. xvi. c. 40.

[4] Harwood's Introd. vol. ii. p. 360. See also Biscoe on the Acts, vol. i. p. 307. and Dr. Clarke's Travels, vol. vii. pp. 21, 22.

[5] Opera et Dies, v. 254—258.

God; which gave St. Paul occasion to deliver that admirable discourse in the Areopagus, which is related in Acts xvii. 23—31.[1]

IX. Very numerous are the allusions in the Sacred Writings to the idolatrous rites of the heathen, and to their persuasions concerning their power and influence. A few only of these can be here noticed.

1. With regard to the opinions which were entertained concerning their gods : —

(1.) The heathens had generally a notion, that all deities were local, and limited to a certain country or place, and had no power any where else, but in that country or place; and thus we read in 2 Kings xvii. 26. that the colonists sent by the king of Assyria to Samaria in place of the Israelites attributed their being plagued with lions to their not knowing the manner of the god of the land. In conformity with this notion, Jonah (who lived in the midst of the mixed multitude of Gentiles, that had forced themselves into the district of Galilee, with their various forms of worship,) seems to have considered Jehovah as the local god of Judæa; and, in order to escape from his presence, *he rose up to flee unto Tarshish, and went down to Joppa.* (Jonah i. 3.) So also in 1 Kings xx. 23. it is said that the servants of the king of Syria persuaded their master, that the gods of the Israelites were gods of the hills; hearing, perhaps, that the law was given on Mount Sinai, that the temple was built on Mount Sion, and that they delighted to worship on high places; and therefore they imagined that they would have the advantage by fighting the Israelites in the plain. It is not unlikely that such of the Israelites who were murmurers in the wilderness (being those among them who were most tainted with idolatry) entertained the same opinion, and believed that God was a local deity and his power limited; for in this manner it is that the Psalmist represents them reasoning with themselves, — *Can God furnish a table in the wilderness? Behold he smote the rock that the waters gushed out, and the streams overflowed, but can he give bread also? Can he provide flesh for his people?* (Psal. lxxviii. 19, 20.)

(2.) All the nations of antiquity, especially in the East, supposed the Deity to be surrounded by light so dazzling as to overpower all mortal vision. This mode of speaking was, in a later age, transferred to the divine majesty and perfections, as being utterly incomprehensible to the human faculties. (Psal. civ. 1—3. Ezek. i. 1 Tim. vi. 16.)[2]

(3.) " Another common opinion which prevailed among the heathens, was, that sometimes the immortal gods, disguised in human form, deigned to visit mortals, and conversed with them. According to their theology, Jupiter and Mercury accompanied each other on these expeditions. Agreeably to this notion, which universally obtained among the Pagans, we find that the Lycaonians, when they saw a miracle performed upon a helpless cripple, immediately cried out in the last astonishment, — *The gods are come down unto us in the likeness of men!* (Acts xiv. 11.) Instantly Paul and Barnabas were metamorphosed, by their imaginations, into Jove and Mercury, who, according to their creed, were inseparable companions in these visits. These heathens (as we have already intimated) recognised Jupiter in

---

[1] On the subject of this altar, see Vol. I. pp. 196, 197.
[2] Robinson's Translation of Wahl's Gr. Lexicon to the New Test. voce Απροσιτος. Bloomfield's Annotations on the New Test. vol. viii. pp. 286, 287.

Barnabas, because, probably, his appearance and person were more specious and striking ; and Paul, whose bodily presence was weak, but whose public talents and rhetoric were distinguished, they persuaded themselves could be no other than Mercury, the eloquent interpreter of the gods." [1]

(4.) Further, when persons were wrongfully oppressed and afflicted, the heathens believed that the gods interfered in their behalf. The tokens of their presence were *earthquakes, the opening of doors, and the loosing of their bonds.*[2] In this manner God bore a miraculous testimony of his approbation to his faithful servants Paul and Silas, when imprisoned at Philippi ; and the knowledge of this fact will account for the extreme fright of the gaoler, which terminated so happily for his salvation. (Acts xvi. 25—29.)[3]

2. Although the priesthood constituted a distinct class of persons among the Jews, yet among the Romans, and it should seem also among the Greeks, they did not form a separate order. Among the Romans they were chosen from among the most honourable men in the state. In the eastern provinces of the Roman empire, persons were annually selected from among the more opulent citizens to preside over the things pertaining to religious worship, and to exhibit annual games at their own expense in honour of the gods, in the same manner as the ædiles did at Rome. These officers received their appellations from the districts to which they belonged, as Syriarch (Συριαρχης), Phœ-niciarch (Φοινιχιαρχης), and the like : of course, in proconsular Asia, they were called Asiarchs (Ασιαρχαι). The temple of Diana at Ephesus was erected at the common expense of all the Grecian cities in Asia Minor. It is evident from Acts xix. 31. that at that very time they were solemnising games [4] in honour of Diana, who was one of the great celestial deities (the *dii majorum gentium* of the Romans), and who was, therefore, called *the* GREAT GODDESS, by the recorder or town-clerk of Ephesus. (Acts xix. 35.)[5] This circumstance will account for St. Paul's being hurried before the tribunal of the Asiarchs.

3. We learn from various profane authors that *High Places,* or eminences, were considered to be the abode of the heathen deities, or at least as the most proper for sacrificing ; and, therefore, sacrifices were offered either on the summits of mountains or in woods. Thus it was the custom of the antient Persians to go up to the tops of the loftiest mountains, and there to offer sacrifices to Jupiter, — distinguishing by that appellation the whole expanse of heaven.[6] Further, as most of these sacrifices were accompanied with prostitution, or other impure rites, they seem to have chosen the most retired spots, to conceal their abominations. On this account, and also to obliterate every vestige of, or temptation to, idolatry, the Israelites were commanded to offer sacrifices to Jehovah, only and exclusively in the place which

---

[1] Dr. Harwood's Introd. vol. ii. p. 359.

[2] Elsner, in his notes on Acts xvi. 26. has shown, by a series of most apposite quotations, that each of these things was accounted a token of the divine appearance in behalf of those who suffered unjustly, and who were dear to the gods. — Observationes Sacræ, vol. i. pp. 441—444.

[3] Biscoe on the Acts, vol. i. p. 313.

[4] Grotius, Hammond, Poole's Synopsis, Wetstein, and Doddrige on Acts xix. 31. Biscoe on the Acts, vol. i. pp. 303, 304. Robinson's Greek Lexicon, voce Ασιαρχης.

[5] See Elsner's Observationes Sacræ, vol. i. pp. 460, 461.

[6] Herodotus, lib. i. c. 131.

he should appoint (Deut. xii. 14.); and were also prohibited from sacrificing in *high places* (Lev. xxvi. 30.), and from placing *a grove of trees*[1] near his altar. (Deut. xvi. 21.) The profligate Manasseh, however, utterly disregarded these prohibitions, when he *built up again the high places, and reared up altars for Baal, and made a grove.* (2 Kings xxi. 3.) Thus Isaiah (lvii. 4, 5.) reproached the Israelites with the like prevarication, when he said, *Are ye not children of transgression, a seed of falsehood, inflaming yourselves with idols under every green tree, slaying the children in the vallies under the clefts of the rocks?* And Jeremiah (iii. 6.) reproaches them with having played the harlot, that is, worshipped idols on every high mountain, and under every green tree. Nor were only mountains, woods, and vallies, appointed for the worship of false gods; almost every thing else, among the Pagans, bore the marks of idolatry. Herodotus[2] says, that the Phœnicians, who were the greatest seamen in the world, adorned the heads and sterns of their ships with the images of their gods: and Luke (Acts xxviii. 11.) has observed, that the vessel which carried St. Paul from Malta to Syracuse had the sign of Castor and Pollux; and it is not improbable, that the vessel in which Europa was carried away had the sign of a bull, which gave occasion to the poets to say, that Jupiter carried her away under that shape.[3]

4. The statues of the deities were carried in procession on the shoulders of their votaries. This circumstance is distinctly stated by Isaiah, in his masterly exposure of the insanity of idolatry. (xlvi. 7.) In this way do the Hindoos at present carry their gods; and, indeed, so exact a picture has the prophet drawn of the idolatrous processions of this people, that he might be almost supposed to be sitting among them, when he delivered his prediction to the Jews.[4] It was also customary to make *shrines* or portable models of the temples of those deities which were the principal objects of worship, and to place a small image therein, when they travelled or went to war, as also for their private devotions at home. From the celebrity of the temple of Diana at Ephesus, it is but natural to suppose, that there would be a great demand for models of it, which would become a kind of substitute for the temple itself, to such of her votaries as lived in distant parts of Greece. It is evident from Acts xix. 24—27. that the manufacture of such shrines proved a source of great emolument to Demetrius, and the artisans employed by him, who might naturally expect a brisk demand for their models, from the vast concourse of worshippers who were present at the annual solemnisation of the games in honour of Diana: which demand not equalling their expectations, Demetrius might ascribe his loss to St. Paul's preaching against idolatry, as the Apostle had now (Acts xix. 8. 10.) been more than two years at Ephesus; so that *all they which dwelt in Asia heard the word of the Lord Jesus, both Jews and Greeks.*[5] The tabernacle of Moloch (Amos v. 26.)

---

[1] In Sir William Ouseley's Travels in the East (vol. i. pp. 359—401.) the reader will find a very learned and very interesting memoir on the *sacred trees* of the antients, which illustrates many important passages of sacred writ.

[2] Hist. l. iii. c. 37.　　　　　　　　　　　[3] Biscoe on the Acts, vol. i. pp. 326, 327.

[4] Ward's History, &c. of the Hindoos, vol. ii. p. 330. Roberts's Oriental Illustrations, p. 577.

[5] Biscoe on the Acts, vol. i. pp. 301, 302. 304.

is supposed to have been a portable temple or shrine, made after the chief temple of that " horrid king," as Milton emphatically terms him.[1]

" When the heathens offered a sacrifice to any of those numerous divinities which they worshipped, it was usual on this sacred solemnity, in which religion and friendship were harmoniously interwoven and united with each other, for all the sacrificers to have their temples adorned with chaplets of flowers, — and the victims, too, that were led to the altar, were dressed with fillets and garlands. Abundant examples of this custom are found in almost every page of the Greek and Roman classics. The Lycaonians, who recognised Jupiter in Barnabas, and Mercury in Paul, and, believing themselves honoured with a visit from these divinities, from the miracle which Paul had wrought in restoring a cripple to the full use of his limbs, intended to show their veneration of this illustrious condescension to them by celebrating a public and solemn sacrifice, and decked themselves, and the victims they intended to immolate, in this manner.[2] The priest, therefore, of Jove, whom it seems they worshipped as the guardian of their city, and whose temple stood a little way[3] out of the town, immediately brought victims and chaplets of flowers to crown the apostles, agreeably to the pagan rites, — and in this manner advanced towards the door of the house, where the apostles lodged, designing to sacrifice to them. This custom, here mentioned, was in conformity with the heathen ritual. All wore garlands at a heathen sacrifice, both the people and the victims."[4]

5. When the victim devoted to the sacrifice was brought before the altar, the priest, having implored the divine favour and acceptance by prayer, poured wine upon its head; and after the performance of this solemn act of religion, which was termed a *libation*, the victim was instantly led to the slaughter. To this circumstance St. Paul, knowing the time of his martyrdom to be very near, has a very striking allusion; representing this rite, which immediately preceded the death of the victim, as already performed upon himself, implying that he was now devoted to death, and that his dissolution would speedily follow. *I am now ready to be offered,* says he (2 Tim. iv. 6.): literally, *I am already poured out as a libation; the time of my departure is at hand.* A similar expressive sacrificial allusion occurs in Phil. ii. 17. *Yea,* says the holy Apostle, *and if I be* POURED OUT *upon the sacrifice and service of your faith, I joy and rejoice with you all.* In this passage he represents the faith of the Philippians as the sacrificial victim, and compares his blood, willingly and joyfully to be shed in martyrdom, to the libation poured out on occasion of the sacrifice.[5]

After the usual portions of the victims had been burnt on the altar,

---

[1] See Dr. Clarke's Travels, vol. vi. pp. 215—218., for some curious information concerning the portable shrines of the antients.

[2] Acts xiv. 13. Then the priest of Jupiter, which was before their city, brought oxen and *garlands* unto the gates, and would have done *sacrifice* unto the people.

[3] Προ της πολεως. Ibid. Το ΠΡΟ ΤΗΣ ΠΟΛΕΩΣ Ασκληπιειον. The temple of Æsculapius which was before the town, or a little way out of the city. Polybius, lib. i. p. 17. edit. Hanov. 1619.

[4] Dr. Harwood's Introduction, vol. ii. p. 301. Wetstein and Dr. A. Clarke on Acts xiv. 11—15.

[5] Parkhurst's Gr. Lexicon, p. 621. Harwood, vol. ii. pp. 219, 220. Drs. Clarke and Macknight on the passages cited.

or given to the officiating priests, the remainder was either exposed by the owner for sale in the market, or became the occasion of giving a feast to his friends, either in the temple or at his own house. Meat of this description, termed ειδωλοθυτα, or meats offered to idols, in Acts xv. 29., was an abomination to the Jews; who held that not only those who partook of such entertainments, but also those who purchased such meat in the market, subjected themselves to the pollution of idolatry. The apostle James, therefore, recommends, that the Gentile Christians should abstain from all meats of this kind, out of respect to this prejudice of Jewish Christians; and hence he calls these meats αλισγηματα, pollution of idols, that is, meats polluted in consequence of their being sacrificed unto idols. (Acts xv. 20., compare also 1 Cor. viii. 1. 4. 7. 10. x. 19. 28.) It appears from Judg. ix. 27. that feasting after sacrifice in the temples of idols was not unknown to the Schechemites.

6. Singing and dancing were the general attendants of some of these idolatrous rites: thus, the Israelites danced before the golden calf. (Exod. xxxii. 19.) To this day, dancing before the idol takes place at almost every Hindoo idolatrous feast. But their sacrifices were not confined to irrational victims: it is well known that the practice of offering human victims prevailed to a great extent [1]; and among the Ammonites and Phœnicians they were immolated to propitiate Moloch and Baal; and children were in some manner dedicated and devoted to them. The idolatrous worshippers are said to make them pass through the fire; denoting some rite of dedication and purification. This was most expressly forbidden to the Israelites. (Lev. xviii. 21.) In this manner Ahaz devoted his son (2 Kings xvi. 3.); but as Hezekiah afterwards succeeded his father on the throne of Judah, it is evident that *he* was not put to death. From the declarations of the psalmist (cvi. 36—40.), and of the prophet Ezekiel (xvi. 21. xx. 26. 31.), it is, however, certain that many human victims were thus barbarously sacrificed.

The adoration or worship which idolaters paid to their gods did not consist barely in the sacrifices which they offered to them, but likewise in prostrations and bowings of the body; thus Naaman speaks of *bowing in the house* of Rimmon. (2 Kings v. 18.) It was also a religious ceremony, to *lift up the hand to the mouth and kiss it*, and then, stretching it out, to throw as it were the kiss to the idol: both this and

---

[1] The Egyptians had several cities, which were termed *Typhonian*, — such as Heliopolis, Idithya, Abarei, and Busiris, — where at particular seasons they immolated men. The objects thus devoted were persons of bright hair and a particular complexion, such as were seldom to be found among that people. Hence we may conclude that they were foreigners; and it is probable that while the Israelites resided in Egypt, the victims were chosen from their body. They were burnt alive upon a high altar, and thus sacrificed for the good of the people: at the conclusion of the sacrifice, the priests collected their ashes, and scattered them upwards in the air, — most likely with this view, that, where any of the dust was wafted, a blessing might be entailed. By a just retribution, Moses and Aaron were commanded to take ashes of the furnace, (which in the Scriptures is used as a type of the slavery of the Israelites, and of all the cruelty which they experienced in Egypt,) and to scatter them abroad *towards the heaven* (Exod. x. 8, 9.), but with a different intention, viz. that where any the smallest portion alighted, it might prove a plague and a curse to the ungrateful, cruel, and infatuated Egyptians. Thus there was a designed contrast in these workings of Providence, and an apparent opposition to the superstition of the times. Bryant, on the Plagues of Egypt, p. 116. On the prevalence of human sacrifices in antient times, see Vol. I. p. 5. and note.

the former ceremony are mentioned in 1 Kings xix. 18. And so Job, in order to express his not having fallen into idolatry, very elegantly says, *If I beheld the sun while it shined, or the moon walking in brightness, and my heart had been secretly enticed, or my mouth hath kissed my hand,* &c. (Job xxxi. 26, 27.); for to *kiss* and to *worship* are synonymous terms in Scripture, as appears from Psal. ii. 12. There is an idolatrous rite mentioned by Ezekiel, called the *putting the branch to the nose* (Ezek. viii. 17.), by which interpreters understand, that the worshipper, with a wand in his hand, touched the idol, and then applied the wand to his nose and mouth, in token of worship and adoration.[1] There appears to be this difference, however, between the idolatry of the Jews and that of other nations, viz. that the Jews did not deny a divine power and providence; only they imagined that their idols were the intermediate causes, by which the blessings of the supreme God might be conveyed to them; whereas the heathens believed that the idols they worshipped were true gods, and had no higher conceptions, having no notion of one eternal, almighty, and independent Being.[2]

In the account of the decisive triumph of true religion over idolatry, related in 1 Kings xviii., we have a very striking delineation of the idolatrous rites of Baal; from which it appears that his four hundred and fifty priests, or prophets, as they are termed, employed the whole day in their desperate rites. The time is divided into two periods, 1. *From morning until noon,* which was occupied in preparing and offering the sacrifice, and in earnest supplication for the celestial fire, (for Baal was unquestionably the god of fire or the sun, and had only to work in his own element,) vociferating, *O Baal, hear us* (1 Kings xviii. 26.); and, 2. *They continued from noon until the time of offering evening sacrifice* (the time when it was usually offered to Jehovah in the temple at Jerusalem), performing their frantic rites.

They leaped up and down at the altar [3], that is, they danced around it with strange and hideous cries and gesticulations, tossing their heads to and fro, with a great variety of bodily contortions, precisely as the Ceylonese do to this day.[4] In like manner the priests of Mars among the Romans danced and leaped around the altars of that divinity, from which circumstance they derived their name, — Salii.[5] *And it came to*

---

[1] Mr. Roberts (to whom biblical students are so greatly indebted for the light he has thrown on hundreds of texts of Scripture by the application of Hindoo customs) is of opinion that to *put the branch to the nose,* was the idolatrous practice of boring a child's nose, and putting a ring therein in order to dedicate it to an idol; and therefore to shew that it was under its protection, rather than that of Jehovah. Oriental Illustrations, pp. 488—493.

[2] On the subject of the idolatrous worship of the heathens, the editor of Calmet's Dictionary has accumulated much interesting information. See the Fragments, particularly Nos. 107. 185. 212, 213.

[3] This is the marginal rendering, and most correct, of 1 Kings xviii. 26.

[4] From the statement of a Ceylonese convert to Christianity (who was formerly one of the principal high priests of Budhoo) Dr. A. Clarke has described the manner and invocations of the pagan inhabitants of that island (Comment. on 1 Kings xviii.), to which we are indebted for part of the present elucidation of the rites of Baal; and his account is confirmed by Dr. John Davy, in his Travels in Ceylon.

[5] Jam dederat Saliis (a saltu nomina ducunt)
    Armaque et ad certos verba canenda modos.— OVID. Fast. iii. 387, 388.
    On the custom of dancing around the altars of the gods, the reader will find much curious information in Lomeier's treatise De veterum Gentilium Lustrationibus, cap. 33. pp. 413. *et seq.*

pass at noon that Elijah mocked them: had not the intrepid prophet of the Lord been conscious of the divine protection, he certainly would not have used such freedom of speech, while he was surrounded by his enemies: *And said, Cry aloud!* Oblige him, by your vociferations, to attend to your suit. — Similar vain repetitions were made by the heathen in the time of our Saviour, who cautions his disciples against them in Matt. vi. 7.[1]— *For he is a god* — the supreme God; you worship him as such; and, doubtless, he is jealous of his own honour, and the credit of his votaries. *Either he is talking* — he may be giving audience to some others: or, as it is rendered in the margin of our larger Bibles, — *he meditateth* — he is in a profound reverie, projecting some godlike scheme — *or he is pursuing* — taking his pleasure in the chase — *or he is on a journey* — having left his audience chamber, he is making some excursions — *or peradventure he sleepeth and must be awaked.* — Absurd as these notions may appear to us, they are believed by the Hindoos, to each of whose gods some particular business is assigned, and who imagine that Vishnoo sleeps for months in the year, while others of their deities are often out on journies or expeditions.[2] Accordingly the priests of Baal *cried aloud, and cut themselves after their manner.* This was not only the custom of the idolatrous Israelites, but also of the Syrians, Persians, Indians, Greeks, Romans, and, in short, of all the antient heathen world. Hence we may see the reason why the Israelites were forbidden to *cut themselves, to make any cuttings in their flesh for the dead,* and *to print any marks upon themselves.* (Deut. xiv. 1. Lev. xix. 28.) For the heathens did these things not only in honour of their gods, but also in testimony of their grief for the loss of any of their neighbours. The Scythians, as we are informed by Herodotus, were accustomed to slash their arms on the death of their kings [3]; and it is not improbable that some similar custom obtained among some one of the neighbouring nations. The modern Persians to this day cut and lacerate themselves, when celebrating the anniversary of the assassination of Hossein, whom they venerate as a martyr for the Moslem faith.[4]

7. The heathens showed their veneration for their deities in various ways, the knowledge of which serves to illustrate many passages of Scripture. Thus nothing was more frequent than the prostitution of

---

[1] The infuriated worshippers of Diana *all with one voice about the space of two hours cried out, "Great is Diana of the Ephesians."* (Acts xix. 34.) Not to multiply unnecessary examples, see an illustration of these vain repetitions in the Heautontimoreumenos of Terence, act. v. scene 1. We are informed by Servius that the antient heathens, after supplicating the particular deity to whom they offered sacrifice, used to invoke all the gods and goddesses, lest any one of them should be adverse to the suppliant. Servius in Virgil. Georg. lib. i. 21. (vol. i. p. 178. of Burmann's edition, Amst. 1746. 4to.) For a remarkable instance of the "vain repetitions" of the modern Mohammedans, see Dr. Richardson's Travels in the Mediterranean, &c. vol. i. pp. 462—464.

[2] Ward's History, &c. of the Hindoos, vol. ii. p. 324.

[3] Herodotus, lib. iv. c. 71.

[4] Mr. Morier has given a long and interesting narrative of this anniversary. " It is," he says, " necessary to have witnessed the scenes that are exhibited in their cities, to judge of the degree of fanaticism which possesses them at this time. I have seen some of the most violent of them, as they vociferated *Ya Hossein !* walk about the streets almost naked, with only their loins covered and their bodies streaming with blood, by the voluntary cuts which they had given to themselves, either as acts of love, anguish, or mortification. Such must have been the cuttings of which we read in Holy Writ." Morier's Second Journey, p. 176.

women, with examples of which the antient writers abound.   According to Justin[1], the Cyprian women gained that portion which their husbands received with them, on marriage, by previous public prostitution.   And the Phœnicians, as we are informed by Augustine, made a gift to Venus of the gain acquired by the same disgusting means.[2] Hence we may account for Moses prohibiting the Israelites from committing any such atrocities.   (Lev. xix. 29.)   The Hindoos often dedicate their daughters to their gods, who at a certain age become prostitutes for life. — Others dedicated to them the spoils of war; others, votive tablets and other offerings in commemoration of supposed benefits conferred on them.[3]

A more frequent and indeed very general custom was the carrying of marks on their body in honour of the object of their worship. This is expressly forbidden in Lev. xix. 28.   To this day, all the castes of the Hindoos bear on their foreheads, or elsewhere, what are called the *sectarian marks*, which not only distinguish them in a civil, but also in a religious point of view, from each other.[4]   Most of the barbarous nations lately discovered have their faces, arms, breasts, &c. curiously carved or *tatooed*, probably for superstitious purposes. Antient writers abound with accounts of marks made on the face, arms, &c. in honour of different idols, — and to this the inspired penman alludes (Rev. xiii. 16, 17.   xiv. 9. 11.   xv. 2.   xvi. 2.   xix. 20. xx. 4.), where false worshippers are represented as receiving in their hands, and in their forehead, the marks of the beast.

The prohibition in Lev. xix. 27. against the Israelites rounding *the corners of their heads*, and *marring the corners of their beards*, evidently refers to customs which must have existed among the Egyptians, during their residence among that people; though it is now difficult to determine what those customs were.   Herodotus informs us, that the Arabs shave or *cut their hair round* in honour of Bacchus, who (they say) wore his hair in this way; and that the Macians, a people of Libya, cut their hair *round*, so as to leave a tuft on the top of the head[5]; in this manner the Hindoos[6], and the Chinese cut their hair to the present day.   This might have been in honour of some idol, and, therefore, forbidden to the Israelites.

The *hair* was much used in divination among the antients; and for purposes of religious superstition among the Greeks; and particularly about the time of the giving of this law, as this is supposed to have been the æra of the Trojan war.   We learn from Homer, that it was customary for parents to dedicate the hair of their children to some god; which, when they came to manhood, they cut off and consecrated to the deity.   Achilles, at the funeral of Patroclus, cut off his golden locks, which his father had dedicated to the river god Sperchius, and threw them into the flood.[7]   From Virgil's account of the

---

1 Hist. lib. xviii. c. 5.
2 Calmet on Lev. xix. 29.   Michaelis's Commentaries, vol. iv. pp. 183—185.
3 See much curious information on this subject in Dr. Clarke's Travels, vol. vi. pp. 444 —448. 8vo. and Mr. Dodwell's Classical Tour in Greece, vol. i. pp. 341, 342.
4 See Forbes's Oriental Memoirs, vol. iii. p. 15.   Roberts's Oriental Illustrations, p. 91.
5 Herod. lib. iii. c. 8. and lib. iv. c. 175.
6 Roberts's Oriental Illustrations, p. 90.
7 Iliad. xxiii. 142, &c.

death of Dido [1], we learn that the *topmost lock* of hair was dedicated to the *infernal gods*. If the hair was *rounded*, and dedicated for purposes of this kind, it will at once account for the prohibition in this verse. [2]

A religion so extravagant as that of paganism could not have subsisted so long, had not the priests by whom it was managed contrived to secure the devotion of the multitudes by pretending that certain divinities uttered oracles. The researches of enlightened travellers have laid open the contrivances by which these frauds were managed, at least, in Greece. [3] Various were the means by which the credulity of the people was imposed upon. Sometimes they charmed serpents, — extracted their poison, and thus rendered them harmless; — a practice to which there are frequent allusions in the Old Testament, and it must have been a gainful and an established traffic.

X. Moses has enumerated seven different sorts of DIVINERS into futurity, whom the Israelites were prohibited from consulting (Deut. xviii. 10, 11.), viz. 1. Those who *used divination,* — that is, who endeavoured to penetrate futurity by auguries, using lots, &c.; — 2. *Observers of times,* those who pretended to foretell future events by present occurrences, and who predicted political or physical changes from the aspects of the planets, eclipses, motion of the clouds, &c.; — 3. *Enchanters,* either those who charmed serpents, or those who drew auguries from inspecting the entrails of beasts, observing the flights of birds, &c.; — 4. *Witches,* those who pretended to bring down certain celestial influences to their aid by means of herbs, drugs, perfumes, &c.; — 5. *Charmers,* those who used spells for the purposes of divination; — 6. *Consulters with familiar spirits,* — Pythonesses, those who pretended to inquire by means of one spirit to get oracular answers from another of a superior order; — and, 7. *Wizards,* or *necromancers,* those who (like the witch at Endor) professed to evoke the dead, in order to learn from them the secrets of the invisible world.

Four kinds of Divination are particularly mentioned in sacred history, viz. by the cup, — by arrows, — by inspecting the livers of slaughtered animals, — and by the staff.

1. *Divination by the cup* appears to have been the most antient: it certainly prevailed in Egypt in the time of Joseph (Gen. xliv. 5.) [4], and it has from time immemorial been prevalent among the Asiatics, who have a tradition (the origin of which is lost in the lapse of ages) that there was a cup which had passed successively into the hands of different potentates, and which possessed the strange property of representing in it the whole world, and all the things which were then doing in it. The Persians to this day call it the *Cup of Jemsheed,* from a very antient king of Persia of that name, whom late historians

---

[1] Æneid. iv. 698.   [2] Calmet, and Dr. A. Clarke on Lev. xix. 27.
[3] See Dr. Clarke's Travels, vol. vi. pp. 479, 480. ; also vol. iii. p. 298.
[4] We have no reason to infer that Joseph practised divination by the cup; although, according to the superstition of those times, supernatural influence might be attributed to *his* cup. And as the whole transaction related in Gen. xliv. was merely intended to deceive his brethren for a short time, he might as well affect divination by his cup, as affect to believe that they had stolen it.

and poets have confounded with Bacchus, Solomon, Alexander the Great, &c. This cup, filled with the elixir of immortality, they say, was discovered when digging the foundations of Persepolis. To this cup the Persian poets have numerous allusions; and to the intelligence supposed to have been received from it they ascribe the great prosperity of their antient monarchs, as by it they understood all events, past, present, and future. Many of the Mohammedan princes and governors affect still to have information of futurity by means of a cup. Thus when Mr. Norden was at Dehr or Derri in the farthest part of Egypt, in a very dangerous situation, from which he and his company endeavoured to extricate themselves by exerting great spirit, a spiteful and powerful Arab in a threatening way told one of their people, whom they had sent to him, that he knew what sort of people they were, that *he had consulted his cup*, and had found by it that they were those of whom one of their prophets had said, that Franks would come in disguise, and passing every where, examine the state of the country, and afterwards bring over a great number of other Franks, conquer the country, and exterminate all.[1] It was precisely the same thing that Joseph meant when he talked of *divining by his cup*.[2]

Julius Serenus tells us, that the method of *divining by the cup* among the Abyssinians, Chaldees, and Egyptians, was to fill it first with water, then to throw into it their plates of gold and silver, together with some precious stones, whereon were engraven certain characters: and, after that, the persons who came to consult the oracle used certain forms of incantation, and so calling upon the devil, received their answers several ways; sometimes by articulate sounds, sometimes by the characters, which were in the cup, arising upon the surface of the water, and by this arrangement forming the answer; and many times by the visible appearing of the persons themselves about whom the oracle was consulted. Cornelius Agrippa[3] tells us likewise, that the manner of some was to pour melted wax into a cup containing water, which wax would range itself into order, and so form answers, according to the questions proposed.[4]

2. *Divination by arrows* was an antient method of presaging future events. Ezekiel (xxi. 21.) informs us that Nebuchadnezzar, when marching against Zedekiah and the king of the Ammonites, and coming to the head of two ways, mingled his arrows in a quiver, that he might thence divine in what direction to pursue his march; and that he consulted teraphim, and inspected the livers of beasts, in order to determine his resolution. Jerome, in his commentary on this passage, says that "the manner of divining by arrows was thus: — They wrote on several arrows the names of the cities against which they intended to make war, and then putting them promiscuously all together into a quiver, they caused them to be drawn out in the manner of lots, and that city, whose name was on the arrow first drawn out, was the first they assaulted."[5] This method of divination was practised by the

---

[1] Trav. vol. ii. p. 150.   [2] Harmer, vol. ii. p. 475.
[3] De occult. Philos. l. i. cap. 57.
[4] Dr. A. Clarke on Gen. xliv. 5. Burder's Oriental Customs, vol. i. p. 54.
[5] On this subject see some curious information in the Fragments supplementary to Calmet, No. 179.

idolatrous Arabs, and prohibited by Mohammed[1], and was likewise used by the antient Greeks, and other nations.[2]

3. *Divination by inspecting the liver* of slaughtered animals was another mode of ascertaining future events, much practised by the Greeks and Romans, by the former of whom it was termed 'Ηπατοσκοπια, or *looking into the liver*. This word subsequently became a general term for divination by inspecting the entrails of sacrifices, because the liver was the first and principal part observed for this purpose. To this method of divination there is an allusion in Ezekiel xxi. 21.[3]

4. *Rabdomancy*, or divination by the staff, is alluded to by the prophet Hosea (iv. 12.); it is supposed to have been thus performed: The person consulting measured his staff by spans, or by the length of his finger, saying, as he measured, " I will go, or, I will not go; I will do such a thing, or, I will not do it;" and as the last span fell out so he determined. Cyril and Theophylact, however, give a different account of the matter. They say that it was performed by erecting two sticks, after which they murmured forth a certain charm, and then, according as the sticks fell, backwards or forwards, towards the right or left, they gave advice in any affair.[4]

In the later period of the Jewish history, we meet with many persons among the Jews, who pretended to be *sorcerers*.[5] This class of persons dealt in incantations and divinations, and boasted of a power, in consequence of their deep science, and by means of certain rites, to evoke the spirits of the dead from their gloomy abodes, and compel them to disclose information on subjects beyond the reach of the human powers: of this description, probably, was the sorcerer

---

[1] Koran, ch. v. 4. (Sale's translation, p. 94. 4to. edit.) In his preliminary discourse, Mr. Sale states that the arrows, used by the idolatrous Arabs for this purpose, were destitute of heads or feathers, and were kept in the temple of some idol, in whose presence they were consulted. Seven such arrows were kept in the temple of Mecca, but generally in divination they made use of three only, on one of which was written, *My* LORD *hath commanded me,* — on another, *My* LORD *hath forbidden me,* — and the third was blank. If the first was drawn, they regarded it as an approbation of the enterprise in question ; if the second, they made a contrary conclusion ; but if the third happened to be drawn, they mixed them and drew over again, till a decisive answer was given by one of the others. These divining arrows were generally consulted before any thing of moment was undertaken — as when a man was about to marry, to undertake a journey, or the like. (Sale's Prel. Disc. pp. 126, 127.)

[2] Potter's Antiquities of Greece, vol. i. pp. 359, 360.

[3] Ibid. vol. i. pp. 339, 340. The practice of " divination from the liver is very old, and was practised by the Greeks and Romans, till Christianity banished it, together with the gods of Olympus. In Æschylus, Prometheus boasts of having taught man the division of the entrails, if smooth, and of a clear colour, to be agreeable to the gods ; also the various forms of the gall and the liver." (Stolberg's History of Religion, vol. iii. p. 436.) Among the Greeks and Romans, as soon as a victim was sacrificed, the entrails were examined. They began with the liver, which was considered the chief seat ; or, as Philostratus expresses himself (Life of Apollonius, viii. 7. § 15.), as the prophecying tripod of all divination. If it had a fine, natural, red colour ; if it was healthy, and without spots ; if it was large and double ; if the lobes turned outwards ; they promised themselves the best success in their undertakings : but it portended evil if the liver was dry, or had a band between the parts, or had no lobes. It was also considered an unfortunate omen if the liver was injured by a cut in killing the victim. (Matern. of Cilano, Roman Antiquities, vol. ii. p. 164.) Rosenmüller. Burder's Oriental Literature, vol. ii. p. 185.

[4] Selden de diis Syris. Synt. l. cap. 2. p. 28. Godwin's Moses and Aaron, p. 216. Pococke and Newcome, in loc. Potter's Antiq. of Greece, vol. i. p. 359. (Edinb. 1804.)

[5] Josephus relates that, at the period above referred to, there were numerous sorcerers and deceivers ; who, pretending to show wonders and prodigies, seduced great numbers of people after them into the wilderness. (Ant. Jud. lib. xx. c. 8. § 6. Bell. Jud. lib. iv. c. 13. § 4.)

Bar-Jesus, mentioned in Acts xiii. 6—11. There also were others, such as Simon the sorcerer (Acts viii. 9.); who having some knowledge of natural philosophy and astrology, abused that knowledge and deceived the common people by pretending to foretell future events, from the motions and appearances of the planets and stars, and to cure certain diseases by repeating certain phrases, &c.[1] So prevalent was the practice of sorcery among the Jews, that many of their elders, judges, or rabbies, are said to have attained such a proficiency in magic or sorcery, as to surpass even those who made it their profession.[2]

The prevalence of magic among the heathen is too well known to require any proofs. Pythagoras and other distinguished Greek philosophers took no small pains to attain the knowledge of this art: the inhabitants of Ephesus in particular were distinguished for their magical skill. And it was no small triumph of the Gospel that many of the Christian converts at Ephesus, who had previously *used curious arts*, (τα περιεργα, which word is used by Greek writers to denote magical arts, incantations, &c.) *brought their books together and burnt them before all men*. (Acts xix. 19.) So celebrated was the city of Ephesus for the magic art, that some particular forms of incantation derived their names from thence, and were called Εφεσια Γραμματα, or *Ephesian Letters*.[3] They appear to have been amulets inscribed with strange characters, which were worn about the person for the purpose of curing diseases, expelling demons, and preserving individuals from evils of different kinds. The "books" above mentioned were such as taught the science, mode of forming, use, &c. of these charms.[4]

SECTION II.

ON THE STATE OF RELIGION AMONG THE JEWS, IN THE TIME OF
JESUS CHRIST.

PREVIOUSLY to the Babylonish captivity there are no vestiges of the existence of any sect among the Jews. Devoted to the study of their law and to the ceremonies of their religion, they neglected those curious studies which were esteemed among other nations. The temple of Jehovah and the houses of the prophets were their principal schools; in which they were taught how to serve the Lord and to observe the ordinances which he had commanded. After the captivity we do not meet with any traces of any sects among them until the time of the Maccabæan princes; when it should seem that the Jewish literati, in

---

[1] Robinson's Gr. Lex. *voce* Μαγος.

[2] If any credit may be given to the Talmuds, twenty-four of the school of rabbi Judah were killed by sorcery; and eighty women sorceresses were hanged in one day by Simon ben Shetah. So greatly did the practice of this art prevail among them, that skill in it was required as a necessary qualification for a person to be chosen a member of their councils, whether that of seventy-one or those of twenty-three; in order that he might be the better able to try and judge the accused; whether they were really guilty of sorcery or not. Lightfoot's Works, vol. i. p. 371. vol. ii. p. 244. (folio edit.) where the passages from the Talmuds are given.

[3] Biscoe on the Acts, vol. i. pp. 290—293.

[4] Dr. A. Clarke on Acts viii. 17. where some curious information relative to the Ephesian letters is collected from the lexicographers, Suidas and Hesychius.

imitation of the sects of the Grecian philosophers, became divided in their opinions, and composed the three celebrated sects of the Pharisees, Sadducees, and Essenes. As these sects are frequently mentioned in the New Testament, it is proposed in this section to give an account of their origin and tenets, together with those of the Herodians, who are repeatedly mentioned by Jesus Christ, and of some other minor denominations of religious parties which were in existence during the period of time comprised in the New Testament history.[1]

---

§1. ACCOUNT OF THE JEWISH SECTS MENTIONED IN THE NEW TESTAMENT.

I. *The Pharisees.* — II. *The Sadducees.* — III. *The Essenes.* — IV. *The Scribes.* — V. *The Lawyers.* — VI. *The Samaritans.* — VII. *The Herodians.* — VIII. *The Galilæans.* — IX. *The Zealots.* — X. *The Sicarii.*

I. The PHARISEES were the most numerous and powerful sect of the Jews. The precise time when they first appeared is not known: but, as Josephus[2] mentions the Pharisees, Sadducees, and Essenes, as distinct sects, in the reign of Jonathan (B. C. 144—139), it is manifest that they must have been in existence for some time. Calmet is of opinion that their origin cannot be carried higher than the year of the world 3820, corresponding with the year 184 before the Christian æra. They derived their name from the Hebrew verb פרש (PHARASH) to separate; because they professed an uncommon separation from the apparel and customs of the world to the study of the law, and an extraordinary devotion to God and sanctity of life, beyond all other men. Hence one of them is represented as thanking God, that he was *not as other men are;* and St. Paul, in his masterly apology before king Agrippa, terms them αχριβεστατη αιρεσις, the most rigorous sect, in our version rendered *the most straitest sect.* (Acts xxvi. 5.) They were not restricted to any particular family or class of men: there were Pharisees of every tribe, family, and condition. The credit which they had acquired by their reputation for knowledge and sanctity of life early rendered them formidable to the Maccabæan sovereigns; while they were held in such esteem and veneration by the people, that they may be almost said to have given what direction they pleased to public affairs.[3] They boasted that, from their accurate knowledge of religion,

---

[1] The authorities principally consulted for this section are Pritii Introductio in Lectionem Novi Testamenti, cc. 33, 34. De Statu Religionis Judæorum tempore Christi, pp. 446—471. Calmet's Dissertation sur les Sectes des Juifs, Dissert. tom. i. pp. 711—743. Godwin's Moses and Aaron, and Jennings's Jewish Antiquities, book i. ch. 10—13. Schulzii Archæologia Biblica, pp. 170—180. Carpzovii Antiquitates Hebr. Gentis, pp. 173—247. Pictet's Theologie Chrétienne, tom. i. pp. 627—630. and tom. iii. pp. 103—117. Jahn, Archæol. Bibl. §§ 316—320. and Ackermann, Archæol. Bibl. §§ 305—311. Beausobre's and L'Enfant's Introd. (Bp. Watson's Tracts, vol. iii. pp. 184—192.)

[2] Ant. Jud. lib. xiii. c. 5. § 9.

[3] The high reputation and influence of the Pharisees are strikingly illustrated by the following anecdote : — When Alexander Jannæus lay on his death-bed, about eighty years before the Christian æra, his queen Alexandra having expressed great anxiety on account of the exposed state in which herself and sons would be left, the dying monarch recommended her to court the Pharisees, and delegate part of her power to them. Alexandra followed this advice ; and the Pharisees, availing themselves of the opportunity, made themselves masters of the government, and disposed of every thing as they pleased. Josephus, Ant. Jud. lib. xiii. c. 15. § 5. c. 16. § 1. Bell. Jud. lib. i. c. 4.

they were the favourites of heaven [1]; and thus, trusting in themselves that they were righteous, despised others. (Luke xi. 52. xviii. 9. 11.)

Among the tenets inculcated by this sect, we may enumerate the following; viz.

1. They ascribed all things to fate or providence, yet not so absolutely as to take away the free will of man, though fate does not cooperate in every action.[2] They also believed in the existence of angels and spirits, and in the resurrection of the dead (Acts xxiii. 8.): but, from the account given of them by Josephus, it appears that their notion of the immortality of the soul was the Pythagorean metempsychosis [3]; that the soul, after the dissolution of one body, winged its flight into another; and that these removals were perpetuated and diversified through an infinite succession, the soul animating a sound and healthy body, or being confined in a deformed and diseased frame, according to its conduct in a prior state of existence. From the Pharisees, whose tenets and traditions the people generally received, it is evident that the disciples of our Lord had adopted this philosophical doctrine of the transmigration of souls; when, having met with a man who had been *born* blind, they asked him whether it were the sins of this man in a pre-existent state which had caused the Sovereign Disposer to inflict upon him this punishment. To this inquiry Christ replied, that neither his vices or sins in a pre-existent state, nor those of his parents, were the cause of this calamity. (John ix. 1—4.) From this notion, derived from the Greek philosophy, we find that during our Saviour's public ministry, the Jews speculated variously concerning him, and indulged several conjectures, which of the antient prophets it was whose soul now animated him, and performed such astonishing miracles. Some contended that it was the soul of Elias; others of Jeremiah; while others, less sanguine, only declared in general terms that it must be the soul of one of the old prophets by which these mighty deeds were now wrought. (Matt. xvi. 14. Luke ix. 19.)[4]

2. The Pharisees contended that God was in strict justice *bound* to bless the Jews, and make them all partakers of the *terrestrial* kingdom of the Messiah, to justify them, to make them eternally happy, and that he could not possibly damn any one of them! The ground of their justification they derived from the merits of Abraham, from their knowledge of God, from their practising the rite of circumcision, and from the sacrifices they offered. And as they conceived works to be meritorious, they had invented a great number of *supererogatory* ones, to which they attached greater merit than to the observance of the law itself. To this notion St. Paul has some allusions in those parts of his

---

[1] Ant. Jud. lib. xvii. c. 2. § 4.

[2] Ibid. lib. xiii. c. 5. § 9. lib. xviii. c. 2. § 3.   De Bell. Jud. lib. ii. c. 8. § 14.   Acts v. 38, 39.

[3] Josephus, Ant. Jud. lib. xviii. c. 1. § 3.   De Bell. Jud. lib. ii. c. 8. § 14. lib. iii. c. 8. § 5.   The author of the Book of Wisdom (ch. viii. 20.) seems to allude to the same doctrine, when he tells us, *that, being good, he came into a body undefiled.*

[4] Dr. Lightfoot's Works, vol. ii. pp. 568, 569.   Dr. Harwood's Introd. to the New Test. vol. ii. p. 355.   To this popular notion of a transmigration of souls, Dr. H. ascribes the alarm of Herod, who had caused John the Baptist to be beheaded, when the fame of Christ's miracles reached his court; but, on comparing Matt. xvi. 6. with Mark viii. 15., it appears that Herod was a *Sadducee*, and, consequently, disbelieved a future state. His alarm, therefore, is rather to be attributed to the force of conscience which haunted his guilty mind in despite of his libertine principles.

Epistle to the Romans, in which he combats the erroneous suppositions of the Jews.[1]

3. The Pharisees were the strictest of the three principal sects that divided the Jewish nation (Acts xxvi. 5.), and affected a singular probity of manners according to their system, which however was for the most part both lax and corrupt. Thus, many things which Moses had *tolerated* in civil life, in order to avoid a greater evil, the Pharisees determined to be morally right; for instance, the law of retaliation, and that of divorce from a wife for *any* cause. (Matt. v. 31. *et seq.* xix. 3—12.) During the time of Christ, there were two celebrated philosophical and divinity schools among the Jews, that of Schammai and that of Hillel. On the question of divorce, the school of Schammai maintained, that no man could legally put away his wife except for adultery : the school of Hillel, on the contrary, allowed of divorce for *any* cause (from Deut. xxiv. 1.), even if the wife found no favour in the eyes of her husband, — in other words, if he saw any woman who pleased him better. The practice of the Jews seems to have gone with the school of Hillel. Thus we read, (in Ecclus. xxv. 26.) " If she go not as thou wouldest have her, cut her off from thy flesh ; give her a bill of divorce and let her go ; " and in conformity with this doctrine, Josephus [2], who was a Pharisee, relates that he repudiated his wife who had borne him three children, because he was not pleased with her manners or behaviour.

4. Further, they interpreted certain of the Mosaic laws most literally, and distorted their meaning so as to favour their own philosophical system. Thus, the law of loving their neighbour, they expounded solely of the love of their friends, that is, of the whole Jewish race; all other persons being considered by them as natural enemies (Matt. v. 43. compared with Luke x. 31—33.), whom they were in no respect bound to assist. Dr. Lightfoot has cited a striking illustration of this passage from Maimonides.[3] An oath, in which the name of God was not distinctly specified, they taught was not binding (Matt. v. 33.), maintaining that a man might even swear with his lips, and at the same moment annul it in his heart ! So rigorously did they understand the command of observing the sabbath-day, that they accounted it unlawful to pluck· ears of corn, and heal the sick, &c. (Matt. xii. 1. *et seq.* Luke vi. 6. *et seq.* xiv. 1. *et seq.*) Those natural laws which Moses did not sanction by any penalty they accounted among the petty commandments, inferior to the ceremonial laws, which they preferred to the former, as being the weightier matters of the law (Matt. v. 19. xv. 4. xxiii. 23.), to the total neglect of mercy and fidelity. Hence they accounted causeless anger and impure desires as trifles of no moment (Matt. v. 21, 22. 27—30.) ; they compassed sea and land to make proselytes [4] to the Jewish religion from among the Gentiles, that they

---

[1] See Rom. i.—xi. Josephus, Ant. Jud. lib. xvii. c. 2. § 4. De Bell. Jud. lib. ii. c. 8. § 4. Justin. Dialog. cum Tryphon. Pirke Aboth.

[2] Life of himself, § 76. Grotius, Calmet, Drs. Lightfoot, Whitby, Doddridge, and A. Clarke (on Matt. v. 30. *et seq.* and Matt. xix. 3. *et seq.*) have all given illustrations of the Jewish doctrine of divorce from rabbinical writers. See also Selden's Uxor Hebraica, lib. iii. c. 22. (Op. tom. ii. col. 782—786.)

[3] " A Jew sees a Gentile fall into the sea, let him by no means lift him out: for it is written, '*Thou shalt not rise up against the blood of thy neighbour.*' But this is NOT thy neighbour." Works, vol. ii. p. 152.

[4] Justin Martyr bears witness to the inveterate malignity of the proselytes of the Pha-

might rule over their consciences and wealth: and these proselytes, through the influence of their own scandalous examples and characters, they soon rendered more profligate and abandoned than ever they were before their conversion. (Matt. xxiii. 15.) Esteeming temporal happiness and riches as the highest good, they scrupled not to accumulate wealth by every means, legal or illegal (Matt. v. 1—12. xxiii. 4. Luke xvi. 14. James ii. 1—8.); vain and ambitious of popular applause, they offered up long prayers [1] in public places, but not without a self-sufficiency of their own holiness (Matt. vi. 2—5. Luke xviii. 11.); under a sanctimonious appearance of respect for the memories of the prophets whom their ancestors had slain, they repaired and beautified their sepulchres (Matt. xxiii. 29.); and such was their idea of their own sanctity, that they thought themselves defiled if they but touched or conversed with *sinners*, that is, with publicans or tax-gatherers, and persons of loose and irregular lives. (Luke vii. 39. xv. 1. *et seq.*)

But, above all their other tenets, the Pharisees were conspicuous for their reverential observance of the traditions or decrees of the elders. These traditions, they pretended, had been handed down from Moses through every generation, but were not committed to writing; and they were not merely considered as of equal authority with the divine law, but even preferable to it. "The words of the Scribes," said they, "are lovely above the words of the law; for the words of the law are weighty and light, but the words of the scribes are ALL weighty." [2] Among the traditions thus sanctimoniously observed by the Pharisees, we may briefly notice the following:—1. *The washing of hands* up to the wrist before and after meat (Matt. xv. 2. Mark vii. 3.), which they accounted not merely a religious duty, but considered its omission as a crime equal to fornication, and punishable by excommunication. 2. The *purification* of the cups, vessels, and couches used at their meals by ablutions or washings (Mark vii. 4.); for which purpose the six large water-pots mentioned by St. John (ii. 6.) were destined. But these ablutions are not to be confounded with those symbolical washings mentioned in Psal. xxvi. 6. and Matt. xxvii. 24. 3. Their *punctilious payment of tithes* (temple-offerings), even of the most trifling thing. (Luke xviii. 12. Matt. xxiii. 23.) 4. *Their wearing broader phylacteries and larger fringes* to their garments than the rest of the Jews. (Matt. xxiii. 5.) He, who wore his phylactery and his fringe of the largest size, was reputed to be the most devout. 5. *Their fasting*

---

risees against the name of Christ, at the beginning of the second century. "Your prose-lytes," says he to Trypho the Jew (p. 350.), "not only do not believe in Christ, but blaspheme his name with *twofold more virulence than yourselves.* They are ready to show their malicious zeal against us; and, to obtain merit in your eyes, wish to us reproach, and torment, and death." See further Dr. Ireland's Paganism and Christianity compared, pp. 21—23.

[1] Bucher, after a very antient Hebrew manuscript ritual, has given a long and curious specimen of the "vain repetitions" used by the Pharisees. See his Antiquitates Biblicæ ex Novo Testamento selectæ, pp. 240—244. Vitembergæ, 1729. 4to.

[2] Jerusalem Berachoth, fol. 3. 2. as cited by Dr. Lightfoot in his Horæ Hebraicæ on Matt. xv. The whole of his Hebrew and Talmudical Exercitations on that chapter is singularly instructive. The collection of these traditions, by which the Jews made the law of God of none effect, is termed the Talmud: of which, and of its use in illustrating the Holy Scriptures, an account has already been given. On the traditions of the modern Jews (which illustrate very many passages of the New Testament), the reader may consult Mr. Allen's Modern Judaism, chap. viii. to xv. pp. 140—280.

twice a week with great appearance of austerity (Luke xviii. 12. Matt. vi. 16.); thus converting that exercise into religion which is only a help towards the performance of its hallowed duties.   The Jewish days of fasting were the second and fifth days of the week, corresponding with our Mondays and Thursdays: on one of these days they commemorated Moses going up to the mount to receive the law, which, according to their traditions, was on the fifth day or Thursday; and on the other his descent after he had received the two tables, which they supposed to have been on the second day, or Monday.

Very surprising effects are related concerning the mortifications of the Pharisees, and the austerities practised by some of them in order to preserve the purity of the body.   Sometimes they imposed these painful exercises for four, eight, or even ten years, before they married. They deprived themselves almost entirely of sleep, lest they should involuntarily become unclean or polluted during sleep.   Some of them are said to have slept on narrow planks, not more than twelve fingers broad; in order that, if they should sleep too soundly, they might fall upon the ground and awake to prayer.   Others slept on small and sharp pointed stones, and even on thorns, in order that they might be laid under a kind of necessity to be always awake.[1]   As, however, none of these austerities were legally commanded, and as the Pharisees were not bound to practice them by any law or other obligation, each seems to have followed his own inclination and the impulse or ardour of his devotion.   The Talmuds mention seven sorts of Pharisees, two of whom appear to be alluded to, though not specified by name, in the New Testament, viz. 1. The Shechemite Pharisees, or those who entered into the sect only from motives of gain; just as the Shechemites suffered themselves to be circumcised.   This order of Pharisees is most probably alluded to in Matt. xxiii. 5. 14.; and, 2. The Pharisees who said, "Let me know what my duty is, and I will do it." — "I have done my duty, that the command may be performed according to it."   Of this sort the young man in the Gospel appears to have been, who came to Jesus Christ, saying, "*Good master*, WHAT GOOD THING SHALL I DO, that I may have eternal *life?*" and who at length replied, — ALL *these have I kept* (or, *observed*) *from my youth up.* (Matt. xix. 16. 20.)[2]

With all their pretensions to piety, the Pharisees entertained the most sovereign contempt for the people; whom, being ignorant of the law, they pronounced to be accursed. (John vii. 49.)   It is unquestionable, as Mosheim has well remarked, that the religion of the Pharisees was, for the most part, founded in consummate hypocrisy; and that, in general, they were the slaves of every vicious appetite, proud, arrogant, and avaricious, consulting only the gratification of their lusts, even at the very moment when they professed themselves to be engaged in the service of their Maker.   These odious features in the character of the Pharisees caused them to be reprehended by our Saviour with the utmost severity, even more than he rebuked the Sadducees; who, although they had departed widely from the genuine principles of re-

---

[1] Epiphanius, Hæres. p. 16.
[2] Jerusalem Talmud, Berachoth, fol. 13. 2. Sotah, fol. 20. 3. Babylonish Talmud, fol. 22. 2.   Dr. Lightfoot has translated the entire passages in his Horæ Hebraicæ on Matt. iii. 7.

ligion, yet did not impose on mankind by pretended sanctity, or devote themselves with insatiable greediness to the acquisition of honours and riches.[1] *All* the Pharisees, however, were not of this description. Nicodemus appears to have been a man of great probity and piety; and the same character is applicable to Gamaliel. If Saul persecuted the church of Christ, he did it out of a blind zeal ; but, not to insist on the testimony which he bears of himself, it is evident, from the extraordinary favour of God towards him, that he was not tainted with the other vices common to the sect of the Pharisees. What he says of it, that it was the strictest of all, cannot admit of any other than a favourable construction.[2]

II. The sect of the SADDUCEES is by some writers considered as the most antient of the Jewish sects ; though others have supposed that the Sadducees and Pharisees gradually grew up together. This sect derives its appellation from Sadok, or Zadok, the disciple and successor of Antigonus Sochæus, who lived above two hundred (Dr. Prideaux says two hundred and sixty-three) years before Christ; and who taught his pupils to " be not as servants, who wait upon their master for the sake of reward, but to be like servants who wait upon their master, not for the sake of reward;" but that they should let the fear of the Lord be in them.[3] Unable to comprehend a doctrine so spiritual, Sadok deduced from it the inference that neither reward nor punishment is to be expected in a future life. The following are the principal tenets of the Sadducees : —

1. *That there is no resurrection, neither angel nor spirit* (Matt. xxii. 23. Acts xxiii. 8.), and that the soul of man perishes together with the body.[4]

2. That there is no fate or over-ruling providence, but that all men enjoy the most ample freedom of action ; in other words, the absolute power of doing either good or evil, according to their own[5] choice ; hence they were very severe judges.[6]

3. They paid no regard whatever to any tradition, adhering strictly to the letter of Scripture, but preferring the five books of Moses to the rest. It has been conjectured by some writers that they rejected all the sacred books but those of Moses. But this hypothesis is no proof: for, in the first place, this sect took its rise at a time when the Jewish canon had been closed ; and it was just as easy for the Sadducees to

---

[1] Mosheim's Commentaries on the Affairs of Christians, vol. i. p. 83.

[2] Beausobre's and L'Enfant's Introd. (Bp. Watson's Tracts,) vol. iii. p. 190.

[3] Lightfoot's Horæ Hebraicæ on Matt. iii. 7.

[4] Josephus de Bell. Jud. lib. i. c. 8. *in fine.* Ant. Jud. lib. xviii. c. 1. § 4. Some learned men have expressed their surprise, that the Sadducees should deny the existence of angels, since they acknowledged the five books of Moses, in which such frequent and express mention is made of the appearance and ministry of angels. To this it is answered, that they believed not the angels, spoken of in the books of Moses, to be of any duration, but looked on them as beings created only for the service they performed, and existing no longer. (Grotius on Matt. xxii. xxiii. &c. Lightfoot's Works, vol. ii. p. 702. Whitby on Acts xxiii. 8. and Matt. xxii. 23.) There seem to have been heretics in the time of Justin Martyr (the second century), who entertained a similar opinion. (Justin. Dial. cum Tryphone, p. 358. b.) And it is evident that this notion was entertained by some among the Jews, so lately as the emperor Justinian's time (the sixth century); for there is a law of his extant (Novel. 146. c. 2.) published against those Jews, who should presume either to deny the resurrection and judgment, or that angels, the workmanship and creatures of God, did subsist. Biscoe on the Acts, vol. i. p. 99.

[5] Josephus, Ant. Jud. lib. xiii. c. 5. § 9. De Bell. Jud. lib. ii. c. 8. § 4.

[6] Ant. Jud. lib. xviii. c. 10. § 6.

make their opinions harmonise with the other books of the Old Testament as with the books of Moses. Secondly, how could any of the Sadducees have sustained the office of high-priest, if they had departed in so important a point from the belief of the nation ? Thirdly, although Josephus frequently mentions their rejecting the traditions of the elders, yet he nowhere charges them with rejecting any of the sacred books; and, as he was himself a Pharisee, and their zealous antagonist, he would not have passed over such a crime in silence. It is further worthy of remark, that our Saviour, who so severely censured the Sadducees for their other corruptions, did not condemn them for such rejection.[1]

In point of numbers, the Sadducees were an inconsiderable sect; but their numerical deficiency was amply compensated by the dignity and eminence of those who embraced their tenets, and who were persons of the first distinction. Several of them were advanced to the high priesthood.[2] They do not, however, appear to have aspired, generally, to public offices. Josephus affirms that scarcely any business of the state was transacted by them; and that, when they were in the magistracy, they generally conformed to the measures of the Pharisees, though unwillingly, and out of pure necessity; for otherwise they would not have been endured by the multitude.[3]

III. Concerning the origin of the ESSENES, who were the third principal sect of the Jews, there is a considerable difference of opinion. By some writers of Jewish antiquities they have been identified with the fraternity of Assidæans, who are mentioned in 1 Macc. ii. 42. as being zealously devoted to the law ; while others trace their descent to the Rechabites. But the latter were a *family* only, and not a sect. Most probably they derived their origin from Egypt, where the Jewish refugees, who fled for security after the murder of Gedaliah, were compelled, on the captivity of the greater part of their body, to lead a recluse life, out of which the Essene institute might have grown. They were dispersed chiefly through Palestine, Syria, and Egypt, though they were to be met with in other countries. The Essenes differed in many respects from the Pharisees and Sadducees, both in doctrines and in practice. They were divided into two classes:—1. The *practical*, who lived in society, and some of whom were married, though it appears with much circumspection. These dwelt in cities and their neighbourhoods, and applied themselves to husbandry and other innocent occupations. 2. The *contemplative* Essenes, who were also called Therapeutæ or Physicians, from their application principally to the cure of the diseases of the soul, devoted themselves wholly to meditation, and avoided living in great towns as unfavourable to a contemplative life. But both classes were exceedingly abstemious, exemplary in their moral deportment, averse from profane swearing, and most rigid in their observance of the sabbath. They held, among other tenets, the immortality of the soul (though they denied the resurrection of the body), the existence of angels, and a state of future rewards and

[1] Schmucker's Biblical Theology, vol. i. p. 264. The reader will find several additional proofs in confirmation of the preceding account of the books received by the Sadducees, in Dr. Jortin's Remarks on Eccl. Hist. Appendix, No. II. vol. i. pp. 368—374. Edit. 1805.
[2] Acts v. 17. xxiii. 6. Josephus, Ant. Jud. lib. xiii. c. 10. §§ 6, 7. lib. xviii. c. 1. § 4.
[3] Ant. Jud. lib. xviii. c. 1. § 4.

punishments.   They believed every thing to be ordered by an eternal fatality or chain of causes.   Although Jesus Christ censured all the other sects of the Jews for their vices, yet he never spoke of the Essenes; neither are they mentioned by name in any part of the New Testament.   The silence of the evangelical historians concerning them is by some accounted for by their eremitic life, which secluded them from places of public resort; so that they did not come in the way of our Saviour, as the Pharisees and Sadducees often did.   Others, however, are of opinion, that the Essenes being very honest and sincere, without guile or hypocrisy, gave no room for the reproofs and censures which the other Jews deserved; and, therefore, no mention is made of them.

But though the Essenes are not expressly named in any of the sacred books, it has been conjectured that they are alluded to in two or three passages.   Thus, those whom our Lord terms eunuchs, who have made themselves such for the kingdom of heaven's sake (Matt. xix. 12.), are supposed to be the contemplative Essenes, who abstained from all intercourse with women, in the hope of acquiring a greater degree of purity, and becoming the better fitted for the kingdom of God.   St. Paul is generally understood to have referred to them, in Col. ii. 18. 23., where "voluntary humility," and "neglecting the body," are peculiarly applicable to the Essenes; who, when they received any persons into their number, made them solemnly swear that they would keep and observe the books of the sect and the names of the angels with care.[1]   What is also said in the above-cited passage, of "intruding into things not seen," is likewise agreeable to the character of the Therapeutic Essenes; who, placing the excellence of their contemplative life in raising their minds to invisible objects, pretended to such a degree of elevation and abstraction, as to be able to penetrate into the nature of angels, and assign them proper names, or rightly interpret those already given them; and also to pry into futurity and predict future events.   On these accounts it is highly probable that they were "vainly puffed up by their fleshly mind."   Further, the tenets referred to by St. Paul (Col. ii. 21. "touch not, taste not, handle not,") are such as the Essenes held, who would not taste any pleasant food, but lived on coarse bread and drank nothing but water, and some of whom would not taste any food at all till after sunset: if touched by any that were not of their own sect, they would wash themselves, as after some great pollution.   It has been conjectured that there might be a sodality of Essenes at Colossæ, as there were in many other places out of Judæa; and that some of the Christians, being too much inclined to Judaism, might also affect the peculiarities of this sect; which might be the reason of the Apostle's so particularly cautioning the Colossians against them.[2]

---

[1] Josephus, de Bell. Jud. lib. ii. c. 8. § 7.

[2] Jennings's Jewish Antiquities, book i. c. 13. Encyclopædia Metropolitana, vol. x. p. 592. Michaelis thinks that Saint Paul alludes to the tenets and practices of the Essenes in his Epistle to the Ephesians, and in his first Epistle to Timothy.   Introd. to the New Test. vol. iv. pp. 79—85.   Dr. Prideaux has collected with great industry and fidelity all that Philo, Josephus, and Pliny have recorded concerning the Essenes.   Connection, vol. ii. book v. sub anno 107 B. C. pp. 343—363. 8th edit.   There is a very interesting description of the institute of the Essenes in vol. ii. pp. 124—150. of "Helon's Pilgrimage to Jerusalem," which contains an admirable and graphic delineation of Jewish manners and customs, such as they most probably were at the time when the advent of the Messiah was at hand.

IV. There is in the Gospels frequent mention of a set of men called SCRIBES, who are often joined with the chief priests, elders, and Pharisees. They seem to have been men of learning, and on that account to have had great deference paid to them (Matt. ii. 4. vii. 29.); but, strictly speaking, they did not form any distinct sect. The Scribes generally belonged to the sect of the Pharisees, in whose traditions and explanations of the law they were profoundly skilled; and on the sabbath-days "they sat in Moses' seat" and instructed the people. Originally, they had their name from their employment, which at first was *transcribing* the law: but in progress of time they exalted themselves into the public ministry and became teachers of it, authoritatively determining what doctrines were or were not contained in the Scriptures, and teaching the common people in what sense to understand the law and the prophets. In short, they were the oracles which were consulted in all difficult points of doctrine and duty; and it is not improbable that they were, for the most part, Levites, whose peculiar business it was to study and read the law.[1] The Scribes were of different families and tribes, and therefore of different sects: hence we read, that there were Scribes of the sect of the Pharisees and also of the Sadducees. (Acts xxiii. 9.) In the New Testament, the Scribes are frequently identified with the Pharisees, because they held both these titles. They were Scribes by office, and Pharisees by religious profession. This explanation will account for the Pharisees in Matt. xxii. 35. being called Scribes in Mark xii. 28.[2]

V. The LAWYERS (νομικοι) or TEACHERS OF THE LAW and Scribes appear to be synonymous terms, importing one and the same order of men; as St. Matthew (xxii. 35.) calls him a lawyer whom St. Mark (xii. 28.) terms one of the Scribes. Dr. Macknight conjectures the Scribes to have been the public expounders of the law, and that the lawyers studied it in private: perhaps, as Dr. Lardner conjectures, they taught in the schools.[3] But M. Basnage is of opinion that they were a distinct class or sect of men, who adhered closely to the text of the law, and totally disregarded all traditions, and that they were the same as the modern Karaites.[4]

VI. The SAMARITANS, mentioned in the New Testament, are generally considered as a sect of the Jews.

For the translation of this very pleasing and instructive work from the German of Frederick Strauss, the lover of sacred literature is indebted to the Rev. John Kenrick, M. A. of York.

1 Dr. Burton's Papists and Pharisees compared, p. 6. (Oxford, 1766. 8vo.)

2 Spanheim's Ecclesiastical Annals, by the Rev. G. Wright, p. 178.

3 Prideaux, vol. ii p. 343. Lardner's Credibility, part i. book i. ch. 4. § 3. (Works, vol. i. p. 126.) Macknight's Harmony, sect. 87. vol. ii. p. 472. 8vo. edit.

4 Basnage's History and Religion of the Jews, book i. ch. 8, 9. pp. 104—114. The Karaites claim a very remote antiquity, some pretending that they are descended from the ten tribes who were carried into captivity by Shalmaneser, while others glory in their descent from Ezra. This sect was reformed by rabbi Anun in the eighth century. They are found in different parts of Russia, Poland, Lithuania, Austria, the Caucasus, Turkey, Egypt, Abyssinia, India, and the Holy Land; but their numbers are not known. The principal point of difference between them and the rabbinists or Pharisaical Jews consists in their rejection of the oral law, and their rigid appeal to the text of Scripture, as the exclusive and only infallible source and test of religious truth. On this account they are called KARAITES (קראים KARAIM) or *Scripturists*, from קרא KARA or *Scripture*. Dr. Henderson's Biblical Researches and Travels in Russia, p. 319. In pp. 315—339. he has given a very interesting account of the principles, &c. of the Karaites in the Crimea. Carpzov has given an abstract of the earlier writers concerning this sect in his Antiquitates Hebrææ Gentis, pp. 168—172.

This appellation is, in the New Testament, given to a race of people who sprang originally from an intermixture of the ten tribes with Gentile nations. When the inhabitants of Samaria and of the adjacent country were carried into captivity by Shalmaneser king of Assyria, he sent in their place colonies from Babylonia, Cuthah, Ava, Hamath, and Sepharvaim; with which the Israelites who remained in the land became intermingled, and were ultimately amalgamated into one people. (2 Kings xvii. 24.) An origin like this would, of course, render the nation odious to the Jews; and the Samaritans further augmented this cause of hatred by rejecting all the sacred books of the Jews, except the Pentateuch, which they had received from the Jewish priest who had been sent to them from Assyria to instruct them in the true religion. (2 Kings xvii. 27, 28.) On the return of the Jews from the Babylonish captivity, when they began to rebuild Jerusalem and the temple, the Samaritans requested to be acknowledged as Jewish citizens, and to be permitted to assist in the work; but their application was rejected. (Ezra iv. 1—4.) In consequence of this refusal and the subsequent state of enmity, the Samaritans not only took occasion to calumniate the Jews before the Persian kings (Ezra iv. 5. Neh. iv. 1—7, 8.); but also, recurring to the directions of Moses (Deut. xxvii. 11—13.), that on entering the promised land the Hebrews should offer sacrifices on Mount Gerizim, they erected a temple on that mountain, and instituted sacrifices according to the prescriptions of the Mosaic law.[1] From all these and other circumstances, the national hatred between the Samaritans and Jews increased to such a height, that the Jews denounced the most bitter anathemas against them (Ecclus. l. 26.), and for many ages refused them every kind of intercourse. Hence the woman of Samaria was astonished that Jesus Christ, who was a Jew, should ask drink of her. (John iv. 9.)[2] Hence also the Jews, when they would express the utmost aversion to Christ, said to him — *Thou art a* SAMARITAN, *and hast a devil.* (John viii. 48.) The temple on Mount Gerizim was destroyed by Hyrcanus, B.C. 129[3] : but the Samaritans, in the time of Jesus, esteemed that mountain sacred, and as the proper place of national worship. (John iv. 20, 21.) At that time, also, in common with the Jews, they expected the advent of a Messiah (John iv. 25.), and many of them afterwards became the followers of Jesus Christ, and embraced the doctrines of his religion. (Acts viii. 1. ix. 31. xv. 3.)[4]

Towards the close of the Jewish polity, the Samaritans suffered much from the Romans; and though they received a little favourable treatment from one or two of the pagan emperors, yet they suffered considerably under some of the professing Christian emperors, par-

---

[1] Josephus, Ant. Jud. lib. xi. c. 8. § 4.

[2] The following incident proves how little change the spirit of the Samaritan women has undergone within the last eighteen centuries. The Rev. Vere Munro, when travelling in the vicinity of Naplous (on the site of the antient Sychar), having descried some Samaritan women drawing water at a well, desired his servant to request them to give him some to drink. But they refused the indulgence, some of them exclaiming, " Shall I give water to a Christian, and make my pitcher filthy, so that I can use it no more for ever?" Summer Ramble in Syria, vol. i. p. 63.

[3] Josephus, Ant. Jud. lib. xiii. c. 10. §§ 2, 3.

[4] Robinson's Gr. Lex. *voce* Σαμαρειτης. Tappan's Lectures on Jewish Antiq. pp. 224— 227. Kuinöel, on John iv. 9, 25.

ticularly Valentinian and Justinian.[1] At present, the Samaritans are very much reduced in point of numbers. Their principal residence is at Sichem or Shechem, now called *Napolose* or *Nablous*. In 1823, there were between twenty and thirty houses, and about sixty males paid the capitation-tax to the Mohammedan government.[2] They celebrated divine service every Saturday. Formerly they went four times a year, in solemn procession, to the old synagogue on Mount Gerizim : and on these occasions they ascended before sunrise, and read the law till noon ; but of late years they have not been allowed to do this. The Samaritans have one school in Napolose, where their language is taught. The head of this sect is stated to reside at Paris.[3] The Samaritans at Napolose are in possession of a very antient manuscript Pentateuch, which they assert to be nearly 3500 years old ; but they reject the vowel points as a rabbinical invention. In order to complete our notice of this sect, we have subjoined their confession of faith, sent in the sixteenth century by Eleazar their high priest to the illustrious critic Scaliger, who had applied to them for that purpose; together with a few additional particulars from the baron de Sacy's Memoir on the Samaritans, and the Rev. W. Jowett's Christian Researches in Syria.[4]

1. The Samaritans observe the Sabbath with all the exactness required in Exodus; for not one of them goes out of the place where he is on the sabbath-day, except to the synagogue, where they read the law, and sing the praises of God. They do not lie that night with their wives, and neither kindle nor order fire to be kindled : whereas the Jews transgress the sabbath in all these points; for they go out of town, have fire made, lie with their wives, and even do not wash themselves after it. — 2. They hold the passover to be their first festival ; they begin at sunset, by the sacrifice enjoined for that purpose in Exodus; but they sacrifice *only* on Mount Gerizim, where they read the law, and offer prayers to God, after which the priest dismisses the whole congregation with a blessing. [Of late years, however, having been prohibited from ascending Mount Gerizim by their oppressors the Turks, they offer the paschal sacrifice within their city, which they consider to be within the precincts of the sacred place.] — 3. They celebrate for seven days together the feast of the harvest, but they do not agree with the Jews concerning the day when it ought to begin; for these reckon the next day after the solemnity of the passover; whereas the Samaritans reckon fifty days, beginning the next day after the sabbath, which happens in the week of the unleavened bread, and the next day after the seventh sabbath following, the feast of the harvest begins. — 4. They observe the fast of expiation on the tenth of the seventh month : they employ the four and twenty hours of the day in prayers to God, and singing his praises, and fasting. All fast,

---

[1] Basnage's History of the Jews, pp. 73—77. In pp. 63—96. he has given minute details respecting the history, tenets, and practices of this sect or people.

[2] Jowett's Christian Researches in Syria, p. 195.

[3] Visit of the Rev. James Connor, in 1819 and 1820, to Candia, Rhodes, Cyprus, and various parts of Syria and Palestine, annexed to the Rev. W. Jowett's Christian Researches in the Mediterranean, p. 425.

[4] Mémoire sur l'Etat actuel des Samaritains, par M. Silvestre de Sacy. Paris, 1812. 8vo. Jowett's Christian Researches in Syria, pp. 196—198. See also Joan. Christoph. Friedrich, Discussionum de Christologia Samaritanorum Liber. Accedit Appendicula de Columba Dea Samaritanorum. Lipsiæ, 1821. 8vo.

except children at the breast, whereas the Jews except children under seven years of age. — 5. On the fifteenth of the same month, they celebrate the feast of tabernacles. — 6. They never defer circumcision beyond the eighth day, as it is commanded in Genesis, whereas the Jews defer it sometimes longer. — 7. They are obliged to wash themselves in the morning, when they have lain with their wives, or have been sullied in the night by some uncleanness; and all vessels, that may become unclean, become defiled when they touch them before they have washed. — 8. They take away the fat from sacrifices, and give the priests the shoulder, the jaws, and the belly. — 9. They never marry their nieces as the Jews do, and have but one wife, whereas the Jews may have many. — 10. They believe in God, in Moses, and in Mount Gerizim. Whereas, say they, the Jews put their trust in others, we do nothing but what is expressly commanded in the law by the Lord who made use of the ministry of Moses; but the Jews swerve from what the Lord hath commanded in the law, to observe what their fathers and doctors have invented. — 11. They receive the Torah or Pentateuch, and hold it as their only sacred book; they reverence the books of Joshua and Judges, but do not account them sacred in the same manner as the Torah, considering Joshua not to have been a prophet, but only the disciple of a prophet, that is, of Moses. — 12. They expect a prophet, whom they term Hathab; but, say they, "there is a great mystery in regard to Hathab, who is yet to come. We shall be happy when he comes." When the Rev. Mr. Jowett, in November, 1823, interrogated the officiating Samaritan priest concerning their expectation of a Messiah, the latter replied that they were all in expectation of him; — "that the Messiah would be a man, not the Son of God,— and that this" (Napolose) "was to be the place which he would make the metropolis of his kingdom : this was the place, of which the Lord had promised, he would place his name there." The report of the Samaritans worshipping a dove is groundless; nor is it true that they deny the resurrection of the dead, or the existence of angels. They admit, however, that they recite hymns and prayers that Jehovah would pardon the dead, and the priest purifies them by prayer.

The Samaritans have a catalogue of the succession of their high priests from Aaron to the present time. They believe themselves to be of the posterity of Joseph by Ephraim, and that all their high priests descended from Phinehas; whereas the Jews have not one of that family. They boast that they have preserved the Hebrew characters which God made use of to promulgate his law; while the Jews have a way of writing from Ezra, which is cursed for ever. And, indeed, instead of looking upon Ezra as the restorer of the law, they curse him as an impostor, who has laid aside their old characters to use new ones in their room, and authorised several books that were written to support the posterity of David.

Several attempts have been made to convert these Samaritans; but they have been oppressed instead of being made Christians, and they are reduced to a small number rather by misery than by the multitude of those who have been converted. Nay, they seem more stubbornly wedded to their sect than the Jews, though these adhere rigorously to the law of Moses. At least Nicon, who lived after the twelfth century, when setting down the formalities used at the reception of heretics, observes, that if a Jew had a mind to be converted, in order to avoid punishment or the payment of what he owed, he was to purify himself, and satisfy his creditors before he was admitted. But the Samaritans were not received before they had been instructed two years, and were required to fast ten or fifteen days before they professed the Christian religion, to attend at morning and evening prayers, and to learn some psalms; others were not used with so much rigour. The term of two years which was enjoined to the Samaritan proselytes is an argument that they were suspected, and the reason why they were so was, that they had often deceived the Christians by their pretended conversion.[1]

VII. The HERODIANS were rather a political faction than a religious sect of the Jews: they derived their name from Herod the Great, king of Judæa, to whose family they were strongly attached. They were distinguished from the other Jewish sects, first, by their concurring in Herod's plan of subjecting himself and his people to the dominion of the Romans; and, secondly, in complying with the latter in many of their heathen practices, such as erecting temples with images for idolatrous worship, raising statues, and instituting games in honour of Augustus; which symbolising with idolatry upon views of interest and worldly policy is supposed to have been a part at least of the *leaven of Herod*, against which Jesus Christ cautioned his disciples (Mark viii. 15.); consequently they were directly opposed to the Pharisees, who, from a misinterpretation of Deut. xvii. 15. maintained that it was not lawful to submit to the Roman emperor, or to pay taxes to him. But Herod and his followers, understanding the text to exclude only a voluntary choice, and not a necessary submission where force had overpowered choice, held an opinion directly contrary, and insisted that in this case it was lawful both to submit to the Roman emperor, and also to pay taxes to him. How keen then must have been the malice of the Pharisees against Christ, when they united with their mortal enemies the Herodians, in proposing to him the ensnaring question, whether it was lawful to give tribute to Cæsar or not? (Matt. xxii. 16.) If our Redeemer had answered in the negative, the Herodians would have accused him to the Roman power as a seditious person; and if in the affirmative, the Pharisees were equally ready to accuse him to the people, and excite their indignation against him, as betraying the civil liberties and privileges of his country. Christ by his prudent reply defeated the malice of both, and at the same time implicitly justified the Herodians in paying tribute to Cæsar. It is further probable that the Herodians, in their doctrinal tenets, were chiefly of the sect of the Sadducees, who were the most indifferent to religion among the whole Jewish nation; since that which is by one evangelist called the *leaven of Herod* (Mark viii. 15.), is by another termed (Matt. xvi. 6.) the *leaven of the Sadducees*.[2]

---

[1] Lewis's Origines Hebrææ, vol. iii. pp. 57—59. In pp. 59—65. he has printed a letter, purporting to have been written by the Samaritans at Shechem in the seventeenth century, and sent by them to their brethren in England, by Dr. Huntington, some time chaplain to the Turkey Company at Aleppo, and afterwards Bishop of Raphoe, in Ireland.

[2] Prideaux's Connection, part ii. book v. (vol. ii. pp. 365—368.) Jennings's Jewish Antiquities, book i. ch. xii. Calmet, Dissertations, tom. i. pp. 737—743. where the different opinions of former writers concerning the Herodians are enumerated; as also in Elsley's Annotations on the Gospels, vol. i. pp. 342—346. vol. ii. p. 15. Parkhurst's Greek Lexicon, voce; Lardner's Credibility, part i. book i. ch. iv. § 4. (Works, vol. i. pp. 126, 127.) Tappan's Lectures on Jewish Antiq. p. 239.]

VIII. The GALILÆANS were a political sect that originated from the Pharisees, A.D. 12, when Archelaus was banished, Judæa reduced into a Roman province, and a census taken by Quirinius or Cyrenius, president of Syria (to which province Judæa was attached). On this occasion, Judas the Galilæan, or Gaulonite, as he is also called[1], exhorted the people to shake off this yoke, telling them, that tribute was due to God alone, and, consequently, ought not to be paid to the Romans; and that religious liberty and the authority of the divine laws were to be defended by force of arms. In other respects his doctrines appear to have been the same as those of the Pharisees. The tumults raised by these pernicious tenets were indeed suppressed (Acts v. 37.); but his followers, who were called Galilæans, continued secretly to propagate them, and to make proselytes, whom they required to be circumcised. As the same restless disposition and seditious principles continued to exist at the time when the apostles Paul and Peter wrote their Epistles, they took occasion thence to inculcate upon Christians (who were at that time generally confounded with the Jews), the necessity of obedience to civil authority, with singular ability, truth, and persuasion. See Rom. xiii. 1. *et seq.* 1 Tim. ii. 1. *et. seq.* 1 Peter ii. 13. *et. seq.*[2]

IX. The ZEALOTS, so often mentioned in Jewish history, appear to have been the followers of this Judas. Lamy is of opinion that the JUST MEN whom the Pharisees and Herodians sent to entangle Jesus in his conversation were members of this sect. (Matt. xxii. 15, 16. Mark xii. 13, 14. Luke xx. 20.)[3] Simon the Canaanite, one of the apostles of Jesus Christ, is called *Zelotes* (Luke vi. 15.); and in Acts xxi. 20. and xxii. 3. (Gr.) we find that there were certain Christians at Jerusalem, who were denominated ZEALOTS. But these merely insisted on the fulfilment of the Mosaic law, and by no means went so far as those persons, termed Zelotæ or Zealots, of whom we read in Josephus's history of the Jewish war.

X. The SICARII, noticed in Acts xxi. 38. were assassins, who derived their name from their using poniards bent like the Roman *sicæ*, which they concealed under their garments, and which was the secret instrument of assassination.[4] The Egyptian impostor, also mentioned by the sacred historian, is noticed by Josephus, who says that he was at the head of 30,000 men, though St. Luke notices only 4000; but both accounts are reconciled by supposing that the impostor (who in the second year of Nero pretended to be a prophet) led out 4000

---

1 He was a native of Gamala, in the province of Gaulonitis.

2 Josephus, Ant. Jud. lib. xviii. c. 1. §§ 1. 6. lib. xx. c. 5. § 2. De Bell. Jud. lib. ii. c. 17. §§ 7—9. lib. vii. c. 8. § 1. The Theudas mentioned in Acts v. 36. must not be confounded with the Theudas or Judas referred to by Josephus. (Ant. lib. xx. c. 5. § 1.) Theudas was a very common name among the Jews; and the person mentioned by the sacred historian was probably one of the many leaders who took up arms in defence of the public liberties, at the time of Cyrenius's enrolment, at least seven, if not ten, years before the speech delivered by Gamaliel. (Acts v. 34—40.) He seems to have been supported by smaller numbers than the second of that name, and (as the second afterwards did) perished in the attempt; but as his followers were dispersed, and not slaughtered, like those of the second Judas, survivors might talk much of him, and Gamaliel might have been particularly informed of his history, though Josephus only mentions it in general terms. See Dr. Lardner's Credibility, part i. book ii. ch. vii. (Works, vol. i. pp. 405—413.) Dr. Doddridge on Acts v. 36.

3 Apparatus Biblicus, vol. i. p. 239.

4 Josephus, Ant. Jud. lib. xx. c. 8. § 10.

from Jerusalem, who were afterwards joined by others to the amount of 30,000, as related by Josephus. They were attacked and dispersed by the Roman procurator Felix.[1]

---

§ 2. ON THE EXTREME CORRUPTION OF THE JEWISH PEOPLE, BOTH IN RELIGION AND MORALS, AT THE TIME OF CHRIST'S BIRTH.

General Corruption of the Leaders of the Jewish Nation — of their Chief Priests, and other Ministers of Religion — its deplorable Effects on the People. — State of the Jews not resident in Palestine.

The preceding chapters[2] will have shown that the political state of the Jews was truly deplorable. Although they were oppressed and fleeced by various governors, who exercised the most rigorous authority over them, in many instances with peculiar avarice, cruelty, and extortion, yet they were in some measure governed by their own laws, and were permitted to enjoy their religion. The administration of their sacred rites continued to be committed to the high priest and the Sanhedrin; to the former the priests and Levites were subordinate as before: and the form of their external worship, except in a very few points, had suffered no visible change. But, whatever comforts were left to them by the Roman magistrates, they were not allowed to enjoy them by their chief priests and popular leaders, whom Josephus characterises as profligate wretches, who had purchased their places by bribes or by acts of iniquity, and maintained their ill-acquired authority by the most flagitious and abominable crimes. Nor were the religious creeds of these men more pure: having espoused the principles of various sects, they suffered themselves to be led away by all the prejudice and animosity of party (though, as in the case of our Saviour, they would sometimes abandon them to promote some favourite measure); and were commonly more intent on the gratification of private enmity, than studious of advancing the cause of religion, or promoting the public welfare. The subordinate and inferior members were infected with the corruption of the head; the priests, and the other ministers of religion, were become dissolute and abandoned in the highest degree; while the common people, instigated by examples so depraved, rushed headlong into every kind of iniquity, and by their incessant seditions, robberies, and extortions, armed against themselves both the justice of God and the vengeance of men.

Owing to these various causes, the great mass of the Jewish people were sunk into the most deplorable ignorance of God and of divine things. Hence proceeded that dissoluteness of manners and that profligate wickedness which prevailed among the Jews during Christ's ministry upon earth; in allusion to which the divine Saviour compares the people to a multitude of lost sheep, straying without a shepherd (Matt. x. 6. xv. 24.), and their teachers, or doctors, to blind guides, who professed to instruct others in a way with which they were totally unacquainted themselves.[3] (Matt. xv. 14. John ix. 39, 40.)

---

[1] Josephus, Ant. Jud. lib. xx. c. 8. § 6.   De Bell. Jud. lib. ii. c. 13, § 5.   Dr. Lardner's Credibility, part i. book ii. ch. viii. (Works, vol. i. pp. 414—419.)

[2] See particularly pp. 107—115. of the present volume.

[3] Mosheim's Eccl. Hist. book i. part i. chap. ii., and also his Commentaries on the

More particularly, in the New Testament [1], "the Jews are described as a most superstitious and bigotted people, attached to the Mosaic ritual and to the whimsical traditions of their elders, with a zeal and fanaticism approaching to madness.   They are represented as a nation of hypocrites, assuming the most sanctimonious appearance before the world, at the corners of crowded streets uttering loud and fervent strains of rapturous devotion, merely to attract the eyes of a weak and credulous multitude, and to be noticed and venerated by them as mirrors of mortification and heavenly-mindedness; devoured with ostentation and spiritual pride; causing a trumpeter to walk before them in the streets, and make proclamation that such a rabbi was going to distribute his alms; publicly displaying all this showy parade of piety and charity, yet privately guilty of the most unfeeling cruelty and oppression; devouring widows' houses, stripping the helpless widow and friendless orphan of their property, and exposing them to all the rigours of hunger and nakedness; clamouring, *The temple of the Lord! The temple of the Lord!* making conscience of paying tithe of mint, anise, and cummin, to the support of its splendour and priesthood, but in practical life violating and trampling upon the first duties of morality, — justice, fidelity, and mercy, — as being vulgar and heathenish attainments, and infinitely below the regard of exalted saints and spiritual perfectionists.   Their great men were to an incredible degree depraved in their morals, many of them Sadducees in principle, and in practice the most profligate sensualists and debauchees; their atrocious and abandoned wickedness, as Josephus testifies [2], transcended all the enormities which the most corrupt age of the world had ever beheld; they compassed sea and land to make proselytes to Judaism from the Pagans, and, when they had gained these converts, soon rendered them, by their immoral lives and scandalous examples, more depraved and profligate than ever they were before their conversion. The Apostle tells them, that by reason of their notorious vices their religion was become the object of calumny and satire among the heathen nations.   *The name of God is blasphemed among the Gentiles through you!* [3] (Rom. ii. 24.)   And in his Epistle to Titus, he informs us that the Jews in speculation, indeed, acknowledged a God, but in practice they were atheists; for in their lives they were abominably immoral and abandoned, and the contemptuous despisers of every thing that was virtuous.   *They profess that they know God, but in works they deny him, being abominable and disobedient, and unto every good work reprobate.* (Titus i. 16.)   This testimony to the religious and moral character of the Jewish people, by Jesus Christ and his apostles,

---

Affairs of Christians before the time of Constantine the Great, vol. i. introd. chap. ii. Pritii Introductio ad Lectionem Novi Testamenti, c. 35.   De summa Populi Judaici corruptione, tempore Christi, pp. 471—473.

[1] For the following picture of the melancholy corruption of the Jewish church and people, the author is indebted to Dr. Harwood's Introduction to the New Testament. (vol. ii. pp. 58. 61.)

[2] Josephus, Bell. Jud. lib. vii. p. 1314. Hudson.   Again, says this historian, " They were universally corrupt, both publicly and privately.   They vied which should surpass each other in impiety against God and injustice towards men."   Ibid.

[3] The superstitious credulity of a Jew was proverbial among the heathens.   Credat Judæus Apella. Horat.   Epictetus mentions and exposes their greater attachment to their ceremonies than to the duties of morality.   Dissertationes, lib. i. p. 115. edit. Upton.   See also Josephus contra Apion. p. 480.   Havercamp.

is amply corroborated by Josephus, who has given us a true estimate of their principles and manners, and is also confirmed by other contemporary historians.[1] The circumstance of their nation having been favoured with an explicit revelation from the Deity, instead of enlarging their minds, miserably contracted and soured them with all the bitterness and leaven of theological odium. They regarded uncircumcised heathens with sovereign contempt[2], and believed them to be hated by God, merely because they were born aliens from the commonwealth of Israel, and lived strangers to their covenant of promise. They would not eat with them (Acts xi. 3.), do the least friendly office for them, or maintain any social correspondence and mutual intercourse with them. The Apostle comprises their national character in a few words, and it is a just one: *They were contrary to all men.*[3] (1 Thess. ii. 15.) The supercilious insolence, with which the mean and selfish notion of their being the only favourites of heaven and enlightened by God inflated them as a people, and the haughty and scornful disdain in which they held the heathens, are in a very striking manner characterised in the following spirited address of St. Paul to them: — *Behold! thou art called a Jew, and restest in the law, and makest thy boast of God: and knowest his will, and approvest the things that are more excellent, being instructed out of the law, and art confident that thou thyself art a guide of the blind, a light of them which are in darkness, an instructor of the foolish, a teacher of babes, which hast the form of knowledge and of the truth in the law.* (Rom. ii. 17—20.) This passage exhibits to us a faithful picture of the national character of this people, and shows us how much they valued themselves upon their wisdom and superior knowledge of religion, arrogating to themselves the character of lights and guides, and instructors of the whole world, and contemptuously regarding all the heathen as blind, as babes, and as fools.

" Another ever memorable instance of the national pride and arrogance of this vain and ostentatious people is, that when our Lord was discoursing to them concerning their pretensions to moral liberty, and representing the ignoble and despicable bondage in which sin detains its votaries, they imagined this to be an indirect allusion to

---

[1] " I cannot forbear," says Josephus, " declaring my opinion, though the declaration fills me with great emotion and regret, that if the Romans had delayed to come against these wretches, the city would either have been ingulfed by an earthquake, overwhelmed by a deluge, or destroyed by fire from heaven, as Sodom was: for that generation was far more enormously wicked than those who suffered these calamities." Bell. Jud. lib. v. c. 13. p. 1256. " These things they suffered," says Origen, " as being the most abandoned of men." Origen contra Celsum, p. 62. Cantab. 1677.

[2] " The Jews are the only people who refuse all friendly intercourse with every other nation, and esteem all mankind as enemies." Diod. Siculus, tom. ii. p. 524. edit. Wesseling, Amstel. 1746. " Let him be to thee as an heathen man and a publican." (Matt. xviii. 17.) Of the extreme detestation and abhorrence which the Jews had for the Gentiles we have a very striking example in that speech which St. Paul addresses to them, telling them in the course of it, that God had commissioned him to go to the Gentiles. The moment he had pronounced the word, the whole assembly was in confusion, tore off their clothes, rent the air with their cries, threw clouds of dust into it, and were transported into the last excesses of rage and madness. " He said unto me, Depart, for I will send thee far hence unto the Gentiles: they gave him audience," says the sacred historian, " until this word, and then lifted up their voice and said, Away with such a fellow from the earth ; for it is not fit that he should live." (Acts xxii. 21.)

[3] This character of the Jewish nation is confirmed by Tacitus, and expressed almost in the very words of the Apostle, " Adversus omnes alios hostile odium." Tacit. Hist. lib. v. § 5. vol. iii. p. 261. edit. Bipont.

the present condition of their country: their pride was instantly in flames; and they had the effrontery and impudence openly to assert, that they had always been free, and were never in bondage to any man (John viii. 33.); though every child must know the history of their captivities, must know that Judæa was at that very time a conquered province, had been subdued by Pompey, and from that time had paid an annual tribute to Rome. Another characteristic which distinguishes and marks this people, was that kind of evidence which they expected in order to their reception of truth. *Except they saw signs and wonders they would not believe!* (John iv. 48.) If a doctrine proposed to their acceptance was not confirmed by some visible displays of preternatural power, some striking phenomena, the clear and indubitable evidences of an immediate divine interposition, they would reject it. In antient times, for a series of many years, this people had been favoured with numerous signal manifestations from heaven: a cloud had conducted them by day, and a pillar of fire by night; their law was given them accompanied by a peculiar display of solemn pomp and magnificence; and the glory of God had repeatedly filled their temple. Habituated as their understandings had been, for many ages, to receive as truth only what should be attested and ratified by signs from heaven, and by some grand and striking phenomena in the sky, it was natural for them, long accustomed as they had been to this kind of evidence, to ask our Saviour to give them some *sign from heaven* (Matt. xvi. 1.), to exhibit before them some amazing and stupendous prodigy in the air to convince them of the dignity and divinity of his character. *The Jews*, says St. Paul, *require a sign* (1 Cor. i. 22.); it was that species of evidence to which their nation had been accustomed. Thus we read that the Scribes and Pharisees came to John, desiring him that he would show them a sign from heaven. Again, we read that the Jews came and said to Jesus, *What sign showest thou unto us, seeing that thou dost these things? Jesus answered and said unto them, Destroy this temple, and in three days I will raise it up!* (John ii. 18, 19.) What kind of signs these were which they expected, and what sort of preternatural prodigies they wanted him to display in order to authenticate his divine mission to them, appears from the following passages: *They said, therefore, unto him, What sign showest thou then, that we may see and believe thee? What dost thou work? Our fathers did eat manna in the desert; as it is written, He gave them bread from heaven!* (John vi. 30, 31.) This method, therefore, of espousing religious doctrines, only as they should be confirmed by some signal and indubitable interposition of the Deity, and their cherishing the vanity and presumption that heaven would lavish its miraculous signs whenever they called for them, constitute a striking and very distinguishing feature in the national character of this people."

So exceedingly great was the fecundity of the Jewish people, that multitudes of them had occasionally been constrained to emigrate from their native country; hence, at the time of our Saviour's birth, there was scarcely a province in the Roman empire in which they were not to be found, either serving in the army, engaged in the pursuits of commerce, or exercising some lucrative arts. They were maintained, in foreign countries, against injurious treatment and violence, by various special edicts of the emperors and magistrates in their favour[1]; though from the peculiarities of their religion and manners, they were held in very general contempt, and were not un-frequently exposed to much vexation and annoyance, from the jealousy and indignation of an ignorant and superstitious populace. Many of them, in consequence of their long residence and intercourse with foreign nations, fell into the error of endeavouring to make their religion accommodate itself to the principles and institutions of some of the different systems of heathen discipline: but, on the other hand, it is clear that the Jews brought many of those among whom they resided to perceive the superiority of the Mosaic religion over the Gentile superstitions, and were highly instrumental in causing them to forsake the worship of a plurality of gods. Although the knowledge which the Gentiles thus acquired from the Jews respecting the only true God, the Creator and Governor of the universe, was, doubtless, both partial and limited, yet it inclined many of them the more readily to listen to the subsequent arguments and exhortations of the apostles of our Saviour, for the purpose of exploding the worship of false deities, and recalling men to the knowledge of true religion. All which, Mosheim observes, with equal truth and piety, appears to have been most singularly and wisely directed by the adorable hand of an interposing Providence: to the end that this people, who were the sole depository of the true religion and of the knowledge of the one supreme God, being spread abroad through the whole earth, might be every where, by their example, a reproach to superstition, contribute in some measure to check it, and thus prepare the way for that fuller display of divine truth which was to shine upon the world from the ministry and Gospel of the Son of God.[2]

---

[1] In proof of this observation, Mosheim refers to Jacobi Gronovii Decreta Romana et Asiatica pro Judæis ad cultum divinum per Asiæ Minoris urbes securè obeundum. Lugd. Bat. 1712. 8vo. See also Dr. Lardner's Credibility, part i. book i. ch. 8. (Works, vol. i. pp. 164—201.) where numerous valuable testimonies are adduced.

[2] Mosheim's Commentaries, vol. i. p. 106. Eccl. Hist. vol. i. p. 52. edit. 1806. Besides the authorities cited in the preceding chapter, the Jewish sects, &c. are largely dis-cussed by Prideaux, Connection, book v. vol. ii. pp. 335—368. Relandi Antiq. Sacr. Hebræorum, pp. 276. *et seq.* Ikenius, Antiq. Hebr. pp. 33—42. Schachtii Dictata in Ikenium, pp. 241. *et seq.* Dr. Macknight's Harmony, vol. i. disc. 1. Lamy's Apparatus Biblicus, vol. i. pp. 225—243. Dr. Lardner's Credibility, part i. book i. ch. 4. Leus-den's Philologus Hebræo-Mixtus, pp. 138—170. Buddei Hist. Philosophiæ Hebræorum, pp. 86. *et seq.*

PART IV.

DOMESTIC ANTIQUITIES

OF THE JEWS, AND OF OTHER NATIONS INCIDENTALLY MEN-
TIONED IN THE SCRIPTURES.

CHAPTER I.

ON THE DWELLINGS OF THE JEWS.

I. *Caves.* — II. *Tents.* — III. *Houses—their Arrangement—Materials— and
Conveniences.* — IV. *Furniture.* — V. *Cities, Markets, and Gates.*

I. AS men, in the primitive condition of society, were unacquainted
with the arts, they, of course, were not able to build themselves houses;
they abode, therefore, necessarily under the shade of trees. It is
probable that when mankind began to multiply on the earth, they
dwelt in CAVES, many of which, in the Holy Land, are both capacious
and dry, and still afford occasional shelter to the wandering shepherds
and their flocks. Thus, Lot and his daughters abode in a cave, after
the destruction of Sodom. (Gen. xix. 30.) Antient historians [1] contain many notices of troglodytes, or dwellers in caves, and modern
travellers have met with them in Barbary and Egypt, as well as in
various other parts of the East.[2] The Horites, who dwelt on Mount
Seir, the Zamzummim, and the Emims or Anakim, are supposed to
have resided in caves.

II. In succeeding ages, they abode generally in TENTS, as the
Arabs of the Desert do to this day. The invention of these is ascribed
to Jabal the son of Lamech, who is, therefore, termed the *father of
such as dwell in tents.* (Gen. iv. 20.) The patriarchs pitched their
tents where they pleased, and, it should seem, under the shade of
trees whenever this was practicable. Thus, Abraham's tent was
pitched under a tree in the plains of Mamre (Gen. xviii. 4.), and
Deborah the prophetess dwelt under a palm tree between Ramah and
Bethel, in Mount Ephraim. (Judg. iv. 5.) In the East, to this day, it
is the custom in many places to plant about and among their buildings
trees, which grow both high and broad, and afford a cooling and refreshing shade. It appears from 1 Kings iv. 25. that this practice
antiently obtained in Judæa, and that vines and fig-trees were com-

---

[1] Herodotus, lib. iii. c. 74. Diod. Sic. lib. iii. c. 31. Quintus Curtius, lib. v. c. 6.
Josephus, Ant. Jud. lib. xv. c. 4. § 1.

[2] The inhabitants of Anab, a town on the east of the river Jordan, (lat. 32. long. 35. E.)
all live in grottoes or caves excavated in the rock. Buckingham's Travels among the Arab
Tribes, p. 61.

monly used for this purpose.   These trees furnished two great articles
of food for their consumption, and the cuttings of their vines would be
useful to them for fuel.   The tents of the emirs and sovereigns of the
East are both large and magnificent, and furnished with costly hangings.   Those of the Turcomans are said to be black [1]; and those of
the Turks green: but, according to D'Arvieux, Dr. Shaw, and M.
Volney, the tents of the Bedouins, or Arabs of the Desert, are universally *black* [2], or of a very *dusky brown*.   To these the bride in the
Canticles compares herself (i. 5.)—*I am black* (or, *tawney*) *as the tents
of Kedar*, but *comely*, or *beautiful* as the curtains of Solomon.   In the
East, those who lead a pastoral life frequently sit (as Abraham did) in
the tent-door in the heat of the day. (Gen. xviii. 1.)   The Arabian
tents are of an oblong figure, supported according to their size, some
with one pillar, others with two or three, while a curtain or carpet,
occasionally let down from each of these divisions, converts the whole
into so many separate apartments.   These tents are kept firm and
steady, by bracing or stretching down their eaves with cords, tied to
hooked wooden pins, well pointed, which they drive into the ground
with a mallet: one of these pins answering to the nail, as the mallet
does to the hammer, which Jael used in fastening the temples of
Sisera to the ground. (Judg. iv. 21.)   In these dwellings the Arabian
shepherds and their families repose upon the bare ground, or with
only a mat or carpet beneath them.   Those who are married have
each of them a portion of the tent to themselves separated by a
curtain. [3]   The more opulent Arabs, however, always have two tents,
one for themselves, and another for their wives, besides others for
their servants; in like manner, a particular tent was allotted to Sarah.

---

[1] Emerson's Letters from the Ægean, vol. i. p. 192.

[2] From Hit, a town on the banks of the Euphrates, to Hillah, the site of antient Babylon,
" the *black tent* of the Bedouin, formed of strong cloth made of goat's hair and wool mixed,
supported by low poles, is almost the only kind of habitation met with." (Capt. Chesney's
Reports on the Navigation of the Euphrates, p. 3. London, 1833. folio.)   The Illyauts, a
wandering tribe of Arabs, have *black* tents. (Hon. Capt. Keppel's Narrative of Travels
from India to England, vol. i. p. 100.)

[3] Shaw's Travels, vol. i. pp. 398, 399.   The description given by the intelligent traveller
Mr. Buckingham of the tent of the Sheik of Barak, who was at the head of a tribe of Turcomans, wandering in the vicinity of Aleppo, will enable us to form some idea of the shape
and arrangement of the tent of the patriarch, Abraham.   " The tent occupied a space of
about thirty feet square, and was formed by one large awning, supported by twenty-four
small poles in four rows of six each, the ends of the awning being drawn out by cords fastened
to pegs in the ground.   Each of these poles giving a pointed form to the part of the awning,
which it supported, the outside looked like a number of umbrella tops, or small Chinese
spires.   The half of this square was open in front and at the sides, having two rows of poles
clear, and the third was closed by a reeded partition, behind which was the apartment for
females, surrounded entirely by the same kind of matting."......" When the three angels are
said to have appeared in the plains of Mamre, he is represented as sitting in the tent-door in
the heat of the day." (Gen. xviii. 1—10.)   " ' And when he saw them, he ran to meet
them from the tent-door, and bowed himself towards the ground....And Abraham hastened
into the tent unto Sarah, and said, Make ready quickly three measures of fine meal, knead it,
and make cakes upon the hearth.   And he took butter, and milk, and the calf which he had
dressed, and set it before them, and *he stood 'by them*, under the tree, and they did eat.'
When inquiry was made after his wife, he replied, ' Behold she is *in* the tent.'   And when
it was promised him that Sarah should have a son, it is said, ' And Sarah heard in the tent-
door which was *behind* him.'......The form of Abraham's tent, as thus described, seems to
have been exactly like the one in which we sit : for in both there was a shaded open front
in which he could sit in the heat of the day, and yet be seen from afar off; and the apartment of the females, where Sarah was, when he stated her to be within the tent, was immediately *behind* this, wherein she prepared the meal for the guests, and from whence she
listened to their prophetic declaration." Travels in Mesopotamia, vol. i. pp. 30. 33, 34.

(Gen. xxiv. 67.) When travelling, they were careful to pitch their tents near some river, fountain, or well. (1 Sam. xxix. 1. xxx. 21.) In countries subject to violent tempests as well as to intolerable heat, a portable tent is a necessary part of a traveller's baggage, both for defence and shelter. To this the prophet Isaiah appears to allude. (iv. 6.) [1]

III. In progress of time men erected HOUSES for their habitations: those of the rich were formed of stone or bricks, but the dwellings of the poor were formed of wood, or more frequently of mud, as they are to this day in the East Indies [2]; which material is but ill calculated to resist the effects of the impetuous torrents, that descended from the mountains of Palestine.[3] Our Lord alludes to this circumstance at the close of his sermon on the mount. (Matt. vii. 26, 27.) In the Indies, also, nothing is more common than for thieves to dig or break through these mud walls, while the unsuspecting inhabitants are overcome by sleep, and to plunder them.[4] To similar depredations Jesus Christ appears to allude, when he exhorts his disciples not to lay up their treasure where *thieves* BREAK THROUGH *and steal.* (Matt. vi. 19, 20.) Job also seems to refer to the same practice. (xxiv. 16.) In the holes and chinks of these walls serpents sometimes concealed themselves. (Amos v. 19.) In Egypt, it appears from Exod. v. 7. that straw antiently entered into the composition of bricks; and some expositors have imagined that it was used (as with us) merely for burning them; but this notion is unfounded. The Egyptian bricks were a mixture of clay, mud, and straw, slightly blended and kneaded together, and afterwards baked in the sun. Philo, in his life of Moses, says, that they used straw to bind their bricks.[5] The straw still preserves its original colour, and is a proof that these bricks were never burnt in stacks or kilns.[6] Part of the bricks of the celebrated

---

1 Bp. Lowth on Isaiah iv. 6.   Pareau, Antiq. Hebr. pp. 353—356.   Bruning, Antiq. Hebr. p. 273.   Jahn et Ackermann, Archæol. Biblica, §§ 26—31.

2 In Bengal and Ceylon, as well as in Egypt, houses are constructed with this frail material.   Dr. Davy's Account of the Interior of Ceylon, p. 256.   See also Harmer's Observations, vol. i. pp. 265. 285.   The houses at Mousul "are mostly constructed of small unhewn stones, cemented by mortar, and plastered over with mud, though some are built of burnt and unburnt bricks."   Buckingham's Travels in Mesopotamia, vol. ii. p. 28.

3 See instances of the frailty of these tenements in Dr. Shaw's Travels, vol. i. p. 250. ; Belzoni's Researches in Egypt, p. 299. ; Ward's View of the History, &c. of the Hindoos, vol. ii. p. 335. ; and Roberts's Oriental Illustrations, p. 538.

4 Ward's History, &c. of the Hindoos, vol. ii. p. 325.   Roberts's Oriental Illustrations, p. 284, 285.

5 Philonis Opera, tom. ii. p. 86. (edit. Mangey.)

6 Shaw's Travels, vol. i. p. 250.   Mr. Belzoni, in his Researches in Egypt, found similar bricks in an antient arch which he discovered at Thebes, and which he has engraved among the plates illustrative of his Researches in Egypt, Nubia, &c.   Plate xliv. No. 2. In and near the ruins of the antient Tentyra, Dr. Richardson also found huts built of sun-dried brick, made of straw and clay. (Travels, vol. i. pp. 185. 259.)   They are thus described by the Rev. Mr. Jowett, as they appeared in February, 1819. — Speaking of the remains of antient buildings in that part of Egypt, he says, — " These magnificent edifices, while they display the grandeur of former times, exhibit no less the meanness of the present. This temple, built of massive stone, with a portico of twenty-four pillars, adorned with innumerable hieroglyphics, and painted with beautiful colours, the brightness of which in many parts remains to this day, is choked up with dusty earth.   Village after village, *built of unburnt brick*, crumbling into ruins, and giving place to new habitations, have raised the earth, in some parts, nearly to the level of the summit of the temple; and fragments of the walls of these mud huts appear, even on the roof of the temple.   In every part of Egypt, we find the towns built in this manner, upon the ruins, or rather the rubbish, of the former habitations.   The expression in Jeremiah xxx. 18. literally applies to Egypt, in the very

tower of Babel (or of Belus, as the Greeks termed it,) were made of clay mixed with chopped straw, or broken reeds, to compact it, and then dried in the sun. Their solidity is equal to that of the hardest stone.[1] Among the ruins discovered on the site of antient Nineveh, are houses, built of sun-dried bricks, cemented with mud; and similarly constructed dwellings were observed by Mr. Buckingham in the village of Karagoosh, near Mousul in Mesopotamia.[2] At this day the town of Busheher (or Bushire), like most of the towns in Persia, is built with sun-dried bricks and mud.[3] There is an allusion to this mode of building in Nahum iii. 14.

At first, houses were small; afterwards they were larger, especially in extensive cities, the capitals of empires. The art of multiplying stories in a building is very antient, as we may conclude from the construction of Noah's ark and the tower of Babel. The houses in Babylon, according to Herodotus[4], were three and four stories high; and those in Thebes or Diospolis[5], in Egypt, were four or five stories. In Palestine they appear to have been low, during the time of Joshua; an upper story, though it *may* have existed, is not mentioned till a more recent age. The houses of the rich and powerful in Palestine, in the time of Christ, were splendid, and were built according to the rules of Grecian architecture.[6]

Of all modern travellers, no one has so happily described the form and structure of the eastern buildings as Dr. Shaw, from whose account the following particulars are derived, which admirably elucidate several interesting passages of Holy Writ.

" The streets of the cities, the better to shade them from the sun, are usually narrow, sometimes with a range of shops on each side. If from these we enter into any of the principal houses, we shall first pass through a porch[7] or gateway, with benches on each side, where the master of the family receives visits, and despatches business; few persons, not even the nearest relations, having admission any farther, except upon extraordinary occasions. From hence we are received into the court, which lying open to the weather, is, according to the

---

meanest sense — *The city shall be builded upon her own heap;* and the expression in Job xv. 28. might be illustrated by many of these deserted hovels — *He dwelleth in desolate cities, and in houses which no man inhabiteth, which are ready to become heaps.* Still more touching is the allusion in Job iv. 19 ; where the perishing generations of men are fitly compared to habitations of the frailest materials built upon the heap of similar dwelling places, now reduced to rubbish — *How much less in them that dwell in houses of clay, whose foundation is in the dust !* " — (Jowett's Researches in the Mediterranean, pp. 131, 132.) — In one place, says the same intelligent traveller, " the people were making bricks, with straw cut into small pieces, and mingled with the clay to bind it. Hence it is, that, when villages built of these bricks fall into rubbish, which is often the case, the roads are full of small particles of straws extremely offensive to the eyes in a high wind. They were, in short, engaged exactly as the Israelites used to be, making bricks with straw ; and for a similar purpose — to build extensive granaries for the bashaw ; treasure-cities for Pharaoh." Exod. i. 11. (Ibid. p. 167.)

[1] Sir R. K. Porter's Travels in Georgia, Persia, Babylonia, &c. vol. ii. pp. 329, 330.
[2] Buckingham's Travels in Mesopotamia, vol. ii. p. 71.
[3] Price's Journal of the British Embassy to Persia, Part I. p. 6. Lond. 1825. folio.
[4] Herodot. lib. i. c. 180.　　　　　　　[5] Diod. Sic. lib. i. c. 45.
[6] Jahn et Ackermann, Archæol. Bibl. § 33.
[7] In Bengal, servants and others generally sleep in the verandah or porch, in front of their master's house. (Ward's History, &c. of the Hindoos, vol. ii. p. 323.) The Arab servants in Egypt do the same. (Wilson's Travels in Egypt and the Holy Land, p. 55.) In this way *Uriah slept at the door of the king's house, with all the servants of his lord.* (2 Sam. xi. 9.)

ability of the owner, paved with marble, or such proper materials, as will carry off the water into the common sewers." This court corresponded to the *cava ædium* or *impluvium* of the Romans; the use of which was to give light to the windows and carry off the rain. " When much people are to be admitted, as upon the celebration of a marriage, the circumcising of a child, or occasions of the like nature, the company is seldom or never admitted into one of the chambers. The court is the usual place of their reception, which is strewed accordingly with mats or carpets, for their more commodious entertainment. The stairs which lead to the roof are never placed on the outside of the house in the street, but usually at the gateway or passage room to the court; sometimes at the entrance within the court. This court is now called in Arabic *el woost*, or the middle of the house, literally answering to the το μεσον of St. Luke. (v. 19.) In this area our Saviour probably taught. In the summer season, and upon all occasions when a large company is to be received, the court is commonly sheltered from the heat and inclemencies of the weather by a vellum umbrella or veil, which, being expanded upon ropes from one side of the parallel wall to the other, may be folded or unfolded at pleasure. The Psalmist seems to allude either to the tents of the Bedouins, or to some covering of this kind, in that beautiful expression, *of spreading out the heavens like a veil or curtain.*" (Psal. civ. 2. See also Isaiah xl. 22.) [1] The arrangement of oriental houses satisfactorily explains the circumstances of the letting down of the paralytic into the presence of Jesus Christ, in order that he might heal him. (Mark ii. 4. Luke v. 19.) The paralytic was carried by some of his neighbours to the top of the house, either by forcing their way through the crowd by the gateway and passages up the staircase, or else by conveying him over some of the neighbouring terraces; and there, after they had drawn away the στεγην or awning, they let him down along the side of the roof through the opening or impluvium *into the midst* of the court *before Jesus.* Στεγη, Dr. Shaw remarks, may with propriety denote no less than *tatlilo* (the corresponding word in the Syriac version), any kind of covering; and, consequently, αποστεγαζειν may signify, the removal of such a covering. 'Εξορυξαντες is in the Vulgate Latin version rendered *patefacientes*, as if further explanatory of απεστεγασαν. The same in the Persian version is connected with κραββατον, and there implies making holes in it for the cords to pass through. That neither απεστεγασαν nor εξορυξαντες imply any force or violence offered to the roof, appears from the parallel passage in St. Luke; where, though δια των κεραμων καθηκαν αυτον, *per tegulas demiserunt illum*, is rendered by our translators, *they let him down through the tiling*, as if that had been previously broken up, it should be rendered, *they let him down over, along the side*, or *by the way of the roof*, as in Acts ix. 25. and 2 Cor. xi. 33., where the like phraseology is observed as in St. Luke: δια is rendered in both places *by*, that is, *along the side*, or *by the way of the wall.* 'Εξορυξαντες may express the plucking away or removing any obstacle, such as awning or part of a parapet, which might be in their way. Κεραμοι was first used for a roof of tiles, but afterwards came to signify any kind of roof. [2]

---

[1] Dr. Shaw's Travels in Barbary, &c. vol. i. pp. 374—376. 8vo. edition.
[2] Ibid. vol. i. pp. 382—384. Valpy's Gr. Test. on Mark ii. 4. " If the circumstances

The following diagram will perhaps give the reader a tolerably accurate idea of the arrangement of an eastern house.

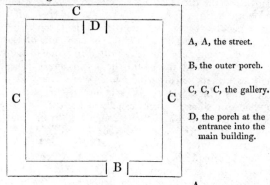

A, A, the street.

B, the outer porch.

C, C, C, the gallery.

D, the porch at the entrance into the main building.

Now, let it be supposed, that Jesus was sitting at D in the porch, at the entrance into the main building, and speaking to the people, when the four men carrying the paralytic came to the front gate or porch, B. Finding the court so crowded that they could not carry him in and lay him before Jesus, they carried him up the stairs at the porch to the top of the gallery, C, C, C, and along the gallery round to the place where Jesus was sitting, and forcing a passage by removing the balustrade, they lowered down the paralytic, with the couch on which he lay, into the court before Jesus. Thus we are enabled to understand the manner in which the paralytic was brought in and laid before the compassionate Redeemer.[1]

" The court is for the most part surrounded with a cloister, as the *cava ædium* of the Romans was with a peristylium or colonnade, over which, when the house has one or more stories (and they sometimes have two or three), there is a gallery erected of the same dimensions with the cloister, having a balustrade, or else a piece of carved or latticed work going round about it, to prevent people from falling from it into the court. From the cloisters and galleries we are conducted into large spacious chambers of the same length of the court, but seldom or never communicating with one another. One of them frequently serves a whole family, particularly when a father indulges his married children to live with him; or when several persons join in the rent of the same house. Hence it is that the cities of these countries, which are generally much inferior in size to those of Europe, are so

---

related by the evangelist had happened in India, nothing could be easier than the mode of letting down the paralytic. A plank or two might be started from the top balcony or viranda in the back court, where the congregation was probably assembled, and the man [be] let down in his hammock." Callaway's Oriental Observations, p. 71.

[1] Mr. Hartley has dissented from the interpretation above given by Dr. Shaw. " When I lived in Ægina" (he relates), " I used to look up not unfrequently above my head, and contemplate the facility with which the whole transaction might take place. The roof was constructed in this manner : — A layer of reeds, of a large species, was placed upon the rafters. On these a quantity of heather (heath) was strewed ; upon the heather earth was deposited, and beat down into a compact mass. Now what difficulty could there be in removing, first the earth, then the heather, next the reeds ? Nor would the difficulty be increased, if the earth had a pavement of tiling ($\kappa\epsilon\rho\alpha\mu\omega\nu$) laid upon it. No inconvenience could result to the persons in the house from the removal of the tiles and earth ; for the heather and reeds would intercept any thing which might otherwise fall down, and would be removed last of all." (Hartley's Researches in Greece, p. 240.)

exceedingly populous, that great numbers of the inhabitants are swept away by the plague, or any other contagious distemper. In houses of better fashion, these chambers, from the middle of the wall downwards, are covered and adorned with velvet or damask hangings, of white, blue, red, green, or other colours (Esth. i. 6.), suspended upon hooks, or taken down at pleasure.[1] But the upper part is embellished with more permanent ornaments, being adorned with the most ingenious wreathings and devices in stucco and fret-work. The ceiling is generally of wainscot, either very artfully painted, or else thrown into a variety of panels, with gilded mouldings and scrolls of their Koran intermixed. The prophet Jeremiah (xxii. 14.) exclaims against the eastern houses that were ceiled with cedar, and painted with vermilion. The floors are laid with painted tiles, or plaster of terrace. But as these people make little or no use of chairs (either sitting cross-legged or lying at length) they always cover and spread them over with carpets, which, for the most part, are of the richest materials. Along the sides of the wall or floor, a range of narrow beds or mattresses is often placed upon these carpets: and for their farther ease and convenience, several velvet or damask bolsters are placed upon these carpets or mattresses; indulgences which seem to be alluded to by *their stretching themselves upon couches,* and *by the sewing of pillows to the armholes,* as we have it expressed in Amos vi. 4. and Ezek. xiii. 18. At one end of the chamber there is a little gallery, raised three, four, or five feet above the floor, with a balustrade in the front of it, with a few steps likewise leading up to it. Here they place their beds; a situation frequently alluded to in the Holy Scriptures; which may likewise illustrate the circumstance of Hezekiah's *turning his face when he prayed towards the wall,* i. e. from his attendants (2 Kings xx. 2.), that the fervency of his devotion might be the less taken notice of and observed. The like is related of Ahab (1 Kings xxi. 4.), though probably not upon a religious account, but in order to conceal from his attendants the anguish he felt for his late disappointments. The stairs are sometimes placed in the porch, sometimes at the entrance into the court. When there is one or more stories, they are afterwards continued through one corner or other of the gallery to the top of the house, whither they conduct us through a door that is constantly kept shut to prevent their domestic animals from daubing the terrace, and thereby spoiling the water which falls from thence into the cisterns below the court. This door, like most others we meet with in these countries, is hung, not with hinges, but by having the jamb formed at each end into an axle-tree or pivot, whereof the uppermost, which is the longest, is to be received into a correspondent socket in the lintel, while the other falls into a cavity of the same fashion in the threshold."[2] Antiently, it was the custom to secure the door of a house, by a cross-bar or bolt, which by night was

---

[1] Similar costly hangings appear to have decorated the pavilion or state tent of Solomon, alluded to in Cant. i. 5.; the beauty and elegance of which would form a striking contrast to the black tents of the nomadic Arabs. The state tents of modern oriental sovereigns, it is well known, are very superb: of this gorgeous splendour, Mr. Harmer has given some instances from the travels of Egmont and Hayman. The tent of the Grand Seignior was covered and lined with silk. Nadir Shah had a very superb one, covered on the outside with scarlet broad cloth, and lined within with violet-coloured satin, ornamented with a great variety of animals, flowers, &c. formed entirely of pearls and precious stones. (Harmer on Sol. Song, p. 186.)

[2] Dr. Shaw's Travels in Barbary, vol. i. pp. 374—379.

fastened by a little button or pin: in the upper part of the door was left
a round hole, through which any person from without might thrust his
arm, and remove the bar, unless this additional security were superadded. To such a mode of fastening the bride alludes in Cant. v. 4.[1]

"The top of the house, which is always flat, is covered with a strong
plaster of terrace, whence in the Frank language it has obtained the
name of *the terrace*.[2] This is usually surrounded by two walls, the
outermost whereof is partly built over the street, and partly makes the
partition with the contiguous houses, being frequently so low that one
may easily climb over it. The other, which may be called the parapet
wall, hangs immediately over the court, being always breast high, and
answers to the מַעֲקֶה, or *lorica*, Deut. xxii. 8., which we render the
battlements. Instead of this parapet wall, some terraces are guarded,
like the galleries, with balustrades only, or latticed work; in which
fashion, probably, as the name seems to import, was the שְׂבָכָה, or net,
or lattice, as we render it, that Ahaziah (2 Kings i. 2.) might be carelessly leaning over, when he fell down from thence into the court.
For upon those terraces several offices of the family are performed,
such as the drying of linen and flax (Josh. ii. 6.), the preparing of figs
or raisins, where likewise they enjoy the cool refreshing breezes of the
evening, converse with one another, and offer up their devotions."[3]
At Tiberias, we are informed that the parapet is commonly made of
wicker-work and sometimes of green branches; which mode of con-
structing booths seems to be as antient as the days of Nehemiah, when
the people went forth, at the feast of tabernacles, *and brought branches
and made themselves booths, every one upon the top of his house.* (Neh.
viii. 16.)[4] "As these terraces are thus frequently used and trampled
upon, not to mention the solidity of the materials with which they are
made, they will not easily permit any vegetable substances to take root
or thrive upon them; which perhaps may illustrate the prophet Isaiah's
comparison of the Assyrians to *the grass upon the house-tops*. (Isaiah
xxxvii. 27.) When any of these cities are built upon level ground, one
may pass along the tops of houses from one end of them to the other,
without coming down into the street."[5] In the mountainous parts of
modern Palestine these terraces are composed of *earth*, spread evenly
on the roof of the house, and rolled hard and flat. On the top of
every house a large stone roller is kept, for the purpose of hardening
and flattening this layer of rude soil, to prevent the rain from pene-
trating; but upon this surface, as may be supposed, grass and weeds
grow freely. Similar terraces appear to have been antiently constructed in that country: it is to such grass that the Psalmist alludes
as useless and bad — *Let them be as the grass upon the house-tops, which*

---

[1] Bp. Percy's Translation of Solomon's Song, p. 76.

[2] On these terraces, the inhabitants of the East sleep, in the open air, during the hot
season. See instances, illustrating various passages of the Scriptures, in the Travels of Ali
Bey, vol. ii. p. 293. Mr. Kinneir's Travels in Armenia, &c. p. 134. Mr. Morier's
Second Journey in Persia, p. 230., where a wood-cut is given explanatory of this practice;
and Mr. Ward's History, &c. of the Hindoos, vol. ii. p. 323.

[3] Thus we read that Samuel communed with Saul upon the house-top (1 Sam. ix. 25.);
David walked upon the roof of the king's house (2 Sam. xi. 2.); and Peter went up upon
the house-top to pray. (Acts x. 9.)

[4] Madden's Travels in Turkey, Egypt, &c. vol. ii. p. 314.

[5] This is particularly the case at Aleppo. Irby's and Mangles' Travels, p. 238. Shaw's
Travels, vol. i. pp. 380, 381. Mr. Lane has given a description of a modern Egyptian
house, which corresponds in all material points with that above given. Manners and Customs of the Modern Egyptians, vol. i. pp. 7. &c. London, 1836. 8vo.

withereth afore it groweth up. (Psal. cxxix. 6.) These low and flat-roofed houses afford opportunities to speak to many *on* the house as well as to many in the court-yard below : this circumstance will illustrate the meaning of our Lord's command to his apostles, *What ye hear in the ear,* that *preach ye* upon the *house-tops.* (Matt. x. 27.)[1] On these terraces incense was antiently burnt (Jer. xix. 13. xxxii. 29.), and the host of heaven was worshipped. (Zeph. i. 5.)

In Barbary, the hills and vallies in the vicinity of Algiers are beautified with numerous country seats and gardens, whither the opulent resort during the intense heats of summer. In all probability, the summer-houses of the Jews, mentioned by the prophet Amos (iii. 15.), were of this description ; though these have been supposed to mean different apartments of the same house, the one exposed to a northern and the other to a southern aspect.

During the Rev. Mr. Jowett's residence at Haivali, in May, 1818, he relates that the house, in which he abode, gave him a correct idea of the scene of Eutychus's falling from the upper loft, while Paul was preaching at Troas. (Acts xx. 6—12.) " According to our idea of houses," he remarks, " the scene of Eutychus's falling from the upper loft is very far from intelligible ; and, besides this, the circumstance of preaching generally leaves on the mind of cursory readers the notion of a church. To describe this house, which is not many miles distant from the Troad, and perhaps, from the unchanging character of oriental customs, nearly resembles the houses then built, will fully illustrate the narrative.

" On entering my host's door, we find the ground floor entirely used as a store : it is filled with large barrels of oil, the produce of the rich country for many miles round : this space, so far from being habitable, is sometimes so dirty with the dripping of the oil, that it is difficult to pick out a clean footing from the door to the first step of the staircase. On ascending, we find the first floor, consisting of a humble suite of rooms, not very high : these are occupied by the family, for their daily use. It is on the next story that all their expense is lavished : here, my courteous host has appointed my lodging : beautiful curtains, and mats, and cushions to the divan, display the respect with which they mean to receive their guest : here, likewise, their splendour, being at the top of the house, is enjoyed, by the poor Greeks, with more retirement and less chance of molestation from the intrusion of Turks : here, when the Professors of the College waited upon me to pay their respects, they were received in ceremony and sat at the window. The room is both higher and also larger than those below : it has two projecting windows ; and the whole floor is so much extended in front beyond the lower part of the building, that the projecting windows considerably overhang the street. In such an upper room — secluded, spacious, and commodious — Paul was invited to preach his parting discourse. The divan, or raised seat, with mats or cushions, encircles the interior of each projecting window : and I have remarked, that when company is numerous, they sometimes place large cushions behind the company seated on the divan ; so that a second tier of company, with their feet upon the seat of the divan, are sitting behind, higher than the front row. Eutychus, thus sitting, would be on a

---

[1] Jowett's Christian Researches in Syria, &c. pp. 89. 95.

level with the open window; and, being overcome with sleep, he would easily fall out from the third loft of the house into the street, and be almost certain, from such a height, to lose his life. Thither St. Paul went down; and comforted the alarmed company, by bringing up Eutychus alive. It is noted, that *there were many lights in the upper chamber.* The very great plenty of oil in this neighbourhood would enable them to afford many lamps: the heat of these and so much company would cause the drowsiness of Eutychus at that late hour, and be the occasion, likewise, of the windows being open."[1]

In most houses, some place must have been appropriated to the preparation of food; but kitchens are for the first time mentioned in Ezek. xlvi. 23, 24. The hearth or fire-place appears to have been on the ground. Chimnies, such as are in use among us, were unknown to the Hebrews, even in the latest times of their polity. The smoke, therefore, escaped through large openings left for that purpose, which in our version of Hos. xiii. 3. are rendered by the equivalent term, chimnies.[2]

It was common, when any person had finished a house, and entered into it, to celebrate the event with great rejoicing, and to perform some religious ceremonies to obtain the divine blessing and protection. The dedication of a *newly-built* house was a ground of exemption from military service. (Deut. xx. 5.) The xxxth Psalm, as appears from the title, was composed on occasion of the *dedication of the house of David;* and this devout practice obtained also among the antient Romans.[3] In Deut. vi. 9. Moses directs the Israelites to write certain portions of his laws on the doors of their houses and the gates of their cities. This direction Michaelis understands not as a positive injunction, but merely an exhortation, to inscribe his laws on the door-posts of their houses. " In Syria and the adjacent countries, it is usual at this day to place inscriptions above the doors of the houses, consisting of passages from the Koran or from the best poets. Among us, where, by the aid of printing, books are so abundantly multiplied, and may be put into the hands of every child, such measures would be quite superfluous; but, if we would enter into the ideas of Moses, we must place ourselves in an age when the book of the law could only come into the hands of a few opulent people."[4]

IV. The FURNITURE of the oriental dwellings, at least in the earliest ages, was very simple: that of the poorer classes consisted of but few articles, and those such as were absolutely necessary. The interior of the more common and useful apartments was furnished with sets of large nails with square heads (like dice), and bent at the head so as to make them cramp-irons. In modern Palestine, the plan is to fix nails or pins of wood in the walls, while they are still soft, to suspend such domestic articles as are required; since, consisting altogether of clay, they are too frail to admit of the operation of the hammer.[5] To this custom there is an allusion in Ezra ix. 8. and Isa. xxii. 23. On these nails were hung their kitchen utensils or other articles. Instead of chairs they sat on mats or skins; and the same

---

[1] Jowett's Christian Researches in the Mediterranean, pp. 66, 67.
[2] Pareau, Antiquitas Hebraica, p. 363.   [3] Bruning, Antiq. Hebr. p. 309.
[4] Michaelis's Commentaries, vol. iii. pp. 371, 372.   In like manner, the antient Egyptians wrote the owner's name, and also a lucky sentence over the entrance of the house; and from these Mr. Wilkinson thinks it probable that the Jews derived the custom of dedicating their houses.   Manners, &c. of the Antient Egyptians, vol. ii. p. 124.
[5] Rae Wilson's Travels, vol. ii. p. 118. 3d edit.

articles, on which they laid a mattress, served them instead of bedsteads, while their upper garment served them for a covering, and sovereigns had chairs of state or thrones with foot-stools.[1] (Exod. xxii. 26, 27. Deut. xxiv. 12.)   This circumstance accounts for our Lord's commanding the paralytic to take up his bed and go unto his house. (Matt. ix. 6.)[2]   The more opulent had (as those in the East still have) fine carpets, couches, or divans, and sofas, on which they *sat*[3], lay, and slept. (2 Kings iv. 10.   2 Sam. xvii. 28.)   They have also a great variety of pillows and bolsters with which they support themselves when they wish to take their ease.   There is an allusion to them in Ezek. xiii. 18., in which verse the marginal rendering, *elbows*, is preferable to that in the text.   In later times their couches were splendid, and the frames inlaid with ivory (Amos vi. 4.), which is very plentiful in the east, and the coverlids rich and perfumed. (Prov. vii. 16, 17.)[4] On these sofas, in the latter ages of the Jewish state, (for before the time of Moses it appears to have been the custom to sit at table, Gen. xliii. 33.) they universally reclined, when taking their meals (Amos vi. 4. Luke vii. 36—38.) : resting on their side with their heads towards the table, so that their feet were accessible to one who came behind the couch, as in the annexed diagram : —

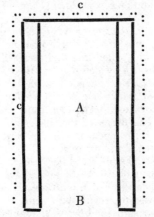

In which A denotes the table, and c, c, c, the couches on which the guests reclined.   B is the lower end, open for servants to enter and supply the guests.   The knowledge of this custom enables us to under-

---

[1] Bp. Lowth on Isa. lii. 2.

[2] " A mat and pillow form all the bed of the common people in the East ; and their rolling up the one in the other has often struck me as illustrating the command to *rise, take up thy bed, and walk*. (Luke v. 19. Mark ii. 4. 11.)   In Acts ix. 34. Peter said to Æneas, *Arise and spread* thy bed *for thyself*.   David's bed (1 Sam. xix. 15.) was probably the duan" (divan) " or raised bench with two quilts, one doubled and serving for a mattress, and the other as a covering.   It was probably not unlike a sailor's hammock, laid on the floor or bench." Callaway's Oriental Observations, p. 21.

[3] A passage in Jeremiah xiii. 22. may in some degree be explained by the oriental mode of sitting — *For the greatness of thine iniquity are thy skirts discovered, and thy heels made bare.*   " I have often been struck," says Mr. Jowett, " with the manner in which a great man sits ; for example, when I visited the bashaw, I never saw his feet : they were entirely drawn up under him, and covered by his dress. This was dignified. To see his feet his skirts must have been discovered : still more so, in order to see the heels, which often serve as the actual seat of an Oriental."   Jowett's Christian Researches in the Mediterranean, p. 169.

[4] Jahn et Ackermann, Archæologia Biblica, § 40.

stand the manner in which John leaned on the bosom of his Master
(John xiii. 23.), and Mary anointed the feet of Jesus, and wiped them
with her hair; and also the expression of Lazarus being carried into
Abraham's bosom (Luke xvi. 22.): that is, he was placed next to
Abraham at the splendid banquet, under the image of which the Jews
represented the happy state of the pious after death.[1]

Antiently, splendid hangings were used in the palaces of the eastern
monarchs, and ample draperies were suspended over the openings in
the sides of the apartments, for the two-fold purpose of affording air,
and of shielding them from the sun. Of this description were the
costly hangings of the Persian sovereigns mentioned in Esther i. 6.;
which passage is confirmed by the account given by Quintus Curtius
of their superb palace at Persepolis.

Other articles of necessary furniture were, at least in the more antient periods, both few and simple. The principal were a hand-mill,
with which they ground their corn, a kneeding-trough, and an oven.
The HAND-MILL resembled the *querns*, which, in early times, were in
general use in this country, and which still continue to be used in
some of the more remote northern islands of Scotland, as well as in
the East. So essential were these domestic utensils, that the Israelites
were forbidden to take them in pledge. (Deut. xxiv. 6.) The KNEAD-
ING-TROUGHS (at least those which the Israelites carried with them
out of Egypt, Exod. xii. 34.) were not the cumbersome articles now in
use among us, but comparatively small wooden bowls, like those of
the modern Arabs, who, after kneeding their flour in them, make
use of them as dishes out of which they eat their victuals. The OVEN
was sometimes only an earthen pot in which fire was put to heat it,
and on the outside of which the batter or dough was spread, and
and almost instantly baked. At other times, however, ovens must
have been built. The ovens of the modern Arabs are formed of
mortar in a conical form, open at the top, and the fire is kindled
inside, according to the literal expression of Scripture, *cast* INTO *the*
oven. (Matt. vi. 30.) Cakes of bread were also baked by being placed
within the oven. The modern Arabs work the dough by hand into a
thin cake, which is then thrown with a little violence against the side
of the oven, and allowed to remain there until it is sufficiently baked.[2]

Besides kneading-troughs and ovens, they must have had different
kinds of earthen-ware vessels, especially pots to hold water for their
various ablutions. While sitting upon the shattered wall which enclosed "the Well oᶠ Cana" in Galilee, in February, 1820, Mr. Rae
Wilson observed six females, having their faces veiled (Gen. xxiv. 66.
Cant. v. 7.), come down to the well, each carrying on her head a pot
(John ii. 6—10.), for the purpose of being filled with water: one of
whom lowered her pitcher into the well and offered him water to
drink, precisely in the same manner in which Rebekah, many centuries
before, had offered water to Abraham's servant. (Gen. xxiv. 18.)
These water-pots are formed of clay, hardened by the heat of the
sun, and are of a globular shape, large at the mouth, not unlike the
bottles used in our country for holding vitriol, but not so large. Many
of them have handles attached to the sides: and it was a wonderful
coincidence with Scripture that the vessels appeared to contain much

---

[1] Robinson's Greek Lexicon, voce Κολπος.
Hardy's Notices of the Holy Land, page 263.

about the same quantity as those which, the evangelist informs us, were employed on occasion of the marriage which was honoured by the Saviour's presence; namely, three firkins, or twelve gallons each.[1]   About twenty years before, the Rev. Dr. E. D. Clarke, while exploring the ruins of Cana in Galilee, saw several large massy stone water-pots, answering the description given of the antient vessels of the country (John ii. 6.); not preserved nor exhibited as relics, but lying about, disregarded by the present inhabitants as antiquities with whose original use they were acquainted.   From their appearance, and the number of them, it was quite evident that the practice of keeping water in large stone pots, each holding from eighteen to twenty-seven gallons, was once common in the country.[2]   In the later times of the Jewish polity, BASKETS formed a necessary article of furniture to the Jews; who, when travelling either among the Gentiles or the Samaritans, were accustomed to carry their provisions with them in κοφινοι, baskets, in order to avoid defilement by eating with strangers.[3] Large sacks are still, as they antiently were (John ix. 11. Gen. xliv. 1—3.), employed for carrying provisions and baggage of every description.[4]

The domestic utensils of the orientals are nearly always of brass; and to these they often refer as a sign of property. (See Ezek. xxvii. 13.)[5] Bowls, cups, and drinking vessels of gold and silver, it appears from Gen. xliv. 2. 5. and 1 Kings x. 21. were used in the courts of princes and great men; but the modern Arabs, as the Jewish people antiently did, keep their water, milk, wine, and other liquors, in BOTTLES made of skins, which are chiefly of a red colour (Exod. xxv. 5.) ; and their mouths are closed by slips of wood, that they may contain milk or other liquids. The Arabs use the skins of sheep or goats tanned with a caustic for this purpose: those of kids or lambs serve for milk, while the larger skins are used either for wine or water.[6] These bottles, when old, are frequently rent, but are capable of being repaired, by being bound up or pieced in various ways. Of this description were the *wine bottles of the Gibeonites, old and rent, and bound up*. (Josh. ix. 4.) As *new* wine was liable to ferment, and consequently would burst the old skins, all prudent persons would put it into new skins. To this usage our Lord alludes in Matt. ix. 17. Mark ii. 22. and Luke v. 37, 38. Bottles of skin, it is well known, are still in use in Spain, where they are called *Borrachas*.[7] As the Arabs make fires in their tents, which have no chimnies, they must be greatly incommoded by the smoke, which blackens all their utensils and taints their skins. David, when driven from the court of Saul, compares himself to a *bottle in the smoke*. (Psal. cxix. 83.) He must have felt acutely, when he was driven from the vessels of gold and silver in the palace of Saul, to live like an Arab, and drink out of a smoky leathern bottle. His language is, as if he had said, — " My present appearance is as different from what it was when I dwelt at court, as the furniture of a palace differs from that of a poor Arab's tent." Apartments were lighted by means of LAMPS, which were fed

---

[1] Rae Wilson's Travels in the Holy Land, &c. vol. ii. pp. 3, 4. 3d edition.
[2] Travels, vol. ii. p. 445.   [3] Kuinöel, on Matt. xiv. 19.
[4] Rae Wilson's Travels, vol. i. pp. 175, 176.
[5] Roberts's Oriental Illustrations, p. 497.
[6] Rae Wilson's Travels, vol. i. p. 176.   Lieut. Wellstead's Travels, vol. i. pp. 89, 90.
[7] Harmer's Observations, vol. i. p. 217.   See also vol. ii. pp. 135—138. for various remarks illustrative of the nature of the drinking vessels antiently in use among the Jews.

with olive oil, and were commonly placed upon elevated stands. (Matt. v. 15.) The *lamps* of Gideon's soldiers (Judg. vii. 16.), and those of the wise and foolish virgins (Matt. xxv. 1—10.), were of a different sort. They were a kind of torches or flambeaux made of iron or earthen-ware, wrapped about with old linen, moistened from time to time with oil.[1]

V. In progress of time, as men increased upon the earth, and found themselves less safe in their detached tents, they began to live in society, and fortified their simple dwellings by surrounding them with a ditch, and a rude breast-work, or wall, whence they could hurl stones against their enemies. Hence arose villages, towns, and CITIES, of which Cain is said to have been the first builder. In the time of Moses, the cities of the Canaanites were both numerous and strongly fortified. (Numb. xiii. 28.) In the time of David, when the number of the Israelites was greatly increased, their cities must have proportionably increased; and the vast population which (we have already seen) Palestine maintained in the time of the Romans is a proof both of the size and number of their cities. The principal strength of the cities in Palestine consisted in their situation : they were for the most part erected on mountains or other eminences which were difficult of access; and the weakest places were strengthened by fortifications and walls of extraordinary thickness.

The STREETS in the Asiatic cities do not exceed from two to four cubits in breadth, in order that the rays of the sun may be kept off; but it is evident that they must have formerly been wider, from the fact that carriages were driven through them, which are now very seldom, if ever, to be seen in the East. The houses, however, rarely stand together, and most of them have spacious gardens annexed to them. It is not to be supposed that the almost incredible tract of land, which Nineveh and Babylon are said to have covered, could have been filled with houses closely standing together: antient writers, indeed, testify that almost a third part of Babylon was occupied by fields and gardens.

In the early ages of the world the MARKETS were held at or near the Gates of the Cities, (which, we have already seen[2], were the seats of justice), generally within the walls, though sometimes without them. Here commodities were exposed to sale, either in the open air or in tents (2 Kings vii. 18. 2 Chron. xviii. 9. Job xxix. 7.) : but in the time of Christ, as we learn from Josephus, the markets were enclosed in the same manner as the modern eastern bazars, which are shut at night, and where the traders' shops are disposed in rows or streets; and (in large towns) the dealers in particular commodities are confined to particular streets.

The GATES of the Cities, and the vacant places next adjacent to them, must have been of considerable size; for we read that Ahab king of Israel assembled four hundred false prophets before himself and Jehoshaphat king of Judah, in the Gate of Samaria. (1 Kings xxii. 10.) And besides these prophets, we may readily conclude that each of these monarchs had numerous attendants in waiting. Over or by the side of many gates there were towers, in which watchmen were stationed to observe what was going on at a distance. (2 Sam. xviii. 24. 33.)[3]

---

[1] Jahn et Ackermann, Archæol. Bibl. § 40.   Calmet's Dictionary, voce Lamps.

[2] See p. 116. *suprà.*

[3] Bruning, Antiq. Hebr. pp. 279—281.   Calmet, Dissertations, tom. i. pp. 313—315. Jahn et Ackermann, Archæol. Bibl. § 41.   Pareau, Ant. Hebr. pp. 367—371.

CHAPTER II.

ON THE DRESS OF THE JEWS.[1]

I. *Dress in the early Ages.* — II. *Tunic.* — III. *Upper Garment.* — *Other Articles of Apparel.* — IV. *Coverings for the Head.* — *Mode of Dressing the Hair.* — V. *Sandals.*—VI. *Seals or Signets, and Rings.*—VII. *Some Articles of Female Apparel elucidated.* — *Complexion of the Women.* — VIII. *Rending of Garments, a Sign of Mourning.* — IX. *Numerous Changes of Apparel, deemed a necessary Part of their Treasure.*

I. IN the early ages, the dress of mankind was very simple. Skins of animals furnished the first materials (Gen. iii. 21. Heb. xi. 37.) [2], which, as men increased in numbers and civilisation, were exchanged for more costly articles, made of wool and flax, of which they manufactured woollen and linen garments (Lev. xiii. 47. Prov. xxxi. 13.) ; afterwards fine linen, and silk, dyed with purple, scarlet, and crimson, became the usual apparel of the more opulent. (2 Sam. i. 24. Prov. xxxi. 22. Luke xvi. 19.)   In the more early ages, garments of various colours were in great esteem: such was Joseph's robe, of which his envious brethren stripped him, when they resolved to sell him.[3] (Gen. xxxvii. 23.)   Robes of various colours were likewise appropriated to the virgin daughters of kings (2 Sam. xiii. 18.), who also wore richly embroidered vests. (Psal. xlv. 13, 14.)[4] It appears that the Jewish garments were worn pretty long ; for it is mentioned as an aggravation of the affront done to David's ambassadors by the king of Ammon, that he cut off their garments *in the middle, even to their buttocks.* (2 Sam. x. 4.)

The dress of the Jews, in the ordinary ranks of life, was simple and nearly uniform.   John the Baptist *had his raiment of camel's hair* (Matt. iii. 4.), — not of the fine hair of that animal which is wrought into camlets, (in imitation of which, though made of wool, is the English camlet,) but of the long and shaggy hair of camels, which in the East is manufactured into a coarse stuff like that antiently worn by monks and anchorets.[5]

It is evident, from the prohibition against changing the dresses of the two sexes, that in the time of Moses there was a difference between the garments worn respectively by men and women ; but in what that difference consisted it is now impossible to determine.   The fashion, too, of their apparel does not appear to have continued always the same ; for, before the first subversion of the Jewish monarchy by

---

[1] The principal authorities for this chapter are Calmet's Dissertation sur les Habits des Hebreux, Dissert. tom. i. pp. 337—371. ; and Pareau, Antiquitas Hebraica, pp. 371 —385.

[2] Mr. Rae Wilson met with some Arabs, residing near the (so called) village of Jeremiah, who were clothed in *sheep* and *goat skins*, open at the neck.   Travels in the Holy Land, &c. vol. i. p. 189. 3d. edition.

[3] A coat of many colours is as much esteemed in some parts of Palestine at this day as it was in the time of Jacob, and of Sisera.   Buckingham's Travels among the Arab Tribes, p. 31.   Emerson's Letters from the Ægean, vol. ii. p. 31.

[4] Jahn et Ackermann, §§ 118, 119.

[5] On this subject see Captain Light's Travels in Egypt, &c. p. 135. and Mr. Morier's Second Journey in Persia, p. 44.   Chardin assures us, that the modern Dervises wear garments of coarse camels' hair, and also great leathern girdles.   Harmer's Obs. vol. ii. p. 487.

Nebuchadnezzar, there were some who delighted to wear *strange* (that is, foreign) apparel. In every age, however, there were certain garments (as there still are in the East) which were common to both sexes, though their shape was somewhat different.

II. The simplest and most antient was the TUNIC, or inner garment, which was worn next the body. At first, it seems to have been a large linen cloth, which hung down to the knees, but which was afterwards better adapted to the form of the body, and was sometimes furnished with sleeves. The tunics of the women were larger than those worn by men. Ordinarily they were composed of two breadths of cloth sewed together; hence those which were woven whole, or without seam on the sides or shoulders, were greatly esteemed. Such was the tunic or coat of Jesus Christ mentioned in John xix. 23. A similar tunic was worn by the high priest.[1] This garment was fastened round the loins, whenever activity was required, by a girdle. (2 Kings iv. 29. John xxi. 7. Acts xii. 8.) The prophets and poorer class of people wore leathern girdles (2 Kings i. 8. Matt. iii. 4.), as is still the case in the East; but the girdles of the opulent, especially those worn by women of quality, were composed of more precious materials, and were more skilfully wrought. (Ezek. xvi. 10. Isa. iii. 24.) The girdles of the inhabitants of the East, Dr. Shaw informs us, are usually of worsted, very artfully woven into a variety of figures, such as the rich girdles of the virtuous virgins may be supposed to have been. (Prov. xxxi. 24.) They are made to fold several times about the body; one end of which being doubled back, and sewn along the edges, serves them for a purse, agreeably to the acceptation of ζωνη in the Scriptures (Matt. x. 9. Mark viii. 6. where it is rendered a purse). The Turks make a further use of these girdles, by fixing therein their knives and poniards : while the Hojias, *i. e.* the writers and secretaries, suspend in the same their inkhorns; a custom as old as the prophet Ezekiel, who mentions (ix. 2.) *a person clothed in white linen, with an inkhorn upon his loins.*[2]

III. Over the tunic was worn a larger vest, or UPPER GARMENT. It was a piece of cloth nearly square, like the hykes or blankets woven by the Barbary women, about six yards long, and five or six feet broad. The two corners, which were thrown over the shoulders, were called the *skirts*, literally, *the wings* of the garment. (1 Sam. xv. 11. xxiv. 4, 5. 11. Hag. ii. 12. Zech. viii. 23.) This garment serves the Kabyles or Arabs for a complete dress in the day; and as they sleep in their raiment (as the Israelites did of old, Deut. xxiv. 13.) it likewise serves them for their bed and covering in the night. " It is a loose, but troublesome kind of garment, being frequently disconcerted and falling to the ground, so that the person who wears it is every moment obliged to tuck it up, and fold it anew around his body. This shews the great use of a girdle whenever they are engaged in any active employment, and the force of the Scripture injunction alluding to it, of *having our loins girded*[3] in order to set

---

1 Josephus, Ant. Jud. lib. iii. c. 7. § 4.

2 Shaw's Travels, vol. i. pp. 409, 410. 8vo. edit.

3 In India, " when people take a journey, they always have their loins well girded, as they believe that they can walk much faster, and to a greater distance ...... When men are about to enter into an arduous undertaking, by-standers say, ' *Tie your loins well up.*' " (Luke xii. 35. ; Eph. vi. 4. ; 1 Pet. i. 13.) Roberts's Oriental Illustrations, p. 72.

about it. The method of wearing these garments, with the use to
which they are at other times put, in serving for coverlids to their
beds, leads us to infer that the finer sort of them (such as are worn
by the ladies and by persons of distinction), are the *peplus* of the antients. Ruth's veil, which held six measures of barley (Ruth iii. 15),
might be of the like fashion, and have served extraordinarily for the
same use; as were also the clothes (τα ιματια, the upper garments) of
the Israelites (Exod. xii. 34.), in which they folded up their kneading-
troughs: as the Moors, Arabs, and Kabyles do, to this day, things of
the like burden and incumbrance in their hykes. Instead of the *fibula*
that was used by the Romans, the Arabs join together with thread or
a wooden bodkin the two upper corners of this garment; and after
having placed them first over one of their shoulders, they then fold
the rest of it about their bodies. The outer fold serves them frequently instead of an apron, wherein they carry herbs, leaves, corn,
&c., and may illustrate several allusions made thereto in Scripture; as
gathering the lap full of wild gourds (2 Kings iv. 39.), rendering seven-
fold, *giving good measure into the bosom* (Psalm cxxix. 7. Luke vi. 38.),
and *shaking the lap.*" (Neh. v. 13.)[1] It was these ιματια, or upper
garments, which the Jewish populace strewed in the road during
Christ's triumphant progress to Jerusalem. (Matt. xxi. 8.) A person
divested of this garment, conformably to the Hebrew idiom, is said to
be *naked.* (2 Sam. vi. 20. John xxi. 7.) By the Mosaic constitution, in
Numb. xv. 37—40., the Israelites were enjoined to put fringes on the
borders of their upper garments, that they might *remember all the
commandments of the Lord to do them.* A similar exhortation is recorded in Deut. vi. 8. compared with Exod. xiii. 16. But in succeeding ages, these injunctions were abused to superstitious purposes; and
among the charges alleged against the Pharisees by Jesus Christ, is that
of enlarging their PHYLACTERIES, and the fringes of their garments
(Matt. xxiii. 5.), as indicating their pretensions to a more studious and
perfect observance of the law. These phylacteries consisted of four
strips or scrolls of parchment, or the dressed skin of some clean
animal, inscribed with four paragraphs of the law, taken from Exod.
xiii. 1—10. and xiii. 11—16. Deut. vi. 4—9. and xi. 13—21. all inclusive; which the Pharisees, interpreting literally (as do the modern
rabbins) Deut. vi. 8. and other similar passages, tied to the fronts of
their caps and on their arms, and also inscribed on their door-posts.
These phylacteries were regarded as amulets, or, at least, as efficacious in keeping off evil spirits, whence their Greek name Φυλακτηρια,
from φυλαττω, to guard or preserve. The practice of inscribing passages of the Koran upon the door-posts of their houses is said to be
still continued by the Mohammedans in Judæa and Syria.[2] The
κρασπεδον, *hem* or *border* of Christ's garment, out of which a healing
power issued to the diseased who touched it (Matt. ix. 20. xiv. 36.

---

[1] Shaw's Travels, vol. i. pp. 404—406.
[2] Calmet's Dictionary, voce *Phylacteries.* Robinson's Greek Lexicon, voce Φυλακτηρια.
Respecting the phylacteries of the modern Jews, Mr. Allen has collected much curious
information. Modern Judaism, pp. 304—318. In the Bibliotheca Sussexiana there is
a description of three Jewish phylacteries, which are preserved among the MSS. in the
library of his Royal Highness the Duke of Sussex. Bibl. Sussex, vol. i. part i. pp. xxxvi.
—xxxix.

Mark vi. 56. Luke viii. 44.), was the fringe which he wore, in obedience to the law.

The Χλαμυς, chlamys, or scarlet robe with which our Saviour was
arrayed in mock majesty (Matt. xxvii. 28. 31.), was a scarlet robe
worn by the Roman soldiers. The Στολη was a flowing robe reaching
to the feet, and worn by persons of distinction. (Mark xii. 38. xvi. 5.
Luke xv. 22. xx. 46. Rev. vi. 11. vii. 9. 13, 14.) The Σινδων was a
linen upper garment, worn by the Orientals in summer and by night,
instead of the usual ιματιον. (Mark xiv. 51, 52.) It was also used as
an envelope for dead bodies. (Matt. xxvii. 59. Mark xv. 46. Luke
xxiii. 53.) The Φαιλονη[1], or cloak (2 Tim. iv. 13.), was the same as
the *penula* of the Romans, viz. a travelling cloak with a hood to protect
the wearer against the weather.[2] The Σουδαριον, or handkerchief,
corresponded to the Καψιδρωτιον of the Greeks, and the *sudarium* of
the Romans, from whom it passed to the Chaldæans and Syrians
with greater latitude of signification, and was used to denote any
linen cloth. (John xi. 44. xx. 7. Acts xix. 12.) The Σιμικιντιον (semi-
cinctium), or apron, passed also from the Romans : it was made of
linen, surrounded half the body (Acts xix. 12.), and corresponded nearly
to the Περιζωμα of the Greeks.[3] Whenever the men journeyed, a staff
was a necessary accompaniment. (Gen. xxxii. 10. xxxviii. 18. Matt.
x. 10. Mark vi. 8.)

IV. Originally, men had no other COVERING FOR THE HEAD than
that which nature itself supplied, — the *hair*. Calmet is of opinion
that the Hebrews never wore any dress or covering on their heads :
David, when driven from Jerusalem (he urges), fled with his head
covered with his upper garment; and Absalom would not have been
suspended among the boughs of an oak by his hair, if he had worn a
covering. (2 Sam. xvi. 30. xviii. 9.) But may not these have been
particular cases? David went up the Mount of Olives, as a mourner
and a fugitive; and Absalom, fleeing in battle, might have lost his cap
or bonnet. It is certain, that the צָנִיף (tsaniph), or turban, was common both to men and women. (Job xxix. 14. Isa. iii. 23.)

Long hair was in great esteem among the Jews. The hair of
Absalom's head was of such prodigious length, that in his flight, when
defeated in battle, as he was riding with great speed under the trees,
it caught hold of one of the boughs; in consequence of which he was
lifted off his saddle, and his mule running from beneath him, left
him suspended in the air, unable to extricate himself. (2 Sam. xviii.
9.) The plucking off the hair was a great disgrace among the Jews;
and, therefore, Nehemiah punished in this manner those Jews who
had been guilty of irregular marriages, in order to put them to the
greater shame. (Neh. xiii. 25.) Baldness was also considered as a
disgrace. (2 Sam. xiv. 26. 2 Kings ii. 23. Isa. iii. 24.) On festive
occasions, the more opulent perfumed their hair with fragrant unguents.
(Psal. xxiii. 5. Eccl. ix. 8. Matt. vi. 17. xxvi. 7.) Among the antient
Egyptians it was customary for a servant to attend every guest as he
seated himself, and to anoint his head.[4] And it should seem, from
Cant. v. 11., that black hair was considered to be the most beautiful.

---

1 Robinson's Lexicon, vocibus.   2 Adam's Roman Antiquities, p. 386.
3 Valpy's Gr. Test. on Luke xix. 20. and Acts xix. 12.
4 Wilkinson's Manners, &c. of the Antient Egyptians, vol. ii. p. 213.

The Jews wore their beards very long, as we may see from the example of the ambassadors, whom David sent to the king of the Ammonites, and whom that ill-advised king caused to be shaved by way of affront. (2 Sam. x. 4.) And as the shaving of them was accounted a great indignity, so the cutting off half their beards, which made them still more ridiculous, was a great addition to the affront, in a country where beards were held in such great veneration.

In the East, especially among the Arabs and Turks, the beard is even now reckoned the greatest ornament of a man, and is not trimmed or shaven, except in cases of extreme grief: the hand is almost constantly employed in smoothing the beard and keeping it in order, and it is often perfumed as if it were sacred. Thus, we read of the fragrant oil, which ran down from Aaron's beard to the skirts of his garment. (Psal. cxxxiii. 2. Exod. xxx. 30.) [1] A shaven beard is reputed to be more unsightly than the loss of a nose; and a man who possesses a reverend beard is, in their opinion, incapable of acting dishonestly. If they wish to affirm any thing with peculiar solemnity, they swear by their beard; and when they express their good wishes for any one, they make use of the ensuing formula — *God preserve thy blessed beard!* From these instances, which serve to elucidate many other passages of the Bible besides that above quoted, we may readily understand the full extent of the disgrace wantonly inflicted by the Ammonitish king, in cutting off half the beards of David's ambassadors. Niebuhr relates, that if any one cut off his beard, after having recited a *fatha*, or prayer, which is considered in the nature of a vow never to cut it off, he is liable to be severely punished, and also to become the laughing-stock of those who profess his faith. The same traveller has also recorded an instance of a modern Arab prince having treated a Persian envoy in the same manner as Hanun treated David's ambassadors, which brought a powerful army upon him in the year 1765.[2] The not trimming of the beard was one of the indications by which the Jews expressed their mourning. (2 Sam. xix. 24.)

" All the Grecian and Roman women, without distinction, wore their hair long. On this they lavished all their art, disposing it in various forms, and embellishing it with divers ornaments. In the antient medals, statues, and basso-relievos, we behold those plaited tresses which the apostles Peter and Paul condemn, and see those expensive and fantastic decorations which the ladies of those times bestowed upon their head-dress. This pride of braided and plaited tresses, this ostentation of jewels, this vain display of finery, the apostles interdict, as proofs of a light and little mind, and inconsistent with the modesty and decorum of Christian women. St. Paul, in his first Epistle to Timothy, in the passage where he condemns it, shows us in what the pride of female dress then consisted. *I will,* says he, *that women adorn themselves in modest apparel, with shamefacedness and sobriety, not with* BROIDERED HAIR, *or* GOLD, *or* PEARLS, *or* COSTLY ARRAY: *but (which becometh women professing godliness) with good works.* (1 Tim. ii. 9.) St. Peter in like manner ordains, that the *adorning* of the fair sex should not be so much *that outward adorning of* PLAITING *the hair, and of wearing of* GOLD, *or* PUTTING ON OF APPAREL: *but let*

---

[1] Rae Wilson's Travels in the Holy Land, &c. vol. i. p. 147. 3d edition.
[2] Descript. de l'Arabie, p. 61.

it be the hidden man of the heart, in that which is not corruptible, even the ornament of a meek and quiet spirit, which is in the sight of God of great price. (1 Pet. iii. 3.) [1] On the contrary, the men in those times universally wore their hair short, as appears from all the books, medals, and statues that have been transmitted to us. This circumstance, which formed a principal distinction in dress between the sexes, happily illustrates the following passage in St. Paul (1 Cor. xi. 14, 15.) : *Doth not even nature itself teach you, that if a* MAN *have* LONG HAIR *it is a* SHAME *to him? But if a* WOMAN *have* LONG HAIR, *it is a* GLORY *to her; for her hair is given her for a covering.*

"The Jewish and Grecian ladies, moreover, never appeared in public without a veil. Hence St. Paul severely censures the Corinthian women for appearing in the church without a veil, and praying to God uncovered, by which they threw off the decency and modesty of the sex, and exposed themselves and their religion to the satire and calumny of the heathens. The whole passage beautifully and clearly exhibits to the reader's ideas the distinguishing customs which then prevailed in the different dress and appearance of the sexes." (Compare 1 Cor. xi. 13—16.) [2]

V. Their legs were bare, and on the feet they wore SANDALS, or soles made of leather or of wood, and fastened around the feet in various ways, after the oriental fashion. (Gen. xiv. 23. Exod. xii. 11. Isa. v. 27. Mark vi. 9. John i. 27. Acts xii. 8.) As luxury increased, magnificent sandals constituted, in the East, a part of the dress of both males and females, who could afford such a luxury. (Cant. vii. 1. Ezek. xvi. 10.) The sandals of Judith were so brilliant, that, notwithstanding the general splendour of her bracelets, rings, and necklaces, these principally succeeded in captivating the ferocious Holofernes. (Judith x. 4. xvi. 9.) [3] On entering a sacred place it was usual to lay them aside (Exod. iii. 5. Josh. v. 15.), as is the practice among the Mohammedans in the East to this day. When any one entered a house, it was customary to take off the sandals, and wash the feet. (Gen. xviii. 4. xix. 2.) A similar custom obtains in India at the present time. [4] Among persons of some rank it was the office of servants

---

1 Mr. Emerson's account of the dress of the younger females in the house of the British consul in the Isle of Milo, in the Levant, strikingly illustrates the above-cited passage of St. Peter. He describes their hair as being PLAITED into long triple bands, and then twisted round the head, interlaced with strings of zechins, mahmoudis, and other GOLDEN COINS, or left to flow gracefully behind them. They also wore four or five gowns and other GARMENTS, HEAPED ON with less taste than profusion, and all are secured at the waist by a velvet stomacher, richly embroidered, and glittering with gilded spangles. (Emerson's Letters from the Ægean, vol. ii. p. 238.)

2 Harwood's Introd. to the New Test. vol. ii. pp. 101—103.

3 Dr. Good's Sacred Idyls, pp. 147. 172. In the East generally, and in the island of Ceylon in particular, "the shoes of brides are made of velvet, richly ornamented with gold and silver, not unlike a pair in the Tower [of London] worn by queen Elizabeth." Callaway's Oriental Observations, p. 47.

4 An intelligent oriental traveller has the following instructive observations on this subject : — " I never understood the full meaning of our Lord's words, as recorded in John xiii. 10., until I beheld the better sort of natives return home after performing their customary ablutions. The passage reads thus : ' He that is washed needeth not save to wash his feet, but is clean every whit.' Thus, as they return to their habitations barefoot, they necessarily contract in their progress some portion of dust on their feet; and this is universally the case, however nigh their dwellings may be to the river side. When therefore they return, the first thing they do is to mount a low stool, and pour a small vessel of water over their feet, to cleanse them from the soil they may have contracted in their journey homewards; if they are of the higher order of society, a servant performs it for them, and then they are ' clean every whit.' " Statham's Indian Recollections, p. 81. London, 1832. 12mo.

to take off the sandals of guests, and (after washing their feet) to return them to the owners on their departure. (Matt. iii. 11. Mark v. 7.
Luke iii. 16. John xiii. 4, 5. 14—16. 1 Tim. v. 10.) Persons who
were in deep affliction, went barefoot (2 Sam. xv. 30. xix. 24. Isa. xx.
2—4.); which, under other circumstances, was considered to be ignominious and servile. (Deut. xxv. 9, 10. Isa. xlvii. 2. Jer. ii. 25.)

VI. Seals or Signets, and Rings, were commonly worn by both
sexes.

Pliny [1] states that the use of *Seals* or *Signets* was rare at the time of
the Trojan war; but among the Hebrews they were of much greater
antiquity, for we read that Judah left his *signet* as a pledge with Tamar.
(Gen. xxxviii. 25.) The antient Hebrews wore their seals or signets,
either as rings on their fingers, or as bracelets on their arms, a custom
which still obtains in the East. Thus the bride in the Canticles (viii.
6.) desires that the spouse would wear her as a seal on his arm. Occasionally, they were worn upon the bosom by means of an ornamental
chain or ligature fastened round the neck. To this custom there is an
allusion in Prov. vi. 21. The expression to *set as a* seal *upon the heart,
as a* seal *upon the arm* (Cant. viii. 6.), is a scriptural expression denoting
the cherishing of a true affection; with the exhibition of those constant
attentions which bespeak a real attachment. Compare also Hag. ii. 23.
Jer. xxii. 24. The *Ring* is mentioned in Isa. iii. 21., and also in the
parable of the prodigal, where the father orders a ring for his returning son (Luke xv. 22.), and also by the apostle James. (ii. 2.) The
compliment of a royal ring was a token that the person to whom it
was given, was invested with the highest mark of favour, power, and
honour: thus Pharaoh took off his ring from his hand, and put it on
Joseph's. (Gen. xli. 42.) And Ahasuerus plucked off his ring from
his finger, and bestowed it on Haman (Esther iii. 10.), and afterwards
on Mordecai. (viii. 2.) The same practice is still common in India. [2]

. VII. Although the garments antiently worn by the Jews were few
in number, yet their ornaments were many, especially those worn by
the women. The prophet Isaiah, when reproaching the daughters of
Sion with their luxury and vanity, gives us a particular account of
their female ornaments. (Isa. iii. 16—24.)[3] The most remarkable
were the following: —

1. The Nose Jewels (ver. 21.), or, as Bishop Lowth translates them,
the jewels of the nostril. They were rings set with jewels, pendent from
the nostrils, like ear-rings from the ears, by holes bored to receive
them. Ezekiel, enumerating the common ornaments of women of the
first rank, distinctly mentions the nose jewel (Ezek. xvi. 12. marg.
rendering); and in an elegant Proverb of Solomon (Prov. xi. 22.)
there is a manifest allusion to this kind of ornament, which shows that
it was used in his time. Nose jewels were one of the love-tokens presented to Rebecca by the servant of Abraham in the name of his
master. (Gen. xxiv. 22. where the word translated *ear-ring* ought to
have been rendered *nose jewel*.) [4] However singular this custom may

---

[1] Nat. Hist. lib. xxxiii. c. 1.
[2] Roberts's Oriental Illustrations, pp. 46, 47.
[3] Schroeder has treated at great length on the various articles of female apparel mentioned
in Isa. iii. 16—24. in his *Commentarius Philologico-Criticus de Vestitu Mulierum Hebræarum.* Lug. Bat. 1735. 4to.
[4] Bp. Lowth on Isaiah, vol. ii. p. 47.

appear to us, modern travellers attest its prevalence in the East among women of all ranks.[1]

2. The EAR-RING was an ornament worn by the men as well as the women, as appears from Gen. xxxv. 4. and Éxod. xxxii. 2.; and by other nations as well as the Jews, as is evident from Numb. xxxi. 50. and Judg. viii. 24. It should seem that this ornament had been heretofore used for idolatrous purposes, since Jacob, in the injunction which he gave to his household, commanded them *to put away the strange gods that were in their hands, and the ear-rings that were in their ears.* (Gen. xxxv. 2. 4.)[2] It appears that the Israelites themselves in subsequent times were not free from this superstition; for Hosea (ii. 13.) represents Jerusalem as having decked herself with ear-rings to Baalim.

3. PERFUME BOXES (in our version of Isa. iii. 20. rendered *tablets*) were an essential article in the toilet of a Hebrew lady. A principal part of the delicacy of the Asiatic ladies consists in the use of baths, and the richest oils and perfumes: an attention to which is in some degree necessary in those hot countries. Frequent mention is made of the rich ointments of the bride in the Song of Solomon. (iv. 10, 11.) The preparation for Esther's introduction to king Ahasuerus was a course of bathing and perfuming for a whole year: *six months with oil of myrrh, and six months with sweet odours.* (Esth. ii. 12.) A diseased and loathsome habit of body, which is denounced against the women of Jerusalem —

And there shall be, instead of perfume, a putrid ulcer —

Isa. iii. 24. Bp. LOWTH's version.

instead of a beautiful skin, softened and made agreeable with all that art could devise, and all that nature, so prodigal in those countries of the richest perfumes, could supply, — must have been a punishment the most severe, and the most mortifying to the delicacy of these haughty daughters of Sion.[3]

4. The TRANSPARENT GARMENTS (in our version of Isa. iii. 23. rendered *glasses*) were a kind of silken dress, transparent like gauze, worn only by the most delicate women, and by such as dressed themselves more elegantly than became women of good character. This sort of garments was afterwards in use both among the Greeks and Romans.[4]

5. Another female ornament was a CHAIN about the neck (Ezek. xvi. 11.), which appears to have been used also by the men, as may be inferred from Prov. i. 9. This was a general ornament in all the eastern countries: thus Pharaoh is said to have put a chain of gold about Joseph's neck (Gen. xli. 42.); and Belshazzar did the same to Daniel (Dan. v. 29.); and it is mentioned with several other things

---

[1] Bp. Lowth on Isaiah, vol. ii. p. 48. Harmer's Observations, vol. iv. pp. 316—320. In the East Indies, a small jewel, in form resembling a rose, ornaments ore nostril of even the poorest Malabar woman. Callaway's Oriental Observations, p. 48.

[2] It is probable that the ear-rings, or jewels, worn by Jacob's household, had been consecrated to superstitious purposes, and worn, perhaps, as a kind of amulet. It appears that rings, whether on the ears or nose, were first superstitiously worn in honour of false gods, and probably of the sun, whose circular form they might be designed to represent. Maimonides mentions rings and vessels of this kind, with the image of the sun, moon, &c. impressed on them. These superstitious objects were concealed by Jacob in a place known only to himself. Grotius on Gen. xxxv. 4. Calmet's Dictionary, voce *Ring.*

[3] Bp. Lowth's Isaiah, vol. ii. pp. 49, 50.   Ibid. p. 49.

as part of the Midianitish spoil. Numb. xxxi. 50.) Further, the arms or wrists were adorned with *bracelets:* these are in the catalogue of the female ornaments used by the Jews (Ezek. xvi. 11.), and were part of Rebecca's present. They were also worn by men of any considerable figure, for we read of Judah's bracelets (Gen. xxxviii. 18.), and of those worn by Saul. (2 Sam. i. 10.)

6. We read in Exod. xxxviii. 8. of the women's Looking Glasses, which were not made of what is now called glass, but of polished brass, otherwise these Jewish women could not have contributed them towards the making of the brazen laver, as is there mentioned. In later times, mirrors were made of other polished metal, which at best could only reflect a very obscure and imperfect image. Hence St. Paul, in a very apt and beautiful simile, describes the defective and limited knowledge of the present state by that opaque and dim representation of objects, which those mirrors exhibited. *Now we see δι' ἐσοπτρον by means of a mirror* [1], *darkly;* not *through a glass,* as in our version of 1 Cor. xiii. 12.; for telescopes, as every one knows, are a very late invention.

7. To the articles of apparel above enumerated may be added Feet Rings. (Isa. iii. 18. in our version rendered tinkling ornaments about the feet.) Most of these articles of female apparel are still in use in the East. The East Indian women, who accompanied the Indo-Anglican army from India to Egypt, wore large rings in their noses, and silver cinctures about their ankles and wrists, their faces being painted above the eye-brows. In Persia and Arabia, also, it is well known that the women paint their faces and wear gold and silver rings about their ankles, which are full of little bells that tinkle as they walk or trip along. Cingalese children often wear rings about their ankles; Malabar and Moor children wear rings, hung about with hollow balls, which tinkle as they run.[2] The licensed prostitutes whom Dr. Richardson saw at Gheneh (a large commercial town of Upper Egypt) were attired in a similar manner.[3]

8. As large black eyes are greatly esteemed in the East, the oriental women have recourse to artificial means, in order to impart a dark and majestic shade to the eyes. Dr. Shaw informs us, that none of the Moorish ladies think themselves completely dressed, until they

---

[1] The 'Εσοπτρον, or metallic *mirror*, is mentioned by the author of the apocryphal book of the Wisdom of Solomon (vii. 26.); who, speaking of Wisdom, says that *she is the brightness of the everlasting light and* 'ΕΣΟΠΤΡΟΝ ἀκαλιδωτον *the unspotted* mirror *of the power of God and the image of his goodness.* The author, also, of the book of Ecclesiasticus, exhorting to put no trust in an enemy, says, *Though he humble himself and go crouching, yet take good heed and beware of him; and thou shalt be unto him ὡς εκμεμαχως* 'ΕΣΟΠΤΡΟΝ, *as if thou hadst wiped a* mirror, *and thou shalt know that his* rust *hath not altogether been wiped away.* (Ecclus. xii. 11.) The mention of rust in this place manifestly indicates the metallic composition of the mirror; which is frequently mentioned in the antient classic writers. See particularly Anacreon, Ode xi. 3. and xx. 5, 6. Dr. A. Clarke, on 1 Cor. xiii. 12.

[2] Dr. Clarke's Travels, vol. v. p. 320. 8vo. edit. Morier's Second Journey in Persia, p. 145. Ward's History, &c. of the Hindoos, vol. ii. pp. 329. 333. Callaway's Oriental Observations, pp. 47, 48.

[3] This is the only place in Egypt where we saw the women of the town decked out in all their finery. They were of all nations and of all complexions, and regularly licensed, as in many parts of Europe, to exercise their profession. Some of them were *highly painted, and gorgeously attired with costly necklaces, rings in their noses and in their ears, and bracelets on their wrists and arms.* They sat at the doors of their houses, and called on the passengers as they went by, in the same manner as we read in the book of Proverbs." [vii. 6—23.] (Richardson's Travels, vol. i. p. 260.) The same custom was observed by Pitts, a century before, at Cairo. See his Account of the Mahometans, p. 99.

have tinged their eye-lids with al-ka-hol, that is, with stibium, or the
powder of lead-ore.   As this process is performed " by first dipping
into this powder a small wooden bodkin of the thickness of a quill,
and then drawing it afterwards through the eye-lids, over the ball of
the eye, we have a lively image of what the prophet Jeremiah (iv. 30.)
may be supposed to mean by *renting the eyes* (not as we render it, *with
painting*, but) *with* פוך, *lead-ore.*   The sooty colour which in this
manner is communicated to the eyes is thought to add a wonderful
gracefulness to persons of all complexions.   The practice of it,
no doubt, is of great antiquity : for, besides the instances already
noticed, we find, that when Jezebel is said to have painted her face
(2 Kings ix. 30.), the original words are תשם בפוך עניה, i. e. *she
adjusted*, or *set off*, *her eyes with the powder of lead-ore.*   So likewise
Ezek. xxiii. 40. is to be understood.   *Keren-happuch*, i. e. the horn of
pouk or lead-ore, the name of Job's youngest daughter, was relative
to this custom or practice." [1]   The custom of staining the eye-lids and
brows with a moistened powder of a black colour, was common in
Egypt from the earliest times ; and it appears to have been followed
by persons of both sexes, though among the Jews it was confined to
women.[2]   The modern Persian, Egyptian, and Arab women, continue
the practice of tinging their eye-lashes and eye-lids.[3]

It was a particular injunction of the Mosaic law that *the women shall
not wear that which pertaineth unto a man, neither shall a man put on
a woman's garment.* (Deut. xxii. 5.)   This precaution was very necessary against the abuses which are the usual consequences of such dis-
guises.   For a woman drest in a man's clothes will not be restrained
so readily by that modesty which is the peculiar ornament of her sex;
and a man drest in a woman's habit may without fear and shame go
into companies where, without this disguise, shame and fear would
hinder his admittance, and prevent his appearing.

In hot countries, like a considerable part of Palestine, travellers
inform us, that the greatest difference imaginable subsists between the
complexions of the women.   Those of any condition seldom go abroad,
and are ever accustomed to be shaded from the sun, with the greatest
attention.   Their skin is, consequently, fair and beautiful.   But women
in the lower ranks of life, especially in the country, being from the
nature of their employments more exposed to the scorching rays of
the sun, are, in their complexions, remarkably tawny and swarthy.
Under such circumstances, a high value would, of course, be set, by
the eastern ladies, upon the fairness of their complexions, as a distinguishing mark of their superior quality, no less than as an enhance-
ment of their beauty.   We perceive, therefore, how natural was the
bride's self-abasing reflection in Cant. i. 5, 6. respecting her tawny

---

[1] Dr. Shaw's Travels, vol. i. p. 413.

[2] Wilkinson's Manners, &c. of the Antient Egyptians, vol. iii. pp. 380—382.

[3] Lane's Manners and Customs, &c. of the Modern Egyptians, vol. i. pp. 41, 42.   In pp. 42,
43, he has given engravings of the apparatus used for tinging the eye-lids.   Harmer's Observations, vol. iv. p. 334.   Shaw's Travels, vol. i. p. 414.   Morier's Second Journey,
pp. 61. 145.   The eyes of the wife of a Greek priest, whom Mr. Rae Wilson saw at Tiberias, were stained with black powder.   (Travels in the Holy Land, &c. vol. ii. p. 17.)
" The Palmyrene women......are the finest looking women of all the Arab tribes of Syria.
...... Like other Orientals of their sex, they dye the tips of the fingers and the palms of the
hands red, and wear gold rings in their ears: and the jet-black dye of the hennah for the
eye-lashes is never forgotten ; they imagine, and, perhaps, with truth, that its blackness gives
the eye an additional languor and interest."   Carne's Letters from the East, p. 592.

complexion (caused by exposure to servile employments) among the fair daughters of Jerusalem; who, as attendants on a royal marriage (we may suppose), were of the highest rank.[1]

VIII. To change habits and wash one's clothes were ceremonies used by the Jews, in order to dispose them for some holy action which required particular purity. Jacob, after his return from Mesopotamia, required his household to *change their garments, and go with him to sacrifice at Bethel.* (Gen. xxxv. 2, 3.) Moses commanded the people to prepare themselves for the reception of the law by purifying and washing their clothes. (Exod. xix. 10.) On the other hand, the RENDING OF ONE'S CLOTHES is an expression frequently used in Scripture, as a token of the highest grief. Reuben, to denote his great sorrow for Joseph, *rent his clothes* (Gen. xxxvii. 29.); Jacob did the like (ver. 34.); and Ezra, to express the concern and uneasiness of his mind, and the apprehensions he entertained of the divine displeasure, on account of the people's unlawful marriages, is said to rend his garments and his mantle (Ezra ix. 3.); that is, both his inner and upper garment: this was also an expression of indignation and holy zeal; the high priest rent his clothes, pretending that our Saviour had spoken blasphemy. (Matt. xxvi. 65.) And so did the apostles, when the people intended to pay them divine honours. (Acts xiv. 14.) The garments of mourners among the Jews were chiefly sackcloth and haircloth. The last sort was the usual clothing of the prophets, for they were continual penitents by profession; and therefore Zechariah speaks of the rough garments of the false prophets, which they also wore to deceive. (Zech. xiii. 4.) Jacob was the first we read of that put sackcloth on his loins, as a token of mourning for Joseph (Gen. xxxvii. 34.), signifying thereby that since he had lost his beloved son he considered himself as reduced to the meanest and lowest condition of life.

IX. A prodigious number of sumptuous and magnificent habits was in antient times regarded as a necessary and indispensable part of their treasures. Horace, speaking of Lucullus, (who had pillaged Asia, and first introduced Asiatic refinements among the Romans,) says, that, some persons having waited upon him to request the loan of a *hundred* suits out of his wardrobe for the Roman stage, he exclaimed — " A hundred suits ! how is it possible for me to furnish such a number? However, I will look over them and send you what I have." — After some time he writes a note, and tells them he had FIVE THOUSAND, to the whole or part of which they were welcome.[2]

This circumstance of amassing and ostentatiously displaying in wardrobes numerous and superb suits, as indispensable to the idea of wealth, and forming a principal part of the opulence of those times, will elucidate several passages of Scripture. The patriarch Job, speaking of riches in his time, says, — *Though they heap up silver as the dust, and prepare raiment as the clay.* (Job xxvii. 16.) Joseph gave his brethren changes of *raiment*, but to Benjamin he gave three hundred pieces of silver, and *five changes* of raiment. (Gen. xlv. 22.)[3]

---

1 Fry's Translation of the Song of Solomon, p. 36.
2 Horat. Epist. lib. i. ep. 6. ver. 40—44.
3 Presenting garments is one of the modes of complimenting persons in the East. See several illustrative instances in Burder's Oriental Literature, vol. i. pp. 93, 94.

Naaman carried for a present to the prophet Elisha ten changes of raiment, that is, according to Calmet, ten tunics and ten upper garments. (2 Kings v. 5.) In allusion to this custom our Lord, when describing the short duration and perishing nature of earthly treasures, represents them as subject to the depredations of moths, from which the inhabitants of the East find it difficult to preserve the large store of garments. *Lay not up for yourselves* TREASURES *on earth, where moth and rust do corrupt.* (Matt. vi. 19.) The illustrious apostle of the Gentiles, when appealing to the integrity and fidelity with which he had discharged his sacred office, said, — *I have coveted no man's gold, or silver, or* APPAREL. (Acts xx. 33.) The apostle James, likewise, (just in the same manner as the Greek and Roman writers, when they are particularising the opulence of those times,) specifies gold, silver, and *garments*, as the constituents of riches : — *Go to now, ye rich men ; weep and howl for your miseries that shall come upon you. Your gold and silver is cankered, and your* GARMENTS *are moth-eaten.* (James v. 1. 3. 2.)[1] The fashion of hoarding up splendid dresses still subsists in Palestine. It appears from Psal. xlv. 8. that the wardrobes of the East were plentifully perfumed with aromatics ; and in Cant. iv. 11. the fragrant odour of the bride's garments is compared to the odour of Lebanon.[2] With robes thus perfumed Rebecca furnished her son Jacob, when she sent him to obtain by stratagem his father's blessing. *And he* (Isaac) *smelled the smell* (or *fragrance*) *of his raiment and blessed him, and said, See! the smell of my son. is as the smell of a field which the* LORD *hath blessed.* (Gen. xxvii. 27.)[3] In process of time, this exquisite fragrance was figuratively applied to the moral qualities of the mind ; of which we have an example in the Song of Solomon, i. 3.

> Like the fragrance of thine own sweet perfumes
> Is thy name, — a perfume poured forth.[4]

CHAPTER III.

JEWISH CUSTOMS RELATING TO MARRIAGE.

I. *Marriage accounted a Sacred Obligation by the Jews.* — II. *Polygamy tolerated.* — *Condition of Concubines.* — III. *Nuptial Contract, and Espousals.* — IV. *Nuptial Ceremonies.* — V. *Divorces.*

I. MARRIAGE was considered by the Jews as an affair of the strictest obligation. They understood literally and as a precept these words uttered to our first parents, *Be fruitful, and multiply, and replenish the earth.* (Gen. i. 28.) Their continual expectation of the coming of the Messiah added great weight to this obligation. Every one lived

---

[1] Harwood's Introd. vol. ii. pp. 247, 248.
[2] Dr. Good's Sacred Idyls, p. 122. In p. 123. he has quoted the following passage from Moschus, in which the same idea occurs with singular exactness : —

——————————— του αμβροτος οδμη
Τελοθι και λειμωνος εκαινυτο λαρον αϋτμην.   Idyl. B. 91.
Whose heavenly fragrance far exceeds
The fragrance of the breathing meads.
                    Dr. Good's translation of Solomon's Song, p. 123.

[3] Jowett's Christian Researches in Syria, &c. pp. 97, 98.
[4] Dr. Good's version.

in the hopes that this blessing should attend their posterity; and therefore they thought themselves bound to further the expectance of him,
by adding to the race of mankind, of whose seed he was to be born,
and whose happiness he was to promote, by that temporal kingdom for
which they looked upon his appearance.

Hence celibacy was esteemed a great reproach in Israel; for, besides
that they thought no one could live a single life without great danger
of sin, they esteemed it a counteracting of the divine counsels in the
promise, that *the seed of the woman should bruise the head of the serpent.*
On this account it was that Jephthah's daughter deplored her virginity,
because she thus deprived her father of the hopes which he might
entertain from heirs descended from her, by whom his name might
survive in Israel, and, consequently, of his expectation of having the
Messiah to come of his seed, which was the general desire of all the
Israelitish women.   For the same reason also sterility was regarded
among the Jews (as it is to this day among the modern Egyptians [1]
and Hindoos[2],) as one of the greatest misfortunes that could befall
any woman, insomuch that to have a child, though the woman immediately died thereupon, was accounted a less affliction than to have
none at all; and to this purpose we may observe, that the midwife
comforts Rachel in her labour (even though she knew her to be at the
point of death) in these terms, *Fear not, for thou shalt bear this son
also.* (Gen. xxxv. 17.)

From this expectation proceeded their exactness in causing the
brother of a husband, who died without issue, to marry the widow he
left behind, and the disgrace that attended his refusing so to do; for,
as the eldest son of such a marriage became the adopted child of the
deceased, that child and the posterity flowing from him were, by a
fiction of law, considered as the real offspring and heirs of the deceased
brother.   This explains the words of Isaiah, that *seven women should
take hold of one man, saying, We will eat our own bread, and wear our
own apparel; only let us be called by thy name, to take away our reproach.*
(Isa. iv. 1.) This was the reason also why the Jews commonly married
very young. The age prescribed to men by the Rabbins was eighteen
years.   A virgin was ordinarily married at the age of puberty, that is,
twelve years complete, whence her husband is called the guide of her
youth (Prov. ii. 17.), and the husband of her youth (Joel i. 8.); and
the not giving of maidens in marriage is in Psal. lxxviii. 63. represented
as one of the effects of the divine anger towards Israel.   In like manner, among the Hindoos, the delaying of the marriage of daughters is
to this day regarded as a great calamity and disgrace.[3]

---

[1] The most importunate applicants to Dr. Richardson for medical advice were those who
consulted him on account of sterility, which in Egypt (he says) is still considered the greatest
of all evils.   " The unfortunate couple believe that they are bewitched, or under the curse of
heaven, which they fancy the physician has the power to remove.   It is in vain that he declares the insufficiency of the healing art to take away their reproach.   The parties hang
round, dunning and importuning him for the love of God, to prescribe for them, that they
may have children like other people.   ' Give me children, or I die,' said the fretful Sarah to
her husband; ' Give me children, or I curse you,' say the barren Egyptians to their physicians."   Dr. Richardson's Travels along the Mediterranean, &c. vol. ii. p. 106.   A nearly
similar scene is described by Mr. R. R. Madden, who travelled in the East between the years
1824 and 1827.   Travels in Turkey, &c. vol. ii. p. 51.

[2] Roberts's Oriental Illustrations, p. 161.

[3] Ward's History, &c. of the Hindoos, vol. ii. p. 327.   Maurice's Indian Antiquities
vol. vii. p. 329.   Home's History of the Jews, vol. ii. pp. 350, 351.

II. From the first institution of marriage it is evident that God gave but one woman to one man; and if it be a true, as it is a common, observation, that there are every where more males than females born in the world, it follows that those men certainly act contrary to the laws both of God and nature who have more than one wife at the same time. But though God, as supreme lawgiver, had a power to dispense with his own laws, and actually did so with the Jews for the more speedy peopling of the world, yet it is certain there is no such toleration under the Christian dispensation, and, therefore, their example is no rule at this day. The first who violated this primitive law of marriage was Lamech, who *took unto him two wives.* (Gen. iv. 19.) Afterwards we read that Abraham had concubines. (Gen. xxv. 6.) And his practice was followed by the other patriarchs, which at last grew to a most scandalous excess in Solomon's and Rehoboam's days. The word concubine in most Latin authors, and even with us at this day, signifies a woman, who, though she be not married to a man, yet lives with him as his wife; but in the Sacred Writings it is understood in another sense. There it means a lawful wife, but of a lower order and of an inferior rank to the mistress of the family; and, therefore, she had equal right to the marriage-bed with the chief wife; and her issue was reputed legitimate in opposition to bastards: but in all other respects these concubines were inferior to the primary wife; for they had no authority in the family, nor any share in household government. If they had been servants in the family, before they came to be concubines, they continued to be so afterwards, and in the same subjection to their mistress as before. The dignity of these primary wives gave their children the preference in the succession, so that the children of concubines did not inherit their father's fortune, except upon the failure of the children by these more honourable wives; and, therefore, it was, that the father commonly provided for the children by these concubines in his own lifetime, by giving them a portion of his cattle and goods, which the Scripture calls *gifts.* Thus Sarah was Abraham's primary wife, by whom he had Isaac, who was the heir of his wealth. But besides her, he had two concubines, namely, Hagar and Keturah; by these he had other children whom he distinguished from Isaac, for it is said, *He gave them gifts, and sent them away while he yet lived.* (Gen. xxv. 5, 6.) A similar custom obtains in the East Indies to this day. In Mesopotamia, as appears from Gen. xxix. 26., the younger daughter could not be given in marriage " before the first-born " or elder, and the same practice continues to this day among the Armenians, and also among the Hindoos, with whom it is considered criminal to give the younger daughter in marriage before the elder, or for a younger son to marry while his elder brother remains unmarried.[1] As Rebekah had her nurse to accompany her (Gen. xxiv. 59.), so, at this day, in India the *aya,* or nurse, who has brought up the bride from infancy, accompanies her to her new home. She is her adviser, assistant, and friend.[2]

III. No formalities appear to have been used by the Jews — at least none were enjoined to them by Moses — in joining man and wife together. Mutual consent, followed by consummation, was deemed

---

[1] Home's History of the Jews, vol. ii. p. 352. Paxton's Illustrations of Scripture, vol. iii. p. 129. 2d edit. Hartley's Researches in Greece and the Levant, pp. 229, 230.

[2] Roberts's Oriental Illustrations of the Scriptures, pp. 28, 29.

sufficient. The manner in which a daughter was demanded in marriage is described in the case of Shechem, who asked Dinah the daughter of Jacob in marriage (Gen. xxxiv. 6—12.) ; and the nature of the contract, together with the mode of solemnising the marriage, is described in Gen. xxiv. 50, 51. 57. 67. There was, indeed, a previous espousal[1] or betrothing, which was a solemn promise of marriage, made by the man and woman each to the other, at such a distance of time as they agreed upon. This was sometimes done by writing, sometimes by the delivery of a piece of silver to the bride in presence of witnesses, as a pledge of their mutual engagements. We are informed by the Jewish writers that kisses were given in token of the espousals (to which custom there appears to be an allusion in Canticles i. 2.), after which the parties were reckoned as man and wife.[2] After such espousals were made (which was generally when the parties were young) the woman continued with her parents several months, if not some years (at least till she was arrived at the age of twelve), before she was brought home, and her marriage consummated.[3] That it was the practice to betroth the bride some time before the consummation of the marriage is evident from Deut. xx. 7. Thus we find that Samson's wife remained with her parents a considerable time after espousals (Judg. xiv. 8.); and we are told that the Virgin Mary was visibly with child before she and her intended husband came together. (Matt. i. 18.) If, during the time between the espousals and the marriage, the bride was guilty of any criminal correspondence with another person, contrary to the fidelity she owed to her bridegroom, she was treated as an adulteress ; and thus the holy Virgin, after she was betrothed to Joseph, having conceived our blessed Saviour, might, according to the rigour of the law, have been punished as an adulteress, if the angel of the Lord had not acquainted Joseph with the mystery of the incarnation.[4] At the present day, when a Jew marries a woman, he throws the skirt or end of his talith over her, to signify that he has taken her under his protection. This practice explains Ezek. xvi. 8. where the prophet, describing the Jewish church as an exposed infant, mentions the care of God in bringing her up with great tenderness, and at the proper time marrying her: which is expressed in the same way as the request of Ruth (iii. 9.) — *I spread my skirt over thee,* and thou becamest mine. At the marriages of Hindoos, the bridegroom folds a silken skirt several times over the rest of the bride's clothes, to intimate that he has married her.[5]

Among the Jews, and generally throughout the East, marriage was

---

[1] " Before the giving of the law (saith Maimonides), if the man and woman had agreed about marriage, he brought her into his house and privately married her. But, after the giving of the law, the Israelites were commanded, that if any were minded to take a woman for his wife, he should receive her, first before witnesses, and henceforth let her be to him to wife, — as it is written, ' If any one take a wife.' This taking is one of the affirmative precepts of the law, and is called ' espousing.' " Lightfoot's Horæ Hebr. on Matt. i. 18. (Works, vol. xi. p. 18. 8vo. edit. 1823.)

[2] Dr. Gill's Comment. on Sol. Song i. 2. The same ceremony was practised among the primitive Christians. (Bingham's Antiquities, book xxii. c. 3. sect. 6.) By the civil law, indeed, the kiss is made a ceremony, in some respects, of importance to the validity of the nuptial contract. (Cod. Justin. lib. v. tit. 3. de Donation. ante Nuptias, leg. 16.) Fry's translation of the Canticles, p. 33.

[3] The same practice obtains in the East Indies to this day. Ward's History of the Hindoos, vol. ii. p. 334.

[4] Calmet, Dissertations, tom. i. p. 279. Pareau, Antiq. Hebr. p. 440.

[5] Roberts's Oriental Illustrations, pp. 156, 157.

considered as a sort of purchase, which the man made of the woman
he desired to marry; and, therefore, in contracting marriages, as the
wife brought a portion to the husband, so the husband was obliged to
give her or her parents money or presents in lieu of this portion.
This was the case between Hamor, the father of Shechem, and the
sons of Jacob, with relation to Dinah (Gen. xxxiv. 12.); and Jacob,
having no money, offered his uncle Laban seven years' service [1], which
must have been equivalent to a large sum. (Gen. xxix. 18.) Saul did
not give his daughter Michal to David, till after he had received a
hundred foreskins of the Philistines. (1 Sam. xviii. 25.) Hosea bought
his wife at the price of fifteen pieces of silver, and a measure and a
half of barley. (Hos. iii. 2.) The same custom also obtained among
the Greeks and other antient nations [2]; and it is to this day the practice in several eastern countries, particularly among the Druses,
Turks, and Christians, who inhabit the country of Haouran, and also
among the modern Scenite Arabs, or those who dwell in tents. [3]

IV. It appears from both the Old and New Testaments, that the
Jews celebrated the nuptial solemnity with great festivity and splendour. Many of the rites and ceremonies, observed by them on this
occasion, were common both to the Greeks and Romans. We learn
from the Misna, that the Jews were accustomed to put crowns or garlands on the heads of newly married persons; and it should seem
from the Song of Solomon (iii. 11.), that the ceremony of putting it on
was performed by one of the parents. Among the Greeks the bride
was crowned by her mother [4]; and among them, as well as among
the Orientals, and particularly the Hebrews, it was customary to wear
crowns or garlands, not merely of leaves or flowers, but also of gold
or silver, in proportion to the rank of the person presenting them;
but those prepared for the celebration of a nuptial banquet, as being
a festivity of the first consequence, were of peculiar splendour and
magnificence. Chaplets of flowers only constituted the nuptial crowns
of the Romans. Some writers have supposed that the nuptial crowns
and other ornaments of a bride are alluded to in Ezek. xvi. 8—12.

We may form some idea of the apparel of the bride and bridegroom
from Isa. lxi. 10., in which the yet future prosperous and happy state
of Jerusalem is compared to the dress of a bride and bridegroom.
The latter was attended by numerous companions: Samuel had thirty
young men to attend him at his nuptials (Judg. xiv. 11.), who in
Matt. ix. 15. and Mark ii. 19. are termed *children of the bride-chamber.*
"At every wedding two persons were selected, who devoted themselves for some time to the service of the bride and bridegroom. The
offices assigned to the paranymph, or שׁוֹשְׁבִין, were numerous and

---

[1] The Crim Tartars, who are in poor circumstances, serve an apprenticeship for their
wives, and are then admitted as part of the family. Mrs. Holderness's Notes, p. 8.
first edit.

[2] Potter's Greek Antiquities, vol. ii. p. 279.

[3] Burckhardt's Travels in Syria, &c. pp. 298. 385. De la Roque, Voyage dans la Palestine, p. 222. See several additional instances in Burder's Oriental Literature, vol. i.
pp. 56—59. Young girls, Mr. Buckingham informs us, are given in marriage for certain
sums of money, varying from 500 to 1000 piastres, among the better order of inhabitants,
according to their connections or beauty; though among the labouring classes it descends as
low as 100 or even 50. This sum being paid by the bridegroom to the bride's father adds
to his wealth, and makes girls (particularly when handsome) as profitable to their parents
as boys are by the wages they earn by their labour. Buckingham's Travels among the Arab
Tribes, pp. 49. 143.

[4] Dr. Good's translation of Solomon's Song, p. 106.

important; and, on account of these, the Baptist compares himself to the friend of the bridegroom.[1] (John iii. 29.) The offices of the paranymph were threefold—before—at—and after the marriage. Before the marriage of his friend it was his duty to select a chaste virgin, and to be the medium of communication between the parties, till the day of marriage. At that time he continued with them during the seven days allotted for the wedding festival, rejoicing in the happiness of his friend, and contributing as much as possible to the hilarity of the occasion. After the marriage, the paranymph was considered as the patron and friend of the wife and her husband, and was called in to compose any differences that might take place between them. As the forerunner of Christ, the Baptist may be well compared to the paranymph of the Jewish marriages. One of the most usual comparisons adopted in Scripture to describe the union between Christ and his Church is that of a marriage. The Baptist was the paranymph[2], who, by the preaching of repentance and faith, presented the church as a youthful bride and a chaste virgin to Christ. He still continued with the bridegroom, till the wedding was furnished with guests. His joy was fulfilled when his own followers came to inform him that Christ was increasing the number of his disciples, and that all men came unto him. This intelligence was as the sound of the bridegroom's voice, and as the pledge that the nuptials of heaven and earth were completed. From this representation of John as the paranymph, of Christ as the bridegroom, and the Church as the bride, the ministers and stewards of the Gospel of God may learn, that they also are required, by the preaching of repentance and faith, to present their hearers in all purity to the head of the Christian church. It is for them to find their best source of joy in the blessing of the most Highest on their labours — their purest happiness in the improvement and perfecting of the Church confided to their care." [3]

Further, it was customary for the bridegroom to prepare garments for his guests (Matt. xxii. 11.), which, it appears from Rev. xix. 8., were white; in these passages the wedding-garment is emblematical of Christian holiness and the righteousness of the saints. It was also usual for the bridegroom, attended by the nuptial guests, to conduct the bride to his house by night, accompanied by her virgin train of attendants, with torches and music and every demonstration of joy.[4] To this custom, as well as to the various ceremonies just stated, our Saviour alludes in the parables of the wise and foolish virgins (Matt. xxv. 1—12.), and of the wedding-feast, given by a sovereign,

---

[1] " Smaller circumstances and coincidences sometimes demonstrate the truth of an assertion, or the authenticity of a book, more effectually than more important facts. May not one of those unimportant yet convincing coincidences be observed in this passage? The Baptist calls himself the friend of the bridegroom, without alluding to any other paranymph, or שושבין. As the Jews were accustomed to have two paranymphs, there seems, at first sight, to be something defective in the Baptist's comparison. But our Lord was of Galilee, and there the custom was different from that of any other part of Palestine. The Galileans had one paranymph only." Townsend's Harmony of the New Testament, vol. i. p. 132.

[2] Exemplo et vitâ, says Kuinöel, communi depromto Johannes Baptista ostendit, quale inter ipsum et Christum discrimen intercedat. Se ipsum comparat cum paranympho, Christum cum sponso; quocum ipse Christus se quoque comparavit, ut patet e locis, Matt. ix. 15. and xxv. 1. Scilicet, ὁ φίλος τοῦ νυμφίου, est sponsi socius, ei peculiariter addictus, qui Græcis dicebatur παρανυμφιος, Matt. ix. 15. υἱος τοῦ νυμφωνος. Heb. שושבין filius lætitiæ. — Com. in lib. N. T. Hist. vol. iii. p. 227.

[3] Townsend's Harmony of the New Test. vol. i. p. 132.

[4] The same custom obtains in India. Roberts's Oriental Illustrations, p. 554.

in honour of his son's nuptials. (Matt. xxii. 2.) In the first of these
parables ten virgins are represented as taking their lamps to meet the
bridegroom; five of whom were prudent, and took with them a supply
of oil, which the others had neglected. In the mean time, *they all
slumbered and slept,* until the procession approached; but, in the
middle of the night *there was a cry made, Behold, the bridegroom
cometh! Go ye out to meet him.*[1] On this, all the virgins arose speedily
to trim their lamps. The wise were instantly ready; but the imprudent virgins were thrown into great confusion. Then, first, they
recollected their neglect: their lamps were expiring, and they had no
oil to refresh them. While they were gone to procure a supply, the
bridegroom arrived: *they that were ready went in with him to the marriage; and the door was shut*[2], and all admittance was refused to the
imprudent virgins.[3] The solemnities here described are still practised by the Jews in Podolia[4], and also by the Christians in Syria[5],
and in Egypt.[6] These companions of the bridegroom and bride are
mentioned in Psal. xlv. 9. 14., and Cant. v. 1. 8. John the Baptist
calls them the *friends of the bridegroom.* (John iii. 29.)

From the parable, " in which a great king is represented as making
a most magnificent entertainment at the marriage of his son, we learn

---

[1] The Rev. Mr. Hartley, describing an Armenian wedding, says, — " The large number
of young females who were present naturally reminded me of the wise and foolish virgins
in our Saviour's parable. These being friends of the bride, the *virgins, her companions*
(Psal. xlv. 14.), had come to *meet the bridegroom.* It is usual for the bridegroom to come
at *midnight;* so that, literally, *at midnight* the *cry* is *made,* Behold, the bridegroom cometh!
Go ye out to meet him. But, on this occasion, *the bridegroom tarried;* it was two o'clock
before he arrived. The whole party then proceeded to the Armenian church, where the
bishop was waiting to receive them; and there the ceremony was completed." Researches
in Greece and the Levant, p. 231.

[2] Mr. Ward has given the following description of a Hindoo wedding, which furnishes a
striking parallel to the parable of the wedding-feast in the Gospel. " At a marriage, the
procession of which I saw some years ago, the bridegroom came from a distance, and the
bride lived at Serampore, to which place the bridegroom was to come by water. After waiting
two or three hours, at length, near midnight, it was announced, as if in the very words of
Scripture, ' Behold, the bridegroom cometh! Go ye out to meet him.' All the persons employed now lighted their lamps, and ran with them in their hands to fill up their stations in
the procession; some of them had lost their lights, and were unprepared; but it was then too
late to seek them, and the cavalcade moved forward to the house of the bride, at which place
the company entered a large and splendidly illuminated area, before the house, covered with
an awning, where a great multitude of friends, dressed in their best apparel, were seated
upon mats. The bridegroom was carried in the arms of a friend, and placed on a superb
seat in the midst of the company, where he sat a short time, and then went into the house,
the door of which was immediately shut, and guarded by Sepoys. I and others expostulated
with the door-keepers, but in vain. Never was I so struck with our Lord's beautiful parable,
as at this moment: — *And the door was shut!*" (Ward's View of the History, &c. of the
Hindoos, vol. iii. pp. 171, 172.)

[3] Alber, Hermeneut. Vet. Test. pp. 200, 201. Bruning, Antiq. Græc. p. 95. Gilpin
on the New Test. vol. i. p. 100.

[4] At Kamenetz-Podolskoi, Dr. Henderson relates, " we were stunned by the noise of a
procession, led on by a band of musicians playing on tambourines and cymbals, which passed
our windows. On inquiry, we learned that it consisted of a Jewish bridegroom, accompanied
by his young friends, proceeding to the house of the bride's father, in order to convey her
home to her future residence. In a short time they returned with such a profusion of lights,
as quite illuminated the street. The bride, deeply veiled, was led along in triumph, accompanied by her virgins, each with a candle in her hand, who, with the young men, sang and
danced before her and the bridegroom. The scene presented us with an ocular illustration
of the important parable recorded in the twenty-fifth chapter of the Gospel of Matthew; and
we were particularly reminded of the appropriate nature of the injunction which our Saviour
gives us to watch and be ready; for the re-procession must have commenced immediately on
the arrival of the bridegroom." Biblical Researches, p. 217.

[5] See Mr. Jowett's Christian Researches in Syria, pp. 87, 88.

[6] See Mr. Rae Wilson's Travels in the Holy Land, Egypt, &c. vol. i. p. 335. third
edition.

that all the guests, who were honoured with an invitation, were expected to be dressed in a manner suitable to the splendour of such an occasion, and as a token of just respect to the new-married couple — and that after the procession in the evening from the bride's house was concluded, the guests, before they were admitted into the hall where the entertainment was served up, were taken into an apartment and viewed, that it might be known if any stranger had intruded, or if any of the company were apparelled in raiments unsuitable to the genial solemnity they were going to celebrate; and such, if found, were expelled the house with every mark of ignominy and disgrace. From the knowledge of this custom the following passage receives great light and lustre. When the king came in to see the guests, he discovered among them a person who had not on a wedding-garment. — He called him and said, *Friend, how camest thou in hither, not having a wedding-garment? and he was speechless:* — he had no apology to offer for this disrespectful neglect. The king then called to his servants, and bade them bind him hand and foot — to drag him out of the room — and thrust him out into midnight darkness." (Matt. xxii. 12.)[1]

"The Scripture, moreover, informs us that the marriage-festivals of the Jews lasted a whole week;" as they do to this day among the Christian inhabitants of Palestine.[2] "*Laban said, It must not be so done in our country to give the younger before the first-born. Fulfil her week, and we will give thee this also.* (Gen. xxix. 26, 27.) And *Sampson said unto them, I will now put forth a riddle unto you: if you can certainly declare it me within the* SEVEN DAYS *of the feast, and find it out, then I will give you thirty sheets, and thirty change of garments.* (Judges xiv. 12.) This week was spent in feasting, and was devoted to universal joy. To the festivity of this occasion our Lord refers: — *Can the children of the bride-chamber mourn, as long as the bridegroom is with them? but the days will come, when the bridegroom shall be taken from them, and then shall they fast.*" (Mark ii. 19, 20.)[3]

The eastern people were very reserved, not permitting the young women at marriages to be in the same apartments with the men; and, therefore, as the men and women could not amuse themselves with one another's conversation, the men did not spend their time merely in eating and drinking; for their custom was to propose questions and hard problems, by resolving which they exercised the wit and sagacity of the company. This was done at Samson's marriage, where he proposed a riddle to divert his company. (Judg. xiv. 12.) At nuptial and other feasts it was usual to appoint a person to superintend the preparations, to pass around among the guests to see that they were in want of nothing, and to give the necessary orders to the servants. Ordinarily, he was not one of the guests, and did not recline with them; or, at least, he did not take his place among them until he had performed all that was required of him. (Ecclus. xxxii. 1.) This officer is by St. John (ii. 8, 9.) termed Ἀρχιτρίκλινος, and Ἡγούμενος by the author of the book of Ecclesiasticus: as the latter lived about the year 190 B.C., and while the Jews had intercourse with the Greeks, especially in Egypt, it is most probable that the custom of choosing a governor

---

[1] Harwood's Introduction, vol. ii. p. 122.
[2] Jowett's Christian Researches in Syria and Palestine, p. 95.
[3] Harwood's Introd. vol. ii. p. 123. Bruning states that the Jews distinguish between a bride who is a *virgin* and one who is a *widow*; and that the nuptial feast of the former lasted a whole week, but for the latter it was limited to three days. Antiq. Hebr. p. 71.

of the feast passed from the Greeks to the Jews.[1] Theophylact's remark on John ii. 8. satisfactorily explains what was the business of the ἀρχιτρικλινος: — "That no one might suspect that their taste was so vitiated by excess as to imagine water to be wine, our Saviour directs it to be tasted by the *governor of the feast*, who certainly was sober ; for those, who on such occasions are intrusted with this office, observe the strictest sobriety, that every thing may, by their orders, be conducted with regularity and decency." [2]

At a marriage-feast to which Mr. Buckingham was invited, he relates that when the master of the feast came, he was "seated as the stranger-guest immediately beside him : and on the ejaculation of ' B' Ism Allah ' being uttered, he dipped his fingers in the same dish, and had the choicest bits placed before him by his own hands, as a mark of his being considered a friend or favourite; for this is the highest honour that can be shown to any one at an eastern feast."

" Two interesting passages of Scripture derive illustration from this trait of eastern manners. The first is that, in which the Saviour says, ' When thou art bidden of any man to a wedding, sit not down in the highest room, [that is, place or station,] lest a more honourable man than thou be bidden of him : and he that bade thee and him come and say to thee, Give this man place : and thou begin with shame to take the lowest room. But when thou art bidden, go and sit down in the lowest room ; that when he that bade thee cometh, he may say unto thee, Friend, go up higher : then shalt thou have worship in the presence of them that sit at meat with thee.' (Luke xiv. 8—10.) In a country, where the highest importance is attached to this distinction, the propriety of this advice is much more striking than if applied to the manners of our own ; and the honour is still as much appreciated throughout Syria, Palestine, and Mesopotamia, at the present day, as it was in those of the Messiah. The other passage is that, in which, at the celebration of the passover, Jesus says (Matt. xxvi. 23.), ' He that dippeth his hand with me in the dish, the same shall betray me.' As there are but very few, and these always the dearest friends, or most honoured guests, who are seated sufficiently near to the master of the feast to dip their hands in the same dish with him (probably not more than three or four out of the twelve disciples at the last supper enjoyed this privilege), the baseness of the treachery is much increased, when one of those few becomes a betrayer ; and in this light the conduct of Judas was, no doubt, meant to be depicted by this pregnant expression." [3]

V. Marriage was dissolved among the Jews by Divorce as well as by death.[4] Our Saviour tells us, that *Moses suffered this because of the hardness of their heart, but from the beginning it was not so* (Matt. xix. 8.); meaning that they were accustomed to this abuse, and to prevent greater evils, such as murders, adulteries, &c. he permitted it : whence it should seem to have been in use before the law ; and we see that Abraham dismissed Hagar, at the request of Sarah. It appears that

---

[1] Robinson's Greek Lexicon, voce 'Αρχιτρικλινος. Alber, Interpretatio Sacræ Scripturæ, tom. ix. p. 83.

[2] Theophylact as cited in Parkhurst's Greek Lexicon, voce 'Αρχιτρικλινος.

[3] Buckingham's Travels in Mesopotamia, vol. i. pp. 406, 407.

[4] Among the Bedouin Arabs, a brother finds himself more dishonoured by the seduction of his sister than a man by the infidelity of his wife. This will account for the sanguinary revenge taken by Simeon and Levi upon the Shechemites for the defilement of their sister Dinah. (Gen. xxxiv. 25—31.) See D'Arvieux's Travels in Arabia the Desart, pp. 243, 244.

Samson's father-in-law understood that his daughter had been divorced, since he gave her to another. (Judg. xv. 2.) The Levite's wife, who was dishonoured at Gibeah, had forsaken her husband, and never would have returned, if he had not gone in pursuit of her. (Judg. xix. 2, 3.) Solomon speaks of a libertine woman, who had forsaken her husband, the director of her youth, and (by doing so contrary to her nuptial vows) had forgotten the covenant of her God. (Prov. ii. 17.) Ezra and Nehemiah obliged a great number of the Jews to dismiss the foreign women, whom they had married contrary to the law (Ezra x. 11, 12. 19.) ; but our Saviour has limited the permission of divorce to the single case of adultery. (Matt. v. 31, 32.) Nor was this limitation unnecessary ; for at that time it was common for the Jews to dissolve this sacred union upon very slight and trivial pretences. A short time before the birth of Christ, a great dispute arose among the Jewish doctors concerning the interpretation of the Mosaic statutes relative to divorce ; the school of Shammai contending that it was allowable only for gross misconduct or for violation of nuptial fidelity, while the school of Hillel taught that a wife might be repudiated for the slightest causes. To this last-mentioned school belonged the Pharisees, who came to our Lord, *tempting him, and saying unto him, Is it lawful for a man to put away his wife for every cause*—for any thing whatever that may be disagreeable in her ? (Matt. xix. 3.) Upon our Lord's answer to this inquiry, that it was not lawful for a man to repudiate his wife, except for her violation of the conjugal honour, the disciples (who had been educated in Jewish prejudices and principles) hearing this, said — *If the case of the man be so with his wife*, if he be not allowed to divorce her except only for adultery, *it is not good to marry !* (Matt. xix. 10.) This facility in procuring divorces, and this caprice and levity among the Jews, in dissolving the matrimonial connection, is confirmed by Josephus, and unhappily verified in his own example : for he tells us that he repudiated his wife, though she was the mother of three children, because he was not pleased with her behaviour.[1]

CHAPTER IV.

BIRTH, NURTURE, ETC. OF CHILDREN.[2]

I. *Child-birth.* — *Circumcision.* — *Naming of the Child.* — II. *Privileges of the First-born.*—III. *Nurture of Children.* — IV. *Power of the Father over his Children.* — Disposition of his Property. — V. Adoption.

I. IN the East (as indeed in Switzerland and some other parts of

---

[1] Josephus de Vita sua, c. 76. Home's History of the Jews, vol. ii. p. 358. Harwood's Introd. vol. ii. p. 125. Calmet's Dissertation sur le Divorce. Dissert. tom. i. pp. 390, 391. The following are some of the principal causes for which the Jews were accustomed to put away their wives, at the period referred to : — 1. " It is commanded to divorce a wife, that is not of good behaviour, and is not modest, as becomes a daughter of Israel." — 2. " If any man hate his wife, let him put her away." — 3. " The school of Hillel saith, If the wife cook her husband's food illy, by over-salting it, or over-roasting it, she is to be put away." — 4. Yea, " If, by any stroke from the hand of God, she become dumb or sottish," &c. — 5. R. Akibah said, " If any man sees a woman handsomer than his own wife, he may put her away ; because it is said, ' If she find not favour in his eyes.' " —(Lightfoot's Horæ Hebraicæ, on Matt. v. 31.—Works, vol. xi. p. 118. 8vo. edit.) This last was the cause assigned by Josephus for repudiating his wife in the passage above cited.

[2] This chapter is compiled from Michaelis's Commentaries, vol. i. pp. 427—430. 443—

Europe, where the women are very robust), child-birth is to this day an event of but little difficulty[1]; and mothers were originally the only assistants of their daughters, as any further aid was deemed unnecessary. This was the case of the Hebrew women in Egypt. (Exod. i. 19.) It is evident from Gen. xxxv. 17. and xxxviii. 28. that midwives were employed in cases of difficult parturition; and it also appears that in Egypt, from time immemorial, the care of delivering women was committed to female midwives. (Exod. i. 15. *et seq.*) From Ezek. xvi. 4. it seems to have been the custom to wash the child as soon as it was born, to rub it with salt, and to wrap it in swaddling clothes. (The Armenians, to this day, wash their new-born infants in salt and water, previously to dressing them.) The birth-day of a son was celebrated as a festival, which was solemnised every succeeding year with renewed demonstrations of festivity and joy, especially those of sovereign princes. (Gen. xl. 20. Job. i. 4. Matt. xiv. 6.) The birth of a son or of a daughter rendered the mother ceremonially unclean for a certain period: at the expiration of which she went into the tabernacle or temple, and offered the accustomed sacrifice of purification, viz. a lamb of a year old, or, if her circumstances would not afford it, two turtle-doves, or two young pigeons. (Lev. xii. 1—8. Luke ii. 22.)

On the eighth day after its birth the son was circumcised, by which rite it was consecrated to the service of the true God (Gen. xvii. 10. compared with Rom. iv. 11.): on the nature of circumcision, see pp. 269 — 271. *supra.* At the same time the male child received a name (as we have already remarked in p. 271.): in many instances he received a name from the circumstances of his birth, or from some peculiarities in the history of the family to which he belonged (Gen. xvi. 11. xxv. 25, 26. Exod. ii. 10. xviii. 3, 4.); and sometimes the name had a prophetic meaning. (Isa. vii. 14. viii. 3. Hos. i. 4. 6. 9. Matt. i. 21. Luke i. 13. 60. 63.)

II. " The First-born, who was the object of special affection to his parents, was denominated, by way of eminence, *the opening of the womb.* In case a man married a widow who by a previous marriage had become the mother of children, the first-born as respected the second husband was the child that was eldest by the second marriage. Before the time of Moses, the father might, if he chose, transfer the right of primogeniture to a younger child, but the practice occasioned much contention (Gen. xxv. 31, 32.), and a law was enacted over-ruling it. (Deut. xxi. 15—17.) *The first-born* inherited peculiar rights and privileges. — 1. He received a double portion of the estate. Jacob in the case of Reuben, his first-born, bestowed his additional portion upon Joseph, by adopting his two sons. (Gen. xlviii. 5—8.) This was done as a reprimand, and a punishment of his incestuous conduct (Gen. xxxv. 22.); but Reuben, notwithstanding, was enrolled as the first-born in the genealogical registers. (1 Chron. v. 1.) — 2. *The first-born* was the priest of the whole family. The honour of exercising the priesthood was transferred, by the command of God communicated through Moses, from the tribe of Reuben, to whom it belonged by right of primogeniture, to that of

447.   Lewis's Origines Hebrææ, vol. ii. pp. 240—310.   Calmet's Dictionary, article *Adoption.*   Bruning, Antiq. Hebr. pp. 1—11.   Pareau, Antiquitas Hebraica, part iv. c. 6. de liberorum procreatione et educatione, pp. 442—446.
[1] Harmer's Observations, vol. iv. p. 433.   Morier's Second Journey, p. 106.

Levi. (Numb. iii. 12—18. viii. 18.) In consequence of this fact, that God had taken the Levites from among the children of Israel, instead of all the first-born, to serve him as priests, the first-born of the other tribes were to be redeemed, at a valuation made by the priest not exceeding five shekels, from serving God in that capacity. (Numb. xviii. 15, 16. compared with Luke ii. 22. *et seq.*)— 3. *The first-born* enjoyed an authority over those who were younger, similar to that possessed by a father (Gen. xxv. 23. *et seq.* 2 Chron. xxi. 3. Gen. xxvii. 29.), which was transferred in the case of Reuben by Jacob their father to Judah. (Gen. xlix. 8—10.) The tribe of Judah, accordingly, even before it gave kings to the Hebrews, was every where distinguished from the other tribes. In consequence of the authority which was thus attached to the first-born, he was also made the successor in the kingdom. There was an exception to this rule in the case of Solomon, who, though a younger brother, was made his successor by David at the special appointment of God. It is very easy to see in view of these facts, how the word first-born came to express sometimes a great, and sometimes the highest dignity." [1] (Isa. xiv. 30. Psal. lxxxix. 27. Rom. viii. 29. Coloss. i. 15—18. Heb. xii. 23. Rev. i. 5. 11. Job xviii. 13.)

III. In the earliest ages, mothers suckled their offspring themselves, and, it should seem from various passages of Scripture, until they were nearly or quite three years old: on the day the child was weaned, it was usual to make a feast. (2 Macc. vii. 27. 1 Sam. i. 22—24. Gen. xxi. 8.) The same custom of feasting obtains in Persia and India to this day. [2] In case the mother died before the child was old enough to be weaned, or was unable to rear it herself, nurses were employed; and also in later ages when matrons became too delicate or too infirm to perform the maternal duties. These nurses were reckoned among the principal members of the family; and, in consequence of the respectable station which they sustained, are frequently mentioned in sacred history. See Gen. xxxv. 8. 2 Kings xi. 2. 2 Chron. xxii. 11.

" *The daughters* rarely departed from the apartments appropriated to the females, except when they went out with an urn to draw water, which was the practice with those who belonged to those humbler stations in life, where the antient simplicity of manners had not lost its prevalence. (Exod. ii. 16. Gen. xxiv. 11. 16. xxix. 10. 1 Sam. ix. 11, 12. John iv. 7.) They spent their time in learning those domestic and other arts, which are befitting a woman's situation and character, till they arrived at that period in life, when they were to be sold, or by a better fortune given away, in marriage. (Prov. xxxi. 13. 2 Sam. xiii. 7.) The daughters of those who by their wealth had been elevated to high stations in life, so far from going out to draw water in urns, might be said to spend the whole of their time within the walls of their palaces. In imitation of their mothers, they were occupied with dressing, with singing, and with dancing; and, if we may judge from the representations of modern travellers, their apartments were sometimes the scenes of vice. (Ezek. xxiii. 18.) They went abroad but very rarely, as already intimated, and the more rarely, the higher they were in point of rank, but they received with

---

[1] Jahn's Archæologia Biblica, by Mr. Upham, § 165.
[2] Morier's Second Journey, p. 107. Roberts's Oriental Illustrations, p. 24.

cordiality female visitants. The virtues of a good woman, of one that is determined, whatever her station, to discharge each incumbent duty, and to avoid the frivolities and vices at which we have briefly hinted, are mentioned in terms of approbation and praise in Prov. xxxi. 10—31.

" *The sons* remained till the fifth year in the care of the women; then they came into the father's care, and were taught not only the arts and duties of life, but were instructed in the Mosaic law, and in all parts of their country's religion. (Deut. vi. 20—25. xi. 19.) Those who wished to have them further instructed, provided they did not deem it preferable to employ private teachers, sent them away to some priest or Levite, who sometimes had a number of other children to instruct. It appears from 1 Sam. i. 24—28. that there was a school near the holy tabernacle, dedicated to the instruction of youth.

IV. "The authority to which a father was entitled extended not only to his wife, to his own children, and to his servants of both sexes, but to his children's children also. It was the custom antiently for sons newly married to remain at their father's house, unless it had been their fortune to marry a daughter, who, having no brothers, was heiress to an estate; or unless by some trade, or by commerce, they had acquired sufficient property to enable them to support their own family. It might of course be expected, while they lived in their father's house, and were in a manner the pensioners on his bounty, that he would exercise his authority over the children of his sons as well as over the sons themselves." In this case the power of the father " had no narrow limits, and, whenever he found it necessary to resort to measures of severity, he was at liberty to inflict the extremity of punishment. (Gen. xxi. 14. xxxviii. 24.) This power was so restricted by Moses, that the father, if he judged the son worthy of death, was bound to bring the cause before a judge. But he enacted, at the same time, that the judge should pronounce sentence of death upon the son, if on inquiry it could be proved, that he had beaten or cursed his father or mother, or that he was a spendthrift, or saucy, or contumacious, and could not be reformed. (Exod. xxi. 15. 17. Lev. xx. 9. Deut. xxi. 18—21.) The authority of the parents, and the service and love due to them, are recognised in the most prominent and fundamental of the *moral laws* of the Jewish polity, viz. the *Ten Commandments.* (Exod. xx. 12.)

" The son, who had acquired property, was commanded to exhibit his gratitude to his parents, not only by words and in feeling, but by gifts. (Matt. xv. 5, 6. Mark vii. 11—13.) The power of the father over his offspring in the antient times was not only very great for the time being, and while he sojourned with them in the land of the living; but he was allowed also to cast his eye into the future, and his prophetic curse or blessing possessed no little efficacy."[1]   (Gen. xlix. 2—28.)

It appears from 1 Kings xx. 1. (marginal rendering) that, in the disposition of his effects, the father expressed his last wishes or will in the presence of witnesses, and probably in the presence of the future heirs, as Jacob did, in Gen. xlviii.; and this, Michaelis is of opinion, seems to be what is called giving the inheritance to his sons, in Deut.

---

[1] Jahn's Archæologia Biblica, by Mr. Upham, §§ 166, 167.

xxi. 16. Testaments were not written until long after that period. The following regulations obtained in the disposition of property: —

1. " As it respected *sons :* — The property or estate of the father, after his decease, fell into the possession of his sons, who divided it among themselves equally; with this exception, that the eldest son received two portions." It appears, however, from Luke xv. 12. that sons might demand and receive their portion of the inheritance during their father's lifetime; and that the parent, though aware of the dissipated inclinations of the child, could not *legally* refuse the application.

2. " As it respected the *sons of concubines :* — The portion, which was given to them, depended altogether upon the feelings of the father. Abraham gave presents, to what amount is not known, both to Ishmael and to the sons whom he had by Keturah, and sent them away before his death. It does not appear that they had any other portion in the estate; but Jacob made the sons whom he had by his concubines, heirs as well as the others. (Gen. xxi. 8—21. xxv. 1—6. xlix. 1—27.) Moses laid no restrictions upon the choice of fathers in this respect; and we should infer that the sons of concubines for the most part received an equal share with the other sons, from the fact that Jephthah, the son of a concubine, complained, that he was excluded without any portion from his father's house. (Judg. xi. 1—7.)

3. " As it respected *daughters:* — The daughters not only had no portion in the estate, but, if they were unmarried, were considered as making a part of it, and were sold by their brothers into matrimony. In case there were no brothers, or they all had died, they took the estate (Numb. xxvii. 1—8.): if any one died intestate, and without any offspring, the property was disposed of according to the enactments in Numb. xxvii. 8—11.

4. " As it respected *servants :* — The servants or the slaves in a family could not claim any share in the estate as a right, but the person who made a will might, if he chose, make them his heirs. (Comp. Gen. xv. 3.) Indeed, in some instances, those who had heirs, recognised as such by the law, did not deem it unbecoming to bestow the whole or a portion of their estates on faithful and deserving servants. (Prov. xvii. 2.)

5. " As it respected *widows :* — The widow of the deceased, like his daughters, had no legal right to a share in the estate. The sons, however, or other relations, were bound to afford her an adequate maintenance, unless it had been otherwise arranged in the will. She sometimes returned back again to her father's house, particularly if the support, which the heirs gave her, was not such as had been promised, or was not sufficient. (Gen. xxxviii. 11. compare also the story of Ruth.) The prophets very frequently, and undoubtedly not without cause, exclaim against the neglect and injustice shown to widows."[1] (Isa. i. 17. x. 2. Jer. vii. 6. xxii. 3. Ezek. xxii. 7. comp. Exod. xxii. 22—24. Deut. x. 18. xxiv. 17.) The condition of widows in the East is very desolate, and has furnished the prophet Jeremiah with affecting similitudes, in order to denote the desolate condition of Jerusalem, after that city had been sacked, and its inhabitants carried into captivity to Babylon. See Lam. i. 1. 17.

---

[1] Jahn's Archæologia Biblica, by Mr. Upham, § 168.

V. Where there were no sons to inherit property, it appears from various passages of the New Testament, that ADOPTION, — or the taking of a stranger into a family, in order to make him a part of it, acknowledging him as a son and heir to the estate, — was very generally practised in the East, in the time of our Saviour. Adoption, however, does not appear to have been used by the elder Hebrews: Moses is silent concerning it in his laws; and Jacob's adoption of his two grandsons, Ephraim and Manasseh (Gen. xlviii. 1.), is rather a kind of substitution, by which he intended, that the two sons of Joseph should have each his lot in Israel, as if they had been his own sons. *Thy two sons, Ephraim and Manasseh, are mine ; as Reuben and Simeon they shall be mine.* But as he gave no inheritance to their father Joseph, the effect of this adoption extended only to their increase of fortune and inheritance; that is, instead of one part, giving them (or Joseph, by means of them) two parts. Two other kinds of adoption among the Israelites are mentioned in the Scriptures; viz.

1. The first consisted in the obligation of a surviving brother to marry the widow of his brother, who had died without children (Deut. xxv. 5. Ruth iv. 5. Matt. xxii. 24.); so that the children of this marriage were considered as belonging to the deceased brother, and went by his name; a practice more antient than the law, as appears in the history of Tamar; but this manner of adopting was not practised among the Greeks and Romans: neither was that kind of adoption intended by Sarah, Leah, and Rachel; when they gave their handmaidens to their husbands. (Gen. xvi. 2. xxx. 3.)

2. Various instances of another kind of adoption are recorded in the Old Testament, viz. that of a father having a daughter only, and adopting *her* children. Thus, in 1 Chron. ii. 21, 22., Machir the grandson of Joseph, who is called *father of Gilead,* (that is, chief of that town,) gave his daughter to Hezron, who married her when he was threescore years old, and she bare him Segub. And Segub begat Jair, who had three and twenty cities in the land of Gilead. Jair acquired a number of other cities, which made up his possessions to threescore cities. (Josh. xiii. 30. 1 Kings iv. 13.) However, both he and his posterity, instead of being reckoned to the family of Judah as they ought to have been by their *paternal* descent from Hezron, are reckoned as sons of Machir the father of Gilead. It further appears from Numb. xxxii. 41. that this very Jair, who was in fact the son of Segub, the son of Hezron, the son of *Judah,* is expressly called Jair the son of *Manasseh,* because his maternal great-grandfather was Machir, the son of Manasseh. In like manner, we read that Mordecai adopted Esther his niece: when her father and mother were dead, *he took* her *for his own* daughter. So the daughter of Pharaoh adopted Moses, *and he became her son.* (Exod. ii. 10.) So we read in Ruth iv. 17. that Naomi had a son: *a son is born to Naomi:* when, indeed, it was the son of Ruth, and only a distant relation (or, in fact, none at all,) to Naomi, who was merely the wife of Elimelech, to whom Boaz was kinsman.

By the propitiation of our Saviour, and the communication of the merits of his death, *penitent* sinners become the adopted children of God. Thus St. Paul writes (Rom. viii. 15.), *Ye have received the spirit of adoption, whereby we cry, Abba, Father. We wait for the adoption of the children of God.* And (Gal. iv. 4, 5.) *God sent forth his Son to re-*

deem them that were under the law, that we might receive the adoption of sons.

Among the Mohammedans the ceremony of adoption is performed, by causing the adopted to pass through the shirt of the person who adopts him.   For this reason, to adopt among the Turks is expressed by saying — to draw any one through one's shirt; and an adopted son is called by them *Akietogli*, the son of another life — because he was not begotten in this.[1]   Something like this is observable among the Hebrews: Elijah adopted the prophet Elisha, by throwing his mantle over him (1 Kings xix. 19.) ; and when Elijah was carried off in a fiery chariot, his mantle, which he let fall, was taken up by Elisha his disciple, his spiritual son, and adopted successor in the office of prophet. (2 Kings ii. 15.)

This circumstance seems to be illustrated by the conduct of Moses, who dressed Eleazar in Aaron's sacred vestments, when that high priest was about to be gathered to his fathers; indicating thereby, that Eleazar succeeded in the functions of the priesthood, and was, in some sort, adopted to exercise that dignity.   The Lord told Shebna, the captain of the temple, that he would deprive him of his honourable station, and substitute Eliakim, the son of Hilkiah, in his room. (Isa. xxii. 21.)   *I will* CLOTHE HIM WITH THY ROBE, *and strengthen him with thy girdle, and I will commit thy government into his hand.* St. Paul, in several places, says, that *real* Christians *put on the Lord Jesus ; and that they put on the new man*, in order to denote their adoption as sons of God. (Rom. xiii. 14. Gal. iii. 26, 27.)

CHAPTER V.

ON THE CONDITION OF SLAVES AND OF SERVANTS, AND THE CUSTOMS RELATING TO THEM, MENTIONED OR ALLUDED TO IN THE NEW TESTAMENT.

I. *Slaves, how acquired.* — II. *Their Condition among the Hebrews.* — III. *And among other Nations.* — IV. *Of hired Servants.* — *Customs relating to them and to Slaves alluded to in the New Testament.*— V. *Different Kinds of Slaves or Servants mentioned in the Scriptures.*

I. SLAVERY is of very remote antiquity ; and when Moses gave his laws to the Jews, finding it already established, though he could not abolish it, yet he enacted various salutary laws and regulations.   The Israelites, indeed, might have Hebrew servants or slaves, as well as alien-born persons, but these were to be circumcised, and were required to worship the only true God (Gen. xvii. 12, 13), with the exception of the Canaanites.

Slaves were acquired in various ways; viz. 1. By *Captivity*, which is supposed to have been the first origin of slavery (Gen. xiv. 14. Deut. xx. 14. xxi. 10, 11.) ; 2. By *Debt*, when persons being poor were sold for payment of their debts (2 Kings iv. 1.   Matt. xviii. 25.) ; 3. By committing a *Theft*, without the power of making restitution (Exod. xxii. 2, 3.   Neh. v. 4, 5.) ; 4. By *Birth*, when persons were born of married slaves.   These are termed *born in the house* (Gen.

---
[1] D'Herbelot Bibl. Orient. p. 47.

xiv. 14. xv. 3. xvii. 23. xxi. 10.), *home-born* (Jer. ii. 14.), and the *sons* or children of *hand-maids*. (Psal. lxxxvi. 16. cxvi. 16.) Abraham had three hundred and eighteen slaves of this description; 5. *Man-stealing* was another mode by which persons were reduced into slavery.[1] The seizing or stealing of a free-born Israelite, either to treat him as a slave or to sell him as a slave to others, was absolutely and irremissibly punished with death by the law of Moses. (Exod. xxi. 16. Deut. xxiv. 7.) Although the Gospel is intended to make no change or difference in the civil circumstances of mankind who are converted from paganism to Christianity, the master and the slave being equally called, as St. Paul argues at length in 1 Cor. vii. 17—24.; yet the same apostle (1 Tim. i. 9, 10.), when enumerating various classes of offenders who are obnoxious to law, expressly denounces *men-stealers*, ἀνδραποδισταις, those who kidnap men, to sell them for slaves: in other words, slave-traders.[2]

II. Slaves received both food and clothing, for the most part of the meanest quality, but whatever property they acquired belonged to their lords: hence they are said to be worth double the value of a hired servant. (Deut. xv. 18.) They formed marriages at the will of their master, but their·children were slaves, who, though they could not call him a father (Gal. iv. 6. Rom. viii. 15.), yet were attached and faithful to him as to a father, on which account the patriarchs trusted them with arms. (Gen. xiv. 14. xxxii. 6. xxxiii. 1.) If a married Hebrew sold himself, he was to serve for six years, and in the seventh he was to go out free, together with his wife and children; but if ·his master had given one of his slaves to him as a wife, she was to remain with her children, as the property of his master. (Exod. xxi. 2—4.) The duty of slaves was to execute their lord's commands, and they were for the most part employed in tending cattle or in rural affairs;

---

[1] Pareau, Antiq. Hebr. pp. 448, 449. Michaelis's Commentaries, vol. i. pp. 158—164.

[2] " The New Testament," says Bishop Horsley, in one of his speeches in the House of Lords, " contains an express reprobation of the slave-trade by name, as sinful in a very high degree. The apostle, St. Paul, having spoken of persons that were lawless and disobedient, ungodly and sinners, unholy and profane, proceeds to specify and distinguish the several cha-racters and descriptions of men to whom he applies those very general epithets; and they are these, — ' murderers of fathers, murderers of mothers, man-slayers, they that defile them-selves with mankind, *men-stealers*.' " ..... " This text condemns and prohibits the slave-trade in one at least of its most productive modes. But I go further; I maintain that this text, rightly interpreted, condemns and prohibits the slave-trade generally in all its modes: it ranks the slave-trade in the descending scale of crime, next after parricide and homicide. The original word, which the English Bible gives men-stealers, is ἀνδραποδιστης. Our translators have taken the word in its restricted sense which it bears in the Attic law; in which the δικη ἀνδραποδισμου was a criminal prosecution for the specific crime of kidnapping, the penalty of which was death. But the phraseology of the Holy Scripture, especially in the preceptive part, is a popular phraseology; and ἀνδραποδιστης, in its popular sense, is a person who ' deals in men,' literally, a *slave-trader*. That is the English word literally and exactly corresponding to the Greek." ..... " The Greek word is so explained by the learned grammarian Eustathius, and by other grammarians of the first authority. Although the Athenians scrupled not to possess themselves of slaves, yet the *trade* in slaves among them was infamous." (Speeches in Parliament, p. 539.) The following observation of a learned modern critic is too important to be withheld from the reader : — " By ἀνδραποδισταις the best commentators are agreed is meant, those who kidnapped and sold into slavery free persons. Now this was regarded by the law as felony of the deepest dye, and was always punished with death. And as all the crimes here mentioned are of the most heinous kind, and as robbery does not elsewhere occur in the list, so ἀνδραποδισταις seems as put for rob-bery of the worst sort. Let then the slave-traders (Christians, alas!) of our times tremble : for *all*, who in *any way* participate in that abominable traffic, are ἀνδραποδισται; since they thereby uphold a system, which perpetually *engenders man-stealing*." (Bloomfield's Annotations on the New Test. vol. viii. p. 201.) — By the act of parliament 3 & 4 Wil-liam IV. chap. 73. slavery was ABOLISHED throughout the British Colonies.

and though the lot of some of them was sufficiently hard, yet under a mild and humane master it was tolerable. (Job xxxi. 13.) When the eastern people have no male issue, they frequently marry their daughters to their slaves; and the same practice appears to have obtained among the Hebrews, as we read in 1 Chron. ii. 34, 35. *Now Sheshan had no sons but daughters; and Sheshan had a servant* (slave), *an Egyptian, whose name was Jarha; and Sheshan gave his daughter to Jarha his servant to wife.* In Barbary, the rich people when childless, have been known to purchase young slaves, to educate them in their own faith, and sometimes to adopt them for their own children. The greatest men of the Ottoman empire are well known to have been originally slaves brought up in the seraglio; and the Mameluke sovereigns of Egypt were originally slaves. Thus the advancement of the Hebrew captive Joseph to be viceroy of Egypt, and of Daniel, another Hebrew captive, to be chief minister of state in Babylon, corresponds with the modern usages of the East

In order to mitigate the conditions of slaves, various statutes were enacted by Moses. Thus, 1. They were to be treated with humanity: the law in Lev. xxv. 39—53., it is true, speaks expressly of slaves who were of Hebrew descent; but, as alien-born slaves were engrafted into the Hebrew church by circumcision, there is no doubt but that it applied to all slaves.—2. If a man struck his servant or maid with a rod or staff, and he or she died under his hand, he was to be punished by the magistrate; if, however, the slave survived for a day or two, the master was to go unpunished, as no intention of murder could be presumed, and the loss of the slave was deemed a sufficient punishment. (Exod. xxi. 20, 21.) — 3. A slave, who lost an eye or a tooth by a blow from his or her master, acquired his or her liberty in consequence. (Exod. xxi. 26, 27.) — 4. All slaves were to rest from their labours on the Sabbath, and on the great festivals. (Exod. xx. 10. Deut. v. 14.)— 5. They were to be invited to certain feasts. (Deut. xii. 17, 18. xvi. 11.)—6. A master who had betrothed a female slave to himself, if she did not please him, was to permit her to be redeemed, and was prohibited from selling her to a strange nation, *seeing he had dealt deceitfully with her.* If he had betrothed her to his son, he was to deal with her after the manner of daughters. If he took another wife, her food, raiment, and duty of marriage, he was not to diminish. *And if he did not these three unto her, then she was to go out free without money.* (Exod. xxi. 7—11.)—7. Hebrew slaves were to continue in slavery only till the year of jubilee, when they might return to liberty, and their masters could not detain them against their wills. If they were desirous of continuing with their masters, they were to be brought to the judges, before whom they were to make a declaration that for this time they disclaimed the privilege of this law; and had their ears bored through with an awl against the door-posts of their master's house [1], after which

---

[1] *Boring of the ear* was an antient custom in the East: it is thus referred to by Juvenal:—

... Libertinus prior est: " Prior," inquit, " Ego adsum,
Cur timeam, dubitemve locum defendere? quamvis
Natus ad Euphratem, molles quod in AURE FENESTRÆ
Arguerint, licet ipse negem."   Sat. i. 102—105.

The freedman bustling through, replies, " First come is still
First served; and I may claim my right, and will,
Though born a *slave* — ('t were bootless to deny
What these ᴮᴼᴿᴱᴰ ᴇᴀʀs *betray to every eye.*")   GIFFORD.

they had no longer any power of recovering their liberty until the next year of jubilee, after forty-nine years. (Exod. xxi. 5, 6.) This very significant ceremony implied that they were closely attached to that house and family; and that they were bound to *hear*, and punctually to *obey*, all their master's orders.—8. If a Hebrew by birth was sold to a stranger or alien dwelling in the vicinity of the land of Israel, his relations were to redeem him, and such slave was to make good the purchase-money if he were able, paying in proportion to the number of years that remained, until the year of jubilee. (Lev. xxv. 47—55.) Lastly, if a slave of another nation fled to the Hebrews, he was to be received hospitably, and on no account to be given up to his master. (Deut. xxiii. 15, 16.)[1]

III. Although Moses inculcated the duty of humanity towards slaves, and enforced his statutes by various strong sanctions, yet it appears from Jer. xxxiv. 8—22. that their condition was sometimes very wretched. It cannot, however, be denied that their situation was much more tolerable among the Hebrews than among other nations, especially the Greeks and Romans.[2] Nor is this a matter of astonishment: for the Israelites were bound to exercise the duties of humanity towards these unhappy persons by weighty sanctions and motives, which no other nation had, whose slaves had no sabbath, no day of rest, no legal protection, and who were subject to the cruel caprice of their masters, whose absolute property they were, and at whose mercy their lives every moment lay.[3] " For the slightest and most trivial offences they were cruelly scourged and condemned to hard labour; and the petty tyrant of his family, when exasperated by any real or apprehended injury, could nail them to a cross, and make them die in a lingering and most miserable manner. These slaves, generally, were wretched captives, who had been taken prisoners in unfortunate battles, or had fallen into their enemies' hands in the siege of cities. These miserable captives, antient history informs us, were either butchered in cold blood, or sold by auction for slaves to the highest bidder. The unhappy prisoners thus bought and enslaved were sometimes thrust into deep mines, to be drudges through life in darkness and despair: sometimes were pent up in private workhouses, and condemned to the most laborious and ignoble occupations: frequently the toils of agriculture were imposed upon them, and the

---

Calmet to whom we are indebted for this fact, quotes a saying from Petronius Arbiter, as attesting the same thing; and another of Cicero, in which he rallies a Libyan who pretended he did not hear him.—" It is not," said the philosopher, " *because your ears are not sufficiently* BORED."—Commentaire Littéral, sur l'Exode xxi. 6. tom. i. p. 501.

[1] Jahn, Archæol. Bibl. § 171.

[2] Among the Romans more particularly, slaves were held — *pro nullis* — *pro mortuis* — *pro quadrupedibus* — for *no men* — for *dead men* — for *beasts;* — nay, were in a much worse state than any cattle whatever. They had no *head* in the state, no *name*, no tribe, or register. They were not capable of being injured, nor could they take by purchase or descent; they had no heirs, and could make no will. Exclusive of what was called their *peculium,* whatever they acquired was their master's; they could neither plead nor be pleaded, but were entirely excluded from all civil concerns; were not entitled to the rights of matrimony, and, therefore, had no relief in case of adultery; nor were they proper objects of cognation nor affinity. They might be sold, transferred, or pawned, like other goods or personal estate; for goods they were, and as such they were esteemed. Taylor's Elements of the Roman Civil Law, p. 429. 4to. Adam's Summary of Roman Antiquities, pp. 38, 39. There is a learned and interesting Essay, by the Rev. B. B. Edwards, on Roman Slavery, especially in the early centuries of the Christian era, in the Andover Biblical Repository for October, 1835, vol. viii. pp. 411—436.

[3] Jahn, Archæol. Bibl. § 172.

severest tasks unmercifully exacted from them [1] : most commonly they were employed in the menial offices and drudgery of domestic life, and treated with the greatest inhumanity. As the last insult upon their wretchedness, they were branded in the forehead, and a note of eternal disgrace and infamy publicly and indelibly impressed upon them ! One cannot think of this most contumelious and reproachful treatment of a fellow-creature without feeling the acutest pain and indignation. To the above-mentioned customs in the treatment of slaves, which obtained among the antients, there are several allusions in the New Testament. Thus St. Paul, in reference to the custom of purchasing slaves, on whose heads a price was then fixed, just as upon any other commodity, and who, when bought, were the entire and unalienable property of the purchaser, by a very beautiful and expressive similitude represents Christians as the servants of Christ ; informs them that an immense price had been paid for them: that they were not at their own disposal; but in every respect, both as to body and mind, were the sole and absolute property of God. *Ye are not your own : for ye are bought with a price : therefore glorify God in your body and in your spirit, which are God's.* (1 Cor. vi. 20.) So also again : *Ye are bought with a price : be not ye the servants of men.* (1 Cor. vii. 23.) St. Paul usually styles himself the servant of Christ ; and in a passage in his Epistle to the Galatians, alluding to the signatures with which slaves in those days were branded, he tells them that he carried about with him plain and indelible characters impressed in his body, which evinced him to be the servant of his master Jesus. *From henceforth let no man trouble me, for I bear in my body the marks of the Lord Jesus."* (Gal. vi. 17.) [2] It was a doctrine of the pharisaic Jews, that proselytes were released from all antecedent, civil, and even natural relations; and it is not improbable that some of the Jewish converts might carry the same principle into the Christian community, and teach that, by the profession of Christianity, slaves were emancipated from their Christian masters. In opposition to this false notion, the same great apostle requires that all who are under the yoke of servitude be taught to yield due obedience to their masters, and animadverts with great severity upon those false teachers, who, from mercenary views, taught a different doctrine. (1 Tim. vi. 1—10.) Against this principle of the judaising zealots, St. Paul always enters his strong protest, and teaches that the profession of Christianity makes no differ-

---

[1] The following passage from Mr. Jowett's Christian Researches in the Mediterranean will give an idea of the rigour with which slaves are treated to this day in the East. The conductor of a nitre factory for the Pasha of Egypt having received commands to prepare a large quantity of nitre in great haste, — "for this purpose he was building small reservoirs and ducts, with old picked bricks, gathered from ruins ; and which are better than the modern baked bricks. A great number of young persons of both sexes were engaged in the work, carrying burdens. To give vivacity to their proceedings, *they are required to sing ;* and to keep them diligent, *there were task-masters standing at intervals of about ten feet, with whips in their hands which they used very freely.* We seemed to behold the manners of the antient Egyptians, Exodus v." Jowett's Researches, p. 130. May not the command to *sing* also explain Psal. cxxxvii. 3, 4. ? " The Mâllems" (or heads of districts of Coptic Christians in Egypt), the same traveller elsewhere remarks, " transact business between the bashaw and the peasants. He punishes them, if the peasants prove that they oppress ; and yet he requires from them that the work of those who are under them shall be fulfilled. They strikingly illustrate the case of the officers, placed by the Egyptian task-masters over the children of Israel ; and, like theirs, the Mâllems often find that their case is evil. See Exod. v. 6—29." Ibid. p. 168. See also Mr. Carne's Letters from the East, pp. 71, 72.

[2] Harwood's Introduction, vol. ii. pp. 144—146.

ence in the civil relations of men. See 1 Cor. vii. 17—24. It appears probable from Isa. xvi. 14. and xxi. 16. that it was the usual practice to hire servants either for one year or for three years. This circumstance may explain the meaning in Deut. xv. 18. of a bondman being *worth a double hired servant to his master, in serving him six years.* Which passage of the law, if thus understood by the Israelites, would teach them that a bondman ought not to be made to work more laboriously than a hired servant, but only to serve for a longer time.[1]

IV. Though slavery was tolerated and its horrors were mitigated by the wise and humane enactments of Moses, yet in the progress of time, as hired servants would be necessary, various regulations were in like manner made by him, to insure them from being oppressed. Like slaves, hired labourers were to partake of the rest of the sabbath, and also to share in the produce of the sabbatical year: their hire was to be paid every day before sunset (Lev. xix. 13. Deut. xxiv. 14, 15.); but what that hire was to be, the Hebrew legislator has not determined, because the price of labour must have varied according to circumstances. From the parable of the proprietor of a vineyard and his labourers, which is related in Matt. xx. 1—15., " we learn these three particulars concerning the servants in Judea, or at least in Jerusalem: — That early in the morning they stood in the market-place to be hired — that the usual wages of a day-labourer were at that time a denarius, or about seven-pence halfpenny of our money — and that the customary hours of working were till six in the evening. Early in the morning the master of a family rose to hire day-labourers to work in his vineyard.[2] Having found a number he agreed to pay them a DENARIUS for the WAGES of the DAY, and sent them into his vineyard. About nine o'clock he went again into the MARKET-PLACE, and found several others unemployed, whom he also ordered into his vineyard, and promised to pay them what was reasonable. At twelve and three in the afternoon, he went and made the same proposals, which were in the same manner accepted. He went likewise about five o'clock, and found a number of men sauntering about the market in idleness, and he said to them, Why do you consume the whole day in this indolent manner? There is no one hath thought fit to give us any employment, they replied. Then go you into the vineyard among my other labourers, and you shall receive what is just. In the evening the proprietor of the vineyard ordered his steward to call the workmen together, beginning from the last to the first, to pay them their wages without any partiality or distinction. When those, therefore, came, who had been employed about five in the afternoon, they received a denarius a piece. When those, who had been hired in the morning, saw them return with such great wages, they

---

[1] Girdlestone's Commentary and Lectures on the Old Testament, vol. i. p. 660.

[2] The same custom obtains to this day in Persia. In the city of Hamadan there is a maidan or square in front of a large mosque. " Here," says Mr. Morier, " we observed every morning before the sun rose, that a numerous band of peasants were collected with spades in their hands, waiting, as they informed us, to be hired for the day to work in the surrounding fields. This custom, which I have never seen in any other part of Asia, forcibly struck me as a most happy illustration of our Saviour's parable of the labourers in the vineyard in the 20th chapter of Matthew, particularly when passing by the same place late in the day, we still found others standing idle, and remembered his words, *Why stand ye here all the day idle?* as most applicable to their situation; for, in putting the very same question to them, they answered us, *Because no man hath hired us.*" Morier's Second Journey through Persia, p. 265.

indulged the most extravagant joy, imagining that their pay would vastly exceed that of the others; but how great was their disappointment, when they received from the steward each man a denarius! This supposed injurious treatment caused them to raise loud clamours against the master. And they complained to him of his usage of them, saying, the last labourers you hired only worked a SINGLE HOUR, and you given them the same wages as you have given us who have been scorched with excessive heat, and sustained the long and rigorous toil of the whole day. He turned to one who appeared the most petulant of them, and directed this reply, Friend, I do thee no injustice; was not our agreement for a denarius? Take what justice entitles thee to, without repining, and calmly acquiesce in the faithful performance of our original agreement— a principle of benevolence disposes me freely to bestow upon the last persons I hired what equity obliged me to give to you.

" It has been observed that slaves were condemned to the mines, where their uncomfortable lives were consumed in the most rigorous and servile drudgery. It is natural to suppose that these wretches, born to better hopes, upon their first entrance into these dismal subterraneous abodes of darkness and despair, with such doleful prospects before them, would be transfixed with the acutest distress and anguish, shed bitter unavailing tears, gnash their teeth for extreme misery, and fill these gloomy caverns with piercing cries and loud lamentations. Our Lord seems to allude to this, and, considered in this view, the imagery is peculiarly beautiful and expressive, when he represents the wicked servant and unfaithful steward bound hand and foot and cast into utter darkness, where there would be weeping, wailing, and gnashing of teeth! (Matt. viii. 12. xxii. 13.) The reader will be pleased with the ingenious remarks of the learned and judicious Dr. Macknight on this passage: — " In antient times the stewards of great families were slaves as well as the servants of a lower class, being raised to that trust on account of their fidelity, wisdom, sobriety, and other good qualities. If any steward, therefore, in the absence of his lord, behaved as is represented in the parable, it was a plain proof, that the virtues on account of which he was raised were counterfeit, and by consequence that he was an hypocrite. Slaves of this character, among other chastisements, were sometimes condemned to work in the mines. And as this was one of the most grievous punishments, when they first entered, nothing was heard among them but weeping and gnashing of teeth, on account of the intolerable fatigue to which they were subjected in these hideous caverns without hope of release. There shall be weeping and gnashing of teeth." [1]

"Crucifixion was a servile punishment, and usually inflicted on the most vile, worthless, and abandoned of slaves. In reference to this it is that St. Paul represents our Lord taking *upon him the form of a servant, and becoming subject to death, even the death of the* CROSS (Phil. ii. 8.); crucifixion was not only the most painful and excruciating, but the most reproachful and ignominious death that could be suffered. Hence it is that the Apostle so highly extols the unexampled love for man and magnanimity of Jesus, *who for the joy set before him endured the* CROSS, *despising the shame* (Heb. xii. 2.) and infamy even of such a death. It was this exit which Jesus made, that insuperably disgusted

---

[1] Dr. Macknight's Harmony, p. 522. 2d edit. 1763.

so many among the heathens; who could never prevail with themselves to believe that religion to be divine, whose founder had suffered such an opprobrious and infamous death from his countrymen. And for men to preach in the world a system of truths as a revelation from the Deity, which were first delivered to mankind by an illiterate and obscure Jew, pretending to a divine mission and character, and who was for such a pretension crucified, appeared to the heathens the height of infatuation and religious delusion. *The preaching of the* cross *was to them foolishness* (1 Cor. i. 23.); and the religion of a crucified leader, who had suffered in the capital of his own country the indignities and death of a slave, carried with it, in their estimation, the last absurdity and folly, and induced them to look upon the Christians, and the wretched cause in which they were embarked, with pity and contempt. Hence St. Paul speaks of the offence of the cross [1], the great and invincible disgust conceived by the men of those times against a religion whose founder was crucified! Hence he speaks of not being ashamed of the Gospel from the circumstance which made such numbers ashamed of it, nay, of glorying in the cross [2] of Christ; though the consideration of the ignominious and servile death he suffered was the very obstacle that made the heathens stumble at the very threshold of Christianity, and filled them with insurmountable prejudices against it." [3]

V. Among the Greeks, slaves were commonly termed δουλοι, in opposition to the ελευθεροι, or those who were free born; and, by some of the comic writers, οἰκεται. They were also frequently termed παιδες. These appellations also occur in the New Testament, where we find them characterised by different names, according to the nature of the services which they performed. Thus in Acts xii. 20. we meet with a *chamberlain;* ... Blastus, ὁ ἐπι τοῦ κοιτωνος, who had charge of the royal bedchamber, or, in modern language, the royal chamberlain. These persons often had great influence with their masters. [4] Those, who had large flocks of sheep and herds of cattle, which they intrusted to ποιμενες, inferior shepherds, appointed a chief shepherd, ἀρχιποιμην, to superintend them. In 1 Pet. v. 4. this appellation is applied to the chief teacher of religion, that is, Jesus Christ, who is to come as judge. Kings are often termed οἱ ποιμενες των λαων, because they watch for the safety and welfare of their subjects; and the same figure is transferred to religious teachers, who strive by their instructions and exhortations to promote the highest interests of mankind. The ἐπιτροπος and οἰκονομος appear to be synonymous terms for him who had the chief charge or oversight of the property or domestic affairs of any one. This class of men had authority over the slaves of a family, and seem to have sometimes been slaves themselves. (Luke xii. 42. 1 Cor. iv. 2.) Besides the general care of affairs, the boys of a family also appear to have been intrusted to their charge; at least in regard to pecuniary matters. (Gal. iv. 4.) Schleusner considers the ἐπιτροπος in this passage as the guardian appointed by the law or by the magistrate, and the οἰκονομος as one who was appointed by will. Opposed to slaves were the Ἐργαται, or hired labourers (Matt. xx. 1.), whether they were Γεωργοι, or cultivators of the soil (Luke xx. 9, 10.),

---

[1] Σκανδαλον του σταυρου. Galat. v. 11.
[2] God forbid that I should glory save in the cross of our Lord Jesus Christ. Galat. vi. 14.   [3] Harwood's Introduction, vol. ii. pp. 147—152.
[4] See Adam's Roman Antiquities, p. 488.

'Αμπελουργοι, or vine-dressers (Luke xiii. 7.); or Θυρωροι, door-keepers. (Mark xiii. 34. John xviii. 16, 17.)   But, whatever was the nature of their service, each was required to prosecute that particular work which was deemed most suitable for him by his master or lord, whether the latter was at home or abroad (Mark xiii. 34. Luke xii. 42. xiv. 17. xvii. 7, 8.), with all honesty and fidelity. (Tit. ii. 9, 10.) [1]

Among the Greeks those slaves who had conducted themselves well were manumitted, or released from bondage.   The Greeks termed those who were thus liberated ἀπελευθερους, or freed men; which word is applied by St. Paul to him who is called into the church of Christ, while a slave, in order to denote that he is free indeed, as being made by Christ a partaker of all the privileges of the children of God. (1 Cor. vii. 22.)   Corinth was long the chief slave mart of Greece: and we may reasonably conclude that many slaves were converted to Christianity.   In some of the Grecian states, the son and heir was permitted to adopt brethren, and communicate to them the same privileges which he himself enjoyed.   To this some commentators have supposed that Jesus Christ refers in John viii. 32.

Lastly, when slaves proved ungrateful to their former masters or patrons, they might be again reduced into bondage, both among the Greeks and Romans.   To this usage St. Paul may refer when he exhorts the Galatian believers in Christ not to suffer the judaising teachers *again to entangle them in the yoke of bondage.* (Gal. v. 1.) [2]

CHAPTER VI.

DOMESTIC CUSTOMS AND USAGES OF THE JEWS.

I. *Forms of Salutation and Politeness.—Reverence to Superiors.—*II. *Mode of receiving Guests or Visitors. —* III. *Conversation and Bathing. —* IV. *Food and Entertainments.—*V. *Mode of Travelling.—*VI. *Hospitality a sacred Duty among the Jews. — Account of the Tesseræ Hospitales of the Greeks and Romans.*

I. "VARIOUS are the modes of address and politeness which custom has established in different nations.   The Orientals were very exact in the observances of outward decorum: and we may collect, from several passages in the Old and New Testament, that their salutations and expressions of regard on *meeting* each other were extremely tedious and tiresome, containing many minute inquiries concerning the person's welfare, and the welfare of his family and friends; and when they *parted*, concluding with many reciprocal wishes of happiness and benediction on each other." [3]   The ordinary formulæ of saluta-

---

[1] Robinson's Gr. Lexicon, in vocibus; Stosch's Compendium Archæologiæ Novi Testamenti, pp. 45, 46.

[2] Bruning, Compendium Græcarum à profanis Sacrarum, p. 86.   Kuinöel, on John viii. 32.

[3] Of the minute, not to say frivolous, inquiries and salutations above mentioned, the following is a striking illustration: — " Every passer by," says the Rev. Mr. Jowett, " has his ' *Alla ybárakek*,' — ' God bless you.'   Conversation is sometimes among strangers made up of a very large proportion of these phrases; for example, — ' Good morning.'   Answer, ' May your day be enriched !' — ' By seeing you.' — ' You have enlightened the house by your presence.' — ' Are you happy ?' — ' Happy; and you, also.' — ' You are comfortable, I am comfortable;' meaning ' I am comfortable, if you are.'   These sentences are often

tion were — *The Lord be with thee! — The Lord bless thee!* — and
Blessed be thou of the Lord! but the most common salutation was
Peace (that is, may all manner of prosperity) *be with thee!* (Ruth ii. 4.
Judg. xix. 20. 1 Sam. xxv. 6. Psal. cxxix. 8.) In the latter ages of
the Jewish polity, much time appears to have been spent in the rigid
observance of these ceremonious forms, for which the modern inhabitants of the East continue to be remarkable.[1] "When our Lord,
therefore, in his commission to the seventy, whom he despatched into
the towns and villages of Judæa to publish the Gospel, strictly ordered
them to *salute no man by the way* (Luke x. 4.), he designed only by
this prohibition that they should employ the utmost expedition; that
they should suffer nothing to retard and impede them in their progress
from one place to another; and should not lavish those precious
moments, which ought to be devoted to the sacred and arduous duties
of their office, in observing the irksome and unmeaning modes of
ceremonious intercourse.   Not that our Lord intended that his disciples should studiously violate all common civility and decency, and
industriously offend against all the rules of courteousness and decorum,
since he commanded them upon their entrance into any house to *salute
it* (Matt. x. 12.), and observe the customary form of civility in wishing
it *peace* (Luke x. 5.) or universal happiness. This injunction, to *salute
no one on the road,* means only that they should urge their course with
speed, and not suffer their attention to be diverted from the duties of
their commission.   There is a passage in the Old Testament parallel
to this, and which beautifully illustrates it.   Elisha, despatching his
servant Gehazi to recover the son of the Shunamite, strictly enjoins
him to make all the expedition possible, which is thus expressed:
*Gird up thy loins and take my staff in thine hand, and go thy way.
If thou meet any man, salute him not, and if any salute thee, answer him
not again.* (2 Kings iv. 29.)

    " In all countries these modes of address and politeness, though
the terms are expressive of the profoundest respect and homage, yet
through constant use and frequency of repetition soon degenerate into
mere verbal forms and words of course, in which the heart has no
share. They are a frivolous unmeaning formulary, perpetually uttered
without the mind's ever annexing any idea to them. To these empty,
insignificant forms, which men mechanically repeat at meeting or
taking leave of each other, there is a beautiful allusion in the following
expression of our Lord in that cónsolatory discourse which he delivered to his apostles when he saw them dejected and disconsolate, on
his plainly assuring them that he would soon leave them and go to the
Father. *Peace I leave with you : my peace I give unto you : — not as
the world giveth, give I unto you.* (John xiv. 27.) Since I must shortly

---

repeated; and, after any pause, it is usual to turn to your neighbour, and resume these
courtesies many times." Jowett's Christian Researches in Syria, p. 90.

[1] Serious and taciturn as the natives of the East usually are, they grow talkative when
they meet an acquaintance, and salute him. This custom has come from Asia with the
Arabs, and spread over the north coast of Africa. A modern traveller relates the reciprocal
salutations with which those are received who return with the caravans. " People go a great
way to meet them : as soon as they are perceived, the questioning and salutation begins,
and continues with the repetition of the same phrases : ' How do you do? God be praised
that you are come in peace ! God give you peace ! How fares it with you ?' The higher
the rank of the person returning home, the longer does the salutation last." See Horne-
man's Journal. Stollberg's History of Religion, vol. iii. p. 183. Burder's Oriental
Literature, vol. i. p. 486.

be taken from you, I now bid you adieu, sincerely wishing you every
happiness; not as the world giveth, give I unto you; not in the unmeaning ceremonial manner the world repeats this salutation: for my
wishes of peace and happiness to you are sincere, and my blessing and
benediction will derive upon you every substantial felicity. This
sheds light and lustre upon one of the finest and most beautiful pieces
of imagery which the genius and judgment of a writer ever created.
In the eleventh chapter of the Epistle to the Hebrews, the author
informs us with what warm, anticipating hopes of the Messiah's future
kingdom those great and good men, who adorned the annals of former
ages, were animated. These all, says he, died in faith, they closed
their eyes upon the world, but they closed them in the transporting
assurance that God would accomplish his promises. They had the
firmest persuasion that the Messiah would bless the world. By faith
they antedated these happy times, and placed themselves, in idea, in
the midst of all their fancied blessedness. They hailed this most
auspicious period: saluted it, as one salutes a friend whose person we
recognise, at a distance. These all died in faith, died in the firm
persuasion that God would accomplish these magnificent promises,
though they themselves had not enjoyed them, but only had seen them
afar off: God had only blessed them with a remote prospect of them.
They were, therefore, persuaded of them, they had the strongest conviction of their reality—they embraced them — with transport saluted [1]
them at a distance, confessing that they were but strangers and pilgrims upon earth, but were all travelling towards a CITY which had
foundations, whose builder and maker is God." [2]

Respect was shown to persons on meeting, by the salutation of
Peace be with you! and laying the right hand upon the bosom: but if
the person addressed was of the highest rank, they bowed to the
earth. Thus *Jacob bowed to the ground seven times until he came near
to his brother Esau.* (Gen. xxxiii. 3.) Such was the piety of antient
times, that masters saluted their labourers with " *The Lord be with
you!* " to which they answered, " *The Lord bless thee!* " [3] Sometimes
the hem of the person's garment was kissed, and even the dust on
which he had to tread. (Zech. viii. 23. Luke viii. 44. Acts x. 26.
Psal. lxxii. 9.) Near relations and intimate acquaintances kissed each
other's hands, head, neck, beard (which on such occasions only could
be touched without affront), or shoulders. (Gen. xxxiii. 4. xlv. 14.
2 Sam. xx. 9. Luke xv. 20. Acts xx. 37.) So, in India, when people
meet after long absence, they fall on each other's shoulder or neck, and
kiss or smell the part. [4] The modern Arabs salute their chiefs by
kissing either cheek alternately. [5] Whenever the common people
approach their prince, or any person of superior rank, it was customary for them to prostrate themselves before him. " In particular,
this homage was universally paid to the monarchs of Persia by those

---

[1] Ἀσπασαμενοι. The word always used in salutations. See Romans xvi. passim.
[2] Harwood's Introduction, vol. ii. pp. 279—283.
[3] Not unlike the above, are the salutations in use at this time among the Turks. " Say
to a Turk, according to custom, ' May your morning be propitious!' he replies, ' May
you be the pledge of God!' Ask a Turk, ' Is your health good?' he answers, ' Glory be
to God!' Salute him as you pass him rapidly in travelling, he exclaims, ' May God be
merciful to you!' At parting, he addresses you, ' To God I commend you!' and is
answered, ' May God be with you.'"—Hartley's Researches in Greece, p. 233.
[4] Roberts's Oriental Illustrations, p. 51.
[5] Irby's and Mangles' Travels, p. 262.

who were admitted into their presence ; — a homage, in which some
of the Greek commanders, possessed of a truly liberal and manly
spirit, peremptorily refused [1] to gratify them.   In imitation of these
proud sovereigns, Alexander the Great exacted a similar prostration.
This mode of address obtained also among the Jews.   When honoured
with admittance to their sovereign, or introduced to illustrious personages, they fell down at their feet, and continued in this servile
posture till they were raised.   There occur many instances of this
custom in the New Testament.   The wise men who came from the
East, when they saw the child Jesus with his mother Mary, *fell down
and worshipped him.*   Great numbers of those who approached our
Saviour *fell down at his feet.*   We read of several of the common
people who *prostrated* themselves before him and worshipped him.
Cornelius, at his first interview with Peter, when he met him, *fell
down* before him and worshipped him, and remained in this submis-
sive attitude till Peter took him up ; saying, *Stand up : I also am a man.*
In the Old Testament we read that Esther *fell down* at the feet of
Ahasuerus.   These prostrations among the eastern people appear to
us to the last degree unmanly and slavish [2]; but it seems that the
inhabitants of the oriental countries have always used more illiberal
and humiliating forms of address and homage than ever obtained in
Europe.

" It was also customary in those times, whenever a popular harangue was about to be delivered, and the people stood convened, for
the orator, before he entered on his discourse, *to stretch forth his hand
towards* the multitude as a token of respect to his audience, and to
engage their candid attention.   Frequent instances of this polite address of an orator to the assembled multitude occur in the classics.
In like manner we read that St. Paul, before he commenced his
public apology to the multitude, bespoke their respect and candour
by *beckoning with his hand* to them.   Paul said, ' I am a man who am
a Jew of Tarsus, a city of Cilicia, a citizen of no mean city; and I
beseech thee suffer me to speak unto the people.   And when he had
given him licence, Paul stood on the stairs and *beckoned with his hand*
unto the people.'   Thus, also, in the account of the tumult which
happened at Ephesus, when the whole city was filled with confusion,
some clamouring one thing, some another, and the mob which Demetrius had raised were instigated to the last excesses of violence and
fury, though, as is usual in mobs, the majority of them, as the sacred
historian tells us, knew not what it was that had brought them
together; in the midst of this confused scene we read that the Jews
pushed forward and placed one Alexander on an eminence.   He being
exalted above the crowd, intended in a formal harangue to exculpate
the Jews from any concern in the present disturbance.   Accordingly

---

[1] Vereor ne civitati meæ sit opprobrio, si quum ex eâ sim profectus, quæ cæteris gentibus
imperare consueverit, potius barbarorum quam illius more fungar? C. Nepos. Conon.
p. 153.   The Athenians punished a person with death for submitting to this slavish prostration.   Athenienses autem Timagoram inter officium salutationis Darium regem more
gentis illius adulatum, capitali supplicio affecerunt; unius civis humilibus blanditiis totius
urbis suæ decus Persicæ dominationi summissum graviter ferentes. Valerius Maximus,
lib. vi. cap. 3. p. 561. Torrenii, Leidæ, 1726.

[2] Qui ubi in castra Romana et prætorium pervenerunt, more adulantium, accepto, credo,
ritu ex eâ regione ex quâ oriundi erant, procubuerunt.   Conveniens oratio tam humili adu-
lationi. Livius, lib. xxx. cap. 16. tom. iii. p. 130. edit. Ruddiman.

he *beckoned to them with his hand* — making use of this respectful customary address to insure their favourable regard, before he delivered
his designed apology. But this specious and popular artifice, it seems,
did not avail the orator; for the moment the mob understood he was
a Jew, they pierced the air with their confused cries, repeating, for
two hours together, *Great is Diana of the Ephesians!*

 " From time immemorial it has also been the universal custom in
the East to send presents one to another. No one waits upon an
eastern prince, or any person of distinction, without a present. This
is a token of respect which is never dispensed with. How mean and
inconsiderable soever the gift, the intention of the giver is accepted.
Plutarch informs us that a peasant happening to fall in the way of
Artaxerxes the Persian monarch in one of his excursions, having
nothing to present to his sovereign, according to the oriental custom,
the countryman immediately ran to an adjacent stream, filled both his
hands, and offered it to his prince. The monarch, says the philosopher,
smiled and graciously received it, highly pleased with the good dispositions this action manifested.[1] All the books of modern travellers
into the East, Sandys, Thevenot, Maundrell, Shaw, Pococke, Norden,
Hasselquist," Light, Clarke, Morier, Ouseley, Buckingham, and
others, "abound with numberless examples, of this universally prevalent
custom of waiting upon great men with presents — unaccompanied
with which, should a stranger presume to enter their houses, it would
be deemed the last outrage and violation of politeness and respect.
It was, therefore, agreeably to this oriental practice which obtains in
all these countries to this day[2], that the wise men, when they entered
the house to which the star had directed them, and saw the child and
his mother, after they had prostrated themselves before him, and paid
him the profoundest homage, as the evangelist informs us, opened
their treasures, and testified their sense of the dignity of his person,
by respectfully making him rich presents, consisting of gold, frankincense, and myrrh."[3]

 II. When any person visited another, he stood at the gate (as is
still usual in India[4]) and knocked, or called aloud, until the person
on whom he called admitted him. (2 Kings v. 9—12. Prov. viii. 34.
Acts x. 17. xii. 13. 16.) If the visitor was a person of extraordinary
dignity, it was customary to send persons of rank, who were followed
by others of still greater rank, to meet him, and do him honour.
Thus *Balak sent princes more and more honourable* to meet Balaam
(Numb. xxii. 15.), and the same custom obtains to this day in Persia.[5]
Visitors were always received and dismissed with great respect. On
their arrival water was brought to wash their feet, water was also poured
upon their hands. (2 Kings iii. 11.[6] Gen. xviii. 4. xix. 2.), and the

---

[1] Plutarch's Morals, vol. i. p. 299. edit. Gr. Stephani.

[2] The common present now made to the great in these countries is a *horse ;* an *ass* might
answer the same purpose, and to this Moses probably alludes in Numb. xvi. 15. as
well as Samuel (1 Sam. xii. 3.), particularly as asses were then deemed no dishonourable
beast for the saddle. See Burder's Oriental Literature, vol. i. p. 243.

[3] Harwood's Introduction, vol. ii. pp. 284—289.

[4] Statham's Indian Recollections, p. 113.

[5] Morier's Second Journey, p. 129.

[6] The Oriental method of washing is universally different from that practised in the
West. Nowhere is water poured previously into a basin ; but the servant pours water from
a pitcher upon the hands of his master. See a confirmation of this remark, and of
2 Kings iii. 11. in Roberts's Oriental Illustrations of Scripture, p. 222. " The custom of

guests were anointed with oil. On all joyful occasions the people of the east anoint the head with oil.[1] David alludes to this in Psal. xxiii. 5. The same practice obtained in our Saviour's time. Thus we find Mary Magdalene approaching him at an entertainment, and, as a mark of the highest respect and honour she could confer, breaking an alabaster vase full of the richest perfume and pouring it on his head.[2] Our Lord's vindication to Simon, of the behaviour of this woman, presents us with a lively idea of the civilities in those times ordinarily paid to guests on their arrival, but which marks of friendship and respect had (it seems) been neglected by this Pharisee, at whose house Jesus Christ then was. *He turned to the woman, and said unto Simon, Seest thou this woman?* *I entered into thine house, and thou gavest me* NO WATER FOR MY FEET, *but she hath* WASHED MY FEET *with her tears, and wiped them with the hairs of her head.* *Thou gavest me no* KISS: *but this woman, since I came in, hath not ceased to* KISS MY FEET. *Mine* HEAD *with* OIL *thou didst not anoint; but this woman hath* ANOINTED MY FEET *with ointment.* (Luke vii. 44—46.) To this practice of anointing, Solomon alludes (Prov. xxvii. 9.); and among the Babylonians it was usual to present *sweet odours.* (Dan. ii. 46.) It is still the custom in Egypt, among the Arabs and other nations, thus to treat their guests, and, when they are about to depart, to burn the richest perfumes.[3] The ceremony of *washing the feet* is still observed among the Christians of Assalt in Palestine, towards all strangers who come amongst them as guests or visitors.[4] An elevated seat, in the corner of the room, was considered as the post of honour. (Isa. xxxviii. 2.)[5] Among the Asiatic sovereigns it is a common custom to give both garments and money to ambassadors, and persons of distinction whom they wish to honour: hence they keep in their wardrobes several hundred changes of raiment ready for presents of this kind. This usage obtained in Egypt, where Joseph gave changes of raiment to his brethren, and to his brother Benjamin three hundred pieces of silver, besides five changes of raiment. (Gen. xlv. 22.) That such were given by way of reward and honour, see Judg. xiv. 12. 19. Rev. vi. 11. and vii. 9. 14.[6]

III. " *Conversation,* in which the antient Orientals indulged like other men, in order to beguile the time, was held in the gate of the city. Accordingly, there was an open space near the gate of the city, as is the case at the present day in Mauritania, which was fitted up with seats for the accommodation of the people. (Gen. xix. 1. Psal. lxix. 12.) Those who were at leisure occupied a position on these seats, and either amused themselves with witnessing those who came in and those who went out, and with any trifling occurrences that might offer themselves to their notice, or attended to the judicial trials,

---

washing hands prevails also to this day. The servant goes round to all the guests, with a pitcher and with a vessel to receive the water falling from the hands, and performs the office attributed to Elisha. The same service is repeated when the repast is ended." Hartley's Researches in Greece, pp. 233, 234.

1 Roberts's Oriental Illustrations, p. 323.

2 It is worthy of remark that Otto of Roses, which is the finest perfume imported from the East at this time, is contained in pots or vases, with covers so firmly luted to the top, that it requires force and breaking to separate them, before the perfume can be poured out. Does not this explain the action of Mary Magdalene?

3 See several instances of this custom in Harmer's Observations, vol. ii. pp. 378—392.

4 Buckingham's Travels among the Arab Tribes, p. 24.

5 Bp. Lowth's Isaiah, vol. ii. pp. 242, 243.

6 Jahn, Archæol. Bibl. §§ 176, 177. Harwood, vol. ii. p. 117.

which were commonly investigated at public places of this kind, viz. the gate of the city. (Gen. xix. 1. xxxiv. 20. Psal. xxvi. 4, 5. lxix. 12. cxxvii. 5. Ruth iv. 11. Isa. xiv. 31.) Intercourse by conversation, though not very frequent, was not so rare among the antient Orientals, as among their descendants of modern Asia, except perhaps in Palestine.[1] Nor is this to be wondered at, since the fathers drank wine, while the descendants are obliged to abstain from it; and we are well assured, that the effect of this exhilarating beverage was to communicate no little vivacity to the characters of the antient Asiatics, at least to that of the Hebrews. (See Isa. xxx. 29. Jer. vii. 34. xxx. 19. Amos vi. 4, 5.) The antient Asiatics, among whom we include the Hebrews, were delighted with singing, with dancing, and with instruments of music. Promenading, so fashionable and so agreeable in colder latitudes, was wearisome and unpleasant in the warm climates of the East, and this is probably one reason why the inhabitants of those climates preferred holding intercourse with one another, while sitting near the gate of the city, or beneath the shade of the fig-tree and the vine. (1 Sam. xxii. 6. Micah iv. 4.) It is for the same reason also that we so frequently hear in the Hebrew Scriptures of persons sitting down, as in the following passage: ‘ Blessed is the man that standeth not in the way of sinners, *nor sitteth in the seat of the scornful.*’ (See Psal. i. 1. cvii. 32. lxxxix. 7. cxi. 1. lxiv. 2. 1. 20. xxvi. 5.)

“ The *bath* was always very agreeable to the inhabitants of the East (Ruth iii. 3. 2 Sam. xi. 2. 2 Kings v. 10.); and it is not at all surprising that it should have been so, since it is not only cooling and refreshing, but is absolutely necessary in order to secure a decent degree of cleanliness in a climate where there is so much exposure to dust. The bath is frequently visited by eastern ladies, and may be reckoned among their principal recreations. Those Egyptians, who lived at the earliest period of which we have any account, were in the habit of bathing in the waters of the Nile. (Exod. ii. 5. vii. 13—25.) It was one of the civil laws of the Hebrews, that the bath should be used. The object of the law, without doubt, was to secure a proper degree of cleanliness among them. (Lev. xiv. 2. xv. 1—8. xvii. 15, 16. xxii. 6. Numb. xix. 7.) We may, therefore, consider it as probable, that public baths, soon after the enactment of this law, were erected in Palestine, of a construction similar to that of those which are so frequently seen at the present day in the East.

“ The Orientals, when engaged in conversation, are very candid and mild, and do not feel themselves at liberty directly to contradict

---

[1] “ It is no uncommon thing,” says the Rev. Mr. Jowett, “ to see an individual, or a group of persons, even when very well dressed, sitting with their feet drawn under them, upon the bare earth, passing whole hours in idle conversation. Europeans would require a chair ; but the natives here prefer the ground: in the heat of summer and autumn it is pleasant to them to while away their time in this manner, under the shade of a tree. Richly adorned females, as well as men, may often be seen thus amusing themselves. As may naturally be expected, with whatever care they may at first sitting down choose their place, yet the flowing dress by degrees gathers up the dust : as this occurs, they from time to time arise, adjust themselves, shake off the dust, and then sit down again.” This usage beautifully illustrates Isa. lii. 2. *Shake thyself from the dust — arise — sit down, O Jerusalem.* The sense of these expressions, to an Oriental, is extremely natural. “ The captive daughter of Zion, brought down to the dust of suffering and oppression, is commanded to arise and shake herself from that dust ; and then, with grace and dignity, and composure and security, to *sit down :* to take, as it were, again, her seat and her rank amid the company of the nations of the earth, which had before afflicted her, and trampled her to the earth.” Jowett’s Christian Researches in Syria, pp. 282, 283.

the person with whom they are conversing, although they may at the same time be conscious that he is telling them falsehoods. The antient Hebrews, in particular, very rarely used any terms of reproach more severe than those of שָׂטָן (saᴛᴀɴ), *adversary* or *opposer*, רקה (ʀᴀcᴀʜ), *contemptible*, and sometimes נָבָל (ɴᴀʙᴀʟ), *fool*, an expression which means a wicked man or an atheist. (Job ii. 10. Psal. xiv. 1. Isa. xxxii. 6. Matt. v. 22. xvi. 23.) When any thing was said, which was not acceptable, the dissatisfied person replied, *let it suffice thee*, (Deut. iii. 26.), or, *it is enough*. (Luke xxii. 38.) In addressing a superior, the Hebrews did not commonly use the pronouns of the first and second person; but, instead of *I*, they said *thy servant*, and instead of *thou*, they employed the words *my lord*. Instances of this mode of expression occur in Gen. xxxii. 4. xliv. 16. 19. xlvi. 34. Dan. x. 17. and Luke i. 38.

"The formula of assent or affirmation was as follows: *Thou hast said*, or *thou hast rightly said*. We are informed by the traveller Aryda, that this is the prevailing mode of a person's expressing his assent or affirmation to this day, in the vicinity of Mount Lebanon, especially where he does not wish to assert any thing in express terms. This explains the answer of the Saviour to the high priest Caiaphas in Matt. xxvi. 64., when he was asked, whether he was the Christ the Son of God, and replied, συ ειπας, *thou hast said*.

"To spit in company in a room, which was covered with a carpet, was an indication of great rusticity of manners; but in case there was no carpet, it was not accounted a fault in a person, provided he spat in the corner of the room. The expression, therefore, in Deuteronomy xxv. 7—9., viz. *she shall spit in his face*, is to be understood literally, the more so on this account, because in other places, where spitting, buffeting, &c. are mentioned, they occur under circumstances, where there existed a great excitement of feeling, and because there are not wanting instances of even greater rudeness and violence, than that of spitting in one's face. (Matt. xxvi. 67. Mark xiv. 65. comp. 1 Kings xxii. 24. Isa. lvii. 4. Ezek. ii. 6. xxv. 6. 2 Sam. xvi. 6, 7.) The Orientals, as is very well known, are fond of taking a nap at noon, to which they are strongly invited by the oppressive heat of their climate. 2 Sam. iv. 5. xi. 2. Matt. xiii. 25.) The phrase, *to cover one's feet*, is used in certain instances to express the custom of retiring to rest or sleeping at this time. (Judg. iii. 24. 1 Sam. xxiv. 4.)" [1]

IV. The Jews rose early, about the dawn of day, when they breakfasted. They dined about eleven in the forenoon, and supped at five in the afternoon. From this circumstance of their breakfasting so early, Dr. Lightfoot endeavours to account for the language of the evangelists John (xix. 14.) and Mark (xv. 25.) concerning our Lord's crucifixion. The former notices the time from the preparation of the passover; and the latter, the time of the day. The preparation began at the dawn or cock-crowing. From this custom, too, the term to *rise early* denotes diligence, either in doing good or evil. Supper appears to have been the principal meal among the Jews, as it was among the Greeks and Romans. [2]

---

[1] Mr. Upham's translation of Jahn's Archæologia Biblica, pp. 194—196.

[2] Compare Mark vi. 21. Luke xiv. 16. and John xii. 2. ; and see Abp. Potter's Antiquities of Greece, vol. ii. p. 353, and Dr. Adam's Summary of Roman Antiquities, p. 433.

From the whole of the sacred history, it is evident that the food of the Jews was of the simplest nature, consisting principally of milk, honey [1], rice, vegetables [2], and sometimes of locusts, except at the appointed festivals, or when they offered their feast-offerings; at these times they ate animal food, of which they appear to have been very fond (Numb. xi. 4.), when (as is done at this day throughout the East) the guests dipped their hands in the dish. (Ruth ii. 14. Matt. xxvi. 23. John xiii. 26.) [3] The pottage of lentiles and bread, which Jacob had prepared, and which was so tempting to the impatient Esau as to make him sell his birthright, shows the simplicity of the *ordinary* diet of the patriarchs. (Gen. xxv. 34.) The same diet is in use among the modern Arabs [4], and in the Levant. [5] Isaac in his old age longed for *savoury meat*, which was accordingly prepared for him (Gen. xxvii. 4. 17.); but this was an unusual thing. The feast with which Abraham entertained the three angels was a calf [6], new cakes baked on the hearth, together with butter (*ghee*) and milk. [7] (Gen. xviii. 6, 7.) We may form a correct idea of their ordinary articles of food by those which were presented to David on various occasions by Abigail (1 Sam. xxv. 18.), by Ziba (2 Sam. xvi. 1.), and by Barzillai. (2 Sam. xvii. 28, 29.)

The most useful and strengthening, as well as the most common, article of food, was, doubtless, *bread*. Frequent mention is made of this simple diet in the Holy Scriptures [8], which do not often mention the flesh of animals: though this is *sometimes* included in the *eating of bread*, or making a meal, as in Matt. xv. 2. Mark iii. 20 vii. 2. Luke xiv. 1. and John vi. 23. Sometimes the ears were gathered and the grain eaten, before the corn was reaped; in the earliest times, after it had been threshed and dried, it was eaten without any further prepar-

---

[1] The antients used honey instead of sugar, and seem to have relished it much. Hence it is figuratively used as an image of pleasure and happiness in Psal. cxix. 103. Prov. xxiv. 13, 14. and Sol. Song iv. 11. When taken in great quantities it causes vomiting, and is consequently used by a figure (Prov. xxv. 16.) to express fastidiousness, or any nauseating sensation. (Jahn's Biblical Archæology, § 77.) In consequence of the too liberal use of honey, as a substitute for sugar, by the modern inhabitants of the Cyclades Islands in the Levant, many of them are affected with scrofulous diseases. May not this effect be alluded to in Prov. xxv. 27. ? (Emerson's Letters from the Ægean, vol. ii. p. 233.)

[2] In later times, when the Jews were dispersed among the heathen nations, they often abstained from eating flesh, as it might have been offered to idols and sold in shambles; they therefore subsisted entirely on *vegetables*. To this circumstance St. Paul alludes in Rom. xiv. 2.

[3] See examples in Shaw's Travels, vol. i. p. 418. and Jowett's Christian Researches in Syria, p. 284.

[4] Irby's and Mangles' Travels, p. 275.

[5] In the island of Santorin, Mr. Emerson speaks of soup made of *lentils ;* which, when stewed, are of a reddish tinge, and so far agree with the *red pottage* of Jacob, mentioned in Gen. xxv. 30. 34. (Letters from the Ægean, vol. ii. p. 127.)

[6] A young kid seethed in milk is to this day a delicacy set before strangers by the Bedouin Arabs. Buckingham's Travels among the Arab Tribes, p. 7.

[7] Milk and honey were the chief dainties of the antients, as they still are among the Arabs, and especially the Bedouins. Hence the land of Canaan is described as a *land flowing* with milk and honey. (Exod. iii. 8.) Butter is also an article much in use, as is attested by all modern travellers. See particularly Burckhardt's Travels in Syria, p. 385. Irby's and Mangles' Travels in Egypt, &c. pp. 263. 481, 482.

[8] Thus, in Gen. xviii. 5. and 1 Sam. xxviii. 22. we read, *I will fetch a morsel of* BREAD. — Gen. xxi. 14. *Abraham took* BREAD, *and a bottle of water, and gave it unto Hagar.* — Gen. xxxvii. 25. *They sat down to* EAT BREAD. — Gen. xliii. 31. *Joseph said,* Set on BREAD. — Exod. ii. 20. *Call him that he may* EAT BREAD. — Exod. xvi. 3. *We did* EAT BREAD *to the full.* — Deut. ix. 9. *I neither did* EAT BREAD, *nor drink water.* — 1 Sam. xxviii. 20. *Saul had* EATEN *no* BREAD *all the day,* &c.

ation. This was called *parched corn.* Subsequently, the grain was
pounded in a mortar, to which practice Solomon alludes. (Prov.
xxvii. 22.) In later times, however, it was in general ground into
flour, fermented with leaven, and made into bread; though on certain
occasions, as at the departure of the Israelites from Egypt, they baked
unleavened bread. (Exod. xii. 34—39.) In the East the grinding of corn
was, and still is, the work of female slaves: it is extremely laborious,
and is esteemed the lowest employment in the house.[1]   The lightest
bread, which was made of the finest flour, and was *made quickly upon
the hearth,* they called *cakes* (Gen. xviii. 6.) ; the larger and coarser sort
were called *loaves.* (1 Sam. xxi. 3.)   The cakes were antiently baked
upon the hearth (Gen. xviii. 6.): afterwards, this was done upon the
coals, being probably laid upon some grate. (1 Kings xix. 6.)   But
the Holy Bread was baked in an oven. (Lev. ii. 4.)   The *fuel,* used
for this and other culinary purposes, consisted of thorns, wood of all
kinds, and in general, as their sure supply, the dung of cows, asses, or
camels[2], dried and collected into heaps (Lam. iv. 5.) : grass, also, was
employed for the same purpose. (Matt. vi. 30.)   The knowledge of
this circumstance illustrates Eccles. vii. 6. Psal. lviii. 9. Amos iv. 11.
Zech. iii. 2. Isa. vii. 4. and especially Ezek. iv. 12.   In order to show
the extremity of distress, to which the Jews would be reduced in the
captivity, the prophet was to prepare the most common provisions and
to bake the bread with *human dung.*   Nothing could paint more
strongly a case of extreme necessity than this ; and the Jews would so
understand this sign.[3]

The Hebrews were forbidden to eat many things which were, and
are, eaten by other nations ; some animals being unclean according to
the Mosaic Law, (those, for instance, which were either actually impure
and abominable, or were esteemed so) ; others being set apart for the
altar, certain parts of which it was, consequently, not lawful to eat.

The regulations concerning clean and unclean animals are principally recorded in Lev. xi. and Deut. xiv.; and according to them, the
following articles are reckoned unclean, and, consequently, are interdicted to the Hebrews ; viz. 1. Quadrupeds, which do not ruminate,
or which have cloven feet ; — 2. Serpents and creeping insects; also
certain insects which sometimes fly, and sometimes advance upon their
feet; but locusts, in all their four stages of existence, are accounted
clean ; — 3. Certain species of birds, many of the names of which are
obscure ; — 4. Fishes without scales, and also those without fins ; —
5. All food, all liquids, standing in a vessel, and all wet seed into
which the dead body of any unclean beast had fallen ; — 6. All food
and liquids, which stood in the tent or chamber of a dying or dead
man, remaining meanwhile in an uncovered vessel. (Numb. xix. 15.);—
7. Every thing which was consecrated by any one to idols (Exod.
xxxiv. 15.) : it was this prohibition, that in the primitive church occasioned certain dissensions, upon which Paul frequently remarks,
especially in 1 Cor. viii. 10. ; — 8. A kid boiled in the milk of its

---

[1] Bp. Lowth's Isaiah, vol. ii. p. 294.

[2] " Mahomet, our camel-driver, made bread: he kneaded the dough in a leathern
napkin ; and, mixing a good deal of salt with it, made a flat round cake, about half an inch
thick, and baked it on *dried camels' dung.*" Irby's and Mangles' Travels, p. 172. A similar
mode of preparing cakes is described by Mr. Rae Wilson.   Travels in the Holy Land, &c.
vol. ii. p. 156. 3d edition.

[3] Boothroyd's translation of the Bible, vol. i. p. 60.

mother. (Exod. xxiii. 19. xxxiv. 26. Deut. xiv. 21.) This was prohibited either to enforce the duty of humanity to animals, or to guard
the Hebrews against some idolatrous or superstitious practice of the
heathen nations.

The consecrated animal substances interdicted to the Hebrews were,
1. Blood (Lev. xvii. 10. xix. 26. Deut. xii. 16—23, 24. xv. 23.) ; —
2. Animals which had either died of disease or had been torn by wild
beasts, though strangers might eat them if they chose (Exod. xxii. 31.
Deut. xiv. 26.) ; — 3. The fat covering the intestines, termed the *net*
or *caul ;* — 4. The fat upon the intestines, called the *mesentery,* &c. ;
— 5. The fat of the kidneys ; — 6. The *fat tail* or rump of certain
sheep. (Exod. xxix. 13—22. Lev. iii. 4—9, 10. ix. 19.)[1]

Many ingenious conjectures have been assigned for these prohibitions; but the Scriptures, which are our safest guide in inquiries of
this kind, expressly inform us, that the design of them was both moral
and political. This is declared in Lev. xx. 24—26. *I am the Lord
your* GOD, *who have separated you from other people ; ye shall therefore
put difference between clean beasts and unclean ; and ye shall not make
yourselves abominable by beast or by fowl, or by any living thing that
creepeth on the ground, which I have separated from you as unclean : and
ye shall be holy unto me, for I the Lord am holy, and have severed you
from other people that ye should be mine.* As if the Almighty had said,
" I have selected you from, and have exalted you far above, the
heathen and idolatrous world. Let it be your care to conduct yourselves worthy of this distinction. Let the quality of your food, as well
as the rites of your worship, display your peculiar and holy character.
Let even your manner of eating be so appropriate, so pure, so nicely
adjusted by my law, as to convince yourselves and all the world, that
you are indeed separated from idolaters, and devoted to me alone."
Agreeably to this declaration Moses tells the Israelites (Deut. xiv. 2,
3. 31.), *The* LORD *hath chosen you to be a peculiar people unto himself,
above all the nations that are upon the earth. Thou shalt not eat any
abominable thing. Ye shall not eat any thing that dieth of itself; ye
shall give it to a stranger or sell it to an alien, for ye are a holy people.*
In other words, " Since God has invested you with singular honour
and favour, you ought to reverence yourselves : you ought to disdain
the vile food of heathen idolaters. Such food you may lawfully give
or sell to foreigners, but a due self-respect forbids you to eat it." The
immediate and primary intention of these and other similar regulations
was to break the Israelites of the ill habits to which they had been
accustomed in Egypt, or which they had indulged while in that
country ; and to keep them for ever distinct from that corrupt people,
both in principles and practices, and by parity of reason from all other
idolatrous nations. Another reason for the distinction was, that, as
the Jews were peculiarly devoted to God, they should be reminded of
that relation by a particularity of diet, which should serve emblematically as a sign of their obligation to study moral purity. Further, it
has been suggested, as a reason for the distinctions between clean and
unclean food, not only that the quality of the food itself is an important consideration (*clean* animals affording a copious and wholesome

---

[1] Jahn, Archæol. Bibl. § 143. The Mosaic ordinances respecting clean and unclean
beasts are fully considered by Michaelis, Commentaries, vol. ii. pp. 219—254.

nutriment, while *unclean* animals yield a gross nutriment, which is often the occasion of scrofulous and scorbutic disorders) ; but also, that to the eating of certain animals may be ascribed a specific influence on the moral temperament.[1]

Their ordinary beverage was water, which was drawn from the public wells and fountains (John iv. 6, 7.), and which was to be refused to no one. (Matt. xxv. 35.) The water of the Nile, in Egypt, after it has been deposited in jars to settle, all modern travellers attest[2], is singularly delicious as well as extraordinarily wholesome, and is drunk in very large quantities; while that of the few wells, which are found in that country, is not potable, being both unpleasant and insalubrious. When the modern inhabitants depart thence for any time, they speak of nothing but the pleasure they shall find on their return, in drinking the water of the Nile. The knowledge of this circumstance gives a peculiar energy to those words of Moses, when he denounced to Pharaoh, that the waters of the Nile should be turned into blood, even in the very filtering vessels ; and that the Egyptians should *loathe to drink of the water of the river.* (Exod. vii. 17—19.) That is, they should loathe to drink of that water which they used to prefer to all the waters of the universe, and so eagerly to long for, and should prefer to drink of well-water, which in their country is so detestable.[3] After the settlement of the Israelites in Canaan, they drank wine of different sorts, which was preserved in skins. Red wine seems to have been the most esteemed. (Prov. xxiii. 31. Rev. xiv. 20.) In the time of Solomon, *spiced wines* were used, mingled with the juice of the pomegranate. (Song viii. 2.)[4] When Judæa was under the dominion of the Romans, *medicated* wines (as we have seen) were given to those who were to be crucified, in order to blunt the edge of pain, and stun the acuteness of sensibility.[5] The *strong drink* שֵׁכָר (sheceR), mentioned in Lev. x. 9., and many other passages of Holy Writ, means any kind of fermented liquors, whether prepared from corn, dates, apples, or any other kind of fruits. One of the four prohibited drinks among the Mohammedans is called *sakar*, which, though it has the same general meaning as the Hebrew word, especially signifies palm wine.[6]

The patriarchs, like the modern inhabitants of the East, were accustomed to take their meals under the shade of trees. Thus Abra-

---

[1] Tappan's Lectures on Heb. Antiq. pp. 260—264. Dr. Harris's Nat. Hist. of the Bible, pp. xxxi.—xxxvii. (American edit.) or pp. xxiv.—xxx. of the London edition. See also the Rev. W. Jones's Zoologia Ethica. (Works, vol. iii. pp. 1—116.)

[2] See particularly Belzoni's Researches in Egypt, p. 325. 4to. edit. Turner's Tour in the Levant, vol. ii. p. 511. and Dr. Richardson's Travels along the Shores of the Mediterranean, vol. i. p. 33.

[3] Harmer's Observations, vol. iii. pp. 564—566. See also a narrative of the Pacha of Egypt's Expedition to Dongola and Sennaar, by an American, pp. 150, 151. (London, 1822. 8vo.)

[4] Spiced wines were not peculiar to the Jews. The celebrated Persian poet, Hafiz, speaks of wine — " richly bitter, richly sweet." The Romans lined their vessels (*amphoræ*) with odorous gums, to give the wine a warm bitter flavour ; and it is said that the Poles and Spaniards adopt a similar method, in order to impart to their wines a favourite relish. (Odes of Hafiz, translated by Nott, p. 30. note.) The juice of the pomegranate tree is often employed in the East, to give a pleasant sub-acid flavour to a variety of beverages ; and where the laws of the Koran are not allowed to interpose, or their prohibitions are disregarded, a delicious wine is frequently manufactured from this juice alone. Harmer's Observations, vol. ii. pp. 145, 146.

[5] See pp. 163, 164 of this volume.

[6] C. B. Michaelis, Dissertatio Philologica naturalia quædam et artificialia codicis sacri ex Alcorano illustrans, § 12. In Pott's and Ruperti's Sylloge Commentationum Theologicarum, tom. ii. pp. 49, 50.

ham *stood* by the angels *under the tree, and they* did eat. (Gen. xviii. 8.)
The antient Hebrews did not eat indifferently with all persons; they
would have been polluted and dishonoured in their own opinion, by
eating with people of another religion, or of an odious profession.   In
Joseph's time, they neither ate with the Egyptians nor the Egyptians
with them (Gen. xliii. 32.) ; nor in our Saviour's time with the Samaritans (John iv. 9.); and the Jews were scandalised at Jesus Christ's
eating with publicans and sinners. (Matt. ix. 11.)   As there were
several sorts of meats, whose use was prohibited, they could not conveniently eat with those who partook of them, fearing some pollution
by touching them, or if by accident any part of them should fall upon
them.   The antient Hebrews at their meals had each his separate
table.   When Joseph entertained his brethren in Egypt, he seated
each of them at his particular table, and he himself sat down separately
from the Egyptians who ate with him : but he sent to his brethren, out
of the provisions which were before him. (Gen. xliii. 31. *et seq.*)   Elkanah, Samuel's father, who had two wives, distributed their portions to
them separately. (1 Sam. i. 4, 5.)   In Homer, each of the guests has
his little table apart; and the master of the feast distributes meat to
each.   We are assured that this is still practised in China ; and many
in India never eat out of the same dish, nor on the same table, and
they believe they cannot do so without sin ; and this, not only in their
own country, but when travelling, and in foreign lands.[1]   The antique
manners which we observe in Homer we likewise perceive in Scripture, with regard to eating, drinking, and entertainments.   We find
great plenty, but little delicacy ; great respect and honour paid to the
guests by serving them plentifully : thus Joseph sent his brother Benjamin a portion five times larger than his other brethren ; and Samuel
set a whole quarter of a calf before Saul.   From Neh. viii. 10. 12. and
Esth. ix. 19. 22. it appears to have been customary to send a portion
of what remained from their public feasts to those for whom nothing
was prepared, or who were by any circumstances prevented from being
present at them.   The women did not appear at table in entertainments with the men.   This would have been then, as it is at this day
throughout the East, an indecency.[2]   Thus *Vashti the Queen made a
feast for the women in the royal house, which belonged to Ahasuerus* (Esther i. 9.), while the Persian monarch was feasting his nobles.

In India, feasts are given in the open halls and gardens, where a
variety of strangers are admitted, and much familiarity is allowed.
This easily accounts for a circumstance in the history of Christ which
is attended with considerable difficulty ;—the penitent Mary coming
into the apartment where he was, and anointing his feet with the ointment, and wiping them with the hairs of her head. (Luke vii. 44.)
This familiarity is not only common, but is far from being deemed
either disrespectful or displeasing.[3]   From the parables of the nuptial
feast (Matt. xxii. 2—4.) and of the Great Supper (Luke xiv. 16, 17.)
it appears antiently to have been the custom for the parties invited not
to go to the entertainment, until it was announced to be ready.   A
similar usage obtains in modern Persia; when Sir Harford Jones,

---

[1] See examples in Ward's View of the History, &c. of the Hindoos, vol. ii. p. 315.
Renaudot, Notes sur le Voyage des deux Arabes à la Chine, pp. 123, 124.
[2] Roberts's Oriental Illustrations, p. 255.
[3] Forbes's Oriental Memoirs, vol. iii. pp. 183. 190.

during his political mission thither in 1808–9, dined with the Khan of Bushire, the envoy and his suite did not go to the Khan's residence, until the latter had sent a messenger to say that the entertainment was *ready* for his reception.[1] In modern India, as well as in antient Judæa, (Matt. xxii. 9.) it is usual for a rich man to give a feast to the poor, the maimed, and the blind. From 1 Sam. xvi. 11. (marginal rendering) and Psal. cxxviii. 3. it should seem that the antient Hebrews sat down round about a mat or low table, cross-legged, in the same manner as is still practised in the East : afterwards, however, they imitated the Persians and Chaldæans, who reclined on table-beds while eating ; some traces of which are observable in the Book of Proverbs (xxiii. 1.), in Amos (vi. 4. 7.), Ezekiel (xxiii. 41.), and Tobit (ii. 4.) ; but this practice was not general. We see expressions in the sacred authors of those times, which prove, that they also sat at table. At Ahasuerus's banquet (Esth. i. 6.) the company lay on couches, and also at that which Esther gave the king and Haman. (Esth. vii. 8.) Our Saviour in like manner reclined at table (as already described in pp. 391, 392), when Mary Magdalene anointed his feet with perfume (Matt. xxvi. 7.), and when John, at the last supper, rested his head on his bosom. (John xiii. 25.) The Orientals have, as the Jews antiently had, all their great feasts in the evening (see Mark vi. 21. John xii. 2. Rev. iii. 20.) Previously to taking food, it was usual to implore the divine blessing, as we see by the example of Samuel, which is alluded to in 1 Sam. ix. 13. ; and it should seem from 1 Tim. iv. 4. that the same laudable practice obtained in the time of the apostle Paul. " In an eastern feast or ceremony, nothing can exceed the particularity, which is observed in reference to the rank and consequent precedence of the guests. Excepting when kings and members of the royal family are present, the floor and seats are always of an equal height ; but the upper part of a room is more respectable, and there the most dignified individual will be placed. Should, however, an inferior presume to occupy that situation, he will soon be told to go to a lower station."[2] This custom eminently illustrates Prov. xxv. 7. and Luke xiv. 8.

The modern Jews, before they sit down to table, after the example of their ancestors, carefully wash their hands. They speak of this ceremony as being essential and obligatory. After meals they wash them again. When they sit down to table, the master of the house, or chief person in the company, taking bread, breaks it, but does not divide it ; then putting his hand on it, he recites this blessing : *Blessed be thou, O Lord our God, the king of the world, who producest the bread of the earth.* Those present answer, *Amen.* Having distributed the bread among the guests, he takes the vessel of the wine in his right hand, saying, *Blessed art thou, O Lord our God, king of the world, who hast produced the fruit of the vine.* They then repeat the 23d Psalm.[3] They take care, that after meals there shall be a piece of bread remaining on the table : the master of the house orders a glass to be washed, fills it with wine, and elevating it, says, Let us bless him of whose benefits we have been partaking ; the rest answer, Blessed be he, who has heaped his favours on us, and by his goodness has now fed us. Then he recites a pretty long prayer, wherein he thanks God for his

---

[1] Morier's Journey through Persia in the Years 1808–9, p. 73. London, 1812. 4to.
[2] Roberts's Oriental Illustrations, p. 375.
[3] See Buxtorf's Synag. and Leo of Modena, part ii. c. 10.

many benefits vouchsafed to Israel : beseeches him to pity Jerusalem and his temple, to restore the throne of David, to send Elias and the Messiah, to deliver them out of their long captivity.   All present answer, *Amen.* They recite Psal. xxxiv. 9, 10.; and then, after passing the glass with a little wine in it round to those present, he drinks what is left, and the table is cleared.[1]

V. The people of the East have a general propensity for associates in all their transactions and journies : hence, in India, if a man has to travel from a distant village on business, he takes with him a large company of his neighbours and friends.[2]   This circumstance may account for the brethren accompanying Peter from Joppa. (Acts x. 23. xi. 12.)

When persons journeyed, they provided themselves with every necessary, as there were no inns for the reception of travellers. Women and rich men frequently travelled on asses or camels, which carried not only their merchandise, but also their household goods and chattels, and queens were carried in palanquins (Cant. iii. 7.)[3]; and it appears that the Jews often travelled in *caravans* or companies (as the inhabitants of the East do to this day), especially when they went up to Jerusalem at the three great annual festivals.   The *Psalms of Ascensions,* or of *Degrees,* as they are commonly entitled (cxx.—cxxxiv.), are supposed to have received this appellation from the circumstance of their being sung by the more devout Jews, when they were *ascending* or travelling up to the Holy City on these occasions.   The *company,* among which Joseph and Mary supposed Jesus to have been on their return from the passover, when he was twelve years old (Luke ii. 42 —44.), was one of these caravans.[4]   The Ceylonese travel in a similar way at festivals to particular places of worship.[5]

VI. In the East, antiently, as well as in modern times, there were no inns, in which the traveller could meet with refreshment.   Shade from the sun, and protection from the plunderers of the night, is all that the caravansaries afford.   Hence hospitality was deemed a sacred duty incumbent upon every one.   The Sacred Writings exhibit several instances of hospitality exercised by the patriarchs, and the writings of modern travellers show that similar hospitality still exists in the East.[6]   Abraham received three angels, invited them, served them himself, and stood in their presence ; Sarah his wife took care of the kitchen, and baked bread for his guests. (Gen. xviii. 2, 3, &c.)[7]   Lot

---

[1] Calmet's Dissertations, tom. i. pp. 342—350.

[2] Roberts's Oriental Illustrations, p. 576.

[3] In our common version מטה (מ‍ATAH) is rendered *bed.* Mr. Harmer first suggested that a palanquin was intended ; and he has been followed by Dr. Good in his version of Solomon's Song. The mode of travelling or taking the air in a couch, litter, or vehicle of this name, supported on the shoulders of slaves or servants, is extremely common all over the East at the present day, and is unquestionably of immemorial date. These palanquins are often of most elegant and superb manufacture, as well as most voluptuously soft and easy. Of this description was the couch or palanquin of Solomon. Good's translation of the Song of Solomon, p. 103.

[4] See the various passages of Harmer's Observations, referred to in his Index, article *Caravans.* Ward's History of the Hindoos, vol. ii. p. 338. Fragments supplementary to Calmet, No. I.

[5] Callaway's Oriental Observations, p. 74.

[6] See Light's Travels in Egypt, &c. p. 82. Belzoni's Researches in Egypt, p. 61. Burckhardt's Travels in Syria, pp. 24. 295. Roberts's Oriental Illustrations, p. 565.

[7] Mr. Buckingham has described an interesting trait of Oriental hospitality in an Arab Sheik of Barak, the chief of a Turcoman tribe dwelling in the vicinity of Aleppo, on the plain of Barak, which is very similar to the hospitable conduct of Abraham, related in Gen. xviii.

waited at the city-gate to receive guests. (Gen. xix. 1.) When the inhabitants of Sodom meant to insult his guests he went out, he spoke to them, he exposed himself to their fury, and offered rather to give up his own daughters to their brutality than his guests. (Gen. xix. 5—9.) The same is observable in the old man of Gibeah, who had received the young Levite and his wife. (Judg. xix. 16, 17.) St. Paul (Heb. xiii. 2.) urges the examples of Abraham and Lot, as an encouragement to the faithful, to exercise hospitality, saying, that they who have practised it have merited the honour of receiving angels under the form of men. In the East, on account of the intense heat of the weather during summer, they were accustomed to travel by night. This circumstance will explain the parable of the importunate guest who arrived at midnight (Luke xi. 5—8.); in which the rites of hospitality, common among the orientals, are generally recognised and supposed to be acted upon, though not in so prompt a manner as was usual.[1]

The primitive Christians made one principal part of their duty to consist in the exercise of hospitality. Our Saviour tells his apostles, that whoever received them received himself; and that whosoever should give them even a glass of water, should not lose his reward. (Matt. xxv. 41. 45.) At the day of judgment, he will say to the wicked, *Depart, ye cursed, into everlasting fire : I was a stranger, and ye received me not ; . . . . . inasmuch as ye have not done it unto the least of these, ye have not done it unto me.* St. Peter (1 Ep. iv. 9.) requires the faithful to use hospitality to their brethren without murmuring and complaint. St. Paul in several of his Epistles recommends hospitality, and especially to bishops. (1 Tim. iii. 2. Tit. i. 8.) The primitive Christians were so ready in the discharge of this duty that the very heathens admired them for it. They were hospitable to all strangers, but especially to those of the same faith and communion. Believers scarcely ever travelled without letters of recommendation, which testified the purity of their faith; and this procured them a hospitable reception wherever the name of Jesus Christ was known. Calmet is of opinion, that the two last epistles of St. John may be such kind of letters of communion and recommendation as were given to Christians who travelled.

Instances of hospitality among the early Greeks abound in the writings of Homer, whose delineations of manners and customs reflect so much light on the Old Testament, especially on the Pentateuch; and that antient hospitality, which the Greeks considered as so sacred and inviolable, is still partially preserved. When the traveller makes

---

" When we alighted at his tent-door, our horses were taken from us by his son, a young man well dressed in a scarlet cloth benish and a shawl of silk for a turban. The Sheik, his father, was sitting beneath the awning in front of the tent itself; and, when we entered, rose up to receive us, exchanging the salute of welcome, and not seating himself until all his guests were accommodated."..... " Soon afterwards, warm cakes prepared on the hearth, cream, honey, dried raisins, butter, lebben, and wheat boiled in milk, were served to the company. Neither the Sheik himself nor any of his family partook with us, but stood around, to wait upon their guests." Buckingham's Travels in Mesopotamia, vol. i. pp. 30. 32. (8vo. edit.)

[1] Captains Irby and Mangles on two occasions partook of Arab hospitality, in a manner which strikingly illustrates the parable above cited. " We arrived at a camp late at night ; and, halting before a tent, found the owner, with his wife and children, had just retired to rest; when it was astonishing to see the good humour with which they all arose again, and kindled a fire, the wife commencing to knead the dough and prepare our supper, our Arabs making no apology, but taking all as a matter of course, though the nights were bitterly cold." Travels in Egypt, Nubia, Syria, &c. p. 278.

a second tour through the country, he can hardly do any thing more offensive to the person by whom he was entertained in his first journey, than by not again having recourse to the kindness of his former host. Travelling would, indeed, be impracticable in Greece, if it were not facilitated by this noble sentiment; for the Protogeroi are not found in all parts of the country, and the miserable khans or caravansaries are generally constructed only in towns or in highways.

Travelling, in the greater part of Greece, seems to have been, antiently at least, as difficult as it is at the present day; and that circumstance gave rise to the laws of hospitality. This reciprocal hospitality became hereditary in families even of different nations; and the friendship which was thus contracted was not less binding than the ties of affinity, or of blood. Those between whom a regard had been cemented by the intercourse of hospitality were provided with some particular mark, which, being handed down from father to son, established a friendship and alliance between the families for several generations; and the engagement thus entered into could not be dispensed with, unless publicly disavowed in a judicial manner, nothing being considered so base as a violation of it. This mark was the σύμβολον ξενικον of the Greeks, and the *tessera hospitalis* of the Latins. The σύμβολον was sometimes an astragal [1], probably made of lead, which being cut in halves [2], one half was kept by the host, and the other by the person whom he had entertained. On subsequent occasions they or their descendants, by whom the symbol was recognised, gave or received hospitality on comparing the two tallies. Mr. Dodwell found some half astragals of lead in Greece, which had probably served for this purpose. [3]

The antient Romans divided a *tessera* lengthwise, into two equal parts, as signs of hospitality, upon each of which one of the parties wrote his name, and interchanged it with the other. The production of this, when they travelled, gave a mutual claim to the contracting parties and their descendants, for reception and kind treatment at each other's houses, as occasion offered. These *tesseræ* were sometimes of stone, shaped in the form of an oblong square; and as they were carefully and privately kept, so that no one might claim the privileges

---

[1] The astragal was a bone of the hinder feet of cloven-footed animals. Plin. Nat. Hist. b. xi. cc. 45, 46.

[2] Jacobi Nicholai Loensis Miscell.   Epiphill. p. 4. c 19.   Samuelis Petiti Miscel. b. 2. c. i.   Note on v. 613.   Euripid. Medea, Ξενοις τε πεμπειν συμβολ', οι δρασουσι σ' ευ.

[3] Mr. Dodwell's Classical Tour in Greece, vol. i. p. 519.   Plautus, in his play called Pænulus (act 5. sc. 2.), represents Hanno, the Carthaginian, as retaining a symbol of hospitality reciprocally with Antidamas of Calydon; but Antidamas being dead, he addresses himself to his son Agorastocles, and says, —
————————————"Si ita est, tesseram
     Conferre, si vis, hospitalem — eccam attuli."
Agorastocles answers : —
     " Agedum hoc ostende, est par probe, nam habeo domum."
To which Hanno : —
     " O mi hospes, salve multum, nam mihi tuus pater
     Pater tuus ergo hospes Antidamas fuit ;
     Hæc mihi hospitalis tessera cum illo fuit."
Agorastocles proceeds : —
     " Ergo hic apud me hospitium tibi præbebitur."
" If this be the case, here is the tally of hospitality, which I have brought; compare it if you please. — Show it me; it is indeed the tally to that which I have at home ; — My dear host you are heartily welcome; for your father Antidamas was my host; this was the token of hospitality between him and me ; and you shall, therefore, be kindly received in my house." Ibid. p. 520.

of them, besides the person for whom they were intended, this circumstance gives a beautiful and natural explanation of the following passage in Rev. ii. 17. where it is said, *To him that overcometh, will I give a white stone, and in the stone a new name written, which no man knoweth, saving he that receiveth it.* In this passage the venerable translators of our authorised version, by rendering it a white *stone*, seem to have confounded it with the *calculus* or small globular stone, which was commonly used for balloting, and on some other occasions. The original words are ψηφον λευκην, which do not specify either the matter or the form, but only the use of it. By this allusion, therefore, the promise made to the church at Pergamos seems to be to this purpose:— " To him that overcometh, will I give a *pledge* of my affection, which shall constitute him my *friend,* and entitle him to privileges and honours, of which none else can know the value or extent." And to this sense the following words very well agree, which describe this stone or *tessera,* as having in it *a new name written, which no man knoweth, saving he that receiveth it.*[1]

CHAPTER VII.

ON THE OCCUPATIONS, LITERATURE, STUDIES, AND SCIENCES OF THE HEBREWS.

SECTION I.

RURAL AND DOMESTIC ECONOMY OF THE JEWS.

I. MANAGEMENT OF CATTLE *by the Jews.* — *Various Animals reared by them.* — II. *Laws of Moses respecting* AGRICULTURE. — III. *Manures known and used by the Jews.* — IV. *Their Mode of ploughing, sowing, and reaping.* — V. *Different Ways of threshing out Corn.* — VI. *Vineyards, and the Culture of the Vine and Olive.*—*Gardens.*—VII. *Allusions in the Scriptures to the rural and domestic Economy of the Jews.*

JUDÆA was eminently an agricultural country; and all the Mosaic statutes were admirably calculated to encourage agriculture as the chief

---

[1] Ward's Dissertations upon several passages of the Sacred Scriptures, pp. 229—232. London, 1759. 8vo. Dr. T. M. Harris's Dissertation on the Tessera Hospitalis of the Antient Romans, annexed to his Discourses on the Principles, Tendency, and Design of Free-Masonry. Charlestown (Massachussetts), Anno Lucis 5801. This writer has also given several proofs of the prevalence of a similar practice among the Antient Christians, who carried the tessera with them in their travels as an introduction to the friendship and brotherly kindness of their fellow-Christians. Afterwards, heretics, to enjoy those privileges, counterfeited the tessera. The Christians then altered the inscription. This was frequently done till the Nicene Council gave their sanction to those marked with the initials of the words Πατηρ, Υιος, Αγιον Πνευμα; which B. Hildebrand calls *Tesseræ Canonicæ.* The impostor Peregrinus, as we learn from Lucian (Op. tom. iii. p. 325. Amst. 1743), feigned himself a Christian, that he might not only be clothed and fed by the Christians, but also be assisted on his travels, and enriched by their generosity; but his artifice was detected and exposed. The procuring of a tessera (Dr. Harris remarks), as a mark of evangelisation, answered all the purposes, and saved all the trouble, of formal written certificates, and introductory letters of recommendation. The danger of its being used by impostors, as in the case of Peregrinus, rendered it necessary to preserve the token with great care, and never to produce it but upon special occasions. Notwithstanding the simplicity of this method, it continued in use until the time of Burchardus, archbishop of Worms, who flourished A.D. 1100, and who mentions it in a visitation charge. (Harris's Sermons, &c. pp. 319, 320.)

foundation of national prosperity, and also to preserve the Jews detached from the surrounding idolatrous nations.

I. After they had acquired possession of the promised land, the Jews applied themselves wholly to agriculture and the tending of cattle, following the example of their ancestors, the patriarchs, who (like the Arabs, Bedouins, Turcomans, and numerous tribes of eastern Asia,) were generally husbandmen and shepherds, and whose chief riches consisted in cattle, slaves, and the fruits of the earth. Adam brought up his two sons to husbandry, Cain to the *tilling of the ground,* and Abel *to the feeding of sheep.* (Gen. iv. 2.) Jabal was a grazier of cattle, of whom it is said, that *he was the father of such as dwell in tents* (ver. 20.), that is, he travelled with his cattle from place to place, and for that end invented the use of tents, which he carried with him for shelter. After the Deluge, Noah resumed his agricultural labours which had been interrupted by that catastrophe. (Gen. ix. 20.) The chief wealth of the patriarchs consisted in cattle. (Gen. xiii. 2. compared with Job i. 3.) Abraham and Lot must have had vast herds of cattle, when they were obliged to separate because the land could not contain them (Gen. xiii. 6.); and strifes between the different villagers and herdsmen of Syria still exist, as well as in the days of those patriarchs.[1] Jacob, also, must have had a greater number, since he could afford a present to his brother Esau of *five hundred and eighty* head of cattle. (Gen. xxxii. 13—17.)[2] It was their great flocks of cattle which made them in those primitive times put such a price upon wells. These were possessions of inestimable value in a country where it seldom rained, and where there were but few rivers or brooks, and, therefore, it is no wonder that we read of so many contests about them.

In succeeding ages, we find, that the greatest and wealthiest men did not disdain to follow husbandry, however mean that occupation is now accounted.[3] Moses, the great lawgiver of the Israelites, was

---

[1] Richardson's Travels along the Mediterranean, vol. ii. p. 196.

[2] The following description of the removal of an Arab horde will afford the reader a lively idea of the primitive manners of the patriarchs:—" It was entertaining enough to see the horde of Arabs decamp, as nothing could be more regular. First went the sheep and goat-herds, each with their flocks in divisions, according as the chief of each family directed, then followed the camels and asses, loaded with the tents, furniture, and kitchen utensils; these were followed by the old men, women, boys, and girls, on foot. The children that cannot walk are carried on the backs of the young women, or the boys and girls; and the smallest of the lambs and kids are carried under the arms of the children. To each tent belong many dogs, among which are some greyhounds; some tents have from ten to fourteen dogs, and from twenty to thirty men, women, and children belonging to them. The procession is closed by the chief of the tribe, whom they called Emir and Father (emir means prince), mounted on the very best horse, and surrounded by the heads of each family, all on horses, with many servants on foot. Between each family is a division or space of one hundred yards, or more, when they migrate; and such great regularity is observed, that neither camels, asses, sheep, nor dogs, mix, but each keeps to the division to which it belongs without the least trouble. They had been here eight days, and were going four hours' journey to the north-west, to another spring of water. This tribe consisted of about eight hundred and fifty men, women, and children. Their flocks of sheep and goats were about five thousand, besides a great number of camels, horses, and asses. Horses and greyhounds they breed and train up for sale: they neither kill nor sell their ewe-lambs. At set times a chapter in the Koran is read by the chief of each family, either in or near each tent, the whole family being gathered round, and very attentive." Parson's Travels from Aleppo to Bagdad, pp. 109, 110. London, 1808. 4to.

[3] Honourable as the occupation of a shepherd was among the Hebrews, it was *an abomination to the Egyptians* (Gen. xlvi. 34.) at the time when Jacob and his children went down into Egypt.—From the fragments of the antient historian Manetho, preserved in Josephus and Africanus, it appears that that country had been invaded by a colony of Nomades or

a shepherd. Shamgar was taken from the herd to be a judge in Israel, and Gideon from his threshing-floor (Judg. vi. 11.), as were Jair and Jephthah from the keeping of sheep. When Saul received the news of the danger to which the city of Jabesh-gilead was exposed, he was coming after the herd out of the field, notwithstanding he was a king. (1 Sam. xi. 5.) And king David, *from feeding the ewes great with young, was brought to feed Jacob his people and Israel his inheritance* (Psal. lxxviii. 71.); and it should seem, from 2 Sam. xiii. 23., that Absalom was a large sheep-owner. King Uzziah is said to be a lover of husbandry (2 Chron. xxvi. 10.); and some of the prophets were called from that employment to the prophetic dignity, as Elisha was from the plough (1 Kings xix. 19.), and Amos from being a herdsman. But the tending of the flocks was not confined to the men[1]: in the primitive ages, rich and noble women were accustomed to keep sheep, and to draw water as well as those of inferior quality. Thus, Rebecca, the daughter of Bethuel, Abraham's brother, carried a pitcher, and drew water (Gen. xxiv. 15. 19.), as the women of Palestine still generally do: Rachel, the daughter of Laban, kept her father's sheep (Gen. xxix. 9.); and Zipporah, with her six sisters, had the care of their father Jethro's flocks, who was a prince or (which in those times was an honour scarcely inferior) a priest of Midian. (Exod. ii. 16.) Repeated instances occur in Homer of the daughters of princes tending flocks, and performing other menial services.[2]

1. Among the larger animals kept by the Hebrews or Jews, NEAT CATTLE claim first to be noticed, on account of their great utility. They are termed collectively בקר (BAKAR), and though they are of small stature in the East, yet they attain to considerable strength. (Prov. xiv. 4.) The bulls of Bashan were celebrated for their strength. (Psal. xxii. 12.) The castration of bulls, or the males of the ox-tribe, as well as of other male animals, which was common among other nations, was prohibited to the Hebrews. (Lev. xxii. 24, 25.) Oxen were used both for draught and for tillage, as is still the case in the East: they were also employed in treading out the corn, during which they were not to be muzzled (Deut. xxv. 4.); and were driven by means of ox-goads (Judg. iii. 31.), which, if they resembled those used in more recent times in the East, must have been of considerable size.[3] Calves

---

Shepherds descended from Cush, who established themselves there, and had a succession of kings. After many wars between them and the Egyptians, in which some of their principal cities were burnt and great cruelties were committed, they were compelled to evacuate the country; but not till they had been in possession of it for a period of nine hundred years. This alone was sufficient to render shepherds odious to the Egyptians; but they were still more obnoxious, because they killed and ate those animals, particularly the sheep and the ox, which were accounted most sacred among them. See Bryant's Analysis of Antient Mythology, vol. vi. pp. 193—211. 8vo. edit.

[1] From Hector's address to his horses, it appears that his wife, Andromache, though a princess, did not think it beneath her dignity to feed those animals herself. Iliad. viii. 185 —189.

[2] See particularly Iliad lib. vi. 59. 78. Odyss. lib. vi. 57. xii. 131.

[3] The intelligent traveller, Maundrell, in his journey from Jerusalem to Aleppo, relates, that when he was near Jerusalem, he came to a certain place, where (says he) " the country people were every where at plough in the fields, in order to sow cotton : it was observable, that in ploughing, they used goads of an extraordinary size ; upon measuring of several, I found them to be about eight feet long, and, at the bigger end, six inches in circumference. They were armed at the lesser end with a sharp prickle, for driving of the oxen, and at the other end with a small spade, or paddle of iron, strong and massy, for cleansing the plough from the clay that incumbers it in working. May we not from hence conjecture, that it was with such a goad as one of these, that Shamgar made that prodigious slaughter related of

or the young of the ox-kind, are frequently mentioned in Scripture, because they were commonly used in sacrifices. The *fatted calf* (1 Sam. xxviii. 24. Luke xv. 23.) was stall-fed, with a special reference to a particular festival or extraordinary sacrifice.

2. So useful to the Hebrews were ASSES, that the coveting of them is prohibited in the decalogue, equally with oxen: in the East they attain to a considerable size and beauty. Princes and people of distinction did not think it beneath their dignity to ride on asses (Numb. xxii. 21. Judg. i. 4. v. 10. x. 4. 2 Sam. xvi. 2.); when, therefore, Jesus Christ rode into Jerusalem on an ass, he was received like a prince or sovereign. (Matt. xxi. 1—9.) The Hebrews were forbidden to draw with an ox and an ass together (Deut. xxii. 10.), probably because one was a clean animal, and, consequently, edible, while the other was declared to be unclean, and, consequently, unfit for food. The habits and speed of wild asses, which antiently were numerous in Arabia Deserta and the neighbouring countries, are described with great force and poetical beauty in Job xxxix. 5—8.

MULES, which animals partake of the horse and ass, were probably unknown in the earlier ages. It is very certain that the Jews did not breed them, because they were forbidden to couple together two creatures of different species. (Lev. xix. 19.) They seem to have been brought to the Jews from other nations; and the use of them was become very common in the time of David, and they formed a considerable part of the royal equipage. (2 Sam. xiii. 29. xviii. 9. 1 Kings i. 33. 38. 44. x. 25. 2 Chron. ix. 24.)

3. HORSES were not used by the Jews for cultivating the soil: indeed, though they abounded in Egypt in the time of Moses (as may be inferred from Exod. ix. 3. xiv. 6, 7. 9. 23—28. xv. 4.), yet we do not find any mention of their being used before the time of David, who reserved only a hundred horses for his mounted life-guard, or perhaps for his chariots, out of one thousand which he captured (2 Sam. viii. 4.), the remainder being houghed, according to the Mosaic injunction. Solomon carried on a trade in Egyptian horses for the benefit of the crown.[1]

4. CAMELS are frequently mentioned in the Scriptures: antiently, they were very numerous in Judæa, and throughout the East, where they were reckoned among the most valuable live stock. The patriarch Job had at first three thousand (Job i. 3.), and, after his restoration to prosperity, six thousand. (xlii. 12.) The camels of the Midianites and Amalekites were *without number, as the sand by the seaside for multitude.* (Judg. vii. 12.) So great was the importance attached

---

him? I am confident that whoever should see one of these instruments, would judge it to be a weapon, not less fit, perhaps fitter, than a sword for such an execution : goads of this sort I saw always used hereabouts, and also in Syria ; and the reason is, because the same single person both drives the oxen, and also holds and manages the plough ; which makes it necessary to use such a goad as is above described, to avoid the incumbrance of two instruments." Maundrell's Travels, p. 110. In January, 1816, Mr. Buckingham observed similar goads in use, at Ras-el-Hin (or Ain), in the vicinity of the modern town of Sour, which stands on the site of ancient Tyre (Travels in Palestine, p. 57.) ; and the Rev. Mr. Hartley, in March, 1828, met with the same kind of goads in Greece. (Missionary Register, May, 1830, p. 223.)

[1] Michaelis's Commentaries, vol. ii. pp. 394, 395. In pp. 431—514. there is an elaborate dissertation on the antient history and uses of horses. For the reason why the Israelitish sovereigns were prohibited from multiplying horses, see p. 86. of the present volume.

to the propagation and management of camels, that a particular officer was appointed in the reign of David to superintend their keepers; and as the sacred historian particularly mentions that he was an Ishmaelite, we may presume that he was selected for his office on account of his superior skill in the treatment of these animals. (1 Chron. xxvii. 30.)

Two species of camels are mentioned in the Scripture, viz. 1. the גמל (GaMaL), or *common camel,* which has two bunches on its back, that distinguish it from, 2. the בכר (BaKaR), or dromedary, which has only one bunch. The dromedary is remarkable for its fleetness. Both species are now, as well as antiently, much used for travelling long journies. The camel's furniture, mentioned in Gen. xxxi. 34., is most probably the large seat or pack-saddle, invariably observed in the East upon the back of camels. When taken off, at the close of a journey, it would equally afford a place of concealment for the images, and a convenient seat for Rachel.[1] The Arabs eat both the flesh and milk of camels, which, however, were forbidden to the Israelites, as being unclean animals. (Lev. xi. 4. Deut. xiv. 7.) A coarse cloth is manufactured of camels' hair in the East, which is used for making the coats of shepherds and camel drivers, and also for the covering of tents. It was, doubtless, this coarse kind which was worn by John the Baptist, and which distinguished him from those residents in royal palaces, who wore soft raiment. (Matt. iii. 4. xi. 8.)

5. Among the smaller cattle, GOATS and SHEEP were the most valuable, and were reared in great numbers on account of their flesh and milk; the latter animals were also of great value on account of their wool, which was shorn twice in the year. Sheep-shearing was a season of great festivity. (2 Sam. xiii. 23—27. 1 Sam. xxv. 2., &c.) Jahn enumerates *three* varieties of sheep, but Dr. Harris specifies only two breeds as being found in Syria; viz. 1. The Bedouin sheep, which differs little in its appearance from our common breed, except that the tail is somewhat longer and thicker; and, 2. A breed which is of more frequent occurrence than the other, and which is much more valued on account of the extraordinary bulk of its tail, which has been noticed by all travellers. The antient Hebrews, like the modern Arabs, were accustomed to give names of endearment to favourite sheep (2 Sam. xii. 3.); the shepherds also called them generally by name, and the sheep knowing the shepherd's voice obeyed the call (John x. 3. 14.), while they disregarded the voice of strangers.[2] They also appear to have numbered them (Jer. xxxiii. 13.), as the shepherds count their flocks in modern Greece, by admitting them one by one into a pen.[3]

It was the duty of the shepherds to conduct the flocks to pasture, and to protect them from the attacks of thieves and wild beasts (John x. 10—12.): for this purpose they were furnished with a crook (Psal. xxiii. 4.) and with a sling and stones.[4] David was equipped with his shepherd's staff and sling when he went forth to encounter the Philistine giant Goliath. (1 Sam. xvii. 40.) And as it sometimes happened

---

[1] Hartley's Researches in Greece, p. 232.
[2] The Icelanders to this day call their sheep by name (Dr. Henderson's Travels in Iceland, vol. i. pp. 189, 190.); so also do the modern Greeks. (Hartley's Journal of a Tour in 1828. Missionary Register, May, 1830, p. 223.)
[3] Hartley's Researches in Greece, p. 238.
[4] In India, the shepherds generally have a sling and stones, by which they correct wanderers, and keep off their foes, dogs being rarely used. Roberts's Oriental Illustrations, p. 432.

that the owners of large flocks made very hard bargains with their shepherds (as Laban did with Jacob, Gen. xxxi. 38—40.), Moses made various enactments in this respect which are equally characterised by their equity and humanity. In guarding and managing their flocks dogs were of great use; though these animals, being declared by the law of Moses to be unclean, were held in great contempt among the Jews. (1 Sam. xvii. 43. xxiv. 14. 2 Sam. ix. 8. 2 Kings viii. 13.) They had them, however, in considerable numbers in their cities, where they were not confined in the houses or courts, but were forced to seek their food where they could find it. The Psalmist compares violent men to dogs, that go about the city by night in quest of food, and growl if they be not satisfied. (Psal. lix. 6. 14, 15.) Being frequently almost starved, they devour corpses. (1 Kings xiv. 11. xvi. 4. xxi. 19.)

When the sheep were pastured in the open country, the shepherds were accustomed to keep watch in turns by night. The shepherds to whom the glad tidings of the Messiah's advent were announced were thus employed. (Luke ii. 8.) The Jews, however, had sheep-folds, which were inclosures without roofs, surrounded by walls, with doors at which the animals entered: here they were confined both at the season of sheep-shearing, as well as during the night. (John x. 1. Numb. xxxii. 16. 2 Sam. vii. 8. Zeph. ii. 6.) [1] In Palestine flocks antiently were, as they still are, tended, not only by the owner, but also by his sons and daughters, as well as servants. Consequently they were exposed to all the vicissitudes of the seasons, which circumstance explains the observation of Jacob, who, in remonstrating with the mercenary Laban, says that *in the day the drought consumed him, and the frost by night, and his sleep departed from his eyes.* (Gen. xxxi. 40.) [2]

II. Moses, following the example of the Egyptians, made AGRICULTURE the basis of the state. He accordingly appointed to every citizen a certain quantity of land, and gave him the right of cultivating it himself, and of transmitting it to his heirs. The person who had thus come into possession could not alienate the property for any longer period than until the next jubilee: a regulation which prevented the rich from coming into the possession of large tracts of land, and then leasing them out to the poor, in small parcels; — a practice which antiently prevailed, and exists to this day in the East. The law of Moses further enacted, that the vendor of a piece of land, or his nearest relative, had a right to redeem the land sold, whenever they chose, by paying the amount of profits up to the year of jubilee (Ruth iv. 4. Jer. xxxii. 7, 8.); and by a third law the Israelites were required (as was the case among the Egyptians after the time of Joseph, Gen. xlvii. 18—26.) to pay a tax of two tenths of their income unto God; whose servants they were to consider themselves, and whom they were to obey as their king. (Lev. xxvii. 30, 31. Deut. xii. 17—19. xiv. 22—29.) The custom of marking the boundaries of lands by stones (though it prevailed a long time before Moses, Job xxiv. 2.), was confirmed and perpetuated by an express law, which prohibited

---

[1] Pareau, Antiq. Hebr. pp. 412—416. Jahn et Ackermann, Archæol. Bibl. §§ 46 —51. Harris's Nat. Hist. of the Bible at the articles, Asses, Mules, Horses, Camels, Sheep, and Dogs.

[2] Rae Wilson's Travels in the Holy Land, vol. i. p. 400. 3d edition.

the removal of such land-marks (Deut. xix. 14.), and denounced a curse against the person who removed them without authority. (Deut. xxvii. 17.) In giving this law, Moses reminded the Israelites, that it was God who gave them the land; thus insinuating that the land-marks should all in some sense be sacred to the giver. Among the Romans, they actually were held sacred. Indeed, they can be so easily removed, and, consequently, a man be so unobservedly deprived of his property, that it becomes necessary to call in the aid of the fear of God to prevent it; and this Moses, who gave his laws by divine command, did with peculiar propriety.

These regulations having been made in respect to the tenure, in-cumbrances, &c. of landed property, Joshua divided the whole country which he had occupied, *first*, among the several tribes, and, *secondly*, among individual Israelites, running it out with the aid of a measuring line. (Josh. xvii. 5—14. compared with Amos vii. 17. Mic. ii. 5. Psal. lxxviii. 55. and Ezek. xl. 3.) From this circumstance the line is fre-quently used, by a figure of speech, for the heritage itself. (See instances in Psal. xvi. 6. and Josh. xix. 9. Heb.) [1]

The fixing of every one's inheritance in the family to which it had been appropriated in the first division of Canaan was doubtless one great reason, which made the Jews chiefly follow husbandry and im-prove their estates; for though (as we have seen) an inheritance might have been alienated for a time, yet it always returned in the year of jubilee. Their being prohibited, also, to take any interest from their brethren for the use of money, and the strict injunctions laid upon them by Jehovah, with respect to their dealings and commerce with foreigners, deprived them so much of the ordinary advantages thence arising, that they were in a manner obliged to procure their living from the fruits and produce of the earth, the improvement of which constituted their chief care.

III. Although the Scriptures do not furnish us with any *details* respecting the state of agriculture in Judæa, yet we may collect from various passages many interesting hints that will enable us to form a tolerably correct idea of the high state of its cultivation. From the parable of the *vineyard let forth to husbandmen* (Matt. xxi. 33, 34.) we learn that rents of land were paid by a part of the produce; a mode of payment formerly practised by the Romans [2], which antiently ob-tained in this country [3], and which is still practised by the Italians. [4]

The soil of Palestine is very fruitful, if the dews and vernal and autumnal rains are not withheld: but the Hebrews, notwithstanding the richness of the soil, endeavoured to increase its fertility in various ways. With the use of MANURES, the Jews were unquestionably acquainted. Doves' dung (2 Kings vi. 25.) appears to have been very highly valued by the Jews, as to this day it is by the Persians. [5] Salt,

---

[1] Jahn et Ackermann, Archæol. Bibl. § 55. Michaelis's Commentaries, vol. iii. pp. 373, 374.

[2] See Plin. Epist. lib. ix. Ep. 37. Horat. Epist. lib. i. Ep. 14. 42.

[3] The *Boldon Book*, a survey of the state of the bishopric of Durham made in 1183, shows what proportion of the rent was paid in cows, sheep, pigs, fowls, eggs, &c., the re-mainder being made up chiefly by manual labour.

[4] See Blunt's Vestiges of Antient Manners and Customs in Modern Italy, p. 220. London, 1823. 8vo.

[5] " The dung of pigeons is the dearest manure which the Persians use ; and as they apply it almost entirely for the rearing of melons, it is probable, on that account, that the melons of Ispahan are so much finer than those of other cities. The revenue of a pigeon house is

either by itself or mixed in the dunghill in order to promote putrefaction, is specially mentioned as one article of manure (Matt. v. 13.
Luke xiv. 34, 35.); and as the river Jordan annually overflowed its
banks, the mud deposited when its waters subsided must have served
as a valuable irrigation and top-dressing, particularly to the pasture
lands. It is probable that, after the waters had thus subsided, seed
was sown on the wet soft ground; in allusion to which Solomon says,
Cast thy bread (corn or seed) *upon the waters : for thou shalt find it
again,* with increase, *after many days.* (Eccles. xi. 1.) And Isaiah,
promising a time of peace and plenty, says, Blessed are ye that sow
beside all waters, and send *forth thither the feet of the ox and the ass.*
(Isa. xxxii. 30.)

In Egypt, such vegetable productions as require more moisture than
that which is produced by the inundation of the Nile are refreshed by
water drawn out of the river, and afterwards deposited in capacious
cisterns. When, therefore, their various sorts of pulse, melons, sugar-
canes, &c. all of which are commonly ploughed in rills, require to be
refreshed, they strike out the plugs which are fixed in the bottom of
the cisterns : whence the water, gushing out, is conducted from one
rill to another by the gardener, who is always ready, as occasion requires, to stop and divert the torrent, by *turning the earth against it by
his foot,* and at the same time opening, with his mattock, a new trench
to receive it. A similar mode of irrigating lands obtains in the island
of Cyprus[1] and also in India.[2] This method of imparting moisture
and nourishment to a land, rarely, if ever, refreshed with rain, is often
alluded to in the Scriptures, where it is made the distinguishing quality
between Egypt and the land of Canaan. *For the land,* says Moses,
*whither thou goest in to possess it, is not as the land of Egypt from whence
ye came out, where thou sowedst thy seed,* and wateredst it with thy foot,
as a garden of herbs : *but the land, whither ye go to possess it, is a land
of hills and valleys, and drinketh water of the rain of heaven.* (Deut. xi.
10, 11.)[3] This mode of irrigation is alluded to in Psal. i. 3., where
the good man is compared to a fruitful tree, *planted by the rivers of
waters* פַלְגֵי מַיִם (PALGEY-MAYIM), that is, *the streams or divisions of the
waters,* meaning those which are turned on and off as above mentioned
by the cultivator.[4] The prophet Jeremiah has imitated, and elegantly
amplified, the passage of the Psalmist above referred to.

> " He shall be like a tree planted by the water-side,
> And which sendeth forth her roots to the aqueduct :
> She shall not fear when the heat cometh,[5]
> But her leaf shall be green ;
> And in the year of drought she shall not be anxious,
> Neither shall she cease from bearing fruit."   Jer. xvii. 8.

---

about a hundred tomauns per annum; and the great value of this dung, which rears a
fruit that is indispensable to the existence of the natives during the great heats of summer,
will probably throw some light upon that passage in Scripture, where, in the famine of Samaria, the fourth part of a cab of dove's dung was sold for five pieces of silver. 2 Kings
vi. 25." Morier's Second Journey through Persia, p. 141. See also Sir R. K. Porter's
Travels in Persia, vol. i. p. 451.
  [1] Rae Wilson's Travels, vol. i. p. 185. 3d. edition.
  [2] Statham's Indian Recollections, p. 429.
  [3] Dr. Shaw's Travels in Barbary, &c. vol. ii. pp. 266, 267.
  [4] Dr. A. Clarke on Psal. i. 3. See also Burder's Oriental Literature, vol. ii. p. 1.
  [5] " To appreciate the beauty of this allusion, it is necessary to think of a parched desert,
where there is scarcely a green leaf to relieve the eye. In the midst of that waste is
perhaps a tank, a well, or a stream, and near to the water's edge will be seen plants, shrubs,

From this image the son of Sirach has most beautifully illustrated the influence and the increase of religious wisdom in a well-prepared heart: —

> " I also came forth as a canal from a river,
> And as a conduit flowing into a paradise.
> I said, I will water my garden,
> And I will abundantly moisten my border;
> And, lo! my canal became a river,
> And my river became a sea."   Eccles. xxiv. 30, 31.

This gives us the true meaning of the following elegant Proverb:—

> " The heart of the king is like the canals of waters in the hand of Jehovah;
> Whithersoever it pleaseth him, he inclineth it."   Prov. xxi. 1.

The direction of it is in the hand of Jehovah, as the distribution of the water of the reservoir, through the garden by different canals, is at the will of the gardener.

Solomon mentions his own works of this kind: —

> " I made me gardens and paradises;
> And I planted in them all kinds of fruit-trees.
> I made me pools of water,
> To water with them the groves flourishing with trees."
>   Eccles. ii. 5. 9.[1]

IV. In the first ages of the world, men were chiefly employed in digging and throwing up the earth with their own hands; but Noah advanced the art of husbandry (Gen. ix. 20.), and contrived fitter instruments for ploughing than were known before. This patriarch is called a *man of the ground*, but in our translation, a *husbandman*, on account of his improvements in agriculture, and his inventions for making the earth more tractable and fruitful. It was a curse upon the earth after the fall, that it should bring forth thorns and thistles: these obstructions were to be removed, which required much labour, and the ground was to be corrected by ploughing.

The earliest mention made in the Old Testament of a PLOUGH is in Deut. xxii. 10. where the Israelites are prohibited from ploughing *with an ox and an ass together;* a plain intimation, that it had been customary with the idolatrous nations of the East to do so. In Syria, the plough is still drawn, frequently by one small cow, at most with two, and sometimes only by an ass.[2] In Persia, Mr. Morier states, that it is for the most part drawn by one ox only, and not unfrequently by an ass.[3] In Egypt they plough with two oxen.[4] The plough appears to have been furnished with a share and coulter, probably not very unlike those which are now in use. (1 Sam. xiii. 20, 21. Isa. ii. 4.

---

and trees covered with the most beautiful foliage. So shall be the man who puts his trust in Jehovah." Roberts's Oriental Illustrations, p. 476.

[1] Bp. Lowth's Isaiah, vol. ii. pp. 24, 25. Maundrell (p. 88.) has given a description of the remains, as they are said to be, of these very pools made by Solomon, for the reception and preservation of the waters of a spring, rising at a little distance from them; which will give us a perfect notion of the contrivance and design of such reservoirs. " As for the pools, they are three in number, lying in a row above each other; being so disposed, that the waters of the uppermost may descend into the second, and those of the second into the third. Their figure is quadrangular; the breadth is the same in all, amounting to about ninety paces: in their length there is some difference between them; the first being one hundred and sixty paces long; the second, two hundred; the third, two hundred and twenty. They are all lined with wall, and plastered, and contain a great depth of water."

[2] Dr. Russel's History of Aleppo, vol. i. p. 73.

[3] Morier's First Travels in Persia, p. 60.

[4] Dr. Richardson's Travels, vol. ii. p. 167.

Joel iii. 10. Mic. iv. 3.) " The plough, in use at Nazareth, is not moved upon wheels. The share, which is small, scarcely grazes the earth; and it has only one handle or shaft, with a small piece of wood across the top, for the husbandman to guide it, resembling the head of a staff or the handle of a spade. The man holds this in his right hand, with which he goads the oxen. The whole machine is made so extremely light, that a person might with facility carry it in his arms. The share is covered with a piece of broad iron pointed at the end, so that it might be converted into a weapon of warfare. In all probability, it is to this peculiarity, that one of the prophets refers; when he calls on the nations to relinquish rural occupations, and convert their ploughs into instruments of battle. (Joel iii. 10.) Another of the sacred writers has reversed this recommendation, and applied it to the tranquillity with which it is prophesied [that] the church shall be ultimately blessed in the latter days." (Isa. ii. 4.) [1]

The method of managing the ground, and preparing it for the seed, was much the same with the practice of the present times; for Jeremiah speaks of ploughing up the fallow ground (Jer. iv. 3.), and Isaiah of harrowing or breaking up the clods (Isa. xxviii. 24.); but Moses, for wise reasons, doubtless, gave a positive injunction, that they should not sow their fields with mingled seed.

The kinds of grain sown by the Jews were fitches, cummin, wheat, barley, and rye. (Isa. xxviii. 25.) The cultivated fields were guarded by watchmen (as they still are in the East) who sit upon a seat hung in a tree, or in a lodge or watch-tower made of planks, and keep off birds, beasts, and thieves. (Jer. iv. 16, 17. Isa. xxiv. 20.) It was lawful for travellers to pluck ears from the standing corn in another's field, and to eat them; but they were on no account to use a sickle. (Deut. xxii. 25. compared with Matt. xii. 1. Mark ii. 23. and Luke vi. 1.) Their corn-fields were infested with a worthless kind of weed resembling corn (ζιζανιον), in our version rendered tares; but it is evident that this is a different production from our tare or vetch, which is a very useful plant. It is supposed to have been the *lolium temulentum*, a species of darnel growing among corn, to which it bears some resemblance. Bread, which may be made from a mixture of darnel ground with corn, will produce giddiness and sickness; an effect which the straw is known to have upon cattle. In India, as in Judæa in the time of Jesus Christ (Matt. xiii. 25.), nothing is more common than for an enemy to come by night and sow tares on the newly ploughed land. [2]

There were three months between their sowing and their first reaping, and four months to their full harvest: their barley harvest was at the Passover, and their wheat harvest at the Pentecost. The reapers made use of sickles, and according to the present custom they filled their hands with the corn, and those who bound up the sheaves their bosom: there was a person *set over the reapers* (Ruth ii. 5.) to see that they did their work, that they had provision proper for them, and to pay them their wages: the Chaldees call him Rab, the master, the

---

[1] Rae Wilson's Travels, vol. i. p. 401. 3d. edition. A similar description of a Syrian plough is given by Mr. Robinson (Travels in Palestine, vol. i. pp. 184, 185.); and also by Mr. Monro. (Summer Ramble in Syria, vol. i. p. 89.)
[2] Roberts's Oriental Illustrations, p. 540.

ruler, or governor of the reapers. Women were employed in reaping as well as the men; and the reapers were usually entertained above the rank of common servants, though in the time of Boaz we find nothing provided for them but bread and parched corn; and their sauce was vinegar (a kind of weak wine), which, doubtless, was very cooling in those hot countries. (Ruth ii. 14.) The poor were allowed the liberty of gleaning, though the landowners were not bound to admit them immediately into the field as soon as the reapers had cut down the corn and bound it up in sheaves, but after it was carried off: they might choose also among the poor, whom they thought most worthy or most necessitous. A sheaf left in the field, even though discovered, was not to be taken up, but to be left for the poor. (Deut. xxiv. 19.) The conclusion of the harvest, or carrying home the last load, was with the Jews a season of joyous festivity, and was celebrated with a harvest feast. (Psal. cxxvi. 6. Isa. xvi. 9, 10.) Hence the "joy of harvest" was a proverbial expression, denoting great joy. (Isa. ix. 3.) [1] The corn being pulled [2], or cut, and carried in waggons or carts (Numb. vii. 3—8. Isa. xxviii. 27, 28. Amos ii. 13.), was either laid up in stacks (Exod. xxii. 6.) or barns (Matt. vi. 26. xiii. 30. Luke xii. 18. 24.); and, when threshed out, was stored in granaries or garners. (Matt. iii. 12.) David had *storehouses in the fields, in the cities, and in the villages, and in the castles.* (1 Chron. xxvii. 25.)

V. After the grain was carried into the barn, the next concern was to thresh or beat the corn out of the ear, which process was performed in various ways. Sometimes it was done by horses (Isa. xxviii. 28.), as is the practice to this day among the Koords [3], and by oxen, that trod out the corn with their hoofs shod with brass. (Mic. iv. 12, 13.) This mode of threshing is expressly referred to by Hosea (x. 11.), and in the prohibition of Moses against *muzzling the ox that treadeth out the corn* (Deut. xxv. 4.), and it obtains in Persia [4] and India [5] to this day, where oxen are employed; as buffaloes are in Ceylon, asses in North Africa, and horses in Crim Tartary. [6] Another mode of threshing was, by drawing a loaded cart with wheels over the corn, backwards and forwards; so that the wheels running over it, forcibly shook out the grain (Isa. xxviii. 28.); but the most common mode appears to have been that which is in use in this country, viz. by flails. Thus the fitches are said to be beaten out with a staff, and the cummin with a rod. In this manner Gideon and Araunah or Ornan threshed out their wheat (Judg. vi. 11. 1 Chron. xxi. 20.); for it is represented as their own personal action.

The threshing floors were places of great note among the antient Hebrews, particularly that of Araunah the Jebusite, which was the

---

[1] The joy of harvest is equally a Hindoo expression to denote great joy. Roberts's Oriental Illustrations, p. 404.

[2] In crossing one of the plains of the Turcomans, "we passed," says Mr. Buckingham, " a party of husbandmen gathering in the harvest, the greater portion of the grain being now fully ripe. *They plucked up the corn by the roots,* a practice often spoken of in the Scriptures, though reaping seems to be made the earliest and most frequent mention of." Travels in Mesopotamia, vol. i. p. 42.

[3] Buckingham's Travels in Mesopotamia, vol. i. p. 418.

[4] Sir R. K. Porter's Travels in Georgia, Persia, &c. vol. ii. p. 90.

[5] See Turner's Embassy to Thibet, p. 184.

[6] Ward's History, &c. of the Hindoos, vol. ii. p. 320. Dr. Davy's Travels in the Interior of Ceylon, p. 275. (London, 1821), where a threshing-floor is delineated. Capt. Lyon's Tour in Mourzouk and Fezzan, p. 169. Mrs. Holderness's Notes on the Crim Taters, p. 97. (London, 1821.) See also Mr. Dodwell's Classical Tour in Greece, vol. ii. p. 10.

spot of ground chosen by king David on which to build the altar of God (2 Sam. xxiv. 25.), and this was the very place where the temple of Solomon was afterwards erected. (2 Chron. iii. 1.) These floors were covered at the top to keep off the rain, but lay open on all sides, that the wind might come in freely for the winnowing of the corn ; which being done, they were shut up at night, with doors fitted to them, that if any body lay there, he might be kept warm, and the corn be secured from the danger of robbers (Ruth iii. 6.) : the time of winnowing, or separating the corn from the chaff, was in the evening or night, when the heat of the day was over, and cool breezes began to rise [1] ; for this purpose, they had the same implements which are in common use ; for Isaiah speaks of winnowing *with the shovel, and with the fan.* (Isa. xxx. 24.) The grain, being threshed, was thrown into the middle of the threshing floor; it was then exposed with a fork, to a gentle wind (Jer. iv. 11, 12.), which separated the broken straw and the chaff: so that the kernels, and clods of earth with grain cleaving to them, and the ears not yet thoroughly threshed, fell upon the ground. The clods of earth, as is customary in the East at the present day, were collected, broken in pieces, and separated from the grain by a sieve ; whence the operation of sifting is, in prophetic language, a symbol of misfortune and overthrows. (Amos ix. 9. Luke xxii. 31.) The heap thus winnowed, which still contained many ears that were broken but not fully threshed out, was again exposed in the threshing floor, and several yoke of oxen were driven over it, for the purpose of treading out the remainder of the grain. At length the grain, mingled with the chaff, was again exposed to the wind by a fan, which bore off the chaff, so that the pure wheat fell upon the floor. (Ruth iii. 2. Isa. xxx. 24.) In the figurative language of prophecy, this process is symbolical of the dispersion of a vanquished people (Isa. xli. 15, 16. Jer. xv. 7. li. 2.), and also of the final separation between the righteous and the wicked. (Job xxi. 18. Psal. i. 4. xxxv. 5. Matt. iii. 12. Luke iii. 17.) The scattered straw, as much at least as was required for the manufacturing of bricks and for the fodder of cattle, was collected; but the residue was reduced to ashes by fire: from this custom the sacred writers have derived a figurative illustration, to denote the destruction of wicked men. (Isa. v. 24. xlvii. 14. Nah. i. 10. Mal. iv. 1. Matt. iii. 12.)

After the corn was threshed, it was dried either in the sun (2 Sam. xvii. 19.), or by a fire, or in a furnace. This is called parched corn (Lev. xxiii. 14. 1 Sam. xvii. 17. and xxv. 18.), and was sometimes used in this manner for food without any farther preparation, but generally the parching or drying of it was in order to make it more fit for grinding. This process was performed either in mortars or mills, both of which are mentioned in Numb. xi. 8. And Solomon speaks of the former, when he compares the braying of a fool in a mortar to the like practice used with wheat. (Prov. xxvii. 22.) But mills were chiefly employed for this purpose; and they were deemed of such use and necessity, that the Israelites were strictly forbidden *to take the nether or upper mill-stone in pledge ;* the reason of which is added, because this

---

[1] Ruth iii. 2. *Behold he* (Boaz) *winnoweth barley* TO NIGHT *in the threshing floor.* In India " much of the agricultural labour is performed in the night. The sun is so hot and so pernicious, that the farmers endeavour as much as possible to avoid its power. Hence numbers plough and irrigate their fields and gardens long after the sun has gone down, or before it rises in the morning." (Roberts's Oriental Illustrations of Scripture, p. 155.)

was taking a man's life in pledge (Deut. xxiv. 6.), intimating that while the mill ceases to grind, people are in danger of being starved.

The grinding at mills was accounted an inferior sort of work, and, therefore, prisoners and captives were generally put to it. To this work Samson was set, while he was in the prison-house. (Judg. xvi. 21.) There hand-mills were usually kept, by which prisoners earned their living. (Lam. v. 13.) The expression in Isa. xlvii. 2. — *Take the mill-stones, and grind meal,* — is part of the description of a slave. In Barbary, most families grind their wheat and barley at home, having two portable mill-stones for that purpose: the uppermost of which is turned round by a small handle of wood or iron, that is placed in the rim. When this stone is large, or expedition is required, a second person is called in to assist; and it is in that country usual for the women alone to be thus employed, who seat themselves over against each other with the mill-stones between them. This practice illustrates the propriety of the expression of sitting *behind the mill* (Exod. xi. 5.), and also the declaration of our Lord, that *two women shall be grinding at the mill; the one shall be taken and the other left.* (Matt. xxiv. 41.) [1] From Jer. xxv. 10. and Rev. xviii. 22., it appears that those who were occupied in grinding beguiled their laborious task by singing, as the Barbary women continue to do to this day.

VI. Palestine abounded with generous wine; and in some districts the grapes were of superior quality. The canton allotted to Judah was celebrated on this account; and it is, perhaps, with reference to this circumstance, that the venerable patriarch said of his son Judah, — *He washed his garments* IN WINE, *and his clothes in the* BLOOD OF GRAPES. (Gen. xlix. 11.) In this district were the vales of Sorek and of Eshcol; and the cluster which the Hebrew spies carried from this last place was so large as to be carried on a staff between two of them. (Numb. xiii. 23.)

The Jews planted their vineyards most commonly on the south side [2] of a hill or a mountain, the stones being gathered out and the space hedged round with thorns or walled. (Isa. v. 1—6. compared with Psal. lxxx. 8—16. and Matt. xxi. 33.) A good vineyard consisted of a thousand vines, and produced a rent of *a thousand silverlings,* or shekels of silver. (Isa. vii. 23.) It required two hundred more to pay the dressers. (Song of Solomon viii. 11, 12.) In these the keepers and vine-dressers laboured, digging, planting, pruning, and propping the vines, gathering the grapes, and making wine. This was at once a laborious task, and often reckoned a base one. (2 Kings xxv. 12. Song of Solomon i. 6. Isa. lxi. 5.) Some of the best vineyards were at Engedi, or perhaps at Baal-hamon, and at Sibmah. (Song of Solomon i. 14. viii. 11. Isa. xvi. 9.) Vines also were trained upon

---

[1] Dr. Shaw's Travels in Barbary, vol. i. p. 416.

[2] The *sides* of the sun-burnt hills near Nablous (the antient Shechem) — the mountains of the *height of Israel* — " seem peculiarly adapted for the training of vines. They are, however, almost totally neglected; forming, doubtless, a remarkable contrast to their state in the days of Israel's prosperity, when the *drunkards of Ephraim* (Isa. xxviii. 1. 3. 7.) prided themselves in the abundance and strength of their wines. How celebrated these parts once were for this article of produce we learn from several notices in the Old Testament: Gideon, by a happy comparison, thus disparages his own services, in the presence of the Ephraimites — *Is not the* GLEANING *of the grapes of Ephraim better than the vintage of Abiezer ?* (Judg. viii. 2.) And the restoration of Israel is described, partly by their return to the rearing of vineyards, which should yield, as formerly they had done, an abundant vintage." (Jer. xxxi. 5.) Jowett's Christian Researches in Syria. &c. p. 304.

the walls of the houses [1] (Psal. cxxviii. 3.), and *purged* or cleaned by lopping off every useless and unfruitful branch, and superfluous excrescence, in order that the fruitful branches might be rendered more productive. (John xv. 2.) [2] *The vines with the tender grapes gave a good smell* early in the spring (Song of Solomon ii. 13.), as we learn, also, from Isa. xviii. 5. *afore the harvest,* that is, the *barley* harvest, *when the bud is perfect, and the sour grape is ripening in the flower.* It was also (as it still is) usual to erect temporary huts [3], made of boughs and reeds, to shelter the servant who was employed to guard the fruit when nearly ripe from birds and other creatures of prey (Isa. i. 8.) [4], and particularly from the ravages of wild boars (Psal. lxxx. 13.), which to this day are as destructive in Greece [5], as they antiently were in Palestine. As soon as the vintage was completed, these sheds were either taken down or suffered to perish. From this circumstance Job derives a beautiful simile, to illustrate the short duration of the prosperity of the wicked. (xxvii. 18.) [6] But it appears from Isa. v. 1, 2. Matt. xxi. 33. and Mark xii. 1., that towers were erected for this purpose, as they still are in some parts of Palestine. [7]

" The *vintage* followed the wheat harvest and the *threshing* (Lev. xxvi. 5. Amos ix. 13.), about June or July, when the clusters of the grapes were gathered with a sickle, and put into baskets (Jer. vi. 9.), carried and thrown into the wine-vat, or wine-press, where they were probably first *trodden* by men and then *pressed.* (Rev. xiv. 18—20.) It is mentioned, as a mark of the great work and power of the Messiah, *I have trodden the* figurative *wine-press alone ; and of the people there was none with me.* (Isa. lxiii. 3. ; see also Rev. xix. 15.) The vintage was a season of great mirth. Of the juice of the squeezed grapes were formed *wine* and *vinegar.* The wines of Helbon [8], near Damascus, and of Lebanon, where the vines had a fine sun, were reckoned most

---

[1] The same mode of culture is practised in Persia to this day. Mr. Morier has given an engraving on wood illustrative of this custom, which beautifully elucidates the patriarch Jacob's comparison of Joseph to a *fruitful bough,* whose *branches run over the wall.* (Gen. xlix. 22.) Second Journey, p. 232.

[2] In modern Greece the vine is cut or purged in the following manner : — " Only two or three of the principal sprouts are permitted to grow up from the root: the rest are cut off, and this practice is often called by the Greeks CLEANING." Rev. John Hartley's Journal of a Tour in Greece, in 1828. (Missionary Register, May, 1830, p. 225.)

[3] Upon different heights among the plantations of fig-trees and vineyards, with which the modern village of Bethlehem was surrounded in 1833, the Rev. V. Munro observed the *lodges,* or *watch* towers, mentioned by Isaiah (i. 8.), stand far apart from each other ; they guard particular districts rather than particular gardens. Summer Rambles in Syria, vol. i. p. 248.

[4] Isa. i. 8. *And the daughter of Zion is left as a* cottage *in a* vineyard, *as a lodge in a garden* of cucumbers. " There is a small species of cucumber of which the natives of India are very fond. ...... Large fields of these are sometimes planted ; which, when nearly arrived to maturity, require incessant watching to protect them from the attacks of man and beast." (Statham's Indian Recollections, p. 90.)

[5] Hartley's Researches in Greece, pp. 234, 235.

[6] Dr. Boothroyd on Job xxvii. 18.

[7] In the route between Jerusalem and the convent of Saint Elias (which is situated about an hour's distance from that city), Mr. Buckingham was particularly struck with the appearance of several small and detached square towers in the midst of the vine-lands. These, his guide informed him, were used as watch-towers, whence watchmen to this day look out, in order to guard the produce of the lands from depredation. This fact will explain the use and intention of the *tower* mentioned in Matt. xxi. 33. and Mark xii. 1. Similar towers were seen by Captains Irby and Mangles, as they passed between numerous vineyards, some of which appeared to be antique. Travels in Egypt, &c. p. 342.

[8] At one time the wine of Helbon (which place Strabo terms Chalybon) was held in such repute, that it was appropriated exclusively to the use of the kings of Persia. Strabon. Geographia, tom. ii. p. 1043. edit. Oxon.

excellent.[1] (Ezek. xxvii. 18. Hos. xiv. 7.) The wines of Canaan being
very heady, were commonly mixed with water for common use, as the
Italians do theirs; and sometimes they scented them with frankincense, myrrh, calamus, and other spices (Prov. ix. 2. 5. Song of
Solomon viii. 2.): they also scented their wine with pomegranates, or
made wine of their juice, as we do of the juice of currants, goose-
berries, &c. fermented with sugar.   Wine is best when old and on the
lees, the dregs having sunk to the bottom. (Isa. xxv. 6.)   Sweet wine is
that which is made from grapes fully ripe. (Isa. xlix. 26.)   The Israelites
had two kinds of *vinegar,* the one was a weak wine, which was used
for the common drink in the harvest field, &c. (Ruth ii. 14.), as the
Spaniards and Italians still do; and it was probably of this that
Solomon was to furnish *twenty thousand baths* to Hiram, for his servants, the hewers that cut timber in Lebanon. (2 Chron. ii. 10.) The
other had a sharp acid taste, like ours; and hence Solomon hints, that
a sluggard vexes and hurts such as employ him in business; *as vinegar*
is disagreeable *to the teeth, and smoke to the eyes* (Prov. x. 26.); and
as vinegar poured *upon nitre* spoils its virtue: *so he that singeth songs
to a heavy heart* does but add to its grief. (Prov. xxv. 20.)   The poor
were allowed to *glean* grapes, as well as corn and other articles
(Lev. xix. 10. Deut. xxiv. 21. Isa. iii. 14. xvii. 6. xxiv. 13. Mic.
vii. 1.); and *the gleaning of the grapes of Ephraim was better than the
vintage of Abiezer.* (Judg. viii. 2.)   The vineyard was not to be
pruned and dressed in the sabbatical year. (Lev. xxv. 3, 4.)   The
vessels in which the wine was kept were, probably, for the most part,
bottles, which were usually made of *leather,* or goat-skins, firmly sewed
and pitched together.   The Arabs pull the skin off goats in the same
manner that we do from rabbits, and sew up the places where the legs
and tail were cut off, leaving one for the neck of the bottle, to pour
from; and in such bags, they put up and carry, not only their liquors
but dry things which are not apt to be broken; by which means they
are well preserved from wet, dust, or insects.   These would in time
crack and wear out.   Hence, when the Gibeonites came to Joshua,
pretending that they came from a far country, amongst other things
they brought *wine bottles old and rent, and bound up where they had
leaked.* (Josh. ix. 4. 13.)   Thus, too, it was not expedient to put new
wine into old bottles, because the fermentation of it would break or
crack the bottles. (Matt. ix. 17.)   And thus David complains, that
he is become like *a bottle in the smoke;* that is, a bottle dried, and
cracked, and worn out, and unfit for service. (Psal. cxix. 83.)   These
bottles were probably of various sizes, and sometimes very large; for
when Abigail went to meet David and his four hundred men, and took
a present to pacify and supply him, *two hundred loaves* and *five sheep
ready dressed,* &c. she took only two *bottles of wine* (1 Sam. xxv. 18.);
a very disproportionate quantity, unless the bottles were large.   But
the Israelites had *bottles* likewise made by the *potters.* (See Isa. xxx.
14. margin, and Jer. xix. 1. 10. xlviii. 12.)   We hear also of vessels
called *barrels.* That of the widow, in which her meal was held (1 Kings
xvii. 12. 14.) was not, probably, very large; but those four in which
the water was brought up from the sea, at the bottom of Mount Carmel, to pour upon Elijah's sacrifice and altar, must have been large.

---

[1] Lebanon and its vicinity still produce excellent wine; — at least a dozen sorts, all of
which are cheap.   Carne's Letters from the East, p. 239.

(1 Kings xviii. 33.) We read likewise of other *vessels,* which the widow of Shunem borrowed of her neighbours, to hold the miraculous supply of oil (2 Kings iv. 2—6.) ; and of the *water-pots,* or jars, or jugs, *of stone,* of considerable size, in which our Lord caused the water to be converted into wine. (John ii. 6.)   Grapes, among the Israelites, were likewise *dried* into *raisins.*   A part of Abigail's present to David was *an hundred clusters of raisins* (1 Sam. xxv. 18.); and when Ziba met David, his present contained the same quantity. (2 Sam. xvi. 1. ; see also 1 Sam. xxx. 12. and 1 Chron. xii. 40.)"[1]

It was a curse pronounced upon the Israelites, that, upon their disobedience, they should plant vineyards and dress them, but they should neither drink of the wine nor eat the grapes, for the worms should eat them. (Deut. xxviii. 39.)   It seems that there is a peculiar sort of worms that infest the vines, called by the Latins Volvox and Convolvulus, because it wraps and rolls itself up in the buds, and eats the grapes up, when they advance towards ripeness, as the Roman authors explain it.[2]

Besides other fruits that were common in Judæa, as dates, figs, cucumbers[3], pomegranates, they had regular plantations of OLIVES, which were a very antient and profitable object of horticulture. So early as the time of Noah (Gen. viii. 11.) the branches of the olive tree were, and since that time have been among all nations, the symbol of peace and prosperity.   Oil is first mentioned in Gen. xxviii. 18. and Job xxiv. 11.; which proves the great antiquity of the cultivation of this tree.   Olives, in Palestine, are of the best growth, and afford the finest oil; whence that country is often extolled in the Scriptures on account of this tree, and especially in opposition to Egypt, which is destitute of good olives. (Numb. xviii. 12. Deut. vii. 13. xi. 14. xii. 17. xviii. 4.)   The olive delights in a barren, sandy, dry, and mountainous soil ; and its multiplied branches (which are very agreeable to the eye as they remain green throughout the winter) have caused it to be represented as the symbol of a numerous progeny, — a blessing which was ascribed to the peculiar favour of God. (Psal. lii. 8. cxxviii. 3. Jer. xi. 16. Hos. xiv. 6.)   The oil, extracted from it by a press, enabled the Jews to carry on an extensive commerce with the Tyrians (Ezek. xxvii. 17. compared with 1 Kings

---

[1] Investigator, No. IV. pp. 307—309. — The pleasing and instructive Essay on the Agriculture of the Israelites (by the Rev. James Plumptre), in the first, third, and fourth numbers of this journal, contains the fullest account of this interesting subject extant in the English language.

[2] Bochart. Hieroz. p. 3. l. iv. c. 27.

[3] On the cultivation of this valuable article of food in the East, Mr. Jowett has communicated the following interesting particulars.   During his voyage to Upper Egypt, in February, 1819, he says, " We observed the people making holes in the sandy soil on the side of the river.   Into these holes they put a small quantity of pigeons' dung and feathers, with the seed of melons or cucumbers.   The value of this manure is alluded to in 2 Kings vi. 25.   The produce of this toil I had an opportunity of seeing, in due season ; that is, the following month of June.   Extensive fields of ripe melons and cucumbers then adorned the sides of the river.   They grew in such abundance, that the sailors freely helped themselves. Some guard, however, is placed upon them.   Occasionally, but at long and desolate intervals, we may observe a little hut made of reeds, just capable of containing one man ; being, in fact, little more than a fence against a north wind.   In these I have observed, sometimes, a poor old man, perhaps lame, feebly protecting the property.   It exactly illustrates Isaiah i. 8.   *And the daughter of Zion is left ...... as a lodge in a garden of cucumbers.*   The abundance of these most necessary vegetables brings to mind the murmurs of the Israelites ; Numb. xi. 5, 6.   *We remember ...... the cucumbers, and the melons, and the leeks, and the onions, and the garlick ; but now our soul is dried away.*"   Jowett's Researches in the Mediterranean, &c. p. 127.

v. 11.); they also sent presents of oil to the kings of Egypt. (Hos. xii. 1.) The berries of the olive tree were sometimes plucked or carefully shaken off by the hand before they were ripe. (Isa. xvii. 6. xxiv. 13. Deut. xxiv. 20.) It appears from Mic. vi. 15. that the presses for extracting the oil were worked with the feet; the best and purest oil, in Exod. xxvii. 20. termed *pure olive-oil beaten*, was that obtained by only beating and squeezing the olives, without subjecting them to the press.

Among the judgments with which God threatened the Israelites for their sins, it was denounced, that though they had olive trees through all their coasts, yet they should not anoint themselves with the oil, for the olive should cast her fruit (Deut. xxviii. 40.); being blasted (as the Jerusalem Targum explains it) in the very blossom, the buds should drop off for want of rain, or the fruit should be eaten with worms. Maimonides observes [1], that the idolaters in those countries pretended by certain magical arts to preserve all manner of fruit, so that the worms should not gnaw the vines, nor either buds or fruits fall from the trees (as he relates their words out of one of their books) : in order, therefore, that he might deter the Israelites from all idolatrous practices, Moses pronounces that they should draw upon themselves those very punishments, which they endeavoured by such means to avoid.

The antient Hebrews were very fond of GARDENS, which are frequently mentioned in the Sacred Writings, and derive their appellations from the prevalence of certain trees ; as the *garden of nuts* and of *pomegranates.* (Sol. Song. vi. 11. iv. 13.) The modern inhabitants of the East take equal delight in gardens with the antient Hebrews, on account of the refreshing shade and delicious fruits which they afford, and also because the air is cooled by the waters of which their gardens are never allowed to be destitute. (1 Kings xxi. 2. 2 Kings xxv. 4. Eccles. ii. 5, 6. John xviii. 1. xix. 41.) The Jews were greatly attached to gardens, as places of burial: hence they frequently built sepulchres in them. (2 Kings xxi. 18. Mark xv. 46.) A pleasant region is called a *garden of the Lord*, or *of God*, that is, a region extremely pleasant. See examples in Gen. xiii. 10. Isa. li. 3. and Ezek. xxxi. 8. [2]

VII. The sacred poets derive many beautiful ALLUSIONS and IMAGES from the rural and domestic economy of the Jews ; and as the same pursuits were cherished and followed by them during the manifestation of our Redeemer, "it is natural to imagine that in the writings of Jews there must occur frequent allusions to the implements and arts of agriculture, and to those rustic occupations which in general formed the study and exercise of this nation. Hence the beautiful images and apt similitudes in the following passages : — No one having *put his hand to the* PLOUGH *and looking back*, is *fit for the kingdom of God.* — *Ye are God's* HUSBANDRY, *or cultivated field.*[3] — *A workman that needeth not to be ashamed, rightly* DIVIDING [4] *the word of*

---

[1] More Nevoch. p. 3. c. 37.

[2] Ikenii Antiquitates Hebr. pp. 583—589. Pareau, Antiq. Hebr. pp. 406—411. Jahn et Ackermann, Archæol. Bibl. §§ 57—70.

[3] 1 Cor. iii. 9. Θεου γεωργιον.

[4] 2 Tim. ii. 15. Εργαlην ορθοτομουντα. A beautiful and expressive image taken from an husbandman (εργατης) drawing his furrow even, and cutting the ground in a direct line. Ernesti says, that the cognate word ορθοτομια is used by Clemens Alexandrinus, Eusebius,

truth. — *Wherefore lay apart all filthiness and superfluity of naughtiness, and receive with meekness the engrafted word.* — *Whatsoever a man* SOWETH, *that shall he* REAP: *he that* SOWETH *to the flesh* — lives a sensual life — *shall from the flesh* REAP *destruction, but he that* SOWETH *to the spirit,* — lives a rational life, — *shall from the spirit* REAP *everlasting life.* — *Consider the ravens, they* SOW *not, neither do they* REAP, *or gather into barns, yet your heavenly Father feedeth them.* — *I am the good* SHEPHERD, *and know my* SHEEP, *and am known of mine.* — *Fear not,* LITTLE FLOCK, *it is your Father's good pleasure to give you the kingdom.*   How striking is the parable of the sower, which, by *seed,* scattered promiscuously, and in every direction by an *husbandman,* and meeting a various fate, according to the respective nature of the soil into which it fell, represents the different reception which Gospel doctrine would experience in the world, according to the different dispositions and principles of that mind into which it was admitted! *He that soweth the* GOOD SEED, *is the Son of Man; the* FIELD *is the world; the* GOOD SEED *are the children of the kingdom; the* TARES *are the children of the wicked one; the enemy that* SOWED *them is the devil; the* HARVEST *is the end of the world; and the* REAPERS *are the angels. As therefore the* TARES *are gathered and burnt in the fire, so shall it be in the end of the world.* — *Whose* FAN *is in his hand, and he will thoroughly* PURGE *his* FLOOR, *and* GATHER *his* WHEAT *into the* GARNER, *but he will* BURN UP *the* CHAFF *with* UNQUENCHABLE FIRE.   By what an apt and awful similitude does St. Paul represent God's rejection of the Jews and admission of the heathens, by the boughs of an olive being lopped off, and the scion of a young olive ingrafted into the old tree!   (Rom. xi. 17. &c.)" — a practice which still obtains in the Morea or Peloponnesus [1]; "and, by continuing the same imagery, how strictly does he caution the Gentiles against insolently exulting over the mutilated branches and cherishing the vain conceit that the boughs were lopped off merely that they might be ingrafted; for if God spared not the native branches, they had greater reason to fear lest he would not spare them; that they should remember that the Jews through their wilful disbelief of Christianity were cut off, and that they, the Gentiles, if they disgrace their religion, would in like manner forfeit the divine favour, and their present flourishing branches be also cut down!   To inspire the Gentile Christians with humility, he concludes with assuring them that the Jewish nation, though they had experienced the severity of God, as he calls it, were not totally forsaken of the Almighty: that the branches, though cut down and robbed of their antient honours, were not abandoned to perish: when the Jews returned from their infidelity they would be ingrafted:—an omnipotent hand was still able to re-insert them into their original stock.   For if thou, O heathen, the scion of an unfruitful wild olive, wert cut out of thy own native barren tree, and, by a process repugnant to the ordinary laws of nature, wert ingrafted into the fruitful generous olive

---

and others, for ορθοδοξια — right doctrine.   Instit. Interp. Nov. Test., p. 109. (Edit. 1792.) A similar remark is also made by Schleusner, voce ορθοτομεω.

[1] The Rev. John Hartley, who travelled in Greece in 1828, says, — " I had my attention directed to the practice of grafting the olive-trees, to which St. Paul alludes (Rom. xi. 17. 20. 23, 24.)   Logothetes" (his friend and guide) " showed me a few wild olives; but by far the greater number are such as have been grafted.   He informs me that it is the universal practice in Greece to graft, from a good tree, upon the wild olive." (Missionary Register, May, 1830, p. 225.)

— how much more will not those, who naturally belong to the antient stock, be, in future time, ingrafted into their own kindred olive! With what singular beauty and propriety is the gradual progress of religion in the soul, from the beginning to its maturity, represented by seed committed to a generous soil, which, after a few successions of day and night, imperceptibly vegetates — peeps above the surface — springs higher and higher — and spontaneously producing, first, the verdant blade — then the ear — afterwards the swelling grain, gradually filling the ear (Mark iv. 27. 28.) [1]; and when the time of harvest is come, and it is arrived at its maturity, it is then reaped and collected into the storehouse. Beautiful illustrations and images like these, taken from rural life, must seal the strongest impressions, particularly upon the minds of Jews, who were daily employed in these occupations, from which these pertinent similes and expressive comparisons were borrowed." [2]

SECTION II.

ON THE ARTS CULTIVATED BY THE HEBREWS OR JEWS.

I. *Origin of the Arts. — State of them from the Deluge to the Time of Moses. — II. State of the Arts from the Time of Moses until the Captivity. — III. State of the Arts after the Captivity.—IV. Account of some of the Arts practised by the Jews. — 1. Writing ; — Materials used for this Purpose ; — Letters ; — Form of Books. — 2. Engraving. — 3. Painting. — V. Music and Musical Instruments. — VI. Dancing.*

I. THE arts, which are now brought to such an admirable state of perfection, it is universally allowed, must have originated partly in necessity and partly in accident. At first they must have been very imperfect and very limited; but the inquisitive and active mind of man, seconded by his wants, soon secured to them a greater extent, and fewer imperfections. Accordingly, in the fourth generation after the creation of man, we find mention made of artificers in brass and iron, and also of musical instruments. (Gen. iv. 21, 22.) Those communities, which, from local or other causes, could not flourish by means of agriculture, would necessarily direct their attention to the encouragement and improvement of the arts. These, consequently, advanced with great rapidity, and were carried to a high pitch so far back as the time of Noah; as we may learn from the very large vessel built under his direction, the construction of which shows that they must have been well acquainted with some at least of the mechanical arts. They had also, without doubt, seen the operations of artificers in other ways besides that of building, and after the deluge imitated their works as well as they could. Hence it is, that shortly after that event, we find mention made of utensils, ornaments, and many other things which imply a knowledge of the arts. Compare Gen. ix. 21. xi, 1—9. xii. 7, 8. xiv. 1—16. xvii. 10. xviii. 4—6. xix. 32. xxxi. 19. 27. 34.

Seminis modo spargenda sunt, quod quamvis sit exiguum, cum occupavit idoneum locum, vires suas explicat, et ex minimo in maximos auctus diffunditur. Senecæ Opera, tom. ii. epist. 38. p. 134. edit. Gronovii. 1672.

Harwood's Introduction, vol. ii. pp. 107—112.

II. Egypt in the early age of the world excelled all other nations in a knowledge of the arts. Although the Hebrews during their residence in Egypt applied themselves to the rearing of cattle, yet they could not remain four hundred years in that country without becoming initiated to a considerable degree into that knowledge which the Egyptians possessed. Among other labours imposed upon them, was the building of treasure cities (Exod. i. 11—14.), and, according to Josephus, they were employed in erecting pyramids.[1] Moses, it is true, did not enact any special laws in favour of the *arts,* nor did he interdict them or lessen them in the estimation of the people; on the contrary, he speaks in the praise of artificers. (Exod. xxxv. 30—35. xxxvi. 1. *et seq.* xxxviii. 22, 23, &c.) The grand object of Moses, in a temporal point of view, was to promote agriculture, and he thought it best, as was done in other nations, to leave the arts to the ingenuity and industry of the people.

Soon after the death of Joshua, a place was expressly allotted by Joab, of the tribe of Judah, to artificers: for in the genealogy of the tribe of Judah, delivered in 1 Chron. iv. 14., we read of a place called the *Valley of Craftsmen,* and (verse 21. 23.) of a family of workmen of fine linen, and another of potters: and when Jerusalem was taken by Nebuchadnezzar, the enemy *carried away all the craftsmen and smiths.* (2 Kings xxiv. 14.) But as a proof that their skill in manufactures, and trade therein, could not be very extensive, we find that the prophet Ezekiel (chap. xxvii.) in describing the affluence of the goods which came to Tyre, makes mention of nothing brought thither from Judæa, except wheat, oil, grapes, and balm, which were all the natural products of their soil. It appears that the mistress of the family usually made the clothing for her husband, her children, and herself, and also for sale. (Exod. xxxv. 25. 1 Sam. ii. 19. Prov. xxxi. 18—24. Acts ix. 39.) Employment, consequently, as far as the arts were concerned, was limited chiefly to those who engaged in the more difficult performances; for instance, those who built chariots, hewed stones, sculptured idols or made them of metal, or who made instruments of gold, silver, and brass, and vessels of clay, and the like. (See Judg. xvii. 4. Isa. xxix. 16. xxx. 14. Jer. xxviii. 13.) In the time of Saul, mention is made of smiths, who manufactured implements of agriculture as well as arms; but who were carried off by the Philistines, in order that they might be enabled to keep the Israelites more effectually in subjection. (1 Sam. xiii. 19—22.) Among the Hebrews, artificers were not, as among the Greeks and Romans, servants and slaves, but men of some rank and wealth: and as luxury and riches increased, they became very numerous. (Jer. xxiv. 1. xxix. 2. 2 Kings xxiv. 14.) Building and architecture, however, did not attain much perfection prior to the reign of the accomplished Solomon. We read, indeed, before the Israelites came into the land of Canaan, that Bezaleel and Aholiab (who were employed in the construction of the tabernacle) excelled *in all manner of workmanship* (Exod. xxxv. 30—35.), but we are there told, that they had their skill by inspiration from God, and it does not appear that they had any successors; for in the days of Solomon, when the Hebrews were at rest from all their enemies, and were perfectly at liberty to follow out improvements of every kind, yet they had no

---

[1] Antiq. lib. ii. c. 9. § 1.

professed artists that could undertake the work of the temple; so that, in the commencement of his reign, Solomon was obliged to send to Hiram king of Tyre for a skilful artist (2 Chron. ii. 7.), by whose direction the model of the temple and all the curious furniture of it was both designed and finished. From the Syrians the Israelites must have learned much, because, long after the reign of Solomon, there were numerous native artisans employed in carpentry and building (2 Kings xii. 11—13. xxii. 4—6.); and among the captives carried away by Nebuchadnezzar, *all the craftsmen and smiths* are generally noticed. (2 Kings xxiv. 14.) But besides these, mention is made of particular manufacturers, as potters (Jer. xviii. 2—4.), fullers (2 Kings xviii. 17. Isa. vii. 3. Mal. iii. 2. Mark ix. 3.), bakers (Jer. xxxvii. 21. Hos. vii. 4.), and barbers. (Ezek. v. 1.)

III. During the captivity many Hebrews (most commonly those to whom a barren tract of the soil had been assigned) applied themselves to the arts and to merchandise. Subsequently, when they were scattered abroad among different nations, a knowledge of the arts became so popular, that the Talmudists taught, that all parents ought to teach their children some art or handicraft. They indeed mention many learned men of their nation, who practised some kind of manual labour, or, as we should say, followed some trade. Accordingly, we find in the New Testament, that Joseph the husband of Mary was a carpenter, and that he was assisted by no less a personage than our Saviour in his labours. (Matt. xiii. 55. Mark vi. 3.) Simon is mentioned as a tanner in the city of Joppa.[1] (Acts ix. 43. x. 32.) Alexander, a learned Jew, was a copper-smith (2 Tim. iv. 14.); Paul and Aquila were tent makers, σκηνοποιοι. Not only the Greeks, but the Jews also, esteemed certain trades *infamous.* The Rabbins reckoned the drivers of asses and camels, barbers, sailors, shepherds, and innkeepers, in the same class with robbers. Those Ephesians and Cretans, who were lovers of gain, αἰσχροκερδεῖς (1 Tim. iii. 8. Tit. i. 7.), were men, as we may learn from antient writers, who were determined to get money, in however base a manner. In the apostolic age, the more eminent Greek tradesmen were united into a society. (Acts xix. 25.)[2]

IV. ACCOUNT OF SOME OF THE PRINCIPAL ARTS, PRACTISED BY THE JEWS.

1. WRITING.—We meet with no notice of this art in the Old Testament before the copy of the law was given by God to Moses, which was *written* (that is, engraven) *on two tables of stone by the finger of God* (Exod. xxxi. 18.), and this is called the *writing of God.* (Exod. xxxii. 16.) It is, therefore, probable that God himself was the first who taught letters to Moses, who communicated the knowledge of them to the Israelites, and they to the other eastern nations.[3] En-

---

[1] The trade of a tanner was esteemed by the Jews so contemptible, that all who followed it were required to mention the same before their marriage, under the penalty of the nuptials being void. It is recorded in the Misna, that, after the death of a man whose brother had exercised the trade of a tanner, the wise men of Sidon determined, that the widow of the deceased was permitted to decline intermarrying with that brother. Townsend's Harmony of the New Test. vol. ii. p. 103.

[2] Jahn's Archæologia Biblica, by Mr. Upham, §§ 80—84. Pareau, Antiq. Hebr. pp. 419—423.

[3] We know that the inhabitants of Yemen or the Southern Arabia were accustomed, in the remotest ages, to inscribe their laws and wise sayings upon stone. See Meidanii

graving or sculpture seems, therefore, to be the most antient way of writing, of which we have another very early instance in Exod. xxxix. 30., where we are told that " holiness to the Lord " was written on a golden plate, and worn on the high priest's head. And we find that the names of the twelve tribes were commanded to be written on twelve rods. (Numb. xvii. 2.) To this mode of writing there is an allusion in Ezek. xxxvii. 16.[1] In later times the Jews made use of broad rushes or flags for writing on, which grew in great abundance

---

Proverb. Arab. p. 45. (cited in Burder's Oriental Literature, vol. i. p. 198.) and Dr. A. Clarke's Commentary, on Exod. xxxii. 15.

[1] Writing on billets or sticks was practised by the Greeks. Plutarch, in his Life of Solon (Vitæ, tom. i. p. 20. ed. Bryan.), and Aulus Gellius (Noct. Att. lib. ii. c. 12.), inform us that the very antient laws of that philosopher, preserved at Athens, were inscribed on tablets of wood called *Axones*. In later times a similar mode of writing was practised by the aboriginal Britons, who cut their letters upon sticks, which were most commonly squared, and sometimes formed into three sides; consequently a single stick contained either four or three lines. (See Ezek. xxxvii. 16.) The squares were used for general subjects, and for stanzas of four lines in poetry; the trilateral ones were adapted to triades, and for a peculiar kind of antient metre, called *Triban* or triplet, and *Englyn Milwyr*, or the warrior's verse. Several sticks with writing upon them were put together, forming a kind of frame, which was called *Peithynen* or elucidator; and was so contrived that each stick might be turned for the facility of reading, the end of each running out alternately on both sides of the frame. The subjoined cut

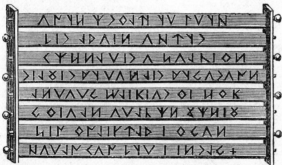

is an engraved specimen of antient British writing, copied from Dr. Fry's elegant work intitled *Pantographia*. (p. 307.) The following is a literal reading in the modern orthography of Wales, with a correct translation : —

> " Aryv y doeth yw pwyll :
> Bid ezain alltud :
> Cyvnewid a haelion :
> Diengid rhywan eid rhygadarn :
> Enwawg meieiad o' i voc :
> Goiaen awel yn nghyving :
> Hir oreistez i ogan :
> Llawer ear byw i Indeg."

TRANSLATION.

> " The weapon of the wise is reason :
> Let the exile be moving :
> Commerce with generous ones :
> Let the very feeble run away ; let the very powerful proceed :
> The swineherd is proud of his swine :
> A gale is almost ice in a narrow place :
> Long penance to slander :
> The frail Indeg has many living relations."

A continuation of this mode of writing may be found in the *Runic* or *Clog* (a corruption of *Log*) Almanacks, which prevailed among the northern nations of Europe so late even as the sixteenth century. See a description and engraving of one in Dr. Plot's Natural History of Staffordshire, pp. 418—422.

in Egypt, and are noticed by the prophet Isaiah when foretelling the confusion of that country. (Isa. xix. 6, 7.) Writing on palm and other leaves is still practised in the East.[1]

The other eastern nations made use chiefly of parchment, being the thin skins of animals carefully dressed. The best was made at Pergamos, whence it was called *Charta Pergamena*. It is probable that the Jews learned the use of it from them, and that this is what is meant by a *roll* (Ezra vi. 2.), and a *roll of a book* (Jer. xxxvi. 2.), and a *scroll rolled together* (Isa. xxxiv. 4.) : for it could not be thin and weak paper, but parchment which is of some consistency, that was capable of being thus rolled up. St. Paul is the only person who makes express mention of parchment. (2 Tim. iv. 13.) In Job xix. 24. and in Jer. xvii. 1. there is mention made of pens of iron, with which they probably made the letters, when they engraved on lead[2], stone[3],

---

[1] In the Sloanian Library, in the British Museum, there are upwards of twenty manuscripts written on leaves, in the Sanskrit, Burman, Peguan, Ceylonese, and other languages. (Ayscough's Catalogue of the Sloane Library, pp. 904—906.) In Tanjore and other parts of India, the palmyra leaf is used. (Dr. C. Buchanan's "Christian Researches in Asia," pp. 70, 71. 8vo. edit.) The common books of the Burmans, like those of the Hindoos, particularly of such as inhabit the southern parts of India, are composed of the palmyra leaf, on which the letters are engraved with a stylus. (Symes's Account of an Embassy to Ava, vol. ii. p. 409. 8vo.) In their more elegant books, the Burmans write on sheets of ivory, or on very fine white palmyra leaves : the ivory is stained black, and the margins are ornamented with gilding, while the characters are enamelled or gilt. On the palmyra leaves the characters are in general of black enamel : and the ends of the leaves and margins are painted with flowers in various bright colours. A hole through both ends of each leaf serves to connect the whole into a volume by means of two strings, which also pass through the two wooden boards that serve for binding. In the finer binding of these kinds of books, the boards are lacquered ; the edges of the leaves are cut smooth and gilt, and the title is written on the upper board. The two boards are by a knot or jewel secured at a little distance from the boards, so as to prevent the book from falling to pieces, but sufficiently distant to admit of the upper leaves being turned back, while the lower ones are read. The more elegant books are in general wrapped up in silk cloth, and bound round by a garter, in which the natives ingeniously contrive to weave the title of the book. (Asiatic Researches, vol. iv. p. 306. 8vo. edit.) The Ceylonese sometimes make use of the palm leaf, but generally prefer that of the *Talipot tree*, on account of its superior breadth and thickness. From these leaves, which are of immense size, they cut out slips from a foot to a foot and a half long, and about two inches broad. These slips being smoothed and all excrescences pared off with the knife, they are ready for use without any other preparation : a fine-pointed steel pencil, like a bodkin, and set in a wooden or ivory handle, ornamented according to the owner's taste, is employed to write, or, rather, to engrave, their characters on these talipot slips, which are very thick and tough. In order to render the characters more visible and distinct, they rub them over with oil mixed with pulverised charcoal, which process also renders them so permanent, that they never can be effaced. When one slip is insufficient to contain all that they intend to write on any particular subject, the Ceylonese string several together by passing a piece of twine through them, and attach them to a board in the same way as we file newspapers. (Percival's Account of the Island of Ceylon, p. 205.) The Bramin manuscripts, in the Telinga language, sent to Oxford from Fort St. George, are written on the leaves of the Ampana, or *Palma Malabarica*. In the Maldive Islands, the natives are said to write on the leaves of the Marcarciquean, which are a fathom and a half (*nine feet*) long, and about a foot broad ; and in other parts of the East Indies, the leaves of the plantain tree are employed for the same purpose.

[2] The eminent antiquary, Montfaucon, informs us that in 1699 he bought at Rome a book wholly composed of lead, about four inches in length, by three inches in width, and containing Egyptian Gnostic figures and unintelligible writing. Not only the two pieces which formed the cover, but also all the leaves (six in number), the stick inserted into the rings which held the leaves together, the hinges, and the nails, were all of lead, without exception. Antiquité Expliquée, tom. ii. p. 378. It is not known what has become of this curious article.

[3] "The most antient people, before the invention of books and before the use of sculpture upon stones and other small fragments, represented things great and noble upon entire rocks and mountains : the custom was not laid aside for many ages. Semiramis, to perpetuate her memory, is reported to have cut a whole rock into the shape of herself. Han-

or other hard substances: but for softer materials they, in all probability, made use of quills or reeds; for we are told of some in the tribe of Zebulun who *handled the pen of the writer.* (Judg. v. 14.) David alludes to the *pen of a ready writer* (Psal. xlv. 1.), and Baruch, as we are told, wrote the words of Jeremiah with ink in a book. (Jer. xxxvi. 18.) It is highly probable that several of the prophets wrote upon tablets of wood, or some similar substance. (Compare Isa. xxx. 8. and Habakkuk ii. 2.) Such tablets, it is well known, were in use long before the time of Homer (who lived about one hundred and fifty years before the prophet Isaiah). Zecharias, the father of John the Baptist, when required to name his son, *asked for a writing-table*, πιναχιδιον (Luke i. 63.); and such tablets were also in use among the Romans and other antient nations, and are yet to be seen in modern Greece, where they are called by the same name.[1] They were not finally disused in western Europe until the fourteenth century of the Christian æra. They were, in general, covered with wax, and the writing was executed with styles or pens, made of gold, silver, brass, iron, copper, ivory or bone, which at one end were pointed for the purpose of inscribing the letters, and smooth at the other extremity for the purpose of erasing.[2] In Barbary the children, who are sent to school, write on a smooth thin board slightly daubed over with whiting, which may be wiped off or renewed at pleasure. The Copts, who are employed by the great men of Egypt in keeping their accounts, &c. make use of a kind of pasteboard, from which the writing is occasionally wiped off with a wet sponge. To this mode of writing there is an allusion in Neh. xiii. 14., and especially in Numb. v. 23.; where, in the case of the woman suspected of adultery, who was to take *an oath of cursing*, it is said that *the priest shall write the curses in a book, and blot them out with the bitter water.* It appears that these maledictions were written with a kind of ink prepared for the purpose, without any calx of iron or other material that could make a permanent dye; and were then washed off the parchment into the water which the woman was obliged to drink: so that she drank the

---

nibal, long after the invention of books, engraved characters upon the Alpine rocks, as a testimony of his passage over them; which characters were remaining about two centuries ago, [that is, in the sixteenth century,] according to Paulus Jovius. It appears particularly to have been the custom of the northern nations, from that remarkable inscription mentioned by Saxo, and several ages after him delineated and published by Olaus Wormius. It was inscribed by Harold Hyldeland, to the memory of his father, and was cut out in the side of a rock, in Runic characters, each letter of the inscription being a quarter of an ell long, and the length of the whole thirty-four ells." (Wise's *Letter to Dr. Mead*, p. 25.) The custom was eastern as well as northern, as appears from that remarkable instance which occurs in Captain Hamilton's *Account of the East Indies*, vol. ii. p. 241. The author, after giving a short history of the successful attack which the Dutch made upon the island of Amoy, in China, A.D. 1645, adds, " This history is written in large Chinese characters on the face of a smooth rock, that faces the entrance of the harbour, and may be fairly seen as we pass out and into the harbour." Burder's Oriental Literature, vol. i. p. 535.

[1] " At Karitena, it is still usual for schoolboys to have a small clean board, on which the master writes the alphabet, or any other lesson, which he intends his scholars to read. As soon as one lesson is finished, the writing is marked out or scraped out; and the board may thus be continually employed for writing new lessons. Not only does this instrument harmonise in its use with the writing-table mentioned Luke i. 63. ; but the Greeks call it by the very same name, πιναχιδιον." Rev. John Hartley's Tour in Greece, in 1828. (Missionary Register, May, 1830. pp. 231, 232.)

[2] On this subject and on the substances generally employed for writing, both in antient and modern times, see an Introduction to the Study of Bibliography, by the author of this work, vol. i. pp. 31—72.

very words of the execration. The ink used in the East is almost all of this kind; a wet sponge will completely obliterate the finest of their writings.[1] The ink was carried in an implement, termed by our translators an inkhorn, which was stuck into the girdle (Ezek. ix. 2, 3.), as it still is in the Levant.[2]

Epistles or Letters, which are included under the same Hebrew word with Books (viz. ‏ספר‎, sepher), are very rarely mentioned in the earlier ages of antiquity. The first notice of an epistle in the Sacred Writings occurs in 2 Sam. xi. 14.: but afterwards they are more frequently mentioned. In the East, letters are to this day commonly sent unsealed: but, when they are sent to persons of distinction, they are placed in a valuable purse, which is tied, closed over with clay or wax, and then stamped with a signet. The same practice obtained in antient times. See Isa. viii. 6. xxix. 11. (marginal rendering), Neh. vi. 5. Job xxxviii. 14. The book which was shown to the apostle John (Rev. v. 1. vi. 1, 2, &c.) was sealed with *seven seals*, which unusual number seems to have been affixed, in order to intimate the great importance and secrecy of the matters therein contained. The most antient epistles begin and end without either salutation or farewell; but under the Persian monarchy it was very prolix. It is given in an abridged form in Ezra iv. 7—10. and v. 7. The apostles, in their epistles, used the salutation customary among the Greeks, but they omitted the usual farewell (χαιρειν) at the close, and adopted a benediction more conformable to the spirit of the Gospel of Christ. When Paul dictated his letters (as he most frequently did), he wrote the benediction at the close, with his own hand. See an instance in 2 Thess. iii. 17.[3]

Books being written on parchment and similar flexible materials, were rolled round a stick or cylinder; and if they were very long, round two cylinders, from the two extremities. Usually, the writing was only on the inside. The writing on Ezekiel's roll (Ezek. ii. 9, 10.) being on *both* sides, indicated that the prophecy would be long.[4] The reader unrolled the book to the place which he wanted, αναπτυξας το βιβλιον, and rolled it up again, when he had read it, πτυξας το βιβλιον (Luke iv. 17—20.); whence the name ‏מגלה‎ (megillah), *a volume*, or thing rolled up. (Psal. xl. 7. Isa. xxxiv. 4. Ezek. ii. 9. 2 Kings xix. 14. Ezra. vi. 2.) The leaves thus rolled round the stick, and bound with

---

[1] Harmer's Observations, vol. iii. p. 127. Dr. A. Clarke on Numb. v. 23.

[2] Emerson's Letters from the Ægean, vol. ii. p. 64. " This implement is one of considerable antiquity; it is common throughout the Levant, and we met with it often in the houses of the Greeks. To one end of a long brass tube for holding pens is attached the little case containing the moistened sepia used for ink, which is closed with a lid and snap, and the whole stuck with much importance in the girdle. This is, without doubt, the instrument borne by the individual, whom Ezekiel mentions as *one man clothed in linen, with a writer's inkhorn by his side.* (Ezek. ix. 2.)" Ibid. p. 64. *note.*

[3] Jahn's Archæol. Hebr. by Mr. Upham, §§ 88, 89. Pareau, Antiq. Hebr. pp. 426 —428.

[4] In the monastery of Megaspelaion, in Greece, the Rev. Mr. Hartley observed two beautiful rolls of the same description with that mentioned in Ezek. ii. 9, 10.; and containing the Liturgies of St. Chrysostom and that attributed by the Greeks to St. James. " You began to read by unfolding, and you continued to read and unfold, till at last you arrived at the stick to which the roll was attached. Then you turned the parchment round, and continued to read on the other side of the roll; folding it gradually up, until you completed the Liturgy. Thus it was *written within and without.*" Hartley's Researches in Greece, p. 238.

a string, could be easily sealed. (Isa. xxix. 11. Dan. xii. 4. Rev. v. 1. vi. 7.) Those books which were inscribed on tablets of wood, lead, brass, or ivory, were connected together by rings at the back, through which a rod was passed to carry them by. In Palestine, when persons are reading privately in a book, " they usually go on, reading aloud with a kind of singing voice, moving their heads and bodies in time, and making a monotonous cadence at regular intervals, — thus giving emphasis; although not such an emphasis, pliant to the sense, as would please an English ear. Very often they seem to read without perceiving the sense; and to be pleased with themselves, merely because they can go through the mechanical act of reading in any way." — This practice may enable us to " understand how it was that Philip should hear at what passage in Isaiah the Ethiopian Eunuch was reading, before he was invited to come up and sit with him in the chariot. (Acts viii. 30, 31.) The Eunuch, though probably reading to himself, and not particularly designing to be heard by his attendants, would read loud enough to be understood by a person at some distance." [1]

2. Though the art of CARVING or ENGRAVING was not invented by the Hebrews, yet that it was cultivated to a considerable extent, is evident not only from the cherubim which were deposited first in the tabernacle and afterwards in Solomon's temple, but from the lions, which were on each side of his throne (1 Kings x. 20.), and from the description which Isaiah (xliv. 13—17.) has given us of the manner in which idols were manufactured.

3. By whomsoever PAINTING was invented, this art appears to have made some progress in the more advanced periods of the Jewish polity. In Ezek xxiii. 14, 15. mention is made of *men pourtrayed upon the wall, the images of the Chaldæans pourtrayed with vermilion, girded with girdles upon their loins, exceeding in dyed attire upon their heads, all of them princes to look to.* Jeremiah mentions apartments which were *painted with vermilion.* (xxii. 14.) But as all pictures were forbidden by the Mosaic law, as well as images (Lev. xxvi. 1. Numb. xxxiii. 52.), it is most probable that these pictures were copied by the Jews from some of their heathen neighbours, after they had been corrupted by intercourse with them.

4. The art of MUSIC was cultivated with great ardour by the Hebrews, who did not confine it to sacred purposes, but introduced it upon all special and solemn occasions, such as entertaining their friends, public festivals, and the like: thus Laban tells Jacob that if he had known of his leaving him, *he would have sent him away with mirth and with songs, with tabret and with harp.* (Gen. xxxi. 27.) Isaiah says, that *the harp and the viol, the tabret and pipe, are in their feasts* (Isa. v. 12.); and, to express the cessation of these feasts, he says, *the mirth of tabrets ceaseth, the joy of the harp ceaseth.* (Isa. xxiv. 8.) It was also the custom at the coronation of kings. (2 Chron. xxiii. 13. And it was the usual manner of expressing their mirth upon their receiving good tidings of victory, and upon the triumphant returns of their generals, as may be seen in Judg. xi. 34. and 1 Sam. xviii. 6. That music and dancing were used among the Jews at their

---

[1] Jowett's Christian Researches in Syria, p. 121.

feasts in latter ages, may be inferred from the parable of the prodigal son. (Luke xv. 25.) Besides their sacred music, the Hebrew monarchs had their private music. Asaph was master of David's royal band of musicians. It appears that in the temple-service female musicians were admitted as well as males, and that in general they were the daughters of Levites. Heman had fourteen sons and three daughters who were skilled in music; and Ezra, when enumerating those who returned with him from the Babylonish captivity, reckons two hundred singing men and singing women. The Chaldee paraphrast on Eccles. ii. 8., where Solomon says that he had *men singers and women singers,* understands it of singing women of the temple.

In the tabernacle and the temple, the Levites (both men and women) were the lawful musicians; but on other occasions the Jews were at liberty to use any musical instruments, with the exception of the silver trumpets which were to be sounded only by the priests, on certain solemn and public occasions. (Numb. x. 1—10.)

The invention of musical instruments is ascribed to Jubal. (Gen. iv. 21.) The following are the principal MUSICAL INSTRUMENTS mentioned in the Sacred Writings [1]: —

(1.) *Pulsatile Instruments.* — These were three in number, viz. The tabret, the cymbal, and the sistrum.

i. The *Tabret, Tabor,* or *Timbrel,* תֹף (TUPH), was composed of a circular hoop, either of wood or brass, which was covered with a piece of skin tensely drawn and hung round with small bells. It was held in the left hand and beaten to notes of music with the right. After the passage of the Red Sea, Miriam the sister of Moses took a timbrel, and began to play and dance with the women (Exod. xv. 20.): in like manner the daughter of Jephthah came to meet her father with timbrels and dances, after he had discomfited and subdued the Ammonites. (Judg. xi. 34.) The ladies in the East, to this day, dance to the sound of this instrument. The earliest notice of the tabret occurs in Gen. xxxi. 27.

ii. The *Cymbal,* צְלְצַל (TSELTSEL), Psal. cl. 5. consisted of two large and broad plates of brass, of a convex form; which being struck against each other, made a hollow ringing sound.[2] They form, in our days, a part of every military band.

iii. The *Sistrum,* מְנַעְנְעִים (MENAANOIM), which in our version of 2 Sam. vi. 5. is mis-rendered *cornets,* was a rod of iron bent into an oval or oblong shape, or square at two corners and curved at the others, and furnished with a number of moveable rings; so that, when shaken or struck with another rod of iron, it emitted the sound desired.

(2.) *Wind Instruments.* — Six of these are mentioned in the Scriptures, viz. The organ, the flute and hautboy, dulcimer, horn, and trumpet.

i. The *Organ,* עֻגָב (OGEB), is frequently mentioned in the Old Testament, and its invention is ascribed to Jubal in Gen. iv. 21.; but it cannot have been like our modern organs. It is supposed to have

---

[1] For some remarks on the titles of certain *Psalms,* which are supposed to have been derived either from musical instruments or the tunes to which they were sung, see Vol. IV. pp. 109—113.

[2] Josephus, Ant. Jud. lib. vii. c. 12.

been a kind of flute, at first composed of one or two, but afterwards of about seven pipes, made of reeds of unequal length and thickness, which were joined together. It corresponded most nearly to the συριγξ or pipe of Pan among the Greeks.

ii. iii. The הליל (CHALIL), and the נקב (NEKEB), which our translators have rendered *pipes*, are supposed to have been the flute and hautboy.

iv. The סומפּוניה (SUMPUNJAH), or dulcimer (Dan. iii. 5.), was a wind instrument made of reeds; by the Syrians called *Sambonjah*, by the Greeks Σαμβυκη, and by the Italians *Zampogna*.

v. The *Horn* or *Crooked Trumpet* was a very antient instrument, made of the horns of oxen cut off at the smaller extremity. In progress of time ram's horns were used for the same purpose. It was chiefly used in war.

vi. The form of the straight *Trumpet* is well known: it was used by the priests (Numb. x. 8. 1 Chron. xv. 24.) both on extraordinary occasions (Numb. x. 10.), and also in the daily service of the temple. (2 Chron. vii. 6. xxix. 26.) In time of peace, when the people or the rulers were to be convened together, this trumpet was blown softly: but when the camps were to move forward, or the people were to march to war, it was sounded with a deeper note.

(3.) *Stringed Instruments.* — These were the harp and the psaltery.

i. The *Harp* כנור (KINOUR), seems to have resembled that in modern use: it was the most antient of all musical instruments. (Gen. iv. 21.) It had ten strings, and was played by David with the hand (1 Sam. xvi. 23.); but Josephus[1] says, that it was played upon or struck with a plectrum.

ii. The *Psaltery* נבל (NEBEL), obtained its name from its resemblance to a leathern bottle, or at least to a vessel in which wine was preserved: it is first mentioned in the Psalms of David, and the invention of it is ascribed to the Phœnicians. In Psal. xxxiii. 2. and cxliv. 9. it is called a *ten-stringed instrument*, but in Psal. xcii. 3. it is distinguished from the latter. Josephus[2] says, that it had twelve sounds (or strings), and was struck or played upon by the fingers.[3]

Effects the most astonishing are attributed in the Scriptures to the Hebrew music, of the nature of which we know but very little. Several examples are recorded, in the sacred history, of the power and charms of music to sweeten the temper, to compose and allay the passions of the mind, to revive the drooping spirits, and to dissipate melancholy. It had this effect on Saul, when David played to him on his harp. (1 Sam. xvi. 16. 23.) And when Elisha was desired by Jehoshaphat to tell him what his success against the king of Moab would be, the prophet required a minstrel to be brought unto him; and when he played, it is said that the *hand of the Lord came upon him* (2 Kings iii. 15.); not that the gift of prophecy was the natural effect of music, but the meaning is, that music disposed the organs, the humours, and in short the whole mind and spirit of the prophet, to receive these supernatural impressions.

---

[1] Ant. Jud. lib. vii. c. 12.   [2] Ibid.

[3] Calmet, Dissertation sur les Instrumens de Musique des Hebreux, prefixed to his Commentary on the Psalms. Jahn, Archæologia Biblica, §§ 94—96. Brown's Antiquities of the Jews, vol. i. pp. 315—321.

(4.) DANCING was an ordinary concomitant of music among the Jews. Sometimes it was used on a religious account: thus Miriam with her women glorified God (after the deliverance from the Egyptians), in dances as well as songs (Exod. xv. 20.), and David danced after the ark. (2 Sam. vi. 16.) It was a thing common at the Jewish feasts (Judg. xxi. 19. 21.) and in public triumphs (Judg. xi. 34.), and at all seasons of mirth and rejoicing. (Psal. xxx. 11. Jer. xxxi. 4. 13. Luke xv. 25.) The idolatrous Jews made it a part of their worship which they paid to the golden calf. (Exod. xxxii. 19.) The Amalekites danced after their victory at Ziklag (1 Sam. xxx. 16.), and Job makes it part of the character of the prosperous wicked, (that is, of those who, placing all their happiness in the enjoyments of sense, forget God and religion,) that their children dance. (Job xxi. 11.) The dancing of the profligate Herodias's daughter pleased Herod so highly, that he promised to give her whatever she asked, and accordingly, at her desire, and in compliment to her, he commanded John the Baptist to be beheaded in prison. (Matt. xiv. 6—8.) Most probably it resembled the voluptuous performances of the dancing girls who still exhibit in the East.[1]

SECTION III.

ON THE LITERATURE AND SCIENCES OF THE HEBREWS.

I. *Schools.— On the Schools of the Prophets in particular.*—II. *Appellations given to the Jewish Doctors or Teachers.*—III. *Their Method of Teaching.* — IV. *Studies of the Jews.* — 1. *History.* — 2. *Poetry.* — 3. *Oratory.*— 4. *Ethics.*— 5. *Physics.*— 6. *Arithmetic.* — 7. *Mathematics.* — 8. *Astronomy.* — 9. *Astrology.* — 10. *Surveying.*—11. *Mechanic Arts.*— 12. *Geography.*

I. SCHOOLS have ever been considered among polished nations as the chief support of states : in them are formed the ministers of religion, judges, and magistrates, as well as the people at large; and there are taught religion, laws, history, and all those sciences, the knowledge of which is of the greatest importance to the well-being of nations, and to the comfort of private life. The Jewish writers pretend that from the earliest ages there have been schools; and that, before the Deluge, they were under the direction of the patriarchs : but these notions have long since been deservedly rejected for want of authority.

Although the Hebrews confined their pursuits to agriculture and the management of cattle, yet we have no reason to conclude that they were a nation of ignorant rustics. Of that which most concerns man to know, — their religious and moral duties, — they could not be ignorant, since the father of every family was bound to teach the laws of Moses to his children. (Deut. xxxii. 6. Psal. lxxvii. 5.) We have, however, no evidence of the existence of any schools, strictly so called, earlier than the time of Samuel : and as the Scriptures do not mention

---

[1] Carne's Letters from the East, p. 165. Pareau, Antiq. Hebr. p. 431. Home's Hist. of the Jews, vol. ii. pp. 339, 340.

the schools of the prophets, before him who was both a judge and a prophet in Israel, we may venture to ascribe those schools to him.   It is
not improbable that the almost total cessation of the spirit of prophecy
under the ministry of Eli, and the degeneracy of the priesthood, first
occasioned the institution of these seminaries, for the better education
of those who were to succeed in the sacred ministry.   From 1 Sam. x.
5. 10. xix. 20. 2 Kings ii. 5. and xxii. 14., it appears that the schools
of the prophets were first erected in the cities of the Levites; which
for the more convenient instruction of the people were dispersed through
the several tribes of Israel.   In these places convenient edifices were
built for the abode of the prophets and their disciples, who were thence
termed the *Sons of the Prophets;* over whom presided some venerable
and divinely-inspired prophet, who is called their father. (2 Kings ii. 12.)
Samuel was one, and, perhaps, the first of those fathers (1 Sam. xix. 20.),
and Elijah was another (2 Kings ii. 12.), who was succeeded by Elisha
in this office. (2 Kings vi. 1.) The sons of the prophets lived together
in a society or community (2 Kings iv. 38.) ; they were instructed in
the knowledge of the law, and of the principles of their religion, as well
as in the sacred art of psalmody, or (as it is termed in 1 Sam. x. 5. and
1 Chron. xxv. 1. 7.) prophesying with harps, psalteries, and cymbals.
At the conclusion of their lectures and religious exercises, they were
accustomed to eat together with their masters.   Calmet is of opinion
that these schools subsisted until the Babylonish captivity : and it
should seem that the captives resorted to such establishments, to hear
the prophets, when there were any, in the places where they resided.
Ezekiel relates various conversations which he had with the elders of
Israel who came to consult him : the people also assembled about him,
apparently for the purpose of hearing him and being instructed by
him ; but they were not very careful to reduce his instructions to practice. (Ezek. viii. 1. xiv. 1. xx. 1.)   It is not improbable that from the
schools of the prophets God chose such persons as he deemed fit to
exercise the prophetic office, and to make known his will to the people.
The greater prophets employed these scholars or young prophets to
carry prophetic messages.   In 2 Kings ix. 1., Elisha sent one of the
sons of the prophets to anoint Jehu king of Israel: and in 1 Kings xx.
15., the young prophet, who was sent to reprove Ahab for sparing
Ben-Hadad, king of Syria, is by the Chaldee paraphrast called one of
the sons or disciples of the prophets.   Hence Amos relates it as an unusual circumstance, that he *was no prophet,* not one of those distinguished men who presided over these seminaries,— *neither a prophet's
son,* educated from his youth in the schools of the prophets; but that
he was *an herdsman and a gatherer of sycamore fruit,* who did not pursue the studies and mode of living peculiar to the prophets, when *the*
LORD *took him as he was following the flock,* and commanded him to go
and prophesy unto his people Israel. (Amos vii. 14, 15.) [1]   To the
schools of the prophets succeeded the synagogues: but it appears that
in the time of Jesus Christ eminent Jewish doctors had their separate

---

[1] Calmet, Dissertation sur les Ecoles des Hébreux, Dissert. tom. i. pp. 372—376., and
Dictionary, voce Schools. Stillingfleet's Origines Sacræ, pp. 92—101. 8th edition, Basnage's
Hist. of the Jews, pp. 410, 411.   Witsii Miscellanea Sacra, lib. i. c. 10. § 10. p. 79.
Bp. Story's Essay concerning the Nature of the Priesthood, pp. 39—42.

schools; as Gamaliel, the preceptor of St. Paul, and probably also Tyrannus.

II. Various APPELLATIONS were antiently given to learned men. Among the Hebrews they were denominated הכמים (HAKAMIM), as among the Greeks they were called σοφοι, that is, *wise men.* In the time of Christ, the common appellative for men of that description was γραμμχτευς, in the Hebrew סופר (SOPHER), *a scribe.* They were ad· dressed by the honorary title of *Rabbi,* רב, רבי (RAB, RABBI), that is, *great* or *master.* The Jews, in imitation of the Greeks, had their seven wise men, who were called *Rabboni,* רבן. Gamaliel was one of the number. They called themselves the children of wisdom; expressions which correspond very nearly to the Greek φιλοσοφος. (Matt. xi. 19. Luke vii. 35.) The heads of sects were called *fathers* (Matt. xxiii. 9.), and the disciples, תלמודים (TALMUDIM), were denominated sons or children.[1] The Jewish teachers, at least some of them, had private lecture-rooms, but they also taught and disputed in synagogues, in temples, and, in fact, wherever they could find an audience. The method of these teachers was the same with that which prevailed among the Greeks. Any disciple who chose might propose questions, upon which it was the duty of the teachers to remark and give their opinions. (Luke ii. 46.) The teachers were not invested with their functions by any formal act of the church or of the civil authority; they were self-constituted. They received no other salary than some voluntary present from the disciples, which was called an *honorary,* τιμη, HONORARIUM. (1 Tim. v. 17.) They acquired a subsistence in the main by the exercise of some art or handicraft. According to the Talmudists they were bound to hold no conversation with women, and to refuse to sit at table with the lower class of people. (John iv. 27. Matt. ix. 11.) The subjects on which they taught were numerous, commonly intricate, and of no great consequence; of which there are abundant examples in the Talmud.[2]

III. After the Jews became divided into the two great sects of Sadducees and Pharisees, each sect had its separate school. The METHOD OF TEACHING in these schools may be easily collected from the Gospels

---

1 " It was antiently the custom of preceptors to address their pupils by the title of *sons :* thus, the disciples of the prophets are called the *sons of the prophets.* (1 Kings xx. 35. 2 Kings ii. 3. iv. 38.) St. Paul styles Timothy his *son.* (1 Tim. i. 2. 2 Tim. i. 2.) St. John styles those to whom his first epistle was sent, his *children* (ii. 1. v. 21.); and thus the royal sage (Prov. i. 8.) addresses his young hearers, exhorting them not to contemn the advice and admonition of their parents; because obedience to parents is a duty, second only in importance to obedience to God." Holden's Translation of Proverbs, p. 88.

2 A sort of academical degree was conferred on the pupils in the Jewish seminaries, which, after the destruction of Jerusalem, were established at Babylon and Tiberias, and of which Basnage has given a copious account in his History of the Jews, book v. c. 5. pp. 410—414. (London, 1708. folio.) The circumstances attending the conferring of this degree are described by Maimonides (Jadchazaka, lib. vi. 4.) as follows:—1. The candidate for the degree was examined, both in respect to his moral character and his literary acquisitions. 2. Having undergone this examination with approbation, the disciple then ascended an elevated seat. Matt. xxiii. 2. 3. A writing tablet was presented to him, to signify, that he should write down his acquisitions, since they might escape from his memory, and, without being written down, be lost. 4. A key was presented, to signify that he might now open to others the treasures of knowledge. (Luke xi. 52.) 5. Hands were laid upon him; a custom derived from Numb. xxvii. 18. 6. A certain power or authority was conferred upon him, probably to be exercised over his own disciples. 7. Finally, he was saluted in the school of Tiberias, with the title of *Rabbi,* רב, in the school of Babylon, with that of *Master,* מר. (Jahn's Archæologia Biblica, by Mr. Upham, 105.)

and Acts. The *Doctors* or *Teachers* generally sat. Thus our Lord
sat down previously to delivering his sermon on the mount (Matt. v.
1.); as Gamaliel also did in his school. (Acts xxii. 3.) Sometimes,
however, the Jewish teachers, like the Greek philosophers, were accustomed to have their disciples around them, wherever they went,
and to discourse, as occasion arose, on things either human or divine.
In this way our Lord delivered some of his most interesting instructions
to his apostles. Allusions to this practice occur in Matt. iv. 20. x. 38.
xvi. 24. Mark i. 18. xvi. 24. The *Pupils* generally sat below their
preceptors. St. Paul tells the Jews, that he sat or studied at the feet
of Gamaliel. (Acts xxii. 3.) Philo relates that the children of the Essenes sat at the feet of their masters, who interpreted the law, and
explained its figurative sense, after the manner of the antient philosophers. The author of the commentary on the first Epistle to the
Corinthians, published under the name of St. Ambrose, says, on ch. xiv.,
that the Jewish rabbins sat on elevated chairs; while scholars who had
made the greatest proficiency sat on benches just below them, and the
junior pupils sat on the ground on hassocks. But in the Talmud[1], it
is stated that the masters sat down while the scholars stood.[2]

IV. The Jews did not become distinguished for their intellectual
acquirements before the time of David, and especially of Solomon, who
is said to have surpassed all others in wisdom; a circumstance which
was the ground of the many visits which were paid to him by distinguished foreigners. (1 Kings v. 9—12.) His example, which was truly
an illustrious one, was, beyond question, imitated by other kings. The
literature of the Hebrews was limited chiefly to religion, the history of
their nation, poetry, philosophy, ethics, and natural history; on which
last subject Solomon wrote many treatises, no longer extant. The
Hebrews made but little progress in science and literature after the
time of Solomon. During their captivity, it is true, they acquired
many foreign notions, with which they had not been previously acquainted : and they, subsequently, borrowed much, both of truth and
of falsehood, from the philosophy of the Greeks. The author of the
book of Wisdom, with some others of the Jewish writers, has made
pretty good use of the Greek philosophy. It is clear, notwithstanding
this, that the Jews after the captivity fell below their ancestors in respect to *History ;* as the published annals of that period are not of a
kindred character with those of the primitive ages of their country.

1. That the art of HISTORICAL WRITING was antiently much cultivated in the East, the Bible itself is an ample testimony; for it not
only relates the prominent events, from the creation down to the fifth
century before Christ, but speaks of many historical books, which have
now perished; and also of many monuments erected in commemoration of remarkable achievements, and furnished with appropriate inscriptions. The Babylonians, also, the Assyrians, the Persians, and
Tyrians, had their Historical Annals. Among the Egyptians there
was a separate order, viz. the priests, one part of whose duty it was to
write the history of their country. In the primitive ages the task of
composing annals fell in most nations upon the priests, but at a later
period the king had his own secretaries, whose special business it was

---

[1] Tit. Megillah.   [2] Calmet, Dissertations, tom. i. pp. 377, 378.

to record the royal sayings and achievements.   The prophets among
the Hebrews recorded the events of their own times, and, in the earliest
periods, the Genealogists interwove many historical events with their
accounts of the succession of families.   Indeed, it should not be forgotten, that antient history generally partakes more of a genealogical
than a chronological character.   Hence the Hebrew phrase for genealogies, תּוֹלְדוֹת (TOLDOTH), is used also for history (Gen. vi. 9. x. 1.);
and hence no epoch more antient than that of Nabonasser is any where
found.   In the Bible, however, this defect, in regard to a regular
chronological system, is in a manner compensated by the insertion in
various places of definite periods of time, and by chronological genealogies.   In giving a concise account of the genealogy of a person, the
Hebrews, as well as the Arabs, took the liberty to omit, according to
their own pleasure, one or more generations.   (Ruth iv. 18—22.   Ezra
vii. 1—5.   Matt. i. 8.)   It was considered so much of an honour to
have a name and a place in these family annals, that the Hebrews
from their first existence as a nation, had public genealogists, denominated שׁוֹטֵר, שׁוֹטְרִים (SHOTer, SHOTeRIM.)

Not only the Hebrews, but, if we may credit Herodotus and Diodorus Siculus, the Egyptians also assigned a certain period to a generation.   According to their estimation, three generations made an hundred years.   In the time of Abraham, however, when men lived to a
greater age, an hundred years made a generation.   This is clear from
Gen. xv. 13. 16., and from the circumstance, that Abraham, Isaac,
and Jacob dwelt two hundred and fifteen years in the land of Canaan,
and yet there were only two generations.

The study of history among the Jews was chiefly confined to the
affairs of their own nation.   Much information, however, may be obtained from their historical and other writings, for the better understanding the states of other foreign nations with which they became
very closely connected : and the most antient historical documents of
the Hebrews throw more light upon the origin of nations, and the
invention and progress of the arts, than any other writings that are
extant.

2. POETRY had its origin in the first ages of the world, when undis-
ciplined feelings and a lively imagination naturally supplied strong
expressions, gave an expressive modulation to the voice, and motion to
the limbs.   Hence poetry, music, and dancing, were in all probability
contemporaneous in their origin.   As the nature and genius of the
poetry of the Hebrews has already been discussed at some length in
the second volume of this work, it is sufficient here to remark, that the
effusions of the inspired Hebrew muse infinitely surpass in grandeur,
sublimity, beauty, and pathos, all the most celebrated productions of
Greece and Rome.   Not to repeat unnecessarily the observations
already offered on this topic, we may here briefly remark, that the
eucharistic song of Moses, composed on the deliverance of the Israelites
and their miraculous passage of the Red Sea (Exod. xv. 1—19.), is
an admirable hymn, full of strong and lively images.   The song of
Deborah and Barak (Judg. v.), and that of Hannah the mother of
Samuel (1 Sam. ii. 1), have many excellent flights, and some noble
and sublime raptures.   David's lamentation on the death of Saul and
Jonathan (2 Sam. i. 19.) is an incomparable elegy.   The gratulatory

hymn (Isa. xii.) and Hezekiah's song of praise (Isa. xxviii.) are worthy of every one's attention. The prayer of Habakkuk (iii.) contains a sublime description of the divine majesty. Besides these single hymns, we have the book of Psalms, Proverbs, Ecclesiastes, Canticles, and Lamentations; all of which are composed by different poets, according to the usage of those times. The Psalms are a great storehouse of heavenly devotion, full of affecting and sublime thoughts, and with a variety of expressions, admirably calculated to excite a thankful remembrance of God's mercies, and for moving the passions of joy and grief, indignation and hatred. They consist mostly of pious and affectionate prayers, holy meditations, and exalted strains of praise and thanksgiving. The allusions are beautiful, the expressions tender and moving, and the piety of the authors is singularly remarkable. The Proverbs of Solomon are a divine collection of many admirable sentences of morality, wonderfully adapted to instruct us in our duty to God and man. The book of Ecclesiastes teaches us, in a very lively manner, the insufficiency of all earthly enjoyments to make a man happy. The Canticles or Song of Solomon, under the parable of a man's affection to his spouse, in very tender yet elegant expressions, shows us the ardent love of Christ to his church and people; and the Lamentations of Jeremiah contain a very mournful account of the state of Jerusalem, as destroyed by the Chaldæans.

3. ORATORY does not appear to have been cultivated by the Hebrews; although the sacred writers, following the impulse of their genius, have left such specimens in their writings, as the most distinguished orators might imitate with advantage. Want of eloquence was objected as a defect against the apostle Paul (1 Cor. i. 17.), who, notwithstanding, possessed a highly cultivated mind, and was by no means deficient in strong natural eloquence.

4. Traces of ETHICS, that is, of the system of prevailing moral opinions, may be found in the book of Job, in the 37th, 39th, and 73d Psalms, also in the books of Proverbs and Ecclesiastes, but chiefly in the apocryphal book of Wisdom, and the writings of the son of Sirach. During the captivity, the Jews acquired many new notions, and appropriated them, as occasion offered, to their own purposes. They at length became acquainted with the philosophy of the Greeks, which makes its appearance abundantly in the book of Wisdom. After the captivity, the language in which the sacred books were written was no longer vernacular. Hence arose the need of an interpreter on the sabbatic year, a time when the whole law was read; and also on the sabbath in the synagogues, which had been recently erected in order to make the people understand what was read. These interpreters learnt the Hebrew language at the schools. The teachers of these schools, who, for the two generations preceding the time of Christ, had maintained some acquaintance with the Greek philosophy, were not satisfied with a simple interpretation of the Hebrew idiom, as it stood, but shaped the interpretation, so as to render it comformable to their philosophy. Thus arose contentions, which gave occasion for the various sects of Pharisees, Sadducees, and Essenes. In the time of our Saviour, divisions had arisen among the Pharisees themselves. No less than eighteen nice questions, if we may believe the Jewish Rabbins, were contested, at that period, between the schools of Hillel

and Shammai. One of which questions was an inquiry, " What cause was sufficient for a bill of divorce ?" If the Shammai and Hillel of the Talmud are the same with the learned men mentioned in Josephus, viz. Sameas and Pollio, who flourished thirty-four years before Christ, then Shammai or Sameas is undoubtedly the same with the Simeon who is mentioned in Luke ii. 25. 34., and his son Gamaliel, so celebrated in the Talmud, is the same with the Gamaliel mentioned in Acts v. 34. xxii. 3.

5. PHYSICS, or NATURAL PHILOSOPHY, has secured but little attention in the East; but a knowledge of the animal, vegetable, and mineral kingdoms, or the science of NATURAL HISTORY, was always much more an object of interest. Whatever knowledge of this science the Hebrews subsequently had, they most probably derived partly from the Canaanitish merchants, partly from the Egyptians, and other nations with whom they had intercourse. The book of Job evinces that its author possessed an intimate knowledge of the works of nature. The agricultural and pastoral habits of the Hebrews were favourable to the acquisition of this science ; and how much they loved it will be evident to any one who peruses the productions of the sacred poets, especially those of David. But no one among the Hebrews could ever be compared to King Solomon; *who spake of trees, from the cedar that is in Lebanon, even to the hyssop that springeth out of the wall, and also of beasts and of fowl, and of creeping things and of fishes.* (1 Kings iv. 33.) The numerous images which our Saviour derived from the works of nature, attest how deeply he had contemplated them.

6. ARITHMETIC. — The more simple methods of arithmetical calculation are spoken of in the Pentateuch, as if they were well known. The merchants of that early period must, for their own convenience, have been possessed of some method of operating by numbers.

7. MATHEMATICS. — By this term we understand Geometry, Mensuration, Navigation, &c. As far as a knowledge of them was absolutely required by the condition and employments of the people, we may well suppose that knowledge to have actually existed; although no express mention is made of these sciences.

8. ASTRONOMY. — The interests of agriculture and navigation required some knowledge of astronomy. An evidence, that an attempt was made at a very early period, to regulate the year by the annual revolution of the sun, may be found in the fact, that the Jewish months were divided into thirty days each. (See Gen. vii. 11. viii. 4.) In Astronomy, the Egyptians, Babylonians, and Phœnicians exhibited great superiority. We are informed there were magicians or enchanters in Egypt (Exod. vii. 11. Lev. xx. 27. xix. 31. Deut. xviii. 20.), denominated in Hebrew מכשפים, because they computed eclipses of the sun and moon, and pretended to the people, that they produced them by the efficacy of their own enchantments. Astronomy does not appear to have been much cultivated by the Hebrews : the laws of Moses, indeed, by no means favoured this science, as the neighbouring heathen nations worshipped the host of heaven ; hence the sacred writers rarely mention any of the constellations by name. See Job ix. 9. xxxviii. 31, 32. Isa. xiii. 10. Amos v. 8. 2 Kings xxiii. 5.

9. ASTROLOGY. — It is by no means surprising that the Hebrews did not devote greater attention to astronomy, since the study of

astrology, which was intimately connected with that of astronomy, and was very highly estimated among the neighbouring nations (Isa. xlvii. 9. Jer. xxvii. 9. l. 35. Dan. ii. 13. 48.), was interdicted to the Hebrews. (Deut. xviii. 10. Lev. xx. 27.) Daniel, indeed, studied the art of astrology at Babylon, but he did not practise it. (Dan. i. 20. ii. 2.) The astrologers (and those wise men mentioned in Matt. ii. 1. *et seq.* appear to have been such) divided the heavens into apartments or habitations, to each one of which apartments they assigned a ruler or president. This fact developes the origin of the word βεελζεβουλ, בַּעַל זְבוּל, *or the Lord of the (celestial) dwelling.* (Matt. x. 25. xii. 24. 27. Mark iii. 22. Luke xi. 15—19.)

10. Measures of length are mentioned in Gen. vi. 15, 16. A knowledge of the method of measuring lands is implied in the account given in Gen. xlvii. 20—27. Mention is made, in the books of Job and Joshua, of a line or rope for the purpose of taking measurements, חֶבֶל, קִי. It was brought by the Hebrews, out of Egypt, where, according to the unanimous testimony of antiquity, Surveying first had its origin, and, in consequence of the inundations of the Nile, was carried to the greatest height. It was here, as we may well conclude, that the Hebrews acquired so much knowledge of the principles of that science, as to enable them, with the aid of the measuring line above mentioned, to partition and set off geographically the whole land of Canaan. The weights used in weighing solid bodies (Gen. xxiii. 15, 16.), provided they were similar to each other in form, imply a knowledge of the rudiments of stereometry.

11. The Mechanic Arts. — No express mention is made of the mechanic arts; but that a knowledge of them, notwithstanding, existed, may be inferred from the erection of Noah's ark, and the tower of Babel; from the use of balances in the time of Abraham; also from what is said of the Egyptian chariots, in Gen. xli. 43. xlv. 19. l. 9. and Exod. xiv. 6, 7.; and from the instruments used by the Egyptians in irrigating their lands. (Deut. xi. 10.) It is implied in the mention of these, and subsequently of many other instruments, that other instruments still, not expressly named, but which were, of course, necessary for the formation of those which are named, were in existence.

12. Geography. — Geographical notices occur so frequently in the Bible, that it is not necessary to say much on this point; but see Gen. x. 1—30. xii. 4 — 15. xiv. 1—16. xxviii. 2—9. xlix. 13., &c. Perhaps, however, it deserves to be repeated, that in the time of Joshua, the whole of Palestine was subjected to a geographical division. (Josh. xviii. 9.) It is evident, then, from their geographical knowledge, as well as from other circumstances already mentioned, that there must have existed among the Hebrews the rudiments, if nothing more, of geographical science[1].

---

[1] Jahn's Archæologia Biblica, by Upham, §§ 98—100. 104. 106. Pareau, Antiquitas Hebraica, pp. 432—438.

SECTION IV.

ON THE COMMERCE AND NAVIGATION OF THE HEBREWS.

I. *Commerce of the Midianites, Egyptians, and Phœnicians.*—II. *Mode of transporting Goods.*—III. *Commerce of the Hebrews, particularly under Solomon and his Successors.*—IV. *Notice of Antient Shipping.*—V. *Money, Weights, and Measures.*

I. THE Scriptures do not afford us any example of trade, more antient than those caravans of Ishmaelites and Midianites, to whom Joseph was perfidiously sold by his brethren. These men were on their return from Gilead, with their camels laden with spices, and other rich articles of merchandise, which they were carrying into Egypt; where, doubtless, they produced a great return, from the quantities consumed in that country for embalming the bodies of the dead. From their purchasing Joseph, and selling him to Potiphar, it is evident that their traffic was not confined to the commodities furnished by Gilead. But the most distinguished merchants of antient times were the Phœnicians, who bought the choicest productions of the East, which they exported to Africa and Europe, whence they took in return silver and other articles of merchandise, which they again circulated in the East. Their first metropolis was Sidon, and afterwards Tyre, founded about 250 years before the building of Solomon's temple, or 1251 before the Christian æra; and wherever they went, they appear to have established peaceful commercial settlements, mutually beneficial to themselves and to the natives of the country visited by them. The commerce of Tyre is particularly described in Isa. xxiii. and Ezek. xxvii. xxviii.

II. The commerce of the East appears to have been chiefly carried on by land: hence ships are but rarely mentioned in the Old Testament before the times of David and Solomon. There were two principal routes from Palestine to Egypt; viz. one along the coasts of the Mediterranean Sea, from Gaza to Pelusium, which was about three days' journey; and the other from Gaza to the Elanitic branch of the Arabian Gulf, which now passes near Mount Sinai, and requires nearly a month to complete it. Although chariots were not unknown to the antient inhabitants of the East, yet they chiefly transported their merchandise across the desert on camels, a hardy race of animals, admirably adapted by nature for this purpose: and lest they should be plundered by robbers, the merchants used to travel in large bodies (as they now do), which are called *caravans;* or in smaller companies termed *kafilés* or *kaflés*. (Job vi. 18, 19. Gen. xxxvii. 25. Isa. xxi. 13.)

III. Although the land of Canaan was, from its abundant produce, admirably adapted to commerce, yet Moses enacted no laws in favour of trade; because the Hebrews, being specially set apart for the preservation of true religion, could not be dispersed among idolatrous nations without being in danger of becoming contaminated with their abominable worship. He therefore only inculcated the strictest justice in weights and measures (Lev. xix. 36, 37. Deut. xxv. 13, 14.); and left the rest to future ages and governors. It is obvious, however, that the three great festivals of the Jews, who were bound to present themselves before Jehovah thrice in the year, would give occasion for much domestic traffic, which the individuals of the twelve tribes would carry on with each other either for money or produce.   From Judg. v. 17. it should seem that the tribes of Dan and Asher had some commercial dealings with the neighbouring maritime nations; but the earliest *direct* notice contained in the Scriptures of the commerce of the Hebrews does not occur before the reign of David.   This wise and valiant prince, by many victories, not only enlarged the boundaries of his empire, but also subdued the kingdom of Edom (which he reduced into a province), and made himself master of the two ports of Elath and Ezion-geber on the Red Sea.   Part of the wealth acquired by his conquests he employed in purchasing cedar-timber from Hiram I. king of Tyre, with whom he maintained a friendly correspondence as long as he lived; and he also hired Tyrian masons and carpenters for carrying on his works.[1]   This prince collected, for the building of the temple, upwards of eight hundred millions of our money, according to Dr. Arbuthnot's calculations.[2]   On the death of David, Solomon his successor cultivated the arts of peace, and was thereby enabled to indulge his taste for magnificence and luxury, more than his father could possibly do.   Being blessed with a larger share of wisdom than ever before fell to the lot of any man, he directed his talents for business to the improvement of foreign commerce, which had not been expressly prohibited by Moses.   He employed the vast wealth amassed by his father in works of architecture, and in strengthening and beautifying his kingdom.   The celebrated temple at Jerusalem, the fortifications of that capital, and many entire cities (among which was the famous Tadmor or Palmyra), were built by him.   Finding his own subjects but little qualified for such undertakings, he applied to Hiram II. king of Tyre, the son of his father's friend Hiram, who furnished him with cedar and fir (or cypress) timber, and large stones, all properly cut and prepared for building; which the Tyrians carried by water to the most convenient landing-place in Solomon's dominions. Hiram II. also sent a great number of workmen to assist and instruct Solomon's people, none of whom had skill to *hew timber like unto the Sidonians* (1 Kings v. 5, 6.), as the Israelites then called the Tyrians, from their having been originally a colony from Sidon.   Solomon, in return, furnished the Tyrians with corn, wine, and oil; and he even received a balance in gold.   (1 Kings v. 9—11. 2 Chron. ii. 10.)   It is not improbable, however, that the gold was the stipulated price for Solomon's cession of twenty cities to the Tyrians; but Hiram, not liking the cities, afterwards returned them to him. (1 Kings ix. 12, 13.)

The great intercourse of trade and friendship, which Solomon had with the first commercial people in the western world, inspired him with a strong desire to participate in the advantages of trade.   His father's conquests, as we have already seen, had extended his terri-

---

[1] Eupolemus, an antient writer quoted by Eusebius (De Præp. Evang. lib. ix.), says that David built ships in Arabia, in which he sent men skilled in mines and metals to the island of Ophir.   Some modern authors, improving upon this rather suspicious authority, have ascribed to David the honour of being the founder of the great East Indian commerce.

[2] Tables of Antient Coins, pp. 35. 208.

tories to the Red Sea or the Arabian Gulf, and had given him the possession of a good harbour, whence ships might be despatched to the rich countries of the south and east. But, his own subjects being totally ignorant of the arts of building and navigating vessels, he again had recourse to the assistance of Hiram. The king of Tyre, who was desirous of an opening to the oriental commerce, the articles of which his subjects were obliged to receive at second hand from the Arabians, entered readily into the views of the Hebrew monarch. Accordingly, Tyrian carpenters were sent to build vessels for both kings at Ezion-geber, Solomon's port on the Red Sea; whither Solomon himself also went to animate the workmen by his presence.

Solomon's ships, conducted by Tyrian navigators, sailed in company with those of Hiram to some rich countries, called Ophir (most probably Sofala on the eastern coast of Africa), and Tarshish, a place supposed to be somewhere on the same coast.[1] The voyage required three years to accomplish it; yet, notwithstanding the length of time employed in it, the returns in this new channel of trade were prodigiously great and profitable, consisting of gold, silver, precious stones, valuable woods, and some exotic animals, as apes and peacocks. We have no information concerning the articles exported in this trade: but, in all probability, the manufactures of the Tyrians, together with the commodities imported by them from other countries, were assorted with the corn, wine, and oil of Solomon's dominions in making up the cargoes; and his ships, like the late Spanish galleons, imported the bullion, partly for the benefit of his industrious and commercial neighbours. (1 Kings vii.—x. 2 Chron. ii. viii. ix.) Solomon also established a commercial correspondence with Egypt; whence he imported horses, chariots, and fine linen-yarn: the chariots cost six hundred, and the horses one hundred and fifty, shekels of silver each. (1 Kings x. 28, 29. 2 Chron. i. 16, 17.)

After the division of the kingdom, Edom being in that portion which remained to the house of David, the Jews appear to have carried on the oriental trade from the two ports of Elath and Ezion-geber, especially the latter, until the time of Jehoshaphat, whose fleet was wrecked there. (1 Kings xxii. 48. 2 Chron. xx. 36, 37.) During the reign of Jehoram, the wicked successor of Jehoshaphat, the Edomites shook off the yoke of the Jewish sovereigns, and recovered their ports. From this time the Jewish traffic, through the Red Sea, ceased till the reign of Uzziah; who, having recovered Elath soon after his accession, expelled the Edomites thence, and, having fortified the place, peopled it with his own subjects, who renewed their former commerce. This appears to have continued till the reign of Ahaz, when Rezin, king of Damascus, having oppressed and weakened

---

[1] It is certain that under Pharaoh Necho, two hundred years after the time of Solomon, this voyage was made by the Egyptians. (Herodotus, lib. iv. c. 42.) They sailed from the Red Sea, and returned by the Mediterranean, and they performed it in three years; just the same time that the voyage under Solomon had taken up. It appears likewise from Pliny (Nat. Hist. lib. ii. c. 67.), that the passage round the Cape of Good Hope was known and frequently practised before his time; by Hanno the Carthaginian, when Carthage was in all its glory; by one Eudoxus, in the time of Ptolemy Lathyrus, king of Egypt; and Cælius Antipater, an historian of good credit, somewhat earlier than Pliny, testifies that he had seen a merchant who had made the voyage from Gades to Æthiopia. Bp. Lowth, however, supposes Tarshish to be Tartessus in Spain. Isaiah, vol. ii. pp. 34, 35.

Judah in conjunction with Pekah, king of Israel, took advantage of this circumstance to seize Elath; whence he expelled the Jews, and planted it with Syrians. In the following year, however, Elath fell into the hands of Tiglathpileser, king of Assyria, who conquered Rezin, but did not restore it to his friend and ally, king Ahaz.[1] Thus finally terminated the commercial prosperity of the kingdoms of Judah and Israel. After the captivity, indeed, during the reigns of the Asmonæan princes, the Jews became great traders. In the time of Pompey the Great there were so many Jews abroad on the ocean, even in the character of pirates, that king Antigonus was accused before him of having sent them out on purpose. During the period of time comprised in the New Testament history, Joppa and Cæsarea were the two principal ports; and corn continued to be a staple article of export to Tyre. (Acts xii. 20.)[2]

During the Babylonish captivity, the Jews seem to have applied themselves much more than they had previously done to commercial pursuits; for though some of them cultivated the soil at the exhortation of Jeremiah (xxix. 4, 5.), yet many others appear to have gained their subsistence by buying and selling. Hence, immediately after their restoration, there were Jewish traders, who, regardless of the rest of the sabbath-day which was enjoined by Moses, not only bought and sold on that sacred day (Neh. xiii. 15.), but also extorted unjust usury. (Neh. v. 1—13.) In later times, foreign commerce was greatly facilitated by Simon Maccabæus, who made the fortified city of Joppa a commodious port (1 Macc. xiv. 5.), and by Herod the Great, who erected the city of Cæsarea, which he converted into a very excellent harbour, which was always free from the waves of the sea by means of a magnificent mole.[3]

IV. Respecting the size and architecture of the Jewish ships, we have no information whatever. The trading vessels of the antients were, in general, much inferior in size to those of the moderns: Cicero mentions a number of ships of burden, none of which were below two thousand amphoræ, that is, not exceeding fifty-six tons[4]; and in a trading vessel, in all probability of much less burden, bound with corn from Alexandria in Egypt to Rome, St. Paul was embarked at Myra in Lycia. From the description of his voyage in Acts xxvii. it is evident to what small improvement the art of navigation had then attained. They had no anchors, by which to moor or secure their vessels; and it is most probable that the crew of the vessel, on board of which the Apostle was embarked, drew her up on the beach of the several places where they stopped, and made her fast on the rocks, as the antient Greeks did in the time of Homer[5], which practice also still obtains in almost every island of Greece.[6] Further, they had no com-

---

[1] During this period, the Jews seem to have had privileged streets at Damascus, as the Syrians had in Samaria. (1 Kings xx. 34.) In later times, during the crusades, the Genoese and Venetians, who had assisted the Latin kings of Jerusalem, had *streets* assigned to them, with great liberties and exclusive jurisdictions therein. See Harmer's Observations, vol. iii. pp. 489—492.

[2] Jahn, Archæol. Hebr. §§ 107—111. Macpherson's Annals of Commerce, vol. i pp. 22—24. 26. Prideaux's Connection, vol. i. pp. 5—10. 8th edit.

[3] Josephus, Ant. Jud. lib. xv. c. 9. § 6. Pareau, Antiq. Hebr. pp. 418, 419.

[4] Epist. ad Familiares, lib. xii. ep. 15.

[5] Iliad, lib. i. 435. et passim.

[6] Emerson's Letters from the Ægean, vol. ii. p. 121. The following passages of Acts

pass by which they could steer their course across the trackless deep; and the sacred historian represents their situation as peculiarly distressing, when the sight of the sun, moon, and stars was intercepted from them. (Acts xxvii. 20.) The vessel being overtaken by one of those tremendous gales, which at certain seasons of the year prevail in the Mediterranean [1] (where they are now called *Levanters*), *they had much work to come by the* ship's *boat*, which appears to have been towed along after the vessel, agreeably to the custom that still obtains in the East, where the skiffs are fastened to the sterns of the ships (16.); *which having taken up*, that is, having drawn it up close to the stern, they proceeded to *under-gird the ship.* (17.) We learn from various passages in the Greek and Roman authors, that the antients had recourse to this expedient in order to secure their vessels, when in imminent danger [2]; and this method has been used even in modern times.[3]

Much ingenious conjecture has been hazarded relative to the nature of the *rudder-bands*, mentioned in Acts xxvii. 40.; but the supposed difficulty will be obviated by attending to the structure of antient vessels. It was usual for all large ships (of which description were the Alexandrian corn ships) to have *two* rudders, a kind of very large and broad oars, which were fixed at the head and stern. The bands were some kinds of fastenings, by which these rudders were hoisted some way out of the water; for as they could be of no use in a storm, and in the event of fair weather coming the vessel could not do without them, this was a prudent way of securing them from being broken to pieces by the agitation of the waves. These bands being loosed, the rudders would fall down into their proper places, and serve to steer the vessel into the creek which they now had in view.[4]

It was the custom of the antients to have images on their ships both at the head and stern; the first of which was called Παρασημος, or the *sign*, from which the vessel was named, and the other was that of the tutelar deity to whose care it was committed. There is no doubt but they sometimes had deities at the head: in which case it is most likely that, if they had any figure at the stern, it was the same; as it is hardly

---

xxvii. will derive elucidation from the above practice: it will be observed that at setting sail there is no mention made of heaving up the anchor; but there occur such phrases as the following:—*And entering into a ship of Adramyttium*, WE LAUNCHED, *meaning to sail by the coasts of Asia.* (verse 2.) *And when the south wind blew softly, supposing that they had obtained their purpose*, LOOSING THENCE, *they sailed close by Crete.* (13.) And again, *And when we had* LAUNCHED FROM THENCE, *we sailed under Cyprus, because the winds were contrary.* (4.) Ibid. pp. 121, 122.

[1] Mr. Emerson has described the phenomena attending one of these gales in his Letters from the Ægean, vol. ii. pp. 149—152.

[2] Raphelius and Wetstein, in loc. have collected numerous testimonies. See also Dr Harwood's Introduction, vol. ii. pp. 239, 240.

[3] The process of under-girding a ship is thus performed:—A stout cable is slipped under the vessel at the prow, which the seamen can conduct to any part of the ship's keel, and then fasten the two ends on the deck, to keep the planks from starting. As many rounds as may be necessary, may be thus taken about the vessel. An instance of this kind is mentioned in Lord Anson's Voyage round the World. Speaking of a Spanish man-of-war in a storm, the writer says, — " They were obliged to throw overboard all their upper-deck guns; and *take six turns of the cable round the ship, to prevent her opening.*" (p. 24. 4to. edit.) Bp. Pearce and Dr. A. Clarke on Acts xxvii. 17. Two instances of under-girding a ship are noticed in the Chevalier de Johnstone's Memoirs of the Rebellion in 1745-6. (London, 1822. 8vo.) pp. 421. 454.

[4] Elsner and Wetstein on Acts xxvii. 40.

probable, that the ship should be called by the name of one deity, and be committed to the care of another. The constellation of the Dioscuri, that is, of Castor and Pollux (Acts xxviii. 11.), was deemed favourable to mariners; and, therefore, for a good omen, they had them painted or carved on the head of the ship, whence they gave it a name, which the sacred historian uses.[1]

The Egyptians commonly used on the Nile a light sort of ships or boats made of the reed papyrus.[2] Isaiah alludes to them (xviii. 2.), in our version rendered *vessels of bulrushes*.[3] Boats of similar frail materials are still in use in the East.[4]

V. Commerce could not be carried on without COIN, nor without a system of WEIGHTS and MEASURES.

Although the Scriptures frequently mention gold, silver, brass, certain sums of money, purchases made with money, current money, and money of a certain weight; yet the use of COIN or stamped MONEY appears to have been of late introduction among the Hebrews. Calmet is of opinion, that the antient Hebrews took gold and silver only by weight, and that they regarded the purity of the metal and not the stamp. The antient Egyptians also settled the price of commodities by weight.[5] The practice of weighing money is stated by M. Volney to be general in Syria, Egypt, and Turkey : no piece, however effaced, is there refused. The merchant draws out his scales and weighs it[6], as in the days of Abraham, when he purchased the cave of Machpelah for a sepulchre. (Gen. xxiii. 16.)[7] The most antient mode of carrying on trade, unquestionably, was by way of barter, or exchanging one commodity for another; a custom which obtains in some places even to this day. In process of time such metals as were deemed the most valuable were received into traffic, and were weighed out; until the inconveniences of this method induced men to give to each metal a certain mark, weight, and degree of alloy, in order to determine its value, and save both buyers and sellers the trouble of weighing and examining the metal. In some cases, the earliest coins bore the impression of a particular figure; in others, they were made to resemble objects of nature. The coinage of money was of late date among the Persians, Greeks, and Romans. The Persians had none coined before the reign of Darius the son of Hystaspes, nor had the Greeks (whom

---

[1] Valpy's Gr. Test. vol. ii. on Acts xxviii. 11.

[2] Ex ipso quidem papyro navigia texunt. Pliny, Hist. Nat. lib. xiii. 11. The same fact is attested by Lucan: conseritur bibula Memphitis cymba papyro. Pharsal. lib. iv. 136.

[3] Bp. Lowth on Isaiah xviii. 2.

[4] The Hon. Capt. Keppel, giving an account of an excursion up the river Tigris, thus describes the boat in which he embarked: — It was in shape like a large circular basket; the sides were of willow, covered over with bitumen, the bottom was laid with reeds. This sort of boat is common to the Euphrates and the Tigris, and is probably best adapted to the strong currents common to these rivers. May not these boats be of the same kind as the *vessels of bulrushes upon the waters* alluded to by Isaiah? (xviii. 2.)" Narrative of Travels from India, vol. i. pp. 197, 198.

[5] Wilkinson's Manners, &c. of the Antient Egyptians, vol. iii. pp. 237, 238.

[6] In a piece of sculpture discovered by Captains Irby and Mangles at El Cab, the antient Eleethias in Egypt, there was represented a pair of scales: at one end was a man writing an account while another was weighing some small articles, probably loaves of bread. The weight was in the form of a cow couchant. Travels in Egypt, Nubia, &c. pp. 130—132.

[7] Volney's Travels in Syria, &c. vol. ii. p. 425. In considerable payments an agent of exchange is sent for, who counts paras by thousands, rejects pieces of false money, and weighs all the sequins either separately or together. (Ibid.) This may serve to illustrate the phrase, *current money with the merchant*, in Gen. xxiii. 16.

the Romans most probably imitated) any before the time of Alexander. We have no certain vestiges of the existence of coined money, among the Egyptians, before the time of the Ptolemies; nor had the Hebrews any coinage until the government of Judas Maccabæus, to whom Antiochus Sidetes, king of Syria, granted the privilege of coining his own money in Judæa. Before these respective times, all payments were made by weight; this will account for one and the same word (*shekel*, which comes from *shakal*, to *weigh*,) denoting both a certain weight of any commodity and also a determinate sum of money.[1] The holy pliancy of temper with which believers should conform to all the precepts of the Gospel is by St. Paul represented by a beautiful allusion to the coining of money, in which the liquid metals accurately receive the figure of the mould or die into which they are poured. (Rom. vi. 17.)[2]

WEIGHTS AND MEASURES were regulated at a very early period in Asia. Moses made various enactments concerning them for the Hebrews; and both weights and measures, which were to serve as standards for form and contents, were deposited at first in the tabernacle, and afterwards in the temple, under the cognisance of the priests.[3] On the destruction of Solomon's temple these standards necessarily perished; and during the captivity the Hebrews used the weights and measures of their masters.

For tables of the weights, measures, and money used in commerce, and which are mentioned in the Bible, the reader is referred to No. I. of the Appendix to this volume.

CHAPTER VIII.

AMUSEMENTS OF THE JEWS. — ALLUSIONS TO THE THEATRES, TO THEATRICAL PERFORMANCES, AND TO THE GRECIAN GAMES IN THE NEW TESTAMENT.

I. *Recreations of the Jews in domestic Life.*—II. *Military Sports.*—III. *Introduction of Gymnastic and Theatrical Exhibitions among the Jews.* — IV. *Allusions to the Theatres and to Theatrical Performances in the New Testament.*—V. *Allusions to the Grecian Games, particularly the Olympic Games.* — 1. *Qualifications of the Candidates.* — *Preparatory Discipline to which they were subjected.*—2. *Foot Race.*— 3. *Rewards of the Victors.* — 4. *Beautiful Allusions to these Games in the New Testament explained.*

THE whole design of the Mosaic institutes, being to preserve the knowledge and worship of the true God among the Israelites, will sufficiently account for their silence respecting recreations and amusements. Although no particular circumstances are recorded on this subject, we meet with a few detached facts which show that the Hebrews were not entirely destitute of amusements.

---

[1] Calmet's Dictionary, vol. ii. article *Money*.   See a full account of the money coined by the Maccabæan princes, in F. P. Bayer's Dissertatio De Nummis Hebræo-Samaritanis, Valentiæ Edetanorum. 1781. 4to.   [2] Cox's Horæ Romanæ, p. 33.

[3] Michaelis has fully discussed the wisdom and propriety of the Mosaic regulations concerning weights and measures, in his Commentaries on the Laws of Moses, vol. iii. pp. 378 —397.

I. The various events incident to DOMESTIC LIFE afforded them occasions for festivity. Thus, Abraham made a great feast on the day when Isaac was weaned. (Gen. xxi. 8.) Weddings were always seasons of rejoicing (see pp. 410—414. *suprà*): so also were the seasons of sheep-shearing (1 Sam. xxv. 36. and 2 Sam. xiii. 23.); and harvest-home. (See p. 456.) To which may be added, the birth-days of sovereigns. (Gen. xl. 20. Mark vi. 21.) Of most of these festivities music (see pp. 471, 472.) and dancing (see p. 474.) were the accompaniments. From the amusement of children sitting in the market-place, and imitating the usages common at wedding feasts and at funerals, Jesus Christ takes occasion to compare the Pharisees to sullen children who will be pleased with nothing which their companions can do, whether they play at weddings or funerals; since they could not be prevailed upon to attend either to the severe precepts and life of John the Baptist, or to the milder precepts and habits of Christ. (Matt. xi. 16, 17.) [1] The infamous practice of gamesters who play with loaded dice has furnished St. Paul with a strong metaphor, in which he cautions the Christians at Ephesus against the cheating *sleight of men* (Eph. iv. 14.), whether unbelieving Jews, heathen philosophers, or false teachers in the church itself, who corrupted the doctrines of the Gospel for worldly purposes, while they assumed the appearance of great disinterestedness and piety.[2]

II. MILITARY SPORTS and exercises appear to have been common in the earlier periods of the Jewish history. By these the Jewish youth were taught the use of the bow (1 Sam. xx. 20. 30—35.), or the hurling of stones from a sling with unerring aim. (Judg. xx. 16. 1 Chron. xii. 2.) Jerome informs us, that in his days (the fourth century) it was a common exercise throughout Judæa for the young men, who were ambitious to give proof of their strength, to lift up round stones of enormous weight, some as high as their knees, others to their navel, shoulders, or head, while others placed them at the top of their heads, with their hands erect and joined together. He further states, that he saw at Athens an extremely heavy brazen sphere or globe, which he vainly endeavoured to lift; and that on inquiring into its use, he was informed, that no one was permitted to contend in the games until, by his lifting of this weight, it was ascertained who could be matched with him. From this exercise, Jerome elucidates a difficult passage in Zech. xii. 3., in which the prophet compares Jerusalem to a stone of great weight, which being too heavy for those who attempted to lift it up, or even to remove it, falls back upon them, and crushes them to pieces.[3]

III. Among the great changes which were effected in the manners and customs of the Jews, subsequently to the time of Alexander the Great, may be reckoned the introduction of GYMNASTIC SPORTS and GAMES, in imitation of those celebrated by the Greeks; who, it is well known, were passionately fond of theatrical exhibitions. These amusements they carried, with their victorious arms, into the various countries of the East; the inhabitants of which, in imitation of their masters, addicted themselves to the same diversions, and endeavoured to distinguish themselves in the same exercises. The profligate high

---

[1] Kuinöel on Matt. xi. 17.   [2] Dr. Macknight on Eph. iv. 14.
[3] Jerome on Zech. xii. 3. (Op. tom. iii. col. 1780. Edit. Benedictin.) W. Lowth on Zech. xii. 3.

priest Jason, in the reign of Antiochus Epiphanes, first introduced public games at Jerusalem, where he erected a gymnasium, or "place for exercise, and for the training up of youth in the fashions of the heathen." (2 Macc. iv. 9.) "The avowed purpose of these athletic exercises was, the strengthening of the body; but the real design went to the gradual change of judaism for heathenism, as was clearly indicated by the pains which many took to efface the mark of circumcision. The games, besides, were closely connected with idolatry; for they were generally celebrated in honour of some pagan god. The innovations of Jason were therefore extremely odious to the more pious part of the nation, and even his own adherents did not enter fully into all his views." [1] They also produced a demoralising effect upon the Jews. Even the very priests, neglecting the duties of their sacred office, hastened to be partakers of these unlawful sports, and were ambitious of obtaining the prizes awarded to the victors. (10—15.) The restoration of divine worship, and of the observance of the Mosaic laws and institutions under the Maccabæan princes, put an end to these spectacles. They were, however, revived by Herod, who, in order to ingratiate himself with the emperor Augustus (b. c. 7.), built a theatre at Jerusalem [2], and also a capacious amphitheatre, without the city, in the plain; and who also erected similar edifices at Cæsarea [3], and appointed games to be solemnised every fifth year with great splendour, and amid a vast concourse of spectators, who were invited by proclamation from the neighbouring countries. Josephus's narrative of these circumstances is not sufficiently minute to enable us to determine with accuracy *all* the exhibitions which took place on these occasions. But we may collect, that they consisted of wrestling, chariot-racing, music, and combats of wild beasts, which either fought with one another, or with men who were under sentence of death:— a barbarous amusement which has happily been abolished by the beneficent influence of the Gospel. Further, the most distinguished wrestlers were invited to attend by the promise of very great rewards to the victors. The Gentiles were highly delighted with these exhibitions, which were so utterly repugnant to the laws and customs of the Jews, that they regarded them with the utmost horror and detestation. [4]

IV. In all countries the stage has ever furnished different languages with some of the most beautiful Metaphors and ALLUSIONS that adorn them. [5] In every tongue we read of the drama of human life [6]: its scenes are described as continually shifting and varying:

---

1 Jahn's Hist. of the Hebrew Commonwealth, vol. i. p. 308.
2 Josephus, Ant. Jud. ib. xv. c. 8. § 1.
3 Bell. Jud. lib. i. c. 21. § 8. The different passages of Josephus are examined in detail by Eichhorn (to whom we are indebted for the facts above stated) in his Commentatio de Judæorum Re Scenica, inserted in the second volume of the Commentationes Societatis Regiæ Gottingensis Recentiores. Gottingæ, 1813. 4to.
4 Josephus, Ant. Jud. lib. xv. c. 8. §§ 1, 2.
5 For the following account of the theatrical representations, and of the Grecian games alluded to in the New Testament, the author is indebted to Dr. Harwood's Introduction, vol. ii. sections 1. and 4., collated with Brüning's Compendium Antiquitatum Græcarum e profanis Sacrarum, pp. 352—376., from which treatise Dr. H. appears to have derived a considerable portion of his materials.

6   Σκηνη πας ὁ βιος, και παιγνιον· η μαθε παιζειν,
     Την σπουδην μεταθεις, η φερε τας οδυνας.   Epigram in Antholog.

Quomodo fabula, sic vita; non quàm diu, sed quàm bene acta sit, refert. Nihil ad rem

mortal life is represented as an intricate plot, which will gradually unfold and finally wind up into harmony and happiness; and the world is styled a magnificent theatre, in which God has placed us,—assigned to every man a character,—is a constant spectator how he supports this character,—and will finally applaud or condemn according to the good or bad execution of the part, whatever it is, he has been appointed to act.[1]   The drama was instituted to exhibit a striking picture of human life, and, in a faithful mirror, to hold up to the spectator's view that miscellany of characters which diversify it, and those interchanges and reverses of fortune which chequer it.[2]   It is scarcely necessary to remark, though the observation is proper for the sake of illustrating a very beautiful passage in one of St. Paul's Epistles, that a variety of scenes is painted, which by means of the requisite machinery are very frequently shifting, in order to show the characters in a variety of places and fortunes.   To the spectator, lively and affecting views are by turns displayed, sometimes, for example, of Thebes, sometimes of Athens[3], one while of a palace, at another of a prison; now of a splendid triumph, and now of a funeral procession,—every thing, from the beginning to the catastrophe, perpetually varying and changing according to the rules and conduct of the drama. Agreeably to this, with what elegance and propriety does St. Paul, whom we find quoting Menander, one of the most celebrated writers of the Greek comedy, represent the fashion of this world as continually passing away[4], and all the scenes of this vain and visionary life as perpetually shifting!   "The imagery," says Grotius, "is taken from the theatre, where the scenery is suddenly changed, and exhibits an appearance totally different."[5]   And as the transactions of the drama are not real, but fictitious and imaginary, such and such characters being assumed and personated, in whose joys or griefs, in whose domestic felicities or infelicities, in whose elevation or depression, the actor is not really and personally interested, but only supports a character, perhaps entirely foreign from his own, and represents passions and affections in which his own heart has no share: how beautiful and expressive, when considered in this light, is that passage of Scripture wherein the Apostle is inculcating a Christian indifference for this world, and exhorting us not to suffer ourselves to be

---

pertinet, quo loco desinas: quocunque voles desine: tantùm bonam clausulam impone. Seneca, epist. lxxvii. tom. ii. p. 306. edit. Elz. 1673.   Οιον ει κωμῳδον απολυει της σκηνης ὁ παραλαβων στρατηγος αλλ' ουκ ειπον τα πεντε μερη, αλλα τα τρια, καλως ειπας· εν μεντοι τῳ βιῳ τα τρια λον το δραμα ἐστι.   Mar. Antoninus, lib. xii. p. 236. edit. Oxon. The words of the Psalmist, — " we spend our days as a tale that is told," — have been supposed to be an allusion to a dramatic fable.   The imagery, considered in this view, would be striking, did we know that the early Jews ever had any scenical representations.

  [1] Epicteti Enchirid. cap. 17. p. 699. Upton.   Epicteti Dissertationes ab Arriano. lib. iv. p. 580. Upton.

  [2] M. Antoninus, lib. xi. § vi. p. 204. edit. Oxon.

  [3] ———— Modò me Thebis, modò ponit Athenis.   Horat. Epist. lib. ii. ver. 213.

  [4] 1 Cor. vii. 31.   Παραγει γαρ το σχημα του κοσμου τουτου.

  [5] Dicitur, παραγειν το σχημα της σκηνης, ubi scena invertitur, aliamque plane ostendit faciem.   Grotius, ad loc.   Mais comme Grotius remarque que cette reflexion de l'Apôtre est empruntée du théâtre, et que le mot Grec σχημα, que l'on traduit la figure, signifie proprement un personnage de théâtre, ou une décoration dans Euripide et dans Aristophane, et que les Grecs disoient pour marquer le changement de scène, ou de décoration du théâtre παραγει το σχημα της σκηνης, on croit qu'il faudroit traduire, La face de ce monde change, ce qui convient parfaitement au dessein de l'Apôtre dans cette conjuncture.   Projet d'une Nouvelle Version, par le Cene, p. 674.   Rotter. 1696.

unduly affected either by the joys or sorrows of so fugitive and transitory a scene! (1 Cor. vii. 29—31.) *But this I say, brethren, the time
is short. It remaineth that both they that have wives be as though they
had none : and they that weep as though they wept not : and they that
rejoice as though they rejoiced not : and they that buy as though they
possessed not : and they that use this world as not abusing it.*[1] *For the
fashion of this world passeth away.* If we keep in mind the supposed
allusion in the text (the fashion of this world passeth away) we shall
discern a peculiar beauty and force in his language and sentiment.
For the actors in a play, whether it be comedy or tragedy, do not act
their own proper and personal concerns, but only personate and mimic
the characters and conditions of other men. And so when they weep
in acting some tragical part, it is as though they wept not; and there
is more show and appearance, than truth and reality, of grief and
sorrow in the case. On the other hand, if they rejoice in acting some
brighter scene, it is as though they rejoiced not; it is but a feigned
semblance of joy, and forced air of mirth and gaiety, which they
exhibit to the spectators, no real inward gladness of heart. If they
seem to contract marriages, or act the merchant, or personate a gentle-
man of fortune, still it is nothing but fiction. And so when the
play is over, they have no wives, no possessions or goods, no enjoyments of the world, in consequence of such representations. In like
manner, by this apt comparison, the Apostle would teach us to
moderate our desires and affections towards every thing in this world;
and rather, as it were, to personate such things as matters of a foreign
nature, than to incorporate ourselves with them, as our own proper
and personal concern.[2]

" The theatre is also furnished with dresses suitable to every age,
and adapted to every circumstance and change of fortune. The persons of the drama, in one and the same representation, frequently
support a variety of characters : the prince and the beggar, the young
and the old, change their dress according to the characters in which
they respectively appear, by turns laying aside one habit and assuming
another, agreeably to every condition and age.[3] The apostle Paul
seems to allude to this custom, and his expressions regarded in this
light have a peculiar beauty and energy, when he exhorts Christians
to PUT OFF the OLD MAN *with his deeds, and to* PUT ON the NEW MAN.
(Coloss. iii. 9, 10. Eph. iv. 22, 23, 24.) *That ye* PUT OFF, *concerning
the former conversation, the* OLD MAN, *which is corrupt according to the
deceitful lusts : and be renewed in the spirit of your minds, and that ye*
PUT ON THE NEW MAN [4], *which after God is created in righteousness and
true holiness.*

---

[1] Καταχρωμενοι is very unhappily rendered abuse. It is here used in a good sense, as the
whole passage requires. From the transiency of human life the Apostle observes, that those
who are now using this world's happiness will soon be as those who had never enjoyed it.
The Greek writers use Παραχραομαι or Αποχραομαι to abuse.

[2] Brekell's Discourses, p. 318.

[3] Ειναι γαρ ομοιον τω αγαθω υποκριτη τον σοφον· ος αν τε Θερσιτου αν τε Αγαμεμνονος προ-
σωπον αναλαβη, εκατερον υποκρινεται προσηκοντως. Diogenes Laertius, lib. vii. p. 468.
edit. Meibomii. 1692.

[4] Mihi quidem dubium non est quin hæc loquendi ratio ducta sit ab *actoribus,* qui, *habitu
mutato,* vestibusque depositis, *alias* partes agunt, *aliosque* se esse produnt, quam qui in *scenâ*
esse videbantur. Krebsii Observationes in Nov. Test. p. 342 Lipsiæ, 1755.

" It is, moreover, well known, that in the Roman theatres and amphitheatres malefactors and criminals were condemned to fight with lions, bears, elephants, and tigers, for which[1] all parts of the Roman dominions were industriously ransacked, to afford this very polite and elegant amusement to this most refined and civilised people. The wretched miscreant was brought upon the stage, regarded with the last ignominy and contempt by the assembled multitudes, made a gazing-stock to the world, as the Apostle expresses it; and a wild beast, instigated to madness by the shouts and light missive darts of the spectators, was let loose upon him, to tear and worry him in a miserable manner. To this sanguinary and brutal custom the following expressions of the author of the Epistle to the Hebrews allude. (x. 32, 33.) *Ye endured a great fight of afflictions, partly whilst ye were made a gazing-stock, both by reproaches and afflictions.* The original is very emphatical; being openly exposed as on a public theatre to ignominious insults and to the last cruelties.[2] In another passage also, St. Paul, speaking of the determined fierceness and bigotry with which the citizens of Ephesus opposed him, uses a strong metaphorical expression taken from the theatre: — *If after the manner of men I have fought with beasts at Ephesus.* Not that the Apostle appears to have been actually condemned by his enemies to combat with wild beasts in the theatre," (because the Roman citizens were never subjected to such a degradation :) " he seems only to have employed this strong phraseology, to denote the violence and ferocity of his adversaries, which resembled the rage and fury of brutes, and to compare his contention with these fierce pagan zealots and fanatics to the common theatrical conflict of men with wild beasts.[3]

---

[1] ——— Quodcunque tremendum est
Dentibus, aut insigne jubis, aut nobile cornu,
Aut rigidum setis capitur, decus omne timorque
Sylvarum, non caule latent, non mole resistunt.　　　　Claudian.

[2] Ονειδισμοις τε και θλιψεσι Θεατριζομενοι, exposed on a public stage. Dispensatorem ad bestias dedit. Hoc est, *seipsum traducere.* Id est, says one of the commentators, ludibrio exponere. Petronius Arbiter, p. 220. edit. Burman. 1709. Εξεθεατρισαν εαυτους. They openly exposed themselves. Polybius, p. 364. Hanov. 1619. Eusebius relates that Attalus, a Christian, was led round the amphitheatre, and exposed to the insults and violence of the multitude. Περιαχθεις κυκλω του αμφιθεατρου. Eusebius, Hist. Eccles. lib. v. p. 206. Cantab. Solebant olim gladiatores et bestiarii, antequam certamen obirent per ora populi circumduci. Valesii not. in loc. There is a striking passage in Philo, where, in the same strong metaphorical imagery the Apostle here employs, Flaccus is represented deploring the public ignominy to which he was now reduced. See Philonis Opera, tom. ii. p. 542. edit. Mangey.

[3] The same metaphors are of frequent occurrence in the New Testament. Herod is called a fox ; Go and tell that fox. (Luke xiii. 32.) Hypocrites are called wolves in sheep's clothing. (Matt. vii. 15.) Rapacious and mercenary preachers are styled wolves, that will enter and ravage the fold : There will enter among you grievous wolves, not sparing the flock. (Acts xx. 29.) The Apostle uses a harsher metaphor to denote the malice and rage of his adversaries : Beware of dogs. (Phil. iii. 2.) Had St. Paul been thus engaged, says Dr. Ward, it is difficult to apprehend how he could have escaped without a miracle. For those who conquered the beasts were afterwards obliged to fight with men till they were killed themselves. It seems most reasonable, therefore, to understand the expression [εθηριομαχησα] as metaphorical, and that he alludes to the tumult raised by Demetrius. He uses the like metaphor, and with respect to the same thing (1 Cor. iv. 9.), and again (13.), alluding to another custom. As to the expression, Κατ' ανθρωπον in 1 Cor. xv. 32. the sense seems to be *humanitus loquendo.* Dr. Ward's Dissertations on Scripture, dissert. xlix. pp. 200, 201. The very same word which the Apostle here employs to denote the violence and fury of his adversaries is used by Ignatius in the like metaphorical sense, Απο Συριας μεχρι Ρωμης ΘΗΡΙΟΜΑΧΩ δια γης και θαλασσης, νυκτος και ημερας. All the way from Syria to Rome, by sea and by land, by night and by day, do I FIGHT WITH WILD BEASTS. Ignatii

Let it be farther observed, for the elucidating a very striking passage in 1 Cor. iv. 9. that in the Roman amphitheatre the *bestiarii,* who in the morning combated with wild beasts, had armour with which to defend themselves, and to annoy and slay their antagonist. But the last who were brought upon the stage, which was about noon[1], were a miserable number, quite naked, without any weapons to assail their adversary — with immediate and inevitable death before them in all its horrors, and destined to be mangled and butchered in the direst manner. In allusion to this custom, with what sublimity and energy are the apostles represented to be brought out last upon the stage, as being devoted to certain death, and being made a public spectacle to the world, to angels and men ! *For I think that God hath set forth us the apostles last, as it were appointed to death : for we are made a spectacle to the world, to angels and men.* Dr. Whitby's illustration of this distinguished passage is accurate and judicious. " Here the Apostle seems to allude to the Roman spectacles, της των θηριομαχων και μονομαχιας ανδροφονου, that of the *bestiarii* and the gladiators, where in the morning men were brought upon the theatre to fight with wild beasts, and to them was allowed armour to defend themselves, and smite the beasts that did assail them : but in the meridian spectacle were brought forth the gladiators naked, and without any thing to defend them from the sword of the assailant, and he that then escaped was only reserved for slaughter to another day; so that these men might well be called επιθανατιοι, men appointed for death; and this being the last appearance on the theatre for that day, they are said here to be set forth εσχατοι, the last."

V. But the most splendid and renowned solemnities, which antient history has transmitted to us, were the Olympic Games. Historians, orators, and poets, abound with references to them, and their sublimest imagery is borrowed from these celebrated exercises. " These games were solemnised every fifth year by an infinite concourse of people from almost all parts of the world.[2] They were celebrated with the greatest pomp and magnificence: hecatombs of victims were slain in honour of the immortal gods; and Elis was a scene of universal festivity and joy. There were other public games instituted, as the Pythian, Nemean, Isthmian ; which could also boast of the valour and dexterity of their combatants, and show a splendid list of illustrious names, who had, from time to time, honoured them with their presence. But the lustre of these, though maintained for a series of years, was obscured,

---

Epist. ad Rom. p. 94. edit. Oxon. 1708. Προφυλασσω δε υμας απο των θηριων ανθρωπομορφων. I advise you to beware of beasts in the shape of men, p. 22. So also the Psalmist, *My soul is among lions, even the sons of men, whose teeth are spears and arrows.* (Psal. lvii. 4.) *Break their teeth, O God, in their mouths. Break out the great teeth of the young lions, O Lord.* (Psal. lviii. 6.) See also Lakemacher's Observationes Sacræ, part ii. pp. 194 —196.

[1] Matutinarum non ultima præda ferarum. Martial. xiii. 95. Casu in meridianum spectaculum incidi — quiquid ante pugnatum est, misericordia fuit, nunc omissis nugis mera homicidia sunt : nihil habent quo tegantur, ad ictum totis corporibus expositi — non galeâ, non scuto repellitur ferrum. Seneca, tom. ii. epist. vii. pp. 17, 18. edit. Gronov. 1672. Απολλυντο μεν θηρια ελαχιστα, ανθρωποι δε πολλοι, δι μεν αλληλοις μαχομενοι, δι δε και υπ' εκεινων αναλομενοι. Dion. Cassius, lib. lx. p. 951. Reimar. See also pp. 971, 972. ejusdem editionis. See also Beausobre's note on 1 Cor. iv. 9. and Lipsii Saturnalia, tom. vi. p. 951.

[2] Josephus, De Bell. Jud. lib. i. cap. 21. § 12. ed. Havercamp. Arriani. Epictetus, lib. iii. p. 456. edit. Upton. 1741.

and almost totally eclipsed, by the Olympic. We find that the most formidable and opulent sovereigns of those times were competitors for the Olympic crown. We see the kings of Macedon[1], the tyrants of Sicily[2], the princes of Asia Minor, and at last the lords of imperial Rome, and emperors of the world[3], incited by a love of glory, the last infirmity of noble minds, enter their names among the candidates, and contend for the envied palm;—judging their felicity completed, and the career of all human glory and greatness happily terminated, if they could but interweave the Olympic garland with the laurels they had purchased in fields of blood.[4] The various games, which the Romans celebrated in their capital and in the principal cities and towns of Italy, with such splendour, ostentation, and expense, seem to have been instituted in imitation of the Grecian; though these were greatly inferior in point of real merit and intrinsic glory: for though the Romans had the gymnastic exercises of the stadium and the chariot race, yet the mutual slaughter of such numbers of gladiators, the combats with lions, bears, and tigers, though congenial to the sanguinary ferocity and brutality of these people,—for no public entertainment could be made agreeable without these scenes,—must present spectacles to the last degree shocking to humanity; for every crown here won was dipt in blood.

1. "The Olympic exercises principally consisted in running, wrestling, and the chariot-race; for leaping, throwing the dart, and discus, were parts of that they called the Pentathlon. The candidates were to be freemen, and persons of unexceptionable morals.[5] A defect in legitimacy or in personal character totally disqualified them. It was indispensably necessary for them previously to submit to a severe regimen.[6] At their own houses they prescribed themselves a particular course of diet; and the laws required them, when they had given in their names to be enrolled in the list of competitors, to resort to Elis, and reside there thirty[7] days before the games commenced; where the regimen and preparatory exercises were regulated and directed by a number of illustrious persons who were appointed every day to superintend them. This form of diet they authoritatively prescribed, and

---

1 Philip. Eadem quoque die nuntium pater ejus [Philippus] duarum victoriarum accepit: alterius, belli Illyrici, alterius, certaminis Olympici, in quod quadrigarum currus miserat. Justin. lib. xii. cap. 16. p. 359. edit. Gronov. 1719. Cui Alexandro tanta omnium virtutum naturâ ornamenta exstitere, ut etiam Olympio certamine vario ludicrorum genere contenderit. Justin. lib. vii. cap. 2. p. 217.

2 Hiero king of Syracuse. See Pindar's first Olympic ode: his first Pythian ode. Theron king of Agrigentum. See the second and third Olympic odes.

3 Nero. See Dion Cassius, tom. ii. pp. 1032, 1033. 1066. edit. Reimar. Aurigavit [Nero] plurifariam, Olympiis etiam decemjugem. Suetonius in Vita Neronis, p. 605. edit. var. Lug. Bat. 1662.

4   Sunt quos curriculo pulverem Olympicum
      Collegisse, juvat: metaque fervidis
      Evitata rotis, palmaque nobilis
      Terrarum dominos evehit ad Deos.   Horat. lib. i. ode i.

5 The candidates were obliged to undergo an examination of another kind, consisting of the following interrogatories:—1. Were they freemen? 2. Were they Grecians? 3. Were their characters clear from all infamous and immoral stains? West's Dissertation on the Olympic Games, p. 152. edit. 12mo.

6 Arriani Epictetus, lib. iii. p. 456. Upton.

7 Philostratus, de Vita Apollonii. lib. v. cap. 43. p. 227. edit. Olearii. Lipsiæ, 1709.

religiously inspected, that the combatants might acquit themselves in the conflict in a manner worthy the Grecian name, worthy the solemnity of the occasion, and worthy those crowds of illustrious spectators by whom they would be surrounded. There are many passages in the Greek and Roman classics which make mention of that extreme strictness, temperance, and continence which the candidates were obliged to observe.

> Qui studet optatam cursu contingere metam,
> Multa tulit fecitque puer ; sudavit et alsit :
> Abstinuit venere et vino. 　　　Hor. Art. Poet. ver. 412.

> A youth, who hopes th' Olympic prize to gain,
> All arts must try, and every toil sustain ;
> Th' extremes of heat and cold must often prove,
> And shun the weak'ning joys of wine and love. 　　　Francis.

The following is a very distinguished passage in Arrian's discourses of Epictetus, which both represents to the reader the severity of this regimen and the arduous nature of the subsequent contention [1] : — "Do you wish to conquer at the Olympic games ? — But consider what precedes and follows, and then if it be for your advantage, engage in the affair. You must conform to rules ; submit to a diet, refrain from dainties, exercise your body whether you choose it or not, in a stated hour, in heat and cold : you must drink no cold water, nor sometimes even wine. In a word, you must give yourself up to your master, as to a physician. Then, in the combat you may be thrown into a ditch, dislocate your arm, turn your ankle, swallow abundance of dust, be whipped, and, after all, lose the victory. When you have reckoned up all this, if your inclination still holds, set about the combat." [2]

2. " After this preparatory discipline, on the day appointed for the celebration, a herald called over their names, recited to them the laws of the games, encouraged them to exert all their powers, and expatiated upon the blessings and advantages of victory. He then introduced the competitors into the stadium, led them around it, and, with a loud voice, demanded if any one in that assembly could charge any of the candidates with being infamous in his life and morals, or could prove him a slave, a robber, or illegitimate. [3] They were then conducted to the altar, and a solemn oath exacted from them, that they would observe the strictest honour in the contention. Afterwards, those who were to engage in the foot-race were brought to the barrier, along which they were arranged, and waited, in all the excesses of ardour and impatience, for the signal. The cord being dropped, they all at once sprung forward [4], fired with the love of glory, conscious that the eyes of all assembled Greece were now upon them, and that the envied palm, if they won it, would secure them the highest honours, and immortalise their memory. It is natural to imagine with what rapidity they would urge their course, and, emulous of glory, stretch

---

[1] Epictetus, lib. iii. c. 15. See also Epicteti Enchiridion. cap. 29. p. 710. edit. Upton.

[2] Mrs Carter's translation of Arrian, pp. 268, 269. London, 1758. 4to.

[3] See West's Dissertation on the Olympic Games, p. 154. 12mo.

[4] ————————————— signoque repente
Corripiunt spatia audito, limenque relinquunt
Effusi, nimbo similes : simul ultima signant. 　　　Virgil, Æneid v. ver. 315

every nerve to reach the goal.   This is beautifully represented in the
following elegant epigram (translated by Mr. West) on Arias of Tarsus, victor in the stadium : —

> The speed of Arias, victor in the race,
> Brings to thy founder, Tarsus, no disgrace ;
> For, able in the course with him to vie,
> Like him, he seems on feather'd feet to fly.
> The barrier when he quits, the dazzled sight
> In vain essays to catch him in his flight.
> Lost is the racer through the whole career,
> Till victor at the goal he re-appear.

In all these athletic exercises the combatants contended naked[1] ;
for though, at first, they wore a scarf round the waist, yet an unfortunate casualty once happening, when this disengaging itself, and en-
tangling round the feet, threw the person down, and proved the
unhappy occasion of his losing the victory, it was, after this accident,
adjudged to be laid aside.[2]

3. " Chaplets composed of the sprigs of a wild olive[3], and branches
of palm, were publicly placed on a tripod in the middle of the stadium[4],
full in the view of the competitors, to inflame them with all the
ardour of contention, and all the spirit of the most generous emulation.
Near the goal was erected a tribunal, on which sat the presidents of
the games, called Hellanodics, personages venerable for their years
and characters, who were the sovereign arbiters and judges of these
arduous contentions, the impartial witnesses of the respective merit
and pretensions of each combatant, and with the strictest justice conferred the crown.

4. " It is pleasing and instructive to observe, how the several particulars here specified concerning these celebrated solemnities, which
were held in the highest renown and glory in the days of the
apostles, explain and illustrate various passages in their writings, the
beauty, energy, and sublimity of which consist in the metaphorical
allusions to these games, from the various gymnastic exercises of
which their elegant and impressive imagery is borrowed.   Thus the
writer of the Epistle to the Hebrews, (an epistle which, in point of
composition, may vie with the most pure and elaborate of the Greek
classics,) says, *Wherefore seeing we also are compassed about with so
great a cloud of witnesses, let us lay aside every weight, and the sin
which doth so easily beset us, and let us run with patience the race that
is set before us ; looking unto Jesus, the author and finisher of our faith,
who for the joy that was set before him, endured the cross, despising the*

---

[1] Thucydides, lib. i. § 6. tom. i. pp. 16, 17 ed. Glasg.

[2] In the xivth Olympiad, one Orsippus, a racer, happened to be thrown down by his
scarf tangling about his feet, and was killed ; though others say that he only lost the victory by that fall ; but whichever way it was, occasion was taken from thence to make a
law, that all the *athletes* for the future should contend naked.   West's Dissertation, p. 66.
12mo.

[3] Το γερας εστιν ουκ αργυρος, ουδε χρυσος, ου μην ουδε κοτινου στεφανος η σελινου.   Josephus contra Apion. lib. ii. § 30. p. 488.   Havercamp.   Strabo, in his geographical description of the Elian territories, mentions a grove of wild olives.   Εστι δ'αλσος αγριελαιων
πληρες.   Strabo, lib. viii. p. 343. edit. Paris, 1620.   Probably from this grove the Olympic
crowns were composed.

[4] To excite the emulation of the competitors, by placing in their view the object of their
ambition, these crowns were laid upon a tripod or table, which during the games was brought
out and placed in the middle of the stadium.   West's Dissertation, p. 174. 12mo.

shame, and is set down at the right hand of the majesty on high. For consider him that endured such contradiction of sinners against himself, lest you be wearied and faint in your minds. Wherefore lift up the hands that hang down, and the feeble knees; and make straight paths for your feet, lest that which is lame be turned out of the way. (Heb. xii. 1—3. 12, 13.) In allusion to that prodigious assembly, from all parts of the world[1], which was convened at Olympia to be spectators of those celebrated games, the Apostle places the Christian combatant in the midst of a most august and magnificent theatre, composed of all those great and illustrious characters, whom in the preceding chapter he had enumerated, the fancied presence of whom should fire him with a virtuous ambition, and animate him with unconquered ardour to run the race that was set before him. *Wherefore seeing we are compassed about with such a cloud of witnesses[2]:* whose eyes are upon us, who expect every thing from the preparatory discipline we have received, and who long to applaud and congratulate us upon our victory: *let us lay aside every weight[3], and the sin that doth so easily beset us[4];* let us throw off every impediment, as the competitors for the Olympic crown did, and that sin that would entangle and impede our steps, and prove the fatal cause of our losing the victory; *and let us run with patience the race set before us;* like those who ran in the Grecian stadium, let us, inflamed with the idea of glory, honour, and immortality, urge our course with unremitting ardour toward the destined happy goal for the prize of our high calling of God, *looking unto Jesus the author and finisher of our faith:* as the candidates for the Olympic honours, during the arduous contention, had in view those illustrious and venerable personages from whose hands they were to receive the envied palm, and who were immediate witnesses of their respective conduct and merit; in imitation of them, let us Christians keep our eyes steadfastly fixed upon Jesus the original introducer and perfecter of our religion, who, if we are victorious, will rejoice to adorn our temples with a crown of glory that will never fade; *who, for the joy set before him[5], endured the cross, despising the shame, and is now set down at the right hand of God:* Jesus himself, to seize the glorious palm which his God and Father placed full in his view in order to inspirit him with ardour and alacrity, in the race he

---

[1] Not merely the inhabitants of Athens, of Lacedæmon, and of Nicopolis, but the inhabitants of the whole world are convened to be spectators of the Olympic exercises. Arriani Epictetus, lib. iii. p. 456. Upton.

[2] Νεφος μαρτυρων. A cloud of witnesses. This form of expression occurs in the politest writers. See Iliad, x. 133. Æneid, vii. 793. Andron. Rhodii Argonauticon, iv. 398. Appian, Pisc. i. 463. and Euripidis Hecuba, ver. 907.

[3] Ογκον αποθεμενοι παντα. A stadio sumpta similitudo : ibi qui cursuri sunt, omnia quæ oneri esse possunt, deponunt. Grot. in loc. Monet ut ογκον abjiciamus, quo vocabulo crassa omnis et tarda moles significatur. Beza.

[4] Ευπεριστατον. Entangled by wrapping round. An allusion to the garments of the Greeks which were long, and would entangle and impede their steps, if not thrown off in the race. See Hallet, in loc.

[5] Προκειμενης αυτω χαρας. The joy placed full in his view. In the Olympic exercises the prize was publicly placed in the view of the combatants to fire their emulation. The following note of Krebsius is very elegant:—Elegantissima metaphora est vocis προκειμενης, e veterum certaminum ratione ducta. Proprie enim προκεισθαι dicuntur τα αθλα, sc. præmia certaminis, quæ publicè proponuntur in propatulo, ut eorum aspectus, certaque eorum adipiscendorum spes, certaturos alacriores redderet ad certamen ineundum, victoriamque reportandam. J. Tob. Krebsii Observat. in N. T. e Joseph. p. 377. Lips. 1755. 8vo.

had set before him, cheerfully submitted to sorrows and sufferings, endured the cross, contemning the infamy of such a death, and, in consequence of perseverance and victory, is now exalted to the highest honours, and placed on the right hand of the Supreme Majesty. *For consider him that endured such contradiction of sinners against himself, lest ye be wearied and faint in your minds*[1] *;* consider him who conflicted with such opposition of wicked men all confederated against him, and let reflections on his fortitude prevent your being languid and dispirited; *therefore lift up the hands which hang down, and the feeble knees.*[2] *And make straight paths for your feet, lest that which is lame be turned out of the way :* exert in the Christian race those nerves that have been relaxed, and collect those spirits which have been sunk in dejection : make a smooth and even path for your steps, and remove every thing that would obstruct and retard your velocity.

"The following distinguished passage in St. Paul's first Epistle to the Corinthians (ix. 24—27.) abounds with agonistical terms. Its beautiful and striking imagery is totally borrowed from the Greek stadium. *Know ye not that they who run in a race, run all, but one receiveth the prize? So run, that ye may obtain. And every man that striveth for the mastery, is temperate in all things. Now they do it to obtain a corruptible crown; but we an incorruptible. I therefore so run, not as uncertainly ; so fight I, not as one that beateth the air : but I keep under my body, and bring it into subjection ; lest that by any means, when I have preached the Gospel to others, I myself should be a cast-away :* know you not that in the Grecian stadium great numbers run with the utmost contention to secure the prize, but that only one person wins and receives ? With the same ardour and perseverance do you run, that you may seize the garland of celestial glory. Every one, also, who enters the lists as a combatant, submits to a very rigid and severe regimen.[3] They do this to gain a fading chaplet[4], that is only composed of the decaying leaves of a wild olive, but in our view is hung up the unfading wreath of immortality.[5] With this in full

---

[1] Ἱνα μη καμητε, ταις ψυχαις ὑμων εκλυομενοι. Hæc duo verba a palæstra et ab athletis desumpta sunt, qui proprie dicuntur καμνειν et ψυχαις εκλυεσθαι, cum corporis viribus debilitati et fracti, omnique spe vincendi abjectâ, victas manus dant adversario —— Neque dubium est quin apostolus eo respexerit. Krebsius, p. 390.

[2] Διο τας παρειμενας χειρας και τα παραλελυμενα γονατα ανορθωσατε. Quemadmodum Paulus sæpissime delectatur loquendi formulis ex re palæstricâ petitis ; ita dubium non est, quin hic quoque respexisse eo videatur. Athletis enim et luctatoribus tribuuntur παρειμεναι χειρες et ϖαραλελυμενα γονατα, cum luctando ita defatigati, viribusque fracti sunt, ut neque manus neque pedes officio suo fungi possint, ipsique adeo victos se esse fateri cogantur. Krebsius, p. 392.

[3] Πας δε ὁ αγωνιζομενος παντα εγκρατευεται. We have already noticed how rigid and severe this regimen was, and what temperance and continence [εγκρατεια] those who entered their names in the list of combatants were previously obliged to observe. Multa tulit fecit-que puer, sudavit et alsit: abstinuit venere et vino, says Horace. See Æliani, Var. Hist. lib. xi. cap. 3. p. 684.   Gronovii. Lug. Bat. 1731, and Plato de'Legibus, lib. viii. pp. 139, 140. edit. Serrani, 1578, and Eustathius ad Hom. Iliad Ω. p. 1472.

[4] Φθαρτον στεφανον. The chaplet that was bestowed on the victor in the Olympic games was made of wild olive, the crowns in the Isthmian games were composed of parsley. These chaplets were fading and transitory Διδους και τοις ϑυμελικοις στεφανου μεν ου χρυσους, αλλ' ὡσπερ εν ολυμπια, κοτινων. Plutarch. Cato, jun. p. 1433. edit. Gr. Steph. 8vo. See also Porphyrius de Antro Nympharum, p. 240. edit. Cantab. 1655. Philonis Opera, tom. ii. p. 463. edit. Mangey. Τους γαρ τα Ισθμια νικωντας οἱ Κορινθιοι των σελινων στεφανουσιν. Those who conquer in the Isthmian games the Corinthians crown with parsley. Polyæni Stratag. lib. v. p. 376. edit. Casaubon. 1589.

[5] Ἡμεις δε, αφθαρτον. With what ardour in the Christian race this glorious crown should inspire us is well represented by Irenæus. Bonus igitur agonista ad incorruptelæ agonem

prospect I run the Christian race, not distressed with wretched uncertainty concerning its final issue.[1] I engage as a combatant, but deal not my blows in empty air.[2] But I inure my body to the severest discipline, and bring all its appetites into subjection: lest, when I have proclaimed[3] the glorious prize to others, I should, at last, be rejected as unworthy[4] to obtain it. This representation of the Christian race must make a strong impression upon the minds of the Corinthians, as they were so often spectators of those games, which were celebrated on the Isthmus, upon which their city was situated. It is very properly introduced with, KNOW YOU NOT; for every citizen in Corinth was acquainted with every minute circumstance of this most splendid and pompous solemnity. St. Paul, in like manner, in his second Epistle to Timothy (ii. 5.), observes, *that if a man strive for mastery, yet is he not crowned, unless he strive lawfully :* he who contends in the Grecian games secures not the crown, unless he strictly conform to the rules prescribed.

"What has been observed concerning the spirit and ardour with which the competitors engaged in the race, and concerning the prize they had in view to reward their arduous contention, will illustrate the following sublime passage of the same sacred writer in his Epistle to the Philippians (iii. 12—14.) :— *Not as though I had already attained, either were already perfect ; but I follow after, if that I may apprehend that for which also I am apprehended of Christ Jesus. Brethren, I count not myself to have apprehended : but this one thing I do, forgetting those things which are behind, and reaching forth unto those things which are before, I press towards the mark, for the prize of the high calling of God in Christ Jesus :* Not that *already* I have acquired this *palm ;* not that I have *already* attained perfection ; but I *pursue my course,* that I may *seize* that *crown* of immortality, to the hope of which I was raised by the gracious appointment of Christ Jesus. My Christian brethren, I do not esteem myself to have obtained this glorious *prize :* but one thing occupies my whole attention ; forgetting what I *left behind,* I *stretch every nerve* towards the *prize* before me, pressing with *eager* and *rapid steps,* towards the *goal,* to *seize* the immortal *palm*[5], which

---

adhortatur nos, uti coronemur, et preciosam arbitremur coronam, videlicet quæ per agonem nobis acquiritur, sed non ultro coalitam. Et quantò per agonem nobis advenit, tantò est preciosior: quantò autem preciosior, tantò eam semper diligamus. Irenæus, lib. iv. p. 377. edit. Grab. The folly also of Christians in being negligent and remiss, when an incorruptible crown awaits their persevering and victorious constancy and virtue, is also beautifully exposed by Justin Martyr. See his Apol. ii. p. 78. edit. Paris, 1636.

[1] So we understand ουκ αδηλως. Mr. West renders it, in the illustration he has given us of this passage ; I so run, as not to pass undistinguished ; and then adds the following note ; Ὡς ουκ αδηλως, may also signify in this place, as if I was unseen, not unobserved, *i. e.* as if I was in the presence of the judge of the games, and a great number of spectators. West's Dissertation, p. 253. 12mo.

[2] Ουτω πυκτευω, ως ουκ αερα δερων. This circumstance is often mentioned in describing the engagements of combatants ; thus, Virgil has, Entellus vires in ventum effudit. Æneid, v. 443. Vacuas agit inconsulta per auras Brachia. Valerius Flaccus, iv. 302. τρις δ' ηερα τυψε βαθειαν. Iliad, Τ. 446. See also Oppian. Piscat. lib. ii. ver. 450. Rittershus. Lug. Bat. 1597.

[3] Αλλοις κηρυξας ; proclaimed, as a herald, the prize to others. A herald, κηρυξ, made proclamation at the games what rewards would be bestowed on the conquerors.

[4] Αδοκιμος γενωμαι. Be disapproved ; be rejected as unworthy ; come off without honour and approbation.

[5] Τα μεν οπισω επιλανθανομενος, τοις δε εμπροσθεν επεκτεινομενος, επι σκοπον διωκω επι το βραβειον. Every term here employed by the Apostle is agonistical. The whole passage

God, by Christ Jesus, *bestows*. This affecting passage, also, of the same apostle, in the *second* Epistle of Timothy, written a little before his martyrdom, is beautifully allusive to the above-mentioned race, to the crown that awaited the victory, and to the Hellanodics or judges who bestowed it :— *I have fought a good fight, I have finished my course*[1], *I have kept the faith. Henceforth there is laid up for me a crown of righteousness, which the Lord, the righteous Judge, shall give me at that day : and not to me only, but to all them also that love his appearing."* (2 Tim. iv. 7, 8.)

CHAPTER IX.

ON THE DISEASES MENTIONED IN THE SCRIPTURES, TREATMENT OF THE DEAD, AND FUNERAL RITES.

SECTION I.

ON THE DISEASES MENTIONED IN THE SCRIPTURES.

I. *Origin and Progress of the Art of Medicine in the East.* — II. *Notice of Remedies in use among the Jews.* — III. *Account of some particular*

---

beautifully represents that ardour which fired the combatants when engaged in the race. Their spirit and contention are in a very striking manner described in the following truly poetical lines of Oppian, which happily illustrate this passage : —

> Ὡς δε ποδωκειης μεμελημενοι ανδρες αεθλων,
> Σταθμης ὁρμηθεντες, αποσσυτοι ωκεα γουνα
> Προπρυτιταινομενοι δολικον τελος εγκονεουσιν
> Εξανυσαι πασιν· δε πονος νυσση τε πελασσαι,
> Νικης τε γλυκυδωρον ἑλειν κρατος, ες τε θυρεθρα
> Αἴξαι, και καρτος αεθλιον αμφιβαλεσθαι.
>
> Oppian Pisc. lib. iv. ver. 101. edit. Rittershusii.

As when the thirst of praise and conscious force
Invite the labours of the panting COURSE,
Prone from the lists the blooming rivals strain,
And spring exulting to the distant plain,
Alternate feet with nimble-measured bound
Impetuous trip along the refluent ground,
In every breast ambitious passions rise,
To seize the goal, and snatch th' immortal prize.

> Jones's Translation.

Instat equis auriga suos vincentibus, illum
Præteritum temnens, extremos inter euntem.

> Horat. Satyr. lib. i. Sat. i. 115, 116.

[1] Τον ΔΡΟΜΟΝ τετελεκα. I have finished my RACE. The whole passage is beautifully allusive to the celebrated games and exercises of those times. Δρομος properly signifies a race. Theocritus, idyl. iii. ver. 41. Sophoclis Electra, ver. 693. See also ver. 686—688. Euripidis Andromache, ver. 599. Euripidis Iphigenia in Aulide, ver. 212. Strabo, lib. iii. p. 155. edit. Paris, 1620. Xenophontis Memorab. pp. 210, 211. Oxon. 1741. So this word ought to be rendered. (Acts xx. 24.) *But none of these things move me, neither count I my life dear unto myself ; so that I might finish my* COURSE *with joy ;* τελειωσαι τον ΔΡΟΜΟΝ μου : finish the short race of human life with honour and applause. It is a beautiful and striking allusion to the race in these celebrated games. — In the fifth volume of Bishop Horne's Works there is an animated discourse on the Christian race ; the materials of which are partly derived from Dr. Harwood's Introduction to the New Testament, vol. ii. sect. 4.

I. THE diseases to which the human frame is subject would naturally lead men to try to alleviate or to remove them : hence sprang
the ART OF MEDICINE. In the early ages of the world, indeed, there
could not be much occasion for an art which is now so necessary to
the health and happiness of mankind. The simplicity of their manners, the plainness of their diet, their temperance in meat and drink,
and their active life, (being generally occupied in the field, and in
rural affairs,) would naturally tend to strengthen the body, and to
afford a greater share of health than what we now enjoy. So long as
our first parents continued in that state of uprightness in which they
were created, there was a tree, emphatically termed the tree of life,
the fruit of which was divinely appointed for the preservation of
health; but after the fall, being expelled from Eden, and, consequently,
banished for ever from that tree, they became liable to various diseases, which, doubtless, they would endeavour to remove, or to mitigate
in various ways. From the longevity of the patriarchs it is evident
that diseases were not very frequent in the early ages of the world,
and they seem to have enjoyed a sufficiently vigorous old age, except
that the eyes became dim and the sight feeble. (Gen. xxvii. 1. xlviii.
10.) Hence it is recorded as a remarkable circumstance concerning
Moses, that in extreme old age (for he was an hundred and twenty
years old when he died) *his eye was* NOT *dim, nor his natural force*
abated. (Deut. xxxiv.7.)

The Jews ascribed the origin of the healing art to God himself
(Ecclus. xxxviii. 1, 2.), and the Egyptians attributed the invention of
it to their god Thaut or Hermes, or to Osiris or Isis.

Antiently, at Babylon, the sick, when they were first attacked by
a disease, were left in the streets, for the purpose of learning from
those who might pass them what practices or what medicines had
been of assistance to them, when afflicted with a similar disease. This
was, perhaps, done also in other countries. The Egyptians carried
their sick into the temple of Serapis; the Greeks carried theirs into
those of Æsculapius. In the temples of both these deities there were
preserved written receipts of the means by which various cures had been
effected. With the aid of these recorded remedies, the art of healing assumed in the progress of time the aspect of a science. It assumed such
a form, first in Egypt, and at a much more recent period in Greece ;
but it was not long before those of the former were surpassed in
excellence by the physicians of the latter country. That the Egyptians,
however, had no little skill in medicine, may be gathered from what
is said in the Pentateuch respecting the marks of leprosy. That some
of the medical prescriptions should fail of bringing the expected relief
is by no means strange, since Pliny himself mentions some which are
far from producing the effects he ascribes to them. Physicians are
mentioned first in Gen. l. 2. Exod. xxi. 19. Job xiii. 4. Some acquaintance with chirurgical operations is implied in the rite of circumcision. (Gen. xvii. 11—14.) There is ample evidence that the

Israelites had some acquaintance with the internal structure of the human system, although it does not appear that dissections of the human body, for medical purposes, were made till as late as the time of Ptolemy. That physicians sometimes undertook to exercise their skill, in removing diseases of an internal nature, is evident from the circumstance of David's playing upon the harp to cure the malady of Saul. (1 Sam. xvi. 16.) The art of healing was committed among the Hebrews, as well as among the Egyptians, to the priests; who, indeed, were obliged, by a law of the state, to take cognisance of leprosies. (Lev. xiii. 1—14. 57. Deut. xxiv. 8, 9.) Reference is made to physicians who were not priests, and to instances of sickness, disease, healing, &c. in the following passages; viz. 1 Sam. xvi. 16. 1 Kings i. 2—4. 2 Kings viii. 29. ix. 15. Isa. i. 6. Jer. viii. 22. Ezek. xxx. 21. The probable reason of king Asa's not seeking help from God, but from the physicians, as mentioned in 2 Chron. xvi. 12., was, that they had not at that period recourse to the simple medicines which nature offered, but to certain superstitious rites and incantations; and this, no doubt, was the ground of the reflection which was cast upon him. About the time of Christ, the Hebrew physicians both made advancements in science, and increased in numbers.[1] It appears from the Talmud[2], that the Hebrew physicians were accustomed to salute the sick by saying, "*Arise from your disease.*" This salutation had a miraculous effect in the mouth of Jesus. (Mark v. 41.) According to the Jerusalem Talmud, a sick man was judged to be in a way of recovery, who began to take his usual food. (Compare Mark v. 43.) The antients were accustomed to attribute the origin of diseases, particularly of those whose natural causes they did not understand, to the *immediate* interference of the Deity. Hence they were denominated, by the antient Greeks, Μαστιγες, or the *scourges of God*, a word which is employed in the New Testament by the physician Luke himself (vii. 21.), and also in Mark v. 29. 34.[3]

II. Concerning the remedies actually employed by the Jews few particulars are certainly known. Wounds were bound up, after applying oil to them (Ezek. xxx. 21. Isa. i. 6.), or pouring in a liniment composed of oil and wine (Luke x. 34.), oil being mollifying and healing, while wine would be cleansing and somewhat astringent. Herod was let down into a bath of oil.[4] Great use was made of the celebrated balm of Gilead. (Jer. viii. 22. xlvi. 11. li. 8.) The comparison in Prov. iii. 8. is taken from the plasters, oils, and frictions, which, in the East, are still employed on the abdomen and stomach in most maladies: the people in the villages being ignorant of the art of making decoctions and potions, and of the doses proper to be administered, generally make use of external medicines, to which in India they give a decided preference.[5] When Jesus Christ authorised his apostles to heal the sick (Matt. x. 8.), the evangelist Mark relates that they *anointed with oil* many that were sick, and healed them. (vi. 13.)

---

[1] Mark v. 26. Luke iv. 23. v. 31. viii. 43.   Josephus, Antiq. Jud. lib. xvii. c. 6. § 5.
[2] Schabbath, p. 110.   See also Lightfoot's Horæ Hebraicæ on Mark v. 41.
[3] Jahn, Archæol. Biblica, by Upham, §§ 105. 184.   Pareau, Antiq. Hebr. pp. 164. 166.
[4] Josephus, Bell. Jud. lib. i. c. 33. § 5.
[5] Bp. Lowth's Isaiah, vol. ii. p. 10.   Roberts's Oriental Illustrations, p. 556.

From the expressions in Prov. iii. 18. xi. 30. xiii. 12. and xv. 4.
Calmet thinks it probable that the Jews had salutary herbs and plants
which they called the tree of life, and which we should now call medicinal herbs and plants, in opposition to such as are poisonous and
dangerous, which they call the tree of death. Some modern neologian
expositors have imagined, that the Pool of Bethesda at Jerusalem was
a bath, the waters of which derived their sanative power from the entrails of the victims offered in sacrifice being washed therein (John
v. 2—7.), and that by the *angel* was simply intended a man, who was
sent to stir up from the bottom the corrupt sediment; which being
distributed through the water, the pores of the person who bathed in
it were penetrated by this matter, and his disorder repelled. " But
this is a miserable evasion, to get rid of the power and goodness of
God, built on the merest conjecture, [and] self-contradictions, and
every way as unlikely as it is insupportable. It has never yet been
proved, that the sacrifices were ever washed; and, could even this be
proved, who can show that they were washed in the Pool of Bethesda?
These waters healed a man in a *moment* of *whatsoever disease* he had.
Now, there is no *one* cause under heaven can do this. Had only one
kind of disorder been cured here, there might have been some countenance for this deistical conjecture — but this is not the case; and we
are obliged to believe the relation just as it stands, and thus acknowledge the sovereign power and mercy of God, or take the desperate
flight of an infidel, and thus get rid of the passage altogether." [1]

III. Various diseases are mentioned in the Sacred Writings, as
cancers, consumption, dropsy, fevers, lunacy, &c. Concerning a few
disorders, the nature of which has exercised the critical acumen of
physicians as well as divines, the following observations may be satisfactory to the reader : —

1. Of all the maladies mentioned in the Scriptures, the most formidable is the disorder of the skin, termed LEPROSY [2], the characteristic symptom of which is patches of smooth laminated scales, of
different sizes and of a circular form. This disease was not peculiar
to the Israelites, but antiently was endemic in Palestine, as it still is
in Egypt and other countries. In the admirable description of the
cutaneous affections to which the Israelites were subject after their
departure from Egypt, given by Moses in the thirteenth chapter of
the book of Leviticus, there are three which distinctly belong to the
leprosy.[3] All of them are distinguished by the name of בהרת
(BEHRAT), or "bright spot;" viz.

i. The בהק (BOHAK), which imports brightness but in a subordinate degree, being a dull white spot : it is not contagious, and does

---

[1] Dr. A. Clarke's Commentary on John v. 3.

[2] This dreadful disorder has its name from the Greek Λεπρα, from λεπις a *scale;* because in this disease the body was often covered with thin white *scales,* so as to give it the
appearance of snow. Hence the hand of Moses is said to have been leprous as *snow*
(Exod. iv. 6.) ; and Miriam is said to have become *leprous, white as snow* (Numb. xii. 10);
and Gehazi, when struck judicially with the disease of Naaman, is recorded to have gone
out from the presence of Elisha, a *leper, as white as snow.* (2 Kings v. 27.) Dr. A. Clarke
on Lev. xiii. 1.

[3] For this account of the leprosy, the author is almost wholly indebted to Dr. Good's
Study of Medicine, vol. v. pp. 587—597. 2d edition.

not render a person unclean, or make it necessary that he should be confined. Michaelis describes a case of bohak from the traveller Niebuhr, in which the spots were not perceptibly elevated above the skin, and did not change the colour of the hair; the spots in this species of leprosy do not appear on the hands or abdomen, but on the neck and face they gradually spread, and continue sometimes only about two months, though in some cases as long as two years, when they gradually disappear of themselves. This disorder is neither infectious nor hereditary, nor does it occasion any inconvenience.[1]

ii. Two species called צרעת (TSORAT,) that is, venom or malignity, viz. the בהרת לבנה (BEHRAT lebena), or bright white behrat (Lev. xiii. 38, 39.), בהרת כהה (BEHRAT CECHA), dark or dusky behrat, spreading in the skin. (Lev. xiii. 3.) Both these are contagious; in other words, render the person affected with it unclean, and exclude him from society.

(1.) In the behrat cecha (the *Leprosis Lepriasis nigricans* of Dr. Good's nosological system) the natural colour of the hair, which in Egypt and Palestine is *black*, is not changed, as Moses repeatedly states, nor is there any depression of the dusky spot, while the patches, instead of keeping stationary to their first size, are perpetually enlarging their boundary. The patient labouring under this form of the disease was pronounced unclean by the Hebrew priest, and, consequently, was sentenced to a separation from his family and friends: whence there is no doubt of its having proved contagious. Though a much severer malady than the common leprosy, it is far less so than the species described in the ensuing paragraph; and on this account it is dismissed by Moses with a comparatively brief notice.

(2.) The behrat lebena, (*Leprosis Lepriasis candida*, or *leuce* of Dr. Good's Nosology,) or *bright white leprosy*, is by far the most serious and obstinate of all the forms which the disease assumes. The pathognomonic characters, dwelt upon by Moses in deciding it, are "a glossy white and spreading scale upon an elevated base, the elevation depressed in the middle, but without a change of colour, the black hair on the patches, which is the natural colour of the hair in Palestine, participating in the whiteness, and the patches themselves perpetually widening their outline." Several of these characters taken separately belong to other lesions or blemishes of the skin, and, therefore, none of them were to be taken alone; and it was only when the whole of them concurred that the Jewish priest, in his capacity of physician, was to pronounce the disease a tsorat, or malignant leprosy.

Common as this form of leprosy was among the Hebrews, during and subsequent to their residence in Egypt, we have no reason to believe that it was a family complaint, or even known amongst them antecedently: whence there is little doubt, notwithstanding the confident assertions of Manetho to the contrary, that they received the infection from the Egyptians, instead of communicating it to them.

---

[1] Michaelis's Commentaries on the Laws of Moses, vol. iii. pp. 233, 234. " That all this," he adds, " with equal force and truth, should still be found exactly to hold, at the distance of 3500 years from the time of Moses, ought certainly to gain some credit to his laws, even with those who will not allow them to be of divine authority." (p. 234.)

Their subjugated and distressed state, however, and the peculiar nature of their employment, must have rendered them very liable to this as well as to various other blemishes and misaffections of the skin: in the productions of which there are no causes more active or powerful than a depressed state of body or mind, hard labour under a burning sun, the body constantly covered with the excoriating dust of brick-fields and an impoverished diet; to all of which the Israelites were exposed, whilst under the Egyptian bondage.

It appears, also, from the Mosaic account, that in consequence of these hardships there was, even after the Israelites had quitted Egypt, a general predisposition to the contagious form of leprosy, so that it often occurred as a consequence of various other cutaneous affections. Eight different blemishes in the skin, which had a tendency to terminate in this terrible disease, are enumerated by Moses, and described by Dr. Good, to whose elaborate treatise the reader is referred. The effects of leprosy, as described by travellers who have witnessed the disorder in its most virulent forms, are truly deplorable.[1] The Mosaic statutes respecting leprosy are recorded in Lev. xiii. and xiv. Numb. v. 1—4. and Deut. xxiv. 8, 9. They are in substance as follows:—

(1.) On the appearance of any one of the cutaneous affections above noticed on any person, the party was to be inspected by a priest, both as acting in a judicial capacity, and also as being skilled in medicine. The signs of the disease, which are circumstantially pointed out in the statute itself, accord with those which have been noticed by modern physicians. "If, on the first inspection, there remained any doubt as to the spot being really a symptom of leprosy, the suspected person was shut up for *seven* days, in order that it might be ascertained, whether it spread, disappeared, or remained as it was; and this confinement might be repeated. During this time, it is probable that means were used to remove the spot. If in the mean time it spread, or continued as it was, without becoming paler, it excited a strong suspicion of real leprosy, and the person inspected was declared unclean. If it disappeared, and after his liberation became again manifest, a fresh inspection took place.

(2.) "The unclean were separated from the rest of the people. So early as the second year of the Exodus, lepers were obliged to reside without the camp (Numb. v. 1—4.); and so strictly was this law enforced, that the sister of Moses herself, becoming leprous, was expelled from it. (Numb. xii. 14—16.) When the Israelites came into their own land, and lived in cities, the spirit of the law thus far operated, that lepers were obliged to reside in a separate place, which was called (בית חפשית) BETH CHOPHSCHITH, or the *house of uncleanness;* and from this seclusion not even kings, when they became leprous, were exempted. (2 Kings xv. 5.) As, however, a leper cannot always be within doors, and may, consequently, sometimes meet clean persons, he was obliged, in the *first* place, to make himself known by his dress, and to go about with torn clothes, a bare head,

---

[1] Mr. Barker, the agent of the British and Foreign Bible Society, when at Damascus in the year 1825, describing the hospital of Christian lepers, says, "How afflicting was their situation and appearance! Some were without noses and fingers, being eaten up by the disease, and others were differently disfigured." Twenty-sixth Report of the Bible Society, App. p. 111.

and his chin covered; and in the *next* place, when any one came too near him, to cry out that he was *Unclean.* (Numb. xiii. 45, 46.)"

(3.) Although a leper, merely meeting and touching a person, could not have immediately infected him, yet, as such a rencontre and touch would have rendered him Levitically unclean, in order to prevent leprosy from spreading, in consequence of close communication, " it was an established rule to consider a leprous person as likewise unclean in a Levitical or civil sense; and, consequently, whoever touched him, became also unclean; not indeed medically or physically so, — that is, *infected* by one single touch, — but still unclean in a civil sense.

(4.) " On the other hand, however, for the benefit of those found clean, the law itself specified those who were to be pronounced free from the disorder; and such persons were then clear of all reproach, until they again fell under accusation from manifest symptoms of infection. The man who, on the first inspection, was found clean, or in whom the supposed symptoms of leprosy disappeared during confinement, was declared clean : only, in the latter case, he was obliged to have his clothes washed. If, again, he had actually had the disorder, and got rid of it, the law required him to make certain offerings, in the course of which he was pronounced clean." [1]

(5.) The leprous person was to use every effort in his power to be healed; and, therefore, was strictly to follow the directions of the priests. This, Michaelis is of opinion, may fairly be inferred from Deut. xxiv. 8.

(6.) When healed of his leprosy, the person was to go and show himself to the priests, that he might be declared clean, and offer the sacrifice enjoined in that case; and, when purified, that he might be again admitted into civil society. (Matt. viii. 4. Lev. xiv. 11—32.)

(7.) Lastly, As this disease was so offensive to the Israelites, God commanded them to use frequent ablutions, and prohibited them from eating swine's flesh and other articles of animal food that had a tendency to produce this disease.

The peculiar lustrations which a person who had been healed of a leprosy was to undergo are detailed in Lev. xiv. — See an abstract of them in p. 335. of this volume.

2. The DISEASE with which the patriarch JOB was afflicted (ii. 7.) has greatly exercised the ingenuity of commentators, who have supposed it to be the contagious leprosy, the small pox, and the ELE-PHANTIASIS, or Leprosy of the Arabians. The last opinion is adopted by Drs. Mead and Good, and by Michaelis, and appears to be best supported. This dreadful malady, which the antient medical writer Paulus Ægineta has accurately characterised as an universal ulcer, was named elephantiasis by the Greeks, from its rendering the skin of the patient like that of an elephant, scabrous and dark coloured, and furrowed all over with tubercles, loathsome alike to the individual and to the spectators. When it attains a certain height, as it appears to have done in this instance, it is incurable, and, consequently, affords the unhappy patient no prospect but that of long-continued misery.[2]

---

[1] Michaelis's Commentaries, vol. iii. pp. 278—287.
[2] Mead's Medica Sacra, pp. 1—11. (London, 1755.) Good's translation of Job, p. 22.

3. The DISEASE OF THE PHILISTINES, mentioned in 1 Sam. v. 6. 12. and vi. 17., has been supposed to be the dysentery; but it was most probably the hæmorrhoids or bleeding piles, in a very aggravated degree. Jahn, however, considers it as the effect of the bite of venomous solpugas.[1]

4. The DISEASE OF SAUL (1 Sam. xvi. 14.) appears to have been a true madness, of the melancholic or atrabilarious kind, as the antient physicians termed it; the fits of which returned on the unhappy monarch at uncertain periods, as is frequently the case in this sort of malady. The remedy applied, in the judgment of experienced physicians, was an extremely proper one, viz. playing on the harp. The character of the modern oriental music is expression, rather than science: and it may be easily conceived how well adapted the unstudied and artless strains of David were to soothe the perturbed mind of Saul; which strains were bold and free from his courage, and sedate through his piety.[2]

5. The DISEASE OF JEHORAM KING OF ISRAEL. — This sovereign, who was clothed with the double infamy of being at once an idolater and the murderer of his brethren, was diseased internally for two years, as had been predicted by the prophet Elijah; and his bowels are said at last to have fallen out by reason of his sickness. (2 Chron. xxi. 12—15. 18, 19.) This disease, Dr. Mead says, beyond all doubt was the dysentery, and though its continuance so long a time was very uncommon, it is by no means a thing unheard of. The intestines in time become ulcerated by the operation of this disease. Not only blood is discharged from them, but a sort of mucous excrements likewise is thrown off, and sometimes small pieces of the flesh itself; so that apparently the intestines are emitted or fall out, which is sufficient to account for the expressions that are used in the statement of king Jehoram's disease.[3]

6. The DISEASE WITH WHICH HEZEKIAH WAS AFFLICTED (2 Kings xx. 7. Isa. xxxviii. 21.) has been variously supposed to be a pleurisy, the plague, the elephantiasis, and the quinsey. But Dr. Mead is of opinion that the malady was a fever which terminated in an abscess; and for promoting its suppuration a cataplasm of figs was admirably adapted. The case of Hezekiah, however, indicates not only the limited knowledge of the Jewish physicians at that time, but also that though God can cure by a miracle, yet he also gives sagacity to discover and apply the most natural remedies.[4]

7. Concerning the nature of NEBUCHADNEZZAR'S MALADY (Dan. iv. 25, 26. 31—33.) learned men are greatly divided, but the most probable account of it is that given by Dr. Mead; who remarks that all the circumstances of it, as related by Daniel, so perfectly agree with hypochondriacal madness that to him it appears evident, that Nebuchadnezzar was seized with this distemper, and under its influence ran wild into the fields; and that fancying himself transformed into an ox, he fed on grass in the manner of cattle. For every sort of madness is a disease of a disturbed imagination: under which this unhappy man laboured full seven years. And through neglect

---

[1] Archæol. Bibl. § 185.   [2] Mead's Medica Sacra, pp. 20—33.
[3] Mead's Medica Sacra, p. 35.   Jahn's Archæol. Bibl. § 187.
[4] Medica Sacra, p. 37.

of taking proper care of himself, his hair and nails grew to an excessive length; by which the latter growing thicker and crooked resembled the claws of birds. Now, the antients called persons affected with this species of madness λυκανθρώπο, (*wolf-men*) or κυνανθρώποι (*dog-men*) ; because they went abroad in the night imitating wolves or dogs; particularly intent upon opening the sepulchres of the dead, and had their legs much ulcerated, either by frequent falls, or the bites of dogs.[1] In like manner are the daughters of Proetus related to have been mad, who, as Virgil says,—

> —— *Implerunt falsis mugitibus agros.*[2]
> —— With mimick'd mooings filled the fields.

For, as Servius observes, Juno possessed their minds with such a species of madness, that fancying themselves cows, they ran into the fields, bellowed often, and dreaded the plough. But these, according to Ovid, the physician Melampus, —

> —— *per carmen et herbas*
> *Eripuit furiis.*[3]
> Snatch'd from the furies by his charms and herbs.

Nor was this disorder unknown to the moderns : for Schenckius records a remarkable instance of it in a husbandman of Padua, *who imagining that he was a wolf, attacked, and even killed several persons in the fields ; and when at length he was taken, he persevered in declaring himself a real wolf, and that the only difference consisted in the inversion of his skin and hair.*[4] But it may be objected to this opinion, that his misfortune was foretold to the king, so that he might have prevented it by correcting his morals; and, therefore, it is not probable that it befell him in the course of nature. But we know that those things, which God executes either through clemency or vengeance, are frequently performed by the assistance of natural causes. Thus, having threatened Hezekiah with death, and being afterwards moved by his prayers, he restored him to life, and made use of figs laid on the tumour, as a medicine for his disease. He ordered king Herod, upon account of his pride, to be devoured by worms. And no one doubts but that the plague, which is generally attributed to the divine wrath, most commonly owes its origin to corrupted air.[5]

8. The PALSY of the New Testament is a disease of very wide import, and the Greek word, which is so translated, comprehended not fewer than five different maladies, viz. (1.) *Apoplexy,* a paralytic shock, which affected the whole body;—(2.) *Hemiplegy,* which affects and paralyses only one side of the body; the case mentioned in Matt. ix. 2. appears to have been of this sort; — (3.) *Paraplegy,* which paralyses all the parts of the system below the neck; — (4.) *Catalepsy,* which is caused by a contraction of the muscles in the whole or part of the body; the hands, for instance. This is a very dangerous dis-

---

1 See Aetius, Lib. Medicin. lib. vi. and Paul. Ægineta, lib. iii. c. 16.
2 Eclog. vi. 48.
3 Metamorph. xv. 325.
4 Observationes Medicæ Rar. de Lycanthrop. Obs. 1.
5 Medica Sacra, pp. 58—61.

ease; and the effects upon the parts seized are very violent and deadly. Thus, when a person is struck with it, if his hand happens to be extended, he is unable to draw it back: if the hand be *not* extended, when he is so struck, he is unable to extend it. It seems to be diminished in size, and dried up in appearance; whence the Hebrews were accustomed to call it a *withered hand.* The impious Jeroboam was struck with catalepsy (1 Kings xiii. 4—6.); the prophet Zechariah, among the judgments he was commissioned to denounce against the *idol shepherd that leaveth the flock,* threatens that *his arm shall be dried up.* (Zech. xi. 17.)   Other instances of this malady occur in Matt. xii. 10. and John v. 3. 5.—(5.) The *Cramp.* This, in oriental countries, is a fearful malady, and by no means unfrequent.   It originates from the chills of the night; the limbs, when seized with it, remain immoveable, sometimes turned in and sometimes out, in the very same position as when they were first seized.   The person afflicted resembles a man undergoing the torture, βασανιζομενῳ, and experiences nearly the same sufferings.   Death follows this disease in a few days.   Alcimus was struck with it (1 Macc. ix. 55—58.), as also was the centurion's servant. (Matt. viii. 6.)

9. The disease, which in Matt. ix. 20. Mark v. 25. and Luke viii. 43. is denominated an ISSUE OF BLOOD, is too well known to require any explanation.   Physicians confess it to be a disorder which is very difficult of cure. (Mark v. 26.)[1]   How does this circumstance magnify the benevolent miracle, wrought by Jesus Christ on a woman who had laboured under it for twelve years !

10. The BLINDNESS of the sorcerer Elymas (Acts xiii. 6—12.) is in the Greek denominated αχλυς, and with great propriety, being rather an obscuration than a total extinction of sight.   It was occasioned by a thin coat or tunicle of hard substance, which spread itself over a portion of the eye, and interrupted the power of vision.   Hence the disease is likewise called σκοτος, or *darkness.*   It was easily cured, and sometimes even healed of itself, without resorting to any medical prescription.   Therefore St. Paul added in his denunciation, that the impostor *should not see the sun for a season.*   But the blindness of the man, of whose miraculous restoration to sight we have so interesting an account in John ix., was total, and being inveterate from his birth, was incurable by any human art or skill.   See an examination of this miracle in Vol. I. pp. 234, 235.

11. Lastly, in the New Testament we meet with repeated instances of what are termed DEMONIACAL POSSESSION.   The reality of such possessions indeed has been denied by some authors, and attempts have been made by others to account for them, either as the effect of natural disease, or the influence of imagination on persons of a nervous habit.   But it is manifest, that the persons, who in the New Testament are said to be *possessed with devils* (more correctly with demons) cannot mean only persons afflicted with some strange disease; for they are evidently here as in other places — particularly in Luke iv. 33—36. 41.—distinguished from the diseased.   Further, Christ's speaking on various occasions to these evil spirits, as distinct from the persons possessed by them, — his commanding them and asking them questions,

---

[1] Jahn's Archæologia Biblica, § 199.

and receiving answers from them, or not suffering them to speak, — and several circumstances relating to the terrible preternatural effects which they had upon the possessed, and to the manner of Christ's evoking them,—particularly their requesting and obtaining permission to enter the herd of swine (Matt. viii. 31, 32.), and precipitating them into the sea; all these circumstances can *never* be accounted for by any distemper whatever. Nor is it any reasonable objection that we do not read of such frequent possessions before or since the appearance of our Redeemer upon earth. It seems, indeed, to have been ordered by a special providence that they should have been permitted to have *then* been more common; in order that He, who came to destroy the works of the Devil, might the more remarkably and visibly triumph over him; and that the machinations and devices of Satan might be more openly defeated, at a time when their power was at its highest, both in the souls and bodies of men; and also, that plain facts might be a sensible confutation of the Sadducean error, which denied the existence of angels or spirits (Acts xxiii. 8.), and prevailed among the principal men both for rank and learning in those days. The cases of the demoniacs expelled by the apostles were cases of real possession; and it is a well known fact, that in the second century of the Christian æra, the apologists for the persecuted professors of the faith of Christ appealed to their ejection of evil spirits as a proof of the divine origin of their religion. Hence it is evident that the demoniacs were not merely insane or epileptic patients, but persons really and truly vexed and convulsed by unclean demons.[1]

SECTION II.

TREATMENT OF THE DEAD. — FUNERAL RITES.

I. *Jewish Notions of Death.* — II. *Mosaic Laws relating to the Dead.* — III. *Preparations for Interment.* — IV. *Rites of Sepulture.* — *Lamentations for the Dead.* — V. *Notice of the Tombs of the Jews.* — *Monumental Inscriptions.* — VI. *Funeral Feasts.* — *Duration of Mourning.*

So strong was the love of life among the Hebrews, that instances of suicide are of extremely rare occurrence in the history of that people. Saul, Ahithophel, and the traitor Judas are the only persons recorded to have laid violent hands upon themselves, in a fit of desperation. (1 Sam. xxxi. 4, 5. 2 Sam. xvii. 23. Matt. xxvii. 3—5.) In the last period of the Jewish state, however, the custom of the Romans appears to have greatly lessened the horror of suicide among the Jews[2]; but that most terrible of all diseases, the leprosy, seems to have rendered its victims utterly regardless of life. (Job vii. 15.)

I. The Hebrews, in common with many other antient nations, especially in the East, were accustomed to represent death by various

---

[1] For a summary of the evidence that the demoniacs, mentioned in the New Testament, were persons *really possessed by evil spirits*, see Bp. Newton's Works, vol. iv. pp. 256—304., and Mr. Townsend's Harmony of the New Test. vol. i. pp. 157—160.

[2] Josephus, De Bell. Jud. lib. iii. c. 8. §§ 4—7.

terms which were calculated to mitigate the appalling image inspired by that last enemy of mankind. Hence they often called death a journey or departure. (Josh. xxiii. 14. 1 Kings ii. 2. Eccles. v. 15. vi. 6. Luke ii. 29.) Frequently also they compared it to sleep, and to rest after the toils of life were over (Gen. xlvii. 30. Job iii. 13. 17—19. Isa. xiv. 8. lvii. 2. Matt. ix. 29. xxvii. 52. John xi. 11. Acts vii. 60. 1 Cor. xi. 30. 1 Thess. iv. 13. 2 Pet. iii. 4. Rev. xiv. 13.); and it was a very common expression to say, that the party deceased had gone, or was gathered to his fathers or to his people. (Gen. xv. 15. xxv. 8. 17. xxxv. 29. xlix. 29. 33. Numb. xx. 24. xxvii. 13. xxxi. 2. Deut. xxxii. 50. Judg. ii. 10. 2 Kings xxii. 20.)[1]

II. By the law of Moses a dead body conveyed a legal pollution to every thing that touched it,—even to the very house and furniture,—which continued seven days. (Numb. xix. 14, 15, 16.) And this was the reason why the priests, on account of their daily ministrations in holy things, were forbidden to assist at any funerals, but those of their nearest relatives (Lev. xxi. 1—4. 10—12.); nay, the very dead bones, though they had lain ever so long in the grave, if digged up, conveyed a pollution to any who touched them. This circumstance will account for Josiah's causing the bones of the false priests to be burnt upon the altar at Bethel (2 Chron. xxxiv. 5.), in order that these altars, being thus polluted, might be held in the greater detestation.[2]

III. After the principle of life was extinguished, the following ceremonies were performed by the Jews: —

1. The eyes of the deceased were closed by the nearest of kin, who gave the parting kiss to the lifeless corpse: thus, it was promised to Jacob, when he took his journey into Egypt, that Joseph should *put his hands upon his eyes* (Gen. xlvi. 4.); and accordingly we read that, when Jacob expired, Joseph *fell upon his face and kissed him.* (Gen. l. 1.) From the Jews, Calmet observes, this practice passed to the heathens, who gave the dying a farewell kiss, and received their last sigh, in token of their affectionate union.

2. The next office was the ablution of the corpse, which (except when it was buried immediately) was laid out in an upper room or chamber. Thus, when Tabitha died, it is said, that they *washed her body, and laid it in an upper chamber.* (Acts ix. 37.) This rite was common both to the Greeks and Romans[3], in whose writings it is frequently mentioned. In Egypt, it is still the custom to wash the dead body several times.

3. The bodies of persons of distinction were embalmed: this process the Jews probably derived from the Egyptians, whose various methods of embalming their dead with spices and nitre are minutely described by Herodotus, and Diodorus Siculus.[4] The patriarch Jacob was embalmed according to the Egyptian process: his remains lay in nitre *thirty* days, for the purpose of drying up all superfluous and noxious

---

[1] Pareau, Antiquitas Hebr. pp. 468, 469.

[2] Home's Hist. of the Jews, vol. ii. p. 362. Michaelis has examined at length the reason and policy of the Mosaic statutes on this subject. Commentaries, vol. iii. pp. 322—330.

[3] Sophoclis Electra, verse 1143. Virgil Æneid, lib. vi. 218, 219.

[4] Herodotus, lib. ii. cc. 86—88. tom. ii. pp. 131, 132. Oxon. 1809. Diodorus Siculus, lib. i. cc. 91—93. edit. Bipont.

moisture; and during the remaining *forty* days, they were anointed with gums and spices, to preserve them; which unction, it appears from Gen. l. 2, 3., was the proper embalming. The former circumstance explains the reason why the Egyptians *mourned for Jacob threescore and ten days;* the latter explains the meaning of the *forty* days, which were fulfilled for Israel.[1]

In later times, where the deceased parties were persons of rank or fortune, after washing the corpse, the Jews "embalmed it, by laying all around it a large quantity of costly spices and aromatic drugs[2], in order to imbibe and absorb the humours, and by their inherent virtues to preserve it as long as possible from putrefaction and decay. Thus we read that Nicodemus brought a mixture of myrrh and aloes, about a hundred pounds weight, to perform the customary office to the dear deceased. This embalming was usually repeated for several days together, that the drugs and spices thus applied might have all their efficacy in the exsiccation of the moisture and the future conservation of the body.[3] They then swathed the corpse in linen rollers or bandages, closely enfolding and wrapping it in that bed of aromatic drugs with which they had surrounded it. Thus we find that Joseph of Arimathea and Nicodemus *took the body of Jesus and wrapt it in linen clothes with the spices, as the manner of the Jews is to bury.* (John xix. 40.) This custom we behold also in the Egyptian mummies, round which, Thevenot informs us, the Egyptians have sometimes used above a thousand ells of filleting, beside what was wrapped about the head. Thus, when our Lord had cried with a loud voice, '*Lazarus come forth!*' it is said, *the dead came forth, bound hand and foot in grave clothes.* (John xi. 44.)[4] We learn from Scripture, also, that about the head and face of the corpse was folded a napkin, which was a separate thing, and did not communicate with the other bandages in which the body was swathed. Thus we read, that the face of Lazarus was bound about with a napkin (John xi. 44.); and when our Lord was risen, Peter, who went into the sepulchre, saw the linen clothes lie, and the napkin that had been folded round his head, not lying with the linen clothes, but wreathed together in a place by itself, lying at some distance from the rollers in which his body had been swathed, and folded up, exactly in the state it was when first wrapped round his head." (John xx. 7.)[5]

---

[1] Paxton's Illustrations, vol. iii. p. 249. 2d. edit.

[2] Matt. xxvi. 12. *For in that she hath poured this ointment on my body, she did it for my funeral,* προς το ενταφιασαι με, to embalm me. The word does not properly signify to bury. The note of Beza is accurate. Ad funerandum me, προς το ενταφιασαι με. Vulg. et Erasmus, ad me sepeliendum, malé. Nam aliud est θαπτειν quam ενταφιαζειν: ut Latinis sepelire est sepulchro condere: funerare vero pollincire, cadaver sepulchro mandandum prius curare. Beza ad Matt. xxvi. 12. Ενταφιασαι est corpus ad funus componere, et ornamentis sepulchralibus ornare. Wetstein, in loc.

[3] Habebat consuetudo, ut carissima capita, et quæ plurimi fierent cadavera, non semel tantum ungerentur, sed sæpius, pluribusque continuis diebus, donec exsiccato, et absorpto vi aromatum omni reliquo humore, immo tabefactâ carne aridâ, et quasi æneâ redditâ, diu servari possint integra et immunia a putrefactione. Lucas Brugensis, in Marc. xvi.

[4] Δεδεμενος—κειριαις. Phavorinus explains Κειρια by calling them επιταφιοι δεσμοι, sepulchral bandages. Κειρια σημαινει τα σχοινια τα ενταφια. Etymol.

[5] He went into the sepulchre, and then he plainly saw the linen clothes, μονα, alone, or without the body, and κειμενα lying, that is, undisturbed, and at full length, as when the body was in them. The cap, or napkin, also, which had been upon our Lord's head, he found separate, or at a little distance from the open coffin; but εντετυλιγμενον, folded up in wreaths, in the form of a cap, as it had been upon our Lord's head. Dr. Benson's Life

Besides the custom of embalming persons of distinction, the Jews commonly used great burnings for their kings, composed of large quantities of all sorts of aromatics, of which they made a fire, as a triumphant farewell to the deceased. In these they were wont to burn their bowels, their clothes, armour, and other things belonging to the deceased. Thus, it is said of Asa, that *they made a very great burning for him* (2 Chron. xvi. 14.), which could not be meant of his corpse in the fire, for in the same verse it is said, *they buried him in his own sepulchre.* This was also done at the funeral of Zedekiah. (Jer. xxxiv. 5.) And it was very probably one reason why, at the death of Jehoram, the people made no burning for him like the burning of his fathers (2 Chron. xxi. 19.), because his bowels being ulcerated by his sickness, they fell out, and to prevent the stench, were immediately interred or otherwise disposed of; so that they could not well be burnt in this pompous manner after his death; though as he was a wicked king, this ceremony might possibly have been omitted on that account also.

The burning of dead bodies in funeral piles, it is well known, was a custom prevalent among the Greeks and Romans, as it is in India to this day[1], upon which occasion they threw frankincense, myrrh, cassia, and other fragrant articles into the fire: and this in such abundance, that Pliny represents it as a piece of profaneness, to bestow such heaps of frankincense upon a dead body, when they offered it so sparingly to their gods. And though the Jews might possibly learn from them the custom of burning the bowels, armour, and other things belonging to their kings, in piles of odoriferous spices, yet they very rarely, and only for particular reasons, burnt the dead bodies themselves. We are told, indeed, that the people of Jabesh-Gilead *took the bodies of Saul and his sons* (from the place where the Philistines had hung them up), *and came to Jabesh, and burnt them there* (1 Sam. xxxi. 12.); but by this time their bodies must have been in such a state, that they were not fit to be embalmed; or, perhaps, they were apprehensive that if they should embalm them, and so bury them, the people of Bethshan might at some future time dig them up, and fix them a second time against their walls; and, therefore, the people of Jabesh might think it more advisable to recede from their common practice, and for greater security to imitate the heathen in this particular. Amos also speaks of the burning of bodies (vi. 10.); but it is evident from the words themselves, and from the context, that this was in the time of a great pestilence, not only when there were few to bury the dead, but when it was unsafe to go abroad and perform the funeral rites by interment, in which case the burning was certainly the best expedient.

In some cases the rites of sepulture were not allowed; and to this it has been thought that there is an allusion in Job xxvii. 19. It was the opinion of the pagan Arabs that, upon the death of any person, a bird, by them called *Manah*, issued from the brain, which haunted the sepulchre of the deceased, uttering a lamentable scream. This

---

of Christ, p. 524. Wrapped together in a place by itself, as if the body had miraculously slipt out of it, which indeed was the real fact. Dr. Ward's Dissertations, p. 149. Harwood's Introduction, vol. ii. pp. 135—137.

[1] Roberts's Oriental Illustrations, pp. 242, 243.

notion, also, the late professor Carlyle thinks, is evidently alluded to in Job xxi. 32., where the venerable patriarch, speaking of the fate of the wicked, says : —

> He shall be brought to the grave,
> And shall watch upon the raised up heap.[1]

The Jews showed a great regard for the burial of their dead; to be deprived of it was thought to be one of the greatest dishonours that could be done to any man : and, therefore, in Scripture it is reckoned one of the calamities that should befall the wicked. (Eccles. vi. 3.) In all nations there was generally so much humanity as not to prevent their enemies from burying their dead. The people of Gaza allowed Sampson's relations to come and take away his body (Judg. xvi. 31.); though one would have thought that this last slaughter which he made among them might have provoked them to some acts of outrage even upon his dead body. But as he stood alone in what he did, none of the Israelites joining with him in his enterprises, they might possibly be apprehensive, that, if they denied him burial, the God of Israel, who had given him such extraordinary strength in his lifetime, would not fail to take vengeance on them in that case, and, therefore, they were desirous, it may be, to get rid of his body (as afterwards they were of the ark), and glad, perhaps, that any one would remove such a formidable object out of their sight. Jeremiah prophesied of Jehoiakim, that he should be buried with the burial of an ass (Jer. xxii. 19.), meaning, that he should not be buried at all, but be cast forth beyond the gates of Jerusalem, exposed to the air and putrefaction above ground, as beasts are, which is more plainly expressed afterwards, by telling us, that *his body should be cast out in the day to the heat, and in the night to the frost.* (Jer. xxxvi. 30.) The author of that affecting elegy, the seventy-ninth psalm, when enumerating the calamities which had befallen his unhappy countrymen, particularly specifies the denial of the rites of sepulture, as enhancing their afflictions. *The dead bodies of thy servants have they given to be meat unto the fowls of heaven ; the flesh of thy saints unto the beasts of the earth.* (Psal. lxxix. 2.)

IV. The RITES OF SEPULTURE were various at different times, and also according to the rank or station of the deceased.

1. Before the age of Moses, the funeral took place a few days after death. (Gen. xxiii. 19. xxv. 9. xxxv. 29.) In Egypt, a longer time elapsed before the last offices were performed for Jacob and Joseph, on account of the time which was requisite for the Egyptian process of embalming, in order that the corpse might be preserved for a long time. (Gen. xlix. 29. l. 3. 24—26.) As it is probable that the Israelites, when in Egypt, had been accustomed to keep their dead for a considerable period, the Mosaic laws, respecting the uncleanness which arose from a dead body, would compel them to a more speedy interment. At length, after the return from the Babylonish captivity, it became customary for the Jews to bury the dead on the same day, and as soon as possible after the vital spark was extinguished. Jahn affirms (but without assigning any authority for his assertion), that the Jews did this in imitation of the Persians; but it is more likely, that the custom

---

[1] Carlyle's Specimens of Arabian Poetry, p. 14. 2d edit.

arose from a superstitious interpretation of Deut. xxi. 22, 23., which law enjoined, that the body of one who had been hanged on a tree should be taken down before night. The burial of Tabitha was delayed, on account of the disciples sending for the apostle Peter. (Acts ix. 37.)

2. The poorer classes were carried forth to interment lying on an open bier or couch, as is the universal practice in the East to this day, not screwed into a coffin. In this way the son of the widow of Nain was borne to his grave without the city: and it should seem that the bearers at that time moved with as much rapidity as they do at the present time among the modern Jews.[1] The rich, and persons of rank, were carried forth on more costly biers. Josephus relates that the body of Herod was carried on a golden bier, richly embroidered[2]; and we may presume, that the bier on which Abner was carried was more costly than those used for ordinary persons. (2 Sam. iii. 31.)

But whatever the rank of the parties might be, the superintendence and charge of the funeral were undertaken by the nearest relations and friends of the deceased. Thus, Abraham interred Sarah in the cave of Macpelah (Gen. xxiii. 19.); Isaac and Ishmael buried Abraham (Gen. xxv. 9.); Esau and Jacob buried Isaac (Gen. xxxv. 29.); Moses buried Aaron on Mount Hor (Numb. xx. 29.); the old prophet laid the disobedient prophet in his own grave (1 Kings xiii. 30.); Joseph of Arimathea interred Jesus Christ in his own new tomb (Matt. xxvii. 59, 60.); and the disciples of John the Baptist performed the last office for their master. The sons and numerous relations of Herod followed his funeral procession.[2] Sometimes, however, servants took the charge of interring their masters, as in the case of Josiah king of Judah. (2 Kings xxiii. 30.) Devout men carried Stephen to his burial. (Acts viii. 2.) The funeral obsequies were also attended by the friends of the deceased, both men and women, who made loud lamentations for the deceased, and some of whom were hired for the occasion. David and a large body of the Israelites *mourned before Abner.* (2 Sam. iii. 31, 32.) Solomon mentions the circumstance of mourners going about the streets (Eccles. xii. 5.); who, most probably, were persons hired to attend the funeral obsequies, to wail and lament for the departed.[3] From Jer. ix. 17. it appears, that women were chiefly employed for this purpose; and Jerome, in his commentary on that passage says, that the practice was continued in Judæa, down to his days, or the latter part of the fourth century.[4] In Jer. xlviii. 36., the use of musical instruments by

---

[1] Not to detail the observations of the earlier travellers, it may suffice to adduce three instances from recent and intelligent English travellers. — At Cairo, says Mr. Carne, " we met an Arab funeral: about twenty men, friends of the deceased, advanced under a row of palm-trees, singing in a mournful tone, and bearing the body. The corpse was that of a woman neatly dressed in white, and borne on an *open bier*, with a small awning of red silk over it." (Letters from the East, p. 109.) At Baghtchisarai in the Crimea, Dr. Henderson saw a corpse conveyed to the public cemetery of the Christians: it "was simply wrapped round with a white cloth, laid upon a *bier* or *board*, and borne by four men to the grave. This mode of performing the funeral obsequies obtains equally among the Jews, Christians, and Mohammedans in these parts, with the exception of the European families, who naturally conform to the rite of their ancestors." (Biblical Researches, p. 304.) Mr. Hartley observed a similar mode of interment in Greece. " The corpse is always exhibited to full view: it is placed upon a bier which is borne aloft upon the shoulders, and is dressed in the best and gayest garments possessed by the deceased." (Researches in Greece, p. 118.)

[2] Josephus, Ant. Jud. lib. xvii. c. 8. § 3. Bell. Jud. lib. i. c. 33. § 9.

[3] Holden's translation of Ecclesiastes, p. 171.

[4] Dr. Blayney's translation of Jeremiah, p. 270. 8vo. edit.

these hired mourners is distinctly recognised; and Amos (v. 17.) alludes to such mourning as a well known custom.

In the time of Jesus Christ and his apostles, the funeral dirges sung by these hired mourners were accompanied by musical instruments. " The soft and plaintive melody of the flute was employed to heighten these doleful lamentations and dirges. Thus we read, that on the death of the daughter of Jairus, a company of mourners, with players on the flute, according to the Jewish custom, attended upon this sorrowful occasion. When Jesus entered the governor's house, he saw the minstrels and the people wailing greatly. (Matt. ix. 23.) The custom of employing music to heighten public and private grief was not in that age peculiar to the Jews. We find the flute also employed at the funeral solemnities of the Greeks and Romans, in their lamentations for the deceased, as appears from numerous testimonies of classic authors."[1] The same custom still obtains among the Moors in Africa, the Turks in Palestine, the Hindoos[2], the Egyptians[3], and the modern Greeks. " At all their principal entertainments," says Dr. Shaw, " and to show mirth and gladness upon other occasions, the women welcome the arrival of each guest, by squalling out for several times together, Loo! Loo! Loo!"[4] At their funerals, also, and upon other melancholy occasions, they repeat the same noise, only they make it more deep and hollow, and end each period with some ventriloquous sighs. The αλαλαζοντας πολλα, or wailing greatly, (as our version expresses it, Mark v. 38.) upon the death of Jairus's daughter, was, probably, performed in this manner. For there are several women, hired to act upon these lugubrious occasions, who, like the *præficæ*, or mourning women of old, are *skilful in lamentation* (Amos v. 16.), and great mistresses of these melancholy expressions: and, indeed, they perform their parts with such proper sounds, gestures, and commotions, that they rarely fail to work up the assembly into some extraordinary pitch of thoughtfulness and sorrow. The British factory has often been very sensibly touched with these lamentations, whenever they were made in the neighbouring houses."[5] The Rev. William Jowett, during his travels in Palestine, arrived at the town of Napolose, which stands on the site of the antient Schechem, immediately after the death of the governor. "On coming within sight of the gate," he relates, " we perceived a numerous company of females, who were singing in a kind of recitative, far from melancholy, and beating time with their hands. On our reaching the gate, it was suddenly exchanged for most hideous plaints and shrieks; which, with the feeling that we were entering a city at no time celebrated for its hospitality, struck a very dismal impression upon my mind. They accompanied us a few paces, but it soon appeared that the gate was their station; to which, having received nothing from us, they returned. We learned in the

[1] Harwood's Introduction, vol. ii. pp. 132. 134. where various passages of classic authors are cited.
[2] Roberts's Oriental Illustrations, pp. 243—249.
[3] Lane's Manners and Customs of the Modern Egyptians, vol. ii. pp. 286, 287.
[4] Dr. Shaw conceives this word to be a corruption of Hallelujah. He remarks, Αλαλη, a word of the like sound, was used by an army either before they gave the onset, or when they had obtained the victory. The Turks to this day call out, Allah! Allah! Allah! upon the like occasion. Travels, vol. i. p. 435. note *. (8vo. edit.)
Ibid. pp. 435, 436.

course of the evening, that these were only a small detachment of a
very numerous body of *cunning women,* who were filling the whole city
with their cries, — *taking up a wailing* with the design, as of old, to make
the eyes of all the inhabitants *run down with tears, and their eyelids
gush out with waters.* (Jer. ix. 17, 18.) For this good service they
would, the next morning, wait upon the government and principal
persons, to receive some trifling fee."[1] The Rev. John Hartley, during
his travels in Greece, relates that, one morning, while taking a solitary
walk in Ægina, the most plaintive accents fell upon his ear which he
had ever heard. He followed in the direction from which the sounds
proceeded, and they conducted him to the newly-made grave of a
young man, cut down in the bloom of life, over which a woman, hired
for the occasion, was pouring forth *lamentation and mourning and woe,*
with such doleful strains and feelings, as could scarcely have been supposed other than sincere.[2]

In proportion to the rank of the deceased, and the estimation in
which his memory was held, was the number of persons who assisted
at his funeral obsequies, agreeably to the very antient custom of the
East. Thus, at the funeral of Jacob, there were present not only
Joseph and the rest of his family, but also the servants and elders (or
superintendents of Pharaoh's house) and the principal Egyptians, who
attended to do honour to his memory, and who accompanied the procession into the land of Canaan. (Gen. l. 7—10.) At the burial of
Abner, David commanded Joab and all the people that were with him
to rend their garments, and gird themselves with sackcloth, and to
mourn before Abner, or make lamentations in honour of that general;
and the king himself followed the bier. (2 Sam. iii. 31.) *All Judah
and the inhabitants of Jerusalem did honour* to Hezekiah *at his death.*
(2 Chron. xxxii. 33.) *Much people of the city were with* the widow of
Nain, who was following her only son to the grave. (Luke vii. 12.)

---

[1] Jowett's Christian Researches in Syria, p. 194. The mourning of the Montenegrins
bears a great resemblance to that of the oriental nations. On the death of any one, nothing
is heard but tears, cries, and groans from the whole family: the women, in particular, beat
themselves in a frightful manner, pluck off their hair and tear their faces and bosoms. The
deceased person is laid out for twenty-four hours, in the house where he expires, with the
face uncovered; and is perfumed with essences, and strewed with flowers and aromatic
leaves, after the custom of the antients. The lamentations are renewed every moment,
particularly on the arrival of a fresh person, and especially of the priest. Just before the
defunct is carried out of the house, his relations whisper in his ear, and give him commissions for the other world, to their departed relatives or friends. After these singular
addresses, a pall or winding-sheet is thrown over the dead person, whose face continues
uncovered, and he is carried to church: while on the road thither, women, hired for the
purpose, chant his praises, amid their tears. Previously to depositing him in the ground,
the next of kin tie a piece of cake to his neck, and put a piece of money in his hand, after
the manner of the antient Greeks. During this ceremony, as also while they are carrying
him to the burial-ground, a variety of apostrophes is addressed to the defunct, which are
interrupted only by mournful sobs, asking him why he quitted them? Why he abandoned
his family? He, whose poor wife loved him so tenderly, and provided every thing for him
to eat! Whose children obeyed him with such respect, while his friends succoured him
whenever he wanted assistance; who possessed such beautiful flocks, and all whose undertakings were blessed by heaven! When the funeral rites are performed, the curate and
mourners return home, and partake of a grand entertainment, which is frequently interrupted by jovial songs, intermixed with prayers in honour of the deceased. One of the
guests is commissioned to chant a "lament" impromptu, which usually draws tears from
the whole company; the performer is accompanied by three or four monochords, whose
harsh discord excites both laughter and tears at the same time. Voyage Historique et
Politique à Montenegro, par M. le Colonel Vialla de Sommières, tom. i. pp. 275—278.
Paris, 1820. 8vo.

[2] Hartley's Researches in Greece, pp. 119, 120.

Josephus informs us that Herod was attended to Herodium (a journey of twenty-five days), where he had commanded that he should be interred, first, by his sons and his numerous relations; next, by his guards, and after them by the whole army, in the same order as when they marched out to war; and that these were followed by five hundred of his domestics, carrying spices.[1]

Further, it was usual to honour the memory of distinguished individuals by a funeral oration or poem: thus David pronounced an eulogy over the grave of Abner. (2 Sam. iii. 33, 34.)   Upon the death of any of their princes, who had distinguished themselves in arms, or who, by any religious actions, or by the promotion of civil arts, had merited well of their country, they used to make lamentations or mournful songs for them: from an expression in 2 Chron. xxxv. 25. *Behold they are written in the Lamentations,* we may infer that they had certain collections of this kind of composition.   The author of the book of Samuel has preserved the exquisitely beautiful and affecting elegy which David composed on occasion of the death of Saul and Jonathan; but we have no remains of the mournful poem, which Jeremiah made upon the immature death of the pious king Josiah, mentioned in the last-cited chapter: which loss is the more to be deplored, because in all probability it was a master-piece in its kind, since never was there an author more deeply affected with his subject, or more capable of carrying it through all the tender sentiments of sorrow and compassion, than Jeremiah.   But no funeral obsequies were conferred on those who laid violent hands on themselves: hence we do not read that the traitor-suicide Judas was lamented by the Jews (Matt. xxvii. 4.), or by his fellow-disciples. (Acts i. 16.)

Among many antient nations, a custom prevailed of throwing pieces of gold and silver, together with other precious articles, into the sepulchres of those who were buried: this custom was not adopted by the Jews.   But in Ezek. xxxii. 27. there is an allusion to the custom which obtained among almost all antient nations, of adorning the sepulchres of heroes with their swords and other military trophies.   The prophet, foretelling the fall of *Meshech and Tubal,* and all her multitude, says that *they are gone down to hell* (or the invisible state) *with their weapons of war; and they have laid their swords under their heads.*   In Mingrelia, Sir John Chardin informs us, they all sleep with their *swords under their heads,* and their other arms by their sides; and they bury them in the same manner, their arms being placed in the same position.   This fact greatly illustrates the passage above cited, since, according to Bochart, and other learned geographers, Meshech and Tubal mean Mingrelia, and the circumjacent country.[2]

V. The most simple Tombs or monuments of old consisted of hillocks of earth, heaped up over the grave, of which we have numerous examples in our own country.   In the East, where persons have been murdered, heaps of stones are raised over them as *signs;* and to this custom the prophet Ezekiel appears to allude. (xxxix. 15.)[3]

The earliest sepulchres, in all probability, were caverns.   Abraham purchased the cave of Machpelah of Ephron the Hittite for a family

---

[1] Josephus, Ant. Jud. lib. xvii. c. 8. § 3.
[2] Harmer's Observations on Scripture, vol. iii. pp. 55, 56.
[3] Shaw's Travels, vol. i. Pref. p. xviii.

L L 4

burial-place. (Gen. xxiii. 8—18.) Here were interred Abraham and Sarah, Isaac and Rebekah; here also Jacob buried Leah, and charged his sons to deposit his remains. (Gen. xlix. 29—32. 1. 13.) The antient Jews seem to have attached much importance to interment in the sepulchre of their fathers, and particularly to being buried in the land of Canaan (Gen. xlvii. 30. xlix. 29. 1. 25.), in which affection for the country of their ancestors they are not surpassed by their descendants, the modern Jews.[1] In Psal. xxviii. 1. cxliii. 7. and Prov. ℩. 12. the grave is represented as a pit or cavern, into which a descent ɪs necessary; containing dormitories or separate cells for receiving the dead (Isa. xiv. 15. Ezek. xxxii. 23.), so that each person may be said to lie in his own house (Isa. xiv. 18.), and to rest in his own bed. (Isa. lvii. 2.) These sepulchral vaults seem to have been excavated for the use of the persons of high rank and their families. The vanity of Shebna, who was reproved for it by Isaiah, is set forth by his being so studious and careful to have his sepulchre on high, in a lofty vault, and, probably, in an elevated situation, that it might be the more conspicuous. (Isa. xxii. 16.)[2] Of this kind of sepulchres there are remains still extant at Jerusalem, some of which are reported to be the sepulchres of the kings of Judah[3], and others, those of the Judges.[4]

The following description of the Tombs of the Kings (as they are termed), which are situated near the village of Gournou, on the west bank of the river Nile, will illustrate the nature of the antient sepulchres, which were excavated out of the mountains. "Further in the recesses of the mountains, are the more magnificent Tombs of the Kings; each consisting of many chambers, adorned with hieroglyphics. The scene brings many allusions of Scripture to the mind; such as Mark v. 2, 3. 5., but particularly Isaiah xxii. 16. *Thou hast hewed thee out a sepulchre here, as he that heweth him out a sepulchre on high, and that graveth a habitation for himself in a rock;* for many of the smaller sepulchres are excavated nearly half way up the mountain, which is very high. The kings have their magnificent abodes nearer

---

[1] The modern Jews, in the time of Rabbi Solomon Jarchi, buried their dead immediately, and put wooden props in the tombs by their side, by leaning on which they would be enabled to arise more easily at the resurrection of mankind from death. They further persuade themselves that all the bodies of Jews dying out of Palestine, wherever they may be interred, will perform a subterraneous journey into Palestine, in order that they may participate in the resurrection. S. Jarchi on Gen. xlvii. — Alber, Inst. Herm. Vet. Test. tom. i. p. 319.

[2] Bp. Lowth on Isaiah, vol. ii. pp. 120. 170. 328, 329.

[3] " Above half a mile from the wall" of Jerusalem, "are the Tombs of the Kings. In midst of a hollow, rocky and adorned with a few trees, is the entrance. You then find a large apartment, above fifty feet long, at the side of which a low door leads into a series of small chambers, hewn out of the rock, of the size of the human body. There are six or seven of these low and dark apartments, in which are hewn recesses of different shapes for the reception of bodies." (Carne's Letters from the East, p. 294. Three Weeks in Palestine, p. 75.)

[4] " The Sepulchres of the Judges, so called, are situated in a wild spot, about two miles from the city. They bear much resemblance to those of the Kings, but are not so handsome or spacions." (Carne's Letters from the East, p. 294.) " No shadow, not even of a rock, is spread over these long enduring relics, in which tradition has placed the ashes of the rulers of Israel. They consist of several divisions, each containing two or three apartments cut out of the solid rock, and entablatures are carved with some skill over the entrance. No richly carved relics, or fragments of sarcophagi remain here, as in the tombs of the kings; and their only use is to shelter the wandering passenger or the benighted traveller, who finds no other resting place in the wild around." (Carne's Recollections of the East, pp. 135, 136.)

the foot of the mountain; and seem, according to Isaiah xiv. 18., to have taken a pride in resting as magnificently in death as they had done in life—*All the kings of the nations, even all of them, lie in glory; every one in his own house.* The stuccoed walls within are covered with hieroglyphics. They cannot be better described than in the words of Ezekiel, viii. 8—10. *Then said he unto me, Son of man, dig now in the wall; and when I had digged in the wall, behold a door. And he said unto me, go in; and behold the wicked abominations that they do here. So I went in, and saw: and behold every form of creeping things and abominable beasts, and all the idols of the house of Israel, pourtrayed upon the wall round about.* The Israelites were but copyists: the master-sketches are to be seen in all the antient temples and tombs of Egypt."[1]

Farther, "it appears from the Scriptures, that the Jews had family sepulchres in places contiguous to their own houses, and generally in their gardens:" and the same usage obtained among the Romans and other nations.[2] " Such was the place in which Lazarus was interred; and such, also, was the grave in which the body of our Lord was deposited. Joseph of Arimathea, a person of distinction, by St. Mark called an honourable counsellor," (Mark xv. 43.) or member of the sanhedrin, "mindful of his mortality, had hewn out of the rock in his garden a sepulchre, in which he intended his own remains should be reposited. *Now in the place where he was crucified there was a garden, and in the garden a new sepulchre, wherein was no man yet laid.* When Joseph, therefore, had taken the body of Jesus, and wrapped it in a clean linen cloth, he carried it into the tomb which he had lately hollowed out of the rock; and rolled a great stone to the low door of the sepulchre, effectually to block up the entrance, and secure the sacred corpse of the deceased, both from the indignities of his foes, and the officiousness of his friends. Sometimes, also, they buried their dead in fields, over whom the opulent and families of distinction raised superb and ostentatious monuments, on which they lavished great splendour and magnificence, and which they so religiously maintained from time to time in their pristine beauty and glory."[3] To this custom our Saviour alludes in the following apt comparison: *Woe unto you scribes and Pharisees, hypocrites! for ye are like unto*

[1] Jowett's Researches in the Mediterranean, p. 133.

[2] Thus, the Mausoleum of Augustus was erected in a garden. Dr. Münter has collected numerous classical inscriptions, which attest the application of gardens to sepulchral purposes. (Symbolæ ad Interpretationem Evangelii Johannis ex Marmoribus, pp. 29, 30.) The modern inhabitants of Mount Lebanon have their sepulchres in gardens. The Rev. Mr. Jowett, during his visit to Deir-el-Kamr, the capital of the Druses on that mountain, says, that while walking out one evening a few fields' distance with the son of his host, to see a detached garden belonging to his father, the young man pointed out to him near it a small solid stone building, very solemnly adding, " *Kabbar Beity* — the sepulchre of our family." It had neither door nor window. " He then" (adds Mr. J.) " directed my attention to a considerable number of similar buildings at a distance; which to the eye are exactly like houses, but which are, in fact, family mansions for the dead. They have a most melancholy appearance, which made him shudder while he explained their use." . . . . " Perhaps this custom, which prevails particularly at Deir-el-Kamr, and in the lonely neighbouring parts of the mountain, may have been of great antiquity, and may serve to explain some Scripture phrases. The prophet Samuel was *buried in his house at Ramah* (1 Sam. xxv. 1.); it could hardly be in his dwelling-house. *Joab was buried in his own house in the wilderness.* (1 Kings ii. 34.)" Jowett's Christian Researches in Palestine, p. 280.

[3] Harwood's Introduction, vol. ii. pp. 139. 141, 142. The sepulchres, described and delineated by Mr. Emerson, completely elucidate the form of the Jewish tombs. Letters from the Ægean, vol. ii. pp. 55—59.

*whited sepulchres, which indeed appear beautiful outward, but are within
full of dead men's bones, and of all uncleanness. Even so ye also outwardly
appear righteous to men, but within ye are full of hypocrisy and iniquity.*
(Matt. xxiii. 27.) [1]   But though the sepulchres of the rich were thus
beautified, the graves of the poor were oftentimes so neglected, that if
the stones by which they were marked happened to fall, they were not
set up again, by which means the graves themselves did not appear;
they were αδηλα, that is, not obvious to the sight, so that men might
tread on them inadvertently. (Luke xi. 44.) [2]   From Jer. xxvi. 23. we
may collect that the populace of the lowest order (Heb. *sons or children
of the people*) were buried in a public cemetery, having no distinct
sepulchre to themselves, as all persons of rank and character, and
especially of so honourable an order as that of the prophets, used to
have.[3]

After the deceased had been committed to the tomb, it was customary among the Greeks and Romans, to put the tears shed by the
surviving relatives and friends into lachrymatory urns, and place these
on the sepulchres, as a memorial of their distress and affection. From
Psal. lvi. 8. it should seem that this custom was still more antiently in
use among the eastern nations, especially the Hebrews. These vessels
were of different materials, and were moulded into different forms.
Some were of glass, and some were of earthen ware [4], being diminutive
in size and of delicate workmanship.

In order to do honour to the memory of the dead, their sepulchres
were sometimes distinguished by monuments. The custom of erecting
these seems to have obtained even from the patriarchal age.   Thus,

---

[1] The following passage from Dr. Shaw's Travels, affords a striking illustration of
Matt. xxiii. 27. " If we except a few persons, who are buried within the precincts of the
sanctuaries of their marabutts, the rest are carried out at a small distance from their cities
and villages, where a great extent of ground is allotted for the purpose. Each family has
a particular part of it walled in, like a garden, where the bones of their ancestors have
remained for many generations. For in these inclosures the graves are all distinct and separated, each of them having a stone placed upright both at the head and feet, inscribed with
the name and title of the deceased; while the intermediate space is either planted with
flowers, bordered round with stones, or paved with tiles. The graves of the principal citizens
are further distinguished, by having cupolas or vaulted chambers of three, four, or more
square yards built over them: and as these very frequently lie open, and occasionally shelter
us from the inclemency of the weather, the demoniac (Mark v. 5.) might with propriety
enough have had his dwelling among the tombs: and others are said (Isa. lxv. 4.) *to
remain among the graves and to lodge in the monuments (mountains).* And as all these different sorts of tombs and sepulchres, with the very walls likewise of their respective cupolas
and inclosures, are constantly kept clean, whitewashed, and beautified, they continue to
illustrate those expressions of our Saviour where he mentions the garnishing of sepulchres,
and compares the scribes, Pharisees, and hypocrites to whited sepulchres, which indeed
appear beautiful outward, but within were full of dead men's bones and all uncleanness."
Shaw's Travels, vol. i. pp. 395, 396.
[2] Macknight's Harmony, sect. 87. vol. ii. p. 473.
[3] Dr. Blayney's Jeremiah, p. 349.
[4] Dr. Chandler's Life of David, vol. i. p. 106. Among the valuable remains of antient
a rt collected by Dr. E. D. Clarke among the ruins of Sicyon, in the Peloponnesus, were
lachrymatories of more antient form and materials than anything he had ever before observed
of the same kind; " the lachrymatory phials, in which the Sicyonians treasured up their
tears, deserve rather the name of *bottles ;* they are nine inches long, two inches in diameter,
and contain as much fluid as would fill a phial of three ounces; consisting of the coarsest
materials, a heavy blue clay or marle. . . . . . Sometimes the vessels found in antient
sepulchres are of such diminutive size, that they are only capable of holding a few drops of
fluid; in these instances there seems to be no other use for which they were fitted.   Small
lachrymal phials of glass have been found in the tombs of the Romans in Great Britain;
and the evident allusion to this practice in the Sacred Scriptures— *Put those my tears into
thy bottle* (Psal. lvi. 8.) — seems decisive as to the purpose for which these vessels were
designed."   Travels in various Countries of Europe, &c. vol. vi. pp. 541, 542.

Jacob erected a pillar upon the grave of his beloved wife Rachel. (Gen. xxxv. 20.) This is the earliest monument mentioned in the Scriptures: it is evident from that passage that it was standing when Moses wrote; and its site seems to have been known in the time of Samuel and Saul. (1 Sam. x. 2.) The monument now shown in the vicinity of Bethlehem, as Rachel's tomb, is a modern and Turkish structure, which *may*, perhaps, be the true place of her interment.[1] In later times, inscriptions appear to have been placed on tombstones, denoting the persons who were there interred. Such was the title or inscription discovered by Josiah, which proved to be the burial-place of the prophet who was sent from Judah to denounce the divine judgments against the altar which Jeroboam had erected more than three centuries before. Simon Maccabæus built a splendid monument at Modin in honour of his father and his brethren. (1 Macc. xiii. 25—30.) In the time of Jesus Christ, it appears that the hypocritical scribes and Pharisees repaired and adorned the tombs of the prophets whom their ancestors had murdered for their faithfulness, under a sanctimonious appearance of respect for their memory. The antient Arabs raised a heap of stones over the body of the dead (Job xxi. 32. marginal rendering), which was guarded. In the year 1820, Mr. Rae Wilson observed on the plain of Zebulun, not far from Cana, piles of stones covering over or marking the place of graves. Similar cairns, also the remains of remote antiquity, exist both in England and in Scotland.[2] Among the Hebrews, great heaps of stones were raised over those whose death was either infamous, or attended with some very remarkable circumstances. Such were the heaps raised over the grave of Achan (Josh. vii. 26.), over that of the king of Ai (viii. 29.), and over that of Absalom (2 Sam. xviii. 17.); all which were sepulchral monuments to perpetuate the place of their interment.

VI. A FUNERAL FEAST commonly succeeded the Jewish burials. Thus, after Abner's funeral was solemnised, the people came to David to eat meat with him, though they could not persuade him to do so. (2 Sam. iii. 35.) He was the chief mourner, and probably had invited them to this banquet. Of this Jeremiah speaks (xvi. 7.), where he calls it the *cup of consolation, which they drank for their father or their mother;* and accordingly the place where this funeral entertainment was made, is called in the next verse the house of feasting. Hosea calls it the *bread of mourners.* (Hos. ix. 4.) Funeral banquets are still in use among the oriental Christians.[3]

The usual tokens of mourning by which the Jews expressed their grief and concern for the death of their friends and relations, were by rending their garments, and putting on sackcloth (Gen. xxxvii. 34.), sprinkling dust on their heads, wearing of mourning apparel (2 Sam. xiv. 2.), and covering the face and the head. (2 Sam. xix. 4.) They were accustomed also in times of public mourning to go up to the roofs or platforms of their houses, there to bewail their misfortunes, which practice is mentioned in Isaiah xv. 3. and xxii. 1. Antiently, there was a peculiar space of time allotted for lamenting the deceased,

---

[1] Maundrell's Journey from Aleppo, p. 117. " It has all the appearance of one of those tombs often erected to the memory of a Turkish Santon." Carne's Letters, p. 277.

[2] Rae Wilson's Travels in the Holy Land, vol. ii. p. 5. third edition.

[3] Harmer's Observations, vol. iii. p. 19.

which they called *the days of mourning.* (Gen. xxvii. 41. and l. 4.)
Thus the Egyptians, who had a great regard for the patriarch Jacob,
lamented his death *threescore and ten days.* (Gen. l. 3.) The Israelites
wept for Moses in the plains of Moab *thirty days.* (Deut. xxxiv. 8.)
Afterwards, among the Jews, the funeral mourning was generally confined to *seven days.* Hence, besides the mourning for Jacob in Egypt,
Joseph and his company set apart *seven days* to mourn for his father,
when they approached the Jordan with his corpse. (Gen. l. 10.) In
the time of Christ, it was customary for the nearest relative to visit
the grave of the deceased, and to weep there. The Jews, who had
come to condole with Mary, on the death of her brother Lazarus, on
seeing her go out of the house, concluded that she was *going to the
grave to weep there.* (John xi. 31.) The Syrian women are still accustomed, either alone[1], or accompanied by some attendants, to visit
the tombs of their relatives, and mourn their loss : and the same usage
obtains almost throughout the East, among Jews as well as Christians
and Mohammedans; and in Persia, Egypt[2], Greece, Dalmatia,
Bulgaria, Croatia, Servia, Wallachia, and Illyria.

It does not appear that there was any general mourning for Saul
and his sons, who died in battle : but the national troubles, which followed upon his death, might have prevented it. David, indeed, and
his men, on hearing the news of their death, mourned and wept for
them until even. (2 Sam. i. 12.) And the men of Jabesh-Gilead *fasted
for them seven days* (1 Sam. xxxi. 13.), which must not be understood
in a strict sense, as if they took *no* food during that time, but that they
lived very abstemiously, ate little, and that seldom, using a low and
spare diet, and drinking water only.

How long widows mourned for their husbands is nowhere told us in
Scripture. It is recorded, indeed, of Bathsheba, that *when she heard
that Uriah her husband was dead, she mourned for him* (2 Sam. xi. 26.) ;
but this could neither be long nor very sincere.

---

[1] " A female, with part of her robe drawn over her head, or veiled, was seen seated
by the tombs of her relatives on the summit of Mount Moriah, or along its sides, just
beneath the walls of Jerusalem." Carne's Letters, p. 332.

[2] " We arrived " (at one of the villages of Elephantina, an island in the Nile,) " just in
time to witness a *coronagh,* or wailing for the dead. A poor woman of the village had that
morning received the melancholy intelligence that her husband had been drowned in the
Nile. He had been interred without her knowledge, near the spot where the body was
found ; and she, along with several of her female friends, was paying the unavailing tribute
of lamentation to his departed shade." (Richardson's Travels, vol. i. p. 355.) " One
morning," says the same intelligent traveller, " when standing among the ruins of the
antient Syene, on the rocky promontory above the ferry, I saw a party of thirteen females
cross the Nile to perform the lugubrious dirge at the mansions of the dead. They set up a
piteous wail on entering the boat, after which they all cowered up together, wrapt in their
dirty robes of beteen. On landing, they wound their way slowly and silently along the
outside of the walls of the antient town, till they arrived at their place of destination, when
some of them placed a sprig of flowers on the grave, and sat down silently beside it ; others
cast themselves on the ground, and threw dust over their heads, uttering mournful lamentations, which they continued to repeat at intervals, during the short time] that I witnessed
their procedure." (Ibid. vol. i. p. 360.) Mr. Jowett witnessed a similar scene at Manfelout,
a more remote town of Upper Egypt. Christian Researches in the Mediterranean, p. 162.
Alber, Inst. Herm. Vet. Test. tom. i. pp. 311—319. Calmet, Dissertation sur les Funé-
railles des Hébreux. Dissert. tom. i. pp. 290—309. Pareau, Antiquitas Hebraica, pp. 472
—477. Jahn, Archæol. Bibl. §§ 204—211. Stosch, Compendium Archæologiæ Œconomicæ Novi Testamenti, pp. 121—132. Brünings, Compendium Antiquitatum Græcarum,
pp. 388—400. ; and his Compendium Antiquitatum Hebræarum, pp. 257—264. The
subject of Hebrew sepulchres is very fully discussed by Nicolai, in his treatise De Sepulchris
Hebræorum (Lug. Bat. 1706), which is illustrated with several curious plates, some of
which, however, it must be confessed, are rather fanciful.

APPENDIX.

No. I.

TABLES OF WEIGHTS, MEASURES, AND MONEY, MENTIONED IN THE BIBLE.

Extracted chiefly from the Second Edition of Dr. Arbuthnot's Tables of Antient Coins, Weights, and Measures.

[Referred to in page 488. of this Volume.]

1. *Jewish Weights reduced to English Troy Weight.*

	lbs.	oz.	pen.	gr.
The gerah, one-twentieth of a shekel —	0	0	0	12
Bekah, half a shekel — — —	0	0	5	0
The shekel — — — —	0	0	9	2$\frac{4}{7}$
The maneh, 60 shekels — —	2	3	6	10$\frac{2}{7}$
The talent, 50 maneh or 3000 shekels —	113	10	1	10$\frac{2}{7}$

2. *Scripture Measures of Length reduced to English Measure.*

							Eng. feet.	inch.	dec.
A digit							0	0	912
4	A palm						0	3	648
12	3	A span					0	10	944
24	6	3	A cubit				1	9	888
96	24	6	2	A fathom			7	3	552
144	36	12	6	1$\frac{1}{2}$	Ezekiel's reed		10	11	328
192	48	16	8	2	1$\frac{1}{3}$	An Arabian pole	14	7	104
1920	480	160	80	20	13$\frac{1}{3}$	10	A schœnus or measuring line	145	11	004

3. *The long Scripture Measures.*

					Eng. miles.	paces.	feet.	dec.
A cubit					0	0	1	824
400	A stadium or furlong				0	145	4	6
2000	5	A sabbath day's journey			0	729	3	0
4000	10	2	An eastern mile		1	403	1	0
12000	30	6	3	A parasang		4	153	3	0
96000	240	48	24	8	A day's journey	33	172	4	0

4. *Scripture Measures of Capacity for Liquids, reduced to English Wine Measure.*

							Gal.	pints.
A caph	-		-		-	-	0	$0\frac{5}{8}$
$1\frac{1}{3}$	A log	-		-		-	0	$0\frac{6}{9}$
$5\frac{1}{3}$	4	A cab		-		-	0	$3\frac{1}{3}$
16	12	3	A hin	-		-	1	2
32	24	6	2	A seah	-	-	2	4
96	72	18	6	3	A bath or ephah	-	7	4
960	720	180	60	30	10	A kor or coros, chomer or homer -	75	5

5. *Scripture Measures of Capacity for dry Things, reduced to English Corn Measure.*

							Pecks.	gal.	pints.
A gachal	-		-		-	-	0	0	$0\frac{17}{120}$
20	A cab	-		-		-	0	0	$2\frac{5}{8}$
36	$1\frac{4}{5}$	An omer or gomer		-		-	0	0	$5\frac{1}{10}$
120	6	$3\frac{1}{3}$	A seah	-		-	1	0	1
360	18	10	3	An ephah	-	-	3	0	3
1800	90	50	15	5	A letech	-	16	0	0
3600	180	100	30	10	2	A chomer, homer, kor, or coros	32	0	1

6. *Jewish Money reduced to the English Standard.*

					£	s.	d.
A gerah	-		-		0	0	$1\frac{59}{160}$
10	A bekah	-		-	0	1	$1\frac{11}{10}$
20	2	A shekel	-	-	0	2	$3\frac{3}{8}$
1200	120	50	A maneh, or mina Hebraica	-	5	14	$0\frac{3}{4}$
60000	6000	3000	60	A talent	342	3	9

	£	s.	d.
A solidus aureus, or sextula, was worth -	0	12	$0\frac{1}{2}$
A siclus aureus, or shekel of gold, was worth -	1	16	6
A pound or mina - -	3	2	6
A talent of gold was worth -	5475	0	0

7. *Roman and Greek Money, mentioned in the New Testament, reduced to the English Standard.*

	£	s.	d.	far.
A (mite Λεπτον or Ασσαριον) -	0	0	0	$0\frac{31}{336}$
A farthing (Κοδραντης) about -	0	0	0	$1\frac{1}{2}$
A penny or denarius (Δηναριον) -	0	0	7	3

In the preceding table, silver is valued at 5s. and gold at £4 per ounce.

No. II.

A CHRONOLOGICAL TABLE

OF THE

PRINCIPAL EVENTS RECORDED IN THE BIBLE.

PART I.

A Table of the most REMARKABLE EVENTS *comprised in the Old Testament, abridged from Archbishop* USHER *and Father* CALMET, *together with the corresponding Dates adopted by the Rev. Dr.* HALES *in his " New Analysis of Chronology," and by the Right Rev. Dr.* GLEIG, *in his new Edition of Stackhouse's History of the Bible.*

** *The true Date of the Birth of Christ is* FOUR YEARS *before the common Æra, or A.D.*

PERIOD I.

From the Creation to the Deluge.

Dr. Hales.	Anno Mundi, or Year of the World		Year before Christ 4000, before A. D.	Dr. Hales.
1	1	THE creation	4004	5411
		Eve, tempted by the serpent, disobeys God, and persuades her husband Adam to disobedience also. God drives them out of paradise.		
100	3	Cain born, Adam's eldest son.	3998	5311
101	4	Abel born, Adam's second son.	3997	5310
201	128	Cain kills his brother Abel.	2876	5210
230	130	Seth born, son of Adam and Eve.	3874	5181
435	235	Enos born, son of Seth.	3769	4996
625	325	Cainan born, son of Enos.	3679	4786
795	395	Mahalaleel born, son of Cainan.	3609	4616
960	460	Jared born, son of Mahalaleel.	3544	4451
1122	622	Enoch born, son of Jared.	3382	4289
1287	687	Methuselah born, son of Enoch.	3317	4124
1474	874	Lamech born, son of Methuselah.	3130	3937
930	930	Adam dies, aged 930 years.	3074	4481
1487	987	Enoch translated : he had lived 365 years.	3017	3914
1142	1042	Seth dies, aged 912 years.	2962	4269
1656	1056	Noah born, son of Lamech.	2948	3755
1340	1140	Enos dies, aged 905 years.	2864	4071
1534	1235	Cainan dies, aged 910 years.	2769	3877
1690	1290	Mahalaleel dies, aged 895 years.	2714	3721
1922	1422	Jared dies, aged 962 years.	2582	3489
2136	1536	God informs Noah of the future deluge, and commissions him to preach repentance to mankind,120 years before the deluge.	2468	3275
2227	1651	Lamech dies, the father of Noah, aged 777 years.	2353	3184
2348	1656	Methuselah dies, the oldest of men, aged 969 years, in the year of the deluge ; and the same year, Noah, being 600 years old, by divine command enters the ark.	2349	3155

Dr. H.	A. M.	PERIOD II. *From the Deluge to the Birth of Abraham.*	B. C.	Dr. H.
2257	1657	Noah and his family quit the Ark. He offers sacrifices of thanksgiving. God appoints the rainbow as a pledge that he would send no more an universal deluge.	2347	3154
2258	1658	Arphaxad born, the son of Shem.	2346	3153
2393	1693	Salah born, son of Arphaxad.	2311	3018
2523	1723	Heber born, son of Salah.	2281	2888
2657	1757	Phaleg born, son of Heber.	2247	2754
2797	1770	The building of the tower of Babel.	2234	2614
2857	1770	The confusion of languages, and dispersion of the nations.		2554
2857	1771	The beginning of the Babylonian or Assyrian monarchy by Nimrod; and of the Egyptian empire by Ham the father of Mizraim.	2233	2554
		The trial of Job, according to Dr. Hales, took place.	2130	2337
2787	1787	Reu born, the son of Phaleg.	2217	2624
2919	1819	Serug born, Son of Reu.	2185	2492
3049	1849	Nahor born, son of Serug.	2155	2362
3128	1878	Terah born, the son of Nahor.	2126	2283
3198	1948	Haran born, the son of Terah.	2056	2213
2606	2006	Noah dies, aged 950 years.	1998	2805
3258	2008	Abram born, the son of Terah.	1996	2153

PERIOD III.

From the Birth of Abraham to the Departure of the Israelites out of Egypt, and their Return into the Land of Canaan.

Dr. H.	A. M.		B. C.	Dr. H.
3268	2018	Sarai born, wife of Abram.	1986	2143
3318	2083	The call of Abram from Ur of the Chaldees to Haran in Mesopotamia, where his father Terah died, aged 205 years.	1917	2093
3333	2083	The second call of Abram from Haran. — He comes into Canaan with Sarai his wife, and Lot his nephew; and dwells at Sichem.	1921	2078
3334	2084	Abram goes into Egypt; Pharaoh takes his wife, but soon restores her again. Abram returns from Egypt; he and Lot separate.	1920	2077
3341	2091	Abram's victory over the five kings, and rescue of Lot.	1913	2070
3344	2094	Sarai gives her maid Hagar, for a wife to her husband Abram. Ishmael born, the son of Abram and Hagar. Abram was 86 years old. (Gen. xvi. 16.)	1910	2067
3357	2107	The new covenant of the LORD with Abraham. (Gen. xvii.) Sodom, Gomorrah, Admah, and Zeboim, burnt by fire from heaven. Lot is preserved; retires to Zoar; commits incest with his daughters.	1897	2054
3358	2108	Abraham departs from the plains of Mamre to Beer-sheba. Isaac born.	1896	2053
3383	2133	Abraham offers his son Isaac for a burnt-offering. Sarah dies, aged 127 years.	1871	2028
3398	2148	Isaac marries Rebekah.	1858	2013
3418	2168	Jacob and Esau born, Isaac being 60 years old.	1836	1993
3438	2186	Abraham dies, aged 175 years.	1818	1973
3495	2245	Isaac blesses Jacob, who withdraws into Mesopotamia, to his uncle Laban; and marries first Leah, and then Rachel.	1759	1916
3526	2276	Joseph, being 17 years old, tells his father Jacob his brethren's faults; they hate him, and sell him to strangers, who take him into Egypt. Joseph sold again, as a slave, to Potiphar.	1728	1885
3539	2289	Pharaoh's dreams explained by Joseph, who is made governor of Egypt.	1715	1872
3548	2298	Joseph's ten brethren come into Egypt to buy corn. Joseph imprisons Simeon. — His brethren return; Joseph discovers himself, and engages them to come into Egypt with their father Jacob, then 130 years old.	1706	1863
3683	2433	A revolution in Egypt. The Israelites persecuted. Moses born; exposed on the banks of the Nile; and found by Pharaoh's daughter, who adopts him.	1571	1728
3723	2473	Moses kills an Egyptian; flees into Midian; marries Zipporah, the daughter of Jethro; has two sons by her, Gershon and Eliezer.	1531	1688
		According to archbishop Usher, the trial of Job took place.	1520	

Dr. H.	A. M.		B. C.	Dr. H.
3763	2513	Moses, commissioned by God, returns into Egypt. Pharaoh refuses to set the Israelites at liberty. Moses inflicts ten plagues on Egypt; after which the Israelites are liberated. Pharaoh pursues the Israelites with his army, and overtakes them at Pi-hahiroth. The waters divided. Israel goes through on dry ground. The Egyptians drowned; 21st of the first month.	1491	1648
3764	2514	The delivery of the law, with various circumstances of terror, &c.	1490	1647
3765	2515	The people resolve on entering Canaan, but are repulsed by the Amalekites and the Canaanites. Establishment of the priesthood, &c.		
		The sedition of Korah, Dathan, and Abiram, is supposed to have happened about this time.		
3803	2553	The Israelites enter Canaan.	1451	1608
		The death of Moses, who is succeeded by Joshua.		
		Joshua sends spies to Jericho.		

Period IV.

From the Return of the Israelites into the Land of Canaan to the Establishment of the Regal State.

Dr. H.	A. M.		B. C.	Dr. H.
3803	2553	The people pass the river Jordan. — Joshua restores circumcision. — Jericho taken. — The Gibeonites make a league with Joshua. — War of the five kings against Gibeon, whom Joshua defeats; the sun and moon stand still.	1451	1608
3804	2554	War of Joshua against the kings of Canaan; conquest and division of that country, &c.	1451	1609
3811	2561	Joshua renews the covenant between the Lord and the Israelites. — Joshua dies, aged 110 years.	1443	1582
		After his death the elders govern about eighteen or twenty years, during which time happen the wars of Judah with Adoni-bezek.		
3849	2599	During the succeeding anarchy happened the idolatry of Micah, and the war of the twelve tribes against Benjamin, to revenge the outrage committed on the wife of a Levite.	1405	1561
		God sends his prophets in vain to reclaim the Hebrews. He permits, therefore, that they should fall into slavery under their enemies.		
3985	2469	Deborah, Barak, and others judge the Israelites.	1535	
4045	2519	Gideon delivers Israel.	1485	1366
4189	2663	Under his judicature God raises up Samson.	1341	1222
		The actions of Samson.		
4259	2723	The birth of Samuel.	1271	1152

Period V.

From the Establishment of the Regal State to the Babylonish Captivity.

Dr. H.	A. M.		B. C.	Dr. H.
4341	2745	The Israelites ask a king of Samuel. — Saul is appointed and consecrated king.	1259	1110
4343	2747	War of the Philistines against Saul, who, having disobeyed Samuel's orders, is rejected by God.	1257	1108
4351	2755	Saul's second offence.	1249	1100
4361	2785	David succeeds to Saul on the throne of Israel.	1219	1070
4375	2819	Absalom's rebellion against his father David quashed. — The restoration of David.	1185	1036
4381	2825	Adonijah aspires to the kingdom. David causes his son Solomon to be crowned, who is proclaimed king by all Israel.	1179	1030
		The death of David, aged 70 years.		
		Solomon reigns alone, having reigned about six months in the lifetime of his father David. He reigned in all 40 years.		
4391	3001	The temple of Solomon finished, being seven years and a half in building. — Its dedication.	1003	1020
4421	3029	The death of Solomon, accession of Rehoboam, and the revolt of the ten tribes. Jeroboam the son of Nebat acknowledged king of the ten tribes.	971	991

Dr. H.	A. M.	*Kings of Judah, for 388 years.*	B. C.	Dr. H.
4422	3030	Rehoboam, intending to subdue the ten tribes, is commanded to forbear.	970	990
4424	3032	Rehoboam gives himself up to impiety.	967	987
4438	3046	Rehoboam dies. Abijam succeeds him; reigns three years.	954	973
4439	3047	Abijam's victory over Jeroboam; who loses many thousands of his troops.	953	972
4441	3049	Abijam dies. Asa succeeds him, and suppresses idolatry in Judah.	951	970
4471	3064	Asa engages Ben-hadad king of Syria to make an irruption into the territories of the kingdom of Israel, to force Baasha to quit his undertaking at Ramah.	936	940
4482	3090	Death of Asa, who is succeeded by Jehoshaphat. He expels superstitious worship.	910	929
		Elijah removed from this world in a fiery chariot.		
4514	3107	Jehoshaphat accompanies Ahab in his expedition against Ramoth Gilead; where he narrowly escapes a great danger.	893	897
4515	3108	Jehoshaphat equips a fleet for Ophir: Ahaziah king of Israel partaking of the design, the fleet is destroyed by tempest.	892	896
4517	3115	Jehoshaphat dies; Jehoram succeeds him.	885	904
4515	3117	Jehoram, at the importunity of his wife Athaliah, introduces into Judah the worship of Baal. He is smitten by God with an incurable distemper in his bowels; makes his son Ahaziah viceroy, or associate in his kingdom. Jehoram dies.	884	896
4515	3117	Ahaziah reigns but one year.	884	896
		Joash or Jehoash born.		
		Homer the Greek poet flourishes.		
4516	3120	Ahaziah accompanies Jehoram king of Israel to the siege of Ramoth Gilead. He is slain by Jehu.	879	895
		Athaliah kills all the royal family; usurps the kingdom. Jehoash is preserved and kept secretly in the temple six years.		
4522	3126	Jehoiada the high priest sets Jehoash on the throne of Judah, and slays Athaliah.	878	889
4562	3164	Zechariah the high priest, son of Jehoiada, killed in the temple by order of Jehoash.	836	849
		Hazael king of Syria wars against Jehoash.		
4563	3165	Hazael returns against Jehoash; and forces large sums from him. (2 Chron. xxiv. 23.)	835	848
		Jehoash dies; and is succeeded by Amaziah.		
4591	3178	Amaziah wars against Jehoash king of Israel; is defeated by him.	822	820
4602	3189	Amaziah dies; Uzziah or Azariah succeeds him. Isaiah and Amos prophesy in Judah under this reign.	810	809

Dr. H.	A. M.	*Kings of Israel, for 254 years.*	B. C.	Dr. H.
4422	3030	Jeroboam, son of Nebat, the first king of Israel, or of the revolted ten tribes.— He abolishes the worship of the LORD, and sets up the golden calves.	970	990
4439	3047	Jeroboam overcome by Abijam, who kills 500,000 men.	953	972
4443	3050	Jeroboam dies; Nadab his son succeeds: reigns two years.	950	968
4445	3052	Nadab dies; Baasha succeeds him.	946	966
4468	3074	Baasha dies; Elah his son succeeds him.	926	943
4469	3075	Elah killed by Zimri, who usurps the kingdom seven days.	925	942
4469	3075	Omri besieges Zimri in Tirzah; he burns himself in the palace.	925	942
4473	3079	Omri builds Samaria; makes it the seat of his kingdom.	921	938
4480	3086	Omri dies; Ahab his son succeeds.	914	981
4503	3096	The prophet Elijah presents himself before Ahab, and causes the false prophets of Baal to be slain. Gives the prophetic unction to Elisha.	904	908
4504	3103	Ben-hadad king of Syria besieges Samaria; is forced to quit it.	901	905
4506	3107	Ahab wars against Ramoth Gilead; is killed in disguise. Ahaziah succeeds.	897	900
4507	3108	Ahaziah falling from the lattice of his house, is dangerously wounded, and dies; Jehoram his brother succeeds him, and makes war against Moab.	896	899
4508	3109	Elisha foretells victory to the army of Israel, and procures water in abundance.	895	898
4515	3119	Samaria besieged by Ben-hadad king of Syria. Ben-hadad and his army seized with a panic, flee during the night.	881	885
4516	3120	Elisha going to Damascus, foretells the death of Ben-hadad, and the reign of Hazael. Jehoram marches with Ahaziah against Ramoth Gilead; is dangerously wounded, and carried to Jezreel. Jehu rebels against Jehoram; kills him, and usurps the throne.	880	884
4544	3148	Jehu dies; Jehoahaz his son succeeds him.	852	867
4561	3165	Jehoahaz dies. Joash, or Jehoash, whom he had associated with himself on the throne A.M. 3162, succeeds him.	835	850
4579	3168	Hazael king of Syria dies; and Ben-hadad succeeds him. Jehoash wars against Ben-hadad.	822	832
4576	3178	Jehoash obtains a great victory over Amaziah king of Judah.	821	834
4577	3179	Jehoash king of Israel dies; Jeroboam II. succeeds him. Jonah, Hosea, and Amos in Israel, prophesy during this reign.	820	833
4640	3232	Jeroboam II. dies; Zachariah his son succeeds him. The chronology of this reign is very perplexed.	779	792
4640	3232	Zachariah killed by Shallum, after reigning six months.	768	771
4641	3233	Shallum reigns one month; is killed by Menahem. Pul (or Sardanapalus) king of Assyria invades Israel; Menahem becomes tributary to him.	767	770

Dr. H.	A. M.	Kings of Judah.	B. C.	Dr. H.
4654	3246	Uzziah dies; Jotham his son succeeds. Isaiah sees the glory of the Lord. (Isa. vi.) Isaiah and Hosea continue to prophesy.	754	757
4669	3261	Rezin king of Syria, and Pekah king of Israel, invade Judah.	737	742
4670	3262	Jotham dies; Ahaz succeeds him. Rezin king of Syria, and Pekah king of Israel, continue their hostilities against Judah.	736	741
4671	3263	Isaiah foretells to Ahaz the birth of the Messiah, and a speedy deliverance from the two kings his enemies. Nevertheless, the year following they return again and spoil his country. Ahaz invites to his assistance Tiglath-pileser king of Assyria, and submits to pay him tribute.	735	740
4686	3278	Ahaz king of Judah dies, and is succeeded by his son Hezekiah, who restores the worship of the Lord in Judæa, which Ahaz had almost entirely subverted.	722	725

Dr. H.	A. M.	Judah alone.	B. C.	Dr. H.
4696	3285	On the death of Shalmaneser, Sennacherib succeeds him, and invades Judah, and takes several cities.	712	715
4702	3291	Hezekiah's sickness and miraculous cure. He gives money to Sennacherib, who still continues his war against him. He sends Rabshakeh to Jerusalem, and marches himself against Tirhakah king of Cush or Arabia. Returning into Judæa, the angel of the Lord destroys many thousands of his army; he retires to Nineveh, where he is slain by his sons.	706	709
4687	3292	Esar-haddon succeeds Sennacherib. Micah the Morasthite, and Nahum, prophesy.	705	708
4715	3306	Hezekiah dies, and is succeeded by Manasseh.	694	696
4734	3323	Esar-haddon becomes master of Babylon; re-unites the empires of Assyria and Chaldæa.	677	677
4740	3329	Manasseh taken by the Chaldæans, and carried to Babylon.	671	671
4758	3347	The war of Holofernes, who is slain in Judæa by Judith.	653	653
4770	3361	Manasseh dies. He returned into Judæa a considerable time before, but the period is not exactly known; Amon succeeds him; reigns two years.	639	641
4772	3363	Amon dies; Josiah succeeds him.	637	639
	3376	Jeremiah begins to prophesy, in the thirteenth year of Josiah.		
4803	3394	Josiah opposes the expedition of Necho king of Egypt against Carchemish, is mortally wounded, and dies at Jerusalem. Jeremiah composes lamentations on his death. Jehoahaz is placed on the throne by the people; but Necho, returning from Carchemish, deposes him, and installs Eliakim, or Jehoiakim, his brother, son of Josiah.	606	608
4809	3398	Nebuchadnezzar besieges and takes Jerusalem; leaves Jehoiakim there, on condition of paying him a large tribute. Daniel and his companions led captive to Babylon.	602	602
4813	3402	Nebuchadnezzar's dream of a great statue explained by Daniel.	598	598

Dr. H.	A. M.	*Kings of Israel.*	B. C.	Dr. H.
4653	3243	Menahem dies; Pekahiah his son succeeds.	757	760
4655	3245	Pekahiah assassinated by Pekah, son of Remaliah.	755	758
4665	3254	Arbaces, governor of Media, and Belesis, governor of Babylonia, besiege Sardanapalus king of Assyria in Nineveh, who, after a siege of three years, burns himself in his palace, with all his riches. Arbaces is acknowledged king of Media, and Belesis of Babylon.	746	756
4673	3264	Tiglath-pileser defeats and slays Rezin king of Damascus; enters the land of Israel, and takes many cities and captives, chiefly from Reuben, Gad, and the half tribe of Manasseh. The first captivity of Israel.	736	738
4683	3265	Hoshea son of Elah slays Pekah, and usurps the kingdom.	735	738
4687	3276	Shalmaneser succeeds Tiglath-pileser king of Nineveh.	724	727
4692	3279	Hoshea makes an alliance with So king of Egypt, and endeavours to shake off the yoke of Shalmaneser, who besieges Samaria; takes it after three years' siege, and carries beyond the Euphrates the tribes that Tiglath-pileser had not already carried into captivity; and puts an end to the kingdom of Israel, after it had subsisted two hundred and fifty-four years.	721	719

Dr. H.	A. M.	*Judah alone.*	B. C.	Dr.
4815	3404	Jehoiakim revolts against Nebuchadnezzar, who sends an army from Chaldæa, Syria, and Moab, which ravages Judæa, and brings away 3023 Jews to Babylon, in the seventh year of Jehoiakim.	596	596
4816	3405	Cyrus born, son of Cambyses and Mandane.	595	595
		Jehoiakim revolts a second time against Nebuchadnezzar; is taken, put to death, and cast to the fowls of the air.		
		Jehoiachin or Coniah, or Jeconiah, succeeds him. Nebuchadnezzar besieges him in Jerusalem, and takes him, after he had reigned three months and ten days. He is carried to Babylon, with part of the people. Mordecai is among the captives.		
		Zedekiah, his uncle, is left at Jerusalem in his place.		
4821	3410	Ezekiel begins to prophesy in Chaldæa.	590	590
4823	3412	Zedekiah takes secret measures with the king of Egypt, and revolts against the Chaldæans. Nebuchadnezzar marches against Jerusalem; besieges it; quits the siege to repel the king of Egypt, who comes to assist Zedekiah; returns to the siege. Jeremiah continues prophesying during the whole of the siege, which continued almost three years. Ezekiel also describes the same siege in Chaldæa.		
4826	3415	Jerusalem taken on the ninth day of the fourth month (July), the 11th year of Zedekiah. Zedekiah, endeavouring to flee by night, is taken, and brought to Riblah, to Nebuchadnezzar; his eyes are put out, and he is carried to Babylon.	588	586
		Jerusalem and the temple burnt; seventh day of the fourth month. The Jews of Jerusalem and Judæa carried captive beyond the Euphrates; the poorer classes only left in the land.		
		Thus ends the kingdom of Judæa, after it had subsisted four hundred and sixty-eight years, from the beginning of the reign of David: and three hundred and eighty-eight years from the separation of Judah and the ten tribes.		

Dr. H.	A. M.	PERIOD VI.	B. C.	Dr. H.
		From the Babylonish Captivity to Nehemiah's Reform.		
4827	3416	The beginning of the seventy years' captivity foretold by Jeremiah. Gedaliah made governor of the remains of the people. He is slain.	587	586

MEDIAN AND PERSIAN DYNASTY.

Dr. H.	A. M.		B. C.	Dr. H.
4858	3447	Darius the Mede.	553	553
4860	3449	Cyrus the Persian.	551	551
4875	3464	Babylon taken by Cyrus, who sets the Jews at liberty, and permits them to return into Judæa under Zorobabel. Joshua, the first high priest, in the same year.	536	536
4876	3465	The second temple begun.	535	535
4882	3471	Death of Cyrus; Cambyses reigns.	529	529
4890	3479	Darius Hystaspes.	521	521
4895	3484	The temple finished.	516	516
4926	3515	Death of Darius; Xerxes succeeds to the throne.	485	485
4928	3517	Jehoiakim high priest.	483	483
4947	3536	Artaxerxes succeeds Darius.	464	464
4948	3537	He stops the rebuilding of Jerusalem.	463	463
4951	3540	Artaxerxes marries Esther.	460	460
4954	3543	He sends Ezra to Jerusalem, with several priests and Levites.	457	457
4958	3547	Eliashib high priest.	453	453
		Nehemiah governor of Judæa.		
4988	3577	Darius Nothus.	423	423
4991	3580	Nehemiah's reform among the Jews.	420	420
		End of the Old Testament canon.		

PERIOD VII.

From Nehemiah's Reform to the Birth of John the Baptist.

PERSIAN DYNASTY.
Jewish High Priests.

Dr. H.	A. M.		B. C.	Dr. H.
4991	3580	Eliashib.		
4998	3587	Joiada or Judas.	420	420
5038	3627	Jonathan or John.	413	413
5070	3659	Jaddua or Jaddus.	373	373
			341	341

MACEDO-GRECIAN DYNASTY.
Jewish High Priests.

Dr. H.	A. M.		B. C.	Dr. H.
5090	3679	Onias I.	321	321
5111	3700	Simon the Just.	300	300
5120	3709	Eleazar.	291	291
5135	3724	Manasses.	276	276
5161	3750	Onias II.	250	250
5194	3783	Simon II.	217	217
5216	3805	Onias III.	195	195
5236	3825	Jesus or Jason.	175	175
5237	3827	Onias or Menelaus.	172	172

ASMONÆAN PRINCES OR MACCABEES.

Dr. H.	A. M.		B. C.	Dr. H.
5247	3837	Judas Maccabæus.	163	163
		Jachim or Alcimus, high priest.	160	160
5251	3840	Jonathan.		
5558	3847	He is appointed high priest.	153	153
5268	3857	Simon.	143	143
5275	3864	John Hyrcanus.	136	136

Dr. H.	A. M.		B. C.	Dr. H.
5305	3894	Aristobulus and Antigonus.	106	106
5306	3895	Alexander Jannæus.	105	105
5333	3922	Queen Alexandra.	78	78
5342	3931	Hyrcanus II.	69	69
5342	3931	Aristobulus II.	69	69
		ROMAN SOVEREIGNTY.		
5348	3937	Pompey takes Jerusalem.	63	63
		Hyrcanus II. again.		
5371	3960	Antigonus.	40	40
5373	3963	Idumæan king, Herod the Great.	37	37
5411	4000	John the Baptist born six months before the birth of Jesus Christ.	4	5
		The birth of our Lord and Saviour Jesus Christ took place A.M. 4000 according to the vulgar æra; but its true date according to Calmet is A.M. 4004, and A.M. 5411 according to Dr. Hales.		

PART II.

A Table of the PRINCIPAL EVENTS *recorded in the New Testament, from the Birth of Christ, to the Destruction of Jerusalem and the Completion of the Canon of the New Testament.*

A. M.		Y. of J. C.	Before the Vulgar Æra
4000	The nativity of Jesus Christ.	1	4
	The circumcision, purification, and presentation of Christ in the temple.		
	Archelaus, Ethnarch of Judæa.		3
			V. Æ. or A. D.
4012	Christ visits the temple.	12	8
4032	The ministry of John the Baptist.	32	29
4033	The baptism and temptation of Christ.	33	30
	FIRST PASSOVER. — Christ purges the temple, and preaches in Judæa. — Imprisonment of John the Baptist.		
4034	SECOND PASSOVER. — The twelve apostles sent forth. John the Baptist beheaded.	34	31
4035	THIRD PASSOVER. — Seventy disciples sent forth.	35	32
	Transfiguration of Jesus Christ.		
4036	FOURTH PASSOVER. — The crucifixion, death, resurrection, and ascension of Christ.	36	33
	Feast of Pentecost. — Descent of the Holy Spirit.		
4037	The church increased.	37	34
4038	The church multiplied.	38	35
4039	The martyrdom of Stephen. — *First* Jewish persecution of the Church.	39	36
4040	Conversion of Paul.	40	37
	The *Hebrew* Gospel of Matthew probably written about this time.		
4044	Herod Agrippa, king of Judæa.	44	39
4047	*Second* Jewish persecution of the church.	47	44
4061	Paul imprisoned at Jerusalem.	61	58
4063	He is sent to Rome, and shipwrecked at Malta.	64	61
4064	He arrives at Rome, and continues there a prisoner two years.		
	The General Epistle of James, and the *Greek* Gospel of Matthew, written about this time.		
4065	Epistle of Paul to the Philippians.	65	62
	Epistles to the Colossians, Ephesians, and Philemon.		
	Martyrdom of James the Less, bishop of Jerusalem.		
4066	Epistle of Paul to the Hebrews, written from Italy soon after he was set at liberty.	66	63
	Luke writes his Gospel and the Acts of the Apostles in this or the following year.		

A. M.		Y. of J. C.	A. D.
4066	Epistle of Paul to Titus, and his first Epistle to Timothy.	66	63
	Mark writes his Gospel about this time.		
4067	Paul comes out of Italy into Judæa: visits the churches in Crete, Ephesus, Macedonia, and Greece.	67	64
	Peter writes his first Epistle, probably, from Rome.		
4068	Peter writes his second Epistle, probably, from Rome, about the beginning of this year.	68	65
	Several prodigies at Jerusalem, this year, during the passover.		
	Paul goes to Rome the last time ; is there put into prison ; also Peter.		
	Second Epistle of Paul to Timothy.		
	The Epistle of Jude written in this or the following year.		
4069	The martyrdom of Paul and Peter at Rome.	69	66
	Cestius Gallus governor of Syria comes to Jerusalem ; enumerates the Jews at the passover.		
	Disturbances at Cæsarea, and at Jerusalem.		
	Florus puts several Jews to death.		
	The Jews rise, and kill the Roman Garrison at Jerusalem.		
	A massacre of the Jews of Cæsarea and Palestine.		
	All the Jews of Scythopolis slain in one night.		
	Cestius governor of Syria comes into Judæa.		
	He besieges the temple of Jerusalem ; retires ; is defeated by the Jews.		
	The Christians of Jerusalem, seeing a war about to break out, retire to Pella, in the kingdom of Agrippa, beyond Jordan.		
	Vespasian appointed by Nero for the Jewish war.		
	Josephus made governor of Galilee.		
	Vespasian sends his son Titus to Alexandria; comes himself to Antioch, and forms a numerous army.		
4070	Vespasian enters Judæa ; subdues Galilee.	70	67
	Tiberias and Tarichea, which had revolted against Agrippa, reduced to obedience by Vespasian.		
	Divisions in Jerusalem.		
	The Zealots seize the temple, commit violences in Jerusalem, and send for the Idumæans to succour Jerusalem.		
4071	Vespasian takes all the places of strength in Judæa about Jerusalem.	71	68
	Simon son of Gioras ravages Judæa and the south of Idumæa.		
	In this or the following year John writes his three Epistles.		
4073	Titus marches against Jerusalem to besiege it.	73	70
	Comes down before Jerusalem some days before the passover.		
	The factions unite at first against the Romans, but afterwards divide again.		
	The Romans take the first inclosure of Jerusalem ; then the second ; they make a wall all round the city, which is reduced to distress by famine.		
	July 17. the perpetual sacrifice ceases in the temple.		
	The Romans become masters of the court of the Gentiles, and set fire to the galleries.		
	A Roman soldier sets the temple on fire, notwithstanding Titus commands the contrary.		
	The Romans, being now masters of the city and temple, offer sacrifices to their gods.		
	The last inclosure of the city taken.		
4074	Titus demolishes the temple to its very foundation.	74	71
	He also demolishes the city, reserving the towers of Hippicos, Phazael, and Mariamne.		
	Titus returns to Rome with his father Vespasian ; they triumph over Judæa.		
4098	John banished to Patmos.	98	95
4100	John liberated from exile.	100	97
	John writes his Gospel and Revelation about this time.		

Grotto at Nazareth, *said to have been the House of* Joseph and Mary.

No. III.

A BIOGRAPHICAL, HISTORICAL, AND GEOGRAPHICAL

INDEX

OF THE PRINCIPAL PERSONS, NATIONS, COUNTRIES,' AND PLACES,

MENTIONED IN THE HOLY SCRIPTURES:

Including also an Index to the PRINCIPAL MATTERS contained in this Volume.

This Index is compiled from the works of Bræm, Calmet, Reland, Wells, Chompré, Gesenius, Rosenmüller, Schleusner, Dr. Robinson (of New York), Serieys, Coquerel, Macbean, Drs. Whitby, Hales, and Parish, M. Anquetil, and various other writers and commentators, who have treated on Sacred History, Biography, and Geography ; and also from the Travels in Palestine, Asia Minor, and Egypt, of Bishop Pococke, Lord Lindsay, Major Sir G. Temple, the Rev. Dr. E. D. Clarke, Lieutenant-Colonel Leake, the Hon. Capt. Keppel, Captains Irby and Mangles, and Capt. Skinner, the Rev. Messrs. W. Jowett, Connor, Hartley, Monro, and Arundell, Messrs. Addison, Buckingham, Carne, Emerson, Lane, Robinson, Wilkinson, Lieut. Wellstead, and of Dr. Robert Richardson, who explored various parts of the East; in company with the Rt. Hon. the Earl of Belmore, in the years 1816—1818. Those names of persons and places only are omitted which occur but seldom in the Bible, and of which nothing more is known than appears in the passages where they occur.

A A

AARON, the son of Amram and Jochebed, of the tribe of Levi (Exod. vi. 20.), was born three years before his brother Moses. The Scripture is silent respecting every thing which preceded his call to be the spokesman or interpreter of Moses before Pharaoh, king

A A

of Egypt. From this time (the eighty-third year of his age), Aaron was the associate of Moses in all the transactions of the Israelites, until his death on Mount Hor, B. C. 1452, in the hundred and twenty-third year of his age, and in the fortieth year after the depart-

A B

ure of the Israelites from Egypt. (Numb. xxxiii. 38, 39.) Aaron was the first high priest of the Jews; and was succeeded in the pontifical office and dignity by his son Eleazar. (Deut. x. 6.) For an account of Aaron's conduct in the affair of the golden calf, see p. 340. of this volume.

AB, the eleventh month of the civil year of the Jews, and the fifth month of their ecclesiastical year. For the festivals and fasts observed by the Jews in this month, see p. 179.

ABADDON (Heb.), or APOLLYON (Gr.), that is, the Destroyer : the name of the angel of the bottomless pit. (Rev. ix. 11.)

ABANA and PHARPAR, two rivers of Damascus, mentioned in 2 Kings v. 12. The valley of Damascus, which lay between Libanus and Anti-Libanus, was watered by five rivers, of which these were the two principal. Both descended from Mount Hermon. The Pharpar flowed by the walls of Damascus : the Abana flowed through the city and divided it into two parts. The latter is supposed to be the principal arm of the river Barada (the Chrysarroas of classical geographers), called Baneas ; and the Pharpar is, not improbably, the same river as is now called the Fidsheh.

ABARIM, mountains of, notice of, 52.

ABDON, one of the judges of Israel ; he succeeded Elon, and governed the Israelites eight years. He had forty sons and thirty grandsons, who rode on seventy asses. He was buried in Pirathon, in the land of Ephraim. (Judg. xii. 13—15.)

ABDON, the name of a Levitical city, situated in the canton allotted to the tribe of Asher, and given to the Levites of the family of Gershon.

ABEDNEGO, a Chaldee name given by the king of Babylon's officer to Azariah, one of Daniel's companions. He was thrown into a fiery furnace, with Shadrach and Meshach, for refusing to adore the statue erected by the command of Nebuchadnezzar; but both he and his companions were miraculously preserved. (Dan. iii.)

ABEL, the second son of Adam, and the first shepherd : he was murdered by his elder brother Cain, through envy ; because his sacrifice, offered in faith, was accepted by God, being (it is supposed) consumed by celestial fire, while the offering of Cain was rejected. (Gen. iv. 2—8. Heb. xi. 4.)

ABEL, the name of several cities in Palestine ; viz.

1. ABEL-BETH-MAACHAH, or ABEL-MAIN, a city in the northern part of the canton allotted to the tribe of Naphtali. Hither fled Sheba the son of Bichri, when pursued by the forces of king David ; and the inhabitants, in order that they might escape the horrors of a siege, cut off Sheba's head, which they threw over the wall to Joab. (2 Sam. xx. 14—22.) About eighty years after, it was taken and ravaged by Benhadad king of Syria. (1 Kings xv. 20.) About two hundred years after this event, it was captured

A B

and sacked by Tiglath-pileser, who carried the inhabitants captive into Assyria. (2 Kings xv. 29.) This place was subsequently rebuilt ; and, according to Josephus, became, under the name of ABILA, the capital of the district of Abilene.

2. ABEL-KERAMIM, the place or *plain of the vineyards* (Judg. xi. 33.), a village of the Ammonites, where they were discomfited by Jephthah. According to Eusebius, it abounded in his time with vineyards, and was six Roman miles from Rabbath Ammon.

3. ABEL-MEHOLAH was the native country of Elisha. (1 Kings xix. 16.) It could not be far from Scythopolis. (iv. 12.) Eusebius places it in the great plain, sixteen miles from Scythopolis, south. Not far from hence Gideon obtained a victory over the Midianites. (Judg. vii. 22.)

4. ABEL-MIZRAIM (the mourning of the Egyptians), was formerly called the floor of Atad. (Gen. l. 11.) Jerome, and some others after him, believe this to be the place afterwards called Bethagla, at some distance from Jericho and Jordan, west.

5. ABEL-SHITTIM was a town in the plains of Moab, beyond Jordan, opposite Jericho. According to Josephus, Abel-Shittim, or Abela, as he calls it, was sixty furlongs from Jordan. Eusebius says, it was in the neighbourhood of Mount Peor. Moses encamped at Abel-Shittim before the Hebrew army passed the Jordan, under Joshua. (Numb. xxxiii. 49. xxv. 1.) Here the Israelites fell into idolatry, and worshipped Baal-Peor, seduced by Balak ; and here God severely punished them by the hands of the Levites. (Numb. xxv. 1, 2, &c.) This city is often called Shittim only. (Antiq. lib. iv. cap. 7. and v. 1., and de Bello, lib. v. cap. 3.)

ABEZ, a town in the canton of the tribe of Issachar. (Josh. xix. 20.)

ABIAH. — 1. The second son of Samuel, who entrusted to him and his brother Joel the administration of justice, which they executed so ill, that the elders of Israel came to the prophet and demanded of him a king. (1 Sam. viii. 2—5.) — 2. A priest of the posterity of Aaron, and the founder of a sacerdotal family. When all the priests were divided into twenty-four classes, the eighth class was denominated from him the class of Abia. (1 Chron. xxiv. 10.) To this class belonged Zechariah, the father of John the Baptist. (Luke i. 5.)

ABIATHAR, the son of Ahimelech, the tenth high priest of the Jews. Escaping from the massacre of the priests at Nob, he joined the party of David, and continued in the pontificate until the reign of Solomon : by whom he was deprived of his office, for having embraced the faction of Adonijah.

ABIB, the name of the seventh month of the Jewish civil year, and the first of their ecclesiastical year. It was also called Nisan. For an account of the fasts or festivals occurring in this month, see p. 178.

ABIGAIL. — 1. The wife of Nabal, of Car-

AB

mel; by her prudence and address, she averted the wrath of David against her husband, who had churlishly refused him succours during his distress in consequence of the persecutions of Saul. On the death of Nabal, she became the wife of David. (1 Sam. xxv.)—2. The sister of David. (1 Chron. ii. 16, 17.)

ABIHU, the son of Aaron and Elisheba, who was consumed together with his brother Nadab, by a flash of fire sent from God, for offering incense with strange fire, instead of taking it from the altar of burnt-offering. (Lev. x. 1, 2.) This severity of punishment was necessary towards the first transgressors of the divine law, in order to deter others from the same offence, and to increase the reverential awe of the Divine Majesty. It would seem that Nadab and Abihu were betrayed into this act of presumption by intemperance at the feast, upon the feast-offerings: for immediately after, and in consequence of their fate, Moses prohibited the priests from drinking wine and strong drink, when they approached the sanctuary. (Mant and D'Oyly, on Lev. x.)

ABIJAH, the son of Jeroboam I. king of Israel, a young prince of promising hopes, who is supposed to have shown himself averse from his father's idolatry, and died early. (1 Kings xiv.)

ABIJAH, or ABIJAM, the son and successor of Rehoboam king of Judah. He reigned 33 years; a wicked prince, who imitated the impiety and misconduct of his father.

ABIJAH, the name of the wife of Ahaz, and the mother of Hezekiah king of Judah.

ABILA. See ABEL-BETH-MAACHAH.

ABILENE, region of, 15.

ABIMAEL, the name of a descendant of Joktan. (Gen. x. 28. 1 Chron. i. 22.) In these passages he and his brethren probably represent different Arabian tribes; though no name has yet been discovered in the Arabian writers which clearly corresponds to Abimael.

ABIMELECH, a common appellative of the Philistine kings, as Pharaoh was of the Egyptian monarchs. Two of this name are mentioned in the Scriptures, viz. 1. Abimelech king of Gerar, the contemporary of Abraham. Struck with the beauty of Sarah, he took her from the patriarch, who had passed her as his sister, but restored her in consequence of a divine command. (Gen. xx.) — 2. Abimelech II. supposed to be the son of the preceding, with whom Isaac entered into an alliance. (Gen. xxvi.)

ABIMELECH, the son of Gideon by a concubine. After his father's death he took possession of the government; procured himself to be acknowledged king; and afterwards put to death all his brethren, except Jotham, who escaped his fury. He was himself subsequently wounded at Thebez by a woman, who hurled a piece of a mill-stone upon his head; and, indignant at the idea of perishing by the hand of a woman, he commanded his

AB

armour-bearer to pierce him with his sword. (Judg. viii.)

ABINADAB. — 1. A Levite of Kirjath-jearim, who received the ark after it had been sent back by the Philistines. It continued in his house until David sent to conduct it thence to Jerusalem. (1 Sam. vii. 2. 2 Kings vi. 3, 4.) — 2. One of Saul's sons, who perished with him at the battle of Gilboa. — 3. The brother of David and the son of Jesse. (1 Chron. ii. 13.)

ABIRAM. — 1. One of those who conspired with Korah and Dathan against Moses, and who perished in the same manner. (Numb. xvi.) — 2. The eldest son of Hiel the Bethelite, who expired as his father was laying the foundation of Jericho, which he had undertaken to rebuild (1 Kings xvi. 34.), as Joshua more than 530 years before had prophetically announced would be the case. (Josh. vi.)

ABISHAG, the name of a beautiful virgin who was sent for to cherish David in his old age. Interpreters are not agreed whether she became the consort of David or was only his concubine. After David's death, she was demanded in marriage by Adonijah: but his request was rejected by Solomon; who, considering that, if it were granted, Adonijah would affect the regal power, caused him to be put to death. (1 Kings i. 3, 4. ii. 13—25.)

ABNER, the son of Ner, uncle to king Saul, and general of his forces. After the death of his sovereign, he preserved the crown for his son Ishbosheth: but, afterwards quarrelling with him, Abner joined David. He was, subsequently, slain by Joab, in revenge for the death of his brother Asahel, who was slain in open battle. David honoured Abner with public obsequies. (2 Sam. iii.)

ABRAHAM, the patriarch and founder of the Israelitish nation, celebrated in the Scriptures for his probity, and for his unshaken confidence in the promises of God. He was the son of Terah, and was born at Ur, a city of Chaldæa. Called by God out of his own country, by faith he went forth into an unknown country where he dwelt with his posterity, resting on the general promise of God for a better inheritance. Having married Sarah, he became the father of Isaac, whom by faith he offered on an altar, though in him he expected a completion of all the promises which God had made to him: but, as at first he had miraculously received a son, he concluded that God could with equal ease, after death, raise him again to life. (Heb. xi. 8—10. 17—19.) The patriarch's first name was Abram, which signifies *the father of elevation*, or *an elevated father;* but on a renewal of the divine covenant with him and of the promises made to him by God, it was changed to Abraham, the import of which is, the *father of a great multitude.* (Gen. xvii.) He died at the age of 175 years, and was interred, with Sarah his wife, in the field and cave at Machpelah. (xxv.)

A C

ABSALOM, the son of king David by Maachah. He rebelled against his father, and was slain by Joab, about 1020 years B. C. (2 Sam. xiii.—xviii.)

ABSTINENCE, vows of, 325.

ACADEMICAL DEGREES, conferred among the Jews, 476. note ².

ACCHO. See PTOLEMAIS.

ACELDAMA, a place without the south wall of Jerusalem, beyond the pool of Siloam. It was called the Potter's Field (Matt. xxvii. 7. 10.), because they dug thence the earth of which they made their pots : and the Fuller's Field, beeause they dried their cloth there; but being afterwards bought with that money by which the high priest and rulers of the Jews purchased the blood of the holy Jesus, it was, by the providence of God so ordering it, called Aceldama, that is, the field of blood. (Acts i. 19. Matt. xxvii. 7, 8.) The place, which in modern times has been shown to travellers as Aceldama, is described by Bishop Pococke as an oblong square cavern about twenty-six paces long, twenty broad, and apparently about twenty feet deep. It is inclosed on every side, either with the rock or by a wall, and covered over. There are six holes in the top, by which a person may look down into it; and through these holes the dead bodies are thrown in. Several sepulchral grottoes are to be seen in the vicinity of this spot.

ACHAIA, in the largest sense, comprehends Greece properly so called. It is bounded on the west by Epirus, on the east by the Ægean Sea, on the north by Macedonia, on the south by Peloponnesus. This seems to be the region intended when St. Paul, according to the Roman acceptation, mentions all the *regions of Achaia*, and directs his second Epistle to all the saints in Achaia. (2 Cor. xi. 10.) Thus, what is Achaia, in Acts xix. 21. is Hellas, that is, Greece. (Acts xx. 2.) Achaia strictly so called, is the northern region of Peloponnesus, bounded on the north by the Gulf of Corinth, on the south by Arcadia, on the east by Sicyonia, and on the west by the Ionian Sea. Of this region CORINTH was the capital.

ACHAN, the son of Charmi, of the tribe of Judah ; who, contrary to the express command of God, had appropriated some valuable articles out of the spoils of Jericho: for which he, together with all his family, was stoned, and all his effects were consumed with fire. (Josh. vii. 22.)

ACHISH, a king of Gath, in whose court David took refuge from Saul ; but, his life being endangered, he feigned madness before the king. When war broke out between Saul and the Philistines, David marched with his army: but the lords of the Philistines, being apprehensive lest he should turn against them in battle, desired Achish to dismiss him, which accordingly he did, with commendations for his fidelity. (1 Sam. xxi.—xxix.)

ACHMETHA. See ECBATANA.

ACHOR, a valley in the territory of Jericho,

A D

and in the canton of the tribe of Benjamin, where Achan was stoned. (Josh. vii. 24.)

ACHSAH, the daughter of Caleb, who promised her in marriage to him who should conquer Kirjathsepher from the Philistines. Othniel took the place and married Achsah. (Josh. xv. 16, 17.)

ACHZIB, a city belonging to the tribe of Asher (Josh. xix. 29.), who were unable to expel the old inhabitants from it. (Judg. i. 31.) It is now called Zib, and is situated on the sea-coast, to the north of Ptolemais. Another Achzib, in the territory of Judah, is mentioned in Josh. xiv. 44. and Micah i. 14.

ACKSHAPH, a city belonging to the tribe of Asher. The king of Ackshaph was conquered by Joshua. (xii. 20.) Some writers are of opinion, that Ackshaph is the same as Ecdippa, on the Mediterranean, between Tyre and Ptolemais ; others, that Ecdippa is described in Josh. xix. 20. under the name of Achzib. It is probable that Ackshaph and Achzib are but different names for the same town. Mr. Buckingham, who visited this place in January 1816, found it a small town situated on a hill near the sea, and having a few palm-trees rearing themselves above its dwellings.

ACQUITTAL, in criminal cases, forms of, 123.

ACTIONS, civil and criminal, how determined among the Jews, 120—125.

ADADA, a city in the southern part of the canton belonging to the tribe of Judah, not far from the boundaries of Idumæa or Edom. (Josh. xv. 27.)

ADAM, the first man, and the father of the human race, was created out of the dust of the earth, by God himself, who animated him with a reasonable soul, and formed him after his moral image, in righteousness and true holiness. Having transgressed the single command imposed on him by God, in token of his dependence upon Him as lord paramount of the creation, Adam forfeited the state of happiness in which he had been created, and entailed a curse on himself and his posterity, had not God made a promise of a future Saviour. (Gen. i. ii. iii.) He died, aged 930 years.

ADAMA, or ADMAH, one of the five cities destroyed by fire from heaven, on account of the profligate wickedness of their inhabitants, and afterwards overwhelmed by the waters of the Dead Sea. (Gen. xix. 24.) It was the most easterly of those which were swallowed up ; and there is some probability, either that it was not entirely sunk under the waters, or that the subsequent inhabitants of the country built a city of the same name on the eastern shore of the Dead Sea ; for Isaiah, according to the LXX, says, *God will destroy the Moabites, the city of Ar, and the remnant of* Adama. (Isa. xv. ult.) Αρω το σπερμα Μωαβ, και Αριηλ, και το καταλοιπον Αδαμα.

ADAR, the twelfth month of the ecclesias-

A D

tical Jewish year, and the sixth of the civil year. For a notice of the festivals, &c. during this month, see p. 177.

ADONI-BEZEK (the Lord of Bezek) was the first Canaanitish king conquered by the Israelites after the death of Joshua. He was taken to Jerusalem, where he died, after his toes and thumbs had been cut off, which he owned to be a just retribution of divine providence in retaliation of what he had himself inflicted upon others. (Judg. i. 7.)

ADONIJAH, the fourth son of king David by Haggith. He aspired to the kingdom before his father's death; but was disappointed of his hopes by the command of David, who ordered Solomon to be proclaimed king. He afterwards desired Abishag, the Shunemite, to wife; this request was not only rejected, but he was ordered to be put to death, as one guilty of treason. (1 Kings ii. 13—25.)

ADONI-ZEDEK (the Lord of Zedek) was king of Zedek, or Jerusalem, and one of the five Canaanitish kings shut up in the cave of Makkedah, whither they fled after their defeat by Joshua; by whose command they were taken out and put to death, and their bodies hung on five trees. (Josh. x.)

ADOPTION, ceremony of, and its effects, 420, 421.

ADORAIM, a town in the southern part of the tribe of Judah, which was fortified by Rehoboam. (2 Chron. xi. 9. 11.)

ADORAM, the chief treasurer of Rehoboam, who was sent by that prince, in the commencement of his reign, to the rebellious tribes, to endeavour to reduce them to their allegiance; and perished, the victim of an infuriated populace. (1 Kings xii. 13.) It is uncertain whether this Adoram was the same as Adoniram, who had filled the same office under Solomon. (1 Kings iv. 6.) He might be his son, and one of the young men who gave evil counsels to Rehoboam. However this may be, it was the height of imprudence to send him to the revolted tribes who had complained of the burden of taxes: and hence some expositors have imagined, that Rehoboam sacrificed his chief treasurer in the vain hope that his death would calm the effervescence of popular fury.

ADRAMMELECH, and SHAREZER, sons of Sennacherib, were probably the children of slaves who had no right to the Assyrian throne, and who assassinated their father on his return from his unsuccessful expedition against Hezekiah, at Nineveh, while worshipping in the temple of Nisroch his god: after which they fled into Armenia.

ADRAMMELECH, an idol (probably the sun), worshipped by the inhabitants of Sepharvaim, who caused their children to pass through the fire to it.

ADRAMYTTIUM, a maritime town of Mysia in Asia Minor, over against the island of Lesbos, situated at the foot of Mount Ida. (Acts xxvii. 1, 2.) It was a colony of the Athenians.

A G

ADRIA is mentioned in Acts xxvii. 27., where, it is to be observed, that when Saint Paul says, that they were tossed in Adria, he does not say in the Adriatic Gulf, which ends with the Illyrian Sea, but in the Adriatic Sea, which, according to Hesychius, is the same with the Ionian Sea; and therefore to the question, How Saint Paul's ship, which was near to Malta, and so, either in the Lybian or Sicilian Sea, could be in the Adriatic? It is well answered, That not only the Ionian, but even the Sicilian Sea, and part of that which washes Crete, was called the Adriatic. Thus, Ptolemy says, that Sicily was bounded on the east by the Adriatic; and that Crete was compassed on the west by the Adriatic Sea: and Strabo says, that the Ionian Gulf is a part of that which, in his time, was called the Adriatic Sea. (*Whitby.*)

ADRIEL, the son of Barzillai, married Merab, the daughter of Saul, (who had first been promised to David, 1 Sam. xviii. 19.) by whom he had five sons, who were given up to the Gibeonites, to be put to death in revenge of Saul's cruelty to them. In 2 Sam. xxi. 8. they are called the sons of Michal; she having adopted them, or else the name ot Michal is by mistake put for Merab.

ADULLAM, a city in the south part of the canton of the tribe of Judah towards the Dead Sea. (Josh. xv. 35.) The king of this place was killed by Joshua. (xii. 15.) In a cave (see p. 51.) in its vicinity David was concealed. (1 Sam. xxii. 1.) Rehoboam rebuilt and fortified this place. (2 Chron. xi. 7.) In the fourth century it was a considerable town, but it has long since been reduced to ruins.

ADULTERY, trial of a woman suspected of, 122, 123.

ADUMMIM, a rising ground at the entrance of the wilderness of Jericho is called the *going up to Adummim*, in Josh. xv. 7.: which name signifies *red* or *bloody*, probably from the sanguinary murders there committed. A town of this name belonged to the tribe of Benjamin.

ÆNON, or ENON, signifies the place or springs, where John baptized. (John iii. 23.) It is uncertain where it was situated, whether in Galilee, Judæa, or Samaria.

ÆRAS, or ERAS (Jewish), account of, 181, 182.

AGABUS, a prophet, who foretold a famine which took place in the land of Judæa, in the fourth year of the reign of Claudius, A. D. 44. (Acts xi. 28.) This famine is mentioned by Suetonius and other profane writers. Agabus also foretold the imprisonment of Paul by the Jews, and his being sent bound to the Gentiles; all which literally came to pass.

AGAG was probably a common appellative for the kings of the Amalekites. One, of this name, was conquered and taken prisoner; and, though condemned according to the law of the interdict, he was spared by Saul. He

A H

was put to death at Gilgal by order of Samuel. The fate of Agag has called forth the verbose pity of infidels; who, while they have affected to deplore his fate, have forgotten only one thing, viz. that he had been a cruel and sanguinary tyrant; and that Samuel reproached him for his cruelty before he commanded him to be put to death. (1 Sam. xv.)

AGED PERSONS, laws concerning, 195.

AGRICULTURE of the Jews, 451—458. Agricultural allusions, 462—464.

AGRIPPA (Herod), } 111.
AGRIPPA (Junior), } 111.

AGUR, a wise man to whom the thirtieth chapter of the book of Proverbs is ascribed, otherwise unknown. As the appellative *Agura*, in Syriac, signifies one who applies himself to the study of wisdom, Gesenius thinks it possible, that the name may be significant and allegorical.

AHAB, a king of Israel, who reigned 22 years, and surpassed all his predecessors in impiety. He was entirely under the influence of his idolatrous wife Jezebel. He died, B. C. 897, of the wounds, which he had received in battle with the Syrians, according to the prediction of Micaiah the son of Imlah. (1 Kings xvii.—xxi.)

AHAD, or ACHAD, a Syrian idol, notice of, 345.

AHASUERUS, or ARTAXERXES LONGIMANUS, a king of Persia, who married Esther. See Vol. IV. p. 66. note.

AHAVA, a river of Babylonia, or of Assyria, where Ezra assembled those captives whom he afterwards brought into Judæa. (Ezra viii. 15.) It is supposed to be that which ran along the region of Adiabene, where a river Diava, or Adiava, is mentioned, on which Ptolemy places the city Abane or Aavane. This is probably the country called Ava (2 Kings xvii. 24. xviii. 34. xix. 13.), whence the kings of Assyria translated the people called Avites into Palestine; and where, likewise, in their room, they settled some of the captive Israelites. Ezra intending to collect as many Israelites as he could, to return with him to Judæa, halted in the country of Ava, or Ahava, whence he sent agents into the Caspian mountains, to invite such Jews as were willing to join him. (Ezra viii. 17.)

AHAZ, king of Judah, son of Jotham, who died, B.C. 726; for his iniquities he was denied a place in the sepulchres of the kings his predecessors. (2 Chron. xxviii.)

AHAZIAH, the son and successor of Ahab, king of Israel: he was as distinguished for his horrid impiety as his father was. He reigned only one year after his father's death. (1 Kings xxii. 52.)

AHAZIAH, king of Judah, the son and successor of Jehoram, by Athaliah; he reigned one year, and received his mortal wound by command of Jehu, and died at Megiddo. (2 Kings viii. 2 Chron. xxiii.)

AHIJAH, a prophet in the reign of Jero-

A J

boam I., who dwelt at Shiloh, and foretold the death of his son Abijah.

AHIMELECH, a priest of Nob, to whom David went, and whom Saul commanded to be put to death with other priests for assisting him. — Also a priest, in the reign of David, the son of Abiathar; who is likewise called Abimelech.

AHITHOPHEL, an eminent counsellor in the reign of David, so distinguished for his prudence and wisdom, that his advice equally obtained the confidence of the people and the monarch. He joined the conspiracy of the rebel Absalom against David: but, finding his profligate but crafty counsel disregarded, he went to his house at Gillo, hanged himself, and was buried in the sepulchre of his fathers. It has been asked, What motive could induce a privy counsellor of David, who was held in such high consideration, to enter into Absalom's conspiracy? The pride of overturning a throne, of which he was the support, and the hope of reigning himself under the name of Absalom, will, perhaps, account for the conspiracy, but not for the incest which he advised Absalom to commit. Ahithophel was the father of Eliam the father of Bathsheba (2 Sam. xxxiii. 34. xi. 3. 1 Chron. iii. 5.): and there is every reason to think, that he wished to revenge his granddaughter; particularly when we consider the infamous advice which he gave, his eagerness for pursuing David, and the desire he expressed to smite the king himself. (2 Sam. xvi. 21. xvii. 1, 2.) His suicide was as deliberate as his hatred: he was one of those men who are as useful friends as they are dangerous enemies, equally able in good and evil, who employ their talents in the service of their passions, do nothing by halves, and are models of guilt or of virtue.

AHOLAH and AHOLIBAH, two fictitious names, employed by the prophet Ezekiel (xxiii. 4.) to denote the two kingdoms of Judah and Samaria. Aholah and Aholibah are represented as two sisters of Egyptian extraction; the former standing for Jerusalem, the latter for Samaria. Both prostituted themselves to the Egyptians and Assyrians, in imitating their abominations and idolatries; for which reason the LORD abandoned them to those very people, for whom they had evinced so improper an attachment, being carried into captivity, and reduced to the severest servitude by them.

AI, or HAI, a city of antient Canaan, near Bethel, which was taken by military stratagem, by the Israelites under Joshua. (Josh. vii.) After the return of the Jews from Babylon, the Benjamites (to whom it belonged) resumed possession of this place. (Neh. xi. 21.)

AILATH. See ELATH, infra.

AJALON, a city in the canton of the tribe of Dan, assigned to the Levites of Kohath's family. It was situated between Timnath and Beth-Shemesh, and is probably the city alluded to in Josh. x. 12. There were three

A L

other cities of this name; one in the canton of Benjamin, another in that of Ephraim, not far from Schechem; and the third in the canton of Zebulun; the situation of which is not known.

AJALON, valley of, notice of, 53.

ALEXANDER. — 1. A man whose father Simon was compelled to bear the cross of Jesus Christ. (Mark xv. 21.) — 2. Another, who had been high priest, and who was present at the interrogation of the apostles Peter and John, concerning the healing of the man who had been lame from his birth. (Acts iv. 6.) Some have imagined, that he was the brother of Philo, the celebrated Jewish writer, who flourished in the reign of Caligula. — 3. A Jew of Ephesus. At the time of the sedition raised in that city by Demetrius against Paul, the populace in their blind fury seem to have confounded the Christians with the Jews: and the latter, being desirous that the mob should direct their vengeance against the believers in Jesus Christ, commissioned Alexander to harangue the Ephesians and to plead their cause, but in vain. The Ephesians, as soon as they knew that he was a Jew, refused to listen to him. Beza and Bolten have conjectured that this was the Alexander δ χαλκευς (the worker in metals, or smith,) who did the apostle "much evil." (1 Tim. iv. 14.) As every male Jew was obliged to learn some trade, this is not improbable. Coquerel, however, thinks that he was one of those venal orators, whose eloquence was always at the command of any that would employ them. — 4. A brazier or smith, *who made shipwreck concerning the faith* (1 Tim. i. 19, 20.), and whom Saint Paul *delivered unto Satan;* that is, expelled him from the communion of the Christian church, to be no longer considered as a Christian, but as a subject of Satan's kingdom.

ALEXANDRIA, a celebrated city of Egypt, built by Alexander the Great, A. M. 3673, B. C. 331, and situated between the Mediterranean Sea and the Lake Moeris. Alexandria at present exhibits no vestiges of its former magnificence, except the ruins that surround it, and which are of very remote antiquity. Under the Arabian dynasty, its splendour gradually declined with its commerce. From the neglect of the canals, which antiently diffused fertility through the surrounding country, and the encroachments of the sand, the city is now insulated in a desert, and exhibits no vestiges of those delightful gardens and cultivated fields, which subsisted even to the time of the Arabian conquest. The commerce of antient Alexandria was very extensive, especially in corn (Egypt being considered the granary of Rome), which was exported in vessels of considerable burden; so that the centurion could easily meet with a *ship of Alexandria*, laden with corn, *sailing into Italy.* (Acts xxvii. 6.) Alexandria was the native place of Apollos. (Acts xviii. 24.)

ALPHÆUS, the father of James the Less

A M

(Matt. x. 3. Mark iii. 18. Luke vi. 15. Acts i. 13.), and the husband of Mary, the sister of the mother of Jesus. He is the same person who is called Cleophas in John xix. 25.; but not the same who in Mark ii. 14. is said to be the father of Levi or Matthew.

ALMODAD, a people or tribe in Yemen, who sprang from Joktan. (Gen. x. 26.)

AMAD, a city belonging to the tribe of Asher. (Josh. xxix. 26.)

AMALEK, the son of Eliphaz by Timnah his concubine, and grandson of Esau. (Gen. xxxvi. 12.) He was the father of the

AMALEKITES, the first and most powerful of the nations in the vicinity of Canaan. They dwelt in Arabia Petræa, living like the present Arabs in hamlets, caves, or tents. They were always the enemies of the Israelites, whom they attacked in the desert, but were repulsed. Afterwards they joined with the Midianites and Moabites in a design to oppress the Israelites; who were delivered by Ehud from Eglon king of the Moabites (Judg. iii.), and by Gideon from the Midianites and Amalekites. (viii.) Balaam predicted that they should *perish for ever.* (Numb. xxiv. 29.) In fact, perpetual wars against their neighbours, and especially the Jews, insensibly ruined them. Saul made a terrible slaughter of them, and was not permitted to save Agag their king, who was hewn in pieces by the prophet Samuel: David exterminated those who had escaped the former massacre. After this terrible execution, we meet no more with the name of Amalek but in the history of Esther; in whose time Haman, an Amalekite, to revenge an affront he imagined himself to have received from the Jew Mordecai, conceived the design of causing to be cut off, in a single night, not only all the Jews dispersed in the states of Ahasuerus king of Babylon, but even those who had been left in Judæa to mourn over the ruins of their country. This dreadful design recoiled on Haman, who was exterminated with all his family; and the Jews received permission to pursue and put to death their enemies wherever they could find them. They made a great slaughter of them; and since this event, nothing more has been certainly known concerning the Amalekites.

AMAM, a city in the southern part of the tribe of Judah. (Josh. xv. 26.)

AMANA, a mountain mentioned in Sol. Song iv. 8. which, some have imagined, was in Cilicia, whither the government of Solomon extended: but it was, most probably, a part of Mount Libanus, as Shenir and Hermon, which are mentioned in the same passage, were parts of the same mountainous range.

AMASA, a nephew of David, whom Absalom appointed general of his army. (2 Sam. xvii. 25.) After the defeat of that prince, David pardoned Amasa and offered him the command in chief of his forces in the room of Joab, by whom he was treacherously murdered. (2 Sam. xx.)

AMAZIAH, the eighth king of Judah, who

A M

succeeded Joash B. C. 839. The commencement of his reign was auspicious; but, after he had subdued the Edomites (2 Kings xiv.), he carried off their idol gods and acknowledged them for his own, by adoration and offering incense. He then proclaimed war against Joash king of Israel, who defeated his forces and took him prisoner. He reigned ingloriously fifteen years after this event; and at length, hated by his subjects, and abandoned by the Almighty, he was assassinated by conspirators at Lachish, whither he had fled.

AMMON. See NO-AMMON, infra.

AMMONITES, a people descended from Ammon, son of Lot; called sometimes Ammanites. They destroyed the giants Zamzummim, and seized their country. (Deut. ii. 19, 20, 21.) God forbad Moses and Israel from attacking the Ammonites, because he did not intend to give their land to the Hebrews. Nevertheless, as, previously to the Israelites entering Canaan, the Amorites had conquered great part of the countries belonging to the Ammonites and Moabites, Moses retook this from the Amorites, and divided it between the tribes of Gad and Reuben. Long after this, in the time of Jephthah (Judg. xi. 13.), the Ammonites declared war against Israel, pretending that Israel detained the country which had been theirs before the Amorites possessed it. Jephthah replied, that this territory being acquired by Israel in a just war, from the Amorites, who had long enjoyed it by right of conquest, he was under no obligation to restore it. The Ammonites being dissatisfied with this reply, Jephthah gave them battle, and defeated them.

The Ammonites and Moabites generally united in attacking Israel. After the death of Othniel, the Ammonites and Amalekites joined with Eglon, king of Moab, to oppress them. Some years after, about A. M. 2799, the Ammonites greatly oppressed the Israelites beyond Jordan; but, in 2817, God raised up Jephthah to deliver them. In the beginning of Saul's reign, A. M. 2909, B. C. 1195, Nahash, king of the Ammonites, having attacked Jabesh-Gilead, reduced it to a capitulation. (1 Sam. xi. 1.) Nahash offered no other conditions, than their submitting to have every man his right eye plucked out, as a reproach upon Israel; but Saul coming seasonably to the succour of Jabesh, delivered the city and people from the intended barbarity of Nahash. David, having been a friend of the king of Ammon, after his death sent compliments of condolence to Hanun his son and successor; who, regarding these ambassadors as spies, treated them in a very affronting manner. David avenged the affront, subdued the Ammonites, the Moabites, and the Syrians, their allies. Ammon and Moab continued under the government of David and Solomon, and after the separation of the ten tribes, were subject to the kings of Israel till the death of Ahab. (2 Kings i. 1. A. M. 3107, B. C. 897.) Jehoram, son of Ahab, and successor of Ahaziah, defeated the Moab-

A M

ites, A. M. 3109. (2 Kings iii. 4, 5, 6, &c.) But it does not appear that this victory reduced them to his obedience. At the same time, the Ammonites, Moabites, and other people, made an irruption into Judah, but were repulsed and routed by Jehoshaphat. (2 Chron. xx. 1, 2. et seq.)

The prophet Isaiah (xv. xvi.) threatens the Moabites with a misfortune which was to happen three years after his prediction; this probably had reference to the war of Shalmaneser against them, about A. M. 3277, B.C. 727. — After the tribes of Reuben, Gad, and the half-tribe of Manasseh were carried captive by Tiglath-pileser, A. M. 3264, B. C. 740, the Ammonites and Moabites took possession of the cities belonging to these tribes, for which Jeremiah reproaches them. (Jer. xlix. 1.) The ambassadors of the Ammonites were some of those to whom that prophet presented the cup of the Lord's fury, and whom he directed to make bonds and yokes for themselves, exhorting them to submit to Nebuchadnezzar; and threatening them if they did not, with captivity and slavery. (Jer. xxvii. 2, 3, 4.) The prophet Ezekiel (xxv. 4. 10.) denounces their entire destruction, and tells them, that God would give them up to the people of the East, who should set their palaces in their country, so that the Ammonites should be no more mentioned among nations; and this as a punishment for insulting the Israelites on their calamities, and the destruction of their temple by the Chaldæans. These calamities happened to them in the fifth year after the taking of Jerusalem, when Nebuchadnezzar made war against all the people around Judæa, A. M. 3420 or 3421, B. C. 583.

It is probable that Cyrus gave to the Ammonites and Moabites the liberty of returning into their own country, whence they had been removed by Nebuchadnezzar; for we see them, in the lands of their former settlement, exposed to those revolutions which included the people of Syria and Palestine; and subject sometimes to the kings of Egypt, and sometimes to the kings of Syria. Antiochus the Great took Rabboth or Philadelphia, their capital, demolished the walls, and put a garrison into it, A. M. 3806. During the persecutions of Antiochus Epiphanes, the Ammonites manifested their hatred to the Jews, and exercised great cruelties against those who dwelt near them. (1 Macc. v. 6—45.) Justin Martyr says (Dialog. cum Tryphone, p. 272.), that in his time — the second century — there were still many Ammonites remaining; but Origen (Comm. on Job) assures us, that in his days, they were only known under the general name of Arabians. Thus was the prediction of Ezekiel accomplished. See a minute account of the fulfilment of prophecies concerning the Ammonites and their country, in Mr. Keith's Evidence of the Christian Religion from Prophecy, pp. 152—160. — Notice of the idols worshipped by the Ammonites, p. 344. of this volume.

AN

AMNON, the son of David and Ahinoam. Having conceived a criminal passion for his sister Tamar, he violated her: and two years after, when he was intoxicated at a feast made by Absalom the uterine brother of Tamar, the servants of the latter assassinated him. (2 Sam. xiii.)

AMON, the fourteenth king of Judah, succeeded Manasseh,whose impieties he imitated: he was assassinated by his own servants after a reign of two years, and in the 24th year of his age, B. C. 640.

AMORITES, a people descended from Amori or Amorrhæus, the fourth son of Canaan. They first peopled the mountains west of the Dead Sea. They likewise had establishments east of that sea, between the brooks Jabbok and Arnon, whence they forced the Ammonites and Moabites. (Josh. v. 1. Numb. xiii. 29. xxi. 29.) Moses wrested this country from their kings, Sihon and Og. A. M. 2553, B. C. 1451. The prophet Amos (ii. 9.) speaks of their gigantic stature and valour. He compares their height to the cedar; their strength to the oak. The name Amorite, is often taken in Scripture for Canaanites in general. The lands which the Amorites possessed on this side Jordan, were given to the tribe of Judah; and those which they had possessed beyond the Jordan, to the tribes of Reuben and Gad.

AMOS, or AMOZ. — 1. The father of the prophet Isaiah; who, according to antient traditions, was the son of Joash and the brother of Amaziah king of Judah. —2. The third of the Minor Prophets, for an account of whom, and an analysis of his predictions, see Vol. IV. pp. 157—159.

AMPHIPOLIS, a city between Macedon and Thrace, but dependent on Macedon, mentioned in Acts xvii. 1. Paul and Silas, being delivered out of prison, left Philippi, went to Thessalonica, and passed through Amphipolis. This city had the name likewise of Chrysopolis.

AMRAPHEL, king of Shinar, an ally of Chedorlaomer, plundered the Pentapolis and took Lot prisoner, who was rescued by Abraham and his associates. (Gen. xiv.)

AMUSEMENTS of the Jews, 488, 489.

ANAB, a city in the mountainous parts of the canton, belonging to the tribe of Judah. (Judg. xv. 50.)

ANAKIM, the descendants of Anak, a gigantic tribe who dwelt in the land of Canaan; in comparison of whom the unbelieving Hebrew spies, that were sent to explore the country, reported that they were but as grasshoppers. (Numb. xiii. 33.) Their capital, Kirjath-Arba or Hebron, was taken, and they were destroyed by Caleb, with the assistance of the tribe of Judah. (Josh xv. 14. Judg. i. 20.)

ANAMMELECH, one of the deities in honour of whom the Sepharvaites caused their children to pass through the fire. It is supposed to have signified the moon.

ANANIAH, a city of Palestine, where the Benjamites dwelt after the captivity. (Neh. xi. 32.)

ANANIAS, the name of several persons mentioned in the Scriptures, of whom the following were the most remarkable : —

1. The son of Nebedæus, who was high priest, A. D. 47. He was sent as a prisoner to Rome by Quadratus, governor of Syria, and Jonathan was appointed in his place; but being discharged by Claudius, in consequence of the protection of Agrippa, he returned to Jerusalem; where, as Jonathan had been murdered through the treachery of Felix the successor of Quadratus, Ananias appears to have performed the functions of the high priest, as sagan or substitute, until Ismael the son of Phabæus was appointed to that office by Agrippa. (Compare Vol. I. pp. 94, 95.) Before this Ananias St. Paul was brought; and the apostle's prediction that God *would smite him* (Acts xxiii. 3.) was subsequently accomplished, when he was murdered in the royal palace by a body of mutineers, at the head of whom was his own son.

2. A Jew of Jerusalem, the husband of Sapphira, who attempted to join the Christians, but died instantly on being convicted of falsehood by Peter. (Acts v. 1. 3. 5.)

3. A Christian of Damascus, who restored the sight of Paul, after his vision. (Acts ix. 10—17. xxii. 12.)

ANATHOTH, a city in the tribe of Benjamin, memorable as being the birth-place of the prophet Jeremiah. (Josh. xxi. 18. Jer. i. 1.) According to Eusebius and Jerome, it was situated about three miles to the north of Jerusalem, though Josephus states it to be twenty furlongs. This city, which was assigned as a residence to the Levites of the family of Kohath, and also as one of the cities of refuge, has long since been destroyed.

ANDREW, one of the twelve apostles. He was a native of Bethsaida in Galilee, and was at first a follower of John the Baptist, but afterwards became a disciple of Jesus Christ. According to ecclesiastical tradition, after the ascension of Jesus Christ, he preached the Gospel to the Scythians, and was crucified at Patræ in Achaia. Epiphanius mentions the *Acts of Andrew*, a spurious book, which was used by the Encratites, Apostolics, and Origenians.

ANDRONICUS, a Jewish Christian, a kinsman and fellow-prisoner of St. Paul, who says that he was *of note* or *in reputation* among the apostles; by which expression we are not to understand that he was one of the number of apostles, but that he was one of those early converts who were highly esteemed by the apostles, before the dispersion occasioned by the death of Stephen.

ANER, one of the levitical cities, situated in the canton of the tribe of Manasseh. (1 Chron. xvi. 70.) Also the brother of Mamre, a confederate of the patriarch Abraham.

AN

ANIM, a city in the mountainous parts of the canton of Judah. (Josh. xv. 50.)

ANIMALS, reared by the Jews, 448—450. Certain animals, why prohibited to be eaten by them, 438—440.

ANNA, a prophetess, the daughter of Phanuel, of the tribe of Asher. This pious widow constantly attended the morning and evening service at the temple; and, at the advanced age of eighty-four years, when the venerable Simeon was uttering his hymn of thanksgiving at the presentation of Christ in the temple, she coming into the temple began to praise God and to speak of the Messiah to all those who were waiting for the redemption of Israel. (Luke ii. 36—38.)

ANNAS, or, according to Josephus, Ananus, was a high priest of the Jews. He obtained the pontificate under Quirinus, proconsul of Syria, but was deprived of it, during the reign of Tiberius, by Valerius Gratus, governor of Judæa. The dignity was transferred, first to Ismael the son of Phabæus, and shortly after to Eleazar. He held the office one year, and was then succeeded by Simon; who, after another year, was followed by Joseph or Caiaphas, the son-in-law of Annas, A. D. 26. As Caiaphas continued in office until A. D. 35, Annas appears to have acted as his substitute or sagan, and enjoyed great influence jointly with him. (Luke iii. 2. John xviii. 13. 24. Acts iv. 6.)

ANNUAL Festivals, important design of, 303, 304.

ANTILIBANUS (Mount), account of, 48, 49. ANTIOCH.

1. *Antioch, the metropolis of Syria,* formerly called RIBLAH, was erected, according to some writers, by Antiochus Epiphanes; according to others, by Seleucus Nicanor, the first king of Syria after Alexander the Great, in memory of his father Antiochus, and was the royal seat of the kings of Syria, or the place where their palace was. For power and dignity it was little inferior to Seleucia or Alexandria; and the inhabitants were celebrated for their luxury, effeminacy and licentiousness. Josephus says, that it was the third great city of all that belonged to the Roman provinces; it was called *Antiochia apud Daphnem,* or Antioch near Daphne, *i. e.* the village where her temple was, to distinguish it from fourteen other cities of the same name. It was celebrated among the Jews, for the *jus civitatis,* which Seleucus Nicanor had given to them in that city, with the Grecians and Macedonians; and for the wars of the Maccabæans with those kings. Among Christians it is memorable for being the place where they first received that name by divine appointment, (Acts xi. 26.) and where both St. Luke and Theophilus were born and inhabited. Modern Antioch and its vicinity were completely destroyed by a tremendous earthquake in the autumnal months of the year 1822. The modern Arabic name of this place is *Antakia.*

2. *Antioch of Pisidia,* a city mentioned

AN

in Acts xiii. 14., was properly situated in Phygia, and is described by the Greek geographer, Strabo, as " near Pisidia." Hitherto, on the authority of D'Anville and other subsequent geographers, this Antioch has been considered to occupy the site of the modern town of Aksher, (the antient Philomelium) but the Rev. F. V. J. Arundell, by whom it was discovered in November 1833, after it had been long lost to the traveller, has proved that it was at Yalobatz, a place several miles to the south of Aksher. The site and present state of this once celebrated city are minutely described by Mr. A. The remains of a splendid aqueduct, twenty-one arches of which are perfect, of massive walls, of a theatre, acropolis, and of a temple of Bacchus, together with the ruins of two if not more extensive Christian churches, attest the antient magnificence of Antioch. (Discoveries, vol. i. pp. 267—312.) Here Paul and Barnabas preached; but the Jews, who were angry at seeing that some of the Gentiles received the Gospel, raised a sedition against Paul and Barnabas, and obliged them to leave the city.

ANTIOCHUS, a common name of the kings of Syria, after the time of Alexander the Great; the actions of many of whom are foretold by the prophets, and related in the books of the Maccabees.

1. ANTIOCHUS SOTER, or Saviour, son of Seleucus Nicanor, began to reign B. C. 276. He conferred many immunities upon the Jews of Asia. He was succeeded by his son,

2. ANTIOCHUS THEOS, or the God, B. C. 257; whose marriage with the daughter of Ptolemy Philadelphus, king of Egypt, is foretold by Daniel. (xi. 6.)

3. ANTIOCHUS THE GREAT, son of Seleucus Callinicus, began to reign B. C. 219. In consequence of the Jews submitting to him, he permitted them throughout his dominions to live according to their own laws.

4. ANTIOCHUS EPIPHANES, or the Illustrious, son of Antiochus the Great, was one of the most sanguinary persecutors of the Jewish nation that ever lived. He is the subject of Daniel's predictions. (Dan. xi. 21—29.) Though his Syrian flatterers gave him the appellation of *Epiphanes,* the epithet of *vile,* or despicable, given him by the prophet (ver. 21.), agrees better with his true character; for he disgraced himself by such profligate conduct that the historian Polybius, his contemporary, and others after him, instead of Epiphanes, more correctly called him *Epimanes,* or the madman. This Antiochus designed nothing less than the utter extirpation of Judaism: he commanded the statue of Jupiter Olympius to be placed upon the altar of the temple at Jerusalem, and a sow to be offered in sacrifice. These profanations, and his other oppressions, aroused the family of the Maccabees, who bravely resisted the forces of Antiochus: who, filled with indignation, was hastening into Judæa, to make Jerusalem (as he menaced) a grave for all

A P

the Jews; but divine vengeance pursued him; and Antiochus, falling from his chariot, bruised his limbs, and died in the most excruciating tortures, B. C. 160. He was succeeded by his son.

5. ANTIOCHUS EUPATOR, who reigned only two years.

6. ANTIOCHUS THEOS, son of Alexander Balas, was treacherously put to death by Tryphon his minister, B. C. 139.

7. ANTIOCHUS PIUS, SOTER, or SIDETES, (that is, the fisher or hunter,) reigned ten years, B. C. 137 to 127; in which last year he was put to death by the Parthians.

ANTIPAS, a *faithful martyr*, mentioned in Rev. ii. 13, is *said* to have been put to death in a tumult at Pergamos by the priests of Æsculapius, who had a celebrated temple in that city.

ANTIPAS (Herod). Biographical notice of, 110.

ANTIPATRIS, a small town which was situated in the road from Jerusalem to Cæsarea, in the beautiful and fertile plain of Sharon. It was formerly called Capharsalma: but being rebuilt and beautified by Herod the Great, it was by him named Antipatris, in honour of his father Antipater. Hither St. Paul was brought after his apprehension at Jerusalem. (Acts xxiii. 31.)

ANTONIA (Tower of,) 23.

APHARSITES, and APHARSACHTHITES, were two tribes or nations in subjection to the king of Assyria, by whom colonies of them were sent to inhabit the country of Samaria in place of the Israelites, who had been removed beyond the river Euphrates. They greatly opposed the building of Jerusalem. (Ezra v. 6. iv. 9.) Some have supposed the Apharsites to be the Parrhasii in the east of Media; others, the Persians; and the Apharsachthites have been compared with Parasitaceni, Parœtaceni, a people of Media.

APHEK. — There are several cities of this name mentioned in Scripture, as,

1. APHEK, in the tribe of Judah. Here the Philistines encamped, when the ark was brought from Shiloh, which was taken in battle by the Philistines. (1 Sam. iv.) Probably this is the Aphekah, mentioned in Josh. xv. 53.

2. APHEK, in the valley of Jezreel. Here the Philistines encamped, while Saul and his army lay near Jezreel, on the mountains of Gilboa. (1 Sam. xxix. 1, &c.)

3. APHEK, a city belonging to the tribe of Asher, near the country of the Sidonians. (Josh. xix. 30. xiii. 4.) Perhaps this was the

4. APHEK, a city of Syria, one of the principal in Ben-Hadad's kingdom, in the vicinity of which the battle was fought between Ahab and Ben-Hadad, when the Syrians were beaten (1 Kings xx. 26, &c.), and as they retreated with precipitation into the city, the city wall fell upon them, and crushed 27,000. Probably in this city Aphek, or Aphaca, situated in Libanus, on the river

A Q

Adonis, stood the famous temple of Venus, the Aphacite. This city lay between Heliopolis and Biblos.

APOLLONIA, a city of Macedonia Prima, situated between Amphipolis and Thessalonica, about a day's journey from the former place. St. Paul passed through this city on his way to Thessalonica. (Acts xvii. 1.)

APOLLOS, a Jewish Christian, born at Alexandria, and distinguished for his eloquence and success in propagating the Gospel. His history and character are given in Acts xviii. 24—28. xix. 1. He preached at Corinth with such eloquence, that the Corinthians, divided in their affections, boasted that they were the disciples of Paul, or of Cephas, or of Apollos. From these vain disputes St. Paul, certain of the humility of his friend, took occasion to write those admirable passages, in which he requires the Corinthian Christians to forget both Paul and Apollos, and to refer every thing to Christ. (1 Cor. i. 12. iii. 4. iv. 6.) It is uncertain whether the apostle alludes in 2 Cor. iii. 1. to the letters of recommendation which Apollos took with him on his departure from Ephesus for Corinth: but it is clear, that the success of the latter in Achaia, and the admiration felt by the Corinthians for his eloquence, excited no envious emotions in the mind of St. Paul, since he earnestly pressed him to return to Corinth (1 Cor. xvi. 12.), and subsequently recommended him in a very particular manner to the friendly attentions of Titus. (Tit. iii. 13.)

APPAREL, royal, notice of, 89.

APPEALS, to superior Jewish tribunals, 118. To the imperial tribunal, 131.

APPHIA, a Christian woman, whom the antient fathers supposed to be the wife of Philemon: a conjecture which is rendered not 'improbable by the circumstance that in the inscription of his epistle to Philemon in favour of Onesimus, St. Paul mentions Apphia before Archippus. (Philem. 2.)

APPII FORUM, a small town on the celebrated Appian Way, constructed by the Roman censor Appius Claudius, and which led from Rome to Capua, and thence to Brundusium. St. Paul passed through this place on his first journey to Rome; whence, according to Antoninus's Itinerary, it was distant 43 Roman miles, or about 40 English miles.

APPLE-TREES, of Palestine, notice of, 68.

AQUILA, a native of Pontus, in Asia Minor, was a Jew by birth, and a tent maker by occupation; who, with his wife Priscilla, was converted by St. Paul to the Christian faith. When the Jews were banished from Rome by the emperor Claudius (the Christian and Jewish religions being confounded by the Romans), Aquila and his wife retired to Corinth, and afterwards became the companions of St. Paul in his labours, by whom they are mentioned with much commendation. (Acts xviii. 2. 18. 26. Rom. xvi. 3. 1 Cor. xvi. 19. 2 Tim. iv. 19.) The most

N N 2

A R

cordial friendship appears to have subsisted between them : Aquila and Priscilla had even saved Paul's life at the risk of their own; which instance of devotedness to the apostle has been referred to the accusation preferred against the apostle before Gallio at Corinth, or to the tumult excited by Demetrius at Ephesus. (Acts xviii. 12. xix. 24.)

AR or ARIEL OF MOAB. See RABBATH-MOAB.

ARABIA, the name of a large region, including the peninsula, which lies between Syria, Palestine, the Arabian and Persian Gulfs, and the Indian Ocean or Sea of Arabia. Its inhabitants are supposed to be principally descended from Ishmael, and in the earlier books of Scripture are termed בני קדם (BENI KEDEM) or children of the east (Judg. vi. 3. 1 Kings v. 10. Isa. xi. 14. Jer. xlix. 28.); and in the later books ערבים (ARABIM), or Arabians. (2 Chron. xxii. 1. Neh. ii. 19.) The Greek geographers divided this country into three parts, Arabia Ευδαιμων or Felix, Πετρωδης or Petræa, and Σκηνιτις or Ερημος, Deserta : but these divisions were not antiently known to the inhabitants of the East, nor are they recognised in any part of the Old or New Testament.

1. ARABIA FELIX lies between the ocean on the south-east, and the Arabian and Persian gulfs. It is a fertile region, especially in the interior, producing various species of odoriferous shrubs and fragrant gums, as francincense, myrrh, cassia, &c. The queen of Sheba is supposed to have reigned over part of this region.

2. ARABIA PETRÆA received its name from the city Petra : it lies on the south and south-east of Palestine, extending to Egypt, and including the peninsula of Mount Sinai. It is remarkable for its mountains and sandy plains.

3. ARABIA DESERTA lies between the other two, and extends northward along the confines of Palestine, Syria, Babylonia, and Mesopotamia ; including the vast deserts which lie between these limits, and which are inhabited only by wandering tribes of savage Arabs. For a description of the horrors of a journey across the great desert of Arabia, see pp. 60—62.

The Scriptures frequently mention the Arabians (meaning those adjoining Judæa) as a powerful people, who valued themselves on their wisdom. Their riches consisted principally in flocks and cattle ; they paid king Jehoshaphat an annual tribute of 7700 sheep, and as many goats. (2 Chron. xvii. 11.) The kings of Arabia furnished Solomon with a great quantity of gold and silver. (2 Chron. ix. 14.) They loved war, but made it rather like thieves and plunderers, than like soldiers. They lived at liberty in the field, or the desert, concerned themselves little about cultivating the earth, and were not very obedient to established governments. This is the idea which the Scripture gives of

them (Isa. xiii. 20.), and the same is their character at this day. Since the promulgation of the Gospel, many Arabians have embraced Christianity; though by far the greater part continue to profess the faith of Mohammed.

ARAD, a Canaanitish royal city in the southern part of Palestine. Its king having opposed the passage of the Israelites, they afterwards took it with its dependencies. (Numb. xxi. 1—3.) In later times, Arad was rebuilt; and is placed by Eusebius in the vicinity of the desert of Kades, at the distance of 20 Roman miles from Hebron.

ARAM, fifth son of Shem, was father of the people of Syria, who, from him, are called Aramæans. The region, which in the Old Testament is denominated ARAM, is a vast tract extending from Mount Taurus south as far as Damascus, and from the Mediterranean Sea in an eastern direction beyond the Tigris into Assyria. Different parts of this region are called by different names ; as — *Aram Naharaïm,* or Syria of the Two Rivers, that is, *Mesopotamia ; Aram of Damascus ; Aram of Soba ; Aram Bethrehob ;* and *Aram of Maacha ;* because the cities of Damascus, Soba, Bethrehob, and Maacha, were in Syria ; or at least, because Syria contained the provinces of Soba, Maacha, Rehob, &c. Homer and Hesiod call Aramæans those whom the more modern Greeks call Syrians. The prophet Amos (ix. 7.) seems to say, that the first Aramæans dwelt in the country of Kir, in Iberia, where the river Cyrus runs; and that God brought them from thence, as he did the Hebrews out of Egypt; but at what time this happened is not known. Moses always calls the Syrians, and inhabitants of Mesopotamia, Aramites. The Aramæans often warred against the Hebrews ; David subdued them, and obliged them to pay him tribute. Solomon preserved the same authority; but, after the separation of the ten tribes, it does not appear that the Syrians were generally subject to the kings of Israel; unless, perhaps, under Jeroboam II., who restored the kingdom of Israel to its antient boundaries. (2 Kings xiv. 25.)

ARARAT, a celebrated mountain in the Greater Armenia, on which Noah's ark rested after the deluge. (Gen. viii. 4.) It is of stupendous height, and was inaccessible to the summit, until Professor Parrot, of the University of Dorpat, on the 27th of September, O. S. 1829, after repeated failures, overcame every impediment. By trigonometrical measurement he ascertained that the larger and principal peak is 16,254 Paris feet above the level of the sea. He describes the summit as being a slightly convex, almost circular platform, about 200 Paris feet in diameter, which at the extremity declines pretty steeply on all sides. He subsequently ascended the little Ararat, which is above 13,100 feet above the level of the sea. The entire upper region of the mountain is covered with perpetual snow and ice : and the mag-

AR

nitude of the great peak is annually increasing in consequence of the continual accession of ice. The eternal snows upon its summit occasionally form vast avalanches, which precipitate themselves down its sides, with a sound not unlike that of an earthquake. *Agridagh,* or the *Great Mountain,* is the name given to this sublime mountain by the Turks; the Armenians call it *Macis,* or the *Mother of the World;* and the Persians in the neighbourhood *Kuhi Nuach,* or the *Mountain of Noah;* but all unite in reverencing it as the haven of the great ship, which preserved the father of mankind from the waters of the deluge. So great is the reverence of the Armenians for this mountain, that, as soon as they can see it, (and from its great height it is visible at the distance of ten days' journey,) they kiss the earth and repeat certain prayers making the sign of the cross. (Sir R. K. Porter's Travels in Persia, vol. i. pp. 183, 184. Stuart's Hebrew Chrestomathy, p. 150. Andover Biblical Repository for January 1832, p. 203., and for April 1836, p. 414.

Arba. See Hebron.

Archelaus, the son and successor of Herod the Great in the government of part of his dominions. See an account of him in p. 109.

Archippus, a Christian, who was either a teacher or a deacon of the church at Colossæ. (Col. iv. 17.)

Αρχισυναγωγος, or ruler of the synagogue, powers and functions of, 253.

Areopagus, tribunal of, 135.

Aretas, the third of the name, a king of Arabia, was the father-in-law of Herod Antipas, against whom he declared war in revenge for repudiating his daughter. Antipas called the Romans to his assistance; but some unaccountable delay in the marching of their forces, and the death of the emperor Tiberius, put an end to the expedition, and saved Aretas. It is supposed that he availed himself of this favourable opportunity to make an incursion into Syria, and obtain possession of Damascus, where he appointed an ethnarch, whose jurisdiction probably extended only over the Jews who dwelt there. Some learned men have supposed this name to have been of Greek origin, and to be derived from ἀρετη, excellence or pre-eminence, but Dr. Pococke is of opinion, that it is an Arabic name (from *al-hareth*) which was common to many of the Arabian kings.

Argob, the capital city of a region of the same name, which was situated beyond the Jordan, in Bashan, the most fruitful country on the other side of that river: it belonged to the half-tribe of Manasseh.

Arimathea, a small town to which Joseph belonged who begged the body of Jesus from Pilate. (Matt. xxvii. 57.) It was about thirty-six or thirty-seven miles distant from Jerusalem, and is now called Ramla. At present it is a wretched dilapidated place, but exhibits vestiges of having once been an extensive and flourishing town. (Three

AR

weeks in Palestine, p. 14.) Its environs are said to be very beautiful.

Aristarchus, a native of Thessalonica, a city of Macedonia, who embraced Christianity, and accompanied St. Paul in several of his journies. He was seized in the tumult at Ephesus, and was afterwards carried with the apostle as a prisoner to Rome, where he shared his imprisonment. (Acts xix. 29. xx. 4. xxvii. 2. Col. iv. 20. Philem. 24.)

Arithmetic of the Jews, 480,

Ark. See Noah.

Armageddon, the name of a place mentioned in Rev. xvi. 16., the position and nature of which are unknown. According to some expositors, it is compounded of two words, signifying the mountain of Mageddo or Megiddo; a place situated at the foot of Mount Carmel, and celebrated in the history of God's people for two memorable slaughters, first of the Canaanites (Judg. v. 19.), and afterwards of the Israelites. (2 Kings xxiii. 29.) Others, however, conjecture that the name Armageddon means a dry, barren, mountainous, and desert country, such as the Jews deemed to be the abode of unclean spirits. This meaning of the word accords with what is said in Rev. xvi. 12—14.

Armies of the Hebrews, levies, divisions, officers, and discipline of, 198—206., and of the Romans, 225—227.

Arms of the Hebrews, 207. Defensive arms, 207—210. Offensive arms, 210, 211. Allusions to the Greek and Roman armour in the New Testament, 223, 224.

Arnon, a brook and valley of the same name, forming the northern boundary of the country of Moab. (Numb. xxi. 13. Deut. iii. 8. 12. 16. iv. 28.) According to the observations of the traveller Seetzen, its present name is Mujeb.

Aroer. — 1. The proper name of a city of the Gadites, on the river Arnon. (Numb. xxxii. 34. Deut. ii. 36. iii. 12. Josh. xii. 2. xiii. 25.) *The cities of,* or *about* Aroer, mentioned in Isa. xvii. 2., Prof. Gesenius is of opinion, may mean the cities beyond Jordan generally. — 2. The name of a place in the canton of the tribe of Judah. (1 Sam. xxx. 28.)

Arpad, a city and country in Syria, near Hamath, with which it is often joined, and which for a time had its own kings. (2 Kings xviii. 34. xix. 13. Isa. x. 9. Jer. xlix. 23.)

Arphaxad, the son of Shem, who is mentioned in the genealogy of Mary, was born two years after the deluge. (Gen. x. 22—24. xi. 12, 13.) The names of his brethren are most of them the names of countries. If this be the case with Arphaxad, the most probable supposition is that of Josephus, viz. that it denotes Chaldæa.

Arrows used by the Hebrews, notice of, 211. Divination by arrows, 359, 360.

Artaxerxes (ארתחששתא Artachschaschtha), a title of several Persian kings. Professor Gesenius derives it from the an-

AS

tient Persian word *Artahshetr*, which is found upon the inscriptions of Nachschi Roustam. The latter part of this word is the Zendish *Khshethro* (also *sherao*), a king. But the syllable *art* (which is found in several Persian names, as Artabanus, Artaphernes, Artabasus), appears to have signified great or mighty. At least the Greeks gave it this interpretation. This signification is now lost in the Persian. From the original *Artahshetr*, the modern Persians formed *Ardeshir* (a name borne by three kings of the dynasty of the Sassanides); the Armenians, *Artashir*; the Greeks, *Artaxerxes*; and the Hebrews *Artachschaschtha*. Two Persian sovereigns, who bore this name, are mentioned in the Old Testament; viz.

1. ARTAXERXES, who at the instigation of the enemies of the Jews issued an edict, prohibiting them from rebuilding Jerusalem. (Ezra iv. 7—22.) This Artaxerxes is generally considered to be the pseudo-Smerdis, one of the Persian Magi, who assumed that name, and pretending to be Smerdis the son of Cyrus and the brother of Cambyses, occupied the throne between the reigns of Cambyses and Darius the son of Hystaspes.

2. ARTAXERXES, who issued a decree extremely favourable to the Jews, which was carried by Ezra to Jerusalem. (Ezra vii. 1. viii. 1.) This sovereign is the Artaxerxes surnamed Longimanus, or the Long-handed, from a trifling deformity. Nehemiah was his cup-bearer, and was permitted by him to return to Jerusalem, with a commission to rebuild its walls, and to be the governor of Judæa.

Αρτεμις. See DIANA.

ARTS, origin of, 464. State of them from the deluge until the time of Moses, *ibid*. And from Moses until after the captivity, 465, 466. Account of some of the arts practised by the Jews, 466—474.

ARUBOTH, or ARABOTH, a city or country belonging to the tribe of Judah. (1 Kings iv. 10.) Its true situation is unknown.

ARVAD, or ARADUS, a small island at the mouth of the river Eleutherus, on the coast of Phœnicia, opposite to Tyre. (Ezek. xxvii. 8.) It is now called *Ruad*, and is quite deserted. The ARVADITE is mentioned in Gen. x. 18. The Arvadites were employed as mariners by the Tyrians.

ASA, king of Judah, succeeded his father Abijam, B. C. 951. He was distinguished for his success in war, and his zeal for the worship of the true God. In the latter part of his reign, the prophet Hanani having reproved him for his distrust in God in forming an alliance with Ben-Hadad king of Syria, he was so exasperated that he put the prophet in chains, and at the same time gave order for the execution of many of his friends. He is supposed to have died of a severe fit of the gout, B.C. 886.

ASAPH, HEMAN, and JEDUTHUN, of the tribe of Levi, were constituted by David chiefs of the sacred singers, of whom their families formed a part. (1 Chron. xxi. 1.) They are all three termed prophets or seers (1 Chron. xxv. 5. 2 Chron. xxix. 30. xxxv. 15.), which appellation is supposed to refer rather to their genius as sacred poets and musicians, than to their possessing the spirit of prophecy. Psalms l. lxxiii.—lxxxiii. were composed by Asaph.

ASENATH, the daughter of Potipherah, and wife of Joseph, was the mother of Ephraim and Manasseh. (Gen. xli. 45. and xlvi. 20.) The etymology, Gesenius observes, is Egyptian (but obscure), and this circumstance furnishes an additional presumption in favour of the authenticity of the writings of Moses; for, according to Coquerel, the name of a woman absolutely analogous to this has been discovered on Egyptian monuments, which is composed of the monosyllable *As* and *Neith*, the name of the Egyptian Minerva.

ASHDOD. See AZOTUS, p. 554. infrà.

ASHER, the son of Jacob and Zilpah, gave his name to one of the tribes of Israel. (Gen. xxx. 13. 1 Chron. ii. 2.) For the limits of the canton assigned to this tribe, see p. 13. But they never expelled the nations of the country, nor did they obtain entire possession of the district allotted to them. Their soil produced abundance of the comforts and luxuries of life, and was rich in mines. The tribe of Asher tamely submitted to the tyranny of Jabin king of Canaan, but assisted Gideon in his pursuit of the Midianites. On the exodus from Egypt, the fighting men of this tribe were 41,500; in the wilderness they amounted to 53,400.

ASHKENAZ, the eldest son of Gomer (Gen. x. 3. Jer. li. 27.), and the father or head of a nation. That a people in northern Asia is intended is evident from its being placed next to Gomer (Cymmeria), in the first instance, and next to Ararat (Armenia), in the second. Hence the conjecture is not improbable, that Ashkenaz itself was also a tribe and province of Armenia, or, at least, lay not far from it, near the Caucasus or towards the Black Sea. Further than this we have no data. The Jews understand by it, Germany, and ignorantly use the word in that signification.

ASHPENAZ, master of the eunuchs, or rather one of the chief chamberlains of Nebuchadnezzar, who was commanded to select certain Jewish captives to be instructed in the literature and sciences of the Chaldæans. In this number he included Daniel and his three companions, whose names he changed into Chaldæan appellations. Their refusal to partake of the provisions sent from the monarch's table filled Ashpenaz with apprehension; he had, however, the generosity not to use constraint towards them. At that time, as in our days, the Asiatic despots frequently punished with death the least infraction of their wills. In acceding to the request of Daniel, Ashpenaz had every thing to apprehend; and the grateful prophet specially

A S

records that God had disposed him to treat him with kindness. (Dan. i. 3—16.)

ASHTAROTH, a Phœnician or Syrian idol, notice of, 345.

ASHUR, the son of Shem (Gen. iii. 11.), who gave his name to ASSYRIA.

ASIA, one of the largest divisions of the Old World, is not mentioned in the Old Testament. In the New Testament it is always taken for Asia Minor, as it includes the proconsular Asia, which comprised the four regions of Phrygia, Mysia, Caria, and Lydia. In this proconsular Asia were the seven churches of Ephesus, Laodicæa, Pergamos, Philadelphia, Sardis, Smyrna, and Thyatira.

ASIARCHS, officers appointed to preside over the worship of the gods, and the sacred games in Asia Minor. See p. 351. In our version of Acts xix. 31. they are termed the *chief of Asia.*

ASKELON, or ASHKELON, a city in the territory of the Philistines, situated between Azotus or Ashdod and Gaza, on the coast of the Mediterranean or Great Sea, about 520 furlongs from Jerusalem. After the death of Joshua, the tribe of Judah took Askelon, which subsequently became one of the five governments belonging to the Philistines. (Judg. i. 18.) This place is frequently mentioned in the Scriptures. During the crusades it was a station of considerable importance. Numerous ruins attest its antient strength; its walls are broken down, and at present not a single inhabitant is to be found there, thus literally fulfilling the prophecies of Jeremiah, Zephaniah, and Zechariah: — *Ashkelon* is *cut off* (Jer. xlvii. 5.), *Ashkelon* shall be *a desolation* (Zeph. ii. 4.), *Ashkelon shall not be inhabited.* (Zech. ix. 5.)

ASMONÆANS, an appellation given to the Maccabees, the descendants of Mattathias, surnamed Asmon. See p. 106.

ASNAPPER, the proper name of an Assyrian king or general. (Ezra iv. 10.) On account of the statement in ver. 2. it is supposed to be only a different name of Esar-haddon.

ASPHAR, a lake mentioned in 1 Macc. ix. 33. which Calmet supposes to be the Lacus Asphaltites, or DEAD SEA. For an account of which see pp. 40—42.

Ass, a well known quadruped, which was declared to be unclean, and consequently not fit to be eaten by the Israelites. (Lev. xi. 26.) Asses were reared by them for draught, 449. For a refutation of the calumny against the Jews, of worshipping an ass, see p. 343. And on the subject of Balaam's ass speaking, see Vol. II. p. 627.

ASSEMBLY at Ephesus, powers of, 135, 136.

ASSOS, a maritime city of Mysia, according to some geographers, but of Troas, according to others. It occupied a commanding situation at some distance from the coast, and was fortified with strong walls. A theatre, and the remains of several temples, and other edifices still attest its antient· splendour. (Cramer's Description of Asia Minor, vol. i.

A S

pp. 122, 123.) Assos is mentioned in Acts xx. 13, 14.

ASSYRIA, a country of Asia, which derived its name from Assur or Asshur, the second son of Shem (Gen. x. 22.), or from a tribe designated after him, who settled in this region. Considerable difficulties exist with respect to its boundaries. It appears to have been situated between the Tigris and the Euphrates, inclosed between those two rivers, from the part where they begin to approach each other on leaving Mesopotamia to that where they join, not far from their mouth, in the Gulf of Persia. Rosenmüller (Bib. Geogr. vol. ii. p. 120.) states that "it nearly corresponded with the modern Kourdistan or land of the Kourds" (a hardy and predatory nomadic tribe), "with the pachalik of Mosul, which contains about sixteen hundred German miles, and was thus about the size of the United Kingdoms of Naples and Sicily. The northern part is very mountainous, but towards the south it is generally level, like the neighbouring country of Babylonia. The culture of the soil is promoted by the number of rivers which traverse the country, and by the pleasant alternation of hill and dale which diversify its surface; while the navigable Tigris" (the Hiddekel of the Hebrews) "presents great facilities for commerce. In different parts of the southern division there are springs of naphtha The country abounds in wheat, and in the more esteemed kinds of fruit, as also in wine, cotton, and manna. It was therefore with truth, that the Assyrian commander Rabshakeh called his native country *a land, where there is corn and wine, bread, and vineyards, olive oil and honey.* (2 Kings xviii. 32. Isa. xxxvi. 17.)" Which account is confirmed by Mr. Rich. (Residence in Kourdistan, vol. i. pp. 132. 142.)

Sketch of the History of ASSYRIA, *illustrative of the Prophetic Writings.*

The empire of Assyria was founded by Ninus, the son of Belus; and, according to Herodotus, it continued five hundred and twenty years. (Herod. lib. i. c. 95.) Ninus reigned one hundred and twenty-two years, according to some historians (Jul. African. and Eusebius in Chron.), though others make his reign to have lasted only seventeen years. (Diod. Sicul. lib. ii. c. i.—iv.) He enlarged and embellished the antient city of Nineveh, which had been built by Nimrod, many ages before his time. (Gen. x. 9, 10.) The commencement of his reign is fixed by Archbishop Usher to the year of the world 2737, B. C. 1267, during the period when Deborah and Barak judged the Israelites.

Ninus was succeeded by his queen Semiramis, who reigned forty-two years. She enlarged the Assyrian empire, which she left in a flourishing state to her son Ninyas, A. M. 2831, B. C. 1173. The Scriptures are totally silent concerning the subsequent history of that celebrated monarchy, and the successors of Ninyas, until the time of the prophet

AS

AS

Jonah, who flourished A. M. 3180, B. C. 824; and even then they do not state the name of the monarch who filled the Assyrian throne. It is evident, however, that Nineveh was at that time a city of immense extent, whose inhabitants, like those of other great cities, abounding in wealth and luxury, were extremely corrupt in their morals. But, at the preaching of Jonah, both sovereign and subjects repented and abandoned their evil ways, and thus for a time delayed the execution of the divine judgments. About fifty years after the time of Jonah, the Scriptures mention a king of Assyria, named PHUL or PUL, who invaded the kingdom of Israel, in the days of Menahem (2 Kings xv. 19. 1 Chron. v. 26.), who gave him a thousand talents of silver to engage him to lend him his assistance, and secure him on his throne. Pul is supposed to have been the father of Sardanapalus, the last king of the Assyrians, in whose reign the crimes of the Ninevites having risen to their utmost height, God raised up enemies to chastise them. Arbaces the Median, indignant at the effeminate and luxurious life which Sardanapalus led in his palace, conspired with Belesis, governor of Babylon, to shake off the yoke of so worthless a sovereign. After various engagements, they compelled him to retreat to Nineveh, where he expected that he should be able to defend himself a long time, because the city was strongly fortified, and the besiegers had not machines to batter the walls. But in the third year of the siege, the river Tigris, being swollen with continual rains, overflowed part of the city, agreeably to the predictions of Nahum (particularly i. 8—10.), and broke down the wall for twenty furlongs. Sardanapalus, that he might not fall into the hands of his enemies, burnt himself in his palace, with his women and all his immense treasures. (Usher's Annals, p. 48. A. M. 3254. Athenæus, lib. xii. c. 12.) Arbaces and Belesis then divided the dominions of Sardanapalus: the former had Media, which he restored to its liberty; the latter had Babylon, where he reigned fourteen years: Nineveh they left to Ninus the younger, who was heir to the antient kings of Assyria, and maintained the *second* Assyrian monarchy with considerable splendour; so that out of the ruins of this vast empire, there were formed three considerable kingdoms, viz. that of Nineveh, that of Babylon, and that of the Medes. We shall briefly consider each of them, separately, according to the share they had in the affairs of the Jews.

Belesis, called BALADAN, by Isaiah (xxxix. 1. 2 Kings xx. 12.), is the Nabonassar of profane historians. He founded the Babylonian empire, of which he made Babylon the metropolis. He was succeeded by his son Merodach Baladan, who cultivated Hezekiah's friendship, as appears from the embassy which he sent to the latter, to congratulate him on his recovery from sickness (2 Kings xx. 12.), A. M. 3291, B. C. 713.

After this time the sacred historians are silent concerning the kings of Babylon, until the time of Esar-haddon, who is noticed in the next column.

The younger Ninus, who was left king of Assyria and Nineveh, is the TIGLATH-PILESER of the Scriptures (2 Kings xv. 29. xvi. 7. 10. 2 Chron. xxviii. 20.), A. M. 3257, B. C. 747. His empire appears to have been the most celebrated in the East; as Ahaz king of Judah sent to request his assistance against Rezin king of Damascus, and Pekah king of Israel. Accordingly, Tiglath-pileser advanced with a numerous army, defeated Rezin, captured Damascus, and put an end to the kingdom erected there by the Syrians, agreeably to the predictions of Isaiah (viii. 4.) and (Amos) i. 5. He also entered the kingdom of Israel, conquered Pekah, and carried away part of the ten tribes beyond the river Euphrates. But Ahaz soon had cause to regret this unhallowed alliance: for Tiglath-pileser exacted from him such immense sums of money, that he was obliged not only to exhaust his own treasures, but also to take all the gold and silver out of the temple. (2 Chron. xxviii. 20, 21. 24.) Ahaz became tributary to the Assyrian monarch, whose successors found abundance of pretexts for entering the kingdom of Judah, which they ultimately ruined and subverted.

SHALMANESER, the successor of Tiglath-pileser, came into Syria, A. M. 3280, B. C. 724. and desolated the country of the Moabites, agreeably to the prophecy of Isaiah (xvi. 1.), delivered three years before. He then attacked Samaria, and completed the misfortunes of the Israelites who remained, by carrying them into captivity beyond the Euphrates. Thus terminated the kingdom of Israel, A. M. 3283, B. C. 721. (2 Kings xvii. 3. xviii. 9—11.) Hezekiah, by the special protection of God, escaped the fury of Shalmaneser, to whom, however, he became tributary, and the Assyrian returned in triumph to Nineveh.

Shortly after these events, most of the maritime cities that were subject to the Tyrians revolted against them, and submitted to the Assyrians. Shalmaneser advanced to their assistance. These cities furnished him with a fleet of sixty or seventy vessels, manned by eight hundred Phœnician rowers. They were attacked by the Tyrians with twelve vessels only; who dispersed their fleet, and took five hundred prisoners. The Assyrian monarch did not venture to lay siege to Tyre; but he left bodies of troops in its vicinity to guard the river and aqueducts whence the Tyrians obtained their supplies of water. His precautions were frustrated by the besieged, who dug wells within their city. It was about this time that Isaiah denounced against them those judgments which are recorded in the twenty-third chapter of his prophecies. And Hezekiah seems to have availed himself of the troubled state of Phœnicia and the whole coast of the Mediter-

A S

ranean, in order to attack the Philistines. (2 Kings xviii. 7, 8.)

SENNACHERIB ascended the throne of Assyria A. M. 3287, B. C. 717, and was immediately involved in war, both in Asia and in Egypt. While he was thus engaged, Hezekiah shook off the yoke of the Assyrians, and refused to pay the tribute exacted from him by Shalmaneser. It appears from some passages of Scripture, that Hezekiah had concluded treaties of mutual alliance and defence with the kings of Egypt and Ethiopia against the Assyrian monarch. (Isa. xx. 1. *et seq.* 2 Kings xviii. 24. xix. 9.) Upon Hezekiah's refusal of the tribute, Sennacherib invaded Judah with a mighty army, and captured the principal cities of that country. It is probable that he took Damascus in his progress. The pious monarch, grieved to see his kingdom pillaged, implored peace of Sennacherib on any terms he would prescribe ; and gave him three hundred talents of silver and thirty talents of gold to withdraw. But the Assyrian, regardless alike of the sanction of oaths and of treaties, continued the war, and prosecuted his conquests more vigorously than ever. Nothing was able to withstand his power ; and of all the strong places of Judah, none remained uncaptured but Jerusalem, which was reduced to the very last extremity. Isaiah, however, encouraged Hezekiah, by promises of divine interposition and deliverance, and announced that the enemy would soon be obliged to return into his own country. (2 Kings xix. 20—34.) Accordingly, after Sennacherib had defeated the allied forces of the King of Egypt and of Tirhakah king of Ethiopia, who had advanced against him to assist Hezekiah, he returned into Judah with immense spoil, and renewed the siege of Jerusalem : but an angel of Jehovah slew one hundred and eighty-five thousand of his troops. (2 Kings xix. 35.) Sennacherib returned to Nineveh, where two of his sons, weary of his tyranny and savage temper, slew him while he was worshipping in the temple of Nisroch his god, and immediately fled into the mountains of Armenia. (2 Kings xix. 37. Tobit i. 21.)

It was during the first year of this war that Hezekiah fell sick, and was cured in a miraculous manner, and that the shadow of the sun went back ten degrees on the dial of the palace, to prove the truth of Isaiah's prediction of his recovery. (2 Kings xviii. xix. xx. Isaiah xxxviii. xxxix.)

A. M. 3294, B. C. 710. On the death of Sennacherib, ESAR-HADDON, another of his sons, reigned in his stead. He is called Sargon by Isaiah. (xx. 1.) He reigned twenty-nine years, during which he waged war with the Philistines, from whom his general, Tartan, took Ashdod. He also attacked Egypt and Ethiopia (Isa. xx.), and Idumæa or Edom (Isa. xxxiv.), in order to avenge the injuries they had committed against his father Sennacherib; and at length he took Jerusalem, and carried Manasseh king of

A T

Judah to Babylon. (2 Chron. xxxiii.) This last war, however, happened long after those above related. Esar-haddon restored the glory of Assyria; and, in addition to his other victories, to the sceptre of Nineveh he united that of Babylon, having availed himself of the intestine troubles and commotions occasioned by the extinction of the royal family, to make himself master of that city, and annex it to his former dominions. Manasseh, having been restored to the divine favour after a deep and sincere repentance, obtained his liberty, and returned to Jerusalem, after a short captivity at Babylon. (Usher's Annals, A. M. 3327.)

Saosduchin or NEBUCHADNEZZAR I. succeeded Esar-haddon, and reigned twenty years, according to Ptolemy. Having conquered Arphaxad king of the Medes (the Deioces of Herodotus, lib. i. cc. 101, 102.), he resolved to subjugate all the neighbouring territories. He therefore despatched Holofernes into Syria and Palestine with an immense army ; but that general was slain, and his army totally discomfited, before Bethulia, in the manner related in the apocryphal book of Judith.

A. M. 3356, B. C. 648, Saracus, otherwise called Chinaldon or Chyna-Ladanus, succeeded Saosduchin in the Assyrian throne. Having rendered himself obnoxious to his subjects by his effeminacy, and the little care he took of his dominions, Nabopolassar, satrap of Babylon, and Cyaxares the son of Astyages king of Media, leagued together against him. He was besieged in Nineveh, which was taken by his enemies, who partitioned his dominions between them ; Nabopolassar becoming master of Nineveh and Babylon, and Cyaxares having Media and the adjacent provinces. (Usher's Annals, A. M. 3378. Calmet, Précis de l'Histoire Profane de l'Orient, §. I. Dissert. tom. ii. pp. 329—333.)

ASSYRIAN IDOLS, worshipped by the Israelites, 346.

ASTARTE, a Phœnician or Syrian idol, notice of, 345.

ASTRONOMY and ASTROLOGY of the Jews, 480, 481.

ATHALIAH, daughter of Omri king of Samaria, and wife of Jehoram king of Judah. Jehu having slain her son Ahaziah, she seized the kingdom, and destroyed all the sons of Jehoram (whom he had by other wives) except Jehoash, who was providentially saved by Jehosheba, and who afterwards succeeded to the throne. Athaliah was slain, after an usurpation of six years. (2 Kings xi.)

ATHENS, a celebrated city of Greece, sometime a very powerful commonwealth, distinguished by the military talents, but still more by the learning, eloquence, and politeness of its inhabitants. St. Paul coming hither, A. D. 52, found them plunged in idolatry, occupied in inquiring and reporting news, curious to know every thing, and divided in opinion concerning religion and happiness. (Acts xvii.) From an altar erected to the

A Z

" Unknown God" (the origin of which see Vol. I. pp. 196, 197.), the great apostle of the Gentiles, taking opportunities here to preach Jesus Christ, was carried before the judges of the tribunal, called the Areopagus; where he gave an illustrious testimony to truth, and a remarkable instance of powerful reasoning. (See an account of the AREOPAGUS in p. 135.) Modern Athens suffered severely during the late war with the Turks. It is intended to be the metropolis of the new kingdom of Greece.: and the plan of the city has been so arranged, that many of the principal remains of antiquity will be brought into view in one long street, which is to pass through the centre, and finish at the antient entrance. The present small population is daily increasing.. An extensive olive grove in the suburbs affords almost the only article of commerce connected with the place. (Hardy's Notices of the Holy Land, pp. 314—317.)

Some of the finest specimens of antient art at Athens now adorn the British Museum. The reader, who is desirous of a full account of the state of Athens, and of its various monuments of former times, is referred to the Travels of Dr. Clarke, to the Classical Tour of Mr. Dodwell, and to Mr. Stewart's Antiquities of Athens.

ATONEMENT, fast of, 317, 318.

ATTALIA, a maritime city of Pamphylia, and the chief residence of the prefect. It derived its name from king Attalus, its founder. Hither St. Paul went from Perga in Pamphylia. (Acts xiv. 25.) It still subsists under the name of *Sattalia*.

AUGUSTUS (Octavius) the first, or, according to some writers, the second emperor of Rome. He commanded the enrolment to be made which is mentioned in Luke ii. 1. — The forty-second year of his reign is that in which Jesus Christ was born. The title of Augustus, which he received from the flattery of the senate, became the personal appellation of his successors; and St. Luke has employed the corresponding Greek word, to designate Nero. (Acts xxv. 21. 25.)

AVEN. See ON, *infrà*.

AVEN (Plain of), a beautiful valley in the part of Syria near to Damascus: according to Gesenius, it is now called *Un*, and is proverbially considered as a delightful valley. As the original word (Bikath-Aven, which is retained in the marginal rendering of Amos i. 5.) signifies the plain of vanity, it is conjectured to have been a place remarkable for idolatry, Bethel being called Beth-Aven in Hos. v. 8. for that reason.

AVIMS, the original inhabitants of the country afterwards possessed by the Caphtorim or Philistines. (Deut. ii. 23.)

AVITES or AVIM, the inhabitants of Aveh or Ava, a city whence colonies were sent into Samaria. (2 Kings xvii. 24. 31.) Ava is supposed to have been situated in the north-west of Chaldæa.

AZARIAH. — 1. The name of a king of Judah, also called UZZIAH (which see *infrà*):

B A

— 2. The name of several high priests among the Jews, — and, 3. The name of a prophet in the time of Asa. (2 Chron. xv. 1, 2.)

AZEKAH, a city in the tribe of Judah, to the south of Jerusalem, and east of Bethlehem. (Josh. xv. 35)

AZOTUS, or ASHDOD, a city of Judæa, was antiently one of the five cities belonging to the princes of the Philistines. (Josh. xiii.3. 1 Sam. vi. 17.) In the division of Palestine by Joshua it was allotted to the tribe of Judah (Josh. xv. 47.); but the possession of it, if not retained, was soon recovered by the Philistines, who three hundred years afterwards, having captured the ark of God, brought it to Ashdod, and deposited it in the temple of their idol-deity Dagon. (1 Sam. v. 1.) Subsequently Uzziah king of Judah, having successfully warred against the Philistines, broke down its walls. (2 Chron. xxvi. 6.) The city was captured by Tartan the Assyrian general, in the time of Hezekiah. (Isa. xx. 1.) After the return of the Jews from the Babylonish captivity, the numerous alliances made by them with the women of Ashdod, introduced the worship of false gods into their families; so that the offspring of these marriages *spake half in the language of Ashdod, and could not speak in the Jews' language, but according to the language of each people.* For this crime against the law of God, that most upright and patriotic of religious governors, Nehemiah, contended with them, and made them swear that they would contract no more such idolatrous unions. (Neh. xiii. 23—26.) Ashdod was afterwards captured by Judas Maccabæus (1 Macc. v. 68.), by whose brother Jonathan it was reduced to ashes. (1 Macc. x. 84.) It was evidently a place of great strength and consequence. By the Greeks it was called AZOTUS. Here Philip the evangelist was found, after he had baptised the Ethiopian eunuch at Gaza, which was about thirty miles distant. (Acts viii. 40.) At present Ashdod is an inconsiderable village called *Esdud*, which exhibits no vestiges of its former splendour. The road to this lies over an undulating surface, partially covered with grain and thistles: it stands on the summit of a grassy hill, with luxuriant pasture around it. (Robinson's Travels in Palestine, vol. i. p. 21.)

———

BAAL, a Phœnician idol, notice of, 345, 346, and of his worship, 355, 356.

BAALAH. See KIRJATH-JEARIM, *infrà*.

BAALBERITH,   ⎫ Phœnician idols, notice
BAALZEBUB,   ⎬ of, 346.
BAALZEPHON,   ⎭

BAAL-GAD, a city which was situated *in the valley of Lebanon, under Mount Hermon* (Josh. xi. 17. xii. 7.): it was one of the places which remained unconquered by the Israelites at the death of Joshua. (Josh. xiii. 5.) By the Greeks and Romans it was afterwards called Heliopolis, and by the

B A

modern natives it is called *Baalbec*, both which names mean the City of the Sun. It is supposed to have been the place called BAAL-HAMON in Sol. Song viii. 11., and also BAALATH in 2 Kings ix. 18. The inhabitants of the country believe that Baal-Gad or Baalbec was erected by Solomon. It stands at the foot of Anti-Libanus, just where the mountain terminates in a plain, and it presents to the traveller a magnificent spectacle of ruins, among which those of the Temple of the Sun are most conspicuous. The splendid work of Messrs. Wood and Dawkins, published at London in 1753, and reprinted in 1827, will convey some idea of the magnificence of these remains of antient art; of which some accurate views will be found in the " Landscape Illustrations of the Bible," edited by the author of this work. The population of Baalbec, which in 1751 was five thousand, in 1835 was reduced to two hundred persons. The modern town consists of a number of mean huts, and a few half-ruined mosques. A description of the ruins of this place, as they appeared in the autumn of 1835, is given by Mr. Addison, in his Damascus and Palmyra, vol. ii. pp. 51—72. ; and by Lord Lindsay, as they appeared in the summer of 1837, in his Letters from Egypt, &c., vol. ii. pp. 191—204.

BAALPEOR, a Canaanitish idol, notice of, 345.

BAASHA, the son of Ahijah, and commander in chief to Jeroboam I. : he treacherously killed his sovereign Nadab, and afterwards usurped his kingdom, B. C. 953—930.

BABEL, the name of a lofty tower, which the descendants of Noah began to build about one hundred and twenty years after the deluge : it was so called (*Babel* signifying *confusion*), because God there confounded the language of those who were employed in the undertaking. (Gen. x. 10. xi. 9.) Their object was to build a city and a tower, in order to prevent their further dispersion over the earth. But, as this was contrary to the divine purpose of replenishing the earth with inhabitants, God caused them to be scattered, the tower was left apparently incomplete : but the foundations of the city were probably laid, and a portion of the builders continued to dwell there. This place afterwards became the celebrated city of

BABYLON, the metropolis of Chaldæa, which was pre-eminently distinguished for the magnificence of its buildings, especially after its enlargement and improvement by Nebuchadnezzar, when it became one of the wonders of the world. It is said to have covered an area of 480 stadia, or nearly 60 miles in circumference ; and the wall by which it was surrounded was 50 cubits in thickness, and 200 in height. The river Euphrates divided the city into two parts, which were connected by means of a noble bridge, about a furlong in length and sixty feet wide. Dr. Hales has given a copious and accurate account of antient Babylon in his Analysis of Chronology, (vol. i. pp. 453—456., 4to edit.)

B A

The banks of the waters of Babylon were planted with willows, which are mentioned in the Scriptures. Thus Isaiah (xv. 7.), describing in prophetic language the captivity of the Moabites by Nebuchadnezzar, says, that *they shall be carried away to the valley of willows.* The territory surrounding the ruins of antient Babylon is at present composed chiefly of plains, whose soil is rich; and the river-banks are still hoary with reeds, and covered with the grey ozier willows, on which the captives of Israel suspended their harps (Psal. cxxxvii. 1—4.), and refused to be comforted, while their conquerors tauntingly commanded them to sing the songs of Sion. (Sir R. K. Porter's Travels in Georgia, &c. vol. ii. p. 297.) The most terrible denunciations were uttered against Babylon by the Hebrew prophets (compare Vol. I. pp. 289, 290.), the literal fulfilment of whose predictions has been shown by various modern travellers who have described the present state of its ruins, which have been discovered in the vicinity of the modern town of Hilleh, in the pashalik of Bagdad. (See particularly Mr. Rich's Two Memoirs on the Ruins of Babylon, the accuracy of whose statements is confirmed by Mr. Buckingham, in the interesting description contained in his Travels in Mesopotamia, vol. ii. pp. 258—394 : Sir R. K. Porter's Travels in Georgia, &c. vol. ii pp. 308—332., 337—400.; and the Hon. Capt. Keppel's Narrative of Travels from India, vol. i. pp. 171—188., who also attests the accuracy of Mr. Rich and has adopted his measurements.) The prophet Isaiah, describing the calamities that were to be inflicted on Babylon by Cyrus, calls this city *the desert of the sea.* Jeremiah to the same purport, says (li. 36. 42.), *I will dry up the sea of Babylon and make her springs dry. — The sea is come up upon her. She is covered with the multitude of the waves thereof.* Megasthenes (in Eusebius De Præp. Evang. lib. ix. c. 41.) states, that Babylon was built in a place which had before so greatly abounded with water, that it was called *the sea.*

Babylon was very advantageously situated, both in respect to commerce and as a naval power. It was open to the Persian Gulf by the Euphrates, which was navigable by large vessels ; and being joined to the Tigris above Babylon, by the canal called *Naharmalca*, or the Royal River, supplied the city with the produce of the whole country to the north of it, as far as the Euxine and Caspian Seas. Semiramis was the foundress of this part also of the Babylonian greatness. She improved the navigation of the Euphrates, and is said to have had a fleet of three thousand gallies. We are not to wonder that, in later times, we hear little of the commerce and naval power of Babylon : for, after the capture of the city by Cyrus, the Euphrates was not only rendered less fit for navigation by being diverted from its course, and left to spread over the country ; but the Persian monarchs, residing in their own country, in order to prevent any invasion by sea on that part of their empire, purposely obstructed the navigation of both rivers by making cataracts in them; that is, by raising dams across the channel, and making artificial falls in them, so that no vessel of any size or force could possibly come up. Alexander began to restore the navigation of the rivers by demolishing the cataracts upon the Tigris, as far up as Seleucia, but he did not live to complete his great designs; those upon the Euphrates still continued. Ammianus Marcellinus mentions them as subsisting in his time. The prophet Ezekiel (xvii. 4.) calls Babylon *the land of merchants :* and Isaiah (xliii. 14.), Bishop Lowth's translation) speaks of the *Chaldæans exulting in their ships ;* which, Bp. L. remarks, he might justly do, in his time, though afterwards they had no foundation for any such boast. (Bp. Lowth, on Isa. xliii. 14.) There is an erudite and valuable memoir, by Mr. F. M. Hubbard, on the commerce of antient Babylon in the seventh and eighth volumes of the Andover Biblical Repository for 1836.

Babylon rapidly declined during the Persian dynasty : Darius Hystaspes broke down the walls and took away the gates, which Cyrus had spared. Alexander the Great designed to rebuild the temple of Belus, which had gone to decay, and actually employed ten thousand labourers for two months in removing the rubbish ; but the attempt was rendered abortive, by his premature death in the flower of his age, and pride of conquest. Seleucus Nicator, his successor in the kingdom of Syria, dismantled and spoiled Babylon, to build Seleucia in its neighbourhood, to which he transplanted the inhabitants; and in Strabo's time, about the Christian era, " the greater part of Babylon was become a desert," which the Parthian kings converted into a park, where they took the recreation of hunting, in Jerome's time, A. D. 340. Its ruins are now the haunts of lions and other beasts of prey, so as often to be inaccessible. Thus gradually have been fulfilled the predictions of Scripture :—" Babylon, the beauty of kingdoms, the glory of the pride of the Chaldæans, shall become as Sodom and Gomorrah, which God overthrew. It shall never be re-established, neither shall it be inhabited from generation to generation. The Arab shall not pitch his tent there, nor shall the shepherd make his fold there : the wild beasts of the desert shall lie there, and howling monsters shall fill their houses : — for her time is near to come, and her days shall not be prolonged." (Isaiah xiii. 19—22.)

The remains of antient Babylon, as described by recent travellers, are so vast, that the whole could never be suspected of having been the work of human hands, were it not for the layers of bricks which are found therein. They are fire-baked, and cemented with zepht, or bitumen; between each layer are found oziers. Here are found those large and thick bricks imprinted with unknown characters, specimens of which are preserved in the British Museum, in the Museum of

the East India Company, and in other depositaries of antiquities. The composition of these bricks corresponds exactly with the account given by the sacred historian of the builders of Babel. *Let us make brick* (said they), *and burn them thoroughly. And they had brick for stone, and slime* [or bitumen] *had they for mortar.* (Gen. xi. 3.) Accurate engravings of the ruins of Babylon are given in the " Landscape Illustrations of the Bible."

The name of Babylon was mystically given to Rome by the apostle Peter, as we have shown at length in the critical preface to his first epistle, in Vol. IV. pp. 435, 436. The BABYLONIAN KINGDOM was founded by the celebrated hunter and hero Nimrod, after the dispersion which followed the unsuccessful attempt to build the tower of Babel. " It extended from Babylon in Mesopotamia towards the north, over Calneh (Ctesiphon), as far as Accad (Nisibis) and Erech (Edessa), including the whole land of Shinar. But, however powerful for those times, we cannot suppose it to have been either populous or well organised. Even the four cities, which are mentioned as the strong holds of this kingdom, were nothing more than small villages slightly fortified. As this was the first attempt to establish an extensive domain, it must have been universally disagreeable to the men of that period. Consequently, it was of short duration ; and Nimrod's Babylon must not be regarded as the germ of that universal monarchy which took its rise in a later age, and among a different people." (Jahn's Hebrew Commonwealth, vol. i. p. 6.)

Sketch of the History of the BABYLONIAN *or* CHALDÆAN EMPIRE, *to illustrate the Predictions of the Prophets.*

A. M. 3398, B. C. 606. Nabopolassar having associated his son NEBUCHADNEZZAR with him in the empire, sent him to reduce the provinces of Syria and Palestine, which had revolted from him. In his way thither, the young prince defeated the army of Pharaoh Necho king of Egypt, and recaptured Carchemish. (Jer. xlvi. 2.) Having penetrated into Judæa, he besieged Jerusalem, and took it, and caused Jehoiakim, the son of Josiah king of Judah, to be put in chains, intending to have him carried to Babylon; but, being moved with his repentance and affliction, he restored him to his throne. (2 Chron. xxxvi. 6.) Great numbers of the Jews, and, among the rest, some children of the royal family, were carried captive to Babylon, whither all the royal treasures, and part of the sacred vessels of the temple, were likewise transported. (2 Chron. xxxvi. 7. Dan. i. 1—7.) Thus was accomplished the judgment which God had denounced to Hezekiah by the prophet Isaiah. (xxxix. 5—7.) From this celebrated period, which was the fourth year of Jehoiakim king of Judah, we are to date the seventy years' captivity of the Jews at Babylon, so often foretold

BA

by Jeremiah. Among the members of the royal family thus taken captives was the prophet Daniel ; Ezekiel followed some time afterwards.

A. M. 3399, B. C. 605. Nabopolassar died, and Nebuchadnezzar began to reign alone; and in the fourth year of his empire he had the memorable vision related and interpreted by the prophet Daniel. (ii.) At this time Jehoiakim revolted from the king of Babylon, whose generals marched against him, and ravaged his country. (2 Kings xxiv. 1, 2.) Jehoiakim "slept with his fathers," neither regretted nor lamented by his subjects, agreeably to the prediction of Jeremiah (xxii. 18, 19.); though the precise manner of its fulfilment is not recorded by the sacred historian. Jehoiachin or Jeconiah, also called Coniah (Jer. xxii. 24.), succeeded to the throne and iniquity of his father ; and in the eighth year of his reign Jerusalem was besieged and taken by the generals of Nebuchadnezzar ; and Jehoiachin, together with part of the nobility, and the princes of the people, were carried into captivity, to Babylon. (2 Kings xxiv. 6—16.) — Mattaniah, also called Zedekiah, who was the uncle of Jehoiachin, was elevated to the throne, and left at Jerusalem, A. M. 3405, B. C. 599. (2 Kings xxiv. 17.)

Nebuchadnezzar did not continue long at Babylon. Having received intelligence that Zedekiah had made an alliance with Pharaoh Hophra king of Egypt, and had violated his oath of fidelity, Nebuchadnezzar marched against him, defeated his forces, and laid siege to Jerusalem, agreeably to the prediction of Jeremiah. (xliv. 30.) The arrival of the Egyptian monarch, at the head of a powerful army, gave the besieged a gleam of hope, but their joy was of short duration. The Egyptians were defeated, and the conqueror returned to Jerusalem, which he took by storm, after a siege of two years, A. M. 3416, B. C. 588. Zedekiah was arrested in his flight, and conducted to Riblath, where Nebuchadnezzar was. After seeing his two children put to death before his face, the Jewish king was deprived of both his eyes, loaded with chains, and carried to Babylon, where he died. Jerusalem was destroyed, the temple pillaged and burnt, and the chief of the people that yet survived were carried into captivity beyond the Euphrates. Only a wretched remnant of the common people was left in Judæa, under the government of Gedaliah the son of Ahikam (Jer. xl. 5.); who being afterwards put to death by Ishmael the son of Nethaniah, part of the people withdrew into Egypt with Jeremiah (xli. xlii.), and the rest were, a few years afterwards, transported to Babylon by Nebuzaradan. (Jer. lii. 30.)

A. M. 3419, B. C. 585. Three years after the capture of Jerusalem, Nebuchadnezzar commenced the siege of Tyre ; he closely invested it for twelve years, and in the thirteenth year of the siege he took that city.

BA

During this interval he waged war with the Sidonians, Ammonites, Moabites, and Edomites, or Idumeans, in conformity with the prophecies of Jeremiah, Ezekiel, and Obadiah. (Jer. xliii. xliv. xlvi. Ezek. xxvi.—xxviii. (Obad. throughout.) Having captured Tyre, Nebuchadnezzar entered Egypt, and laid waste the whole country. (Ezek. xxix.—xxxi.) Pharaoh Hophra (the Apries of profane historians) was put to death by his enemies (Jer. xliv. 30. Ezek. xxxii.); and Amasis, his rival for the throne, was left to govern that country in his stead. Nebuchadnezzar carried a great number of captives from Egypt to Babylon.

After his return from these successful expeditions, Nebuchadnezzar employed himself in embellishing Babylon ; but, to humble his pride, God sent him the memorable admonitory dream, recorded by the prophet Daniel (iv. 1—27.); and twelve months afterwards he was bereft of his senses, precisely in the manner that had been foretold. (28—33.) At length he recovered his understanding (34—37.), and shortly after died, in the forty-third year of his reign, A. M. 3442, B. C. 563. He was succeeded by EVIL-MERODACH, who reigned only two years. He liberated Jehoiachin king of Judah, who had been detained in captivity nearly thirty-seven years. (Jer. lii. 31.) Evil-Merodach becoming odious to his subjects in consequence of his debaucheries and iniquities, his own relations conspired against him, and put him to death. Neriglissar, one of the conspirators, reigned in his stead ; and after a short reign of four years, being slain in battle, he was succeeded by Laborosoarchod, a wicked and inglorious prince, whom his subjects put to death for his crimes. To him succeeded BELSHAZZAR, called by Berosus, Nabonidus, and by Herodotus, Labynitus. He is supposed to have been the son of Evil-Merodach, and consequently the grandson of Nebuchadnezzar, to whom, according to the prophecy of Jeremiah, all the nations of the East were to be subject, as also to his son and grandson. (Calmet, Précis de l'Histoire Prophane de l'Orient, § II. Dissertations, tom. ii. pp. 333—335.)

BABYLONIAN IDOLS, notice of, 348.

BAITHYLIA, or consecrated stones, notice of, 347.

BALAAM, the son of Beor, dwelt at Pethor in Mesopotamia, not far from the river Euphrates. He was sent for by Balak king of Moab to curse the Israelites ; but, instead of curses, he pronounced only blessings. (Numb. xxii.—xxiv.) It is a question much debated among commentators, whether Balaam was a true prophet of the Lord, or only a magician and diviner or fortune-teller : and the arguments on each side are so strong, as to lead to the conclusion that he was both —a Chaldæan priest, magician, and astrologer by profession, a prophet by accident. He dwelt in a country, which, from time immemorial, was celebrated for the observation of the stars; and the astronomy of antiquity was never, perhaps, free from astrology. His fame, in every thing which at that time formed the science of Chaldæa, filled Asia: the honours and presents which he received, show the high estimation in which he was held. It is a circumstance, moreover, worthy of remark, that his religion was not a pure idolatry. He knew and served the LORD: the knowledge and worship of the true God did not simultaneously disappear among the nations; as is evident from the circumstances recorded of Melchisedek, Jethro, and, perhaps, Abimelech. The history of Balaam presents the last trace of the knowledge of the true God, which is found out of Canaan. If the rites celebrated by him were not devoid of superstition; if it be difficult to put a favourable construction upon the enchantments which Moses seems to attribute to him, it only follows that Balaam, like Laban, blended error and truth. The mixed religion, thus professed by him, furnishes a key to his mysterious history. Sacerdotal maledictions were at that time regarded as inevitable scourges, and the people of Moab and Midian thought that they should find in Moab an adversary, who was capable of opposing Moses; and it was only opposing a prophet to a prophet, a priest to a priest. In the judgment of these nations, Moses was a formidable magician; and, as Pharaoh had done forty years before, they sought out, on their part, a magician, to defend them : they wished to curse the Israelites in the very name of Jehovah, whom they supposed to be a more powerful deity than their own god. These circumstances will enable us without difficulty to conceive how Balaam received the gift of prophecy. The terms employed by the sacred historian are so express, as to leave no doubt that he, occasionally, at least, was inspired. Besides, his predictions are extant; nor does it avail to say, that Balaam was a wicked man. The gift of prophecy did not always sanctify the heart. (See Matt. vii. 22.) If, then, we refer to the circumstances of that memorable day, we shall find in that dispensation reasons worthy of the divine wisdom. The Hebrews had arrived on the borders of Canaan, which country they were on the point of entering; they knew that Moses would not enter it ; and in order to encourage the people to effect the conquest of the promised land, even without Moses, God caused one who was hostile to them to utter predictions of their victory. How encouraging must this circumstance have been to the Hebrews, at the same time that it would prove to them (who were about to come into continual contact with the Canaanites) how vain and useless against them would be the superstitions of those idolatrous nations. The three hills on which Balaam offered sacrifices in the presence of the Israelitish camp, remind us of one of the prejudices of ancient times. The antients believed that a change of aspect induced a

change of condition. On this subject compare p. 214.

BALADAN, or MERODACH-BALADAN, the Belesis and Nabonassar of profane historians, and the founder of the Babylonian empire. Originally only governor of Babylon, he entered into a conspiracy with Arbaces, governor of Media, against Sardanapalus, king of Assyria ; on whose death he had Babylon for his share of the dominions of Sardanapalus, as already related in p. 552.

BALAK, king of Moab, is known only by the circumstance of his having invited Balaam to his assistance against the Israelites. See BALAAM.

BALM of Gilead, 66, 67.

BANISHMENT, a Jewish punishment, notice of, 150.

BAPTISM of Proselytes, 266. Analogy between Circumcision and Baptism, 270. and note.

BARABBAS, the name of a seditious robber, whose release the Jews demanded of Pilate. (John xviii. 40.)

BARACHIAS, the father of Zacharias, mentioned in Matt. xxiii. 35., is supposed to have been Jehoiada the high priest ; it being not uncommon among the Jews to have two names.

BARAK, the son of Abinoam, who, in conjunction with Deborah, delivered the Israelites from the oppression of the Canaanites. (Judg. iv. v. Heb. xi. 32)

BARBARIAN, one who belongs to a different nation, and uses a different language. In this sense the word was used by the Greeks, Romans, and Jews. Under the terms " Greeks" and " Barbarians " Saint Paul comprehends all mankind. In Acts xxviii. 2. 4. the inhabitants of Melita (Malta) are termed " Barbarians," as speaking a dialect of the Phœnician language.

BARGAINS and SALES, how made and ratified, 192.

BAR-JESUS, a Jewish magician in the island of Crete ; who, opposing Paul and Barnabas, and endeavouring to prevent Sergius Paulus from embracing Christianity, was by St. Paul struck blind. (Acts xiii. 6.) On the nature of this blindness, see p. 510. The same miracle, which punished the impostor, converted the proconsul. St. Luke calls him Elymas, an Arabic name signifying sorcerer. He is supposed to have been one of the proconsul's council, who was apprehensive of losing his credit, if the Roman became a Christian.

BAR-JONAH, a patronymic appellation of the apostle Peter. (Matt. xvi. 17.)

BARNABAS, a surname of Joses, a Levite by descent, and born of parents who lived in the Isle of Cyprus. Having embraced Christianity, he became St. Paul's principal associate in his labours for propagating the Gospel. He is supposed to have received the name of Barnabas, which signifies a *son of consolation,* after his conversion to the faith of Jesus Christ. (Acts iv. 36. ix. 27. xi. 22. 25. 30. xii. 25. xiii. 1, 2.)

BE

BARTHOLOMEW, one of the twelve apostles, is supposed to have been Nathaniel, who was one of Christ's first disciples. According to ecclesiastical tradition, after preaching the Gospel in Persia and Arabia, he suffered martyrdom at Albanopolis.

BARTIMÆUS, or the son of Timæus, a blind beggar of Jericho, to whom Jesus Christ miraculously imparted the gift of sight. (Mark x. 46.)

BARUCH, the son of Neriah, descended from an illustrious family of the tribe of Judah, was the scribe or secretary and faithful friend of the prophet Jeremiah, whom he accompanied into Egypt. (Jer. xxxvi.) For an analysis of the apocryphal book of Baruch, see Vol. IV. p. 245.

BASHAN, or BATANÆA, district of, 16. Forest of Bashan, 66.

BASKETS of the Jews, 393.

BATH, much used in the East, 435.

BATH-KOL, or voice from heaven. See Vol. IV. p. 149.

BATHSHEBA, or BATHSHUA, the daughter of Eliam or Ammiel, and the wife of Uriah the Hittite. After his murder she became the wife of David, who had previously committed adultery with her. She subsequently was the mother of Solomon.

BATTLE, order of, 213.

BEARD, reverence of, in the East,' 398, 399. The corners of, why forbidden to be marred, 357.

BEATING TO DEATH, punishment of, 157.

BEATITUDES, Mount of, notice of, 50.

BEAUTIFUL GATE of the Temple, 239.

BEELZEBUB or BELZEBUB, a Phœnician idol, 346.

BEEROTH, a city belonging to the Gibeonites, which was afterwards given up to the tribe of Benjamin. (Josh. ix. 7. 2. Sam. iv. 2.) According to Eusebius, it was seven Roman miles distant from Jerusalem, on the road to Nicopolis.

BEERSHEBA (the well of an oath, or the well of seven), because here Abraham made an alliance with Abimelech, king of Gerar, and gave him seven ewe-lambs, in token of that covenant to which they had sworn. (Gen. xx. 31.) Beersheba was given by Joshua to the tribe of Judah; afterwards it was transferred to Simeon. (Josh. xv. 28.) It was twenty miles from Hebron, south; here was a Roman garrison, in Eusebius's and Jerome's time. The limits of the Holy Land (as we have already remarked) are often expressed in Scripture, by the terms — "From Dan to Beersheba" (2 Sam. xvii. 11, &c.), Dan being the northern, Beersheba the southern extremity of the land.

BEGGARS, treatment of, 196.

BEHEADING, punishment of, 156.

BEL, a Babylonish idol, 348.

BELSHAZZAR, the last monarch of Babylon, grandson of Nebuchadnezzar, who was slain while carousing with his officers; the city being taken, and the empire translated to Cyaxares, whom the Scriptures call Darius the Mede.

BE

BELT, or Girdle (Military) Notice of, 209.

BENHADAD I. king of Syria, who, gained by the presents of Asa king of Judah, broke off his alliance with Baasha king of Israel, and assisted him against the latter. (1 Kings xv. 18.) He was succeeded by his son,

BENHADAD II., who made war against Ahab king of Israel, and was defeated. He also made war against Jehoram the son of Ahab; but by means of the prophet Elisha was obliged to return into his country again, as related in 2 Kings vi. Shortly after he besieged Samaria, which city he reduced to the utmost distress (2 Kings vii.); but, his army being seized with a panic, they deserted the besieged city, and returned home. In the following year, Benhadad was murdered by Hazael, who succeeded to the throne of Syria. (2 Kings viii.)

BENJAMIN, the youngest son of Jacob and Rachel, one of the twelve patriarchs. From him was descended the tribe of Benjamin; for the situation, &c. of the canton allotted to which, see p. 12.

BERACHAH, Valley of, 53.

BEREA, a city of Macedonia, where Paul preached the Gospel with great success. The historian Luke gives an honourable character to the Bereans, in Acts xviii. 10.

BERNICE, notice of, 111.

BEROTHAI, a town in the territory of Hadadezer, king of Syria, which was conquered by David, and from which he took away much brass. (2 Sam. viii. 8.) Hence it has been inferred that there were mines in its vicinity. It is impossible now accurately to determine its situation. "The similarity of the name would lead us to conjecture that Berothai or Berothah was not different from Berytus, the modern Beirūt (Beyroot), a seaport town which is still of importance." (Rosenmüller's Bibl. Geogr. vol. ii. p. 266.)

BESOR, Brook, 38.

BETHABARA, the place of the ford or passage, viz. of the Jordan. It is mentioned in John i. 28., where the best manuscripts, the Vulgate, Saxon, and both the Syriac versions, as well as the Greek paraphrase of Nonnus, read Βηθανια. The reading Βηθαβαρα seems to have arisen from the mere conjecture of Origen; who, in travelling through that region, found no such place as Βηθανια, but saw a town called Βηθαβαρα, and therefore changed the common reading. (Campbell and Bloomfield on John i. 20.)

BETHANY.

1. A town of Judæa, where Lazarus dwelt, and where he was raised from the dead, was fifteen furlongs east from Jerusalem, on the way to Jericho (John xi. 8.), and was situated on the retired and shady side of Mount Olivet. It is now a miserable little village, consisting of a cluster of mud hovels. It is, however, a sweet retired spot. "The path to Jerusalem," from this village, "winds round the mount and through the vale of Jehoshaphat, precisely, to all appearance, as it did, when the Messiah rode thither in regal

BE

but humble triumph, and the people strewed their garments and branches in the way." (Lord Lindsay's Letters from Egypt, vol. ii. p. 63.) Somewhere on this side of that mountainous tract, which reached within eight furlongs of Jerusalem, from which it was only a sabbath-day's journey, Mr. Jowett, with great probability, places the scene of the Ascension: "for it is said (Luke xxiv. 50, 51.), that Jesus Christ led his disciples out as far as to Bethany, and then was parted from them and carried up into heaven. The previous conversation, as related in the beginning of the Acts of the Apostles (i. 6—9.), would probably occupy some time while walking toward Bethany; for we must not judge of the length of our Lord's discourses, by the brevity with which the evangelists record them. Here the last sparks of earthly ambition were extinguished in the bosoms of the apostles; and they were prepared to expect that purer fire which was ere long to burst forth upon the day of Pentecost. Here their Head was taken from them; and two of the ministering spirits of his train, becoming visible to their eyes, interrupted their mute astonishment, and dismissed them to their proper stations." At present the cultivation around Bethany is much neglected; though it is a pleasant, romantic spot, abounding in trees and long grass. Various supposed sites of the houses of Lazarus, of Martha, of Simon the leper, and of Mary Magdalene, are pointed out to credulous and ignorant Christians. (Jowett's Christian Researches in Syria, pp. 256—258. Richardson's Travels, vol. ii. p. 371.)

2. A village on the eastern side of Jordan, where John baptised. (John i. 28.) Its exact position is not known. See Bethabara.

Beth-aven, a city not far from Ai, the same as Bethel, where Jeroboam I. set up his golden calves: whence the prophet Hosea (iv. 15.) in derision calls it Beth-Aven, that is, the *House of Vanity,* or *of Idols ;* instead of *Bethel,* or the *House of God,* which name had been given to it by the patriarch Jacob after his memorable vision, related in Gen. xxvii.

Bethesda, pool of, 24.

Bethlehem, now called Beit-Lahhm, was a celebrated city, about six miles southwest from Jerusalem: it was formerly called Ephrath or Ephrata (Gen. xxv. 19. xlviii. 7. Mic. v. 2.) It was a city in the time of Boaz (Ruth iii. 11. iv. 1.), and was fortified by Rehoboam. (2 Chron. xi. 6.) In Matt. ii. 1. 5. it is called Bethlehem of Judæa, to distinguish it from another town of the same name situated in Lower Galilee, and mentioned in Josh. xix. 15. In Luke ii. 4., it is called the *city of David,* because David was born and educated there. (Compare John vii. 42. and 1 Sam. xvi. 1. 18.) This city, though not considerable for its extent or riches, is of great dignity as the appointed birth-place of the Messiah (Matt. ii. 6. Luke

BE

ii. 6—15.) Modern Bethlehem is a village, pleasantly situated on the brow of an eminence, in a very fertile soil, which only wants cultivation to render it what the name Bethlehem imports — *a house of bread.* Between the clefts of the rock, where the soil is cultivated, vines, figs, and olives, grow in great luxuriance. Bethlehem is said to be nearly as large as Nazareth, and to contain from a thousand to fifteen hundred inhabitants, who are almost wholly Christians, and are a bold, fierce race of men, of whom both Turks and Arabs stand in awe. They maintain themselves by the manufacture of beads, crucifixes, and other articles which they work in mother of pearl or in the fruit of the dome-palm. On the north-eastern side of it is a deep valley, where tradition says that the angels appeared to the shepherds of Judæa, with the glad tidings of our Saviour's nativity (Luke ii. 8—14.); and in this valley Dr. Clarke halted at the identical fountain for whose delicious water David longed. (2 Sam. xxiii. 15—18.) Of the various pretended holy places which are here shown to Christians, the cave of the nativity is the only spot verified by tradition from the earliest ages of Christianity. Between one and two miles from this place, on the road to Jerusalem, stood the site of Rachel's tomb (Gen. xxxv. 19, 20. 1 Sam. x. 2.), which is now covered by a small square Mohammedan building, surmounted by a dome, and resembling in its exterior the tombs of saints and sheiks in Arabia and Egypt. In the vicinity of Bethlehem are the pools of Solomon, which are described in p. 45. suprà. (Dr. Clarke's Travels, vol. iv. pp. 408—420. See also Hasselquist's Travels, p. 144.; Buckingham's Travels in Palestine, pp. 218 — 222; Carne's Letters from the East, p. 277.; Three Weeks in Palestine, p. 49.; Monro's Summer Ramble in Syria, vol. i. p. 248.) On the age of the children massacred at Bethlehem, see Vol. III. p. 181. Historical evidence of that fact, II. pp. 620. 621.

Bethphage, a tract of land and also a small village at the foot of the Mount of Olives, between Bethany and Jerusalem. It derived its name from the abundance of figs which grew there. This tract seems to have run along so near to Jerusalem, that the utmost street within the walls was called by that name. It is mentioned in Matt. xxi. 1. and the parallel passages in the other evangelists.

Bethsaida. There were two cities of this name in Palestine.

1. Bethsaida *of Galilee* (John xii. 21.) was a city beyond Jordan, on the western coast of the sea of Tiberias, near the place where the river enters that sea. It was originally a village, and was enlarged into a city and beautified by Philip the Tetrarch, who called it Julia, in honour of the emperor's daughter. It was one of the cities against which Christ denounced a woe (Matt. xi. 21.) for her impenitence and infidelity, after the mighty

BE

works he had done in her. It also was the residence of the apostles Philip, Andrew, and Peter. (John i. 44.) At present Bethsaida exists in little more than the name. (Jowett's Christ. Researches in Syria, p. 178.)

2. The other Bethsaida lay in the region of Gaulonitis, on the eastern side of the sea of Tiberias, and near the place where the river Jordan enters it. This city was enlarged by Philip, who was Tetrarch of that region (Luke iii. 1.), and who called it *Julias*, in honour of Julia the daughter of the emperor Augustus, though it is not known by that name in the New Testament. This Bethsaida is mentioned in Luke ix. 10, where Jesus is said to have withdrawn himself to a desert place belonging to Bethsaida, after the murder of John the Baptist by Herod; and whence also he is said to have returned across the lake to Capernaum, after he had miraculously fed five thousand men with five loaves and two small fishes. (Matt. xiv. 22—34. John vi. 17.

BETH-SHAN or BETH-SHEAN, a city belonging to the half-tribe of Manasseh, not far from the western bank of the Jordan. (1 Sam. xxxi. 10.) After the defeat of the Israelites and the death of Saul and his sons, the Philistines fastened the body of Saul to the walls of this place, whence the men of Jabesh-Gilead took it down and carried it away. In the fourth century, it was a considerable town, and bore, as it had done for several ages, the names of Scythopolis.

BETHSHEMESH.

1. A levitical city in the tribe of Judah, whither the ark was brought after it had been sent back by the Philistines. Some of the inhabitants, having looked into it with vain curiosity, fell down dead, to the number of seventy. (1 Sam. vi. 19.)

2. A city in the tribe of Issachar. (Josh. xix.)

3. A city in the tribe of Naphtali. Josh. xix. 38. Judg. i. 33.)

4. A city in Egypt. See ON, infra.

BETHUEL, the son of Nahor and Milcha, and nephew of Abraham, was the father of Rebekah. (Gen. xxii.)

BETHULIA, a small city, not far from the mountain known by the name of the *Mountain of the Beatitudes*. It is generally supposed to be the *city set on a hill*, mentioned in Matt. v. 14. It stands on a very eminent and conspicuous mountain, and is seen far and near: it is at present called SAFET, and is a very strong position, and might well defy the power of Holofernes and his army. It answers exactly to the description given in the apocryphal book of Judith. (Carne's Letters, p. 367.) Safet is said to have been peopled by about four hundred Jewish families: for the modern town was destroyed by a calamitous earthquake on January 1, 1837. "Not a house remains standing," according to Mr. E. Scott Colman's interesting "Description of part of the scene of the late great earthquake in Syria." (p. 6.)

BO

"Even the castle, which has many times withstood the violence of man, has given way completely to the impetuosity of the shock." The prospect from this eminence is very extensive. "The view," says the Rev. Mr. Jowett, "to the south and on either side, comprehending about one third of the circle, presents the most surprising assemblage of mountains which can be conceived. It is, if such an expression may be allowed, one vast plain of hills. To a distance of 20 or 30 miles toward Nazareth, and nearly the same toward Mount Tabor and Mount Hermon, the far-spreading country beneath is covered with ranges of mountains; which, having passed over them, we know to be ascents and descents far from inconsiderable; but which, from the eminence of Safet, appear only as bold undulations of the surface of the earth. To the left are the inhospitable and unvisited mountains, eastward of the river Jordan. In the centre of the distant scene appears the beautiful lake of Tiberias, fully seen from one extremity to the other; and in the background, stretching beyond the utmost power of vision, are the mountains of Gilead. On a clear day, the view in that direction must be more than 40 miles." (Jowett's Researches in Syria, p. 184.)

BETROTHING in marriage, ceremony of, 409.

BEVERAGE of the Jews, 440.

BIBLE, chronological table of events mentioned in, 527—536.

BIRTH of children, and privileges of the first born, 415, 416.

BITHYNIA, a region of Asia Minor, bounded on the north by the Euxine sea, on the south by Phrygia, on the west by the Propontis, and on the east by Galatia. Saint Peter addressed his first Epistle (among others) to the Hebrew Christians who were scattered throughout Bithynia. (1 Pet. i. 1.)

BLASPHEMY, punishment of, 138.

BLESSING, valley of, notice of, 53.

BLINDNESS of Elymas, observations on, 510. Jewish law concerning blind persons, 195.

BLOOD-AVENGER, office of, 152, 153.

BLOOD. Offerings of, account of, 288—293. Issue of blood, 510.

BOCHIM, valley of, notice of, 54.

BOOKS, antient, form of, 470, 471.

BOTTLES, form of, 393. 460.

BOUNDARIES of the Holy Land, 4—6.

Bows of the Hebrews, notice of, 211.

BOZRAH, a celebrated city of Edom' or Idumæa, which was afterwards called Bostra by the Greeks and Romans. It is now "for the most part a heap of ruins, a most dreary spectacle. Here and there the direction of a street or alley is discernible, but that is all: the modern inhabitants, a mere handful, are almost lost in the maze of ruins." Lord Lindsay's Letters from Egypt, &c., vol. ii. p. 151. In pp. 135—150. his lordship has given a very interesting description of the remains of this once celebrated city, together with a sketch of its antient history.

C Æ

BRASEN ALTAR and LAVER, 233.
BRASEN SERPENT, worship of, 341, 342.
BREAD, how prepared, 438.
BREAST-PLATE of the High Priest, 280.
and of the Jewish soldiers, 207.
BRICKS, antient, form of, 383. and note.
BRIDES and BRIDEGROOMS, customs relating to explained, 410—414.
BRITONS (antient) writing of, 467. note.
BRUISING in a mortar, punishment of, 156.
BUL, a Chaldæan name of the eighth month of the Jewish civil year.
BURIAL, rites of, 515—521.   Not always permitted to capital prisoners by the Romans, 166.
BURNING to death, punishment of, 155, 156.
BURNING of the dead, 514.
BURNT-OFFERINGS, account of, 291, 292.

CÆSAR, originally the surname of the Julian family. After being dignified in the person of Julius Cæsar, it became the usual appellation of those of his family who ascended the imperial throne. The last of these was Nero; but the name was still retained by his successors, as a sort of title belonging to the imperial dignity. In the New Testament the reigning emperor is called Cæsar, without any other distinguishing appellation. The persons mentioned or alluded to by this title are Augustus (Luke ii. 1.), Tiberius (Luke iii. 1. xx. 22. 24, 25.), Claudius (Acts xi. 8.), and Nero. (Acts xxv. 8.   Phil. iv. 22.)

CÆSAREA.

1. *Cæsarea of Palestine,* so called as being the metropolis of Palestine and the residence of the Roman proconsul, was a city on the coast of the Mediterranean Sea, southward from Mount Carmel. Formerly it was named the Tower of Strato; but its harbour being extremely incommodious, Herod the Great erected a spacious mole, and greatly enlarged and beautified the city, which he denominated Cæsarea, in honour of the emperor Augustus, his great patron, to whom he dedicated it in the twenty-eighth year of his reign, with games and other ceremonies, in a most solemn manner, and with a profusion of expense. It is very frequently mentioned in the New Testament; and is sometimes called, by way of eminence, Cæsarea. Here Peter converted Cornelius and his kinsmen, the first fruits of the Gentiles (Acts x.); here lived Philip the Evangelist (Acts xxi. 8.); and here St. Paul so admirably defended himself against the Jews and their orator Tertullus. (Acts xxiv.) Josephus states that it was one of the largest cities in Palestine, and was inhabited principally by Greeks. (Bell. Jud. lib. iii. c. 9. § 1.) After the destruction of Jerusalem, Cæsarea became the capital of Palestine; but at present it retains nothing of its former splendour. The whole of the surrounding country,

C A

on the land side, is a sandy desert: the waves wash the ruins of the moles, the towers, and the port, which antiently were both its ornament and its defence, towards the sea. Not a creature (except jackals and beasts of prey) resides within many miles of this silent desolation: and its ruins, which are very considerable, have long been resorted to as a quarry whenever building materials were required at Acre. (Dr. Clarke's Travels, vol. iv. pp. 446—448.   Mr. Buckingham has a long and interesting description of the antient history, and present state of Cæsarea. See his Travels, pp. 126—138.)

2. *Cæsarea Philippi* (formerly called Paneas) was situated near the springs of the river Jordan. It was first called Laish or Lechem (Judg. xviii. 7.), and after it was subdued by the Danites (v. 29.), it received the appellation of Dan. Cæsarea was a day's journey from Sidon; a day and a half from Damascus. Philip the Tetrarch built it, or, at least, embellished and enlarged it, and named it Cæsarea, in honour of Tiberius; afterwards, in compliment to Nero, it was called Neronias. The woman who was troubled with an issue of blood, and healed by our Saviour (Matt. ix. 20. Luke viii. 43.), is said to have been of Cæsarea Philippi. The present town of Paneas is small; and the ground it stands on is of a triangular form. From this compressed situation the antient city could not have been of great extent. (Irby's and Mangles' Travels, p. 289.)

CAIAPHAS, also called Joseph, was high priest of the Jews at the time Jesus was crucified, and was a principal agent in that transaction. (Matt. xxvi. 3. 57. Luke iii. 2. John xi. 49. xviii. 13, 14. 24. 28. Acts iv. 6.) He was of the sect of the Sadducees.

CAIN, the eldest son of Adam and Eve. He was the first husbandman, and also the first homicide. (Gen. iv.) He slew Abel, because his own works were evil, and his brother's righteous. (1 John iii. 12.)

CAINAN is mentioned in the genealogy of Jesus Christ by St. Luke (iii. 35, 36.) as the son of Arphaxad, and father of Salah; while in the genealogies preserved in Gen. x. 24. xi. 12. and 1 Chron. i. 24. the son of Arphaxad is denominated Salah, and no mention is made of this Cainan. Various suppositions have been offered to reconcile the seeming contradiction. The simplest solution is always the most certain. St. Luke wrote for those Christians who read the Septuagint Greek version more than the original Hebrew; and, consequently, he preferred their version, which adds the name of Cainan to the genealogy of Shem.

CALAMITIES, with which Palestine was visited, 72—77.

CALEB, a celebrated Jewish warrior, of the tribe of Judah; who, as a reward for his fidelity, when sent, together with Joshua, to explore the country of Canaan, was permitted to enter the promised land, where he obtained possessions. (Josh. xiv. 6—13.)

C A

A district belonging to the tribe of Judah was called after his name. (1 Sam. xxx. 14.)

CALENDAR, Jewish, 175—180.

CALF, golden, worshipped by the Israelites, 340. Account of the golden calves of Jeroboam I. 341.

CALVARY, notice of, 19.

CAMELS, notice of, 449, 450.

CAMPS of the Hebrews, form of, 204—206.

CANA, a small town of Galilee, situated on a gentle eminence to the west of Capernaum. This circumstance distinctly proves how accurately the writings of the evangelists correspond with the geography and present appearance of the country. The ruler of Capernaum, whose child was dangerously ill, besought Jesus to *come down* and heal his son. (John iv. 47—51.) About a quarter of a mile from the small and poor village (for such it now is) on the road from Nazareth, there is a well of delicious water close to the road, whence all the water is taken for the supply of the inhabitants. At this well, which is supplied by springs from the mountains about two miles distant, it is usual for pilgrims to halt, as being the source of the water, which our Saviour, by his first public miracle, converted into wine. (John ii. 11.) In consequence of this miracle, both the Christian and Turkish inhabitants of Cana cherish the singular notion that, by drinking copiously of the water of this spring, intoxication is produced. This place is called Cana of Galilee, to distinguish it from Cana or Kanah (Josh. xix. 28.) which belonged to the tribe of Asher, and was situated in the vicinity of Sidon. Here are shown the ruins of a church, which is said to have been erected by the empress Helena, over the spot where the marriage-feast was held. (Dr. Clarke's Travels, vol. iv. pp. 185—188.) Modern Cana is a village, consisting of not more than twenty miserable huts. (Monro's Summer Ramble in Syria, vol. i. p. 304.)

CANAAN, the son of Ham and the progenitor of the Canaanites. For an account of the land called after him, see pp. 2. 6. How divided by Joshua among the twelve tribes, 9—13. Populousness of Canaan, 70, 71. Idols worshipped by the Canaanites, 344, 345. Their extirpation considered, Vol. II. pp. 593 —595.

CANDACE, a queen of Ethiopia mentioned in Acts viii. 27., was probably queen of Meröe, the chief city of Ethiopia Proper, where a succession of females reigned, all of whom bore this name. (Pliny, Nat. Hist. lib. vi. c. 29.) According to Eusebius, Ethiopia continued to be governed by women, even to his time, — the fourth century. (Eccl. Hist. lib. ii. c. 1.)

CANDLESTICK, golden, in the Temple at Jerusalem, 241.

CAPERNAUM, a town of Galilee, situated on the coast of the lake of Gennesareth, on the borders of the tract occupied by the tribes of Zebulon and Nephthalim. This place is celebrated for the *many mighty works* and discourses performed by our Saviour, which brought a heavy woe upon the inhabitants for their infidelity. (Matt. xi. 23.) In the vicinity of this town or city our Lord delivered his admirable sermon; and near it also was the custom-house, at which Matthew the publican was sitting when Jesus called him to the apostleship. (Matt. ix. 1. 9.) Here the Jews had a synagogue (Mark i. 23. Luke iv. 33.), as the Christians afterwards had a church. Mr. Buckingham in 1817 found various remains of some antient settlement in its vicinity; but in 1823 scarcely a relique remained to attest its former existence. Recent travellers describe the appearance of the Lake of Gennesareth from Capernaum as singularly grand and impressive. This place is now called *Tal-hhewn* or *Tal-hhewm*, as it is differently pronounced. (Buckingham's Travels in Palestine, pp. 469, 470. Jowett's Researches in Syria, p. 168.)

CAPHTOR (Jer. xlvii. 4. Amos ix. 7.) and CAPHTORIM (Gen. x. 14. Deut. ii. 23.), the name of a country and people whence the Philistines are said to have originated. According to the passages above referred to, the Caphtorim came originally from Egypt and settled in Caphtor, which word most of the antient versions have rendered Cappadocia; but some have supposed it to be Cyprus, or Crete; which last both Calmet and Gesenius consider to be the place most probably intended. From Caphtor, a colony migrated and settled in the southern part of Canaan.

CAPITAL Punishments of the Jews, account of, 152—158.

CAPPADOCIA, a kingdom of Asia, bounded on the east by Armenia, on the west by Paphlagonia and Galatia, on the north by the Euxine Sea, and on the south by that part of Mount Taurus which looks towards Cilicia. It was famed for mules and horses, of which it gave yearly to the Persians, horses 1500, mules 2000. The Cappadocians are said to have been a nation so servile, that when the Romans offered them their freedom to live by their own laws, they said they could not endure liberty. This country is mentioned in Acts ii. 9. and also by the apostle Peter, who addresses his first Epistle to the Hebrew Christians who were dispersed through Pontus, Galatia, *Cappadocia*, Bithynia, and Asia Minor.

CAPTAIN of the LORD'S HOST, authority and influence of, 202.

CAPTIVES, cruel treatment of, 216—218.

CAPTIVITY (Babylonish), state of the Hebrews during, 104, 105.

CARAVANS, mode of travelling by, 304, note 1. 443.

CARCHEMISH, a fortified city on the Euphrates belonging to the Assyrians, commanding the pass into the northern part of Mesopotamia, from Syria. Necho king of Egypt took it, and left a strong garrison in it; which was taken and cut in pieces, in the fourth year of Jehoiachin king of Judah, by Nebuchadnezzar king of Babylon. (2 Chron.

C L

pose that he was the treasurer or overseer of Herod's revenue.

CILICIA, a country of Asia Minor, between Pamphylia on the west, and Pieria on the east, Mount Taurus on the north, and the Cilician Sea on the south, celebrated on the account of Cicero, proconsul there, but more on the account of St. Paul's birth at Tarsus, a city of Cilicia. (Acts xxii. 3.)

CINNERETH, or CINNEROTH, a city in the canton of the tribe of Nephtali: it is supposed to be the same, which was afterwards called TIBERIAS; as the Lake of Gennesareth, which in Hebrew is calleh the *Sea of Cinnereth*, is unquestionably the Lake or Sea of Tiberias : for an account of which see pp. 38—40.

CIRCUMCISION of proselytes, 266.; how and when performed, 269, 270.

CISLEU. See CHISLEU.

CISTERNS in Palestine, notice of, 45.

CITATION of parties, in legal proceedings, 121.

CITIES, Jewish, 394. How besieged, 214. Treatment of, when captured, 215, 216. Gates of, seats of justice, 116.

CITIES OF REFUGE, 10, 11.

CITIZENS of Rome, privileges and treatment of, when prisoners, 129, 130.

CLASSES of the Jewish priests, 276.

CLAUDA, an island near Crete, situated near the southern and western sea. It is mentioned in Acts xxvii. 16.

CLAUDIUS.

1. Tiberius Claudius Nero Germanicus, the fifth emperor or Cæsar of Rome. He was the son of Nero Drusus, and obtained the imperial dignity principally through the exertion of Herod Agrippa. (Josephus, Ant. Jud. l. xix. c. 4. § 1. Bell. Jud. l. ii. c. 11. § 2.) In the fourth year of his reign occurred the famine predicted by Agabus. (Acts xi. 28. and Kuinöel in loc.) In the first part of his reign he was favourable to the Jews (Jos. Ant. Jud. l. xx. c. 1. § 2.); but in his ninth year he banished, by edict, all those who had taken up their residence at Rome. (Acts xviii. 2. Suetonius, in Claud. c. 25.) He died, A. D. 54, after a weak and inglorious reign of 14 years, of poison administered by his wife Agrippina, who wished to raise her son Nero to the throne. (Robinson, voce Κλαυδιος.)

2. Claudius Lysias, a Roman tribune, who preserved Paul from a conspiracy of the Jews. (Acts xxiii. 23—35. xxiv. 1—9.)

CLEAN and Unclean Animals, Regulations concerning, 438—440.

CLEOPAS, one of the two disciples who went to Emmaus. (Luke xxiv. 18, &c.) The name is of Greek extraction, being contracted from Cleopatros, like Antipas from Antipatros. He is sometimes confounded with

CLOPAS, the husband of Mary, also called Alpheus. (John xix. 25.) By comparing this passage with Luke xxiv. 10., it appears that the wife of Clopas is the same as the

C O

mother of James the Less (compare Matt. xxvii. 56. with Mark xv. 40.) ; but in Matt. x. 3. and Mark iii. 18. James is said to be the son of Alpheus.

CLIMATE of the Holy Land, 28.

CLOTHES, leprosy of, 335. Rending of, a sign of mourning, 405. — See DRESS.

CNIDUS (Acts xxvii. 7.), was a city and promontory of Caria, memorable for the worship of Venus.

COCK-CROWING, a division of time, 169.

COELO-SYRIA. See SYRIA; 9. infra.

COHORTS (Roman), notice of, 221, 222.

COIN, antiquity of, 487.

COLD SEASON of Palestine, 31.

COLOSSÆ (or Colassæ) was a city of Phrygia Pacatiana in Asia Minor, situated near the conflux of the Lycus and the Meander. It was formerly a large and populous place, but in the time of Saint Paul had lost much of its antient greatness, and stood nearly equidistant from Laodicea and Hierapolis. According to Eusebius, all these cities were destroyed by an earthquake in the tenth year of the emperor Nero, about a year after the writing of Saint Paul's Epistle to the Colossians. A few ruins are all that remain of this once opulent city. The modern name of Khóna or Khónas, which is given to it by the Turks of Asia Minor, serves to identify its site ; as we learn from the Greek historian and emperor Constantine Porphyrogennetus, that in his time (the tenth century) Colossæ was called Chonæ, Χωναι. Const. Porph. de Thematibus, lib. i. Th. 3.) The Bishops of Chonæ subscribed to the second Nicene Council in the year 787, one hundred and fifty years before the time of Porphyrogennetus. (See a description of Colossæ and its vicinity, in Mr. Arundell's Visit to the Seven Churches of Asia, pp. 92—101., and his Discoveries in Asia Minor, vol. ii. pp. 183—185. Col. Leake's Journal of a Tour in Asia Minor, p. 254.)

COMMERCE of the Midianites, Phœnicians, and Egyptians, 482. Of the Hebrews, particularly under Solomon and his successors, 482—485. Of Babylon, 555, 556.

COMPENSATION, in what cases allowed, 147.

CONCUBINES, condition of, 408.

CONQUERORS, reception of, among the Jews, 218, and their triumphs, 220. Triumphs of, among the Romans, 227, 228.

CONTRACTS for disposing of property, how made, 192. Contracts of marriage, 409.

CONVERSATION of the Orientals, 432—436.

Coos, an island in the Ægean or Icarian Sea, near Myndos and Cnidus, which had a city of the same name, from which Hippocrates the celebrated physician, and Apelles the famous painter, were called Coi. Here was a large temple of Æsculapius, and another of Juno. It abounded in rich wines, and here were made those Coæ vestes, which were transparent, and are so often noticed by the classic poets. It is mentioned in Acts xxi. 1.

CORBAN, nature of, explained, 295, 296.

o o 3

CORINTH, the metropolis of Achaia Proper, and the ornament of Greece, was situated on an isthmus between the Ægean and Ionian Seas. From the convenience of its situation for commerce, it abounded in riches, and was furnished with all the accommodations, elegances, and superfluities of life. In the Achæan war, it was destroyed by the Romans under the consul Memmius, about 146 years before the Christian æra, and was rebuilt about one hundred years afterwards by Julius Cæsar, who planted a Roman colony here, and made this city the residence of the proconsul of Achaia. Favoured by its situation between two seas, the new city soon regained its antient splendour : commerce produced an influx of riches, and the luxury and voluptuousness which followed in consequence, corrupted the manners of its inhabitants, who became infamous to a proverb. In the vicinity of this city were celebrated the Isthmian games, to which Saint Paul alludes in different parts of his Epistles. Corinth also possessed numerous schools, in which philosophy and rhetoric were taught by able masters, and strangers resorted thither from all quarters to be instructed in the sciences. The number of sophists in particular was very great. The knowledge of these circumstances affords a key to St. Paul's exhortations against fornication, lasciviousness, and covetousness (1 Cor. vi. 9, 10.), and also his defence of the Christian doctrine against the sophists, to whom the fathers attribute all the strifes and contentions that sprang up in this church. In consequence of the war between the Greeks and Turks, Corinth has been reduced to a miserable heap of ruined hovels, affording very insufficient shelter to some wretched outcasts of the province of Roumelia. (Missionary Register, 1828, p. 388.)

CORN, culture and harvesting of, 455, 456. How threshed out, 456, 457 ; and ground, 457, 458.

CORNELIUS, a devout Roman centurion, who was converted to Christianity by the apostle Peter. (Acts x.)

CORNET, notice of, 472.

CORPORAL injuries, how punished among the Jews, 143.

CORRUPTION (Mount of), 49. Extreme corruption of the Jews at the time of Christ's birth, 376—380.

CORSLET of the Jewish soldiers, 207.

COUNCIL (Great) of the Jews, 118.

COUP-DE-SOLEIL in Palestine, effects of, 33.

COURTS OF JUDICATURE (*Jewish*), and proceedings before them, 115—125. (*Roman*), proceedings in, 125—132.

COURTS of Kings, allusions to, 90—94. Principal officers of, 96.

COURTS OF THE TEMPLE, 239—241.

COVENANTS, how made, 189—191. Covenant of salt, 191.

CRETE, an island in the Mediterranean Sea. A Christian church was planted here, pro-

C Y

bably by St. Paul, who committed it to the charge of Titus. (Acts xxvii. 7. 12, 13. 21. Tit. i. 5.) Its inhabitants were celebrated archers, but infamous for their falsehood, debaucheries, and piracies. The Cretans of the present day are precisely what they were in the days of St. Paul,—*always liars, evil beasts, slow bellies.* They are notoriously, whether Turks or Greeks, the worst characters in the Levant. (Hartley's Researches in Greece and the Levant, p. 108.) See the testimonies of profane writers to the immoral character of the Cretans, in Vol. I. p. 172.

CRIMINAL LAW of the Jews, principles of the, 136—144.

CRIMINALS, Jewish mode of treating, and punishing. See pp. 121—125. 129, 130. The Roman mode of punishing them, 132, 133.

CRISPUS, the chief of a synagogue at Corinth, who embraced the Christian faith, and was baptised by St. Paul. (Acts xviii. 8. 1 Cor. i. 14.)

CROSS, form of, 158. Reproach of, explained, 159, 160.

CRUCIFIXION, mode of, 158. Prevalence of, among antient nations, 159. Lingering nature of this punishment, 159. The circumstances of our Saviour's crucifixion considered and illustrated, 160—167. Solution of supposed difficulties as to the *hour* when he was crucified. Vol. II. p. 576.

CUP, Divination by, 358, 359.

CUTTING asunder, punishment of, 157. Cutting off the hair, 150.

CUSH, or Ethiopia, usually rendered Ethiopia in our English Bible, has a very extensive signification. It comprehends all the southern and eastern borders of Egypt. In some parts of the prophecies of Ezekiel, it plainly denotes African Ethiopia, or Nubia and Abyssinia, and in many other passages. (Isa. xviii. 1. xx. 3. Ezek. xxx. 5, &c.) But in others it must signify Asiatic Ethiopia, or Arabia, as in the description of the garden of Eden. (Gen. ii. 13.) The wife of Moses was contemptuously styled a " Cushite," or Ethiopian of Arabia. (Numb. xii. 1.) And where " Persia, Ethiopia, and Libya," are recited in order, the second must denote Arabia. (Ezek. xxxviii. 5.) Herodotus, in his curious catalogue of the various nations composing the army of Xerxes, distinguishes the long-haired Eastern or Asiatic Ethiopians from the woolly-headed Western or African ; both being descendants of Cush, a roving and enterprising race, who gradually extended their settlements from Chusistan, " the land of Cush," on the coasts of the Persian Gulf, through Arabia, to the Red Sea ; and thence crossed over to Africa, and occupied its eastern coast, and gradually penetrated into the interior of Abyssinia. (Dr. Hales's Analysis of Chronology, vol. i. p. 379.)

CYPRUS, an island in the Mediterranean Sea, situated between Cilicia and Syria, and antiently celebrated for the profligacy of its

D A

inhabitants, whose principal deity was the impure goddess Venus. Here Paul and Barnabas landed, A. D. 44, and successfully preached the Gospel. (Acts xiii. 4. *et seq.* xxi. 3.) Cyprus proved to have been a proconsulate, Vol. I. p. 195. The climate of Cyprus is said to be very unhealthy, especially in the summer, when the heat is intense and suffocating.

CYMBAL, a musical instrument, notice of, 472.

CYRENE, the principal city of the province of Libya in Africa, which was thence sometimes denominated Cyrenaica, and which by the evangelist Luke is called *Libya about Cyrene.* (Acts ii. 10.) Simon, whom the Jews compelled to bear our Saviour's cross (Matt. xxvii. 32. Luke xxiii. 26.), was a native of this place. At Cyrene resided many Jews, who were protected by the Ptolemies and by the Roman power, and who had a synagogue at Jerusalem. Among the Christians who were scattered abroad, in consequence of the *persecution that arose about Stephen,* Luke enumerates those of Cyrene. (Acts xi. 20.)

CYRENIUS, in Latin Quirinus. (Luke ii. 2.) Publius Sulpicius Quirinus was sent from Rome as governor of Syria, with which province Judæa was connected after the banishment of Archelaus to Vienne in Gaul, in order to take a census of the whole province. For the various opinions of commentators concerning that census, see Vol. II. pp. 621 —623.

CYRUS, king of Persia, the son of Cambyses a Persian satrap or grandee, and Mandane, was the liberator of the Jews from the Babylonish captivity. The prophet Isaiah (xliv. 28.) mentioned him by name two hundred years before he was born. See PERSIA, infra.

———

DAGON, a Phœnician idol, notice of, 346.

DALMANUTHA. See MAGDALA, infra.

DALMATIA, a province of Europe on the east of the Adriatic Sea, and forming part of the antient Illyricum. In this province, Titus preached the Gospel. (2. Tim. 4. 10.)

DAMASCUS, a most antient city, where Eliezer the servant of Abraham dwelt, was built, according to Josephus (Antiq. l. i. c. 7. § 15.), by Uz, the son of Aram, mentioned in Gen. x. 23., and situated in the valley between Libanus and Antilibanus, watered by the rivers Abana and Pharphar. (2 Kings v. 12.) It was made tributary to to David (2 Sam. viii. 6.); afterwards it was the capital city of the kings of Syria. (Isa. vii. 8.) It is celebrated for its antiquity, and for being still one of the richest and most magnificent cities of the Levant, but most of all for being the place of the miraculous conversion of St. Paul. At that period, Damascus was properly under the Roman dominion, but it was held for a time

D A

by Aretas. It is situated in a beautiful plain. The street, still called *Straight,* where St. Paul dwelt, is entered from the road by Jerusalem : it is as straight as an arrow, a mile in length, broad, and well paved. (Irby's and Mangles' Travels, pp. 281, 282. Carne's Letters, p. 375.) The region around this city is in the Old Testament called *Syria of Damascus.* The manufactures and commerce of modern Damascus are very extensive.

DAN.

1. The son of Jacob and Bilhah, gave his name to one of the tribes of Israel. For the limits of the district assigned to this tribe, see p. 12.

2. The name of a city in the northern extremity of Judæa, in the tribe of Nephtali ; it was situated at the foot of Mount Libanus, not far from the source of the river Jordan. Here Jeroboam I. set up one of the golden calves. In Rev. vii. 6. the name of the tribe of Dan is omitted, either through the mistake of the transcribers, who mistook ΔΑΝ for MAN, and so wrote Manasseh ; or because the tribe had become extinct ; or, by its early apostasy, had become the common receptacle of idols and corrupter of the rest. (See Judg. xviii.) Dr. Robinson thinks that the first opinion is the most probable, because the tribe of Joseph is afterwards mentioned, which included Manasseh and Ephraim. There appears to have been an antient tradition in the church, that, when Antichrist should come, he should be a Jew, and of the tribe of Dan. (Woodhouse on Rev. vii. 6)

DANCING of the Jews, 474. Idolatrous dances of the heathens, 354.

DANIEL, a distinguished Jewish prophet, who lived and wrote at Babylon during the captivity. For a further account of Daniel and his predictions, see Vol. IV. pp. 205—220.

DARIUS, the common name of several Persian kings, three of whom are mentioned in the Old Testament ; viz.

1. *Darius the Mede,* or Cyaxares. (Dan. vi. 1.)

2. *Darius the son of Hystaspes,* whom archbishop Usher supposes to be the Ahasuerus that married Esther.

3. *Darius Codomannus,* who is mentioned in Neh. xii. 22. See PERSIA, infra.

DARTS, fiery, explained, 224, note 1.

DATHAN, one of those who, with Korah, Abiram, and On, conspired against Moses ; and, with his accomplices, was swallowed up in the earth. (Numb. xvi.)

DAUGHTERS, education of, 417. Portions of, 412.

DAVID, the second king of Israel, was the son of Jesse, of the tribe of Judah, and the town of Bethlehem. He was the founder of the Jewish dynasty ; and from him, in the fulness of the time appointed by God, descended the Messiah, of whom he is considered as an illustrious type. A military

o o 4

order established by him, III. 220. In what sense David was " the man after God's own heart," see Vol. II. p 559.; and for the Psalms ascribed to him, see Vol. IV. pp. 101. 104—106.

DAVID, City of, 18.

DAY, how reckoned by the Jews and Romans, 167, 168.

DAY of atonement, how solemnized, 317, 318.

DEAD, law of Moses concerning, 512. Preparation of, for interment, 512—515. Funeral rites of, 515—523.   Duration of mourning for the dead, 523, 524.

DEAD SEA, description of, 40—42. Chemical analysis of its waters, 41. *note.*

DEAF persons, law concerning, 195.

DEATH, Jewish notions of, 511, 512.

DEBORAH.

1. The name of Sarah's nurse, who attended her into Canaan, and continued to reside in the family of Isaac, until her death in the vicinity of Bethel, where she was interred with much lamentation, under an oak, from that circumstance termed Allon Bachuth, or the Oak of Weeping. (Gen. xxiv. 57. xxxv. 8.)

2. A prophetess, the wife of Lapidoth, and the fourth judge of Israel. She was the only woman who ever filled that high office. (Judg. iv. v.)

DEBTORS, laws concerning, 141, 142.

DECAPITATION, punishment of, 156.

DECAPOLIS, district of, 17.

DEDICATION, Feast of, 319.   Vow of Dedication, 325.

DEFENSIVE arms of the Israelites, 207—210.

DEGREES, Academical, conferred in Jewish seminaries, 476, note 2.

DEMAS, for some time, was a companion of St. Paul, in propagating the Gospel; but he afterwards deserted him when a prisoner at Rome, and returned to Thessalonica, which was at that time a very flourishing commercial city. (Col. iv. 14. Philem. 24. 2 Tim. iv. 10.)

DEMETRIUS.

1. A silversmith at Ephesus, whose chief business consisted in making little models of the temple in that city, with the image of Diana included in them. He excited a tumult against St. Paul. (Acts xix.)

2. A Christian, and it should seem a Christian teacher, who is mentioned with much commendation in 3 John, 12.

DEMONIACAL possessions, reality of, 510, 511.

DERBE, a city of Lycaonia, near Isauria, not far from the Cilician range of Mount Taurus. It was the country of Timothy, and is mentioned in Acts xiv. 6. Various ruins of this place are said still to exist, but they have not been described by any modern traveller.   (Col. Leake's Tour in Asia Minor, pp. 100, 101.)

DESERTS in Palestine, account of, 59. Horrors of the Great Arabian Desert described, 60—62.

" DEVOUT MEN," who they were, 269

DEWS, heavy, in Palestine, 34.

DIANA (Αρτεμις), a heathen goddess, the fabled daughter of Jupiter and Latona, and the twin sister of Apollo. She presided over forests and hunting, and also over childbirth ; and was especially worshipped at EPHESUS, where a temple was erected in her honour, which, for its extent and magnificence, was antiently reputed to be one of the wonders of the world. (Acts xix. 24. 27, 28. 34, 35.)

DICHOTOMY, an oriental punishment, 157.

DINAH was the daughter of Jacob and Leah, at the time the patriarch dwelt not far from the country occupied by the Hivites.   Prompted by curiosity, she *went out to see the daughters of the land,* most probably to a festival, when she was ravished by Schechem, a prince of the Hivites. It is not known what became of her, after the extermination of the Schechemites (Gen. xxxiv.) ; but it appears from Gen. xlvi. 15. that she was living in the patriarch's family, and accompanied him into Egypt.

DIONYSIUS, a member of the tribunal of the Areopagus at Athens, who was induced by the preaching of St. Paul to embrace the Christian religion. (Acts xvii. 34.)

DIOSCURI, or the Twins (Διοσκουροι), Castor and Pollux, the fabled sons of Jupiter and Leda, were supposed to have some peculiar power over storms : hence they became the patron deities of seamen. (Acts xxviii. 11.)

DIOTREPHES, a professing Christian, who (it appears) did not receive with hospitality those whom the apostle John sent to him, or permit others to do so. (3 John, 9.)

DISEASES mentioned in the Scriptures, and their treatment, see pp. 504—511.

DISPERSION, Jews of the,who they were, 268.

DIVINATION, by the cup, 358, 359. By inspecting the liver of victims, 360.   By arrows, 359, 360. By the staff, 360. How punished among the Jews, 138.

DIVORCES, Jewish, account of, 414, 415.

DODANIM, the youngest son of Javan. (Gen. x. 4.)   The country peopled by his descendants cannot be exactly ascertained. The Samaritan text and Septuagint version of Gen. x. 4. read *Rhodanim,* which some interpret of the island of Rhodes ; but Bochart refers it to the river Rhodanus, or Rhone.

DOEG, an Idumæan proselyte who was Saul's chief herdsman: he put to death the priests at Nob, whom Saul imagined to be in conspiracy with David, and to supply him with provisions. (1 Sam. xxii. 9—19.)

DOR. or DORA, the capital of Nephet-Dora, a district in Canaan which was conquered by Joshua (Judg. xii. 23.) It is supposed to have been situated on the coast, not far from Mount Carmel.

DORCAS, a charitable and pious Christian widow of Joppa, whom Peter restored to life. (Acts ix. 36—41.) Like the Syriac name Tabitha, it signifies a gazelle.

E D

DRESS, of the Priests, 277, 278. Of the High Priest, 279, 280. Of the Jews, description of, 395—404. Allusions to theatrical dresses, 405, 406.

DRINK, medicated, given to Christ, nature of, 165.

DRINK-OFFERINGS, account of, 294.

DROWNING, a Jewish punishment, 156.

DRUSILLA, notice of, 111.

DULCIMER, notice of, 473.

DURA, a plain in the Babylonian empire, mentioned in Dan. iii. According to the historian Polybius, with whom Professor Gesenius agrees, it was situated in Mesopotamia, at the mouth of the river Chaboras.

DWELLINGS of the Jews, account of, 381—394.

EAR-RINGS of the Jewish women, 402.

EARTH, frequently denotes the land of Judæa, 1, 2.

EARTHQUAKES, frequent in Palestine, 72.

EBAL, the northern peak of Mount Ephraim, a naked, unfruitful rock near Schechem, and over against Mount GERIZIM. These two mountains are separated by a narrow valley. From Ebal the curses were pronounced. (Deut. xi. 29. Josh. viii. 30.)

ECBATANA, the Achmetha of Ezra (vi. 2.), was the principal city of Media, on the site of which stands the modern Hamadan. It was remarkable for the coolness of its temperature; on which account it was chosen to be the summer residence of Cyrus and the succeeding kings of Persia. It was built and fortified by Deioces, king of the Medes. The tombs of Esther and Mordecai are said to be still preserved here; and a colony of Jews, who have been resident at Hamadan from time immemorial, protect their remains. (Alcock's [unpublished] Travels in Russia, Persia, and Greece, in 1828-29, p. 80. London, 1831. 8vo)

EDEN.

1. The name of the country in which the *Garden* of our first parents was placed. (Gen. ii. 8. 15. iii. 23, 24. iv. 16.) It has been variously supposed to have been situated in Syria, in Babylonia, near the mouth of the Euphrates and in Armenia, whence issue the heads of the Euphrates and Tigris, two of the paradisaical rivers well ascertained; and two others, whose springs are in the neighbourhood, agree in many respects with the third and fourth rivers mentioned by Moses. This last opinion is the most probable, and has been chiefly adopted. A synoptical view of the nine principal hypotheses respecting the site of the terrestrial paradise, is given by the Rev. N. Morren, with illustrative notes, in his valuable translation of Rosenmüller's Biblical Geography of Central Asia, vol. i. pp. 91—98.

E G

2. A pleasant city of Syria, situated on Mount Lebanon. In our authorised version of Amos i. 5. it is rendered the *house of Eden* (marg. rendering *Beth-Eden.*). A beautifully situated village, called *Ehden* still exists on Lebanon.

3. A country of Mesopotamia or Assyria, under the power of the Assyrians. (2 Kings xix. 12. Isa. xxxvii. 12.) In Ezek. xxvii. 23. it is joined with Asshur. Prof. Gesenius conjectures that it may be Maedon in Diarbekir, towards the Tigris.

EDOMITES, notice of. See p. 8., and Idumæa, p. 17.

EDUCATION of children among the Jews, 417, 418.

EGLON, a king of the Moabites, who oppressed the Israelites for eighteen years. (Judg. iii. 12.) At length Ehud, a Benjamite, was raised up to deliver them from their oppression, who slew him in the manner related in Judg. iii. 15—26.

EGYPT, (in Hebrew called Mizraim, after Mizraim the son of Ham.) a country of Africa, the length of which was very disproportionate to its breadth : its extent from the mouths of the Nile to Syene, the border of Nubia, under the tropic of Cancer, was about 500 miles; but it was little wider than the valley through which the Nile ran, in Upper Egypt, until it reached the Lower Egypt, at some distance above the head or vertex of the Delta, where the valley expanded itself. The Upper Egypt or Thebaid seems to be called Pathros in Scripture, as distinguished from the Lower properly called Caphtor, or Egypt. (Compare Isa. xi. 11. with Ezek. xxix. 14. ; and Jer. xliv. 1. with Ezek. xxx 14—16. Deut. ii. 23. Jer. xlvii. 4.) Its population, during the reigns of the Pharaohs, Mr. Lane is of opinion was about six or seven millions. (Manners and Customs of the Modern Egyptians, vol. i. p. 27.) This country seems to have attained an earlier and a higher degree of civilisation and refinement than any other in the world. Even in Abraham's days we find it the seat of a royal government, and a princely court, abounding with provisions, while the neighbouring countries, and even the fertile regions of Palestine, were exposed to frequent famines. (Gen. xii. 10.) In his grandson Jacob's time, there was a settled caravan trade carried on through Palestine from Arabia and the East, for spicery, balm, and myrrh, and probably also for slaves. (Gen. xxxvii. 25.)[1] Its superior fertility, indeed, was occasioned by the annual inundation of the Nile, the rising of which has furnished the prophet Jeremiah (xlvi. 7, 8.) with a fine image[2], and by the irrigation of their lands (Deut. xi. 10.); and wherever this is still practised, the land now literally brings forth by handfuls, as it did in the

---

[1] There is a valuable " Inquiry into the Commerce of Antient Egypt," by Mr. F. M. Hubbard, in the tenth Volume of the Andover Biblical Repository, (July 1837), pp. 33—66.

[2] At Molubis, on the banks of the Nile, Mr. Jowett observed a cattle-fair. Several

time of the patriarch Joseph. (Gen. xli. 47.) In every age of the world, Egypt has been celebrated for those stupendous monuments of antient art, — the pyramids; several of which have been successfully explored by the enterprising traveller, Mr. Belzoni. The countless multitude of date trees, which form even forests about some of the villages, furnish a great source of subsistence to the people. To cut these down (as it is said the French were proceeding to do, and would have done, but that the people surrendered at the prospect of this utter ruin) would be to cut off the support of the present, and the hopes of a future generation. Nothing could be more terrible than this denunciation of Jeremiah (xlvi. 22, 23.) against Egypt: — *They shall march with an army, and come against her with axes as hewers of wood : they shall cut down her forest, saith the Lord, though it cannot be searched ; because they are more than the grasshoppers, and are innumerable.* (Jowett's Christian Researches in the Mediterranean, pp. 167. 170.) On the prophecies concerning Egypt, and their fulfilment, see Vol. I. p. 288.

The Egyptians boasted of being the most antient people in the world ; the inventors of arts and sciences : they communicated to the Greeks the names of the gods, and their theology : they exceeded in superstition and idolatry, worshipping stars, men, animals, and even plants. Moses informs us, that the Hebrews sacrificed beasts, whose slaughter was considered by the Egyptians as an abomination (Exod. viii. 26.), likewise that they would not eat with the Hebrews, because they abhorred all shepherds. Concerning the motives of this aversion, opinions are divided. Some believe it to be founded on the invasion of Egypt by the shepherd kings from Arabia, who reigned here a long time, according to Manetho. Others think that the Egyptians, after their king Sesostris, being accustomed to a soft and idle life, detested shepherds, whose profession was more active and laborious. Others, that the Egyptians were so averse to shepherds, because of their killing and eating sheep, kids, and goats, which were objects of their worship.

The antiquity of the Egyptian empire is indisputable, though its origin is involved in impenetrable obscurity. The common name of the Egyptian kings was Pharaoh, which signified sovereign power, (though each had another name peculiar to himself,) and by this appellation they are generally called in the Scriptures until the time of Solomon; after which they are designated by their proper names. History has preserved the names of several kings of Egypt, and a succession of their dynasties : but the inclination of these historians to magnify the great antiquity of their nation has injured their credibility. It is certain that the Egyptian dynasties were not all successive, but many of them were collateral : and the greatest part of the kings who are placed one after the other, were contemporary, one reigning in one part of Egypt, another in another. After the captivity, Egypt became a place of resort to great numbers of the Jews, who settled there either of their own accord, or in consequence of the invitations and encouragements held out to them by Alexander the Great and the Ptolemies: so that in the reign of Ptolemy Philometer, they were enabled to erect a temple at Leontopolis, similar to that at Jerusalem, and to establish in it all the rites of their paternal worship. (Josephus, Ant. Jud., lib. xiii. c. 3. § 1—3.)

Sketch of the History of the Egyptian Empire as connected with that of the Israelites.

No intercourse subsisted between the Israelites and Egyptians, from the departure of the former out of Egypt, until the reign of Solomon, who having married a daughter of Pharaoh (1 Kings iii. 1 vii 8.), and established a considerable trade between Egypt and Palestine, the two kingdoms became intimately connected. By way of dowry to

---

buffaloes were swimming from the opposite side across the water. Their unwieldy body sinks deep into the water, so that only a part of the neck is level with the surface; while their uplifted heads just raises the snorting nostrils above the water. Often, a little Arab boy takes his passage across the Nile upon the back of this animal ; setting his feet on the shoulders, holding fast by the horns, and thus keeping his balance. As the buffaloes rose out of the water on the bank, I was struck with their large bony size, compared with the little that had appeared of them while in the water. Their emerging brought to mind the passage, Gen. xli. 1, 2. — *Behold he stood by the river : and behold there came up out of the river, seven well-favoured kine and fat fleshed ; and they fed in a meadow.* It was the very scene, and the very country. (Jowett's Christian Researches in the Mediterranean, p. 166.) Mr. J., speaking of the boat in which he crossed the river Nile, says that it " was ballasted with earth taken from the river-banks—very stiff and rich soil, without stones. With this same mud the sides of the boat were plastered, at those parts in the fore-half of the vessel were moveable planks were placed, in order to raise the gunnel higher : the mud filled up the crevices, and prevented the water from gushing in, as would otherwise be the case. This mud was so rich and slimy, and when dry so firm and impervious, that, together with the strong reed that grows on the banks, it is easy to conceive how the mother of Moses constructed a little ark, which would float ; she then placed it among the flags, in order that the stream might not carry it down, Exod. iii. 3," (Ibid. p. 167.)

E G

his daughter, the king of Egypt gave Solomon several cities which he had taken from the Philistines. (1 Kings ix. 16.) Afterwards, however, this intimacy declined, as Pharaoh afforded shelter, even during the life of Solomon, to Jeroboam the son of Nebat (1 Kings ix. 26. 40.), and to Hadad the son of the king of Edom or Idumæa. (Ibid. 18, 19.) The connection was totally broken off in the reign of Rehoboam, the son and successor of Solomon: Shishak king of Egypt invaded the kingdom of Judah, and despoiled the temple of its treasures. (xiv. 25, 26.)

Towards the end of the kingdoms of Israel and Judah, the sovereigns of those countries, finding themselves too weak to resist the Assyrian and Babylonian monarchs who pressed them closely, had frequent recourse to the kings of Egypt for succour. But these applications were always fatal to them. The vain confidence of the people of God in these heathen princes is a frequent subject of reproof in the writings of the prophets. (Isa. xxx. 2. xxxvi. 6. Ezek. xxix. 6, 7. Hosea, *passim*, particularly chapters vii. viii. and ix.) Hezekiah derived no advantage from his alliance with the king of Egypt (2 Kings xviii. 21.); neither was Hoshea king of Israel benefited by his alliance with So, king of the same country. (Hosea vii. 11. viii. 13. ix. 3. xii. 9. Jer. ii. 18. 2 Kings xvii. 4.) Josiah king of Judah was slain in the vain attempt to oppose the passage of Pharaoh Necho through his territories, when marching against the Assyrians. (2 Kings xxiii. 29.) Pharaoh pushed on beyond the Euphrates, and took Carchemish, which place he garrisoned; and on his return through Judæa he deposed Jehoahaz, whom the people had raised to the throne, and placed Eliakim or Jehoiakim in his stead, on whom he imposed a tribute.

The governor of Syria and Phœnicia, who held those provinces in behalf of the king of Babylon, having put them under the dominion of the king of Egypt, Nabopolassar, king of Assyria, sent his son Nebuchadnezzar against him; who first retook Carchemish, and afterwards reduced the whole of the country between the Euphrates and the Nile to his father's sceptre. (Jer. xlvi. Josephus, Ant. Jud. lib. x. c. 6.)

A. M. 3334, B. C. 670. Psammetichus succeeded his father Pharaoh-Necho king of Egypt, and reigned six years. (Herodotus, lib. ii. c. 159—161. After his death, Apries (the Pharaoh-Hophra of the Scriptures) ascended the throne. He made an alliance with Zedekiah king of Judah, and with the king of Ethiopia against Nebuchadnezzar. The latter marched against them, and besieged Jerusalem. The king of Egypt came to the assistance of Zedekiah, but was repulsed and obliged to retire into his own country, whither he was pursued by Nebuchadnezzar, who after taking the cities of Jerusalem and Tyre, conquered and ravaged Egypt, whence

E L

he carried away great numbers of captives, agreeably to the predictions of Jeremiah (xliii. xliv. xlvi.) and Ezekiel (xxix.— xxxi.). Apries was put to death, and Amasis, his enemy and rival for the Egyptian sceptre, was elevated to the throne, A. M. 3435, B. C. 569.

Egypt continued subject to Nebuchadnezzar and his successors until the time of Cyrus the Great. This power rebelled towards the close of his reign. Cambyses, his son and successor, conducted an immense army into Egypt. That country was again subdued, and suffered every excess which the cruel victor could possibly inflict upon it, A. M. 3479, B. C. 525. In the reign of Darius, the son of Hystaspes, the Egyptians once more shook off the Persian yoke, but were reduced to a more oppressive bondage than before by his son and successor Xerxes. In those two invasions the predictions of Isaiah (xxix.), and Jeremiah (xliii. 11—13.), were most signally fulfilled.

A. M. 3544, B. C. 460. During the reign of Artaxerxes Longimanus, the Egyptians once more took up arms, and with the assistance of the Greeks, their allies, protracted the war for six years. Again reduced to the Persian yoke they continued dependent on the Persian monarchs, though governed by their kings, until the reign of Artaxerxes surnamed Ochus, who, in order to punish for a fourth revolt, totally destroyed the kingdom of Egypt, and made it a province of the Persian empire, A. M. 3654, B. C. 350. (Calmet, Hist. Profane de l'Orient, § V. Dissert. tom. ii. pp. 341—343.)

EHUD, the second judge of the Israelites, whom he delivered from the oppression of EGLON king of Moab. (Judg. iii. 15—26.)

EKRON, a city and government of the Philistines, allotted to Judah by Joshua (xv. 45.); but afterwards given to Dan. (Josh. xix. 43.) It was near the Mediterranean, between Ashdod and Jamnia. Ekron was a powerful city; and it does not appear that the Jews ever peaceably possessed it: the Ekronites were the first who proposed to send back the ark, to be delivered from those calamities which it brought on their country. (1 Sam. v. 10.) Beelzebub was adored at Ekron. (2 Kings i. 2.) The site of this city is not known, thus attesting the literal fulfilment of the prophet Zephaniah (ii. 4.), that *Ekron shall be* ROOTED UP.

ELAH, the fourth king of Israel, succeeded his father Baasha, and reigned two years at Tirza, where he was assassinated by Zimri at an entertainment given to him by one of his officers. (1 Kings xvi. 6—10.)

ELAH, Valley of, notice of, 54.

ELAM, the eldest son of Shem, who settled in a country in the south of Media, called after him Elam. Strictly, Elam denotes ELYMAIS, a district of Persia, near the bottom of the Persian Gulf between Media and Babylonia, and forming part of the region of Susiana: but in a wider sense, it is used

E L

generally for Media itself, as in Dan. viii. 2. Gen. x. 22. xiv. 1. Isa. xi. 11. xxii. 6. Jer. xlix. 34—39. Ezek. xxxii.34. In most of these passages, Elam is represented as a contentious people, causing disturbance to the neighbouring nations. Strabo says as much concerning the inhabitants of Elymais. In Jer. xxv. 25, and Acts ii. 9. the inhabitants of this country are mentioned in conjunction with the Medes.

ELATH, ELOTH, or AILATH, a town and port of Idumæa, situated on the Red Sea. On the conquest of Edom by David, he took possession of this place, and there established a trade to all parts of the then known world. Solomon built ships here, and sent them to Ophir. (2 Sam. viii. 14. 2 Chron. viii. 17, 18.) Elath continued in possession of the Israelites about 150 years, until, in the reign of Joram, it was recovered by the Edomites (2 Kings viii. 20.), from whom it was retaken by Azariah. (2 Kings xiv. 22.) Under his grandson Ahaz it was recaptured by the Edomites (xvi. 6.); from whom, after many changes under the Ptolemies, it finally passed into the possession of the Romans. It was antiently a great emporium for the Tyrians.

EL-BETHEL. (Gen. xxxv. 7.), and EL-ELOHE-ISRAEL (Gen. xxxiii. 20.), the name of two altars erected by Jacob after his return to Canaan. The first signifies that God was still the God of Bethel to him in performing the promises there made; the second implies, that the mighty God was still the object of worship to him and his offspring.

ELDAD and MEDAD were two of the seventy elders appointed by Moses; who received the temporary gift of prophesying, or of forming divine hymns, and singing them to God. (Numb. xi. 26.)

ELDERS of the Israelites, 83. Elders of the gate, 116.

ELEAZAR.

1. The third son of Aaron, whom he succeeded in the pontificate. Having been born in the desert, he entered the land of Canaan, in the division of which he assisted Joshua. After executing the office of high priest about 23 years, he died and was buried in the mountains of Ephraim.

2. The son of Abinadab: he was sanctified or set apart to keep the ark of God, which was deposited in his father's house, after it had been sent back to the Israelites, by the Philistines. (1 Sam. vii. 1.)

3. The son of Dodo, the second of David's mighty men, who distinguished himself by his brave achievements. He was one of the three warriors who forced their way through the Philistine forces, to procure water for David from the well of Bethlehem, at the imminent hazard of their lives. (1 Chron. xi. 17—19.)

ELECT LADY, more correctly, the Lady Electa, a pious Christian matron, commended by St. John in his second Epistle. Compare Vol. IV. p. 472.

E L

ELEPHANTIASIS, the disease of Job, 507.

ELHANAN.

1. Another son of Dodo, and one of David's warriors. (1 Chron. xi. 26.)

2. The son of Jair, or Jaare-oregim, another warrior, who slew the giant Lahmi, the brother of Goliath. (2 Sam. xxi. 19.)

ELI.

1. The seventh high priest of the Israelites, whom he judged forty years: he was descended from Ithamar. It is not known why the pontifical dignity was transferred to him from the family of Eleazar. He was severely reproved for his false indulgences to his profligate sons, Hophni and Phinehas: he died suddenly on hearing tidings of the capture of the ark, and the total discomfiture of the Israelites by the Philistines. (1 Sam. ii, iii.)

2. The name of a man, who was the father of Joseph, the husband of Mary. (Luke iii. 23.)

ELIAKIM.

1. A governor of the royal household under Hezekiah; by whom he was deputed, with others, to receive the proposals of Rabshakeh, on the part of Sennacherib. He succeeded Shebna in this office, agreeably to the prediction of Isaiah; who highly eulogised his character, and, under images borrowed from the genius of oriental poetry, promised that he should enjoy unbounded confidence and authority.

2. A king of Judah, the son of Josiah, whose name was afterwards changed by Pharaoh-Necho king of Egypt into JEHOIAKIM (which see).

ELIAS. See ELIJAH.

ELIASHIB, grandson of Joshua the high priest, rebuilt part of the wall of Jerusalem. He was allied, by marriage, to Tobiah the Ammonite, to whom he gave spacious apartments in the second temple, to the scandal of his religion, and the great damage of the country. (Neh. xii. 10. iii. 1. xiii. 4—9.)

ELIEZER.

1. The chief of Abraham's servants, and eminent for the confidence reposed in him by the patriarch, as well as for the piety and prudence with which he executed the commission of procuring a wife for Isaac. (Gen. xxiv.) Before the birth of Isaac, it should seem that Abraham had designed to make him his heir. (Gen. xv. 2.)

2. The son of Dodavah, a prophet, who foretold to Jehoshaphat, that the trade-fleet, which he had fitted out in conjunction with the unworthy Ahaziah, should be wrecked, and prevented from sailing to Tarshish. (2 Chron. xx. 37.)

ELIHU, one of the interlocutors in the book of Job, was "the son of Barachel the Buzite, of the kindred of Ram," or Aram. (Job xxxii. 2. Gen. xxii. 21.) He was of the family of the patriarch Abraham, and was descended from Buz the son of Nahor and Milcah: it is most probable that that branch of the patriarchal family settled in Idumæa.

E M

ELIJAH, or ELIAS, after Moses, was the most celebrated prophet of the Old Testament, surnamed the Tishbite, from Thisbe the place of his birth. He was a strenuous vindicator of the worship of the true God, in opposition to the idolatrous kings under whom he lived. (1 Kings xvii—xix.) He was miraculously translated to heaven (2 Kings ii. 1—11.); and many ages after a still more distinguished honour awaited him. Elijah and Moses are the only men whose history does not terminate with their departure out of this world. Elijah appeared, together with Moses, on Mount Tabor, at the time of Christ's transfiguration, and conversed with him respecting the great work of redemption, which he was about to accomplish. (Matt. xvii. 1—3. and the parallel passages in Mark and Luke.) For an illustration of the conduct of Elijah towards the prophets of Baal, see pp. 355, 356.

ELIM, the seventh encampment of the Hebrews, in the north skirt of the desert, where they found twelve fountains and seventy palm-trees. When this place was visited by Dr. Shaw, in the early part of the eighteenth century, he found here nine wells or fountains, and 2000 palm-trees. (Exod. xv. 27.)

ELIPHAZ, surnamed the Temanite, one of the friends of Job, was most probably descended from Eliphaz the son of Esau, to whom the city or district of Teman was allotted. (Dr. Good, on Job ii. 11.)

ELISHA, the successor of Elijah in the prophetic office: he wrought numerous miracles in the kingdom of Israel, which are related in 2 Kings ii.—xiii. See Vol. II. p. 601. where the destruction of forty-two young persons by this prophet is vindicated from the cavils of sceptics.

ELISHAH, ISLES of ELISHAH, a Grecian province whence purple was brought to Tyre. (Gen. x. 4. Ezek. xxvii. 7.) According to Prof. Gesenius, the name is most probably akin to Elis, which in a wider sense is used for the whole Peloponnesus. According to others, it is Hellas, or Greece. This country most probably derived its name from Elishah the son of Javan, whose descendants peopled part of Greece.

ELKOSH, the birth-place of the prophet Nahum (i. 1.): it is either 1. *Elkosh* or *Alkosh* in Assyria, where he is supposed to have died: his reputed grave is visited in pilgrimage by the Jews. Or 2. according to Jerome, it is *Helcesei* a village in Galilee.

ELUL, the sixth month of the Jewish ecclesiastical year, and the twelfth month of the civil year. The etymology of this word is obscure. For a notice of the festivals in this month, see p. 180.

ELYMAIS. See ELAM.

ELYMAS. See BAR-JESUS, p. 558.

EMBALMING, Egyptian and Jewish processes of, 512, 513.

EMIMS, the antient inhabitants of the land of Canaan, to the east and north-east of the

E N

Dead Sea. They were a numerous, warlike, and gigantic race, probably descended from Ham. They were defeated by Chedorlaomer in Shaveh Kiriathaim, or the Plain of Kiriathaim. (Gen. xiv. 5.)

EMMAUS, a small village of Judæa, distant sixty furlongs from Jerusalem. It is memorable for the very interesting conversation between Jesus Christ and two of his disciples in the evening of the day of his resurrection. (Luke xxiv.) "The mean and trifling village, all that now exists, of Emmaus, stands on an eminence, in the midst of hills. The people, who live here, are poor and wretched; they are chiefly Christians." (Carne's Recollections of the East, p. 213.)

ENCAMPMENTS of the Jews, 204—206.

EN-DOR, a city belonging to the half-tribe of Manasseh on the west side of the Jordan : according to Eusebius, it was four Roman miles to the south of Mount Tabor. Here dwelt the sorceress, who was consulted by Saul a short time before the fatal battle of Gilboa.

EN-EGLAIM, or the fountain of calves, a place situated on the northern point of the Dead Sea. (Ezek. xlvii. 10.)

EN-GEDDA, mountains of, 50.

EN-GEDI, or the *Fountain of the Kid*, antiently called Hazazon Tamar, was a city in the tribe of Judah, not far from the southern point of the Dead Sea. In the vicinity of this place is a cistern, which has existed from the earliest times: here it was the custom to water the flocks, (whence most probably originated its name,) Monro's Summer Ramble in Syria, vol. i. p. 269. Its surrounding district abounded with palm-trees and vines. (Josh. xv. 62. 2 Chron. xx. 2. Song of Sol. i. 14.) Not far from this place was the cave of En-gedi; for a notice of which, see p. 56.

ENGRAVING, art of, among the Jews, 471.

EN-MISPHAT, or the *Fountain of Judgment*, the same as the waters of Meribah, or contention, the name of a fountain in the desert of Sin, otherwise called Kadesh.

EN-ROGEL, or the *Fountain of the Spy*, a fountain on the south-east of Jerusalem : it is supposed to be the same as the fountain of SILOAM ; for a notice of which, see p. 43.

ENOCH.

1. The son of Cain, in honour of whom the first city mentioned in Scripture was called Enoch by his father, who erected it. (Gen. iv. 17.) It is supposed to have been situated on the east of Eden, but its precise site cannot now be ascertained.

2. The father of Methuselah, memorable for his piety. Having lived 365 years, he was translated and did not see death. (Gen. v. 18. 24. Heb. xi. 5.) The memory of which event is confirmed by heathen traditions, Vol. I. p. 147. According to the modern Jews, and the Arabians (who call him *Idris the learned*), he was the inventor of letters, arithmetic, and astronomy; probably from the etymology of the name, which signifies initiated or initiating. For a notice of

E P

the apocryphal prophecy of Enoch, see Vol. II. p. 347.

ENON, a place or fountain, not far from Salim, where John baptised many persons. According to Eusebius, it was eight Roman miles from Scythopolis, and fifty-three north-east of Jerusalem.

ENOS, the son of Seth and grandson of Adam, was born A.M. 235, and died at the age of 905 years: consequently he was contemporary with Adam 695 years, and 84 years with Noah. After the birth of Enos, divine worship, which till that time had been confined to private families, became public. The descendants of Seth separated themselves from the descendants of Cain, and invoked the name of God, probably on fixed days, and in assemblies where every one was admitted. (Gen. v. 6. 1 Chron. i. 1. Gen. iv. 26.)

ENTERTAINMENTS of the Jews, 441, 442.

EPÆNETUS, the first person in proconsular Asia who embraced the Christian faith. (Rom. xvi. 5.) In which passage, many modern versions, and among them our authorised version, read Achaia, which is a mistake in the copy whence they were made: for the Alexandrian and Vatican manuscripts, the Codices Ephrem, Claromontanus, Augiensis, and Boernerianus, and the readings in the Codex Vindobonensis Lambecianus 34. (No. 37. of Griesbach's notation), together with the Memphitic, Armenian, Ethiopic, and Vulgate versions, besides many Latin fathers,—all read 'Aσιas instead of 'Aχαιas; which lection Griesbach considers as certainly equal, if not preferable, to the received reading. That it *is* preferable to that reading is clear from 1 Cor. xvi. 15., where the family of Stephanas is said to be " *the first-fruits of Achaia.*"

EPAPHRAS, the coadjutor of St. Paul in his labours, was reputed to be the first bishop of the church at Colossæ, to which he was affectionately attached. (Col. i. 17. iv. 12. Philem. 23.) He was with St. Paul during his first imprisonment; and has sometimes, but without proof, been confounded with

EPAPHRODITUS, whom that apostle styles a fellow-labourer and fellow-soldier, as having participated in his labours and dangers. He appears to have been the minister of the Philippian church, by which he was sent to carry pecuniary aid to St. Paul, who speaks of him in terms of great respect. (Phil. iv. 18. ii. 25—30.)

EPHESDAMMIM, a place between Shochoh and Azekah on the west of the valley of Elah. Here the army of the Philistines was encamped, when Goliath insulted the hosts of Israel: and here also they were found after David's coronation, and suffered a great slaughter.

EPHESUS was the metropolis of proconsular Asia. (On the powers of the " assembly " held in this city, see pp. 135, 136.) This celebrated city, the remains of which give a high idea of its former beauty, extent, and magnificence, was situated in that part of Asia which was antiently called Ionia (but

E P

now Natolia), about five miles from the Ægean Sea, on the sides and at the foot of a range of mountains overlooking a fine plain that was watered and fertilised by the river Caÿster. Ephesus was particularly celebrated for the temple of Diana, a most magnificent and stately edifice, which had been erected at the common expense of the inhabitants of Asia Proper, and was reputed one of the seven wonders of the world: but the very site of this stupendous and celebrated edifice is now undetermined. Widely scattered ruins attest the splendour of the theatre mentioned in Acts xix. 31.; the elevated situation of which, on Mount Prion, accounts for the ease with which an immense multitude was collected, the loud shouts of whose voices, reverberated from the neighbouring Mount Corissus, would not a little augment the uproar which was occasioned by the populace rushing into the theatre. In the time of Saint Paul, Ephesus was the metropolis of Asia Minor: it abounded with orators and philosophers; and its inhabitants, in their Gentile state, were celebrated for their idolatry and skill in magic, as well as for their luxury and lasciviousness. The present state of Ephesus affords a striking illustration of the accomplishment of prophecy. Ephesus is the first of the apocalyptic churches addressed by the evangelist in the name of Jesus Christ. " His *charge* against her is a declension in religious fervour (Rev. ii. 4.), and his *threat* in consequence (Rev. ii. 5.), a total extinction of her ecclesiastical brightness. After a protracted struggle with the sword of Rome, and the sophisms of the Gnostics, Ephesus at last gave way. The incipient indifference, censured by the warning voice of the prophet, increased to a total forgetfulness; till, at length, the threatenings of the Apocalypse were fulfilled, and Ephesus sunk with the general overthrow of the Greek empire in the fourteenth century." (Emerson's Letters from the Ægean, vol. i. pp. 212, 213.) Ephesus is now under the dominion of the Turks, and is in a state of almost total ruin. The plough has passed over the city; and in March, 1826, when visited by the Rev. Messrs. Hartley and Arundell, green corn was growing, in all directions, amidst the forsaken ruins: and *one* solitary individual only was found who bore the name of Christ, instead of its once flourishing church. Where once assembled thousands exclaimed, " Great is Diana of the Ephesians," now the eagle yells and the jackal moans. The soil of the plain, on which the ruins of Ephesus lie, appears rich: in the summer of 1835, when visited by Mr. Addison, it was covered with a rank burnt up vegetation. This place (he states,) is a dreary uncultivated spot: a few corn-fields were scattered along the site of the antient city, which is marked by some large masses of shapeless ruins and stone walls. (Hartley's Journal, in Missionary Register, 1827, pp. 290—292. Arundell's Visit to the Seven Churches, pp. 27—

E S

56., and his Discoveries in Asia Minor, vol. ii. pp. 252—260. Addison's Damascus and Palmyra, vol. i. pp. 340, 341.)

EPHOD of Gideon, 342. ; and of the High Priests, 279, 280.

EPHRAIM.

1. The youngest son of Joseph by Asenath, was adopted and blessed by Jacob; who laid his right hand on Ephraim, and his left on the head of Manasseh, to intimate that the youngest son should be greater than the eldest, and his posterity more numerous. He gave his name to one of the tribes of Israel; for the limits allotted to which, see p. 12. The Ephraimites were unable to utter the sound *sh,* to which they gave the sound of *s.* (Judg. xii. 6.) It is a singular circumstance, that the modern Greeks have not the sound of *sh* in their language. Hence they are liable to be detected like the Ephraimites. (Hartley's Researches in Greece, p. 232.)

2. A considerable city of Judæa, eight Roman miles north of Jerusalem, according to Eusebius, and near a desert of the same name; to which Jesus Christ retired after he had raised Lazarus from the dead. (John xi. 54.)

3. Ephraim, Forest of, 66.

4. Ephraim, Mountains of, 51.

EPHRATAH.

1. Another name for the town of Bethlehem. (Mic. v. 2.)

2. The lot of Ephraim. (Psal. cxxxii. 6.)

EPICUREANS, the followers of Epicurus, a celebrated Athenian philosopher: they acknowledged no gods, except in name only, and absolutely denied that they exercised any providence over the world. For an illustration of Saint Paul's masterly address to them at Athens, see Vol. IV. p. 341.

EPISTLES, Antient, form of, 470.

EPOCHAS of the Jews, account of, 181.

ERASTUS, treasurer of the city of Corinth, who embraced Christianity and became the fellow-labourer of Saint Paul.

ESAR-HADDON, the son and successor of Sennacherib king of Assyria; for a notice of whose reign, see ASSYRIA, p. 553.

ESAU, or EDOM, the eldest son of Isaac, and the twin brother of Jacob. He delighted much in hunting; while Jacob, being of a more domestic turn, became the favourite of his mother Rebekah, by whose counsel and direction he surreptitiously obtained his father's blessing in preference to Esau; who found no place or scope for a change of purpose in his father, though he sought it carefully with tears. (Gen. xxvii. 1—34. Heb. xii. 17.) On Jacob's return into Canaan from Mesopotamia, whither he had fled to avoid his brother's resentment, Esau received him with great kindness; and on Isaac's death he returned to Mount Seir. Concerning the remainder of his life or the manner of his death the Scriptures are silent. In the historical and prophetical books, Esau and Edom respectively denote Idumæa and the

E U

Idumæan tribes. In Rom. ix. 13. where St. Paul cites Mal. i. 2, 3., the apostle is evidently treating only of the posterities of Jacob and Esau.

ESDRAELON, Plain of, account of, 57.

ESCHOL, Valley of, a fertile vale in the land of Canaan and in the southern part of Judah. Here the Hebrew spies, while exploring the country, cut a very large cluster of grapes, which was carried back by two men, as a specimen of the delicious fruit produced by the country.

ESPOUSALS, Jewish, form of, 409.

ESSENES, Sect of, account of, 368, 369.

ESTHER, or HADASSAH, the great niece of Mordecai, by whom she was adopted. On the divorce of Vashti, she became the queen consort of Ahasuerus: her history is related in the book of Esther; for an analysis of which, see Vol. IV. pp. 64—67.

ETAM.

1. A city in the tribe of Judah between Bethlehem and Tekoah, which was rebuilt and fortified by Rehoboam. (2 Chron. xi. 6.) Josephus says, that there are very pleasant gardens, abounding with water, at Etham, about fifty furlongs or six miles from Jerusalem, to which Solomon used to resort. (Ant. Jud. lib. viii. c. 7.) It is highly probable, that this was the site of one of King Solomon's houses of pleasure, where he made him *gardens and orchards, and pools of water.* (Eccles. ii. 5, 6.) In the vicinity of this place was

2. The rock Etam, to which Samson retired after he had burned the harvest of the Philistines. (Judg. xv. 8.)

ETHAM, the third station of the Israelites after their departure from Egypt. (Numb. xxiii. 6. Exod. xiii. 20.) It is now called *Etti.*

ETHAN, the Ezrahite, was one of the philosophers, to whom Solomon was compared for wisdom in 1 Kings iv. 31. and 1 Chron. ii. 6. The 89th psalm is ascribed to him.

ETHANIM, the antient name of the first month of the Jewish civil year. For a notice of the festivals, &c. in this month, see p. 175.

ETHICS cultivated by the Jews, 479.

ETHIOPIA. See CUSH, p. 566. On the prophecy concerning Ethiopia, and its fulfilment, see Vol. I. pp. 288, 289.

EUNICE, the mother of Timothy, and the wife of a Greek proselyte. She was early converted to the Christian faith. St. Paul has pronounced a high eulogium on her piety. (Acts xvi. 1. 2 Tim. i. 5.)

EUNUCH.

1. One who has been emasculated. Such persons antiently were (as in the East they still are) employed to guard the harems of oriental kings and nobles. See p. 98. of this volume.

2. Since, in the East, eunuchs often rose to stations of great power and trust, the word at length came to signify a *minister of a court,* without necessarily including the idea of emasculation. Such was the officer of Can-

EY

dace, queen of Ethiopia, whose conversion is related in Acts viii. 27—39.

EUODIAS and SYNTICHE were Christian women at Philippi, and probably deaconesses of the church in that city. From Phil. iv. 2. it is evident that a difference of opinion subsisted between them: most probably it was respecting the necessity of retaining the Mosaic ceremonies under the Gospel dispensation and worship.

EUPHRATES, a large and celebrated river of Western Asia: it rises in Armenia Major near Mount Aba, and, after flowing by Syria, Mesopotamia, and the site of Babylon, it empties itself into the Persian Gulf. In Gen. xv. 18. it is called "the great river," which distinctive appellation it deserves in contrast with rivers generally, though not with the Nile. (Buckingham's Travels in Mesopotamia, vol. i. p. 54.) Like the Nile, at certain seasons of the year, the Euphrates inundates the flat countries on its banks, and renders them extremely fertile.

EUROCLYDON, a tempestuous wind common in the Mediterranean, and well known to modern mariners by the name of a *Levanter*. It is not confined to any one single point, but blows in all directions from the north-east, round by the north, to the southeast. The great wind, or mighty tempest, or vehement east wind, described by the prophet Jonah (i. 4. iv. 8.), appears to have been one of these Levanters. Of this description was the violent or tempestuous wind mentioned in Acts xxvii. 14. (Shaw's Travels, vol. ii. pp. 127, 128.)

EVE, the wife of Adam, and the common mother of the human race. (Gen. ii. iii.) The character of Eve is only known to us by her sin; in the commission of which we may observe the two fundamental passions, of which all the others are modifications; viz. pride—*ye shall be as gods;* and sensuality— *the tree was good for food, and its fruit was pleasant to the eyes.* (Gen. iii. 5, 6.)

EVIL-MERODACH, the son and successor of Nebuchadnezzar, king of Babylon. He delivered Jehoiakim king of Judah out of prison, upon whom he conferred many favours. (2 Kings xxv. 27. Jer. lii. 31.) According to Archbishop Usher, he reigned only one year, and was succeeded by his son Belshazzar.

EUTYCHUS, circumstances of the death of, explained, 389, 390.

EXCOMMUNICATION, punishment of, and its effects, 151, 152. 260.

EXECUTION of sentences, how and by whom performed, 124, 125.

EXPIATION, day of, how solemnised, 317, 318.

EXPOSITION of Scripture, part of the synagogue worship, 258, 259.

EXPOSURE to wild beasts, a capital punishment, 157. St. Paul not thus actually exposed, 493.

EYES, putting out, a Jewish punishment, 150. Painting of the eyes described, 403, 404.

FO

EZEKIEL, the son of Buzi, of the house of Aaron (Ezek. i. 1.) was carried captive to Babylon by Nebuchadnezzar, with Jehoiakim king of Judah. He is the third of the greater prophets. See a further account of Ezekiel, and an analysis of his predictions in Vol. IV., pp. 221—231.

EZION-GEBER, a port in Idumæa, on the Elanitic gulf, whence Solomon sent ships to Ophir. (1 Kings ix. 26.) In later times it was called Berenice. Dr. Shaw supposes it to be the same port which is now called by the Arabs *Meenah-el-Dsahab*, or *the port of gold.* (Travels, vol. ii. pp. 118, 119.

EZRA, or ESDRAS, the son (or, according to Coquerel and others, the grandson or great-grandson) of Seraiah, was a priest and scribe or doctor of the law; who, returning from captivity, with a full commission from Artaxerxes, to settle the church and state of the Jews, zealously exerted himself in rectifying all the disorders which had crept into their affairs during their captivity. See a further account of Ezra, and an analysis of the historical book which bears his name, in Vol. IV. pp. 64—66.

———

FAIR HAVENS, a place so called on the coast of Crete, most probably because it had good anchorage. (Acts xxvii. 8.) In the fourth century, according to Jerome, it was a large town.

FAMILIES, Heads of, 81, 82.

FAMINES in the Holy Land, 76.

FASTS of the Jews, public and private, how solemnised, 331, 332. Fast of the atonement, 317, 318.

FATHERS, Jewish, power of, over their families, 418.

FEASTS or FESTIVALS of the Jews, account of, 300—322. Benefits resulting from them, 304. Notice of their ordinary feasts, 441, 442. And of their funeral feasts, 523. See DEDICATION, EXPIATION, JUBILEE, NEW MOON, PASSOVER, PENTECOST, PURIM, SABBATH, SABBATICAL YEAR, TABERNACLES, TRUMPETS.

FEET, washing of, 433, 434. Female ornaments of, 403.

FELIX, procurator of Judæa, account of, 114, 115. and IV. 342.

FERTILITY of Palestine, account of, 63—72.

FESTUS, procurator of Judæa, notice of, 115.

FIG-TREES of Palestine, 68.

FINES, various, imposed by the Jews, 147.

FIRE-SACRIFICES, different kinds of, 291—293.

FIRST-BORN, privileges of, 416, 417.

FIRST-FRUITS, presentation of, 296, 297.

FLORUS, procurator of Judæa, notice of, 115.

FOOD and entertainments of the Jews, 436—442. Particular kinds of food, why

GA

allowed or prohibited to them, 439. Locusts, an article of food, 76.

FOOT-RACE, allusions to, explained, 495—500.

FOREST of Cedars, 65. ; of Ephraim, 66. ; of Hareth, 66. ; of Oaks on Bashan, 66.

FORMS of salutation and politeness, 429, 430.

FORTIFICATIONS of the Jews, 211.

FOUNTAINS in the Holy Land, account of, 42—44.

FREEDOM of Rome, how acquired, and its privileges, 127—180.

FREED MEN, condition of, 429.

FUNERAL RITES of the Jews, 515—519.

FURNITURE of oriental houses, 392. 394.

GAAL, the son of Ebed, who raised a revolt in Schechem against Abimelech the son of Gideon; but, being defeated by the latter, he was compelled to flee. (Judg. ix. 26—41.) It is not known who he was or what afterwards became of him.

GAASH, a hill in the inheritance of Ephraim, on the north side of which stood Timnath-Serah, memorable as being the place where Joshua was buried. (Josh. xxiv. 30.) At the foot of this hill, probably, were the brooks (or valleys) of Gaash mentioned in 2 Sam. xxiii. 30.

GABBATHA. See p. 23.

GAD.

1. Gad, or Good Fortune, a Syrian idol, notice of, 344.

2. Seventh son of Jacob, born of Zilpah : he gave his name to one of the twelve tribes; for the limits of whose allotment, see p. 11.

3. A prophet, the friend of David, whom he faithfully followed during his persecutions by Saul. After David's establishment on the throne of Israel, Gad was commissioned to propose to him one of three scourges, which was to punish the sinful numbering of the people ; and afterwards directed him to build an altar in the threshing-floor of Ornan or Araunah, (1 Sam. xxii. 5. 2 Sam. xxiv.) Gad also wrote a history of David's reign, whence, perhaps, was taken the narrative of that census ; and he transmitted to that monarch the divine commands concerning the establishment of public worship. (2 Chron. xxix. 25.)

GADARA was, according to Josephus (Bell. Jud. lib. iv. c. 24), the metropolis of Peræa, or the region beyond Jordan : it was one of the cities of the district of Decapolis, and consequently under heathen jurisdiction, on which account, perhaps, it was destroyed by the Jews, but was rebuilt by Pompey, in favour of Demetrius Gadarensis, his manumitted servant, according to Josephus. The inhabitants of this city being rich, sent legates to Vespasian when he advanced against Judæa, and gave up this strong city to him ; both the city and the villages belonging to it

GA

lay within the region of the Gergesenes, whence Christ going into the country of the Gadarenes (Mark v. 1.), is said to go into the region of the Gergesenes. (Matt. viii. 28.) The remains of the warm baths for which this place was antiently celebrated, and also of the tombs (among which the Gadarene demoniac is supposed to have abode) are still to be seen : they are almost all inhabited, and the massive stone doors, usually about five or six inches thick, which originally clothed them, still move on their hinges, and open or shut at the option of their present owners. Gadara is now called Oomkais, or Omkeis. The ruins of the antient city are very considerable. " Besides the foundations of a whole line of houses, there are two theatres on the north and west sides of the town,— the former quite destroyed, but the latter in very tolerable preservation, and very handsome. Near it the antient pavement, with wheel-tracks of carriages, is still visible. Broken columns and capitals lie in every direction." The modern inhabitants of this place are as inhospitable as they were in the time of Jesus Christ. (Lord Lindsay's Letters from Edom, &c. vol. ii. p. 97. Quarterly Rev. vol. xxvi. p. 389. Irby's and Mangles' Travels, pp. 297, 298. Madden's Travels in Turkey, &c. vol. ii. p. 311.)

GAIUS.

1. A Macedonian, and fellow-traveller of Saint Paul, who was seized by the populace at Ephesus. (Acts xix. 29.)

2. A native of Derbe, who accompanied Paul in his last journey to Jerusalem. (Acts xx. 4.) To him St. John is supposed to have addressed his third epistle.

3. An inhabitant of Corinth, with whom Paul lodged, and in whose house the Christians were accustomed to meet. (Rom. xvi. 23. 1 Cor. i. 14.)

GALATIA, a province of Asia Minor, bounded on the west by Phrygia, on the east by the river Halys, on the north by Paphlagonia, and on the south by Lycaonia. This country derived its name from the Gauls, two tribes of whom (the Troemi and Tolistoboii) with a tribe of the Celts, or, according to Prof. Hug, Germans (the Tectosages), finding their own country too small to support its redundant population, migrated thither after the sacking of Rome by Brennus; and mingling with the former inhabitants, and adopting the Greek language, the whole were called Gallo-Græci. During the reign of Augustus (A. U. C. 529, B. C. 26), Galatia was reduced into a Roman province, and was thenceforth governed by the Roman laws, under the administration of a proprætor. The Galatians seem to have preserved their native religion, to which they superadded the worship of the great mother of the gods. Their principal cities were Ancyra, Tavium, and Pessinus; the latter of which carried on some commerce. Callimachus (Hymn. in Delum. 5. 184.) and Hilary (Hymn. Hieron. pref. in ep. ad

G A

Galat.), who was himself a Gaul, represent them as a very foolish people ; whence St. Paul says, (iii. 1.) O FOOLISH Galatians, who hath bewitched you ? This church was so dangerously perverted, and almost overturned by the Judaisers there, that the apostle, in his epistle to them, does not call them saints. See an analysis of his epistle to the Galatians in Vol. IV. pp. 370, 371. Galatia was also the seat of colonies from various nations, among whom were many Jews; and from all of these St. Paul appears to have made many converts to Christianity. (Gal. i. 2. 1 Cor. xvi. 1. 2 Tim. iv. 10. 1 Pet. i. 1.) According to Josephus (Ant. Jud. lib. xvi. c. 6.), the Jews here enjoyed considerable privileges. (Robinson, voce Γαλατια; Hug's Introd. vol. ii. pp. 363 —365.)

GALILEE, Upper and Lower, 14, 15. The Galilæans were accounted brave and industrious, though the other Jews affected to consider them as not only stupid and unpolished, but also seditious, and therefore proper objects of contempt. (John i. 47. vii. 52.) They were easily distinguished from the Jews of Jerusalem by a peculiar dialect; for a notice of which, see 14. and note 2.

GALILÆANS, sect of, principles of, 374, 375.

GALILEE OF THE NATIONS, 15.

GALILEE, Sea of, account of, 38—40.

GALLIO, a proconsul of Achaia, was the elder brother of the philosopher Seneca, and was called Marcus Annæus Novatus; but took the name of Gallio, after being adopted into the family of Lucius Junius Gallio. Before his tribunal St. Paul was dragged at Corinth. His conduct on that occasion exhibits him in the character of a mild and amiable man; and St. Luke's account is confirmed by profane writers. See Vol. I. pp. 168, 169.

GAMALIEL, a Pharisee and an eminent doctor of the law, under whom St. Paul was educated. (Acts v. 24. xxii. 3.) He possessed great influence among the Jews, and is said by some to have presided over the sanhedrin during the reigns of Tiberius, Caligula, and Claudius.

GAMES, Olympic, allusions to, explained. 494—501. Gymnastic games in imitation of them among the Jews, 489, 490.

GARDENS of the Hebrews, notice of, 462.

GARMENTS of the priests, 277. Of the high priest, 279, 280. Rending of, a sign of mourning, 405. Great wardrobes of, *ibid.* 406.

GATES of cities, 394.; were seats of justice, 116. Gates of Jerusalem, 20. Proselytes of the Gate, 265, 266.

GATH, a city of the Philistines one of their five principalities (1 Sam. vi. 17.), famous for having given birth to Goliath. David conquered it in the beginning of his reign over all Israel (1 Sam. xvii. 4.): it continued subject to his successors till the declension of the kingdom of Judah. Rehoboam rebuilt

G A

or fortified it. (2 Chron. xi. 8.) Uzziah reconquered it ; as did Hezekiah. Josephus makes it part of the tribe of Dan; but Joshua takes no notice of it. Calmet thinks, that Mithcah mentioned by Moses (Numb. xxxiii. 29.), is the Metheg in 2 Sam. viii. 1. In our authorised version it is rendered, David took Metheg-Ammah, that is, *Metheg the Mother,* which, in 1 Chron. xviii. 1., is explained by—He took Gath and her daughters (or towns); Gath being the mother, and Metheg the daughter. But it may be that the district of Gath and its dependencies was called in David's time Metheg-Ammah; but this being unusual, or becoming obsolete, the author of the Chronicles explains it to be Gath and its villages. According to this idea, Gath of the Philistines, the birth-place of giants (2 Sam. xxi. 20. 22.), must lie far in Arabia Petræa, towards Egypt, which is confirmed by the author of the first book of Chronicles, who says, that the sons of Ephraim being in Egypt, attacked the city of Gath, and were there slain. (1 Chron. vii. 21.)

Jerome says, there was a large town called Gath, in the way from Eleutheropolis to Gaza; and Eusebius speaks of another Gath, five miles from Eleutheropolis, toward Lydda (consequently different from that which Jerome speaks of) ; also another Gath, or Gattha, between Jamnia and Antipatris. Jerome likewise, speaking of Gath-Hephir, the place of the prophet Jonah's birth, says, it was called Gath-Hepher, or Gath, in the district of Hepher, to distinguish it from others of the same name.

Gath was the most southern city of the Philistines, as Ekron was the most northern; so that Ekron and Gath are placed as the boundaries of their land. (1 Sam. vii. 14. xvii. 52.) Gath lay near Mareshah (2 Chron. xi. 8. Micah i. 14. Heb.), which nearly agrees with Jerome, who places Gath on the road from Eleutheropolis to Gaza. Gath was a place of strength, in the time of the prophets Amos and Micah, independent of the kings of Judah (Amos vi. 2. Micah i. 10. 14.) ; but was taken by Uzziah, king of Judah, while Amos was living ; and afterwards by Hezekiah, in Micah's time. Gethaim (2 Sam. iv. 3. Neh. xi. 33.) is Gath. David had a company of Gittite guards.

GATH-HEPHER, the birth-place of the prophet Jonah (2 Kings xiv. 25.), was a town in the allotment of the tribe of Zabulon. (Josh. xix. 13.) It was probably situated in the land of Hepher mentioned in 1 Kings iv. 10.

GAULONITIS, District of, 16.

GAZA, a very celebrated city of the Jews, distant about 60 miles south-west from Jerusalem : it was one of the five cities of the Philistines, which fell by lot to the tribe of Judah (Josh. xv. 47.), and which offered their golden emerods to the God of Israel for a trespass-offering. (1 Sam. vi. 17.) Its gates were carried away by Samson (Judg. xvi. 2.),

GA

and hither he was conducted when taken by the Philistines (v. 21.), three thousand of whom, both men and women, were assembled on the roof of the temple of their god Dagon (27.), and perished when Samson pulled it down. (30.) " If any one should question the possibility of 3000 people being upon the roof of the temple in question, he may be referred to the accounts of the temples at Thebes in Upper Egypt, which have been given by all recent travellers ; accounts, which, while they come to us authenticated in such a manner as to admit of no doubt in regard to their verity and correctness, at the same time present things apparently incredible, and contrary to all the philosophising of most speculative and theoretical historians. The ruins of antient Greece and Rome, so far as vastness and extent are concerned, dwindle into insignificance when compared with the astonishing remains of early architecture at Thebes. What is most confounding of all to that philosophising, in which historians of a sceptical cast are prone to indulge in, is, that these mighty ruins are, beyond all doubt, the relics of architecture designed and executed in ages, when (as some popular writers admonish us to believe) men were not yet weaned from contending with the beasts of the forest for their lairs and for their acorns, nor but very little elevated above them. The ruins at Thebes present evidences of control over physical power ; of skill in architecture on a scale of surprising magnitude ; and of art in mixing and laying on colours that are fresh as if painted but yesterday, after having been laid on for more than thirty centuries ; which confound and put to shame all that the arts and sciences, and the experience of three thousand years, have since been able to accomplish. So much for the rudeness, and barbarity, and ignorance of the *primitive* ages. The Philistines, the near neighbours of the Egyptians, and their hearty coadjutors in polytheism, might well have, and doubtless had, large temples as well as they ; large enough to afford room for three thousand, and some of them not improbably for many more, to stand upon the roof. As to the strength of Samson, in tearing away pillars on which such enormous weight rested ; — those, who disbelieve any thing which is miraculous, will of course regard the whole as a mythos (or fable) ; those who admit the reality of miracles, will doubtless be ready to believe, that there was some supernatural aid afforded him in the case under consideration. A heavy blow was inflicted upon polytheism by the event in question, and on its votaries, who were the enemies of God's chosen people." (Stuart's Hebr. Chrestomathy, pp. 189,190.) Antient Gaza was a great, powerful, and opulent city : it is not improbable that it was the emporium of the inhabitants of the Desert, who brought thither their booty in caravans.

After destroying Tyre, Alexander the Great besieged Gaza, which was at that time

GE

held by a Persian garrison, and took it after a siege of two months. He appears to have left the city standing ; but afterwards, b. c. 96, Alexander Jannæus, reigning prince of the Jews, took it after a siege of a year and destroyed it. Thus was Gaza *made desolate* agreeably to the prediction of Zephaniah. (ii. 4.) Subsequently Gabinius rebuilt this city, which Augustus bestowed on Herod the Great, after whose death it was annexed to Syria. (Schleusner and Robinson, voce Γαζα.) The city of Gaza is mentioned in Acts viii. 26. with the parenthetical remark, — that αὐτη ἐστιν ἐρημος — it [or the *same*] *is desert :* which has greatly exercised the ingenuity of commentators, some of whom refer αὐτη to ὁδος, and translate it by *unfrequented ;* while others, referring it to the city, explain it by *deprived of fortifications :* others again suppose the antient city to have remained desolate, and that which flourished in the days of St. Luke to have occupied a somewhat different site nearer to the sea ; and others consider these words to be a mere gloss which has found its way into the text. A passage, however, in Josephus, which has escaped the researches of most of the learned men, clears up the difficulty, and shows the minute fidelity of the sacred historian. A short time before the siege of Jerusalem, in consequence of a massacre of the Jews at Cæsarea, the whole nation became greatly enraged, and in revenge laid waste many villages and cities ; and among these were Anthedon and *Gaza*, which they utterly demolished. Gaza therefore was actually ἐρημος, a desert, at the time St. Luke wrote. (Josephus, Bell. Jud. lib. ii. c. 18. § 1. Hug's Introd. vol. i. p. 25.) The neighbourhood of modern Gaza is described by Captains Irby and Mangles as being richly wooded with olives, sycamores, mulberries, cedars, fir-trees, &c. &c. The country is inclosed by hedges of prickly pears, the hills, gently rising to the view beyond each other, and the whole has a beautiful appearance. Excepting the perishable materials, with which the houses are constructed, stone being substituted for mud, the town partakes of the wretched appearance of those in Egypt. (Travels, p. 178.)

Gebal.

1. *Gebal*, Mount, see p. 51.

2. *Gebal*, a Phœnician city between Tripoli and Beyroot, situated on a hill, and inhabited by mariners and builders. Its *caulkers* are specially mentioned in Ezek. xxvii. 9.), where its chiefs are termed *wise men*. The Arabs still call it *Djeble* and *Djobail*.

3. *Gebal* (the Gebalene of the Romans), was a mountainous district, inhabited by the Edomites, and extending from the Dead Sea southwards to Selah or Petra. It is mentioned in Psal. lxxxiii. 8. By the Arabs it is called *Djebâl*.

Gedaliah, the son of Ahikam, was left by Nebuchadnezzar in Palestine, after the destruction of Jerusalem, to govern the remainder of the people who continued there. He was treacherously slain by Ishmael the son of Nethaniah. (2 Kings xxv. 22—25.)

GEHAZI, the servant of the prophet Elisha, who, contrary to his master's intention, fraudulently obtained presents of Naaman, the Syrian general, and was smitten with leprosy for his wickedness (2 Kings v. 20—27.); a judgment which ought to warn us not only of the curse which cleaves to ill-gotten wealth, but above all, of the just vengeance of God, which pursues all who, for purposes of worldly gain, bring a scandal and reproach upon their religion.

GEHINNON, or the Valley of Hinnom, 54.

GENEALOGIES of the Hebrews, 186, 187. ; of the Herodian family, 109.

GENNESARETH, a region 50 furlongs in length, and 20 in breadth ; a very pleasant and fruitful place, abounding in the gardens of great men, whence it had its name from Gen and Sar, as being the garden of princes ; it lay at the bottom of the lake of Gennesareth, and gave that name to it. (Luke v. 1.)

GENNESARETH, Sea of, 38—40.

GENTILES, court of, in the temple, 239.

GEOGRAPHY, not unknown to the Jews as a science, 481. 'Sketch of the historical and physical geography of Palestine, 1—77.

GERGESA, or GERASA, a city in the region of DECAPOLIS, so called, either from the Girgashites, the posterity of Canaan, (for neither did Zebulon nor Naphtali drive out all the Canaanites, Judg. i. 30. 33.), or from Gergishta, signifying clay, the soil being clay ; it gave name to a region so called, which comprehended in it Gadara, Hippo, and Magdala. Messrs. Burckhardt, Buckingham, and other modern travellers consider the ruins of *Djerash* to be those of the antient Gergesha or Gerasa. They are very magnificent. Lord Lindsay (who, however, supposes them to be the ruins of Pella, also a city of the Decapolis,) has given a brief but very interesting description of these remains of antient art. (*Letters from Edom, &c.* vol. ii. pp. 103—108.) A beautiful view of the ruins of Gergesha is given in the " Landscape Illustrations of the Bible."

GERIZIM (Mount), a rugged limestone mountain, forming part of the ridge called Mount Ephraim, over against Mount Ebal ; between the two the city Schechem was situated. (Deut. xi. 29. xxvii. 11, 12.) In subsequent times this mountain became the seat of the religious worship of the Samaritans, who erected a temple there ; for a notice of which, see pp. 245, 246. Considerable fragments of antient edifices are stated to be found on its summit, which are supposed to be the foundation, or other remains of this Samaritan temple.

GERSHOM and ELIEZER, the sons of Moses and Zipporah, were only simple Levites, while their relations, the sons of Aaron, enjoyed the highest honours of the pontificate.

GERSHON, a son of Levi, who gave his name to one of the three great branches of the Levites. The office of the Gershonites was, to carry the veils and curtains of the tabernacle, on the western side of which they encamped.

GESHUR, a district of Syria, bordering north of the Hebrew territory (2 Sam. xv. 8. 1 Chron. ii. 23.), and situated on the eastern side of the river Jordan, between Mount Hermon, Maachah, and Bashan. (Deut. iii. 13, 14. Josh. xii. 3, 4.) The Geshurites and Maachathites were not expelled by the Israelites under Joshua. (Josh. xiii. 2. 13.) They must, however, have returned subsequently ; since, in the reign of David, Geshur had its own king Talmai, whose daughter Maachah was the mother of the rebel Absalom. (2 Sam. iii. 3. xiii. 37. xv. 8.) The word *Geshur* signifies a bridge, and corresponds to the Arabic *Djisr :* and in the same region, where (according to the above data,) we must place Geshur, there still exists an antient stone bridge of four arches over the river Jordan, called *Djisr-Beni-Jukub*, or the Bridge of the Children of Jacob.

GESSIUS FLORUS, the procurator of Judæa, notice of, 115.

GETHSEMANE, a garden beyond Kedron, at the foot of Mount Olivet, so called from the wine-presses in it : it is memorable in the evangelical history, as being the scene of our Saviour's agony. It is described by recent travellers, as being a small plat of ground, with a low hedge or inclosure of stones ; no verdure growing on it, save eight magnificent and venerable-looking olive-trees, which have stood there for many centuries : they are highly venerated by the Christians here, who consider any attempt to cut or injure them as amounting to an act of profanation. Although we are informed by Josephus that Titus cut down all the trees within one hundred furlongs of the city, yet it is not improbable that these trees, which are unquestionably of remote antiquity, may have arisen from the roots of the antient trees ; because the olive is very long-lived, and possesses the peculiar property of shooting up again, however frequently it may be cut down. The trees now standing in the garden of Gethsemane are of the species known to botanists as the Olea Europæa. Mrs. Bracebridge, from whose sketch the beautiful drawing was made, which is given in the " Landscape Illustrations of the Bible," states that they are wild olives, and appear pollarded from extreme age ; and their stems are very rough and knarled. " The soil between these trees is bare, without a flower, vegetable, or verdure of any kind growing on it. A footpath intersects the place in an oblique direction, which is walled off from the rest, and is looked upon as accursed ; being that (as it is said,) in which Judas walked when he betrayed his divine Master with a kiss." The view from the garden of Gethsemane is one of the most pleasing in the vicinity of Jerusalem. (Missionary Register for 1824, p. 504. Jowett's Researches in Syria, p. 303. Carne's Letters, p. 290. Rae Wilson's Travels, vol. i. p. 212. third edition. Robinson's Travels in Palestine, vol. i. p. 122. Lord Lindsay's Letters from Egypt, &c. vol. ii. p. 61.)

GIBEAH, a city in the tribe of Benjamin, not far from Jerusalem: it is frequently called *Gibeah of Saul*, from being the birthplace of the first Hebrew monarch.

GIBEON, the capital city of the Gibeonites, who took advantage of the oaths of Joshua, and of the elders of Israel, on an artful representation which they made of their belonging to a very remote country. (Josh. ix.) Joshua and the elders had not the precaution to consult God on this affair, and inconsiderately made a league with these people: they soon discovered their mistake, and without revoking their promise of giving them their lives, they condemned them to carry wood and water to the tabernacle, and other servile work, as a mark of their pusillanimity and duplicity, as slaves and captives; in which state of servitude they remained, till the entire dispersion of the Jewish nation, A. M. 2553, B. C. 1451. Three days after the Gibeonites had surrendered to the Hebrews, the kings of the Canaanites being informed of it, came and besieged the city of Gibeon. (Josh. x. 3, &c.) The Gibeonites came to Joshua, and desired speedy help. Joshua attacked the five kings early in the morning, put them to flight, and pursued them to Bethoron.

The Gibeonites were descended from the Hivites, the old inhabitants of that country, and possessed four cities; Cephirah, Beeroth, Kirjath-jearim, and Gibeon, the capital, afterwards given to Benjamin, excepting Kirjath-jearim, which fell to Judah. The Gibeonites continued subject to those burdens which Joshua had imposed on them, and were very faithful to the Israelites. Nevertheless Saul, through what mistaken zeal we cannot tell, destroyed a very great number of them (2 Sam. xxi. 1, 2, 3, &c.); but God, as a punishment of his cruelty, in the reign of David, sent a great famine, which lasted three years (A. M. 2983, B. C. 1017); and the prophets told David that this calamity would continue so long as that cruelty remained unrevenged, which Saul had exercised against the Gibeonites. David asked the Gibeonites, what satisfaction they desired? They answered, " *Seven of Saul's sons we will put to death, to avenge the blood of our brethren.*" The Gibeonites hung them up before the Lord. This happened early in the spring, when, in Palestine, they begin barley-harvest. From this time there is no mention of the Gibeonites, as composing a sort of separate people. But it is probable that they were included among the Nethinim or Given, who were public slaves, appointed for the service of the temple. (1 Chron. ix. 2.) Afterwards, those of the Canaanites, who were subdued,

and had their lives spared, were added to the Gibeonites. We see (Ezra viii. 20. ii. 58. 1 Kings ix. 20, 21.) that David, Solomon, and the princes of Judah, gave many of them to the Lord; these Nethinim being carried into captivity with Judah and the Levites, many of them returned with Ezra, Zerubbabel, and Nehemiah, and continued as before, in the service of the temple, under the priests and Levites. Gibeon was seated on an eminence, as is evidenced by its name. It was forty furlongs from Jerusalem (according to Josephus) north. It is called Gabaa. (2 Sam. v. 25. compared with 1 Chron. xiv. 16.) There is mention of the fountain and pool of Gibeon. (2 Sam. ii. 13.)

We neither know when, nor by whom, nor upon what occasion, the tabernacle and altar of burnt sacrifices made by Moses, in the wilderness, were removed to Gibeon; but this we certainly know, that toward the end of David's reign, and in the beginning of Solomon's, they were there. (1 Chron. xxi. 29, 30.) David seeing the angel of the Lord at Araunah's threshing-floor, was so terrified, that he had not time or strength to go so far as Gibeon, there to offer sacrifice, but Solomon being seated on the throne, went to sacrifice at Gibeon, because this was the most considerable of all the high places, where sacrifices were then tolerated, the temple being not yet built. (1 Kings iii. 4.)

GIDEON, the fifth judge of the Israelites, whom he delivered from the oppression of the Midianites. (Judg. vii. viii.) He was the son of Joash of the tribe of Manasseh; and, having destroyed the worship of Baal, was surnamed JERUBBAAL. (Judg. vi. 25—32.)

GIDEON, Ephod of, 342.

GIHON.

1. One of the four rivers of Paradise; which Bishop Patrick and Dr. Wells suppose to be the easterly channel of the two, into which the Euphrates is divided after its junction with the Tigris. Others, however, (and among them, Gesenius and Rosenmüller,) more probably, suppose it to be the Oxus or Araxes. Josephus considers it to be the Nile. (Ant. Jud. lib. i. c. 1. § 3.) which is said to be called *Guyon* by the modern Abyssinians.

2. A fountain or watercourse near Jerusalem, where Solomon was anointed king by Zadok the priest and Nathan the prophet. (1 Kings i. 32—40.) It is supposed to be the same which was afterwards called SILOAM; for a notice of which, see p. 43.

GILBOA, Mountains of, notice of, 50.

GILEAD, Mountains of, notice of, 52. Balm of, 66.

GILGAL, a celebrated place on the east of Jericho, and on this side Jordan, where the Israelites encamped for some time after their passage over that river. A city was afterwards built there, which became memorable for many events. It was a seat of justice (or, as we should now term it, an assize-town): Samuel, when travelling in circuit

G O

through the land, went yearly to Gilgal. (1 Sam. vii. 16.) Here Saul was crowned king of the Hebrews. In subsequent times it was the seat of idolatry. (Hos. iv. 15. Amos v. 5.) Near it is a broad and sloping plain, which derives its name from this place.

GIRDLES, notice of, 396. Military girdle, 209.

GIRGASHITES, an antient people of Canaan, whose habitation was beyond the sea of Tiberias, where we find some vestiges of their name in the city of GERGESA or Gergasa, upon the sea of Tiberias.

GOATS, bred by the Jews, notice of, 450.

GOD, crimes against, how punished by the Jews, 136—138.

GOËL, or blood-avenger, office of, 152, 153.

GOG and MAGOG, the accurate chronologer, Dr. Hales, thinks, are the general names of the northern nations of Europe and Asia, or the districts north of Caucasus, or Mount Taurus, colonised by Gog, or Magog, another of the sons of Japhet (Gen. x. 2.), called by the Arabian geographers, Jajuie and Majuje. (Rennel. Herod. p. 112.) Gog rather denotes the people, Magog the land. Thus Balaam foretold that Christ would be "a king higher than Agag," or rather " Gog," according to the more correct reading of the Samaritan Hebrew Text, and of the Septuagint version of Numb. xxiv. 7. : and Ezekiel, foretelling a future invasion of the land of Israel by these northern nations, Meshech, Tubal, and Togarmah, styles "Gog their chief prince," and describes their host precisely as Scythian or Tartarian ; "coming out of the north, all of them riding on horses ; " "bows and arrows" their weapons; " covering the land, like a cloud, and coming like a storm," in the "latter days." (Ezek. xxxviii. 1—17.) He also describes their immense slaughter, in the valley of the passengers on the east of the sea, thence called the valley of Hamon Gog, "the multitude of Gog." (Ezek. xxxix. 1—22.) This prophecy seems also to be revived in the Apocalypse, where the hosts of Gog and Magog are represented as coming to invade "the beloved city," and perishing with immense slaughter likewise in Armageddon, "the Mount of Mageddo," or Megiddo. (Rev. xvi. 14—16. xx. 7—10.) Dr. Hales's Analysis of Chronology, vol. i. p. 463. (first edition).

GOLDEN CALF, worship of, 340. Golden calves of Jeroboam, 341.

GOLGOTHA, notice of, 19.

GOLIATH, a Philistine giant, a native of Gath, well known for his combat with David. (1 Sam. xvii.)

GOMER, the son of Japhet (Gen. x. 2, 3. Ezek. xxxviii. 6.), whose posterity peopled Galatia, according to Josephus ; Phrygia, according to Bochart ; but, according to Calmet and Gesenius, they were the Cimmerians or Cimbri, a little known and barbarous northern nation.

G R

GOMORRAH, one of the four cities in the vale of Siddim, which were sunk in the Dead Sea. (Gen. x. 19. xiii. 10.)

GOODS, how conveyed antiently, 482.

GOSHEN (Land of), was the most fertile pasture ground in the whole of Lower Egypt : thence called Goshen, from Gush, in Arabic, signifying "a heart," or whatsoever is choice or precious. There was also a Goshen in the territory of the tribe of Judah, so called for the same reason. (Josh. x. 41.) Hence Joseph recommended it to his family as "the best of the land " (Gen. xlvii. 11.), and "the fat of the land." (Gen. xlv. 18.) The land of Goshen lay along the most easterly branch of the Nile, and on the east side of it ; for it is evident, that at the time of the Exodus, the Israelites did not cross the Nile. In antient times, it was considerably more extensive, both in length and breadth, in consequence of the general failure of the eastern branches of the Nile ; the main body of the river verging more and more to the west continually, and deepening the channels on that side. (Dr. Hales's Chronology, vol. i. p. 374. Madden's Travels in Turkey, &c. vol. ii. p. 182.)

GOVERNMENT of the Jews, under the patriarchs, 78, 79. Under Moses and the judges, 79—84. Under the kings, 85—99. During the Babylonian captivity, 104, 105. Under the Asmonæan and Herodian princes, 106—112. Under the Roman procurators, 112—114.

GOVERNOR of the Palace, office of, 97.

GOZAN, a city or country in northern Mesopotamia. (2 Kings xvii. 6. xviii 11. xix. 12. Isa. xxxvii. 2.) By the geographer Ptolemy it is called *Gauzanitis*, now *Kausehan*.

GRAIN, different sorts of, cultivated, 455. ; threshing of, 456, 457.

GRAPES, 64, 65. Culture of, 458—461.

GREAT PLAIN, account of, 57.

GREAT SEA, 43.

GREAVES (Military), use of, 209, 210.

GREECE, in the Scriptures, often comprehends all the countries inhabited by the descendants of Javan, as well in Greece as in Ionia and Asia Minor. Since the time of Alexander the Great, the name of Greeks is taken in a more uncertain and enlarged sense, because, the Greeks being masters of Egypt and Syria, of the countries beyond the Euphrates, &c. the Jews called all those Gentiles Greeks. In the Maccabees, the Gospels, and Paul's writings, a Greek commonly signifies a Gentile. In the Old Testament, Greece and Greeks are named Javan. Isaiah says (lxvi. 19.) *that the Lord shall send his ambassadors to Javan, to the isles afar off.* Ezekiel tells us (xxvii. 13. 19.) that Javan, Tubal, and Meshech, came to the fairs at Tyre. Daniel (xi. 2.) speaking of Darius, says, "that he shall stir up all against the realm of Javan." Alexander the Great is described by the name of King of Javan. (Dan. viii. 21. x. 20.)

GRINDING of corn, 457, 458.

H A

GUARD, Military, of the Temple, 244.
GUESTS, reception of, 433, 434.
GYMNASTIC exercises of the Jews, 489, 490.

HABAKKUK, the eighth of the twelve minor prophets, who foretold the captivity and restoration of the Jews. For an analysis of his predictions, see Vol. IV. pp. 204, 205.

HADRACH (Land of). This land, which is mentioned in Zech. ix. 1., occurs in no other part of the Old Testament. But a Syrian king, who is called Rehob in 2 Sam. viii. 3., is by Josephus named Αραος or Αραχος, which Dr. Blayney thinks was his proper and real name; that of Rehob or the charioteer having been added characteristically on account of the number of his chariots. (2 Sam. viii. 4.) This prince reigned over that part of Syria which was called Zobah; so that, if by the land of Hadrach or Arach be meant the kingdom of Zobah, the three capital kingdoms of Syria, Zobah, Damascus, and Hamath, will then be cited for the whole. (Blayney on Zechariah, p. 37.)

HAGAR, an Egyptian woman, handmaid of Sarah, and mother of Ishmael. (Gen. xvi. 1. xxv. 12.) In Gal. iv. 24, 25. St. Paul applies this name by allegorical interpretation to the inferior condition of the Jews under the law, as compared with that of Christians under the Gospel.

HAGARITES or HAGARENES, the descendants of Ishmael. (1 Chron. v. 10.) They constituted a tribe of Arabians, who are supposed to have settled in the vicinity of Mount Sinai.

HAGGAI, the tenth of the minor prophets: he exhorted the Jews to rebuild the temple. For an analysis of his predictions, see Vol. IV. pp. 232, 233.

HAI. See AI, p. 542.

HAIR, Jewish mode of dressing, 398–400. Plucking off, a punishment, 150. Forbidden to be cut in certain forms, 357. Was used in divination by the heathens, 357, 358.

HALAH, a province of Assyria, into which Shalmaneser transported part of the ten tribes. (2 Kings xvii. 6. xviii. 11.)

HAM.

1. The youngest son of Noah, from whom, according to Gen. x. 6—20., most of the southern nations were descended. According to Gesenius, the name literally denotes warm or southern.

2. *Land of Ham*, a poetical name for Egypt, probably (says Gesenius) of Egyptian derivation, but to the Hebrew presenting the same signification as above. (Psal. lxxviii. 51. cv. 23. 27. cvi. 22.)

HAMAN, a Persian nobleman, celebrated as the persecutor of the Jews: he was an Amalekite by nation, and descended from the posterity of Agag. (Esth. iii.—ix.)

HAMATH, on the northern boundary of Canaan, a colony of Phœnicians, and the chief town of a small principality or state,

whose sovereign was in friendship with David. (Numb. xiii. 21. Judg. iii. 3. 2 Sam. viii. 9.) In Amos vi. 2. it is called Hamath the Great, and in 2 Chron. viii. 3. Hamath-Zobah. In Gen. x. 8. the inhabitants are called Hamathites. This town retains its name, and is still a considerable place of traffic with the Arabs, who here purchase the cloth and furniture of their tents.

HANANEEL, a prophet in the reign of Asa king of Judah, by whom he was imprisoned for his fidelity in reproving the monarch for forming an alliance with Benhadad king of Syria. 2 Chron. xvi. 7—10.)

HANDMILLS of the Jews, 392.

HANGING, a Jewish punishment, 157.

HANNAH, the wife of Elkanah, and the mother of the prophet Samuel, whom she consecrated to the service of God. (1 Sam. i. ii.)

HANUN, the son of Nahash, king of the Amorites. By the advice of evil counsellors, he maltreated, contrary to the law of nations, the ambassadors whom David had sent to congratulate him on his accession. (See p. 399.) This transaction led to a war, which terminated fatally for Hanun, whose army was utterly discomfited, his capital taken, and his subjects destroyed. (2 Sam. x. xi. 1. xii. 26—30.) Hanun is supposed to have perished during the war.

HAPHTOROTH, or sections of the prophets read in the synagogues, 255. Table of them, 257.

HARAN.

1. The eldest son of Terah, and brother of Abraham and Nahor, and the father of Lot, Milcah, and Iscah. He is said by Moses to have died before his father (Gen. xi. 28.), a circumstance which to us may appear too minute to be recorded; but, in those days, when life was longer, and subject to fewer diseases than at present, the death of a son before his father was an event of sufficient importance to be distinctly noticed. With the exception of Abel, Haran is the first man mentioned in the sacred history, whose father beheld him depart this life.

2. HARAN or CHARRAN, a city in the northern part of Mesopotamia, where Abraham sojourned for a time in his passage to the land of Canaan. It is enumerated among the towns which had been taken by the predecessors of Sennacherib king of Assyria (1 Kings xix. 12. Isa. xxxvii. 12.), and it is also mentioned by Ezekiel (xxvii. 23.), among the places which traded with Tyre. Haran was favourably situated for commerce, inasmuch as the great road, which led from the Euphrates to the countries of the east, branched off in two directions, eastward to Nisibis and Assyria, and southward into Babylonia. (Rosenmüller's Bib. Geogr. vol. ii. p. 187.) It was the same city, which the Greeks afterwards called Καρραι and the Romans Carræ, and which became celebrated for the defeat and death of Crassus.

HAREM (Royal), notice of, 98.

HARETH, Forest of, 66.

HAROSHETH *of the Gentiles,* a city near Lake Merom, which probably derived its name from the number of Gentiles who resided in its vicinity. Here Sisera dwelt, whose troops were discomfited and pursued by the Israelites to its very gates.

HARP, form of, 473.

HARVESTS of Palestine, account of, 31, 32. 455, 456.

HAVILAH.

1. Two districts in Yemen, the one inhabited by the descendants of Havilah, the son of Cush and grandson of Ham (Gen. x. 7.), the other by descendants of Shem. (ver. 29.)

2. A gold country, mentioned in Gen. ii. 11.: probably the antient Colchis, an extensive country which reached from the Black Sea to Georgia.

HAURAN, a district in the north-eastern part of Canaan, which derived its name from the town or city of Hauran. (Ezek. xlvi.18.) It is the same with the Auranitis of Josephus and the ITURÆA of St. Luke. (iii. 1.) For its limits, &c. see p. 16.

HAZAEL, a general officer of Benhadad king of Syria, whom he treacherously murdered and usurped his kingdom. During a reign of more than forty years, he was the vigilant and successful enemy of the Hebrew princes, whose territories he laid waste, and at length he laid siege to Jerusalem, whence he consented to withdraw, only on condition of the treasures of the temple and of the palace being delivered up to him.

HEAD, coverings for, 398.

HEADS of tribes or families, 81, 82.

HEATHEN NATIONS, account of the deities worshipped by, 349, 350. Allusion to their idolatrous rites explained, 350—358.

HEAVENLY BODIES, the first objects of idolatrous worship, 337.

HEBER.

1. The son of Salah (Gen. xi. 14.), from whom some critics and commentators have supposed that his descendants the Hebrews derived their name.

2. A descendant of Hobab, the brother-in-law of Moses, and husband of Jael, who killed Sisera.

HEBREWS, state of, during the Babylonish captivity, 104, 105. Their commerce, particularly under Solomon and his successors, 482—485. See JEWS.

HEBREWS OF THE HEBREWS, who they were, 264, 265.

HEBRON, antiently called ARBA, and KIR-JATH-ARBA, a city of Judæa, was situated on an eminence, twenty miles southward of Jerusalem, and twenty miles north from Beersheba. The country around it, which is termed " the hill country of Judæa," is but little cultivated. Abraham, Sarah, and Isaac, were buried near Hebron, in the cave of Machpelah. (Gen. xxiii. 7, 8, 9.) Near this place was the oak or turpentine-tree, under which Abraham received three angels.

(Gen. xviii. 1.) Hebron was allotted to Judah. The Lord assigned it to Caleb for inheritance. (Josh. xiv. 13.) Joshua first took Hebron, and killed its king (Josh. x. 3. 23. 37.), but afterwards Caleb again conquered it, assisted by the troops of his tribe, and the valour of Othniel. It was appointed for a dwelling of the priests, and a city of refuge. David, after the death of Saul, settled the seat of his kingdom here. At Hebron, Absalom began his rebellion. During the captivity of Babylon, the Edomites, having invaded the south of Judah, took Hebron ; wherefore in Josephus it is sometimes made a part of Edom. Here Zachariah and Elizabeth resided, and John the Baptist was born. It is described, in 1823, as being a large town, containing about four hundred Arab families, with a Turkish mosque erected over the supposed burial-place of the patriarchs. (Carne's Letters, p. 280.)

HELBON, a city of Syria, celebrated for its wines, which formed an important article of commerce. (Ezek. xxviii. 18.) In the apocryphal second book of Maccabees (xiii. 4.), it is mentioned under the name of Beroea, which had been given to it by Seleucus Nicator, who greatly embellished this city. It is the same as the present *Haleb,* or, as it is termed by Europeans, Aleppo. In 1822 it was almost annihilated by the tremendous earthquake which devastated Syria.

HELIOPOLITAN Temple, notice of, 245.

HELLENES and HELLENISTS, distinction between, 204, 205. note [4]

HELLENISTIC JEWS, who they were, 268.

HELMET of the Jews, 207.

HENA, a city of Mesopotamia, the same probably which was afterwards called *Arah :* it was situated on a ford of the river Euphrates. (2 Kings xviii. 34. xix. 13. Isa. xxxvii. 13.)

HERMOGENES, the name of a man who at first was Saint Paul's companion, but afterwards deserted him. (2 Tim. i. 15.)

HERMON, Mount, 48.

HEROD the Great, account of, 107. Massacre of the infants at Bethlehem by his order, 108. II. 620, 621.

HEROD Agrippa, I. and II. account of, 111.

HEROD Antipas, account of, 110. Why he was at war with Aretas king of Arabia, I. 93.

HERODIAN FAMILY, genealogy of, 109.

HERODIANS, sect of, account of, 374.

HERODIAS, the grand-daughter of Herod the Great, and sister of Herod Agrippa I. She was first married to her uncle Philip (Herod); but afterwards abandoned him, and connected herself with his brother Herod Antipas, whom she persuaded to put John the Baptist to death, because he had boldly denounced their incestuous union. (Matt. xiv. 3. 6. Mark vi. 17. 19. 22. Luke iii. 19.)

HESHBON, the capital city of the kingdom of Sihon, situated about 20 miles eastward of the river Jordan : it was given to the tribe of Reuben. It is supposed to be the same place which is now called Hhubhzān. Numerous ruins attest its antient splendour. This town is situated on so commanding a position, that the view from it extends at least 30 miles in every direction; and, to the southward, where the prospect is most extensive, the eye ranges, probably, a distance of 60 miles in a direct line. (Buckingham's Travels among the Arab Tribes, p. 106.)

HEZEKIAH, the son and successor of Ahaz king of Judah : he was a wise and pious prince, who extirpated idolatry, and restored the worship of the true God throughout his dominions. For a notice of the disease with which he was afflicted, see p. 508.

HIDDEKEL, one of the four rivers which watered Paradise. (Gen. ii. 14.) It is generally supposed to be the same as the Tigris, which flowed through the antient country of ASSYRIA.

HIEL, of Bethel, rebuilt Jericho, notwithstanding the malediction denounced in Josh. vi. 26. ; the effects of which he felt in his own family; his eldest son dying when the foundations of the walls were laid, and his youngest son when the gates were set up. (1 Kings xvi. 34.)

HIERAPOLIS, a city of Phrygia, in the vicinity of Colossæ and Laodicea (Col. iv. 13.), celebrated for its mineral waters, which now flow disregarded by the Turcomans. " Once there existed on the self-same spot a life-giving stream : but Epaphras and his successors, who said to the then countless multitudes of Hierapolis, — ' Whosoever will, may come and take of the water of life freely,' have ages ago been silent in the grave." (Arundell's Seven Churches of Asia, p. 83.) The ruins of Hierapolis are still considerable; they are described by Mr. A. (Ibid. pp. 79—82.) This place is now called Pambouk Kalesi.

HIEROGLYPHIC STONES, forbidden to be worshipped by the Israelites, 347.

HIGH PLACES, account of, 246—248. 351.

HIGH PRIESTS, functions, dress, and privileges of, 279—281. Their succession, 281—284.

HINNOM, a person who is known only from the circumstance of his having given his name to a VALLEY, situated at a very short distance from Jerusalem; for a notice of which, see p. 54.

HIRAM I. king of Tyre, the ally or tributary of David, to whom he sent ambassadors to congratulate him on his accession to the throne. The dominions of Hiram are supposed to have extended over the western part of the chain of Mount Lebanon. When David was building a palace, Hiram sent him cedar timber and able artificers. (2 Sam. v. 11. 1 Chron. xiv. 1.)

HIRAM II., the son and successor of the preceding, who congratulated Solomon on succeeding his father on the throne of Israel. He also furnished Solomon with timber, stone, and artificers for his magnificent buildings, especially the temple at Jerusalem. He

is known under the same name by profane historians.

HIRAM or HURAM, a celebrated artificer, was the son of a widow, belonging to the tribe of Dan, and a Tyrian. He was sent by Hiram II. to Solomon, for whom he executed the principal work in the interior of the temple, as well as several of the sacred utensils. (1 Kings vii. 1. 3. 2 Chron. ii. 14. iv. 11.)

HISTORICAL Geography of the Holy Land, 1—27.

HISTORICAL WRITING, art of, cultivated by the Jews, 477, 478.

HITTITES, the descendants of Heth, the second son of Canaan. They dwelt in the south part of the promised land, near Hebron.

HIVITES, a tribe of the Canaanites. They seem to have been the same with the Avim, whom the Philistines expelled. Driven from the south-west of Canaan, part of them appear to have settled about Avim, Gibeon, and Schechem, whose inhabitants are called Hivites in Josh. ix. 11. 19. xvii. 23. Gen. xxxiv. 2. ; and another part seem to have settled near Mount Hermon. (Josh. xi. 3.)

HOBAB, the son of Jethro, and the brother-in-law of Moses, at whose earnest request he accompanied the Israelites as a guide through the wilderness. His family dwelt among them during the time of the first judges.

HOLOCAUSTS, account of, 291, 292.

HOLY LAND, the country of the Jews, why so called, 2. Sketch of its historical geography, 1—27. Physical geography and productions, 28—69. Testimonies of antient and modern geographers to its fertility, 69—72. Calamities, 72—77. Its present degraded state accounted for, 72. Its government in the patriarchal times, 78, 79. Under Moses, 79—83. Under Joshua and the Judges, 84. Under the Kings, 84—98. Reason why the kingdom of Judah subsisted longer than that of Israel, 102—104. Its condition under the Asmonæan princes and sovereigns of the Herodian family, and under the Roman procurators, 106—114.

HOLY OF HOLIES, account of, 232. 242.

HOMICIDE, proceedings in case of, 142, 143.

HONEY of Palestine, 64.

HOPHRAH. See PHARAOH-HOPHRAH.

HOR.

1. A mountain on the confines of Edom where Aaron died (Numb. xx. 22—28.), whose pretended tomb is still shown to travellers; but, from its appearance, it should seem to have been rebuilt at no very distant period. The view from this mountain is extensive. Irby's and Mangles' Travels, pp. 433—438.)

2. A mountain in Lebanon. (Numb. xxxiv. 7, 8.)

HOREB, a mountain in Arabia Petræa, so near Mount Sinai that Horeb and Sinai seem to be two hills of the same mountain, Sinai lies east, Horeb west : so that when

H U

the sun rises, the latter is covered with the shadow of Sinai. There are springs and fruit-trees on Horeb, but only rain-water on Sinai. At Horeb God appeared to Moses in the burning bush. (Exod. iii. 1, 2, 3.) At the foot of this mountain Moses struck the rock, and drew water from it. (Exod. xvii. 6.) Elijah retired here to avoid the persecution of Jezebel (1 Kings xix. 8.); and the cave or grotto, in which the prophet found shelter, is yet pointed out by tradition, the truth of which is confirmed by the appearance of the surrounding scenery. This cave " is as desolate a place of refuge as the fancy can conceive : — no brook or pool is nigh, to quench the burning thirst; not a shrub grows on the soil, but sad and useless precipices are on every side. Every part of the way was strewed with broken fragments of rocks." (Carne's Recollections of the East, p. 345.) It is frequently said in the Old Testament, that God gave the law at Horeb, though other places expressly name Sinai; because Horeb and Sinai in some sort form but one mountain. From its lofty summit nothing is to be seen on every side, as far as the eye can reach, but ranges of naked mountains succeeding each other, like waves of the sea. This mountain is now called St. Catherine's. (Carne's Letters from the East, pp. 197, 198.)

HORITES, a people who dwelt in Mount Seir (Gen. xiv. 6.), whence they were subsequently expelled by the Edomites. (Deut. ii. 12. 22.)

HORSES, notice of 449.

HORTICULTURE of the Jews, account of, 461, 462.

HOSEA.

1. The earlier name of JOSHUA, the servant and successor of Moses. (Numb. xiii. 8. 16.)

2. The last king of Israel, who, having conspired against Pekah, slew him and usurped his throne. In his reign Shalmaneser king of Assyria invaded Israel, took Samaria, which he reduced to a heap of ruins, and removed the Israelites beyond the river Euphrates.

3. The first of the minor prophets. For an analysis of whose prediction, see Vol. IV. pp. 160—163.

HOSPITALITY of the Jews, 443, 444. Notice of Tesseræ Hospitales, 445, 446.

HOT SEASON in Palestine, 32—34.

HOURS of the Jews and Romans, 168.

HOUSES of the Jews arrangement of, and their furniture, 383—394. Leprosy of houses, 335, 336.

HULDAH, a prophetess, the wife of Shallum, who was consulted by Josiah concerning the book of the law, which was found in the treasury of the temple. (2 Kings xxii. 14.)

HUR, whom some have supposed to be the husband of Miriam, and the brother-in-law of Moses, appears to have been one of the most intimate friends of the latter. During the battle between the Hebrews and the Amalekites, he upheld the weary arms of Moses, and when he was absent he shared with

I N

Aaron the authority over the Israelites. (Exod. xvii. 10. xxiv. 14.)

HUSBANDRY of the Jews, account of, 446. 458.

HUSHAI, the friend of David; who, during the rebellion of Absalom, remained with that prince, and was of eminent service to David by infatuating the counsels of Absalom. (2 Sam. xvi.)

HYMENÆUS is supposed to have been a citizen of Ephesus; who being converted by St. Paul, afterwards fell into the heresy of those who denied the resurrection of the body, or, rather, who maintained that the term was to be understood figuratively in reference to conversion, as being a resurrection from their former death in trespasses and sins; and that no other resurrection was to be expected. (Valpy on 2 Tim. ii. 17.)

HYSSOP, notice of, 65. note 1.

IBZAN, the eighth judge of Israel, governed seven years. His prosperity is indicated by the circumstance of his having thirty sons, and as many daughters; and his riches, by all of them being married. (Judg. xii. 8.)

ICONIUM, a city of Lycaonia, the chief of the fourteen belonging to that tetrarchy. Here was a synagogue of Jews and proselytes, to whom Paul and Barnabas preaching, and confirming their doctrine by miracles, converted many to the Christian faith (Acts xiv. 1, 2, 3.); and here the unbelieving Jews and Gentiles made an assault upon them, *to use them despitefully, and to stone them.* (ver. 5.) It is now called Konieh.

IDOLATRY, origin and progress of, 337. History of it among the Israelites, 338—340. Different kinds of, and its punishment, 136, 137. Idols worshipped by them, 340—349. Idols of Greeks and Romans mentioned in the New Testament, 349, 350. Allusions in Scripture to the idolatrous rites of the heathen explained, 350—358.

IDUMÆA, or EDOM, country of, 17.

ILLYRICUM, a province lying to the north and north-west of Macedonia, along the eastern coast of the Adriatic Sea or Gulf of Venice. It was divided into two parts, Liburnia to the north (now called Croatia), which is not mentioned in the New Testament; and Dalmatia to the south, which region still retains the same name. Hither, St. Paul informs Timothy, Titus went (2 Tim. iv. 10.); and in Rom. xv. 19, he says that he preached the Gospel *from Jerusalem round about unto Illyricum.*

IMMOLATION of victims, 290.

IMPRISONMENT, Jewish modes of, 148, 149, 150.

Ιματια, or Upper Garments, described, 396, 397.

IMPURITIES, legal, purifications of 336.

INAUGURATION of the kings of Israel and Judah, ceremonial of, 88, 89.

INCENSE, offering of, 295.

I S

INJURIES (corporal), punishment of, 143, 144.

INTERCALARY Month, notice of, 174.

INTERMENT, rites of, 512—519.

IRRIGATION practised by the Jews, 453, 454.

ISSAAC, the son of Abraham by Sarah, and one of the patriarchs of the Israelitish nation. He married Rebekah, and was the father of ESAU and JACOB, by whom he was honourably interred in the cave of Machpelah, about ten years before Jacob went into Egypt.

ISAIAH, a celebrated Hebrew prophet, distinguished for the strength and sublimity of his conceptions and language. For a further account of Isaiah, and an analysis of his predictions, see Vol. IV. pp. 164 — 185. In Acts viii. 28. 30. Esaias or Isaiah is metonymically put for the book or prophecy of Isaiah.

ISHBOSHETH, or ISHBAAL, the son and successor of Saul. He reigned only two years ; his whole party being thrown into confusion on the death of Abner, and himself being assassinated by two captains of his own troops. (2 Sam. ii. 1 Chron. viii. 33. ix. 39.)

ISCARIOT. See JUDAS, p. 594. *infra.*

ISHMAEL, the son of Abraham and Hagar. On the birth of Isaac, Hagar and her son were expelled from the house of Abraham, at the desire of Sarah, and dwelt in the wilderness of Paran, to the south of Palestine. Of Egyptian origin by his mother, Ishmael married an Egyptian woman, by whom he had two daughters, one of whom Esau married, and twelve sons, who gave their names to as many tribes of Arabians, conformably to the predictions concerning Ishmael. (Gen. xvii. 20. xxv. 9. xxviii. 9. xxxvi. 5.) For a notice of these predictions and their fulfilment, see Vol. I. pp. 280, 281. Ishmael died, aged 137 years.

ISLES OF THE GENTILES (Gen. x. 5.), probably mean many of the maritime countries washed by the Mediterranean Sea. The Hebrews also used the word *isles* to signify all those countries which were divided from them by the sea. (Isa. xi. 10, 11. xl. 15. Jer. ii. 10.)

ISRAEL, (that is, a *prince of God*, or a mighty prince,) the name given by the angel to the patriarch Jacob at Peniel. (Gen. xxxii. 24.) By Israel, in the Scriptures, is sometimes meant the person of Jacob, and sometimes his whole progeny, including both the kingdom of Judah and the kingdom of Israel, or the ten tribes as distinct from Judah.

ISRAEL, Land of, 2. Kingdom of, 13. Latent causes of the schism between it and the kingdom of Judah, 99—101. Its duration, 101. Mountains of, 51.

ISRAELITES, the descendants of Israel. At first they were called Hebrews, from the patriarch Abraham, surnamed the *Hebrew*, from his having passed over the Euphrates into the land of Canaan. After the exodus from Egypt, they were generally called Israelites ; and on their return from the

J A

Babylonish captivity, they were denominated JEWS, from the tribe of Judah, the most considerable of the twelve tribes. Their political state from the time of Moses to the subversion of their kingdom by the Assyrians, 78—105, Idols worshipped by them, 340—349. Court of the Israelites, 240.

ISSACHAR, the fifth son of Jacob and Leah, and the head of one of the twelve tribes of Israel. For the limits of the canton allotted to which, see p. 12.

ISSUE of blood, 510.

ITALY, an extensive and fertile region of Europe, bounded on the north by the Alps, on the east by the Adriatic Sea or the Gulf of Venice, and on the west aud south by the Ligustine and Tyrrhene Seas, which names were formerly applied to parts of the Mediterranean Sea. ROME was its capital, and the seat of almost universal empire in the time of the writers of the New Testament. (Acts xviii. 2. xxvii. 1. 6. Heb. xiii. 24.)

ITURÆA, region of, 16.

JABBOK, Brook, notice of, 37.

JABESH, a city in the half-tribe of Manasseh beyond Jordan, generally called Jabesh-Gilead, because it lay in Gilead, at the foot of the mountains so named. According to Eusebius it was six miles from Pella towards Gerasa ; consequently, it must have been east of the sea of Tiberias. Jabesh-Gilead was sacked by the Israelites, because its inhabitants refused to join in the war against the tribe of Benjamin. (Judg. xxi. 8.) Nahash, king of the Ammonites, laying siege to Jabesh, proposed hard conditions to the inhabitants, from which Saul delivered them, A. M. 2909, B. C. 1094. They ever after showed great gratitude to Saul and his family : they carried off his and his sons' bodies which the Philistines had hung upon the walls of Bethshan, and buried them honourably in a wood near their city. (1 Sam. xxxi. 11—13.)

JABIN I. king of Hazor, one of the most powerful Canaanitish chieftians, ruled over the northern part of the land of promise. After the ruin of the confederation formed against the Israelites by Adonizedek, Jabin assembled his tributaries near the waters of Merom, and summoned all their forces to arms. This coalition was destroyed, as well as the preceding ; and Jabin himself perished at the destruction of his capital, Hazor. (Josh. xi. 1—12.)

JABIN II. king of Hazor, was probably descended from the preceding sovereign. During one or other of the servitudes of Israel under Cushan or Eglon, the kingdom of Hazor which Joshua had destroyed, appears to have been re-established ; and Jabin must have possessed a powerful dominion, since he is said to have brought into the field 900 chariots armed with scythes. This Jabin oppressed the Israelites for twenty years.

After the death of his general Sisera, who had been conquered by Barak, the war was prolonged for some time, but it was finally terminated by the ruin of Jabin. (Judg. iv.)

JACOB, the second son of Isaac and Rebekah, and the father of the twelve tribes of Israel. Having surreptitiously obtained his father's blessing (Gen. xxvii.), to avoid his brother's resentment, Rebekah sent him away alone into Mesopotamia, to Laban her brother, whose daughters, Leah and Rachel, he married. After serving Laban many years, he returned into the land of Canaan ; having during his journey had an amicable interview with his brother Esau. He afterwards dwelt at Schechem, in a field which he had purchased of the Hivites ; but being apprehensive of the resentment of the people, for the slaughter of the Schechemites by Simeon and Levi on account of the violation of their sister Dinah by Schechem, Jacob removed to Bethel, where he offered sacrifice, and God renewed his promises. Many years after this he went down to Egypt to his son Joseph, where he resided seventeen years, and died in a good old age, after giving his prophetic blessing to his sons. Jacob is, in Scripture, frequently put metonymically for his posterity, that is, for the Israelitish nation.

JACOB'S WELL, notice of, 43.

JAEL, the wife of Heber the Kenite. She killed Sisera, general of the Canaanitish army, whom she had received into her tent, by driving a nail into his temples : concerning this transaction, see Vol. II. p. 597.

JAFFA. See JOPPA p. 592. *infra.*

JAIR, a Gileadite, who judged the Israelites for twenty-two years. He had thirty sons who governed thirty towns, which also bore the name of the towns of Jair.

JAIRUS, a ruler or presiding officer of a synagogue, whose daughter Jesus Christ restored to life by a miracle : the circumstances of which are considered in Vol. I. p. 236.

JAMES.

1. JAMES, *the son of Zebedee*, and the brother of the apostle John : he was put to death by Herod Agrippa, about A. D. 44. (Matt. iv. 21. x. 2. Mark iii. 17. Luke vi. 14. Acts. i. 13. xii. 2.)

2. JAMES, surnamed *the Less.* (Mark xv. 40.) He was the son of ALPHÆUS, and wrote the epistle which bears his name. For an analysis of which, and a further account of James, see Vol. IV. pp. 427—431.

JANNES and JAMBRES, two of the principal Egyptian magicians ; who withstood Moses and Aaron by attempting to imitate the miracles which they actually performed. (Exod. vii. 11, 12. viii. 7. 18. 19.) As these names are not found in the Old Testament, the apostle probably derived them from tradition (2 Tim. iii. 8.), as they are often mentioned in the rabbinical books.

JAPHET, the eldest son of Noah, was a witness of the deluge, and one of those who

were saved in the Ark. His descendants first settled in the isles of the Mediterranean Sea, and on the coasts of Asia Minor and of Europe, whence they spread into the north and west.

JARHAH, the Egyptian slave of an Israelite named Sheshan, who gave him his daughter in marriage, and consequently gave him his liberty. It is not improbable that Jarhah was a proselyte to the religion of Israel. (1 Chron. ii. 34.)

JAVELINS of the Hebrews, notice of, 210.

JAZER, a city beyond the Jordan, given to the tribe of Gad : it afterwards became one of the levitical cities. (Josh. xxi 30. xiii. 25.) The SEA OF JAZER, mentioned in Jer. xlviii. 32.), Dr. Blayney is of opinion, is the Dead Sea, Jazer being in the north border of Moab.

JEBUS, the son of Canaan, and father of the JEBUSITES (Gen. ii. 16.), who dwelt in and around Jerusalem in the mountains, where they continued until the time of David, when Joab took the place. (2 Sam. v. xxiv.)

JEDUTHUN, a Levite, one of David's choristers. (1 Chron. ix. 16. xvi. 38. 41, 42. xxv. 1.) His sons were employed as musicians. (2 Chron. xxxv. 15. Neh. xi. 17.

JEHOAHAZ.

1. JEHOAHAZ, or Shallum, the second son of Josiah king of Judah, whom he succeeded on the throne. He reigned only three months, being taken captive and carried into Egypt by Pharaoh-Necho. (2 Kings xxiii.)

2. JEHOAHAZ, the son and successor of Jehu king of Israel. He followed the evil example of Jeroboam I. during a reign of 17 years. His dominions were ravaged first by Hazael, and afterwards by Ben-hadad, kings of Syria ; but, Jehoahaz humbling himself before God, he and his people were delivered by his son Joash.

JEHOASH. See JOASH.

JEHOIAKIM or Eliakim, son and successor of Jehoahaz, king of Judah. After a wicked and inglorious reign of 11 years, Jerusalem was taken, and Jehoiakim carried as a prisoner to Babylon by Nebuchadnezzar. (2 Kings xxiii. 34—37. 1 Chron. iii. 15.) He was succeeded by his son

JEHOIACHIN, who was also called Coniah and Jechoniah. (1 Chron. iii. 16. Jer. xxii. 24. xxiv. 1.) After a reign of three months he was carried to Babylon by Nebuchadnezzar, together with a multitude of his people, and all the spoils of the city and temple. (2 Kings xxiv. 8. 2 Chron. xxxvi. 9.) Through the kindness of Evil-merodach, the son and successor of Nebuchadnezzar, he was restored to his personal liberty, and was supported at Babylon by the king's bounty. (2 Kings xxv. 27. Jer. lii. 31.)

JEHOIADA, the successor of Azariah in the pontificate ; who with his wife JEHOSHEBA, preserved his nephew Joash from the massacre of the royal family by Athaliah, and placed him on the throne of Judah. He reached the advanced age of 130 years, and was honoured with a burial among the kings, in consideration of his piety and disinterested patriotism. (2 Kings xi. 4, &c. xii. 1, 2. 2 Chron. xxii. 10—12. xxiii. xxiv. 1—3. 15, 16.)

JEHOIARIB, the head of the first of the twenty-four classes of priests established by David (1 Chron. xxiv. 7.), from whom the family of the Maccabees were descended. (2 Macc. ii. 1.)

JEHORAM.

1. JEHORAM, the son of Jehoshaphat king of Judah, with whom for a short time he was associated on the throne, and then succeeded him as sole monarch, B. C. 889. He married Athaliah, the daughter of Ahab, who seduced him into idolatry. He began his reign by murdering his brothers, and was succeeded by Ahaziah, after a wicked reign of eight years. (2 Chron. xxi.) On the nature of his disease, see p. 508. *supra.*

2. JEHORAM or JORAM, king of Israel, the son and successor of Ahab, whose impieties he followed. He was slain in the twelfth year of his reign by Jehu, B. C. 884.

JEHOSHAPHAT, the son and successor of Asa king of Judah: he was a pious prince; and in the third year of his reign he sent some of the chief officers of his court, together with certain Levites and priests, throughout his dominions, to instruct the people in the book of the law and their consequent duties. After a reign of 25 years, he died in peace, B. C. 889. (2 Chron. xvii.—xx. 1—34.)

JEHOSHAPHAT, Valley of, account of, 55.

JEHOVAH, the incommunicable name of the self-existent Being, for which the Jews substituted Adonai, in conformity with an antient superstition. In our authorised translation, this word is rendered "the LORD," in order to distinguish it from Lord, signifying a governor. Concerning the pronunciation of Jehovah, see Gesenius's Hebrew Lexicon, voce יהוה. — Land of Jehovah, 2.

JEHU.

1. A prophet, the son of Hanani, who was sent to denounce the divine judgments against Baasha king of Israel. (1 Kings xvi. 7.)

2. The son of Jehoshaphat, and grandson of Nimshi, who conspired against Jehoram king of Israel, B. C. 884, and reigned 28 years.

JEMIMA, KEZIA, and KEREN-HAPPUCH, the three daughters of Job, born after his restoration to prosperity. They obtained a portion of their father's inheritance, — a privilege which in those days could be conferred only by very rich parents.

JEPHTHAH, the ninth judge of Israel, succeeded Jair in the government of the people, whom he delivered from the Ammonites. Concerning his vow, see Vol. II. p. 598. His administration lasted six years.

JEREMIAH, the second of the four greater prophets, was the son of Hilkiah, of the sacerdotal race, and a native of Anathoth. He was distinguished for an ardent love of his country, for the pathetic tenderness with which he deplored her fate, and for the ungrateful treatment which he received from his countrymen. The time and manner of his death are unknown. For a further account of Jeremiah, and an analysis of his Prophecies and Lamentations, see Vol. IV. pp. 192—204.

JERICHO, a celebrated city in the tribe of Benjamin, of which frequent mention is made in the New Testament. It was the first city taken from the Canaanites by Joshua, who rased it to the ground, and denounced a severe curse on the person who should rebuild it. (Josh. vi. 20. 26. Heb. xi. 30.) This curse was literally fulfilled, in the days of Ahab, upon Hiel the Bethelite, by whom the city was rebuilt. (1 Kings xvi. 34.) After this event it was ennobled by the schools of the prophets, which were established there (2 Kings ii. 5.); and near it was a large but unwholesome spring, the waters of which rendered the soil unfruitful, until they were cured by the prophet Elisha (2 Kings ii. 21.); since which time they have become exceedingly wholesome and fertilising. In the time of our Saviour, Jericho yielded only to Jerusalem for its size and the magnificence of its buildings: it was situated in a *bottom*, in that vast plain which was named the *great plain* (which marks the propriety of the expression *going down from Jerusalem* Luke x. 30.); and is 150 furlongs, about nineteen miles distant from the capital of Judæa. The country around Jericho was the most fertile part of Palestine, abounding in roses and palm-trees (whence in Deut. xxxiv. 3. it is called the *city of palm-trees*), and yielding also great quantities of the opobalsamum or balm of Gilead, so highly esteemed in oriental courts even to the present day; and which being an article of commerce accounts for the mention of publicans and of a chief publican in that region. (Luke xix. 2.) Jericho was one of the cities appropriated for the residence of the priests and Levites, 12,000 of whom dwelt there; and as the way thither from Jerusalem was rocky and desert, it was, as it still is, greatly infested with thieves. Not a living creature is to be seen on it, nor any thing which indicates the habitation of man, or the mark of his hand on the soil. Lord Lindsay, who passed through this road in the summer of 1837, states, that " it runs between bleak stony mountains," and " is dreariness itself." A country more favourable for the attacks of banditti, and caves better adapted for concealment, than those presented on this road, can scarcely be imagined.[1] This circumstance marks the admirable propriety with which our Lord made it the scene of his beautiful narrative of the

---

[1] " The whole of this road," says Mr. Buckingham, " from Jerusalem to the Jordan, is held to be the most dangerous about Palestine, and, indeed, in this portion of it, the very

good Samaritan. (Luke x. 30—37.) Jericho is, at present, a wretched village, consisting of about thirty miserable huts, (compared with which the worst Irish cabin is a palace,) so low, that, at night, one might almost ride over them, without being aware of the fact. The once celebrated " City of Palms" cannot now boast of one of those beautiful trees in its vicinity. The plain that surrounds it (through which the Jordan flows) is watered by a beautiful fountain, called the *Fountain of Elisha:* it has ever been venerated as the same which the prophet Elisha healed (2 Kings ii. 19—22.), the *water* of which was *naught* (or bitter) *and the ground barren.* (Carne's Letters, pp. 322, 323. Three Weeks in Palestine, p. 83. Robinson's Travels in Palestine, vol. i. p. 56. Lord Lindsay's Letters on Egypt, &c. vol. ii. p. 63.)

JEROBOAM I., son of Nebat, and the first king of Israel. He was a wicked prince, who from political motives established idolatry (see p. 341.), and changed the order of the Hebrew calendar. He is never mentioned in the Old Testament, but in terms of detestation. He died after a reign of 22 years.

JEROBOAM II., the thirteenth king of Israel, succeeded his father Jehoahash. He reigned 41 years; and is recorded to have done evil in the sight of God, following the example of Jeroboam I.

JERUBBAAL. See GIDEON.

JERUSALEM (city), situation of and the names by which it was called, 17—19. Fortifications and walls, 19, 20. Its state before the war of the Jews with the Romans, 21. Remarkable buildings, 22, 23. Temple, 236 —244. Successive captures of this city, 24. Its present state and population, 25, 26.

JESUS, that is the Saviour, the name of the Messiah, the Son of God, and the Divine Author of the Christian religion, who is constituted by God the Lord of all things. He is called Jesus, because he came to save his people from their sins. (Matt. i. 21. Eph. i. 21, 22. Heb. i. 2.) The history of his life, miracles, doctrine, death, resurrection, and ascension, is related in the four Gospels. In 2 Cor. i. 19. Jesus is, metonymically, put for the Gospel or religion of Jesus.

JETHRO, or Raguel, a priest of Midian, and the father-in-law of Moses, to whom he gave the wise counsel, of instituting inferior judges (from him sometimes termed *Jethronian prefects*), to hear and determine minor causes; while questions of moment were brought before the Hebrew legislator himself. See pp. 82, 83.

JEWS. — After the captivity, most of those persons who returned and rebuilt Jerusalem and the temple, and restored the rites of the Mosaic worship, having sprung from the kingdom of Judah, the term JEWS became a general appellation for all the inhabitants of Palestine, and afterwards for those descended from them. (Dan. iii. 8. Esth. iii. 10. 2 Macc.

---

aspect of the scenery is sufficient, on the one hand, to tempt to robbery and murder, and, on the other, to occasion a dread of it in those who pass that way. It was partly to prevent any accident happening to us in this early stage of our journey, and partly, perhaps, to calm our fears on that score, that a messenger had been despatched by our guides to an encampment of their tribe near, desiring them to send an escort to meet us at this place. We were met here accordingly, by a band of about twenty persons on foot, all armed with matchlocks, and presenting the most ferocious and robber-like appearance that could be imagined. The effect of this was heightened by the shouts which they sent forth from hill to hill, and which were re-echoed through all the valleys, while the bold projecting crags of rock, the dark shadows in which every thing lay buried below, the towering height of the cliffs above, and the forbidding desolation which every where reigned around, presented a picture that was quite in harmony throughout all its parts. It made us feel most forcibly the propriety of its being chosen as the scene of the delightful tale of compassion which we had before so often admired for its doctrine, independently of its local beauty. (See Luke x. 30—34.) One must be amid these wild and gloomy solitudes, surrounded by an armed band, and feel the impatience of the traveller who rushes on to catch a new view at every pass and turn; one must be alarmed at the very tramp of the horses' hoofs rebounding through the caverned rocks, and at the savage shouts of the footmen, scarcely less loud than the echoing thunder produced by the discharge of their pieces in the valleys; one must witness all this upon the spot, before the full force and beauty of the admirable story of the Good Samaritan can be perceived. Here, pillage, wounds, and death would be accompanied with double terror, from the frightful aspect of every thing around. Here, the unfeeling act of passing by a fellow-creature in distress, as the Priest and Levite are said to have done, strikes one with horror, as an act almost more than inhuman. And here, too, the compassion of the Good Samaritan is doubly virtuous, from the purity of the motive which must have led to it, in a spot where no eyes were fixed on him to draw forth the performance of any duty, and from the bravery which was necessary to admit of a man's exposing himself, by such delay, to the risk of a similar fate to that from which he was endeavouring to rescue his fellow-creature."—(Buckingham's Travels in Palestine, pp. 292, 293. See a good illustration of the nature of the road to Jericho, and of the banditti who infest it, in Sir F. Henniker's Notes during a Visit to Egypt, Nubia, &c. pp. 289—291. London, 1823, 8vo.)

J O

J O

ix. 17.) For the political state of the Jews, from the patriarchal times to their final dispersion, see pp. 78—114. Their courts of judicature, legal proceedings, criminal law and punishments, 115—125, 136—167. Their mode of computing time, 167—182. Tributes and taxes paid by them, 183—186. Their genealogical tables and memorials of events, 186—188. Treaties, covenants, and contracts, 188—192. Oaths, 192—194. The whole nation why accounted holy, 263. Account of the Jewish church and its members, 264—272. All male Jews required to be at Jerusalem at the three great annual festivals, 303. Whither they travelled in caravans, 304. note. Corruptions of religion among them, and their idolatry, 337—360. Did not worship an ass's head, 343. State of religion and sects in the time of Jesus Christ, 361—375. Their private life, manners, custom, arts and sciences, 381—481. Commerce and navigation, 482—488. Amusements, 488, 489. Their treatment of the dead, and funeral rites, 511—524. Their extreme corruption during the time of Christ, 375—380.

In the New Testament, the term "Jews" is employed.

(1.) With reference both to nation and religion. Matt. xxviii. 15. Mark vii. 3.)

(2.) With reference to religion only. (Rom. ii. 28, 29. Rev. ii. 9. iii. 9.)

(3.) With reference to nations only. (Acts xix. 34. xxi. 39. xxii. 3. Gal. ii. 13.)

JEWS OF THE DISPERSION, who they were, 268.

JEZEBEL.

1. The daughter of Ethbaal or Ithobalus king of the Zidonians, and wife of Ahab king of Israel. She was infamous for her idolatries, and for her cruel persecutions of the worshippers of the true God, particularly the prophets. She at length perished miserably, according to a prediction of the prophet Elijah. (1 Kings xvi. 31. xviii. 4. 13. xxi. 23. 2 Kings ix. 30—37.)

2. In Rev. ii. 20. Jezebel is put as a generic term for an idolatrous and infamous woman, the emblem of corrupt teachers. Compare Vol. IV. pp. 524, 525.

JEZREEL, a celebrated city, situated in a valley of that name, in the canton of the half-tribe of Manasseh, on the west of the river Jordan, and on the confines of the tribe of Issachar. (Josh. xix. 18.) Here Ahab had a palace ; and here the retributive justice of God overtook Jezebel. (2 Kings ix. 30—37.)

JEZREEL, Plain of, account of, 57.

JOAB.

1. JOAB, the son of Seraiah and the grandson of Kenaz (1 Chron. iv. 13, 14.), nephew of Othniel the first judge of the Hebrews, was the founder of a colony of artisans, or "craftsmen," at Ono in the tribe of Benjamin, not far from the river Jordan. The valley, where he settled, obtained the name of the Valley of Craftsmen, an appellation which shows, that the arts practised by them were of the first utility ; and Nehemiah gave it the same appellation. (xi. 35.) The establishment of Joab, towards the time of the first judge, from whom he was descended, proves that the Hebrews had not forgotten the arts which they had acquired in Egypt, and shows in what estimation trades were held. The people, who had erected the tabernacle in the wilderness, we may readily conceive, would, in no long time, form establishments of this kind, after they were settled in Canaan.

2. JOAB, the son of Zeruiah, and nephew of David. With his brothers Abishai and Asahel, he commanded his uncle's troops against Abner. He was one of the greatest generals and most valiant men in David's army, but was of an imperious and revengeful disposition. Having conspired to raise Adonijah to the throne of his father David, Joab was put to death by command of Solomon.

JOANNA, the wife of Chuza, steward of Herod Antipas. She is enumerated among those women, who having been healed by Jesus, followed him out of Galilee, and assisted in supporting him. (Luke viii. 3. xxiv. 10.)

JOASH, the eighth king of Judah, was the son of Ahaziah. On the massacre of his family by Athaliah, he was preserved by Jehoiada the high priest and his wife Jehosheba, and secreted for six years in one of the apartments of the temple, where he was brought up. At the age of seven years, the courageous fidelity of the high priest placed him on the throne of his ancestors. During the life of Jehoiada, he ruled well ; but on the death of that wise and pious counsellor, he listened to the advice of some of his courtiers ; fell into gross idolatry ; and at length put to death the son of his benefactor. From this time, his reign became disastrous ; his kingdom was invaded by the Syrians under Hazael ; his armies were totally discomfited by very inferior forces; and he could only save his capital, by delivering to the Syrians the treasures which had been consecrated by his predecessors, and those which he had himself offered in the temple. A lingering illness seized him : the blood of Zechariah, the son of Jehoiada, found avengers ; and after reigning 40 years, Joash was assassinated by three of his servants. (2 Kings xi. xii. 2 Chron. xxiv.)

JOASH or JEHOASH, king of Israel, the son and successor of Jehoahaz. Possessed of more talents than virtues, by his fortunate wars he prepared the splendid reign of his son Jeroboam II. ; and wanted nothing but piety. He reigned sixteen years, during which he "did evil in the sight of the Lord, and departed not from all the sins of Jeroboam the son of Nebat, who made Israel to sin." (2 Kings xii. 10—12. xiv.

JOB, an inhabitant of the land of Uz, or Idumæa, whose piety and afflictions are celebrated in the poetical book which bears his name; for an account of which, and of the patriarch himself, see Vol. IV. pp. 67—96. For a notice of the disease with which he was afflicted, see pp. 507, 508. of this volume.

JOEL, the son of Pethuel, and the second of the minor prophets. His history is entirely unknown. See an analysis of his predictions, in Vol IV. pp. 185,186.

JOHN.

1. JOHN the Baptist, the son of Zecharias and Elizabeth, was the kinsman and precursor of Jesus Christ, and distinguished for the simplicity and integrity of his life. Notice of his dress, see p. 395. He was beheaded by order of Herod Antipas, whom he had reproved for his incestuous marriage. (Matt. iii. 1. xiv. 2—4. 8. 10.)

2. JOHN the Apostle and Evangelist, was the son of Zebedee and Salome, brother of James the elder, and originally a fisherman. He seems to have been of a mild and affectionate disposition, and peculiarly dear to Jesus Christ. His name is prefixed to the fourth Gospel, to three Epistles, and to the Apocalypse; for an analysis of which, see Vol. IV. pp. 304—317. 442—474. 478—491.

3. JOHN, surnamed MARK, the companion of Paul and Barnabas in their journies.

4. JOHN, one of the chief men among the Jews, a member of the Sanhedrin, and perhaps related to the high priest. (Acts iv. 6.)

JOKTAN, the eldest son of Eber, from whom many Arabian tribes were descended. (Gen. x. 25—30.)

JOKTHEEL.

1. A city belonging to the tribe of Judah. (Josh. xv. 38.)

2. The name which Amaziah king of Judah gave to Selah, an Arabian city which he took. (2 Kings xiv. 7.) See SELAH, infra.

JONAH.

1. JONAH, the son of Amittai, and the fifth of the minor prophets, who was swallowed by a large fish, and continued three days and three nights in the stomach of the monster. See an analysis of his prophecy in Vol. IV. pp. 156, 157.

2. JONAH or JONAS, the father of the apostle Simon Peter. He was a fisherman. (John i. 42. xxi. 15—17.)

JONATHAN, the son of Saul, and the faithfully attached friend of David in all his persecutions. Jonathan displayed signal valour in the wars with the Philistines. He perished in battle with his father on Mount Gilboa; and his death is pathetically lamented by David in a funeral elegy which he composed in honour of both. (2 Sam. i.)

JOPPA, a sea-port of Palestine, on the Mediterranean, called also Japha, and now universally Jaffa, owes all the circumstances of its celebrity, as the principal port of Judæa, to its situation with regard to Jerusalem. It is situated on the side of a low hill, over the sea. "As a station for vessels, its harbour is

one of the worst in the Mediterranean: ships generally anchor about a mile from the town, to avoid the shoals and rocks of the place. In antient times it was the only place resorted to as a sea-port in all Judæa. Hither Solomon ordered the materials for the temple to be brought from Mount Libanus, previous to their conveyance by land to Jerusalem." (Clarke's Travels, vol. iv. p. 442. Jolliffe's Letters from Palestine, p. 198. Irby's and Mangles' Travels, pp. 186—188.) It is a place of very great antiquity; and it appears from the Acts of the Apostles (ix. x. xi.) that the Gospel was received here soon after Christ's ascension. Here also St. Peter restored Dorcas to life (Acts ix. 40.) and from this place it was that the prophet Jonah, many centuries before, had embarked for Nineveh. (Jonah i. 3.) Modern Joppa or Jaffa, stands on a promontory, which rises about 150 feet above the level of the sea: it commands varied and picturesque views on every side. The streets are very narrow, uneven, and dirty, and the houses are crowded closely together. The population is between 4000 and 5000, 600 of whom are Christians, of the Romish, Greek, Maronite, and Armenian communions; the remainder are Mohammedans. Except in the immediate vicinity, where a few palm-trees raise their stately heads, the country is remarkably dreary, consisting for the most part of a few low naked sand-hills. There is very little trade here, the only business of the place being derived from the supplies necessary for the pilgrims going to and returning from Jerusalem. The house of the British vice-consul (signor Damiani), in 1831, stood on the reputed site of the house which had been Simon the Tanner's, the host of the apostle Peter; and a portion of an ancient wall therein was pointed out, as a genuine relic of the original mansion. (Three Weeks in Palestine, pp. 6—10. London, 1833. Robinson's Travels in Palestine and Syria, vol. i. pp. 18, 19.)

JORAM. See JEHORAM, 2. p. 589.

JORDAN, River, account of, pp. 36, 37. Region round about, p. 58. Thickets of, p. 66.

JOSEPH.

1. JOSEPH, the eleventh son of Jacob, born of Rachel. Hated by his brethren, he was sold by them as a slave to some Midianitish merchants, by whom he was carried into Egypt, and again sold to Potiphar. He subsequently became governor over all the land of Egypt, and sent for his father and brethren to Egypt, where he provided for them. On the departure of the Israelites, pursuant to his command, the remains of Joseph, which had been embalmed according to the Egyptian process, were carried into Canaan. (Heb. xi. 22.), and, it should seem from Josh. xxiv. 31., after the conquest by Joshua, were interred in Jacob's field near Schechem. (Gen. xxxvii.—l.) Joseph is sometimes, metonymically, put for his descendants, that is, the half-tribe of Ephraim.

2. The *husband of Mary*, and the reputed father of Jesus. (Matt. i. 16. 18—20. 24. ii. 13. 19. Luke i. 27. ii. 4. 16. 33. 43. iii. 23. iv. 22. John i. 46. vi. 42.)

3. JOSEPH *of Arimathea*, a member of the Jewish sanhedrin, and privately a disciple of Jesus Christ. After his death, Joseph requested his body of Pilate, and honourably entombed it in his own new sepulchre. (Matt. xxvii. 57—60. Mark xv. 43—45. Luke xxiii. 50. John xix. 38.)

4. One of the seventy disciples of Jesus, also called Barsabas and Justus. He was nominated as one of the two candidates for the apostleship in place of the traitor Judas. (Acts i. 23.)

JOSES.

1. A brother of James the Less, and a kinsman of Jesus. (Matt. xiii. 55. xxvii. 56. Mark vi. 3. xv. 40. 47.) He is the only one of the sons of Cleopas and Mary who did not become an apostle; which circumstance has been accounted for by Coquerel, who supposes that Joses was one of those brethren or kinsmen of Jesus Christ who distinguished himself by his want of faith in him (compare John vii. 5.), and therefore was deemed unfit for the apostleship. As it appears from Acts i. 14. that the brethren of Jesus were present at the meetings of his disciples, which were held between the ascension and the day of Pentecost, it is not improbable that Joses was converted after the resurrection.

2. JOSES, surnamed BARNABAS, the companion of St. Paul. (Acts iv. 36.)

JOSHUA, the son of Nun, of the tribe of Ephraim, called Jesus by the Greeks. He was the minister or servant, and the successor of Moses; an office which he deserved to fill on many accounts: for not only had Moses discovered in him distinguished talents, but God himself had destined Joshua to be the commander-in-chief of his people, in which capacity Moses presented him to them a short time before his death. Joshua had displayed both knowledge and courage during the life of Moses, whom he accompanied to Mount Sinai at the giving of the law. In the battle with the Amalekites, he had bravely commanded the Israelites, and had been blessed with victory. He had been one of the twelve spies, whom Moses had sent to explore the land of Canaan; and as Caleb and he were the only persons out of that number who had encouraged the people when intimidated by the report of the other spies, so they were the only Israelites who were more than twenty years of age that survived their forty years' wandering in the desert, and participated in the conquest of Canaan. Joshua died at the age of 110 years, after he had for seventeen years governed the Israelites. His earlier name was Hoshea, which Moses changed to Joshua, or, as it is pronounced in Hebrew, Jehoshuah, the import of which is *the Salvation of God.* Joshua has been considered as a type of our Saviour. As the Hebrew general vanquished the impious Canaanites by the aid

of God, and introduced His people into the rest of the promised land, so Jesus (whose name in Greek is the same as Jehoshuah) will one day subdue and exterminate the enemies of his name and disciples, and will introduce his people into that place of rest, in which they will enjoy perfect and eternal happiness. For an analysis of the book of Joshua, see Vol. IV. pp. 33—39.; and for an account of the division of the Holy Land by him, see pp. 8—13. of this volume; and for his government of the Israelites, see p. 84. Observations on the pile of stones raised by Joshua at Gilgal, I. 223.

JOSIAH, the son of Amon and Jedidah, succeeded his father on the throne of Judah, at the early age of eight years, and during a reign of thirty-one years he endeavoured, with much success, to restore the worship of God to its original purity. Being a tributary or ally of Nabopolassar, the founder of the Chaldeo-Babylonian empire, and in all probability bound by treaty to assist him, Josiah, in the discharge of his duty to his liege-superior, refused a passage through his dominions to Pharaoh-Necho, king of Egypt, who was marching into Assyria. The two armies met at Megiddo, where Josiah, entering into the battle in disguise, was mortally wounded by an arrow: he died at Jerusalem, deeply regretted by all his subjects. Jeremiah composed Lamentations in his honour. (2 Kings xxii. xxiii. 2 Chron. xxxiv.)

JOTHAM, the eleventh king of Judah, exercised the regal authority during the leprosy which terminated the life of his father Uzziah, whom he succeeded on the throne. He is recorded to have done that which was right in the sight of God, and to have imitated his father's piety. "*He became mighty, because he prepared his ways before the* LORD *his God.*" He discomfited the Ammonites, and for three years received of them a rich tribute in silver, barley, and corn, which his father had imposed; but which that people had refused to pay. Magnificent erections distinguished his reign. The principal gate of the temple was enlarged and embellished; the hill of Ophel received new fortifications; and various buildings, both for habitation and defence, were erected in the mountains of Judah. After a reign of sixteen years he died, much regretted by his people, and was interred in the sepulchres of the kings, B. C. 742.

JUBAL, the son of Lamech and Adah: *he was the father of all such as handle the harp and organ.* (Gen. iv. 21.) In other terms, he was the inventor of musical instruments. By comparing his discoveries with those of Jabal, the institutor of the nomadic life, and of Tubal-Cain, *the instructor of every artificer in brass and iron,* we may perceive how soon the agreeable followed the useful arts.

JUBILEE, Feast of, how celebrated, 321. Was a proof of the divine legation of Moses, *ibid.* Reason and design of the law concerning the Jubilee, 322.

JU

KA

JUDAH.

1. JUDAH, the fourth son of Jacob and Leah, gave his name to the most numerous of the tribes of Israel ; for the limits of the canton assigned to which, see p. 12. At the time of the revolution under Rehoboam and Jeroboam, this tribe also gave its name to that part of the kingdom of Israel which continued faithful to the house of David.

2. DESERT OF JUDAH, account of, 60.

3 KINGDOM OF JUDAH, 13. Causes of its duration for a longer time than the kingdom of Israel, 102—104.

4. LAND OF JUDAH, notice of, 3.

5. MOUNTAINS OF JUDAH, notice of, 51.

JUDÆA, Country of, 15.

JUDAS.

1. JUDAS, surnamed Iscariot, (Heb. איש קריות, ISH KARIOTH,) that is, a man of Karioth or Carioth, one of the apostles of Jesus Christ. He seems to have possessed the full confidence of his fellow-apostles, by whom he was entrusted with all the presents which were made to them, and with all their means of subsistence : and, when the twelve were sent out to preach and to work miracles, Judas appears to have been among them, and to have received the same powers. He was accustomed, however, even at this time, to appropriate part of the common stock to his own use (John xii. 6.), and at length sealed his infamy by betraying his Lord for money to the Jews. Judas perished miserably, being driven by remorse to hang himself; but the cord broke, and he fell (probably from some elevated place) with such violence as to rupture the abdomen, and dash out his intestines upon the ground. (Matt. xxvii. 5. Acts i. 18.)

2. JUDAS, a Christian teacher, also called Barsabas, who was sent from Jerusalem to Antioch with Paul and Barnabas. Judas and Silas are termed prophets as well as Agabus: which title is given them in a two-fold sense, as zealous preachers of the Gospel, and as ministers of God, who were divinely inspired, according to the exigencies of the church, to predict future events. (Acts xv. 22. 27. 32.)

3. JUDAS, surnamed the Galilæan in Acts v. 37. and also by Josephus (Ant. Jud. lib. xviii. c. 1. § 6. xx. c. 5. § 2. Bell. Jud. lib. ii. c. 8. § 1.), who further calls him a Gaulonite (Ant. Jud. lib. xviii. c. 1. § 1.), was born at Gamala, a city of Lower Gaulonitis, near the south-eastern shore of the lake of Tiberias. In company with one Sadok or Sadducus, he attempted to excite a sedition among the Jews, but was destroyed by Quirinus, at that time governor of Syria and Judæa.

4. JUDAS or JUDE, one of the apostles, also called Lebbeus and Thaddeus, the son of Alphæus and Mary, own brother of James the Less and cousin of our Lord. He was author of the epistle which bears his name ; for an analysis of which, as well as a further account of Jude, see Vol. IV. pp. 474—478.

5. JUDAS MACCABÆUS, son of Mattathias,

whom he succeeded in the office of captain of the Jews, during the persecution of Antiochus Epiphanes. (1 Macc. iii. 1.) After performing many heroic and glorious actions, he at length fell nobly in the field of battle, in an engagement with the Syrian army under the command of Bacchides, the general of Demetrius, the successor of Antiochus. (1 Macc. ix. 18.)

JUDGES of the Israelites, powers and functions of, 84. Judges appointed by Moses, powers of, 82, 83.

JUDICATURE (Jewish), courts of, and proceedings therein, 115—125.

JUDICATURE (Roman), account of, 125—134.

JULIA, a female Christian at Rome, who is supposed to have been the wife of Philologus. (Rom. xvi. 15.) It is not improbable that she was a freed-woman of the family of the Cæsars.

JULIUS, a centurion of the Augustan cohort, who conducted Paul to Rome, and treated the apostle with great courtesy and humanity. (Acts xxvii.)

JUNIAS or JUNIA, a Jewish Christian, who is supposed to have been the wife of Andronicus. (Rom. xvi. 7.)

JUPITER, the supreme god of the antient Greeks and Romans. He had a temple in the suburbs of LYSTRA (which see).

JURISDICTION of Moses, 79—84. ; of Joshua, and the judges, 84. ; of the kings, 85—94.

JUSTICE, seat of, 116. Summary justice, when clamorously demanded, 123, 124.

JUSTUS.

1. The surname of Joseph-Barsabas, who was one of those nominated to be an apostle. (Acts i. 23.) See BARSABAS.

2. A Christian at Corinth, who hospitably received St. Paul. (Acts xviii. 7.)

3. JUSTUS, also called JESUS, appears to have been known to the Jews by the former name, and to the Romans by the latter. He was a Jew by descent, and the friend and coadjutor of Saint Paul. (Col. iv. 11.)

JYAR, the eighth month of the civil year of the Jews ; and the second of their ecclesiastical year. For a notice of the festivals &c. occurring in this month, see p. 178.

KADESH, KADESH-BARNEA, or EN-MISHPAT, a city celebrated for several events. Here Miriam, the sister of Moses, died (Numb. xx. 1.), and the Israelites murmured against God. (xxvii. 14.) It belonged to the tribe of Judah, and is supposed to have been situated about 25 miles to the south of Hebron. But Dr. Wells is of opinion that the Kadesh in the wilderness of Zin was a different place from Kadesh-Barnea in the wilderness of Paran. (Compare Numb. xiii. 26. and Deut. i. 19.) Dr. Lightfoot, however, considers them as one and the same place. In the fourth century, the pretended sepulchre of Miriam was shown.

KADMONITES, antient inhabitants of the land of Canaan, who dwelt beyond the Jor-

K I

dan, to the east of Phœnicia, about Mount Lebanon. (Gen. xv. 19.) They derived their name from their eastern situation.

KANAH, Brook, 38.

KARIOTH or KERIOTH, a town belonging to the tribe of Judah. (Josh. xv. 25.) Also, a town belonging to the tribe of Benjamin. (Josh. xviii. 28.) Of one or other of these places, the traitor Judas was a native. See JUDAS, 1.

KEDAR, a tribe of Arabian nomades, descended from Kedar, the son of Ishmael. (Gen. xxv. 13.) They were rich in flocks of rams, lambs, and goats, in which they traded with the Tyrians (Ezek. xxvii. 21. Jer. xlix. 29.): and they were also celebrated for their skill in the use of the bow. (Isa. xxi. 17.) The manners and habits of the Turcomans, a nomadic tribe who infest the inland portions of Asia Minor, are precisely those of the wandering hordes of Kedar, as described in the books of the Old Testament; and their black tents would fully suit the simile of Solomon (Song i. 5.), while their pastoral traffic is in every respect that adverted to in Ezek. (xxvii. 21.), in his denunciations of destruction against Tyre. (Emerson's Letters from the Ægean, vol. i. p. 192.)

KEDRON, KIDRON, or CEDRON, Brook, account of, 38.

KENITES, a Cananitish people, who, according to 1 Sam. xv. 6., compared with Numb. xxiv. 20, 21., dwelt among the Amalekites. According to Judg. i. 16. iv. 11., they appear to have been descended from Hobab the brother-in-law of Moses.

KENIZZITES, an antient Canaanitish people, who may have been descended from Kenaz, a grandson of Esau. Their place of residence cannot now be determined. (Gen. xv. 19. Numb. xxxii. 12.)

KETURAH, the second wife of Abraham, who married her after the death of Sarah; she bore him six sons. (Gen. xxv.)

KINGS, person of, sacred, 89. Their powers, functions, and revenues, 85—95. Influence of the king's friend, 97.

KINGDOMS of Israel and Judah, 13. Latent causes of the schism between, 99—101. Causes of the longer duration of the kingdom of Judah, 102—104.

KIR (or Cyrus), a country through which flows the river Kur, as it is called by the Russians, or Kier, as it is called by the Persians, the Kuros (Cyrus) of the Greeks; whither Tiglath-Pileser, king of Assyria, sent the principal inhabitants of Syria, whom he had taken captive. (2 Kings xvi. 9.) This river unites its waters to the Aras or Araxes, and empties itself into the Caspian Sea, under the 39th degree of north latitude. A people of foreign aspect, called *Usbecks*, dwell there to this time, who (Prof. Jahn thinks) may be the descendants of these captives. (Hist. of Heb. Commonwealth, vol. i. p. 140.)

KIR-HERES. See RABBATH-AMMON.

KIRJATH or KIRIOTH (קרית), a Hebrew word denoting a city. There was a place of

K O

this name in the canton of the tribe of Benjamin. (Josh. xviii. 28.)

The following proper names of cities are compounded of it; viz.

1. KIRJATH-AIM, or the *Double City.*
(1.) The proper name of a city in the tribe of Reuben. (Numb. xxxii. 37. Josh. xiii. 19.) It was afterwards possessed by the Moabites. (Jer. xlviii. 1. 3. Ezek. xxv. 9.)
(2.) A city in the canton of the tribe of Naphtali. (1 Chron. vi. 61.)

2. KIRJATH-ARBA, or the *City of Arba :* an antient name of HEBRON, which see in p. 580.

3. KIRJATH-HUZOTH, or the *City of Streets,* a royal city of Balak king of Moab. (Numb. xxii. 39.)

4. KIRJATH-JEARIM, (the *City of Forests,*) or BAALAH, (Josh. xv. 9.) also called KIRJATH-BAAL, (xv. 60.) and simply KIRJATH (xviii. 38.) was a town situated on the confines of the allotments to the tribes of Benjamin and Judah. Hence it is reckoned among the cities of both tribes. (Josh. xv. 60. xviii. 28.) But in Judges xviii. 12., it is called Kirjath-jearim in Judah. Here the ark of the covenant remained twenty years after its removal from Beth-shemesh (1 Sam. i. 2.) until David, having obtained possession of Jerusalem, fixed the sanctuary in that city. (1 Sam. vi. 21. 1 Chron. xiii. 6.) Urijah the prophet was a native of this place.

5. KIRJATH-SANNAH, or the *City of the Law,* was a city in the tribe of Judah. (Josh. xv. 49.)

6. KIRJATH-SEPHER, or the *City of Writing,* otherwise called DEBIR; a city in the tribe of Judah, which was captured from the Canaanites by Othniel. (Josh. xv. 15, 16. Judg. i. 10—13.) Concerning the import of its name there is a difference of opinion; some supposing it to have been a seat of learning, while others, from Debir, signifying an oracle, imagine that it was a seminary for the education of priests.

KISH, the son of Abdiel, who was also called Ner, and the father of Saul, of an obscure family in the tribe of Benjamin, was both a shepherd and a warrior, conformably to the custom of those antient times. The Scripture eulogises his valour. He sent his son in pursuit of some lost asses, and he returned to his father the first king of Israel. (1 Chron. viii. 30. ix. 39. 1 Sam. xiv. 51. ix. 1. and x. 2.)

KISHON, Brook, notice of, 38.

KNEADING-TROUGHS of the Israelites, 392.

KOHATH, the son of Levi. (Gen. xlvi. 11.) He was the head of the Kohathites, who were appointed to carry the ark and sacred vessels of the tabernacle, during the marches of the Israelites. (Numb. iv. 1—15.)

KORAH, the son of Izhar, and grandson of Levi, who conspired against Moses. (Exod. vi. 21. Numb. xvi.) From him were descended the sons of Korah, a Levitical family of singers, whom David appointed to guard the doors of the temple. (1 Chron. ix. 19.)

Q Q 2

L A

Eleven psalms are inscribed "for the sons of Korah;" on the probable import of which title, see Vol. IV. p. 102.

KORBAN, nature of the vow of, 295, 296.

LABAN, the son of Bethuel, grandson of Nahor, brother to Rebekah, and father of Rachel and Leah. (Gen. xxviii.)— Also, the name of a place beyond the Jordan, in the plains of Moab; it is otherwise unknown. (Deut. i. 1.)

LAKES in the Holy Land, account of, 38—42.

LAMB, Paschal, ceremonies of offering, &c. See pp. 306—312.

LAMPS, notice of, 393.

LAMENTATIONS for the dead, account of, 516, 517.

LAND of Canaan, 2. Of Israel, 2. Of Jehovah, 3. Of Promise, 2. Of Judah, 3. Holy Land, 2, 3. The Jewish mode of cultivating land, described, 452—456.

LAND-SURVEYING, known to the Jews, 481.

LAODICEA, the chief city of Phrygia Pacatiana in Asia Minor, about 42 miles to the south of Ephesus, and in the vicinity of Colossæ and Hierapolis. Its earlier name was Diospolis or Cæsarea, but after being enlarged by Antiochus II. it was called Laodicea in honour of his wife Laodice. This city was often damaged by earthquakes, and restored either by the opulence of its inhabitants, or by the munificence of the Roman emperors. From the researches of modern travellers, it appears to have been seated on a volcanic hill, of moderate height, but of considerable extent. Its ruins attest that it was large, opulent, and splendid; and there are still to be seen the remains of an amphitheatre, an aqueduct, and many other buildings. In the primitive times of Christianity, as appears from St. Paul's Epistle to the Colossians, in which the Laodiceans are frequently mentioned, this place possessed a flourishing church. But the doom of Laodicea seems to have been more severe and terrible than that of the other six apocalyptic churches: and its present condition is in striking conformity with the rebukes and threatenings of God. Not a single Christian resides at Laodicea! It is even more solitary than Ephesus: the latter has a prospect of a rolling sea, or a whitening sail, to enliven its decay; the former sits in widowed loneliness. Its temples are desolate; the stately edifices of antient Laodicea are now peopled with wolves and jackals. The prayers of the mosque are the only prayers heard near the still splendid ruins of the city, on which the prophetic denunciation seems to have been fully executed, in its utter rejection as a church. "Its crime was pride; its punishment, desolation. The threatening is accomplished: it now stands, rejected of God and deserted by men; its glory, a ruin; its name, a reproach." (Hartley's Visit to the Apocalyptic Churches, in 1826. Mission. Register, July, 1827, p. 296. Arundell's Visit to

L I

the Seven Churches, pp. 84—90. Emerson's Letters from the Ægean, vol. i. pp. 180. 219. Monro's Summer Rambles in Syria, vol. i. pp. 128, 129.)

LASÆA, a maritime city of Crete (Acts xxvii. 8.), which is not mentioned by any of the antient geographers. Its exact site cannot now be ascertained.

LAW and the Prophets, tables of the sections of, as read in the Jewish synagogues, 256, 257. The Mosaic law perverted by the Pharisees, 364, 365.

LAWS, how promulgated, 98, 99.

LAWYERS (Jewish), account of, 370.

LAZARUS.

1. The brother of Martha and Mary, whom Jesus loved, and miraculously raised him from the dead. For an examination of the circumstances of this miracle, see Vol. I. pp. 237—239.

2. The name of a person introduced by Jesus into a very instructive narrative or parable, to represent the poor and distressed in this world. (Luke xvi. 19—25.)

LEAH, the daughter of Laban, and the wife of Jacob, on whom her father imposed her in lieu of Rachel. (Gen. xxix.)

LEARNED MEN, different appellations of, 476.

LEBANON (Mount), account of, 46—48.

LEBBÆUS, a proper name of the apostle JUDE, who was also called Thaddeus. (Matt. x. 3.)

LEGAL PROCEEDINGS of the Jews, account of, 120—125.; and of the Romans, 125—134.

LEGIONS (Roman), notice of, 221.

LEPROSY (Disease of). Symptoms and treatment of, 504—507. Purification of lepers, 335. Leprosy of clothes and houses, 335, 336.

LETTERS or Epistles, form of, 470.

LEVI.

1. The third son of Jacob and Leah. (Gen. xxix. 34.) He is known only as having participated in the revenge of Simeon against the Schechemites, for the violation of Dinah (xxxiv. 25.), and for having given his name to the tribe that was set apart for the priesthood and worship of God.

2. One of the twelve apostles, also called MATTHEW. See p. 599. *infra.*

LEVIES, Military, how raised, 199.

LEVITES, functions, &c. of, 272—274.

LIBERTINES, account of, 251, 252, 268. I. 170.

LIBYA, among the Greeks, was used as another name for Africa, as it imports a part of it. It was divided into Libya Interior and Exterior: but the Libya mentioned by Saint Luke (Acts ii. 10.) is that by Ptolemy called Libya Cyrenaica: and by Pliny, Pentapolitana Regio, from its five chief cities, viz. Berenice, Arsinöe, Ptolemais, Apollonia, and Cyrene. It is noted in the Old Testament, for its chariots and horses used in fight. (2 Chron. xvi. 8.) But it is mentioned by St. Luke, on account of the Jews,

L Y

who, living in such vast numbers in Alexandria, that 50,000 of them were slain at one time, may well be thought to have had some colonies and proselytes in this neighbouring country.

LIFE-GUARDS of the kings of Israel, 97.

LILIES, notice of, 65, and note 2.

LINUS, a disciple whose salutations Saint Paul addresses to Timothy. (2 Tim. iv. 21.) He is commonly supposed to have been the first bishop of Rome.

LITERATURE of the Jews, 474—481.

LIVER, divination by the inspection of, 360.

LOCUSTS, natural history of, and of their devastations, 74, 75. Were eaten by the inhabitants of Palestine, 76.

LOIS, a Christian matron and the grandmother of Timothy, of whose faith the apostle speaks with great commendation. (2 Tim. i. 5.)

LORD'S SUPPER, points of resemblance between, and the Passover, 306—314. It is a perpetual memorial of the vicarious atonement of Jesus Christ, I. 137.

LOT, the son of Haran and nephew of Abraham; after separating from whom, on account of the increase of their cattle, he chose the city of Sodom for his abode. On its destruction, Lot and his two daughters escaped with their lives; but his wife, looking back, perished. (Gen. xix. Luke xvii. 28.) The Moabites and Ammonites descended from Lot.

LOTS, when used judiciously, 122. Notice of the *Feast of Lots*, 320, 321.

LUBIM, the Libyans. (2 Chron. xii. 3. xvi. 8. Nah. iii. 9.)

LUCIUS, a Cyrenian, one of the prophets or teachers of the Christian church at Antioch. (Acts xiii. 1. Rom. xvi. 21.) By some he has been erroneously confounded with the evangelist LUKE.

LUD, the fourth son of Shem, whose descendants peopled the province of LYDIA. (Gen. x. 22.)

LUDIM, a people of Africa, frequently mentioned in Scripture; probably the Ethiopians or Abyssinians.

LUKE (Λουκας, contracted from the Latin *Lucanus*), was a Gentile proselyte who had embraced Christianity. He was the friend and companion of St. Paul in most of his journies, and wrote the Gospel that bears his name and the Acts of the Apostles; for analysis of which, see Vol. IV. pp. 287—303. 317—325.

LUST, crimes of, 143, 144.

LYCANTHROPY, the malady of Nebuchadnezzar, 508, 509.

LYCAONIA (Acts xiv. 6.), a province in Asia Minor, accounted the southern part of Cappadocia, having Isauria on the west, Armenia Minor on the east, and Cilicia on the south. Its chief cities are all mentioned in this chapter, viz. Iconium, Lystra, and Derbe. *They spake* (ver. 11.) *in the Lycaonian tongue,* which is generally understood to have been a corrupt Greek, intermingled

M A

with many Syriac words: but Jablonski supposes it to have been derived from the Assyrian tongue. Why they were disposed to worship Paul and Barnabas, 353. Paul's address to them illustrated, IV. 339.

LYDDA, which in later times was called Diospolis, and is now known by the name of Loudd, was a large village, and, according to Josephus, little inferior to a city for its size. This place is celebrated in the Acts of the Apostles for the miraculous cure of Eneas by the apostle Peter (Acts ix. 32. 34.): it was situated at no great distance from Joppa (ix. 38.), on the way from the latter place to Jerusalem. The soil of the surrounding country is said to be very rich.

LYDIA, a woman of Thyatira, who traded in purple cloths, for which that place was celebrated. She was a Jewish proselyte, of a sincere and pious character, and prompt in acknowledging and professing the truth. She was converted to the Christian faith in consequence of the preaching of St. Paul. (Acts xvi. 14. 40.) Coquerel and others suppose that Lydia, in this place, is merely a patronymic appellation, that is, a Lydian woman; — most probably from the circumstance of Thyatira being situated on the confines of Lydia, a province on the western coast of Asia Minor.

LYSTRA, a city of Lycaonia, chiefly celebrated for the miraculous cure there wrought upon the lame man, which made the Lycaonians think the gods were come down to them in the likeness of men (Acts xiv. 10, 11.), and also for the circumcision of Timothy. (xvi. 1.)

———

MAACAH or MAACHAH. See ABEL-BETH-MAACHAH, p. 538.

MACCABEES, government of, 106, 107. Origin of their name, 106. *note.*

MACEDONIA, a province of Greece, formerly called Æmathia; and from the kings of Macedon, Macedonia. It was bounded on the north by the mountains of Hæmus, on the south by Epirus and Achaia, on the east by the Ægean, on the west by the Ionian and Adriatic Seas; and it is celebrated in all histories for being the third kingdom, which, under Alexander the Great, obtained the empire of the world, and had under it 150 nations. To this country, whose metropolis was then Thessalonica, St. Paul was called by a vision (Acts xvi. 9.); and the churches by him planted in it, are celebrated for their great charity, and ready contribution to the distressed Jews in Judæa (2 Cor. viii. ix.), when they themselves lay under the extremest poverty.

MACHÆRUS, a city and fortress east of the Jordan, between six and nine miles from that river, and not far from its mouth. Here John the Baptist was imprisoned, and subsequently put to death by order of Herod Antipas. (Matt. ix. 2. xiv. 3—12.) This

M A

place is not mentioned by name in the New Testament.

MACHPELAH, the name of the cave purchased by Abraham of Ephron the Hittite, for a burial-place for his wife Sarah. (Gen. xxxiii. 8.) This cave has been covered by the Turks, "by a large and antient mosque; and all around the soil is held inviolable. The cave is in the middle of the interior of the edifice; its dark and deep entrance only is visible, and it is rarely entered. ..... The cave is said by the Turks to be deep and very spacious, cut out of the solid rock, and that the resting-places of the patriarchs still exist, and are plainly to be discerned." (Carne's Recollections of the East, pp. 158, 159.)

MAGDALA, a city and territory on the western side of the lake of Gennesaret, not far from Capernaum and Gamala; it is supposed to have contained within its precincts Dalmanutha; hence, while Matthew says (xv. 39.), *Christ came into the coasts of Magdala,* St. Mark says more particularly (viii. 10.), that *he came into the parts of Dalmanutha.* Burckhardt found here a miserable village called *El Madjdel.*

MAGI, an appellation given among the Persians to priests, wise men, philosophers, and others who devoted themselves to the study of the moral and physical sciences, and who particularly cultivated astrology and medicine. They enjoyed the highest consideration. The *wise men from the east,* who came to worship the infant Messiah, were philosophers of this description; according to some, they came from Persia, or, in the opinion of others, from Arabia, as the precious gums which they offered were the productions of Arabia.

MAGIC, prevalence of, 360, 361.

MAGISTRATES, persons of, sacred, 89. Crimes against them, how punished among the Jews, 140. Magistrates under the Jewish monarchy, 97.

MAGOG. See GOG, p. 582.

MAHANAIM, a city beyond the Jordan in the tribe of Gad, near the tribe of Manasseh; it was assigned to the Levites. (Josh. xiii. 26. 30. xxi. 38.) Here two hosts or camps of angels met Jacob (Gen. xxxii. 2.), whence the name is derived.

MAJESTY, chief distinctions of, among the Jews, 89, 90.

MALACHI, the last of the twelve minor prophets. For an account of him, and an analysis of his predictions, see Vol. IV. pp. 237, 238.

MALCHUS, a servant of Caiaphas the high priest, whose name St. John has very naturally preserved, since he was acquainted with Caiaphas. Malchus was one of the company that was commanded to seize Christ in the garden of Gethsemane: Peter cut off his right ear, which was instantly restored and the wound healed by the omnipotent touch of Jesus, who thus conferred upon him a signal benefit at a most critical time. The miraculous healing of Malchus presents a

M A

union of justice, power, and goodness; and could not fail to convince the apostles of the truth of our Lord's declaration, that no man could take his life from him, and that he could lay it down and resume it again. (John x. 17.) It has indeed been asked, how such a miracle made so little impression upon the company which Judas conducted. The reply is easy. The whole transaction took place in an instant. Peter struck Malchus with a sword. Jesus stood still, with one hand stopped the apostle, and with the other healed the servant; while those who were present, in the middle of the night and by the pale light of torches, scarcely had time to perceive what was passing.

MALICE, crimes of, how punished, 144.

MALTA. See MELITA, p. 600. *infra,*

MAMRE, Valley of, notice of, 53.

MANAEN, the name of a person who was educated with Herod Agrippa I. (Acts xiii. 1.) Perhaps he was the son of that Manaem (Μαναημος) mentioned by Josephus, who predicted the future greatness of Herod. (Ant. Jud. lib. xv. c. 10. § 5.)

MANASSEH.

1. The eldest son of Joseph; who, being adopted by his grandfather, inherited equally with the sons of Jacob. (Gen. xlviii.) For the limits of the territory allotted to the tribe of Manasseh, see pp. 11, 12.

2. MANASSEH, the fourteenth king of Judah, succeeded his father Hezekiah, at the early age of twelve years. In the early part of his reign, most probably misled by the profligate counsels of those who detested the reformation introduced by the pious Hezekiah, Manasseh was a most wicked and idolatrous prince; and for his various crimes was carried captive into Babylon, about the twenty-second year of his reign. But, upon his penitent confession of his sins, he was delivered out of captivity and restored to his country (it has been conjectured after about a year's absence), perhaps in consequence of some revolution in the Assyrian empire. The remainder of his life and reign was as exemplary as its commencement had been inauspicious and profligate. The worship of God was restored; the fortifications of Jerusalem were repaired and strengthened; and military officers were placed in all the fenced cities of Judah. (2 Chron. xxxiii.)

MAN-SLAUGHTER, punishment of, 142.

MAN-STEALING, punishment of, 141.

MANURES of the Jews, notice of, 452—454.

MARAH, a place in the desert of Arabia, so called from the bitterness of its waters. When the Israelites came out of Egypt, on their arrival in the wilderness of Etham, they found the water so bitter that neither themselves nor their cattle could drink it: on which account they gave the name of Marah or bitterness to this encampment. (Exod. xv. 23. Numb. xxxiii. 8.) Most travellers attest that there are several bitter fountains not far from the Red Sea; and Dr. Shaw fixes these

M A

waters at Corondel, a place where there is a small rill, which, unless it be diluted by dews and rain, still continues to be brackish. (Travels, vol. i. p. 104.) A later traveller, who visited this region a century after Dr. S., describing these waters, says, that "the Pool of Marah is of a circular form, about sixty feet round : it gushes forth from a rock at the foot of a barren mountain, and one or two palm trees spread their shade over it. This pool, the only one found for a great distance around, in spite of its clear and tempting appearance, is brackish and bitter to the taste, offering one of the greatest disappointments to the weary traveller, whose thirst indeed may be quenched, though the hope of a sweet and delicious draught is baffled." (Carne's Recollections of the East, p. 348.)

MARESHA, a fenced city in the plain of the tribe of Judah. (Josh. xv. 44.) Jerome and Eusebius call it Morasthi. The prophet Micah was a native of this city, near which was fought the memorable battle between Zerah king of Cush or Ethiopia, and· Asa king of Judah, who obtained a most signal victory. (2 Chron. xiv. 8—10.)

MARK, or John-Mark, the author of the second Gospel, was the nephew of Barnabas, and also the companion of Paul and Barnabas in their journey through Greece (Acts xiii. 5. Col. iv. 11.), and afterwards of Barnabas alone. (Acts. xv. 37. 39.) He afterwards accompanied Peter. (1 Pet. v. 13.) As he was the son of that Mary, at whose house in Jerusalem the apostles were accustomed to meet, it has been conjectured, with great probability, that he was particularly instructed in the doctrines of the Gospel by Peter, who therefore terms him his son. (1 Tim. v. 13. compared with 1 Tim. i. 2. and 2 Tim. i. 2.) For a further account of Mark and of his Gospel, see Vol. IV. pp. 278—286.

MARKETS, where held, 394.

MARRIAGES of the Jews, ceremonies of, 406—414. How dissolved, 414, 415.

MARTHA, the sister of that Lazarus who was raised from the dead by Jesus Christ. (Luke x. 38. 40, 41. John xi. 1, &c. vii. 2.)

MARY, the name of several women mentioned in the New Testament; viz.

1. The Virgin-mother of our Lord and Saviour Jesus Christ : she was of the tribe of Judah, and of the royal house of David, as also was her husband Joseph. After the crucifixion of Christ, who had commended her to the filial care of John, she found an asylum in the house of the beloved apostle ; and when the disciples and apostles were met together in an upper room, she united with them in prayer. (John xix. 25. 27. Acts i. 15.) The time, place, and circumstances of her death are uncertain.

2. A woman of Magdala is supposed to be the same, out of whom Christ expelled seven demons. (Luke vii. 36, 37.) She was one of those who followed him and contributed to his maintenance.

M E

3. One of the sisters of Lazarus. (Luke x. 39—42. John xi. 1, &c.)

4. The mother of James the Less and of Joses : she was sister to the mother of Jesus, and was the wife of Alpheus or Clopas. (Matt. xxvii. 56. 61. xxviii. 1. Mark xv. 40. 47. xvi. 1. John xix. 25.)

5. The mother of the evangelist Mark, at whose house the Christians in Jerusalem were wont to convene. (Acts xi. 12.)

6. Mary, an unknown disciple resident at Rome, to whom St. Paul sent his salutation, with this eulogy— she *bestowed much labour on us* (Rom. xvi. 6.), or, *on you*, according to the Alexandrian and other MSS., and the Syriac, Ethiopic, Coptic, and Arabic versions. It is, therefore, uncertain, whether the apostle here speaks of services actually rendered to himself, or to the believers at Rome.

MATTHEW, also called LEVI, the son of Alpheus, was a collector of the imposts when our Saviour called him to follow him and be an apostle. He wrote the first Gospel ; for an account of which, see Vol. IV. pp. 256—278.

MATTHIAS, one of the disciples who was chosen by lot to fill up the vacancy occasioned by the death of the traitorous apostle Judas Iscariot. (Acts i. 23. 26.) Of his subsequent labours and history, nothing certain is known.

MEASURES of the Jews and other nations mentioned in the Bible, tables of, 527, 528.

MEAT-OFFERINGS, notice of, 294.

MECHANIC ARTS of the Jews, 481.

MEDEBA, a city in the tribe of Reuben, situated in a plain of the same name. (Numb. xxi. 30. Josh. xiii. 9. 16.) According to Eusebius, it was not far from Heshbon. Here Joab gained a memorable victory over the Ammonites and Syrians. (1 Chron. xix. 7—14.) According to Isa. xv. 2. it afterwards belonged to Moab.

MEDIA (Acts ii. 9.) was a vast region of Asia, having on the north the Caspian Sea, on the west Armenia and Assyria, on the south Persia, on the east Hyrcania and Parthia. It had its name from Madai the son of Japhet, mentioned in Gen. x. 2. In the Babylonian captivity, the Jews were carried captive into Assyria, and placed in the cities of the Medes. (2 Kings xvii. 6. and xviii. 11.) Hence we find many of them and their proselytes at Jerusalem, when the Holy Ghost fell on the apostles. The Medes or Medians were subject to the Assyrian monarchs until the reign of Sardanapalus. Arbaces conspired against him, compelled him to burn himself in Nineveh, and restored the Medes to liberty, A.M. 3257, B.C. 747. He is considered as the founder of the Median monarchy, to which Justin assigns a duration of three hundred and fifty years, but Herodotus only one hundred and twenty years. (Justin. Hist. lib. i. c. 6. ed. Bipont. Herod. lib. i. cc. 95—107. ed. Oxon. 1809.) The last-mentioned historian has recorded the names of only four Median sovereigns, viz. Dejoces,

Phraortes, Cyaxares, and Astyages. Diodorus Siculus (lib. ii. c. 32. edit. Bipont.)
enumerates ten kings; Eusebius and Syn-
cellus, eight. Herodotus, however, acknowledges that the Medes had enjoyed their liberty for some time before they elected Dejoces
to be their king, A. M. 3294, B. C. 710. He
caused the city of Ecbatana to be built, and
is said to have reigned fifty-three years.
Phraortes his successor subjugated the Persians to the Median empire, and reigned
twenty-two years, A.M. 3347—3369, B.C. 657
—635. Phraortes was succeeded by Cyaxares, who took Nineveh, and considerably
enlarged the Median empire, A. M. 3369—
3409, B. C. 626—595. His son and successor Astyages reigned thirty-five years, A.M.
3409—3444, B. C. 595—560. No particulars
of his reign, however, are recorded by profane
historians, excepting his repulsing an invasion
of his territories made by the Babylonians
under Evil-merodach, the son of Nebuchadnezzar. On the death of Astyages, the crown
devolved on his son Cyaxares II., whom the
Scriptures call Darius the Mede, A. M. 3444,
B. C. 560. Media is now called Irak Adjami,
and forms (as it also antiently did form) part
of the kingdom of Persia.

MEDICINE, State of, among the Jews, 501
—511.

MEDITERRANEAN SEA, 43. Plain of, 57.

MEGIDDO, a fortified town of the tribe of
Manasseh in the territory of Issachar: it was
formerly a royal city of the Canaanites. The
Water of Megiddo (Judg. v. 19.) is conjec-
tured by Prof. Gesenius to be the river
Kishon. Compare Judg. v. 21. and iv. 13.

MELCHISEDEK, king of Salem (which was
afterwards called Jerusalem), a contemporary
of Abraham, whom he met with refreshments
on his return from the pursuit of Cherdor-
laomer and his allies. (Gen. xiv.) After the
manner of the patriarchal ages, he appears, as
the head of his tribe or family, to have discharged the functions of priest, and to have
offered sacrifices to the true God. By paying him tithes Abraham acknowledged him
to be a priest of the Most High God. In
Heb. vii. St. Paul exhibits the resemblance
between Melchisedek as the type and Jesus
Christ the antitype.

MELCOM, an Ammonitish idol, notice of,
344.

MELITA, or MALTA, an island in the Mediterranean Sea, on which St. Paul and his
companions were wrecked. (Acts xxviii. 1.)
Mr. Bryant, Dr. Hales, and some other eminent critics and commentators, have endeavoured to show that this island was in the
Adriatic Sea, on the coast of Illyricum,—
the same which is now called Meleda. That
MALTA is the island intended by St. Luke
will be evident from the following consider-
ations:— The apostle left the island in a
ship of Alexandria, which had wintered there,
on her voyage to Italy; and after touching at
Syracuse and Rhegium, landed at Puteoli,
thus sailing in a direct course. The other

Melita would be far out of the usual track
from Alexandria to Italy; and, in sailing
from it to Rhegium, Syracuse also would be
out of the direct course. The fact, that the
vessel was tossed all night before the shipwreck in the Adriatic Sea, does not militate
against the probability of its afterwards being
driven upon Malta; because the name ADRIA
(see page 541.) was applied to the whole
Ionian Sea, which lay between Sicily and
Greece. (Robinson's Lexicon, voce Μελίτη.)

MEMORIALS of events, account of, 187, 188.

MEMPHIS. See NOPH, p. 606. *infra.*

MENAHEM, the sixteenth king of Israel:
he murdered the usurper Shallum, and in his
turn usurped the throne. He was a wicked
and cruel prince, who followed the impious
example of Jeroboam I. He died after reigning about ten years.

MENI, or the Moon; a Syrian idol, worshipped in Palestine during the time of the
prophet Isaiah. See pp. 344.

MEN-STEALERS, denunciations against, 420,
and *note.*

MEPHIBOSHETH, a son of Jonathan, whom
David took under his protection, when he
was peaceably seated on his throne.

MERCURY, in heathen mythology, the son
of Jupiter and Maia. He was the fabled
patron of eloquence (on which account the
people of Lystra supposed Paul to be Mercury in disguise, Acts xiv. 12.), the god of
travellers, shepherds, &c. &c., and the conductor of the souls of the dead into the infernal regions.

MERIBAH, the name of a spring in the
desert of Sin, where the Israelites contended
against God. (Numb. xx. 13. 24.) See RE-
PHIDIM.

MERODACH, the name of an idol of the
Babylonians. Lowth and other commentators (on Jer. l. 2.) suppose him to have
been an antient monarch of Babylon, whom
his subjects deified and worshipped. See
BALADAN, p. 558.

MEROM, waters or lake of, notice of, 40.

MESHECH, the sixth son of Japheth (Gen.
x. 2.), who is supposed to have been the
father of the Moschi, a people inhabiting the
mountainous region between Iberia, Armenia,
and Colchis.

MESOPOTAMIA, a region of country, situated
between the rivers Tigris and Euphrates,
extending from the Persian Gulf to Mount
Taurus. The Hebrews call it Aram Naha-
raim, or Aram of the two rivers, because it
was first peopled by Aram, father of the
Syrians, and is situated between two rivers.
This country is celebrated in Scripture as the
first dwelling of men after the deluge; and
because it gave birth to Phaleg, Heber, Terah,
Abraham, Nahor, Sarah, Rebekah, Rachel,
Leah, and to the sons of Jacob. Babylon
was in the antient Mesopotamia, till by vast
labour and industry the two rivers Tigris and
Euphrates were reunited in one channel.
The plains of Shinar were in this country.
It was often called *Mesopotamia Syriæ*, be-

M E

cause it was inhabited by the Aramæans, or Syrians; and sometimes PADAN-ARAM (Gen. xxviii. 2.), or the plains of Aram: or *Sede-aram*, the fields of Aram; to distinguish them from the barren and uncultivated mountains of the same country. Balaam, son of Beor, was of Mesopotamia. (Deut. xxiii. 4.) Chushanrishathaim, king of Mesopotamia, subdued the Hebrews. (Judg. iii. 8.) Some Jews or proselytes from Mesopotamia were at Jerusalem on the day of Pentecost. (Acts ii. 9.) For an interesting description of the modern state of this country, see Mr. Buckingham's Travels in Mesopotamia. London, 1827. 2 vols. 8vo.

MESSIAH, (Heb. משיח, that is, *anointed*,) the same as CHRIST in Greek, the name given to Jesus our Saviour, by way of excellence; he being anointed by his Father, to execute for us the offices of Prophet, Priest, and King, for all which offices persons were anointed with oil, as being symbolical of the graces of the Holy Spirit, which qualified them for their respective duties. Jesus, indeed, was not anointed with material oil, such as was used under the law, but with *the Holy Ghost and with power*. (Acts x. 38.) For a view of the predictions respecting the Messiah, see Vol. I. pp. 291—297. 497—507. As a *Prophet*, whose office was to teach and reprove, Jesus has perfectly instructed us in the will of God, and has shown himself to be the teacher of the most sublime religion ever promulgated to mankind: and he wrought numerous illustrious miracles in proof of his divine mission. As a *Priest*, (whose office it was to offer sacrifices for the expiation of the sins of the people, to bless them, and pray for them,) Jesus, who was both priest and victim, offered himself a sacrifice to God, in order to expiate our sins; for in him we have redemption through his blood, even the forgiveness of sins, according to the riches of his grace. (Eph. i. 3.) He has blessed us, in turning every one of us from our sins: and he ever liveth to intercede for us with God as our Mediator: for, if any man sin, we have an advocate with the father, Jesus Christ the righteous. (Rom. viii. 34. 1 Tim. ii. 5. 1 John ii. 1.) As a *King*,— not like the earthly sovereign whom the Jews expected to deliver them from the yoke of the Romans, which they detested, and who (they believed) would make them the most powerful people upon earth,— Jesus reigns over souls illuminated by the light of his doctrine, and over hearts called to holiness. To his people, whom he hath purchased to himself out of all the nations of the world, he gives for their government laws which are calculated to make them permanently happy both here and hereafter; he defends them against their spiritual enemies, and he will judge them at the last day. His mediatorial kingdom commenced after his resurrection, when he entered into his glory (Luke xxiv. 26.): but it will not be eternal. The authority which he exercises as Mediator and Judge, is only a temporary dispensation

M I

referring to the actual state of the church, and which will cease when he shall have fulfilled his office, that is, after the last judgment. This Saint Paul teaches in a very striking and precise manner, which deserves the greatest attention. See 1 Cor. xv. 24, 25. 28.

METEMPSYCHOSIS, doctrine of, believed by the Pharisees, 363.

MICAH, the sixth of the minor prophets, was contemporary with Isaiah, Joel, Hosea, and Amos. See an analysis of his predictions in Vol. IV. pp. 187—189.

MICHMASH, a town in the tribe of Ephraim, about nine miles from Jerusalem, to the east of Beth-Aven. Contiguous to this place was a ledge of sharp rocks, two of which, named Bozez and Seneh, faced Michmash and Gibeah; the one north, the other south. One of these was ascended by Jonathan and his armour-bearer, who routed the garrison of the Philistines that defended the pass of Michmash. (1 Sam. xiii. 5. 23. xiv. 4—13.) In the vicinity of this place were caves, thickets, rocks, and pits, in which the Israelites concealed themselves from their enemies. (1 Sam. xiii. 6.) Rocks and pits answer to the present appearance of the place to which tradition has given the name of Michmash; but no thickets or bushes are to be seen. A succession of low and barren hills leads up to the higher one of Michmash, which commands a fine and extensive view. There are also several caves on the spot. (Carne's Letters, pp. 330, 331.) At present, this place is distinguished by the name of *Beer*, signifying a well; most probably from its containing a very delicious spring of water. (Rae Wilson's Travels, vol. i. p. 364. Third Edition.)

MIDIAN, the land into which Moses fled from the Egyptians. (Acts vii. 29.) Here Jethro lived (Exod. xviii. 1.), and the people were descended from Madian the son of Abraham by Keturah (Gen. xxv. 2.), whence we have reason to believe they still retained the worship of the true God. It was in Arabia Petræa.

MIDIANITES, commerce of, 482. Account of this people, 7.

MIGDOL, a frontier-town of Lower Egypt, towards the Red Sea, between which and that sea the Israelites encamped. (Exod. xiv. 1.) It is there rendered by the Septuagint Magdolus; and there also Herodotus represents Nekus, or Pharaoh-Necho, as gaining a great victory over the Jews, when Josiah was killed; mistaking Magdolus for Megiddo. Jeremiah represents it as belonging to Egypt Proper (xlvi. 14.), and in the neighbourhood of Tahpanes, or Daphnæ.

MILETUS, a sea-port of Asia Minor, and a city of Ionia, where Saint Paul delivered to the elders of the church of Ephesus that affecting discourse which is recorded in Acts xx. 17—35. Some remains of its ancient and capacious theatre still exist. In this city were born Thales, one of the seven wise men, Anaximander his disciple, Timotheus the celebrated musician, and Anaximenes the philosopher. There was another Miletus in Crete, where St. Paul left Trophimus sick. (2 Tim. iv. 20.)

MILITARY DISCIPLINE of the Jews, 197—218. And of the Romans, 225—227. Military Schools, 206. Military Sports, 489. A military order established by David, 220.

MILLS, oriental, notice of, 392.

MINES of Palestine, 69.

MIRAGE, effects of, 62. and *notes.*

MIRRORS of the Jews, notice of, 403. and *note.*

MITYLENE, was a large and beautiful city of the island of Lesbos, where Pittacus, one of the wise men, Alcæus the poet, Diophanes the orator, and Theophanes the historian, were born. The whole island was also called by that name; as also Pentapolis, from the five cities in it, viz. Issa or Antissa, Pyrrha, Eressos, Arisba, Mitylene. If it had that name in St. Luke's time, we may understand either the island or the city, when he says (Acts xx. 14.), *We came to Mitylene.* Some remains of the antient city are found near Castro, the principal place on the island: its population is estimated at 7,000 ; of whom two or three thousand are Greeks, and the remainder are Mohammedans, besides forty Jewish families.

MIZAR, a small hill not far from Zoar, once a place of resort for David ; and where it appears from Psal. xlii. 6. that he experienced some peculiar manifestations of the divine goodness.

MIZPEH, a high place affording an extensive prospect. (Isa. xxi. 8.) Several places in Palestine bore this name, most probably from being situated on elevated grounds or hills; of which the following were the principal : —

1. MIZPEH, *a city in the tribe of Judah,* to the south of Jerusalem (whence it was distant about eighteen or twenty miles), and to the north of Hebron. (Josh. xv. 33.)

2. MIZPEH, a place in Gilead beyond the Jordan. (Judg. x. 17. xi. 34.) In Judg. xi. 29. it is called *Mizpeh of Gilead,* to distinguish it from other towns or places of the same name.

3. MIZPEH, *a city in the tribe of Benjamin,* where assemblies of the Israelites were often convened : here Samuel dwelt, and here Saul was anointed king. (Judg. xxi. 1. 1 Sam. vii. 5—7. x. 1. 17.) King Asa strengthened it for a frontier fortification against the kingdom of Israel (1 Kings xv. 22. 2 Chron. xvi. 6.): and afterwards the governor Gadaliah had his residence here. (Jer. xl. 6. compared with Neh. iii. 7. 19.)

4. MIZPEH, *a valley in the region of Mount Libanus,* which was inhabited by the Hivites. (Josh. xi. 3. 8.)

MIZRAIM (Gen. x. 6.), a son of Ham, whose descendants are supposed to have peopled Egypt, which country derived its Hebrew name from him. Josephus makes the name to be of Coptic origin (Antiq. l. i. c. 6. § 2.): but Gesenius observes that no-

thing resembling it is found in the present remains of the Coptic language, in which this country bears the name of Χημι.

MOABITES, a people descended from Moab, the incestuous offspring of Lot. Their habitation was beyond Jordan and the Dead Sea, on both sides of the river Arnon. Their capital city was situated on that river, and was called Ar, or Rabbath-Moab, that is, the capital of Moab, or Kirheres, that is, a city with brick walls. This country was originally possessed by a race of giants, called Emim. (Deut. ii. 11, 12.) The Moabites conquered them, and afterwards the Amorites took a part from the Moabites. Moses conquered that part which belonged to the Amorites and gave it to the tribe of Reuben. The Moabites were spared by Moses, for God had restricted them (Deut. ii. 9.): but there always was a great antipathy between the Moabites and Israelites, which occasioned many wars between them. Balaam seduced the Hebrews to idolatry and uncleanness, by means of the daughters of Moab (Numb. xxv. 1, 2.): and Balak, king of this people, endeavoured to prevail on Balaam to curse Israel. God ordained that the Moabites should not enter into the congregation of his people, even to the tenth generation (Deut. xxiii. 3.), because they had the inhumanity to refuse the Israelites a passage through their country, and would not supply them with bread and water in their necessity.

Eglon, king of the Moabites, was one of the first that oppressed Israel, after the death of Joshua. Ehud killed Eglon, and Israel expelled the Moabites. (Judg. iii. 12, &c.) A. M. 2679, B. C. 1325. Hanun, king of the Ammonites, having insulted David's ambassadors, David made war against him, and subdued Moab and Ammon ; under which subjection they continued, till the separation of the ten tribes. The Ammonites and Moabites continued in subjection to the kings of Israel to the death of Ahab. Very shortly after the death of Ahab, the Moabites began to revolt. (2 Kings iii. 4, 5.) Mesha, king of Moab, refused the tribute of an hundred thousand lambs, and as many rams, which till then had been customarily paid, either yearly or at the beginning of every reign, — which of these two is not clearly expressed in Scripture. The reign of Ahaziah was too short to make war with them ; but Jehoram, son of Ahab, and brother to Ahaziah, having ascended the throne, thought of reducing them to obedience. He invited Jehoshaphat, king of Judah ; who, with the king of Edom, then his vassal, entered Moab, where they were in danger of perishing with thirst, but were miraculously relieved. (2 Kings iii. 16, &c.) It is not easy to perceive what were the circumstances of the Moabites from this time ; but Isaiah, at the beginning of the reign of king Hezekiah, threatens them with a calamity, which was to happen three years after his prediction, and which probably referred to the war that

M O

Shalmaneser, king of Assyria, made with the ten tribes, and the other people beyond Jordan. Amos (i. 13, &c.) also foretold great miseries to them, which, probably, they suffered under Uzziah and Jotham, kings of Judah; or under Shalmaneser (2 Chron. xxvi. 7, 8. xxvii. 5.): or, lastly, during the war of Nebuchadnezzar, five years after the destruction of Jerusalem : we believe this prince carried them captive beyond the Euphrates, as the prophets had threatened, (Jer. ix. 26. xii. 14, 15. xxv. 11, 12. xlviii. 74. xlix. 3. 6.), and that Cyrus sent them home again, as he did the rest of the captives. After their return from captivity, they multiplied and fortified themselves as the Jews did, and other neighbouring people; still in subjection to the kings of Persia, afterwards conquered by Alexander the Great, and in obedience to the kings of Syria and Egypt successively, and finally to the Romans. There is a probability, also, that in the later times of the Jewish republic, they obeyed the Asmonæan kings, and afterwards Herod the Great. (Calmet, Hist. des Peuples Voisins des Juifs, &c. Art. IV. Dissert. tom. ii. pp. 410—413.) For an account (by recent travellers) of the fulfilment of the predictions concerning Moab, see Keith's Evidence of the Truth of the Christian Religion from Prophecy, pp. 158—172.

Moloch or Molech, an idol of the Ammonites, worshipped by the Israelites. See p. 344.

Monarchs. See Kings.

Money (Jewish and Roman), mentioned in the Scriptures, tables of, 526. Antiquity of Money, 487, 488.

Money-changers, notice of, 184.

Montenegrins, funeral rites of, 518, *note.*

Months of the Hebrews, see pp. 171, 172. 175—180. Intercalary Months, 174.

Monuments, and Monumental Inscriptions, account of, 519—523.

Moon (New), feast of, 303.

Mordecai, son of Jair, of the tribe of Benjamin, was descended from one of the captives, who were carried into Babylon, and resided at Shushan. He was the foster-father of Esther, through whose influence with Ahasuerus, on the fall of Haman, he became vizier, or prime minister to the Persian monarch. Prof. Gesenius thinks that this name, like that of Esther, is probably of Persian origin.

Moriah, Mount, 18.

Moses, the son of Amram and Jochebed, and great grandson of Levi, was born in Egypt, A. M. 2433. Providentially delivered from the general destruction of all the Hebrew male children, commanded by Pharaoh, and adopted by the daughter of the Egyptian king, Moses was instructed in all the literature and sciences of Egypt. In the eightieth year of his age, he was appointed the leader and legislator of the Hebrews, whom he delivered from their bondage. Division of

N A

Canaan by him among the twelve tribes, 9—13. An account of his jurisdiction, as the viceroy of Jehovah, is given in pp. 79—84. After conducting the Hebrews through their wanderings in the desert during 40 years, he died on the confines of the land of Canaan, aged 120 years, "when his eye was not dim, nor his natural force abated." For an analysis of the Pentateuch, or five books of Moses, see Vol. IV. pp. 1—26. In Exod. ii. 10. there is given a Hebrew derivation of the name Moses, viz. *drawn out,* because the ark in which his mother had deposited him was *drawn out* of the river Nile : but his education among the Egyptians, Gesenius observes, would lead us to regard it as of Egyptian origin; and so it is interpreted by Josephus. (Ant. Jud. l. ii. c. 9. § 6.)

Mountains of the Holy Land, 46—51. In the immediate vicinity of Jerusalem, 18, 19.

Mourning for the dead, duration of, and how expressed, 517. 523, 524. Rending of garments, a sign of mourning, 405.

Mules, notice of, 449.

Murder, laws concerning, 142.

Music and Musical Instruments of the Jews, 471—473.

Myra was one of the six great cities of Lycia, situated near the sea ; whence St. Luke says (Acts xxvii. 5.), that, *sailing over the sea of Cilicia and Pamphylia* they *came to Myra in Lycia.* It still preserves its ancient name; and there are many remains of its former greatness.

Mysia, (Acts xvi. 7, 8.) a country of Asia, was bounded on the north by Bithynia, on the east by Phrygia Minor, on the west by Troäs, on the south by the river Hermus; there, perhaps, St. Paul attempted not to stay, because, as Cicero notes, in his oration for Flaccus (cc. 51, 52.), they were a people despicable and base to a proverb.

Naaman, general of the forces of Ben-Hadad king of Syria. Being afflicted by a leprosy, he was healed by washing seven times in the river Jordan, according to the command of the prophet Elisha. (2 Kings v.)

Nabathæans. See Nebaioth, p. 604.

Nadab.

1. the son of Aaron and the brother of Abihu ; who, offering incense with strange or common fire, instead of that which had miraculously been kindled upon the altar of burnt-offering, was consumed together with his brother. (Lev. x. 12.)

2. The son of Jeroboam I. king of Israel, a wicked prince, who followed the evil example of his father. After reigning two years, he was assassinated by Baasha. (2 Kings xv. 25—27.)

Nahash, a king of the Ammonites, who laid siege to Jabesh-Gilead, shortly after the election of Saul to be king of Israel. He refused to the besieged any terms of accommodation, but on the ignominious condition of every one losing his right eye, thereby for ever incapacitating him from using the bow. This barbarous capitulation was rejected; the besieged obtained a truce of seven days, on condition of surrendering if they did not receive succour : but Saul arrived, and Nahash, after seeing his army totally discomfited, made a shameful retreat. (1 Sam. xi.) Subsequently Nahash rendered some services to David, most probably by giving him an asylum : we may easily conceive, that the enemy of Saul would be the friend of David. (2 Sam. x. 2. 1 Chron. xix. 2.)

NAHUM, a native of Elkosh, the seventh of the minor prophets, is known only by his prophetic denunciations against the Assyrian empire, and particularly Nineveh ; for an account of which, see Vol. IV. p. 190.

NAILS of the Jewish Houses, 390.

NAIN, a small city or town of Galilee, not far from Capernaum, at the gates of which Jesus Christ raised to life a widow's only son (Luke vii. 11—15.); for an examination of which miracle, see Vol. I. pp. 226. 236. Nain derived its name from its pleasant situation: it is now a decayed village, containing between one and two hundred inhabitants. From its situation on the declivity of a mountain " the scene of that miracle must have been rendered more striking as the funeral procession passed slowly out of the gate down the steep, on the bold breast of which the remains of the place now stand." (Carne's Recollections of the East, p. 55.)

NAKED, the Jewish notion of being, explained, 397.

NAMES, various, of the Holy Land, 1—4. of Jerusalem, 17—19. When given to the Jewish children, 271. 416.

NAPHTALI, or NEPHTHALIM, the name of the sixth son of Jacob, born of Bilhah. For the limits of the canton allotted to this tribe, see p. 13.

NARCISSUS, a freed-man and favourite of the emperor Claudius, who possessed great influence at court. (Sueton. in Claud. c. 28. Tacit. Annal. lib. xii. c. 57.) In his family or among his clients were some Christians whom St. Paul salutes in Rom. xvi. 11. It does not appear that Narcissus embraced the Christian faith, though the Greeks have made him bishop of Athens and a martyr, and have even placed him in the number of the 70 disciples.

NATHAN, an illustrious prophet in the reign of David, whom he convinced and reproved by a beautiful and pathetic parable of the heinousness of his guilt in the affair of Bathsheba and Uriah. (2 Sam. xii.) He is supposed to have been the preceptor of Solomon, at whose court his sons held distinguished offices, and of whose reign, as well as that of David, Nathan wrote memoirs which have long since perished. (1 Kings iv. 5. 1 Chron. xxix. 29. 2 Chron. ix. 29.) In the book of Zechariah (xii. 12.) the house of Nathan represents the descendants or family of the prophets.

NATHANAEL, or NATHANIEL, one of the disciples of Christ, who is supposed to be the same person as the apostle BARTHOLOMEW. (John i. 46—50. xxi. 2.)

NATURAL PHILOSOPHY, cultivated by the Jews, 480.

NAZAREATE, vow of.   } See pp. 325,
NAZARITES, account of.   }   326.

NAZARETH, a small city of Lower Galilee, celebrated as having been the place where our Saviour was educated, where he preached, and whence he was called a Nazarene. In the time of Christ it did not possess the best of characters. (John i. 46.) Nazareth, which is at present called Nassara, stands on the side of a barren rocky eminence, or hill, facing the south-east, which is environed by mountains. It was from this hill which overlooks the town, the inhabitants would have precipitated him headlong. (Luke iv. 29.) When visited by Dr. Clarke, in 1801, he found it much reduced. The town was in the most wretched state of indigence and misery ; the soil around might bid defiance to agriculture ; and to the prospect of starvation were added the horrors of the plague ! In 1827, the population amounted to about 2000 persons, principally Christians. Here are numerous reputed holy places to which pilgrims are conducted. Nazareth suffered much less from the terrible earthquake of January 1, 1837, than many other places. Only six persons were killed here, and but few houses were injured. (Lord Lindsay's Letters from Edom, &c. vol. ii. p. 83.) The church belonging to the Spanish convent is very handsome, but inferior to those at Bethlehem and Jerusalem. The vignette in p. 537. represents the grotto at Nazareth, which is *said* to have been the house of Joseph and Mary. (Carne's Letters, pp. 251, 252. Madden's Travels, vol. ii. p. 294.) The Rev. Mr. Jowett has given a very interesting description of the site of Nazareth, together with some observations, to account for the bad character which it bore in the time of Jesus Christ. (See his Christian Researches in Syria, &c. pp. 165—169. In a valley near Nazareth is a fountain, which bears the name of the Virgin Mary, and where the women are seen passing to and fro, with pitchers on their heads, as in former times.

NEAPOLIS, or Shechem. See SICHEM, *infra.*

NEAT Cattle, management of, 448, 449.

NEBAIOTH, the son of Ishmael, from whom the NABATHÆAN tribe of Arabs is supposed to have been descended. (Gen. xxv. 13. xxviii. 9. Isa. lx. 7.) During the several wars maintained by the Jews against the Syrians, under the Maccabæan princes, the Nabathæans were the only neighbouring people who showed them any friendship. (1 Macc. v. 24—27.)

NEBO.

1. A mountain beyond the river Jordan, where Moses died. (Deut. xxxii. 49.) It is now completely barren.

2. A city belonging to the tribe of Reuben. (Numb. xxxii. 38.) It being in the vicinity

of the country of Moab, the Moabites became masters of it ; and it was in their possession in the time of Jeremiah. (xlviii. 1.) The site of this antient city can no longer be traced. *Nebo is spoiled.* (Jer. xlviii. 1.)

3. A city in the tribe of Judah (Ezra ii. 29. x. 43.), which, in Neh. vii. 33., is, by way of distinction, called *the other* Nebo.

4. A Babylonish idol (Isa. xlvi. 1.), which Calmet supposes to be the same as Bel or Baal, see p. 348.

NEBUCHADNEZZAR, king of Babylon, who destroyed Jerusalem, and carried the Jews into captivity. (See p. 563. col. 2.) Like other Assyrian and Babylonian names, this word is best explained from the Persian. According to Gesenius, after Lorsbach, it is the same as *Nebu-godan-sar,* that is, Nebo the chief of the gods. Concerning the nature of Nebuchadnezzar's malady, see pp. 508, 509.

NECHO. See PHARAOH-NECHO.

NEDER, or Common Vow, account of, 225.

NEHEMIAH the son of Hachaliah, was born at Babylon during the captivity, but his family and tribe are not known. Raised to the distinguished office of cup-bearer to Artaxerxes Longimanus, whose favour he enjoyed, Nehemiah forgot not his desolated country. Having obtained a royal commission, he went to Jerusalem for a limited time, to repair its walls and gates, and to regulate many abuses which had crept into the administration of public affairs. He subsequently returned to Babylon; whence, by permission of Artaxerxes, he proceeded a second time to Jerusalem, where he died B.C. 420; having governed the Jews about 30 years. For an account of the book which bears his name, see Vol. IV. pp. 66, 67.

NERGAL, an idol of the Cuthites (2 Kings xvii. 30.), which some suppose to be the planet Mars ; and others, to be the sun.

NETHINIMS, office of, 275.

NEW MOON, feast of, 303.

NIBHAZ, an idol of the Avites (2 Kings xvii. 31.), which, some Hebrew interpreters think, had the shape of a dog ; but other expositors suppose it to have been the sun. The former opinion is the most probable, as vestiges of the antient worship of an idol in the form of a dog have been discovered in Syria in modern times. (Ikenii, Dissert. pp. 149. et seq. 1749. 4to.)

NICANOR, one of the seven primitive deacons chosen by the church at Jerusalem and ordained by the apostles. (Acts vi. 5.)

NICODEMUS, a Pharisee and member of the Jewish sanhedrin, who came by night to Jesus, probably as a serious though timid enquirer. (John iii. 1. 4. 9.) He afterwards took the part of Jesus before the sanhedrin (vii. 50.); and at last joined with Joseph of Arimathea to give his body an honourable burial. (xix. 39.)

NICHOLAS, a proselyte of Antioch, who was chosen one of the seven deacons of the primitive church. (Acts vi. 5.) Many per-

sons have supposed him to be the head of the NICOLAITANS, a sect mentioned in Rev. ii. 6. 15., who held that the divine nature of Christ descended upon him at his baptism, and redescended at his crucifixion, and who abandoned themselves to gross impurity and profligacy of life. Another Nicholas has also been supposed to be the founder of this sect. A better opinion, however, seems to be, that the appellation here is not a proper name, but symbolical ; and that it refers to the same persons who are mentioned in Rev. ii 14. as holding the doctrine of Balaam : since the Greek name Νικολαος corresponds to the Hebrew בִּלְעָם, which is formed from בָּלַע, that is νικαω, to conquer, and עַם, that is λαος, the people. The allusion, according to Dr. Robinson, to whom we are indebted for this article, is, to false and seducing teachers like Balaam, and perhaps refers more particularly to such as opposed the decree of the apostles. The Nicolaitans are conjectured to have been alluded to in 2 Pet. ii. and in Jude 7—19.

NICOPOLIS, a city of Epirus, upon the Ambracian Gulf, mentioned by St. Paul in Tit. iii. 12. Others, however, suppose it to be Nicopolis of Thrace, on the confines of Macedonia, near the river Nessus.

NIGHT, Jewish and Roman divisions of, 169.

NILE, a celebrated river of Egypt, which formed one of the boundaries of the Holy Land. See p. 6. In Gen. xli. 1. Exod. i. 22. ii. 5. iv. 9. vii. 18. and viii. 3. 9. 11., it is termed *the River* without any addition. The existence of Egypt depends upon the Nile, without the annual inundation of which the whole land would be a desert. Its inundation appears to be alluded to in Amos viii. 8. On the turning of the waters of the Nile into blood, see Vol. IV. p. 11.

NIMROD, the son of Cush, and founder of the kingdom of BABYLON. (Gen. x. 8. 10.) In consequence of the protection which he afforded to the people against wild beasts, he may by their own consent have become their leader and chief; or turning his weapons of hunting against men, he may have compelled them to submit to his dominion. His name (which signifies a rebel) seems to favour the latter supposition. (Jahn's Hebr. Commonwealth, vol. i. p. 5.) In Mic. v. 6. Babylonia is called the *Land of Nimrod.*

NINEVEH, the capital of the Assyrian empire, could boast of the remotest antiquity. It was founded by Nimrod, or (as the text of Gen. x. 11. may be rendered) by Asshur the son of Shem : by the Greeks and Romans it was called Ninus. It stood on the eastern bank of the Tigris above Babylon. This city was very splendid, and of great extent : according to Diodorus Siculus, it was 480 stadia or 48 English miles (others estimate it 60 miles) in circumference : in the time of Jonah, it was *an exceeding great city of three*

N O

days' journey, containing *more than six-score thousand persons that could not discern between their right hand and their left.* (Jon. iii. 3. iv. 11.) " As this is a proverbial expression denoting children under the age of three or five years, we may, according to the usual rate of calculation, estimate the entire population at two millions of souls. This number may appear too small in proportion to the vast extent of ground occupied, especially when compared with the population of our European cities : but it is to be kept in view that the antient cities of the east, (as Pekin, Ispahan, Moscow, and others at the present day,) comprehended in their circuit many gardens and large spaces of ground. The walls of Nineveh were a hundred feet high, and so broad that three waggons might be driven on them abreast. Upon the walls stood fifteen hundred towers, each two hundred feet in height; and the whole was so strong as to be deemed impregnable." (Rosenmüller's Bibl. Geogr. vol. ii. pp. 123, 124.) The destruction of Nineveh within forty days, which the prophet Jonah had denounced, was averted by the general repentance and humiliation of the inhabitants (iii. 4—10.), and was suspended for nearly 200 years, until *their iniquity came to the full ;* and then the prophecy (see Vol. I. p. 289.) was literally accomplished, in the third year of the siege of the city, by the combined forces of the Medes and Babylonians; the king, Sardanapalus, being encouraged to hold out in consequence of an antient prophecy that Nineveh should never be taken by assault, till the river became its enemy ; when a mighty inundation of the river, swollen by continual rains, came up against a part of the city, and threw down twenty stadia of the wall in length; upon which the king, conceiving that the oracle was accomplished, burnt himself, his concubines, eunuchs, and treasures, and the enemy entering by the breach, sacked and razed the city, about B. C. 606. (For a copious description of antient Nineveh, see Dr. Hales's Analysis of Chronology, vol. i. pp. 448—450.) Four mounds, the largest running north and south, and the most southerly called after the prophet Jonah, whose tomb it is *supposed* to contain, exhibit all that can now be traced of the metropolis of Asia. They are situated in the immediate vicinity of the modern town of Mousoul. An accurate view and description of these remains of antient Nineveh is given in the second volume of the " Landscape Illustrations of the Bible."

NISROCH, a Babylonish Idol, notice of, 348.

No, No-AMON, or No-AMUN, the Thebes of antient geographers, was the metropolis of Upper Egypt. It is mentioned in Jer. xlvi. 25. Ezek. xxx. 14—16. and Nahum iii. 8. In the Septuagint version of Ezekiel, No is rendered Διοσπολις, the city of Jupiter ; in Nahum, No-Amon is rendered Μερις Αμμων The latter appears to be an etymological explanation of the word after the Coptic. In

O A

that language *N O H* signifies a *cord,* or *measuring line,* hence a *portion measured out ;* and No-Amon, *portio, possessio Amonis,* that is, the seat of the god Amon, or the place where he was principally worshipped. (Jablonskii Opuscula, tom. i. pp. 163—168. Gibbs's Hebr. Lex. p. 406.) Accurate delineations of portions of the ruins of No are given in the first volume of the " Landscape Illustrations of the Bible."

NOAH, the son of Lamech, and the father of the post-diluvian world, was born A. M. 1056. Being the only righteous man of his time, he was preserved together with his family in the ark, during the deluge. (For a refutation of sceptical objections to which, see Vol. I. pp. 158—161.) Noah lived 350 years after that catastrophe, dying at the age of 950 years, A. M. 2006. He left three sons, Shem, Ham, and Japheth, by whom the whole earth was overspread or peopled. (Gen. ix. 18, 19. x. 32.) The seven precepts of Noah, see 266. note 2.

NOD, Land of : — " When Cain after the murder of his brother *went forth from the presence of Jehovah,* he settled in the land of Nod, which lay to the east of Eden. (Gen. iv. 16.) The word *Nod* signifies, in Hebrew, *wandering, flight, banishment :* and the region doubtless obtained that name from the circumstance of the fratricide having been condemned by God (Gen. iv. 14.) to wander as a fugitive or exile." (Rosenmüller's Biblical Geography, vol. i. p. 85.) It is now impossible to ascertain its precise situation.

NOPH, or MEMPHIS, a very celebrated city, the same as Thebes, and the capital of Egypt, until the Ptolemies removed the seat of government to Alexandria. By the modern Copts it is called MENΦ, MENOΥΦ, and NOΥΦ : whence we may explain both the Hebrew forms נף (NOPH) and מף (MEMPH), and also the Greek name Μεμφις. Plutarch (de Isid. et. Osirid. p. 639. ed. Stephani) interprets the name ὁρμον ἀγαθων, from the Coptic *meh,* full, and *nouphi,* good ; or ταφον Οσιριδις, from the Coptic *mhau,* a grave, and *onphi, ενεργετης* a benefactor, as Osiris is called. (Jablonskii, Opusc. tom. i. pp. 137. 150. 179. tom. ii. p. 131. Gibbs's Hebr. Lex. p. 381.) The prophets often mention this city ; and predict the calamities which it was to suffer from the kings of Chaldæa and Persia, &c. (See Isa. xix.13. Jer. xliv. 1. Hos. ix. 6. Ezek. xxx. 13. 16.) Its ruins are very splendid. Jeremiah had foretold, ages before, that Noph should *be waste and desolate, without an inhabitant* (xlvi. 19.), and not a family or cottage is said to remain.

NOSE-JEWELS, of the Jewish Women, notice of, 401.

NUPTIAL CEREMONIES of the Jews, 410—414.

NURTURE of Children, 417, 418.

OAKS, forest of, 66.

P A

PAPHOS, the metropolis of the island of Cyprus (Acts xiii. 4. 6.), and the residence of the pro-consul. It was memorable for the impure worship paid to Venus, the tutelar deity of the island. Here Saint Paul struck blind Elymas the sorcerer, and converted Sergius the pro-consul. The Jews dwelt here in great numbers. (ver. 6.) Twenty-five or thirty miserable huts are all that remain of this once most distinguished city of Cyprus. See CYPRUS.

PARADISE, a word of Persian original, signifying a park, garden, or inclosure full of all the valuable productions of the earth. The word passed into the Hebrew form פרדס (PARDES), which occurs in Sol. Song iv. 13. Neh. ii. 8. Eccles. ii. 5.; and in those passages it is rendered Παραδεισος in the Septuagint version, and denotes a garden of trees of various kinds, a pleasure-park, a delightful grove. In the New Testament, Paradise is applied to the state of faithful souls between death and the resurrection; where, like Adam in Eden, they are admitted to immediate communion with God in Christ, or to a participation of the tree of life, which is in the midst of the paradise of God. (Luke xxiii. 43. Rev. ii. 7.) Of this blessed state St. Paul had a foretaste. See 2 Cor. xii. 2. 4., where he states that he was caught up to the third heaven; and again, that he was caught up to Paradise. He was caught up to the third heaven, that he might contemplate that scene of supreme felicity, which awaits the just after the resurrection; and he was caught up to paradise, that his mind might be contented with a view of their nearer consolations. (Valpy's Gr. Test. on Luke xxiii. 43.)

PARAN, Desert of, notice of, 59.

PARASCHIOTH, or antient divisions of the Pentateuch, read in the Synagogues, 254. Table of them, 256.

PARCHMENT, notice of, 468.

PARENTS, crimes against, how punished, 138, 139.

PARTHIANS are mentioned in Acts ii. 9. in conjunction with the Medes. The empire of Parthia subsisted four hundred years, and disputed for the dominion of the East with the Romans. The Parthians were celebrated for their veneration of their kings, and for their way of fighting by flight, and shooting their arrows backwards. They dwelt between Media and Mesopotamia; in all which trans-Euphratensian places, except some parts of Babylon, and of some other small prefectures, the Jews abounded, and some of them were at Jerusalem when the Holy Ghost fell on the apostles.

PASSOVER, feast of, how celebrated, 304—312. Its spiritual import, 312—314. A proof of the credibility of the Old Testament, I. 135.

PATARA (Acts xxi. 1.), a sea-port town of Syria, antiently of considerable note. Extensive ruins mark its former magnificence and extent. Its port is now entirely

P E

choked up by encroaching sands. (Col. Leake's Tour in Asia Minor, pp. 182, 183.)

PATHROS, a city and district of Egypt, mentioned by the prophets Jeremiah (xliv. i. 15.), and Ezekiel (xxix. 14. and xxx. 14.). The inhabitants of this country are called Pathrusim in Gen. x. 14.

PATMOS, an island in the Ægean Sea, whither the apostle and evangelist John was banished, A. D. 94, and where he had the revelations which he has recorded in the Apocalypse. It is not known how long his exile continued. The soil of Patmos appears to be of volcanic origin, the ruins of its acropolis or citadel were discovered in 1817. Here are very numerous churches, many of which are opened only on the anniversary festival of the saints, to whom they are dedicated. The population is about 4000. (Emerson's Letters from the Ægean, vol. ii. pp. 17—21.)

PATRIARCHAL government, nature of, 78, 79.

PAUL, who was also called Saul, the distinguished apostle of the Gentiles. A Pharisee by profession, and a Roman citizen by birth, he was at first a furious persecutor of the Christians; but after his miraculous conversion, he became a zealous and faithful preacher of the faith which he had before laboured to destroy. See a copious account of the life and apostolic labours of Saint Paul in Vol. IV. pp. 325—346.

PAY of Jewish Soldiers, 206.

PEACE-OFFERINGS, notice of, 292.

PEAR, prickly, of Palestine, 69.

PEKAHIAH, the seventeenth king of Israel, succeeded his father Menahem, and followed the example of his predecessors in maintaining the idolatrous institutions of Jeroboam I. After reigning about two years, he was assassinated at Samaria by

PEKAH, an officer of his guards, who held the throne about twenty years. He also "did evil in the sight of the LORD; he departed not from the sins of Jeroboam the son of Nebat, who made Israel to sin." (2 Kings xv. 27, 28.) Towards the close of his reign, his dominions were overrun by Tiglath-pileser king of Assyria, who carried his subjects into captivity; and Pekah himself was assassinated by Hoshea. (2 Kings xv. 29, 30.

PELETHITES, notice of, 93. 206.

PENTECOST, feast of, how celebrated, 315. A proof of the credibility of the Old Testament, I. 136.

PEOR, or BAAL-PEOR, notice of, 345.

PERÆA, district of, 16.

PERFUME boxes of the Hebrew women, 402.

PERGA, a city of Pamphylia (Acts xiii. 13.), memorable among the heathens for a temple of Diana built there; and among the Christians for the departure thence of John-Mark from Barnabas and Paul, to Jerusalem, which occasioned the rupture between them for a season. (Acts xv. 37. 40.)

PERGAMOS or PERGAMUS was the antient metropolis of Mysia, and the residence of the

P E

Attalian kings: it still preserves many vestiges of its antient magnificence. Against the church at Pergamos, was adduced the charge of instability (Rev. ii. 14, 15.); but to its wavering faith was promised the all-powerful protection of God. " The errors of Balaam, and the Nicolaitanes have been purged away. Pergamos has been preserved from the destroyer ; and three thousand Christians" (out of a population of about 15,000 inhabitants) " now cherish the rites of their religion in the same spot where it was planted by the hands of St. Paul." (Emerson's Letters from the Ægean, vol. i. p. 216.) Of these Christians, about 200 belonged to the Armenian communion ; the remainder are members of the Greek Church. They have each *one* church, but the other churches of Pergamos have been converted into mosques, and are profaned with the blasphemies of the pseudo-prophet Mohammed. There are also about 100 Jews, who have a synagogue. Pergamos, or Bergamo, as it is now called, lies about sixty-four miles north of Smyrna. Its present state is described by Mr. Arundell, in his visit to the Seven Asiatic Churches, pp. 281—290. And in his Discoveries in Asia Minor, vol. ii. pp. 302—304.

PERIZZITES, the antient inhabitants of Palestine, mingled with the Canaanites. It is very probable that they were Canaanites, who had no fixed habitations, and lived sometimes in one country, sometimes in another, and were thence called Perizzites, which term signifies scattered or dispersed. The Perizzites did not inhabit any certain portion of the land of Canaan. In several places of Scripture the Canaanites and Perizzites are mentioned as the chief people of the country. Thus, we read that, in the time of Abraham and Lot, *the Canaanite and Perizzite were in the land.* (Gen. xiii. 7.) Solomon subdued the remains of the Canaanites and Perizzites, which the children of Israel had not rooted out, and made them tributary. (1 Kings ix. 20, 21. 2 Chron. viii. 7.) There is mention of the Perizzites by Ezra, after the return from Babylon; and several Israelites had married wives of that nation. (Ezra ix. 1.)

PERJURY, punishment of, among the Jews, 138.

PERSIA, a country of Asia, bounded on the west by Media and Susiana; on the south by the Persian Gulf; on the north by the great desert that lay between it and Parthia Proper ; and on the east by another still greater, that lay between it and the river Indus. Until the time of Cyrus, and his succession to the Median empire, it was an inconsiderable country, always subject to the Assyrians, Babylonians, or Medes. Its capital city was Persepolis, now Chelminar : lat. 30 degrees. In the neighbourhood of which, to the south-east, was Passagardæ, where was the tomb of Cyrus.

The ruins of Persepolis are remarkable, among other things, for the figures, or symbols, to be seen on the walls and pillars of the

VOL. III.

P E

temple. Sir John Chardin observed there rams' heads with horns, one higher, and th,e other lower, exactly corresponding to Daniel s vision of the Medo-Persian empire : the lower horn denoting the Medes, the higher, which came up last, the Persians. (Dan. viii. 3.) A winged lion, with a crown on his head; alluding, perhaps, to the symbolical representation of the Assyrian empire, by "a lion, with eagle's wings;" denoting their ferocious strength and cruelty, and the rapidity of their conquest. (Dan. vii. 4.)

Sketch of the History of the Persian Empire, illustrative of the Prophetic Writings.

CYRUS, who is deservedly called the Great, both on account of his extensive conquests, and also for his liberation of the captive Hebrews, was the son of Cambyses, a Persian grandee, and Mandane the daughter of Astyages, king of the Medians. He was born A.M. 3405, B.C. 599, one year after his uncle Cyaxares the brother of Mandane. Weary of obeying the Medians, Cyrus engaged the Persians to revolt from them. He attacked and defeated Astyages his maternal grandfather, whose life he spared, and gave him the government of Hyrcania, satisfied with having liberated the Persians, and compelled the Medes to pay him tribute. Not long after, the latter rebelled against him ; and involved Cyrus in a protracted war. His original Persian name was *Agradad;* which, after he had become the sovereign of the Persian empire, he exchanged for *Khorshid* (the splendour of the sun), which the Hebrews abridged to Koresh, the Greeks to *Kuros*, and the Romans to Cyrus. (Rosenmüller's Biblical Geography, vol. i. p. 212.) After his subjugation of the Medes, Cyrus directed his arms against the Babylonians, whose ally Crœsus king of Lydia, having come to their assistance, was defeated and obliged to retire into his own country. Cyrus continued to prosecute the war against the Babylonians, and having settled every thing in that country, he followed Crœsus into Lydia, whom he totally discomfited, and over-ran his territories. Thus far we have followed the narrative of Justin (lib. i. c. 7.): Herodotus relates events nearly in the same order (lib. i. c. 178.), but places the Babylonian war after the war with Crœsus, and the entire reduction of Lydia. He says that Labynitus (the Belshazzar of Scripture) was at that time the king of Babylon, and that Cyrus, having subdued his other enemies, at length attacked and defeated the Babylonians, who withdrew into their city, which was both strongly fortified and amply stored with provisions. Cyrus finding that the siege would be protracted, diverted the course of the Euphrates, by causing great ditches to be dug on both sides of the city, above and below, that its waters might flow into them : the river being thus rendered passable, his soldiers entered the city through its channel. Babylon was taken, and the impious Belshazzar was put to death. (Dan. v. 30.) So extensive was that city,

R R

PE

that the inhabitants of each extremity were ignorant of its capture, though the enemy was in its very centre; and as a great festival had been celebrated on that day, the whole city was absorbed in pleasure and amusements. Cyrus constituted his uncle Cyaxares (or Darius the Mede) king of the Chaldeans. (Dan. v. 31.) Cyrus immediately restored the captive Jews to liberty (2 Chron. xxxvi. 22. Ezra i. 1.), and commanded pecuniary assistance to be given to those who stood in need of it. He died A. M. 3475, B. C. 529, in the seventieth year of his age, though historians are by no means agreed concerning the manner of his death.

Cambyses, the successor of Cyrus, was one of the most cruel princes recorded in history. As soon as he was seated on the throne, he invaded and conquered Egypt, and reigned there three years. At the same time he detached part of his army against the Ethiopians, and commanded his generals to pillage the temple of Jupiter Ammon. Both these expeditions were unfortunate. The army which had been sent against the latter perished in the sands of the deserts; and that which he led against the former, for want of provisions, was compelled to return with great loss. Mortified at his disappointments, Cambyses now gave full vent to the cruelty of his disposition. He killed his sister Meröe, who was also his wife; he commanded his brother Smerdis to be put to death, and killed many of his principal officers; he treated the gods of the Egyptians with the utmost contempt, and committed every possible outrage against them. Hearing at length that his throne was filled by an usurper, who pretended to be his brother Smerdis, and reigned at Babylon, he set out on his return to his dominions, but died at Ecbatana, a town in Syria, situated at the foot of Mount Carmel.

A. M. 3482, B. C. 522. After the death of Cambyses the Persian throne was usurped by seven Magi, who governed for some time, making the people believe that their sovereign was Smerdis the brother of Cambyses. The Samaritans, who were always jealous of the prosperity of the Jews, obtained an edict from the pseudo-Smerdis (called ARTAXERXES in the Scriptures), prohibiting them from rebuilding the temple and fortifications of Jerusalem. (Ezra iv. 7. 16.) This interruption continued until the second year of Darius the son of Hystaspes.

A. M. 3483, B. C. 521. The imposition of the Magi being at length discovered, the pseudo-Smerdis was put to death, after a short reign of eleven months, by seven Persian nobles, and DARIUS the son of Hystaspes was acknowledged king. Having been informed of the permission which Cyrus had granted to the Jews to rebuild their temple, he allowed them to resume the work (Ezra iv. 24. vi. 1.), which they had commenced by the exhortations and encouragement of the prophets Haggai (i. 1.) and Zechariah (i. 1. Ezra v. 1.). This Darius is the Ahasuerus

PH

who married Esther and granted various privileges to the Jews. (See the book of Esther, throughout.)

A. M. 3519, B. C. 485. Xerxes succeeded Darius in the Persian throne; but as no particulars are recorded of him as connected with the Jews, we pass on to the reign of his successor ARTAXERXES, who greatly favoured them, first sending Ezra into Judæa (Ezra vii. viii.), and afterwards Nehemiah, to rebuild the walls of Jerusalem. (Neh. ii. iii.) The Persian monarchy subsisted for many centuries after this event; but, as its history is not connected with that of the Jews, it would be foreign to the plan of this abstract to give the succession of its sovereigns. (Calmet, Histoire Prophane de l'Orient, § IV. Dissert. tom. ii. pp. 336—341.)

PERSON, crimes against, how punished, 142—144.

PESTILENCE or PLAGUE, 72.

PESTILENTIAL BLAST or WIND, 76, 77.

PETER, one of the apostles, formerly called Simon: he was of Bethsaida, and was the son of Jonas, a fisherman, which occupation he also followed. When he was called to the apostleship by our Saviour, he received the name of Πετρος, which signifies a stone (John i. 43.), probably in reference to the boldness and firmness of his character, and his zeal and activity in promoting his Master's cause. See a further account of Peter and an analysis of the two epistles which bear his name, in Vol. IV. pp. 438—442.

PHARAOH, a common appellation of the antient kings of Egypt, who after the age of Alexander were in like manner termed Ptolemy. Jablonski states, that PHOURO, in the common Egyptian dialect, and PHARRO, in the very antient dialect, spoken in the Thebaid, respectively denote *a king*. (Opuscula, tom. i. p. 376.) In Hebrew this name is written פרעה (PHRAH); and Mr. Wilkinson derives it from the antient Egyptian word PHRE (pronounced PHRA), signifying the sun. (Manners and Customs of the antient Egyptians, vol. i. p. 43.) By the Greeks it was rendered Φαραω. The following are the principal sovereigns of this name, who are mentioned in the Old Testament: —

1. PHARAOH, king of Egypt, and contemporary with Abraham. His officers having eulogised the beauty of Sarah, the patriarch's wife, Pharaoh sent for her to his harem, and conferred many presents on her husband, whom he imagined to be her brother. Pharaoh and his family being "plagued with great plagues" by the Almighty, he discovered his error, and restored Sarah to Abraham, whom he sent out of Egypt. (Gen. xii. 10—20.)

2. PHARAOH (Osirtasen I.), the contemporary of Joseph; who, having interpreted his prophetic dreams, was rewarded with distinguished honours, and raised to the office of "ruler throughout all the land of Egypt." (Gen. xli.) Pharaoh participated in Joseph's joy, at his reconciliation with his brethren, and with his noble generosity permitted him to

invite his family into Egypt. On the arrival of Jacob and his sons, he gave them a hospitable reception, notwithstanding shepherds were held in abomination by the Egyptians, and assigned them a residence in the land of Goshen. And on Jacob's decease, he permitted Joseph to make a journey into Canaan, to bury him. (Gen. xlv. 16. xlvii. 1. l. 4.) This Pharaoh is the sovereign alluded to by Stephen in Acts vii. 10. 13.

3. PHARAOH, a king of Egypt, gave one of his daughters in marriage to Mered, a descendant of Judah. (1 Chron. iv. 18.) This remarkable alliance must have taken place while the Hebrews were the guests and not the slaves of the Egyptians; and this prince must certainly have been one of the first successors of the master of Joseph, perhaps Amun-m-gori I. or II. according to Mr. Wilkinson's Catalogue of Egyptian Sovereigns.

4. PHARAOH, king of Egypt, the contemporary of Moses, reigned at the period when Jacob's descendants had already become a great people. The genealogical lists of that period, which are extant, in harmony with the sacred historians, show how rapidly the race of Israel had multiplied. (1 Chron. iv.1—27.) Being the head of a new dynasty, he is called the *king who knew not Joseph.* This prince adopted the false policy of oppressing the Hebrews in the manner related in Exod. ii. little thinking that his own daughter would save from the waters of the Nile the future avenger and deliverer of the Israelites. " Affecting some alarm at their numbers, he suggested that so numerous a body might avail themselves of the absence of the Egyptian troops, and endanger the safety and tranquillity of the country (Exod. i. 10.), and that prudence dictated the necessity of obviating the possibility of such an occurrence. They were in consequence treated like captives taken in war, and were forced to undergo the gratuitous labour of erecting public granaries and other buildings for the Egyptian monarch." (Wilkinson's Manners, &c. of the Antient Egyptians, vol. i. pp. 49, 50.)

5. PHARAOH, the contemporary of Moses, had reigned about eighteen years,when Moses was commanded to return into Egypt, Ramses-Mei-Amoun and his personal enemies being dead. (Exod. iv. 19.) His history is contained in Exod. vi.—xii. : he perished with his army in the Red Sea. (xiv. 5—31.) This Pharaoh is Amenophis or Ramses V. the last king of the eighteenth dynasty, and the father of Ramses VI. or Sesostris.

6. PHARAOH, the contemporary of David, received at his court, and honourably entertained Hadad, prince of Idumæa (to whom he gave his wife's sister in marriage), after the conquest of that people by the Hebrews. (1 Kings xi. 17—19.) He was one of the last kings of the twenty-first or Tanite dynasty, and most probably was a different person from the Pharaoh who is next to be noticed, because it is difficult to conceive how the

protector of Hadad could be the father-in-law of Solomon.

7. PHARAOH, the contemporary of Solomon, gave the Hebrew king his daughter in marriage, with the city of Gezer as a portion. (1 Kings ix. 16.) This prince, the last sovereign of the twenty-first or Tanite dynasty, was probably dethroned and put to death by Shishak, who was contemporary with Rehoboam. M. Coquerel (to whom we are indebted for this account of the Pharaohs) thinks that Eccl. iv. 14. may allude to this event.

8. PHARAOH-NECHO, the contemporary of Josiah king of Judah, took up arms against the new empire of the Chaldæans, which was rapidly advancing and threatening Asia. He resolved to carry the war across the Euphrates into the very centre of the Chaldæan empire; but being opposed in his passage by Josiah, an ally of the Chaldæan monarch, to whom he in vain offered terms of peace, he totally discomfited the forces of the Jewish king near Megiddo. He then marched to Jerusalem, which city he entered by force or by capitulation; and, deposing Jehoahaz who had just succeeded his father upon the throne, he gave the crown of Judah to his elder brother Jehoiakim, and levied a heavy military contribution on the kingdom of Judah. Encouraged by these successes, Necho proceeded on his Asiatic expedition, taking with him Jehoahaz, whom he left prisoner at Riblah. He made himself master of Carchemish on the Euphrates; where, after three years' warfare with various success, he was defeated by Nebuchadnezzar, and forced to return into Egypt with the wreck of his army. On his return, he took the captive Jehoahaz with him. (2 Kings xxiii. 29—34. xxiv. 7. 2 Chron. xxxv. 20—24. xxxvi. 1—4.) The Scripture account of the war carried on by Pharaoh-Necho against the Jews and Babylonians is confirmed by an antient monument discovered in Egypt by the late enterprising traveller Belzoni. (See Vol. I. pp. 193—195.) Pharaoh-Necho, the son of Psammetichus, and the sixth king of the twenty-sixth dynasty, that of the Saïtes, is celebrated in profane history, for his project of digging a canal, to join the Nile to the Red Sea, and by the voyage of discovery which his vessels, manned by Phœnician sailors, made round Africa.

9. PHARAOH-HOPHRA, the Apries or Vaphres of profane historians, was the son of Psammis, and grandson of Pharaoh-Necho. He was the eighth king of the twenty-sixth dynasty, and contemporary with Zedekiah king of Judah, with whom he formed an alliance against Nebuchadnezzar. During the last siege of Jerusalem, Hophra took arms, and advanced to succour his ally. This diversion was useful for a short time; but, agreeably to the predictions of Jeremiah, the Egyptians, notwithstanding their brilliant promises, withdrew without fighting, or at least without making any resistance. After the destruction of Jerusalem, when, deaf to

PH

the counsels of Jeremiah, Azariah and Johanan took refuge in Egypt, the prophet predicted to them the deplorable end of Hophra. (Ezek. xvii. 15. Jer. xxxvii. 5. xliii. 9. xliv. 30. xlvi. 26.) The prophet Ezekiel (xxix.) reproaches Pharaoh with his base conduct towards the king of Judah, and foretels that Egypt should be reduced to a desert, and that the sword should cut off both man and beast. This prediction was afterwards accomplished, first in the person of Pharaoh-Hophra, who was deprived of his kingdom by Amasis who usurped his throne, and subsequently by the conquest of Egypt by the Persians.

PHARISEES, tenets of the sect of, 362—367.

PHARPAR, river. See ABANA, p. 538.

PHILADELPHIA, a city of Asia Minor, derived its name from its founder, Attalus Philadelphus, and is situated about twenty-seven miles to the south-east of Sardis, in a fertile plain, which at present is but little cultivated. Not long before the date of the Apocalyptic Epistle in Rev. iii. 7—22., this city had suffered so much from earthquakes, that it had been in a great measure deserted by its inhabitants; which may in some degree account for the poverty of this church as described in this epistle. And its poverty may also in some degree account for its virtue, which is so highly commended. "Philadelphia appears to have resisted the attacks of the Turks in 1312 with more success than the other cities. At a distance from the sea, forgotten by the emperor, encompassed on all sides by the Turks, her valiant citizens defended their religion and freedom about fourscore years, and at length capitulated with the proudest of the Ottomans (Bajazet) in 1390. Among the Greek colonies and churches of Asia, Philadelphia is still erect — a column in a scene of ruins!" (Gibbon's Decline and Fall, vol. xi. p. 438. 8vo. edit.) Whatever may be lost of the spirit of Christianity, there is still the form of a Christian church in this city; which is now called *A'lah-Shehr,* or the *City of God,* and is a considerable town spreading over the slopes of three or four hills. It contains about 1000 Christians, chiefly Greeks, most of whom speak only the Turkish language. They have twenty-five places of public worship, five of which are large and regular churches, with a resident bishop and inferior clergy: in these five churches divine service is performed once every week; in the larger number it is celebrated only once in the course of the year: a solitary fragment is shown as the last relic of the church of the Apocalypse dedicated to the apostle John. The remains of heathen antiquity here are not numerous. (Hartley's Visit to the Apocalyptic Churches, in Missionary Register, July 1827, pp. 324 —326. Arundell's Visit, pp. 167—174.)

PHILEMON, an opulent Christian at Colossæ; whose slave Onesimus having fled from him to Rome, where he was converted by Saint Paul, the Apostle sent him back to his master

PH

with the admirable letter, which now forms the epistle to Philemon : for an analysis of which, see Vol. IV. pp. 398—403.

PHILIP.

1. The son of Herod, misnamed the Great, by his wife Cleopatra; who, in the division of his father's kingdom, was made tetrarch of Batanæa, Trachonitis, and Ituræa. (Luke iii. 1.) He enlarged and embellished the city of Paneas, to which he gave his own name, and called it CÆSAREA, in honour of the emperor Tiberius. See CÆSAREA, 2. p. 562. *supra.*

2. Another son of the same Herod by Mariamne, daughter of Simon the high priest. He was the husband of Herodias, who was taken from him by his brother Herod Antipas. Having been disinherited by his father, he lived a private life. (Matt. xiv. 3. Mark vi. 7. Luke iii. 19.) As Josephus calls this prince Herod, and the evangelist Philip, it is not improbable, that, after the custom of the Herodian family, he bore *both* those names.

3. One of the apostles of Jesus Christ, a native of Bethsaida. (Matt. x. 3. Mark iii. 18. Luke vi. 14. John i. 44—47. 49. vi. 5. xii. 21, 22. xiv. 8, 9.) He was with the rest of the apostles and disciples who assembled for prayer in an upper room at Jerusalem, after the ascension. (Acts i. 13, 14.) Of the subsequent history of this apostle, nothing certain is known. He is *said* to have preached the Gospel in Scythia and Phrygia, and to have been interred at Hierapolis in Phrygia Pacatiana, where he suffered martyrdom.

4. One of the seven deacons of the church at Jerusalem. (Acts vi. 5.) He preached the Gospel at Samaria, where he performed many miracles, and converted many to the faith of Christ. Afterwards he received a divine command to go towards the south, to the road leading from Gaza to Jerusalem : here he met an eunuch of Candace, queen of Ethiopia, whom he likewise converted to the Christian faith. (Acts viii. 5—38.) After baptizing the eunuch, Philip stopped some time at Azotus; and "passing through, he preached in all the cities until he came to Cæsarea," where he appears to have fixed his residence. He had four daughters; who, like Agabus, according to circumstances, received the gift of prophecy. (Acts viii. 40. xxi. 8, 9.)

PHILIPPI was a city of Macedonia *Prima,* or the first of the four parts into which that province was divided. (See Vol. I. p. 196.) It was of moderate extent, and situated on the confines of Thrace. It was formerly called Crenides, from its numerous springs, and afterwards Datus from the coal mines in its vicinity. The name of Philippi it received from Philip the father of Alexander, who fortified it, and made it a frontier town against the Thracians. Julius Cæsar planted a colony here, which was afterwards enlarged by Augustus, and hence its inhabitants were considered as freemen of Rome. Christianity was first planted at Philippi, by Saint Paul,

P H

A. D. 50, the particulars of which are related in Acts xvi. 9—40.

PHILISTINES, Land of, 7. Account of, 7. Nature of the disease inflicted upon them, 508.

PHILOLOGUS, a Christian at Rome, whom St. Paul salutes in his epistle to the Romans. (xvi. 6.) M. Coquerel is of opinion that he was probably a slave who had been restored to liberty, and who received the name of Philologus, in consequence of his having been instructed in literature and the sciences.

PHINEAS, the son of Eleazar, and grandson of Aaron, was the third high priest of the Jews. He is greatly commended for his zeal for the glory of God in the affair of Zimri and Cosbi (Numb. xxv. 7.): for which God promised that the priesthood should be given to his posterity by a perpetual covenant; this condition being included (as interpreters observe), that his children should continue faithful and obedient. The time of his death is not known.

PHŒBE, a deaconess in the church at Cenchrea, whom St. Paul strongly recommends to the Christians at Rome in his epistle (xvi. 1, 2.), for her hospitality to himself. The deaconesses in the primitive church were sometimes married women, but most frequently widows advanced in years, and who had been the wife of one man; that is, one who had not parted with one husband and married another, a practice which at that time was usual both among the Jews and heathens. (1 Tim. vi. 9, 10.) Their functions consisted in taking care of the sick and poor of their own sex, visiting the prisoners and martyrs, instructing catechumens, assisting at the baptism of women, and various other inferior offices. Phœbe is supposed to have been the bearer of St. Paul's epistle to the Romans.

PHŒNICE, or PHŒNICIA, a province of Syria, which extended from the Gulf of Issus, where it bounded Cilicia on the north, along the coast southwards, to the termination of the ridges of Libanus and Antilibanus, near Tyre, where it met the border of Palestine. In breadth it only comprehended the narrow tract between the continuation of Mount Libanus and the sea. The country was exceedingly fertile, but being extremely limited, they early became a colonising people; extending their colonies to the very extremity of the Mediterranean Sea. Of these, Carthage was one of the most distinguished; and as a commercial nation, the Phœnicians are the most celebrated people of antiquity. The principal cities of Phœnicia were PTOLEMAIS, SIDON, and TYRE, of which a notice is given in the subsequent part of this index. For an account of the idols worshipped by them, see pp. 345—347.

PHŒNICIARCHS, notice of, 351.

PHRYGIA is a province of Asia Minor, divided into the Greater and Lesser. The former had Bithynia on the north, Galatia on the east, Pamphylia and Lycia on the

P I

south, Lydia and Mysia on the west. Its chief cities mentioned in Scripture (Col. ii. 1.) are Laodicea, Hierapolis, and Colossæ. St. Luke seems to speak of Phrygia Major in Acts ii. 10. because he joins it with Pamphylia below it. In Acts xvi. 6. he means Phrygia Minor. The inhabitants are said to have been a servile people, kept in their duty best by stripes, and made wise only by sufferings. In all these parts of Asia Minor, even to Bithynia and the Euxine Sea, the Jews antiently were very numerous.

PHUT or PUT, the name of an African people. According to Josephus (Ant. Jud. l. i. c. 7.) they were the inhabitants of Mauritania, where there is a river called Phut. (Plin. Nat. Hist. l. v. c. 1.) According to the Septuagint and Vulgate versions they were the Libyans. (Jer. xlvi. 9. Ezek. xxvii. 10. xxxviii. 5. Nah. iii. 9.) They are supposed to have been the descendants of Phut, the third son of Ham. (Gen. x. 6.)

PHYGELLUS, a Christian of Asia, who being at Rome during Paul's second imprisonment, A. D. 65, basely deserted him, with Hermogenes. in his necessity. (2 Tim. i. 15.)

PHYLACTARIES described, 397.

PHYSIC. or Medicine, state of, 502—510.

PHYSICS, or natural philosophy of the Jews, 480.

PIHAHIROTH or HIROTH, without the prefix, a place on the Red Sea, where the Israelites made their second encampment. (Exod. xiv. 2. 9. Numb. xiii. 7.) As the Israelites were properly delivered at this place from their captivity, and fear of the Egyptians (Exod. xiv. 5.), Dr. Shaw thinks that it derived its name from that circumstance. (Travels, vol. ii. p. 98.)

PILATE, Pontius, notice of, 114.

PISGAH, Mount, 52.

PISIDIA (Acts xiv. 24.), a country in Asia Minor, having Pamphylia on the south, Galatia on the north, Isauria on the east, and Phrygia on the west. Its chief city was Antioch in Pisidia (Acts xiii. 14.), so called to distinguish it from Antioch in Syria.

PISON, one of the four great rivers which watered the garden of Eden. (Gen. ii. 11, 12.) The author of the apocryphal book of Ecclesiasticus, speaking of a wise man, says, that "he filleth all things with his wisdom," or spreads it on every side, "as Phison and Tigris" spread their waters "in the time of the new fruits," that is, when they are swollen by the melting of the winter-snows. Calmet, Reland, Rosenmüller, and others, suppose it to be the Phasis, a celebrated river of Colchis; Eusebius and Jerome, after Josephus, make it to be the Ganges, which passing into India falls into the ocean.

PITHOM, one of the cities built by the Israelites for Pharaoh. (Exod. i. 11.) Sir John Marsham imagines it to be Pelusium; but it is most probably the πατουμος of Herodotus (Hist. l. ii. c. 158.), who places it on the canal made to join the Red Sea with the Isthmus of Suez. By the Arabians in

P O

later times it is called Fijum or Faijum (pronounced *Faioum*), which name is also applied to the province.

PLAGUE, not unknown in Palestine, 72.

PLAINS of the Holy Land, account of, 57.

PLEADING, form of, among the Jews, in civil and criminal cases, 120—123.

PLOUGHING, Jewish mode of, 454, 455.

POETRY, cultivated by the Hebrews, 478, 479.

POLITENESS, Jewish forms of, 429—432.

POLITICAL Divisions of the Holy Land, 6—17. Political state of the Israelites and Jews from the patriarchal times to the destruction of their polity by the Romans, 78—114.

POLYGAMY, why tolerated among the Jews, 408.

POMEGRANATE trees of Palestine, 68.

PONTUS, a province of Asia Minor, having the Euxine Sea on the north, Cappadocia on the south, Paphlagonia and Galatia on the east, and the Lesser Armenia on the west. It is supposed that Saint Peter preached in Pontus, because he addresses his first Epistle to the believing Hebrews, who were scattered throughout this and the neighbouring provinces.

POOLS of Solomon, 45. Pool of Bethesda, 24. And of Siloam, 24.

POOR, Jewish laws concerning, 195, 196.

POPULATION of the Holy Land, 70. Of Jerusalem, 25, 26.

PORCH of Solomon, 239.

POSSESSIONS, demoniacal, reality of, 510, 511.

POTIPHAR, the captain of Pharaoh's body guard, who purchased Joseph of some Midianitish merchants, and made him superintendent of his house. Afterwards, however, listening to the false charges of his wife, who accused Joseph of attempting to seduce her, he threw Joseph into prison, where he was rigorously confined. It should seem that this rigour was not of very long continuance ; and that he restored Joseph to all his confidence, and entrusted him with the management of the prison. (Gen. xxxvii. 36. xxxix. 19—23.) Potiphar is an Egyptian proper name, which has been explained by the Coptic ΠΙΩΤ ΦΡΡΟ *father*, that is, prime minister of PHARRO, or Pharaoh. Some expositors have made a distinction between the master of Joseph and the keeper of the prison into which he was thrown. Others, however, have conjectured, with more probability, that Potiphar, after having punished Joseph in a transport of wrath and jealousy, acknowledged his innocence ; but that, in order to avoid disgracing his wife, instead of restoring Joseph to his former office, he confided to him the command of the state-prison.

POTIPHERAH, governor, or, more correctly, priest of On, is known only from the circumstance of his having given his daughter in marriage to Joseph. (Gen. xli. 45. xlvi. 20.) Jablonski supposed it to be the same as the Coptic ΠΗΟΝΤ-ΦΡΗ, priest of the sun ; and

P T

the recent discoveries among the Egyptian monuments have shown that his conjecture was not altogether without foundation. PE-THEPH-RE signifies that which belongs to RE, or the Sun : this name was peculiarly suitable for a priest of On or Heliopolis, the city of the sun. Undesigned coincidences like these strongly corroborate the antiquity and authenticity of the Mosaic narrative.

POTTER'S FIELD. See ACELDAMA, page 540.

PRAYERS of the Jews, various appellations of, 326, 327. Public prayers, 327. Private prayers, 327. How offered in the synagogues, 253. Attitudes in prayer, 327—330. Forms of prayer in use among the Jews, 330. The nineteen prayers now used by them, 260—263.

PREACHING, a part of the synagogue service, 258, 259.

PRECIPITATION, a Jewish punishment, 156.

PREPARATION of the Passover, 305. Of the Sabbath, 302.

PRESENTS offered to superiors, 433.

PRIESTS, privileges and functions of, 275—278. Court of the Priests in the Temple, 240.

PRINCES of tribes and families, 81, 82.

PRISCA or PRISCILLA, the wife of Aquila, a converted Jew of Pontus. See AQUILA, p. 547.

PRISONERS (Roman), treatment of, 129, 130. 132, 133. Oriental mode of treating prisoners, 149, 150. Probable origin of one being released at the Passover, 305. Eyes of, put out, 150.

PRISONS (Jewish), notice of, 148—150.

PRIVILEGES of the first-born, 416, 417.

PROCEEDINGS, judicial, forms of, 120—124.

PROCURATORS (Roman), powers of, 112. State of the Jews under them, 113—115.

PRODUCTIONS of the Holy Land, 64—69.

PROMISE, Land of, 2.

PROMULGATION of laws, 98, 99.

PROPERTY, crimes against, how punished, 140—142. Disposal of property, 418, 419.

PROPHETS, notice of, 196. 286. Punishment of false prophets, 138. Schools of the prophets, 475. (See further the General Index of Matters in Vol. IV. article *Prophets*.) " *The Prophets*" an antient division of the Old Testament, p. 255. of this volume. Table of the sections of the prophets as read in the Jewish Synagogue, 257.

PROSELYTES, account of, 265—267. Conditions of proselytism, 267, 268.

PROSEUCHÆ, or oratories of the Jews, 249.

PSALTERY, a musical instrument, 473.

PTOLEMAIS, antiently called Accho (Judg. i. 31.), and now known by the name of ACRE, is a port and town situated on the shore of the Mediterranean Sea, on the confines of Lower and Upper Galilee. Here Saint Paul rested for one day on his journey from Ephesus to Jerusalem. (Acts xxi. 7.) As this port must always have been of great importance in time of war, the town has, consequently, undergone great changes.

PU

During the croisades this city suffered exceedingly both from infidels and Christians, between whom it was the scene of many sanguinary conflicts: at length it fell under the dominion of the late Djezzar Pacha, under whose government and that of his successor it has revived, and is now one of the most considerable towns on the coast. Acre has a beautiful appearance, when beheld from a short distance. This place is celebrated for the repulse there given to Napoleon Buonaparte, by the Turks under the command of Sir Sydney Smith, who, after a long and memorable siege, compelled the French to retire with great loss, and ultimately to abandon Syria. "Acre looks nobly from a distance, but, within its walls, is most wretched; houses in ruins and broken arches" [are] "in every direction." (Ld. Lindsay's Letters from Edom, &c. vol. ii. p. 81.

PUBLICANS, or collectors of the revenue, account of, 185. Why odious to the Jews, *ibid.*

PUBLIUS, an opulent governor of Malta, at the time of St. Paul's shipwreck, who miraculously healed his father of a dangerous malady. The bay in which the vessel was wrecked was contiguous to his estate; and he most probably entertained the apostle during his three months' residence on that island. (Acts xxiii. 7, 8.) An antient inscription found at Malta designates its governor by the same appellation—ΠΡΩΤΟΣ or *chief man*—which St. Luke gives to Publius, (Bloomfield and Kuinöel on Acts xxviii. 7, 8.)

PUL, or PHUL.

1. The proper name of a people remote from Palestine. (Isa. lxvi. 19.) The Latin Vulgate renders it Africa; according to Bochart, it was Philæ, an island of the Nile in Upper Egypt. Vitringa supposes it to be a place in the extremity of Egypt; it being the prophet's object, in the passage just cited, to designate the most remote parts.

2. The name of the first king of Assyria, who is mentioned in the Scriptures. He invaded the kingdom of Israel shortly after Menahem had usurped the throne, who gave him a thousand talents of silver to support him in his kingdom. (2 Kings xv. 19, 20.)

PUNISHMENTS (Hebrew), design of, 145. Inferior punishments, 145—152. Capital punishments, 152—158.

PUNISHMENTS (Roman), mentioned in the Bible, account of, 158—167.

PURIFICATIONS of the Hebrews, account of, 332—334. Purifications of the leprosy, in persons, garments, and houses, 334—336. Purifications in case of minor impurities, 336.

PURIM, or feast of Lots, account of, 318, 319.

PUTEOLI, a maritime town of Campania, in Italy, between Baiæ and Naples, founded by a colony from Cumæ. It was originally called Dicæarchia, and afterwards Puteoli,

RA

from the great number of wells (*putei*) which were in the neighbourhood. It is now called Puzzoli or Puzzuolo. It was a favourite place of resort for the Romans, on account of the adjacent mineral waters and its hot baths: and its harbour was defended by a celebrated mole, the remains of which are still to be seen. St. Paul landed and abode here seven days, by the favour of the centurion, on his first journey to Rome. (Acts xxviii. 13.) It appears from Acts xxviii. 11. that Puteoli was the destination of this vessel from Alexandria; and we learn from the independent testimony of the Jewish historian, Josephus, corroborated by the geographer Strabo, that this was the port of Italy to which ships from Egypt and the Levant commonly sailed. (Antiq. Jud. lib. xviii. c. 7. § 4. c. 8. § 2. Strabo, Geogr. l. xvii. p. 793. ed. Casaub.)

QUARTUS, a Christian resident at Corinth, whose salutations Saint Paul transmitted to Rome. He was probably a Roman, whom commercial affairs had led into Greece. (Rom. xvi. 23.)

QUICKSAND (Συρτις). Two syrtes or sand-banks on the northern coast of Africa, were particularly celebrated among the antients, by whom they were so called as being drawn together by the currents of the sea. One of these, called the *Syrtis Major*, lay between Cyrene and Leptis, and is most probably THN Συρτιν, THE *Quicksand*, alluded to in Acts xxvii. 17.; since a vessel bound westward, after passing Crete, might easily be driven into it by a strong north-easterly wind. The other (*Syrtis Minor*) lay near Carthage. (Kuinöel on Acts xxvii. 17. Robinson's Lexicon, voce Συρτις.)

QUIRINUS or CYRENIUS (Κυρηνιος, in Latin Quirinus), that is, Publius Sulpicius Quirinus, a Roman senator; who, after the banishment of Archelaus to Vienne in Gaul, and the annexation of Judæa to the province of Syria, was sent from Rome, as governor of Syria, to take a census of the whole province with a view to taxation. (Compare Acts v. 37.) This census he completed A.D. 8. This enrolment is alluded to in Luke ii. 2.; for an elucidation of which, see Vol. II. pp. 621—623.

RAAMSES or Rameses, a city erected by the Hebrews during their bondage in Egypt. (Gen. xlvii. 11. Exod. i. 11.) It was situated in the Land of Goshen, and appears to have been the capital of that country. Most probably it was the same with Heroopolis, which stood on the great canal between the Nile and Suez.

RABBATH.

1. *Rabbath, Rabbath-Ammon, or Rabbath of the children of Ammon*, afterwards called Philadelphia, the capital of the Ammonites,

was situated beyond Jordan. It was a place of considerable note in the time of Moses. When David declared war against the Ammonites, his general Joab laid siege to Rabbath-Ammon, where the brave Uriah lost his life, by a secret order given by this prince, that Uriah should be forsaken in a place of danger. And when the city was reduced to the last extremity, David himself went thither, that he might have the honour of taking it. From this time it became subject to the kings of Judah. Afterwards the kings of Israel became masters of it, with all the rest of the tribes beyond Jordan. But towards the conclusion of the kingdom of Israel, Tiglath-pileser having taken away a great part of the Israelites from that country, the Ammonites were guilty of many cruelties against those who remained, in consequence of which the prophets Jeremiah and Ezekiel pronounced very severe prophecies against Rabbath, the capital city of the Ammonites, and against the rest of the country, which probably had their completion five years after the destruction of Jerusalem. Antiochus the Great took the city of Rabbath-Ammon about A.M. 3786. Some time before this, Ptolemy Philadelphus had given it the name of PHILADELPHIA (which see in this index). Various ruins, lying on both sides of a stream, attest its ancient splendour. "The dreariness of its present aspect" (says Lord Lindsay) "is quite indescribable. It looks like the abode of death : the valley stinks with dead camels; one of them was rotting in the stream ; and though we saw none among the ruins, they were absolutely covered in every direction with their dung. That morning's ride would have convinced a sceptic how runs the prophecy. *I will make Rabbah a stable for camels, and the Ammonites a couching-place for flocks.* (Ezek. xxv. 5.) Nothing but the croaking of frogs and the screams of wild birds broke the silence as we advanced up this valley of desolation." (Letters from Egypt, &c. vol. ii. p. 112.) In pp. 113—117. Lord Lindsay has graphically described the ruins of Rabbath-Ammon, which is now deserted except by the Bedouins, who water their flocks at its little river.

2. *Rabbath-Moab,* or *Rabbath of the children of Moab,* the capital of the Moabites, otherwise AR, or ARIEL of Moab, and KIRHERES, or the city with brick walls. (Jer. xlviii. 31. 36.) This city was situated on the river Ar: it underwent many revolutions, and the prophets denounced heavy judgments against it.

RABBI, or RABBONI, import of, 476.

RABDOMANCY, or divination by the staff, 360.

RABSHAKEH, an officer of Sennacherib king of Assyria, who was sent with Rabsaris and Tartan to summon Hezekiah to surrender to his master. (2 Kings xviii. 17.)

RACA, a Syriac word of contempt, meaning a worthless person. (Matt. v. 22.) Those who applied this term to another were ob-noxious to punishment by the COUNCIL of twenty-three. See p. 119. *supra.*

RACHEL, the youngest daughter of Laban, and the wife of Jacob. She was the mother of Joseph and Benjamin. In Jer. xxxi. 15. the prophet introduces Rachel as bewailing the exile of her posterity, that is, Ephraim ; by quoting which language the evangelist Matthew (ii. 18.) in a similar manner introduces her as bemoaning the fate of the children who were massacred at Bethlehem. (Compare Vol. II. p. 342.) The tomb of Rachel is still shown to travellers, near the ruins of the village of Ramah. " It is one of the few places where the observer is persuaded that tradition has not erred. . . . . The spot is as wild and solitary as can well be conceived ; no palms or cypresses give their shelter from the blast ; not a single tree spreads its shade where the beautiful *mother* [wife] of Israel rests." (Carne's Recollections of the East, p. 157.) Mr. Maundrell is of opinion that this may be the true place of Rachel's interment : but the present sepulchral monument cannot be that which Jacob erected ; for it appears to be plainly a modern and Turkish structure. The graves of the Moslems lie thickly strewn around this tomb.

RAHAB.

1. A woman of Jericho, who received into her house, and afterwards concealed, the two spies, whom Joshua had sent to explore that city and its contiguous territory. On the capture of Jericho, Rahab, with her parents, brethren, and all that she had, under the conduct of the two spies, quitted her house in safety. She subsequently married Salmon, one of the chief men in the tribe of Judah, and became the mother of Boaz. (Josh. ii. vi. 17. 22, 23. Ruth iv. 21. Matt. i. 5.) Much discussion has taken place respecting Rahab, whether she were a harlot or one who kept a house of entertainment for strangers. The same word in the Hebrew language denotes persons of both professions : for the same reason, the appellation of harlot is given to Rahab in the Septuagint version, from which the apostles Paul (Heb. xi. 31.) and James (ii. 25.) make use of the same expression : but the Chaldee paraphrast calls her by a word which signifies a woman who keeps a public house, without any mark of infamy. Since those apostles cite her as an eminent example of faith in God, and have ranked her with Abraham, we shall be justified in putting the most charitable construction upon the appellation given to her.

2. A poetical name of Egypt. (Isa. xxx. 7. li. 9. Psal. lxxxvii. 4. lxxxix. 11.) The Hebrew word signifies *proud;* and the name seems to have been given to Egypt, from the pride and insolence of its princes and inhabitants.

RAINS, early and latter, importance of, in Palestine, 31.

RAMA, RAMAH, or RAMATHAIM, was a small town or village in the tribe of Benjamin, about six miles north of Jerusalem : it

R A

is frequently mentioned in the Old Testament. As it stood in a pass between the kingdoms of Israel and Judah, Baasha king of Israel seized it, and began to fortify it, to prevent his subjects from passing that way into the kingdom of Judah. (1 Kings xv. 17. 21.) Here Nebuzaradan, the Chaldæan general, disposed of his Jewish prisoners after their capital was taken, which occasioned a great lamentation among the daughters of Rachel. (Jer. xl. 1—3.) And as Rachel was buried in the vicinity of this place, she is represented in Jer. xxxi. 15. as having issued from her tomb, and lamenting the loss of her children, who were either slain or carried into captivity. A modern Turkish structure here is called the tomb of Rachel, which it evidently is not. Maundrell however thinks that it may have been erected on the site of the spot where she was interred. (Gen. xxxvi. 19.) Oriental geographers speak of Ramah as having formerly been the metropolis of Palestine; and Mr. Buckingham informs us, that every appearance of its ruins even now confirms the opinion of its having been once a considerable city. "Its situation, as lying immediately in the high road from Jaffa to Jerusalem, made it necessarily a place of great resort; and from the fruitfulness of the country around it, it must have been equally important as a military station or a depôt for supplies, and as a magazine for the collection of such articles of commerce as were exported from the coast. In its present state, the town of Ramah is about the size of Jaffa, in the extent actually occupied. The dwellings of this last, however, are crowded together around the sides of a hill, while those of Ramah are scattered widely over the face of the level plain on which it stands. The style of building here is that of high square houses, with flattened domes covering them; and some of the old terraced roofs are fenced around with raised walls, in which are seen pyramids of hollow earthenware pipes, as if to give air and light, without destroying the strength of the wall itself. The inhabitants are estimated at little more than five thousand persons, of whom about one third are Christians of the Greek and Catholic communion, and the remaining two thirds Mohammedans, chiefly Arabs; the men of power and the military being Turks, and no Jews residing there. The principal occupation of the people is husbandry, for which the surrounding country is highly favourable; and the staple commodities produced by them are corn, olives, oil, and cotton, with some soap and coarse cloth made in the town. There are still remains of some noble subterranean cisterns at Ramah, not inferior either in extent or execution to many of those at Alexandria; they were intended for the same purpose, namely, to serve in time of war as reservoirs of water." (Buckingham's Travels in Palestine, p. 168.)

RAMOTH, a famous city in the mountains of Gilead, often called Ramoth-gilead, some-

R E

times Ramoth, and sometimes Ramoth-mizpeh, or the Watch-tower. (Josh. xiii. 26.) This city belonged to the tribe of Gad. It was assigned to the Levites, and was one of the cities of refuge beyond Jordan. (Deut, iv. 43. Josh. xx. 8. xxi. 38.) It became celebrated during the reigns of the later kings of Israel, and was the occasion of several wars between these princes and the kings of Damascus, who had conquered it, and from whom the kings of Israel endeavoured to regain it. (1 Kings xxii. 3—36. 2 Kings viii. 28, 29. 2 Chron. xxii. 5.) Jehoram, king of Judah, was dangerously wounded at the siege of this place; and Jehu, the son of Nimshi, was here anointed king of Israel, by a young prophet sent by Elisha. (2 Kings ix. 1—10.) Ahab, king of Israel, was killed in battle with the Syrians before this place. (2 Chron. xviii. 3, 4, 5. et seq.) It is now called Ramza.

READING, oriental mode of, 471.
REAPING, notice of, 455.
REBELS' BEATING, what, 154, 155.
RECEPTION of visitors, 433, 434.
RECHABITES, account of, 285, 286.
RECORDER, office of, 96.
RECREATIONS of the Jews, 489.
RED SEA, that branch of the southern sea which interposes itself between Egypt on the west, Arabia Felix and some part of Arabia Petræa on the east, while its northern extremities touch on the coast of Edom. Edom, it is well known, in the Hebrew tongue signifies *Red*, and was the name given to Esau for selling his birthright for a mess of pottage. Both the country which was possessed by his posterity (Gen. xxv. 30. xxxvi. 31—40.), and the sea which was contiguous to it, were called after his name; but the Greeks, not understanding the reason of the appellation, translated it into their tongue, and called it Θαλασσα Ερυθρα, whence the Latins termed it *Mare Rubrum*, and we the Red Sea. It is also called *Yam Suph*, "the weedy sea," in several passages (Numb. xxxiii.10. Psal. cvi. 9, &c.) which are improperly rendered "the Red Sea." Some learned authors have supposed, that it was so named from the quantity of weeds in it. But Mr. Bruce, who had seen and examined the whole extent of it, states that he never saw a weed of any sort in it; and remarks that a narrow gulf, under the immediate influence of monsoons blowing from contrary points six months each year, would have too much agitation to produce such vegetables, seldom found but in stagnant water, and seldomer, if ever, found in salt water. He is of opinion that the sea derives its name from the large trees, or plants, of white coral perfectly in imitation of plants on land. One of these, which he saw, from a root nearly central, threw out ramifications measuring twenty-six feet in diameter every way. (Travels, vol. ii. p. 138.) This seems to be the most probable solution that has been hitherto proposed of the name. The tides in this sea are but moderate. At Suez, the dif-

ference between high and low water did not
exceed from three to four feet, according to
Niebuhr's observations on the tides in that
gulf, during the years 1762 and 1763. (Voyage en Arabie, p. 363.) This sea is navigable at all seasons; and the idea entertained
by some modern writers, that it is rapidly
filling up, is quite chimerical. (Lieut.
Wellsted's Travels in Arabia, vol. ii. p. 300.)
Every one knows the celebrated miracle
of the passage over the Red Sea, when God
opened this sea, dried it up, and made the
Israelites pass through it, dry-shod, to the
number of 600,000, without reckoning old
men, women, or children. The rabbins, and
many of the antient fathers, relying on Psal.
cxxxvi. 13. (to him which divided the Red
Sea into parts), have maintained that the Red
Sea was so divided as to make twelve passages; that each of the twelve tribes passed
through a different passage. But other authors have advanced, that Moses having
lived long near the Red Sea, in the country of Midian, had observed that it kept
its regular ebbing and flowing like the
ocean; so that taking the advantage of the
time of the ebb, he led the Hebrews over;
but the Egyptians, not knowing the nature of
the sea, and rashly entering it just before the
return of the tide, were all swallowed up and
drowned, as Moses relates. Thus the priests
of Memphis explained it, and their opinion
has been adopted by a great number of moderns, particularly by the learned critic and
philologer, John David Michaelis, who in the
queries which he sent to the Danish traveller
M. Niebuhr, while in Egypt, proposed to
him to inquire upon the spot, "Whether there
were not some ridges of rocks where the
water was shallow so that an army at particular times may pass over? Secondly, Whether the Etesian winds which blow strongly
all summer from the north-west, could not
blow so violently against the sea as to keep it
back on a heap; so that the Israelites might
have passed without a miracle?" and a copy
of these queries was left also for Mr. Bruce,
to join his inquiries likewise, his observations
on which are excellent. "I must confess,"
says he, "however learned the gentlemen
were who proposed these doubts, I did not
think they merited any attention to solve
them. This passage is told us by Scripture
to be a miraculous one; and if so, we have
nothing to do with natural causes. If we do
not believe Moses, we need not believe the
transaction at all, seeing that it is from his
authority alone we derive it. If we believe
in God that he made the sea, we must believe
he could divide it when he sees proper reason; and of that he must be the only judge.
It is no greater miracle to divide the Red
Sea than to divide the river Jordan. If the
Etesian winds, blowing from the north-west

in summer, could keep up the sea as a wall
on the right, or to the south, of fifty feet high,
still the difficulty would remain of building
the wall on the left hand or to the north.
Besides, water standing in that position for
a day must have lost the nature of fluid.
Whence came that cohesion of particles which
hindered that wall to escape at the sides?
This is as great a miracle as that of Moses.
If the Etesian winds had done this once, they
must have repeated it many a time before and
since, from the same causes. Yet Diodorus
Siculus (lib. iii. p. 122.) says, the Troglodytes, the indigenous inhabitants of that very
spot, had a tradition from father to son, from
their very earliest ages, that once this division
of the sea did happen there; and that, after
leaving its bottom some time dry, the sea
again came back, and covered it with great
fury.[1] The words of this author are of the
most remarkable kind: we cannot think this
heathen is writing in favour of Revelation:
he knew not Moses, nor says a word about
Pharaoh and his host; but records the miracle of the division of the sea in words nearly
as strong as those of Moses, from the mouths
of unbiassed undesigning pagans. Were all
these difficulties surmounted, what could we
do with the pillar of fire? The answer is,
We should not believe it. Why, then, believe the passage at all? We have no authority for the one but what is for the other: it
is altogether contrary to the ordinary nature
of things; and if not a miracle, it must be a
fable." (Vol. ii. pp. 135—137.)
Still, such sceptical queries have their use;
they lead to a stricter investigation of facts,
and thereby tend strongly to confirm the veracity of the history they meant to impeach.
Thus it appears, from the accurate observations of Niebuhr and Bruce, that there is no
ledge of rocks running across the gulf any
where, to afford a shallow passage. And the
second query, about the Etesian or northerly
wind, is refuted by the express mention of a
strong easterly wind blowing across, and
scooping out a dry passage, not that it was
necessary for Omnipotence to employ it there
as an instrument, any more than at Jordan;
but it seems to be introduced in the sacred
history by way of anticipation, to exclude the
natural agency that might in after times be
employed for solving the miracle; and it is
remarkable that the monsoon in the Red Sea
blows, the summer half of the year from the
north, the winter half from the south, neither
of which could produce the miracle in question. Wishing to diminish, though not to
deny the miracle, Niebuhr adopts the opinion
of those who contend for a higher passage
near Suez. "For," says he, "the miracle
would be less if they crossed the sea there,
than near Bedea. But whosoever should suppose that the multitude of the Israelites could

---

[1] Diodorus attributes this to an "extraordinary high tide." The fact, however, that "the
ground was bare to the very bottom of the gulf" is admitted by this curious tradition.

R E

be able to cross it here without a prodigy would deceive himself; for even in our days, no caravan passes that way to go from Cairo to Mount Sinai, although it would shorten the journey considerably. The passage would have been naturally more difficult for the Israelites some thousands of years back, when the gulf was probably larger, deeper, and more extended towards the north; for in all appearance the water has retired, and the ground near this end has been raised by the sands of the neighbouring desert." (p. 354.) But it sufficiently appears, even from Niebuhr's own statement, that the passage of the Israelites could not have taken place near Suez: for, 1. He evidently confounded the town of Kolsum, the ruins of which he places near Suez, and where he supposed the passage to be made, with the bay of Kolsum, which began about 45 miles lower down; as Mr. Bryant has satisfactorily proved, from the astronomical observations of Ptolemy and Ulug Beigh, made at Heroum, the antient head of the gulf. (See his treatise on the Plagues of Egypt, pp. 371, 372.)

2. Instead of crossing the sea at or near Ethan, their second station, the Israelites "turned" southwards along the western shore; and their third station at Pihahiroth, or Bedea, was at least a full day's journey below Ethan, as Mr. Bryant has satisfactorily proved from Scripture. (Exod. xiv. 2.) And it was this unexpected change in the direction of their march, which intimated an intention in the Israelites to quit Egypt; and the apparently disadvantageous situation in which they were then placed, " entangled in the land, and shut in by the wilderness," with a deep sea in front, the mountains of Attaka on the sides, and the enemy in their rear, that tempted the Egyptians to pursue them through the valley of Bedea, by the direct road from Cairo; who " overtook them encamping by the sea, beside Pihahiroth, opposite to Baalzephon." (Exod. xiv. 2—9.)

Niebuhr wonders how the Israelites could suffer themselves to be brought into such a disadvantageous situation, or be led blindfold by Moses to their apparent destruction : "one need only travel with a caravan," says he, " which meets with the least obstacle, viz. a small torrent, to be convinced that the Orientals do not let themselves be led, like fools, by their Caravan Baschi," or leader of the caravan. (p. 350.) But the Israelites went out of Egypt with "a high hand," though led by Moses, yet under the visible guidance and protection of "THE LORD GOD of the Hebrews," who went before them by day in a pillar of a cloud, and by night in a pillar of fire; and who, for their encouragement to enter the passage of the sea miraculously prepared for them, removed the cloud which went before the camp of Israel hitherto, and placed it behind them. (Exod. xiv. 8—20.) " And it came between the camp of the Egyptians and the camp of Israel; and it was a cloud and darkness to the one,

but give light by night to the other; so that the one came not near the other all the night." (Dr. Hales's Analysis of Chronology, vol. i. pp. 388—391.) The preceding elaborate view of this subject furnishes a most clear and satisfactory answer to the cavils of modern infidels.

Various antient traditions among the heathen historians attest the reality of the miraculous passage of the Red Sea by the Israelites : to which we may add that it is *manifest*, from the text of Moses and other sacred authors, who have mentioned this miraculous passage, that no other account is supportable but that which supposes the Hebrews to cross over the sea from shore to shore, in a vast space of dry ground which was left void by the waters at their retiring. (Exod. xiv. 16, 17, &c.) To omit the numerous allusions in the book of Psalms, Isaiah says (lxiii. 11, &c.) that the Lord divided the waves before his people, that he conducted them through the bottom of the abyss, as a horse is led through the midst of a field Habakkuk says (iii. 15.), that the Lord made himself a road to drive his chariot and horses across the sea, across the mud of great waters. Lastly, in the apocryphal book of Wisdom we read (xix. 7, 8. x. 17, 18.), that the dry land appeared all on a sudden in a place where water was before; that a free passage was opened in a moment through the midst of the Red Sea; and that a green field was seen in the midst of the abyss.

REFUGE, cities of, 11.

REGAL GOVERNMENT of the Israelites and Jews, 84—95. Its duration, 102—104.

REGION round about Jordan, notice of, 58.

REHOBOAM, the son and successor of Solomon. In his reign the kingdom of David was divided, the tribes of Judah and Benjamin retaining their allegiance to Rehoboam, while the other ten tribes became subject to Jeroboam the son of Nebat. Rehoboam died after reigning 17 years, and was succeeded on the throne of Judah by his son ABIJAH or ABIJAM, B. C. 954.

RELIGION, corruptions of, among the Jews, 337—361. Particularly in the time of Christ, 376—380.

REMEDIES in use among the Jews, notice of, 503, 504.

REMPHAN, a Coptic name of Saturn, who was also worshipped under the name of MoLOCH. (Acts vii. 43. Compare p. 344.)

RENDING of garments, a sign of mourning, 405.

REPHAIM or RAPHAIM, the sons of Rapha (2 Sam. xxi. 16. 18. Heb. and marginal rendering), a Canaanitish race of giants that dwelt beyond the Jordan (Gen. xiv. 5. xv. 20. Josh. xvii. 15.), from whom the gigantic Og, king of Bashan, was descended. (Deut. iii. 11.) In a wider sense, this word seems to have included all the giant tribes of Canaan. (Deut. ii. 11. 20.) In subsequent times, the sons of Rapha appear to have been men of extraordinary strength among the

Philistines. (2 Sam. xxi. 16. 18. marg. rend.)
The Valley of the Rephaim (for an account of which, see p. 53.) derives its name
from this tribe.

Rephidim, a station or encampment of the
Israelites in the desert (Exod. xvii. 1.) where
the Israelites were miraculously supplied with
water out of the rock of Meribah. It is an
insulated rock, at the foot of Mount Sinai,
about six yards square, according to Dr.
Shaw, but Mr. Carne says that it is about
five yards long, five in height, and four yards
wide. This rock, which is of granite, is in
Deut. viii. 15. rightly called a *rock of flint*,
in consequence of its hardness : it lies, tot-
tering, as it were, and loose, near the middle
of the valley, and seems formerly to have
been a part or cliff of Mount Sinai. *The
waters* which *gushed out, and the stream* which
flowed withal (Psal. vii. 8. 21.), have hollowed
across one corner of this rock a channel about
two inches deep, and twenty inches wide.
There are also four or five fissures, one above
the other, on the face of the rock, each of
them about a foot and a half long, and a few
inches deep, "the lively and demonstrative
evidence of their having been formerly so
many fountains." A remarkable circumstance
is, that they run along the *breadth* of the rock,
and are not sent downwards : they are more
than a foot asunder. Neither art nor chance
could be concerned, says Dr. Shaw, in the
contrivance ; inasmuch as every circumstance
points out to us a miracle ; and, in the same
manner with the rent in the rock of Calvary
at Jerusalem, never fails to produce the
greatest seriousness and devotion in all who
see it. (Shaw's Travels, vol. ii. pp. 109, 110.
Carne's Letters, pp. 198, 199.)

Restitution, in what cases enjoined, 146,
147.

Retaliation among the Jews, 146.

Reuben, the eldest son of Jacob and Leah,
gave his name to one of the twelve tribes of
Israel ; for the canton assigned to which, see
p. 11.

Revenues of the kings of Israel and Judah, 95. Of the Levites, 275. And of the
priests, 277, 278.

Reverence of the Jews for their temple,
243, 244. Of inferiors to superiors, 431, 432.

Rezin, king of Syria, an able prince who
knew how to avail himself of the divisions of
his neighbours, in order to aggrandise himself. He formed an alliance with Pekah
king of Israel against Ahaz king of Judah,
whose dominions he invaded ; and, after obtaining considerable advantages, he took a
great number of prisoners, whom he sent to
Damascus, and then proceeded to lay siege
to Jerusalem, in which he failed. (2 Kings
xv. 37. xvi. 5. 2 Chron. xxxviii. 5.) This
check, which had been foretold by Isaiah
(vii. 1—8.), frustrated the project formed by
the allied princes for overthrowing the dynasty of David. Rezin was more successful
in Idumæa, where he made himself master of
the port of Elath on the Red Sea ; an im-

portant conquest which gave him the command of the neighbouring country and sea.
(2 Kings xvi. 6.) His successes were of
short duration : in the following year, agreeably to the predictions of Isaiah (viii. 4. ix.
10.), Damascus was taken by Tiglath-pileser
king of Assyria, who carried its inhabitants
into bondage, and put to death Rezin, with
whom the kingdom of Syria terminated.

Rhegium, a maritime city, near the south-
western extremity of Italy, opposite to Messina in Sicily. Here St. Paul stayed one day,
on his first voyage to Rome. (Acts xxviii. 13.)
It is now called Rheggio.

Rhodes, an island and city in the Levant,
which is said to have derived its name from
the abundance of roses which grew there.
When St. Paul went to Jerusalem, a. d. 58,
he went from Miletus to Coos, from Coos to
Rhodes, and thence to Patara in Lycia. (Acts
xxi. 1.)

Riblah, a city of Syria, in the country of
Hamath, which, according to Jerome, was
the same with what was afterwards called
Antioch in Syria ; but Rosenmüller observes,
that Antioch lay too far north from the borders of Palestine to be the site of Riblah.
The Babylonians were accustomed to pass
through this place in their irruptions into,
and departures from, Palestine. Pharaoh-
Necho stopped here on his return from the
battle of Megiddo. (2 Kings xxiii. 33.)
Traces of it would seem to be found in the
modern town of Reblah or Rablah, situated
about forty miles south of Hamath, on the
river Orontes, and mentioned by Mr. Buckingham in his "Travels among the Arab
Tribes." (p. 481. London, 1825. 4to.)

Rimmon signifies a pomegranate tree.

1. An idol of the Syrians, supposed to be
the Jupiter of the antients, or, according to
some writers, the sun. (2 Kings v. 8.)

2. A city in the tribe of Simeon, on the
southern boundary of Palestine. (Josh. xv.
32. xix. 7. Zech. xiv. 10.)

3. A rock not far from Gibeah, whither
the children of Benjamin retreated after their
defeat. (Judg. xx. 45. 47. xxi. 13.) Hither
also Saul and his men went. (1 Sam. xiv. 2.)

4. Rimmon-Methoar (*a round pomegranate*), a city in the tribe of Zebulun (Josh.
xix. 13.), which is supposed to be the same
as Rimmono, which is mentioned in 1 Chron.
vi. 62.

5. Rimmon-parez (*split pomegranate*), the
sixteenth encampment of the Israelites in the
wilderness. (Numb. xxxiii. 19.)

Rings worn by the Jews, notice of, 401.

Riphath, the second son of Gomer, and
grandson of Japhet (Gen. x. 3. 1 Chron. i.
6.) The region peopled by his descendants
is supposed to be the mountainous range extending from the west of Europe to that part of
Asia which is situated on the east of the Black
Sea. "But" (Rosenmüller is of opinion)
"it is impossible to fix with precision upon
any one chain of hills, or tribe of people,
with which the Riphath of Scripture may

certainly be identified." (Biblical Geography, by Morren, vol. i. p. 113.)

RIVERS of the Holy Land, 35—38.

ROGEL, or EN-ROGEL, fountain of, 43.

ROME, the metropolis of the world during the period comprised in the New Testament history. According to the chronology of Archbishop Usher, this city was founded by Remus and Romulus, A. M. 3966 of the Julian period, in A. M. 3256, B. C. 748, towards the close of the reign of Hezekiah, king of Judah. This city is so well known, that it is needless to give any account of it here. The later sacred authors of the Old Testament have not mentioned it ; but it frequently occurs in the books of the Maccabees and in the New Testament. Saint Peter (1 Ep. v. 13.) has denoted it by the figurative name of Babylon. *The church that is at Babylon, elected together with you, saluteth you.* Saint John, in his Revelation (xiv. 8. xvi. 19. xvii. 5. xviii. 2. 10. 21.), points it out by the same name, and describes it in such a manner as can only agree to Rome ; 1. By its command over all nations ; 2. By its cruelty towards the saints ; and, 3. By its situation upon seven hills. (Rev. xvii. 9.) St. Paul came twice to Rome : first, A. D. 61, when he appealed to Cæsar ; and, secondly, A. D. 65, a year before his martyrdom, which happened in A. D. 66. Account of the judicature of the Romans, 125—132. Roman tribunals 133, 134. Powers of the Roman procurators, 112. Roman punishments, 158—167. Roman mode of computing time, 168—170. Discipline and military triumphs, 225—229. Tribute reluctantly paid to the Romans by the Jews, 134. Roman idols mentioned in the New Testament, 349.

ROOFS of houses, 388, 389.

ROSH (Ezek. xxxviii. 2, 3. xxxix. 1.), the proper name of a northern nation, mentioned together with Tubal and Meshech ; by whom (Gesenius says) are doubtless to be understood the Russians ; who are described by the Byzantine writers of the tenth century, under the name of 'Ρῶς, as inhabiting the northern parts of Taurus ; and also by Ibn Fosslan, an Arabian writer of the same period, under the name *Rûs*, as dwelling upon the river *Rha*, that is, the Wolga.

ROYAL APPAREL, 89.

RUDDER-BANDS, nature of, 486.

RURAL AND DOMESTIC ECONOMY of the Jews, 446—464.

RUTH, a Moabitish woman, who returned with her mother-in-law Naomi to the land of Israel, and became the wife of Boaz. (Matt. i. 5.) See an analysis of the Book of Ruth in Vol. IV. pp. 43—45.

———

SABBATH of the Jews, how observed, 300, 301. Jewish worship on that day, 302, 303.

SABBATICAL YEAR, account of, 320.

SABTECHAH, a people or country of the

Cushites ; most probably Sabatha or Sabota, a considerable city of Arabia Felix, according to Pliny (Nat. Hist. l. vi. c. 28. § 32.), the principal city of the Atramites, a tribe of Sabæans, on the Red Sea.

SACKBUT, an antient musical instrument, used in Chaldæa, supposed to consist of four strings, and to emit a shrill sound.

SACRAMENT of the Lord's Supper, points of resemblance between and the Jewish Pass-' over, 310, 311.

SACRED OBLIGATIONS and DUTIES of the Jews, 323—337.

SACRED PERSONS among them, account of, 263—286.

SACRED PLACES, account of, 230—263.

SACRED THINGS, account of, 287—298.

SACRED TIMES and SEASONS, account of, 299—323.

SACRIFICES of the Jews, divine origin of, 288. Selection of, and how offered, 289— 291. Different kinds of, 291—298. Their fitness and propriety, 298, 299. Meat and drink offerings, 294. Sacrifice offered at the admission of proselytes into the Jewish church, 267. Fitness and utility of the Jewish sacrifices, 298, 299. Allusions to the sacrifices of the heathens explained, 350 —358.

SADDUCEES, sect of, tenets of, 367, 368.

SAGAN, or substitute of the high priest, 279.

SALAMIS, the chief city of the island of Cyprus, where the Gospel was early preached. (Acts xiii. 5.) It was situated on the southeast side of the island, and was afterwards called Constantia.

SALEM.

1. A name of the city of JERUSALEM. (Psal. lxxvi. 2.)

2. Or SALIM, a place on the banks of the Jordan, where John baptised. (John iii. 23.) Its situation cannot now be ascertained.

SALMONE, a maritime city and promontory, which forms the eastern extremity of the island of Crete. (Acts xxvii. 7.)

SALOME, the wife of Zebedee, and the mother of the apostles James and John. She was one of those who attended Jesus Christ on his journeys, and ministered to him. (Mark xv. 40. xvi. 1. Matt. xx. 20. xxvii. 56.)

SALT, covenant of, 191.

SALT SEA, account of, 40—42.

SALT, Vale of, notice of, 53.

SALUTATIONS, forms of, 429—432.

SAM or SAMIEL wind, notice of, 76, 77.

SAMARIA denotes

1. *The antient capital of the kingdom of Israel,* which is very frequently mentioned in the Old Testament. It was situated on a hill which derived its name from Semer or Shemer, of whom it was purchased by Omri king of Israel, B.C. 921, who made it the seat of his government, and called it Samaria (Heb. *Shomeron*), from its former owner. By his successors it was greatly improved and fortified ; and, after resisting the repeated attacks of the kings of

S A

Assyria, it was destroyed by Shalmaneser, B. c. 717, who reduced it to a heap of stones. (Micah i. 6. 2 Kings xvii. 6.) Samaria seems to have arisen again from its ruins during the reign of Alexander, B. c. 549, after whose death it was subject to the Egyptian and Syrian kings, until it was besieged, taken, and rased to the ground by the high priest Hyrcanus, B. c. 129 or 130. It was afterwards wholly rebuilt, and considerably enlarged by Herod, surnamed the Great, who gave it the name of *Sebaste,* and erected a temple there in honour of the emperor Augustus (Sebastos) Cæsar. Various ruins of Herod's edifices yet remain. Modern Samaria is a small and poor village, steep of approach, but strong by nature, and beautifully situated on a fine, large, insulated hill, surrounded by a broad deep valley; which is environed by four hills, one on each side, that are cultivated with terraces up to the top, sown with grain, and (as the valley also is) planted with fig and olive trees. The hill of Samaria likewise rises in terraces to a height equal to any of the adjoining mountains. (Richardson's Travels, vol. ii. pp. 412, 413.) For a notice of the idols worshipped in Samaria during the captivity, see p. 348. And for an account of the tenets, &c. of the Samaritans, see p. 371—374.

2. *The Region of Samaria,* the district of which Samaria was the chief city. (Luke xvii. 11. John iv. 4, 5. 7. Acts i. 8. viii. 1. 9. ix. 31. xv. 3.) It was situated between Judæa and Galilee and the Plain of Esdraelon. For the state of this region in the time of Christ, see p. 15.

Samaria, Mountains of, p. 46.

Samos, an island of the Archipelago on the coast of Asia Minor. The Romans wrote to the governor of Samos in favour of the Jews, in the time of Simon Maccabæus, A. M. 3685, B. c. 139. (1 Macc. xv. 23.) St. Paul went ashore on the same island, as he was going to Jerusalem, A. D. 58. (Acts xx. 15.)

Samothracia or Samothrace, an island of the Ægean Sea. St. Paul, departing from Troas for Macedonia, arrived first at Samothracia, then landed in Macedonia. (Acts xvi. 11.) It was antiently called Dardana and Leucania, and afterwards Samos; and in order to distinguish it from the other Samos, the epithet Thracian was added, which passed into the name Samothrace.

Samson or Sampson, the thirteenth judge of Israel, the son of Manoah, of the tribe of Dan. Before his birth, he was consecrated to be a Nazarite, and was chosen to deliver the Israelites from the yoke of the Philistines. He was celebrated for his vast physical strength, and for the bravery and success with which he defended his country against its enemies. (Judg. xiii.—xvi.) He judged the Israelites twenty years.

Samuel, a celebrated Hebrew prophet, the son of Elkanah and Hannah, of the tribe of Levi. Having been consecrated to God

S A

from his birth, he received divine communications even in his childhood : he was the fifteenth and last judge of the Israelites. By divine direction, he converted the Hebrew commonwealth into a kingdom; and anointed Saul as the first king, and afterwards David. He is supposed to have been the first institutor of schools for the education of the sons of the prophets. He died at the age of ninety-eight years, about two years before the death of Saul. For an analysis of the two books of Samuel, see Vol. IV. pp. 45—50. ; and on the appearance of Samuel to Saul at Endor, see Vol. I. p. 209.

Sanctuary of the temple described, 241, 242.

Sandals of the Hebrews, notice of, 400.

Sanhedrin, or great council of the Hebrews, powers and functions of, 118, 119.

Sapphira, the wife of Ananias, who, together with him, was struck with instant death, for attempting to deceive God the Holy Spirit. (Acts v. 1. 3. 9, 10.)

Sarah, the wife of Abraham, and the mother of Isaac, whom she bore at an age when she could little expect such a blessing. (Gen. xxi.) She died at the advanced age of 127 years, at Kirjath-arba, afterwards called Hebron. (Gen. xxiii. 1. 9.)

Sardis, the metropolis of the region of Lydia, in Asia Minor, was situated at the foot of Mount Tmolus, which commands an extensive view over the surrounding country. It was celebrated for the great opulence and for the voluptuous and dissipated manners of its inhabitants. This once celebrated capital of Crœsus and the Lydian kings is now reduced to a wretched village called Sart, consisting of a few mud huts occupied by Turkish herdsmen. "A great portion of the ground once occupied by the imperial city is now a smooth grassy plain, browsed over by the sheep of the peasants, or trodden by the camels of the caravan; and all that remains to point out the site of its glory are a few disjointed pillars, and the crumbling rock of the Acropolis." No Christians reside on the spot: two Greek servants of a Turkish miller, in 1826, were the only representatives of the church at Sardis, the present state of which affords a most striking illustration of the accomplishment of the prophetic denunciations against the church in that city. (Emerson's Letters from the Ægean, vol. i. pp. 201. 216—218. ; Hartley's Visit, Missionary Register, 1827, p. 326. ; Arundell's Visit, pp. 176—182.) "If I should be asked" (says the last-cited traveller, who revisited Sardis in 1833,) "what impresses the mind most strongly on beholding Sardis, I should say its indescribable *solitude,* like the darkness in Egypt, darkness that could be felt. So the deep solitude of the spot, once the 'lady of kingdoms,' produces a corresponding feeling of *desolate abandonment* in the mind which can never be forgotten. Connect this feeling with the message, in the Apocalypse, to the church of Sardis : —

S C

Thou hast a name, that thou livest and art dead . . . I will come on thee as a thief, and thou sha't not know at what hour I will come upon thee. (Rev. iii. 1. 3.) And then look around and ask, where are the churches, where are the Christians of Sardis? The tumuli beyond the Hermus reply, 'All dead;' suffering the infliction of the threatened judgment of God, for the abuse of their privileges." (Arundell's Discoveries in Asia Minor, vol. i. p. 28.)

SAREPTA, or ZAREPHATH (Luke iv. 26.), was a city in the territory of Sidon, between that city and Tyre. It was the place where the widow dwelt to whom the prophet Elijah was sent, and was preserved by her cruise of oil and barrel of meal that wasted not. (1 Kings xvii. 9.) Antiently its wines were held in great estimation: at present it is a small village called Zarfa.

SARGON (Isa. xx. 1.), a king of Assyria, whom some critics and expositors have supposed to have been the predecessor of Sennacherib; while others have conceived him to have been Sennacherib himself.

SARON or SHARON, a town adjoining to Lydda, which gave name to the spacious and fruitful valley between Cæsarea and Joppa. Peter's miraculous healing of the paralytic Eneas at Lydda was the means of bringing the inhabitants of Saron to the knowledge of the Gospel. (Acts ix. 35.)

SAUL.
1. The son of Kish, of the tribe of Benjamin, and the first king of Israel. In consequence of his disregarding the divine commands, he was rejected by God, and David the son of Jesse anointed to be sovereign in his stead. Saul, after persecuting David for many years, was slain, together with his two sons, on Mount Gilboa, fighting against the Philistines. (2 Sam. i.) On the nature of his malady, see p. 508.

2. The Jewish name of the apostle PAUL.

SCAPE-GOAT, typical reference of, 318.

SCEPTRE of the kings of Israel, 89.

SCEVA, a Jew, one of the chief priests, whose seven sons went from city to city, as many Jews did, to exorcise those who were possessed by demons. At Ephesus, pretending to invoke the name of Jesus over the possessed, they were so severely treated by these spirits for their presumption, that they were forced to flee out of the house naked and wounded. (Acts xix. 14—17.)

SHECHEM. See SICHEM, p. 625. *infra.*

SCHOOLS of the Jews, 259. Particularly of the prophets, 474, 475. Military Schools, 206.

SCIENCES cultivated by the Jews, account of, 477—481.

SCORPION, the largest of all the insect tribe, sometimes being several inches in length. It is shaped somewhat like a small lobster, and its tail is furnished with a venomous sting producing inflammation and swelling, though it is rarely fatal except through neglect. The malignity of its sting

S E

is proportioned to its size. Scorpions are found only in hot countries, where they lurk in decayed buildings and among the stones of old walls. The body of this insect is said to be much like an egg; which circumstance explains the contrast drawn by Jesus Christ between a scorpion and an egg. (Luke xi. 12.) For a notice of the *Scorpions of the Desert,* see p. 60. *note* 1.

SCOURGING, punishment of, how inflicted among the Jews, 145, and among the Romans, 146. Could not be inflicted on a Roman citizen, 129.

SCRIBES, account of, in the time of Moses, 83, 84.; and in the time of Christ, 370. Royal scribes, 96.

SCRIPTURES, reading of, in the Synagogues, 254 — 257. Exposition of, a part of the Synagogue-Service, 258.

SEALS or SIGNETS of the Jews, 401.

SEAS mentioned in the Scriptures. See pp. 38—43.; and RED SEA, pp. 617—619.

SEASONS of Palestine, 29—34.

SECTS of the Jews, account of, 362—370.

SEED-TIME, notice of, 29.

SEIR.
1. Mountains of Seir, a ridge to the south of the Dead Sea, inclining towards Elath and Ezion-geber upon the Red Sea. This region was first inhabited by the Horites (Gen. xiv. 6. Deut. ii. 12.), from one of whose chiefs (Gen. xxxvi. 20. 30.), it may have derived its name; afterwards by Esau (Gen. xxxii. 4. xxxiii. 14. 16.), and by his posterity. (Deut. ii. 4, 5. 2 Chron. xx. 10.)

2. A mountain upon the frontiers of the tribes of Judah and Dan.

SEIRATH, the place where Ehud stopped after the death of Eglon king of Moab. It is supposed to have been near Bethel. (Judg. iii. 26.)

SELAH, the capital of the Edomites, which Amaziah captured, and changed its name into JOKTHEEL. (2 Kings xiv. 7.) It is supposed to have derived its name (which signifies a rock) from its rocky situation; and lies between the Dead Sea and the Elanitic gulf, in a deep valley surrounded by lofty rocks, so that great part of the dwellings were hewn out of the rock itself. The ruins of this antient city, the Petra of profane geographers, still exist under the Arab name of *Wady Mousa,* or the *Valley of Moses,* and are among the most splendid remains of antient art. Views of them will be found in the "Landscape Illustrations of the Bible," edited by the author of this work.

SELEUCIA, a fortified city of Syria, situated on the sea-coast, a little north of the mouth of the river Orontes: it derived its name from Seleucus Nicator, and was sometimes called *Seleucia ad mare,* to distinguish it from seven or eight other cities in Syria of the same name. (Acts xiii. 4.)

SELEUCIDÆ, æra of, 182. and *note* 1.

SELF-INTERDICTION, vows of, 325.

SENATE of Seventy in the wilderness, notice of, 83.

S H

SENNACHERIB, a king of Assyria, who invaded the kingdom of Judah in the reign of Hezekiah. See ASSYRIA, 553. col. 1.

SENTENCES (Judicial), how performed among the Jews, 124, 125.

SEPHARAD, a country or place where some of the Jewish captives dwelt. In the Latin Vulgate, it is rendered *Bosphorus :* in the Syriac and Chaldee versions, and by modern Hebrew commentators, it is rendered *Spain.* Both these explanations, says Gesenius, are undoubtedly false ; but nothing more certain can be substituted in their place.

SEPHARVAIM, a small district or state governed by its own king (2 Kings xix. 13. Isa. xxxvii. 13.), and most probably situated in Mesopotamia. When Shalmaneser, king of Assyria, carried the Israelites into captivity from Samaria beyond the Euphrates, he sent a colony thither, among which were the Sepharvaim. (2 Kings xvii. 24. 31.)

SEPULCHRES of the Jews, account of, 519— 522.

SEPULTURE, rites of, 515—519.

SERÂB, nature of, 63. and *note* 2.

SERGIUS PAULUS, the Roman proconsul or governor of Cyprus, who was led by the preaching of Paul and Barnabas to embrace the Christian faith. (Acts xiii. 7.)

SERPENT, Brasen, worshipped by the Jews, 341, 342.

SERVANTS, different kinds of, mentioned in the Scriptures, 428, 429. How hired and paid in Judæa, 426.

SETH, the son of Adam and Eve, and father of Enos, was born after the death of Abel. He lived 912 years. His posterity, who were distinguished from the descendants of Cain by the appellation of the sons of God, preserved the patriarchal religion in its purity until the time of the deluge, after which it was transmitted by the race of Shem. (1 Chron. i. 1. Luke iii. 1. Gen. iv 25. v. 3. vi. 2.)

SHADOW OF DEATH, Valley of, notice of, 60. *note* 2.

SHALMANESER or SALMANESER, king of Assyria. See ASSYRIA, 552. col. 2.

SHARON, Vale of, notice of, 55.

SHAVEH, Valley of, notice of, 53.

SHEBA, probably the Saba of the Greek geographer Strabo, was a region situated towards the southern part of Arabia at a distance from the coast of the Red Sea. The queen of Sheba who visited Solomon (1 Kings, x. 2 Chron. ix.) appears to have been the sovereign of this region. The tradition of her visit has maintained itself among the Arabs, who call her Balkis, and affirm that she became the wife of Solomon. In Matt. xii. 42. she is said to have come from the *uttermost parts of the earth,* to indicate (according to the Jewish idiom) that Sheba was a remote country from Judæa.

SHECHEM. See SICHEM, 625.

SHEEP-HUSBANDRY of the Jews, 450, 451.

SHELIACH-ZIBBOR, office of, 253.

SHEM or SEM, the second son of Noah.

(Gen. v. 32.) According to the genealogical table in Gen. x. the nations in south-western Asia, as the Persians, Assyrians, Syrians, Hebrews, and part of the Arabians, were descended from him.

SHEMER, the name of the possessor of the mountain on which the city of SAMARIA was erected by Omri king of Israel, to whom he sold that territory for two talents of silver. From the circumstance of that city being called after his name, as well as from the very small sum given by way of purchase money, it has been conjectured that Shemer made it one of the conditions of sale that his name should be given to the new city. As the law of Moses prohibited the irredeemable cession of estates, and as Shemer's name is mentioned without any notice of its genealogy, it is not improbable that he was descended from the Canaanites, whom the Israelites had not been able to expel.

SHEMONEH ESRAH, or Jewish Prayers, 260—263.

SHENIR, Mount, 48.

SHEPHERDS, duties of, 450, 451.

SHESHACH, another name for Babylon. (Jer. xxv. 26. li. 41.) This is evident from the connection ; but the derivation of the word is obscure. Calmet supposed Sheshach to be a Pagan idol, worshipped at Babylon ; and that Jeremiah gave to that city the name of its tutelar deity.

SHEWBREAD, table of, notice of, 242. 294.

SHIELDS of the Hebrews, and of the Romans, 208, 209.

SHIELD-BEARERS, office of, 208.

SHILOH, a celebrated city in the tribe of Ephraim, where the people assembled (Josh. xviii. 1.) to set up the tabernacle of the congregation, which continued there until the time of Eli. (1 Sam. iv. 3.) It was situated on a high mountain to the north of Bethel.

SHINAR, the territory of Babylon. (Gen. x. 10. xi. 2. xiv. 1. Isa. xi. 11. Dan. i. 2. Zech. v. 11.) The boundaries of this country are defined in Gen. x. 10., and depend on the interpretation given to the names of cities mentioned in that verse.

SHIPS, of the antients, notice of, 485— 487.

SHISHAK, a king of Egypt who was contemporary with Solomon and Rehoboam. He first gave an asylum to the malecontent Jeroboam (1 Kings xi. 40.); and afterwards, as soon as he saw that Rehoboam's power was weakened by the revolt of the ten tribes, he invaded Judæa, and advanced against Jerusalem with an immense army, composed of Egyptians, Ethiopians, Lybians, and Sukkim or Troglodytes. But, satisfied with the submission of the Jewish monarch and with the spoils of his capital, including the treasures of the temple, he left him his throne, and drew off his forces. (1 Kings xiv. 25, 26. 2 Chron. xii. 2—9.) Shishak is the Sesonchis of profane historians, and the head of the Bubastite or twenty-second dynasty of the Egyptian kings. His name has been discovered on the

S I

S I

recently explained Egyptian monuments (compare Vol. I. p. 192.); and he is supposed to have been an Ethiopian, who, supported by the military caste, dethroned the Pharaoh who was Solomon's father-in-law.

SHOES of the Hebrews, 400.

SHOTERIM, office of, 79.

SHUNEM, a city in the tribe of Issachar. (Josh. xix. 18. 2 Sam. xxviii. 4.) Here the prophet Elisha was hospitably entertained by a benevolent woman; whose son dying, he miraculously restored him to life. (2 Kings iv.) According to Eusebius, there was a place called *Sulem* (by a commutation of *l* and *n*) five Roman miles south of Mount Tabor.

SHUR (now called *Djofur*), Wilderness of, notice of, 59.

SHUSHAN, the capital of Susiana, a province of Elam or Persia, which Daniel terms the palace (viii. 2.), because the Chaldæan monarchs had a royal palace here. After Cyrus, the kings of Persia were accustomed to pass the winter there, and the summer at Ecbatana. The winter was very moderate at Shushan, but the heat of the summer was so great, that the very lizards and serpents, if surprised by it in the streets, are said to have been burned up by the solar rays. This city stands on the river Ulai, or Choaspes. In this city, and on this river, Daniel had the vision of the ram with two horns, and the goat with one horn, &c. in the third year of the reign of Belshazzar (Dan. viii. 1—3, &c.), A. M. 3447, B. C. 557. In this city of Shushan, the transactions took place which are related in the book of Esther. Here Ahasuerus, or Darius the son of Hystaspes, generally resided and reigned. (Esth. i. 1, 2. 5, &c.) He rebuilt, enlarged, and adorned it. Nehemiah was also at Shushan, when he obtained from king Artaxerxes permission to return into Judæa, and to repair the walls of Jerusalem. (Neh. i. 1.) Benjamin of Tudela, and Abulfaragius, place the tomb of Daniel at Chuzestan, which is the antient city of Shushan; and a tomb is still shown to travellers, as the tomb of the prophet. Dr. Lightfoot says, that the outward gate of the eastern wall of the temple was called the gate of Shushan; and that upon this gate was carved the figure (more probably the arms or insignia) of Shushan, in acknowledgment of the decree there granted by Darius son of Hystaspes, which permitted the rebuilding of the temple. The site of this once noble metropolis of the antient sovereigns of Persia is now a mere wilderness; no human being residing there excepting one poor dervise, who keeps watch over the supposed tomb of the prophet Daniel. See an account of the ruins and the present state of Shushan, in Sir R. K. Porter's Travels in Georgia, Persia, &c. vol. ii. pp. 411—418.

SICARII, or assassins mentioned in the New Testament, notice of, 375.

SICHEM, SYCHAR or SHECHEM, a city in the allotment of the tribe of Benjamin, near which Jacob bought a field which he gave to Joseph, who was buried there. (Gen. xlviii.

22. Josh. xvii. 7. xxiv. 32. Acts vii. 16.) In its vicinity was Jacob's well or fountain, at which Jesus Christ conversed with a woman of Samaria. (John iv. 5.) After the ruin of Samaria by Shalmaneser, Shechem became the capital of the Samaritans, a remnant of whose sect, now reduced to a very small number, still reside there. It is about forty miles north of Jerusalem. Shechem stands in a delightful situation at the foot and on the lowest slope of Mount Gerizim, and is "embowered in groves of the richest verdure — figs, mulberries, olives; one solitary palm tree towering over them; and hedges of the prickly pear, with its fantastic boughs and yellow blossoms guarding every plantation." (Ld. Lindsay's Letters from Egypt, &c. [in 1837] vol. ii. p. 74.) This place is now called Napolose or Nablous (a corruption of its Greek name Neapolis): contiguous to it lies a valley, which opens into a plain watered by a fruitful stream, that rises near the town. This is universally allowed to be the *parcel of a field* mentioned by Saint John (iv. 5.) which *Jacob bought at the hand of the children of Hamor*. (Gen. xxxiii. 19.) Dr. Clarke (Travels, vol. iv. pp. 260 — 280. 8vo.) has given a minute and very interesting account of the antiquities of Shechem. (See also Mr. Jolliffe's Letters from Palestine, pp. 44 —48.) The few Samaritans, who still reside here, rigidly follow the religion of their ancestors: a few Jewish families are also found here.

SICK, healing of, why deemed unlawful by the Jews, on the Sabbath-day, 301. Treatment of, 502, 503.

SIDDIM, Vale of, notice of, 58.

SIDON, or ZIDON, a celebrated city of Palestine, reputed to have been founded by Sidon the eldest son of Canaan, from whom, according to Josephus, it derives its name; but other authorities derive the name Sidon from the Hebrew or Syrian word צידן (TSÎDEH), which signifies fishing. If the primitive founder was a fisherman, the two accounts may be easily reconciled. Joshua (xi. 8.) calls it Sidon the *Great*, by way of eminence; whence some have taken occasion to say, that in his time there were two Sidons, a greater and a lesser: but no geographer has mentioned any other Sidon than Sidon the Great. Joshua assigned Sidon to the tribe of Asher (Josh. xix. 28.), but this tribe could never get possession of it. (Judg. i. 31.) It is situated on the Mediterranean, one day's journey from Paneas, or from the fountains of Jordan, in a fine level tract of land, the remarkably simple air of which suits with that touching portion of the Gospel, which records the interview of Jesus Christ on this very spot — *the coasts of Tyre and Sidon* — with the Syro-Phœnician woman. (Matt. xv. 21—28. Mark vii. 24—30.) Abulfeda places it sixty-six miles from Damascus. This city has been always famous for its great trade and navigation. Its inhabitants were the first remarkable merchants in the world, and were very early celebrated on account of their luxury; for, in the days of the judges of Israel, the inhabitants of Laish are said to have dwelt careless and secure after the manner of the Zidonians. (Judg. xviii. 7.) The men of Sidon being great shipwrights, were particularly eminent, above all other nations, for hewing and polishing timber, there being *none who were skilled how to hew timber like the Sidonians.* (1 Kings v. 6.) This place is now called *Seide* or *Saide:* its port is small, and nearly filled up with the accumulation of mud. (Irby's and Mangles' Travels, p. 201.) The population is said to be about 7000; of whom 1600 are Christians, 200 are Jews, and the rest are Mohammedans. The city, as it exists at present, rises immediately from the strand; and, when seen from a slight distance, presents a rather imposing appearance. The interior, however, is most wretched and gloomy. "About half-way between Saide (or Sidon) and Sour (or Tyre) are very extensive ruins of towns which once connected these two cities; but of these ruins there is now scarcely one stone left upon another. They consist chiefly of lines which show, rased even with the soil, the foundation of houses — many stones irregularly scattered — a few cisterns with half-defaced sculpture on them; and, at a considerable distance from the path, there are at one spot several low columns either mutilated or considerably sunk in the earth. These reliques show, what it needed indeed no such evidence to prove, that in peaceable and flourishing times, on this road between two such considerable cities as Tyre and Sidon, there must have been many smaller towns for business, pleasure, and agriculture, delightfully situated by the seaside; but peaceful security has long been a blessing unknown to these regions; and we may apply to them the language of Judges v. 7. — *The villages ceased; they ceased in Israel.*" (Jowett's Christ. Researches in Syria, pp. 129, 130.)

SIEGES, how conducted, 211.

SIGNETS, notice of, 401.

SIHON, a king of the Amorites, who refused a passage through his territories to the Hebrews; and, coming to attack them, was himself slain. (Numb. xxi. 21.)

SIHOR, River, 37.

SILAS or SILVANUS (the former name being a contraction of the latter), an eminent Christian teacher, who was Saint Paul's companion in his journeys through Asia Minor and Greece.

SILOAM, Fountain or Pool of, 24. 43. Just over against this pool, near the bottom of the valley, through which its waters flow with an almost imperceptible current, and on the slope of a lofty mountain on the opposite side, is a village called Siloa: it has a miserable aspect, many of the habitations being no better than excavations from the rock, and the rest very meanly built houses and dilapidated stone huts; though it once could boast the palace of Pharaoh's daughter and Solomon's queen. The population is said not to ex-

ceed 200 persons. (Jowett's Researches in Syria, p. 262. Three Weeks in Palestine, p. 45.)

SIMEON, the son of Jacob and Leah: he was the head of one of the twelve tribes; for the limits of whose allotment, see p. 12.

SIMON or SIMEON, the name of several persons mentioned in the New Testament; of whom the following are the most remarkable:—

1. SIMON, surnamed Peter, who was also called Simon Bar-Jona. See PETER, p. 610.

2. SIMON, surnamed the *Canaanite* (perhaps because he was a native of Cana in Galilee), and also Zelotes or the Zealous, probably because he had been of the ZEALOTS. (See p. 375. for a notice of their principles.) He is supposed to have been the brother of James the Less and Jude: the particulars of his life are unknown.

3. SIMON, surnamed the *Cyrenean*, from Cyrene in Libya (where many Jews were settled), who was compelled to assist in bearing the cross of Jesus. (Matt. xxvii. 32.) Why he was so compelled, see p. 162. *supra.*

4. SIMON, surnamed *Bar-jesus*, a sorcerer. (Acts viii. 9. 13.) See BAR-JESUS, p. 558.

SIMOOM Wind, pestilential effects of, 76, 77.

SIN.

1. A strong city in Egypt (Ezek. xxx. 15, 16.) according to Jerome, Pelusium: it was situated on the eastern boundary of Egypt, and was defended by the swamps which lay around it.

2. Desert of Sin, a part of Arabia Deserta, towards Egypt, between Elim and Mount Sinai. (Exod. xvi. 1. xvii. 1. Numb. xxxiii. 12.)

SIN-OFFERINGS, notice of, 292, 293. Were, in certain cases, in the nature of punishments, 147, 148.

SINAI.

1. DESERT OF SINAI, 59.

2. MOUNT SINAI, a mountain in Arabia Petræa, where the law was given. It had two summits; the lower one, called Horeb, or the Mount of God (Exod. iii. 1.), when he appeared to Moses in a flame of fire in a bush. (See HOREB, p. 585. col. 2.) This Horeb is therefore called Sinai by Saint Stephen. (Acts vii. 30.) Mount Sinai is an enormous mass of granite rocks, with a Greek convent at the bottom, called the Convent of St. Catharine. It is the highest of a chain of mountains called by the Arabians Djibl Moosa (or the mountains of Moses), and which requires a journey of several days to go entirely round it. This chain is partly composed of sand-stone: it contains several fertile valleys, in which are gardens producing grapes, pears, dates, and other excellent fruits. These are taken to Cairo, where they are sold at a high price; but the general aspect of the peninsula of Mount Sinai is that of a frightful sterility. (Malte-Brun's System of Geography, vol. ii. p. 200.)

SINIM, a land very distant from Palestine. From the context of Isa. xlix. 12. it appears to have been situated towards the south or

S M

east. Some expositors have supposed it to be Pelusium or Syene ; but these are only cities, and not sufficiently remote. It were better (says Gesenius) to understand it of an eastern country, perhaps *China ;* of the name of which the Hebrews *may* have heard, as well as of Scythia and India.

SION or SIRION, a name of Mount HERMON, 48.

SIVAN or SIUVAN, the third month of the ecclesiastical year of the Jews ; and the ninth of their civil year. For a notice of the festivals, &c. in this month, see pp. 178, 179.

SLAVES, how acquired, 421, 422. Their condition and treatment among the Hebrews, 422 — 424 ; and heathens, 424, 425. Explanation of customs relating to them, mentioned in the New Testament, 426 — 428. Different kinds of, 428.

SLAYING with the sword, a Jewish punishment, 152. 154.

SLINGS of the Hebrews, notice of, 210.

SMYRNA, a city of Asia Minor, was situated between forty and forty-five miles to the north of Ephesus, of which city it was originally a colony. It was antiently frequented by great numbers of Jews, and it is now celebrated for the number, wealth, and commerce of the inhabitants. Of its population, which is estimated at about 77,000 inhabitants, 45,000 are Turks ; 15,000 Greeks ; 8000 Armenians ; 8000 Jews ; and less than 1000 Europeans. (Hartley's Visit, p. 289.) The angel of the church of Smyrna, addressed in the second apocalyptic epistle, is supposed to have been Polycarp, the disciple of Saint John, by whom he was appointed bishop of Smyrna. As he afterwards suffered much, being burnt alive at Smyrna, A. D. 166, the exhortation in Rev. ii. 10. would be peculiarly calculated to support and encourage him. The condition of the Christians residing here is said to be better than in any of the sites of the seven churches mentioned in the Apocalypse ; as if the promise was still in some measure made good to Smyrna. *Fear none of those things which thou shalt suffer. Be thou faithful unto death, and I will give thee a crown of life.* (Rev. ii. 10.)

So, an Egyptian king, contemporary with Hoshea, with whom he formed an alliance. (2 Kings xvii. 4.) He appears, however, to have been too weak to succour Hoshea against the Assyrians, one of whose kings, named Sargon, obtained signal advantages over him. (Isa. xx. 1.) According to Jablonski, So means a *chief prince,* or *prince of the dwelling.* For a long time the Pharaoh, who is named So in the Scriptures, was taken for the Sabacho of profane history, the head of the twenty-fifth or Ethiopian dynasty, who invaded Egypt, caused its monarch Bocchoris to be thrown into the flames, and usurped the throne. More recent and correct researches have shown that So is the Sewe of the Egyptians, and the Sevechus of profane history. (Coquerel, Biog. Sacr. tom. iv.

S P

p. 223. Hoskins's Travels in Ethiopia, pp. 304, 305.)

SODOM, the chief of the Pentapolitan cities, or five cities of the plain, gave the name to the whole land. It was burnt, with three other cities, by fire from heaven, for the unnatural lusts of their inhabitants, the truth of which is attested by numerous heathen writers. See pp. 40—42. *supra.*

SOLDIERS (Jewish), levies of, how made, 199, 200. Mosaic statutes concerning them, 200, 201. How commanded, 201 — 203. Their encampments, 204—206. Their pay and training, 206. Arms of, 207—211.

SOLDIERS (Roman), allusions to the officers, armour, and discipline of, 221—227. Their treatment of Jesus Christ, 161. They watched at the execution of criminals, 166.

SOLOMON, the son of David and Bathsheba, and the third king of Israel, renowned for his wisdom and riches, and for the magnificent temple which he caused to be erected at Jerusalem. The commencement of his reign was characterised by piety and justice ; but afterwards he abandoned himself, through the influence of his heathen wives, to gross and shameful idolatry. Temple of, 236, 237. Extent of his dominions, 13. His commerce, 482—484. He died B.C. 975, after a reign of forty years. For analyses of the books of Proverbs, Ecclesiastes, and Canticles, which were composed by him, see Vol. IV. pp.119—140.

SOLOMON'S Pools, notice of, 45, 46.

SOLOMON'S Porch, notice of, 239.

SONS, education of, 418. Parental authority over them, 418, 419.

SORCERERS, notice of, 360, 361.

SOSTHENES, a chief ruler of a synagogue at Corinth. (Acts xviii. 17.) Concerning the interpretation of which passage the learned differ greatly. Some suppose him to have been at this time an enemy to the apostle Paul, and his accuser, though subsequently a convert to the Christian faith ; and that he was beaten by the unbelieving Greeks, in consequence of the opinion given by the judge, and because he had troubled the proconsul with so impertinent an affair. Others are of opinion, that, at this time, he favoured Christianity, and suffered on that account, the Greeks beating him at the instigation of the unbelieving Jews. However this may have been, Sosthenes afterwards joined with Saint Paul in sending the first Epistle to the Corinthians. (Biscoe on the Acts, vol. i. p. 417.)

SOWING of corn, Jewish mode of, 455.

SPAIN, an extensive region of Europe, which antiently comprehended the country forming the modern kingdoms of Spain and Portugal. In the time of St. Paul it was frequented by Jews, and was subject to the Romans. In Rom. xv. 24. 28. he expresses his intention of visiting Spain ; but it does not appear that he was able to fulfil his design.

SPEARS of the Hebrews, notice of, 210.

SPOIL, how distributed by the Jews, 219.

S Y

mascus were more or less powerful. It was conquered by David. (2 Sam. viii. 5, 6.)

3. SYRIA OF ZOBAH, or Soba, or Sobal, as it is called by the Septuagint, was probably Cœle-Syria, or Syria the hollow. Its capital was Zobah, a city unknown, unless it be Hoba or Hobal, north of Damascus. (Gen. xiv. 15.)

4. SYRIA OF MAACHAH, or of Bethmaacah, was also towards Libanus. (2 Sam. x. 6. 8. 2 Kings xv. 29.) It extended beyond Jordan, and was given to Manasseh. (Deut. iii. 14.)

5. SYRIA OF ROHOB or REHOB, was that part of Syria of which Rehob was the capital. But Rohob was near the northern frontier of the land of promise (Numb. xiii. 21.), on the way or pass that leads to Emath or Hamath. It was given to the tribe of Asher, and is contiguous to Aphek, which was in Libanus. (Josh. xix. 28. 30. and xxi. 31.) Laish, otherwise called Dan, situate at the fountains of Jordan, was in the country of Rohob. (Judg. i. 31.) Hadadazer, king of Syria of Zobah, was son of Rehob or Rohob, or perhaps a native of the city of this name. (2 Sam. viii. 3. 12.) The Ammonites called to their assistance, against David, the Syrians of Rehob, of Zoba, of Maachah, and of Ishtob. (2 Sam. x. 6. 8.)

6. SYRIA OF TOB, or of Ishtob, or of the land of Tob, or of the Tubieni, as they are called in the Maccabees, was in the neighbourhood of Libanus, the northern extremity of Palestine. (Judg. xi. 3. 1 Macc. v.13. 2 Macc. xii. 17.) When Jephthah was banished by his brethren from Gilead, he withdrew into the land of Tob.

7. SYRIA OF EMATH, or Hamath, that of which the city Hamath, on the Orontes, was the capital. The extent and boundaries of this district are uncertain.

8. SYRIA, without any other appellation, stands for the KINGDOM OF SYRIA, of which Antioch became the capital after the reign of the Seleucidæ.

9. CŒLO-SYRIA, or *Cœle-Syria*, or the Lower Syria, occurs in several places of the Maccabees. (1 Macc. x. 69. 2 Macc. iii. 5. 8. iv. 4. viii. 8.) The word Cœle-Syria, in the Greek, signifies *Syria Cava*, or Syria the Hollow, or Deep. It may be considered, says Strabo, either in a proper and restrained sense, as comprehending only the tract of land between Libanus and Antilibanus: or in a larger signification, and then it will comprehend all the country in obedience to the kings of Syria, from Seleucia or Arabia and Egypt.

Syria at first was governed by its own kings, each of whom reigned in his own city and territories. David subdued them about A. M. 2960, B. C. 1044 (2 Sam. viii. 6.), on occasion of his war against the Ammonites, to whom the Syrians gave assistance. (2 Sam. x. 6. 8. 13. 18, 19.) They continued in subjection till after the reign of Solomon, when they shook off the yoke, and could not be re-

T A

duced again till the time of Jeroboam II. king of Israel, A.M. 3179, B.C. 820. Rezin, king of Syria, and Pekah, king of Israel, having declared war against Ahab, king of Judah, this prince found himself under the necessity of calling to his assistance Tiglathpileser, king of Assyria, who put Rezin to death, took Damascus, and transported the Syrians out of their country beyond the Euphrates. From that time Syria continued in subjection to the kings of Assyria. Afterwards it came under the dominion of the Chaldæans; then under that of the Persians; lastly, it was reduced by Alexander the Great, and was subject to all the revolutions that happened to the great empires of the East. After his death Syria became a powerful kingdom, under the dominion of the Seleucidæ, of which at a later period Antioch was the capital. It was subdued by Pompey as far as the Euphrates; and became a Roman province, including also Phœnicia and Judæa. In the time of Christ it was governed by a proconsul, to whom the procurator of Judæa was amenable.

SYRIAN IDOLS, notice of, 344, 345.

SYRO-PHŒNICIA is Phœnicia properly so called, of which Sidon, or Zidon, was the capital ; which having by right of conquest been united to the kingdom of Syria, added its old name Phœnicia to that of Syria. The Canaanitish woman is called a Syrophœnician (Mark vii. 26.), because she was of Phœnicia, which was then considered as making part of Syria. St. Matthew calls her a Canaanitish woman (Matt. xv. 22. 24.), because this country was really peopled by the Canaanites, Sidon being the eldest son of Canaan. (Gen. x. 15.) The Syro-Phœnicians were so called to distinguish them from the Phœnicians of Africa, who were called Liby-Phœnicians. Both were of the same Canaanitish stock or original.

TABERAH (or *burning*), an encampment of the Israelites in the wilderness. (Numb. xi. 3. Deut. ix. 22.) It derives its name from the circumstance that fire went forth from the tabernacle, and burnt a considerable part of their camp, as a punishment for their murmurings.

TABERNACLES, feast of, how celebrated, 315 — 317. A proof of the credibility of the Old Testament, I. 136.

TABERNACLES, various, in use among the Israelites, 231. Form and construction of the tabernacle of Moses, 231—234. Its migrations, 235.

TABITHA, the Aramæan name of a female Christian, otherwise called Dorcas, whom St. Peter miraculously restored to life. (Acts ix. 36. 40.)

TABLE, antient mode of reclining at, explained, 391, 392.

TABLES of weights, measures, and money,

T A

mentioned in the Bible, 525, 526. Chronological Table, 527—536.

TABLETS, for writing, form of, 469.

TABOR, or THABOR, Mount, account of, 50.

TABRET, notice of, 472.

TACTICS, military, of the Jews, 214—216.

TADMOR, a city of Syria, erected by king Solomon, who placed a garrison here to prevent the predatory incursions of the Arabs. It was situated in the wilderness of Syria, on the borders of Arabia Deserta, whence it is called *Tadmor in the Wilderness*, in 1 Kings ix. 18. Josephus places it at two days' journey from the Upper Syria, one day's journey from the Euphrates, and six days' journey from Babylon. He says that there is no water in the wilderness but in this place. (Ant. Jud. lib. viii. c. 6. § 1.) If we may form any conjecture of this city by the ruins of it, which later travellers have described, it must have been one of the first and most magnificent in the East; and it is somewhat surprising that history should give us so little account, when or by whom it was reduced to the melancholy condition in which it now appears. The reason why Solomon erected Tadmor in so desolate a place, was, probably, the commodiousness of its situation, to cut off all commerce between the Syrians and Mesopotamians, and to prevent them from conspiring against him as they had done against his father David. This city preserved its name of Tadmor to the time of Alexander. It then received the name of PALMYRA, which it preserved for several ages. About the middle of the third century, it became celebrated as the seat of the empire of Odenatus and Zenobia. When the Saracens became masters of the East, they restored its antient name of Tadmor, which has continued to the present time. Its situation between two powerful empires, that of the Parthians on the east, and that of the Romans to the west, often exposed it to danger from their contests. In time of peace, however, it soon recovered itself, by its trade with both empires; for the caravans of Persia and of the Indies, which now unload at Aleppo, then used to stop at Palmyra: thence they carried the merchandise of the East, which came to them by land, to the ports of the Mediterranean, and returned the merchandise of the West after the same manner. Mr. Addison has described the ruins of Palmyra, as they appeared in 1835, in his "Damascus and Palmyra," vol. ii. pp. 284—326.; and Lord Lindsay, as they appeared in 1837, in his " Letters from Egypt," &c. vol. ii. pp. 168—178. But the reader who would see these superb remains of antient art accurately delineated and described is referred to Messrs. Wood and Dawkins's " Ruins of Palmyra," which were first published at London in 1753, in one volume folio. The modern village of Tadmor, or (as the Arabs call it) Thadmor, contains 12 or 15 families, among whom there are not more than 20 able-bodied

T E

men: their chief wealth consists of a few herds of goats and dromedaries, with poultry. (Addison, vol. ii. p. 333.)

TAHPANES.

1. TAHAPANES, TAHPANHES (Jer. ii. 16.), or TEHAPHNEHES. was a celebrated city of Lower Egypt: antiently it was a royal city, of considerable note, and is supposed to have been situated near Pelusium or Sin. (Jer. ii. 16. xliii. 7—9. xlvi. 14. Ezek. xxx. 18.) Jeremiah, and the Israelites with him, retired to this place; and here it was revealed to the prophet, that Nebuchadnezzar should take this city, and set up his throne in the very place where Jeremiah had hidden stones. (Jer. xliii. 7—11. xliv. 1.)

2. A queen of Egypt, the wife of that Pharaoh who was contemporary with David, and who gave her sister in marriage to Hadad the Edomite. Tahpanhes educated her sister's son among the royal family of Egypt, perhaps from the mingled motives of affection and of politics.

TAMMUZ, or THAMMUZ.

1. The tenth month of the civil year of the Jews, and the fourth of their ecclesiastical year. For a notice of the festivals, &c. in this month, see p. 179.

2. An Egyptian and Syrian idol, worshipped by the Israelites, notice of, 347.

TANIS. See ZOAN, p. 637. *infra.*

TARES, notice of, 455.

TARSHISH, or TARTESSUS, a city and country in Spain, the most celebrated emporium in the West, to which the Hebrews traded; the *ships of Tarshish* (Isa. xxiii. 1. 4. lx. 9.) denote large merchant ships bound on long voyages (perhaps distinguished by their construction from the common Phœnician ships), even though they were sent to other countries instead of Tarshish. (Gibb's Hebrew Lexicon, pp. 713, 714. where the proofs are adduced at length.)

TARSUS, the metropolis of Cilicia (Acts xxi. 39.), was celebrated for being the place whither Jonah designed to flee, and where St. Paul was born. It was a very rich and populous city, and had an academy, furnished with men so eminent, that they are said to have excelled in all arts of polite learning and philosophy. From the number of its schools and learned men, it was ranked by the side of Athens and Alexandria. Even the academies of those cities and of imperial Rome itself were indebted to it for their best professors. It is now called Tersoos; has no good buildings; and is but ill supplied with the necessaries of life. (Irby's and Mangles' Travels, p. 503.)

TAXES paid by the Jews, 183. 186.

TEACHERS, Jewish, appellations of, 476. Academical degrees conferred on them, *ibid. note.* Manner of teaching, 477.

TEKOAH, a village south-east of Jerusalem, not far from which the Great Desert commenced: it was the birth-place of the prophet Amos. (i. 1.)

TEL-ABIB, a place to which some of the

Israelites were carried captive (Ezek. iii. 15.) Gesenius and Rosenmüller think it not improbably to be the place now called Thelabba, in Mesopotamia, on the river Chebar.

Telasar. See Thelasar.

Temple at Jerusalem, plan of, 236. Account of the *first* temple erected by Solomon, 236, 237. and of the *second* temple erected after the captivity, 237—242. Reverence of the Jews for it, 243. Account of the temple-guard, 244., and of the ministers of the temple, 272—282. The temple-worship described, 302, 303. Annual payments made for its support, 183. Feast of the dedication of the temple, 319, 320.

Temples at Heliopolis and Gerizim, 245, 246.

Tenths, when and of what things paid, 297, 298.

Tents of the Hebrews, account of, 381—383.

Teraphim, notice of, 342, 343.

Terraces (Oriental), notice of, 388.

Tertius, a Christian whom St. Paul employed as his amanuensis in writing his epistle to the Romans. (Rom. xvi. 22.)

Tertullus, a Roman orator or advocate, whom the Jews employed to bring forward their accusation against St. Paul, before the Roman procurator at Cæsarea; probably because they were themselves unacquainted with the modes of proceeding in the Roman courts. (Acts xxiv. 1, 2.)

Tesseræ Hospitales, notice of, 445, 446.

Tetrarch, office of, 110., *note* 4.

Thaddeus. See Jude.

Thammuz. See Tammuz.

Theatres and Theatrical Performances, allusions to, explained, 490—494.

Thebeth, or Tebeth, the fourth month of the civil year of the Jews, and the tenth of their ecclesiastical year. For a notice of the festivals, &c. in this month, see pp. 176, 177.

Thebez, a city in the tribe of Ephraim, at the siege of which Abimelech was killed. (Judg. ix. 50—55.) Eusebius says, that in the fourth century there was a village called Thebez, thirteen Roman miles from Shechem.

Theft, punishment of, among the Jews, 140.

Thelasar, or Telasar, a province of Assyria, mentioned in 2 Kings xix. 12. and Isa. xxxvii. 12. Its precise situation has not been ascertained: but it is supposed to be towards Armenia and Mesopotamia, and about the sources of the rivers Tigris and Euphrates, from the circumstance of the children of Eden inhabiting that country.

Theocracy of the Hebrews, nature of, 79, 80. It subsisted under the kings, 87.

Theophilus, the name of the person to whom Luke inscribed his Gospel and the Acts of the Apostles. (Luke i. 3. Acts i. 1.) He was most probably some Gentile of rank, who had abjured paganism and embraced the Christian faith.

Thessalonica, a large and populous city and sea-port of Macedonia, the capital of one of the four districts into which the Romans divided that country after its conquest by Paulus Æmilius. It was situated on the Thermæan Bay, and was antiently called Thermæ; but, being rebuilt by Philip the father of Alexander, after his victory over the Thessalians, it then received the name of Thessalonica. At the time of writing the Epistle to the Thessalonians, Thessalonica was the residence of the proconsul who governed the province of Macedonia, and of the quæstor who had the charge of the imperial revenues Besides being the seat of government, this port carried on an extensive commerce, which caused a great influx of strangers from all quarters; so that Thessalonica was remarkable for the number, wealth, and learning of its inhabitants. The Jews were extremely numerous here. The modern name of this place is Salonichi: it is the chief port of modern Greece, and has a population of sixty thousand persons, twelve thousand of whom are Jews. According to Dr. Clarke, who has given a very interesting account of the antiquities, present state, and commerce of Thessalonica, this place is the same now it was then; a set of turbulent Jews constituted a very principal part of its population: and when St. Paul came hither from Philippi, where the Gospel was first preached, to communicate the "glad tidings" to the Thessalonians, the Jews were sufficient in number to "set all the city in an uproar."

Theudas, a seditious person, who excited popular tumults among the Jews, probably during the interregnum which followed the death of Herod the Great, while Archelaus was at Rome; at which time Judæa was agitated with frequent seditions. (Acts v. 36.) Compare Vol. II. p. 623.

Thickets on the banks of the Jordan, 66.

Thisbe, a town in the tribe of Naphtali, to the south of Kadesh, the chief city belonging to that tribe. The prophet Elijah is supposed to have been a native of this city, though he might afterwards have dwelt in the land of Gilead. (1 Kings xvii. 1.)

Thomas, called Didymus, one of the twelve apostles: of the circumstances of whose life very little is known.

Thorns, of which Christ's crown was made, 65., *note* 4., 161. *note.*

Three Taverns, a small place or village on the Appian Way to Rome, where travellers stopped for refreshment. According to the Itinerary of Antoninus, it was thirty-three Roman (rather less than thirty-three English) miles from Rome. (Acts xxviii. 15.)

Threshing, and Threshing-floors, account of, 456, 457.

Thyatira, a city of Asia Minor, was a considerable city in the road from Pergamos to Sardis, and about forty-eight miles eastward of the former. It is called by the Turks *Ak-hissar,* and is embosomed in cypresses and poplars. It is now, as antiently it was, celebrated for dyeing: the scarlet cloths which are dyed here being considered superior to any others manufactured in Asia Minor, large quantities of them are sent weekly to Smyrna for the purposes of commerce. In 1826, the population was estimated at 300 Greek houses, 30 Armenian, and 1000 Turkish. (Hartley's Visit, Miss. Reg. pp. 326, 327. Arundell's Visit, pp. 189—191.)

TIBERIAS (John vi. 1—23. xxi. 1.), still called by the natives Tabaria or Tabbareeah, was antiently one of the principal cities of Galilee : it was built by Herod Antipas, tetrarch of Galilee, and so called in honour of the emperor, Tiberius. The privileges conferred upon its inhabitants by Herod caused it in a short time to become a place of considerable note : it was situated in a plain near the Lake of Gennesareth, which is thence termed the *Lake* or *Sea of Tiberias.* (See it described in pp. 38—40.) After the destruction of Jerusalem, this city became eminent for its Academy, over which a succession of Jewish doctors presided until the fourth century. On every side ruins of walls, columns, and foundations, indicate its antient splendour. The modern population of Tiberias is from fifteen hundred to two thousand : it is principally inhabited by Jews, who are said to be the descendants of families resident there in the time of our Saviour. Dr. Clarke conjectures that they are a remnant of refugees who fled hither after the capture of Jerusalem by the Romans. Tiberias is about ninety miles distant from Jerusalem : the modern town, which is very small, and is walled round, with towers at equal distances, stands close to the lake, upon a plain surrounded by mountains ; and is celebrated for its hot baths, which are much frequented. Tiberias had the most imposing appearance, from without, of any town in Syria; but within, it was as wretched as any other. This town was left in ruins by the earthquake which devastated Syria, on Jan. 1, 1837 : its walls were cast down to the ground, its towers split asunder, and their galleries laid open. (Lord Lindsay's Letters from Egypt, &c. [in 1837], vol. ii. p. 88.) About a mile from this town, and exactly in front of the lake, is a chain of rocks, in which are distinctly seen cavities or grottoes, that have been proof against the ravages of time. These have uniformly been represented to travellers as the places referred to in Scripture, which were frequented by miserable and fierce demoniacs, upon one of whom our Lord wrought a miraculous and instantaneous cure. Matt. viii. 28. Mark v. 2, 3. Luke viii. 27. (Dr. Clarke's Travels, vol. iv. pp. 219—233. 8vo. Light's Travels in Egypt, &c. &c. p. 203. Jolliffe's Letters from Palestine, pp. 32—34. Burckhardt's Travels in Syria, &c. pp. 320—330. Travels in Egypt and Nubia, &c. by Captains Irby and Mangles, p. 294. Jowett's Researches in Syria, pp. 171. 173. Carne's Letters, pp. 361, 362. Rae Wilson's Travels in the Holy Land, vol. ii. p. 25. Third Edition.)

TIBERIUS, Claudius Drusus Nero, emperor of Rome, succeeded his step-father Augustus : he died A. D. 37, after reigning 22½ years. In the 14th year of his reign, John the Baptist first appeared ; and the crucifixion of Jesus Christ took place in the third or fourth year after. (Luke iii. 1.)

TIGLATH-PILESER, king of Assyria, the son and successor of Sardanapalus. See ASSYRIA, p. 552. col. 1.

TIMBRELS, notice of, 472.

TIME, Jewish and Roman modes of computing, 167—175. Calendar of the Jewish year, 175—180. Parts of a period of time reckoned for the whole, 180, 181. Æras of time in use among the Jews, 181, 182.

TIMON, the name of one of the seven primitive deacons of the church at Jerusalem. (Acts vi. 5.)

TIMOTHEUS, commonly called Timothy, a Christian of Derbe, whose mother was of Jewish descent, and eminent for her piety, while his father was a Gentile. He was selected by St. Paul, as his chosen companion in his journies ; and was left by him at Ephesus to take the charge of the church there. He appears to have possessed in a high degree the confidence and affection of St. Paul, by whom he is often mentioned in terms of warm commendation. For analyses, &c. of the two epistles addressed to Timothy by the apostle, see Vol. IV. pp. 385—395.

TINKLING ORNAMENTS of the Jewish women, notice of, 403.

TIPSAH, an important city on the western bank of the river Euphrates, which was the frontier town of the north-eastern extremity of Solomon's dominions : it is a day's journey to the east of Tadmor or Palmyra. Here was a celebrated passage or ferry over the Euphrates. (1 Kings iv. 24.) By the antients it was called Thapsacus : its modern name is *El Deir.*

TIRHAKA, a king of Egypt or Ethiopia, is known in Scripture only by the powerful diversion which he made in behalf of Hezekiah, king of Judah, when pressed by the forces of Sennacherib, king of Assyria. (2 Kings xix. 9. xviii. 21. Isa. xxxvi. 6. xxxvii. 9.) Although, under this prince, Egypt appears to have recovered some of the advantages which it had lost under So, the predecessor of Tirhakah ; it is not clear whether we are to understand in the passages just cited a mere report of an invasion which was circulated, and which deceived the Assyrians, or an actual war in which they were engaged with the Egyptian monarch. Some expositors are of opinion that he carried his arms into Assyria, while Sennacherib was in Judæa. Tirhaka, the third sovereign, of the Ethiopian or twenty-fifth dynasty, whose name is confirmed by antient Egyptian monuments and inscriptions, is the Taracus of profane historians. (Compare Vol. I. p. 193.) The researches of our learned countryman Mr. Salt, there referred to, have been confirmed by the subsequent researches of signor Rosellini and ot

T R

Mr. Hoskins. (Travels in Ethiopia, p. 300.) If the predictions contained in the thirtieth and following chapters of Isaiah relate to Hezekiah, Tirhaka must be the Pharaoh intended in those passages; which some commentators refer to anterior times. The prophecies contained in the nineteenth chapter of Isaiah, particularly verses 2. and 4., have been supposed to announce the events which followed Tirhaka's death, the supplanting or removal of the Ethiopian dynasty by that of the Saïtes, and the revolutions which are recorded to have taken place in that period of the history of Egypt.

TIRZAH, a delightful city of Ephraim, the royal seat of the kings of Israel, from Jeroboam I. to Omri, who built the city of Samaria, which then became the capital of his kingdom. (Josh. xii. 24. 1 Kings xiv. 17. xv. 21. 2 Kings xv. 14.) Its situation is represented as pleasant in Sol. Song vi. 4.

TISRI or TIZRI, the first month of the civil year of the Jews, and the seventh of their ecclesiastical year. For a notice of the festivals, &c. occurring in this month, see p. 175.

TITHES, when and of what things paid, 297, 298.

TITUS, a Christian teacher, by birth a Gentile but converted by St. Paul, who therefore calls him his son (Gal. ii. 3. Tit. i. 4.), and whose companion and fellow-labourer he became. In 2 Tim. iv. 10: the apostle speaks of him as having gone to Dalmatia; and in Tit. i. 5. he assigns the reason of his leaving Titus in Crete, viz. to perfect the work which Paul had there begun, and to establish and regulate the churches. For an analysis of St. Paul's Epistle to Titus, see Vol. IV. pp. 395 —398.

TOGARMAH, the name of a northern region and people sprung from Gomer the son of Japhet. (Gen. x. 3.) This country abounded in horses, which were sold to the Tyrians. (Ezek. xxvii. 14.) Most probably it was Armenia, part of which country was celebrated for its horses. Such also is the opinion of the modern Armenians themselves, who claim Torgom the son of Gomer as the founder of their nation, and call themselves the *House of Torgom.*

TOLA, the tenth judge of Israel, of the tribe of Issachar. He succeeded Abimelech, and died after an administration of 23 years. (Judg. x. 1, 2.)

TOMBS of the Hebrews, account of, 519—522.

TORNADOES frequent in Palestine, 73.

TOWER of Antonia, 23.

TRACHONITIS, district of, 16.

TRADITIONS of the elders concerning the Sabbath, exposed, 300, 301.; were preferred by the Pharisees, to the Law of Moses, 365, 366.

TRANSFIGURATION, Mount of, 51. and *note.*

TRANSMIGRATION of souls, believed by the Jews, 363.

T U

TRANSPARENT GARMENTS of the Jewish women, 402.

TRAVELLING, Jewish mode of, 304. *note* 1. 443. Horrors of travelling across the Great Desert of Arabia, 60—62.

TREATIES, nature of 188. How made and ratified, 189—191.

TREES of Palestine, notice of, 65—68.

TRESPASS-OFFERINGS, notice of, 147, 148. 293.

TRIALS, proceedings of, among the Jews, 120—124.

TRIBES, allotments of, 9—13. Heads or princes of, 81.

TRIBUNAL (Imperial) appeals to, 131. Roman tribunals, 125—130. Jewish tribunals, 117—120.

TRIBUTE paid by the Jews, account of, 183. Reluctantly paid to the Romans, 184.

TRIUMPHS (military) of the Romans, allusions to, explained, 227—229.

TROAS, a maritime city of Mysia, situated on the western coast, at some distance to the southward of the supposed site of antient Troy. It is now called *Eski-Stamboul.* The adjacent region is also called Troas or the Troad. (Acts xvi. 8. 11. xx. 5, 6. 2 Cor. ii. 12. 2 Tim. iv. 13.)

TROGYLLIUM (Acts xx. 15.), a promontory at the foot of Mount Mycale, opposite to, and about five miles from Samos.

TROPHIES, military, of the Jews, 221.

TROPHIMUS, a Christian disciple, of Ephesus, who accompanied St. Paul on his departure from Greece for Judæa, and at Jerusalem was the innocent cause of the dangers to which he was there exposed. Recognised by some Jews from Asia Minor, who had seen him with St. Paul, they took occasion to accuse the apostle of having taken Greeks with him into the temple. (Acts xx. 4. xxi. 29.) After this time we find no mention made of Trophimus in the New Testament, until after his master's first imprisonment at Rome. In one of the voyages which followed the apostle's liberation, Trophimus was " left at Miletum sick." (2 Tim. iv. 20.) This circumstance proves, if further proof were wanting, that St. Paul was twice a prisoner at Rome; for Trophimus, at the time of his first journey to Miletus, had not been left there, since we read of his arrival in Judæa. (Acts xx. 15.)

TRUMPETS, form of, 473 ; feast of, 317.

TRUST, violations of, how punished, 141.

TRYPHÆNA and TRYPHOSA, two Christian women resident at Rome, where they laboured in diffusing the knowledge of the Gospel, and in succouring their fellow-believers. The mention of both their names by Saint Paul has led some to conjecture that they were sisters. (Rom. xvi. 12.)

TUBAL, or THUBAL, the fifth son of Japhet (Gen. x. 2.), whose descendants are supposed to have peopled a region of Asia Minor, near the Euxine Sea, on the west of MESHECH. Compare Rosenmüller's Biblical Geography, vol. i. pp. 130, 131

Tubal-Cain, the son of Lamech and Zillah, invented the art of working metals: there is great reason to believe that he was the Vulcan of antient mythology.

Τυμπανισμος, or beating to death, account of, 157.

Tunics of the Jews, form of, 396.

Tychicus, a Christian, probably of Ephesus, who was the friend and associate of St. Paul, and is mentioned by him in the most affectionate terms. (Acts xx. 4. Eph. vi. 21. Col. iv. 7. 2 Tim. iv. 12. Tit. iii.12.)

Tyrannus, a person at Ephesus, in whose house, or school, St. Paul proposed and defended the doctrines of the Gospel. (Acts xix. 9.) By some he is thought to have been a Jewish doctor or rabbi, who had a public school at Ephesus; while others, with more probability, suppose that he was a Greek sophist, because the apostle taught for two successive years in his school, after he had ceased to preach in the synagogues. (Acts xix. 9.)

Tyre, a celebrated city and sea-port of Phœnicia, that boasted of a very early antiquity, which is recognised by the prophet Isaiah (xxiii. 7.), but which is variously estimated by profane writers, whose discordant accounts this is not the place to adjust and determine. Even in the time of Joshua it was strongly fortified; for it is called the *strong city Tyre.* (Josh. xix. 29.) Tyre was twofold, insular and continental. Insular Tyre was certainly the most antient, for it was noticed by Joshua; the continental city, however, as being more commodiously situated, first grew into consideration, and assumed the name of Palæ-tyrus, or Old Tyre. Want of sufficient attention to this distinction has embarrassed both the Tyrian chronology and geography. Insular Tyre was confined to a small rocky island, eight hundred paces long and four hundred broad, and could never exceed two miles in circumference. But Tyre, on the opposite coast, about half a mile from the sea, was a city of vast extent, since, many centuries after its demolition by Nebuchadnezzar, the scattered ruins measured nineteen miles round, as we learn from Pliny and Strabo. Of these, the most curious and surprising are, the cisterns of Ras-el-Ain, designed to supply the city with water; of which there are three still entire, about one or two furlongs from the sea; so well described by Maundrell, for their curious construction and solid masonry. "The fountains of these waters," says he, after the description, "are as unknown as the contriver of them. According to common tradition, they are filled from a subterraneous river, which king Solomon discovered by his great sagacity; and he caused these cisterns to be made as part of his recompence to king Hiram, for the materials furnished by that prince towards building the temple at Jerusalem. It is certain, however, from their rising so high above the level of the ground, that they must be brought from some part of the mountains, which are about a league dis-

tant; and it is as certain that the work was well done at first; seeing it performs its office so well, at so great a distance of time; the Turks having broken an outlet on the west side of the cistern, through which there issues a stream like a brook, driving four corn mills between it and the sea." From these cisterns there was an aqueduct which led to the city, supported by arches, about six yards from the ground, running in a northerly direction, about an hour, when it turns to the west, at a small mount, where antiently stood a fort, but now a mosque, which seems to ascertain the site of the old city; and thence proceeds over the isthmus that connects Insular Tyre with the main, built by Alexander, when he besieged and took it.

Old Tyre withstood the mighty Assyrian power, having been besieged in vain, by Shalmaneser, for five years, although he cut off their supplies of water from the cisterns, which they remedied by digging wells within the city. It afterwards held out for thirteen years against Nebuchadnezzar, king of Babylon, and was at length taken; but not until the Tyrians had removed their effects to the insular town, and left nothing but the bare walls to the victor, which he demolished. What completed the destruction of the city was, that Alexander afterwards made use of these materials to build a prodigious causeway, or isthmus, above half a mile long, to the insular city, which revived, as the phœnix, from the ashes of the old, and grew to great power and opulence, as a maritime state; and which he stormed after a most obstinate siege of five months. Bp. Pococke observes, that "there are no signs of the antient city; and as it is a sandy shore, the face of every thing is altered, and the great aqueduct is in many parts almost buried in the sand." (Vol. ii. p. 81.) Thus has been fulfilled the prophecy of Ezekiel: *Thou shalt be built no more: though thou be sought for, yet shalt thou never be found again!* (xxvi. 21.)

The fate of Insular Tyre has been no less remarkable: when Alexander stormed the city, he set fire to it. This circumstance was foretold: "Tyre did build herself a stronghold, and heaped up silver as the dust, and fine gold as the mire of the streets. Behold the Lord will cast her out, and he will smite her power in the sea, and she shall be devoured with fire." (Zech. ix. 3, 4.) After this terrible calamity, Tyre again retrieved her losses. Only eighteen years after, she had recovered such a share of her antient commerce and opulence, as enabled her to stand a siege of fourteen months against Antigonus, before he could reduce the city. After this, Tyre fell alternately under the dominion of the kings of Syria and Egypt, and then of the Romans, until it was taken by the Saracens, about a. d. 639, retaken by the Crusaders, a. d. 1124; and at length sacked and rased by the Mamelukes of Egypt, with Sidon, and other strong towns, that they might no longer harbour the Chris-

U R

tians, A. D. 1289. (Dr. Hales's Analysis of Chronology, vol. i. pp. 442—444.)

The following description of the modern town of Surat, by a recent intelligent traveller, will give the reader a lively idea of the splendour of antient Tyre in the days of her commercial prosperity, as delineated by the prophet Ezekiel (xxvii. 3.) : — " The bazaars, filled with costly merchandise, picturesque and interesting groups of natives on elephants, camels, horses, and mules; strangers from all parts of the globe, in their respective costume; vessels building on the stocks, others navigating the river; together with Turks, Persians, and Armenians, on Arabian chargers ; European ladies in splendid carriages, the Asiatic females in hackeries drawn by oxen; and the motley appearance of the English and Nabob's troops on the fortifications, remind us of the following description of Tyre: *O thou that art situate*, &c. (Ezek. xxvii. 3.) This is a true picture of Oriental commerce in antient times; and a very exact description of the port, and the bazaars of Surat at the present day." (Forbes's Oriental Memoirs, vol. i. p. 244.)

From Sidon to Tyre is generally one continued plain, varying from 300 to 1000 yards in width. Nearer to Tyre, it becomes considerably wider; and forms to the east of that city, on every side, a rich and pleasing country. About Ras-el-Ain, in particular, the meadows, variegated by streamlets, are very picturesque, and capable of being rendered highly productive. (Jowett's Christian Researches in Syria, p. 297.)

"Numerous beautiful columns, stretched along the beach, or standing in fragments half buried in the sand that has been accumulating for ages, the broken aqueduct, and the ruins which appear in its neighbourhood, exist, as an affecting monument of the fragile and transitory nature of earthly grandeur." (Jowett's Christian Researches in the Mediterranean, Appendix, p. 422. See also his Christian Researches in Syria, pp. 131—141.; and for other testimonies of modern travellers relative to the actual state of Tyre, see Vol. I. pp. 285—288. A considerable part of modern Tyre was destroyed by an earthquake, on Jan. 1. 1837. On the commerce of the Tyrians with the Hebrews, see pp. 483, 484. of this volume.

UNBLOODY OFFERINGS, 294.

UNCLEAN PERSONS, who were such, 334.

UPHAZ, a country rich in gold, the situation of which is no where pointed out. Calmet supposed it to be the same with Ophir. (Dan. x. 5. Jer. 9.)

UPPER GARMENTS, form of, 396.

UR of the Chaldees, a city of Mesopotamia, the dwelling-place of Terah and Abraham; which the latter was ordered to quit. (Gen. xi. 28.) "By faith he obeyed, and went out, not knowing whither he was going." (Heb. xi. 8.) Ur was subsequently called Edessa, by the

W E

Macedonians; and by the Tyrians Urhoi, which the Arabs have corrupted into Urfáh or Orfáh. Mr. Buckingham has given a long and interesting description of its present state. (Travels in Mesopotamia, vol. i. pp. 121—191. Ainsworth's Remarks on Assyria, Babylon, and Chaldæa, p. 152.)

URIM and THUMMIM, what, 280.

Uz, land of (Job i. 1.), the residence of the patriarch Job, is supposed to have been the northern part of Arabia ; though some are of opinion that it is Edom or Idumæa. Compare Vol. IV. p. 79.

UZZIAH, also called Azariah, a king of Judah, who succeeded his father Amaziah, when he was only sixteen years of age. The commencement of his reign was auspicious for his piety and zeal for the worship of God ; but, afterwards, presuming to take upon him the sacerdotal office, he was struck with a leprosy ; and he continued without Jerusalem, separated from other men, until his death, B. C. 758. (2 Kings xiv. 21, 22. xv. 1—7.)

VALLEY of Ajalon, 53. Berachah or Blessing, 53. Bochim, 54. Elah, 54. Hinnom, 54. Jehoshaphat, 55. Mamre, 53. Rephaim, 53. Salt, 53. Sharon, 55. Shaveh, 53. Siddim, 53.

VEGETABLES, grown in Palestine, 64—68.

VEILS of the Hebrew women, 400.

VESTMENTS of the priests, 277, 278. Of the high priest, 279, 280.

VICTIMS, different kinds of, 289. How selected, 289. Manner of presenting them, 290. and of immolating them, among the Jews, 290. and among the heathen nations, 353, 354.

VICTORS, reception of, 218. Triumphs of, among the Romans, 227, 228.

VINES and VINEYARDS of the Jews, culture and management of, 458—461.

VISITORS, how received, 433, 434.

VOLUNTARY Oblations, 295.

Vows, nature and different kinds of, 323 —326. Vow of consecration and of engagement, 295, 296.

WARS, the earliest, were predatory excursions, 197. Wars of the Hebrews, 198. 212 —218.

WASHING, different sorts of, 333.

WATCHES of the Night, 169, 170.

WATER, importance of, in the East, 35. 44. Fetched by women, 45. 333. *note* 2. 392. The waters of the Nile singularly delicious, 444.

WATER-POTS of the Jews, notice of, 392, 393.

WATERS OF MEROM, notice of, 40.

WEAPONS (Military) of the Jews, 207— 211. Allusions to the Greek and Roman weapons in the New Testament, 223, 224.

WEDDINGS of the Jews, 406—414.

WEEKS, account of, 170.

WEIGHTS, table of, 525.

Z I

ZERUBBABEL or ZOROBABEL, the son of Salathiel, of the royal house of David, was appointed chief of those Jews who, by the permission of Cyrus, came from Babylon, at the commencement of that prince's reign. He laid the foundation of the temple, and restored the Mosaic worship. It is not known when this great man and pious ruler died.

ZIDON. See SIDON, p. 625. *supra.*

ZIF, the eighth month of the civil year of the Jews, and the second of their ecclesiastical year. For a notice of the festivals, &c. in this month, see p. 178.

ZIKLAG, a city which Achish, king of Gath, gave to David while he took shelter in the land of the Philistines, and which afterwards remained as a domain to the kings of Judah. (1 Sam. xxvii. 6.) It was taken and plundered by the Amalekites during David's absence: it was situated in the extreme parts of the tribe of Judah, southward.

ZIMRI, the fifth king of Israel, commander of one half of the cavalry of Elath, assassinated his master, usurped his throne, and destroyed all the branches of the royal family. His reign lasted only a week: in consequence of his having neglected to secure the army, they chose Omri king of Israel, who besieged him in Tirzah; and Zimri, finding his capital taken, set the royal palace on fire, and perished in the flames. (1 Kings xvi. 9—20.)

ZIN, a desert in the south of Palestine,

Z O

towards Idumæa. (Numb. xiii. 21. xx. 1. xxxiv. 3, 4. Josh. xv. 1. 3)

ZION, the more elevated southernmost mountain, and upper part of the city of Jerusalem. In the poetical and prophetical books it is often used for Jerusalem itself.

ZIPH, a city of Judah (Josh. xv. 24.), near Hebron, eastward. Its modern name is Sephoury. It was a place of rendezvous for armies during the crusades; and at a short distance from it is a celebrated fountain. (Rae Wilson's Travels, vol. ii. p. 40.)

ZIPH, wilderness of, 59.

ZOAN, an antient city in Lower Egypt; according to the Septuagint and Targums, it is TANIS on the eastern mouth of the Nile. (Numb. xiii. 22. Isa. xix. 11. 13. xxx. 4. Ezek. xxx. 14.)

ZOAR, a city on the southern extremity of the Dead Sea. (Gen. xiii. 10. xix. 22. 30. Isa. xv. 5. Jer. xlviii. 34.) Its more antient name was Bela.

ZOBAH or ARAM-ZOBAH, was the name of a city and petty kingdom of Syria, whose sovereign carried on war with Saul and David. (1 Sam. xiv. 47. 2 Sam. viii. 3. x. 6.) It seems to have been situated near Damascus, and to have included the city Hamath (2 Chron. viii. 3.); but also to have extended towards the Euphrates. (2 Sam. viii. 3.)

ZOROBABEL. See ZERUBBABEL.